CRAIES ON LEGISLATION

AUSTRALIA
Law Book Co.
Sydney

CANADA and USA
Carswell
Toronto

HONG KONG
Sweet & Maxwell Asia

NEW ZEALAND
Brookers
Wellington

SINGAPORE and MALAYSIA
Sweet & Maxwell Asia
Singapore and Kuala Lumpar

CRAIES ON LEGISLATION

A PRACTITIONERS' GUIDE TO THE NATURE, PROCESS, EFFECT AND INTERPRETATION OF LEGISLATION

Eighth Edition

EDITOR
*Daniel Greenberg, of Lincoln's Inn, Barrister;
Parliamentary Counsel*

CONSULTANT EDITOR
*Michael J. Goodman MA PhD, Solicitor;
formerly Professor of Law at the University of Durham,
and a Social Security Commissioner*

LONDON
SWEET & MAXWELL
2004

Founded on Hardcastle on *Statutory Law*

First Edition (1907) By W.F. Craies
Second Edition (1911) By W.F. Craies
Third Edition (1923) By J.G. Pease and J.P. Gorman
Fourth Edition (1936) By W.S. Scott
Fifth Edition (1952) By Sir Charles E. Odgers
Sixth Edition (1963) By S.G.G. Edgar
Seventh Edition (1971) By S.G.G. Edgar
Second Impression (1976)
Third Impression (1978)

Published in 2004 by
Sweet & Maxwell Limited of
100 Avenue Road, London NW3 3PF
Typeset by Interactive Sciences Ltd, Gloucester
Printed and bound by MPG Books Ltd, Bodmin, Cornwall

No natural forests were destroyed to make this product:
only farmed timber was used and re-planted.

ISBN 0 421 859 601

ISBN 0-421-85960-1

9 780421 859609

FOREWORD

On being asked to write this foreword to a new edition of *Craies*, my first reaction was to wonder what there was to justify a new edition. Statutes have been with us from the beginning of English law and, although the emphasis of judgments varies over the years, give or take a little, the basic principles remain much the same.

If I had paused to think, it would have immediately become clear that exactly the opposite was the case. There can have been few sectors of the law that have been so fundamentally altered in the last 30 years as the law affecting the making and construction of legislation affecting the United Kingdom. When the last edition (called *Craies on Statute Law*) was published, in practice there was only one legislative body that could make original law—the Queen in Parliament. In the 30 years which have passed since, laws made by the European Union have become an ever increasing source of United Kingdom legislation. Admittedly, in strict law European law is only part of English law by virtue of s.2(1) of the European Communities Act 1972 but if and so long as that section remains unrepealed, European law has the force of law in the United Kingdom. A Directive which has direct effect is enforceable in the United Kingdom without any intervention of the United Kingdom Parliament. Even where a Directive requires to be given effect by an enactment of the United Kingdom Parliament, the principles of European Union law are of basic importance in construing the enabling Act.

Nor is the impact of European law the only major change that has occurred in this field. The creation of a devolved legislature for Scotland (and to a lesser extent the powers of the National Assembly for Wales) introduced new legislatures and new problems of delimiting the powers devolved to them. In the circumstances it is not surprising that this enormous change in the range of the book has led to it being renamed *"Craies on Legislation"* to reflect the much wider field that it now has to encompass.

In addition to all this, Human Rights have arrived as a major focus of Parliamentary debate and court litigation. As an advocate in 1970, you had to be a brave man to mention the European Convention of Human Rights as a possible aid to construction of an English Statute. Over the years the courts became gradually more willing to approach the construction of legislation on the basis that Parliament should be taken to have intended to comply with the nations' treaty obligations. It was this Judge made presumption that was eventually adopted by Parliament in the Human Rights Act 1998. Since the Act came into force, this statutory presumption that legislation complies with the Human Rights Convention has become ever more common a feature of litigation. Sometimes it seems that we could get rid of all other causes of action. There is no doubt that the Act has basically affected the rights of the individual against the State and its operation is one of the central problems of the moment.

v

All that I have said so far relates to changes in the effect of legislation produced by new statutory provisions. In addition, there have been changes due to judicial decision. In the longer run, judicial rumblings as to the existence of rights so fundamental that not even a sovereign Parliament can ignore them may prove to be the most emotive developments of our day. But currently the biggest judicially introduced change has been the controversial decision in *Pepper v Hart* enabling the court to look at Parliamentary proceedings for the purpose of construing an ambiguous statutory provision.

I have by now said enough to show that the editor of the new edition has been faced with formidable difficulties. The legal world is very fortunate that Mr Greenberg has grappled with these problems with a masterly command. He has dealt with all the points that I have mentioned and a great many more besides. This edition is more of a rewriting than an editing of the last edition but it draws on the authority of the last edition and illuminates all the material which is new since that date. It is a masterly piece of work which could only have been written by a man with a profound and perspicacious knowledge of his subject. It will be indispensable.

Lord Browne-Wilkinson
May 2004

EDITOR'S PREFACE

The aim of *Craies*

It is more than 30 years since *Craies* was last revised. When the last edition was published the United Kingdom did not belong to the European Communities, there was neither a Scottish Parliament nor a National Assembly for Wales, and the European Convention on Human Rights had not been incorporated into the law of the United Kingdom. In these and other ways, legal and political changes have made it necessary to alter the scope of the work considerably.

The essence of the work has not, however, changed. The purpose remains to provide practical guidance about legislation in the United Kingdom. The method remains to concentrate on providing answers to questions that are likely to occur to the users of legislation and to rely where possible on concise quotation from judicial decisions and other relevant documents.

Europe

Craies remains a work about legislation in the United Kingdom.

This edition, however, pays particular attention where necessary to that portion of legislation in the United Kingdom that implements obligations arising out of membership of the European Union. And the final Part of this edition aims to provide sufficient information about legislation emanating from the Treaties and institutions of the European Union for the reader both to put implementing legislation into its proper context and also to understand something about the effects in the United Kingdom, direct and indirect, of legislation of the Communities.

Subordinate legislation

The relative importance of forms of legislation other than Acts of Parliament has continued to grow since the last edition of *Craies*, and this is reflected by a change of emphasis in this edition.

The Appendix

The Appendix to this work is used to permit, without unduly disrupting the flow of the text, the inclusion of both a certain amount of historical material and also some lengthy extracts of judgments and other documents which expound important ideas or principles in a manner likely to be helpful to a reader who requires to look into them in particular depth.

Editorial capacity

The lapse of time since the last edition has made it necessary to rewrite rather than merely to revise. But much of the material is drawn from the last edition, as well as from a variety of other sources. Expressions of opinion should not be imputed to the present editor, and it should be noted that he writes in an exclusively private capacity.

Date of work

This edition aims to present the law as at the end of April 2004.

In many places, examples of legislation are given in order to illustrate what is feasible or precedented: they are not exclusively drawn from legislation presently in force.

Copyright acknowledgments

Certain extracts from judgments are—

(1) given in this work as they appear in publications of the Incorporated Council of Law Reporting for England and Wales, whose assistance is gratefully acknowledged,
(2) taken from the database of judgments maintained by the Court Service, whose Crown Copyright is acknowledged, or
(3) taken from the All England Law Reports and reproduced by kind permission of Reed Elsevier (UK) Limited trading as LexisNexis UK, whose copyright is acknowledged.

Information about and references to European legislation have been taken from *Europa*, a website maintained by the European Commission: the copyright of the European Communities in respect of that information is acknowledged.

Parliamentary copyright material from Hansard and other publications is reproduced with the permission of the Controller of Her Majesty's Stationery Office on behalf of Parliament.

Crown copyright is acknowledged in respect of material taken from a number of sources including, in particular, texts of legislation made available on the internet website of Her Majesty's Stationery Office.

Other acknowledgments

I thank God for enabling me to accomplish this task, and my wife Julia and my children Yisroel, Avi, Shira and Elisheva, for their love, encouragement and support.

The revision of *Craies* after such a long interval was entirely the idea of its consultant editor, Michael Goodman. I am deeply indebted to him both for his original idea and also for his constant encouragement and support.

I also thank the publishers for their kind and attentive treatment.

Invitation to comment

It is hoped that this work will now be revised regularly and frequently. With that in mind, I will welcome comments, criticisms and suggestions, which may be sent to the publishers.

Daniel Greenberg
London
May 2004

CONTENTS

PART 1

THE NATURE OF LEGISLATION

PART 2

THE LEGISLATIVE PROCESS

PART 3

THE EFFECT OF LEGISLATION

PART 4

INTERPRETATION OF LEGISLATION

PART 5

EUROPEAN LEGISLATION

TABLE OF CASES

References in this Table are to paragraph numbers and in some instances followed by a note number where the case appears in footnotes

Part 1

THE NATURE OF LEGISLATION

CHAPTER 1

CONCEPTS AND CLASSES

SECTION 1

TERMINOLOGY

Introduction

This Section explores a number of expressions which are in sufficiently common **1.1.1**
usage in relation to legislation to be worth exploring at the outset.

United Kingdom legislation

The expression "United Kingdom legislation" is not a term of art and is used in **1.1.2**
this work merely as a convenient shorthand for primary legislation passed, and
subordinate legislation made, in the United Kingdom.

As will be seen,[1] legislation passed or made in the United Kingdom may
extend to one or more of the constituent parts of the United Kingdom, and it may
apply only to things done in one or more of those parts or also to things done
abroad.

So the expression "United Kingdom legislation" is a wide one: in particular,
it includes Acts of Parliament, statutory instruments made under powers
conferred by Act, prerogative legislation and legislation made by the devolved
legislatures.

Enactment

The word "enactment" is commonly and colloquially used to describe an Act, a **1.1.3**
provision of an Act, a Church Measure,[2] a provision of a Church Measure, or a
provision of a statutory instrument.[3]

---

[1] Chapter 11, Section 1.
[2] As to which see Chapter 3, Section 7.
[3] It seems less common to find an entire statutory instrument referred to as an enactment. And some
would say that the expression cannot accurately be used in relation to a provision of an instrument,
or indeed in relation to anything other than an Act which is "enacted" upon receipt of Royal
Assent, as shown by the use of the enactment formula "Be it enacted . . . " (see Chapter 2).
Whatever merit there may be in this "purist" approach, the courts have quite simply not adopted
it.

As to its precise legal meaning, it is, rather unhelpfully, true both that "enactment" does not have a single technical meaning within legislation as a whole and also that it does have a single technical meaning on each occasion on which it is used. In other words, it is necessary each time one encounters a legislative reference to an "enactment" to construe the word in the context of the reference.

It is clear that "enactment" is not a mere synonym for "Act". As Ridley J. said in *Wakefield and District Light Railways Corporation v Wakefield Corporation*[4]—

"The word 'enactment' does not mean the same thing as 'Act'. 'Act' means the whole Act, whereas a section or part of a section in an Act may be an enactment."

1.1.4 The question arises, however, whether instruments emanating from Acts, and portions of them, can also amount to enactments. The underlying proposition is enunciated, and the method of construction illustrated, in the following passage of the judgment of Ashworth J. in *Rathbone v Bundock*[5]—

"In some contexts, the word 'enactment' may include within its meaning not only a statute but also a statutory regulation but, as it seems to me, the word does not have that wide meaning in the [Road Traffic Act 1960[6]]. On the contrary, the language used in a number of instances strongly suggests that, in this particular Act, the draftsman was deliberately distinguishing between an enactment and a statutory regulation; see, for example, section 267 and Schedule 18. Accordingly, I am of opinion that, unless the offence alleged against the driver was an offence under Part 1 of the Act within the meaning of paragraph (a) of section 232(1), section 232 was not applicable."

The question of whether a reference to "enactments" includes a reference to subordinate instruments is frequently complicated. This is amply illustrated by the following passage of a Report of the Joint Committee on Statutory Instruments[7]—

"The Committee understands [section 9 of the Finance Act 1994] to mean that conduct may attract a section 9 penalty only if an enactment says it does. The question which arises is whether regulations and orders (rather than Acts of Parliament) are to be understood to be 'enactments' in this

---

[4] [1906] 2 K.B. 140, 145, DC. The decision was upheld on appeal (without direct reference to this point, but with implied acquiescence) at [1907] 2 K.B. 256, CA and at [1908] A.C. 293, HL.
[5] [1962] 2 All E.R. 257, 261, QBD.
[6] 1960 c.16.
[7] Joint Committee on Statutory Instruments, Session 1994–95, 24th Report, para.3 (HL Paper 75, HC 8-xxiv).

context.... The Committee notes that Schedule 4 to the 1994 Act specifically amends only enactments in Acts of Parliament so that they attract section 9 penalties ... It is therefore not clear from the 1994 Act that regulations under the 1992 Act can be considered to be 'enactments' for the purpose of section 9.... In their second memorandum the Commissioners of Customs and Excise quote two cases in which the term 'enactment' has been taken to include regulations and orders.[8] However, of these the first is not an authority for such a proposition and the second acknowledges that the answer to the question depends on the context.... Since, in the context of section 9, it appears to the Committee that 'enactment' does not include enactments in regulations or orders (or other subordinate legislation) the Committee therefore considers that there must be some doubt whether regulation 14 is intra vires."

Because it is sometimes so difficult to determine whether subordinate instruments are intended to be included in a general reference to "enactments", it is now common for legislation using the term "enactment" to define it. The definition is sometimes short, merely to include or exclude subordinate legislation. But the definition can sometimes be more encyclopaedic: for example— **1.1.5**

" 'enactment' includes an Act of the Scottish Parliament, Northern Ireland legislation and an enactment comprised in subordinate legislation, and includes an enactment whenever passed or made" (Enterprise Act 2002,[9] s.129(1)).

" 'enactment' includes an enactment comprised in—

    (a) an Act of the Scottish Parliament;
    (b) subordinate legislation, whether made under an Act or an Act of the Scottish Parliament" (Co-operatives and Community Benefit Societies Act 2003,[10] s.1(9)).

" 'enactment' includes any provision of a Measure of the Church Assembly or of the General Synod of the Church of England" (Trustee Act 2000,[11] s.39(1)).

The Scotland Act 1998[12] amended[13] Sch.1 to the Interpretation Act 1978[14] so that it includes the following definition—

---

[8] *Wicks v Director of Public Prosecutions* [1946] A.C. 362 and *Rathbone v Bundock* [1962] 2 Q.B. 260.
[9] 2002 c.40.
[10] 2003 c.15.
[11] 2000 c.29.
[12] 1998 c.46.
[13] Sch.8, para.16(3).
[14] 1978 c.30.

> " 'Enactment' does not include an enactment comprised in, or in an instrument made under, an Act of the Scottish Parliament."

The purpose of that amendment is to avoid provisions of Westminster legislation inadvertently having an effect on devolved legislation, by making provision by reference to "enactments" without expressly excluding Acts of the Scottish Parliament and their derivative instruments. It is therefore merely a rebuttable presumption and does not establish any kind of principle against the inclusion of Scottish Acts and instruments within the expression "enactment" where appropriate. So where necessary legislation can provide expressly for "enactment" to include Scottish Acts and instruments.[15]

1.1.6   As to whether a reference to "enactments" in general will include future enactments—that is to say enactments not passed or made when the reference is made—it is sometimes appropriate to include express provision to that effect.[16] But in other circumstances the intention is sufficiently clear from the context in which the reference appears to make an express gloss unnecessary.[17]

A particularly interesting recent expansion of the potential breadth of the expression "enactment" is to be found in *R. v Sissen*[18] where the Court of Appeal held that a Regulation of the Council of the European Communities is an enactment for the purposes of s.170(2) of the Customs and Excise Management Act 1979[19] (fraudulent evasion of prohibition or restriction in respect of goods under an enactment).

Other similar expressions are sometimes used in place of "enactment". The expressions "statutory provision" and "legislative instrument" are both found, the former being defined in one place as meaning—

> "any provision made by or under an Act of Parliament, an Act of the Scottish Parliament or any Northern Ireland legislation" (Finance Act 2003,[20] s.121).

The expansion of the meaning of expressions of this kind tends to produce a trend which from time to time has surprising and regrettable results. So, for example, the definition of "subordinate legislation" in s.21(1) of the Human Rights Act 1998[21] clearly caught the Rules of the Royal Society for the Prevention of

---

[15] See, for example, s.117 of the Railways and Transport Safety Act 2003 (c.20): "In this Act "enactment" includes—(a) an Act of the Scottish Parliament, (b) an instrument made under an Act of the Scottish Parliament, and (c) Northern Ireland legislation."

[16] See, for example, s.26(4) of the Data Protection Act 1984 (c.35) which prevented other enactments from interfering with the "subject access provisions" of that Act—"enactment" was glossed by s.41 so as to include future enactments.

[17] See, for example, the Employment Protection (Consolidation) Act 1978 (c.44), Sch.9, para.1(5)(a); see also the related discussion of s.20(2) of the Interpretation Act 1978 (c.30) in Chapter 22.

[18] [2001] 1 W.L.R. 902, CA.

[19] 1979 c.2.

[20] 2003 c.14.

[21] 1998 c.42.

Cruelty to Animals, being rules made under a private Act of 1932[22]: but in deciding accordingly Lightman J. observed "I have however some difficulty accepting that the rules are the sort of 'instrument' which the legislation was intended to cover".[23]

Statute

The word "statute" has had a long history during the course of which its meaning **1.1.7** has developed considerably.[24] This development was remarked upon as long ago as 1857 when Lord Campbell C.J. had to decide, in the case of *R. v Bakewell*[25] the extent of the phrase "under or by virtue of any of the statutes relating to Her Majesty's revenue of excise"[26]: he said[27]—

> "I read the word 'statute,' in the section, as if it were written 'enactment'. The word 'statute' has several meanings. It may mean what is popularly called an Act of Parliament, or a code such as the statute of Westminster, or all the Acts passed in one Session, which was the original meaning of the word. But the question is, what is the meaning of it [in the Act under consideration] . . . The sensible interpretation of section 35 is, that it leaves the revenue officers to follow their ancient mode of conducting proceedings which are to be instituted and pursued by them, but that all other proceedings before magistrates may be conducted in the new and useful form".

The result is that neither "statute" nor "the statute book" has a sufficiently exact technical meaning to be used in legislation, in which context the normal procedure is to refer to enactments or instruments.[28]

The expression "the statute book" is frequently used as a loose way of referring to the extant corpus of legislation having effect in some or all of the United Kingdom at a given time.

This being a purely colloquial expression it is useless to try to attribute to it a precise technical meaning of a kind not intended by those who habitually use it: in particular, whether it includes only primary legislation or also delegated legislation under powers in Acts depends entirely on the circumstances of its use.

Similar considerations apply to the expression "statute law".

---

[22] 1932 c.xxxix.

[23] *R.S.P.C.A. v Attorney-General* [2002] 1 W.L.R. 448 Ch.

[24] In its earliest uses it was used to mean the whole municipal law of the state, from whatever source emanating, and not only legislation. See Sedgwick's *Statutory and Constitutional Law* (2nd ed., 1874) p.33.

[25] 7 El. & Bl. 847, 851.

[26] As used in 11 & 12 Vict. c.43, s.35.

[27] At 851.

[28] As to the meaning of which terms see above.

The useful pretence that there is a single entity known as the statute book which gives rise to the possibility of textual amendments—instructions to a notional editor of the corpus of statute law—is discussed below.[29] In essence, the idea of a "statute book" is a convenient notation when it comes to amending the law, making it possible to express changes concisely by addressing fictitious editorial commands to a non-existent editor. So long as one remembers that this is no more than a convenient way of expressing the intended change of the law, no harm is done and a good deal of ink and paper saved.

Subordinate legislation, &c.

1.1.8 A number of expressions are used colloquially as if they were synonyms of the term subordinate legislation: principal are "secondary legislation", "delegated legislation" and "statutory instruments".

Of these, delegated legislation is a real synonym for subordinate legislation, since it is the delegation of power by primary legislation that gives authority to legislation subordinate to it.

The expression "secondary legislation" is less helpful, since as will be seen[30] it is not apt to describe the entire class of subordinate legislation. The same is true of "statutory instruments", which again describes only a sub-class.[31]

Some kinds of legislation are strictly speaking tertiary, since they owe their authority to an instrument which in turn owes its authority to an Act of Parliament. Although the expression is rarely used, and certainly carries with it no body of law or lore, the following could accurately be described as tertiary forms of legislation—

(1) Legislation made under a power conferred by an instrument made in reliance on s.2(2) of the European Communities Act 1972 (c.68). Section 2(4) allows an instrument under s.2(2) to make any such provision "as might be made by Act of Parliament". Paragraph 1 of Sch.2 to the 1972 Act restricts considerably, but not entirely, the extent to which this can be used to make provision conferring a power to legislate. Broadly speaking, it leaves it possible to confer powers to make procedural rules for a court or tribunal, to give directions "as to matters of administration" and to extend a power "to purposes of the like nature as those for which it was conferred".

(2) An instrument made under an Act of the Scottish Parliament, since Acts of the Scottish Parliament owe their authority to the Scotland Act 1998.[32]

---

[29] See Chapter 14, Section 3, para.14.3.1.
[30] Section 2.
[31] See Chapter 3, Section 2.
[32] 1998 c.46.

(3) Legislation made under a power conferred by a Measure of the National Assembly of the Church of England.[33]

SECTION 2

PRIMARY AND SUBORDINATE LEGISLATION

The distinction

All legislation can be classified as either primary or subordinate.[34] Quite simply, **1.2.1** legislation is subordinate if it owes its existence and authority to other legislation: if it does not, it is primary.

By far the most common and important kind of primary legislation is the Act of Parliament.[35] The only other form of primary legislation of practical modern significance is the prerogative Order in Council.[36] There are a number of other instruments which, although of limited modern significance, will require mention and which, to the extent that they deserve to be classified as legislation at all, are primary rather than secondary.[37]

While forms of primary legislation other than Acts are of little modern practical significance, that does not mean that the Act is the sole source of modern executive power, or even in all respects the most important. It should be remembered that much of government is achieved without legislation at all, and that the prerogative remains a significant source of executive power.[38]

It is sometimes necessary to define subordinate legislation as a class for the purposes of the application of a legislative provision. A helpful definition is provided by s.21(1) of the Interpretation Act 1978[39]—

> "In this Act . . . 'subordinate legislation' means Orders in Council, orders, rules, regulations, schemes, warrants, byelaws and other instruments made or to be made under any Act."

Other definitions of the term are found, and have occasionally been found to have undesired effect.[40]

---

[33] See Chapter 3, Section 7, para.3.7.6.

[34] As to synonymous and quasi-synonymous expressions for subordinate legislation, see Section 1.

[35] As to which see, in particular, Chapter 2.

[36] See Chapter 3, Section 2: since most modern Orders in Council are subordinate, the Order in Council is considered in that Chapter under the heading of subordinate legislation—but with reference also to the occasions on which Orders are prerogative and therefore primary.

[37] See Chapter 3, Section 7 and, in particular, those parts addressing Royal Charters, Proclamations, &c. and Resolutions of Parliament.

[38] Much can be done by the Crown under the Royal Prerogative without legislative authority of any kind. A list of prerogative powers was prepared as a Government Paper submitted to and published by the House of Commons Select Committee on Public Administration (Session 2002–03, Press Notice No.19 of October 27, 2003). And see also the discussion of the Royal Prerogative in Chapter 14, Section 2.

[39] 1978 c.30.

[40] See Section 1, footnote 23.

Significance of the distinction

1.2.2 Broadly speaking, legislation has to be treated in the same way whether it is primary or subordinate. Certainly, the public are no less obliged to comply with requirements of subordinate legislation than with requirements of primary legislation, and the courts are obliged to enforce rights and duties under the two equally.

It might therefore be thought that the distinction between the two kinds of legislation relates principally to the method of their being made, and is therefore of little interest to the citizen at any stage and of no interest at all after the event.

While that is true for most practical purposes, it ceases to be true in the case of legislation that is perceived as being unreasonably burdensome or in some other sense unfair. If the legislation is primary the opportunities for challenging it are severely limited, although there are some.[41] If the legislation is subordinate there is a far wider range of procedures through which and grounds on which it may be challenged.[42]

Other relatively minor distinctions between primary and subordinate legislation exist in matters relating to effect or construction, and these will be adverted to at the relevant places in this work.

Balance between primary and subordinate legislation

1.2.3 Much has been written and said over the years about the difficulty of achieving an ideal balance between primary and secondary legislation.[43] In essence, the aim in striking a balance is to avoid leaving too much of significance to be determined by the executive or the courts while at the same time preventing the principal purpose of the primary legislation from being obscured by an excess of complicated detail.[44] [45] Like many balances between conflicting desiderata, this is both easy to state and impossible to achieve to everybody's satisfaction.

---

[41] See Chapter 11, Section 3.

[42] See Chapter 3, Section 6.

[43] A useful summary of the arguments will be found in *Making the Law*, the Report of the Hansard Society Commission on the Legislative Process, The Hansard Society for Parliamentary Government, November 1992, paras 253 to 260 and the evidence referred to there.

[44] The division of an Act between clauses and Schedules is, of course, one way of preserving the flow of the main legislative story, relegating relatively minor details to the end. But that does not have the other advantages of secondary legislation, principally flexibility.

[45] Incidentally, although this is sometimes presented as if it were a modern tension arising from a new willingness of Parliament to dictate general ideas and leave details of execution to the executive, an interesting historical parallel can be drawn with the origins of statutory drafting, whereby petitions were passed in general terms by Parliament and the legislative details were left to a non-Parliamentary committee—see Chapter 5, Section1, footnote 1.

There are two principal advantages of the use of subordinate legislation: that it relieves pressure on Parliamentary time and that it offers flexibility.[46] There are a number of disadvantages of the use of subordinate legislation that have to be borne in mind in striking the correct balance. The advantages and disadvantages are discussed further below.

First advantage—relieving pressure on Parliamentary time

Almost every Bill in Parliament nowadays relegates a substantial amount of subordinate detail to be settled by the executive in subordinate legislation. The range of matters left to be settled in this way ranges from the amount of fees for specific services to, in effect, putting all the flesh on the statutory bones of an area of law. **1.2.4**

Two examples of the latter are Sch.4 to the Employment Relations Act 1999[47] and Pt 1 of the Commonhold and Leasehold Reform Act 2002.[48] Of these, the former consists entirely of enabling powers, of enormous breadth, providing for the regulation of complicated and important areas of employment law by subordinate legislation. The latter does give some idea of the intended structure of a commonhold system; but it does no more than that, leaving all the details to be provided by subordinate legislation.

The passage of the provisions about commonhold through Parliament was relatively uncontentious, but still occupied many hours of scrutiny in each House. If one tries to imagine how much scrutiny would have been thought necessary had the legislation occupied not thirty pages of principle but three-hundred or more pages of fine detail, it is easy to appreciate that the use of delegated legislation on a large scale is indispensable if Parliament is to pass the number of measures in each Session that is thought necessary by the executive to satisfy the nation's appetite for legal reform.

Length aside, it is clear that there are many matters of fine technical detail that have to be addressed in modern legislation that will be neither efficiently nor

---

[46] A departmental memorandum by the Department for Education and Employment to the House of Lords Select Committee on Delegated Powers and Deregulation on the Education Bill 1996–97 listed four acceptable purposes of secondary legislation in the following terms, approved by the Committee (Session 1996–97, 16th Report (HL Paper 43—February 12, 1997), para.2, footnote 2—

"avoiding too much technical and administrative detail on the face of the legislation, and keeping Bills shorter than they would otherwise be;

"ensuring flexibility in responding to changing circumstances, and a measure of ability to make changes quickly in the light of experience without the need for primary legislation;

"allowing detailed administrative arrangements to be set up and kept up-to-date within the basic structures and principles set out in the primary legislation, subject to Parliament's right to challenge any inappropriate use of powers; and

"allowing flexible timing to get legislation right, to consult, and to change it when circumstances change."

[47] 1999 c.26: Schedule 4 inserts into legislation elsewhere provisions granting wide enabling powers in relation to entitlement to time off from work for maternity and other domestic reasons.

[48] 2002 c.15.

adequately scrutinised by the mechanisms used for the passing of Bills. Statutory instruments are generally referred to committees for both technical[49] and substantive examination.[50]

Second advantage: flexibility

1.2.5 Subordinate legislation can be amended without any, or in some cases without much,[51] expenditure of Parliamentary time, so that anything which is likely to have to be altered in the light of experience or in order to react to changing circumstances is likely, *ceteris paribus*, to be more suited to secondary than to primary legislation.[52] The idea is that once Parliament has approved the fundamental principles of a legal change, it is not necessary to return, and occupy precious Parliamentary time, whenever the details require to be altered.

This has been understood and accepted for many decades. As the First Parliamentary Counsel, Sir Henry Jenkyns, wrote in an official minute in 1893—

> "Statutory rules are in themselves of great public advantage because the details . . . can thus be regulated after a Bill has passed into an Act with greater care and minuteness and with better adaptation to local or other special circumstances than they can possibly be in the passage of a Bill through Parliament. Beside, they mitigate the inelasticity which would otherwise make an act unworkable and are susceptible of modifications . . . as circumstances arise. . . . The method of delegated legislation permits of the rapid utilisation of experience and enables the results of consultation with interests affected by the operation of new Acts to be translated into practice. . . . It also permits of experiment being made and thus affords an opportunity, otherwise difficult to ensure, of utilising the lessons of experience."

---

[49] See Chapter 6, Section 2. The secretariat of the Joint Committee on Statutory Instruments is provided by the Counsel to the Speaker and lawyers working under him. These roles are commonly filled by former members of the Government Legal Service (and it has been common in the past for the Counsel to the Speaker to be a former Parliamentary Counsel). There is therefore a "poacher turned gamekeeper" element in the scrutiny offered to instruments by the Joint Committee's advisers, since having been occupied themselves for many years in the preparation of statutory instruments they are aware of the pressures and temptations to which the executive is subject and are admirably placed to control the technical aspects of subordinate legislation.

[50] See Chapter 6, Section 2. In the House of Lords statutory instruments are not generally referred for substantive examination in committee, and motions for approval or annulment are taken on the floor of the House—but often during the "dinner-hour", that is to say at a convenient break during the main business of the day and therefore at a time when the Chamber is expected to be attended only by those with particular interest and expertise in the substance of the instrument.

[51] See Chapter 6, Section 2.

[52] S.14 of the Interpretation Act 1978 (c.30) implies a power in the case of the most significant kinds of subordinate legislation to amend, revoke and re-enact.

An additional and essential aspect of the flexibility afforded by subordinate legislation is that while Parliament is not always in session, and indeed is unavailable during the summer months for a number of weeks at a time,[53] Ministers of the Crown are always available[54] for the making of emergency legislation.[55]

Dangers and disadvantages of subordinate legislation

One of the most thorough examinations of the dangers of the use of subordinate legislation is to be found in the report of the Committee on Ministers' Powers in 1932.[56] That Committee was particularly concerned by— **1.2.6**

(1) The extension of delegated powers to matters of principle and, particularly, to the imposition of taxation.[57]

(2) The delegation of power to amend Acts.

(3) The conferring of powers so wide that it is impossible to know what limits Parliament intended to impose.[58]

(4) The prohibition of control or inquiry by the courts.[59]

---

[53] Recall is, of course, always a possibility in the case of emergency legislation that is not suitable for subordinate legislation or for which the necessary legislative powers do not exist. Parliament was, for example, recalled in the summer of 1998 following the Omagh bomb for the purpose of passing the Criminal Justice (Terrorism and Conspiracy) Act 1998 (c.40). Although a Bill normally takes a number of months to pass into an Act, the entire process can be conflated into a few days or even hours where necessary: the 1998 Act, for example, was introduced on September 2, 1998 and received Royal Assent on the following day.

[54] Even in a general election campaign, when much of the normal business of government is suspended, Ministerial posts remain occupied and Ministers retain their full powers. The transition from one government to another is for all practical purposes seamless, with new senior Ministers being appointed and ready to sign legislation within a very few hours of the previous Ministry resigning in response to electoral defeat.

[55] For this reason it is common for provisions requiring legislation to be subject to affirmative resolution—as to which see Chapter 6, Section 2—to permit legislation to be made without prior scrutiny where the Minister making it thinks it necessary by reason of urgency—see, for example, s.13 of the European Parliamentary Elections Act 2002 (c.24).

[56] The "Donoughmore Committee"—(1932) Cmd. 4060; see, in particular, p.31.

[57] This is, however, a pass that has now been thoroughly sold. Cursory examination of an annual Finance Bill will reveal the width and variety of powers delegated in fiscal contexts.

[58] There are, of course, many powers conferred in very wide terms. But paradoxically the wider and more general the words of an enabling statute the less it can safely be relied on by the executive to do anything that the courts might find objectionable. In particular, if it is intended to confer a power to impose taxation, to make retrospective legislation, to create an offence or to confer jurisdiction—in short to do any of the things as to which a judicial rebuttable presumption exists as explored in Chapter 19 and in the other passages listed in the chart at the beginning of that Chapter—it will be imperative to confer express power, because without it the courts are likely to infer an absence of sufficient power irrespective of the generality and breadth of the general enabling words.

[59] As to ousters generally see Chapter 19; the considerations expressed there apply, and with even greater force, to subordinate legislation.

What is clear is that, whatever the theoretical considerations, subordinate legislation plays an increasingly important role. This is in part due to specific factors, such as the fact that a very large proportion of the legislative obligations that fall on the United Kingdom every year as a result of membership of the European Union both can be and, in practice, have to be implemented by statutory instrument under the European Communities Act 1972.[60]

There will remain certain matters that are thought inherently more suitable for primary than for secondary legislation.[61]

Specific instances apart, the more complex the world becomes, the more complex becomes the form of regulation required to control activities in accordance with social and political policy, the less suited that regulation becomes to primary legislation and the more necessary it becomes to confer and exercise enabling powers.[62]

Primary legislation referring to or amending secondary legislation

1.2.7 There is much to be said for keeping primary and secondary legislation apart. Differences both in the procedural and legal considerations which apply to each kind of legislation can cause difficulties when the two try to mix. But sometimes it is unavoidable.

There are an increasing number of areas of law in which the primary legislation cannot be more than, in effect, a skeletal set of powers to make subordinate legislation, either because the details of the legislation are simply too complicated and lengthy to pass in an Act, or because the details are constantly having to change to reflect a rapidly changing world.

When that is the case in one area of law, references to it in primary legislation dealing with other areas of law cannot avoid referring to, and if necessary amending, the secondary legislation that embodies the first area. A prime example is the Financial Services and Markets Act 2000,[63] much of which consists of broad powers, the exercise of which is often wholly or principally a matter of giving effect at United Kingdom law to legislation emanating from the

---

[60] 1972 c.68; see further Chapter 3, Section 10.

[61] See, for example, "As a general principle we believe that primary legislation and not secondary legislation is the appropriate tool by which to establish electoral rights."—18th Report of the House of Lords Select Committee on Scrutiny of Delegated Powers (on the Bill for the Northern Ireland (Entry to Negotiations) Act 1996 (c.11)) para.7; note also, for example, the observation of the House of Lords Select Committee on Delegated Powers and Deregulation that a particular power was too wide even if governed by affirmative resolution, and that the matter should be addressed in a different way on the face of the Bill (the Social Security Bill 1997–98)—Session 1997–98, 10th Report, (HL Paper 58, January 14, 1998).

[62] The resultant increasing importance of subordinate legislation is evident from the fact that the Tax Law Rewrite project (as to which see Section 10), set out intending to reproduce primary fiscal legislation, but found itself diverted into secondary legislation of particular importance: see the draft Income Tax (Pay as You Earn) Regulations published by the Tax Law Rewrite in April 2003, the foreword to which by the Paymaster General records that "Representatives of business and tax practitioners asked me to extend the Tax Law Rewrite Project to the PAYE regulations. I was happy to do so."

[63] 2000 c.8.

European Communities.[64] The result is that, for example, s.250 of and Sch.18 to the Enterprise Act 2002,[65] which deal with administrative receivership after the reconstruction by Pt 10 of that Act of the concept of companies going into administration as an alternative to insolvency, are forced in referring to concepts of financial transactions to operate predominantly by reference to provisions of secondary legislation made under the 2000 Act.

There are two principal practical difficulties about express references in **1.2.8** primary legislation to secondary legislation.

The first is the possibility that the secondary legislation will be revoked and re-enacted. Section 17(2)(a) of the Interpretation Act 1978[66] will help to convert references to the old provisions into references to the new where the conversion is straightforward: but it will not always be sufficiently clear, in the case of a re-enactment with modifications, to precisely what the old references should now refer. This difficulty is ameliorated somewhat by the fact that powers to make secondary legislation frequently include power to make consequential modification of primary legislation, although this is not achieved without controversy.[67]

The second difficulty is that of knowing precisely what the effect of the reference to secondary legislation is intended to be. In particular, where primary legislation glosses or modifies the effect of secondary legislation, it can be difficult to know whether it intends to rebut the presumption created by s.14 of the Interpretation Act 1978[68] that the power to make secondary legislation includes power to revoke and amend. Primary legislation certainly has the power to override secondary legislation, and it may therefore be that the amendment by the former of the latter is intended to oust the inherent jurisdiction of the person with power to make the secondary legislation to undo the amendment made by Parliament itself. The result is that it will often be necessary for the primary legislation to specify what degree of freedom it intends to leave to the person with power to make the affected secondary legislation to undo or alter what Parliament has done.[69]

Amendment of primary legislation by secondary legislation

The term "Henry VIII power" is commonly used to describe a delegated power **1.2.9** under which subordinate legislation is enabled to amend primary legislation.[70]

---

[64] As to which in general see Pt 5 of this work.

[65] 2002 c.40.

[66] 1978 c.30; see further Chapter 22.

[67] See below.

[68] 1978 c.30; see further Chapter 22.

[69] See, for example, s.14(2) of the Education Act 1994 (c.30): "The above amendment [of the Education (Teachers) Regulations 1993 (SI 1993/543)] shall not be taken as prejudicing the power to make further regulations revoking or amending the provision inserted."

[70] The House of Lords Select Committee on Delegated Powers and Deregulation defined a Henry VIII power as "a provision in a bill which enables primary legislation to be amended or repealed by subordinate legislation with or without further parliamentary scrutiny" (Report June 1997, Session 1997–98).

These powers attract particular scrutiny of the House of Lords when that House is considering the passage of new primary legislation.

The origin of the term as a description of powers of this kind is not entirely clear.[71]

The conferring by Parliament of Henry VIII powers is frequently criticised in Parliament itself. The following statements are representative—

"The question of the Henry VIII clauses, which arises in relation to clause 92 in particular, concerns me a great deal. . . . Such clauses crop up in far too many Bills. I described the European Representation Bill, which was introduced in the name of the Lord Chancellor, as having more of a Cardinal Wolsey clause than a Henry VIII clause. No doubt such measures are intended to try to reduce the range and extent of primary legislation, but we are already subjected to a considerable number of what are being described as knives, guillotines and programme motions. On top of that, we find that the draconian arrangements in clause 92 make this important Bill much more complicated, and much less democratic, because it can be amended by resolutions of the House, by regulation and by order."[72]

"As the Minister knows, I have no liking for Henry VIII clauses. . . . We are seeing them far too frequently."[73]

"I now invite the Committee's attention to paragraph 15 which relates to power to amend the Schedule. That is what we call a Henry VIII clause giving the Secretary of State power to amend primary legislation made by Parliament. We should try to avoid that wherever possible."[74]

"A Henry VIII clause properly so called—and perhaps we have previously misused the phrase—attempts to take out of the purview and jurisdiction of the court that decision as to the application of the law in the Act of Parliament and give it to a Minister. One thought that one had seen the end of crude Henry VIII clauses. Paragraphs (b) and (c) of Clause 33(7) are crude Henry VIII clauses. They purport to give to the Minister the power to decide whether the law has been complied with or not. As such, we object to them, and we believe, too, that they are highly suspect if one applies

---

[71] See Lord Dahrendorf in a House of Lords debate on delegated legislation (HL Deb. January 14, 2003 cc.166–167)—"After all, Henry VIII's infamous Statute of Proclamations—enabling the king to legislate by royal proclamation rather than due parliamentary process—was issued in 1539. It had a relatively early sunset as it was repealed on the King's death in 1547. The statute was not then called a Henry VIII power. In fact, I had some difficulty tracing the origin of this intriguing 'nickname' as the then Chairman of Committees, Lord Donoughmore, called it in his 1932 report by a committee on Ministers' powers."
[72] HC Deb. April 1, 2003 c.832—William Cash M.P., Crime (International Co-operation) Bill [Lords].
[73] HL Deb. March 17, 2003 c.59—Baroness Anelay of St Johns, Crime (International Co-operation) Bill [HL].
[74] HL Deb. July 15, 2002 c.1015—Lord Renton, Nationality, Immigration and Asylum Bill.

Article 6 of the European Convention on Human Rights, now incorporated by the Human Rights Act.

"Perhaps I may explain. To say that the Secretary of State can decide what is compliance is, in our submission, improper under the most elementary principles of the rule of law. Our amendment does not attempt to exclude the Secretary of State entirely. Our amendment says that the Secretary of State should not have the power to decide what is a completion in a particular case, or set of cases, but should have the right—since the Government wish to interpose the Secretary of State's view on these matters—to issue a code of practice for guidance on the matter. That, as I understand it, is unexceptionable. Tribunals can look at the code of practice and take account of it in deciding the judicial question of whether or not the Act has been contravened. In both cases, and in both paragraphs, we propose that the power to decide this judicial matter should not rest with the executive but that a power to give guidance—if that is what the Government want —should be introduced instead."[75]

A number of specific matters in relation to Henry VIII clauses are addressed by the Third Report of the House of Lords Select Committee on Delegated Powers and Regulatory Reform, Session 2002–03,[76] a Special Report which arose out of controversy during Third Reading in the House of Lords of the Bill for the Nationality, Immigration and Asylum Act 2002,[77] where the clause which became s.157 was introduced.[78] The substantive part of the Report is brief and can be given here in full— **1.2.10**

"The case for Henry VIII powers to make incidental, consequential and similar provision

"We were critical of the reasons given by the Government for the late inclusion of the Henry VIII powers in section 157 of the Nationality,

---

[75] HL Deb. March 25, 2002 C.W.H. 354—Lord Wedderburn of Charlton, Employment Bill.
[76] HL Paper 21; see also the Debate on the Report, HL Deb. January 14, 2003 cc.165–188.
[77] 2002 c.41.
[78] S.157 is a Henry VIII power thought by some, even in its final form, to be of unusual breadth—

"157 Consequential and incidental provision
  (1) The Secretary of State may by order make consequential or incidental provision in connection with a provision of this Act.
  (2) An order under this section may, in particular—
    (a) amend an enactment;
    (b) modify the effect of an enactment.
  (3) An order under this section must be made by statutory instrument.
  (4) An order under this section which amends an enactment shall not be made unless a draft has been laid before and approved by resolution of each House of Parliament.
  (5) Any other order under this section shall be subject to annulment pursuant to a resolution of either House of Parliament."
See also Chapter 14, Section 3.

Immigration and Asylum Act. We have no doubt, however, that there are occasions when Henry VIII powers to make incidental, consequential and similar provision are justified: for example, when the number of incidental, consequential etc. amendments would cause a disproportionate increase in the length of a bill or when, as a matter of practicality, it would be difficult to anticipate the full extent of such amendments during the passage of a bill.

"Standard words

"We note that of the twelve examples we considered each is worded differently. We think that it is debatable whether there should be a presumption that standard wording should be used (with a requirement that any departure from that wording should be explicitly justified). We recognise that such an arrangement would have the benefit of making legislation clearer and simpler. We note, however, the point raised by the First Parliamentary Counsel that standard wording would have to be comprehensive and would therefore run the risk of being broader than necessary in a particular case. In the light of the comments by the First Parliamentary Counsel, we are persuaded that the Government should, in the Explanatory Notes accompanying any new bill, as well as in their memorandum to this Committee, offer an explanation of the reasons why a particular form of wording has been adopted in each case.

"Parliamentary scrutiny

"We note again with regard to the twelve appended examples that, as with their wording, the level of Parliamentary scrutiny varies. In some cases the negative procedure is used; in some the affirmative; and in others the affirmative procedure is used if an enactment is to be amended but otherwise negative. We are not surprised that this is the case. We recognise that in some instances the negative procedure provides a sufficient level of Parliamentary scrutiny. We take the view, however, that there should be a presumption in favour of the affirmative procedure and that reasons for any departure from the affirmative procedure should be set out in full in the Explanatory Notes accompanying a bill and in the memorandum submitted to this Committee."

1.2.11   A Henry VIII power may not be sufficient to permit amendment of the Act which confers it unless it does so expressly.[79]

As to the kind of amendment that is permitted to be made under a Henry VIII power, as with all delegated powers the only rule for construction is to test each proposed exercise by reference to whether or not it is within the class of action

---

[79] See, for example, the Enterprise Act 2002 (c.40), s.277(2).

that Parliament must have contemplated when delegating. Although Henry VIII powers are often cast in very wide terms, the more general the words used by Parliament to delegate a power, the more likely it is that an exercise within the literal meaning of the words will nevertheless be outside the legislature's contemplation.

A statutory provision conferring a power will be subject to the same rebuttable presumptions as other statutory provisions. These presumptions may be creations of the common law[80] or of statute.[81] It will be rare that it is safe to assume, in the absence of express provision, that Parliament intended to permit textual or non-textual interference with a general presumption.

In respect of the class of "constitutional" enactments identified by Laws L.J. in *Thoburn v Sunderland City Council*[82] which, not by reason of purported entrenchment through a rebuttable presumption but by reason of importance, are to be regarded as having a particular strength which puts them, for example, beyond the reach of the traditional doctrine of implied repeal, again it will probably be rarely safe to assume, in the absence of express provision, that Parliament intended to permit textual or non-textual interference.[83]

In respect both of presumptions and constitutional enactments, however, it **1.2.12** may be safe to assume power to interfere under a general Henry VIII power if the proposed interference is either—

(a)   trivial in so far as it concerns the substance of the presumption or the constitutional enactment, or

(b)   so much of the essence of the effective use of the delegated power that the delegation would be nugatory were the interference not permitted.

While a Henry VIII power may be of enormous width, there are certain matters that are generally felt to be unsuitable for delegation in this way. Note, for example, the following comment of the House of Lords Select Committee on Delegated Powers and Deregulation in relation to a power in the Hunting Bill 2000–01 to remove a defence from the Bill by subordinate instrument[84]—

"We do not accept that it is appropriate to delegate a power which allows such a fundamental change to be made—if there should come a time when ministers are of opinion that a defence is allowing activities which they believe Parliament had intended the bill to stop, then the appropriate way to change the law is by bill."

---

[80] As to which see Chapter 19.
[81] For example, s.2(4) of the European Communities Act 1972 (c.68), s.3(1) of the Human Rights Act 1998 (c.42), s.5 of the Oaths Act 1978 (c.19) and the Interpretation Act 1978 (c.30).
[82] [2003] Q.B. 151; see further Section 4.
[83] See Section 4, para.1.4.3, footnote 38.
[84] Session 2000–01, 13th Report March 7, 2001, para.3.

In similar vein, irrespective of the legal width of the power conferred there may be things that Parliamentarians will feel ought not to be done in reliance on the power, being more appropriate for primary legislation.[85]

1.2.13   As is noted elsewhere[86] as a general rule affirmative resolution is thought appropriate for the exercise of a Henry VIII power. But there are exceptional cases where the power is so trivial, or the likely basis on which it will be exercised is so lacking in contention, that it is neither necessary nor desirable to occupy Parliamentary time with motions for approval.[87]

It is unlikely ever to be generally thought acceptable to have a Henry VIII power subject to no form of Parliamentary scrutiny at all.[88]

An unusual and extreme form of Henry VIII power is the power for the executive to repeal all or some of an Act.[89]

SECTION 3

PUBLIC AND PRIVATE LEGISLATION; GENERAL, LOCAL AND PERSONAL LEGISLATION

Introduction

1.3.1   Most Acts of Parliament of modern significance are described as public general Acts,[90] and this is certainly the kind of Act of Parliament with which people

---

[85] Hence, for example, " ... the power to modify was intended to be used to accommodate the provisions of the Road Traffic Act 1991 to local circumstances. We regard this use of it, to remedy defects in a public general act in a piecemeal way as opportunity may arise, as unusual and unexpected"—Joint Committee on Statutory Instruments, Session 1995–96, 25th Report, para.2, (HL Paper 98, HC 34-xxiv) in relation to the Road Traffic (Permitted Parking Area and Special Parking Area) (County of Hampshire, City of Winchester) Order 1996 (SI 1996/1171).

[86] Chapter 6, Section 2.

[87] See, for example, the following comment from the Second Report for Session 1996–97 of the House of Lords Select Committee on Delegated Powers and Deregulation (HL Paper 7, November 7, 1996, paras 2 to 4)—"The power is limited to amending the text of an international convention to give effect to action taken under it and is well precedented. We are satisfied that negative procedure is appropriate." (in relation to s.182C of the Merchant Shipping Act 1995 (c.21) inserted by the Merchant Shipping and Maritime Security Act 1997 (c.28)).

[88] Note "The Committee believes that this is the first Henry VIII provision which it has considered which is not subject at least to negative resolution procedure. Indeed, the Government's evidence to this Committee in 1993 stated that 'Ministers have undertaken that such [*i.e.* Henry VIII] powers will not be sought without the most careful consideration, and they invariably attract the special attention and scrutiny of Parliament'. In the view of this Committee, a Henry VIII provision can never be so trivial as not to justify some Parliamentary scrutiny."—House of Lords Select Committee on Delegated Powers and Deregulation, Session 1996–97, 16th Report, (HL Paper 43, February 12, 1997).

[89] See, for example, s.18(3) and (4) of the Deep Sea Mining (Temporary Provisions) Act 1981 (c.53)—

"(3) If it appears to the Secretary of State that an international agreement on the law of the sea which has been adopted by a United National Conference on the Law of the Sea is to be given effect within the United Kingdom the Secretary of State may by order provide for the repeal of this Act.

(4) An order under subsection (3) above shall not be made unless a draft thereof has been approved by resolution of each House of Parliament."

[90] This has been the case at least for centuries: and for the reason for a recent accelerated diminution in the number of local Acts see below.

nowadays are most familiar and concerned. They form part of the law of one or more of the constituent parts of the United Kingdom[91] and deal with matters which, at least in theory, are of general application.

Historically, "Before 1797 there were only two categories of Acts of Parliament, public and private; the private Act series commenced in 1539. In 1797 public Acts were divided into two series, public general Acts and public local Acts. After 1948 private Acts were known as personal Acts."[92]

The non-public series is actually a series of local and personal Acts, but has come to be styled simply as the series of Local Acts.

The description "public general" in relation to an Act contains two notions, the notion of public-ness and the notion of generality.[93] The distinctions to be drawn are therefore—

(a) whether an Act is public or private, and

(b) whether an Act is general, on the one hand, or local or personal, on the other.

This Section explains the nature of these distinctions and introduces the concept of Acts other than public general Acts.

Irrelevance of classification of Parliamentary Bills

A source of potential confusion to be dismissed at the outset is the fact that whether a Parliamentary Bill is public or private is not determinative of whether the resultant Act is public or private.   **1.3.2**

In relation to Bills the concepts of being public or private relate to the application of two sets of procedures. In essence, the proceedings on a public Bill are designed to focus on the consideration of issues thought to be of general

---

[91] As explained above, for convenience of expression this work will refer frequently to "the law of the United Kingdom". It should be remembered, however, and will be of particular importance in relation to the extent of statutes—as to which see Chapter 11, Section 1—that there is strictly speaking no such corpus of law. There are instead three bodies of law, the law of England and Wales, the law of Scotland and the Law of Northern Ireland. A reference to the law of the United Kingdom is however a useful shorthand the meaning, and limitations, of which will be readily apparent.

[92] Report by Chairmen of Law Commission and Scottish Law Commission on chronological table of local legislation to Lord Chancellor's Advisory Committee on Statute Law (ACSL (96) 3) 21.xii.95, para.6, note 1.

[93] It should be noted at the outset that an Act which is classified as both public and general may in practice affect only a very limited class of persons directly. An obvious example would be those Acts which concern a particular profession. An Act of this kind may be brought in on a private Bill, private in the sense that it is sponsored and proposed by the profession concerned to achieve a particular purpose. But an Act concerning a profession would be general if it sought to regulate the activities of members of that profession for the assumed benefit of those members of the public who seek to benefit from their services: see, for example, the Osteopaths Act 1993 (c.21). The former class of Act, although technically private prior to enactment, may be of very widespread interest. While the latter class, although technically public both as a Bill and as an Act, may in practice concern only a very small proportion of the population.

public political interest, while the procedures on a private Bill are designed to facilitate the expression and consideration of particular private interests that are affected by the legislation proposed. So a Parliamentary Bill is public, in the sense of being subjected to the procedures of the two Houses relating to public Bills, if it deals with matters of public interest, while a Bill will be subjected to the procedures for private Bills if it affects only the interests of particular people or places.

This picture is further complicated by the fact that a Bill presented in either House by a Minister of the Crown is treated as a public Bill, although if it affects particular private interests in certain ways it may be deemed "hybrid" for the purposes of the rules of the House and subjected to a procedure which partakes partly of the characteristics of private Bill procedure and partly of the characteristics of public Bill procedure.

1.3.3   A public Bill always becomes a public Act on receiving Royal Assent. A private Bill may become either a public or a private Act; but, as mentioned below, for many decades it has been the rule that all Bills become public Acts unless they expressly provide to the contrary.

These days an Act is likely to contain provision for classification as private only if it is personal in nature. But a wide range of Bills that result in public Acts (but not public general Acts) are introduced and treated as private Bills in Parliament.

A private Bill that is purely local in nature—the most common kind nowadays—will result in a public Act.

A private Bill that is personal in nature will result in a private Act. These have long been a rarity and have all but become extinct.[94] Their most common purpose is to enable a marriage between otherwise forbidden relationships, something which is still very occasionally necessary[95] but which for the most part has been rendered unnecessary by changes in general legislation.[96] At one stage personal Acts were used to effect divorce: the last divorce Act was passed in 1922.[97]

---

[94] Although as will be seen their occasional revival for particular matters is possible. The classes of matter for which personal and private Acts have been used—some of which continue to have potential relevance for occasional use—include: annuities and grants of money; divorce; estates; change of name; naturalisation; patents; restoration of dignities; and there is no fixed limitation on the range of matters for which a personal Act could be used. While some of these areas have clearly been entirely transferred to regulation by public and general Act, others have not, and in other cases the transfer may turn out to have been less complete than was thought.

[95] See, for example, the Edward Berry and Doris Eilleen Ward (Marriage Enabling) Act 1980 (c.1), the John Ernest Rolfe and Florence Iveen Rolfe (Marriage Enabling) Act 1987 (c.1) and the George Donald Evans and Deborah Jane Evans (Marriage Enabling) Act 1987 (c.2) which were Acts designed to permit the marriage of a parent-in-law to a child-in-law or of a step-parent to a step-child.

[96] See, in particular, the Marriage (Enabling) Act 1960 (c.29) and the Marriage (Prohibited Degrees of Relationship) Act 1986 (c.16); and note, for historical purposes, the following two Acts replaced by the 1960 Act: the Deceased Brother's Widow's Marriage Act 1921 (c.24) and the Deceased Wife's Sister's Marriage Act 1907 (c.47).

[97] *Babington, Hume and Dorothy M* (12–13 GV—not printed or numbered).

Irrelevance of division of public and private law

It should also be noted at the outset that the distinction between public and **1.3.4** private legislation is separate from and unaffected by the division of law into public law and private law.[98] Public legislation frequently deals with matters of private law. Private legislation could have effects at public law.

Distinction between public and private legislation

In fact, almost all Acts nowadays are public, meaning that they form part of the **1.3.5** corpus of law of which the courts will take judicial notice (that is to say, will take for granted and regard as not requiring proof) and which are, generally speaking, to be regarded as within the knowledge of all citizens.[99] It is now, and has been for many decades, a rule[1] that "every Act is a public Act to be judicially noticed as such, unless the contrary is expressly provided by the Act".[2]

Before the enactment of this rule[3] it could be a matter of some difficulty to determine whether an Act were public or not. The criteria to be applied and the manner of their application, as well as something of the historical development of the concepts, are expounded in the judgments of Lord Esher M.R. and Bowen L.J. in *The Queen On The Prosecution Of The St. Giles Board Of Work And Others v London County Council*,[4] in passages which are appended to this work[5] because of their authoritative exposition of a distinction which, while principally of historical importance, is fundamental to a still-used classification of primary legislation (and which may still be of occasional importance in relation to legislation which while old is still effective).

A public Act may on occasion deal entirely with private matters, that is to say the appropriation and management of specific land[6]: see, for example, the

---

[98] Taking a definition along the lines of that provided by Professor Glanville Williams in *The Divisions of the Law*, Appendix III to the Tenth Edition of *Salmond on Jurisprudence*, London 1947—"After the Introduction comes the body of Private Law as opposed to that of Public Law. By general consent this Roman distinction between *jus privatum* and *jus publicum* is accepted as the most fundamental division of the *corpus juris*. Public law comprises the rules which specially relate to the structure, powers, rights, and activities of the state. Private law includes all the residue of legal principles. It comprises all those rules which specially concern the subjects of the state in their relations to each other, together with those rules which are common to the state and its subjects."

[99] See further Chapter 9, Section 1.

[1] Interpretation Act 1978 (c.30), s.3 (derived from the Interpretation Act 1889 (c.63).

[2] As in, for example, s.9 of the Lucas Estate Act 1963 (c.1)—"This Act shall not be a public Act but shall be printed by the several printers to the Queen's most Excellent Majesty duly authorised to print the statutes of the United Kingdom and a copy thereof so printed by any of them shall be admitted as evidence thereof by all judges, justices and others." It is unclear what would be the benefit of including a provision of this kind in an Act nowadays.

[3] Which dates from Lord Brougham's Act of 1850, s.7.

[4] [1893] 2 Q.B. 454, 458–60, CA.

[5] Appendix, Extract 1.

[6] "An Act to appropriate certain lands for the purposes of the National Gallery and the National Portrait Gallery and for other purposes connected therewith, and to make provision with respect to certain Crown lands forming part of or adjacent to St. James' Park." (Long Title).

National Gallery and St. James's Park Act 1911.[7] And a public Act may repeal or amend a private Act.[8]

It should be noted that the term "private" may be used in various ways as a legislative term itself describing legislation, and the reader needs to have regard to the context and to any express definition.[9]

Distinction between general legislation and local or personal legislation

1.3.6   The second distinction inherent in the concept of the public general Act of Parliament is that between legislation which is general in its effect and that which is purely local or personal. The criteria are easy to state in theory but can be difficult to apply in practice. The position remains as expressed more than a century ago by Bowen L.J.[10]—

> "Now, a general Act, *prima facie*, is that which applies to the whole community. In the natural meaning of the term it means an Act of Parliament which is unlimited both in its area and, as regards the individual, in its effects; and as opposed to that you get statutes which may well be public because of the importance of the subjects with which they deal and their general interest to the community, but which are limited in respect of area—a limitation which makes them local—or limited in respect of individuals or persons—a limitation which makes them personal."

It can readily be appreciated from reading this definition that there will be occasions on which it is difficult to say whether an Act is of general application or not for the purposes of this classification. For example, an Act which deals with specific property interests for the purpose of constructing a facility which will be importance to the public generally.[11] Acts of this kind introduced by the Government are treated as partly private during their Parliamentary proceedings[12] but are classified as public and general when they receive Royal Assent.

---

[7] 1911 c.23: note that the Bill for this Act was presented in the House of Lords, referred to the Examiners (as to which see Chapter 5, Section 4), certified by the Examiners (May 22, 1911), passed, sent to the Commons, referred to the Examiners and reported (July 18, 1911) and passed.

[8] See, for example, the repeal of s.53 of the British Transport Commission Act 1949 (c.xxix) by Sch.8 to the Railways and Transport Safety Act 2003 (c.20); or the amendments by Sch.2 to the Commonwealth Institute Act 1958 (c.16) of the Imperial Institute Act 1925 (c.xvii).

[9] S.121(4) of the Local Government etc. (Scotland) Act 1994 (c.39), for example, provides—
> "(4) In paragraph (b) of subsection (1) above, 'private legislation in Parliament' includes—
> (a) a provisional order and a Confirmation Bill relating to such an order; and
> (b) any local or personal Bill."

[10] *R. v London County Council* [1893] 2 Q.B. 454, 462, CA.

[11] As in the case, for example, of the Channel Tunnel Rail Link Act 1996 (c.61).

[12] See Chapter 5, Section 4.

It is worth noting at this point that matters relating to London are generally regarded as being of general interest, so that legislation that applies exclusively to London is treated as general.[13]

Diminishing significance of private Bills and of local and personal Acts

As recently as 50 years ago private Bills and local and personal Acts were of immense importance in almost every area of life. The significance is well illustrated by a passage from the writings of a former Clerk in the House of Commons in an extract appended to this work[14] and by a passage from a Law Commission Report also appended to this work.[15] And the public took much note of the passage of private Bills through Parliament, the progress of which was often seen as being of immense social and commercial significance.[16]

    Since that time, the importance of private Bills and local and personal Acts has fast dwindled, through two causes.[17] First, a number of subjects which were once thought to be of a private or localised nature are now thought of as fit for public legislation.[18] For example—

(1) Matters of health and safety are no longer dealt with for the most part by local by-laws but under the extensive delegated powers under the Health and Safety at Work etc. Act 1974.[19]

(2) The extensive powers of the Transport Police grew originally out of a series of local enactments (relating to individual enterprises and forces) and were not fully and finally handed over to the province of public general legislation until the Railways and Transport Safety Act 2003.[20]

    The second reason for the diminishing importance of private Bills is the rise of a number of procedures designed to fulfil some or all of the function previously performed by private legislation.[21]

1.3.7

1.3.8

---

[13] So the Greater London Authority Act 1999 (c.29) is listed as a public general Act and the Bill for it was treated as neither private nor hybrid.

[14] Appendix, Extract 2.

[15] Appendix, Extract 3.

[16] See the fictitious, but highly realistic and atmospheric, description of the Committee proceedings on the Limehouse and Rotherhithe Bridge Bill, and their effect on the share prices of related commercial undertakings, in Trollope's *The Three Clerks* (1859).

[17] "A few years ago, the private business of the House reduced considerably after both an inquiry into private business and the changes that, by and large, took transport and works business out of the private Bill procedure."—HC Deb. June 16, 1997 c.70 *per* Simon Hughes M.P.

[18] There are also trivial matters that were legislated for originally by private legislation and have since been amended by public legislation: see, for example, the Imperial Institute Act 1925 (c.xvii) amended by the Commonwealth Institute Act 1958 (c.16).

[19] 1974 c.37.

[20] 2003 c.20: see, in particular, ss.18 and 72 and Sch.5 (the first paragraph of which repeals s.53 of the British Transport Commission Act 1949 (c.xxix)).

[21] See, in particular, Chapter 3, Section 8.

There are still, however, occasional instances, of considerable significance for those involved, of matters that cannot be dealt with except by a Bill becoming a Local Act of Parliament. Of the five Local Acts of 2003, for example, one dealt with a quirk of international company law,[22] three dealt with municipal powers[23] and one dealt not with the purchase of land but with information in relation to interests in land.[24]

Clauses Acts

1.3.9 In the nineteenth century in particular private Acts dealing with particular kinds of matter proliferated, notably in relation to the incorporation of bodies and the purchase of land for railways and other kinds of development. There were

---

[22] The preamble to the Transas Group Act 2003 (c.v) explains the need for the Act in the following terms—

"... (11) Having regard to the fact that the area of operation of the Companies (except for Transas Marine Limited) is mainly outside the United Kingdom, certain advantages would accrue to certain of the Companies if their incorporations and undertakings were transferred to the Republic of Ireland:

(12) No procedure exists whereby the incorporation of a company to which the Companies Act 1985 (c.6) applies can be transferred from England to another country:

(13) Under and subject to the law relating to corporations in the Republic of Ireland each of the Companies whose incorporations would be transferred to the Republic of Ireland under this Act will be able, on the passing of this Act, to become incorporated by way of universal transfer in Transas Limited and duly registered in that state:

(14) It is expedient that the other provisions in this Act should be enacted:

(15) The objects of this Act cannot be attained without the authority of Parliament."

[23] The preamble to the Nottingham City Council Act 2003 (c.ii) explains the need for the Act in the following terms—

"WHEREAS—

(1) The Nottingham City Council ("the council") was established under the Local Government Act 1992 (c.19) as a unitary authority for the city of Nottingham ("the city"):

(2) The council wishes to reduce the incidence of offences under the Theft Act 1968 (c.60) by regulating trade in second-hand goods:

(3) It is expedient that the council should have the power to register dealers in second-hand goods within the city:

(4) It is expedient that the council should have the power to obtain information about occasional sales and squat trading:

(5) It is expedient that the other provisions contained within this Act should be enacted:

(6) The purposes of this Act cannot be effected without the authority of Parliament:

(7) In relation to the promotion of the Bill for this Act the requirements of section 239 of the Local Government Act 1972 (c.70) have been observed:"

See also the London Local Authorities and Transport for London Act 2003 (c.iii) and the Hereford Markets Act 2003 (c.iv).

[24] The preamble to the London Development Agency Act 2003 (c.i) explains the need for the Act in the following terms—

"WHEREAS—

(1) It is expedient that in carrying out its functions the London Development Agency should be enabled to require information as to interests in land:

(2) In relation to the promotion of the Bill for this Act the London Development Agency have complied with the requirements of section 26A of and Schedule 6A to the Regional Development Agencies Act 1998 (c.45):

(3) The objects of this Act cannot be attained without the authority of Parliament."

obvious advantages to be gained from having a certain amount of standardisation among these Acts, and this was achieved to some extent by the enactment of Clauses Acts, each of which set out common-form provisions which were thereby made available for incorporation in the individual private Acts. The result was to promote brevity in private Acts while at the same time enhancing their legal certainty.

The demise of the private Act as a tool of primary importance has led to the gradual abandonment of Clauses Acts, most of which are now repealed, although in most cases with savings that could still be of occasional significance. There are one or two that are still of occasional practical utility.[25]

Subordinate legislation

The distinction between public instruments on the one hand and local instruments on the other is broadly the same as for Acts. There are, as would be expected, a significant number each year of instruments of a purely local character.[26] There is no class of personal or private statutory instruments, although it is of course possible to have an instrument which affects only specific individuals or private interests.[27]   **1.3.10**

Hybridity, as expounded in relation to Acts in Chapter 5, Section 4, has very limited relevance to statutory instruments. In the House of Commons hybridity

---

[25] See the Cemeteries Clauses Act 1847 (c.65), the Commissioners Clauses Act 1847 (c.16), the Companies Clauses Act 1863 (c.118), the Companies Clauses Consolidation Act 1845 (1845 c.16), and the Lands Clauses Consolidation Act 1845 (c.18).

[26] For example, in connection with the designation of particular roads or other traffic matters. See, for example, the M2 Junction 2 to A228 Link Road (Trunking) Order 2003 (SI 2003/1600), the A500 Trunk Road (Stoke Pathfinder Project) and Slip Roads Order 2003 (SI 2003/1601), the Alconbury Airfield (Rail Facilities and Connection to East Coast Main Line) Order 2003 (SI 2003/3364) or the Road Traffic (Permitted Parking Area and Special Parking Area) (County of Carmarthenshire) Order 2004 (SI 2004/104(W.11)).

[27] See, for example, art.4 of the Education (School Curriculum and Assessment Authority) (Transfer of Functions) Order 1995 (SI 1995/903) (made under s.252 of the Education Act 1993 (c.35))—

"**Supplementary, incidental and consequential provisions—transfer of staff**

4.—(1) This article applies in relation to the [School Curriculum and Assessment Authority]'s employee Robin Bateman if he is employed under a contract of employment with the Authority immediately before the coming into force of this Order.

(2) That contract of employment shall have effect as if originally made between Robin Bateman and ACAC [Awdurdod Cwricwlwm Ac Asesu Cymru or the Curriculum and Assessment Authority for Wales].

(3) Without prejudice to paragraph (2), all the Authority's rights, powers, duties and liabilities under or in connection with that contract of employment shall by virtue of that paragraph be transferred to ACAC on the day on which this order comes into force and anything done before that day by or in relation to the Authority in respect of that contract or Robin Bateman shall be deemed from that day to have been done by or in relation to ACAC.

(4) Paragraphs (2) and (3) above are without prejudice to any right of Robin Bateman to terminate his contract of employment if a substantial change is made to his detriment in his working conditions, but no such right shall arise by reason only of the change in employer effected by paragraph (2) above."

See also the Education (Chief Inspector of Schools in Wales) Order 1992 (SI 1992/1739) and note the following comment of the Joint Committee on Statutory Instruments (Session 1992–93, 10th

27

has no place in the procedures relating to statutory instruments, and in the House of Lords the concept is relevant only to instruments which are required by statute to receive an affirmative resolution of each House.[28]

Construction

1.3.11 The question of differential construction of private and public Acts is discussed in Chapter 29.

Introduction to Sections 4 to 10

Descriptive Classes of Legislation

1.4.0 There is, of course, no limit to the number of different ways in which it is possible to divide and classify legislation. Apart from those of fundamental importance already described, this work discusses in Sections 4 to 10 below a number of descriptions of legislation that appear likely to be of particular relevance to readers of modern statutes, and which could occasionally be useful for the purposes of classification.

Some methods of classification that may once have been of interest are now of little or no utility. Earlier editions of this work, for example, discuss an ancient classification of remedial Acts[29]: by the time of the last edition this class had already ceased to have much significance because of the displacement of the common law in an increasing number of areas of law.[30] Similarly, the concept of the enabling Act[31] is of little utility as a method of classification now that almost no statute is passed without conferring a range of powers on the executive or on others.[32]

While there is no end to the number of different ways of classifying legislation whether by substance, form or procedure, there are few substantive forms of descriptive classification that serve much in the way of practical purpose.

Report, para.2, HL Paper 33, HC 51-x)—"the name . . . of the person appointed . . . is given . . . but no other means of identification is provided. Many of the names are likely to be common to a number (in some cases a large number) of people. There is therefore a need for something to identify further the individuals intended."

[28] Standing Orders of the House of Lords relating to Public Business, S.O. 72(1)(c).
[29] See 7th ed. (1971) p.60.
[30] As to which see Chapter 14, Sections 1 and 2.
[31] See 7th ed. (1971) p.61.
[32] As to which see Chapter 12.

Section 4

Constitutional Legislation

Introduction

A category of constitutional legislation has been identified in recent years[33] in the context of the discussion of the application of the doctrine of implied repeal.[34] In essence, it has been established that certain statutes are intended by Parliament to alter the fabric of the constitutional arrangements of the United Kingdom in a way that, of their nature, are not to be altered or abrogated by Parliament except by clear and unequivocal legislative words.

1.4.1

Nature of the class

The nature of the class is established in the following extract of the judgment of Laws L.J. in *Thoburn v Sunderland City Council*[35]—

1.4.2

"62. . . . In my opinion a constitutional statute is one which (a) conditions the legal relationship between citizen and State in some general, over-arching manner, or (b) enlarges or diminishes the scope of what we would now regard as fundamental constitutional rights. (a) and (b) are of necessity closely related: it is difficult to think of an instance of (a) that is not also an instance of (b). The special status of constitutional statutes follows the special status of constitutional rights. Examples are the Magna Carta, the Bill of Rights 1689, the Act of Union,[36] the Reform Acts which distributed and enlarged the franchise, the Human Rights Act 1998, the Scotland Act 1998 and the Government of Wales Act 1998. The European Communities Act 1972 clearly belongs in this family. It incorporated the whole corpus of substantive Community rights and obligations, and gave overriding domestic effect to the judicial and administrative machinery of Community law. It

---

[33] Compare the following passage from A. V. Dicey, *The Law of the Constitution*, 7th ed. 1908, pp.22–23—"Constitutional law, as the term is used in England, appears to include all rules which directly or indirectly affect the distribution or the exercise of the sovereign power in the state. . . . The one set of rules are in the strictest sense 'laws' since they are rules which (whether written or unwritten, whether enacted by statute or derived from a mass of custom, tradition, or judge-made maxims known as the common law) are enforced by the courts; these rules constitute 'constitutional law' in the proper sense of that term, and may for the sake of distinction be called collectively 'the law of the constitution.' The other set of rules consist of conventions, understandings, habits, or practices which, though they may regulate the conduct of the several members of the sovereign power, of the ministry, or of other officials, are not in reality laws at all since they are not enforced by the courts. This portion of constitutional law may, for the sake of distinction, be termed the 'conventions of the constitution,' or constitutional morality."

[34] See Chapter 14, Section 4.

[35] [2003] Q.B. 151.

[36] Which is no longer to be treated as a treaty in international law (see proceedings in House of Lords Committee for Privileges in respect of Lord Gray's Motion on the House of Lords Bill 1999–2000 [2000] 2 W.L.R. 664, HL Committee for Privileges).

may be there has never been a statute having such profound effects on so many dimensions of our daily lives. The European Communities Act 1972 is, by force of the common law, a constitutional statute."

Consequences of the doctrine

1.4.3   The consequences of the doctrine of constitutional statutes, and the relationship of this notion with the fundamental doctrine of Parliamentary supremacy, is explored in the lengthy extract of Laws L.J.'s judgment in *Thoburn* appended to this work.[37]

In essence, the principal effects of the establishment of the class are—

i. that members of the class will be assumed not to be substantively amended or repealed by reason only of inconsistency with later enactments, and

ii. that the members of the class will be more carefully protected by the judges from interference of various kinds (such as amendment under statutory powers expressly permitting amendment of legislation in general) than will other statutes.[38]

---

[37] Appendix, Extract 4.

[38] Hence the following observations of the passage of the Government's Response to the Report of the Joint Committee on the Draft Civil Contingencies Bill (January 2004, Cm. 6078, para. 34)—"We have sought advice from Parliamentary Counsel as to the scope of the power to "modify or disapply an enactment", and in particular whether it would permit regulations under Part 2 of the Bill to modify an enactment which has constitutional importance—such as the Human Rights Act 1998 or the Bill of Rights Act 1689. They have advised that each proposed exercise of such a power must be assessed by reference to whether or not it is within the class of action that Parliament must have contemplated when conferring the power. There are certain rebuttable presumptions as to what Parliament must have intended in conferring a power of this kind. These may be presumptions of common law (for example, the presumption against the imposition of taxation) or presumptions based on statute (for example, s.2 of the European Communities Act 1972 or s.3 of the Human Rights Act 1998). These presumptions apply even where Parliament has used general language. The courts have also suggested rules in relation to provisions of particular constitutional importance, requiring statutory modification to be express. The Bill does not contain any express provision that enables regulations under Part 2 of the Bill to modify or disapply a constitutional enactment. While the specific powers listed in the Bill are very wideranging, they are capable of being exercised without interfering with a constitutional enactment. In particular, they are capable of being exercised in accordance with the Convention rights. Nor is the permission to do anything that an Act could do sufficiently precise to displace the general approach detailed above. In light of this, Parliamentary Counsel have advised that, in exercising the power conferred under Part 2 of the Bill, in the unlikely event of needing to use this power, Parliament will not permit interference either with a general presumption or with a "constitutional" enactment. However, it may be safe to assume that Parliament intended to confer the power to interfere with such a statute if the interference is trivial in so far as it concerns the substance of the presumption or the constitutional enactment. Given the inherent limits on the scope of the power, Parliamentary Counsel have advised that if we wished to be able to modify or disapply a constitutional enactment, we should take an express power to do so. We do not propose to do this. Without such an express power, we cannot presently envisage circumstances in which this power would lawfully enable us to make a substantive amendment to a constitutional enactment. In light of this, the Government does not consider that it is appropriate expressly to protect the enactments cited by the Committee from modification or disapplication. The effect of the current drafting appears to achieve the right result in a less inflexible way."

It is likely that now that the class has been identified other purposes for it, or characteristics of it, will be found. In relation to Acts passed before *Thoburn*, however, it will be necessary to have in mind that when they were framed there was no concept that one Act was more important or less vulnerable than any other. Draftsmen of new Acts will, of course, turn their minds to whether the courts are likely to construe them as constitutional enactments, and it is conceivable that in a borderline case where the Act's status was likely to be of particular importance it would be thought necessary to state expressly that it was or was not a member of the class.

SECTION 5

CRIMINAL LEGISLATION

Distinction between criminal and civil law

Once there was rarely difficulty in knowing whether a matter before the courts was civil or criminal.[39] Recently there has been a proliferation of procedures of hybrid appearance that make the question difficult.[40] **1.5.1**

---

[39] In the sense, at least, that criminal and civil procedures were easily distinguishable. As to the substance, however, it is apparent that there have always been difficulties in providing a neat and serviceable distinction. See, for example, the following exposition by Professor Glanville Williams in *The Divisions of the Law*, Appendix III to the Tenth Edition of *Salmond on Jurisprudence*, London 1947: "Within the domain of private law the division which calls for primary recognition is that between civil and criminal law. Civil law is that which is concerned with the enforcement of rights, while criminal law is concerned with the punishment of wrongs. We have examined and rejected the opinion that crimes are essentially offences against the state or the community at large, while civil wrongs are committed against private persons. According to the acceptance or rejection of this opinion, criminal law pertains either to public or to private law. Our classification of it as private is unaffected by the fact that certain crimes, such as treason and sedition, are offences against the state. As already explained, logical consistency in the division of the law is attainable only if we are prepared to disregard the requirements of practical convenience. Greater weight is wisely attributed to the fact that the one is an offence against the state and the other an offence against an individual. Just as the law which is common to both state and subject is considered under the head of private law alone, so the law which is common to crimes and to civil injuries is dealt with under the had of civil law alone. It is obvious that there is a great body of legal principles common to the two departments. The law as to theft involves the whole law as to the acquisition of property in chattels, and the law of bigamy involves a considerable portion of the law of marriage. The arrangement sanctioned by usage and convenience is, therefore, to expound first the civil law in its entirety, and thereafter, under the title of criminal law, such portions of the law of crime as are not already comprehended in the former department."

[40] See, for example, the "civil penalties" in s.9 of the Finance Act 1994 (c.9)—
"9 Penalties for contraventions of statutory requirements
    (1) This section applies, subject to section 10 below, to any conduct in relation to which any enactment (including an enactment contained in this Act or in any Act passed after this Act) provides for the conduct to attract a penalty under this section.
    (2) Any person to whose conduct this section applies shall be liable—
        (a) in the case of conduct in relation to which provision is made by subsection (4) below, or by or under any other enactment, for the penalty attracted to be calculated by reference to an amount of, or an amount payable on account of, any duty of excise, to a penalty of whichever is the greater of 5 per cent of that amount and £250; and
        (b) in any other case, to a penalty of £250.

The courts have had to consider a variety of new forms of procedure and to determine for different purposes whether they amount to criminal or civil procedures. So—

In *B v Chief Constable of the Avon and Somerset Constabulary*[41] the Divisional Court found that the civil standard of proof could be applied to applications relating to sex offender orders, on the grounds that those orders are not criminal proceedings because there is no new charge or finding of guilty.

In *Gough v Chief Constable of Derbyshire Constabulary*[42] the Court of Appeal concluded that proceedings for a banning-order under s.14B of the Football

---

(3) Subject to section 13(3) and (4) below, in the case of any conduct to which this section applies which is conduct in relation to which provision is made by subsection (4) or (5) below or any other enactment for that conduct to attract daily penalties, the person whose conduct it is—
    (a) shall be liable, in addition to an initial penalty under subsection (2) above, to a penalty of £20 for every day, after the first, on which the conduct continues, but
    (b) shall not, in respect of the continuation of that conduct, be liable to further penalties under subsection (2) above.
(4) Where any conduct to which this section applies consists in a failure, in contravention of any subordinate legislation, to pay any amount of any duty of excise or an amount payable on account of any such duty, then, in so far as that would not otherwise be the case—
    (a) the penalty attracted to that contravention shall be calculated by reference to the amount unpaid; and
    (b) the contravention shall also attract daily penalties.
(5) Where—
    (a) a contravention of any provision made by or under any enactment consists in or involves a failure, before such time as may be specified in or determined in accordance with that provision, to send a return to the Commissioners showing the amount which any person is or may become required to pay by way of, or on account of, any duty of excise, and
    (b) that contravention attracts a penalty under this section, that contravention shall also attract daily penalties.
(6) Where, by reason of any conduct to which this section applies, a person is convicted of an offence, that conduct shall not also give rise to liability to a penalty under this section.
(7) If it appears to the Treasury that there has been a change in the value of money since the passing of this Act or, as the case may be, the last occasion when the power conferred by this subsection was exercised, they may by order substitute for any sum for the time being specified in subsection (2) or (3) above such other sum as appears to them to be justified by the change.
(8) The power to make an order under subsection (7) above—
    (a) shall be exercisable by statutory instrument subject to annulment in pursuance of a resolution of the House of Commons; but
    (b) shall not be exercisable so as to vary the penalty for any conduct occurring before the coming into force of the order.
(9) Schedule 4 to this Act (which provides for the conduct to which this section applies, repeals the summary offences superseded by this section and makes related provision with respect to forfeiture) shall have effect."

And for an example of a section which as a result of amendment mixes the new form of civil penalty with the traditional offence in similar circumstances, see s.14 of the Hydrocarbon Oil Duties Act 1979 (c.5).

[41] [2001] 1 W.L.R. 340, QBD, DC.
[42] [2002] 3 W.L.R. 289, CA.

Spectators Act 1989 are civil and not criminal, since they do not require proof that a criminal offence has been committed and do not involve the imposition of a penalty.

In *R. (McCann) v Manchester Crown Court*[43] the House of Lords held that proceedings for an anti-social behaviour order under s.1 of the Crime and Disorder Act 1998 are not criminal proceedings and require to be distinguished in this respect from criminal proceedings to enforce the order.

In *McIntosh v Lord Advocate*[44] the Privy Council held that a person is not charged with a criminal offence for the purposes of Art.6(2) of the European Convention on Human Rights[45] where an application is made against him for a confiscation order under the Proceeds of Crime (Scotland) Act 1995.[46] **1.5.2**

In *Government of the United States of America v Montgomery*[47] the House of Lords concluded that an order under s.77 of the Criminal Justice Act 1988[48] restraining a person from removing or disposing of assets is civil in character and is not a criminal cause or matter for the purpose of s.18(1)(a) of the Supreme Court Act 1981[49] (jurisdiction of the Court of Appeal) despite the fact that it is granted in consequence of criminal proceedings.

In *Han v Commissioners of Customs and Excise*[50] the Court of Appeal laid down rules for establishing whether an ostensibly civil penalty is in fact a criminal charge for the purposes of Art.6(1) of the European Convention on Human Rights, determining that certain procedures described as civil penalties were in fact criminal charges for that purpose.

In *R. v H.*[51] the House of Lords concluded that a determination under s.4A of the Criminal Procedure (Insanity) Act 1964[52] whether a defendant had done acts alleged against him is not the determination of a criminal charge for the purposes of Art.6 of the European Convention on Human Rights.[53] **1.5.3**

In *R. (West) v Parole Board*[54] the Court of Appeal concluded that the exercise by the Parole Board of powers under s.39 of the Criminal Justice Act 1991[55] to

---

[43] [2002] 3 W.L.R. 131, HL (as judgment in *Clingham (formerly C (a minor) v Royal Borough of Kensington and Chelsea (on Appeal from a Divisional Court of the Queen's Bench Division)* and *Regina v Crown Court at Manchester Ex p. McCann*).
[44] [2003] 3 W.L.R. 107, PC.
[45] The European Convention for the Protection of Human Rights and Fundamental Freedoms (Rome, November 4, 1950; TS 71 (1953); Cmd 8969).
[46] 1995 c.43.
[47] [2001] 1 W.L.R. 196, HL.
[48] 1988 c.33.
[49] 1981 c.54.
[50] [2001] 1 W.L.R. 2253, CA.
[51] [2003] 1 W.L.R. 411, HL.
[52] 1964 c.84.
[53] But compare the Powers of Criminal Courts (Sentencing) Act 2000 (c.6), s.10(8)(a).
[54] [2003] 1 W.L.R. 705, CA.
[55] 1991 c.53 (as amended by the Crime and Disorder Act 1998 (c.37)).

recall a person to prison for breach of conditions of release on licence is not the determination of a criminal charge for the purposes of Art.6 of the European Convention on Human Rights.

In *Customs and Excise Commissioners v City of London Magistrates' Court*[56] the court held that an application by the Customs and Excise Commissioners for an access order under para.11 of Sch.11 to the Value Added Tax Act 1994[57] was not criminal proceedings, because no formal accusation is made and no proceedings begun which could lead to conviction, although the taxpayers may indeed be suspected by the Commissioners of the commission of an offence.

In his speech in *McCann* Lord Steyn made a number of observations about the reasons for the development towards non-traditional forms of penalties, and about the nature and method of classification. Relevant extracts from Lord Steyn's speech are appended to this work.[58]

As is to be expected, the fact that the legislature in providing for a particular procedure describes it as civil or criminal will be relevant but not conclusive as a matter of law.[59]

Express words required to create offence

1.5.4   It is now a fixed principle that legislation creating a criminal offence must do so by express words. In some statutes of a few decades ago one finds that the express words are limited to providing for a punishment of a criminal nature, without the statute creating an offence in terms.[60] But even so, the statutes still use express words.[61] Whether ancient statutes may have imposed positive or negative duties expecting that failure to comply would be punishable, without

---

[56] [2000] 1 W.L.R. 2020, QBD.

[57] 1994 c.24.

[58] Appendix, Extract 5.

[59] *R. (Mudie) v Dover Magistrates' Court* [2003] 2 W.L.R. 1344, CA; but it would, of course, be open to Parliament by express legislative provision to require the courts to treat a specified procedure as civil or criminal for specified purposes, subject to the possible application of the European Convention on Human Rights.

[60] See, for a particularly interesting example, section Betting, Gaming and Lotteries Act 1963 (c.2)—

   "2 Restriction on bookmaking except under bookmaker's permit

   (1) No person shall act as a bookmaker on his own account unless he is the holder of a permit authorising him so to act (in this Act referred to as a "bookmaker's permit") which is for the time being in force; and if any person acts as a bookmaker in contravention of this subsection he shall be guilty of an offence: . . .

   (3) If the holder of a bookmaker's permit, on being required by a constable to produce his permit for examination, refuses or without reasonable cause fails so to do, he shall be liable on summary conviction to a fine not exceeding level 1 on the standard scale."

So subs.(1) makes express provision for an offence but no express provision for the penalty (for which general provision is made by s.52(1)) while subs.(3) makes express provision for a penalty but does not use the expression "offence".

[61] But see, however, as to the question of what is sufficiently express for this purpose, *Sales-Matic Ltd v Hinchcliffe* [1959] 3 All E.R. 401.

any provision in the statute, under a common law doctrine of criminal contempt of statute, is an open question.[62] But as to modern statutes the position is clear. As Lloyd L.J. said in *R. v Horseferry Road Justices Ex p. Independent Broadcasting Authority*[63]—

> "I start with the trite observation that, where Parliament intends to create a criminal offence, it invariably, or almost invariably, says so in terms. That is certainly so in modern statutes."

It is also clear that the fact that behaviour would seriously frustrate the intentions underlying a statute is insufficient to render it criminal or otherwise unlawful. As Lord Diplock said in *Director of Public Prosecutions v Bhagwan*[64]—

> "My Lords, I know of no authority which would justify your Lordships in holding it to be a criminal offence for any person, whether or not acting in concert with others, to do acts which are neither prohibited by Act of Parliament nor at common law, and do not involve dishonesty or fraud or

---

[62] Deriving, however, considerable support from Hawkins' *Pleas of the Crown* as cited in the following passage of the judgment of Charles J. in *R. v Hall* [1891] 1 Q.B. 747, 753–754—

> "Before referring to the statutes it is desirable that I should state the principle which should govern a case of this description, and it is nowhere given better, I think, than in Hawkins' Pleas of the Crown, Bk. 2, c.25, s.4. The passage is as follows:
>
> 'It seems to be a good general ground that wherever a statute prohibits a matter of public grievance to the liberties and security of a subject, or commands a matter of public convenience, as the repairing of the common streets of a town, an offender against such statute is punishable, not only at the suit of the party aggrieved, but also by way of indictment for this contempt of the statute, unless such method of proceeding do manifestly appear to be excluded by it. Yet, if the party offending have been fined to the king in the action brought by the party, as it is said that he may in every action for doing a thing prohibited by statute, it seems questionable whether he may be afterwards indicted, because that would be to make him liable to a second fine for the same offence . . . Also where a statute makes a new offence which was no way prohibited by the common law, and appoints a peculiar manner of proceeding against the offender as by commitment, or action of debt, or information, &c., without mentioning an indictment, it seems to be settled to this day that it would not maintain an indictment, because the mentioning the other methods of proceeding seems impliedly to exclude that of indictment. Yet it hath been adjudged that, if such a statute give a recovery by action of debt, bill, plaint, or information, or otherwise, it authorizes a proceeding by way of indictment. Also where a statute adds a further penalty to an offence prohibited by the common law, there can be no doubt but that the offender may still be indicted, if the prosecutor think fit, at the common law. And if the indictment for such offence conclude contra formam statuti, and cannot be made good as an indictment upon the statute, it seems to be now settled that it may be maintained as an indictment at common law.'
>
> This is a full statement of the principle which must guide me as regards the decision of this case. The inquiry to which I have to address myself is - first, whether the offence charged is a statutory offence simply; secondly, whether, if it be so, the statute creating the offence has prescribed a particular remedy in such terms as to exclude either expressly or by implication the remedy by indictment."

[63] [1987] Q.B. 54, DC.
[64] [1972] A.C. 60, 80–82, HL.

deception, merely because the object which Parliament hoped to achieve by the Act may be thereby thwarted. . . .

"The actual decision in *Rex v Manley*[65] is no authority for the proposition that it can be a criminal conspiracy to defeat the intention of an Act of Parliament by using means which are neither prohibited by the Act itself nor criminal or tortuous at common law. Nor should the decision be treated as authority for the proposition that it is an offence at common law to agree to 'act to the prejudice of the state' unless the means adopted are unlawful or the prejudice likely to be caused falls within one of the established categories of public mischief which have been held by previous decisions of the courts to be so contrary to public policy as to justify the imposition of penal sanctions. The public policy disclosed by an Act of Parliament, which derogates from the freedoms previously enjoyed by citizens of this country under the common law, cannot fall within any of these established categories, for *ex hypothesi* it is a new policy."

1.5.5 None of this means that a clear implication, and not merely one arising because of the absence of other express means of enforcement, will not suffice for the creation of a criminal offence. But the circumstances in which an implication will be relied on for this purpose in modern drafting will be very rare. An example, however, is the case of legislation implementing European Community obligations by the creation of an offence, where it may be left to necessary implication that the offence is to be extended in relation to changes in the European legislation. As Lord Nicholls of Birkenhead said in *Department for Environment, Food and Rural Affairs v Asda Stores Ltd*[66]—

"26. I agree that offence-creating provisions must always be expressed with sufficient clarity and precision. But the mechanism chosen by Parliament for implementing Community obligations is a matter of legislative choice for Parliament. Particularly where Community legislation may be changed frequently, Parliament may choose to adopt an approach which does not involve making new implementing regulations whenever Community legislation changes. Courts should not approach the interpretation of implementing statutes or regulations as though there were a presumption that they do not embrace future changes in Community legislation. There is no such presumption. There might have been a place for such a presumption if it were inherently unlikely that implementing statutes or implementing statutory instruments would be intended to embrace future changes in Community legislation, but that is not always so."

---

[65] [1933] 1 K.B. 529.
[66] [2004] 1 W.L.R. 105, 111, HL.

Offences created by subordinate legislation

A variety of kinds of subordinate legislation are able to create or extend criminal **1.5.6** offences, either because they are empowered to do anything that an Act of Parliament can do[67] or because the enabling provision expressly permits the creation or extension of offences.[68] There is, however, a strong presumption against the creation of offences by subordinate legislation rebuttable only by express provision or clear inference.[69]

Presumption of mental element—strict liability

An offence which is committed by an action or omission irrespective of intent is **1.5.7** referred to as an offence of strict liability. There is a presumption that in all cases of serious and "truly criminal" offences created by legislation there is a requirement of intent, but not in relation to "less serious offences".[70] The present state of the presumption is expressed as follows by Dyson L.J. in *R. v Muhamad*[71]—

"The question, whether the presumption of law that *mens rea* is required applies, and, if so, whether it has been displaced, can be approached in two ways. One approach is to ask whether the act is truly criminal, on the basis that, if it is not, then the presumption does not apply at all. The other approach is to recognise that any offence in respect of which a person may be punished in a criminal court is prima facie sufficiently 'criminal' for the presumption to apply. But the more serious the offence, the greater the weight to be attached to the presumption, and conversely, the less serious the offence, the less weight to be attached. It is now clear that it is this latter approach which, according to our domestic law, must be applied.

---

[67] As in the case of s.2(2) of the European Communities Act 1972 (c.68).

[68] As in the case, for example, of s.141(3)(g) of the Nationality, Immigration and Asylum Act 2002 (c.41).

[69] See, for example, "There is nothing to suggest that Parliament, in passing the 1997 Act, intended to authorise the creation of criminal offences as sanctions for breaches of regulations under section 9 (the Act does itself create offences in relation to other provisions). In the Committee's view there are no compelling arguments, given the nature of the plant breeders' rights and the means of enforcing them . . . to support the view that a power to create offences to enforce the regulations must necessarily be applied. In any case there is a persistent and strong current of precedent in legislative practice that, if the creation by delegated legislation of criminal offences is to be authorised, specific provision is included in the Act and, further, that the standard supplemental and incidental power is not a sufficient authorisation. This practice is strong evidence of an implicit principle that the creation of offences (or their authorisation) is something that Parliament reserves for itself. The Committee therefore reports regulation 10 because there is a serious doubt as to whether it is intra vires."—Joint Committee on Statutory Instruments, Session 1997–98, 34th Report, para.4 (HL Paper 105, HC 33-xxxiv).

[70] To see how and in what cases this presumption applies, see *R. v Warner* [1969] 2 A.C. 256, HL, *Sweet v Parsley* [1970] A.C. 132, HL, *B. (A Minor) v Director of Public Prosecutions* [2000] 2 A.C. 428, HL and *R. v Salter* [1968] 2 Q.B. 793.

[71] [2003] 2 W.L.R. 1050, 1054, CA.

"The starting point, therefore, is to determine how serious an offence is created by section 362(1)(a) [of the Insolvency Act 1986[72]], and accordingly how much weight, if any, should be attached to the presumption, but in our judgment it can readily be displaced. As we have said, the maximum sentence indicates that Parliament considered this to be an offence of some significance, but not one of the utmost seriousness. This is not surprising. We do not believe that great stigma attaches to a conviction of this offence. (We note the Government's proposal to repeal the provision altogether and deal with it as misconduct leading to a bankruptcy restriction order . . .) . . . "

1.5.8   The present approach of English jurisprudence to the concept of strict liability, including the application of the presumption, is conveniently summarised by Elias J. in *Barnfather v Islington Education Authority*[73]—

"In general, English law has set its face against offences of strict liability. There is a presumption that mens rea is an element of a criminal offence, although the nature of a presumption of this nature is that it has to give way to Parliament's clearly expressed intention—whether express or implied—to the contrary. In *Gammon (Hong Kong) Ltd v Attorney General of Hong Kong*,[74] Lord Scarman set out the following five propositions when giving the opinion of the Privy Council:

'In their Lordships' opinion, the law relevant to this appeal may be stated in the following propositions (the formulation of which follows closely the written submission of the appellants' Counsel, which their Lordships gratefully acknowledge):

'(1) there is a presumption of law that mens rea is required before a person can be held guilty of a criminal offence;

'(2) the presumption is particularly strong where the offence is 'truly criminal' in character;

'(3) the presumption applies to statutory offences, and can be displaced only if this is clearly or by necessary implication the effect of the statute;

'(4) the only situation in which the presumption can be displaced is where the statute is concerned with an issue of social concern, and public safety is such an issue;

'(5) even where a statute is concerned with such an issue, the presumption of mens rea stands unless it can also be shown that the creation of strict liability will be effective to promote the

---

[72] 1986 c.45.
[73] *Barnfather v Islington Education Authority* [2003] 1 W.L.R. 2318, 2332–33, QBD, DC.
[74] [1985] A.C. 1, PC.

objects of the statute by encouraging greater vigilance to prevent the commission of the prohibited act.'

"The strength of this presumption was strongly emphasised by the House of Lords in *B (a Minor) v D.P.P.*[75] The facts of that case were far removed from this; the defendant had been charged with inciting a girl under the age of 14 to commit an act of gross indecency. The issue was whether a genuine belief that she was over that age was a defence. Their Lordships held that it was, and that it was immaterial whether the defendant had reasonable grounds for his belief or not. Their Lordships relied upon the presumption. Lord Steyn referred with approval to a passage from *Cross on Statutory Interpretation*,[76] where he referred to such presumptions as 'constitutional principles which are not easily displaced by a statutory text'. Lord Hutton emphasised that the test is not whether it is a *reasonable* implication that Parliament has ruled out mens rea as a constituent part of the offence, but whether it is a *necessary* implication."

While the concept of strict liability is frequently criticised, it is generally accepted that it does not necessarily amount to a violation of the principles of Art.6(2) of the European Convention on Human Rights (right to a fair trial and presumption of innocence until proved guilty according to law).[77]

The fact that in general it will be assumed that action is criminal only if deliberate means only that the person must know what he is doing and intend to do it: it does not require that he should know that it is a crime.[78]

Presumption of guilt

A number of criminal statutes provide, in effect, that a person shall be treated as being guilty of an offence in certain circumstances unless he proves some specified matter. **1.5.9**

There is nothing in principle repugnant, or unlawful in the light of the European Convention on Human Rights, in a provision of this kind. As Lord Nicholls said in *R. v Johnstone*[79]—

"The European Court of Human Rights has recognised that the Convention does not, in principle, prohibit presumptions of fact or law. What Article 6(2) requires is that they must be confined within reasonable limits which

---

[75] [2000] 2 A.C. 428, HL.

[76] 3rd ed. 1995 p.166.

[77] *Barnfather v Islington Education Authority* [2003] 1 W.L.R. 2318, QBD, DC.

[78] "First, the principle that ignorance of the law is no defence in crime is so fundamental that to construe the word 'knowingly' in a criminal statute as requiring not merely knowledge of the facts material to the offender's guilt, but also knowledge of the relevant law, would be revolutionary and, to my mind, wholly unacceptable."—*Grant v Borg* [1982] 2 All E.R. 257, 262, HL *per* Lord Bridge of Harwich.

[79] [2003] 3 All E.R. 884, 898–899, HL.

take into account the importance of what is at stake and maintain the rights of the defence ... Thus, as elsewhere in the convention, a reasonable balance has to be held between the public interest and the interests of the individual.

" ... Identifying the requirements of a reasonable balance is not as easy as it might seem. One is seeking to balance incommensurables.

" ... The relevant factors to be take into account when considering whether such a reason exists have been considered in several recent authorities, in particular the decisions of the House in *R. v Director of Public Prosecutions, ex parte Kebeline, R. v Director of Public Prosecutions, ex parte Rechachi*[80] and *R. v Lambert*.[81] And there is now a lengthening list of decisions of the Court of Appeal and other courts in respect of particular statutory provisions.

" ... In evaluating these factors the court's role is one of review. Parliament, not the court, is charged with the primary responsibility for deciding, as a matter of policy, what should be the constituent elements of a criminal offence.

" ... The court will reach a different conclusion from the legislature only when it is apparent the legislature has attached insufficient importance to the fundamental right of an individual to be presumed innocent until proved guilty."

Defences placing burden on accused

1.5.10 It is common for statute to provide a defence for a person charged with an offence where he is able to prove a particular matter.

In relation to summary offences, the burden of proving any defence or exception falls on the defendant by virtue of s.101 of the Magistrates' Courts Act 1980,[82] which provides as follows—

"Where the defendant to an information or complaint relies for his defence on any exception, exemption, proviso, excuse or qualification, whether or not it accompanies the description of the offence or matter of complaint in the enactment creating the offence or on which the complaint is founded, the burden of proving the exception, exemption, proviso, excuse or qualification shall be on him; and this notwithstanding that the information or complaint contains an allegation negativing the exception, exemption, proviso, excuse or qualification."

---

[80] [2000] 2 A.C. 326.
[81] [2001] U.K.H.L. 37.
[82] 1980 c.43.

Other specific examples in the context of indictable or either way offences are also found. Section 11 of the Terrorism Act 2000[83] is an example. It provides—

"(1) A person commits an offence if he belongs or professes to belong to a proscribed organisation.

"(2) It is a defence for a person charged with an offence under subsection (1) to prove—

> (1) that the organisation was not proscribed on the last (or only) occasion on which he became a member or began to profess to be a member, and
> (2) that he has not taken part in the activities of the organisation at any time while it was proscribed."

As to exceptions generally, the common law produced in relation to indictable offences a position similar to that achieved by s.101 of the Magistrates' Courts Act 1980. The former understanding of the position was expressed by Lawton L.J. in *R. v Edwards*[84] as follows— **1.5.11**

"In our judgment this line of authority establishes that over the centuries the common law, as a result of experience and the need to ensure that justice is done both to the community and to defendants, has evolved an exception to the fundamental rule of our criminal law that the prosecution must prove every element of the offence charged. This exception, like so much else in the common law, was hammered out on the anvil of pleading. It is limited to offences arising under enactments which prohibit the doing of an act save in specified circumstances or by persons of specified classes or with specified qualifications or with the licence or permission of specified authorities. Whenever the prosecution seeks to rely on this exception, the court must construe the enactment under which the charge is laid. If the true construction is that the enactment prohibits the doing of acts, subject to provisos, exemptions and the like, then the prosecution can rely upon the exception. In our judgment its application does not depend upon either the fact or the presumption, that the defendant has peculiar knowledge enabling him to prove the positive of any negative averment. . . . Two consequences follow from this view we have taken as to the evolution and nature of this exception. First, as it comes into operation upon an enactment being construed in a particular way, there is no need for the prosecution to prove a prima facie case of lack of excuse, qualification or the like; and, secondly, what shifts is the onus: it is for the defendant to prove that he was entitled

---

[83] 2000 c.11.
[84] [1975] 1 Q.B. 27, CA 39–40.

to do the prohibited act. What rests on him is the legal or, as it is sometimes called, the persuasive burden or proof. It is not the evidential burden."

The question of the nature of the burden on the accused was closely examined in a number of cases in the context of the passing of the Human Rights Act 1998.[85] One of the most recent examinations of the position is found in the context of s.11 of the Terrorism Act 2000[86] in *Attorney-General's Reference (No. 4 of 2000).*[87] Since the judgment of the court as given by Latham L.J. contains a detailed survey of the relevant precedents and guidelines for the application of the relevant principles, a lengthy extract of his judgment is given in the Appendix to this work.[88] The essence of Latham L.J.'s judgment is that each statute must be construed on its own terms, and that compliance with the European Convention of Human Rights is not impossible for a provision of this kind, provided that the circumstances warrant it.

1.5.12   It should be noted, incidentally, that the Terrorism Act 2000 contained express provision on the matter of the burden of proof in relation to a defence, but only in relation to specified offences (of which s.11(2) was not one). As Latham L.J. said[89]—

"The final statutory provision to which it is necessary to refer is section 118 of the Act which deals expressly with defences provided to a person charged with certain offences under the Act. It provides:

'(1) Subsection (2) applies where in accordance with the provisions mentioned in subsection (5) it is a defence for a person charged with an offence to prove a particular matter.

'(2) If the person adduces evidence which is sufficient to raise an issue with respect to the matter the court or jury shall assume that the defence is satisfied unless the prosecution proves beyond reasonable doubt that it is not. . . . '

"This section was clearly enacted in order to deal with the possibility that certain of the statutory provisions providing for such defences might be considered an unjustified infringement of a person's rights under Article 6(2) of the Convention. It is likely that this was a response to the views expressed by both the Divisional Court and the House of Lords in *R. v D.P.P. ex parte Kebilene,*[90] a decision in relation to section 16(A) of the Prevention of Terrorism (Temporary Provisions) Act 1989.[91] The important point for our purposes is that the defence in section 11(2) of the Act with

---

[85] 1998 c.42.
[86] 2000 c.11.
[87] [2003] 3 W.L.R. 1153, CA.
[88] Appendix, Extract 6.
[89] At 1160.
[90] [2000] 2 A.C. 326, HL.
[91] 1989 c.4.

which we are concerned is not one to which the provisions of section 118 apply."

It has not become common for statutes to replicate s.118 of the Terrorism Act 2000. As Latham L.J. says in *Attorney-General's Reference (No. 4 of 2000)* it appears to have been a temporary expedient designed to ensure the effectiveness of certain provisions of that Act despite the effect of *Kebilene*, before the courts had developed the *Lambert* jurisprudence sufficiently to establish the guidelines above for determining what degree of burden on the accused would be compatible with the Convention in a particular case.

How far the apparent breadth of s.101 of the Magistrates' Courts Act 1980 can survive the Human Rights Act 1998[92] and the cases cited above remains to be seen.   **1.5.13**

These principles as to defences hold good for other instances where a defendant is not provided with a defence in specified circumstances but is able to avail himself of a specified facility. In *R. (O) v Crown Court at Harrow*,[93] for example, the court held that compliance with the European Convention on Human Rights made it necessary that the provision in relation to the grant of bail, requiring the court to be satisfied of the existence of exceptional circumstances (in s.25(1) of the Criminal Justice and Public Order Act 1994[94]), be read down[95] so as to impose only an evidential burden on the defendant.

Duplication

Section 18 of the Interpretation Act 1978[96] provides—   **1.5.14**

"Where an act or omission constitutes an offence under two or more Acts, or both under an Act and at common law, the offender shall, unless the contrary intention appears, be liable to be prosecuted and punished under either or any of those Acts or at common law, but shall not be liable to be punished more than once for the same offence."

As to the general presumption against double punishment, see Chapter 19.

Waiver and disposal

As a general rule, criminality is established by statute as a matter of protecting the public interests, and it is not in the power of any individual to dispense with that protection by excusing a wrong done or threatened. Occasionally, however, the legislature may provide that specified activity is unlawful unless done with   **1.5.15**

---

[92] 1998 c.42.
[93] [2003] 1 W.L.R. 2756, QBD.
[94] 1994 c.33.
[95] In accordance with s.3 of the Human Rights Act 1998 (c.42), as to which see Chapter 25.
[96] 1978 c.30.

the permission of a person interested. See, for example, s.193(4) of the Law of Property Act 1925—

> "(4) Any person who, without lawful authority, draws or drives upon any land to which this section applies any carriage, cart, caravan, truck, or other vehicle, or camps or lights any fire thereon, or who fails to observe any limitation or condition imposed by the Minister under this section in respect of any such land, shall be liable on summary conviction to a fine not exceeding level 1 on the standard scale for each offence."[97]

SECTION 6

FINANCIAL LEGISLATION

Introduction

1.6.1 Most activities undertaken by Government cost significant amounts of public money. The decision to use or withhold money derived from public funds[98] is one of the fundamental prerogatives of the Government. This is recognised in particular in a number of features of the supply or financial procedures of the House of Commons.[99] The most significant are—

(1) Standing Order 50[1] which has the effect in practice that only a Minister of the Crown can introduce a Bill which is primarily concerned with public expenditure, and

---

[97] See further *Bakewell Management Ltd v Brandwood* [2004] 2 W.L.R. 955, 973–974, HL *per* Lord Walker of Gestingthorpe.

[98] Primarily the Consolidated Fund (as to the nature of which see below) and the National Loans Fund (as to the nature of which see below). The National Insurance Fund is not regarded for the purposes of the rules of the House of Commons supply procedures, or for the law of Money Bills under s.1(2) of the Parliament Act 1911 (c.13), as a source of public funds: but the House authorities would be expected to resist an attempt to circumvent the rules relating to charges on public funds by charging to the National Insurance Fund expenditure not referable to the purposes for which the fund is primarily intended.

[99] As between the House of Commons and the House of Lords, the House of Commons asserts a privilege in respect of financial matters that has a number of practical effects. The most significant nowadays is that established by s.1 of the Parliament Act 1911 (c.13), whereby a Bill certified by the Speaker of the House of Commons as a Money Bill—which broadly speaking amounts to a Bill wholly concerned with taxation or expenditure—must be passed by the House of Lords without amendment within one month, and if not it is presented for Royal Assent bypassing the Lords. This contrasts with the two Sessions required for the Lords to be bypassed in relation to non-Money Bills under s.2 of the Act.

[1] "50.—(1) A bill (other than a bill which is required to be brought in upon a ways and means resolution) the main object of which is the creation of a public charge may either be presented, or brought in upon an order of the House, by a Minister of the Crown, and, in the case of a bill so presented or brought in, the creation of the charge shall not require to be authorised by a resolution of the House until the bill has been read a second time, and after the charge has been so authorised the bill shall be proceeded with in the same manner as a bill which involves a charge that is subsidiary to its main purpose.

(2) The provisions of paragraph (1) of this order shall apply to any bill brought from the Lords, of which a Minister of the Crown has informed the Clerks at the Table of his intention to take charge."

(2) Standing Orders 48[2] and 49,[3] the combined effect of which is that a Bill imposing a charge upon public funds requires a resolution which in turn requires the assent of the Government, through a process known as the signification of the Queen's recommendation.[4]

"Sink" clauses

The most common form of financial provision in Acts is a proposition to the effect that expenditure of a Minister in connection with the Act shall be paid out of money provided by Parliament.[5] Strangely enough, despite its peremptory form a provision of this kind has no legislative purpose whatsoever. In particular, the proposition is not in itself sufficient to authorise release of funds from the Consolidated Fund[6]: that must be done in the appropriate Consolidated Fund Act or Appropriation Act as described below. **1.6.2**

The explanation for the inclusion of these ineffectual provisions can be found in the procedure of the House of Commons. When a Bill is introduced in that House, any provision which would involve the raising of money by way of taxation or the expenditure of money from the Consolidated Fund is printed in italics.[7] The reason is that until the provision has been authorised by a money resolution or a ways and means resolution of the House, it is not authorised to form part of the Bill, and it is in effect printed only contingently on the assumption that it will in due course be validated by the passing of a resolution.[8] The italics disappear when the Bill is next printed, which is normally when the Bill leaves Committee.

---

[2] "48. This House will receive no petition for any sum relating to public service or proceed upon any motion for a grant or charge upon the public revenue, whether payable out of the Consolidated Fund or the National Loans Fund or out of money to be provided by Parliament, or for releasing or compounding any sum of money owing to the Crown, unless recommended from the Crown."

[3] "49. Any charge upon the public revenue whether payable out of the Consolidated Fund or the National Loans Fund or out of money to be provided by Parliament including any provision for releasing or compounding any sum of money owing to the Crown shall be authorised by resolution of the House."

[4] To be distinguished from Queen's Consent, which does not concern public money (and is discussed in Chapter 5, Section 2).

[5] A provision of this kind is found in many Acts each year, commonly located in a separate section towards the end of the Act. There are minor variations in wording which are for the most part merely a matter of taste on the part of the draftsman.

[6] The Consolidated Fund is established by section see s.1 of the Consolidated Fund Act 1816 (c.98) (see further footnote 12 below). There are now also Consolidated Funds of Scotland (established by s.64 of the Scotland Act 1998 (c.46) and of Northern Ireland (established by s.57 of the Northern Ireland Act 1998 (c.47): but these are, in effect, merely hypothecated funds fed from the Consolidated Fund and by the diversion of certain receipts that would otherwise end up in the Consolidated Fund.

[7] The exception is those Bills—the principal example being the annual Finance Bill—which so fundamentally concern the raising of taxes that they are required to be brought in on a ways and means resolution.

[8] This is required to happen before the relevant provision is considered at the Committee stage. If a resolution has not been passed covering a clause before it is reached in Committee, the Chairman must decline to put the question that the clause stand part of the Bill.

A Bill which gives rise to expenditure in a number of different places would need to contain italics in each of those places. And it could be difficult to identify all provisions of the Bill which would give rise to expenditure. So the practice has arisen of having what is referred to as a "sink clause", amounting to a general proposition that expenditure under the Bill is to be paid out of money provided by Parliament.[9] The convention is then to italicise the sink clause and to leave the rest of the Bill without italics, with the exception of any provision which contains an express mention of expenditure, such as a power to make grants or loans.

Because they have no legal effect, sink clauses are not found in Acts the Bills for which originated in the House of Lords,[10] and are not reproduced when the provisions of an Act are replicated in a consolidation Act.[11]

Statutory charges on particular funds

1.6.3   In some Acts is found a proposition that a particular expense shall be charged on and paid out of the Consolidated Fund.[12]

---

[9] This is also sometimes referred to, although not in the text of legislation, as payment "out of Votes", which simply refers to the fact that the Appropriation Act categories of expenditure are traditionally divided into separate Votes, by Department and subject.

[10] To safeguard the financial privilege of the House of Commons (as to which see para.1.6.1, footnote 99) where a Bill originates in the House of Lords the Lords authorities insert, as a book entry made on Third Reading of the Bill, a proposition known as the "privilege amendment" stating that "Nothing in this Act shall impose any charge on the people or on public funds, or vary the amount or incidence of or otherwise alter any such charge in any manner, or affect the assessment, levying, administration or application of any money raised by any such charge". This statement, which is often at clear variance with the effect of the provisions of the Bill, is then removed by amendment as the Bill passes through the House of Commons. The inclusion of the privilege amendment means that, technically speaking, there is nothing in the Bill when it reaches the Commons which could require a money resolution or a ways and means resolution, and there is therefore nothing to italicise: so a sink clause would serve no purpose.

[11] So, for example, s.233 of the Education Reform Act 1988 (c.40) (expenses) is simply omitted in the Destination Table for the Education Act 1996 (c.56).

[12] For the nature of the Consolidated Fund see s.1 of the Consolidated Fund Act 1816 (c.98)—

"**1 Consolidated funds of Great Britain and Ireland shall become one general consolidated fund**

All rates, duties, taxes, receipts, sums of money, and revenues of what nature or kind soever, which under or by virtue of any Act or Acts in force in Great Britain or Ireland respectively at the time of passing of this Act, and immediately before the said fifth day of January one thousand eight hundred and seventeen, shall or may constitute or form part of or be directed to be carried to the several funds called the consolidated fund of Great Britain and the consolidated fund of Ireland respectively, shall be carried to and shall be and become and shall form and constitute one general fund, to be called the consolidated fund of the United Kingdom of Great Britain and Ireland; and that the said consolidated fund of the United Kingdom of Great Britain and Ireland, whether the same or any part thereof shall be in the Exchequer of Great Britain or in the Exchequer of Ireland, shall in the first place, be charged and chargeable with and shall from time to time be applied indiscriminately to the payment of the whole of the interest of the national debts of Great Britain and Ireland, and the sinking funds applicable to the reduction thereof, as one joint consolidated national debt, interest, and sinking fund; and in the next place the said consolidated fund of the said United Kingdom shall in like manner be charged and chargeable with and shall be applied to the payment of the salaries and other charges of his Majesty's civil list establishments in Great Britain and Ireland; and in the next place the said consolidated fund of the said United Kingdom shall be in like manner charged and chargeable with and shall be applied in payment of all other

Unlike the sink clause, a proposition of this kind this has a very definite legal effect and purpose. In effect, it provides the necessary authority for the release of funds for a specified purpose from the Consolidated Fund, thereby circumventing the Appropriation Act procedure and making it unnecessary to secure a Vote of the House of Commons before obtaining money.[13]

This procedure is reserved for matters in respect of which it is thought undesirable that the House of Commons should be able to exercise operational financial control. The continuity of the salaries of the judiciary, for example, is guaranteed in this way,[14] as is certain expenditure in connection with referendums and elections[15] and in connection with the systems for the authentication of propriety in relation to public expenditure.[16]

Certain matters are also charged on the National Loans Fund.[17] [18]

Provision for payment into the Consolidated Fund

It is common to find a proposition that receipts of money by a Minister are to be paid into the Consolidated Fund. This is entirely without substantive effect, since **1.6.4**

---

charges whatsoever made payable out of the consolidated funds of Great Britain or Ireland respectively, under or by virtue of any Act or Acts in force immediately before the said fifth day of January one thousand eight hundred and seventeen; and after payment and satisfaction of all the aforesaid charges the said consolidated fund of the United Kingdom shall be in like manner indiscriminately applied to the service of the United Kingdom of Great Britain and Ireland, or any part thereof, as shall be directed by Parliament, and shall be issued and applied accordingly, in manner and under the authority herein-after mentioned and directed.";

The Consolidated Funds of Scotland and Northern Ireland are derivative funds fed, for the most part, from the Consolidated Fund.

[13] For the procedure to be adopted see s.13 of the Exchequer and Audit Departments Act 1866 (c.39) as substituted by the Government Resources and Accounts Act 2000 (c.20), s.29(1) and Sch.1.

[14] See s.12(5) of the Supreme Court Act 1981 (c.54)—"(5) Salaries payable under this section shall be charged on and paid out of the Consolidated Fund.". Note that the amount of salaries is determined "by the Lord Chancellor with the concurrence of the Minister for the Civil Service" (s.12(1)) and that allowances in addition to salary are to be "paid out of money provided by Parliament" (s.12(6)) and are therefore controllable directly by Parliament, not being so essential to the independence of the judiciary.

[15] See ss.29 and 200A of the Representation of the People Act 1983 (c.2).

[16] See s.1(4) of the Exchequer and Audit Departments Act 1957 (c.45).

[17] For the nature of the National Loans Fund see s.1 of the National Loans Fund Act 1968 (c.13)—

"**1 The National Loans Fund**
(1) The Treasury shall have an account at the Bank of England, to be called the National Loans Fund.
(2) Money paid into the National Loans Fund shall form one general fund to meet all the outgoings from the Fund, and daily statements of all money paid into and out of the Fund, in such form as the Treasury may direct, shall be sent by the Bank of England to the Comptroller and Auditor General.
(3) The Comptroller and Auditor General shall from time to time at the request of the Treasury grant credits on the National Loans Fund for sums payable out of the Fund under this or any other Act and, subject to section 18 of this Act, all payments out of the National Loans Fund shall be made by the Treasury in accordance with credits so granted. ... "

[18] See, for example, s.1 of the International Monetary Fund Act 1979 (c.29) (payments to International Monetary Fund) or s.13 of the National Loans Act 1968 (c.13) (existing national debt).

there would be nothing else that a Minister could do with surplus money in his departmental accounts.[19] Nevertheless, it is customary to include a provision along these lines.

"Unnecessary" legislation for expenditure: The Baldwin Convention

1.6.5 The statute book contains numerous provisions, and even whole Acts, which serve no legislative purpose because they confer express power for a Minister to do something that he could do anyway without statutory power.[20]

In 1932 the Public Accounts Committee, a select committee of the House of Commons, expressed concern at the possibility of significant expenditure being incurred without express Parliamentary authority.[21] Although payment out of the Consolidated Fund eventually requires the authority of an Appropriation Act, the Act deals in large tranches of activity rather than specific functions, and it can be difficult to discern precise expenditure on particular functions even from the accompanying documents traditionally laid by the Treasury before Parliament to support the Bill for an Appropriation Act.

After a certain amount of correspondence, the Government gave an undertaking[22] that as a general rule new heads of expenditure would be authorised by

---

[19] He could not, in particular, use the surplus to fund expenditure not authorised by the Appropriation Act. Even appropriation of receipts in aid of permitted expenditure requires authorisation under that Act—see the Government Resources and Accounts Act 2000 (c.20). See also s.10 of the Exchequer and Audit Departments Act 1866 (gross revenues) and s.1 of the Exchequer Extra Receipts Act 1868 (c.9) (payment of casual receipts to the Exchequer).

[20] This notion rests on the idea that a Minister is a natural person and almost all senior Ministers are also legal persons, being corporations sole: as such they can do anything that a natural or legal person could do, subject to the constraint that they will be able to pay for it only if statute or Parliament allows them the money. This is the so-called *Ram* doctrine, named after one of its principal exponents, Sir Granville Ram, former First Parliamentary Counsel, who embodied the doctrine in a memorandum dated November 2, 1945. The doctrine, which underpinned Government thought on the subject since the middle of the twentieth-century, became a matter of public record in 2003 with the publication of a series of Parliamentary Answers in the House of Lords on the subject: see the House of Lords Written Answers appended to this work (Appendix, Extract 7); see also the judgment of Lord Phillips of Worth Matravers M.R. in *R. (Hooper) v Secretary of State for Work and Pensions* [2003] 1 W.L.R. 2623, CA (but note that as this work went to press *Hooper* was pending appeal to the House of Lords); and, as to the *Ram* doctrine generally, see also [2003] Public Law 415.

Note, however, that an express provision permitting expenditure may have the effect of rendering unlawful decisions of a Minister to make payments "in circumstances where this conflicts with the intention of Parliament" as manifested in the express provision—see para.1.6.8.

[21] The particular case causing concern was reliance on the Appropriation Act alone by the Ministry of Labour to authorise continuing expenditure in relation to the training and resettlement of unemployed men and women.

[22] The nature of the undertaking appears from the following extract of *Government Accounting 2000* (H.M. Treasury, available on the Internet)—

"1. In 1932 the Public Accounts Committee (PAC) considered how far the annual Appropriation Act could be regarded as sufficient authority for the exercise of functions by a government department in cases where no other specific statutory authority exists. The Committee was of the opinion that, as a matter of general principle:

'where it is desired that continuing functions should be exercised by a government department, particularly where such functions may involve financial liabilities extending

substantive provision in an Act, except where the expenditure was expected to be insignificant or transitory.

The result is that it is accepted as a matter of Parliamentary convention that legislation, and not just the general cover of an Appropriation Act, is required for anything significant in the way of expenditure from public funds. This is sometimes known as the *Baldwin Agreement* or *Baldwin Convention* or as the *1932 Public Accounts Committee Concordat*.

Legislative authority for expenditure

As to the position in law, the question is discussed in the judgment of Lord **1.6.6** Phillips of Worth Matravers M.R. in *R. (Hooper) v Secretary of State for Work and Pensions*[23]—

> " . . . we are here dealing with a suggestion that the court can grant relief against the Crown on the basis that the Crown has both the power under common law and the duty under section 6(1) of the [Human Rights Act 1998[24]], to put in place an ex gratia regime of paying bereavement benefits to widowers when Parliament has made express statutory provision as to the circumstances in which such benefits should be paid to widows and, under the [Contributions and Benefits Act 1992[25]] as amended by the [Welfare Reform and Pensions Act 1999[26]], to widowers. In this context it is necessary to have regard to this injunction of Lord Bridge in *Steele Ford & Newton (a firm) v CPS*[27]—

> beyond a given financial year, it is proper, subject to certain recognised exceptions, that the powers and duties to be exercised should be defined by specific statute.'
>
> "2. In reply to the Committee, the Treasury said that:
>> 'while they think the Executive Government must continue to be allowed a certain measure of discretion in asking Parliament to exercise a power which undoubtedly belongs to it, they agree that practice should normally accord with the view expressed by the Committee that, where it is desired that continuing functions should be exercised by a government department (particularly where such functions involve financial liabilities extending beyond a given year) it is proper that the powers and duties to be exercised should be defined by specific statute. The Treasury will, for their part, continue to aim at the observance of this principle.'
>
> "3. In 1932 the Treasury restated its view that:
>> 'while it is competent to Parliament, by means of an annual vote embodied in the Appropriation Acts, in effect to extend powers specifically limited by statute, constitutional propriety requires that such extensions should be regularised at the earliest possible date by amending legislation, unless they are of a purely emergency or non-continuing character.' "

[23] [2003] 1 W.L.R. 2623, 2669, CA; note that as this work went to press *Hooper* was pending appeal to the House of Lords.
[24] 1998 c.42.
[25] 1992 c.4.
[26] 1999 c.30.
[27] [1994] 1 A.C. 22, 33, HL.

'But still more important, in the present context, is the special constitutional convention which jealously safeguards the exclusive control exercised by Parliament over both the levying and the expenditure of the public revenue. It is trite law that nothing less than clear, express and unambiguous language is effective to levy a tax. Scarcely less stringent is the requirement of clear statutory authority for public expenditure. As it was put by Viscount Haldane in *Auckland Harbour Board v R.*[28]: "It has been a principle of the British Constitution now for more than two centuries . . . that no money can be taken out of the Consolidated Fund into which the revenues of the state have been paid, excepting under a distinct authorisation from Parliament itself." '

"130 The rules governing the circumstances in which ministers can properly make payment out of public funds are rules of constitutional law of some complexity. We shall try to provide a summary, simplified so far as is possible to meet the needs of this judgment.

1.6.7

"131 The fundamental principle is that any expenditure of public funds must be authorised by statute . . . *Auckland Harbour Board v R*[29]; *R. v Secretary of State for Foreign Affairs, ex parte World Development Movement Ltd*[30]—the Pergau Dam case. The complication arises out of the fact that Parliament authorises expenditure of public funds by two different types of statute. Statutes dealing with a particular area of government make provision for specific expenditure for a defined purpose. We shall here describe these as 'specific statutes'. The 1992 and the 1999 Acts are examples of such legislation. Such statutes do not, however, of themselves provide ministers with access to the public funds. Revenues raised by taxation or otherwise are, in general, paid into the Exchequer Account at the Bank of England, where they constitute the Consolidated Fund. Parliamentary authorisation is required for issues from the Consolidated Fund and this is provided each year by the second type of statute. A series of Consolidated Fund Bills are brought before Parliament founded upon supply resolutions. The final such Bill is the Consolidated Fund (Appropriation) Bill, which becomes the Appropriation Act. We shall describe this type of legislation as appropriation legislation. Such legislation authorises the issue to government departments of the funds that they have demonstrated that they require to perform their executive functions. In some instances the funds will be required to make the payments already authorised by specific statutes. In other instances the funds will be required to enable the government departments to make payments pursuant to prerogative or common law powers which are not the subject of any specific statute. Whether expenditure should be authorised by specific statutes, or merely by appropriation

---

[28] [1924] A.C. 318, 326, HL.
[29] [1924] A.C. 318.
[30] [1995] 1 W.L.R. 386.

statutes is a question of constitutional law on which the views of the Treasury and the Public Accounts Committee have differed."

Lord Phillips went on to describe the controversy leading to the Baldwin Convention discussed above.[31]

The quotation from *Hooper* above[32] illustrates the notion that both taxation and expenditure require clear statutory sanction. The point is qualified by the continuation of the speech of Lord Bridge of Harwich in *Steele Ford & Newton*[33] cited above in *Hooper*—

"Before considering whether, in spite of these apparent difficulties, an unexpressed power to order payment of costs out of money provided by Parliament can properly be implied in any of the sections in question, it is necessary, if tedious, to consider in some detail the nature, context and provenance of the legislative provisions in which jurisdiction is specifically conferred to award payment of costs out of central funds. . . . "

The gap between the law as expounded in *Hooper* and *Steele Ford*, on the one hand, and the practice as demanded by the Baldwin Convention relates simply to the effectiveness of the Consolidated Fund Acts and Appropriation Acts. So far as the law is concerned, authorisation by Consolidated Fund Act is authorisation by Act and suffices for all purposes. The reason behind the Baldwin Convention is that for practical purposes it is too easy to "hide" expenditure within an entry in a Consolidated Fund Act, and even if displayed prominently an entry in an Act of that kind does not make it possible for the principle and practicalities of the service to which the expenditure relates to be debated and amended. So that what suffices for legal constitutional purposes is insufficient for the purpose of practical political control, and a provision expressly authorising the substance of the service is required.   **1.6.8**

Although an Appropriation Act suffices as cover for expenditure for legal purposes, for practical purposes and for the purposes of the Baldwin Convention, "where a minister proposes to make payments in circumstances where this conflicts with the intention of Parliament, as manifested in a specific statute, the decision will be unlawful as an abuse of power, even, it seems, if Parliament has authorised the issue of funds for that purpose in an appropriation statute—see *R. v Secretary of State for the Home Dept Ex p. Fire Brigades Union*".[34] [35] Put another way, the authorisation provided by a Consolidated Fund Act or Appropriation Act is restricted to the question of the legality of expending funds, it does not make lawful an activity that would otherwise be unlawful: and in a

---

[31] Para.1.6.5.
[32] Para.1.6.6.
[33] [1994] 1 A.C. 22, 33, HL (on appeal from *Holden & Co. v Crown Prosecution Service (No.2)*); see also *R. v Moore* [2003] 1 W.L.R. 2170, 2173, CA *per* Rose J.
[34] [1995] 2 A.C. 513, 554—and see Chapter 10, Section 1.
[35] *Hooper* at 2671.

case where the mere fact of the expenditure is itself unlawful as conflicting with Parliament's enacted intentions (in the *Fire Brigade Unions* case, because Parliament had required the replacement of a system of informal payments with a new statutory scheme) the authorisation by Consolidated Fund Act or Appropriation Act will not suffice to render the expenditure lawful.

Consolidated Fund and Appropriation Acts

1.6.9 Every year a small number of Consolidated Fund Bills are introduced in the House of Commons. The last one of each Session becomes, on receiving the Royal Assent, and is citable as, an Appropriation Act.

These Acts achieve nothing as a matter of substantive law, except in so far as they provide the distinct authorisation referred to by Viscount Haldane above. Their purpose and effect can be understood only in the context of the supply or financial procedure of the House of Commons and the accounting procedures of the Government. A full understanding of these can be obtained from specialist works on the subject.[36] This Section offers only the briefest of outlines.

Originally, the notion of Consolidated Fund Bills was extremely simple: they were the way for the Government to acquire authority from Parliament for obtaining cash from the Consolidated Fund. The notion of appropriation as set out in the Appropriation Act was a little more difficult to grasp, but amounted in essence to a system of attributing sums advanced to particular services of the Government (*i.e.* showing what sums were appropriated to what services) for the purpose of establishing whether the Estimates presented to Parliament were reflected in the eventual pattern of expenditure.

1.6.10 The situation has become more complicated since the adoption by the Government in 2000 of a system of resource accounting. Instead of focusing purely on the traditional notions of cash and expenditure, the Government's accounts now reflect modern accounting practice by looking at the use of resources.[37]

This was recognised in the Government Resources and Accounts Act 2000,[38] which replaced some very long-standing legislative concepts with ones tailored so far as possible to fit the new concepts of resource accounting. This was not entirely easy, and the notion of appropriation-in-aid was particularly difficult to

---

[36] The supply procedure of the Commons is thoroughly explored in the relevant chapters of Erskine May's *Parliamentary Practice* (23rd ed. 2004). The accounting practices of the Government are explained in *Government Accounting* and the *Resource Accounting Manual*, both available from Her Majesty's Treasury.

[37] In this context "use" has a highly specialised meaning which relates to the change in value of resources. So, for example, depreciation is regarded as a kind of use of a resource, because the value of the resource has diminished. As to this, see s.27 of the Government Resources and Accounts Act 2000 (c.20)—"In this Act a reference to the use of resources is a reference to their expenditure, consumption or reduction in value."

[38] 2000 c.20.

adjust to reflect the new system.[39] At the same time as the 2000 Act, the form of Consolidated Fund and Appropriation Acts was altered to reflect the new financial systems.[40]

Financial regulation is operated by the House of Commons in relation to each Parliamentary Session. One result of that is that if Parliament is dissolved unexpectedly early because of a sudden call of a general election, one of the pieces of business that requires to be taken in the final few days of the last session of the Parliament to be dissolved is the passing of an emergency Appropriation Act.[41]

Appropriation in aid

Originally, the concept of appropriation in aid was simply the notion that where **1.6.11** a Government Department received income it might, instead of surrendering it into the Consolidated Fund, expend it on a service for which expenditure was authorised or to be authorised, that is to say to appropriate the income in aid of the service.

With the introduction of resource accounting as discussed above[42] the concept has become more difficult to explain. Section 2 of the Government Resources and Accounts Act 2000 provides as follows—

"**2 Appropriation in aid**

(1) The Treasury may, subject to any relevant limit set by an Appropriation Act, direct that resources may be applied as an appropriation in aid of resources authorised by Parliament to be used for the service of a particular year.

(2) A direction under subsection (1) shall be—

(a) made by minute, and
(b) laid before Parliament.

(3) Subsections (4) and (5) apply where money is received in connection with an appropriation in aid which has been or is expected to be directed under subsection (1).

---

[39] Originally this concept too was relatively straightforward, the idea being that instead of receiving cash for the full amount of their estimated expenditure and returning all receipts to the Consolidated Fund, Departments could hold on to certain receipts and apply them to items of authorised expenditure. Now the concept, as set out in s.2 of the Government Resources and Accounts Act 2000, is obscure. Occasional problems are bound to arise—see, for example, the Appropriation (No.2) Act 2002 (c.44)—"An Act to modify limits on non-operating appropriations in aid set for the year that ended with March 31, 2002."
[40] These Acts are as a rule drafted not by Parliamentary Counsel but, following standard forms, by collaboration between the Treasury and the Clerk of Supply in the Public Bill Office of the House of Commons.
[41] See, for example, the Appropriation (No.2) Act 1997 (c.57).
[42] Para.1.6.10.

(4) Where the money is received in the year for the service of which the appropriation in aid is authorised—

    (a) the appropriation in aid is authority for the money to be used in accordance with the Treasury's direction, and

    (b) in so far as it is not used for that purpose it shall be paid into the Consolidated Fund.

(5) Where the money is received in a year other than that for the service of which the appropriation in aid is or is to be authorised, it shall be—

    (a) retained and applied as a use of resources authorised by Appropriation Act for the service of the year in which the money is received, or

    (b) paid into the Consolidated Fund. . . . "

The result of this is that appropriation in aid may still refer to the simple application of a flow of income to a class of expenditure. But the concept may also be applied in the context of the wider classes of resources[43] and use of resources with which the new accounting procedures are concerned.

Presumption against taxation

1.6.12   The presumption against taxation can be formulated succinctly in the words of the Judicial Committee of the Privy Council in *Oriental Bank v Wright*[44]—

    "The rule is that the intention to impose a charge upon a subject must be shown by clear and unambiguous language."[45]

---

[43] There is no definition of resources in the 2000 Act (although "use" is defined in s.27). But the Act provides for generally accepted accounting practice to be adopted in relation to what amounts to resources and their application. See, in particular, the following provisions of s.5 (resource accounts: preparation)—
    "(2) Resource accounts shall be prepared in accordance with directions issued by the Treasury.
    (3) The Treasury shall exercise the power to issue directions under subsection (2) with a view to ensuring that resource accounts—
      (a) present a true and fair view,
      (b) conform to generally accepted accounting practice subject to such adaptations as are necessary in the context of departmental accounts, and
      (c) accord with guidance issued by the Treasury about the inclusion of an explanation of the difference between an item appearing in a department's estimate and a corresponding item appearing in or reflected in the department's resource accounts.
    (4) For the purpose of subsection (3)(a) and (b) the Treasury shall in particular—
      (a) have regard to any relevant guidance issued by the Accounting Standards Board Limited or any other body prescribed for the purposes of section 256 of the Companies Act 1985 (accounting standards), and
      (b) require resource accounts to include, subject to paragraph (a), a statement of financial performance, a statement of financial position and a cash flow statement."
[44] (1880) 5 App. Cas. 842, 856.
[45] See also *Simms v Registrar of Probates* [1900] A.C. 323, 337 and *Re Earl Fitzwilliam's Agreement* [1950] Ch. 448.

The width of this formulation shows that it matters not whether the charge ought strictly to be described as a tax or as a payment for services or in some other way.[46] Hence, for example, Lord Tenterden C.J. on the subject of rates in *Dock Co. at Kingston-upon-Hull v Browne*[47]—

> "These rates are a tax upon the subject and it is a sound general rule that a tax shall not be considered to be imposed (or, at least, not for the benefit of a subject) without a plain declaration of the legislature to impose it."[48]

The presumption against taxation is relevant to the discussion elsewhere in this work[49] about the difference between evasion and avoidance in the context of statutory duties. In the case of a statutory duty to pay a tax or other charge, the words of Rowlatt J.[50] express the position—

> "In a taxing Act one has to look at what is clearly said. There is no room for any intendment. There is no equity about a tax. There is no presumption as to a tax.[51] Nothing is to be read in, nothing is to be implied. One can only look fairly at the language used."[52]

For recent judicial pronouncements on this presumption and its extent see *R. (Edison) v Central Valuation Officer*[53] and the many cases cited therein.

As to the presumption against double taxation, see Chapter 19.

Presumption against imposition of fees and charges

Whether or not as a result of the presumption against taxation, it has long been established that neither the Crown nor any other public authority may impose a

1.6.13

---

[46] This is a distinction of some importance in the technical context of the House of Commons' rules about ways and means resolutions—as to which see Chapter 5, Section 2. Broadly speaking, and subject to certain specific exceptions, a charge for, and reflecting the cost of, a service is not regarded under those rules as the imposition of a tax requiring a ways and means resolution, even if the service is provided compulsorily. The distinction is, however, of little practical importance today even in that context, since the practical implications of requiring a ways and means resolution are rarely significant.

[47] (1831) 2 B. & Ad. 43, 58, cited with approval by Vaughan Williams L.J. in *Assheton-Smith v Owen* [1906] 1 Ch. 179, 205.

[48] See also *Gildart v Gladstone* (1810) 11 East 675, 685 (dock dues), *Stockton and Darlington Railway v Barrett* (1844) 11 Cl. & F. 590, 601 (railway charges), *Pryce v Monmouthshire Canal Co.* (1879) 4 App. Cas. 205 (canal charges), *R. v Sedgley* (1831) 2 B. & Ad. 65 (poor rates) and *Tomkins v Ashby* (1827) 6 B. & C. 541, 542 (stamp duty).

[49] Chapter 12, Section 5.

[50] *Cape Brandy Syndicate v Inland Revenue Commissioners* [1921] 1 K.B. 64, 71, cited with approval by Viscount Simon L.C. in *Canadian Eagle Oil Co. v R.* [1946] A.C. 119, 140.

[51] That is to say, no presumption in favour of a tax.

[52] See also *Inland Revenue Commissioners v Ross & Coulter* [1948] 1 All E.R. 616, 625, HL *per* Lord Thankerton, *Lord Advocate v Fleming* [1897] A.C. 145, 151, HL *per* Lord Halsbury, *Tennant v Smith* [1892] A.C. 150, 154, HL *per* Lord Halsbury, *In Ormand Investment Co. v Betts* [1928] A.C. 143, 158, and *Inland Revenue Commissioners v Saunders* [1958] A.C. 285 *per* Lord Reid.

[53] [2003] 4 All E.R. 209, HL.

charge for a service provided without express authority to do so.[54] It is immaterial for this purpose whether the service is one which individuals are obliged, whether by law or as a matter of practice, to use, and whether the charge is limited to the direct cost of providing the service or includes an element of cross-subsidisation or profit.[55]

A power to charge a fee should not be presumed to permit the charging of different levels of fee for different classes of case in the absence of express authority.[56]

Although the level of fee is generally left to the discretion of the charging authority, Parliament takes an interest in the level of fees set and, in particular, in the level of increases.[57] On occasion the enabling statute imposes some kind of limitation on the level of fee that may be charged.[58]

There is also a presumption that where a fee is charged it will relate in some recognisable way to the direct and indirect costs of providing the service for which the fee is charged. If the intention is to set a rate of fee that will make a profit for use on some other activity, or to permit a significant degree of cross-subsidisation of the service offered to one person by the fee charged to another, it will generally be wise to take express provision.[59] Express provision of a

---

[54] *Attorney-General v Wilts United Dairies* (1922) 91 L.J.K.B. 897, 66 Sol. Jo. 630, 127 L.T. 822, 38 T.L.R. 781, HL.

[55] For the purposes of the House of Commons' rules about taxation requiring a ways and means resolution, a charge for a service is generally exempt from the requirement, unless, for example, the charge includes a significant element of cross-subsidisation or profit, or relates to a service that was previously provided without charge.

[56] See Joint Committee on Statutory Instruments, Session 1994–95, 16th Report, para.2 (HL Paper 47, HC 8-xvi).

[57] See, for example, objections by the Joint Committee on Statutory Instruments to the nature of an increase in a fee—Session 1992–93, 35th Report, June 29, 1993 (HL Paper 102, HC 51-xxxv), p.4; note also the Joint Committee on Statutory Instruments requiring (and annexing to Report) a Schedule of previous fees—Session 1994–95 7th Report January 31, 1995 (HL Paper 26, HC 8-vii); and note the Joint Committee on Statutory Instruments requiring and printing a justification of certain increases in fee—Session 1994–95 24th Report June 27, 1995 (HL 75, HC 8-xxiv).

[58] A reference to a "reasonable fee" is common, particularly when the charging body is non-Ministerial—see, for example, s.4 of the Access to Medical Reports Act 1988 (c.28) or s.30 of the Agricultural Tenancies Act 1995 (c.8). But a more precise formula is possible. So, for example, a fee may be limited to the cost of providing a service, while expressly permitting inclusion of an element to reflect general overheads—"(3) A local authority may not specify a fee under sub-paragraph (2) which exceeds the reasonable cost of providing the service sought (but in calculating the cost of providing a service to a person the authority may include a reasonable share of expenditure which is referable only indirectly to the provision of that service." (Sch.8, para.50(3) to the Draft Gambling Bill published by the Department for Culture, Media and Sport in November 2003).

[59] See, for example, s.42 of the Asylum and Immigration (Treatment of Claimants, etc.) Act 2004—

"In prescribing a fee for an application or process under a provision specified in subsection (2) the Secretary of State may, with the consent of the Treasury, prescribe an amount which is intended to—
    (a) exceed the administrative costs of determining the application or undertaking the process, and
    (b) reflect benefits that the Secretary of State thinks are likely to accrue to the person who makes the application, to whom the application relates or by or for whom the process is undertaken, if the application is successful or the process is completed. . . . "

general kind for this purpose (to a limited extent) is provided by s.102 of the Finance (No. 2) Act 1987.[60]

Finance Acts

The House of Commons regards fiscal legislation as falling within its financial privilege. The annual Finance Acts are the most important example, and their

1.6.14

---

[60] 1987 c.51.The text of section 102 is as follows—

"**102 Government fees and charges**

(1) This section applies where a Minister of the Crown or any other person has power under any enactment (whenever passed) to require the payment of, or to determine by subordinate legislation the amount of, any fee or charge (however described), which is payable to the Minister or to any other person who is required to pay the fee or charge into the Consolidated Fund (whether the obligation is so expressed or is expressed as a requirement to make the payment into the Exchequer).

(2) In the following provisions of this section, a power falling within subsection (1) above is referred to as a "power to fix a fee" and, in relation to such a power,

(a) "fee" includes charge;

(b) "the appropriate authority" means, if the power is exercisable by a Minister of the Crown or any Commissioners, that Minister or those Commissioners and, in any other case, such Minister of the Crown as the Treasury may determine; and

(c) "the recipient" means the Minister or other person to whom the fee is payable.

(3) In relation to any power to fix a fee, the appropriate authority or any Minister of the Crown with the consent of the appropriate authority may, by order made by statutory instrument, specify functions, whether of the recipient or any other person and whether arising under any enactment, by virtue of any Community obligation or otherwise, the costs of which, in addition to any other matters already required to be taken into account, are to be taken into account in determining the amount of the fee.

(4) In relation to any functions the costs of which fall to be taken into account on the exercise of any power to fix a fee (whether by virtue of subsection (3) above or otherwise), the appropriate authority or any Minister of the Crown with the consent of the appropriate authority may, by order made by statutory instrument, specify matters which, in addition to any matters already required to be taken into account, are to be taken into account in determining those costs, and, without prejudice to the generality of the power conferred by this subsection, those matters may include deficits incurred before as well as after the exercise of that power, a requirement to secure a return on an amount of capital and depreciation of assets.

(5) No order shall be made under subsection (3) or subsection (4) above unless a draft of the order has been laid before, and approved by a resolution of, the House of Commons.

(6) An order under subsection (3) or subsection (4) above has effect in relation to any exercise of the power to fix the fee concerned after the making of the order; but no earlier exercise of that power shall be regarded as having been invalid if, had the order been made before that exercise of the power, the exercise would have been validated by the order.

(7) In this section—

(a) "Minister of the Crown" has the same meaning as in the Ministers of the Crown Act 1975;

(b) "Commissioners" means the Commissioners of Customs and Excise or the Commissioners of Inland Revenue;

(c) "enactment" does not include Northern Ireland legislation, as defined in section 24(5) of the Interpretation Act 1978; and

(d) subject to paragraph (c) above, "subordinate legislation" has the same meaning as in the Interpretation Act 1978.

(8) . . . "

"Most Gracious Sovereign" enactment formula[61] encapsulates the idea that matters of taxation are arranged between the House of Commons and the Sovereign alone, excluding the House of Lords (although the Lords are permitted, subject to certain procedural constraints[62] and self-denying conventions, to hold proceedings on Finance Bills and other Bills that are purely about money).

The basic rule about the scope of the annual Finance Bill[63] is that it is limited to the raising of revenue to meet central expenditure, either by taxation or by borrowing, and to closely related matters.

It is well established that contributions to the National Insurance Fund are not regarded as revenue raising, or as taxation.[64] It is also well established that the fact that a proposal relates to the Inland Revenue or to Customs and Excise does not of itself make it a candidate for inclusion in a Finance Bill.

Hereditary revenues of the Crown

1.6.15 A number of sources of hereditary revenue of the Crown have been transferred to or converted into public funds, in return for annual returns through the civil list system. The nature of the arrangements is illustrated by the preamble to, by way of example, the Civil List Act 1910[65] (c.28)—

> "Whereas Your Majesty has been graciously pleased to signify to your faithful Commons in Parliament assembled that Your Majesty placed unreservedly at their disposal those hereditary revenues which were so placed by Your Majesty's predecessor, and that Your Majesty is desirous that competent provision should be made for Her Majesty the Queen in the event of Her surviving Your Majesty, . . . Now therefore we, Your Majesty's most dutiful and loyal subjects, the Commons of the United Kingdom in

---

[61] "Most Gracious Sovereign, WE, Your Majesty's most dutiful and loyal subjects, the Commons of the United Kingdom in Parliament assembled, towards raising the necessary supplies to defray Your Majesty's public expenses, and making an addition to the public revenue, have freely and voluntarily resolved to give and to grant unto Your Majesty the several duties hereinafter mentioned; and do therefore most humbly beseech Your Majesty that it may be enacted, and be it enacted by the Queen's most Excellent Majesty, by and with the advice and consent of the Lords Spiritual and Temporal, and Commons, in this present Parliament assembled, and by the authority of the same, as follows".

[62] See in particular the rules about Money Bills adverted to in Chapter 5, Section 2.

[63] As illustrated by a typical long title, that of the Finance Act 2003—"An Act to grant certain duties, to alter other duties, and to amend the law relating to the National Debt and the Public Revenue, and to make further provision in connection with finance."

[64] Hence "The convention is that national insurance is outside the scope of Finance Bills, and must be dealt with in social security legislation. . . . the responsibility for national insurance policy has been transferred to the Treasury through the Contributions Agency transfer legislation . . . However, this is still a matter for social security legislation."—(Minister of State, Department of Social Security, HC Deb. May 7, 1999 c.759).

So, for example, in 2002 there was a Finance Act (c.23) and a National Insurance Contributions Act 2002 (c.19).

[65] 1910 c.28.

Parliament assembled, have freely and voluntarily resolved to make such provision as herein-after appears for the purposes aforesaid, and we do most humbly beseech Your Majesty that it may be enacted."

SECTION 7

DECLARATORY LEGISLATION

Introduction

There are two kinds of declaratory legislation, express and implied. Express declarations, which are less common than they were once, are introduced by words along the lines of "for the avoidance of doubt it is hereby declared that ... ". By implied declaratory legislation is meant merely a proposition contained in legislation that does not itself purport to change the law but merely to express what the position is about a specified matter.[66] **1.7.1**

Blackstone describes an Act as declaratory "where the old custom of the realm is almost fallen into disuse or become disputable, in which case Parliament has thought proper, *in perpetuum rei testimonium*, and for avoiding all doubts and difficulties, to declare what the law is, and ever hath been".[67]

Whether an Act is merely declaratory of the previous law or effects a change is sometimes a matter of dispute, even if it purports to be merely for the avoidance of doubt.[68]

"For the avoidance of doubt"

It is still relatively common to find propositions in legislation introduced by the statement that they are included only for the avoidance of doubt.[69] And there have been entire Acts whose long title declares them to be enacted only for the purpose of removing doubt.[70] **1.7.2**

---

[66] In the drafting of some legislation it is possible to distinguish material of this kind by the use of the indicative rather than "shall". So, for example, s.130 of the Terrorism Act 2000 (c.11) uses the straight indicative in subs.(1) to record that certain parts of the Act extend to the whole of the United Kingdom—since that would be the position even if the Act said nothing—but says "shall extend" in subss.(2) and (3) which limit the extent of certain provisions. But as the use of the legislative "shall" is becoming less widespread—as to which see further Chapter 8, Section 1—this distinction can no longer be assumed.

[67] 1 Comm. 86.

[68] Compare Richmond J. in *Aldridge's case* (1897) 15 N.Z.L.R. 361, 369 and Sir Jocelyn Simon P. in *Adams' case* [1971] P. 188, 213; and see *Fawdry & Co. v Murfitt* [2003] 4 All E.R. 60, 69–70, CA.

[69] See, for example, the Electricity (Miscellaneous Provisions) Act 2003 (c.9), s.2(2); s.171ZF(2) of the Social Security Contributions and Benefits Act 1992 (c.4) inserted by the Employment Act 2002 (c.22), s.2; the Land Registration Act 2002 (c.9), s.116; and the Export Control Act 2002 (c.28), s.1(6).

[70] See, for example, the Act "to remove doubts as to the interpretation of subs.(4) of s.5 of the Representation of the People Act, 1918"—Representation of the People Act 1920 (c.15).

59

There are other legislative propositions that are included only for the avoidance of doubt although they do not say so expressly. The question arises whether this is a legitimate use of legislation. The argument that it is not legitimate rests on the assertion that the sole purpose of legislation is to change the law. But if there is a real doubt as to the state of the law in respect of a particular matter, removing the doubt by express provision does effect a change in the law, even if it does no more than to restore as the sole construction what would probably have been the better construction in the face of doubt.

When declaratory provisions of this kind were more common than they are today there was a rule of thumb that the expression "for the avoidance of doubt" was used for the purpose of guarding against misconstruction of the legislation in which the expression appeared, while the expression "for the removal of doubt" indicated the resolution of a doubt outside that legislation. Whether or not that distinction was ever applied rigidly, it is applied no longer.

Straight declaration

1.7.3   A provision of legislation may declare something to be the case without stating expressly whether it is thereby intending to change the law or merely to assert it. The effect of such a declaration will depend on the circumstances. It will, however, be construed strictly "against the Crown" if it comes to be argued that it has the effect of doing any of the things against which there is a rebuttable presumption.[71]

So in the case of *Sales-Matic Ltd v Hinchcliffe*[72] the courts had to construe s.21 of the Betting and Lotteries Act 1934 which read—

> "Subject to the provisions of this Part of this Act, all lotteries are unlawful."

Lord Parker C.J. said[73]—

> "Going back to section 21, it is, in general terms, declaring all lotteries to be unlawful. It is, to my mind, a novel way of declaring something to be an offence. One may test it in this way: Always supposing that the intention was to create an offence or offences by those words, what are they? Is it saying that anybody who conducts a lottery or promotes a lottery is guilty of an offence? Is it saying that anybody who partakes in a lottery is guilty of an offence? It seems to me that the proper construction of the section is that it is a declaration that all lotteries are unlawful, and then, owing to the difficulty of saying what is meant by promoting or conducting or being concerned with a lottery, the legislature goes on, by section 22, to declare a

---

[71] See Chapter 19.
[72] [1959] 3 All E.R. 401.
[73] At 402.

number of matters, which are connected with the promotion and form part of the promotion and conducting of a lottery, to be offences. Whether if the appellants had been charged under section 22 they could have been held guilty, I do not know. I suspect that in the normal way the appellants would have been charged under section 22(1)(f) in that they used premises for purposes connected with the promotion or conduct of a lottery, but that whoever was considering the matter thought that it was difficult to say that part of a pavement outside a shop was premises, and, therefore, fell back then on the general provisions of section 21. In my opinion, section 21 does not create an offence, and, accordingly, this appeal succeeds."

No power to make implied declaration

Parliament has unconstrained power to direct what the law is to be and how the courts are to construe it. But that power must be exercised by clear words. The mere fact that it is clear from the way a piece of legislation is framed that the legislature must have been assuming a particular interpretation of another law is not enough to make that interpretation the law or to require the courts to adopt it. As Lord Morris of Borth-y-Gest said in *Davies Jenkins & Co Ltd v Davies (Inspector of Taxes)*[74]— **1.7.4**

> "I understand that it is accepted that when Parliament enacted section 18 of the Finance Act, 1954, it must have proceeded on the basis that it was not necessary for the purposes of section 20 of the Finance Act, 1953, that the recipient company should be trading at the time of receipt of a subvention payment. This, in my view, neither relieves the courts from giving free and untrammelled consideration to the interpretation of section 20, nor does it furnish material for their guidance in so giving it. It is well accepted that the beliefs and assumptions of those who frame Acts of Parliament cannot make the law."

This is a principle of some antiquity,[75] fundamental in distinguishing the roles of Parliament and the courts. As Parke B. said in *Russell v Ledsam*[76]—

> "The province of the legislature is not to construe, but to enact, and their opinion, not expressed in the form of law as a declaratory provision would be, is not binding on courts whose duty is to expound the statutes [the legislature] have enacted."

---

[74] [1967] 1 All E.R. 913, 922, HL.

[75] But not going back to the roots of our system. In the early days of the English legal system the line between the judiciary and the legislature was not rigidly defined. In particular, the courts were subordinate to Parliament in ways other than being required to give effect to statutes duly enacted. See Sedgwick's *Statutory and Constitutional Law* (2nd ed. 1874) pp.18 and 174.

[76] (1845) 14 M. & W. 574, 589.

In construing legislation the courts will, however, "assume that the legislature knows the existing state of the law".[77] So where a matter of law is relevant to the application of a provision of legislation the courts will assume that the legislation was founded on an accurate understanding of that matter of law. But if it be apparent that the legislature's understanding was in fact deficient in some way, the courts will not defer to the legislature's deficient understanding but will act upon their own.

And it is of course open to the legislature expressly to enact that a particular construction of a matter of law shall itself have effect in law.[78]

The use of declaratory legislation

1.7.5 By the standard of Blackstone's definition[79] the Magna Carta is largely declaratory. The Treason Act 1351 purports to be wholly declaratory. More recently, the Bastardy (Witness Process) Act 1929 was declaratory, as was s.1(2) of the Ireland Act 1949. The latter provision survives, still in declaratory form, in s.1(1) of the Northern Ireland Act 1998.[80] For other recent examples, see s.26 of the Administration of Justice Act 1964[81] (Inner and Middle Temples), s.33 of the Betting And Gaming Duties Act 1981[82] (interpretation), para.4 of Sch.1 to the British Technology Group Act 1991[83] and s.23 of the Broadcasting Act 1996[84] (enforcement of digital programme licences).

Section 1 of the Interpretation Act 1978

1.7.6 Section 1 of the Interpretation Act 1978[85] provides that—

> "Every section of an Act takes effect as a substantive enactment without introductory words."

This provision is not, however, intending to draw a distinction between substantive and declaratory effect of a provision. It simply confirms the abolition of the ancient practice of repeating "Be it enacted" or "Be it further enacted" at the start of every substantive proposition of an Act.

---

[77] *Young & Co. v Mayor, &c. of Leamington* (1883) 8 App. Cas. 517, 526.

[78] But see the caveat to the note on s.34 of the Anti-terrorism, Crime and Security Act 2001 (c.24) at Chapter 2, para.2.2.1, footnote 18.

[79] Cited above.

[80] 1998 c.47: "It is hereby declared that Northern Ireland in its entirety remains part of the United Kingdom and shall not cease to be so without the consent of a majority of the people of Northern Ireland voting in a poll held for the purposes of this section in accordance with Sch.1." Since one Parliament cannot bind another (or even itself)—see Chapter 2, Section 2—even the latter part of this provision is no more than a declaration of the present intention of the present Parliament.

[81] 1964 c.42.

[82] 1981 c.63.

[83] 1991 c.66.

[84] 1996 c.55.

[85] 1978 c.30.

Danger of declaratory legislation

The dangers inherent in declaratory legislation are revealed by consideration of a particularly common form of declaration (which may or may not refer expressly to declaring)—the provision saving the effect of a particular right or situation from interference by legislation that might be thought to affect it although strictly construed it does not.[86] As Lord Halsbury said in *McLaughlin v Westgarth*[87]— **1.7.7**

> "The misfortune in the framing of these statutes [private Acts] is that any body of persons, seeing a possibility of liability on their part, apply to Parliament to have special provisions inserted for their protection. That application is occasionally complied with and then the argument arises, which their Lordships have heard today—namely, that anybody who is not included in the enumeration of the particular persons so inserted must be taken to be excluded by the operation of the statute from protection, just because they are not included and others are. A great many things are put into a statute *ex abundanti cautela*."

This gives rise to a general principle of drafting, discussed in Chapter 8, Section 1, paras 8.1.12 and 8.1.13.

Subordinate legislation

Everything said in this Section is as relevant to subordinate legislation as it is to primary legislation.[88] **1.7.8**

Section 8

Consolidation Legislation

Introduction

From time to time an area of statute law becomes excessively complicated as a result of the proliferation of pieces of legislation that relate to it. It can be immensely difficult for users of legislation to construct a coherent picture of the present state of the law on a particular matter if different aspects of it are addressed in a large number of different statutes or instruments. **1.8.1**

---

[86] If the interference were found on a proper construction of the legislation, then the provision saving the right would be, of course, substantive and not declaratory.

[87] (1906) 75 L.J.P.C. 117, 118, HL.

[88] There is at least one instance of the entirety of an instrument being devoted to the avoidance of doubt—see the Minister of Education (Transfer of Functions) (Removal of Doubt) Order 1950 (SI 1950/520).

Commercial publications that present all the legislation relevant to a particular matter can be extremely helpful: but they cannot without an inordinate amount of editorial refinement present a clear picture of each aspect of a wide area of law that has become fragmented over the years.

Even where the new legislation has wherever possible tried to take the form of textual amendment of the old, the result will not always be a coherent picture in a single amended statute: the structure of the earlier statutes may well be unavoidably falsified by later amendments; or the language of later amendments, necessarily adapted to the needs of the law at the time when the amendment is made, may cast doubt upon some of the provisions in parts of the earlier Act unaffected by the amendment.[89] And it is often not practicable to proceed by textual amendment, either because of the structure of the earlier legislation or because it would be unacceptably obscure for readers of the amending Bill and Act.

As a result of this, from time to time it may be helpful to replace the existing law on a particular matter with a new Act which makes no substantive change but presents the entire material in a newly organised structure and in language that is both modern and internally consistent. This is the process of consolidation.

This Section is principally concerned with the process of the production of Consolidation Bills.[90]

Responsibility for consolidation

1.8.2   The primary responsibility for the production of Consolidation Bills rests with the three Law Commissions.[91]

At any given time a small team of Parliamentary Counsel work in the Law Commission[92] on secondment from the Office of the Parliamentary Counsel.[93] They divide their time between drafting Bills to be exhibited with reports of the Commission on projects for law reform and working on consolidation. The senior draftsman of the team will from time to time draw up a programme of areas of law thought by draftsmen and others to be most urgently in need of consolidation, which is then approved by the Commissioners. One or more draftsmen are then assigned to the production of a Consolidation Bill on the

---

[89] Even where the solution to that might be a relatively simple amendment to another part of the earlier statute, that is likely to be precluded by the question of relevance (in the House of Lords) or scope (in the House of Commons): the Government may not feel able to expose other substantive areas of the law with which the earlier statute deals to amendment during proceedings on the amending legislation without risking its safe passage.

[90] As to consolidation of subordinate legislation, see para.1.8.9.

[91] The Law Commission and the Scottish Law Commission are established by the Law Commissions Act 1965 (c.22). Consolidation is one of the express duties conferred—see s.3(1)(d). For the similar nature and duties of the Northern Ireland Law Commission see ss.50 and 51 of the Justice (Northern Ireland) Act 2002 (c.26).

[92] The Commission responsible for the law of England and Wales is simply known as "the Law Commission"—Law Commissions Act 1965, s.1(1).

[93] See Chapter 5, Section 1.

topic, working with, and on the instructions of, the Government Department responsible for the substance of that area of law.

Consolidation projects vary greatly in their size and complexity. The Petroleum Act 1998[94] is an example of a relatively short Consolidation Act in a tightly defined area that will not have taken undue time or effort to produce, although doubtless matters of complexity arose during the process. At the other end of the spectrum are projects like the Education Act 1996[95] or the Powers of Criminal Courts (Sentencing) Act 2000[96] each of which took several years to produce.

Minor amendments

The essence of consolidation is to reorganise and restate so as to improve clarity **1.8.3** and intelligibility without altering the substance of the law. So the draftsman is expected to assure the Joint Committee, subject to what follows, that in his or her judgment the Bill makes no change to the substance of the law at all.

But there are three ways in which minor changes may be made to the law by a Consolidation Bill.

(1) The draftsman may become aware in the course of preparing the Bill that a very minor change requires to be made to correct an obvious error or anachronism of no practical significance. In such a case the draftsman may on his own initiative make the change in the Bill as introduced and draw the attention of the Joint Committee to the change by way of a Note submitted to the Committee along with the Bill.

(2) For something a little more substantial but still falling short of significant change of policy or substance, the Bill as introduced may be accompanied by a Law Commission Recommendation that a particular minor change be made.[97]

---

[94] 1998 c.17.

[95] 1996 c.56.

[96] 2000 c.6.

[97] This procedure is used fairly frequently. See, for recent examples, the Education Act 1996 (c.56) ("An Act to consolidate the Education Act 1944 and certain other enactments relating to education, with amendments to give effect to recommendations of the Law Commission"), the Highways Act 1980 (c.66) ("An Act to consolidate the Highways Acts 1959 to 1971 and related enactments, with amendments to give effect to recommendations of the Law Commission") or the Power of Criminal Courts (Sentencing) Act 2000 (c.6) ("An Act to consolidate certain enactments relating to the powers of courts to deal with offenders and defaulters and to the treatment of such persons, with amendments to give effect to recommendations of the Law Commission and the Scottish Law Commission"). The Joint Committee's Fifth Report for Session 1976–77 suggested that recommendations "should be for the following purposes: to tidy up errors of the past, to remove ambiguities and generally to introduce common sense on points where the form of drafting in the past appeared to lead to a result which departed from common sense; though not to introduce any substantial change in the law or one that might be controversial—indeed nothing that Parliament as a whole would wish to reserve for its consideration".

(3) There is also a statutory procedure under which "corrections and minor improvements" may be certified as such by the Lord Chancellor and, at the discretion of the Joint Committee, proceeded with and incorporated into the consolidation.[98]

Each of these procedures is right for a different class of case. Sometimes closely related Bills fall naturally to be dealt with under different procedures: so, for example, of the six consolidation Social Security Acts of 1992[99] those dealing with Great Britain were accompanied by Law Commission Recommendations while those dealing with Northern Ireland used the statutory procedure.[1]

Durability

1.8.4   The process of consolidating a sizeable and technically complicated area of law that has been much amended and glossed can be enormously arduous and time-consuming. It requires immense patience, meticulous attention to detail and an encyclopaedic, although often hastily acquired, knowledge of the relevant law. The result, however, can be very satisfying, when what was previously a confusing and unhelpful maze has been straightened out into a logical and helpful series of propositions.

---

[98] See the Consolidation of Enactments (Procedure) Act 1949 (c.33), s.1. This is an elaborate procedure which is little used; but for recent examples see the National Debt Act 1972 (c.65), the Juries Act 1974 (c.23), the British Airways Board Act 1977 (c.13), the Commonwealth Development Corporation Act 1978 (c.2), the Social Security Contributions and Benefits (Northern Ireland) Act 1992 (c.7), the Social Security Administration (Northern Ireland) Act 1992 (c.8) and the Radioactive Substances Act 1993 (c.12). The idea is to permit amendments where the Lord Chancellor thinks that "in order to facilitate the consolidation of those enactments, corrections and minor improvements ought to be made in such enactments" (s.1(1)). The procedure requires that there be prior publication of a memorandum of the desired improvements in the London Gazette (or Edinburgh or Belfast Gazette, or a combination, as appropriate), and that representations made on the memorandum should be referred to the Joint Committee (s.1(2) and (3)). The amendments have to be approved by the Joint Committee, the Lord Chancellor and the Speaker, all of whom must be satisfied that "the corrections and minor improvements do not effect any changes in the existing law of such importance that they ought, in their or his opinion, to be separately enacted by Parliament" (s.1(5)). The class of improvements that may be made is restricted to "amendments of which the effect is confined to resolving ambiguities, removing doubts, bringing obsolete provisions into conformity with modern practice, or removing unnecessary provisions or anomalies which are not of substantial importance, and amendments designed to facilitate improvement in the form or manner in which the law is stated," and related transitional provisions (s.2).

[99] 1992 cc.4 to 9.

[1] Explained by the Attorney General, speaking to the Bills in the House of Commons, in the following terms: "In preparing the three Great Britain Bills, the Law Commission and the Scottish Law Commission have, in accordance with normal practice, issued a report on the consolidation in which they make a number of recommendations for minor amendments that are necessary in order to produce a satisfactory consolidation. For the Northern Ireland Bills, the Lord Chancellor laid before Parliament in November last year a memorandum containing a number of corrections and minor amendments that were needed in order to facilitate the consolidation. That was in accordance with the Consolidation of Enactments (Procedure) Act 1949." (HC Deb. February 12, 1992 c.1030).

All the more agonising, therefore, when the painstakingly prepared structure is quickly obscured or even fundamentally falsified by new substantive changes to the law. Ideally, of course, one would choose as the subject for a consolidation an area of law which has changed considerably in the immediate past but is thought unlikely to be significantly amended in the near future. But it is often impossible to predict whether an area of law is likely to change in the next few years, and many areas of technical complexity or social importance appear to be subject to almost constant change.

The Education Act 1996 provides a serviceable example of an area of law that changed considerably both before and shortly after a major consolidation project. But examination of the number of Education Acts will show that there was no time within the few years before or after 1996 that would have been more suitable for a consolidation.

By way of an extreme example of the precarious nature of consolidation it may be noted that Chaps 8 and 9 of Pt 3 of the Income Tax (Earnings and Pensions) Act 2003[2] were repealed by Sch.22 to the Finance Act 2003,[3] and a number of other significant amendments were made by that Act, the repeals and amendments coming into force only a few days after the provisions repealed or amended.

Procedure for passing Consolidation Bills

The Parliamentary procedures for the passing of Consolidation Bills are discussed in Chapter 5, Section 3. **1.8.5**

Interpretation

Considerations apply to the interpretation of consolidation measures that do not apply to the interpretation of other legislation. They are explored in Chapter 29. **1.8.6**

Derivation and destination tables

It can be of enormous use to practitioners to be able to identify quickly and accurately the derivation of a provision of a Consolidation Act—that is to say the repealed provision the effect of which it replicates—or the destination of a repealed provision—that is to say the provision of the Consolidation Act that replicates its effect. **1.8.7**

The former is of use, in particular, in order to be able to search for decided cases on the meaning of the repealed provision by way of elucidating the meaning of the provision derived from it.

---

[2] 2003 c.1: a product of the Tax Law Rewrite Project—a kind of consolidation with special features, discussed in Section 10 below.
[3] 2003 c.14.

The latter is of use to the practitioner who knows that a particular provision of the old law is of relevance to a matter before him and needs to track it into the new legislation so as to be able to cite its modern equivalent. This may be far from a simple task, since in the reorganisation of material involved in a consolidation a single proposition in one of the Acts being consolidated may have to be divided so as to appear as a subordinate proposition within a number of disparate propositions of the Consolidation Bill.

For these reasons the draftsman of a Consolidation Bill prepares tables of destinations and derivations which are published at the time of the Bill's introduction.[4] These are reproduced, if necessary in a revised version, in the Annual Volumes of Statutes printed by The Queen's Printer.[5]

Of course there are likely to be individual paragraphs, subsections, or even sections of the legislation being consolidated that do not require replication at all, there being no need for them as a result of the structure adopted by the consolidating Bill.[6] In those cases the destination table will simply record that the provision is not replicated. Equally, the consolidating Bill may find it necessary or expedient to incorporate propositions that were not needed, or at any rate are not found, in the legislation being consolidated. In those cases the derivation table records the derivation of the provision as "drafting".

Pre-consolidation amendment

1.8.8 It sometimes happens that anomalies or peculiarities of an area of law are likely substantially to impede the effectiveness of a consolidation measure, being of too serious substantive effect to be addressed by any of the three procedures mentioned above. If the need for and prospect of consolidation is known at a time when a substantive Bill dealing with the area of law concerned is before Parliament, it may be possible, subject to the demands of the Government's legislative programme, to include in the substantive Bill certain pre-consolidation amendments, designed to facilitate the eventual consolidation.[7]

---

[4] In the case of Consolidation Bills before the Scottish Parliament (as to which see Chapter 7, Section 1) the production of these tables is a requirement of Standing Orders (Rule 9.18.2). No such formal rule exists in the Westminster Parliament, but the production of the tables is an unvarying practice.

[5] As to which see Chapter 9, Section 2.

[6] Or because they had only a transitional effect that is now spent, or were never of any legal effect (see, for example, Section 6 above, para.1.6.2).

[7] So, for example the Home Office's *Introductory Guide to the Crime and Disorder Act 1998* has the following to say about s.106—"Section 106 introduces Schedule 7 which makes a number of pre-consolidation amendments necessary before a Consolidation Bill can be introduced in a future session of Parliament. These are all amendments to various laws relating to the powers of the courts to deal with offenders or defaulters."; and note that Sch.15 to the Finance Act 1987 (c.16) was entitled Pre-consolidation Amendments: Income Tax and Corporation Tax (leading to the Income and Corporation Taxes Act 1988 (c.1)).

Subordinate legislation

Consolidation of subordinate legislation is rare[8] although it does occur.[9] Where **1.8.9** consolidation is thought necessary for subordinate legislation, there is no special procedure necessary, since the more flexible nature of subordinate legislation makes it a relatively simple matter to exercise a power to legislate by revoking and re-enacting an earlier exercise of the power rather than by making textual amendments or free-standing glosses on the earlier legislation.[10] Social security regulations provide an example of technically complex and crowded area of subordinate legislation thought to need consolidation (and an example of pre-consolidation amendment of subordinate legislation).[11]

There are precedents for incorporating subordinate legislation in a Consolidation Bill.[12]

SECTION 9

STATUTE LAW REVISION AND REFORM

Statute law revision

The first proposals for the revision of the statute law in a way which would **1.9.1** improve its form without altering its substance were made by Edward VI, James I and Lord Bacon.[13] But the process of revision did not begin until the repeal in 1856 of a series of obsolete Acts.[14] In 1868 the establishment of the Statute Law

---

[8] The nature of subordinate legislation means that there is less pressure to make minor textual amendments and glosses of the kind that can leave an area of statute law in disarray. There are few if any disadvantages when amending subordinate legislation of revoking and replacing whole instruments or parts of instruments at a time, avoiding the need for eventual wholesale consolidation.

[9] See, for example, the Continental Shelf (Designation of Areas) (Consolidation) Order 2000 (SI 2000/3062), the Dangerous Substances and Preparations (Safety) (Consolidation) Regulations 1994 (SI 1994/2844) and the Teachers Superannuation (Consolidation) Regulations 1988 (SI 1988/1652).

[10] For example, see reg.15(4) of, and Sch.3 to, the Harbour Works (Environmental Impact Assessment) Regulations 1999 (SI 1999/3445) which substitutes a new Sch.3 to the Harbours Act 1964 (c.40) rather than making piecemeal amendments: and note that the consolidation aspect of that approach was thought to fall within s.2(2)(b) of the European Communities Act 1972 (c.68)—as to which see Section 10 below.

[11] See Appendix 1 to the Seventh Report of the Joint Committee on Statutory Instruments, Session 2000–01.

[12] See, for example, the Employment Rights Act 1996 (c.18); but note that the Parliamentary proceedings for the Bill for this consolidation in the 1995–96 Session show that difficulties can arise if a consolidation is intended to include the effect of negative resolution subordinate legislation the period for praying against which has not yet expired.

[13] See Ruffhead, *Statutes*, Vol.1. Pref. P. 20.

[14] See Ilbert, *Legislative Methods and Forms*, 1901, p.57.

Committee[15] inspired an irregular but fairly frequent series of Statute Law Revision Acts.[16]

Responsibility for statute law revision was passed to the Law Commissions upon their establishment in 1965.[17] The provision which confers on the Law Commissions the duty of preparing a programme of consolidations[18] also requires the Commissions—

> "to prepare from time to time at the request of the Minister comprehensive programmes of . . . statute law revision, and to undertake the preparation of draft Bills pursuant to any such programme approved by the Minister".[19]

1.9.2   The work formerly performed by Statute Law Revision Acts is now performed by Statute Law (Repeals) Acts. The scope and intention of these Acts is adequately explained by the long title of the most recent Act[20]—

> "An Act to promote the reform of the statute law by the repeal, in accordance with recommendations of the Law Commission and the Scottish Law Commission, of certain enactments which (except in so far as their effect is preserved) are no longer of practical utility, and to make other provision in connection with the repeal of those enactments."

Between 1969 and 1978 there was a Statute Law (Repeals) Act every year or two. Since then there have been gaps of as much as four or five years between Acts.

The courts have commented that the task of keeping the statute book in repair, including the removal of clearly obsolete material, while not an attractive priority for the executive or Parliament is nevertheless their responsibility, and not a process with which the courts can or should interfere.[21]

---

[15] See para.9.2.16, footnote 56.

[16] See also comments on the number of statutes of little or no practical utility calling for repeal made in the *Report relating to Criminal Law and Procedure*, 1878 (HL) No.178 and the report of the House of Commons Select Committee on the first Statute Law Revision Bill of 1890 (Parl. Rep. (1890) C. 100, p.iii.

[17] For the similar nature and duties of the Northern Ireland Law Commission see ss.50 and 51 of the Justice (Northern Ireland) Act 2002 (c.26).

[18] As to which see s.8 above.

[19] Law Commissions Act 1965 (c.22), s.3(1)(d).

[20] Statute Law (Repeals) Act 1998 (c.43); note that a Statute Law (Repeals) Bill was before Parliament when this work went to print, and was expected to become the Statute Law (Repeals) Act 2004.

[21] "In an ideal world the statute book would always be up-to-date and contain only those Acts and provisions which are needed at present. In practice, that has never been the case. At any given moment you can find statutes which have become out of date and which should be repealed or amended but which linger on untouched since, in a crowded Parliamentary timetable, governments have had other priorities. . . . It is not the function of the courts to keep the statute book up to date. That important responsibility lies with Parliament and the executive. As long ago as 1977 the Law Commission recommended reform of the law of treason and allied offences. Parliament has not so

Preparation of Statute Law Repeal Acts

Statute Law Repeal Acts are today prepared by a small team of lawyers working **1.9.3**
within the Law Commission. The principles on which material is selected for
inclusion remain as they always have been. The aim is to remove from the statute
book provisions, which may amount to whole Acts, sections or even a few words
within a provision, which have no possible further utility in any future
circumstances that can realistically be imagined. The exercise is not to remove
material which has become of less utility than when it was first enacted, or which
Parliament might have come to regret having regard to modern circumstances.
As Sir Cecil Carr put it in a memorandum[22] to the Joint Committee on
Consolidation Bills in relation to what became the Statute Law Revision Act
1948—

> "Statute law revision is a crematorium for dead bodies of law, but not a
> lethal chamber for tiresome invalids who are still alive."

Before a Bill for a Statute Law (Repeal) Act is presented to Parliament a report
is prepared and published by the Law Commission and the Scottish Law
Commission, explaining in detail the proposed repeals, including both the nature
of the provisions to be repealed and the reasons for their obsolescence.[23]

Authorised omissions

Certain provisions of Statute Law Revision Acts authorise the omission of **1.9.4**
specified unnecessary material from "any revised edition of the statutes published by authority". For example, s.3 of the Statute Law Revision Act 1948[24]
permits the omission of words of enactment, while s.3 of the Statute Law
Revision Act 1950[25] permits the omission of material relating to certain foreign
territories. These provisions are of little or no modern significance, since the
Government would be likely to feel entitled to determine its own terms of
reference in the publication of revised statutes, in whatever form, without
statutory authority.

Revival

Occasionally it transpires that a provision, thought to have been of no practical **1.9.5**
utility and included for that reason in a Statute Law Revision Bill, remains of

---

far found the time to enact legislation to give effect to that recommendation. Successive Home
Secretaries have given a higher priority to other reforms. While that might seem unfortunate, it is
ultimately a matter for the political judgment of the executive and Parliament."—*R. v Attorney
General Ex p. Rusbridger* [2003] U.K.H.L. 38, *per* Lord Rodger of Earlsferry, paras 52 & 58.

[22] June 22, 1948.
[23] See, for example, *Statute Law Revision: Sixteenth Report* (published jointly by the two Law
Commissions in May 1998.
[24] 1948 c.62.
[25] 1950 c.6.

practical significance. When this happens it may be necessary to have reviving legislation.[26]

Procedure

1.9.6 The Parliamentary procedures applicable to Statute Law (Repeals) Acts are discussed in Chapter 5, Section 3.

Effect of Statute Law Revision or Repeal Act

1.9.7 The fundamental proposition relating to the effect of Statute Law Revision or Repeal Acts is that they are not intended to change the substantive law. As Viscount Finlay said in *Leeds Industrial Co-operative Society Ltd v Slack*[27]—

> "It is a truism that a Statute Law Revision Repeal was never intended to alter the law, but merely to remove from the Statute Book enactments which were obsolete or unnecessary."

Law reform Acts

1.9.8 Most Bills for Acts are brought into Parliament, whether by the Government or by a private peer or Member, for the purpose of changing some substantive aspect of the way in which society is regulated. As has been seen[28] a small number of Bills are introduced not for the purpose of changing the law but merely for the purpose of reorganising it so as to make it easier for practitioners and other readers.

A few Bills fall between these two extremes. They do aim to change the law, but not in such a way as to make any difference of significant substance. They effect technical improvements where the law has become inconvenient in some way, but are not designed to effect social or policy change.

These Bills are generally the product of work done in one or other of the Law Commissions. Their terms of reference as established by the Law Commissions Act 1965[29] include the duties—

> "to prepare and consider any proposals for the reform of the law which may be made or referred to the Commission,

> "to prepare and submit to the Lord Chancellor from time to time programmes for the examination of different branches of the law with a

---

[26] See, for example, (1) the Statute Law Revision Act 1888 and the Finance Act 1897, s.7, and (2) 10 Geo. 4, c.44, s.9 and the Magistrates' Courts Act 1952.

[27] [1924] A.C. 851, 862, HL.

[28] In the last Section, this Section (and the following Section).

[29] 1965 c.22.

view to reform, including recommendations as to the agency by which any such examination should be carried out, and

"to undertake, pursuant to any such recommendations approved by the Lord Chancellor, the examination of particular branches of the law and the formulation, by means of draft Bills or otherwise, of proposals for reform therein."[30]

It is not always clear, however, what will prove to be a matter of significant social controversy and what will be regarded as mere technical improvement.[31]

The Parliamentary procedures applied to law reform Bills are discussed in Chapter 5, Section 3.

SECTION 10

TAX LAW REWRITE

Introduction

Legislation is often criticised for being too complicated, both in form and in substance. While one can debate endlessly both the causes of this and the limitations on its resolution,[32] it is clear both that some of the complexity cannot be avoided and that some of it can be.

1.10.1

The role of consolidation in bringing renewed structural clarity to an area of law obscured by successive layers of amendment and modification has already been discussed.[33] But there is a limit to what can be achieved by the kind of re-structuring provided by consolidation alone.

As a result of a great deal of public criticism and debate[34] the Government determined in 1995 to consider whether anything could practically be done about the enormous complexity of tax legislation, often singled out as being the worst field of legislation for obscurity and prolixity. In December 1995 the Inland Revenue presented a report to Parliament about the scope for simplifying the tax system of the United Kingdom by rewriting the direct tax primary legislation in

---

[30] S.3(1)(a) to (c).

[31] See, for example, the story of the Family Homes and Domestic Violence Bill 1994–95. Having completed its passage in the House of Lords and made initial progress in the House of Commons the Bill started to attract criticism. "The Family Homes and Domestic Violence Bill was timetabled to complete its stages in the House of Commons on the basis that it was uncontentious. This has proved not to be so. Contentious points have arisen during the last stages of this parliamentary Session. My right hon. and noble Friend the Lord Chancellor has listened to the concerns expressed about the Bill, and he is considering them. The timetable is such, however, that it is now impossible to make further progress this session. My right hon. and noble Friend will continue to work on the Bill with a view to bringing it back before Parliament as soon as possible."—Parliamentary Secretary, Lord Chancellor's Department, HC Deb. November 2, 1995 W.A. 415.

[32] See Chapter 8, Section 1 and the reports there referred to.

[33] See Section 9 above.

[34] See, in particular, the *Interim Report on Tax Legislation* of the Tax Law Review Committee of the Institute for Fiscal Studies, published by the Institute on November 23, 1995.

clearer, simpler language. The scope of the project was to exceed mere consolidation but would fall short of major substantive revision of fiscal policy.

Following this report, in the budget speech of November 1996 the Chancellor of the Exchequer announced that the Inland Revenue would propose detailed arrangements for a project of this kind. The arrangements were published in December 1996.

The scope of the project

1.10.2 The scope of the tax law rewrite project is described in the following terms by the Inland Revenue—

> "Our overall aim is to rewrite the United Kingdom's primary direct tax legislation to make it clearer and easier to use, without changing the law.
>
> "Underlying our overall aim are six critical success factors, all of which must be fully achieved if the project is to succeed—
>
>> 'The rewritten legislation must be accepted by all the main users as clearer and easier to apply and as preserving the effect of the present legislation apart from minor agreed changes in policy.
>>
>> 'Parliament must be able to continue to scrutinise and enact the rewritten legislation in accordance with the clearly defined and appropriate parliamentary procedures to an agreed timetable.
>>
>> 'The main users, both inside and outside the Inland Revenue, must be kept fully informed about progress throughout the life of the project and, when appropriate, properly consulted in good time for their views to influence the rewrite work.
>>
>> 'The operational implications of the rewrite work for the Inland Revenue must be identified and properly addressed.
>>
>> 'The lessons learned from the experience of successfully rewriting the legislation should be developed, in close consultation with the users, into new best practice for producing tax legislation in the future.
>>
>> 'The project—including all the people in the Project Team—must be managed effectively and efficiently and the project's objectives must be achieved within the agreed programme and budget.' "[35]

The project has been extended to include certain subordinate legislation which was considered by commercial interests to be of particular importance and to be

---

[35] Inland Revenue *Tax Law Rewrite: Plans for 2003/2004*, Pt 2 and Appendix A.

likely to benefit particularly from the kind of treatment accorded by the project.[36]

Organisation of the project

The rewrite project is an enormous undertaking involving a large number of **1.10.3**
people and, indeed, many different kinds of person.

The drafting is overseen by a team of draftsmen on secondment from the
Office of the Parliamentary Counsel[37] headed by a senior member of that Office.
But the project team includes a wide variety of kinds of professional, including
specialists in tax law drawn from the private sector.

A Steering Committee[38] provides strategic guidance to the project. Its aim is
to ensure that the project meets its objectives of clarity and user-friendliness,
taking full account of concerns of the private sector. The members of the
Committee are drawn from both Houses of Parliament, the judiciary, the legal
and accountancy professions, consumer interests and business. There is also a
standing Consultative Committee, whose role is to ensure continuous consultation on the rewritten law with all the main private sector interests.

The project frequently publishes draft Bills for comment by interested parties.
As a rule, each Bill is published once in provisional form and once in more
settled, but still consultative, form, before being introduced into Parliament.

Approach and techniques

The approach and techniques of the project are summarised in its reports along **1.10.4**
the following lines[39]—

(1) A new, more logical, structure for the rewritten legislation.

(2) Use of modern language, in so far as this can be achieved without changing
the law or making its effect less certain.

(3) Use of shorter sentences and use of definitions.

(4) Use of signposts and similar rules grouped together, to make the rules easier
to find.

(5) A new format and layout to make it easier to read.[40]

---

[36] See the draft Income Tax (Pay as You Earn) Regulations published by the Tax Law Rewrite in April
2003. The foreword by the Paymaster General records that "Representatives of business and tax
practitioners asked me to extend the Tax Law Rewrite Project to the PAYE regulations. I was happy
to do so."

[37] As to which see Chapter 5, Section 1.

[38] Presently under the chairmanship of the Rt. Hon. the Lord Howe of Aberavon C.H., Q.C.

[39] Drawn from the Inland Revenue *Tax Law Rewrite: Plans for 2003/2004*, Pt 2 and Appendix B.

[40] But since the inception of this project the format for Bills and Acts has changed—see Chapter 2,
Section 5—and the two forms now coincide.

In essence, the project does not aim to make any changes in the underlying fiscal policy. But the project is able to propose minor changes which would improve the rewritten legislation without sacrificing any significant point of principle or policy.

Parliamentary handling

1.10.5   As with Consolidation Bills, the purpose of the rewrite project would be frustrated if the Bills introduced into Parliament were treated as an opportunity to debate, and table amendments to, every aspect of the policy of the tax legislation being rewritten. It was clear at the outset that Bills produced by the project would require some kind of protection and expedition if they were to make progress (without absorbing so much Parliamentary time as to make their introduction practically impossible for the Government).

This is achieved by special arrangements in each House, described in Chapter 5, Section 3.

Progress of the project

1.10.6   The project has so far produced the Capital Allowances Act 2001[41] and the Income Tax (Earnings and Pensions) Act 2003.[42] The aim appears to be to produce a significant addition to the rewritten code each year or two.

The tax law rewrite suffers from the same difficulty as other forms of consolidation in its vulnerability to being quickly rendered ineffective by new substantive amending enactments. The rewrite is, indeed, particularly vulnerable in this respect because, unlike any other area of law, there is expected to be at least one significant Act each year altering substantive tax law.[43] So, for instance, a large part of the Income Tax (Earnings and Pensions) Act 2003 was repealed and re-enacted, almost before it had come into force, by the Finance Act 2003.[44] Part of the aim of the project is to reform the approach to the formulation of tax law generally, with the aim that later Finance Acts should not wholly undermine the clarification and simplification achieved by the rewrite. But there are limits to what can be achieved in this respect, for a number of reasons—

An amending Finance Act is likely to be forced to falsify the structure of the rewrite Act, simply because it is impossible to predict what kind of

---

[41] 2001 c.2.

[42] 2003 c.1.

[43] The Finance Act incorporating the measures announced in the annual budget. This is more than a Parliamentary political convention: at present it is a legal necessity, since income tax is an annual tax, requiring express confirmation by Parliament in order to continue in force. See, for example, s.26 of the Finance Act 2002 (c.23): "Income tax shall be charged for the year 2002–03, and for that year [the rates shall be ...]".

[44] 2003 c.14: see Pt 3(4) of the Repeal Schedule (Sch.43).

substantive expansions or modifications may be later required, so as to allow for them in the construction of the original structure.

Provisions of the annual Finance Acts are determined, drafted and taken **1.10.7** through Parliament in conditions wholly unlike those of the rewrite Bill. The pressures and constraints on the process, including the possible requirement of amendments at a late stage, frequently result in legislation that is less simple than could have been achieved by starting with a blank page, using open consultation, ignoring pressure of time, and performing a consolidation exercise of the kind undertaken by the rewrite project.

The aim of the rewrite project is to introduce or at least maintain substantive simplicity wherever possible. One of the most significant tasks undertaken by the annual Finance Bill is to produce legislation in response to actual or threatened action on the part of the commercial community seen by the Government as abusing or undermining the fiscal system. Inevitably, legislation of this kind—the closing of "loopholes"—introduces further complexity into the system.[45]

Despite this, it is reasonable to hope that the tax law rewrite project will produce Acts that will be relatively enduring, and relatively robust under the strain of minor amendment, in much the same way as the major consolidation of the income and corporation tax legislation in 1988,[46] the essential structure of which has stood the test of time impressively.

---

[45] There has for some time been a debate about whether a general provision prohibiting anything done for the purpose of the avoidance of tax would enable the details of the legislation to be minimised. This is not the place for a thorough exposition of the two sides of this debate, which will be found in specialist tax journals and textbooks. But it is thought unlikely that a general anti-avoidance provision would be construed sufficiently tightly for the Government to feel able to rely on it and to resist making express provision where a particular avoidance opportunity could be identified. Apart from anything else, it is frequently very difficult to determine whether a particular commercial arrangement has been made for legitimate fiscal reasons, for evasive fiscal reasons, for accounting reasons, for commercial reasons or for a mixture of reasons. So although the courts have developed certain limited anti-avoidance doctrines themselves, and although there are specific anti-avoidance provisions of limited effect found in particular tax provisions, the hope that a single anti-avoidance provision of general application would significantly reduce the complexity of the tax code is unlikely ever to be realised. See also Chapter 8, Section 1, paras 8.1.20 and 8.1.21.
[46] The Income and Corporation Taxes Act 1988 (c.1).

CHAPTER 2

ACTS OF PARLIAMENT

SECTION 1

AUTHORITY OF AN ACT

An Act of Parliament owes its authority as law to the fundamental doctrine, one **2.1.1** of the foundation stones of the constitution of the United Kingdom, of the supremacy of Parliament. That doctrine can be summarised as the notion that "the Queen or King in Parliament"—meaning the two Houses of Parliament presided over by the Sovereign—can make any legislation of any kind. As Dicey has it—

> "The one fundamental dogma of English constitutional law is the absolute legislative sovereignty or despotism of the King in Parliament."[1]

This is reflected in the traditional enactment formula set out at the beginning of every Act of Parliament—

> "Be it enacted by the Queen's most Excellent Majesty, by and with the advice and consent of the Lords Spiritual and Temporal, and Commons, in this present Parliament assembled, and by the authority of the same, as follows:—"

It is this formula which in effect records the Royal Assent to the provisions **2.1.2** agreed to by the two Houses of Parliament.[2]

Until the granting of Royal Assent, the text of a proposed Act proceeding through the Houses of Parliament is described as a Bill.[3][4] For the effect or non-effect of a Bill, see Section 2 below.

---

[1] Dicey, *The law of the constitution*, (7th ed., (1908)), p.141.

[2] The formula is varied only for two kinds of legislation: Finance Acts, as to which see Chapter 1, Section 6 and Acts passed without the co-operation of the House of Lords in reliance on the Parliament Act 1911 (c.13), as to which see Chapter 5, Section 2.

[3] For the origin of the term as expressing a response to a petition see Chapter 5, footnote 1.

[4] It is common to use the word "Bill" with an initial capital letter in this context, for the convenience of distinguishing it from other kinds of bill. In many (but not all) Parliamentary documents, however, the customary usage is to refer to "bill" without an initial capital. This work follows the colloquial convention and uses an initial capital, except where quoting a text that does not.

Section 2

Potential Scope of Act

2.2.1 The result of the doctrine of supremacy of Parliament[5] is that an Act can do anything that Parliament chooses. In particular, an Act—

a. can effect fundamental constitutional change,[6]

b. can deem something to be the case for legal purposes when it clearly is not the case for any other purpose,[7]

c. can make law with retrospective effect,[8]

---

[5] As to the origin of the supremacy of Parliament, the matter has recently been discussed in a Written Question in the House of Lords (following the Written Question about the extent of Parliamentary supremacy referred to in Section 3 below) in the following terms (HL Deb. March 31, 2004 WA 160)—

"Lord Lester of Herne Hill asked Her Majesty's Government:

What is their understanding of the legal sources from which the legislative powers of Parliament are derived; and what are those sources.

Lord Goldsmith:

The source of the legislative powers is the common law.";

While it is, of course, possible to debate the point, it may be that much of the debate will amount to little more than semantic disagreement as to what is and is not meant by the common law in this context.

[6] " 'In England,' writes Tocqueville, 'the Parliament has an acknowledged right to modify the constitution; as, therefore, the constitution may undergo perpetual changes, it does not in reality exist; the Parliament is at once a legislative and a constituent assembly.' . . . The description of the English Parliament as at once a legislative and a constituent assembly supplies a convenient formula for summing up the fact that Parliament can change any law whatever. Being a legislative assembly it can make ordinary laws, being a constituent assembly it can makes laws which shift the basis of the constitution."—A. V. Dicey, *The Law of the Constitution*, (7th ed., 1908), p.84; as to special considerations in the case of constitutional statutes, see Chapter 1, Section 4.

[7] So, for example, s.10(5) of the Building Societies Act 1986 (c.53) provided that "An advance shall be treated for the purposes of this Act as secured by a mortgage of a legal estate in registered land in England and Wales or Northern Ireland notwithstanding that the advance is made before the borrower is registered as proprietor of the estate." And s.8 of the Pensions Act 1995 (c.26) provided for certain sums to be treated as debts due from the employer to the trustees of a scheme. And s.72 of the Terrorism Act 2000 (c.11) imposed time limits in respect of preliminary criminal proceedings and provided, in subs.(3), that "where an overall time limit expires before the completion of the stage of proceedings to which the limit applies, the accused shall be treated for all purposes as having been acquitted of the offence to which the proceedings relate." There are, of course, limits on the efficacy of the deeming which Parliament may choose to indulge in: as a draftsman once put it in connection with a privatisation exercise, "a United Kingdom statute can, at least as a proposition of United Kingdom law, deem there to be an apple tree in Trafalgar Square: but it is unlikely that there will be much of a market for the deemed apples."; for an example of a deeming provision treated as being absolute and irrebuttable, and the courts considering that to be justified, both by reference to the Human Rights Act 1998 and generally, by the interests of legal certainty, see para.19.1.23, footnote 61.

[8] As is explored in Chapter 10, Section 3, a presumption against retrospectivity is applied as a rule of construction. And there is a reluctance to legislate retrospectively because of the perceived inherent unfairness of, in particular, proclaiming people to have behaved unlawfully at a time when they could not have known that what they were doing was unlawful (because at the time it was not). But sometimes retrospectivity is unavoidable. And it is often necessary to avoid abuse: in Finance Acts, for example, it is common to backdate the effect of a measure to the budget day when it was first announced, despite the fact that Royal Assent will be some months later. And

d. can interfere with the lives of citizens in any way it chooses (including depriving them of liberty,[9] privacy[10] or property[11]),[12]

e. can permit an assault or battery of a kind that would otherwise be unlawful,[13]

f. can repair an irregularity or invalidity,[14]

g. can create rights and duties of any kind, and can abolish rights and duties of any kind whether their origin be from legislation, from the common law or from an exercise of the prerogative,[15]

---

sometimes a Minister will make an announcement about a proposal to change the law—perhaps by way of an answer in Parliament—and announce that when the change is effected it will be back-dated to the date of the announcement. See, for example, s.102A of the Finance Act 1986 (c.41) inserted by s.104 of the Finance Act 1999 (c.16).

[9] Not just by the creation of an offence punishable by the courts with imprisonment, but by conferring a power to detain—see, for example, s.34 of, and Sch.3 to, the Northern Ireland (Emergency Provisions) Act 1991 (c.24) (detention of suspected terrorists).

[10] As, for example, requiring births or deaths to be registered under the Births and Deaths Registration Act 1953 (c.20) or permitting information supplied to a public official for one purpose to be disclosed to another official for another purpose (as in, for example, s.3 of the Agricultural Statistics Act 1979 (c.13)).

[11] See, for example, the Distribution of German Enemy Property Act 1949 (c.85) or Pt V of the Housing Act 1985 (c.68) (the tenant's "right to buy").

[12] But, again, as a rule of construction it will be presumed that Parliament does not intend to deprive a person of liberty or property in the absence of the expression of a clear intention to the contrary—see Chapter 19.

[13] Obvious examples being the Road Traffic Act 1988 (c.52), s.6 (permitting the, in effect, compulsory administering of breath tests) and the Family Law Reform Act 1969 (c.46), ss.20–23 (permitting the administering of blood tests).

[14] See, for example, the National Health Service (Invalid Direction) Act 1980 (c.15): s.1 provides—
"The instrument dated 1st August 1979 and purporting to be a direction given by the Secretary of State for Social Services with respect to the functions of the Lambeth, Southwark and Lewisham Area Health Authority (Teaching) shall have effect and be deemed to have had effect as if it had been a valid direction under s.86 of the National Health Service Act 1977 specifying as the period during which those functions were to be performed by others the period beginning on 1st August 1979 and ending on 31st March 1980."

[15] So, for an extreme example, Lord Cranworth in the *Montrose Peerage Claim* (1853) 1 Macq. H.L. (Sc.) 401, 404 "I take it to be a matter admitting of no controversy that .. the effect of [the Act] was to destroy that creation [*i.e.* the Dukedom of Montrose]. It was not necessary that there should be any attainder.Parliament was omnipotent." (and see the Earldom of Mar Restitution Act 1855); see also Cockburn C.J. in *R. v Twiss* (1869) L.R. 4 Q.B. 407, 412—"Nothing short of an Act of Parliament can divest consecrated ground of its sacred character", and the Judicial Committee of the Privy Council in *Duranty v Hart* (1864) 2 Moore P.C. (N.S.) 289, 313, note (b)—"Nothing short of an Act of Parliament can displace a decision of the Supreme Court", and *Re Bishop of Natal* (1865) 3 Moore P.C. (N.S.) 115, 148—"After the establishment of an independent legislature in a colony, there is no power in the Crown by virtue of its prerogative, and without an Act of Parliament, to create a bishopric or other ecclesiastical corporation." and *The Prince's Case* (1606) 8 Co. Rep. 1a—"a course of inheritance which is against the rules of the common law cannot be created by charter without the force and strength of an Act of Parliament". See also Chapter 14, Section 2.

h. can abolish or modify ancient principles of the common law,[16]

i. can alter or disregard principles of fundamental public policy,[17]

j. can require the courts to exercise their functions in any given way,[18] or not to exercise their functions,[19] and

k. can make provision by reference to any other law, document or thing.[20]

The only thing that an Act of Parliament cannot do is constrain the freedom of action of a future Parliament.[21]

There are, of course, certain legal, procedural or practical constraints on the supremacy of Parliament. These are discussed in detail in their proper place, but for present purposes they can be listed as follows—

(1) Judicial presumptions of common law in construing Acts.[22]

---

[16] See, for example, s.34 of the Crime and Disorder Act 1998 (c.37) *"Abolition of rebuttable presumption that a child is doli incapax.* The rebuttable presumption of criminal law that a child aged 10 or over is incapable of committing an offence is hereby abolished."; see also Chapter 14, Sections 1 and 2.

[17] "Until Parliament intervened by legislation in 1990 it was always considered to be contrary to public policy, and therefore unlawful, in this jurisdiction for the financial reward which a lawyer received for his services in connection with litigation to vary depending on the outcome of the litigation. In 1988 the Report of the Review Body on Civil Justice (Cm 394), paras 384–389 encouraged the Lord Chancellor to re-examine the prohibition on what it described as 'contingency fees and other forms of incentive scheme'. In 1989 the Government took this suggestion forward, first in a green paper and then in a white paper later that year.These developments led in turn to the enactment of the Courts and Legal Services Act 1990. In s.58 of that Act Parliament decided to permit conditional fee agreements in relation to the provision of advocacy or litigation services in certain narrowly prescribed circumstances."—*Hollins v Russell* [2003] 1 W.L.R. 2487, 2497 CA *per* Brooke L.J.

[18] For an extreme example see s.34 of the Anti-terrorism, Crime and Security Act 2001 (c.24) which purports to require the courts to construe an international Convention, the Refugee Convention, in a particular way. The parameters of the effect of the section are of course open to discussion: clearly Parliament can decree the meaning of the Convention as a matter of the law of the United Kingdom, but Parliament cannot unilaterally change the meaning at international law of a Convention to which the United Kingdom is party (and the meaning at international law could become relevant in a judicial review or other domestic context). See also Chapter 1, Section 7, para.1.7.4.

[19] Although the jurisdiction of the High Court is not owed entirely to statute (despite the Supreme Court Act 1981 (c.54)—see s.19(2)(b)) it is open to Parliament to modify or curtail it: but see Chapter 19, paras 19.1.17—19.1.23.

[20] So, for example, the Merchant Shipping 1995 (c.23), s.173(10) contains the following definition: "'fuel oil' means heavy distillates or residues from crude oil or blends of such materials intended for use as a fuel for the production of heat or power of a quality equivalent to the 'American Society for Testing and Materials' Specification for Number Four Fuel Oil (Designation D396–69)', or heavier". And the Northern Ireland (Entry to Negotiations, etc) 1996 (c.11), s.1 operated by reference to "the negotiations referred to in Command Paper 3232 presented to Parliament on 16th April 1996"; and an Act can permit or require subordinate legislation to make provision by reference to any other instrument or document—see Chapter 3, Section 5.

[21] "That Parliaments have more than once intended and endeavoured to pass Acts which should tie the hands of their successors is certain, but the endeavour has always ended in failure"—A.V. Dicey, *The Law of the Constitution*, (7th ed., 1908), pp.62 and 63; but note what is said below about practical constraints.

[22] See Chapter 19.

(2) Constraints imposed by Parliament in previous Acts.[23]

(3) Obligations of international law.[24]

(4) Territorial restrictions on the jurisdiction of the United Kingdom Parliament.[25]

Even these restrictions and limitations, however, are effective only because they are either established or tolerated by Parliament. And they are subject to Parliament's power to abrogate them by express provision either generally or in specific contexts. The point is expressed forcefully in relation to human rights—the preservation of which is both a long-standing judicial presumption at common law and, since the Human Rights Act 1998,[26] an international obligation of this country expressly transposed into statutory law—by Lord Hoffmann in *R. v Secretary of State for the Home Department, Ex p. Simms*[27]—   **2.2.2**

> "I add only a few words of my own about the importance of the principle of legality in a constitution which, like ours, acknowledges the sovereignty of Parliament.
>
> "Parliamentary sovereignty means that Parliament can, if it chooses, legislate contrary to fundamental principles of human rights. The Human Rights Act 1998 will not detract from this power. The constraints upon its exercise by Parliament are ultimately political, not legal. But the principle of legality means that Parliament must squarely confront what it is doing and accept the political cost."

It is particularly important to emphasise that even the fundamental principles of law that the courts apply in construing Acts are applied not because they are superior to the authority of Parliament but because Parliament permits the courts to apply them and has not until now interfered. Were Parliament to do so—by, for example, expressly enacting a provision that was clearly in breach of the principles of fairness—the courts would be obliged to give effect to Parliament's will. As Lord Reid put it in *British Railways Board v Pickin*[28]—

> "In earlier times many learned lawyers seem to have believed that an Act of Parliament could be disregarded in so far as it was contrary to the law of God or the law of nature or natural justice, but since the supremacy of

---

[23] See Chapter 14, Section 5.
[24] See Chapters 25 and 29.
[25] See Chapter 11, Section 1.
[26] 1998 c.42.
[27] [1999] 3 All E.R. 400, 411–12, HL; and note that this passage was cited with particular approval by Lord Steyn in *R. (Anufrijeva) v Secretary of State for the Home Department* [2003] 3 W.L.R. 252, 265, HL.
[28] [1974] A.C. 765, 781, HL.

Parliament was finally demonstrated by the Revolution of 1688 any such idea has become obsolete."[29]

The suggestion is sometimes advanced that laws of an extreme unconstitutional nature might be disregarded by the courts even if enacted by Parliament. But, as Willes J. said in *Lee v Bude, &c. Railway*[30]—

> "I would observe, as to these Acts of Parliament, that they are the law of this land; and we do not sit here as a court of appeal from parliament. It was once said,—I think in Hobart [*Day v Savadge*[31]]—that, if an Act of Parliament were to create a man judge in his own case, the Court might disregard it. That dictum, however, stands as a warning, rather than an authority to be followed. We sit here as servants of the Queen and the legislature. Are we to act as regents over what is done by parliament with the consent of the Queen, lords, and commons? I deny that any such authority exists."

2.2.3   Despite this and other authorities to similar effect the suggestion is made from time to time that the courts would be right to disregard provision of one kind or another.[32] The question was raised recently in the following exchange by way of Written Question in the House of Lords[33]—

---

[29] As to the historical point referred to, it was observed in *Day v Savadge* that "even an Act of Parliament made against natural equity, as, to make a man judge in his own case, is void in itself; for, *jura naturae sunt immutabilia*, and they are *leges legum.*" (HOB. 87); But see *Lee v Bude and Torrington Railway Company* (1871) L.R. 6 C.P. at 582 *per* Willes J.—"it is further urged, that the company is a mere nonentity, and there never were any shares or shareholders. That resolves itself into this, that Parliament was induced by fraudulent recitals to pass the Act which formed the company. I would observe, as to these Acts of Parliament, that they are the law of this land; and we do not sit here as a court of appeal from Parliament. It was once said—I think in Hobart—that if an Act of Parliament were to create a man judge in his own case, the court might disregard it. That dictum, however, stands as a warning, rather than an authority to be followed. We sit here as servants of the Queen and the legislature. Are we to act as regents over what is done by Parliament with the consent of the Queen, Lords, and Commons? I deny that any such authority exists.If an Act of Parliament has been obtained improperly, it is for the legislature to correct it by repealing it: but, so long as it exists as law, the courts are bound to obey it. The proceedings here are judicial, not autocratic, which they would be if we could make laws instead of administering them."

[30] (1871) L.R. 6 C.P. 576, 580 C.C.P.

[31] (1614) Hob. 85.

[32] Judicial comments on the proposed ouster of the jurisdiction of judicial review in the Asylum and Immigration (Treatment of Claimants, etc.) Bill 2003–04—as to which see further Chapter 19, Section 1, footnote 50—have been presented in that light. It may be, however, that the comments amounted more to a warning that the provisions concerned were likely to be ineffective than that they were likely to be disregarded. See, for example, para.2(7) of the written evidence submitted by the Honourable Mr Justice Collins, former President, Immigration Appeal Tribunal to the House of Commons Select Committee on Constitutional Affairs (Second Report of Session 2003–04 (HC 211-I & 211-II).

[33] HL Deb. March 31, 2004 W.A. 160.

"Lord Lester of Herne Hill asked Her Majesty's Government:

Whether, in preparing legislative proposals to introduce into Parliament, they operate on the basis that the legislative powers of Parliament are, as a matter of British constitutional law, unlimited powers.

The Attorney-General (Lord Goldsmith): The Government consider that it is a fundamental principle of British constitutional law that the competence of Parliament to legislate on any matter is unlimited."

Having said which, the political restraints mentioned by Lord Hoffmann above may in some cases prove to be so compelling as to be absolute for all practical purposes.

In relation to an Act granting independence to a former British possession, for **2.2.4** example, although it remains theoretically possible for Parliament to repeal the Act and re-assert sovereignty over the possession—just as in theory it is open to Parliament to declare sovereignty afresh over a territory that was never before under United Kingdom control—the political and practical considerations (including, but not confined to, those forming part of the corpus of that which is called public international law) are of such strength that even to assert the possibility of repeal as a proposition of legal theory is more misleading than illuminating.

The point is well expounded in the passage of the judgment of Lord Denning in *Blackburn v Attorney-General*[34] appended to this work.[35]

SECTION 3

EFFECT OF ACT

Once Parliament has enacted a provision, every person[36] on whom the statute **2.3.1** places any duty—whether positively to do something or to refrain from doing something—is bound to comply; and the sanction for failure to comply is the panoply of enforcement mechanisms, criminal and civil made available to the courts.[37] The duty to comply is absolute, as is the duty on the courts to enforce:

---

[34] [1971] 2 All E.R. 1380, 1381–82, CA.

[35] Appendix, Extract 8.

[36] This means any legal person, whether a natural individual or a body given legal identity by the rules of law. And Parliament frequently places duties on groups of persons jointly, by virtue of the fact that the standard statutory definition of "person" includes bodies unincorporated—see Chapter 22. Nor is the power of Parliament confined to citizens of the United Kingdom or legal persons incorporated in the United Kingdom: it is open to Parliament to legislate for persons who happen to be in, or to be doing anything in relation to, the United Kingdom, or indeed for persons doing anything anywhere in the world—but the enforcement of the law will in practice depend upon there being some practical connection with the United Kingdom sufficient to bring the matter within the sanctions available to the courts of the United Kingdom or within the rules by which foreign courts will give effect to laws of the United Kingdom.

[37] Whether by statute or by the common law.

the courts cannot choose to regard an Act as undeserving of rigid enforcement. As Ungoed-Thomas J. said in *Cheney v Conn (Inspector of Taxes)*[38]—

> "What the statute itself enacts cannot be unlawful, because what the statute says and provides is itself the law, and the highest form of law that is known to this country. It is the law which prevails over every other form of law, and it is not for the court to say that a parliamentary enactment, the highest law in this country, is illegal."

As Dicey puts it[39]—

> "There is no legal basis for the theory that judges, as exponents of morality, may overrule Acts of Parliament. . . . The plain truth is that our tribunals uniformly act on the principle that a law alleged to be a bad law is *ex hypothesi* a law, and therefore entitled to obedience by the courts."

Just as the courts cannot decline to enforce, nor can they apply equitable or other doctrines for the purpose of granting relief from the effect of the application of the clear meaning of an Act.[40] As Holder L.J. said in *Gibbs v Guild*[41]—

> "Acts of Parliament are omnipotent, and are not to be got rid of by declarations of courts of law or equity."[42]

2.3.2   Even where the consequences of an Act are clearly absurd in a particular case, the courts cannot refuse to give effect to it. In accordance with this principle in *Young & Co. v Mayor, &c. of Leamington*,[43] for example, the Court of Appeal declared one party not bound by a contract that failed to comply with the formal requirements of s.174 of the Public Health Act 1875[44] despite the fact that the party had received the benefit of the contract, on the ground that otherwise the section would be deprived of all effect. Lindley L.J. said[45]—

> "It may be that this is a hard and narrow view of the law; but my answer is, that Parliament has thought it expedient to require this view to be taken, and

---

[38] [1968] 1 All E.R. 779.
[39] A.V. Dicey, *The Law of the Constitution*, (7th edn., 1908).
[40] The old doctrine of construing legislation by proceeding upon the "equity of the statute" was common and appropriate for the manner in which earlier Acts were framed (see *Hay v Lord provost of Perth* (1863) 4 Macq. H.L. (S.C.) 535, 544 *per* Lord Westbury) but is no longer used (see *Edwards v Edwards* (1876) 2 Ch. D. 291, 297 *per* Mellish L.J.).
[41] (1882) 9 Q.B.D. 59, 75.
[42] See further *Curtis v Perry* (1802) 6 Ves.739. And, as to waiver of statutory rights, &c. see Chapter 12, Section 3.
[43] (1882) 8 Q.B.D. 579; (1883) 8 App. Cas. 517.
[44] 1875 c.55.
[45] At 585.

it is not for this or any other court to decline to give effect to a clearly expressed statute because it may lead to apparent hardship."

Despite the principles enunciated above, it is not impossible that the courts will refuse to allow a statute to be used to produce a result which is not merely beyond the probable contemplation of the legislature but actually repugnant as a matter of public policy. So, for example, in *Whiston v Whiston*[46] the Court of Appeal declined to permit a bigamist to make a claim for financial relief under the Matrimonial Causes Act 1973.[47] As will be seen from the reasoning of the Court of Appeal in *Whiston*, as well as from the cases considered in the judgments in that case, this is essentially a matter of assuming that Parliament does not intend to produce a result which is contrary to a fundamental principle, such as that which prevents a person from benefiting from his own wrong-doing. The assumption could therefore be rebutted by clear words, as in the case of other presumptions of the common law.[48]

As to the cases in which a particular construction may be put upon an Act in order to avoid injustice or absurdity, see Chapter 19.

See also Chapter 12, Section 5.

The dicta as to the breadth of Parliamentary sovereignty have had to be **2.3.3** qualified somewhat for practical purposes as a result of the constraints and limitations listed above. But these constraints and limitations are there only because Parliament either imposed them or tolerates their continuance. So the strength of the theory remains.

Although it might seem too obvious to require to be stated, the proposition that an Act is of no effect in law until it has been enacted has been doubted sufficiently often to make its rebuttal a matter of judicial precedent. In *Willow Wren Canal Carrying Co. Ltd v British Transport Commission*[49] Upjohn J. said—

"It is plain, however, that it is not right for this court either now or at the hearing to take into account the possible effect of a Bill which is at present before Parliament and which, so far as this court is concerned, may never become law, or, if passed into law, may contain provisions which ultimately do not affect the rights of the parties before the court. In other words, it is a matter of speculation on which this court will not embark whether a Bill at present before Parliament will be passed into law in its present form."

A mere expression by the Government of an intention to legislate at some **2.3.4** future time should not be accorded legal effect, such as, for example, to determine the construction of existing legislation where the Government's

---

[46] [1995] Fam. 198, CA.
[47] 1973 c.18.
[48] See Chapter 19.
[49] [1956] 1 All E.R. 567, 568 Ch.

intention purports to be based on an understanding of a deficiency in the existing legislation.[50]

For further discussion of the effect of rights and duties conferred or imposed by Act, see Chapter 12.

A right under an Act is a specialty.[51]

SECTION 4

IRREGULARITIES

2.4.1   Once an Act has been passed and duly promulgated[52] any irregularity that may have occurred in respect of the proceedings to which Parliament subjected the Bill for the Act is of no effect, and the courts will not interfere with the Act however apparently material the irregularity and however one might imagine it to have affected the intention of the legislature. The extent of the doctrine and the reasons for it are described in the following passage of the speech of Lord Reid in *British Railways Board v Pickin*[53]—

> "The function of the court is to construe and apply the enactments of Parliament. The court has no concern with the manner in which Parliament or its officers carrying out its Standing Orders perform these functions. Any attempt to prove that they were misled by fraud or otherwise would necessarily involve an inquiry into the manner in which they had performed their functions in dealing with the Bill which became the British Railways Act 1968. . . .

> "For a century or more both Parliament and the courts have been careful not to act so as to cause conflict between them. Any such investigations as the respondent seeks could easily lead to such a conflict, and I would only support it if compelled to do so by clear authority. But it appears to me that

---

[50] See, for example, "True it is . . . that the Law Commission's Report on Limitation of Acts has recently recommended an end to the *Walkley* principle and that the Government has accepted that recommendation in principle and stated in Parliament that it will introduce legislation when a suitable opportunity arises. It by no means follows, however, and I cannot accept, that whilst the *Walkley* Principle continues to hold good under domestic law the United Kingdom is to be regarded as violating the art.6 rights of those affected by it."—*Young v Western Power Distribution plc* [2003] 1 W.L.R. 2868, 2883, CA *per* Simon Brown L.J.

The courts also resist invitations to construe proposals for legislation, in accordance with the general principle against considering hypothetical questions—see, for example, "38. There is a provision in the Communications Bill (clause 311(7)(b)) which some have read as showing an intention to exclude PEBs from the standards of taste and decency. I do not propose to try to construe it; first, because it is not yet law and secondly because the Department of Culture, Media and Sport has written to the BBC to confirm that it is the government's intention that such standards should continue to apply to PPBs and PEBs and that the clause may be amended to make this clear." (*R. v British Broadcasting Corporation (Appellants) Ex p. Prolife Alliance* [2004] 1 A.C. 185, 227, HL *per* Lord Hoffmann).

[51] See further Chapter 12, Section 2.

[52] As to which see Chapter 5 and Chapter 9, Section 2.

[53] [1974] A.C. 765, 786–87, HL.

the whole trend of authority for over a century is clearly against permitting any such investigation.

> "The respondent is . . . not entitled to go behind the Act to show that section 18 should not be enforced. Nor is he entitled to examine proceedings in Parliament in order to show that the appellants by fraudulently misleading Parliament caused him loss."

This extract and the case in which it appears show that this doctrine of the finality of an Act applies not only in public general Acts but even in the case of private legislation.[54] In relation to private legislation the procedures of Parliament are specifically designed to protect private interests from fraudulent or unjustified tampering.[55] Even so, and even where there might be clear evidence that the purpose of those procedures was undermined, the doctrine of Parliamentary supremacy is both too important and too potentially fragile for the courts to permit themselves to interfere. **2.4.2**

Of course, if real fraud or injustice can be shown to the courts it can also be shown to Parliament, and there would be ample and unconstrained mechanisms by which Parliament could redress any wrong that had been suffered as a result of a deliberate misapplication, evasion or abuse of her procedures. As Willes J. said in *Lee v Bude, &c. Railway*[56]—

> "If an Act of Parliament has been obtained improperly, it is for the legislature to correct it by repealing it: but, so long as it exists as law, the Courts are bound to obey it. The proceedings here are judicial, not autocratic, which they would be if we could make laws instead of administering them. The Act of Parliament makes these persons shareholders, or it does not. If it does, there is an end of the question."

Having said all that, and although a public Act of Parliament needs no proof for the judges to be required to take judicial notice of it, the judges are entitled to inquire whether something purporting to be an Act of Parliament is indeed an Act of Parliament[57] (without, as shown above, being entitled to inquire into the legitimacy or application of the procedures followed before enactment). In relation to any Act other than one of great age, however, it is hard to imagine this being a practical issue today. In particular, complicated rules of law as to the validity of the Royal Assent to Acts, and as to the effect of preambles and recitals to an Act, can now be regarded as obsolete.[58] **2.4.3**

---

[54] As to which see Chapter 1, Section 3.
[55] See Chapter 5, Section 4.
[56] (1871) L.R. 6 C.P. 576, 580 C.C.P.
[57] 8 Co. Rep. 18a.
[58] They can be found in thorough exposition in the 7th Edition of this work (1971) at pp.40 to 43. So far as they remain relevant to recitals to private Acts, and preambles where found, see Chapter 26.

In relation to the enactment of an Act in accordance with the provisions of the Parliament Act 1911,[59] s.3 of that Act provides that a certificate of the Speaker of the House of Commons as to compliance with the requirements of the Act "shall be conclusive for all purposes, and shall not be questioned in any court of law".[60]

SECTION 5

FORM OF ACTS

Format

2.5.1 The layout of Acts of Parliament and the fonts used for their printing were changed in 2000 following a working party established under the auspices of the House of Lords Select Committee on Procedure. The Committee presented the principal findings of the working party to the House of Lords in its Second Report for the Session 1998–99[61] in the following terms—

> "The Procedure Committee agrees to the recommendations of the working group. The principal changes proposed are:
>
> 1. a new format for clauses, with bold clause titles instead of side notes;
> 2. Schedules in the same type size as clauses;
> 3. more informative headers at the top of each page;
> 4. some left alignment of internal headings, especially in Schedules;
> 5. new format for Repeal Schedules.[62] . . .
>
> "The Committee also considered a number of additional changes proposed by Lord Howe of Aberavon, chairman of the Tax Law Rewrite Project's Steering Committee. Generally the Committee preferred the original recommendations of the working group, but agreed improved layout of indentations and a modification to the style of Part, Chapter and Schedule headings which should be printed in bold type."

Following an exchange between the House of Commons Select Committee on

---

[59] 1911 c.13—see Chapter 5, Section 2.

[60] It is an open question, however, whether the courts might permit themselves to question, for example, the giving of advice in relation to a certificate, or a decision of Government taken in relation to the use of the Parliament Act 1911 or a particular process under it. And the breadth of s.3 may not be sufficient to prevent a ruling of an *Anisminic* kind.

[61] April 13, 1999.

[62] The only change was to abandon the three column format, in which the title, chapter number and repealed provisions were each displayed in a separate column for a two column format. The suggestion that this improves the lot of readers is more illusory than real, since it is only technical editors of statutory publications, and others with special technical interest in statutes, who are likely to read Repeal Schedules at all frequently, and they are unlikely to find the number of columns significant. Because any repeal of substance is founded elsewhere in the Act, the Schedule is merely a resume of repeals already effected, with the addition of a few purely technical repeals which having no legal substance do not require to be founded. See Chapter 14, Section 4.

Modernisation and the House of Lords Select Committee on Procedure of the House, the latter Committee made a further recommendation[63] overriding the original working party's preference for *Times New Roman* typeface in favour of the larger typeface *Book Antiqua*.

These changes were introduced for Bills and Acts during the Session 2000–01, having been approved by both Houses of Parliament.[64]

Divisions and components

Acts are divided between sections and Schedules.[65] A Schedule is as much a part **2.5.2** of the Act to which it belongs as is a section.[66] Schedules are relegated to the end of the Act in order to prevent technical matters or minor supporting detail from preventing a logical and easily navigable flow of the principal material.

A Schedule is generally introduced by a provision in a section that the Schedule "shall have effect": but it may be introduced merely by a passing reference in a section, along the lines of "in accordance with the provisions of Schedule X".[67]

A section is described as being "of" an Act, while a Schedule is described as being "to" an Act.

---

[63] Fourth Report for Session 1998–99, July 6, 1999.

[64] HL Deb. July 22, 1999 c.1183; and the First Special Report of the House of Commons Select Committee on Modernisation, Session 1998–99.
See the following exchange by way of Written Answer in the House of Commons (HC Deb. December 13, 2000 W.A. 183–184)—

> "Mr.Levitt: To ask the President of the Council when primary legislation will be printed in the new format agreed by both Houses in 1999.
>
> Mrs.Beckett: The new format is being introduced this Session, using new computer software which has had to be developed. The change will be staged, to allow everyone involved to become accustomed to working in the new format and to minimise the risk of disruption should there turn out to be flaws in the software.
>
> For the time being, Bills will continue to be introduced in the old format apart from any Bill originating from the Tax Law Rewrite. Each Bill will be published in the new format in the second House, once it has completed its passage through the first.
>
> So, Bills introduced in this House will be in the old format during their stages in this House; but Bills brought from the other place will be in the new format throughout our consideration of them. Similarly, the other place will deal with Bills introduced there in the old format, but deal with Bills brought from this House in the new format.
>
> All Acts passed after 1 January 2001 will be in the new format.
>
> When we are fully confident that the new format and software are problem-free, it will be used for all Bills at all stages."

A similar question was answered in the same terms in the House of Lords on the same date.

[65] The modern convention is to use an initial capital for Schedule, Part and Chapter but not for section, clause, rule, regulation or paragraph: as to articles, practice varies—the normal domestic convention is to use no capital for an article of an order, but that is not the case for European practice in relation to Directives and other documents sub-divided into articles, or for Northern Ireland instruments.

[66] "With respect to calling it a schedule, a schedule in an Act of Parliament is a mere question of drafting—a mere question of words.The schedule is as much a part of the statute, and is as much an enactment as any other part."—*Attorney-General v Lamplough* (1877–788) L. R. 3 Ex. D. 214, 229, CA, *per* Brett L.J.

[67] See, for example, Sch.9 to the Value Added Tax Act 1994 (c.23) (exempt supplies) which is given effect only by oblique references in ss.8 and 31.

Sections of an Act may be, but need not be, grouped in numbered[68] Parts.[69] This enables the reader to navigate around an Act more easily. And it provides an easy way for provisions about interpretation, extent, commencement or other technical matters to identify groups of provisions to which particular propositions apply.

Parts are occasionally divided into Chapters.[70]

2.5.3 It is not usual for sections of an Act to be grouped into divisions larger than Parts or smaller than Chapters. But the former happens occasionally with very large Acts.[71]

As an alternative to the formal division of an Act into Parts, provisions on related subjects may be grouped together and headed by an italic cross-heading.[72]

A section of an Act is preceded by a heading,[73] and a group of sections (or fasciculus) may be preceded by an italic cross-heading. Sections are numbered by Arabic numerals.[74]

The principal sub-division of a section is a subsection, numbered by Arabic numerals within brackets—(1), (2) . . . A subsection is a separate sentence, not a subordinate proposition begun at section level. As a general rule, only one sentence is found within a subsection.[75]

2.5.4 Where opening words precede a sub-division, whether of a section or otherwise, they are sometimes referred to as the chapeau. Where words follow a sub-division, returning to the margin, they are sometimes referred to as the tail (or, less elegantly, as the "full-out" words).

---

[68] Parts were originally numbered by capital Roman numerals but since the format changes in 1999 mentioned above they have been numbered by Arabic numerals.

[69] A definition or other provision which operates by reference to "this Part" of an Act undoubtedly applies to any Schedule introduced by a section within the Part.

[70] See, for example, the Communications Act 2003 (c.21), the Crime (International Co-operation) Act 2003 (c.32) or the Housing Act 1996 (c.52). It is possible for an Act to have some but not all its Parts sub-divided into Chapters—see, for example, the Criminal Justice Act 2003 (c.44).

[71] So the Insolvency Act 1986 (c.45) is divided into Groups of Parts as well as Parts.

[72] A group of provisions presented in this way can be described as a fasciculus: see, for example, *R. v Johnstone* [2003] 1 W.L.R. 1736, 1739 *per* Lord Nicholls of Birkenhead.

[73] These used to be known as shoulder headings (or side-notes), being placed by the side of the section in the outer margin of the page. This format, which made the headings easy to spot and the flow of the material within a statute easy to follow, was abandoned when a new format for the printing of Bills and Acts was adopted in 1999 (as to which see above).

[74] In the case of old Acts there are sometimes discrepancies as to the numbering of sections as between different editions. S.19(1) of the Interpretation Act 1978 (c.30) establishes that section references are to be read as referring to the latest version of a statute as published by authority, unless the contrary intention appears.

[75] It occasionally happens that a second un-numbered sentence is found within a subsection. This can be useful for a subordinate proposition which belongs as a qualification on the principal proposition in the subsection and which would disturb the symmetry of the section if presented as a separate subsection. But it has the obvious disadvantages that it can cause confusion where another piece of legislation has to refer to a proposition within the subsection and that it can add to the apparent complexity of the section as a whole.

The principal sub-division of a subsection is a paragraph. This is invariably preceded by introductory words at subsection level and is ordered using small letters within brackets—

"(1) In this subsection—

    a. ...,
    b. ..."

The principal sub-division of a paragraph is a sub-paragraph. This is invariably preceded by introductory words at paragraph level and is numbered using lower-case roman numerals in brackets: as in the following—

"(1) For the purposes of this section—

    (a) a dog shall be treated as a domesticated animal only if—

        (i) it has never bitten a postman, or
        (ii) any postman which it has bitten has forgiven it in writing, and

    (b) a hippopotamus shall not be treated as a domesticated animal, irrespective of whether or not it has been trained to perform tricks."[76]

2.5.5 After a paragraph or sub-paragraph it is permissible to return to the margin and add a tail which completes the subsection or paragraph and applies equally to all the paragraphs or sub-paragraphs: as in the following—

"(1) A person may not take into a public park—

    (a) a cat, or
    (b) a dog;

but this subsection does not apply to a dead cat or a dead dog."[77]

The principal division within a Schedule is the paragraph, numbered by Arabic numerals. A group of paragraphs within a Schedule may be presented as a Part of a Schedule, or introduced as a fasciculus by an italic cross-heading.

The principal division of a paragraph is a sub-paragraph, which is numbered and treated structurally as if it were a subsection of a section (so that the first sub-division is a paragraph and a division of the paragraph is a sub-paragraph).

---

[76] It will be seen from this example that the sub-paragraph inevitably imports a degree of structural complexity which some draftsmen regard as generally unacceptable.

[77] Again, some draftsmen consider that as a general rule this imports an unacceptable degree of complexity and that it is generally preferable to make the qualification or exception a separate subsection or paragraph.

The numbering of interpolated provisions poses distinct problems, addressed briefly below.[78]

2.5.6   Other components of Acts, such as footnotes, tables or formulae, may be inserted if the draftsman finds them a helpful way of presenting material. There is no doubt that these are to be treated as being fully part of the Act.[79]

An Act of any size[80] is normally printed with a prefatory table showing (and entitled as) the Arrangement of Sections. This table, which is first supplied when the Bill for the Act[81] is presented and is updated each time the Bill is printed, has no status in law and is no more than a list of the headings for each of the sections and Schedules.

Information about the use of components of Acts in interpretation will be found in Chapter 26. Discussion of the informality of headings will also be found in that Chapter.

Titles

2.5.7   An Act of Parliament has two titles, a short title and a long title.

(1) Short title

The short title of an Act is established by a provision, found at or near the end of the sections, to the effect that the Act "may be cited" by a particular name.

There is no legal requirement that the short title of an Act should be an accurate description of the entirety of its contents, nor would that be possible without often requiring a very unwieldy "short" title. A short title that was positively misleading would, however, be likely to be deprecated.[82]

---

[78] Chapter 8, Section 2.

[79] See, in the context of footnotes, *Erven Warnink B.V. v J. Townend & Sons (Hull) Ltd* [1982] 3 All E.R. 312, CA.

[80] As a rule of thumb, an arrangement is generally provided for a Bill of more than eight clauses and is unlikely to be of much assistance in the case of a Bill of less.

[81] As an Arrangement of Clauses.

[82] The short title is chosen by the draftsman of the Bill. Sometimes it is discussed with the Department with principal responsibility for the Bill, and sometimes aspects of it are discussed with the House authorities. But, as the Parliamentary Under-Secretary in the Home Office said of the Disqualifications Bill 1999–2000, "The title of the Bill is a matter for parliamentary draftsmen; Ministers have not been involved in decisions of that kind."—HC Deb. January 25, 2000 c.480.

While it is frequently impossible to find a short description that gives a clear indication of all the contents of the Bill, the aim should be to avoid a title which through apparent accuracy misleads by omitting reference to one or more provisions of the Bill. Necessarily unhelpful generality is to be preferred in this context (and many others) to false accuracy. It is also important to avoid a short title which amounts to propaganda in the sense of an attempt to praise or justify the policy of the Bill: in an extreme case the Speaker of the House of Commons might refuse to print a Bill with a short title which was thought to mislead or to amount to an abuse of the procedures of the House.

The sole stated purpose of an Act's short title is to facilitate references to it in other documents (referred to as "citation"). Incidentally, of course, it also serves the purposes of giving a general indication of the area with which the Act deals and a precise indication of the year in which it was passed.

A short title may be used to refer to an Act despite the fact that the entire Act (including the provision appointing the short title) has been repealed.[83]

The short title is a relatively modern invention. A number of Acts have provided earlier Acts with short titles for the purposes of citation.[84] [85] There remain a small number of Acts which have effect and do not have short titles—they must be cited by a combination of regnal year and chapter number[86] or by a self-explanatory reference to their provisions. **2.5.8**

The normal form of a short title is "The X Act" followed by the year of enactment.[87] This is not, however, invariable.[88] Originally, a comma preceded the year in a short title, but this practice was discontinued in 1962[89] and by general consent the comma is omitted even in citations of Acts given their short title before that year.

Provision is made in some cases for collective citation of a number of Acts forming a code on a particular topic. Collective citations may be provided for in the specific legislation concerned[90] or in the Interpretation Act 1978[91]; and the

---

[83] Interpretation Act 1978 (c.30), s.19(2).

[84] See, in particular, the Short Titles Acts 1892 and 1896 (c.14) and s.5 of the Statute Law Revision Act 1948 (c.62).

[85] Where this is done, "Where any Act cites or refers to another Act otherwise than by its short title, the short title may, in any revised edition of the Statutes printed by authority, be printed in substitution for such citation or reference"—Statute Law Revision Act 1893 (c.14), s.3.

[86] There may be discrepancies between different records of years and chapters. So s.19(1)(a), (b) and (c) of the Interpretation Act 1978 gives statutory authority to "any revised edition of the statutes printed by authority", to "the edition prepared under the direction of the Record Commission" and to Acts printed "by the Queen's Printer, or under the superintendence or authority of Her Majesty's Stationery Office".

[87] Since the provision establishing the short title is a substantive provision of the Act, the Bill for an Act must include the citation provision on introduction. But, of course, it is normal for a Bill introduced at the start of a Session towards the end of one calendar year to receive Royal Assent in the following calendar year. The proportion of Bills introduced and enacted in the same calendar year is small. If a Bill is introduced giving as its short title "The X Act Year 1" and it is enacted in Year 2, the authorities of either House will alter the citation provision so as to refer to Year 2 as an editorial change when printing the Bill (or the House of Lords authorities will do so when arranging for the printing of the Act) and a formal amendment will not be required. But it is normal for a Bill to be introduced already referring in the citation provision to the following year. This avoids the possibility of the need for change being overlooked on enactment—if the Bill happened to be passed more quickly than had been expected, a reference to Year 1 could be substituted, again as a matter of printing without formal amendment.

[88] Significant exceptions being the Statute of Westminster 1931 (c.4) (s.12 of which gives the short title) and the Bill of Rights (given that short title by the Short Titles Act 1896 (c.14)).

[89] See the note by a former First Parliamentary Counsel, Sir Noel Hutton Q.C., *The Citation of Statutes* 82 L.Q.R. 24–25.

[90] See, for example, the definition of the Immigration Acts in s.158 of the Nationality, Immigration and Asylum Act 2002 (c.41).

[91] 1978 c.30: see Sch.1, which contains definitions of the Corporation Tax Acts, the Income Tax Acts, the Lands Clauses Acts, and the Tax Acts.

Short Titles Act 1896[92] provided for a number of collective citations of previous Acts.[93] [94]

(2) *Long title*

2.5.9 Every Act has a long title, which starts life as the long title to the Bill for the Act and is preserved automatically on Royal Assent as the long title to the Act.

A long title may be amended in certain circumstances during the passage of a Bill through Parliament, but not as freely as the substantive provisions of the Bill.

The purpose of the long title is to give a general indication of the contents of the Act. Unlike the short title, it must be comprehensive[95] and its form is likely to have been influenced heavily by the rules of the two Houses both as to the form of long titles[96] and as to scope or relevance.[97]

Each of the previous two paragraphs is a matter worth bearing in mind when considering how much weight to attach to a long title in construing an Act.[98]

While there can be procedural reasons for making a long title relatively lengthy and specific[99] there is clear support both within Parliament and outside[1] for long titles being[2] sufficiently concise to convey a helpful sense of the general subject matter of the Act.

It is common for long titles to end with the phrase "and for connected purposes". This is designed simply to ensure that the inclusion of a small amount of miscellaneous matter, generally arising from or related to the main substance in some way but not directly consequential on it, need not be mentioned

---

[92] 1896 c.14.

[93] s.2 and Sch.2.

[94] See also, as to construction of a number of Acts as if they were one, Chapter 24.

[95] It would be perfectly reasonable to give an Act that was primarily about insolvency the short title Insolvency Act despite the fact that it also included provisions about a kindred matter such as, for example, receivership or administration. But the long title would be expected to include the other matters, either by express reference, or by reference to the legislation in which they are contained or by use of the common "and for connected purposes" at the end—see, for illustration, the long title to the Enterprise Act 2002 (c.40) ("An Act to establish and provide for the functions of the Office of Fair Trading, the Competition Appeal Tribunal and the Competition Service; to make provision about mergers and market structures and conduct; to amend the constitution and functions of the Competition Commission; to create an offence for those entering into certain anti-competitive agreements; to provide for the disqualification of directors of companies engaging in certain anti-competitive practices; to make other provision about competition law; to amend the law relating to the protection of the collective interests of consumers; to make further provision about the disclosure of information obtained under competition and consumer legislation; to amend the Insolvency Act 1986 and make other provision about insolvency; and for connected purposes").

[96] As to, for example, what reliance can properly be placed on the "and for connected purposes" limb.

[97] See Chapter 5, Section 2.

[98] As to which see Chapter 26.

[99] So as to assist in limiting scope.

[1] See, in particular, HL Deb. June 21, 1994 cc.200–204.

[2] Or, at least, starting out as.

explicitly in the long title but will still be within the scope of the Bill.[3] Scope aside, after enactment it puts the reader on notice that there may be minor but non-consequential changes contained within the Act.

Other components

It was once the norm for an Act of Parliament to be preceded by a preamble setting out the social or legal background to the Act. For public Acts this is now a rarity.[4] The use of the preamble for construction of legislation is discussed in Chapter 26. Although the decline of the preamble has been judicially deprecated[5] the Government's stated policy is firmly set against the reintroduction of the preamble as a general measure.[6]

2.5.10

A preamble can certainly be a useful way of setting the provisions of an Act into context.[7] But a similar role might be served today, depending on the context, by introductory material in Explanatory Notes.[8]

Preambles are required for Acts which start life as Bills subject to the private Bill procedure: the purpose of the preamble is to recite[9] allegations as to the purpose of the Bill and its justification for the Bill each aspect of which must be proved during the examination of the Bill in Committee.[10]

---

[3] As to which see Chapter 5, Section 2.

[4] For relatively recent examples see the Canada Act 1982 (c.11) (reciting the fact that Parliament is legislating for Canada with the consent of and at the request of the Canadian legislatures) and the Endangered Species (Import and Export) Act 1976 (c.72) (reciting the expediency of giving effect to the Washington Convention on International Trade in Endangered Species of Wild Fauna and Flora).

[5] See *L.C.C. v Bermondsey Bioscope Co.* [1911] 1 K.B. 445, 451 *per* Lord Alverstone C.J.

[6] The Leader of the House of Lords, Baroness Jay of Paddington, said in replying to an amendment inserting a preamble to the House of Lords Bill (HL Deb. October 26, 1999 cc.275–76)—"We have already been round this course several times in relation to purpose clauses. I can only repeat what I have said before. Acts of Parliament are legislative vehicles that are supposed to do something. They are not places for uttering aspirations. I accept that in the past—I recognise the noble Lord's point about the preamble to the 1911 Act—this practice was more common. There was a preamble to the Parliament (No. 2) Bill in 1968 that dealt with some of the same proposals now before us. But, on the whole, in 1999 that is not how legislation is drafted. We rely on the operative words of an Act to tell us what the legislation means, while the Long Title informs Peers and Members of Parliament about its subject-matter and purpose. Words that do not mean anything have no place in modern legislation, and that practice certainly predates the present Government."; note also that the Renton Report ((*Report on the Preparation of Legislation*) (Cmnd. 6053)) did not favour the use of preambles for Acts—see the speech of Lord Renton HL Deb. January 21, 1998 c.1583.

[7] See, for example, the preamble to the Territorial Waters Jurisdiction Act 1878 (c.73), an Act designed to reverse the decision in *The Queen v Keyn (The Franconia)* 1876–77 L.R. Ex. D. II 63 C.C.R. (as to which see para.11.2.9, footnote 54), which makes it clear precisely what part of the law was thought to need rectification after that decision.

[8] As to which see Chapter 9, Section 5.

[9] A recital, although in itself a mere allegation, may after the enactment of the Act be treated as having some evidential weight: "It is true that a recital in a private Act is not conclusive evidence of the truth of the recital . . . Nevertheless, such a recital, in the absence of evidence to the contrary, must be very strong evidence of the truth of a matter long beyond the reach of living memory."—*Wyld v Silver* [1963] Ch. 243, 261, CA, *per* Harman L.J.

[10] See Standing Order 142(2) of the Standing Orders of the House of Commons relating to Private Business and para.7.46 of the *Companion to the Standing Orders and Guide to the Proceedings of the House of Lords*.

Citation

2.5.11   Acts may be cited by reference to the chapter number assigned to them.

For public general Acts the standard notation is "(c.1), (c.2), ... ". For Acts published in the local series the standard notation is "(c.i), (c.ii), ... ". For personal Acts the standard notation is "(c.*1*), (c.*2*), ... ".

For Acts passed before 1963, chapter numbers were assigned in a series starting again with each Session of Parliament by reference to the regnal year or years in which that Session wholly or partly fell. Section 1 of the Acts of Parliament Numbering and Citation Act 1962[11] provided that—

> "The chapter numbers assigned to Acts of Parliament passed in the year nineteen hundred and sixty-three and every subsequent year shall be assigned by reference to the calendar year, and not the Session, in which they are passed".

While this rule applies only to Acts enacted from 1963 onwards, the practice of citing regnal years in relation to earlier Acts has largely died out by general consent.[12] In particular, the standard practice for parenthetical citations within Acts is to use only the calendar year and chapter number. Chapter numbers are assigned to Acts on, and in the order of, receiving Royal Assent.

OTHER ASPECTS OF ACTS

2.5.12   The following aspects of Acts are dealt with in some detail elsewhere in this work—

Drafting and preparation	Chapter 5, Section 1
Passage of Bill through Parliament	Chapter 5, Sections 2 to 4
Explanatory Notes	Chapter 9, Section 5
Invalidity (human rights)	Chapter 11, Section 3 and Chapter 25

In addition to those specific passages, any passage in this work that relates to legislation generally will, of course, apply to Acts of Parliament.

---

[11] 10 & 11 Eliz. 2 c.34.

[12] While the use of regnal years is still technically important for distinguishing between two Acts passed in the same calendar year but in different regnal years, in practice even in such a case a person referring to only one of the Acts using the calendar year and chapter number alone would be unlikely to cause much in the way of practical confusion.

CHAPTER 3

SUBORDINATE LEGISLATION: INTRODUCTION

OVERVIEW

This Chapter deals with general introductory matters in relation to subordinate   **3.0.1**
legislation. Specific aspects of the subject are addressed, in this Chapter or
elsewhere in this work, as follows—

SECTION 1

HISTORY AND NATURE OF SUBORDINATE LEGISLATION

History

The notion of delegating legislative authority to the executive goes back many   **3.1.1**
centuries. Two of the earliest examples are the statute of 1337[1] which made it a
felony to export wool, subject to provision to be made by the King and his
Council, and the Statute of the Staple of 1388, by which the Sheriff of Kent was

---

[1] 11 Edw. 3, c.1.

99

directed to move the staple market from Middlesbrough to Calais. Since then occasional instances are found over the centuries,[2] but it was not until the nineteenth century that the use of delegated legislation became commonplace.

From early on it was accepted that there is nothing inherently improper in the cautious delegation of legislative power: as Lord Selborne said in *The Queen v Burah*[3]—

> "Legislation, conditional on the use of particular powers, or on the exercise of a limited discretion, entrusted by the Legislature to persons in whom it places confidence, is no uncommon thing; and, in many circumstances, it may be highly convenient."

In the last few decades the use of subordinate legislation has increased enormously, with a seemingly ever-increasing rate of acceleration, until there are generally between three and four thousand new statutory instruments made every year.[4] Some of these deal with trivial matters or matters of specialised or local interest, such as the setting of technical standards.[5] But others make lengthy and complicated codes about matters of supreme importance.[6] It is true to say that today hardly any Act of social significance is passed that does not confer significant powers to amplify its provisions.

---

[2] See, for example, the Statute of Sewers in 1531, the Statute of Proclamations in 1539 and the Mutiny Act 1717.

[3] (1878) 3 App. Cas. 889, 898, PC.

[4] The totals for the last few years are as follows: 1995–3345; 1996–3291; 1997–3114; 1998–3323; 1999–3705; 2000–3887; 2001–4642; 2002–3849; 2003–3399. As to earlier years, note the following House of Lords Written Answer (HL Deb. May 4, 1995 W.A. 126)—

> Lord Pearson of Rannoch asked Her Majesty's Government: How many statutory instruments were made (a) in each of the last five years; and (b) in 1946, 1956, 1966, 1976 and 1986.
>
> The Lord Privy Seal (Viscount Cranborne): The number of statutory instruments made in each of the years requested is as follows: (a) 1990: 2,667, 1991: 2,953, 1992: 3,359, 1993: 3,279, 1994: 3,334, and (b) 1946: 2,271, 1956: 2,124, 1966: 1,641, 1976: 2,245, 1986: 2,356."

The trend therefore shows marked acceleration, but it also shows that the number of instruments has been in the thousands for many years. There have occasionally been suggestions that instruments have been unnecessarily proliferated by the use of more than one instrument where one would have sufficed—see, for example, Joint Committee on Statutory Instruments Session 1992–93, 35th Report, June 29, 1993 (HL Paper 102, HC 51-xxxv) p.6.

[5] See, for example, the A55 Trunk Road (St Asaph, Rhuddlan, Denbighshire) (Temporary Prohibition of Vehicles and 40 mph Speed Limit) Order 2003 (SI 2003/3), the A63 Trunk Road (South Cave Interchange to North Cave Interchange) and The M62 Motorway (North Cave Interchange) (Temporary Prohibition of Traffic) Order 2003 (SI 2003/18), the ABRO Trading Fund (Amendment) Order 2003 (SI 2003/105), the Sea Fishing (Restriction on Days at Sea) Order 2003 (SI 2003/229), the Air Passenger Duty and Other Indirect Taxes (Interest Rate) (Amendment) Regulations 2003 (SI 2003/230) or the Social Security (Work-focused Interviews for Lone Parents) Amendment Regulations 2003 (SI 2003/400). While apparently of trivial interest, however, it will be noticed that each of these instruments contains matter that could be of immense importance to those individuals who happen to be directly affected.

[6] See, for example, the Income Support (General) Regulations 1987 (SI 1987/1667), the Immigration (European Economic Area) Regulations 2000 (SI 2000/2326), the Care Homes Regulations 2001 (SI 2001/3965) or the British Nationality (General) Regulations 2003 (SI 2003/548).

Of some Acts it can be said that they are little more than "skeleton Acts", providing a skeleton illustrating the general shape and structure of the intended law in relation to a matter but leaving all the detail to be provided by subordinate legislation.[7] And, skeleton Acts apart, there are innumerable individual provisions of other Acts whose entire effect depends upon the making of subordinate legislation, not merely in order to administer the provision but actually in order to give it substance.[8]

Risk of abuse

When a power is conferred on the executive there is inevitable scope for the power to be abused. And the wider the power the greater the nature of the potential abuse. But the courts have always confronted the possibility of abuse as a risk inherent in the nature of the delegation of powers, and have defended Parliament's right to legislate in this way. As Lord Dunedin said in *R. v Halliday*[9]—   **3.1.2**

"It is pointed out that the powers, if interpreted as the unanimous judgment of the Courts below interprets them, are drastic and might be abused. That is true. But the fault, if fault there be, lies in the fact that the British Constitution has entrusted to the two Houses of Parliament, subject to the assent of the King, an absolute power untrammelled by any written instrument obedience to which may be compelled by some judicial body. The danger of abuse is theoretically present; practically, as things exist, it is in my opinion absent. Were a regulation to be framed, as my noble friend who is to follow me suggests, to intern the Catholics of South Ireland or the Jews of London the result would, I think, be the speedy repeal of the Act which authorises the regulation. That preventive measure in the shape of interment of persons likely to assist the enemy may be necessary under the circumstances of a war like the present is really an obvious consideration. Parliament has in my judgment, in order to secure this and kindred objects, risked the chance of abuse which will always be theoretically present when absolute powers in general terms are delegated to an executive body; and

---

[7] What amounts to a skeleton is, however, very much a matter of opinion—see, for example, HL Deb. March 29, 2001 cc.531–531. See also the Oral Question on delegated legislation HL Deb. June 28, 1995 cc.750–751. The question of the proper balance between primary and subordinate legislation is addressed in Chapter 1, Section 2.

[8] See, for an extreme example, Part 2 of the Nationality, Immigration and Asylum Act 2002 (c.41). A number of key provisions of that Part operate by reference to the concept of a "dependant". But the definition of that concept in s.20 provides that "For the purposes of this Part a person is a "dependant" of an asylum-seeker if (and only if) that person—(a) is in the United Kingdom, and (b) is within a prescribed class." ("prescribed" meaning "prescribed by the Secretary of State by order or regulations"—s.39(1)). So it will be impossible to know the effect of Pt 2 in relation to many cases without recourse to the subordinate legislation.

[9] [1917] A.C. 260, 270–271, HL.

has thought the restriction of their powers to the period of the duration of the war to be a sufficient safeguard."

Since the time of *Halliday* a number of new mechanisms for controlling and preventing abuse of delegated powers have emerged, and it is no longer true that repeal of the enabling legislation is the most likely practical method of control.

Power or duty

3.1.3   While it is the predominating rule to confer a mere power to make an instrument, there are occasions on which a duty to legislate is conferred.

This is likely to happen in particular where the practicalities of a system set out in an Act are likely to need adjustment to make them work in the light of transitional circumstances or changing events.[10]

But a duty may be imposed in more general circumstances simply because the legislature wishes to ensure that arrangements are made for a system of a particular kind that cannot practicably be set out on the face of primary legislation.[11]

As to the question whether a power may take on certain aspects of a duty, see Chapter 10, Section 1 and Chapter 12, Section 2.

---

[10] See, for example, s.173(1) of the Health and Social Care (Community Health and Standards) Act 2003 (c.43)—"(1) The appropriate authority shall by order make transitional provision in respect of persons who, immediately before the coming into force of s.172, are providing services under s.35 of the 1977 Act (general dental services)."; or s.294(4) of the Income Tax (Earnings and Pensions) Act 2003 (c.1)—"(4) The Treasury shall by order make such amendments of the definition in subs.(3) as are necessary to secure that the countries listed are those that are from time to time candidates for membership of the European Union."

[11] See, for example, s.80A of the Employment Rights Act 1996 (c.18) (Entitlement to paternity leave: birth) inserted by s.1 of the Employment Act 2002 (c.22)—"(1) The Secretary of State shall make regulations entitling an employee who satisfies specified conditions—(a) as to duration of employment, (b) as to relationship with a newborn, or expected, child, and (c) as to relationship with the child's mother, to be absent from work on leave under this section for the purpose of caring for the child or supporting the mother. (2) The regulations shall include provision for determining—(a) the extent of an employee's entitlement to leave under this section in respect of a child; (b) when leave under this section may be taken. (3) Provision under subs.(2)(a) shall secure that where an employee is entitled to leave under this section in respect of a child he is entitled to at least two weeks' leave. (4) Provision under subs.(2)(b) shall secure that leave under this section must be taken before the end of a period of at least 56 days beginning with the date of the child's birth. (5) Regulations under subsection (1) may—(a) specify things which are, or are not, to be taken as done for the purpose of caring for a child or supporting the child's mother; (b) make provision excluding the right to be absent on leave under this section in respect of a child where more than one child is born as a result of the same pregnancy; (c) make provision about how leave under this section may be taken. . . . "; or s.6 of the Railways and Transport Safety Act 2003 (c.20) (Annual report)—"(1) The Secretary of State shall make regulations requiring the Chief Inspector of Rail Accidents to produce once in each calendar year a report in connection with the activities of the Rail Accident Investigation Branch. (2) Regulations under subs.(1) may, in particular, make provision about—(a) timing of reports; (b) content of reports; (c) publication and other treatment of reports."; see also, for an interesting variation on the theme, s.3(3) of the Statutory Sick Pay 1994 (c.2) "(3) The Secretary of State—(a) shall lay before each House of Parliament the draft of an order under s.159A(1) of the Social Security Contributions and Benefits Act 1992 (inserted by subs.(1) above) framed so as to come into force on or before April 6, 1995, and (b) if the draft order

Statutory instruments

The most common kind of subordinate legislation is the class referred to as **3.1.4** statutory instruments. Strictly speaking, however, the expression "statutory instrument" does not describe a kind of legislation, but a particular method by which different kinds of secondary legislation can be made.

The term derives from section 1 of the Statutory Instruments Act 1946[12] which provides as follows—

"1 Definition of "Statutory Instrument"

(1) Where by this Act or any Act passed after the commencement of this Act power to make, confirm or approve orders, rules, regulations or other subordinate legislation is conferred on His Majesty in Council or on any Minister of the Crown then, if the power is expressed—

(a) in the case of a power conferred on His Majesty, to be exercisable by Order in Council;

(b) in the case of a power conferred on a Minister of the Crown, to be exercisable by statutory instrument,

any document by which that power is exercised shall be known as a "statutory instrument" and the provisions of this Act shall apply thereto accordingly.

(1A) The references in subsection (1) to a Minister of the Crown shall be construed as including references to the National Assembly for Wales.

(2) Where by any Act passed before the commencement of this Act power to make statutory rules within the meaning of the Rules Publication Act 1893 was conferred on any rule-making authority within the meaning of that Act, any document by which that power is exercised after the commencement of this Act shall, save as is otherwise provided by regulations made under this Act, be known as a 'statutory instrument' and the provisions of this Act shall apply thereto accordingly."

Most importantly, therefore, the term "statutory instrument" applies to Orders **3.1.5** in Council and to the exercise by a Minister of the Crown of any power to make subordinate legislation where the power provides for exercise by statutory instrument.

---

is approved by a resolution of each House of Parliament, shall make the order in the form of the draft, unless before December 1, 1994 he lays before each House of Parliament a report explaining why he does not intend to make such an order."

[12] 1946 c.36.

The principal significance of whether a piece of subordinate legislation takes the form of a statutory instrument or not is the application of the provisions for printing and publication.[13]

Legislation conferring power to make secondary legislation routinely provides for the power to be exercised "by statutory instrument". But where an order, for example, is entirely administrative in nature, and it is not thought that anyone other than the persons to whom the order is addressed would be interested in it, the legislation may say nothing about the form of the order, in which case it will not be a statutory instrument.[14] Orders made by a court or tribunal are not made by statutory instrument.

SECTION 2

COMMON FORMS OF SUBORDINATE LEGISLATION

Orders in Council

3.2.1   Orders in Council are described colloquially as being made by the Privy Council. A more accurate technical description is that they are made by "The Queen in Council", which means that they are made by the Queen acting on the advice of the Privy Council.[15]

An Order "in" Council may be made as an exercise of the Royal Prerogative or by virtue of powers conferred by Parliament.

An Order "of" Council is an order made by the Council itself, acting through a small number of Councillors, in exercise of powers conferred on the Council.[16]

---

[13] As to which see Chapter 9, Section 3.

[14] See, for example, s.1(3) of the Commonwealth Development Corporation Act 1999 (c.20).

[15] Hence the old form adopted by, for example, s.2 of the Emergency Powers Act 1920 (c.55): " . . . it shall be lawful for His Majesty in Council, by Order, to make regulations . . . ". Nor is this form entirely obsolete: see, for example, s.4(4) of the Northern Ireland Act 1998 (c.47).

[16] The distinction between Orders in and of Council is marked by their preambles. Compare, for example—

(1) the preamble to the General Optical Council (Disciplinary Committee (Constitution) Amendment Rules) Order of Council 2004 (SI 2004/259) ("Whereas, in pursuance of s.5(2) of the Opticians Act 1989, the General Optical Council have made the Disciplinary Committee (Constitution) Amendment Rules 2004 as set out in the Schedule to this Order: And whereas by s.34 of the said Act such rules shall not come into force until approved by order of the Privy Council: Now, therefore, Their Lordships, having taken the said rules into consideration, are hereby pleased to approve the same."),
with

(2) the preamble to the Liberia (United Nations Sanctions) (Isle of Man) Order 2004 (SI 2004/305) ("Whereas under Article 41 of the Charter of the United Nations the Security Council of the United Nations has, by a resolution adopted on 22nd December 2003 called upon Her Majesty's Government in the United Kingdom and all other States to apply certain measures to give effect to decisions of that Council in relation to Liberia: Now, therefore, Her Majesty, in exercise of the powers conferred on Her by s.1 of the United Nations Act 1946, is pleased, by and with the advice of Her Privy Council, to order, and it is hereby ordered, as follows: . . . ") (Editor's emphases).

Powers conferred in relation to professional bodies are frequently conferred not on the Queen in Council but on the Council itself.[17]

The Privy Council is an ancient institution, dating back to the early days of the Monarchy and being the origin of the system of Cabinet government.[18] Privy Councillors are appointed by the Sovereign.[19]

Some Orders in Council are primary legislation, being made as an exercise of **3.2.2** the Royal Prerogative. Others are subordinate, being made under specific statutory powers. The nature and relative size of each class is illustrated in the following Written Answer given in the House of Commons[20]—

"Mr. Gordon Prentice: To ask the President of the Council[21] how many Orders in Council in 2002 were made under (a) the prerogative and (b) an Act of Parliament.

"Mr. Robin Cook: A total of 526 Orders in Council were made in 2002, of which 372 were made under an Act or Measure and 154 were made under the Prerogative. The Orders approved at each Council meeting are listed on the Privy Council Office website and copies are placed in the Library of the House. The majority of Prerogative Orders related to the appointment of Ministers and Privy Counsellors, the private affairs of Chartered bodies, and Channel Islands business. The majority of statutory Orders were confirmations of Church Commissioners' schemes under the Pastoral Measure 1983."

The range of areas of law still open to regulation and control under the Royal Prerogative is extensive and includes some matters of fundamental importance.[22]

---

[17] See, for example, s.33 of the Opticians Act 1989 (c.44) (default powers of Privy Council).

[18] "Historically, the Cabinet is a private meeting of those Privy Councillors in whom the Sovereign has particular 'confidence' for the time being"—*Cabinet Government*, Sir Ivor Jennings K.B.E., &c., Third Edition, 1959, p.228.

[19] For the most part these appointments are political appointments made at the behest of the Government of the day. In particular, all Cabinet Ministers are on their appointment to the Cabinet also appointed to the Privy Council unless they are already members. But some appointments are honorific.

[20] HC Deb. March 13, 2003 W.A. 397.

[21] The office of President of the Council—until 1997 commonly styled Lord President of the Council whether or not held by a peer—is nowadays a Ministerial Office largely of the nature of a sinecure. It is held by a Minister who performs other duties, generally in relation to "central" or Cabinet Office functions, and who frequently also holds the office of Leader of the House of Commons (or, less frequently, the Leader of the House of Lords) and as such chairs the Ministerial Cabinet Committee on the Legislative Programme and exercises general responsibility for the Government's primary legislative programme.

[22] A list of prerogative powers was prepared as a Government Paper submitted to and published by the House of Commons Select Committee on Public Administration (Session 2002–03, Press Notice No.19 of October 27, 2003).

The remaining powers of the Sovereign to make provision in relation to certain territories abroad is also a significant area in which the Prerogative Order in Council is of importance. See, for example, the preamble to the Gibraltar Constitution Order 1969 (May 23, 1969)—

"Whereas Gibraltar is part of Her Majesty's dominions and Her Majesty's Government have given assurances to the people of Gibraltar that Gibraltar will remain part of Her Majesty's dominions unless and until an Act of Parliament otherwise provides, and furthermore that Her

One of the most significant domestic areas of the prerogative that results in regulation by Order in Council is the appointment and administration of the civil service.[23]

An Order in Council which is primary legislation is sometimes referred to as a "prerogative order".

3.2.3 The Privy Council meets approximately once each month. Councils are held by The Queen and are attended by Ministers and the Clerk of the Council. Meetings are used for, amongst other things, obtaining the Queen's formal approval to Orders which have been discussed and approved by Ministers.

The place and time of meetings and the business transacted at each one are matters of public record. Orders in Council made under statutory powers are statutory instruments[24] and are therefore subject to the standard arrangements for the printing and publication of statutory instruments.[25]

Other Orders in Council, and Orders of Council, are not statutory instruments. But in the case of matters relating to professions or Chartered bodies, the profession or body concerned with each order is likely to make arrangements for its publication. In other cases the secretariat of the Privy Council are likely to be able to assist with inquiries as to the contents of orders.

3.2.4 In the case of Orders of Council which are not statutory instruments, the statute conferring the power to make an order may also make provision about the conduct of the Privy Council's proceedings in making an order and about authentication of orders.[26]

The power to make an Order in Council is today generally conferred through the formula "Her Majesty[27] may by Order in Council make provision ... ".

Despite this imposing formality the reality is that this is a form of executive order as much under the control of the normal departments of Government as any other.

The Government department responsible for the substance of an Order in Council prepares it and submits it to the Clerk to the Privy Council; its being

---

Majesty's Government will never enter into arrangements under which the people of Gibraltar would pass under the sovereignty of another state against their freely and democratically expressed wishes:

And whereas Her Majesty is pleased to make provision for a new Constitution for Gibraltar:

Now, therefore, Her Majesty, by virtue and in exercise of all the powers enabling Her in that behalf, is pleased, by and with the advice of Her Privy Council, to order, and it is hereby ordered, as follows:— ... "

[23] See, in particular, the Civil Service Order in Council 1991 and 1995, and the Civil Service Amendment Orders amending each of those Orders.

[24] By virtue of s.1(1)(a) of the Statutory Instruments Act 1946 (c.36).

[25] As to which see Chapter 9, Section 3.

[26] See, for example, s.35 of the Opticians Act 1989 (c.44).

[27] The Regency Acts 1937–53 apply, so that, for example, the Naval and Marine Pay and Pensions (Deductions for Maintenance) Order 1959 (July 28, 1959, No.32) was made by the Queen Mother and Princess Alexandra of Kent on behalf of the Queen, who was absent from the United Kingdom, in accordance with Letters Patent.

made at the next available meeting of the Privy Council is no more a matter of substance than is the submission of an Act of Parliament to the Queen for Royal Assent.

Orders in Council were once regarded as the most proper form of legislation to be used for anything with a constitutional flavour. They are still commonly used, for this reason, for powers to extend United Kingdom legislation to Crown territories outside the United Kingdom itself (most commonly the Channel Islands and the Isle of Man). They are also used, for the same reason, for the power to transfer functions among Ministers (see Section 12 below). **3.2.5**

The Privy Council used to have a very pronounced role in the control of certain medical and scientific professions, and it retains a significant role in this regard: as a result legislation about professions is often delegated to the Council.[28] The Privy Council also has a strong role in relation to all bodies that hold a Royal Charter.[29]

It may also be thought convenient or appropriate to use Order in Council as the form of legislation where more than one Minister is centrally responsible for the subject matter concerned. This, however, is a factor less likely to have weight now that almost all senior departmental Ministers are Secretaries of State[30] and it is therefore generally open to legislation to confer a power on "the Secretary of State".[31]

There is, however, no obligation to use Orders in Council for a particular class of matter; nor does their form confer any substantive degree of control over the executive or differ in any other real sense from that of the simple executive order. And Orders in Council are more burdensome procedurally for Government departments; partly because of additional formalities and administrative requirements, but mainly because of timing—the Council generally meets only once in each month, and in the summer there is sometimes no meeting for a long period. So, bearing in mind the ever-increasing speed of legislative change, it would not be surprising if certain things once effected by Order in Council came to be effected by simple executive order when the relevant powers came to be replicated. **3.2.6**

In relation to devolution[32] the Privy Council exercises a significant jurisdiction, principally in relation to the resolution of disputes. Although there are

---

[28] For example, Sch.4 to the Medical Act 1983 (c.54) provides for rules in relation to proceedings of committees of the General Medical Council not to come into force until approved by order of the Privy Council; and s.34 of the Opticians Act 1989 (c.44) provides for rules of the General Optical Council not to come into force until approved by order of the Privy Council.

[29] As to which, see generally Section 7 below. Incorporation of a body by Royal Charter involves a surrender to the Privy Council of significant aspects of control of the body's internal affairs.

[30] See Section 12 below.

[31] Defined by Sch.1 to the Interpretation Act 1978 (c.30) as "one of Her Majesty's Principal Secretaries of State" and therefore supplying sufficient flexibility for most purposes.

[32] As to which see Chapter 4.

certain matters of delineation dealt with by Order in Council,[33] the principal jurisdiction is in respect of disputed legislative matters and is exercised through the Judicial Committee of the Privy Council.[34]

Orders, regulations and rules

3.2.7 The three most common forms of subordinate legislation are orders,[35] regulations and rules. The normal way of signalling which is to be used is for an Act to say—

"the Secretary of State may by order provide . . . ",

"the Secretary of State may make regulations providing . . . ", or

"the Secretary of State may make rules about . . . ".[36]

It used to be asserted that there was in general a clear distinction between the use of rules, regulations and orders. Rules are most appropriate for provisions determining the procedure of a body or process. Regulations are most appropriate for amplification of the details of a system the general principles of which are established by an Act. An order is the most appropriate form for making legislation which is not merely filling out details but is, in effect, establishing a new rule of law; and it is also the most appropriate form for legislation which amends an Act.

Rules are still used almost entirely in this way. But the distinction between regulations and orders, which was never rigid, has become very indistinct. In any event, nothing turns on it for practical purposes, except that a power to make one kind of instrument is not exercised in the same statutory instrument as the power to make another kind of instrument.[37]

3.2.8 Acts occasionally permit or require a Minister of the Crown to make informal rules about something. Procedural rules for courts and tribunals are made by

---

[33] See, for example, s.126(2) of the Scotland Act 1998 (c.46) which confers power to distinguish between Scottish and non-Scottish parts of the United Kingdom's territorial sea—and similar powers exist under other devolution legislation. And powers to modify provisions about legislative competence are generally exercisable also by Order in Council—see, for example, s.30(2) and (3) of the Scotland Act 1998.

[34] Which sits principally as an appellate court with a membership drawn from the senior judicial ranks.

[35] It is conventional to use "order" with a lower case initial letter for statutory orders of a general kind, but "Order" with an initial capital when referring to an Order in Council, whether specifically or generically.

[36] Occasionally the Act will leave to the executive a choice of determining what kind of instrument to make. The primary example is s.2(2) of the European Communities Act 1972 which permits the legislative power to be exercised either by Order in Council or by regulations, partly in order to make it easier to combine provisions made under the 1972 Act with provisions made under some other domestic *vires*.

[37] And a power to make rules or regulations will always attract the implied powers in s.14 of the Interpretation Act 1978 (c.30), whereas a power to make orders will do so only if expressed to be made by statutory instrument.

statutory instrument and are, at least for courts, generally subject to specific provision requiring the involvement of a specialist committee established for the purpose. But other administrative matters may also be left to be regulated by rule, without provision for the rule to be made by statutory instrument.

Perhaps the most significant example of the use of informal rules, and of the use of informal subordinate legislation generally, is provided by the Immigration Rules. Under s.3 of the Immigration Act 1971[38] the Secretary of State is obliged to—

> "from time to time (and as soon as may be) lay before Parliament statements of the rules, or of any changes in the rules, laid down by him as to the practice to be followed in the administration of this Act for regulating the entry into and stay in the United Kingdom of persons required by this Act to have leave to enter, including any rules as to the period for which leave is to be given and the conditions to be attached in different circumstances".

These rules are made wholly informally and are not embodied in a statutory instrument.[39] But there is provision in s.3 of the 1971 Act enabling either House of Parliament to make a resolution disapproving a statement laid under the section, in which case the Secretary of State is obliged by the section to make "such changes or further changes in the rules as appear to him to be required in the circumstances".

The result is that a piece of legislation addressing rights of particular human importance is made informally by rule, subject to an *ad hoc* process of Parliamentary scrutiny. Nor are the rules confined to matters of minor administration. In effect, they establish the parameters of the discretion by reference to which crucial rights of entry will be granted or withheld. They may rightly be described as being at the heart of immigration law.

3.2.9

The nature of these rules and the arrangements for their dissemination, as well as their legal effect, has been the subject of comment in the courts and in Parliament.[40]

---

[38] 1971 c.77.

[39] There is a perception that an instrument which is not a statutory instrument can be drafted in a more flexible and generalised way than one which is. The truth is that the degree of precision of language required in an instrument depends on the nature of its substance, and in particular the consequences of non-compliance, than on the form of the instrument.

[40] See *R. v Chief Immigration Officer, Heathrow Airport, ex p. Salamat Bibi* [1976] 3 All E.R. 843, CA *per* Roskill L.J.; see also Motion on the Adjournment *Immigration Rules* HC Deb. June 12, 2003 cc.919–926, including the statement by the Minister for Citizenship and Immigration (c.924) that "The Government need the flexibility to act in this area without delay, when that is necessary in the public interest. The current format of the immigration rules provides that flexibility in the most appropriate way. That flexibility would be diminished to an unacceptable level if the immigration rules had to be produced as a statutory instrument. As the House will know, as a general rule, statutory instruments subject to negative resolution must be laid at least 21 days

Combination of forms

3.2.10 An Order in Council cannot be combined in one instrument with any other form of subordinate legislation, because the Queen in Council can make only those provisions in respect of which power has been conferred on Her. Although the Queen appoints and dismisses Ministers and could accordingly be seen as the source of their power, a power conferred on a Minister cannot be exercised by the Queen, whether in Council, personally or through any other Minister.

As to the combination of other forms of subordinate legislation, there is nothing in theory to prevent a Minister who has a power to make an order about a subject and a power to make regulations about the same or a related subject from exercising both powers in a single instrument, just as there is nothing to prevent—and it is very frequently done—two powers to make an order, or two powers to make regulations, from being exercised in a single instrument. The only theoretical constraint arises where different powers are subject to different kinds of Parliamentary scrutiny.[41] In practice, however, different forms are not combined in one instrument.[42]

SECTION 3

COMPONENTS AND DIVISIONS OF SUBORDINATE INSTRUMENTS

Divisions

3.3.1 The primary division of an order, or of an Order in Council, is an article.[43]

The primary division of a set of regulations is a regulation.

The primary division of a set of rules is a rule.

The primary division of a code or any other instrument not mentioned above is a paragraph.

The first sub-division of a primary division (other than a paragraph[44]) is a paragraph. The sub-division of a paragraph is a sub-paragraph and the sub-division of a sub-paragraph reverts to being a paragraph.[45]

---

before they come into force. Such a delay could have serious implications when we had to introduce a new visa regime, for example. As I have said, there are mechanisms to ensure that the Government are accountable to Parliament in respect of changes made to the immigration rules."

[41] As to which see Chapter 6, Section 2.

[42] And there might certainly be minor (and not insuperable) practical problems in relation to a combination, the most obvious being that of knowing what to call the combined instrument.

[43] The prevailing convention in Great Britain legislation is to use lower case for article. Northern Ireland legislation commonly favours Article (as does European legislation).

[44] For which all the divisions are simply moved one stage up.

[45] Although, as stated above in relation to Acts (Chapter 2, Section 5), it is rare that it is proper to expect a reader to cope with this degree of sub-division: in anything other than a very simple kind of list it is likely to be necessary to recast as a series of higher divisions.

Schedules are used in subordinate legislation in the same way as in Acts[46] and are divided in the same way.

Headings

There is a conventional series of headings at the start of a statutory instrument, used for classification and printing purposes. With one exception,[47] none of these has legal status or is essential to the validity of the instrument.[48]   **3.3.2**

A headnote appears at the top of the first page of certain instruments indicating the nature of the instrument and the form of Parliamentary scrutiny to which it is subject.[49] A headnote may also be used to indicate any other kind of procedure to which an instrument is subject.[50] Where an instrument is issued to replace one printed previously containing an error, a headnote normally declares its status.

The first heading of a statutory instrument is STATUTORY INSTRUMENTS, simply to indicate that the instrument is issued as a statutory instrument within the meaning of the Statutory Instruments Act 1946[51] and not as a prerogative instrument or other document in similar form.

The next heading contains the serial number of the instrument, made up of the year and a number, as in "2004 No. 1" and so on throughout the year. Statutory instruments are numbered in a separate series for each calendar year. A separate serial number appears after the main serial number in brackets where the instrument forms part of a sub-series. At present, the annual sub-series are as follows—   **3.3.3**

The "(C [number])" series, for commencement orders (including appointed day orders).[52]

The "(L [number])" series for legal instruments relating to fees or procedures in the courts of England and Wales.

The "(S [number])" series, for instruments[53] applying to Scotland only and dealing with reserved matters.[54]

The "(NI [number])" series for statutory instruments made in relation to Northern Ireland only.[55]

---

[46] As to which see Chapter 2, Section 5.

[47] See below.

[48] Their usage is, however, expected by Parliament and departure from the conventions would be likely to be noted and deprecated by, in particular, the Joint Committee on Statutory Instruments.

[49] As to which see Chapter 6, Section 2.

[50] Such as proceedings in a devolved legislature.

[51] As to which see Section 1 above.

[52] See Chapter 10, Section 1.

[53] Not to be confused with instruments made by the Scottish Ministers under devolved powers.

[54] See Chapter 7, Section 1.

[55] See Chapter 7, Section 2.

The "(W [number]") series, for instruments made by the National Assembly for Wales and applying to Wales only.[56]

These numbers are assigned by the Statutory Instrument Registrar, an official of Her Majesty's Stationery Office, at the time when the instrument is registered with that Office.

After the serial number heading comes the subject heading or headings, assigned by the Department in accordance with the instructions of the Statutory Instrument Registrar.

3.3.4   If an instrument relates only to England, to England and Wales, to Scotland, to Wales or to Northern Ireland, the subject heading will carry a reference to the relevant territory as a qualifying suffix (as in "**HOUSING, ENGLAND**").

Underneath the subject headings is found the title of the instrument. The title, which is provided for in the citation provision of the text, is assigned by the Department responsible for drafting the instrument. The title includes the year in which the instrument is made.

The title will generally indicate if an instrument is one of a series in relation to a particular matter, commencement being the obvious example.

Underneath the title are found italic cross-headings giving the date on which the instrument was made, the date on which it was laid before Parliament[57] and the date on which it comes into force.[58] These headings fulfil a statutory obligation found in s.4(2) of the Statutory Instruments Act 1946.[59]

The final heading, found only in a lengthy instrument, is a tabular arrangement of contents.

Preamble

3.3.5   Following its headings, every statutory instrument is introduced by a preamble. These do not serve the same function as those once used commonly for Acts[60] or as those routinely used for European instruments, both of which introduce the policy underlying the legislation. Instead, the preamble of a statutory instrument is generally confined to a recital of the powers under which it is made and the fulfilment of any statutory pre-conditions (such as consultation or the publication of notices). The preamble is not part of the text of an instrument and has no legal

---

[56] These instruments will generally have an alternate Welsh form in which the subsidiary number is shown as "Cy [number]".

[57] Or before the House of Commons only, if appropriate.

[58] If the commencement provision is complicated, the italic cross-heading will merely refer to the relevant provision—"*Coming into force—In accordance with article X.*"

[59] "(2) Every copy of any such statutory instrument sold by or under the authority of the King's printer of Acts of Parliament shall bear on the face thereof—(a) a statement showing the date on which the statutory instrument came or will come into operation; and (b) either a statement showing the date on which copies thereof were laid before Parliament or a statement that such copies are to be laid before Parliament."

[60] See Chapter 2, Section 5 and Chapter 26.

effect: in particular, failure to cite a relevant enabling provision would not result in the invalidity of the instrument.

Opening provisions

It is normal for the first provision of a statutory instrument to contain the citation and commencement provisions. Interpretation provisions are also often found near the beginning.[61]   **3.3.6**

Footnotes

Another feature of the composition of statutory instruments that is not found in Acts of Parliament is the footnote. A considerable body of lore has grown up, mostly instigated and enforced by the Joint Committee on Statutory Instruments, as to the use of footnotes in statutory instruments. Their primary purpose is to provide the reader with information on where he will find a law or other document referred to within the text of the instrument, and to record relevant amendments to laws referred to there.[62]   **3.3.7**

As to the Explanatory Notes to statutory instruments, see Chapter 6, Section 1 and Chapter 9, Section 6.

SECTION 4

VIRES

Introduction

Subordinate legislation has already been defined[63] as legislation that owes its existence and authority to other legislation. Implicit in this is the proposition that   **3.4.1**

---

[61] It was once an almost invariable rule that in an Act the interpretation provisions would be found at the end and in a statutory instrument (or in a Schedule to an Act) at the beginning. This is still common in either case, but the exceptions are numerous. In particular, it is common now for an Act, or a provision of an Act, to open with a series of defined terms. While that was once frowned upon as delaying the reader's exposure to the active provisions, in a technical provision it is often true both that the reader will make nothing of the substance without having some definitions explained first, and also that the definitions themselves will impart to the reader a helpful notion as to the substance of the provision as a whole. See, for example, the provisions about the fiscal treatment of rent-factoring arrangements, ss.43A to 43F of the Income and Corporation Taxes Act 1988 (c.1) which begin with the following—

"**43A Finance agreement: interpretation**

  (1) A transaction is a finance agreement for the purposes of sections 43B to 43F if in accordance with normal accounting practice the accounts of a company which receives money under the transaction would record a financial obligation (whether in respect of a lease creditor or otherwise) in relation to that receipt. . . . "

[62] This feature, which was of course once of enormous utility, is of considerably less importance now that up-dated versions of statutory instruments are as readily available through commercial electronic publication as are up-dated versions of Acts.

[63] Chapter 1, Section 2.

113

the potential scope of the subordinate legislation is limited by the extent of authority delegated.

So whereas in the case of an Act of Parliament one starts with the assumption that Parliament can do anything that it wishes to do, subject to certain limitations established by way of judicial presumptions or legislative control,[64] in the case of subordinate legislation one starts with the opposite assumption, namely that the Minister or other office-holder can do nothing by way of legislating unless it is clearly within the contemplation of the power conferred.[65]

The result is that while Acts of Parliament are immune from challenge in the courts except to the extent that Parliament has expressly provided,[66] subordinate legislation may be challenged on the grounds that it is not an exercise of the kind that was contemplated when the relevant power[67] was conferred.

3.4.2   The classic expression of the position is that of Lord Chancellor Herschell in *Institute of Patent Agents v Lockwood*[68]—

> "The effect of an enactment is that it binds all subjects who are affected by it. They are bound to conform themselves to the provisions of the law so made. The effect of a statutory rule if validly made is precisely the same that every person must conform himself to its provisions, and, if in each case a penalty be imposed, any person who does not comply with the provisions whether of the enactment or the rule becomes equally subject to the penalty. But there is this difference between a rule and an enactment, that whereas apart from some such provision as we are considering, you may canvass a rule and determine whether or not it was within the power of those who made it, you cannot canvass in that way the provisions of an Act of Parliament. Therefore, there is that difference between the rule and the statute. There is no difference if the rule is one within the statutory authority, but that very substantial difference, if it is open to consideration whether it be so or not."

The commonly used technical term for powers conferred by statute is *vires*, and a provision which is within the ambit of the powers is described as being *intra vires*, while one that is not is described as being *ultra vires*.

---

[64] As to which see Chapter 2, Section 2.

[65] As to the possibility of the Royal Prerogative being used—nominally by the Queen but in reality by the executive—to legislate, see Sections 2 and 7. That, of course, is primary legislation.

[66] The chief examples being challenge for incompatibility with the United Kingdom's obligations as a member of the European Union—challenge of a kind which the Westminster Parliament has permitted by virtue of the propositions in s.2(1) of the European Communities Act 1972 (c.68)—and challenge for incompatibility with the European Convention on Human Rights, as to which see Chapter 11, Section 3.

[67] For the purposes of this work it will be assumed that a duty to make subordinate legislation—relatively rare but by no means unheard of—contains an implicit power to make the legislation required and can therefore properly be covered by a proposition expressed in terms of legislative powers.

[68] [1894] A.C. 347, 360–361, HL.

For the relationship between *vires* and the concepts considered by the Joint Committee on Statutory Instruments see Chapter 6, Section 2.

Once a court has found that a particular purported exercise of a power to legislate is ineffective as being *ultra vires*, it is open to Parliament to remedy the situation by conferring expanded *vires*.[69]

Requirement of certainty

Subordinate legislation must be cast in terms which are sufficiently precise for **3.4.3** the persons on whom rights and duties are conferred to be able to know the parameters of the rights and duties and the effects of infringement or non-compliance. As Mathew J. put it in relation to by-laws in *Kruse v Johnson*[70]—

> "From the many decisions upon the subject it would seem clear that a by-law to be valid must, among other conditions, have two properties—it must be certain, that is, it must contain adequate information as to the duties of those who are to obey, and it must be reasonable."

Having said that subordinate legislation requires to be certain in order to be valid, and if insufficiently certain will be dismissed as invalid, the courts recognise that there may be some matters as to which it is impossible to legislate without leaving a margin of uncertainty.

Delineation of a geographical area for administrative purposes, for example, is **3.4.4** likely to involve an inevitable element of uncertainty at the edges, and the legislation will not be enforced in respect of any place where there is a real doubt as to whether or not it applied there: but the marginal uncertainty will not be allowed to defeat the entire legislative object, and the legislation will be applied

---

[69] For an example of which see the following observation of Lord McIntosh of Haringey in moving the Second Reading of the Insolvency Bill 1999–2000 (HL Deb. April 4, 2000 c.1252)—"When the Administration of Insolvent Estates of Deceased Persons Order was brought into effect at the end of 1986, it was generally believed that all the assets that a debtor owned immediately before his death would be available to his creditors in any insolvency proceedings which took place after his death. It was also believed that that would include his share in any jointly-owned property. That would have provided a level playing field for the treatment of the estates of all insolvents, whether living or deceased; otherwise, the assets available to creditors would have differed, depending on whether the debtor was alive or dead. However, a decision in the Court Appeal in the case of *Palmer (deceased)* has established that the order-making power contained in Section 421 of the Insolvency Act is not sufficient to bring about that result. The consequence is that the provisions in the 1986 Order are ineffective. As a result, in some cases what may appear to be the main, if not the only, asset—namely, the deceased debtor's interest in the matrimonial home—passes under the survivorship rules to the joint owner and is therefore beyond the reach of his creditors. We are taking this opportunity to amend the order-making power in Section 421 and by so doing we will, as far as is possible, restore a level playing field and give a certainty of outcome for creditors irrespective of whether the insolvent is living or deceased."; as to when it might be proper to legislate in this way with retrospective effect, see Chapter 10, Section 3.

[70] [1898] 2 Q.B. 91, 108, DC.

in relation to areas as to which there can be no doubt as to the intended application.[71]

In the end, the test of what is a reasonable margin of uncertainty is a practical one. If, and to the extent that, the person to whom legislation is addressed clearly knows what is required of him, the legislation is enforceable. If he does not, or to the extent that he does not, the legislation is unenforceable.[72]

Apparently open discretionary power

3.4.5 As to implied limitations on an apparently unconstrained statutory power (whether to make legislation or otherwise) see Chapter 12, Section 2, paras 12.2.5—12.2.7 and Chapter 1, Section 4.

Test of *vires*: subjective or objective

3.4.6 In determining whether a purported exercise of a subordinate power is *intra vires* it is frequently necessary to know whether the constraints or conditions established by the statute for the exercise of the power are to be construed objectively or subjectively. For example, if a Minister has power to legislate where he has reasonable cause to believe that a state of emergency exists, does the validity of the legislation depend on whether there is an emergency or only whether the Secretary of State thinks that there is?

This was the point at the heart of *Liversidge v Anderson*[73] in which the House of Lords decided that it was not for the courts to determine the accuracy or reasonableness of the Minister's belief. That decision was rapidly glossed and adapted in a number of ways, so that the present position was established by which, as with much else, the degree of objectivity or subjectivity to be applied in assessing the breadth of *vires* depends on the expression used in conferring the power and on the context in which it is conferred.

3.4.7 So, for example, as early as 1951 Lord Radcliffe said in *Nakkuda Ali v Jayaratne*[74]—

"Indeed, it would be a very unfortunate thing if the decision of *Liversidge's case* came to be regarded as laying down any general rule as to the construction of such phrases when they appear in statutory enactments. It is an authority for the proposition that the words 'if A.B. has reasonable cause to believe' are capable of meaning 'if A.B. honestly thinks that he has

---

[71] *Percy v Hall* [1997] Q.B. 924, CA.

[72] As Chief Justice Vaughan put it in *Sheppard v Gosnold* (Vaughan, 159, 166)—"A duty impossible to be known can be no duty; for civilly, what cannot be known to be, is as that which is not." See *Barrow v Arnaud* [1846] (8 Q.B. 595, 608).

[73] [1942] A.C. 206, HL; the decision has survived in frequent usage more because of the powerful dissenting speech of Lord Atkin than because of the majority decision—see, for example, Chapter 21, footnote 12.

[74] [1951] A.C. 56, 76–77, PC.

reasonable cause to believe' and that in the context and attendant circumstances of Defence Regulation 18B they did in fact mean just that. But the elaborate consideration which the majority of the House gave to the context and circumstances before adopting that construction itself shows that there is no general principle that such words are to be so understood; and the dissenting speech of Lord Atkin at least serves as a reminder of the many occasions when they have been treated as meaning 'if there is in fact reasonable cause for A.B. so to believe'. After all, words such as these are commonly found when a legislature or law-making authority confers powers on a minister or official. However read, they must be intended to serve in some sense as a condition limiting the exercise of an otherwise arbitrary power. But if the question whether the condition has been satisfied is to be conclusively decided by the man who wields the power the value of the intended restraint is in effect nothing. No doubt he must not exercise the power in bad faith: but the field in which this kind of question arises is such that the reservation for the case of bad faith is hardly more than a formality. Their Lordships therefore treat the words in reg 62, 'where the Controller has reasonable grounds to believe that any dealer is unfit to be allowed to continue as a dealer' as imposing a condition that there must in fact exist such reasonable grounds, known to the Controller, before he can validly exercise the power of cancellation."

Similarly, in *Secretary of State for Education and Science v Tameside Metropolitan Borough Council*[75] Lord Wilberforce said— **3.4.8**

"The section is framed in a 'subjective' form—if the Secretary of State 'is satisfied'. This form of section is quite well known, and at first sight might seem to exclude judicial review. Sections in this form may, no doubt, exclude judicial review on what is or has become a matter of pure judgment. But I do not think that they go further than that. If a judgment requires, before it can be made, the existence of some facts, then, although the evaluation of those facts is for the Secretary of State alone, the court must enquire whether those facts exist, and have been taken into account, whether the judgment has been made on a proper self direction as to those facts, whether the judgment has not been made on other facts which ought not to have been taken into account. If these requirements are not met, then the exercise of judgment, however bona fide it may be, becomes capable of challenge . . .

"The section has to be considered within the structure of the 1944 Act. In many statutes a Minister or other authority is given a discretionary power and in these cases the court's power to review any exercise of the discretion, though still real, is limited. In these cases it is said that the courts cannot

---

[75] [1977] A.C. 1014, HL.

substitute their opinion for that of the Minister; they can interfere on such grounds as that the Minister has acted right outside his powers or outside the purpose of the Act, or unfairly, or on an incorrect basis of fact. But there is no universal rule as to the principles on which the exercise of a discretion may be reviewed: each statute or type of statute must be individually looked at. This Act of 1944, is quite different from those which simply create a ministerial discretion. The Secretary of State, under s 68, is not merely exercising a discretion; he is reviewing the action of another public body which itself has discretionary powers and duties. He, by contrast with the courts in the normal case, may substitute his opinion for that of the authority: this is what the section allows, but he must take account of what the authority, under the statute, is entitled to do. The authority—this is vital—is itself elected, and is given specific powers as to the kind of schools it wants in its area. Therefore two situations may arise. One is that there may be a difference of policy between the Secretary of State (under Parliament) and the local authority: the section gives no power to the Secretary of State to make his policy prevail. The other is that, owing to the democratic process involving periodic elections, abrupt reversals of policy may take place, particularly where there are only two parties and the winner takes all. Any reversal of policy if at all substantial must cause some administrative disruption; this was as true of the 1975 proposals as of those of Tameside. So the mere possibility, or probability, of disruption cannot be a ground for issuing a direction to abandon the policy. What the Secretary of State is entitled, by a direction if necessary, to ensure is that such disruptions are not 'unreasonable', *i.e.* greater than a body, elected to carry out a new programme, with which the Secretary of State may disagree, ought to impose on those for whom it is responsible. After all, those who voted for the new programme, involving a change of course, must also be taken to have accepted some degree of disruption in implementing it.

"The ultimate question in this case, in my opinion, is whether the Secretary of State has given sufficient, or any, weight to this particular factor in the exercise of the judgment."

3.4.9   So the position today is clearly that in determining how far, if at all, to interfere with the exercise of a discretionary judgment (whether to make legislation or to do some other thing) the courts will consider the context rather than applying any rigid rules. As Lord Salmon said in *Attorney General of Saint Christopher, Nevis and Anguilla v Reynolds*[76]—

"Whilst their Lordships consider it unnecessary, for the reasons given by the Attorney General, to express any view about what Lord Reid in *Ridge v*

---

[76] [1979] 3 All E.R. 129, PC.

Baldwin[77] described as 'the very peculiar decision of this House in *Liversidge v Anderson*', they do consider it necessary to deal with the passage in Lord Atkin's speech on which the Attorney General did rely. No doubt that passage supports the argument that the words 'The Secretary of State is satisfied, etc' may confer an absolute discretion on the Executive. Sometimes they do, but sometimes they do not."

It is normal in modern statutory drafting to make the intended degree of subjectivity or objectivity as clear as possible. A number of different expressions are still used, however, (such as "is satisfied", "has reason to believe", "reasonably believes", "thinks", &c.) and difficulties can arise in attempting to distinguish different shades of meaning.[78]

The gradual development of the use and strength of the mechanisms for judicial review of administrative action has produced a position in which in most circumstances a requirement of reasonableness will be implied.[79] That being so, it is often thought unnecessary when conferring powers to legislate (or to do other things) to require that the powers must be exercised reasonably or only when a belief is reasonably held. It is increasingly the norm to confer powers on bodies susceptible to judicial review without express qualification, leaving it to be implied.[80] There are, however, some exceptions.[81]

Power to make incidental or supplemental provision

It is common for a power to legislate to be conferred in terms permitting the making of incidental or supplemental provision. This is often achieved for all powers in an Act in a general provision towards the end of the Act. **3.4.10**

---

[77] [1964] A.C. 40, 73.

[78] See, however, Chapter 8, Section 1, footnote 29. The examples used above are probably more or less synonymous in intention for the modern draftsman, and differences of meaning should therefore be implied from the context rather than imputed to different choices of word.

[79] See further Chapter 12, Section 2, paras 12.2.5—12.2.7.

[80] See, for example, the following passage from the Government's Response to the Report of the Joint Committee on the Draft Civil Contingencies Bill (January 2004, Cm. 6078, para.4)—"The Government has considered carefully the Committee's recommendation to provide expressly that the person making the regulations must act reasonably. As the Committee acknowledge (at para.206 of its Report), the absence of this word does not mean that the decision-maker can act unreasonably or that judicial review is prevented. Both Her Majesty (in this capacity) and a senior Minister of the Crown are subject to a duty to act reasonably by virtue of public law. It is therefore unnecessary to provide specifically that they must do so in the Bill. To make express provision of this kind in this Bill could be positively harmful; it might imply that action might be taken under other enactments that do not specify that the decision-maker must act reasonably which is unreasonable. So while the Government wholly agrees with the sentiment of the Committee on this point, it does not agree that it is necessary or appropriate to make express provision on the face of the Bill."

[81] It is common to find powers conferred on police constables qualified by a requirement for reasonable belief. While police constables are presently susceptible to judicial review, the practice may owe something to the independent status of the constabulary in its origins as an appointment held of the Crown, and the usage was determined in and has been continued from days before the existence of much of the jurisdiction in judicial review presently enjoyed by the courts.

What amounts to incidental or supplemental provision is, of course, difficult to determine. The two expressions are found sometimes together and sometimes apart, in the latter case with sometimes the one and sometimes the other being used apparently interchangeably. Probably, they have to be taken to mean something very similar to each other. Supplemental must mean more, or rather less, than simply additional: it must mean something along the lines of required to supplement the provisions of the instrument or of the Act in order to make it work. Incidental must similarly refer to something that is a necessary or expedient incident of the principal business of the instrument: something that is required to make it work. In this vein Viscount Dilhorne said of "supplemental" in *Daymond v South West Water Authority*[82]—

> "In that section 'supplementary' means, in my opinion, something added to what is in the Act to fill in details or machinery for which the Act itself does not provide—supplementary in the sense that it is required to implement what was in the Act."

As a general rule it can be expected that anything at all significant, and certainly anything involving significant intrusion on the liberty of the subject, will not reliably be effected in reliance on a mere power to make incidental or supplemental provision.[83]

"As if enacted in this Act"

3.4.11   It was once common for a statute to provide that subordinate legislation made under it would have the same effect "as if enacted in this Act". The formula was used in former times to emphasise the fact that both ordinances and proclamations were to be as effective as the statute would have been. In other words, it owes its origin to times when subordinate legislation was little used and the reader could be expected to require positive assurance from the legislature as to the nature and effect of the power conferred.

---

[82] [1976] A.C. 609, 644, HL; for "incidental" being construed in the same way and by reference to the *Daymond* exposition of "supplementary" see *R. v Customs and Excise Commissioners ex p. Hedges and Butler* [1986] 2 All E.R. 164, QBD.

[83] Note, for example, " . . . the Ministry of Agriculture, Fisheries and Food contend that the requirement for the premises to be inspected is reasonably incidental to the power to grant approvals . . . The Committee notes, however, that if Acts of Parliament intend that subordinate legislation should be able to confer powers of entry and inspection, they do so expressly and that they usually provide these sorts of powers in the Act itself . . . The Committee does not accept that such an important power is included in a power to make incidental provision and considers that the presence of a power of entry and inspection in the Act itself indicates that Parliament did not intend that regulations under the Act could include such powers."—Joint Committee on Statutory Instruments, Session 1995–96, 3rd Report, para.5 (HL Paper 16, HC 34-iii).

The formula is insufficient to amount to an ouster of the courts' jurisdiction to examine into the *vires* of purported exercises of the power.[84]

The formula is no longer used.[85]

SECTION 5

SUB-DELEGATION

As a general rule[86] the person on whom a power to legislate is conferred cannot use that power to confer a further power to legislate.[87] But Parliament can, of course, provide for departures from this rule by express power to sub-delegate.[88] **3.5.1**

It can be difficult to know what amounts to sub-delegation.[89] Does, for example, a provision of subordinate legislation fixing an interest rate at 2 per cent above the Retail Prices Index for a given period amount to the delegation of power to the authorities responsible for assessing or publishing the Retail Prices Index? Common sense suggests that it does not, principally on the grounds that the Retail Prices Index is determined wholly without reference to the referential use made of it in the subordinate legislation concerned. But there may be other cases where the point is more difficult to determine: as, for example, where a reference is made in subordinate legislation to something done by a professional body in circumstances where it would not be unrealistic to expect the professional body to be both aware of and influenced by the existence of the reference. And there will be cases where the purpose of a document to which subordinate legislation wishes to refer is so clearly linked to the purpose of the

---

[84] That is the sense in which it was construed by Lord Herschell in *Institute of Patent Agents v Lockwood* [1894] A.C. 347, HL, but see the speech of Lord Dunedin in *R. v Minister of Health, ex p. Yaffe* [1931] A.C. 494 HL. In any event, it is not to be expected that an ouster of jurisdiction in a modern statute would use language of this degree of generality—see Chapter 19.

[85] Its demise doubtless owes a great deal to the well-argued hostility of Sir William Graham-Harrison, former Second Parliamentary Counsel, expressed in his *Notes on the Delegation by Parliament of Legislative Powers, with a Particular Examination of the Case of* The Institute of Patent Agents v Lockwood, *and some Considerations with respect to the Future Granting, Exercise and Control of such Powers*, London, November 1931.

[86] Encapsulated in the Latin maxim *delegatus non potest delegare*.

[87] See also Chapter 13, Section 3, para.12.3.2.

[88] This may be either by specific power to confer a discretion, see for example s.45(10) of the Communications Act 2003 (c.21) or s.106(2)(p) of the Nationality, Immigration and Asylum Act 2002 (c.41), or by a general power to make provision of a kind that could be made by primary legislation, see for example s.2 of the European Communities Act 1972 (c.68) or in some other general breadth of expression, see for example ss.28 and 29 of the Scotland Act 1998 (c.46). But the latter two forms of power to sub-delegate are subject to express restrictions, see the considerable restrictions in para.1(1)(c) of Sch.2 to the 1972 Act (as to which see Section 10 below) and the particular restriction in s.29(2)(a) of the 1998 Act; see also para.1(1)(b) and (4) of Sch.2 to the Human Rights Act 1998 (c.42).

[89] See also Chapter 13, Section 3, para.12.3.2.

legislation that the element of sub-delegation is indubitable.[90] The question will be one of fact and degree, and when in any doubt the draftsman of the primary legislation will confer express power to sub-delegate.[91]

It can also be difficult to distinguish between the use of agents to carry out the administration of a scheme established by subordinate legislation and the conferring of legislative power on those agents. As Scott L.J. said in *Jackson Stansfield & Sons v Butterworth*[92]—

> "The regulation authorised the Minister of Works and no one else to operate its provisions. Those provisions, of course, authorised him to choose his own servants for the detailed tasks involved, but they did not authorise him to transfer his own functions either to the Minister of Health or to the local authorities, and it is interesting to observe in the letter from the Treasury Solicitor's office, which I have quoted, that a denial appears of any such transfer to local authorities. But, in my opinion, both the 'circulars' to the local authorities from the Minister of Health and the 'notes' for their guidance from the Minister of Works in fact do that; for they confer a very wide discretion on the local authorities themselves, and in the circulars and 'notes,' throughout the series, and especially in those of 1947, the function of prosecuting is plainly entrusted to the local authorities. For these reasons I am satisfied, in spite of the argument of the Attorney General, that some of the directions there contained were intended to have legislative effect, although I accept the Attorney General's contention that the regulation contained no such power of delegation. If it be argued that the Minister of Works could choose his licensing officers, I reply that he could have, but did not purport to do so. The delegation to another Minister or to local authorities of powers of administration and discretion was not within the authority of the Minister of Works. *Delegatus delegare non potest*, but the intention to delegate power and discretion to the local authorities is clear. The method chosen was convenient and desirable, but the power so to legislate was, unfortunately, not there."

3.5.2   Nowadays the unlawfulness of sub-delegation is so widely recognised amongst government lawyers that it is unlikely that anything approaching the *Stansfield* instance would be attempted without express authority in the relevant

---

[90] Hence the express permission in s.124(3) of the Education Act 2002 (c.32) for orders about teachers' pay to operate by reference to a document produced in an informal but conventional method—"(3) An order under s.122 may make provision by reference to a document; and—(a) an order which makes provision by reference to a document must include provision about publication of the document, and (b) a reference in this section to an order includes a reference to a document referred to by an order."; contrast with the earlier provision (s.2(3) of the School Teachers' Pay and Conditions 1991 (c.49)—"An order . . . shall contain the provision to be made or refer to provisions set out in a document published by Her Majesty's Stationery Office and direct that those provisions shall have effect or, as the case may be, be amended in accordance with the order."

[91] Provided, of course, that he is made aware in time of the possible wish to sub-delegate.

[92] [1948] 2 All E.R. 558, 564–565, CA.

primary legislation. Express authority to confer a discretionary function is now commonplace.[93]

But instances still arise where the delicate distinction between agency and delegation causes confusion. The issue was brought sharply into focus by the following item in a report of the Joint Committee on Statutory Instruments in connection with a statutory instrument which provided an instrument of government for a school where the instrument gave a power of delegation to officers or committees, without there having been express *vires* to provide for delegation[94]—

> "The Department argued that . . . the corporation would have an implied power to delegate to the principal because Parliament cannot have intended the board of governors to take every decision in relation to the institution. The Committee still finds these arguments unconvincing. . . . there is no need for a statute to express the common law principle that a corporation must, by its artificial nature, act through its human instruments. Paragraph 5(1) confers a true power to delegate functions."

In essence the distinction between delegation and agency is reasonably simple to state, although not always easy to apply in practice. A statutory corporation or other corporate body must act through its agents, because it has no corporeal existence and can act in no other way. Delegation arises only when the corporation establishes a system which gives a pre-determined field of discretion to a person (whether part of, or otherwise acting as agent of, the corporation) and within that field leaves it to the person to exercise a function of the corporation. While the corporation retains complete control of the exercise of the function, the function is not delegated. A similar test is likely to apply in the case of an individual.[95]

3.5.3 In principle it makes no difference to the lawfulness or unlawfulness of a sub-delegation on whom the sub-delegated power is conferred. In particular, for the Minister exercising a power to legislate to seek to arrogate to himself power to legislate further is just as much an unlawful sub-delegation as if he were conferring power on someone else. Parliament has enabled him to legislate by means of a statutory instrument subject, generally, to particular procedures and possibly to compliance with specified conditions. It is not open to him to broaden

---

[93] See, for example, the Education Act 2002 (c.32), s.131 (appraisal)—"(3) The regulations may—(a) require or permit an appraisal to be carried out in a manner which confers a discretion on a person specified by or chosen or determined in accordance with the regulations; (b) permit a person on whom a duty is imposed under subs.(2) to delegate that duty in whole or in part."; or the Railways and Transport Safety Act 2003 (c.20), s.9(5) (regulations)—"(5) Regulations under this section may— . . . (b) confer a discretionary function; . . . ".

[94] Joint Committee on Statutory Instruments, Session 1998–99, 14th Report, paras 8 & 9, HL Paper 46, HC 50-xiv.

[95] See further para.12.4.4, footnote 64.

the nature and width of the power conferred by taking power to legislate informally.[96]

Unnecessary sub-delegation has been deprecated in the following terms by the Joint Committee on Statutory Instruments—

> "The Committee fully appreciate that the justification for the granting of delegated legislative powers is to remove subsidiary or procedural details from the Statute Book and to afford the Executive flexibility and the ability to alter detailed provisions to fit changing circumstances, without the need to enact a new Statute. The corollary of this, however, must be that the delegated legislation itself should be detailed, specific and self-explanatory and should not depend on the exercise of ministerial or departmental discretion unless provision to that effect is expressly contained in the enabling statute."[97]

SECTION 6

CHALLENGING SUBORDINATE LEGISLATION

3.6.1 The principal practical mechanism for challenging subordinate legislation before the courts is by proceedings in the High Court for judicial review on the grounds that the legislation is *ultra vires* or otherwise improper. As Lord Irvine of Lairg L.C. said in *Boddington v British Transport Police*[98]—

> "Challenge to the lawfulness of subordinate legislation or administrative decisions and acts may take many forms, compendiously grouped by Lord Diplock in *Council of Civil Service Unions v Minister for the Civil Service*[99] under the headings of illegality, procedural impropriety and irrationality."

There are a number of specialist works about administrative law generally and judicial review of administrative action in particular that deal at length with the practicalities of challenges of this kind. This work will therefore attempt to do no more than adumbrate some of the principal features of the process.

3.6.2 While Parliament will in various ways[1] scrutinise the *vires* for purported exercises of subordinate legislative authority, the availability of judicial review

---

[96] For an example of objection being taken to a provision on the grounds of purported sub-delegation to the delegate himself see the following observations of the Joint Committee on Statutory Instruments in relation to an instrument making provision subject to the reservation "save as the Commissioners may otherwise allow"—"But it does not appear to the Committee that s.2(2) [of the Finance (No.2) Act 1992 (c.48)] enables the Commissioners to impose the conditions in the Regulations but allow for them to be dispensed with from outside the Regulations." Joint Committee on Statutory Instruments Session 1994–95, 24th Report (HL Paper 75, HC 8-xxiv).

[97] *First Special Report of the Joint Committee on Statutory Instruments*, Session 1977–78 (HL 51, HC 169).

[98] [1999] 2 A.C. 143, 152, HL.

[99] [1985] A.C. 374, HL.

[1] See Chapter 6, Section 2.

provides the most effective protection against abuse of power. As Farwell L.J. put it in *Dyson v Attorney-General*[2] "as it is, the courts are the only defence of the liberty of the subject against departmental aggression".

A number of aspects of *vires* are discussed in the context of the exercise of statutory powers in Chapter 12.

The grounds on which subordinate legislation may be challenged in the courts are as follows[3]—

That the purported exercise of the power is *ultra vires*.

That the purported exercise of the power is unreasonable.[4]

That the purported exercise of the power is insufficiently certain.

That there has been procedural deficiency or irregularity.

---

[2] [1911] 1 K.B. 410, 424.

[3] For an early example of a case enumerating all of these grounds except that of procedure see *Slattery v Naylor* (1888) 13 App. Cas. 446, PC.

[4] For which purpose the notion of reasonableness is that familiar in administrative law, as to which the leading case remains that of *Associated Provincial Picture Houses Limited v Wednesbury Corporation* [1948] 1 K.B. 223, CA. See, in particular, the following passage from the judgment of Lord Greene M.R. (at 228–229)—"When discretion of this kind is granted the law recognizes certain principles upon which that discretion must be exercised, but within the four corners of those principles the discretion, in my opinion, is an absolute one and cannot be questioned in any court of law. What then are those principles? They are well understood. They are principles which the court looks to in considering any question of discretion of this kind. The exercise of such a discretion must be a real exercise of the discretion. If, in the statute conferring the discretion, there is to be found expressly or by implication matters which the authority exercising the discretion ought to have regard to, then in exercising the discretion it must have regard to those matters. Conversely, if the nature of the subject matter and the general interpretation of the Act make it clear that certain matters would not be germane to the matter in question, the authority must disregard those irrelevant collateral matters.

"There have been in the cases expressions used relating to the sort of things that authorities must not do, not merely in cases under the Cinematograph Act but, generally speaking, under other cases where the powers of local authorities came to be considered. I am not sure myself whether the permissible grounds of attack cannot be defined under a single head. It has been perhaps a little bit confusing to find a series of grounds set out. Bad faith, dishonesty—those of course, stand by themselves—unreasonableness, attention given to extraneous circumstances, disregard of public policy and things like that have all been referred to, according to the facts of individual cases, as being matters which are relevant to the question. If they cannot all be confined under one head, they at any rate, I think, overlap to a very great extent. For instance, we have heard in this case a great deal about the meaning of the word 'unreasonable'.

"It is true the discretion must be exercised reasonably. Now what does that mean? Lawyers familiar with the phraseology commonly used in relation to exercise of statutory discretions often use the word 'unreasonable' in a rather comprehensive sense. It has frequently been used and is frequently used as a general description of the things that must not be done. For instance, a person entrusted with a discretion must, so to speak, direct himself properly in law. He must call his own attention to the matters which he is bound to consider. He must exclude from his consideration matters which are irrelevant to what he has to consider. If he does not obey those rules, he may truly be said, and often is said, to be acting 'unreasonably'. Similarly, there may be something so absurd that no sensible person could ever dream that it lay within the powers of the authority. Warrington L.J. in *Short v Poole Corporation* gave the example of the red-haired teacher, dismissed because she had red hair. That is unreasonable in one sense. In another sense it is taking into consideration extraneous matters. It is so unreasonable that it might almost be described as being done in bad faith; and, in fact, all these things run into one another . . . ".

125

3.6.3   It is, of course, possible to imagine many specific kinds of ground upon which particular subordinate legislation may be challenged. New principles of law will arise, including principles of European or international law which by reason of the context of the legislation concerned have to be given effect or taken into consideration in determining the validity of United Kingdom law. But, except where the legislature requires the courts to have regard to a particular matter in determining legality of subordinate legislation,[5] these particular yardsticks are all likely to fall within one of the broad concepts above. As Lord Bridge of Harwich said in *Brind v Secretary of State for the Home Department*[6]—

> "The reality is that judicial review is a jurisdiction which has been developed and is still being developed by the judges. It has many strands and more will be added, but they are and will always be closely interwoven. But however the cloth emerges from the loom, it must never be forgotten that it is a supervisory and not an appellate jurisdiction. As Watkins LJ pointed out, acceptance of 'proportionality' as a separate ground for seeking judicial review rather than a facet of 'irrationality' could easily and speedily lead to courts forgetting the supervisory nature of their jurisdiction and substituting their view of what was appropriate for that of the authority whose duty it was to reach that decision.
>
> "I therefore propose to consider the submission that the directives were disproportionate to the needs of the situation as being an aspect of the submission that the directives were 'perverse' or, as I would put it, 'Wednesbury unreasonable' or, as Lord Diplock would have put it, 'irrational.' "

It is possible to impugn the validity of a piece of subordinate legislation irrespective of whether or not it has been approved by the Houses of Parliament under the procedure described in Chapter 6, Section 2, because in such a case the approval is a matter of confirming and consenting to the policy, not of providing either a variation of or an authoritative construction of the power purported to be exercised. Until it is challenged by someone with a proper ground for doing so, however, the legislation will be presumed to be effective. Both these points are made, together with an exposition of the essential nature of challenge of this kind, in the following passage of the speech of Lord Diplock in *F. Hoffmann-la Roche & Co. v Secretary of State for Trade and Industry*[7]—

> "My Lords, in constitutional law a clear distinction can be drawn between an Act of Parliament and subordinate legislation, even though the latter is contained in an order made by statutory instrument approved by resolutions

---

[5] The obvious examples being the Human Rights Act 1998 (c.42), as to which Chapter 11, Section 3 and the European Communities Act 1972 (c.68), as to which see Chapter 32.

[6] [1991] 1 A.C. 696, 747–748, HL.

[7] [1975] A.C. 295, HL.

of both Houses of Parliament. Despite this indication that the majority of members of both Houses of the contemporary Parliament regard the order as being for the common weal, I entertain no doubt that the courts have jurisdiction to declare it to be invalid if they are satisfied that in making it the Minister who did so acted outwith the legislative powers conferred upon him by the previous Act of Parliament under which the order purported to be made, and this is so whether the order is ultra vires by reason of its contents (patent defects) or by reason of defects in the procedure followed prior to its being made (latent defects). . . .

"Under our legal system, however, the courts as the judicial arm of government do not act on their own initiative. Their jurisdiction to determine that a statutory instrument is ultra vires does not arise until its validity is challenged in proceedings inter partes either brought by one party to enforce the law declared by the instrument against another party or brought by a party whose interests are affected by the law so declared sufficiently directly to give him locus standi to initiate proceedings to challenge the validity of the instrument. Unless there is such challenge and, if there is, until it has been upheld by a judgment of the court, the validity of the statutory instrument and the legality of acts done pursuant to the law declared by it are presumed. It would, however, be inconsistent with the doctrine of ultra vires as it has been developed in English law as a means of controlling abuse of power by the executive arm of government if the judgment of a court in proceedings properly constituted that a statutory instrument was ultra vires were to have any lesser consequence in law than to render the instrument incapable of ever having had any legal effect upon the rights or duties of the parties to the proceedings (*cf. Ridge v Baldwin*[8]). Although such a decision is directly binding only as between the parties to the proceedings in which it was made, the application of the doctrine of precedent has the consequence of enabling the benefit of it to accrue to all other persons whose legal rights have been interfered with in reliance on the law which the statutory instrument purported to declare."

The courts will approach the exercise of a power to make subordinate **3.6.5** legislation by presuming that the delegate of the power to legislate was entitled to exercise it as he chose, subject to the limitations expressed above. The nature of the balance to be struck is illustrated graphically in the judgment of Lord Alverstone C.J. in *Scott v Pilliner*[9]—

"I think that this Court ought not to interfere with a by-law made by a local authority if it can be supported on reasonable grounds; but I also think that it is desirable for the good government of a locality that by-laws should be

---

[8] [1964] A.C. 40.
[9] [1904] 2 K.B. 855, 858–859, DC.

clear and definite and free from ambiguity, and also that such by-laws should not make unlawful things which are otherwise innocent. Of course a local authority may make a by-law for stopping street betting by means of tipsters, and if that was all that this by-law did it would, in my opinion, be valid. I do not wish to be understood to say that a by-law cannot be made to that effect. But it seems to me that the main objection to this by-law is that it is too wide, and that it would include cases where the sale of the paper was not in aid of street betting or of any betting at all.

"If the paper were conducted or the office of the paper were used on behalf of persons carrying on street betting as a fact, then a by-law striking at the evil might be perfectly reasonable; but the by-law in its present form brings within its purview papers which may be found to be mainly devoted to giving information as to the probable results of competitions on which there might be no betting at all. There may be perfectly innocent sales of such papers, and their publication and distribution might not conduce to any betting offence at all, and yet they would fall within this by-law. I think, however, that a by-law might be framed so as to hit the real mischief, and so as to be confined to it.

"Therefore, both on the ground of uncertainty, and mainly on the ground that it may strike at perfectly innocent sales of papers, I think that this by-law is bad and cannot be supported."[10]

---

[10] See also the following passage of the judgment of Lord Russell of Killowen C.J. in *Kruse v Johnson* [1898] 2 Q.B. 91, 99–100—"But, when the Court is called upon to consider the by-laws of public representative bodies clothed with the ample authority which I have described, and exercising that authority accompanied by the checks and safeguards which have been mentioned, I think the consideration of such by-laws ought to be approached from a different standpoint. They ought to be supported if possible. They ought to be, as has been said, 'benevolently' interpreted, and credit ought to be given to those who have to administer them that they will be reasonably administered. This involves the introduction of no new canon of construction. But, further, looking to the character of the body legislating under the delegated authority of Parliament, to the subject-matter of such legislation, and to the nature and extent of the authority given to deal with matters which concern them, and in the manner which to them shall seem meet, I think courts of justice ought to be slow to condemn as invalid any by-law, so made under such conditions, on the ground of supposed unreasonableness. Notwithstanding what Cockburn C.J. said in *Bailey v Williamson* ((1873) L. R. 8 Q. B. 118, 124), an analogous case, I do not mean to say that there may not be cases in which it would be the duty of the Court to condemn by-laws, made under such authority as these were made, as invalid because unreasonable. But unreasonable in what sense? If, for instance, they were found to be partial and unequal in their operation as between different classes; if they were manifestly unjust; if they disclosed bad faith; if they involved such oppressive or gratuitous interference with the rights of those subject to them as could find no justification in the minds of reasonable men, the Court might well say, 'Parliament never intended to give authority to make such rules; they are unreasonable and ultra vires.' But it is in this sense, and in this sense only, as I conceive, that the question of unreasonableness can properly be regarded. A by-law is not unreasonable merely because particular judges may think that it goes further than is prudent or necessary or convenient, or because it is not accompanied by a qualification or an exception which some judges may think ought to be there. Surely it is not too much to say that in matters which directly and mainly concern the people of the county, who have the right to choose those whom they think best fitted to represent them in their local government bodies, such representatives may be trusted to understand their own requirements better than judges. Indeed, if the question of the

It has been suggested that there is a difference between procedural and **3.6.6** substantive defects in subordinate legislation, the former causing the legislation to be voidable, and therefore retaining force until declared void, and the latter causing it to be void, and having no force at all. In *Bugg v Director of Public Prosecutions*[11] Woolf L.J. said[12]—

> "So far as procedural invalidity is concerned, the proper approach is to regard byelaws and other subordinate legislation as valid until they are set aside by the appropriate court with the jurisdiction to do so. A member of the public is required to comply with byelaws even if he believes they have a procedural defect unless and until the law is held to be invalid by a court of competent jurisdiction. If before this happens he contravenes the byelaw, he commits an offence and can be punished. Where the law is substantively invalid, the position is different. No citizen is required to comply with a law which is bad on its face. If the citizen is satisfied that that is the situation, he is entitled to ignore the law."

It is probable that this, like everything else in statutory construction, may serve as a useful guide and starting point but must give way where necessary to the logic and probable policy intentions of the Act conferring the power under which the legislation is made.[13]

Where a person is charged with an offence which derives from or rests on subordinate legislation, it is now established that it is in general open to him to raise the invalidity of the legislation as a defence; if he establishes invalidity he has committed no crime.[14] There are some exceptions to this principle but they are limited in their effect.[15]

Effect of successful challenge

As Lord Browne-Wilkinson said in *Boddington v British Transport Police*[16]— **3.6.7**

> "I adhere to my view that the juristic basis of judicial review is the doctrine of ultra vires. But I am far from satisfied that an ultra vires act is incapable of having any legal consequence during the period between the doing of that act and the recognition of its invalidity by the court. During that period

---

validity of by-laws were to be determined by the opinion of judges as to what was reasonable in the narrow sense of that word, the cases in the books on this subject are no guide; for they reveal, as indeed one would expect, a wide diversity of judicial opinion, and they lay down no principle or definite standard by which reasonableness or unreasonableness may be tested."

[11] [1993] Q.B. 473, DC.
[12] At 500.
[13] See *R. v Wicks* [1998] A.C. 92, HL, *per* Lord Nicholls and Lord Hoffmann.
[14] *Boddington v British Transport Police* [1999] 2 A.C. 143, HL; see also *R. v Wicks* [1998] A.C. 92, HL.
[15] See *R. v Searby* [2003] 3 C.M.L.R. 15, CA.
[16] [1999] 2 A.C. 143, 164, HL.

people will have regulated their lives on the basis that the act is valid. The subsequent recognition of its invalidity cannot rewrite history as to all the other matters done in the meantime in reliance on its validity. The status of an unlawful act during the period before it is quashed is a matter of great contention and of great difficulty: see *Percy v Hall*[17] per Schiemann L.J. and the authorities there referred to; de Smith, Woolf and Jowell, Judicial Review of Administrative Action, 5th ed. (1995), paras 5.044–5.048 and *Calvin v Carr*.[18]"

Severance

3.6.8 It is now accepted as a general rule that when faced with subordinate legislation of any kind a court will, in holding that the legislation is invalid as to any part or aspect, where possible and where productive of a sensible and just result, contrive to save such part of the legislation as is valid on its own terms.

From being "a branch of the law which was in danger of becoming stifled by technicalities"[19] the proposition stated above has emerged as a general rule to be applied wherever practicable and fair without undue deference to technical distinctions.[20]

The rule requiring severance of tainted parts of legislation so as to preserve the remainder emanates from a basic principle of construction[21] requiring the courts to lean towards validity. As Stephenson L.J. said in *Thames Water Authority v Elmbridge Borough Council*[22]—

"For some centuries our courts have been applying to the benevolent interpretation of written instruments of all kinds, including statutes, the common sense principle preserved in Latin as '*ut res magis valeat quam pereat*': Coke upon Littleton 36a; Broom's Legal Maxims, 10th ed. (1939), p.361.

---

[17] [1997] Q.B. 924, 950–952.

[18] [1980] A.C. 574, 589–590.

[19] *Thames Water Authority v Elmbridge Borough Council* [1983] Q.B. 570, 581, CA *per* Dunn L.J.

[20] "Much of the difficulty in the case seems to me to have been caused by the very use of the word 'severance' which, in relation to the construction of documents and in particular of covenants in restraint of trade, has acquired a special and technical meaning. Its use in this case demonstrates the danger of using such words in their general or ordinary meaning to describe a process in which the court is in fact considering the validity of the purported exercise of power by a local authority. The label given to the process tends to confuse the reality of the process itself by imposing rules of law designed to deal with quite different situations. I would echo the words of Ormrod L.J. in *Dunkley v Evans* [1981] 1 W.L.R. 1522, 1524–1525, that the court should not strive officiously to kill to any extent greater than it is compelled to do. If, as here, it is perfectly plain that the urban district council had no power to do what it purported to do in respect of an easily identifiable parcel of land, it would not be conducive to good public administration for the court officiously to hold that the whole document, including that part which was within the power of the council, was invalid."—*Thames Water Authority, per* Dunn L.J. at 580–581.

[21] See Chapter 19.

[22] At 585.

"By applying that principle they have been able, not only to make sense of **3.6.9** near nonsense but also to give effect to what is good and enforce what is valid, while refusing to enforce what is bad and giving no effect to what is invalid. This latter exercise can be carried out, and can, of course, be carried out only, where the good and bad parts are clearly identifiable and the bad part can be separated from the good and rejected without affecting the validity of the remaining part. But this ought to be done whenever the good and bad parts can be so identified and separated and what remains is clearly valid in the sense that there is nothing inherently unenforceable about it and all the surrounding circumstances indicate that common sense and the intention of the maker of any document which includes both good and bad parts would give effect to it.

"There will be cases where no such identification and separation of good from bad is possible and the invalidity of one part will taint and invalidate the whole. (The curate's egg was such a tainted whole, whatever its deferential consumer may have intended to hint to the contrary.) But I cannot see why this should be so in every case where the document which confronts the court does not itself identify the invalid part. To treat every such document as the egg of the curate would disable the court, by a matter of form only, from dividing what is clearly divisible into its component parts . . . ".

Section 7

Rarer Forms of Subordinate Legislation and Quasi-Legislation

By-laws

By-laws were once of sufficient practical importance to be regarded as a form of **3.7.1** legislation deserving of consideration in their own right. But as the incidence of other forms of subordinate legislation has multiplied over the years, and perhaps as the balance of control in many social matters has shifted from local by-laws to central regulation, the body of by-law legislation has for all practical purposes become merged into that of delegated legislation generally.

As to the definition of a by-law, that propounded by Lord Russell of Killowen C.J. in *Kruse v Johnson*[23] remains sufficient—

"But first it seems necessary to consider what is a by-law. A by-law, of the class we are here considering, I take to be an ordinance affecting the public, or some portion of the public, imposed by some authority clothed with statutory powers ordering something to be done or not to be done, and accompanied by some sanction or penalty for its non-observance. It

---

[23] [1898] 2 Q.B. 91, 96–97, DC.

131

necessarily involves restriction of liberty of action by persons who come under its operation as to acts which, but for the by-law, they would be free to do or not do as they pleased. Further, it involves this consequence—that, if validly made, it has the force of law within the sphere of its legitimate operation."

Codes of practice

3.7.2 Legislation frequently allows a Minister to give directions or to issue guidance or a code of practice.[24] Sometimes a Minister or other body is required to issue a code of practice regulating the performance of a particular function.[25]

The terms "code of conduct" and "code of practice" are synonymous and interchangeable, although the latter is the more usual nowadays.

It is presently common for legislation conferring a power or duty to issue codes of practice to confer an express power or duty to revise the code from time to time.[26]

Codes of practice were at one stage a controversial form of subordinate legislation on the grounds that they have the effect of delegating legislative power to the executive to be exercised in a most informal and unregulated manner.[27] But they are now a familiar and accepted part of the legislative scene.

There are two instances of particular social significance where important practical details on which a system depends are regulated by code of practice—

(1) The Highway Code, made under section 38 of the Road Traffic Act 1988,[28] deals with general and vital matters relating to the proper practice for traffic on the roads. Section 38(7) provides that a failure to observe the code does not itself produce criminal or civil liability "but any such failure may in any proceedings (whether civil or criminal . . .) be relied upon by any party to the proceedings as tending to establish or negative any liability which is in question in those proceedings."

(2) The Police and Criminal and Criminal Evidence Act 1984 delegates a number of matters of enormous social significance, including search and

---

[24] See, for example, the Local Government and Housing Act 1989 (c.42), s.31, the Regulatory Reform Act 2001 (c.6), s.9 or the Railways and Transport Safety Act 2002 (c.20), s.47.

[25] See, for example, the Architects Act 1997 (c.22), s.13, the Ethical Standards in Public Life etc. (Scotland) Act 2000 (asp 7), the Immigration and Asylum Act 1999 (c.33), s.32A or the Police and Criminal Evidence Act 1984 (c.60), s.113.

[26] See, for example, the Police (Northern Ireland) Act 1998 (c.32), s.38, the Anti-Terrorism, Crime and Security Act 2001 (c.24), s.102 or the General Teaching Council For Wales (Functions) Regulations (SI 2000/1979), reg. 13.

[27] See, for example, HL Deb. January 15, 1986 cc.1075–1104.

[28] 1988 c.52.

detention of persons and seizure of property, to regulation by code of practice.[29]

Codes of practice are also of importance in the deregulatory regime of the **3.7.3**
Regulatory Reform Act 2001.[30]
Many other Acts use codes of practice to a lesser degree.[31]
Codes of practice can also be agreed informally between parties responsible for some statutory or contractual duty. For example, the local highway authorities maintain a Code of Practice for Maintenance Management which is agreed amongst themselves and endorsed by central and devolved government. A code of this kind is certainly not legislation, having no statutory authority. But that does not necessarily deprive it of all legal effect: it may well be considered by the courts as helpful or even crucial in establishing whether a statutory or contractual function has been performed according to the standard that can reasonably be expected having regard to norms within an industry (and, therefore, whether or not negligence has occurred).

Guidance

It is common for an Act to require or permit a Minister of the Crown to issue **3.7.4**
guidance about how something under the Act, or connected with its subject matter, is to be done.[32] And it is also common for an Act to require an authority performing a function under the Act to have regard in the performance of the function to guidance issued by a Minister for that purpose.[33] Whether or not that gives the guidance the status and effect of subordinate legislation is open to—probably futile—debate. What is indisputable is that guidance of this kind is capable of having legal effect both as a result of the provisions of the statute that

---

[29] See, in particular, s.66—
    "66 Codes of practice
       (1) The Secretary of State shall issue codes of practice in connection with—
          (a) the exercise by police officers of statutory powers—
             (i) to search a person without first arresting him; or
             (ii) to search a vehicle without making an arrest;
          (b) the detention, treatment, questioning and identification of persons by police
             officers;
          (c) searches of premises by police officers; and
          (d) the seizure of property found by police officers on persons or premises.
       (2) Codes shall (in particular) include provision in connection with the exercise by police
          officers of powers under section 63B above [drug testing]."
    See also ss.60 and 60A (recording of interviews).
[30] 2001 c.6: see ss.9 to 11.
[31] For example, ss.99 and 100 of the Terrorism Act 2000 (c.11) (codes of practice on exercise of police powers, seizure and retention of property, exercise of powers by members of armed forces, and video recording of interviews by police).
[32] See, for example, the Firearms (Amendment) Act 1997 (c.5), s.22(2).
[33] See, for example, the Football Spectators Act 1989 (c.37), s.19(5).

authorises its issue and as a result of the application by the courts of the ordinary principles of administrative law.[34]

Statute sometimes allows or requires a Minister to give guidance or advice in a context in which there is no duty to comply with it.[35] That guidance or advice cannot properly be regarded as legislation, although it is not impossible that the courts would have regard to it in determining whether a duty of care or some other kind of duty had been fulfilled.

There is also now a plethora of different kinds of power or duty to give advice and guidance of a more or less informal kind. Despite the fact that this advice or guidance does not create directly enforceable legal rights or duties, its practical importance is indubitable. As an extreme example of this, s.33 of the Wildlife and Countryside Act 1981[36]—which requires Ministers to prepare "codes containing such recommendations, advice and information as they consider proper for the guidance of" persons exercising specified statutory functions and persons affected by those functions—requires the code to be approved by both Houses of Parliament before being issued, despite the absence of direct legal consequences flowing from it.[37]

Directions

3.7.5 Acts frequently require or allow a Minister to give directions, generally in respect of some administrative matter. So long as there is a duty to comply with the direction it can be seen as a form of subordinate legislation. Generally the duty to comply will be express, but, particularly where the direction is given to a public body that is susceptible to the administrative law process of judicial review, it may be appropriate for the duty to comply to be left to be implied.

---

[34] For this reason the role of guidance is not uncontroversial, principally on account of the lack of standard systems for publication or Parliamentary scrutiny. See, for example, the following statement by a former Lord Chancellor, Lord Mackay of Clashfern, on the Report Stage of the Courts Bill 2002–03 (HL Deb. May 8, 2003, cc.1191–92): "To my mind, a perhaps completely novel procedure—if it is not completely novel it is certainly exceptional—has been adopted for modifying the statutory functions of the boards as prescribed in new Clause 5. It provides that the Lord Chancellor can by guidance supplement the functions conferred on the boards by the statute. I am not aware of any other situation in which guidance has been used as an instrument for amending primary legislation. There is a good deal of talk, as there has been over the years, about the propriety of amending statutes by secondary legislation, but this is a step further, Without the ordinary process for such change, in practical terms, it is difficult to know how a person who is not very familiar with the statutes can in years to come find out the current functions of these boards. I do not think that it would occur to one to look through the guidance issued to find the changes."

[35] For example, see s.39 of the Road Traffic Act 1988 (c.52) which allows the Secretary of State to disseminate information or advice relating to the use of roads.

[36] 1981 c.69.

[37] Subs.(2). And see, for example, HL Deb. April 4, 2003 cc.1581–96. See also s.182 of the Licensing Act 2003 (c.17) (guidance).

Church Measures

Measures passed by the General Synod of the Church of England[38] are **3.7.6** technically subordinate, since their authority derives from s.4 of the Church of England Assembly (Powers) Act 1919.[39] But they are treated very much like Acts, being presented for Royal Assent and printed by the Queen's Printer's of Acts of Parliament, numbered as a separate series for each calendar year and published at the end of the annual volumes of statutes.

This treatment is justified by the width of the power to make Measures. Section 19(6) of the 1919 Act provides that—

> "A measure may relate to any matter concerning the Church of England, and may extend to the amendment or repeal in whole or in part of any Act of Parliament, including this Act:
> Provided that a measure shall not make any alteration in the composition or powers or duties of the Ecclesiastical Committee, or in the procedure in Parliament prescribed by section four of this Act."

Unusually, the Parliamentary procedures for the handling of a Measure are regulated to a considerable extent by statute. Section 2 of the 1919 Act requires the establishment of a joint Ecclesiastical Committee of the two Houses.[40] Section 3(1) then requires that "Every measure passed by the Church Assembly shall be submitted by the Legislative Committee[41] to the Ecclesiastical Committee, together with such comments and explanations as the Legislative Committee may deem it expedient or be directed by the Church Assembly to add." The

---

[38] This is "the Assembly constituted in accordance with the constitution set forth in the Appendix to the Addresses presented to His Majesty by the Convocations of Canterbury and York on the tenth day of May nineteen hundred and nineteen": Church of England Assembly (Powers) Act 1919 (c.76), s.1(1). It was renamed the General Synod of the Church of England by s.2 of the Synodical Government Measure 1969 (No.2).

[39] 1919 c.76.

[40] **"2 Establishment of an Ecclesiastical Committee**
   (1) There shall be a Committee of members of both Houses of Parliament styled "The Ecclesiastical Committee."
   (2) The Ecclesiastical Committee shall consist of fifteen members of the House of Lords, nominated by the Lord Chancellor and fifteen members of the House of Commons nominated by the Speaker of the House of Commons, to be appointed on the passing of this Act to serve for the duration of the present Parliament and thereafter to be appointed at the commencement of each Parliament to serve for the duration of that Parliament. . . .
   (3) The powers and duties of the Ecclesiastical Committee may be exercised and discharged by any twelve members thereof, and the Committee shall be entitled to sit and to transact business whether Parliament be sitting or not, and notwithstanding to vacancy in the membership of the Committee. Subject to the provisions of this Act, the Ecclesiastical Committee may regulate is own procedure."
   For the regulation of the Ecclesiastical Committee's proceedings see the resolution of March 22, 1921 adopting the procedure of other Joint Committees.

[41] *i.e.* the Legislative Committee of the Church Assembly.

Ecclesiastical Committee then consider and report to Parliament.[42] The final part of the process is determined by s.4 as follows—

3.7.7   "When the Ecclesiastical Committee shall have reported to Parliament on any measure submitted by the Legislative Committee, the report, together with the text of such measure, shall be laid before both Houses of Parliament forthwith, if Parliament be then sitting, or, if not, then immediately after the next meeting of Parliament, and thereupon, on a resolution being passed by each House of Parliament directing that such measure in the form laid before Parliament should be presented to His Majesty, such measure shall be presented to His Majesty, and shall have the force and effect of an Act of Parliament on the Royal Assent being signified thereto in the same manner as to Acts of Parliament: . . . [43]"

Consideration of a Measure is routinely referred by the House of Commons to a Standing Committee,[44] leaving the final decision to the House, but without further opportunity for debate.

---

[42] Section 3(2) to (5)—

"(2) The Ecclesiastical Committee shall thereupon consider the measure so submitted to it, and may, at any time during such consideration, either of its own motion or at the request of the Legislative Committee, invite the Legislative Committee to a conference to discuss the provisions thereof, and thereupon a conference of the two committees shall be held accordingly.

(3) After considering the measure, the Ecclesiastical Committee shall draft a report thereon to Parliament stating the nature and legal effect of the measure and its views as to the expediency thereof, especially with relation to the constitutional rights of all His Majesty's subjects.

(4) The Ecclesiastical Committee shall communicate its report in draft to the Legislative Committee, but shall not present it to Parliament until the Legislative Committee signify its desire that it should be so presented.

(5) At any time before the presentation of the report to Parliament the Legislative Committee may, either on its own motion or by direction of the Church Assembly, withdraw a measure from further consideration by the Ecclesiastical Committee; but the Legislative Committee shall have no power to vary a measure of the Church Assembly either before or after conference with the Ecclesiastical Committee."

[43] Proviso for splitting of Measure.

[44] See Standing Order 118(4) to (6)—

"(4) Where a Member has given notice of—

(a) . . . , or

(b) a motion that a measure under the Church of England Assembly (Powers) Act 1919 be presented to Her Majesty for her Royal Assent, or a motion relating to an instrument made under such a measure,

a motion may be made by a Minister of the Crown at the commencement of public business, that the instrument be referred to such a committee, and the question thereon shall be put forthwith; and if, on the question being put, not fewer than twenty Members rise in their places and signify their objection thereto, the Speaker shall declare that the noes have it.

(5) Each committee shall consider each instrument referred to it on a motion, 'That the committee has considered the instrument'; and the chairman shall put any question necessary to dispose of the proceedings on such a motion, if not previously concluded,

There are recorded instances of Parliament failing to approve a Measure.[45]

Royal Charter

Royal Charter[46] is no longer[47] much used as a mechanism for conferring **3.7.8** significant rights or duties of a public nature. But Parliament can recognise and preserve by statute the system of granting status by Charter, thereby in effect converting it into a form of subordinate legislation.[48] Statute may also operate by reference to a body created by Charter[49] or may expressly preserve the effect of a provision of a Charter.[50]

A Royal Charter is granted, generally in response to a petition requesting a Charter, as an exercise of the Royal Prerogative.[51] In that sense it is a primary instrument, but it confers rights and duties of a general nature only in a very limited and indirect sense, and is perhaps, subject to the previous paragraph, best not described as legislation.[52]

---

when the committee shall have sat for one and a half hours (or, in the case of an instrument relating exclusively to Northern Ireland, two and a half hours) after the commencement of those proceedings; and the committee shall thereupon report the instrument to the House without any further question being put.

(6) If any motion is made in the House of the kind specified in paragraphs (3) or (4) of this order, in relation to any instrument reported to the House in accordance with paragraph (5) of this order, the Speaker shall put forthwith the question thereon and such question may be decided at any hour, though opposed."

[45] See, for example, proceedings in the House of Commons on the Prayer Book Measure in 1927 and 1928.

[46] A Royal Charter is a written instrument made in the form of Letters Patent: there is always to be found in the concluding sentences of every Royal Charter the following:—"IN WITNESS whereof We have caused these Our Letters to be made Patent".

[47] At one stage a Charter could be used for certain purposes to create rights having the same authority as those conferred by Act of Parliament. See, for example, the Charter of 1337 (Edward III) creating and vesting in the Black Prince the Duchy of Cornwall and making provision for succession by the Sovereign's eldest son, being also heir apparent, immediately upon his birth. (See further Chapter 5, Section 2, para.5.2.23).

[48] The most significant modern example is s.245 of the Local Government Act 1972 (c.70) which empowers the Sovereign to confer certain kinds of municipal status by charter. And as early as 1837 the Chartered Companies Act empowered the grant of charters of incorporation to trading companies, a power that had particular continuing significance in relation to banks.

[49] See, for example, Disability (Grants) Act 1993, s.1 "The Secretary of State may make grants to . . . (c) Motability (a body corporate constituted by Royal Charter), for such purposes as the Secretary of State may determine", or the references to the British Broadcasting Corporation in the Broadcasting Act 1990 (c.42) or 1996 (c.55).

[50] See, for example, s.24 of the Municipal Corporations Act 1883 (c.18): "Nothing in this Act shall deprive the lord of the manor of Corfe of any title enjoyed by him under any charter."

[51] Although in certain cases nowadays it may be the exercise of a delegated power.

[52] The principal effect of the grant of a Royal Charter is to incorporate the body to which the Charter is granted. The ease with which bodies have been able, for several decades, to become incorporated through registration under legislation relating to companies has made the grant of new Charters a rare event, although new grants are occasionally made in respect of professional or charitable bodies, where that is thought to be in the public interest. There are presently about 400 active Chartered bodies.

Royal Proclamation

3.7.9 A Royal Proclamation is no longer a primary source of law. It appears that there was once power to legislate by proclamation but—

> "In 1610, however, a solemn opinion or protest of the judges established the modern doctrine that Royal Proclamations have in no sense the force of law; they serve to call the attention of the public to the law, but they cannot of themselves impose upon any man any legal obligation or duty not imposed by common law or by Act of Parliament."[53] [54]

Certain parliamentary business is transacted by Royal Proclamation. A proclamation in this context is essentially an exercise of primary prerogative power, particularly in the matter of the summoning of a Parliament, although it is now both referred to in statute and, to some extent at least, controlled by statutory authority.[55]

Letters Patent[56]

3.7.10 Again, there is no modern force of primary legislation in Letters Patent but they can be used as a mechanism for the delegation of power (although not normally legislative power). For example, section 6 of the Data Protection Act 1998[57] provides for the Information Commissioner to be appointed "by Her Majesty by Letters Patent".[58]

Royal Warrant

3.7.11 Warrants have also historically been used to have effects of various kinds. One of the most significant is the Royal Warrant of King Edward VII establishing the official roll of the baronetage. A Warrant could be used today to grant privileges of various kinds,[59] but none that amounted to or were to be enforced through legal rights or duties. So, again, it does not deserve to be classified as a primary legislative instrument.

---

[53] A.V. Dicey, *The Law of the Constitution*, 7th ed. 1908, p.51.
[54] See also "In Mr. Justice Blackstone's Commentaries, Book I., Ch.7, Of the King's Prerogative, Vol.i., p.270, it is stated that the King's Proclamations are binding upon the subjects where they do not either contradict the old laws or tend to establish new ones." *Attorney-General v Brown* [1920] 1 K.B. 773 *per* Sankey J.
[55] See Meeting of Parliament Act 1797 (c.127), s.1 and references in Sch.1 to the Representation of the People Act 1983 (c.2) (timetable for Parliamentary elections).
[56] Other than Charters.
[57] 1998 c.29.
[58] Subs.(2).
[59] Such as in relation to precedence or titles.

Resolution, &c. of Parliament

A resolution of either House of Parliament has by itself no legal effect.[60]   **3.7.12**

But in a small number of cases Parliament has delegated to the House of Commons or to both Houses the power to, in effect, make legislation by resolution.[61]

In relation to financial matters appertaining to either House of Parliament itself, such as the remuneration of Members, it is usual for the House to pass resolutions[62] which are primary in the sense that they are not exercising any delegated power: but they would not in themselves suffice to authorise the release of money from public funds without the confirmation of provision in an Appropriation Act.[63]

The most regular and significant example of legislative power delegated to be exercised by Parliamentary resolution is a fundamental part of the annual budget process, but although the public regularly feel its effects there are probably few who are aware that they derive from a resolution. The Budget Speech by the Chancellor of the Exchequer marks the introduction into the House of Commons of a Bill which will in the ordinary course of events take several weeks to pass.[64] The fear is, of course, that once the Bill is published people will take advantage of the period before Royal Assent to take full advantage of the old law, often in a way which will undermine the effectiveness of the new.

So the Provisional Collection of Taxes Act 1968[65] allows the Government to   **3.7.13**
obtain a resolution of the House of Commons at the end of the budget debate

---

[60] Even in relation to matters of the Houses' own procedures, while the Houses may regulate themselves by resolution or any other method that they choose, even the Houses accept that a resolution may be decisive for their own internal purposes but will have no effect in law. See, for example, the following statement from para.381 of the First Report of the Joint Committee on Parliamentary Privilege Session 1998–99 (March 30, 1999)—

"Ever since *Stockdale v Hansard* (1839), the courts have refused to accept that either House, by resolution, can determine the legal effect of its privileges. Never, since that case, has the House of Commons refused to admit the jurisdiction of the courts when matters of privilege arise in the course of court proceedings."

[61] And it is common for an Act to enable either House of Parliament—or in the case of certain financial instruments just the House of Commons—to annul a piece of secondary legislation by resolution. The effect of a resolution on a motion to annul a statutory instrument is set out in s.5(1) of the Statutory Instruments Act 1946 (c.36).

[62] See, for example, the original resolution for the payment of a salary to Members—Commons Journals (1911) 400, 406. Revising resolutions and resolutions for allowances are passed every few years. Ministerial salaries, and the salaries of certain non-Ministerial office-holders, are paid under the Ministerial and other Salaries Act 1975 (c.27).

[63] As to which see Chapter 1, Section 6.

[64] Like other Bills, however, in emergency it is possible to accelerate the process and have a Bill, in the most extreme case, introduced and passed through all stages in both Houses on a single day. When a Session of Parliament comes to an unexpectedly early close with the calling of a general election, it is sometimes necessary to pass a Finance Act with some degree of urgency to ensure that the necessary annual authority is given for income tax. See, for example, the Finance Act 1992 (c.20) which was introduced on March 12, 1992 and received Royal Assent on March 16 that year.

[65] 1968 c.2.

giving provisional effect to certain provisions of the Finance Bill[66]: provided that the Bill is proceeded with in accordance with conditions specified in the 1968 Act, the resolutions "have statutory effect as if contained in an Act of Parliament"[67] until replaced by the provisions of the Finance Act in due course. And for those provisions which are thought essential to have effect before the end of the (normally four-day) budget debate, s.5 of the Provisional Collection of Taxes Act 1968 allows the Commons to agree at the start of the budget debate a resolution giving immediate provisional effect to specified resolutions.[68]

Another important example of power delegated to Parliament to be exercised by instrument, while control is nominally vested in the Crown, is the dismissal of judges of the Supreme Court.[69] In this case the power is to be exercised by address to the Sovereign.

There are also a few other particular cases of provisions in relation to which it is thought appropriate to delegate power to be exercised by the House of Commons by resolution.[70]

Treasury Minute

3.7.14   Section 2 of the Government Resources and Accounts Act 2000[71] delegates power to the Treasury to direct by Treasury Minute that resources may be applied

---

[66] The relevant provisions are signified, in the ways and means resolutions on which the Finance Bill is founded, by the inclusion of the formula "And it is hereby declared that it is expedient in the public interest that this Resolution should have statutory effect under the provisions of the Provisional Collection of Taxes Act 1968".

[67] Section 1(2)—

"... where the House of Commons passes a resolution which—

(a) provides for the renewal for a further period of any tax in force or imposed during the previous financial year (whether at the same or a different rate, and whether with or without modifications) or for the variation or abolition of any existing tax, and

(b) contains a declaration that it is expedient in the public interest that the resolution should have statutory effect under the provisions of this Act,

the resolution shall, for the period specified in the next following subsection, have statutory effect as if contained in an Act of Parliament and, where the resolution provides for the renewal of a tax, all enactments which were in force with reference to that tax as last imposed by Act of Parliament shall during that period have full force and effect with respect to the tax as renewed by the resolution. ... "

[68] This is traditionally used for increases in duty on petrol and other hydrocarbon oils or on alcoholic drinks: the idea being to avoid a rush of stock-piling prior to the increase taking effect.

[69] Supreme Court Act 1981 (c.54), s.11—

"(1) This section applies to the office of any judge of the Supreme Court except the Lord Chancellor.

. . .

(3) A person appointed to an office to which this section applies shall hold that office during good behaviour, subject to a power of removal by Her Majesty on an address presented to Her by both Houses of Parliament."

Note that this provision antedates, and will be overtaken by, the establishment of a new Supreme Court proposed by the Government at the time when this work went to print.Note also that the Information Commissioner "may be removed from office by Her Majesty in pursuance of an Address from both Houses of Parliament"—Data Protection Act 1998 (c.29), Sch.5, para.2(3).

[70] For example, the salary of the Information Commissioner is specified by resolution of the House of Commons—Data Protection Act 1998 (c.29), Sch.5, para.3(1).

[71] 2000 c.20.

as an appropriation in aid of resources authorised by Parliament to be used for the service of a particular year.

Extra-statutory concession

An "extra-statutory concession" is not strictly speaking a form of legislation, **3.7.15** being by definition something that is outside statute. Since, however, it is of a certain amount of importance as, in effect, a relaxation of legislation, particularly in the fiscal field, it deserves some treatment in this work.

As a general rule, the executive is as much bound by the legislation of Parliament (or even of the executive under power delegated by Parliament) as anyone else. There is no power in the executive to excuse a citizen from compliance with the law.[72]

Having said that, however, the various branches of the executive charged with duties of enforcing the law are frequently given the discretion, whether expressly or implicitly, to fail to enforce in a particular case where it would be counter-productive or contrary to principle.[73]

The most common instance of the exercise of this kind of power is the extra-statutory concession in the fiscal field.

The Inland Revenue describes an extra-statutory concession in the following terms—

> "An extra-statutory concession is a relaxation which gives taxpayers a reduction in tax liability to which they would not be entitled under the strict letter of the law. Most concessions are made to deal with what are, on the whole, minor or transitory anomalies under the legislation and to meet cases of hardship at the margins of the code where a statutory remedy would be

---

[72] "Neither the police, nor customs, nor any other member of the executive have any power to alter the terms of the Ordinance forbidding the export of heroin, and the fact that they may turn a blind eye when the heroin is exported does not prevent it from being a criminal offence."—*Yip Chiu-Cheung* [1995] 1 A.C. 111, 118 HL *per* Lord Griffiths.

[73] The Crown Prosecution Service, for example, has a discretion whether or not to prosecute in any particular case—see the Code for Crown Prosecutors established under s.10 of the Prosecution of Offences Act 1985 (c.23). And this may sometimes be used to reflect not only efficiency and effectiveness but implicit obsolescence—"At any given moment you can find statutes which have become out of date and which should be repealed or amended but which linger on untouched since, in a crowded Parliamentary timetable, governments have had other priorities. Such statutes pose a familiar problem for those who have to decide whether to prosecute, especially when social circumstances have changed. Recent history provides examples. Should breaches of the Sunday trading laws be prosecuted when the shops appear to meet a public demand? Should corner shop owners be prosecuted if, to their customers' satisfaction, they stay open long after the statutory closing time, that was introduced to save fuel during the First World War? Should people be prosecuted for participating in consensual homosexual acts in private? When these and similar issues have arisen, prosecutors have done what they always do: they have had regard to the public interest in deciding whether to prosecute. See, for instance, paras 6.1–6.3 of the Code for Crown Prosecutors issued by the Crown Prosecution Service. If the prosecutors mistake the public interest, any resulting prosecution is liable to provoke public criticism or even ridicule, while placing a martyr's crown on the defendant's head."—*R. v Attorney General, ex parte Rusbridger* [2003] U.K.H.L. 38, para.52, HL *per* Lord Rodger of Earlsferry.

difficult to devise or would run to a length out of proportion to the intrinsic importance of the matter.

"The concessions [listed by the Revenue] are of general application, but it must be borne in mind that in a particular case there may be special circumstances which will need to be taken into account in considering the application of the concession. A concession will not be given in any case where an attempt is made to use it for tax avoidance."[74]

Although it is the fiscal field in which extra-statutory concessions are of principal importance, the general idea would remain the same in any other area of law involving enforcement by the government of rights vested in the Crown by legislation.

3.7.16   The extent to which the Inland Revenue may use extra-statutory concessions as ways of changing the substance of the law rather than as ways of enhancing the efficiency of the system of tax-collection as a whole came under particular scrutiny in the case of *R. (Wilkinson) v Inland Revenue Commissioners.*[75] The conclusion of the Court of Appeal is summarised by Lord Phillips of Worth Matravers M.R., after discussion of authorities, as follows[76]—

"[45] It seems to us that the effect of these authorities is plain. One of the primary tasks of the commissioners is to recover those taxes which Parliament has decreed shall be paid. Section 1 of the [Taxes Management Act 1970[77]] permits the commissioners to set about this task pragmatically and to have regard to principles of good management. Concessions can be made where those will facilitate the overall task of tax collection. We draw attention, however, to Lord Diplock's statement that the commissioners' managerial discretion is as to the best manner of obtaining for the national exchequer the highest net return that is practicable.

"[46] No doubt, when interpreting tax legislation, it is open to the commissioners to be as purposive as the most pro-active judge in attempting to ensure that effect is given to the intention of Parliament and that anomalies and injustices are avoided. But in the light of the authorities that we have cited above and of fundamental constitutional principle we do not see how s.1 of the 1970 Act can authorise the commissioners to announce that they will deliberately refrain from collecting taxes that Parliament has unequivocally decreed shall be paid, not because this will facilitate the overall task of collecting taxes, but because the commissioners take the view that it is objectionable that the taxpayer should have to pay the taxes in question."

---

[74] Inland Revenue Leaflet I.R.1 (Practitioners Series), *Extra-statutory Concessions.*
[75] [2003] 1 W.L.R. 2683, CA.
[76] At 731–732.
[77] 1970 c.9.

Even if the reason for the Commissioners' view is a matter of law arising since the enactment of the legislation imposing the tax in question (such as the Human Rights Act 1998[78]) it is for Parliament, and not the Commissioners, to effect any amendment of the law required. The Commissioners must enforce the law as it is.[79]

International treaties

An international treaty is not self-executing—that is to say that it is not competent on its own to confer rights or duties within the law of any part of the United Kingdom.[80] The mere fact that Her Majesty's Government are a party to an international agreement, be it Treaty or Convention, cannot in itself confer rights or duties as a matter of the law of the United Kingdom.

3.7.17

As Lord Oliver of Aylmerton said in *Maclaine Watson & Co. Ltd v Department of Trade and Industry, Maclaine Watson & Co. Ltd v International Tin Council*[81]—

" . . . as a matter of the constitutional law of the United Kingdom, the royal prerogative, whilst it embraces the making of treaties, does not extend to altering the law or conferring rights on individuals or depriving individuals of rights which they enjoy in domestic law without the intervention of Parliament. Treaties, as it is sometimes expressed, are not self-executing. Quite simply, a treaty is not part of English law unless and until it has been incorporated into the law by legislation. So far as individuals are concerned, it is *res inter alios acta* from which they cannot derive rights and by which they cannot be deprived or rights or subjected to obligations; and it is outside the purview of the court not only because it is made in the conduct of foreign relations, which are a prerogative of the Crown, but also because, as a source of rights and obligations, it is irrelevant."

In order to convert an international treaty into a form in which it confers rights and duties within the United Kingdom—which will generally be necessary in order to comply with the obligations imposed on Her Majesty's Government as a result of entering into the treaty—legislation will be required. There being no general power vested in the executive to legislate for this purpose, primary

---

[78] 1998 c.42.

[79] See also Chapter 1, Section 6, paras 1.6.6—1.6.8.

[80] Hence Lord Wilberforce in *Fothergill v Monarch Airlines* [1981] A.C. 251, 271, HL—"The Warsaw Convention of 1929, which contained an article 26 in similar form, was agreed to in a single French text, deposited with the Government of Poland. It was introduced into English law (not being, of course, self-executing) by the Carriage by Air Act 1932. This set out in Schedule 1 a translation of the Convention into English and provided (section 1) that the provisions of the Convention as so set out should have the force of law in the United Kingdom."

[81] [1990] 2 A.C. 418, 500, HL; see also *European Roma Rights Centre v Immigration Officer at Prague Airport (United Nations High Commissioner for Refugees intervening)* [2003] 4 All E.R. 247, CA.

legislation will be required, although it may itself confer power to make subordinate legislation.[82]

3.7.18   Where an international agreement concluded by Her Majesty's Government does not purport to confer or require the conferring of legal rights and duties, it may still be necessary to make legislative provision within the United Kingdom for the purpose of giving full effect to the intentions of the agreement.[83]

Legislation to give effect to an international treaty may either make free-standing provision—replicating provisions of the treaty or making such other provision as is necessary to give effect to it—or it may simply state as a legislative proposition that certain provisions of a specified treaty are to have force of law within the United Kingdom (in which case it is usual, where feasible, to append to the Act the English text of such parts of the treaty as confer rights and duties). The latter approach is common for obvious reasons, saving legislative words and avoiding unnecessary confusion as a result of possible failure to reproduce accurately the effect of the treaty's provisions. Its efficacy depends, to a large extent, on the form in which the treaty has been negotiated, whether it is a series of propositions ready to be given legal effect within the relevant jurisdictions, or whether it has more the character of an underlying policy or framework document. The effectiveness of the approach where it is adopted is well established.[84]

---

[82] The most significant example is s.2 of the European Communities Act 1972 (c.68), discussed in s.10 below. Other examples are frequent: for a recent and wide-ranging one, see section 103 of, and Sch.6 to, the Railways and Transport Safety Act 2003 (c.20), which in connection with the Convention concerning International Carriage by Rail signed at Berne on May 9, 1980 both confers free-standing powers and provides certain extensions of the powers under s.2 of the European Communities Act 1972.

[83] See, for example, s.7 of the Northern Ireland Arms Decommissioning Act 1997 (1997 c.7) which merely refers to a Commission as "an independent organisation established by an agreement, made in connection with the affairs of Northern Ireland between Her Majesty's Government in the United Kingdom and the Government of the Republic of Ireland, to facilitate the decommissioning of firearms, ammunition and explosives". The section does not purport to establish the Commission, that having been effected by the agreement itself, but it does go on to permit the making of an order conferring legal capacity on the Commission and granting immunities in relation to it, so as to facilitate its effective operation in accordance with the underlying intention of the international agreement.

[84] Lord Denning M.R. in *The Hollandia* [1982] Q.B. 872, CA—"Section 1(2) said that: 'The provisions of the Rules, as set out in the Schedule to this Act, shall have the force of law.' What does this mean? In my opinion it means that, in all courts of the United Kingdom, the provisions of the Rules are to be given the coercive force of law. So much so that, in every case properly brought before the courts of the United Kingdom, the Rules are to be given supremacy over every other provision of the bill of lading. If there is anything elsewhere in the bill of lading which is inconsistent with the Rules or which derogates from the effect of them, it is to be rejected."; and Sir Sebag Shaw in the same case—"For myself, I find it difficult to see how these two subsections can be read otherwise than as adopting the Rules as part of the Act itself so as to imbue them with the character of a statutory enactment."; and Lord Diplock in the same case in the House of Lords ([1983] 1 A.C. 565, 571)—"My Lords, the provisions in section 1 of the Act that I have quoted appear to me to be free from any ambiguity perceptible to even the most ingenious of legal minds. The Hague-Visby Rules, or rather all those of them that are included in the Schedule, are to have the force of law in the United Kingdom: they are to be treated as if they were part of directly enacted statute law."

Foreign legislation

For the purposes of this work it is worthy of note that foreign legislation, while **3.7.19** it can never confer or impose rights or duties within the law of a part of the United Kingdom, may be of persuasive value in relation to the interpretation of our own legislation in some way. This is particularly likely in two cases—

Where the foreign legislation emanates from and is designed to give effect to an international obligation by which the United Kingdom has become bound.

Where the legislature has a close connection with the United Kingdom, for example an Overseas Territory or a Commonwealth country, whose legal and legislative practice is similar to ours for good historical reasons.[85]

Judicial notice will not be taken of foreign legislation, which will therefore require to be proved. Generally, some kind of ad hoc expert evidence will be sufficient.

Where legislation contemplates that an issue relating to foreign legislation is likely to arise in the application of our legislation it may make special provision for the proof of the relevant foreign legislation.[86]

Legislation of certain Overseas Territories is treated as foreign legislation but benefits from special provision as to proof under s.6 of the Colonial Laws Validity Act 1865.[87]

SECTION 8

CONSTRUCTION OF WORKS, &c.

Introduction

Before 1992 a private Bill was an indispensable part of any large-scale industrial **3.8.1** development that needed to acquire rights over or in relation to too large or too fragmented an area of land to make it practical to proceed entirely by a series of private agreements. But the process of promoting a private Bill was (and

---

[85] As to the doctrine of comity as applied by the Judicial Committee of the Privy Council in construing legislation in the exercise of its ultimate appellate role from foreign courts and tribunals, see Chapter 20, paras 20.1.41 and 20.1.42.

[86] So, for example, s.25 of the Immigration Act 1971 (c.77) (assisting illegal entry), as substituted by s.143 of the Nationality, Immigration and Asylum Act 2002 (c.41) makes provision by reference in part to "a law which has effect in a member State and which controls, in respect of some or all persons who are not nationals of the State, entitlement to—(a) enter the State, (b) transit across the State, or (c) be in the State." Section 25(3) therefore provides that "A document issued by the government of a member State certifying a matter of law in that State—(a) shall be admissible in proceedings for an offence under this section, and (b) shall be conclusive as to the matter certified."

[87] 1865 c.63.

145

remains) expensive and slow, and not all aspects of the procedure for the passage of the Bill were thought satisfactory.

In 1992 the Transport and Works Act[88] introduced a new procedure designed to allow certain construction projects that would previously have required a private Bill to proceed without one. The result has been some diminution in the number of private Bills being promoted: there were 23 local Acts in 1991, 11 in 1995, eight in 2000 and five in 2003.

It should be noted at the outset that the 1992 Act applies only to England and Wales. Scotland has had for some years a similar system.[89]

It should also be noted that the 1992 Act system is capable of application in relation to Crown land.[90]

Scope of transport and works orders

3.8.2 Section 1 of the 1992 Act enables the Secretary of State[91] to make by statutory instrument an order relating to, or to matters ancillary to, the construction or operation of a railway or similar transport system in England and Wales.

Section 3 of the 1992 Act enables the Secretary of State to make by statutory instrument an order relating to, or to matters ancillary to—

(1) the construction or operation of an inland waterway in England and Wales, or

(2) the carrying out of certain works which interfere with rights of navigation in waters within or adjacent to England and Wales.[92]

3.8.3 Orders under s.1 or 3 of the 1992 Act can interfere with the application of legislation, particularly legislation of local effect and can, broadly speaking, do anything that the Secretary of State considers necessary to achieve their primary objectives.[93] In particular, an order may make provision about any of the following matters[94]—

(1) The construction, alteration, repair, maintenance, demolition and removal of railways and certain other transport systems, waterways, roads, watercourses, buildings and other structures.

(2) The carrying out of any other civil engineering or other works.

---

[88] 1992 c.42.

[89] See Chapter 5, Section 3.

[90] s.25.

[91] It should be noted that the National Assembly for Wales now exercises these powers, and most but not all powers under the 1992 Act, in relation to Wales—see the National Assembly for Wales (Transfer of Functions) Order 1999 (SI 1999/672), art.2 and Sch.1.

[92] The Secretary of State may not make an order under s.3 if in his opinion the primary object of the order could be achieved by means of an order under the Harbours Act 1964 (c.40)—s.3(2).

[93] s.5.

[94] Sch.1.

(3) The acquisition of land, whether compulsorily or by agreement.

(4) The creation and extinguishment of rights over land (including rights of navigation over water), whether compulsorily or by agreement.

(5) The abrogation and modification of agreements relating to land.

(6) The conferring on persons providing transport services of rights to use systems belonging to others.

(7) The protection of the property or interests of any person.

(8) The imposition and exclusion of obligations or of liability in respect of any acts or omissions.

(9) The making of agreements to secure the provision of police services.

(10) The carrying out of surveys and the taking of soil samples.

(11) The payment of compensation.

(12) The charging of tolls, fares (including penalty fares) and other charges, and the creation of summary offences in connection with non-payment (or in connection with a person's failure to give his name or address in accordance with provisions relating to penalty fares).

(13) The making of byelaws by any person and their enforcement, including the creation of summary offences.

(14) The payment of rates.

(15) The transfer, leasing, discontinuance and revival of undertakings.

(16) The submission of disputes to arbitration.

(17) The imposition of requirements to obtain the consent of the Secretary of State.

An order under s.1 or 3 may not, however, extinguish a public right of way over land unless the Secretary of State is satisfied that an alternative right of way has been or will be provided, or is not required.[95]

Procedure

The process of obtaining an order under the 1992 Act begins with the making of an application to the Secretary of State.[96] In addition to prescribing what information is to be included in applications for orders under the 1992 Act, rules **3.8.4**

---

[95] s.5(6).
[96] s.6(1).

under the Act can require steps, such as publication of notice and consultation, to be taken before an application is made.[97]

The present rules under the Act[98] prescribe a considerable procedure to be complied with before an application may be made. These include the publication of notices, the provision of environmental information, environmental statements, environmental impact assessments and plans. Not all requirements are applicable to every application. The rules can also require the provision of a draft order with an application, and the Secretary of State is empowered to prescribe model clauses that are to be included in draft orders submitted for this purpose.[99]

Once an application has been made the rules prescribe additional requirements for the giving of notices and the publication of information.

Additional requirements are prescribed by the 1992 Act itself[1] in cases with a European aspect, in the sense that another Member State[2] would be affected by the project in question. This might be because the project would be likely to have significant effects on the environment in another Member State, or because the authorities of the other Member State consider that their State is likely to be significantly affected by the project and request information relating to the application. In these cases the Act provides for the provision by the Secretary of State to the Member State of documents and information relating to the application, consultation by the Secretary of State with the Member State in connection with the application, and notification by the Secretary of State to the Member State of the decision, or of matters relating to the decision, on the application.

The 1992 Act makes provision for an order to be made under s.1 or 3 in a case without an application being made to the Secretary of State for certain military and defence purposes, and also where the Secretary of State considers it necessary for certain reasons in the interests of safety.[3]

Objections

3.8.5 The most important feature of the private Bill procedure is the provision of opportunity for persons adversely affected by the proposed legislation to petition against it and to explain to a Parliamentary committee why it ought not to be enacted. The 1992 Act preserves the essence of this facility by creating a

---

[97] s.6(2)(c) and (d).
[98] The Transport and Works (Applications and Objections Procedure) (England and Wales) Rules 2000 (SI 2000/2190); amended by the Transport and Works (Applications and Objections Procedure) (England and Wales) (Amendment) Rules 2002 (SI 2002/1965).
[99] s.8.
[1] s.6A, inserted by the Transport and Works (Assessment of Environmental Effects) Regulations 1998 (SI 1998/2226).
[2] For this purpose a reference to a Member State includes not only states that are members of the European Union but also states that are contracting parties to the Agreement on the European Economic Area.
[3] s.7.

procedure for the making of objections. The details of the procedure for the making of objections are prescribed by the rules.

Provided the prescribed procedure is correctly complied with in making an objection, the Secretary of State may not make a decision on the application for a s.1 or 3 order without first taking the objection into consideration.[4] The effect of that obligation is that if an objector felt able to show that a decision to make an order was clearly unreasonable given the strength of his interest and the likely harm that the order would do to it, he would be able to apply to the High Court for a judicial review of the Secretary of State's decision in accordance with the normal procedures of administrative law. The Secretary of State is not, however, obliged to consider an objection which he thinks raises only issues that can properly be addressed at the stage of determining proper compensation.[5]

If the Secretary of State feels that an issue raised by an application for an order under s.1 or 3 of the 1992 Act (or by a proposal of his own to make an order in reliance on s.7) requires consideration in the form of a local inquiry he can cause one to be established.[6]

The Secretary of State may also give a person who makes an objection to an application an opportunity of appearing before and being heard by a person appointed by the Secretary of State for the purpose.[7]

Certain classes of objector receive a preferential treatment under the Act to the extent that if they make an objection they can also insist on its either being referred to a local inquiry or being heard by an appointed person. This special class of objectors consists of local authorities affected by the proposal and certain people whose property would in effect be the subject of a compulsory purchase if the order under s.1 or 3 were made.

Determination of an application

Where an application has been made to the Secretary of State for an order under s.1 or 3 of the 1992 Act (or he proposes to make one on his own initiative in reliance on s.7) he has three options: he can make the order as requested in the application; he can make an order giving effect to those proposals with modifications; or he can simply reject the application.[8]   **3.8.6**

A particular ground expressed by the Act for rejecting an application is that the Secretary of State believes that the proposals can be achieved by other means.[9] The Secretary of State can also grant part only of an application.[10]

---

[4] s.10(2).
[5] s.10(3)(b).
[6] s.11(1).
[7] s.11(2).
[8] s.13.
[9] s.13(2): it is, however, presumably unlikely that an application would be allowed to proceed through all its stages (including the preliminary procedures) without the question of alternative powers having been raised and determined at an early stage.
[10] s.13(3).

If the Secretary of State proposes to make an order which gives effect to proposals with substantial modifications which will make a substantial change in the proposals, he has to notify persons likely to be affected by the modifications and give them an opportunity to make representations.[11]

Special procedure orders

3.8.7 The Statutory Orders (Special Procedure) Act 1945[12] establishes a procedure, devised as a variation on the provisional order Bill,[13] the aim of which is to accentuate the local consultation and other procedures and to limit the Parliamentary proceedings.

The scope of the procedure is established by s.1(1) of the Act as follows—

> "(1) Where, by any Act passed after the passing of this Act, power to make or confirm orders is conferred on any authority, and provision is made requiring that any such order shall be subject to special parliamentary procedure, the provisions of this Act shall apply in relation to any order so made or confirmed."

The procedure is invoked relatively infrequently.[14] Orders subject to the special Parliamentary procedure are therefore correspondingly rare, but they are made from time to time.[15]

3.8.8 The essence of the special procedure provided for by the 1945 Act is as follows—

An order is made and laid before Parliament.[16]

But "No order . . . shall be laid before Parliament until the requirements of the empowering enactment with respect to the publication or service of notices, the consideration of objections, and the holding of inquiries or other proceedings preliminary to the making or confirmation of the order have been complied with, or, where no such requirements are imposed by that enactment, until the requirements of [Schedule 1 to the 1945 Act—default procedures] have been

---

[11] s.13(4).

[12] 1945 c.18.

[13] As to which see Chapter 5, Section 4.

[14] For recent examples see ss.17 to 21 of the Acquisition of Land Act 1981 (c.67), s.44 of the Civil Aviation Act 1982 (c.16) or s.38 of the Channel Tunnel Act 1987 (c.53).

[15] See, for example, the South West Water Limited Ilsham Pumping Station Compulsory Purchase Order 2000.

[16] s.1(2).

complied with; and after any such requirements . . . have been complied with, notice of the Minister's intention to lay the order before Parliament shall be published in the London Gazette not less than three days before the order is so laid."[17]

Once the order is laid before Parliament, there is an opportunity for petitions to be brought against it (whether opposing it generally or seeking specific amendment).[18]

After the end of the period during which petitions may be brought, either House may cause the order to lapse by resolving for its annulment.[19]

If no annulment order is passed, any petitions outstanding are referred to a Joint Committee (unless the House has ordered otherwise).[20]

If the order is neither annulled nor petitioned against, it comes into force.[21]

The Joint Committee considers a petition against the order and reports the order with or without specified amendments.[22]

If reported unamended, the order comes into force. If reported with amendments, the order comes into force with those amendments, unless the relevant Minister prefers to withdraw the order altogether or to bring before Parliament a Bill confirming the order without the amendments.[23]

Although a relatively rare occurrence, the use of the 1945 Act can still be of considerable commercial and local significance and can cause controversy.[24]

In certain circumstances an order under the Transport and Works Act 1992[25] can be subject to special Parliamentary procedure under the 1945 Act.[26]

---

[17] s.2(1).
[18] s.3.
[19] s.4(1).
[20] s.4(2).
[21] s.4(3).
[22] s.5.
[23] s.6; the only confirming Bills ever to have been brought were the Mid-Northamptonshire Water Order Confirmation (Special Procedure) Bill 1948–49 and the Okehampton By-pass (Confirmation of Orders) Bill 1985–86.
[24] See, for example, the Lords Written Question *Special Procedure Orders: Identity of Petitioners* HL Deb. March 11, 1997 W.A. 22.
[25] 1992 c.42—see above.
[26] s.12(1) (special parliamentary procedure)—"An order under section 1 or 3 above authorising a compulsory purchase shall be subject to special parliamentary procedure to the same extent as it would be, by virtue of section 18 or 19 of the Acquisition of Land Act 1981 (or by virtue of paragraph 5 or 6 of Schedule 3 to that Act) (National Trust land, commons etc), if the purchase were authorised by an order under section 2(1) of that Act."

SECTION 9

REGULATORY REFORM

Introduction

3.9.1   The Regulatory Reform Act 2001[27] enables two kinds of thing to be done.

(1) It enables provision to be made "for the purpose of reforming legislation which has the effect of imposing burdens affecting persons in the carrying on of any activity".[28]

(2) It enables "codes of practice to be made with respect to the enforcement of restrictions, requirements or conditions".[29]

In introducing the Second Reading of the Bill which became the 2001 Act the Minister of State for the Cabinet Office,[30] speaking in the House of Lords, explained the underlying policy of the Bill. An extract of his speech is appended to this work.[31]

This Section focuses on the first of the two activities made possible by the Act, regulatory reform orders, and explains the scope and nature of the orders and something of the process by which they are made.[32]

Scope

3.9.2   The fundamental power under the 2001 Act is to make regulatory reform orders "for the purpose of reforming legislation which has the effect of imposing burdens affecting persons in the carrying on of any activity".[33] The legislation sets out a number of things which the reform can be designed to achieve—

(1) removing or reducing a burden,

(2) re-enacting a burden that is "proportionate to the benefit which is expected to result from the re-enactment",[34]

(3) imposing a new burden which is "proportionate to the benefit which is expected to result from its creation",[35] and

(4) removing inconsistencies and anomalies.

---

[27] 2001 c.6.
[28] The phrase used in the Long Title of the Act.
[29] Same.
[30] Lord Falconer of Thoroton.
[31] Appendix, Extract 9.
[32] For examples of use made of the regulatory reform procedure see below.
[33] s.1(1).
[34] s.1(1)(b).
[35] s.1(1)(c)(ii).

Subject to the constraints mentioned below, the potential power of a regulatory reform order is very wide. It can, in particular, amend or repeal enactments and impose burdens on the executive.[36]

The scope of the power turns on the notion of a burden, which the Act defines[37] so as to include, broadly speaking—

(1) any kind of restriction, requirement or condition (or the consequences of failing to observe a restriction, requirement or condition), and

(2) any limit on a person's statutory powers.

Constraints on the use of the power

Since s.1 of the Act is cast in terms of such potential width, giving the executive **3.9.3** very considerable powers in matters first thought suitable for primary legislation by Parliament, the Act also imposes a number of constraints on the exercise of the power designed to ensure that it is not abused, or used to do things that should be done by Parliament itself.

The regulatory reform order procedure may be used only in relation to an Act that was passed at least two years before the date of the order.[38] This is because the procedure is not designed to give the executive a veto over provisions recently enacted by Parliament. Rather it is intended to provide a mechanism by which the executive can carry out a continual programme of repairing and renewing legislation minor aspects of which have become outdated as a result of changes in the surrounding legal, social or political environment. If Parliament wishes to rethink a provision that it has enacted within the last two years, it must do so itself.[39]

The Act also requires[40] that a Minister proposing to make a regulatory reform order should satisfy himself that the order will not—

(1) remove any necessary protection, or

(2) prevent a person from continuing to exercise any right or freedom which he might reasonably expect to continue to exercise.

In the case of a regulatory reform order that would itself impose a burden on the performance of a particular activity by a person the Act requires[41] that the Minister proposing to make the order be satisfied—

---

[36] s.1(6).

[37] s.2.

[38] s.1(2)(a).

[39] This prohibition extends to the reform of a provision which although passed more than two years previously has been substantively amended within the last two years (s.1(4)). Again, the thought is that had Parliament felt the provision to be in need of modernisation it would have done what was necessary as part of the substantive change.

[40] s.3(1).

[41] s.3(2).

(1) "that the provisions of the order, taken as a whole, strike a fair balance between the public interest and the interests of the persons affected by the burden being created", and

(2) that the extent to which the order removes or reduces a burden, or has other beneficial effects for persons affected by existing legislative burdens, makes it desirable for the order to be made.

There are also specific limitations, by way of maximum punishments, on the power of a regulatory reform order to create a criminal offence.[42] And a regulatory reform order may not generally provide for forcible entry, search or seizure, or compel the giving of evidence.[43]

Procedure

3.9.4   Regulatory reform orders are statutory instruments and they are subject to the affirmative resolution procedure.[44] For procedural purposes a distinction is drawn between regulatory reform orders which make substantial provision and those which only modify "subordinate provisions"[45] of an earlier order: the latter are subject to a less strict procedure.

The first procedural requirement is for consultation. Before making a regulatory reform order a Minister is obliged to consult, in particular, appropriate representative organisations and any statutory body directly affected.[46] The Law Commissions are also to be consulted in appropriate cases.[47] If the result of consultation is to inspire modification of the original proposals, the modified proposals have to be made the subject of renewed consultation.[48]

Following the preliminary consultation, if the Minister determines to proceed with his proposals he must lay before Parliament a draft of the proposals and a statement showing—

---

[42] s.3(4).
[43] s.3(5).
[44] As to which see Chapter 6, Section 2.
[45] A regulatory reform order may designate certain of its provisions as subordinate provisions: s.4(3).
[46] s.5.
[47] s.5(1)(c).
[48] s.5(3): although it is common to find a legislative requirement to consult on proposals that may be modified as a result of the responses to consultation, it is unusual to find an express requirement to renew the consultative process on modification. Although such a requirement would be implied by the courts where necessary to give full effect to the requirement to consult, its express statement in relation to regulatory reform orders is a reflection of Parliament's desire to establish effective and apparent safeguards on what is perceived both as a generally significant delegation of power to the executive and, in particular, as one which is particularly likely to impinge both upon specific interests—making it particularly necessary to ensure that those specially affected are involved throughout the process—and upon matters of general legal significance, as to which the Law Commissions are well placed to play a safe-guarding advisory role.

a. the burdens which the existing law affected by the proposals has the effect of imposing,

b. how the Minister's proposals remove or reduce those burdens,

c. what else the proposals achieve,

d. whether the existing law affected by the proposals affords any necessary protection and, if so, how that protection is to be continued,

e. whether any of the proposals could prevent a person from continuing to exercise a right or freedom which he might reasonably expect to continue to exercise and, if so, how he is to be enabled to continue to exercise that right or freedom,

f. whether the proposals would have the effect of creating a burden affecting the carrying on of an activity and, if so—

   i. that the burden is proportionate to the benefit which is expected to result from its creation,

   ii. that the proposals strike a fair balance between the public interest and the interests of the persons affected by the burden being created, and

   iii. that the extent to which the order removes or reduces one or more burdens, or has other beneficial effects for persons affected by the burdens imposed by the existing law, justifies the proposals,

g. whether any provisions of the proposed order are being designated as subordinate provisions, and if so why,

h. whether any savings or increases in cost are expected to result from the proposals and, if so, why and how much,

i. any other benefits which are expected to flow from the implementation of the proposals,

j. consultation undertaken,

k. representations received as a result of that consultation, and

l. the changes (if any) which the Minister has made to his original proposals in the light of those representations.[49]

3.9.5 Provision is made for protecting the confidentiality, as between the Minister and his consultees, of representations made in commercial confidence.[50]

The Act makes special provision for the Parliamentary scrutiny of the draft proposals and statement proposals laid under s.6.[51] This is an ad hoc procedure

---

[49] s.6.
[50] s.7.
[51] s.8.

invented for the purpose of these orders[52] designed to permit a very thorough scrutiny where appropriate, but without taking up time as a routine measure for provisions not thought to need it.

The essence of the procedure is that the Minister is not permitted to give effect to proposals laid under s.6 until the expiry of a two month period.[53] During this period it is open to anyone to make representations to the Minister about the proposals and he has a statutory duty to have regard to representations made[54]: he is particularly and expressly required to have regard to any resolution or report of, or of any committee of, either House of Parliament.[55]

The House of Commons has a perpetual Select Committee for the purpose of examining proposals and making reports.[56]

3.9.6 The House of Lords has a Select Committee on Delegated Powers and Regulatory Reform[57] one of the functions of which is to examine proposals for regulatory reform orders.

If the Minister does determine to proceed with proposals after the end of the two month period for Parliamentary consideration, he is required to lay a draft instrument for affirmative resolution.[58] Together with the draft order he is required to lay before Parliament a statement giving details of—

---

[52] Although based on practice for the earlier deregulation orders.

[53] Strictly speaking, a period of 60 days, ignoring periods of more than four days during which either House of Parliament does not meet, whether through dissolution, prorogation or adjournment—s.8(2) and (3).

[54] s.8(4).

[55] This is not, of course, a legal duty to abide by any recommendation of Parliament or to give effect to any resolution of Parliament. Indeed, as a matter of law it adds nothing to the general requirement to have regard to representations, and it is open to the Minister concerned to say that having had regard to representations he has concluded to ignore them. It would, however, be open to anyone aggrieved by this decision to seek a judicial review of the Minister's decision to proceed with his proposals. The Minister would, in accordance with the normal principles of judicial review, have to show that he had given careful consideration to the matters raised by Parliament—or indeed by any other objector—and that it was not wholly unreasonable in the circumstances to proceed despite the objections made. While the courts would, of course, be reluctant to substitute their judgment for the Minister's in a matter of this kind, equally it might in certain circumstances be hard to show that a reasonable Minister could properly fail to abide by a resolution of either House or of a Joint or Select Committee.

[56] Standing Order No.141—the Regulatory Reform Committee. The terms of reference are to consider and report to the House of Commons on proposals for regulatory reform orders under the Regulatory Reform Act 2001 and, subsequently, any ensuing draft regulatory reform order. The Committee also considers subordinate provisions orders made under the 2001 Act.

[57] The Committee is established by Sessional Order of the House of Lords. The present terms of reference are "to report whether the provisions of any bill inappropriately delegate legislative power, or whether they subject the exercise of legislative power to an inappropriate level of parliamentary scrutiny; to report on documents and draft orders laid before Parliament under the Regulatory Reform Act 2001; and to perform, in respect of such documents and orders and subordinate provisions orders laid under that Act, the functions performed in respect of other instruments by the Joint Committee on Statutory Instruments".

See House of Lords Standing Order 65 for the authority for the continuation of this Select Committee.

[58] s.4: except in the case of the minor exceptions already alluded to.

1. any representations, resolution or report made during the two month period, and

2. any changes made to the original proposals in the light of any such representations, resolution or report.[59]

The ability to have amendments suggested and made during the consultation and scrutiny process is considered to be one of the principal strengths of the regulatory reform process.[60]

Use of power to make regulatory reform orders

A considerable number of orders have been made under the powers in s.1 of the Regulatory Reform Act 2001. Seven were made in 2002 and eight in 2003. They cover a very broad range of subjects.[61]   **3.9.7**

---

[59] s.8(5).

[60] So, for example, the following passage of the House of Commons Select Committee on Regulatory Reform's First Special Report for Session 2002–03 (October 28, 2003)—

"7 . . . The ability to provide for amendments to be made to draft orders between stages is one of the strengths of the 'super-affirmative' procedure, which makes provision for a form of pre-legislative scrutiny of regulatory reform orders. As the Minister states, it would be odd if a Department identified a defect in an order after the first stage of scrutiny, but was not able to make a change to improve the working of the order or to close a loophole because representations had not been made to that effect.

"8. We are nevertheless concerned that departments should not be able to make changes to draft orders between first and second stage which alter the nature or scope of the order. The Minister has stated that if a suggested change is likely to affect the persons consulted on the proposal for the order so that they might have expressed a different view in response to the consultation, then the department concerned would be expected to undertake further consultation on the issue. He has indicated that if departments are unclear as to the substantive effect of the proposed changes, they should seek without prejudice advice from the Parliamentary committees on the specific amendments proposed, the reason for making the changes and their potential effect. . . .

"9. We strongly agree with the Minister's view that Departments should be expected to get their orders right first time. We nevertheless consider that it may be sensible to allow for minor changes to be made to draft orders between first and second-stage scrutiny on the Department's own initiative, if it is clear that those changes would improve the working of the order and would not involve changes of principle on which consultees would be expected to have a view. We consider that all such changes should be identified as such, and explained in full, in the explanatory statement laid before Parliament alongside the draft order. If, in our view, the amendments are of sufficient substance that the department concerned should have consulted upon their likely effect, we will decline to recommend approval of the draft order until such consultation has taken place."

[61] See the Regulatory Reform (Sunday Trading) Order 2004 (SI 2004/470), the Regulatory Reform (Gaming Machines) Order 2003 (SI 2003/3275), the Regulatory Reform (Business Tenancies) (England and Wales) Order 2003 (SI 2003/3096), the Regulatory Reform (British Waterways Board) Order 2003 (SI 2003/1545), the Regulatory Reform (Sugar Beet Research and Education) Order 2003 (SI 2003/1281), the Regulatory Reform (Schemes under s.129 of the Housing Act 1988) (England) Order 2003 (SI 2003/986), the Regulatory Reform (Housing Management Agreements) Order 2003 (SI 2003/940), the Regulatory Reform (Assured Periodic Tenancies) (Rent Increases) Order 2003 (SI 2003/259), the Regulatory Reform (Credit Unions) Order 2003 (SI 2003/256), the Regulatory Reform (Special Occasions Licensing) Order 2002 (SI 2002/3205), the Regulatory Reform (Removal of 20 Member Limit in Partnerships etc) Order 2002 (SI 2002/3203), the Regulatory Reform (Housing Assistance) (England and Wales) Order 2002 (SI 2002/1860), the Regulatory Reform (Vaccine Damage Payments Act 1979) Order 2002 (SI 2002/1592), the

The House of Commons Select Committee on Regulatory Reform published a First Special Report for Session 2002–03[62] considering various matters of a general nature concerning the use of the 2001 Act. Amongst the Committee's conclusions were the following, relating to the use of the new procedure—

"Identifying appropriate reforms in proposed Bills and Acts of Parliament

"38. The [Regulatory Impact Unit[63]] currently assesses departmental bids for proposed Bills in order to identify any proposed reforms that could instead be achieved by way of a regulatory reform order. The [Government's] memorandum indicates that, in general, if a reform can be achieved by way of either primary legislation or the regulatory reform procedure, the Government's position is that the latter method is to be preferred. The RIU also has a commitment to reviewing major items of legislation after they are enacted, in order to identify proposals for reducing regulatory burdens, including by way of regulatory reform order.

3.9.8

"39. We commend the RIU for taking the initiative in assessing both Bill bids and enacted legislation. We consider that this work should not prevent the RIU from continuing to focus its energies on raising awareness of the regulatory reform procedure across Government. Clearly, it is preferable that measures suitable for enactment by way of the regulatory reform procedure should be identified early in the policy-making process, rather than at the stage where they have already progressed to inclusion in Bill bids.

"Seeking proposals for regulatory reform orders from Members of Parliament

"40. In our October 2002 report,[64] we urged other Members of Parliament to come forward with suggestions for potential regulatory reform orders:

'We would strongly encourage any of our colleagues who thinks that he or she has identified a reform which might be suitable for implementation by means of a regulatory reform order to act as the Government has suggested [in its May 2002 memorandum], in gathering the initial evidence and lobbying the responsible Minister for action. As the regulatory reform procedure becomes established, we look forward to seeing many more proposals generated, not only by the Government and

---

Regulatory Reform (Carer's Allowance) Order 2002 (SI 2002/1457), the Regulatory Reform (Golden Jubilee Licensing) Order 2002 (SI 2002/1062), the Regulatory Reform (Voluntary Aided Schools Liabilities and Funding) (England) Order 2002 (SI 2002/906) and the Regulatory Reform (Special Occasions Licensing) Order 2001 (SI 2001/3937).

[62] October 28, 2003.
[63] A group of officials within the Cabinet Office.
[64] HC (2001–02) 1272, para.41.

Members of Parliament (including select committees) but also by those outside interest groups who so often criticise the effect of overly burdensome legislation.'

"At the same time, we emphasised our belief that the primary responsibility for identifying potential regulatory reform orders must remain with the Government.

3.9.9

"41. The Government told us that no such proposals have been forthcoming from Members. The Minister stated that the Government has 'a number of different forums in which we ask not just individual MPs but actually a wide range of interest groups to participate in the [better regulation] agenda. I have been somewhat disappointed to discover the level of uptake.' The memorandum notes that the Government initially anticipated Members coming forward with proposals for how the law might be reformed. The Government now considers that it is better to expect Members to identify areas where Government intervention is creating unnecessary burdens, and for the Government to decide on the most appropriate means to remove the burdens.

"42. From our own knowledge and experience as Members, we conclude that many of our colleagues remain unaware of the purpose of the regulatory reform procedure. . . .

"43. Despite the fact that work remains to be done in raising awareness amongst Members, we are disappointed that our colleagues appear not to have informed themselves of the opportunities offered by the regulatory reform procedure. The procedure gives Members the opportunity to put to the Government a proposal to reform a particular regulatory burden in primary legislation, where that reform would probably not otherwise merit a place in the Government's legislative programme. At present, Members have a range of methods at their disposal for raising awareness of a regulatory burden in legislation and pressing for action to remove it: presentation bills, Ten Minute Rule bills, early day motions and oral and written questions. If Members are serious in their wish to remove a regulatory burden, they ought to be aware that the regulatory reform procedure exists and press for the relevant Minister to use it. We urge Members to consider making greater use of the potentially powerful tool for legislative reform created by the Regulatory Reform Act.

3.9.10

"44. We also draw to Members' attention the possibility that the Government could be asked to consider taking forward an unsuccessful proposal for a Private Member's Bill in the form of a regulatory reform order, where appropriate. The Cabinet Office has stated that it also examines bids for 'hand-out' bills[65] in order to identify clauses which might be delivered by

---

[65] See para.5.2.2, footnote 86.

regulatory reform order, and will then discuss with Departments whether the provisions might be delivered by regulatory reform order. We are pleased to note that systematic scrutiny of 'hand-out' bills for clauses which might be delivered by Regulatory Reform Order is taking place. We nevertheless consider that Departments should be further encouraged to develop bids to reform regulation in legislation as RROs in the first instance.

3.9.11   **"Including draft regulatory reform orders in Law Commission proposals**

"45. The Minister drew to our attention the work of the Law Commission, the statutory body charged with keeping the law under review and making recommendations for law reform, in promoting regulatory reform orders. Where appropriate, the Commission is increasingly opting to include draft regulatory reform orders in its proposals for law reform, rather than draft Bills. According to the latest bulletin from the Commission, 29 Commission reports await implementation by the Government. At least four of these are presently being taken forward, or are intended to be taken forward, by means of regulatory reform order.

"46. We are encouraged to hear of the Law Commission's work in promoting regulatory reform orders. . . . "

So there is some Parliamentary pressure for the continued and expanded use of the regulatory reform order, as a result of which it could become a very significant source of legislation.[66]

Deregulation and contracting out orders

3.9.12   As has already been mentioned[67] the procedure under the Deregulation and Contracting Out Act 1994[68] has to a considerable extent been overtaken by the procedures under the Regulatory Reform Act 2001.[69] But the 1994 Act retains some degree of importance, chiefly in relation to orders for contracting out under Part II.

Section 69(1) and (2) of the Deregulation and Contracting Out Act 1994, taken together, permit a Minister of the Crown to make an order providing that a function of a Minister or an office-holder "may be exercised by, or by employees of, such person (if any) as may be authorised in that behalf by the office-holder or Minister whose function it is".

---

[66] A Government review of progress was awaited when this work went to print.
[67] See above.
[68] 1994 c.40.
[69] 2001 c.6.

The power extends to "any function of a Minister or office-holder which is conferred by or under an enactment and which, by virtue of an enactment or rule of law, could be exercised by an officer of the Minister or office-holder.[70]

Section 70 of the Deregulation and Contracting Out Act 1994 permits a Minister of the Crown to provide that certain functions of a local authority "may be exercised by, or by employees of, such person (if any) as may be authorised in that behalf by the local authority whose function it is". **3.9.13**

There are some exceptions to both the power under s.69 and the power under s.70.[71] Put simply, they are that it is not permitted to make an order for contracting out of—

(1) the jurisdiction of a court or judicial tribunal,

(2) a function which affects the liberty of individuals,

(3) a power or right to enter property or to search or seize property, or

(4) a power or duty to make subordinate legislation.

As one would expect, the exceptions are themselves subject to a number of detailed qualifications.[72]

An authorisation to contract out under the 1994 Act can last for a period of up to ten years, subject to earlier revocation.[73] **3.9.14**

The use of the power to permit contracting out of a person's function does not prevent that person from continuing to exercise the power himself.[74]

The simple effect of contracting out in accordance with arrangements under the 1994 Act is that anything done by the contractor is treated (except in so far as the criminal law is concerned) as if done by the Minister, office-holder or local authority by whom the function is contracted out.[75]

A contracting out order is subject simply to the normal affirmative resolution procedure.[76] An order under s.70 requires prior consultation with local government organisations.[77]

A small but steady stream of orders under the contracting out provisions of the 1994 Act has been made since its enactment and continues to be made.[78]

---

[70] In other words, it does not apply in relation to a function which, in the circumstances, is clearly intended to be exercised personally by the person in whom it is vested.
[71] Set out in s.71.
[72] Set out in s.71.
[73] s.69(5)(a) and (b) (which are applied for the purposes of s.70 by s.70(4)).
[74] s.69(5)(c) (which is applied for the purposes of s.70 by s.70(4)).
[75] s.72(2).
[76] s.77(2)—as to affirmative resolution procedure, see Chapter 6, Section 2.
[77] s.70(3).
[78] See SI 1999/2106, 1999/2128, 2000/353, 2000/898, 2001/3539, 2001/4061, 2002/445, 2002/928, 2002/1888, 2002/3052, 2003/1668, 2003/1908 and 2003/2704.

INSTRUMENTS IMPLEMENTING COMMUNITY OBLIGATIONS

Introduction

3.10.1 When the European Communities Act 1972[79] was passed upon the United Kingdom becoming a member of the European Communities, it was clear both that there was more needed by way of adjustment of our primary and subordinate legislation than could conveniently be effected in a single Act, and also that membership of the Communities would continually give rise to obligations that would require implementation by adjustment of, and additions to, our primary and subordinate legislation.

For this reason, the 1972 Act conferred broad powers on the executive to give effect to initial and future obligations arising out of the United Kingdom's membership of the Communities.

There have been many hundred instruments under this power[80] passed since the power was conferred, and more are passed, in an increasingly wide range of areas of social importance, each year.[81] Their scope, nature and effect therefore deserve to be exposed in a little detail, which is the purpose of this Section.

Scope

3.10.2 Section 2(2) of the European Communities Act 1972 is an extremely broad power, permitting the making of provision—

"(a) for the purpose of implementing any Community obligation of the United Kingdom, or enabling any such obligation to be implemented, or of enabling any rights enjoyed or to be enjoyed by the United Kingdom under or by virtue of the Treaties to be exercised; or

(b) for the purpose of dealing with matters arising out of or related to any such obligation or rights or the coming into force, or the operation from time to time, of [section 2(1)][82]".

The extreme width of this formulation is confirmed by section 2(4) as including the power to make "any such provision (of any such extent) as might be made

---

[79] 1972 c.68.

[80] Some instruments are made partly in reliance on the 1972 Act and partly on other wholly domestic *vires*.

[81] Note, for example, the Employment Equality (Sexual Orientation) Regulations 2003 (SI 2003/1661) and the Employment Equality (Religion or Belief) Regulations 2003 (SI 2003/1660).

[82] s.2(1) provides—"(1) All such rights, powers, liabilities, obligations and restrictions from time to time created or arising by or under the Treaties, and all such remedies and procedures from time to time provided for by or under the Treaties, as in accordance with the Treaties are without further enactment to be given legal effect or used in the United Kingdom shall be recognised and available in law, and be enforced, allowed and followed accordingly; . . . ".

by Act of Parliament" subject to a few express exceptions. The exceptions are that an instrument under section 2(2) may not—

(1) impose or increase taxation,

(2) make provision having retrospective effect,

(3) confer "any power to legislate by means of orders, rules, regulations or other subordinate instrument, other than rules of procedure for any court or tribunal", or

(4) create a new criminal offence punishable with imprisonment for more than two years or punishable on summary conviction with imprisonment for more than three months or with a fine of more than level 5 on the standard scale (if not calculated on a daily basis) or of more than £100 a day.[83]

Of these exceptions, the third is itself subject to a significant qualification, that **3.10.3** it does not prevent "the modification of a power to legislate conferred otherwise than under section 2(2), or the extension of any such power to purposes of the like nature as those for which it was conferred; and a power to give directions as to matters of administration is not to be regarded as a power to legislate".[84]

The result of these provisions taken together is that the power to legislate under s.2(2) is of enormous breadth. In particular, the generality of the notion of what is a matter "arising out of or related to" the United Kingdom's obligations under the European Treaties should be noted.[85]

---

[83] European Communities Act 1972 (c.68), Sch.2, para.1(1)(a) to (d).

[84] Sch.2, para.1(2).

[85] For illustrations and discussions of the breadth of this power see: *Pickstone and other v Freemans* [1988] 2 All E.R. 803; *R v Secretary of State for Employment, ex parte Equal Opportunities Commission* [1992] 1 All E.R. 545; *Equal Opportunities Commission and another v Secretary of State for Employment* [1994] 1 All E.R. 910; *Betts and others v Brintel Helicopters Ltd (t/a British International Helicopters)* [1997] 2 All E.R. 840; and *Thoburn v Sunderland City Council* [2002] 4 All E.R. 156.

For an instance of reliance on this power to effect a complete restatement with minor modifications of a set of provisions, rather than a piecemeal implementation of only those changes required by the relevant European law, see reg.15(4) of and Sch.3 to the Harbour Works (Environmental Impact Assessment) Regulations 1999 (SI 1999/3445).

But note that Parliament watches closely purported use of s.2(2)(b) and protests occasionally—see, for example, "In their second memorandum, the Department restate their view that s.2(2)(b) of the 1972 Act enables provision to be made for a 'uniform system of recognition in the UK of qualifications applying without discrimination to EEA nationals and third-country nationals, and to EEA qualifications and third-country qualifications' as matters 'related to' the Community obligation to make provision in relation to EEA nationals with EEA qualifications. Whilst recognising the expediency of a single specialist register covering all such persons, the Committee does not agree that that constitutes a sufficient connection with the Community obligation to make such provision a matter which is 'related to' the obligation for the purposes of section 2(2)(b) of the 1972 Act. . . . . The Committee believes that crucial assistance as to the width of the power conferred by section 2(2)(b) is to be derived from the reference, in the last limb of that subsection, to the 'objects of the Communities'."—Joint Committee on Statutory Instruments, Session 1995–96, 13th Report, para.2 (HL Paper 53, HC 34-xiii).

The courts will, however, give s.2(2)(b) a very wide construction based primarily on whether there is a substantive connection between what is proposed to be done and the underlying Community obligation: see, for example, Otton L.J. in *R v Secretary of State for Trade and*

The nature of the exceptions to the s.2(2) power is mostly apparent. But the exception preventing the delegation of power is not entirely clear, particularly because of the qualification permitting modification of existing powers and delegation on "administrative" matters. Whether a particular matter amounts to administration or legislation is something that can be assessed only in relation to each set of circumstances.

Procedure

3.10.4   The power in s.2(2) of the European Communities Act 1972 is exercisable in either of two forms, the choice being for the Government to make on each occasion. The first form is the Order in Council.[86] The second form is that of regulations made by a Minister of the Crown designated for the purpose by Order in Council. There is no difference of significance or substance between the two forms. As a general rule, regulations will be used unless the constitutional or professional significance of the instrument is such as to make an Order in Council seem more appropriate.

Unusually, it is for the Government to decide in respect of each instrument made under the power in s.2(2) of the European Communities Act 1972 whether or not to obtain the approval of the two Houses of Parliament by reference to a draft before the instrument is made. If the Government chooses not to obtain approval of a draft, the instrument—whether it be an Order in Council or regulations—is subject to the negative resolution procedure and can be annulled.[87]

Although the choice of affirmative or negative resolution is one for the Government, the Joint Committee on Statutory Instruments and other Parliamentary or other bodies will feel free to comment if it appears that an inappropriate choice has been made. As a general rule, anything of major substantive novelty is likely to be done by affirmative resolution, as is anything which involves significant amendment of primary legislation.[88]

Industry, ex parte Unison—"Against this analysis I am satisfied that the applicants have not advanced a sound basis for limiting the scope of the phrase 'relating to' in s.2(2)(b). I reject the alternative meaning suggested by [Counsel] of 'tangential to or consequential'. This is not the language of the Directive or the UK legislation. I see no reason not to give the phrase 'relating to' or 'related to' any meaning other than its natural, everyday meaning. Thus I am satisfied that the obligation to consult a Trade Union in regard to one redundancy is related to a Community obligation, and not distinct, separate or divorced from it."

For an example of s.2(2)(b) relied upon to permit an element of consolidation, see reg.15(4) of, and Sch.3 to, the Harbour Works (Environmental Impact Assessment) Regulations 1999 (SI 1999/3445) which substitutes a new Sch.3 to the Harbours Act 1964 (c.40) rather than making piecemeal amendments.

[86] As to which see Chapter 3, Section 2.

[87] European Communities Act 1972, Sch.2, para.2(2).

[88] See, for example, "However, the Committee considers that the content of these Regulations is so significant in embodying a policy choice in the formulation of the new exception from the 1975 Act

Distinguishing section 2(2) instruments

Despite the constitutional importance and breadth of the power under s.2(2) of the European Communities Act 1972 there is nothing unusual or specific about the form of an instrument made under it which enables it to be readily identified. On its face it is the same as any other Order in Council or set of regulations made by statutory instrument.[89] **3.10.5**

The preamble to the instrument will, of course, cite s.2(2) as the power under which the instrument is made. But that may not be the only provision cited, as it is both permitted and common for an instrument to be made partly under the powers in s.2(2) and partly under domestic *vires*.[90]

Where an instrument is made for the principal purpose of giving effect to a Community obligation, the Explanatory Note to the instrument will record that fact and briefly explain the nature and effect of the obligation concerned.[91]

As to whether a single instrument can be made partly under the powers in s.2(2) and partly under free-standing domestic powers, while there is nothing to prevent this as a matter of law, there are clear advantages in avoiding it as a general rule. Unless it is clear on the face of the instrument which provisions are made under which power, it may be difficult on a later occasion to work out what amendments can be made under the domestic *vires* alone. And if the European instrument being implemented is annulled, it might be difficult to know what to do about the instrument (again, unless the "European" provisions were clearly severable). Later amendment apart, it may be important for readers to be able to identify which provisions are founded on European obligations, because those are likely to have to be approached (and possibly construed) in a different way from those resting only on domestic *vires*.[92]

---

that it would have been more appropriate to have made the Regulations subject to draft affirmative procedure. The Committee therefore reports to both Houses that an inappropriate choice of procedure for Parliamentary control has been made for these Regulations."—Joint Committee on Statutory Instruments, Session 1994–95, 8th Report, para.7 (HL Paper 27, HC 8-viii).

[89] In particular, there is no separate sub-series for Statutory Instrument numbering, as there is for commencement orders and certain other kinds of instrument.

[90] There is a mild convention that it is preferable to use domestic powers granted by Parliament to the executive for specific purposes in so far as possible, and to reserve reliance on s.2(2) for matters that cannot be accomplished in that way. And the domestic powers may sometimes be more far-reaching than s.2(2): they may, for example, contain no limitation, or a lesser limitation, on the kind of offence that may be created.

[91] As will the Explanatory Notes in a case where a European obligation is implemented by primary legislation.

[92] Hence, in relation to SI 1995/288, note the report of the Joint Committee on Statutory Instruments—"The recital of powers states that these Regulations are made in exercise of powers conferred by certain provisions of the Environmental Protection Act 1990 and also by s.2(2) of the European Communities Act 1972. The Committee asked the Department to specify the provisions made under s.2(2) of the 1972 Act. Their memorandum states that paragraphs . . . . of regulation 3 are made in reliance of that power. The Committee accordingly reports the Regulations for the elucidation provided by the memorandum"—Joint Committee on Statutory Instruments, Session 1994–95, 13th Report, para.4 (HL Paper 39, HC 8-xiii).

The "copy-out" debate

3.10.6 For the most part the drafting of instruments under the powers in s.2(2) of the European Communities Act 1972 is the same as the drafting of any other statutory instrument.

But one problem regularly arises where the Directive or other European instrument being implemented uses a term which is neither entirely bereft of meaning nor sufficiently precise for normal purposes of the drafting of law in the United Kingdom. The problem is whether simply to replicate the term (the "copy out" approach) and rely on the fact that the courts will be bound to have regard to the intended meaning within the context of the underlying European legislation—having regard to any relevant decision of the European Court of Justice and if necessary having recourse to a reference to that court for the purpose of elucidating that intended meaning—or whether to attempt to render into precise English (the "interpretive" approach) the understood intention of the underlying European legislation.

Each approach has something to be said for it, and each has its limitations.

The interpretive approach aims to produce law of the same degree of precision as that with which our domestic courts regularly deal, and to make it unnecessary for the courts or the citizens to whom the legislation is primarily addressed to have to discover the terms and probable intention of the underlying European legislation.

3.10.7 The principal argument for the copy-out approach is that the interpretive approach, while well-intentioned, can sometimes lead to a false accuracy that can seriously mislead the courts and citizens. If it is beyond all doubt what the intention is of the term as used in the European legislation, then no harm will be done by interpreting it and rendering it into precise English. But very often that is not the case: European Directives are negotiated through a political process wholly unlike the way in which domestic legislation is framed, and the text has to be rendered into a form which is acceptable to each of the negotiating delegations, and in a number of different languages at the same time. Even where the precise policy intention is clear, it may be difficult or impossible to find expressions in each of the Community languages that contain precisely the right nuances and convey the intended meaning exactly.

This exposure of the benefits and dangers of each approach indicates in what circumstances each is most justifiably used. Where the intention of an expression is clear, perhaps because of the context of the Directive or its purposes as stated in the preamble,[93] it is indeed helpful to make that intention clear on the face of the implementing legislation. But where there is a significant doubt, an attempt

---

[93] While the preamble has more or less died out as a tool of English law, being extinct for public general primary legislation and used only for specific formal and procedural purposes in secondary legislation, it is alive and well in Europe. Directives and other instruments are routinely preceded by a lengthy preamble—sometimes as long as the instrument itself or even longer—in a form which often conveys the legislative intention more clearly than the instrument itself.

to resolve the doubt by using an expression which has a clear meaning at English law is merely misleading: the change effected by the additional precision has no effect as a matter of European law, and therefore the courts will be obliged to ignore it[94] and attempt to discover for themselves the intention of the underlying European instrument, should the implementing legislation be challenged. So in those circumstances the interpretive approach merely conceals the doubt and thereby creates a trap for the unwary or inexperienced.[95]

The question of whether or not provisions of a Directive being implemented should be merely copied out or expanded upon has attracted the attention of the Joint Committee on Statutory Instruments on more than one occasion.[96] In particular, there are some striking instances in which the Committee has had great sympathy for the principle of copy-out, and has agreed that it is practically unavoidable in the circumstances as a matter of European law, while still considering that as a matter of the law of the United Kingdom the copy-out approach does not result in sufficiently precise law to be justiciable according to the principles applied by the domestic courts.[97] **3.10.8**

---

[94] Because of the obligation in s.2(1) of the 1972 Act to give full effect to Community law.

[95] Which is probably what Jacob J. alluded to in referring to the "customary unhelpful way of 're-write' rather than 'copy-out' " in *Apple Computer Incorporated v Design Registry* October 24, 2001 Ch.

[96] So, for example, "However, the Committee considers that no difference in wording should be used when no difference in meaning is intended, and considers that the wording used in the definition in the Directive should, in this case, have been directly followed. As it was not, the Committee reports the Regulations as being defectively drafted."—Joint Committee on Statutory Instruments Session 1994–95 7th Report 31.i.95 (HL Paper 26 HC 8-vii) para.7.

[97] Note "The Directive describes the relevant category of vessels in terms of vessels 'staying very close to shore'. Accordingly, regulation 2 of the present Regulations amends the Table to regulation 4(1) of the 1995 Regulations so that the term 'no more than 30 nautical miles from shore' is replaced by the term 'very close to shore'. Breach of the relevant requirement would constitute an offence under regulation 12(1) of the 1995 Regulations and would attract a summary fine of up to £5,000. The Committee asked the Department by what criteria a vessel would be regarded, for the purposes of bringing criminal proceedings against its owner, as being of a description which stays, or does not stay, 'very close to the shore'. The Department reply in a memorandum printed in Appendix I that the phrase is not defined in the Directive, and that 'it will ultimately be for the European Court of Justice to interpret it'. They go on to explain, that, as a general rule, the Department would not consider a vessel operating more than 60 miles out to sea as being one 'very close to shore' and that whether one operating within that distance would be considered 'very close to shore' would depend on the circumstances. The Committee recognises that the Department have been constrained to legislate in these imprecise terms only as a result of a similarly imprecise Directive and the requirement of European Community law to secure the uniform application of a Directive's provisions. However, the amendment made by regulation 2 produces a formulation of an obligation so imprecise as to be unacceptable by reference to normal United Kingdom legislative practice in a context such as this in which the obligation carries a criminal sanction for failure to comply with it. The Committee therefore considers that it must, without implying any criticism of the Department, report the regulation to both Houses of Parliament on the ground that the provision is defectively drafted."—Joint Committee on Statutory Instruments, Session 1996–97, 8th Report, para.2 (HL Paper 32, H.C. 29-viii).

See also the similar report of the Joint Committee on Statutory Instruments, Session 1996–97, 11th Report, para.5 (HL Paper 39, HC 29-xi).

See also "The Committee asked the Department to explain what coverage is meant by 'etc.' in sub-paragraph (d) of that Schedule. The Department state that the wording is taken from Council Directive 94/55/EC. The Committee restates that it does not consider that copying-out from

Lapsing

3.10.9   As to the effect on a s.2(2) instrument where the European legislation which it implements ceases to have effect, see para.32.2.11.

Construction of Community Treaties, &c.

3.10.10   As for the rules established by s.3 of the 1972 Act for the construction of Community Treaties and instruments, see Chapters 29 and 32.

SECTION 11

REMEDIAL ORDERS

Introduction

3.11.1   In certain circumstances it may come to the attention of the Government that the effect of a provision of legislation is contrary to the United Kingdom's obligations as a signatory to the European Convention on Human Rights.

Section 10[98] of the Human Rights Act 1998[99] confers a power on the Government to take remedial action where—

Directives excuses Departments from a duty to be specific in making legislation, and so reports Schedule 3 for defective drafting."—Joint Committee on Statutory Instruments, Session 1997–98, 16th Report, para.7 (HL Paper 48, HC 33-xvi).

See also "The Committee takes this opportunity to remind Departments that European directives must be properly transposed into domestic law, and that repeating the words of a Directive is no substitute for framing implementing regulations in terms which fit United Kingdom law- in this case that it is not 'intervention' which is being authorised but a power to give directions."—Joint Committee on Statutory Instruments, Session 1997–98, 20th Report, para.3 (HL Paper 62, HC 33-xx).

[98] The full text of section 10 is as follows—

   "**10 Power to take remedial action**

   (1) This section applies if—

       (a) a provision of legislation has been declared under section 4 to be incompatible with a Convention right and, if an appeal lies—

           (i) all persons who may appeal have stated in writing that they do not intend to do so;

           (ii) the time for bringing an appeal has expired and no appeal has been brought within that time; or

           (iii) an appeal brought within that time has been determined or abandoned; or

       (b) it appears to a Minister of the Crown or Her Majesty in Council that, having regard to a finding of the European Court of Human Rights made after the coming into force of this section in proceedings against the United Kingdom, a provision of legislation is incompatible with an obligation of the United Kingdom arising from the Convention.

   (2) If a Minister of the Crown considers that there are compelling reasons for proceeding under this section, he may by order make such amendments to the legislation as he considers necessary to remove the incompatibility.

   (3) If, in the case of subordinate legislation, a Minister of the Crown considers—

       (a) that it is necessary to amend the primary legislation under which the subordinate legislation in question was made, in order to enable the incompatibility to be removed, and

       (b) that there are compelling reasons for proceeding under this section, he may by

---

(1) a provision is declared under section 4 of the Act to be incompatible with a Convention right,[1] or

(2) a judgment of the European Court of Human Rights in proceedings brought against the United Kingdom makes a Minister think that a provision if legislation is incompatible with the Convention.

The limitations on this section are significant and the necessity for them not immediately apparent. In particular—

a. It is hard to see why a judgment of the European Court in proceedings brought against a country other than the United Kingdom should not be allowed to trigger the power to take remedial action here, if we have legislation in the same terms as that other country. Where a person with international interests or a group of persons in a number of countries are affected by legislation that they believe to be incompatible with their Convention rights, it may be a matter of mere convenience or practicality as to which State is made the defendant in action before the European Court, in the expectation that a successful judgment will obviate the need for others to take proceedings (as is common in domestic litigation where a number of people have a similar cause of action).   **3.11.2**

b. There may well be changes in circumstances, other than a judgment of the European Court, that lead the Government to conclude that a piece of legislation that was previously defensible in terms of compatibility with the Convention has ceased to be so.

Of course, there is nothing to stop the Government from amending legislation to ensure conformity with the Convention whenever it pleases.[2] But the normal

---

order make such amendments to the primary legislation as he considers necessary.

(4) This section also applies where the provision in question is in subordinate legislation and has been quashed, or declared invalid, by reason of incompatibility with a Convention right and the Minister proposes to proceed under paragraph 2(b) of Schedule 2.

(5) If the legislation is an Order in Council, the power conferred by subsection (2) or (3) is exercisable by Her Majesty in Council.

(6) In this section "legislation" does not include a Measure of the Church Assembly or of the General Synod of the Church of England.

(7) Schedule 2 makes further provision about remedial orders."

[99] 1998 c.42.

[1] As to s.4 of the 1998 Act see Chapter 11, Section 3.

[2] For an example of a legislative opportunity being taken to restore compliance see the following observation of Lord McIntosh of Haringey in moving the Second Reading of the Insolvency Bill 1999–2000 (HL Deb. April 4, 2000 c.1252)—"In addition, section 219 of the Insolvency Act currently allows answers obtained by use of compulsory power to be used in evidence. That is contrary to the decision of the European Court of Human Rights in the case of *Saunders v the United Kingdom*. Therefore, we are taking the opportunity to put right that situation."

pressures on the legislative programme,[3] and the normal requirements of passage through both Houses,[4] make the use of an order-making power obviously the most likely way of ensuring prompt and effective amendment of legislation that becomes incompatible.

Scope of remedial orders

3.11.3 The most significant aspect of the scope of a remedial order is the ability to amend primary or secondary legislation.[5] More generally, an order may do anything necessary to remedy the perceived incompatibility with the Convention rights.

A remedial order may be made so as to have retrospective effect[6] but not for the purpose of conferring retrospective criminal liability.[7]

A remedial order may sub-delegate.[8]

Procedure

3.11.4 Schedule 2 to the Human Rights Act 1998 provides the procedure to be followed in relation to a remedial order.[9]

In general, a remedial order requires to be laid in draft before Parliament for 60 days, approved by resolution of each House and then made. Before the draft is laid the relevant Minister must lay before Parliament a proposal and supporting information[10]; and where representations are made about the proposals the Minister must when laying the eventual draft summarise the representations and the changes, if any, resulting from them.[11]

In cases of urgency there is power to disregard the provisions for laying in draft.[12] The order then has to be laid after making, representations have to be considered, and the order lapses unless confirmed by resolution of each House.[13]

---

[3] See Chapter 5, Section 1.
[4] See Chapter 5, Section 2.
[5] Human Rights Act 1998, Sch.2, para.1(2).
[6] Sch.2, para.1(1)(b).
[7] Sch.2, para.1(4).
[8] Sch.2, para.1(1)(c)—"A remedial order may . . . make provision for the delegation of specific functions."
[9] "2. No remedial order may be made unless—
   (a) a draft of the order has been approved by a resolution of each House of Parliament made after the end of the period of 60 days beginning with the day on which the draft was laid; or
   (b) it is declared in the order that it appears to the person making it that, because of the urgency of the matter, it is necessary to make the order without a draft being so approved."
[10] Sch.2, para.3(1).
[11] Sch.2, para.3(2).
[12] Sch.2, para.2(b).
[13] Sch.3, para.4.

The Joint Committee on Human Rights[14] has a role in considering and reporting on proposals for remedial orders.[15]

Use of power

The power to make remedial orders has, not surprisingly, been used only rarely. For examples see the Mental Health Act 1983 (Remedial) Order 2001[16] and the Naval Discipline Act 1957 (Remedial) Order 2004.[17] Each of those orders was made without prior affirmation by the Houses and carries a statement of urgency by the Minister.[18] The 2001 Order responded to a declaration of incompatibility[19] while the 2004 Order responded to a judgment of the European Court of Human Rights.[20]   **3.11.5**

---

[14] Appointed by the two Houses of Parliament "to consider matters relating to human rights in the United Kingdom (but excluding consideration of individual cases); proposals for remedial orders, draft remedial orders and remedial orders".

[15] See, for example, the Sixth Report for Session 2001–02 (HL 57, HC 472) which considers the Mental Health Act 1983 (Remedial) Order 2001 and concludes, in para.7—"We consider that the Order made on 18 November remedies the incompatibility in the provisions of the Mental Health Act 1983 identified by the Court of Appeal in its declaration of 4 April 2001. We recommend that the Mental Health Act 1983 (Remedial) Order 2001 should be approved by each House in the form in which it was originally laid before Parliament."

[16] SI 2001/3712.

[17] SI 2004/66.

[18] "Whereas . . . it appears to the Secretary of State that, because of the urgency of the matter, it is necessary to make the order without a draft being approved by resolution of each House of Parliament;".

[19] The Explanatory Note says—
> "In the case of The Queen on the application of H v Mental Health Review Tribunal North & East London Region (Secretary of State for Health Intervening) (4 April 2001) the Court made a declaration under section 4 of the Human Rights Act 1998 that—
> "Sections 72(1) and 73(1) of the Mental Health Act 1983 are incompatible with Articles 5(1) and 5(4) of the European Convention of Human Rights in that, for the Mental Health Review Tribunal to be obliged to order a patient's discharge, the burden is placed upon the patient to prove that the criteria justifying his detention in hospital for treatment no longer exist; and that Articles 5(1) and 5(4) require the Tribunal to be positively satisfied that all the criteria justifying the patient's detention in hospital for treatment continue to exist before refusing a patient's discharge.".
> "In order to remove the incompatibility, the Order amends sections 72(1) and 73(1) of the 1983 Act to provide that a Mental Health Review Tribunal shall direct the discharge of a patient if they are not satisfied that the criteria justifying his detention in hospital for treatment continue to exist. The Order also makes a consequential amendment to subsection (2) of section 73 of the 1983 Act."

[20] The Explanatory Note says—
> "In the case of Mark Grieves v United Kingdom (Application No 57067/00), the Grand Chamber of the European Court of Human Rights held that there had been a violation of Article 6(1) of the Convention in that the position of the judge advocate in the applicant's trial by court-martial did not provide a sufficient guarantee of the independence of the court-martial because, among other reasons, he had been appointed by the Chief Naval Judge Advocate, a serving naval officer.
> "In order to remove this incompatibility, the Order amends sections 47M(1) and (2)(c), 52FG(1), 52FJ(3), 53B(1), 53C(2) and 59(4A) of the Act to provide that the Judge Advocate

The principles relevant to the decision whether to use a remedial order or a Bill were discussed by the Joint Committee on Human Rights in its Seventh Report for Session 2001–02[21] in the following terms—

> "32. As a matter of general constitutional principle, it is desirable for amendments to primary legislation to be made by way of a Bill. This is likely to maximize the opportunities for Members of each House to scrutinize the proposed amendments in detail. It would allow amendments to be made to the terms of the proposed amendments to the law during their parliamentary passage. (The procedure under section 10 of and Schedule 2 to the Human Rights Act 1998 does not allow for Parliament directly to amend either a draft remedial order or a remedial order—only to suggest amendments.) In many cases it may be easy to remove an incompatibility by means of a short Bill which could be drafted quickly and passed speedily through both Houses. Such a Bill may often be politically uncontroversial. Proceeding by way of a Bill may result in the incompatibility being removed far more quickly than would be possible using the non-urgent remedial order procedure, which (as we point out in our Sixth Report) could allow eleven months or so to elapse between the making of the declaration of incompatibility and the coming into effect of the necessary amendment to the law. Sometimes there may be good reasons for proceeding by Bill even where the matter is more complex. For example, if it is necessary to establish a regime of inspection, regulation, appeal or compensation in order to remove the incompatibility, or to authorize significant expenditure, in order to provide adequate and continuing safeguards for Convention rights, it might be preferable (constitutionally and practically) for those arrangements to be set out in a Bill rather than effected by way of subordinate legislation.

3.11.6
> "33. On the other hand, we accept that other factors sometimes militate in favour of using the Remedial Order procedure. We make no attempt to enumerate these exhaustively, but they include the following—

>> 'Where the amendment relates to a body of legislation which is under review with a view to major legislative reform in (say) two or three years time, it might be difficult or considered inappropriate to find time in the legislative timetable for an earlier Bill covering just part of the field to be dealt with later by the larger Bill. (For example, the Remedial Order on which we reported in our Sixth Report dealt with a small area of mental

---

of Her Majesty's Fleet, a civilian, will appoint judicial officers and judge advocates. The Order also makes consequential changes to the Courts-Martial (Royal Navy) Rules 1997, the Naval Custody Rules 2000, the Summary Appeal Court (Navy) Rules 2000 and the Administration of Oaths (Summary Appeal Court) (Navy) Order 2000."
[21] HL 58, HC 473—paras 32 to 34.

health law, the whole of which is due to be the subject of major reform in a Bill intended to be introduced to Parliament in 2003 or so.)

'The legislative timetable might be fully occupied by other important, or even emergency, legislation. (For example, had it been decided to remedy the incompatibility with the Mental Health Act 1983, sections 72 and 73, by way of a Bill, its passage might well have been significantly delayed by the priority which would probably have been given to the Anti-terrorism, Crime and Security Bill and—perhaps—the Proceeds of Crime Bill as part of a package of anti-terrorism measures.)

'The need to remedy incompatibilities with Convention rights should be given a high priority. If waiting for a slot in the legislative timetable might cause significant delay (for example, for one of the reasons outlined above), and the Remedial Order procedure would be likely to cause less delay, we take the view that the Minister would be entitled to consider that there were compelling reasons for proceeding by means of a Remedial Order.

'The need to avoid undue delay is particularly pressing when the **3.11.7** incompatibility affects, or might affect, the life, liberty, safety, or physical or mental integrity of the individual. In such cases, we consider that there would be compelling reasons for using the Remedial Order procedure in order to secure even a small acceleration in the speed with which an incompatibility could be removed.'

"34. Ultimately, the Minister's judgment must balance these (and other) relevant factors in the light of the situation giving rise to the particular incompatibility. The Committee will look to the Minister to ensure that the need to remove incompatibilities as speedily as possible, and factors affecting the impact of the incompatibilities on particular individuals, are given full weight when making the decision. In any case, however, our view is that final decisions about how to remedy incompatibilities should be made no later than six months after the end of legal proceedings."

SECTION 12

TRANSFER OF FUNCTIONS ORDERS

Introduction

Transfer of Functions Orders are made under the Ministers of the Crown Act **3.12.1** 1975[22] and their purpose is to effect or facilitate change in ministerial respon-sibilities.

---

[22] 1975 c.26: this was a Consolidation Act, the power having existed for some decades previously.

Transfer of functions orders partake in part of the nature of buses and in part of the nature of elementary carpentry tools.

They are like buses because they are gregarious by nature and rarely arrive singly, long gaps frequently occurring between groups. As a general rule a number of orders are likely to accompany any reshuffle of Ministerial positions which involves serious structural alterations in the machinery of government.

They are like elementary carpentry tools because a small number of very broad powers are provided, with which it is possible to secure complicated and effective adaptation of the statute book.[23]

Scope of power

3.12.2 All orders under the 1975 Act are known colloquially as Transfer of Functions Orders, although as will be seen they may not provide for the transfer of any function and they may not even be directly connected with the transfer of any function.

The range of things that may be done under the 1975 Act is as follows—

(1) An order may provide that a function previously exercisable by Minister X be exercisable in future by Minister Y.[24]

(2) An order may provide for the dissolution of a department of government and the redistribution of its functions.[25]

(3) An order may provide for a function of Minister X to be exercisable concurrently with Minister Y, or to cease to be exercisable concurrently with Minister Y.[26]

(4) An order may make provision in connection with a change in the departments of the office of Secretary of State, or a change in the functions of a Secretary of State.[27]

---

[23] Prompting a former First Parliamentary Counsel, Sir John Fiennes, KCB, QC to write to a colleague—"When I first married I bought myself at Woolworths a screwdriver and a pair of pincers, and with these as my only tools performed prodigies of carpentry: transfer of functions orders are much like that."

[24] s.1(1)(a). This power is available in respect of any function, whether vested in Minister X by virtue of statute or by prerogative (which in this sense generally means no more than purely informal and administrative arrangement). But generally speaking a function vested informally can also be transferred informally. So one would not expect to need to make a Transfer of Functions Order in respect of a function vested other than by virtue of statute, unless it were desired to make in connection with the change any consequential or incidental provision. In such a case the transfer by order serves in effect merely as a hook on which to hang the consequential or incidental provision.

[25] s.1(1)(b): this is rare, but see, for example, the Ministry of Agriculture, Fisheries and Food (Dissolution) Order 2002 (SI 2002/794).

[26] s.1(1)(c).

[27] s.2. It is open to the Queen as an exercise of the Royal Prerogative to create new Secretaries of State, or to allow Secretarial offices to fall into abeyance by appointing nobody to them. These matters are arranged entirely at the behest of the Prime Minister of the time.

(5) An order may change the title of a Minister.[28]

An order under any of the first three categories may include incidental, **3.12.3** consequential and supplemental provision for the purpose of giving full effect to the order.[29] The range of provision that may be made by way of supplementary provision of this kind is extremely wide[30] and includes—

(1) provision for the transfer of property, rights and liabilities held in connection with any functions transferred or distributed;

(2) provision for the carrying on and completion by or under the authority of the Minister to whom any functions are transferred of anything commenced by or under the authority of a Minister of the Crown before the date when the Order takes effect;

(3) provision adapting enactments relating to any functions transferred so as to enable them to be exercised by the Minister to whom they are transferred and his officers;

(4) provision for the substitution of the Minister to whom functions are transferred for any other Minister of the Crown in any instrument, contract, or legal proceedings made or commenced before the date when the Order takes effect.

The provision that may be made by orders making provision in connection with a change in the Secretarial departments includes the matters listed as possible consequential provision under the previous paragraph, and includes in addition the power to make a Secretary of State a corporation sole.[31]

These powers are of course extremely wide. Here as elsewhere,[32] however, the **3.12.4** very breadth of the power makes it unsafe to rely upon it to do anything that is likely to have significant effect of a kind that could be argued not to fall within the general legislative contemplation. In this context, indeed, as a general rule it is unlikely to be safe to use these very general powers to do anything that might be challenged by someone on the grounds that it interferes with private interests.

For example, it is common for a Transfer of Functions Order to alter references in "instruments", adopting a wide definition of that expression sufficient to

---

[28] s.4.
[29] As explained in para.3.12.7, these apparently supplementary provisions may be the entire point of the order.
[30] See footnote 23 above.
[31] A corporation sole means simply an entity that, while not being a body, is invested with legal personality and perpetual succession—and from that arises the ability of the office-holder from time to time to conduct commercial transactions without incurring personal liability (or acquiring personal rights).
[32] See, for example, Chapter 1, Section 2 and Chapter 2, Sections 2 and 3.

include certain contracts and other private agreements.[33] That is generally reasonable and sensible because it is purely beneficial for those who have contracted with a Government Department to have the contract automatically up-dated so as to refer to the relevant Minister from time to time. In the case, however, of an instrument accompanying the splitting of a department into two,[34] since the division is likely to involve the employment of additional officials to handle establishment functions, a person who has contracted to provide health or other services to personnel of the original department might object to having the contract impliedly amended so as to refer to personnel of both new departments. In such a case, general words construing references to the old department as including references to the two new departments would be unlikely to be construed as being intended to operate so as to increase the contractor's substantive obligations.

Use of power

3.12.5 More than one hundred orders have been made under the 1975 Act and its principal predecessor.[35] As stated above it is usual to have a number of orders made at or around one time and then an interval of some years before the next, although individual orders are also sometimes made. For obvious reasons, the clusters of orders tend to be concentrated around changes of Government or major Cabinet reshuffles.[36]

Joint exercise versus concurrent exercise

3.12.6 The 1975 Act treats concurrence and joint-exercise of functions differently. As has been seen, an order under s.1 may make provision creating or terminating an arrangement whereby one Minister's functions may be exercisable concurrently with another. Joint exercise is not mentioned in s.1 of the Act. But any reference in the 1975 Act to a Minister includes a reference to Ministers acting jointly.[37]

The difference between a function that is exercisable jointly and one that is exercisable concurrently can be expressed concisely. Where a function is vested

---

[33] See, for example, art.2 of the Transfer of Functions (Registration and Statistics) Order 1996 (SI 1996/273)—"In this Order "instrument", without prejudice to the generality of that expression, includes in particular Royal Charters, Orders in Council, Letters Patent, judgments, decrees, orders, rules, regulations, directions, schemes, bye-laws, awards, contracts and other agreements, memoranda and articles of association, warrants, certificates and other documents".

[34] See, for example, the Transfer of Functions (International Development) Order 1997 (SI 1997/1749).

[35] Ministers of the Crown (Transfer of Functions) Act 1946 (c.6).

[36] Following the formation of a new administration in 1997, for example, there were 14 orders between then and 2003. And there were 7 orders in 1992 following a significant re-structuring of the existing administration.

[37] s.5(6).

in two Ministers jointly[38] each exercise requires the involvement of both Ministers, acting together. Where a function is vested in two Ministers concurrently, either may perform it, acting alone, on any occasion.

The result of the position outlined above is that although s.1(1) does not expressly permit the making of an order providing for a function to be exercisable jointly or to cease to be exercisable jointly, that result can be achieved using the existing powers of s.1(1) construed in accordance with s.5(6). To provide for joint exercise of what is presently a function vested in Minister X alone, an order can rely on s.1(1)(a) to transfer the function from Minister X to Ministers X and Y acting jointly. To deprive Minister Y of responsibility for a function vested in Ministers X and Y jointly, an order can transfer the function from Ministers X and Y jointly to Minister X.[39]

Section 1 orders versus section 2 orders

In essence, s.1 of the 1975 Act permits the transfer of functions and con-   **3.12.7**
sequential provision, while s.2 permits the making consequential provision in relation to transfers of functions between Secretaries of State, where the transfer has been effected informally. It is often a matter of administrative convenience whether to effect a transfer between Secretaries of State informally and make a related s.2 order or to effect the transfer by s.1 order.

References to Ministers in legislation

The need for a transfer of functions order can of course be obviated if legislation   **3.12.8**
conferring powers or making other references to ministers uses as non-specific as possible a form of reference.

Originally there were only two Secretaries of State,[40] and other new ministerial positions that arose were designated as Minister of a particular matter.[41] The

---

[38] As is the case, for political reasons, for functions of the First Minister and deputy First Minister in Northern Ireland—see, for example, s.23(4) of the Northern Ireland Act 1998 (c.47) ("The First Minister and deputy First Minister acting jointly may by prerogative order under subsection (3) . . . ". Or a power may be exercisable jointly by any number of Ministers or by a combination of Ministers and other authorities—see, for example, s.325(1) of the Criminal Justice Act 2003 (c.44) (" 'responsible authority', in relation to any area, means the chief officer of police, the local probation board for that area and the Minister of the Crown exercising functions in relation to prisons, acting jointly").

[39] It might be argued that this appears to be an abuse of the process. But the argument is not strong. Since it is indubitable that the power in s.1(1)(a) would be sufficient to transfer the sole function from Minister X to Ministers A and B and then from Ministers A and B to Minister Y—or to transfer a joint function of Ministers X and Y to Minister A and then to Minister X—it seems unreasonable to object to the transition being made in a single step. In any event, the manoeuvre has been successfully attempted—see, for example, art.5 of the Transfer of Functions (Transport, Local Government and the Regions) Order 2002 (SI 2002/2626) (transfer of joint highways functions) or art.3 of the Transfer of Functions (National Heritage) Order 1992 (SI 1992/1311) (transfer of functions relating to museums, libraries, the arts etc.).

[40] Home and Foreign Affairs.

[41] There always were, and still are, a number of other offices, such as Lord Privy Seal, Chancellor of the Duchy of Lancaster and Lord President of the Council—but although there are some legislative references to them, they are and always have been relatively rare.

result was that legislative provisions conferring powers or making other references to Ministers of the Crown were generally specific as to the particular ministerial office concerned, referring to it by title.

With the increase over time in the number of Secretarial departments of State it has become increasingly possible to refer simply to "the Secretary of State",[42] and the result is a diminished importance in the transfer of functions by order. Most changes of departmental responsibility can now be effected by administrative redistribution in the responsibilities of the Secretaries of State, without having to amend legislation which vests powers or property in "the Secretary of State".[43] There are still occasional references to particular Secretaries in subordinate legislation or non-legislative instruments that concern a particular Department: and there are even occasional references in primary legislation, but they are now rare.[44]

Non-Ministerial Transfer of Functions Orders

3.12.9 Acts other than the 1975 Act occasionally confer powers to transfer undertakings between non-Ministerial public bodies. Orders exercising these functions can generally be distinguished easily from orders under the 1975 Act because their title begins with reference to the substantive area concerned and mentions transfer of functions parenthetically, while orders under the 1975 Act do the reverse.[45]

The content and form of powers under these *ad hoc* provisions is often similar to the structure of the 1975 Act, and the same is true of the derivative

---

[42] Which is defined by Sch.1 to the Interpretation Act 1978 (c.30) as meaning one of Her Majesty's Principal Secretaries of State.

[43] The last major departmental ministerial head who is not a Secretary of State is the Lord Chancellor, who is the subject of a considerable number of legislative references: but at the time when this work went to print there were Government plans to abolish that office, and it was being held concurrently with the office of Secretary of State (as a new instance of that office styled the Secretary of State for Constitutional Affairs). Until recently there was also the Minister of Agriculture, Fisheries and Food, but he too was transformed into a Secretary of State—see the Ministry of Agriculture, Fisheries and Food (Dissolution) Order 2002 (SI 2002/794).

[44] For a recent example see s.31(1) of the Government of Wales Act 1998 (c.38).

[45] Contrast, for example, the National Institutions of the Church of England (Transfer of Functions) Order 1998 (SI 1998/1715) made under s.5 of the National Institutions Measure 1998 or the Social Security Contributions (Transfer of Functions, etc) (Northern Ireland) Order 1999 (SI 1999/671) made under s.24 of the Social Security Contributions (Transfer of Functions, etc) Act 1999 (c.2) with the Transfer of Functions (Insurance) Order 1997 (SI 1997/2781) or the Transfer of Functions (Road Traffic) Order 1999 (SI 1999/3143), both made under the 1975 Act. For a particularly stark contrast compare the Transfer of Functions (Education and Employment) Order 1995 (SI 1995/2986) made under the 1975 Act with the Education (School Curriculum and Assessment Authority) (Transfer of Functions) Order 1995 (SI 1995/903) made under s.252 of the Education Act 1993 (c.35).
Note, however, that orders wholly under s.4 of the 1975 Act (change of title of Ministers) are given a title referring to the Minister concerned without mentioning transfer of functions—see, for example, the Secretary of State for Culture, Media and Sport Order 1997 (SI 1997/1744) and orders wholly dissolving Ministries are generally given a title referring the Ministry being dissolved—see, for example, the Ministry of Agriculture, Fisheries and Food (Dissolution) Order 2002 (SI 2002/794): but such orders are rare.

instruments. But there are generally subject-specific additions, sometimes of some complexity.

Transfer of liability

It is common for transfer of functions orders, whether under the Ministers of the Crown Act 1975 or under specific legislation for transfer, to transfer liability from one body to another. This is generally intended to relate only to civil liability. While it would not be impossible to confer power to transfer criminal liability, it is not to be assumed either that a general power is sufficient to permit such a transfer or that a transfer of liability in general terms intends to effect it.[46]

3.12.10

---

[46] *R. v Pennine Acute Hospitals NHS Trust* [2004] 1 All E.R. 1324, CA.

CHAPTER 4

DEVOLVED LEGISLATION

The legislative system of the United Kingdom has become considerably more **4.1.1**
complicated as a result of the devolution legislation of 1998,[1] under which a high
degree of legislative competence has been devolved to the Scottish Parliament[2]
and to the Northern Ireland Assembly,[3] and a lesser but still significant degree of
competence has been devolved to the National Assembly for Wales.[4]

This Chapter gives an idea of the scope and procedures for legislation to be
made by or concerning the devolved administrations and institutions.

There are presently no regional assemblies for England enjoying devolved
powers,[5] but the idea is occasionally raised and discussed in Parliament.[6]

The three Acts presently providing for devolution are the Scotland Act 1998,[7]
the Northern Ireland Act 1998[8] and the Government of Wales Act 1998.[9]

Preservation of powers of UK Parliament

The most important introductory point to make in relation to devolution is that, **4.1.2**
at least as a matter of legal structure which may or may not entirely reflect the

---

[1] Consisting of the Scotland Act 1998 (c.46), the Government of Wales Act 1998 (c.38) and the
Northern Ireland Act 1998 (c.47).
[2] Established by s.1 of the Scotland Act 1998 (c.46); see Section 2 below.
[3] See Section 3 below.
[4] See Section 4 below.
[5] Although of course local authorities and other councils have limited powers to make bylaws under
the Local Government Acts.
[6] See, for a recent statement of Government policy, HL Deb. April 8, 2003 W.A. 35–36: it is not clear
that regional assemblies for England would have any legislative powers.
[7] 1998 c.46: "An Act to provide for the establishment of a Scottish Parliament and Administration
and other changes in the government of Scotland; to provide for changes in the constitution and
functions of certain public authorities; to provide for the variation of the basic rate of income tax
in relation to income of Scottish taxpayers in accordance with a resolution of the Scottish
Parliament; to amend the law about parliamentary constituencies in Scotland; and for connected
purposes." (Long title).
[8] 1998 c.47: "An Act to make new provision for the government of Northern Ireland for the purpose
of implementing the agreement reached at multi-party talks on Northern Ireland set out in
Command Paper 3883." (Long title).
[9] 1998 c.38: "An Act to establish and make provision about the National Assembly for Wales and
the offices of Auditor General for Wales and Welsh Administration Ombudsman; to reform certain
Welsh public bodies and abolish certain other Welsh public bodies; and for connected purposes."
(Long title).

political reality at any given time, it represents a delegation of power from the Parliament of the United Kingdom (sometimes referred to in this context as "the Westminster Parliament") to the regional institutions, but it does not diminish the potential power of that Parliament.

Even in matters for which primary responsibility has been devolved to a regional institution, the Westminster Parliament remains competent to legislate.[10]

4.1.3   The use of the Westminster Parliament's legislative powers is constrained in practice, although not of course in theory, by the Sewel Convention. The nature and origin of the convention are described adequately for present purposes by the following passages from replies given by Secretary of State for Scotland in Written Answers in the House of Commons—

> "The 'Sewel Convention' is a commitment made by the Government during the passage of the Scotland Bill that 'the UK Parliament would not normally legislate with regard to devolved matters except with the agreement of the devolved legislature. The Devolved Administrations will be responsible for seeking such agreement as may be required for this purpose on an approach from the UK Government'. Proposals for the inclusion of provisions relating to devolved matters in a UK Bill, and therefore the need to invoke the Sewel Convention, arise at the initiative of either the UK Government or the Executive, but in every case, require a process of discussion and agreement between the two Administrations. That process normally involves an exchange of correspondence between the UK Minister who is in charge of the Bill and the First Minister, or the relevant portfolio Minister." [11]

> "The Memorandum of Understanding indicates there will be consultation with the Scottish Executive on policy proposals affecting devolved matters whether or not they involve legislative change. In practice, this means that there is ongoing dialogue between the Scottish Executive and Government departments, including the Scotland Office. For this reason it is impossible to determine at whose initiative discussions about the use of the Sewel convention begin, as they usually take place in the context of wider and on-going discussions. As a matter of principle, either the Government or the Scottish Executive can take the initiative in establishing whether Sewel consent is needed. It is for the Scottish Executive to indicate the view of the Scottish Parliament and to take whatever steps are appropriate to ascertain that view. The Scottish Parliament has agreed to 39 Sewel motions since its inception." [12]

---

[10] Scotland Act 1998, s.28(7) and Northern Ireland Act 1998, s.5(6).
[11] HC Deb. February 5, 2003 WA 291.
[12] HC Deb. February 13, 2003 WA 904.

Introduction

The Scotland Act 1998[13] implemented the policy of Scottish devolution. The **4.2.1**
central features of the devolution of power are the creation of a Scottish
Parliament, a Scottish Administration (consisting of Scottish Ministers and a
civil service) and a separate Scottish Consolidated Fund. This Section considers
the principal legislative implications of Scottish devolution.

Acts of the Scottish Parliament

Section 28 of the Scotland Act 1998 provides as follows—   **4.2.2**

> ### "28 Acts of the Scottish Parliament
>
> (1) Subject to section 29, the Parliament may make laws, to be known as
> Acts of the Scottish Parliament.
>
> (2) Proposed Acts of the Scottish Parliament shall be known as Bills; and
> a Bill shall become an Act of the Scottish Parliament when it has
> been passed by the Parliament and has received Royal Assent.
>
> (3) A Bill receives Royal Assent at the beginning of the day on which
> Letters Patent under the Scottish Seal signed with Her Majesty's own
> hand signifying Her Assent are recorded in the Register of the Great
> Seal.
>
> (4) The date of Royal Assent shall be written on the Act of the Scottish
> Parliament by the Clerk, and shall form part of the Act.
>
> (5) The validity of an Act of the Scottish Parliament is not affected by
> any invalidity in the proceedings of the Parliament leading to its
> enactment.
>
> (6) Every Act of the Scottish Parliament shall be judicially noticed.
>
> (7) This section does not affect the power of the Parliament of the United
> Kingdom to make laws for Scotland."

The essence of this is that the Scottish Parliament is given the power[14] to **4.2.3**
legislate by Act, and once an Act is passed it is to be judicially noticed in the

---

[13] 1998 c.46.

[14] A delegation which results in its Acts being technically delegated legislation and not primary
legislation—see Chapter 1, Section 2. The use of the expression "Act" is, of course, designed to
indicate that within the devolved competence the Scottish Parliament has an area of complete
control and sovereignty very similar to, although derived from, that of the Westminster Parliament.
In particular, the Acts of the Scottish Parliament are expected to sub-delegate powers to make
subordinate instruments, which are to be treated for many purposes in a manner similar to
instruments made under Acts of the Westminster Parliament.

same manner as an Act of the Westminster Parliament (that is to say it can be cited to the courts anywhere in the United Kingdom as a matter of fact and does not require proof of authenticity).[15] Nor are the courts to inquire into the validity of the proceedings leading up to the passing of an Act of the Scottish Parliament: even an acknowledged deficiency or irregularity in the proceedings in that institution does not affect the validity of an Act of the Scottish Parliament to which Royal Assent has been given.[16]

The procedure for producing an Act of the Scottish Parliament is broadly speaking the same, as a matter of legal structure, as the procedure for Acts of the Westminster Parliament. In particular, an Act starts life as a Bill and becomes an Act when it receives the Royal Assent, which is effected when "Letters Patent under the Scottish Seal[17] signed with Her Majesty's own hand signifying Her Assent" are recorded in the Register of the Great Seal.[18]

Legislative competence

4.2.4 The essentially devolved nature of legislation by the Scottish Parliament is reflected in the notion of legislative competence, very much akin to the notion of *vires* in relation to traditional forms of delegated legislation.

Section 29(1) and (2) enact the fundamental restriction of the powers of the Scottish Parliament by reference to the notion of legislative competence—

> "(1) An Act of the Scottish Parliament is not law so far as any provision of the Act is outside the legislative competence of the Parliament.
>
> (2) A provision is outside that competence so far as any of the following paragraphs apply—
>
> > (a) it would form part of the law of a country or territory other than Scotland, or confer or remove functions exercisable otherwise than in or as regards Scotland,[19]
> >
> > (b) it relates to reserved matters,[20]
> >
> > (c) it is in breach of the restrictions in Schedule 4,[21]

---

[15] Scotland Act 1998, s.28(6).

[16] Scotland Act 1989, s.28(5).

[17] This is the seal appointed by the Treaty of Union to be kept and used in place of the Great Seal of Scotland—Scotland Act 1998, s.2(6).

[18] Scotland Act 1998, s.28(3).

[19] This does not prevent an Act of the Scottish Parliament from amending a provision of an Act of the Westminster Parliament in so far as it has effect in relation to Scotland—see, for example, section 60 of the Local Government in Scotland Act 2003 (asp 1) (consequential amendments and repeals).

[20] The reservations are set out in Sch.5 to the Scotland Act 1998, and do not prevent legislation which is merely incidental to or consequential on a provision within the legislative competence. The reservations are digested below.

[21] Sch.4 to the Act contains specific protected and entrenched provisions (principally constitutional enactments). The Schedule is digested in the Appendix to this work (Extract 10).

(d) it is incompatible with any of the Convention rights[22] or with Community law,

(e) it would remove the Lord Advocate from his position as head of the systems of criminal prosecution and investigation of deaths in Scotland."

The most extensive and complicated restriction of the Scottish Parliament's **4.2.5** legislative competence is that of the reservation of specified matters. The reservations are set out in the very detailed provisions of Sch.5 to the Act. It is impracticable to list them all in this work, partly because of the level of detail[23] and partly because they are subject to change by Order in Council.[24] But a flavour of the area of legislative incompetence can be given by setting out the present principal heads of reservation—

(1) the constitution;

(2) political parties;

(3) foreign affairs;

(4) the civil service;

(5) defence;

(6) treason;

(7) fiscal, economic and monetary policy, currency, financial services, financial markets and money laundering;

(8) home affairs: misuse of drugs, data protection, elections, firearms, entertainment, immigration and nationality, scientific procedures on live animals, national security, betting, emergency powers, extradition, access to information and lieutenancies;

(9) trade and industry: business associations, insolvency, competition, intellectual property, import and export control, sea fishing, consumer protection, product standards, product safety, product liability, weights and measures, telecommunications, postal services, research councils and industrial development;

(10) energy: electricity, oil, gas, coal, nuclear energy and energy conservation;

(11) transport: road transport, railways, marine transport and aviation;

---

[22] The European Convention for the Protection of Human Rights and Fundamental Freedoms (Rome, 4 November 1950; TS 71 (1953); Cmd 8969).
[23] The Queen's Printer's version of the Scotland Act 1998 takes 18 A4 pages to set out the reservations.
[24] Scotland Act 1998, s.30(2).

(12) social security (including child support, occupational and personal pensions and war pensions);

(13) regulation of the following professions: architect, health professions and auditor;

(14) employment: employment rights and duties, industrial relations, health and safety at work, and job search and support;

(15) health: abortion, xenotransplantation, embryology, surrogacy, genetics, medicines and poisons;

(16) media: broadcasting and public lending right;

(17) judicial remuneration;

(18) equal opportunities;

(19) control of weapons;

(20) ordnance survey;

(21) time;

(22) outer space.

4.2.6   These broad heads are subject to a number of qualifications and exceptions.

Probably the most politically significant exceptions are in relation to tax. The Scottish Parliament has a limited power, exercisable by resolution, to vary the basic rate of income tax for Scottish taxpayers.[25] And it may by legislation raise "local taxes to fund local authority expenditure (for example, council tax and non-domestic rates)".[26]

Tax apart, the qualifications and exceptions in relation to almost every head are of serious significance, and no assumptions should be made at any time about the state of legislative competence of the Scottish Parliament without checking both the details of Schs 4 and 5 to the 1998 Act and, in particular, whether any recent amendment has been made of them.[27]

It will of course frequently happen that the competence of the Scottish Parliament in relation to a particular matter comes into question. Sch.6 to the Scotland Act 1998 provides a mechanism for the resolution of devolution issues generally, which include questions of legislative competence and also questions about the functions of the Scottish Ministers and the Scottish Executive and about compatibility with the European Convention on Human Rights and with the law of the European Communities.[28] [29]

---

[25] Scotland Act 1998, s.73.

[26] Exception to Section A1 of Part II of Sch.5 to the Scotland Act 1998.

[27] For early orders made amending Schs 4 and 5 see SI 1999/1748, 1999/1749, 2000/1563, 2000/1831, 2000/3252, 2000/3253, 2001/1456 and 2001/3649.

[28] The expression "devolution issue" is defined in para.1 of Sch.6.

[29] For an example of a devolution issue concerning the compatibility of the Scottish system with the European Convention on Human Rights see *Clark (Procurator Fiscal, Kirkcaldy) v Kelly* [2003] 1 All E.R. 1106 PC.

On introducing a Bill into the Scottish Parliament the member of the Scottish **4.2.7**
Executive in charge of the Bill must state that in his view the Bill is within the
Parliament's legislative competence.[30] The Presiding Officer then has to form
and state a view as to legislative competence.[31] The Advocate General, Lord
Advocate or Attorney General may refer the question whether a Bill is within the
Parliament's legislative competence to the Judicial Committee of the Privy
Council.[32] If the Judicial Committee decide that a Bill is outside the Parliament's
competence, the Presiding Officer may not submit the Bill for Royal Assent.[33]

The Secretary of State may also prevent the Presiding Officer of the Scottish
Parliament from presenting a Bill for Royal Assent if he thinks the Bill—

(1) is incompatible with an international obligation of the United Kingdom,

(2) is against the interests of the defence or national security of the United
Kingdom, or

(3) modifies the law in relation to a reserved matter undesirably.[34]

Use made of legislative power

The number of Acts of the Scottish Parliament passed in each of the first years **4.2.8**
of the Scottish Parliament is as follows—

1999	1
2000	12
2001	15
2002	17
2003	19

The subjects addressed cover a wide range dealing, for example, with local
government,[35] land law,[36] children[37] and animal welfare.[38]

There is an annual Budget (Scotland) Act.[39]

---

[30] s.31(1) of the Scotland Act 1998.
[31] s.31(2).
[32] s.33(1).
[33] s.32(3).
[34] S.35.
[35] 2001 asp 9, 2002 asp 1 and 2003 asp 1.
[36] 2000 asp 5, 2001 asp 5 and 2003 asp 2.
[37] 2001 asp 14 and 2003 asp 5.
[38] 2002 asp 6 and asp 10.
[39] See, for example, the Budget (Scotland) Act 2002—"An Act of the Scottish Parliament to make
provision, for financial year 2002/03, for the use of resources by the Scottish Administration and
certain bodies whose expenditure is payable out of the Scottish Consolidated Fund, for authorising
the payment of sums out of the Fund, for the maximum amount of relevant expenditure for the
purposes of section 94(5) of the Local Government (Scotland) Act 1973 (c.65) and the maximum
amounts of borrowing by certain statutory bodies; to make provision, for financial year 2003/04,
for authorising the payment of sums out of the Fund on a temporary basis; and for connected
purposes".

As well as dealing with subjects addressed for England and Wales by public general Acts, an Act of the Scottish Parliament may deal with a matter of local or private interest. See, for example, the University of St. Andrews (Postgraduate Medical Degrees) Act 2002.[40]

4.2.9   In the first Session of the Scottish Parliament (1999–2003) of the 62 Bills passed by the Parliament 50 were Executive Bills (that is to say Bills introduced by Scottish Ministers), eight were Members' Bills (that is to Bills introduced by private Members), three were Committee Bills (that is to say Bills introduced by a Committee[41] and one was a Private Bill. Of the Executive Bills, four were Budget Bills.

The convention has arisen of citing Acts of the Scottish Parliament by "asp" and the number of the Act for that calendar year.[42]

The convention appears to be for short titles of Acts of the Scottish Parliament to include the words (Scotland), except where the connection with Scotland is apparent from the other words of the title.[43]

Subordinate legislation

4.2.10   An Act of the Westminster Parliament or an Act of the Scottish Parliament may confer a function on the Scottish Ministers.[44] The Minister may not, however, make subordinate legislation which—

(1) is incompatible with a provision of the European Convention on Human Rights that is incorporated into the law of the United Kingdom, or

(2) is incompatible with the law of the European Communities.[45]

If a Scottish Minister makes subordinate legislation which the Secretary of State believes to be incompatible with an international obligation, to be contrary to the United Kingdom's national security and defence interests, or to deal with a reserved matter undesirably, the Secretary of State may by order revoke the legislation.[46]

A large number of subordinate powers not conferred by Act of the Scottish Parliament but by Act of the Westminster Parliament (whether passed before or

---

[40] 2002 asp 15—"An Act of the Scottish Parliament to permit the University of St. Andrews to grant postgraduate research degrees in medicine to qualified medical practitioners".
[41] See Chapter 7, Section 1.
[42] No full stop is used by convention. There are not known to be any plans to have the Westminster Acts published as an annual series of vipers.
[43] Hence, for example, the Scottish Local Government (Elections) Act 2002 (asp 1) and the School Education (Amendment) (Scotland) Act 2002 (asp 2). And, of course, the mere fact that a short title contains the word "(Scotland)" does not mean that it is certainly an Act of the Scottish Parliament—many Westminster Acts from before devolution, and some after devolution in relation to reserved matters, will contain that word in the title.
[44] Scotland Act 1998, s.52.
[45] s.57(2).
[46] s.58(4).

after 1998) are now exercisable in respect of Scotland by the Scottish Ministers.[47] These now account for a significant part of the annual production of statutory instruments.[48]

SECTION 3

NORTHERN IRELAND

Introduction

The policy of devolution in Northern Ireland is presently given effect to **4.3.1** principally by the Northern Ireland Act 1998.[49] Unlike Scotland and Wales, there had before 1998 been in place a system for the devolution of power in Northern Ireland, although it had been in suspension for some time, and legislation for Northern Ireland was being made either by ordinary Act of the Westminster Parliament or by a separate system of subordinate legislation.[50]

The structure of devolution in relation to Northern Ireland recognises the particular political volatility there.[51] Accordingly the devolution of power can be turned on and off by suspension and revival under ss.1 and 2 of the Northern Ireland Act 2000.[52] While devolution is in place the principal method of legislating for Northern Ireland on devolved matters is Act of the Northern Ireland Assembly.[53] While devolution is suspended the principal method of legislating for Northern Ireland on matters that would be devolved is Order in Council.[54]

One result of the political instabilities in Northern Ireland over many decades is that there is a bewildering array of kinds of legislation that have been able to be passed in relation to Northern Ireland at different times. Although the principal mechanisms now are intended to be Act of the Northern Ireland Assembly and Act of the Westminster Parliament, not only are the procedures for legislation during the suspension of devolution of continuing importance, but there are relics of earlier periods both of devolution and direct rule that are of considerable continuing importance in some contexts. This Section focuses on the principal present mechanisms: but readers should be aware that they may

---

[47] See ss.53 to 58 of the Scotland Act 1998.
[48] The numbers for recent years are: 1999 (first full year of devolution)—203; 2000–453; 2001–494; 2002–570; 2003–623: so there appears to be a significant acceleration.
[49] 1998 c.47.
[50] Under Sch.1 to the Northern Ireland Act 1974 (c.28).
[51] When this work went to print the Northern Ireland Assembly was in a state of suspension, having been suspended by the Northern Ireland Act 2000 (Suspension of Devolved Government) Order 2002 (SI 2002/2574) made under s.2(2) of the Northern Ireland Act 2000 (c.1) and revoking the previous restoration order (the Northern Ireland Act 2000 (Restoration of Devolved Government) (No.2) Order 2001 (SI 2001/3231).
[52] 2000 c.1.
[53] Under s.5 of the Northern Ireland Act 1998.
[54] Under para.1(1) of the Sch. to the Northern Ireland Act 2000.

encounter in relation to Northern Ireland any of the following that may still have force[55]—

(1) Acts of the Parliament of Ireland,

(2) Acts of the Parliament of Northern Ireland,

(3) Orders in Council under s.1(3) of the Northern Ireland (Temporary Provisions) Act 1972,[56]

(4) Measures of the Northern Ireland Assembly established under s.1 of the Northern Ireland Assembly Act 1973,[57]

(5) Orders in Council under Sch.1 to the Northern Ireland Act 1974,[58]

(6) Acts of the Northern Ireland Assembly, and

(7) Orders in Council under s.85 of the Northern Ireland Act 1998.[59]

Act of the Assembly

4.3.2 The Northern Ireland Assembly[60] may, by virtue of s.5 of the Northern Ireland Act 1998, pass Bills which become Acts when they have been passed by the Assembly and have received Royal Assent.

The principal constraint on the scope of legislation made by the Assembly is the concept of legislative competence established by s.6 of the Northern Ireland Act 1998. A provision is outside the Assembly's legislative competence if it—

(1) extends outside Northern Ireland,

(2) affects functions to be exercised otherwise than in relation to Northern Ireland,

(3) deals with an excepted matter (other than in a merely ancillary way),

(4) is incompatible with those parts of the European Convention on Human Rights incorporated into the law of the United Kingdom,

---

[55] The list may be cited as a whole as "Northern Ireland legislation", see Interpretation Act 1978 (c.30), s.24(5) and Sch.1.
[56] 1972 c.22.
[57] 1973 c.17.
[58] 1974 c.28.
[59] 1998 c.47.
[60] Unlike the Scottish and Welsh devolved bodies, the Northern Ireland Assembly was not first established by the 1998 legislation. A Parliament of Northern Ireland was established by s.1(1) of the Government of Ireland Act 1920 (c.67). This was replaced by an Assembly established by the Northern Ireland Constitution Act 1973 (c.36). That was replaced by the New Northern Ireland Assembly established under the Northern Ireland (Elections) Act 1998 (c.12), the title of which was converted to the Northern Ireland Assembly by s.4(5) of the Northern Ireland Act 1998.

(5) is incompatible with the law of the European Communities,

(6) is discriminatory on the grounds of religious belief or political opinion,[61] or

(7) would interfere with an entrenched enactment.

The excepted matters are set out in Sch.2 to the 1998 Act. The principal classes of exception are— **4.3.3**

(1) The Crown and the constitution,

(2) The United Kingdom Parliament,

(3) International relations,

(4) Defence,

(5) Honours,

(6) National security,

(7) Nationality,

(8) Immigration and asylum,

(9) Taxes and duties,

(10) National insurance,

(11) Judges,

(12) Elections,

(13) Coinage,

(14) Nuclear energy,

(15) Sea fishing outside a specified Northern Ireland zone,

(16) Outer space, and

(17) Certain provisions of the 1998 Act itself.

The Assembly may legislate in respect of an excepted matter in a way which is merely incidental to other matters, but only with the consent of the Secretary of State.[62]

The entrenched enactments, listed in s.7 of the 1998 Act, with which the Assembly's legislation may not interfere are the European Communities Act

---

[61] This is unlike anything found in the Scotland or Wales Acts and reflects particular political sensitivities in Northern Ireland.

[62] s.8(a).

1972,[63] the Human Rights Act 1998[64] and certain provisions of the 1998 Act itself.

4.3.4   As well as excepted matters, Sch.3 to the 1998 Act defines a class of reserved matter. The Assembly may legislate in respect of a reserved matter, but only with the consent of the Secretary of State.[65] The class of reserved matters can be varied by Order in Council,[66] but an Order in Council for this purpose requires approval in draft by resolution of each House of Parliament, and a draft may not be laid except in response to a resolution of the Assembly, passed with cross-community support,[67] praying for the alteration of the class of reserved matters. The principal reserved matters presently are—

(1) Conferring functions in relation to Northern Ireland on a Minister of the Crown,

(2) Crown property,

(3) Navigation at sea,

(4) Civil aviation,

(5) The foreshore and sea bed,

(6) Domicile,

(7) Postal services,

(8) Qualification for membership of the Assembly and its privileges and immunities,

(9) Criminal law,

(10) Public order,

(11) The police,

(12) Firearms and explosives,

(13) Civil defence,

(14) Courts,

(15) Import and export,

(16) The minimum wage,

(17) Financial services and markets,

(18) Competition,

[63] 1972 c.68.
[64] 1998 c.40.
[65] s.8(b).
[66] s.4(2).
[67] As defined in s.4(5).

(19) Intellectual property,

(20) Weights and measures,

(21) Telecommunications,

(22) The National Lottery,

(23) Genetics and embryology,

(24) Consumer safety,

(25) Data protection, and

(26) Oaths.

When a Bill is introduced into the Assembly the Minister in charge of it must **4.3.5** make a statement that the Bill is within the Assembly's legislative competence.[68] The Presiding Officer must also scrutinise a Bill and may not permit its introduction or progress if a provision is outside the Assembly's legislative competence.[69]

The Attorney General for Northern Ireland may refer to the Judicial Committee of the Privy Council the question whether a provision of a Bill is within the Assembly's judicial competence.[70] If the Judicial Committee decide that a provision of a Bill is outside the Assembly's legislative competence, the Secretary of State may not present the Bill for Royal Assent.[71]

If a Bill passes the Assembly in reliance on the Secretary of State's consent (either because it deals with ancillary excepted matters or because it deals with reserved matters[72]) the Secretary of State may not submit it for Royal Assent unless it has been laid before the Westminster Parliament and no motion is passed within a specified period that the Bill should not be presented for Royal Assent.[73] There are certain exceptions to this, including a modified procedure in case of urgency.

Orders in Council

During any period when the Northern Ireland Assembly is suspended by order of **4.3.6** the Secretary of State under s.1 of the Northern Ireland Act 2000, an Order in Council may do anything that could be done by Act of the Assembly, by virtue of the Schedule to that Act.

The Northern Ireland Act 1998 also confers power to make provision by Order in Council dealing with a certain number of reserved matters (the most significant

---

[68] s.9.
[69] s.10.
[70] s.11.
[71] s.14(2).
[72] s.8.
[73] s.15.

being criminal law, public order, the police, firearms, civil defence, emergency powers and the courts).[74] An Order in Council of this kind requires to have been approved in draft by resolution of each House of Parliament,[75] and the draft may not be laid unless the Assembly has been consulted.[76] There is a modified scrutiny procedure for cases of urgency.[77]

There are also a large number of Orders in Council under Sch.1 to the Northern Ireland Act 1974[78] that still have effect, mostly replicating for Northern Ireland provision made for Great Britain by Act of the Westminster Parliament.

While it is open to the Westminster Parliament to legislate directly for Northern Ireland, the feeling is that the Order in Council procedure acknowledges the distinctive jurisdiction in Northern Ireland and gives a desirable degree of control to the officials in Northern Ireland over their own affairs. It is therefore generally preferred to direct legislation, even where the Order in Council is expected to do little or nothing more than transpose in the law of Northern Ireland provisions identical to those contained in the Bill for Great Britain.[79]

Subordinate legislation

4.3.7 An Act of the Westminster Parliament or an Act of the Northern Ireland Assembly may confer a function on a Northern Ireland Minister or on a Northern Ireland department.[80] The Minister or department may not, however, make subordinate legislation which—

is incompatible with a provision of the European Convention on Human Rights that is incorporated into the law of the United Kingdom,

is incompatible with the law of the European Communities,

is discriminatory on the grounds of religious belief or political opinion, or

interferes with an entrenched enactment.[81]

---

[74] s.85(1).
[75] s.85(3).
[76] s.85(4).
[77] s.85(7).
[78] 1974 c.28.
[79] Hence, for example, "It has become normal for us to allow our colleagues in Northern Ireland to implement matters in that unique way—by Orders in Council. Now is not the time to overturn that process. However, I undertake to write to my opposite number in the Northern Ireland Office to draw attention to the proceedings on the Bill in House and in Committee and to express my Hon. Friend's view, which I am happy to endorse, that Northern Ireland should consider the measures proposed in the Bill and hasten to implement as many of them as are relevant to Northern Ireland. I hope that my Hon. Friend will accept that undertaking."—Activity Centres (Young Persons' Safety) Bill—Minister speaking in Standing Committee C March 8, 1995 c.88.
[80] s.22.
[81] s.24.

If a Minister or a Northern Ireland department makes subordinate legislation which deals with an excepted or reserved matter, the Secretary of State may by order revoke the legislation (and may do so retrospectively).[82]

SECTION 4

WALES

Introduction

The Government of Wales Act 1998[83] gave effect to the policy of Welsh devolution. The principal difference between the nature of the devolution of power to Wales and the devolution of power to Scotland and to Northern Ireland is the absence of a body with power to initiate legislation of a character akin to primary legislation. There is a National Assembly for Wales,[84] but it does not consider Bills and pass Acts.[85]   **4.4.1**

Subordinate legislation

The Assembly may exercise powers transferred to it under the 1998 Act[86] or conferred on it directly by primary legislation enacted since July 1998.[87] A variety of functions were conferred by the National Assembly for Wales (Transfer of Functions) Order 1999,[88] including functions under statutes relating to—   **4.4.2**

(1) agriculture,

(2) animals,

(3) building,

(4) burial,

---

[82] s.25.

[83] 1998 c.38.

[84] Established by s.1.

[85] Extension of the Assembly's powers in various ways is sometimes discussed but has not at present been effected.

[86] s.22.

[87] The 1998 Act received the Royal Assent on July 31. Since that time it has been possible to arrange for a power to be exercised by the Assembly in relation to Wales either by having the enabling primary legislation confer it to that extent expressly on the Assembly, or by conferring it on one or more Ministers of the Crown and leaving transfer to the Assembly to be effected by Order in Council under s.22.

[88] SI 1999/672; see also the National Assembly for Wales (Transfer of Functions) (No.2) Order 1999 (SI 1999/2787), the National Assembly for Wales (Transfer of Functions) Order 2000 (SI 2000/253), the National Assembly for Wales (Transfer of Functions) (No 2) Order 2000 (SI 2000/1830), the National Assembly for Wales (Transfer of Functions) (Variation) Order 2000 (SI 2000/1829) and the National Assembly for Wales (Transfer of Functions) Order 2001 (SI 2001/3679).

(5) children,

(6) countryside,

(7) disability,

(8) discrimination,

(9) education,

(10) environment,

(11) fire services,

(12) fisheries,

(13) food safety,

(14) forestry,

(15) historic buildings and monuments,

(16) housing,

(17) industry,

(18) land law,

(19) libraries,

(20) licensing,

(21) local government,

(22) mines,

(23) planning,

(24) pollution,

(25) public health,

(26) tourism,

(27) transport, and

(28) water.

This list is included only to give a general idea of the areas in which functions are transferred to the Assembly. But by no means every function in each of these areas was transferred, and since 1999 there have been a number of varying orders,[89] and a number of Acts have conferred functions expressly on the Assembly.[90] So specific research is required in order to determine the precise area of competence of the Assembly at a given time.

---

[89] SI 2000/253, 1829, 1830 and 2001/3679.
[90] See, for example, ss.23, 42 and 50 of the Anti-social Behaviour Act 2003 (c.38).

A number of functions under private Acts or subordinate legislation have also **4.4.3** been transferred to the Assembly.

In certain cases, subordinate legislation falls to be made by the Assembly and a Minister of the Crown or Government department, acting jointly.

As a general rule, where subordinate legislation is made by the Assembly no Parliamentary procedure applies to the making of the legislation, even in a case where Parliamentary procedure is prescribed for the exercise of the same power by a Minister.[91]

There is a committee of the Assembly that has the statutory duty of scrutinising, and where necessary reporting to the Assembly about, subordinate legislation made, confirmed or approved, or proposed to be made, by the Assembly.[92] The criteria against which the committee considers the legislation referred to it are set out in the Standing Orders of the Assembly[93] as follows—

"The grounds for inviting the Assembly to pay special attention to a proposed Assembly Order or other subordinate legislation are:

(a) if there appears to be doubt whether the subordinate legislation is within the Assembly's powers or it appears to make unusual or unexpected use of the powers under which it is made;

(b) if the Act of Parliament or other instrument which gives the Assembly the power to make the subordinate legislation contains specific provisions excluding it from challenge in the courts;

(c) if it appears to have retrospective effect where the Act of Parliament or other authorising instrument does not give express authority for this;

(d) if for any particular reason its form or meaning needs further explanation;

(e) if its drafting appears to be defective or the instrument fails to fulfil statutory or other legal requirements; or

(f) if there appear to be inconsistencies between the English and Welsh texts."[94]

The procedures for the making, confirmation or approval of subordinate **4.4.4** legislation by the Assembly are prescribed partly by the Standing Orders of the Assembly[95] and partly by the Government of Wales Act 1998.[96] The most notable point about the procedures for present purposes is that under section

---

[91] Government of Wales Act 1998, s.44.
[92] Government of Wales Act 1998, s.58.
[93] Made by the Secretary of State under s.50(3) of the Government of Wales Act 1998.
[94] Standing Order 11(5). These matters are similar to those set out in the terms of reference of the United Kingdom Parliament's Joint Committee on Statutory Instruments, as to which see Chapter 6, Section 2.
[95] By virtue of s.64 of the Government of Wales Act 1998.
[96] ss.65 to 68.

68(1) of the Act they are required to include provision which in effect replicates the rule of the House of Commons[97] that legislation giving rise to significant expenditure from public funds may be initiated only on the recommendation of the Government (represented in this context by the Executive Committee of the Assembly).[98]

Subordinate legislation made by the Assembly is generally made in both English and Welsh, and the two texts have equal authority.[99] [1] The Assembly has power to make orders requiring a particular Welsh word or phrase to be construed in accordance with a specified English equivalent.[2] (It is rare but not unknown for primary legislation particularly affecting Wales to use the Welsh language.[3])

In addition to any limitation on vires imposed by the provision conferring the power to make subordinate legislation, legislation made by the Assembly is subject to the additional constraints of compatibility with European Community law[4] and with the European Convention on Human Rights.[5] There is also a procedure by which a Minister of the Crown may interfere if he believes that for the Assembly to take or to omit to take legislative (or other) action would breach any other international obligation of the United Kingdom (or where a Minister believes that legislation made by the Assembly or within its control breaches an international obligation).[6]

Schedule 8 to the Government of Wales Act 1998 establishes a procedure whereby questions as to the legislative or other competence of the Assembly may be referred to the courts, with ultimate authority lying with the Judicial Committee of the Privy Council.

Primary legislation

4.4.5 Although the Assembly has no power to pass Acts itself, it has a statutory right to be consulted by the Secretary of State for Wales about the Government's primary legislative programme.[7]

Private Bills

4.4.6 While not having the power to enact its own Acts, the Assembly has a limited power to promote or oppose private Bills in the Westminster Parliament.[8]

---

[97] As to which see Chapter 1, Section 6.

[98] s.68(1).

[99] By virtue of s.122(1) of the Government of Wales Act 1998.

[1] Despite the provision for equal authority, discrepancies in the two versions would of course cause difficulties: hence s.122(2).

[2] s.122(2).

[3] See, for example, Sch.2 to the Referendums (Scotland and Wales) Act 1997 (c.61) (form of ballot paper) and Sch.3, Table 5 (amendment of regulations); or provisions providing for a Welsh alternative title for a position.

[4] s.106(7).

[5] s.107(1).

[6] s.108.

[7] Government of Wales Act 1998, s.31.

[8] Government of Wales Act 1998, s.37.

Europe-inspired legislation

In certain circumstances the Assembly may make legislation under section 2(2) **4.4.7**
of the European Communities Act 1972[9] for the purpose of implementing an
obligation of the United Kingdom under the Community Treaties.[10]

Welsh language

While not originally anything to do with the devolution of legislative power as **4.4.8**
such, it is worth mentioning the effect of the Welsh Language Act 1993[11] in
relation to statutory modification to reflect the use of the Welsh language.
Sections 25 and 26 of that Act provide as follows—

"25 Powers to give Welsh names to statutory bodies etc

"(1) Where a name is conferred by an Act of Parliament on any body,
office or place, the appropriate Minister may by order confer on the
body, office or place an alternative name in Welsh.

"(2) Where an Act of Parliament gives power, exercisable by statutory
instrument, to confer a name on any body, office or place, the power
shall include power to confer alternative names in English and
Welsh.

"(3) Subsection (1) above does not apply in relation to a name conferred
on any area or local authority by the Local Government Act 1972.

"26 Powers to prescribe Welsh forms   4.4.9

"(1) This section applies where an Act of Parliament specifies, or confers
power to specify—

(a) the form of any document, or
(b) any form of words,

which is to be or may be used for an official or public purpose or for
any other purpose where the consequences in law of any act depend
on the form used.

"(2) Where the Act itself specifies the form of the document or the form
of words, the appropriate Minister may by order prescribe—

(a) a form of the document in Welsh, or partly in Welsh and partly
in English or, as the case may be,
(b) a form of words in Welsh,

for use in such circumstances and subject to such conditions as may
be prescribed by the order.

---

[9] 1972 c.68.
[10] Government of Wales Act 1998, s.29.
[11] 1993 c.38.

4.4.10   "(3) Where the Act confers a power to specify the form of the document or the form of words, the power shall include power to prescribe—

(a) separate forms of the document, or separate forms of words, in Welsh and in English, and

(b) in the case of a document, a form partly in Welsh and partly in English,

for use in such circumstances and subject to such conditions as may be prescribed by the instrument by which the power is exercised.

"(4) Where the powers conferred by this section are exercised in relation to the form of a document or a form of words, a reference in an Act or instrument to the form shall, so far as may be necessary, be construed as (or as including) a reference to the form prescribed under or by virtue of this section.

"(5) This section shall not apply in relation to a provision which—

(a) confers, or gives power to confer, a name on any body, office or place, or

(b) requires specified words to be included in the name of any body, office or place."

Orders under s.25(1) or 26(2) are made by statutory instrument subject to negative resolution procedure.[12] The powers under ss.25 and 26 are now exercisable concurrently by the appropriate Minister and the National Assembly for Wales.[13] Each of them has been used on a number of occasions.[14] The powers under each section are available in relation to Acts passed after the 1993 Act itself.[15] Provision is made for determining the appropriate Minister.[16]

---

[12] s.27(3).

[13] See art.2 of, and Sch.1 to, the National Assembly for Wales (Transfer of Functions) Order 1999 (SI 1999/672).

[14] For examples of the use of s.25 see the Velindre National Health Service Trust (Establishment) Amendment Order 1999 (SI 1999/826), the Swansea (1999) National Health Service Trust (Change of Name) Order 1999 (SI 1999/1321) and the Cardiff and Vale National Health Service Trust Establishment Order 1999 (SI 1999/3451). For examples of the use of s.26 see the National Assembly for Wales (Oath of Allegiance in Welsh) Order 1999 (SI 1999/1101), the European Parliamentary Elections (Welsh Forms) (Amendment) Order 1999 (SI 1999/1402), the Legal Aid in Criminal and Care Proceedings (General) (Amendment) (No.3) Regulations 1999 (SI 1999/2123), the Legal Aid in Criminal and Care Proceedings (General) (Amendment) (No.5) Regulations 1999 (SI 1999/2737), the Powers of Attorney (Welsh Language Forms) Order 2000, (SI 2000/215), the Non-Domestic Rating (Demand Notices) (Amendment) (Wales) Regulations 2000 (SI 2000/793), the Elections (Welsh Forms) Order 2001 (SI 2001/1204), the National Assembly for Wales (Elections: Nomination Papers) (Welsh Form) Order 2001 (SI 2001/2914), the Local Elections (Declaration of Acceptance of Office) (Amendment) (Wales) Order 2001 (SI 2001/2963), the Education (Budget Statements) (Wales) Regulations 2002 (SI 2002/122), the Penalties for Disorderly Behaviour (Form of Penalty Notice) Regulations 2002 (SI 2002/1838), the Attestation of Constables (Welsh Language) Order 2002 (SI 2002/2312) and the Non-Domestic Rating (Demand Notices) (Amendment) (Wales) Regulations 2003 (SI 2003/414).

[15] s.27(4).

[16] s.27(4) and (5).

Part 2

THE LEGISLATIVE PROCESS

CHAPTER 5

PRIMARY LEGISLATION

SECTION 1

PREPARATION

Responsibility for the drafting of Bills

The Bills for almost all Acts of Parliament are drafted by lawyers working, as civil servants, in the Office of the Parliamentary Counsel.[1] There are presently about fifty draftsmen in the Office, divided into teams of two or three. Each team

5.1.1

---

[1] Historically, statutes have been drafted at different times in different ways. Before 1487 a committee composed of judges, counsellors and officials routinely drafted the statutes in Latin or Norman French, taking as their instructions the Parliament Rolls which were not engrossed until the conclusion of Each Parliament. In other words either or both Houses of Parliament petitioned for remedy of a particular grievance but left the terms of the remedial Act to the King in Council. The statutes when drafted were engrossed on the statute roll. In this way "Parliament recognised that those who administered the law were supposed to have a real, and not a merely nominal, hearing in the making of laws" (Y. B. 14 & 15 Edw. 3, Pref. By Pike, p.lxii; and see Stubbs, *Constitutional History*, Vol.2, pp.571 and 575, and Anson, *Law and Custom of the Constitution*, Vol.1, 5th ed., 1922, p.260). This practice led to difficulties and controversies between the Commons and the Crown—in a manner not entirely dissimilar to difficulties about the delegation of legislative powers today—and was (see 1 Clifford, *History of Private Bill Legislation*, 1885, p.326) finally discontinued in the reign of Henry VIII (who is, ironically, credited with the invention of the mechanism by which powers may be delegated to the executive to amend primary legislation) by the regularising of the practice of appending a Bill to demands send to the King and by the addition in 1433 of the words "by authority of Parliament" to the words of enactment. From the reign of Henry VIII onwards petition ceased to be the method of instigating laws in relation to public matters and the use of the Bill became uniform (see *Stubbs* and *Anson* cited above). According to Redlich and Ilbert's *The Procedure of the House of Commons* (London, 1908, Vol.I, p.15), the principal reason for the tension in relation to and the eventual abandonment of the practice of having Bills drawn by the judges in response to a petition was the perception that the Bills insufficiently matched the petitions to which they were addressed, so that Bills produced by Parliament became used as a way of expressing a precise demand for action rather than requesting that a solution be found by the judges. Again according to Redlich and Ilbert, Henry V in essence surrendered on this point in 1414. In the reign of Richard III began the sessional publication of printed statutes in a statute roll which from 1487 was produced, in English rather than Latin or Norman French, by conveyancers. It is, however, apparent that certain judges have played a role in advising or assisting in the matter of legislative drafting from time to time over the years: see, for example, the quotation from Stephen J. at Chapter 8, Section 1, para.8.1.6; and for a recent example, note that between 1994 and 1996 Lord Saville of Newdigate chaired a committee of officials which considered arbitration legislation and was closely involved in the production of the Bill for the Arbitration Act 1996. As to the common drafting of statutes by judges in past centuries, note Hengham CJ to Counsel in a case on the 2nd Statute of Westminster—"Ne glossez point le Statut: nous le savons meuz de vous, qar nous le feimes." (Do not expound the statute to us: we know it better than you because we made it) (33–35 Ed. 1, (R.S.) 83).

203

is at any one time responsible for one or more Bills or discrete parts of a Bill. Although originally principally associated with the Treasury,[2] the Office is now part of the Cabinet Office, but headed by its own Permanent Secretary, the First Parliamentary Counsel.

A small number of Bills not drafted by Parliamentary Counsel find their way onto the statute book. The kind of Bill that is often thought to provide the most significant example of this, Law Commission Consolidation Bills and Law Reform Bills, is not in fact an example at all: these are drafted by Parliamentary Counsel working on secondment to the Law Commission. Counsel are also routinely seconded to the Tax Law Rewrite Project,[3] and are often involved in other Government projects.[4]

5.1.2　　Almost all primary legislation starts life as a Bill presented by the Government of the day to Parliament, whether in the House of Lords or the House of Commons.

Large numbers of Bills are presented by non-Government members in both Houses, but few of these reach the statute book. Indeed they are generally presented without any real hope that they will become law but with the hope only that they will attract attention in Parliament and outside, with the eventual aim of creating sufficient pressure on the Government to produce their own legislation on the subject in due course.[5] This is particularly effective in the House of Lords, where by convention the Government does not enjoy anything like the close degree of control over the Order Paper that it has in the House of Commons[6]: the result is that a peer who introduces a Bill can normally arrange that it is debated on a number of occasions.[7]

A small number of private Members' or peers' Bills will reach the statute book. This will be for one of three reasons—

---

[2] The Office was established by Treasury Minute on February 8, 1869. A graphic, although dated, account of life in the Office can be found in the autobiography of Sir Harold S. Kent GCB, QC, DCL, *In on the Act—Memoirs of a Lawmaker*, Macmillan, 1979. The nature and problems of the Office are also discussed in detail in *The Preparation of Legislation*, Report of a Committee appointed by the Lord President of the Council, chaired by the Rt. Hon Sir (later Lord) David Renton, May 1975, Cmnd. 6053.

[3] This is a Government project within the Inland Revenue, initiated by a report to Parliament in December 1995, which aims to rewrite the direct tax legislation of the United Kingdom in clearer and simpler language. There is a special procedure for handling Bills produced as part of this project—see House of Commons Standing Orders No.60. See further Chapter 1, Section 10.

[4] Most significantly, they routinely supervise the drafting of subordinate legislation that amends the text of primary legislation.

[5] To give one recent example, the issue of fox-hunting was brought back to prominent attention in the House of Commons by Mr. Michael Foster M.P.'s private Member Bill in 1997. That Bill failed, but it was succeeded in the following Session by a Government Bill presenting a number of options to the two Houses. That Bill also failed and was followed in the Session 2002–03 by a single-option Government Bill (which did not pass through the House of Lords).

[6] In the House of Commons the Government controls the business on each day's Order Paper with the exception of Opposition Days, private Members' Fridays and days named by the Chairman of Ways and Means for private Business—all of which are allocated and regulated by the Standing Orders.

[7] Two for a Bill that has a second reading and then passes straight to third reading, three or four for a Bill which goes into Committee between second and third readings.

At some stage before or during the passage of a Bill the Government may reach the conclusion that it favours the principle of the Bill and is prepared to support it, or even to provide some time to debate it.[8]

The Bill may have gained a high place in the ballot for private Members' Bills in the House of Commons.[9]

There may be a majority against the Government on a particular topic.[10]

A private Member's or private peer's Bill will generally have been drafted **5.1.3** either by the private Member or peer[11] or by a lawyer working for or remunerated by a pressure group anxious to secure the passage of the Bill.

In many Bills there are provisions that apply wholly or principally to things in or done in Northern Ireland or Scotland. And it is not unknown for a Bill to extend solely to Scotland or Northern Ireland. This is less common after devolution than it was before, but there are still a large number of matters in respect of which provision in a Westminster Act, or a whole Westminster Act, is either required or likely to be thought desirable.[12] Provisions or Bills that wholly affect Scotland or Northern Ireland are generally drafted by officials in Scotland and in Northern Ireland, liasing (except in the case of an entirely Scottish or Northern Irish Bill) with the Parliamentary Counsel in charge of the Bill.

---

[8] An example is the Activity Centres (Young Persons' Safety) Act 1995 (c.15) which started life as a private Member's Bill in the Commons but was accorded Government support and technical assistance. See the following passage of the speech of the proposer of the Bill, David Jamieson M.P., on the Third Reading of the Bill (HC Deb. March 24, 1995 c.645)—"With your permission, Mr. Deputy Speaker, I should like to thank one or two people who have assisted me with the Bill. I pay tribute to the Minister of State, Department for Education for his support in getting the Bill through the House. Had it not been for his support, we would not be participating in the Third Reading debate today. I thank him for his contribution in getting the Bill through the House. I also thank the silent ones behind him, his civil servants, who have been so helpful in seeing the Bill through Parliament. The Minister did them credit today by reading out the brief that they had written for him—and excellent it was too."

[9] The ballot, held under Standing Orders, has the effect of giving twenty Bills each Session priority in the allocation of time on private Members' Fridays. In the normal order of events, a Bill in one of the first seven places has a reasonable chance of passing through the Commons even in the face of spirited opposition, provided that there is a majority in favour of the principle of the Bill. Once the Bill has passed the House of Commons, even if it fails to pass the House of Lords s.2 of the Parliament Act 1911 (c.13) would allow the Lords to be by-passed and the Bill to proceed for Royal Assent if it were successfully re-introduced in the Commons in the following Session. Bills brought in by Members not successful in the ballot, or only securing a low place, will pass only if there is no opposition.

[10] It is rare that this results in the passage of an entire Bill, because of the number of stages and amount of time in each House required. But it is by no means rare for this to result in the addition to a Bill of a provision, or the making of an amendment, that the Government did not support.

[11] A limited amount of assistance for this purpose is provided by the clerks in the Public Bill Office in each House, although they are not lawyers and are unlikely to feel able to draft on any technical or complicated matter, or to guarantee the effectiveness of subsidiary provisions on enforcement or the like. And a small grant is made to cover the employment of professional assistance. For recommendations on the development of these facilities see the Fourth Report of the House of Commons Select Committee on Procedure of the House for Session 2002–03 (HC 333), para.50.

[12] See Chapter 4.

The process of drafting a Bill

5.1.4   A Bill assigned to Parliamentary Counsel is drafted by him or her on instructions from lawyers[13] working within the Department responsible for the subject matter of the Bill. Sometimes collaboration between two or more Departments is necessary, either with each being responsible for instructing on separate parts of the Bill or with shared responsibility for some or all of the instructions. The departmental lawyers are, in turn, acting on instructions from their administrative clients within the department.

For the most part the process of turning the instructions into draft legislation is conducted by correspondence, with drafts passing between the draftsman and the Department until both are satisfied. Meetings are sometimes necessary, and on a particularly complicated or politically sensitive Bill many meetings, sometimes involving Ministers, may be necessary.

The principles to be applied in drafting are discussed in Chapter 8.

There is a tendency to regard Parliamentary Counsel as the root of all legislative evil, or at least as the source of all legislative obscurity and prolixity. In debates in Parliament one will frequently hear the drafting nominally attacked where the speaker is actually taking exception to the substance of the provision concerned. That apart, it is true that Parliamentary Counsel are subject to a number of constraints that can result in provisions being less satisfactory than either Counsel or the reader would like.[14] These include the time pressures under which Bills are often required to be prepared, the framework within which Acts are required to be drafted[15] and sometimes the need to make changes during the passage of a Bill with, for reasons of economy with Parliamentary time, as little structural change as possible.[16] But the difficulty of the exercise and its occasional successes are also sometimes recognised, whether generally or specifically.[17]

---

[13] It is rare for administrators to instruct Counsel directly, although it is common for lawyers and administrators to meet Counsel together to discuss matters arising during the preparation or progress of a Bill. The principal exception is in relation to the annual Finance Bill, where it is usual for administrative specialists within the Inland Revenue to instruct Counsel directly.

[14] And this is generally recognised even by some of the most tenacious critics of legislative drafting: see, for example, the following observation by Lord Simon of Glaisdale, one of the peers most closely interested in matters of legislative drafting—"Even by present standards this is a very prolix Bill. It must not be thought that I blame the parliamentary draftsmen who are generally fine lawyers and people of great skill. They are working under very great pressure. Members of the Committee will remember that Bernard Shaw once apologised for writing a long letter because he did not have time to write a short one. Any draftsman . . . will know that it is much easier to draft loosely and discursively rather than economically. So your Lordships are fully entitled to satisfy themselves that the provisions in the Bill are really necessary."—HL Deb. January 19, 1999 cc.490–491 re the Access to Justice Bill 1998–99.

[15] See Chapter 8, Section 1, para.8.1.10.

[16] See further Chapter 8, Section 1, para.8.1.5.

[17] Note, for example, "First, I am grateful to the hon. Gentleman for the tribute that he has paid to Parliamentary Counsel. The Government—and, in that sense, the House—get an absolutely first-class service from these people, who are a somewhat insufficiently sung part of the legislative and governmental process."—Leader of the House of Commons HC Deb. July 11, 1996 c.639.

The legislative programme

Before each Parliamentary Session the Government prepares a list of Bills that **5.1.5** are intended to be introduced during the Session. Some of these, but not necessarily all, will be announced in the Queen's Speech at the State Opening of Parliament. The list is approved by the Cabinet as a whole, but responsibility for its preparation is delegated to the Cabinet Ministerial Committee currently[18] known as the Legislative Programme Committee (commonly referred to simply as LP).

Membership of the Legislative Programme Committee varies slightly over the years, but the Committee includes and principally consists of those Ministers with responsibility for Business Management in each House[19] and Ministers with legal or constitutional responsibility.

The present terms of reference of the Legislative Programme Committee are as follows—

> "To prepare and submit to Cabinet drafts of the Queen's speeches to Parliament and proposals for the legislative programme; to monitor the progress of Bills in preparation and during their passage through Parliament; to review the programme as necessary; to examine all draft Bills; to consider the Parliamentary handling of Government Bills, EC documents, and Private Members' business, and such other related matters as may be necessary; and to keep under review the Government's policy in relation to issues of Parliamentary procedures."

By far the most time-consuming part of the Committee's work is the **5.1.6** consideration of draft Bills and their approval for introduction. The official secretariat of the Committee liase with the department responsible for a Bill and with Parliamentary Counsel throughout the preparation of the Bill. Papers are circulated around the Committee reporting on progress from time to time. Finally, in a typical case, shortly before introduction the Bill will be considered at a meeting of the Committee and approved for introduction. At that Committee

---

[18] The name of this Committee has changed over the years, but its essential functions have not: except that until 2000 there were separate Committees, one dealing with the preparation of the Queen's Speech for the next Session and one dealing with the management of the Parliamentary legislative business of the current Session—the two committees were merged and all the functions are now performed by LP.

[19] In 2003 membership of LP was as follows: Leader of the House of Commons, Lord Privy Seal and Secretary of State for Wales (Chair); Deputy Prime Minister and First Secretary of State; Secretary of State for Transport and Secretary of State for Scotland; Secretary of State for Northern Ireland; Leader of the House of Lords and Lord President of the Council; Chief Secretary, Treasury; Parliamentary Secretary, Treasury and Chief Whip; Minister without Portfolio; Secretary of State for Constitutional Affairs; Chief Whip (House of Lords) and Captain of the Gentleman-at-Arms; Minister for the Cabinet Office and Chancellor of the Duchy of Lancaster; Attorney General; Advocate General; Deputy Leader of the House of Commons; Parliamentary Under Secretary of State, Wales Office. A Minister in the Foreign and Commonwealth Office was also, although not a full member of the Committee, a regular recipient of Committee papers.

meeting a Minister from the responsible department will be invited to attend, unless already a member of the Committee, to present the Bill and discuss its Parliamentary handling. The Parliamentary Counsel drafting the Bill also attends the Committee to advise about readiness and any procedural or handling matters of particular interest.

The Legislation Committee is not a policy committee: the policy of each Bill brought to the Committee must already have been approved by the relevant Ministerial Cabinet Committee[20]—the Committee is concerned only with the Parliamentary handling aspects of the Bill (sometimes referred to as the Business Management aspects).

The Legislation Committee monitors the progress of a Bill through Parliament. In particular, the Committee is responsible for approving significant proposals for the amendment of the Bill.

5.1.7   In order to manage effectively and efficiently a programme of primary legislation that Parliament can scrutinise properly in the time available[21] it is necessary to limit the area with which each Bill deals fairly rigorously.

Here the Parliamentary rules of scope[22] assist. They prevent the tabling of amendments on, or the discussion of matters relating to, issues not within the scope of the Bill as introduced.[23] The Government can be reasonably sure that a Bill designed to make one set of changes in the law will not be swamped by the actual or attempted introduction of a large number of entirely new matters.[24]

It occasionally happens that the Government wish to change the law in a particular respect but have no available vehicle in the legislative programme for effecting the change. One of the Bills already assigned to the programme might be able to deal with some of the issue, but not the whole, without the effect being an unacceptable expansion of the Bill's scope. That will explain why certain legislative provisions appear narrower than one might expect.[25]

---

[20] Most frequently that on Domestic Affairs (DA).

[21] Particularly bearing in mind that, subject to the procedures for carry-over discussed in Section 2 below, every Bill introduced in one Session has to pass through all its Parliamentary stages in that Session.

[22] Technically referred to in the House of Lords as relevance.

[23] See further Section 2 below.

[24] The rules are not, of course, particularly rigorous, especially in the House of Lords. But they do provide significant protection, and the tighter the scope of the Bill as introduced the more effective that protection is likely to be. In particular, a Bill restricted to one or two distinct issues will be strongly protected from the introduction of others (the "one-topic" and "two-topic" rules). Once a Bill has three or more topics, the scope of the Bill becomes the area of substance of which those topics are examples, which can be a difficult concept to apply in relation to a Bill. In the case of certain "portmanteau" Bills—the best example being the occasional Criminal Justice Bills—scope can be so wide that more or less any change in the law that a person wanted to introduce could be crafted as a selectable amendment.

[25] s.145 of the Nationality, Immigration and Asylum Act 2002 (c.41), for example, addresses the issue of traffic in prostitution. But in order to preserve the already wide scope of the Bill for the 2002 Act the section is limited to traffic which involves an international element. See the Ministerial comments (Lord Bassam of Brighton) in the debate on the clause which became s.145—HL Deb. July 23, 2002 c.301.

Supporting documents

The team of officials responsible for the preparation and passage of a Bill will in the course of their activities prepare a considerable amount of material of different kinds, some of which is intended only for the briefing of Ministers but some of which will or may find its way into the public domain. **5.1.8**

Explanatory notes

Explanatory Notes are discussed at length in Chapter 9, Section 5. All that need be said about them here is that their preparation commonly begins at an early stage of the drafting of a Bill and may occupy a good deal of the time of the departmental division responsible for the Bill. **5.1.9**

Explanatory Notes replaced for the most part the old system of notes on clauses, which were produced as a clause-by-clause commentary for the use of Ministers, but were often distributed, in whole or in part, to people with particular interest in the content of the Bill, such as members of the Standing Committee on the Bill in the House of Commons. In most cases notes on clauses were not found to be particularly illuminating.[26]

Regulatory impact assessment

A Regulatory Impact Assessment is now routinely prepared and published for every Bill.[27] Briefly, this is "an assessment of the impact of policy options in terms of the costs, benefits and risks of a proposal." A fuller description of the nature and purpose of the document is provided by the extract of *Better Policy Making: A guide to Regulatory Impact Assessment*[28] appended to this work.[29] **5.1.10**

Keeling Schedule

A Keeling Schedule[30] is a Schedule to a Bill setting out how the text of provisions of another piece of legislation will appear once textually amended by the Bill. It is obviously of considerable assistance to readers of any Bill which **5.1.11**

---

[26] A notable exception is the annual Finance Bill where it was routine, long before the introduction of the Explanatory Notes for other Bills, to prepare and make publicly available detailed technical commentaries on each provision by way of notes on clauses.

[27] According to a policy announced by the Government in March 1998.

[28] *Better Policy Making: A guide to Regulatory Impact Assessment*—a Cabinet Office publication published in January 2003 and available on the Cabinet Office website.

[29] Appendix, Extract 11.

[30] So called because "it was adopted as a trial in 1938 to meet a complaint by several Members of the House of Commons headed by Mr. E.H. Keeling (later Sir Edward Keeling) and Mr. R.P. Croom-Johnson (later Mr Justice Croom-Johnson, father of the present judge) that there was far too much legislation by reference which Members could not understand without the texts of the principal Acts referred to as they would appear if amended."—Renton Report (*Report on the Preparation of Legislation*) (Cmnd. 6053), para.13.21.

209

contains many textual amendments of an Act, particularly if, as frequently happens, the amendments do not follow in the Bill the same sequence as the provisions which they amend in the Act.

It is rare nowadays for a Keeling Schedule to be incorporated in a Bill. But they are still widely used as informal methods of explaining the effect of a Bill or of subordinate legislation.[31]

SECTION 2

PASSAGE OF PUBLIC BILL THROUGH PARLIAMENT

NORMAL PROCEDURE

Introduction

5.2.1   It is not the role of this work to attempt a thorough description of the procedures and practices in accordance with which a Bill proceeds through Parliament and becomes an Act. The authoritative description of the process will be found in Erskine May's *Treatise on the Law, Privileges, Proceedings and Usage of Parliament* which under the auspices of the Erskine May Memorial Trust is from time to time revised by officials of the two Houses of Parliament.[32] Additional information can be had by referring to the Standing Orders of each House and other abbreviated information made available by each House on its website.

What follows is merely a brief summary of the passage of a Bill, designed to serve the purpose of setting the scene for those readers whose interest in the matter arises as background to the study of legislation and for whom comprehensive technical details of the process are therefore unnecessary.

The procedures for consideration of a Bill are broadly similar in each House of Parliament, but there are some variations of significance. This Section begins

---

[31] See, for example the following exchange in the House of Lords (HL Deb. December 10, 2003 c.750)—

> "**Baroness Anelay of St Johns:** My Lords, is not my noble friend Lord Renton right to have brought the House's attention to the fact that it is important to have consolidation of statute so that there is information which is clear to all about what the law actually means? While welcoming the very constructive answer of the noble and learned Lord, may I invite him to go further? As a first stage towards this review, on each and every occasion that a Bill is presented to this House, could we not have a Keeling schedule so that all matters may be properly debated and the public may see those matters?
>
> **Lord Goldsmith:** My Lords, as the noble Baroness will recall, during passage of the Bill—certainly during passage of the part for which I was responsible—I made available to noble Lords taking part in the debate not quite a Keeling schedule, which would appear in the Act, but a print of what the statute would look like if the amendments were made.".

Or see the Written Ministerial Statement by the Secretary of State for Culture, Media and Sport February 10, 2004—"The Department for Culture, Media and Sport has today published a draft Community Radio Order, associated Keeling Schedule and Explanatory Memorandum for public consultation. Copies of these documents are available in the House Libraries, or from the department's website."

[32] When this work went to print the current edition was the 23rd ed. 2004.

by describing the procedure in the House of Commons, and then summarises the differences that affect procedure in the House of Lords.

Certain classes of public Bill are subjected to significant variations from the normal procedure. These are described in Section 3. The passage of non-public Bills is considered in Section 4.

Status of Bill

A Bill is of no legal effect until such time as it has been given the royal Assent and become an Act of Parliament.[33] Until that time it is merely a proposal for legislation.

5.2.2

Parts of a Bill

The only difference between the terminology for Bills and that for their resulting Acts is that the principal sub-division of a Bill is a clause, which becomes a section on enactment.

The principal sub-division of a clause is a subsection: there is no such thing as a "sub-clause", although the term is sometimes used colloquially (occasionally even by Parliamentarians).

Other divisions are as for Acts.[34]

5.2.3

Pre-legislative scrutiny

It is now generally agreed that an opportunity for committees of each House, or a Joint Committee of both Houses, to consider a draft of a Bill in advance of its introduction, and therefore at a time when substantive comments and suggestions can be accommodated with comparative ease, produces benefits for Government, Parliament and citizens alike.[35]

5.2.4

---

[33] But see further Chapter 2, Section 1.

[34] See Chapter 2, Section 5.

[35] See in particular the following passage of the Report of the House of Commons Select Committee on the Modernisation of the House of Commons, First Report, Session 1997–98, July 23, 1997, paras 19 & 20—"The present Government's declared intention to build on its predecessor's policy of publishing a number of Bills in draft form provides a real chance for the House to exercise its powers of pre-legislative scrutiny in an effective way. Although it is unrealistic to expect all or most major bills to be published in draft, it can reasonably be hoped that such a practice will grow wherever appropriate. There is almost universal agreement that pre-legislative scrutiny is right in principle, subject to the circumstances and nature of the legislation. It provides an opportunity for the House as a whole, for individual backbenchers, and for the Opposition to have a real input into the form of the actual legislation which subsequently emerges, not least because Ministers are likely to be far more receptive to suggestions for change before the Bill is actually published. It opens Parliament up to those outside affected by legislation. At the same time such pre-legislative scrutiny can be of real benefit to the Government. It could, and indeed should, lead to less time being needed at later stages of the legislative process; the use of the Chair's powers of selection would naturally reflect the extent and nature or previous scrutiny and debate. Above all, it should lead to better legislation and less likelihood of subsequent amending legislation."

Note also the following passages from the speech of the Deputy Leader of the House of Commons (Mr. Phil Woolas M.P.) in a Westminster Hall debate on pre-legislative scrutiny (HC Deb. February 24, 2004 17WH—20WH)—" . . . Pre-legislative scrutiny gives Parliament and

What was once a rarity has therefore become relatively common-place.[36] But as is generally acknowledged, there will still be many Bills for which pre-legislative scrutiny is not appropriate or possible, whether because of the urgency with which they have to be prepared and introduced for practical or political reasons, or because of the politically or commercially sensitive nature of their content, or for some other reason.[37]

There is a range of options for the way in which pre-legislative scrutiny is performed. A Bill can be referred to one of the existing permanent Select

---

stakeholders in the wider society an opportunity to influence the Bill's content when the Government's views have not been firmly set—the so-called set-in-stone stage. Examples given include the Civil Contingencies Bill, which is a good one, the Gambling Bill and the Communications Bill. Hon. Members on both sides of the House have acknowledged that all were improved by the process of pre-legislative scrutiny. . . .

"One purpose of pre-legislative scrutiny and draft publication is to connect better the process of law making with the public. It cannot be right that the intent of Parliament, which it is the purpose of law making to reflect, should more often be subject to interpretation by the courts rather than the clarity of the laws that are passed in this place. If we wish to connect the public with Parliament and encourage public consent for, and better understanding of, the laws that we pass, we must ensure that people have an opportunity to influence the law, either directly or through their various representatives in the form of pressure groups and interest groups, as well as their MP. We must ensure, first, that they believe that they can have an input and, secondly, that they better understand the law and its intent.

"All MPs regularly experience in their constituency criticisms of the law, of what is believed to be the law and of what is believed to be the intent of Parliament. Unless the courts and the public have an opportunity clearly to understand that intent, the consent for Parliament will diminish and the political process will be damaged. Pre-legislative scrutiny is an opportunity to improve the law in its intent and clarity. That is the important point."

[36] "I should like to move towards a position where we can announce in future a two-year legislative programme and, so far as possible, publish draft Bills and consult on the second year's Bills before they are introduced. That will take time to bring about, but I think that it is a worthwhile reform which will deliver better legislation. We have begun to move in that direction this year, with two draft Bills set out in the Gracious Speech, In future years, I anticipate steadily increasing the number of draft Bills brought before the House."—The Prime Minister speaking in the Debate on the Address HC Deb. October 23, 1996 c.3.

And note the following passage from the speech of the Deputy Leader of the House of Commons (Mr Phil Woolas M.P.) in a Westminster Hall debate on pre-legislative scrutiny (HC Deb. February 24, 2004 17WH–20WH)—"It is, I think, widely accepted that the Government are committed to [pre-legislative scrutiny]. We have shown that by our actions and have greatly increased the number of Bills that are published in draft form. Hon. Members may be interested in the figures: there were three draft Bills in 1997–98, followed by six in each of the following two years, two in the election year, six in 2001–02, nine in the last Session and, as has been said, possibly 12 in the current Session. We are committed to increasing the number of draft Bills."

[37] See the following passages from the speech of the Deputy Leader of the House of Commons (Mr Phil Woolas M.P.) in a Westminster Hall debate on pre-legislative scrutiny (HC Deb. February 24, 2004 17WH–20WH)—"It is not always possible in the sausage factory production of legislation to be precise. I am happy to place on the record that Departments rightly have to take advice from parliamentary counsel, whose function it is to probe and to seek clarification of intent. Sometimes there are unforeseen consequences in the preparation and sometimes it is not always possible to publish in draft form. That is a long-winded way of saying that it is not a perfect world.

" . . . the House must understand that our legislative programme must have some flexibility and that the provisional list of draft Bills will be subject to change. The Government's proposals are subject to discussion in the usual channels in both Houses of Parliament—the Lords and the Commons—both of which we must take into account. For example, following such discussions it

Committees charged with monitoring the activities of the Government department which has principal responsibility for the substance of the Bill. Or a Select Committee can be constituted expressly for the purpose of considering the draft Bill. Or a Joint Committee of both Houses can be established for that purpose.

In any case the committee will have the usual powers to call witnesses and hear evidence, which, apart from the inevitably greater substantive flexibility when the Bill is still in an early draft form, is the principal advantage which the pre-legislative scrutiny process has over the methods routinely used to consider Bills once introduced.

The Joint Committee route is particularly favoured for obvious reasons. It enables members of each House to benefit from the particular expertise, experience and interests of members of the other House. And it provides a single, and therefore efficient, forum for exposing the background of the policy of the Bill to each House, thereby preparing for more informed and focused debate once the Bill is introduced.[38]

5.2.5

Provided that a draft Bill is described as such, and does not purport to be an advance copy of that which Parliament will publish as a Bill, there is no breach of privilege or propriety in making a draft Bill available either for consultation well in advance of introduction or for more limited exposure shortly before introduction.[39]

---

was agreed to introduce the civil partnerships Bill in this Session rather than as a draft Bill as the Government originally proposed. . . .

"Drafting resources may need to be diverted to other priorities and slippage may mean that there is insufficient time for publication in draft.

" . . . My view and, more importantly, the Government's view is that a Bill should be published in draft form unless there are good reasons for not doing so. Such reasons may be broader than my hon. Friend suggested. He talked about the need to respond to emergencies and about the 11 September tragedy, but other forces majeures may require a legislative response from the Government. There may also be financial pressures, and the financial year is a key determinant in planning the legislative programme. I can also reveal that the business managers set about the timetable for the Higher Education Bill because of demands by the printers of university prospectuses.It was therefore a real-world timetable, which had little to do with the parliamentary timetable.

"Some Bills are timetabled in response to decisions by our courts and the European courts. The timetable for the Gender Recognition Bill, which had its Second Reading yesterday, was drafted in response to the need to protect the British taxpayer against liabilities as a result of the judgment by the European Court of Human Rights. Those are examples of real-world pressures on timetables. Famous 'events' can also change things. However, on the basis of a shared understanding of that framework, the Government's objective is to move towards the presumption of a draft Bill."

[38] For an example of a motion establishing a joint committee to consider a draft Bill see the motions for the Civil Contingencies Draft Bill, Lords Journals June 12, 2003 and July 11, 2003 and Commons Journals July 10, 2003.

[39] "The Government are frequently encouraged to print Bills in advance so that their contents may be widely known and circulated. Also, many hon. Members apply to introduce a ten-minute Bill and give details to the press. I can see no objection to that. Such Bills are simply in draft form at that stage, and I take no exception to the practice . . . "—Madam Speaker replying to Point of Order HC Deb. June 6, 1996 c.728.

Introduction

5.2.6 A Bill can be introduced into either House of Parliament. In the case of a Government Bill, the choice is made by the Government.[40] A peer or a Member of Parliament can introduce a Bill only into the House to which he or she belongs.

Bills of a principally or significantly financial nature are likely to start in the House of Commons.[41] This is one aspect of the Commons financial privilege, the notion that it is for the Commons alone to propose and control public expenditure and taxation. The doctrine of the Commons financial privilege is now both significantly eroded and regarded in part as an obscure technicality. But it is still honoured both procedurally and substantively to some extent, both in rules as to introduction and as evidenced in particular by the minimal degree of scrutiny which by convention is given in the House of Lords to certain financial Bills.[42] There was a time, however, when the Commons' financial prerogative was considered both inside and outside Parliament as being of the essence of the balance between the two Houses, and the application of the prerogative and its importance was a matter of common public knowledge and frequent reference.[43]

5.2.7 In the House of Commons the normal method of introducing a Government Bill is for Notice of Presentation to be handed in on one day to appear on the Order Paper of the next day, and for the Bill to be introduced on that next day,

---

[40] There is a Ministerial Committee of the Cabinet, known as the Legislative Programme Committee and chaired by the Leader of the House of Commons and President of the Council, which considers into which House a Bill should be introduced. See further Section 1 above.

[41] And a Bill "of aids and supplies" (broadly speaking, taxation) can start only in the House of Commons.

[42] This is a matter of occasional controversy in relation to Consolidated Fund Bills, where a minority of peers have sometimes suggested substantive debate should be permissible. But the majority of the House of Lords has consistently declined to alter the convention by which these Bills are not considered (see the First Report from the House of Lords Select Committee on Procedure of the House Session 1995–96 (HL Paper 8) and the debate on the Report HL Deb. December 13, 1995 cc.1279–1288).

[43] See, by way of piquant illustration, the following passage from the Editorial of the Beccles & Bungay Weekly News for Tuesday May 22, 1860 (entitled *The Lords, The Commons and the Paper Duty*)—"The Paper Duty Abolition Bill has received the sanction of the Commons, has been sent upto the Lords for approval, and the Lords threaten rejection. Now this bill is a money bill. . . . So that the Lords, by rejecting this bill would directly and indirectly interfere with the prerogatives of the House of Commons. It is a question of taxation, and so long ago as 1678 it was resolved by the House of Commons: 'That all aids and supplies, and aids to his Majesty in parliament, are the sole gift of the Commons; and all bills for the granting of any such aids and supplies ought to begin with the Commons; and that it is the undoubted and sole right of the Commons to direct, limit, and appoint in such bills, the ends, purposes, considerations, conditions, limitations, and qualifications of such grants,which ought not to be changed or altered by the House of Lords'. . . . The bill is a money bill—being a money bill it belongs of right to the Commons, and there is no sufficient cause for the Lords to deviate from the usual course.".

It was the same Bill that Trollope realistically made the subject of a local debating club in *The Struggles of Brown, Jones and Robinson* (1861–62).

with publication either on that day or on the third day.[44] Certain Bills relating to financial matters are preceded by resolutions authorising that provision be made for the substance of the Bill concerned: the Finance Bill is the obvious and annual example, being preceded by the resolutions on which the Budget debate is held.[45]

First Reading (Commons)

A Bill is deemed to be read a first time on introduction. There is no substance to this process, and no debate.   **5.2.8**

The Bill is presented by one Member of Parliament, who may be supported by a number of others: nominally the supporters assist in the preparation of the Bill, but their contribution is generally limited to permitting their names to appear as supporters on the back of the Bill.[46] A Government Bill is generally presented by the senior Minister of the department with principal responsibility for the subject matter of the Bill, supported by a small number of other senior Ministers (frequently including the Prime Minister) and one or two junior Ministers.[47]

Human Rights Act Statement

The statement required to be made before Second Reading in respect of   **5.2.9**
compliance with the Human Rights Act 1998 is discussed in Chapter 11, Section 3.

Second Reading (Commons)

The first debate about a Bill takes place on a motion that it be read a Second   **5.2.10**
Time. The second reading is the opportunity for a general debate about the

---

[44] It used to be the norm to have publication on the day after introduction, with publication on the day of introduction being available for cases of particular urgency. In recent years, however, the expedited case has become very common. The main practical significance of the timing of publication is that Departments often like to hold a press conference to coincide with introduction, in which case they like to be able to make copies of the Bill publicly available at the press conference. On the expedited route, the Bill is printed overnight before the day of introduction and embargoed, for release on introduction. The other significance of the time of publication is that by convention for Government Bills two weekends are allowed to elapse between the time when the Bill is published and second reading. For private Members' Bills there is no such convention, although the Speaker has urged the importance of publication as far in advance of Second Reading as is reasonably practicable and the Bill must at all events have been published before second reading (Standing Order 14(9)).

[45] As to the provisional legal effect of the Budget resolutions see Chapter 3, Section 7.

[46] Which is why supporters of a Bill are sometimes referred to as its "backers". (There is, however, no evidence to suggest that the Parliamentary use of the expression "backer" is responsible for its wider colloquial use; early usage seems to derive from sporting and financial usage, which in turn appears to derive simply from the notion of a person who stands behind another ready to indemnify or support him.)

[47] Normally the junior Minister or Ministers who is or are expected to lead for the Government in the Standing Committee on the Bill.

fundamental principles of a Bill. Details may be addressed in so far as they elucidate issues of importance, but many of the speeches will focus entirely on the general level. Most importantly, there is no opportunity to move amendments to the Bill.[48]

In rare cases, the second reading debate in the House of Commons can be "sent upstairs" to a second reading committee, in order to preserve time on the floor of the House for what are seen as more important matters: this procedure can be operated only with general consensus.[49]

Financial resolutions (Commons)

5.2.11 As has been explained above[50] the financial initiative of the Government is preserved by the requirement[51] that a proposal that would involve an expenditure from (most sources of) public money is recommended by the Crown. A Bill that would require public expenditure requires that expenditure to be approved by a resolution of the House of Commons known as a money resolution, and in proposing the motion for that resolution the Government indicates[52] the Crown's approval.

A Bill that raises sums by way of taxation is required to have the taxation approved by a resolution of the House of Commons known as a ways and means resolution.

A Bill cannot proceed in Committee (or at least the provisions involving money cannot be taken in Committee) unless the necessary financial resolutions have been obtained. The resolutions are therefore required for all practical purposes to be taken between Second Reading and Committee. For Government Bills the norm is now for the financial resolutions to be taken immediately after Second Reading.[53]

5.2.12 It is possible to have a Bill that does not require financial resolutions to be amended by the inclusion of provisions that do require a resolution. Even where a Bill does have financial resolutions taken for it, a provision added by amendment may be outside the terms of the original resolutions. In either case it is possible to take a supplemental resolution to cover the additional financial implications.

---

[48] In the House of Commons it is usual for what is known as a "reasoned amendment" to be moved on a small number of Bills in each Session which the Opposition find particularly objectionable. And the procedure is available in the House of Lords also. But these are amendments to the motion that the Bill be read a second time, and are of a general nature: they do not address or alter the detailed text of the Bill.

[49] Standing Order No. 90; for an example of a technical Bill sent to second reading Committee in the House of Commons having already been taken in Public Bill Committee in the House of Lords, see the Law of Property (Miscellaneous Provisions) Bill 1993–94 (the second reading proceedings on which took four minutes on July 18, 1994); see also the Civil Evidence Bill 1994–95.

[50] See Chapter 1, Section 6.

[51] Standing Order No. 48.

[52] By the inclusion on the Order Paper of the words "Queen's recommendation signified".

[53] In order to gain the procedural advantage of having the question on the motion for the resolution put without the possibility of debate—Standing Order No. 52(1)(a).

Committee Stage (Commons)

If the motion for the second reading of a Bill is rejected, the Bill falls. If it passes, **5.2.13** as is normally the case, the Bill has to be committed to a committee to be read through, and have amendments proposed and debated, clause by clause and Schedule by Schedule.

In the House of Commons, the normal procedure[54] is for a Bill to be committed to one of the seven or so Standing Committees appointed by the Speaker for this purpose. The membership of each Standing Committee varies from Bill to Bill and is arranged by the Usual Channels[55] so that it includes people interested in the Bill concerned and with an overall membership which, as a general rule, reflects the balance of power of the parties in the Chamber.

A Bill may, normally on a motion moved by the Government, be committed to a Committee of the Whole House.[56] The result is that the Committee stage takes place in the Chamber, which enables every Member of the House of Commons to participate in the clause-by-clause examination of the Bill and in tabling amendments. While the Chamber is in Committee on a Bill no other business can, of course, be taken: so having a Committee of the Whole House can, depending on the length of the Bill and the number of amendments tabled, create considerable pressure on the time available to the Government for its other legislative and non-legislative business. The procedure is therefore reserved for Bills of particular political or constitutional importance[57] or for Bills that are so short and uncontroversial that they can conveniently be taken through all their

---

[54] Standing Order No. 63(1).

[55] In either House of Parliament the phrase "the usual channels" is used to describe discussions between the business managers, sometimes known as the Whips, of each political party. Even in times of a large government majority a considerable degree of cooperation by both the Official Opposition—the party with the largest number of seats in the House of Commons after the Government—and by the other parties, is necessary if the Government is to get all its business through in good order. And even in times of bitter political hostility between the parties it is normally possible to achieve this necessary level of cooperation through these usual channels. In the House of Lords the position is complicated further by the large number of peers who do not "accept the Whip" of any party, meaning that they do not undertake to vote in accordance with the directions of any one party even as a general rule. These peers, collectively known as the Cross-bench peers, generally appoint a Convenor who, without any authority to direct them on matters of voting, has sufficient authority to enter into negotiations with the usual channels to secure the orderly progress of business.

[56] Standing Order No. 63(2).

[57] Such as the Bills for giving effect to the Maastricht Treaty in the European Union, for the expulsion of the hereditary peers from the House of Lords or for the holding of referendums on devolution. As to the general principle, see the following exchange in the House of Commons (HC Deb. March 4, 1997 c.708)—"Sir Patrick Cormack 'Does my right hon. Friend agree with the proposition propounded by the post-war Labour Government that constitutional measures should always be taken in Committee on the Floor of the House?'. Prime Minister 'Yes, I do. That has been the constitutional position in this House. It is the way in which matters have normally been handled. I cannot conceive that anyone would wish to change the long-established tradition.'"

stages at a single sitting.[58] It is possible for a Bill to be committed in part to a Standing Committee and in part to a Committee of the Whole House, and this kind of split committal is routinely used for the Finance Bill.[59]

5.2.14   Other special kinds of committal are also available, although used only relatively rarely. A Bill may be committed to a Select Committee,[60] the format of which enables the Committee to call witnesses and to examine evidence about and discuss the policy background to the Bill in a way not available in a Standing Committee.[61] It is also possible to commit a Bill to a Special Standing Committee,[62] which partakes partly of the character of a Select Committee and partly of the character of a Standing Committee.[63]

The Committee examining a Bill does, broadly speaking, two kinds of thing.

---

[58] For example, see the Bill for the Hong King (Economic and Trade Office) Act 1996 which had all its Commons stages on October 31, 1996; and this is the process commonly adopted to allow private Members' Bills to proceed through all stages by way of "call-over", unanimous agreement without debate, at the end of a private Members' Friday sitting.

[59] This is the annual Bill giving effect to the Budget. The standard practice is for the Opposition to nominate, through the usual channels, a number of measures of particular interest to them that they wish to have debated on the Floor of the House, and for the remainder to be committed to a Standing Committee.

[60] Standing Order No. 63(2).

[61] This process is generally used for the quinquennial Armed Forces Bill.

[62] Standing Order No. 63(2).

[63] This process was used, for example, for the Adoption and Children Bill 2001–02. The Minister introducing the debate on Third Reading (HC Deb. May 20, 2002 c.97) described the use of the Special Standing Committee in the following terms: "The Bill was referred to a Special Standing Committee, which gave Members the opportunity to hear from key stakeholders in the adoption community and acknowledged experts in the field. That consultative approach was a very positive experience, and it provides an example for the future. Following the evidence sessions, the Bill was considered in detail by the Special Standing Committee. I am extremely grateful to my hon. Friends, particularly those who brought their considerable expertise to the Committee. May I say what a pleasure it was to be surrounded by so many ex-social workers? Other hon. Members brought to the proceedings important experience of constituency casework and even personal experience of adoption. It was invaluable to take part in such an informed debate, and the Bill has undoubtedly benefited from it."; see also "In a motion on the Order Paper some of us have suggested that it would be entirely appropriate for the Bill to go to a Special Standing Committee. The more I have heard of the critique that has developed during the day, the more I have felt that to be right. It is essential that we spend some time exploring the rationale for the Bill in a bipartisan way, teasing out some of the issues, before we start the usual, line by line, ministerial defence of the Bill that is the disabling feature of so much legislation that is created in this place. Few measures have passed through the Special Standing Committee procedure since it started in 1980—the Mental Health (Amendment) Bill in the 1981–82 Session, the Matrimonial and Family Proceedings Bill in the 1983–84 Session and now the Children (Scotland) Bill. Those are similar measures to the one before us, in that they needed thorough, bipartisan scrutiny. I shall conclude by quoting what the distinguished then Leader of the House, Norman St. John Stevas, said when introducing that raft of procedural changes, including the Special Standing Committee arrangements. Speaking about Special Standing Committees, he said that—'Government Bills which raise substantial issues, not of acute party controversy' [Official Report, October 30, 1980; Vol.991, c.725.] should be subject to that type of arrangement. The case for that has been made in today's debate. We need a few sessions in which Members who are interested in all that can explore further the aspects that we have begun to discuss today, before we start the usual progress of the Bill."—Dr. Tony Wright M.P. speaking on the Medical (Professional Performance) Bill 1994–95 HC Deb. April 25, 1995 cc.719–720.

First, the Committee goes through the Bill clause by clause and Schedule by Schedule and debates a motion that each clause "stand part of the Bill". While in practice a number of clauses may be taken together, or certain clauses of no interest to the Committee may be stood part of the Bill on a motion moved formally and without either explanation or debate, this is the principal opportunity for a detailed examination of the workings of the Bill. Even on matters where there is no controversy between the political parties, the Minister will routinely give some explanation of the purpose and effect of each provision, and Members may wish to ask for clarification or amplification.

While the Committee will by default consider the Bill's provisions in order, it is possible to arrange for particular provisions to be taken earlier or later than would otherwise be the case. The motion to achieve this is called an Order of Consideration Motion. In the case of a Bill covered by a programme motion[64] the order of consideration is generally provided for by the resolution of the programming sub-committee.[65]

The procedure in Committee, particularly in the Standing Committee, is **5.2.15** relatively relaxed and informal, and there are no restrictions on the number of times a Member may speak on a particular motion or matter (as there are in the Chamber). The result is that it is the norm for the Minister's explanation to be interrupted frequently with requests for expansion, whether from Members of his own party or opposition Members. A team of officials from the Minister's Department are positioned sufficiently near to him to be able to pass him additional briefing, which they do in response to requests for clarification. The result of that is that proceedings in the Standing Committee can, at their best, be extremely constructive and enlightening. It is at this stage of a Bill's progress that a Minister is most likely to make a statement of the Government's intentions or understanding of the kind to which the courts will have regard under the rule in *Pepper v Hart*.[66]

The second principal activity of the Committee on a Bill is the consideration and making of amendments to the text of the Bill. Amendments may do one of three things[67]—

(1) They may add text.

(2) They may remove text.

---

[64] As to which see below.

[65] But because of the timing involved, with the Programming sub-Committee generally meeting shortly before the beginning of the Committee, it is common for an order of consideration motion to be tabled by the Minister in charge of the Bill in Committee a few days before the beginning of the Committee, to enable the marshalling of the amendments on the Order Papers in accordance with what is expected to be directed by the eventual resolution of the sub-Committee. When the sub-Committee eventually reports, the motion is withdrawn.

[66] See Chapter 28.

[67] It is also possible to transpose clauses from one place in the Bill to another or to divide one clause into a number of clauses—technically these are done by way of motion rather than by way of amendment, but the process is indistinguishable for all practical purposes.

(3) They may substitute one set of words for another.

Any Member[68] may table[69] an amendment to any part of the Bill and he will have an opportunity to "move" the amendment, being an opportunity to explain its intention to the Committee and invite them to vote that it be made. There are, however, a number of constraints upon this process—

(1) The rules of the House secure that an amendment will be out of order (in which case it will not be called by the Chairman for moving by the Member who tabled it) if it is outside the scope of the Bill,[70] or not covered by a Money Resolution for the Bill,[71] or if it is frivolous or vexatious.

(2) Even where an amendment is not disorderly, the Chairman has the discretion whether or not to select it for debate, and if selected whether and how to group it for debate with other amendments. There are a number of reasons why an amendment might not be selected for debate, ranging from its being defective or trivial to questions of the overall structure and progress of the debate in Committee.

(3) It is now routine for Bills to be subject to programme motions, that allocate time for different stages of the Bill.[72] In particular, a programme motion generally requires the Standing Committee on a Bill to conclude its proceedings on or by a particular date. Again in general, the time available to a Standing Committee under a programme motion is allocated by a Programming Sub-Committee of the Standing Committee. The result is that at various points during the proceedings of the Committee it may come up

---

[68] Even one who is not a Member of the relevant Standing Committee, although in that case he will have to find a Member of the Committee who is prepared to move the amendment for him.

[69] The expression "table" in relation to an amendment is used at all stages in both Houses. It reflects the notion that the amendment is placed on the table of the House so as to be available for perusal by all Members. In fact, of course, no such thing happens. Amendments are handed in to a particular office known in each House as the Public Bill Office, which arranges for them to be printed. Lists of amendments are published by Her Majesty's Stationery Office and are available through that Office to members of the public; and they are published by each House on the internet. In the case of a stage of a Bill which is taken with little or no notice, "manuscript amendments" are sometimes permitted, in which case ad hoc and informal arrangements are made for circulating the text of the amendments to interested members of the House concerned, but the text of the amendments will not as a rule be available in advance to members of the public.

[70] This is a technical concept, determined in practice by the Chairman or Speaker on the advice of the Clerks to the House: in some cases it will be immediately apparent what the scope of a particular Bill is, but in others the question may be both difficult to determine and also of considerable political importance. The long title of the Bill will be of some influence in determining scope, although it is no longer determinative (whether to exclude or to include matters) in either House. In the House of Lords the notion of scope is strictly referred to as the notion of the area of relevance of a Bill, although the term scope is also used colloquially.

[71] See above.

[72] By virtue of Sessional Orders agreed to by the House of Commons in November 2000, renewed with modifications on June 28, 2001 and preserved since. A Bill which is not the subject of a Programme Motion may, in cases of urgency or controversy, be controlled by an Allocation of Time Motion ("guillotine") under Standing Order No. 83.

against a deadline[73] set by the Programming Sub-Committee at which point the Committee is required to conclude proceedings on a certain part of the Bill. Amendments to that part of the proceedings that have not yet been debated will not be moved for debate, although usually in the case of Government amendments, and occasionally in the case of selected non-Government amendments, it is possible to have the amendments moved formally for a decision.

It is common to have amendments tabled to a provision of a Bill in Committee not because the Member tabling the amendment definitely wants to have the provision amended in a particular way, but because he finds obscure the precise purpose of the provision, or the Government's underlying intentions in relation to it; the amendment is designed merely to elicit further clarification or information. Amendments of this kind are colloquially referred to as "probing amendments". They are generally not pressed to a vote but after discussion are withdrawn with the permission of the Committee. An amendment will also be withdrawn with the permission of the Committee if the Member who moved it wishes to reflect on what the Government have said in response to it, or to allow the Government to reflect on what he and his supporters have said, before deciding whether to press the amendment to a vote at a later stage of proceedings on the Bill (whether in that House or, through colleagues, in the next House).

5.2.16

The Government's response to an amendment moved by a non-government member of the Committee—whether he be a member of the Government party or not—may be to resist it outright, which is the norm, or to accept it. Where the Government accepts an amendment it still has to be voted on, but the combination of the Government's vote and the votes of the amendment's proposers and supporters will normally be sufficient to secure its passing.

It is relatively rare, although by no means unheard of, for the Government to accept a non-Government amendment as drafted, principally because even where the substantive purpose of the amendment is acceptable to the Government there are likely to be technical defects which would prevent it from being effective law. In those cases the Government generally indicates its acceptance of the principle of the amendment and undertakes to table a Government amendment at a later stage of the Bill achieving the desired result in a technically accurate way.[74]

It is common for the Government to table amendments to its own Bills, drafted by Parliamentary Counsel. On a long and complicated Bill as many as several hundred Government amendments may be made to a Government Bill in the course of all its Parliamentary stages. These may—

5.2.17

---

[73] These are sometimes colloquially referred to as the "knives", a term deriving from practice in relation to Allocation of Time Motions (colloquially referred to as guillotines) which were the forerunner of the programme motion.

[74] Sometimes, where the intention of the amendment is known well in advance and the Government has had correspondence with the member concerned, the Government arrange for Parliamentary Counsel to draft an amendment achieving the desired effect and then arrange for the amendment to be "handed out" for tabling by the member concerned.

(1) reflect matters which there was insufficient time to perfect prior to the introduction of the Bill,

(2) effect changes which the Government think right having listened to points made in debate, or

(3) reflect changes in circumstance since introduction.

Proceedings in Committee on a Bill of any size are generally spread over a number of weeks. It is usual for Standing Committees to meet on two days each week, with a morning and afternoon sitting, each of about two and a half hours, on each day.[75] It is standard for a lengthy Bill to have between ten and twenty sittings in Standing Committee, and it is not unusual to have more than that.

It is technically possible[76] for a procedure resolution to prevent the tabling of amendments to a Bill, although the only circumstances in which such a resolution is likely to be passed are those in which a Bill is introduced very shortly after a previous Bill on the same subject was lost, as when a Bill is re-introduced in the Commons with a view to being passed under the Parliament Act 1911.[77]

Report (Commons)

5.2.18   Following Committee, progress depends on the nature and result of consideration in Committee. A Bill which has been committed to a Committee of the Whole House and has not been amended there proceeds straight to Third Reading.[78] Where a Bill has been amended in Committee of the Whole House, or has been considered in a Standing Committee whether amended there or not, the Committee is required to make a report of the amendments to the House, the Bill is printed as amended in the Committee,[79] and the House proceeds to Consideration on Report of the Bill as amended.[80]

At the Report stage the Bill is not before the House clause by clause as it is in Committee.[81] But nor is the House constrained to examine only those changes made by the Committee. Instead, it is open to Members to table amendments to any part of the Bill, and the consideration proceeds through the amendments.

---

[75] But if it is considered through the usual channels desirable to accelerate process through Committee without depriving the Committee of opportunity to debate the Bill it is possible to arrange for the Committee to sit on additional days and to extend the afternoon sittings.

[76] Precedents are rare: but see Aircraft and Shipbuilding Industries Bill HC Deb. December 1, 1976.

[77] As to which see below.

[78] As to which see below.

[79] Although this is sometimes impossible in practice, where a Bill considered in Committee of the Whole House proceeds to have its remaining stages taken on the Floor of the House that same day. In such a case ad hoc arrangements will be made by the Clerks.

[80] Standing Order Nos 71 and 73.

[81] The principal significance of this being that there is neither debate nor vote on each clause of the Bill, only on the amendments proposed at Report.

Order of Consideration motions are available on Report as they are in Committee.

Just as the Chairman in Committee has the discretion to decide which of the tabled amendments are worthy of being debated and how they should be grouped together for discussion, so does the Speaker at the Report Stage. And this discretion will be exercised, in part, to ensure that the Report Stage does not simply retrace the steps of the discussion in Committee, except in the case of a matter of sufficient significance to be worth debating again before the wider House.

Recommittal (Commons)

A Bill that has come out of Committee can be sent back to that stage by a motion agreed to by the House.[82] This can be done before the Report stage has commenced, at some point during the Report stage or between Report and Third Reading.[83] The principal purpose of recommittal is to enable a complicated matter that has arisen to be dealt with in accordance with the more relaxed and flexible procedures of the Committee stage. It is relatively rare but by no means unheard of.[84]   **5.2.19**

Third Reading (Commons)

The final stage in considering a Bill is the motion that the Bill be read a third time. As a rule this motion is considered immediately after the conclusion of proceedings on Report[85] and takes the form of a fairly brief resume of the principal points of policy of the Bill and of the earlier proceedings on it.   **5.2.20**

For all practical purposes, no amendments may be moved on Third Reading.[86]

---

[82] Standing Order No. 74.

[83] It is normal for a Bill to proceed straight from Report to Third Reading; but this is not invariable—see further below.

[84] See, for a recent example, the Planning and Compulsory Purchase Bill 2002–03. A more controversial example is that of the Hunting Bill 2002–03: the recommittal motion for that Bill was moved by the Government immediately after the Consideration on Report on June 30, 2003. Amendments had been carried against the Government which substantially altered the principal effect of the Bill, and as a result the entire Bill was recommitted "to the Standing Committee to which it previously stood committed for the purpose of making such amendments as the Committee consider to be necessary or expedient in consequence of the addition to the Bill of New Clause 11 [which prohibited the registration of fox-hunting—and therefore in the opinion of the Government rendered the entire registration system futile] on Consideration".

[85] Although this is not invariable, and where proceedings on Report produce a dramatic result the Government may wish to have an interval between Report and Third Reading for recommittal or reflection—see, for example, the Hunting Bill 2003–03.

[86] The rule as expressed by Standing Order No. 77 is that no amendment "not being merely verbal" may be made. Since all amendments are verbal, and it being unclear what if anything is added by the qualification "merely", it may be assumed for all practical purposes that no amendment may be made. But the exception could be relied upon to permit the correction of a minor technical error.

Grouping and selection of amendments (Commons)

5.2.21 At all amendable stages tabled amendments are subject to the authority of the Speaker (in Committee of the Whole House or on Report) or the Chairman (in Standing Committee) in two ways. An amendment will be called for debate and for a vote as to whether it should be made only if it is selected for that purpose by the Speaker or Chairman. And the Speaker or Chairman will group together amendments for debate (but not vote) at one time. These powers emanate from the inherent authority of the Chair[87] and are exercised in the interests of ensuring orderly and helpfully-focused debate. The Speaker or Chairman acts on the advice of the Clerks, who in turn routinely invite informal observations from Parliamentary Counsel.[88]

Selection of amendments is entirely a matter for the Chair's discretion, although strictly speaking there is a distinction between ruling an amendment out of order[89] and merely declining to select it in the interests of debate. While the general principles according to which this discretion is exercised are well-known, reasons are not given.[90]

The fact that an issue has been determined at one stage in a Bill's proceedings does not prevent it being re-opened by amendment at a later stage.

For the relationship between the Chair's power of selection and grouping and the order of consideration as arranged by motion, see below (in relation to programme motions).

5.2.22 As a general rule, it is necessary to give notice of amendments[91] and failure to do so results in their not being selected. But where proceedings on a Bill follow each other very fast[92] or where there are special reasons for Members' having been unable to give notice, "manuscript" amendments are commonly selected.[93]

---

[87] See also Standing Order 32.

[88] In this respect Parliamentary Counsel put their technical knowledge of the subject-matter of the Bill at the disposal of the House authorities for the purpose of facilitating orderly debate: in performing this function, and other advisory functions in relation to matters of Parliamentary procedure, Counsel act not as mere advocates for the Government, but as independently discharging a responsibility to Parliament at the standing request of the Government.

[89] The principal examples being where it is outside the scope of the Bill or not covered by the financial resolutions for the Bill. The fact that an amendment would hybridise the Bill is not a reason for failing to select it.

[90] "If the hon. Gentleman is asking me why I have not selected some of the amendments that he has tabled, the answer is that the Speaker never gives reasons for the non-selection of amendments." —Speaker HC Deb. June 24, 1996 c.49.

[91] That is to say, to hand them in for printing in advance of the stage at which they will be taken. On the first occasion on which an amendment is printed it appears with a star, and starred amendments are generally considered as not having been given with sufficient notice for selection.

[92] Which can sometimes be on the same day.

[93] In this context "manuscript" means simply not printed on the day's Order Paper. Nowadays it is unheard of for an amendment to be moved, even during the "to-and-fro" stages (as to which see below), without a typescript copy of the amendment having been handed to the House authorities at least a few minutes before the amendment comes to be moved, whereupon the House authorities will arrange for copies of the amendment to be made available to Members in the Vote Office.

Where an amendment is carried to a Government Bill against the Government's wishes, two conventions apply.

(1) The Government will not resist (in the sense of forcing a Division on) any amendment consequential on the first amendment—as a rule of thumb this is likely to mean any amendment grouped with the first amendment.

(2) The Government acquire a duty to make such other amendments to the Bill as are required to give effect to the obvious intention of the amendment carried against it. That may amount to tabling an amendment to perfect the first amendment or to tabling other amendments elsewhere in the Bill to deal with consequential matters. As a matter of theory, where the first amendment was made in the Bill's first House these additional amendments ought to be tabled by the Government before the Bill passes to its second House: but the convention is by general consent disregarded in cases where it would serve no useful purpose or might actually confuse, as, for example, in the case where the Government intends to reverse the effect of the first amendment in the next House within the following few days.[94]

Queen's or Prince's Consent (Commons & Lords)

A Bill requires the Queen's Consent if any provision of it affects—   **5.2.23**

(1) the Royal prerogative, or

(2) the private interests of the Sovereign.

A Bill requires the Consent of the Prince of Wales if it affects the private interests of the Duchy of Cornwall.[95]

---

[94] Hence, for example, the Explanatory and Financial Memorandum for the Police Bill 1996–97 as printed for the House of Lords—"As a result of conflicting amendments made at Report Stage in the House of Lords, Part III of the Bill is technically defective."

[95] The reason for this is that the Duchy of Cornwall vests in the Prince of Wales while there is one, but in the case of a vacancy in that position would revert to the Sovereign: the Sovereign therefore has a residuary personal interest in matters that affect the property of the Duchy of Cornwall, and that interest is protected by a requirement for the incumbent beneficiary to give Consent. It will be seen from this that the title of the Duke of Cornwall (presently held by the Prince of Wales) and the inheritance of the Duchy are in a peculiar position. They were created in 1337 by Edward III and vested in the Black Prince by a charter having the authority of an Act of Parliament: by virtue of that charter they pertain to the Sovereign's eldest son, being also heir apparent, immediately upon his birth, and in the event of his death without leaving issue the next surviving son of the Sovereign succeeds; if, however, the heir apparent dies leaving issue, the Duchy reverts to the Crown. That is why alone among non-Crown land the Crown's prerogative attaches to the lands of the Duchy of Cornwall, for the reason that they never entirely cease to be Crown lands.
Note also HC Deb. April 30, 1996 W.A. 417—"To ask the Prime Minister in what circumstances the Prince of Wales's Consent is needed for a Bill."—"Bills whose provisions affect the hereditary revenues, personal property or interests of the Duchy of Cornwall require the consent of the Prince of Wales to be signified in both Houses before they are passed. The same would apply to any Bill which affected the interest of the Prince of Wales in his capacity as Prince and Steward of Scotland."

Consent is generally signified on behalf of the Crown[96] at Third Reading. But if a matter affecting the prerogative is fundamental to the Bill it may be required that Consent be signified at Second Reading.[97]

The issue of Consent is a matter entirely of House procedure. It has no bearing on the legal issue of the application of legislation to the Crown.[98] In particular, once a Bill has received Royal Assent and has become an Act, the question of Consent is redundant.

Passing from one House to the other

5.2.24   Once a Bill has been given a Third Reading in its first House it automatically passes to the other House. Nothing is required to achieve this and, indeed, nothing can be done to stop it happening.

The Bill passes automatically to the second House and is printed, but will not make any progress there unless it is taken up by a Member of that House. In the case of Government Bills this is arranged automatically by the Government Whips[99] in each House. In the case of other Bills it is necessary for the Member in Charge of the Bill in the first House to find someone in the second House prepared to take up the Bill in that House and to be responsible for its progress there.

There is no way in which either House can force the other to take any steps on a Bill sent from the first House, unless a member of the second House takes charge of it.[1] The result is that it is common for non-Government Bills to originate in the House of Lords, where the allocation of time is both more flexible and more consensual than in the House of Commons, pass through and from that House without difficulty, but fail in the House of Commons, either for want of a Member prepared to take charge of the Bill or for lack of time to make progress.

---

[96] By one of the many Ministers and other Members of either House who are members of the Privy Council. The process of obtaining Consent is supervised by the Government and conducted by correspondence between the Government and the Palace or Duchy.

[97] As was the case for, for example, the Chemical Weapons Bill 1995–96 (HC Deb. November 23, 1995 c.810)—

"The President of the Board of Trade and Secretary of State for Trade and Industry (Mr. Ian Lang): I have it in Command from the Queen to acquaint the House that Her Majesty having been informed of the purport of the Chemical Weapons Bill has consented to place her Prerogative, so far as it is affected by the Bill, at the disposal of Parliament for the purposes of the Bill.

"Order for Second Reading read."

In such cases Consent is notified in full and not merely by a token assent from a Privy Councillor as is the case for Third Reading Consent.

[98] As to which see Chapter 11, Section 5.

[99] The name colloquially given to the Ministers in each House with responsibility for the management of Government Business. Taken together with the Leader of the House of Commons and the Leader of the House of Lords they are sometimes referred to collectively within Government as the "Business Managers".

[1] But, as will be seen below, in certain circumstances the House of Commons can dispense with the participation and cooperation of the House of Lords under the Parliament Act 1911.

When a Bill is given a Third Reading in its second House, one of two **5.2.25** situations will appertain. If the Bill has not been amended in the second House, on passing its second House it has completed every required Parliamentary stage for its enactment and is now officially described as awaiting Royal Assent.[2]

If the Bill has been amended in the second House, the amendments made there have to be sent back for consideration by the House in which the Bill originated. This process[3] can be complicated. The second House sends to the first House a list of amendments by reference to the print of the Bill as it arrived from the first House.[4] The first House then considers the amendments. In relation to each of the amendments made by the second House the first House may—

(1) accept it outright,

(2) reject it outright,

(3) propose an amendment to it,

(4) reject it but propose an alternative amendment,[5] or

(5) accept it and propose a consequential amendment to the Bill.

The first House then sends to the second House a list of the first House's responses to the second House's amendments. Where the list includes an outright rejection of an amendment it is accompanied by reasons.[6] That is then considered by the second House. In each case it may accept what the first House says, insist on its original position or suggest a compromise. The Bill then goes back to the first House, where a similar process takes place. The essence is that the process continues until either—

(1) both Houses agree on every amendment, or

(2) a stalemate occurs, in which case the Bill is lost.[7]

---

[2] As to which see below.

[3] Sometimes described colloquially as "to-and-fro" or "ping-pong".

[4] This can itself be difficult to compile where text amended at one stage has been amended at a later stage.

[5] Known as an amendment in lieu.

[6] The reasons, which are nowadays concise and stylised and are not designed to be particularly informative, are drafted by Parliamentary Counsel and submitted by a Minister to a small Committee appointed to draw up reasons. In the Commons this takes place behind the Speaker's Chair in a small room next to the Lobby and known as the Reasons Room.

[7] Although this is a question of some technical complexity, broadly speaking a stalemate occurs where each House has had one chance to reconsider its position on a matter and has refused to do so.

The disastrous consequences of a stalemate mean that a number of devices have been developed by which a dispute may be kept technically alive as the Bill passes backwards and forwards between the two Houses. The European Parliamentary Elections Bill 1997–98 is believed to hold the record, having passed between the Houses eleven times (culminating in proceedings "on Consideration of Lords Reasons for Disagreeing to a further Amendment Proposed by the Commons in lieu of Lords Amendments to which the Commons have Disagreed"): the process resulted in stalemate, and the Bill was lost.

On one occasion the stalemate rule came into play (in the opinion of the Lords authorities) in circumstances where there was still a political will to effect a compromise. The House of Lords

Programme motions (Commons)

5.2.26 Since November 1997[8] it has been the norm for a Government Bill to be the subject of one or more motions agreed to by the House of Commons for the programming of its stages in that House.[9] The verdict of the House of Commons Select Committee on Modernisation of the House of Commons on recent experience of the programming process is given in the extract of a Report of that Committee appended to this work.[10]

The essence of the programming of Bills is that it is intended to be more or less a consensual process, at least so far as the Usual Channels are concerned,[11] although that has not always been the apparent reality.

The initial programme motion for a Bill will usually specify a date by which the Standing Committee is required to complete consideration of the Bill and a number of days for consideration on Report.

5.2.27 For the present, programming of Bills is still regarded by the House of Commons as an experiment. It is regulated, therefore, not by Standing Orders but by Sessional Orders[12] renewed each Session.[13]

A programme motion itself is generally considered without debate although in certain circumstances a short debate is permissible.[14] The first programme motion for a Bill is generally taken at the close of Second Reading at the same time as any financial resolutions, and supplementary motions may be taken from time to time.[15] The Commons proceedings on Consideration of Lords Amendments are generally programmed by a separate motion.

Where a programmed Bill is committed to a Standing Committee—which is the norm for all public Bills—the Sessional Orders require the appointment of a

---

accordingly passed a motion—"that it is desirable to vary the normal practice of the House when considering Commons Reasons and Amendments, whereby no further consideration of a bill can take place in the event that—

    (i)   the Lords insist on an amendment;

    (ii) the Commons insists on its disagreement to that amendment; and

    (iii) neither House has offered alternative proposals;

to allow the House to consider the Commons Reason and Amendment to the bill"—see HL Minutes of Proceedings May 11, 2004, Planning and Compulsory Purchase Bill 2003–04.

[8] See Commons Journals (1997–98) 219.

[9] For a full history of the emergence of the programme motion as a norm see the First Report of Session 2002–03 of the House of Commons Select Committee on Modernisation of the House of Commons (*Programming of Bills*) (HC 1222—November 3, 2003).

[10] Appendix, Extract 12.

[11] That is to say, that it is intended to represent agreement between the front benches both as to how much time can sensibly be allocated to the Bill in order for the opposition to debate points of controversy and for the Government to make sufficient progress with its Bills and also as to how that time should be allocated among the different provisions of the Bill. Each front bench will then hold its own informal discussions with its back-benchers as to the allocation among them of time available to debate the Bill.

[12] Sessional Orders A to I on the Programming of Bills, June 28, 2001.

[13] See, for example, renewal for Session 2003–04, Commons Journals November 6, 2003.

[14] Sessional Order A(6).

[15] For example, if it becomes clear that the Standing Committee requires a little more time to consider the Bill.

sub-committee of the Standing Committee to agree a timetable for the Committee's consideration of the Bill within the overall time limit set by the House in the programme motion.[16] The sub-committee proposes a timetable, generally including "knives" allocating time to particular provisions of the Bill, and the Standing Committee votes on the sub-committee's proposals at the beginning of its proceedings. The sub-committee's resolution can be varied by supplementary resolutions presented to the Committee during its proceedings.

A similar Business Committee procedure is available for allocation of proceedings on Report. But the relative brevity of those proceedings often results in that procedure being disapplied by the Programme Motion. **5.2.28**

The relationship between orders of consideration provided for by programme motion or sub-committee or Committee resolution, on the one hand, and the Chair's grouping and selection[17] on the other hand, is as follows. The Chair may group amendments (or motions, including motions that a clause or Schedule Stand Part) for debate together, irrespective of where they come in the Bill. Once an amendment or motion has been called, anything grouped with it by the Chair will be discussed. The grouped amendments or motions will not be voted upon, however, until the point for considering them is reached, which will be in accordance either with the default order of the Bill or with the order of consideration as set out in the programme motion or resolution.

Guillotines (Commons)

The programming motion is a relatively new device aimed at producing an essentially consensual form of regulation of the progress of Government Bills. An alternative, and entirely non-consensual, process that has been available to Governments since 1887[18] is the guillotine, or, as it is more properly called, the allocation of time motion. **5.2.29**

This has the same purpose as the programming motion already described, but is passed generally against fierce opposition on the strength of the Government's majority in the House of Commons. It has been used extensively but intermittently over the years,[19] with periods of frequent use being interspersed with periods of years during which it was used seldom or never.

The guillotine procedure is controlled, in so far as it is controlled at all, by precedent and experience rather than being regulated by Standing or Sessional

---

[16] The Sub-Committee has a Government majority, as does the Standing Committee itself, and its proceedings are generally, but not necessarily, brief and informal.

[17] As to which see above.

[18] The guillotine motion was first used on the Criminal Law Amendment (Ireland) Bill of 1887.

[19] 36 Bills were guillotined between 1881 and 1921, 14 between 1921 and 1945, and 30 between 1945 and 1975. Between 1989 and 1999 there were 68 guillotines. Since 1999 the programme motion has more or less taken over the from the guillotine, with 105 programme motions in the two Sessions 2000–01 and 2001–02 (and only three guillotines in those Sessions).

Orders. It does, however, have protection from the Standing Orders against itself being filibustered.[20]

House of Lords procedure

5.2.30   The procedures in the House of Lords for consideration of a Bill are broadly the same as in the House of Commons, but with the following significant variations.

Allocation of time

5.2.31   In general, time is less tightly controlled in the House of Lords than in the House of Commons. There is no Speaker with powers of selecting amendments[21] or curtailing or controlling debate. And the allocation of days is not at the disposal of the Government in the same way as it is in the House of Commons: almost all aspects of the control of business have to be arranged by consensus and negotiation within the Usual Channels. Allocation of time motions and programme motions are not used.[22] One result of all this is that it is common for debate in Committee of the Whole House on a lengthy Bill to be spread over two, three or four days, and even Report often takes more than one day.[23]

Where debate on a Bill has been curtailed, or can be argued to have been curtailed, in the House of Commons by the use of either of a programme motion or an allocation of time motion, it is common for peers to advance that as a reason for prolonging debate in the Lords, particularly on provisions that have not been reached in debate at all owing to the descent of a knife at an earlier stage of Committee or Report.[24]

Second reading

5.2.32   It is rare for a Bill to be denied a Second Reading in the House of Lords, and the vote on the motion for second reading is in particular influenced by a Convention

---

[20] Standing Order 83—"83. If a motion be made by a Minister of the Crown providing for an allocation of time to any proceedings on a bill the Speaker shall, not more than three hours after the commencement of the proceedings on such a motion, put any question necessary to dispose of those proceedings."

[21] They are generally grouped for debate by agreement through the Usual Channels, but unlike in the House of Commons the groupings are purely informal suggestions and it is open to any peer to depart from them during the debate.

[22] Although it is common to have procedure motions disapplying rules or conventions of the House to permit Bills to proceed with unusual expedition.

[23] For example, the Nationality, Immigration and Asylum Bill 2001–02, a Bill of moderate length (about 100–150 pages) but attracting considerable political and social interest, occupied eight days in Committee of the Whole House (including one on re-commitment) and three for Report (including one following re-commitment).

[24] See, for example, HL Deb. July 3, 2003 c.1119.

that the House of Lords does not reject a Bill that effects a legislative change announced in the manifesto of the Governing party.[25]

Committee

There are no Standing Committees in the House of Lords, whether for the scrutiny of Bills in Committee, subordinate legislation or for any other purpose.[26] The exceptional approach in the House of Commons for committee stage of a Bill—Committee of the Whole House taken on the floor of the Chamber—is the normal approach in the House of Lords.

5.2.33

The principal alternative in the House of Lords to Committee of the Whole House is the Grand Committee. This was once a rarity, but in the last few years it has come to be used more extensively, being used for a small number of Bills each Session.[27] The Grand Committee is held, generally at the same time as the House is sitting in the Chamber, in a small room near the Chamber.[28] The aim is to relieve pressure on the time of the Chamber without denying a Bill a thorough scrutiny: so the proceedings follow a similar pattern to those in the Chamber, and are reserved for Bills on which it is thought[29] that only a small number of peers are likely to wish to participate in Committee. The nature of proceedings in Grand Committee are described by the Chairman at the opening of consideration of each Bill along the following lines[30]—

"Before I put the Question that the Title be postponed, it may be helpful to remind your Lordships of the procedure for today's Committee stage.

---

[25] This convention, known as the Salisbury or Salisbury/Addison Convention, owes its origins to what was perceived as a perpetual Conservative majority in the House of Lords as a result of the preponderance of the hereditary peers. The convention was an act of self-restraint thought necessary if the elected House of Commons were not to be frustrated by the unelected House of Lords in the implementation of the manifesto upon which the government was elected and given its majority in the House of Commons (which it was thought might make the temptation to create a new Labour majority by the creation of life peers politically irresistible). The Convention is frequently discussed and alluded to, and its significance and effect since the expulsion of the hereditary peers from the House of Lords has been the subject of particular attention. See, in particular, HL Deb. May 19, 1993 cc.1780–1813; HL Deb. December 7, 1993 c.839 and c.901–02; HC Deb. February 3, 1969 c.150; letter to *The Times* by Lord Denham (a former Conservative Whip) February 9, 1996; [1998] Public Law 371–77; and HL Deb. January 24, 2001 cc.264–300.

[26] That does not, of course, mean that there are no Committees that are appointed regularly each Session and are, in effect, permanent. But although such committees exist in the Lords they are not permanent creations of the Standing Orders, as is the case in the Commons, and they are not available for the scrutiny of Bills in Committee.

[27] 5 Bills were sent to Grand Committee in the Session 2002–02. For a recent example, see the Bill for the European Parliament (Representation) Act 2003 (c.7).

[28] Normally the Moses Room, so called after the large picture of Moses receiving the Law on Mount Sinai which hangs at one end of the room.

[29] In discussion within the Usual Channels.

[30] This quote being taken from the words of the Deputy Chairman of Committees (Lord Skelmersdale) on the European Parliament (Representation) Bill 2002–03 HL Deb. March 13, 2003 c.G.C. 29.

Except in one important respect, our proceedings will be exactly as in a normal Committee of the Whole House. We shall go through the Bill clause by clause; noble Lords will speak standing; all Lords are free to attend and participate; and the proceedings will be recorded in Hansard. The one difference is that the House has agreed that there shall be no Divisions in a Grand Committee. Any issue on which agreement cannot be reached should be considered again at the Report stage when, if necessary, a Division may be called. Unless, therefore, an amendment is likely to be agreed to, it should be withdrawn."

5.2.34   There are a number of other options for Committee stage in the Lords, none of them used frequently.

It is possible to commit a Bill to a Public Bill Committee, being a select committee with between 12 and 16 appointed members and the Chairman of Committees. Votes may be taken in a Public Bill Committee, and although any peer may attend and speak, and even move amendments to the Bill, only the appointed peers may take part in Divisions. This procedure is designed principally for government Bills of a technical and non-controversial nature on which it is generally thought that it is unnecessary to occupy the time of the Chamber, while leaving peers with a particular interest in and knowledge of the subject matter of the Bill to give it a thorough scrutiny in the normal way.[31]

5.2.35   For a Bill which, while not sufficiently controversial to make Committee on the Floor of the House a necessity, requires detailed examination of technical matters, it is possible to use a slight variant of the last-named procedure, the Special Public Bill Committee. The only difference is that the Special committee is able to take written and oral evidence on the Bill, before proceeding to examine it provision by provision in the ordinary way.[32]

Finally, it is possible to commit a Bill to a select committee convened for that purpose or to a joint committee of the two Houses.[33]

---

[31] In discussion within the Usual Channels.

[32] See the First Report of the House of Lords Select Committee on Procedure of the House Session 1995–96 and the debate on the Report at HL Deb. November 13, 1995 cc.1279–1288.

[33] But note that a motion to commit a Bill to a Select Committee for the taking of evidence and the conduct of a detailed investigation has been seen as an attempt to wreck a Bill. See, for example, the following exchange between the Lord President of the Council, Leader of the House of Lords (Baroness Amos) and the Leader of Her Majesty's Opposition in the Lords (Lord Strathclyde) HL Deb. March 8, 2004 cc.1110–1111 following a successful non-Government motion to commit the Constitutional Reform Bill 2003–04 to a Select Committee—

"Baroness Amos: My Lords, this House has taken a very serious step. By this vote, this House—the unelected House—has made it impossible for the democratically elected House of Commons to receive this Bill promised in the Queen's Speech in November in time to consider it this Session. That is very serious indeed, and the Government will consider what the consequences may be.

Lord Strathclyde: My Lords, I am grateful for the noble Baroness the Leader of the House having made that short statement. I am sorry that she has not been able to tell us what the consequences might be this evening. Surely one of the consequences must be that this Bill

Order of consideration

Order of Consideration motions are available in the House of Lords both in Committee and on Report. **5.2.36**

Report

Where, as is the norm, a Bill has its Committee stage on the Floor of the House, there will be no substantive Report stage unless amendments are made in Committee. This is the same as the position in the House of Commons (but a rarity there and the norm in the House of Lords). **5.2.37**

Third reading

In the House of Lords there is generally a significant interval of days between Report and Third Reading, in which the Bill is reprinted as amended on Report. The Third Reading is, unlike in the Commons, a further stage at which substantive amendments may be made to the Bill It was once the case that amendments on Third Reading were restricted to matters requiring to be put right from earlier developments, or responding to undertakings given or points raised in earlier debate, and the like: but this rule has become so relaxed in recent years that it has ceased to be recognisable as a rule for any practical purpose.[34] **5.2.38**

Re-commitment

Recommittal is called re-commitment in the House of Lords and is perhaps slightly more common there than in the Commons, although still rare. **5.2.39**

Intervals

Whereas in the House of Commons it is common to have more than one stage of a Bill taken in one day, and that is the norm for Report and Third Reading, in the House of Lords the rule is that two stages of one Bill may not be taken on the same day.[35] And there are recommended minimum intervals which ought to be allowed to elapse between stages.[36] **5.2.40**

---

should be carried over into the next Session. Carryover was not a proposal put forward by the Conservative Party; it is part of the programme of modernisation introduced by the Labour Government. Why do they not now use their own tools to get this Bill on the statute book, if that is what Parliament wishes?"

[34] But note the rule against reversing defeats described below.

[35] Standing Order No. 47: the rules can be displaced in the case of a Bill of particular urgency, but only by a resolution on a motion of which notice has been given.

[36] As approved by the Second Report of the House of Lords Select Committee on Procedure of the House Session 1976–77: two weeks between Second Reading and Committee and between Committee and Report, and three days between Report and Third Reading.

Money

5.2.41 There are no financial resolutions in the House of Lords.

Strictly, it is not for the Lords to pass any measure that would raise money by way of taxation or impose a charge upon public funds. It is however routine nowadays for a Bill with significant financial implications to be introduced in the House of Lords.[37] The fiction of the House of Commons' exclusive prerogative in relation to these matters is preserved[38] by the insertion by the Lords Clerks on the Third Reading of the Bill of words known as the Privilege Amendment, disclaiming all intention of the Bill's having financial implications, notwithstanding their being apparent on the face of the provisions. The Privilege Amendment is then removed by the House of Commons in Committee.[39]

Selection and grouping of amendments

5.2.42 There is no selection of amendments in the House of Lords.[40] Amendments are grouped for debate, but the grouping is a matter of convenience and not of authority, and is agreed through the Usual Channels.

Matters already decided

5.2.43 The general rule that the determination of an issue at one stage in a Bill's proceedings does not prevent it being re-opened by amendment at a later stage is subject in the House of Lords to an exception in the case of Third Reading where by convention earlier decisions are not re-opened.[41] There is also not a

---

[37] Although it would be extraordinary—and some would say improper—for a Bill wholly concerned with expenditure or taxation to be introduced in the House of Lords.

[38] See House of Commons Standing Order No.80(a).

[39] No similar procedure is required for Bills originating in the House of Commons because by the time the Bill reaches the House of Lords the money has been authorised by resolution of the Commons. It may, however, be necessary for an amendment in the House of Lords that introduces new spending or fiscal implications to be authorised by supplementary resolution before the amendment is considered by the House of Commons.

[40] Although where a tabled amendment is disorderly in the sense of being outside the area of relevance of the Bill the Lords authorities may advise against its being moved for debate, and the Leader of the House may intervene on the advice of the Lords authorities for the same purpose: but whether or not the advice is listened to is a matter for the peer concerned, and for the House. There is also a rule of pre-emption operated by the occupant of the Chair, whereby it will be announced before an amendment is moved if it would have the effect of rendering it impossible to put the question on a later amendment (because, for example, the words to which the later amendment relates will no longer appear).

[41] While the rules in the House of Lords tend to be generally more flexible and more subject to the pleasure of the House than in the House of Commons, this rule is applied strictly—see, for example, Mental Health (Amendment) Bill, HL Deb. March 4, 1982. But note Business of the House Motion April 29, 1996—"That, notwithstanding the practice of the House relating to consideration on Third Reading of amendments which have been fully debated and decided at a previous stage of the bill, an amendment to insert a new clause (Evidence concerning proceedings in Parliament) may be considered on Third Reading of the Defamation Bill [HL]"; see also HL Deb. April 29, 1996 c.1405.

convention but a customary self-denying ordinance (of relatively recent origin) practiced by the Government that they do not seek to reverse on Report defeats in Committee.

Private Peer's Bills

The House of Lords operates a convention whereby the Government do not stand **5.2.44** in the way of the debate of matters brought to the House by way of private peer's Bill. As well as time generally being found for the consideration of private peers' Bills in a much more generous way than is the case in the House of Commons, it is a convention in the House of Lords that the Government takes other self-denying steps to permit a private peer's Bill to proceed, such as not voting against amendments to the Bill whether the Government supports their effect or not.[42]

House of Lords Select Committee on Delegated Powers and Deregulation

The House of Lords has a Select Committee[43] one of the functions of which is **5.2.45** to scrutinise Bills before the House, and amendments before the House where appropriate.[44] The role of the Committee is stated in the opening paragraph of their Special Report for Sessions 2001–02 and 2002–03[45]—

---

[42] Hence, for example, "For those reasons, I am not in favour of the amendment and the Government cannot support it; although in line with the convention which exists in your Lordships' House, I shall not vote against it."—Baroness Blatch, Sexual Offences (Amendment) Bill HL Deb. April 3, 1995 c.73.

[43] The Committee is established by Sessional Order of the House of Lords. The present terms of reference are "to report whether the provisions of any bill inappropriately delegate legislative power, or whether they subject the exercise of legislative power to an inappropriate level of parliamentary scrutiny; to report on documents and draft orders laid before Parliament under the Regulatory Reform Act 2001; and to perform, in respect of such documents and orders and subordinate provisions orders laid under that Act, the functions performed in respect of other instruments by the Joint Committee on Statutory Instruments".

The history of the establishment of the Committee is summarised as follows in the Committee's Special Report for Sessions 2001–02 and 2002–03 (December 17, 2003—*The Work of the Committee*) See House of Lords Standing Order 65 for the authority for the continuation of this Select Committee—

"In February 1992, the Select Committee on the Committee Work of the House, under the chairmanship of Lord Jellicoe,—'the Jellicoe Committee'—noted that 'in recent years there has been considerable disquiet over the problem of wide and sometimes ill-defined order-making powers which give Ministers unlimited discretion'. The Jellicoe Committee recommended the establishment of a delegated powers scrutiny committee in the House of Lords which would, it suggested, 'be well suited to the revising function of the House'. As a result, the Select Committee on the Scrutiny of Delegated Powers was appointed in the following session, initially as an experiment for a limited period. It was established as a sessional committee from the beginning of Session 1994–95."

[44] While the Committee aim to produce a report on each Bill before it is considered in detail by the House, it is obviously possible to have highly significant delegated powers inserted by way of amendment as a Bill goes through the House. Where that appears to be the case, the Committee aim to produce a supplementary report.

[45] December 17, 2003—*The Work of the Committee.*

"Over recent decades, Government activity has become increasingly complex and, as a result, delegated (or secondary) legislation has increased both in volume and importance. Parliament recognises that detailed implementation of legislation needs to be undertaken by powers delegated (to the executive, the National Assembly for Wales or some other body or person) by primary legislation if the Parliamentary process is to remain workable. It is also recognised, however, that a principal function of Parliament is to scrutinise the ambit of powers granted by primary legislation and to provide some control over their exercise. The Delegated Powers and Regulatory Reform Committee contributes to the effective performance of that function."

5.2.46   Reports of the Committee are published and are generally available to the House before the commencement of proceedings on the Bill. The Department responsible for a Bill routinely submits a memorandum to the Committee explaining the purpose of each power to make subordinate legislation conferred by the Bill, and setting out any special considerations relevant to the nature of the power or the level of scrutiny chosen for it. The Committee's Report on a Bill will often append some or all of a departmental memorandum. Where the Government has responded to an earlier Report, the response may be appended to a later Report.[46]

It is common for peers during debate on a Bill to refer to recommendations or observations of the Committee made in a Report on the Bill, and it is also common for amendments to be tabled by non-Government peers, or sometimes by Government amendment, for the purpose of implementing a recommendation of the Committee, perhaps by raising the level of scrutiny of the exercise of a power from negative resolution to affirmative resolution.

There is no equivalent to this Committee in the House of Commons, although the idea has been occasionally suggested.[47] There is some reason to think that a Joint Committee could sensibly consider the matters addressed by the Lords Delegated Powers Committee, as is the case for the Joint Committee on Statutory Instruments.[48]

Joint Committee on Human Rights

5.2.47   The Joint Committee on Human Rights[49] has a role in considering and reporting on Bills before either House. The Committee's present approach to its role is

---

[46] See, for example, Annex 3 to the Fifth Report of Session 2003–04 (January 29, 2004).
[47] See, in particular, HC Deb. May 4, 1995 cc.451–2.
[48] As to which see Chapter 6, Section 2.
[49] Appointed by the two Houses of Parliament "to consider matters relating to human rights in the United Kingdom (but excluding consideration of individual cases); proposals for remedial orders, draft remedial orders and remedial orders".

explained in the following passage from the Summary of its Third Report for Session 2003–04[50]—

> "The Joint Committee on Human Rights examines every Bill presented to Parliament. With Government Bills its starting point is the statement made by the Minister under section 19 of the Human Rights Act 1998 in respect of its compliance with Convention rights as defined in that Act. However, it also has regard to the provisions of other international human rights instruments which bind the UK.
>
> "The Committee does not in general publish separate reports on each Bill which raises human rights questions,[51] but publishes regular progress reports on its scrutiny of Bills, setting out any initial concerns it has about Bills it has examined and, subsequently, the Government's responses to these concerns and any further observations it may have on these responses. The aim is to complete the cycle of consideration of a Bill before its second reading in the second House."

The Committee will draw aspects of a Bill to the special attention of either House where it considers it right to do so, and reference is likely to be made to the Committee's reports during debate on a Bill. A report of the Committee has no other procedural effect (and no legal effect).

Royal Assent

Once a Bill has been passed by both Houses with only such amendments as are agreed to by both Houses, nothing remains but for it to receive Royal Assent. It is for the Government to determine when to submit Bills for Royal Assent, that being a matter like most others in respect of which the Sovereign acts upon the advice of Ministers. It is normal to wait until a few Bills are ready for Royal Assent and to submit them at one time. But Bills could be presented singly if urgency so demanded. It would probably be contrary to convention, however, for the Government to choose between Bills that were ready for Royal Assent, presenting some and delaying others.

    It is no longer conceivable, as it once was, that Royal Assent would be withheld.[52]

5.2.48

---

[50] January 2004—HL 23, HC 252.

[51] But there have already been exceptions: see, for example, the Committee's Fifth Report of Session 2003–04 (HL 35, HC 304) which amounts to a supplemental report in relation to the Asylum and Immigration (Treatment of Claimants, etc.) Bill 2003–04.

[52] Royal Assent is given by the Sovereign acting on the advice of Ministers. It is inconceivable today that either Ministers would advise against the giving of Royal Assent or that the Sovereign would ignore advice to give Royal Assent. The Royal Assent was last refused to a Bill passed by both Houses of Parliament when Queen Anne on March 11, 1708 refused to Assent to a Bill for settling the militia in Scotland on the grounds of invasion of Her prerogative and following an example set by King Charles II on November 30, 1678. In this respect Royal Assent is unlike Queen's Consent (discussed above): in that process the aim is partly to take account of the Sovereign's private interests, in respect of which she acts on the advice of personal advisers and not on the advice of

It was once commonplace for Assent to be signified by the Sovereign in person, but this has not occurred since 1854. The manner in which Assent is signified is today controlled by the Royal Assent Act 1967,[53] section 1(1) of which provides as follows—

"An Act of Parliament is duly enacted if Her Majesty's Assent thereto, being signified by Letters Patent under the Great Seal signed with Her Majesty's own hand,—

(a) is pronounced in the presence of both Houses in the House of Lords in the form and manner customary before the passing of this Act[54]; or

(b) is notified to each House of Parliament, sitting separately, by the Speaker of that House[55] or in the case of his absence by the person acting as such Speaker."

5.2.49   Once the Royal Assent is signified to the Bill it becomes an Act, and will come into force either in accordance with its provisions or, where they say nothing about commencement, as from the beginning of the day on which Royal Assent is given.[56]

The timing of the giving of Royal Assent is formally endorsed in accordance with the following provision of the Acts of Parliament (Commencement) Act 1793[57]—

Ministers—but even so it is inconceivable for practical purposes that Consent would be refused, although it is not inconceivable that the Government might refuse to facilitate a request for Consent where it was thought that the measure requiring Consent had no realistic prospect of even being debated, let alone being enacted.

[53] 1967 c.23.

[54] This refers to the pronouncement of Royal Assent by Commission. This commonly occurs when Commissioners are appointed to prorogue Parliament (to bring to an end a Session of Parliament, whether or not prior to a dissolution). Before the Commissioners perform their duty of prorogation, it is normal for them to deal with the signification of Assent to all Bills at that time awaiting Royal Assent. The ceremony takes place in the House of Lords, but the Commons are summoned to attend at the Bar to observe. The original authority for Assent by Commission is the Royal Assent by Commission Act 1541 (33 Hen. 8. c.21), ss.(3) and (5)—"be it declared by authority of this present Parliament that the King's royal assent by his letters patent under his Great Seal, and signed with his hand, and declared and notified in his absence to the Lords Spiritual and Temporal and the Commons assembled together in the House, is and ever was of as good strength and force as though the King's person had been there personally present and had assented openly and publicly to the same".

[55] Although it is sometimes asserted that the House of Lords does not have a Speaker, what is meant is that it does not have a Speaker with regulatory powers as do the Commons. But the House of Lords does have a Speaker, being presently the Lord Chancellor—see Standing Orders 18 and 19. The arrangements for Speaker after the presently proposed abolition of the position of Lord Chancellor remain to be determined.

[56] Interpretation Act 1978 (c.30), s.4(b); see further Chapter 10, Section 1.

[57] 1793 c.13; the underlying purpose of this provision in its original form (which included provision for default commencement at the date endorsed) is indicated by its long title—"An Act to prevent Acts of Parliament from taking effect from a time prior to the passing thereof".

"The clerk of the Parliaments shall endorse (in English)[58] on every Act of Parliament which shall pass after the eighth day of April one thousand seven hundred and ninety-three, immediately after the title of such Act, the day, month and year when the same shall have passed and shall have received the royal assent; and such endorsement shall be taken to be a part of such Act."

The Parliament Acts

The relationship between the House of Lords and the House of Commons has been a matter of political controversy and difficulty for many decades. The ascendancy of the House of Commons, and the superior legitimacy of its authority as the elected Chamber, was given statutory recognition by the Parliament Act 1911.[59]

    The Parliament Act 1911 contains two principal provisions for the purposes of this work.

    Section 1 of the Parliament Act 1911[60] imposes particular constraints on the House of Lords in respect of its examination of Bills sent from the House of Commons that exclusively concern public financial matters.[61] The House of

5.2.50

---

[58] This quaint qualification is inserted on account of the Clerks' penchant, which they have still not entirely conquered, for conducting business in Norman French or Latin.

[59] 1911 c.13; the Act was amended significantly by the Parliament Act 1949 (c.103). For this reason it is common to refer to the application of "the Parliament Acts" although it is in fact only the Parliament Act 1911, as amended, that applies. As to the legitimacy or otherwise of the 1949 amendment of the 1911 Act see the debate on the Second Reading of Lord Donaldson of Lymington's private peer's Bill on the subject—HL Deb. January 19, 2001 cc.1308–32.

[60] The full text of section 1 is as follows—

"1 Powers of House of Lords as to Money Bills

    (1) If a Money Bill, having been passed by the House of Commons, and sent up to the House of Lords at least one month before the end of the session, is not passed by the House of Lords without amendment within one month after it is so sent up to that House, the Bill shall, unless the House of Commons direct to the contrary, be present to His Majesty and become an Act of Parliament on the Royal Assent being signified, notwithstanding that the House of Lords have not consented to the Bill.

    (2) A Money Bill means a Public Bill which in the opinion of the Speaker of the House of Commons contains only provisions dealing with all or any of the following subjects, namely, the imposition, repeal, remission, alteration, or regulation of taxation; the imposition for the payment of debt or other financial purposes of charges on the Consolidated Fund, the National Loans Fund or on money provided by Parliament, or the variation or repeal of any such charges; supply; the appropriation, receipt, custody, issue or audit of accounts of public money; the raising or guarantee of any loan or the repayment thereof; or subordinate matters incidental to those subjects or any of them. In this subsection the expressions 'taxation', 'public money', and 'loan' respectively do not include any taxation, money, or loan raised by local authorities or bodies for local purposes.

    (3) There shall be endorsed on every Money Bill when it is sent up to the House of Lords and when it is presented to His Majesty for assent the certificate of the Speaker of the House of Commons signed by him that it is a Money Bill. Before giving his certificate, the Speaker shall consult, if practicable, two members to be appointed from the Chairmen's Panel at the beginning of each Session by the Committee of Selection."

[61] The definition of this is complex and not without points of uncertainty—see s.1(2) of the Parliament Act 1911.

Commons asserts a privilege in respect of matters relating to the public finance[62] which, in essence, results in the position that while it is seen as not unreasonable for the House of Lords to wish to consider the terms of a Bill which relates exclusively to public money, it is thought unreasonable for that House either to seek to delay the passing of the Bill significantly or to seek to insist upon amendments to it.

5.2.51   Section 1 therefore requires that if a Bill sent from the House of Commons is certified by the Speaker as a Money Bill, the House of Lords must pass it within one month and without amendment. If they fail to do this, the Act requires that the Bill is to be presented for Royal Assent[63] without the involvement of the House of Lords, unless the House of Commons decide otherwise.[64]

Although there is nothing under the Parliament Act 1911 Act to prevent the House of Lords from considering a Money Bill in detail, and indeed passing amendments for the consideration of the Commons, as a general rule proceedings in the House of Lords on a Money Bill are perfunctory and, in particular, do not include a detailed examination in Committee.

Section 2[65] of the Parliament Act 1911 applies to a Bill of any kind and again imposes constraints, although of a lesser nature, on the House of Lords'

---

[62] See above.

[63] For which purpose the normal enactment formula is varied—see s.4(1) of the Parliament Act 1911.

[64] s.1(1).

[65] The full text of s.2 is as follows—

"2 Restriction of the powers of the House of Lords as to Bills other than Money Bills

(1) If any Public Bill (other than a Money Bill or a Bill containing any provision to extend the maximum duration of Parliament beyond five years) is passed by the House of Commons in two successive sessions (whether of the same Parliament or not) and, having been sent up to the House of Lords at least one month before the end of the session, is rejected by the House of Lords in each of those sessions, that Bill shall, on its rejection for the second time by the House of Lords, unless the House of Commons direct to the contrary, be presented to His Majesty and become an Act of Parliament on the Royal Assent being signified thereto, notwithstanding that the House of Lords have not consented to the Bill: Provided that this provision shall not take effect unless one year has elapsed between the date of the second reading in the first of those sessions of the Bill in the House of Commons and the date on which it passes the House of Commons in the second of those sessions.

(2) When a Bill is presented to His Majesty for assent in pursuance of the provisions of this section, there shall be endorsed on the Bill the certificate of the Speaker of the House of Commons signed by him that the provisions of this section have been duly complied with.

(3) A Bill shall be deemed to be rejected by the House of Lords if it is not passed by the House of Lords either without amendment or with such amendments only as may be agreed to by both Houses.

(4) A Bill shall be deemed to be the same Bill as a former Bill sent up to the House of Lords in the preceding session if, when it is sent up to the House of Lords, it is identical with the former Bill or contains only such alterations as are certified by the Speaker of the House of Commons to be necessary owing to the time which has elapsed since the date of the former Bill, or to represent any amendments which have been made by the House of Lords in the former Bill in the preceding session, and any amendments which are certified by the Speaker to have been made by the House of Lords in the second session and agreed to by the House of Commons shall be inserted in the Bill as presented for Royal Assent in pursuance of this section:

Provided that the House of Commons may, if they think fit, on the passage of such a Bill through the House in the second session, suggest any further amendments without inserting

consideration. The general idea here is that it is considered reasonable for the House of Lords to be able to challenge the House of Commons on a Bill other than a Money Bill, and if necessary to delay it for an entire Session, but no longer.

Section 2 therefore provides that if a Bill[66] is sent by the House of Commons to the House of Lords in each of two successive Sessions of Parliament, the House of Lords is obliged to pass the Bill, without insisting on any amendment, in the second Session. The sanction is the same as in the case of a Money Bill, namely that the Bill if not passed without amendment is simply presented for Royal Assent. The substantive terms of the Bill in each Session must be identical.

The Parliament Act 1911 is not relied upon frequently: but it has been used on a few occasions in recent years.[67]

Timing: general

It is normal for the passage of a Bill through its Parliamentary stages to take several months. Most Parliamentary Sessions begin in the late autumn,[68] and a Bill introduced between the start of the Session and Christmas is likely to receive Royal Assent before the summer long adjournment.[69] A number of Bills are

5.2.52

---

the amendments in the Bill, and any such suggested amendments shall be considered by the House of Lords, and, if agreed to by that House, shall be treated as amendments made by the House of Lords and agreed to by the House of Commons; but the exercise of this power by the House of Commons shall not affect the operation of this section in the event of the Bill being rejected by the House of Lords."

[66] Apart from a Money Bill or a Bill to extend the length of a Parliament beyond five years—s.2(1).

[67] The following Acts have been presented for Royal Assent under the Parliament Act 1911: the Government of Ireland Act 1914, the Welsh Church Act 1914, the Parliament Act 1949, the War Crimes Act 1991, the European Parliamentary Elections Act 1999 (an earlier Bill in the same terms having fallen only after an unprecedented and not-so-far repeated number of exchanges between the two Houses), and the Sexual Offences (Amendment) Act 2000. On a number of other occasions Bills have been re-introduced in the House of Commons in circumstances in which they would have been presented for Royal Assent under the Parliament Act 1911 had the Lords not agreed to them, but in the event the Lords have agreed to them: see the Temperance (Scotland) Bill 1913, the Trade Union and Labour Relations Bill 1975–76, and the Aircraft and Shipbuilding Industries Bill 1976–77.

The use of the Parliament Act 1911 to pass the 1949 Act amending it has given rise to extensive argument over the years about the validity of the 1911 Act as amended. See, for example, the debate on the Second Reading of Lord Donaldson of Lymington's private peer's Bill on the subject—HL Deb. January 19, 2001 cc.1308–32. But while the argument has a number of passionate adherents, it has never found favour with a Government of any political persuasion, nor has it been successfully tested in the courts (as to which s.3 of the 1911 Act imposes a significant restraint—"Any certificate of the Speaker of the House of Commons given under this Act shall be conclusive for all purposes, and shall not be questioned in any court of law.").

[68] The obvious exception being Sessions which start after a spring General Election, in which case the first Session of the new Parliament is likely to last for about a year and a half.

[69] But not necessarily—the progress of a government Bill is determined by the Government's Business Managers (the Whips and the Leaders of each House) and they may hold back a Bill begun early in the Session either in order to allow other Bills to make urgent progress or because a matter arising in relation to the Bill makes its delay desirable.

generally begun in each House at the start of the Session, with others being fed in from time to time as the Session progresses.[70]

In cases of need, however, a Bill can pass through all its stages in a matter of just a few weeks, a few days or even in a single day.[71] Where a Bill has failed in one Session and is re-introduced in the next (whether or not with a view to being passed under the Parliament Acts) there are precedents for expediting its progress by curtailing proceedings.[72]

Timing: carry-over of Bills

5.2.53 The general—and once invariable—rule is that a Bill that has not been given Royal Assent before the end of the Session in which it was introduced lapses.

This rule is routinely relaxed for private and Hybrid Bills,[73] both because the need for them is less likely to be either dictated by or accommodated to the Parliamentary calendar and also because of the difficulty in finding time for them to make progress in accordance with their particularly lengthy procedures. The relaxation of the rule is achieved by a motion in the House in which the Bill stands when the Session closes providing, in effect, for a Bill in identical terms introduced at the start of the following Session to be accorded expedited treatment.

In 1998 the two Houses agreed in principle that certain Government Bills of a public general nature might be accorded similar treatment by way of carry over from one Session to another.[74] This has since been implemented.[75] The original intention was that this procedure would be used for Bills that had been introduced late in the Session—particularly as a result of an extended pre-legislative scrutiny by a select or joint committee prior to introduction—and had not managed

---

[70] The Queen's Speech made in opening the Parliamentary Session announces a number of Bills which are expected to form part of the programme, and some but not all of these are likely to be introduced at the start of the Session. But Bills not announced in the Speech are also introduced during a Session, either because the need for them has arisen since the Speech or simply because the Government thought it unnecessary to mention them expressly in the Speech.

[71] See, for example, the Imprisonment (Temporary Provisions) Bill 1980–81 (October 28 and 29, 1980), the Northern Ireland Bill 1971–72, the Prevention of Terrorism (Additional Powers) Bill 1995–96, the Criminal Justice (Terrorism and Conspiracy) Bill 1997–98 (for which Parliament was recalled, following the Omagh bomb) and the Football (Disorder) Bill (July 13, 2000).

[72] See, for example, HC Deb. December 9, 1975 cc.371–418 (re Trade Union and Labour Relations Bill 1975–76), Commons Journals vol.247 p.253 (March 12, 1991 (re War Crimes Bill 1990–91) or HL Deb. May 20, 1992 c.606 (re three Consolidation Bills).

[73] As to which see Section 4 below; and see "When a Session of Parliament is brought to an end by a Dissolution, it is the practice of the House to enable those private Bills that were before it to resume their passage in the new Parliament."—HC Deb. June 16, 1997 c.70 *per* Peter Brooke M.P. moving standard carry-over motion.

[74] House of Lords Select Committee on Procedure of the House, 3rd Report Session 1997–98; House of Commons Select Committee on Modernisation of the House, 3rd Report Session 1997–98.

[75] In the House of Commons by Sessional Order or Temporary Order—see now Temporary Order of October 29, 2002. For the Lords the procedure is informal and arranged ad hoc through the Usual Channels—see paragraphs 6.06 to 6.08 of the *Companion to the Standing Orders and Guide to Procedure*, 2003 Edition.

to complete passage through the first House by the end of the Session. As yet little use has been made of this new procedure.[76]

Withdrawal of Bill

There are, as would be expected, rules about the circumstances in which a Bill once started in either House may be withdrawn or abandoned at different stages.   **5.2.54**

  To give a general flavour of the effect of the rules it will be sufficient to state the following—

> The rate at which a Bill makes progress is in each House entirely a matter for the member in charge of the Bill,[77] subject to the availability of time as decreed by Standing Orders in the House of Commons or as arranged by the Usual Channels in the House of Lords.

> So it is open to a member in charge of a Bill to decline to name a day for its further progress,[78] or to name a day a long way ahead. No other member (including a supporter of the Bill in the House of Commons[79]) can force the pace.[80]

> Once a particular motion has been made to either House by way of or in the course of proceedings on a Bill, however, it is generally not open to any one person, including the person who made the motion (whether or not the member in charge of the Bill) to abort proceedings.[81] They must be brought to a conclusion in the ordinary way, by a vote where appropriate, unless they stand adjourned in accordance with the rules of the House or unless the motion is withdrawn with, generally, the leave of the House.

Private Members' and private peers' Bills

For the most part, a Bill presented by a private Member in the House of Commons or by a private peer in the House of Lords has to pass through the same   **5.2.55**

---

[76] But for an early example of its use see the Planning and Compulsory Purchase Bill 2002–03 carried over to 2003–04.

[77] That is, the person who presents it or who takes it up on its passing from the other House.

[78] Which will generally result in the House's papers recording the Bill as dropped.

[79] Bills presented in the House of Commons note on the back both a presenter and a small number of supporters: but for the purposes of the rules of the House the supporters have no special status in relation to proceedings on the Bill. As to Government Bills, however, the Government acts and is treated as one, and so any Minister, whether a supporter of the Bill or not, can take any step in relation to a Government Bill.

[80] Attempts to hijack a Bill by having an opponent take charge of it on its transmission from one House and then refuse to name a date for its progress would doubtless be thwarted in some manner or another, probably informally: ultimately it is for each House to preserve and adapt as necessary its rules of procedure, and no procedural innovation is impossible if the House sufficiently wishes to achieve it.

[81] It is not, therefore, generally open to a member of either House to "test the water" by embarking on a process and then retreat without injury if the going gets rough: he must be prepared to submit to defeat.

stages, and is subject to the same principles, as a Bill presented by the Government. In practice, of course, the differences of procedure while minor in theory are of enormous practical importance.

The principal difference is strictly speaking nothing to do with the procedures of either House for the passing of public Bills, but arises from the principle that in the House of Commons almost all of the time available for debate and progressing of Bills is at the disposal of the Government. The Order Paper is at the Government's disposal every day except for a few opposition days,[82] a small amount of time for the consideration of private Bills[83] and 13 Fridays each Session[84] for private Members' Bills.

Within those 13 Fridays priority is given, in effect,[85] to the Bills introduced by the Members coming in the top 20 places in a ballot held for the purpose soon after the commencement of each Session. The effect of the allocation of time on the Order Paper is that only those in the top five or so places in the ballot have a realistic prospect of making progress in the face of any significant opposition, while even the top one or two places cannot guarantee success to a Bill opposed even by a small minority, if serious and well-organised. Bills that command general support[86] may make progress if introduced by a Private Member even if he does not secure a top-twenty ballot place.[87]

---

[82] Presently 20 per Session—Standing Order 14(2).

[83] See Section 4 below.

[84] Standing Order No. 14(4).

[85] By preventing earlier introduction of other private Members' Bills.

[86] The Government may support a non-contentious private Member's Bill passively, by not whipping a vote against it, or even actively with the provision of a certain amount of Government time to complete its stages. Sometimes the Government prepare a Bill on a non-contentious matter of insufficient importance or urgency for inclusion in the Government's legislative programme and make it available to a private Member who secures a top-twenty ballot place and who may happen to be interested in the reforms proposed in the Bill: these Bills are known as "handout Bills".

[87] Private Members' Bills are "called over" at the end of debating time on a private Members' Friday with a view to having all or a number of stages taken "on the nod"—that is to say without debate—at that time: while the practice is sometimes deprecated and for long periods has been prevented by the single objecting voice sufficient to prevent a stage from being taken on the nod, over the years there have been a large number of Bills passing multiple stages (sometimes including the making of amendments) on the nod in this way—see, for example, the Bail (Amendment) Bill 1992–93 HC Deb. May 7, 1993 c.470, the New Towns (Amendment) Bill [Lords] and the Mental Health (Amendment) Bill [Lords] HC Deb. March 11, 1994, the Road Traffic Regulation (Special Events) Bill 1993–94 HC Deb. March 11, 1994, the Olympic Symbol etc. (Protection) Bill 1994–95 (second reading, Committee and third reading all on the nod) HC Deb. February 10, 1995 c.636, the Non-Domestic Rating (Information) Bill 1995–96 and the Law Reform (Year and a Day Rule) Bill 1995–96 HC Deb. February 9, 1996 c.624, the Marriage Ceremony (Prescribed Words) Bill 1995–96 HC Deb. March 29, 1996 c.1358, the Party Wall etc. Bill 1995–96 (second reading, Committee, Queen's Consent, Prince's Consent and third reading HC Deb. July 12, 1996 c.760, the Public Order (Amendment) Bill 1995–96 and the Hong Kong (War Wives and Widows) (No.2) Bill 1995–96 HC Deb. July 12, 1996 c.760–1, the Local Government (Gaelic Names) (Scotland) Bill 1996–97 HC Deb. December 13, 1996 c.586, and the Theft (Amendment) Bill [Lords] 1996–97 HC Deb. December 13, 1996 c.586 (despite a statement by the Deputy Speaker reminding the House that the Chair has deprecated going into Committee forthwith when the Bill has only just been published). In recent years there has been sufficient opposition to the principle of passing Bills without debate to prevent much use of the "on the nod" procedure.

A Bill introduced by someone with a top-twenty place in the Session's ballot **5.2.56** is often referred to as a Ballot Bill.

It is possible for a private Member to introduce a Bill that would place a charge upon public funds.[88] Where a money resolution is required[89] the Government will usually[90] arrange for one to be provided, so as not to stifle debate by the use of a technicality: that does not, of course, prevent the Government from opposing the substance of the Bill and whipping a vote against it.

In similar vein, if Queen's Consent is required for a private Member's Bill the Government will usually make the necessary arrangements, again so as not to be seen to stifle debate by use of a technicality.

A statement under s.19 of the Human Rights Act 1998[91] is not required for a **5.2.57** private Member's or private peer's Bill. But—

> "Where the Bill is directly assisted by the Government, however, the Minister responsible for the policy should, as a matter of good practice, express the Government's views on compatibility with the Convention rights during the Second Reading debate."[92]

No hybrid private Member's or private peer's Bill has ever successfully passed through all its Parliamentary stages. The requirements of the procedure applying to hybrid Bills are so time-consuming that by the time they were satisfied and the Bill was able to make progress it would be impossibly far behind other private Members' Bills for that Session.

SECTION 3

PASSAGE OF PUBLIC BILL THROUGH PARLIAMENT

SPECIAL PROCEDURES

Introduction

The normal process of passing a Bill through both Houses of Parliament is, of **5.3.1** course, time consuming, being designed to afford ample opportunity for both the principles and the details of the Bill to be properly scrutinised, and if necessary altered, in each House. The result is that there is enormous pressure on the time available in each Parliamentary Session for the passage of Bills, and even the Government, with most of the time of the House of Commons at least at its

---

[88] But not if that is the principal purpose or effect of the Bill—House of Commons Standing Order 50 permits such Bills to be proceeded upon without a founding financial resolution only if presented by a Minister.

[89] See above.

[90] But not necessarily; and the matter is wholly at the Government's discretion—see HC Deb. April 25, 1995 cc.754–756.

[91] 1998 c.42, as to which see Chapter 11, Section 3.

[92] Home Secretary, Written Answer HC Deb. May 5, 1999.

disposal, is generally hard pressed to achieve the passage of all the primary legislation that it wants to enact.

In the ordinary course of the legislative programme, therefore, it would be almost impossible to find time for Bills which were merely matters of "tidying up" the law without making any change that was substantive or, from a social point of view, significant. In particular, a Bill that is not of practical significance may still have to be of great length—as in the case of a Consolidation Bill—or of considerable technical complexity—as in the case of a Law Reform Bill: in neither case would it be appropriate or realistic to expect Parliament to allow these Bills through without scrutiny of any kind, perhaps by way of Private Members' "back of the chair" Bills.[93] Equally, however, it is not realistic to expect the Government to devote several days of the time available to it in each House to debating and scrutinising a measure which while possibly of considerable importance to the users of the statute book in simplifying and clarifying the form of the law, does not make any substantive contribution to the achievement of the Government's policies.

This is why each House has developed procedures designed to enable Bills of technical importance or merit, but which are not expected to raise issues of party-political or social controversy, to make expedited progress.

Consolidation Bills

5.3.2 If Consolidation Bills were subjected to the same degree of substantive consideration as other Bills it is obvious that there would be time for few if any to make progress in an average Session of Parliament. The Bill for the Education Act 1996, for example, had more than 500 clauses and covered almost every area of the law of education: had it been used as an opportunity to propose and debate by way of amendment innovations in the substance of the law, it would have been impossible to have the Bill passed without occupying an enormous percentage of the Government's available time for legislation. The result of that would be that Governments would be extremely reluctant to introduce consolidation legislation at all and would confine themselves to Bills implementing new policy.

Since it is, however, in the interests of the public in general that Consolidation Bills should be prepared and passed, the two Houses have ordered matters in such a way as to make it possible for Consolidation Bills to be given a fair wind, whilst protecting the system from abuse by building in safeguards to ensure that substantive change is not brought forward in the guise of consolidation.

---

[93] This refers to the practice of introducing a Bill by placing it in a bag on the back of the Speaker's Chair in the House of Commons. As a private Member's Bill without any priority for private Member's time, it can be expected to make progress only if agreed to "on the nod" without debate or objection. For further details of the allocation of time to private Members' Bills, see Section 2 above.

The most important feature of the procedure for the passing of Consolidation Bills, and that which is most responsible for securing their efficient passage, is the use of a Joint Committee of the two Houses of Parliament for their scrutiny. A joint committee for this purpose was first established in 1894 and is renewed by Standing Orders of each House.[94] The committee presently consists of 12 members of each House, with a Law Lord as its Chairman.[95]

It is usual for a Consolidation Bill to be introduced in the House of Lords **5.3.3** under the authority of the Lord Chancellor.[96] Second Reading is generally unlikely to take long, since it is recognised on all sides of each House that it is important to welcome Consolidation Bills and to allow them to make progress. After Second Reading the Bill will stand referred to the Joint Committee.

Proceedings in the Joint Committee are thorough, but principally confined to technical aspects of the Bill rather than to the merits of the substance of the law being consolidated. The Committee routinely takes oral evidence on the Bill from the draftsman and from the relevant Government Department.

The Joint Committee is able to make amendments to the Bill which would have the effect of improving the consolidation.

At the conclusion of their consideration of the Bill the Joint Committee will **5.3.4** make a report to Parliament, either simply confirming that the Bill is a pure consolidation measure which represents the existing law, or drawing the attention of Parliament to any point of special interest in the Bill.

On leaving the Joint Committee the Bill is likely to go through its remaining stages in the House of Lords with expedition and with little or no discussion.

On entering the House of Commons the Bill becomes subject to an expedited procedure under Standing Orders.[97] The essence of the procedure is that no debate is permitted on second or third reading of a Consolidation Bill and the House is simply asked, on the strength of its earlier involvement through its delegates on the Joint Committee, to approve the Bill or to reject it.

It is unusual for a Consolidation Bill to be extensively amended during its passage, partly because of the arrangements for scrutiny, partly because of the absence of substantive controversy and partly because of the greater than usual care and length of time available for the preparation of the Bill before introduction. But a major consolidation is likely to have been subjected to similar time and other constraints in its preparation as other Bills and may require more amending during its passage.[98]

---

[94] House of Commons Standing Order No. 52; House of Lords Standing Order No. 140.

[95] For a discussion of the role and responsibilities of the Joint Committee see [1983] Statute Law Review 133.

[96] Who has ministerial responsibility for the Law Commissions and also, in a general sense, for the state of the statute book. How this responsibility will be assigned with the establishment of the Secretary of State for Constitutional Affairs and the abolition of the office of Lord Chancellor remained to be seen when this work went to print.

[97] Standing Order No. 58.

[98] See, for example, the Bill for the Income and Corporation Taxes Act 1988 (c.1).

Statute Law (Repeals) Bills

5.3.5   The Standing Orders which establish the Joint Committee on Consolidation, &c. Bills[99] give the committee jurisdiction over "bills prepared by one or both of the Law Commissions to promote the reform of the statute law by the repeal, in accordance with Law Commission recommendations, of certain enactments which (except in so far as their effect is preserved) are no longer of practical utility, whether or not they make other provision in connection with the repeal of those enactments, together with any Law Commission report on any such bill".[1]

Since Statute Law (Repeals) Bills are prepared to give effect to a report of the two Law Commissions[2] they attract the provisions of House of Commons Standing Order 59. The result is that they are referred to a second reading committee (or the Scottish Grand Committee, where appropriate) unless the House orders otherwise. Following proceedings in the second reading committee the normal proceedings apply for Bills referred to second reading committee.[3]

Tax-law rewrite Bills

5.3.6   Bills emanating from the Tax Law Rewrite Project[4] require the same kind of protection as Consolidation Bills and for the same reasons.

In the House of Commons Standing Order No. 60 makes the following arrangements—

(1) The procedure is engaged by a Minister presenting a Bill as a tax law rewrite Bill, and obtaining a resolution of the House that the Bill be treated as such.

(2) Second Reading of a tax law rewrite bill is taken in Committee and not on the floor of the House.[5]

(3) On being read a second time a tax law rewrite bill is committed not to an ordinary Standing Committee but to the Joint Committee on Tax Law Rewrite Bills.[6] This Joint Committee proceeds a little like a Standing Committee, with it being possible to table amendments.

(4) On being reported from the Joint Committee a tax law rewrite Bill is committed to a Committee of the Whole House—where it can be expected to be passed swiftly—unless the House orders otherwise. The House can

---

[99] House of Commons Standing Order 140; House of Lords Standing Order 52.
[1] Standing Orders 140(1)(e) and 52(5).
[2] See Chapter 1, Section 9.
[3] Standing Order 90; and see Section 2 above.
[4] See Chapter 1, Section 10.
[5] The procedure in Second Reading Committees is prescribed by Standing Order No. 90.
[6] Established, in so far as the House of Commons is concerned, by Standing Order No. 152C.

agree to a motion dispensing with further Committee proceedings and moving directly to Third Reading.

Proceedings on a tax law rewrite Bill in the House of Lords are affected by the fact that rewrite Bills are invariably introduced into the House of Commons and will generally be certified by the Speaker as Money Bills.[7] The requirement for expedited treatment is therefore imposed by the Parliament Act 1911[8] and does not require to be created by procedure. As a Money Bill, the usual practice in the House of Lords is to have no consideration in Committee at all. But the House of Lords has, of course, representatives on the Joint Committee who will be able to report any matter that they think requires the attention of the House. The House of Lords procedure for tax law rewrite Bills is discussed in the Fourth Report of the Select Committee on Procedure of the House for Session 1999–2000.[9]

---

[7] See Section 1 above.

[8] 1911 c.13.

[9] The relevant part of the report, which was approved by the House (HL Deb. November 13, 2000 cc.11–12), is as follows—

"Tax Simplification Bills

Tax simplification Bills are a new form of legislation proposed by the Tax Law Rewrite Project. They are intended to make the language of tax law simpler, but they preserve the effect of the existing law, subject to any minor changes which may be desirable. Such Bills will normally be introduced into the House of Commons, and it is expected that the Speaker will certify them as money Bills. It is proposed that a Joint Committee of the two Houses should consider the Bills after Second Reading in the Commons and that the Joint Committee's report should be laid before both Houses.

Given the subject matter of tax simplification Bills, the Committee recommends that when the House deals with such Bills:

procedure in the Joint Committee should follow the procedure of Select Committees of the Commons when such procedure differs from that of Select Committees in the Lords, and the chairman of the Joint Committee should have power to select amendments to the Bill; the Committee stage of a tax simplification Bill, being a money Bill, should normally be negatived.

It is intended that the first tax simplification Bill should he introduced early next Session. The Committee therefore recommends that the Joint Committee on Tax Simplification Bills should have the following orders of reference:

Joint Committee on Tax Simplification Bills

(1) That a Select Committee he appointed to join with a committee appointed by the Commons as the Joint Committee on Tax Simplification Bills to consider tax simplification Bills, and in particular to consider whether each Bill committed to it preserves the effect of the existing law, subject to any minor changes which may be desirable;

(2) That the quorum of the committee shall be two;

(3) That the committee have leave to report from time to time;

(4) That the committee have power to appoint specialist advisers;

(5) That the minutes of evidence taken before the committee shall, if the committee think fit, be printed and delivered out; and

(6) That the procedure of the Joint Committee shall follow the procedure of Select Committees of the House of Commons when such procedure differs from that of Select Committees of this House, and shall include the power of the chairman to select amendments."

Law Commission Bills

5.3.7   In the House of Commons there are expedited arrangements for the consideration of Government Bills "the main purpose of which is to give effect to proposals contained in a report by either of the Law Commissions".[10] This provision was introduced in 1995[11] and has remained since, although little used.

It is not always, however, possible to predict accurately what measures of law reform will be regarded as uncontroversial by everyone. Even the fact that a Bill has started and made considerable progress under the expedited procedures for Law Commission Bills is no guarantee that it will not suddenly become the focus of controversy sufficient to prevent its successful passage.[12]

Bills relating exclusively to Scotland or Northern Ireland

5.3.8   The procedures available for separate consideration of Bills relating exclusively to Scotland or Northern Ireland are of less importance since devolution than they were. Select Committees are available for particular consideration of territorial matters where necessary.

SECTION 4

PASSAGE OF NON-PUBLIC BILLS THROUGH PARLIAMENT

Introduction

5.4.1   It will be rare for the practitioner or lay reader to be much concerned in the passage through Parliament of primary legislation other than a public general Bill. And if a person becomes intimately concerned with a particular measure that is not public and general he will need specialised technical advice of a kind not appropriate to be provided here. What follows is therefore merely a brief description of the principal classes of primary legislation other than public general Bills and how their treatment in Parliament differs from that already described in relation to public general Bills.[13]

---

[10] Standing Order 59. The essence of the procedure is referral to a Second Reading Committee—as to which see Section 1 above.

[11] HC Deb. November 2, 1995 c.405.

[12] See, for example, the story of the Family Homes and Domestic Violence Bill 1994–95. Having completed its passage in the House of Lords and made initial progress in the House of Commons the Bill started to attract criticism. "The Family Homes and Domestic Violence Bill was timetabled to complete its stages in the House of Commons on the basis that it was uncontentious. This has proved not to be so. Contentious points have arisen during the last stages of this parliamentary Session. My right hon. and noble Friend the Lord Chancellor has listened to the concerns expressed about the Bill, and he is considering them. The timetable is such, however, that it is now impossible to make further progress this session. My right hon. and noble Friend will continue to work on the Bill with a view to bringing it back before Parliament as soon as possible." Parliamentary Secretary, Lord Chancellor's Department, HC Deb. November 2, 1995 W.A. 415.

[13] See Section 2 above.

This Section deals with the Parliamentary passage of the following kinds of Bill—

Part (1)	Private Bills
Part (2)	Personal Bills
Part (3)	Hybrid Bills
Part (4)	Order Confirmation Bills, &c.

PART (1)

PRIVATE BILLS

Introduction

The nature of a private Bill has been explained earlier in this work.[14]   **5.4.2**
The arrangements for the passage of a private Bill through Parliament are different in three particularly significant respects from those for the passage of a public Bill—

1. There are extensive arrangements made for challenge by those with a particular private interest affected by the Bill.

2. The amount of time available for the consideration of private Bills is severely limited, which can make it difficult or impossible for an opposed private Bill to pass.

3. In determining whether to pass a private Bill each House exercises a role which is as much judicial as it is political, determining not merely whether the provisions sought are politically desirable but whether it has been established by the promoters that they are practically necessary.

This Section sets out the principal features of the private Bill procedure. As in the case of the Section on the procedures for public Bills, this Section provides a legal practitioners' introduction rather than an exhaustive technical guide.
It should be noted that both Houses of Parliament have separate sets of Standing Orders for Private Business.[15]

Introduction of private Bill

As was originally the case for all Bills,[16] a private Bill is introduced on a petition   **5.4.3**
made by the person who wants the Bill to pass into law.[17] That could be an

---

[14] Chapter 1, Section 3.
[15] Undifferentiated references in other Sections of this work to a numbered Standing Order are to the Standing Orders for Public Business. A reference in this Section to a numbered Standing Order is to the Standing Orders for Private Business.
[16] See Section 1 above.
[17] Standing Orders HC 2, HL 2.

individual, but is generally an organisation. A unique feature of the private Bill procedure is therefore that someone other than a Member of Parliament or peer plays a proprietary role in relation to the Bill.

The handling of the Parliamentary procedures is entrusted to a Parliamentary Agent. Certain firms of Parliamentary agents are accredited by the Speaker of the House of Commons as having sufficient expertise to handle the progress of a private Bill through Parliament.

A petition cannot be presented in the House of Commons after November 27 in any year without, in effect, the permission of the Chairman of Ways and Means.[18] Since the promoters will wish to have as long as possible in the Session to attempt to have their Bill passed in one Session, that in effect means that the most suitable window of opportunity for the presentation of a private Bill petition is between the opening of a Session[19] and November 27.

Notice of promotion of Bill, &c.

5.4.4   The Standing Orders require publication in newspapers and the official Gazettes[20] of intention to bring in a private Bill. The notice must "contain a concise summary of the purposes of the bill, but without detailed particulars and without any reference to provisions of an ancillary, subsidiary, or consequential nature intended to give effect to any such purpose".[21] The notice must also state arrangements for inspection and purchase of copies of the Bill and the deadline and arrangements for the deposit of objections to the Bill.

There are also detailed provisions for notice to be given to particular kinds of person in the case of particular kinds of Bill.[22] The promoters are obliged to deposit copies of the Bill with a number of interested authorities,[23] depending on the nature of the Bill, and to arrange for copies to be available to each House.

The promoters are obliged to make arrangements whereby interested parties can obtain copies of the Bill, and they are also obliged to deposit copies of the Bill with various authorities.

---

[18] Standing Order HC 3.

[19] Which can be as late as November: in 2003 it was on November 26!

[20] The London Gazette in any case, and, where the provisions sought affect Scotland or Northern Ireland, the Edinburgh Gazette or the Belfast Gazette.

[21] Standing Orders HC 4, HL 4.

[22] See, for example, "On or before 5th December in the case of a bill whereby it is proposed to authorise the construction of gas works or sewage works, or works for the manufacture or conversion of the residual products of gas or sewage, or a station for generating electricity, or the making, construction or extension of a sewage farm, cemetery, burial ground, crematorium, destructor, or hospital for infectious diseases, notices in writing of the proposal shall be given to the owner, lessee and occupier of each dwelling house situate within 275 metres of the land intended to be used for any such purpose"—Standing Order HC 17 (and see Standing Order HL 17).

[23] Including Government departments in the case of the construction of public works such as railways (but this category has become particularly rare since the advent of the Transport and Public Works Orders, as to which see Chapter 3, Section 8).

In certain cases the promoters are obliged to obtain preliminary consents.[24]

The copies of the Bill made available in accordance with the Standing Orders for preliminary notification are required to be covered by an explanatory memorandum. And the Bill opens with a preamble which states the grounds upon which the promoters believe it necessary for them to obtain the powers and other provisions in the Bill in order to complete the project to which the Bill relates.

The Examiners

The requirements for notice, deposits of plans, consents and the like are lengthy and complicated.[25] Each House therefore appoints Examiners of Petitions for Private Bills.[26] The task of an Examiner is—

> "[to] report to the House whether Standing Orders 4 (Contents of notice) to 59[27] (Cross sections of roads, etc.), so far as applicable, have or have not been complied with; and, when they have not been complied with, he shall also report to the House the facts upon which his decision is founded, and any special circumstances connected with the case."[28]

5.4.5

The examination is obviously a matter of considerable importance, because on the Examiner's report depends the promoters' ability to bring in their Bill. The examination is therefore a formal stage and the promoters have a right to appear or be represented,[29] as have parties alleging non-compliance with the Standing Orders.[30]

Once the Examiner has completed his examination of a private Bill he certifies to both Houses that any Standing Orders applicable to the Bill have, or have not, been complied with. Where there is any deficiency in compliance the report explains the facts and any relevant circumstances.

Cases of non-compliance with the Standing Orders, or cases where there is doubt as to compliance, are referred by each House to its Standing Orders (Private Bills) Committee.[31]

Introduction

The Government cannot introduce a private Bill. Where the Government wish to promote a Bill that affects private rights as well as furthering a public object, the

5.4.6

---

[24] Standing Orders HC 25 and 25A—tramways and London.
[25] Standing Orders HC 4 to 68, HL 4 to 68.
[26] These appointments are generally held by officials of the two Houses.
[27] The remaining preliminary Standing Orders require compliance only after Second Reading.
[28] Standing Orders HC 70, HL 72.
[29] Standing Order HC 74A.
[30] Standing Order HC 75, HL 76.
[31] As to which see Standing Orders HC 103 to 108, HL 84 to 89.

Bill is hybrid and is dealt with in accordance with a procedure composed of elements of the procedures for private Bills and elements of the procedures for public Bills.[32]

Perhaps surprisingly, it is not for the promoters to choose in which House of Parliament to introduce their Bill. The allocation between the two Houses is determined by consultation between the Chairman of Ways and Means in the House of Commons[33] and the Lord Chairman of Committees in the House of Lords.[34] The promoters are usually invited to express views on the House of introduction.

While there are no rigid criteria for allocation, lengthy Bills, particularly technically complicated ones, are likely to be allocated to the House of Lords, and any Bill likely to raise a matter of political contention, or which raises significant financial issues, is likely to be allocated to the House of Commons. If a Bill is substantially for the same purpose as a Bill rejected by one House in a previous Session it is likely to be required to return to that House for introduction. If two Bills are in competition, in the sense that it is unlikely to be desirable to grant the provisions sought in both, they are likely to be required to start in the same House.

Objections by Members of Parliament or peers are taken in the ordinary way of opposition to the progress of the Bill once introduced. But the major difference between private and public Bills in this respect is that whether or not a private Bill is to be opposed determines the procedural steps to be taken in relation to it, as described below.

Human rights

5.4.7 While not falling within the requirements of s.19 of the Human Rights Act 1998,[35] the Standing Orders of each House require the promoters of a private Bill to include in the memorandum attached to the Bill "a statement of opinion, by or on behalf of the promoters, as to the compatibility of the provisions of the bill with the Convention rights (as defined in the Human Rights Act 1998".[36] The Standing Orders then require that a Minister of the Crown prepare a report about the promoters' statement and present it to the House.[37]

---

[32] See Section 2 above.

[33] The title refers to an aspect of the House of Commons supply procedure; but in modern times the Chairman of Ways and Means has become, in effect, the senior assistant to the Speaker, and therefore handles a good deal of non-financial business.

[34] Although the Lord Chancellor is formally the Speaker of the House of Lords, but without disciplinary or regulatory powers, it is the Chairman of Committees who most closely approximates to the Speaker of the House of Commons for many administrative purposes.

[35] As to which see Chapter 11, Section 3.

[36] Standing Order HC 38(3), HL 38.

[37] Standing Order HC 169A, HL 98A; see also, for example, HL Minutes for January 29, 2003—"It was reported by the Chairman of Committees, pursuant to Private Business Standing Order 91

Bill promoted by charity, &c.

A private Bill affecting the constitution or management of a charity or of an **5.4.8**
educational institution cannot be proceeded with in the House of Commons
unless the Attorney-General has made a report to Parliament on the Bill.[38]

Objecting to a private Bill

There are two routes for a person who seeks to object to a private Bill. The first **5.4.9**
is to become personally a formal objector to the Bill. The second is to attract the
attention of a Member of Parliament or a House with a view to their opposing the
Bill during its passage.

Objections to a private Bill may be presented by way of petition by an
individual or organisation that has a genuine interest in the content of the Bill.
Since even a single objection can seriously prejudice a Bill's chances of passing
into law, it would clearly be undesirable to allow people to object merely
capriciously without having a personal or direct interest in the matter.[39] An entire
community can object through the medium of a representative body such as a
parish council. Disputes between the promoters and a potential objector about the
objector's right to petition are referred to the Court of Referees in the case of a
Bill in the House of Commons[40] or determined by the opposed private Bill
Committee to which the Bill is referred in the case of a Bill in the House of
Lords.

Passage of a private Bill

Subject to what follows, the procedures for passing a private Bill are the same as **5.4.10**
for a public Bill.

In the House of Commons, there are regular and frequent opportunities for a
private Bill to pass a stage of its Parliamentary passage where it is unopposed.
But if even a single Member objects to a Bill making progress, the relevant stage
cannot be passed without debate and a vote. Once opposed, therefore, the private

---

(Special circumstances), that he had received a report on the bill from Tony McNulty M.P.,
Minister for Housing, Planning and Regeneration, stating that, in the Minister's opinion, the
promoters had failed to undertake an adequate assessment of the compatibility of their proposals
with European Convention on Human Rights in respect of clause 4(1)."
[38] Standing Order HC 158(1).
[39] It is routine for objections to be deal with at an early stage, before the presentation of a petition,
by negotiations between the promoters and the objectors: which makes it even more desirable to
avoid artificial and groundless objections being used as a form of blackmail to extort money from
the promoters. Hence the control over who may petition. But anyone who falls outside the technical
arrangements for personal objection is still able to pursue any perceived grievance through the
alternative route of encouraging a Member of Parliament or a peer to object to the Bill.
[40] Standing Orders HC 89–102: the Court is composed of (probably back-bench) Members of
Parliament assisted by the House authorities.

Bill has to compete for a share of the very limited time available for debating private business.

The other procedural effect of objections is to determine the nature of the Committee to which a private Bill is committed.[41]

5.4.11   If there are no petitions against a private Bill outstanding at the time when it comes to be committed[42] it is referred to an unopposed Bill committee. This is a relatively small Committee of four plus the Chairman, whose task is to determine whether the promoter of the Bill has established that the Bill is necessary.

Where there are petitions against a private Bill it is committed to an opposed Bill committee.[43] This committee is also composed of four members plus the Chairman, but each Member has to be impartial to the interests concerned in the Bill and has to make a declaration that he or she has neither a personal interest nor a local constituency interest in the Bill.

Both kinds of Committee, but particularly the opposed Bill committees, have more the feel of a judicial inquiry than of other Parliamentary proceedings relating to Bills. In essence, they are indeed inquiries to determine whether the promoters have established to the satisfaction of the House that a Bill is necessary. The promoters are usually represented by Counsel, and objectors may appear through Counsel or in person. In establishing their case for the necessity of the Bill the promoters are likely to call witnesses and adduce evidence.[44]

5.4.12   Objectors to the Bill may seek to have a Bill rejected outright or to have it amended.

Having heard representations and evidence the Committee deliberates in private and determines either that the case for the Bill as expressed in its preamble has been proved or that it has not been proved.[45] The latter finding kills the Bill. If the Committee finds the case for the Bill proved, it goes on to consider the desirability of amendment, particularly for purposes relating to protection of interests of petitioners against the Bill if there are any. Generally, the Committee will consider amending the Bill to reduce the extent of powers granted to the promoters if the Committee concludes that the objects of the Bill can be achieved satisfactorily without taking such broad powers.[46]

The Committee stages are distinct in each House, as in the case of public Bills, and it is therefore possible for a private Bill to have to face two opposed Bill Committees.

---

[41] Before committal certain Bills may have to be re-referred to the Examiners to certify compliance with Standing Orders requiring consents after Second Reading.

[42] *i.e.* at the conclusion of its second reading, as for all Bills.

[43] In the House of Lords referred to as the Select Committee.

[44] In many respects the proceedings can be reminiscent of the private business proceedings graphically described by Anthony Trollope in Chapter XXXII of *The Three Clerks*.

[45] Even an unopposed private Bill committee is entitled to find the case for the Bill not proved—see, for example, the Crossrail Bill 1994–95. In the House of Lords the form of the finding is that "it is not expedient to proceed further with the Bill".

[46] In the House of Lords an opposed private Bill if approved by the Select Committee is returned to an unopposed private Bill Committee.

In other respects the Parliamentary stages of private Bills are the same as for public Bills, including the requirement to be presented for Royal Assent, at which point they become law.

Carry-over

Because of the length of time that can be taken up both with the preliminary arrangements in compliance with Standing Orders and with the passage of an opposed Bill through its Parliamentary stages, and the enormous costs to which the promoters would be put if they had to start completely afresh in each Session having failed to complete the passage of the Bill in the previous Session, it has long been established that private Bills are an exception to the rule against carry-over from one Session to another.[47] Towards the end of each Session the promoters of a private Bill that is in progress in either House will seek motions permitting suspension and revival in the following Session: the effect of the motion is to treat certain stages in the second Session as having been already completed.

5.4.13

PART (2)

PERSONAL BILLS

Personal Bills

The private Bills considered in the preceding passages of this Chapter are those which seek powers in relation to the execution of certain building or other works, or provisions relating to the conduct of institutions, and other matters that may affect private interests but in their purpose and effect go beyond purely personal matters relating to individuals. It is also possible, however, to have a private Bill which is designed to achieve a purpose purely in relation to an individual's personal status or affairs.[48]

5.4.14

Bills relating to the "estate, property, status, or style, or otherwise relating to the personal affairs, of an individual"[49] are brought in upon a petition as for other private Bills, and are all started in the House of Lords.

The petition is referred to the Personal Bills Committee of the House of Lords, who make a report to the House prior to the Bill's being granted a first reading. The promoters are required to satisfy the Committee that "the objects of the Bill are proper to be enacted by a personal Bill".[50] In particular, the Committee will require to be satisfied that—

5.4.15

---

[47] Even before the current experimental provisions in relation to Government Bills—as to which see Section 2 above.
[48] See Chapter 1, Section 3.
[49] Standing Orders HL 3.
[50] Standing Orders HL 154.

(1) the Bill is necessary,

(2) there is no objection of public policy to the provisions of the Bill,

(3) it does not affect public interests, and

(4) all individuals affected by the provisions of the Bill have consented and that proper provision is made for protecting the interests of any children who may be affected.

The Committee can amend the Bill.

Special provision is made for notification of a personal Bill which affects property rights.

Other than as outlined above, the procedure for a personal Bill is broadly the same as for any other private Bill.

PART (3)

HYBRID BILLS

Nature of hybridity

5.4.16 Hybridity is a concept relevant only to Parliamentary procedure and not to the Acts emanating from Bills: that is to say, all hybrid Bills become public general Acts indistinguishable in treatment or effect from any other public general Acts.

The classic definition of a hybrid Bill was provided in the following terms by the Speaker of the House of Commons[51]—

"a public bill which affects a particular private interest in a manner different from the private interests of other persons or bodies of the same category or class".

5.4.17 The precise applications and limits of this definition are technical, being determined both by a system of precedent established over many years and by a practical application of the rules and procedures of each House of Parliament. Whether a particular Bill is hybrid is therefore something that can be advised about only by the officials of the two Houses and others[52] and often only at an advanced stage of preparation of the Bill.

Particular difficulties can be caused by the notion of differentiation among members of the class, it being often unclear what amounts to the relevant class for the purpose. London is now an established exception, whereby a Bill that

---

[51] Mr. Speaker Hylton-Foster speaking on the Bill for the London Government Act 1963.
[52] Notably Parliamentary Counsel.

relates only to matters concerning London will not be considered hybrid merely on that account and will proceed as a public general Bill.

A useful rule of thumb for acquiring a general flavour for the kind of Bill likely to be hybrid is to consider whether the nature of the Bill is such that it is theoretically likely that there would be a class of person with sufficient private interest in the matters affected by the Bill to wish, and be entitled, to petition against the Bill in the event of their private interests not being properly safeguarded or compensated by the promoters of the Bill.

Application of hybridity rules

Ultimately the question whether a Bill is hybrid is determined by the Examiners if referred to them by either House.   **5.4.18**

Introduction

Hybrid Bills are generally introduced by the Government. They are relatively rare,[53] and many Sessions pass without even one being introduced.[54]   **5.4.19**

A hybrid Bill may be introduced into either House, and unlike private Bills it is for the promoter, generally the Government, to choose the House of introduction.

Passage of hybrid Bill

Where the Examiners conclude that that provisions of the Standing Orders relating to Private Bills apply to a public Bill—in other words once the Bill has been found to be hybrid—it will proceed more or less as if it were a Private Bill until after the end of the special Committee proceedings, after which its treatment reverts to that for public general Bills.   **5.4.20**

The early stages are generally handled by a Parliamentary agent in the normal way, while the stages after the conclusion of the special proceedings are generally handled by a government Department in more or less the normal way. Hybrid Bills are generally drafted by Parliamentary Counsel in the normal way.

In both Houses, committal is to a Select Committee.

---

[53] For one thing, the cost, delay and uncertainty associated with the passage of a hybrid Bill make it a highly unattractive option, with the result that the Government are likely to go to considerable lengths to avoid having to introduce a hybrid Bill. This may include abandoning or adjusting policies thought worthwhile in themselves but which are not judged to justify the difficulties associated with hybridity (particularly where a relatively small aspect of a larger set of measures would hybridise what would otherwise be a straightforward government Bill).

[54] Since 1985 the following hybrid Bills have been introduced: Museum of London 1985–1986, Channel Tunnel 1986–1987, Norfolk and Suffolk Broads 1986–1988, Chevening Estate 1986–1987, Dartford-Thurrock Crossing 1987–1988, Caldey Island 1989–1990, Agriculture and Forestry (Financial Provisions) 1990–1991, Severn Bridges 1990–1992, Cardiff Bay Barrage 1991–1993 and Channel Tunnel Rail Link 1994–1996.

Hybrid Bills have been recognised, along with private Bills and for the same reasons, as an exception to the traditional rules against carrying a Bill over from one Session to another.

Bill becoming hybrid

5.4.21   It is possible for an amendment to be tabled to a Bill containing provisions which would render the Bill hybrid if incorporated. In itself that is not a reason for failing to select the amendment in the Commons or for failing to address it in the Lords. If an amendment of that kind were carried in either House, the Bill would be referred at that stage to the Examiners and the provisions relating to private Bills would then be required to be complied with in the ordinary way.

Disapplication of procedure

5.4.22   Since hybridity is a matter only of the rules of procedure of the two Houses, it is open to each House to agree to modify or disapply the application of those rules in a particular case.

So either House could resolve to treat a hybrid Bill as thought it were not hybrid[55] although this is unlikely to be a practical solution except in a case where the Standing Orders were complied with in relation to a recent Bill in the same or very similar terms, or in relation to a Bill where for some reason the prospect of reasonable opposition is remote.

PART (4)

ORDER CONFIRMATION BILLS, &C.

Bills confirming orders under the Private Legislation Procedure (Scotland) Act 1936

5.4.23   The Private Legislation Procedure (Scotland) Act 1936[56] consolidated earlier legislation of 1899 which was originally designed principally to spare promoters of private Bills relating wholly to railways or other public utilities in Scotland the trouble and expense associated with having to travel to London, and to bring their witnesses and evidence, in order to satisfy the requirements of taking a private Bill through the Westminster Parliament.

In essence, the following is the system established by the Act—

The Act establishes a system of non-parliamentary local enquiries for the preliminary stages of the procedure, very much along the lines of the

---

[55] As was done in 1976 in relation to the Aircraft & Shipbuilding Industries Bill.
[56] 1936 c.52.

preliminary proceedings established for private Bills by the Standing Orders described in Part 1 of this Chapter.

Following the enquiries, the Secretary of State can issue a provisional order, but in deciding whether or not to do so he has regard to a report of the Chairman of Committees in the House of Lords and the Chairman of Ways and Means in the House of Commons, who in turn have regard to the weight of opposition to the proposals and to other matters.[57]

If the Secretary of State does make a provisional order, it has effect only if confirmed by Parliament.

Confirmation is achieved by a Government Bill, normally presented in the House of Commons. Despite being presented by the Government, an order confirmation Bill is treated as a private Bill, having to compete with private Bills for debating time and being, if passed, printed in the local and personal Act series. **5.4.24**

Expedited procedures are provided for a Bill confirming an order as to which there was no inquiry—and which is therefore treated as having been effectively unopposed. In the case of a Bill confirming an order as to which an inquiry was held, it is possible—although unusual—to have further objections referred to a Joint Committee.

The advent of devolution[58] means that this procedure will now be required only for matters as to which legislative power is reserved to the Westminster Parliament.[59] But the Transport and Works Act 1992[60] does not apply in Scotland and has not therefore diminished the number of order confirmation Bills in the same way as it has diminished the number of private Bills in relation to works in England and Wales.

Provisional Order Confirmation Bills

The Provisional Order Confirmation Bill procedure, having been used commonly in the late nineteenth and early twentieth centuries, is now moribund.[61] **5.4.25**

---

[57] "If it appears from the report of the Chairmen that in their opinion the provisions or some of the provisions of the draft Order relate to matters outside Scotland to such an extent, or raise questions of public policy of such novelty and importance, that they ought to be dealt with by Private Bill and not by Provisional Order, the Secretary of State shall, without further inquiry, refuse to issue the Provisional Order, so far as the same is objected to by the Chairmen."—s.2(2).

[58] As to which see Chapter 4.

[59] See Chapter 4, Section 2.

[60] 1992 c.42: as to orders under which see Chapter 3, Section 8.

[61] Having been overtaken, in particular, by the Statutory Orders (Special Procedure) Act 1945 procedure discussed above. The only recent examples of use of this procedure are the presentation of two Bills in the 1979–80 Session under the General Pier and Harbour Acts 1861 and 1862 (now repealed by the Transport and Works Act 1992—as to which see Chapter 3, Section 8) and of one Bill under the Public Health Act 1936 in the 1976–77 Session.

The essence of the system is that an Act[62] lays down a framework procedure for action in relation to some kind of public work, enabling local authorities or others to adopt a procedure and have their adoption confirmed by Act. The system of confirmation is broadly similar to that adumbrated above for orders under the Private Legislation Procedure (Scotland) Act 1936.

Statutory Orders (Special Procedure) Act 1945

5.4.26 The Statutory Orders (Special Procedure) Act 1945[63] can in particularly contentious cases give rise to confirmation Bills of a kind similar to that discussed above for Provisional Orders. But it is very rare.[64]

Orders under the 1945 Act are described in Chapter 3, Section 8.

---

[62] See, in particular, the Commons Act 1876 (c.56), the Public Health Act 1936 (c.49) and the Public Health (Drainage of Trade Premises) Act 1937 (c.40).

[63] 1945 c.18.

[64] The only examples being the Mid-Northamptonshire Water Order Confirmation (Special Procedure) Bill 1948–49 and the Okehampton By-pass (Confirmation of Orders) Bill 1985–86.

CHAPTER 6

SUBORDINATE LEGISLATION

Introduction

Works about legislation and statutory interpretation have traditionally focused principally on the Act of Parliament, particularly in the context of the process of drafting and passing legislation. But statutory instruments are of increasing importance to the practitioner, with more and more Acts doing little more than providing a skeleton to be fleshed out by subordinate legislation.[1] It is therefore important for anyone who wants to understand the process by which legislation comes to be produced to understand as much about the process of producing subordinate legislation as about the process of enacting primary legislation. **6.1.1**

Responsibility for the making of subordinate legislation

Powers to make subordinate legislation are generally delegated to Ministers of the Crown. **6.1.2**

The most common recipient of a power nowadays is "the Secretary of State" by which is meant[2] any of those persons who hold the office of Secretary of State.

---

[1] Perhaps the most extreme example of this is the Financial Services and Markets Act 2000 (c.8), which could be said to consist almost entirely of a scheme of enabling powers. This is for the powerful reason that both the practical matters with which the act deals, and the European legislation which permeates the control of those matters, are too fluid to be capable of capturing in primary legislation. Or to give another example, the Employment Relations Act 1999 (c.26) deals in ss.7, 8 and 19 with the highly socially significant matters of part-time employment, paternity leave, maternity leave and domestic leave; and it does so entirely by conferring a range of very broad powers, again because of the fluidity inherent in the subject matter and in the European legislation that increasingly controls it. While these are extreme examples, there are many other Acts which would serve almost as well to illustrate the shift of emphasis towards subordinate legislation. Indeed there are few if any Acts passed nowadays of significance that do not at some point legislate by enacting at most the broad principle and leaving the essential details to subordinate legislation. See further Chapter 1, Section 2, and Chapter 3, Section 1.

[2] Interpretation Act 1978 (c.30), Sch.1.

Almost every senior Minister[3] is now a Secretary of State.[4] Powers are also occasionally vested in other senior Ministers.[5]

Powers are not vested in junior Ministers[6] and could not properly be so vested. A power should vest in the senior Minister of a department, and be exercised by him through the agency of officials and junior Ministers as appropriate under the rule in *Carltona*.[7]

In addition to special instances dealt with elsewhere in this work of the delegation by Parliament of power other than to a Minister,[8] there are a number of particular occasions on which legislative power is delegated to a person other than a Minister of the Crown. The most significant examples are the common delegation of powers by Finance Acts to the Commissioners of Inland Revenue or to the Commissioners of Customs and Excise[9] and the delegation of powers in relation to procedural rules of courts and tribunals to committees.[10] There are also occasional less significant instances of delegation to other non-Ministerial persons.[11]

---

[3] By which is meant, in this context, a Minister to whom are assigned by the Prime Minister responsibilities for substantive aspects of government and who heads a department of officials and, normally, junior ministers, dedicated to addressing those responsibilities under his control. There is no necessary correlation between seniority in this sense and membership of the Cabinet. While a Secretary of State is normally a member of the Cabinet, there are other Ministers who may be appointed to "sinecure" positions such as Chancellor of the Duchy of Lancaster or Lord Privy Seal whose political importance is such that they occupy Cabinet seats. And it is has been known for Ministers of State—junior departmental Ministers—to sit in Cabinet.

[4] See further Chapter 3, Section 12.

[5] See, for example, the commencement power vested in the Lord Privy Seal by s.5 of the Chevening Estate Act 1987 (c.20) or the power of the Lord President of the Council under s.15 of the Copyright Act 1911 (c.46) (transferred to him by SI 1986/600). While powers are transferred both to and from these "sinecure" offices by Transfer of Functions Orders, it is possible to identify a general trend over the years of the more substantive functions away from these offices to the Secretary of State—for example, the once extensive functions of the Lord President of the Council under the Atomic Energy Authority Act 1954 (c.32) were transferred to the Secretary of State.

[6] That is to say Ministers of State and Parliamentary Under-Secretaries of State, being Ministers responsible to (and historically appointed by or at the request of) senior Ministers in charge of a Department.

[7] As to which see Chapter 12, Section 4.

[8] Orders in Council, Resolutions of either House, the Scottish Parliament, the National Assembly for Wales, the Northern Ireland Assembly and the Church Assembly.

[9] These are both statutory boards which are to some extent independent of Ministers in the performance of their functions, although for many purposes they come under the regulation and control of the Treasury. As to the Treasury, the original ministerial office of Lord High Treasurer of England has been in commission for many years and the functions are exercised by the Commissioners of Her Majesty's Treasury who act to all intents and purposes as a single ministerial office, the senior minister being nominally the Prime Minister but in practice the Chancellor of the Exchequer.Statutory references to the Treasury are references to the Commissioners—see Interpretation Act 1978 (c.30), Sch.1. A number of the junior commissioner posts are used for non-financial political purposes, including Whips and other business managers in both Houses.

[10] See, for example, s.2 of the Civil Procedure Act 1996 (c.12).

[11] See, for example, the delegation to (*inter alia*) the Forestry Commissioners by s.13 of the Channel Tunnel Act 1987 (c.53); or the power in the Public Health (Control of Disease) Act 1984 (c.22), s.16 for local authorities by order subject to the approval of the Secretary of State to direct notifiable diseases; or the Registration of Births, Deaths and Marriages (Miscellaneous Amendments) Regulations 1995 (SI 1995/744) made by the Registrar General with the approval of the

It is common for an instrument to be made by more than one Minister. Where a power is conferred on two Ministers concurrently, either may exercise it. Where it is conferred on two Ministers jointly, it may be made only by the two Ministers acting jointly. And where a power is conferred on "the Secretary of State" it may be thought appropriate, particularly for instruments having a significant territorial effect in relation to Scotland, Wales or Northern Ireland, for more than one Secretary of State or junior Minister to exercise the power.[12]

Consultation

It is common for the Minister in whom a power to make delegated legislation is vested to be under a statutory duty to consult before he exercises it.[13] Failure to consult will generally render voidable any purported exercise of the delegated power. While a duty to consult falls far short of a duty to comply with the wishes of the consultee, it is also more than a pure formality, requiring the person consulting to give his mind in a genuine way to matters raised by those consulted.[14]   **6.1.3**

Other conditions

The power to make subordinate legislation is often conferred subject to the prior satisfaction of specified conditions. Consultation, already discussed, is the most common.   **6.1.4**

Another frequent requirement is to obtain Treasury consent in the case of an instrument having significant financial implications.[15] Where Treasury consent is required it is signified by two Commissioners of Her Majesty's Treasury.[16]

Secretary of State for Health. A particularly striking instance is s.7 of the Public Schools Act 1868 (c.118) which empowered the governing bodies of certain schools to amend existing statutes of those schools whether having force by virtue of an Act or otherwise: while striking, the force of this example is moderated both by its localised effect and also by the fact that the result has to be approved by Order in Council.

[12] See, for example, the Scallop Fishing Order 2004 (SI 2004/12)—"The Secretary of State for Environment, Food and Rural Affairs, in exercise of the powers conferred by s.1 of the Sea Fish (Conservation) Act 1967, and now vested in her, and she and the Secretary of State concerned with the sea fishing industry in Northern Ireland, in exercise of the powers conferred by ss.3, 15(3) and 20(1) of that Act, and now vested in them, make the following Order . . . ".

[13] See, for example, s.25(2) of the Access to Justice Act 1999 (c.22)—"Before making any remuneration order relating to the payment of remuneration to barristers or solicitors the Secretary of State shall consult the General Council of the Bar and the Law Society".

[14] "The essence of consultation is the communication of a genuine invitation, extended with a receptive mind, to give advice"—*Agricultural, Horticultural and Forestry Industry Training Board v Aylesbury Mushrooms Ltd* [1972] 1 All E.R. 280, 284 QBD *per* Donaldson J.

[15] It was once common for instruments authorising significant expenditure to require Treasury consent. In recent years the requirement for Treasury consent has been imposed more sparingly, and is now found particularly, although not exclusively, in relation to powers with a financial flavour (such as powers to give directions about remuneration or accounts).

[16] In accordance with s.1 of the Treasury Instruments (Signature) Act 1849 (c.89).

Failure to have consent signified where required is fatal and renders an instrument a nullity.[17]

Satisfaction of consultation or other conditions prior to the making of an instrument ought, as a matter of good legislative practice, to be recorded in the preamble or recitals to the instrument itself, so that the reader is made aware both of the requirements to be satisfied before the relevant power can be exercised and that it has been exercised in the manner recited. Failure to comply with this practice is likely to attract the criticism of the Joint Committee on Statutory Instruments.[18]

Drafting responsibility

6.1.5 With few exceptions, statutory instruments are drafted not by Parliamentary Counsel but by departmental lawyers,[19] acting on the instructions of their policy clients, the departmental administrators. As a general rule there is likely to be less formality about the process than in the case of primary legislation, and the separation of roles between the formulation of policy and its implementation through drafting is likely to be less strictly observed. But the precise nature of the process will depend on a number of factors, including general working practices in the department concerned and the nature of the statutory instrument concerned.

Again as a rule, the process of drafting is only one part of the role of departmental lawyers, and they will be called on to draft any statutory instrument which is required in the area of law for which they have advisory responsibility at the time. The result is that the draftsman of a statutory instrument may be relatively inexperienced in the art of drafting (although he or she may be a highly experienced expert in the art) but he or she will certainly be thoroughly versed in the technicalities of the area of law concerned, and will generally have acquired considerable expertise in its application to practical and substantive

---

[17] Note, for example, "The Department reply . . . that due to an oversight the Order did not receive the consent of the Treasury and is therefore invalid. When the error was drawn to the attention of the Department by the Committee they set in motion the making of a new Order, which was made (with the consent of the Treasury) on 12th November, laid before Parliament on that day and came into force on 13 November."—Joint Committee on Statutory Instruments, Session 1998–99, 1st Report, para.9 (HL Paper 4, HC 50-i).

[18] See, for example, "Section 3(3) of the Opticians Act 1989 required certain consultations to be carried out before this Order could be made. The recitals to this instrument make no reference to that consultation. In a memorandum printed in Appendix VI the Privy Council confirm that the required consultation was in fact carried out, but admit that 'it would have been an improvement to the drafting' of the present Order to have included a reference to consultation in the recitals. The Committee considers that such a reference should indeed have been made, and in its absence reports the instrument for defective drafting as acknowledged by the Department."—Joint Committee on Statutory Instruments, Session 1994–95, 4th Report, para.7 (HL Paper 17, HC 8-iv).

[19] Most large Government Departments have a permanent staff of lawyers working under the departmental legal adviser. Some of the smaller departments are served by lawyers from the Treasury Solicitor's department, either on secondment or by arrangement with the Treasury Solicitor.

matters. Although some areas of law require less legislation than others, in the course of a typical career a departmental lawyer will acquire considerable experience of drafting. In addition, all departments have arrangements, of greater or lesser formality, for the scrutiny of draft statutory instruments by a departmental lawyer of particular experience in drafting.

Statutory instruments that amend primary legislation are by a rule of government shown in draft to Parliamentary Counsel, as are Deregulation Orders and Regulatory Reform Orders.[20]   **6.1.6**

A few statutory instruments are drafted by Parliamentary Counsel on instructions from departmental lawyers. The most significant class of these nowadays is Transfer of Functions Orders.[21] Apart from a number of other kinds of less common instrument, an instrument may be drafted or settled by Parliamentary Counsel, by *ad hoc* agreement between a department and the First Parliamentary Counsel.

Instruments appertaining to particular professional or other organisations may be drafted by lawyers or others employed by the organisation. Where this occurs it is important that the Government department responsible for the area within which the organisation operates makes arrangements to scrutinise the drafting of the instrument before it is approved or submitted to the Privy Council to be made.[22]

Explanatory Notes

Unlike the Explanatory Notes for Bills and Acts which are a recent innovation,[23]   **6.1.7** it has been the practice for many decades to append to a statutory instrument a note which describes its principal effects for the benefit of easy assimilation of the instrument's purport.

The explanatory note to an order is appended to the instrument and is introduced by the heading Explanatory Note followed by the italic words *"This note is not part of the Order"*.[24] These words, which would probably be implied were they not expressed, are designed simply to warn the reader not to construe the finer points of the note and compare it with the text: or, rather, to accord precedence to the text of the instrument should there be any apparent conflict between it and the note. The words do not, of course, prevent the courts from having regard to the note in so far as it may illuminate the legislative purpose of the instrument and aid construction.[25]

---

[20] As to which see Chapter 3, Section 9.
[21] See Chapter 3, Section 12.
[22] See the comments of the Joint Committee on Statutory Instruments Session 1992–93, 37th Report, July 13, 1993 (HL Paper 108, HC 51-xxxvii) para.2.
[23] See Chapter 9, Section 5.
[24] Before 1965 the formula was *"This Note is not part of the Order, but is intended to indicate its general purport."*
[25] As to the extent to which the courts will use the note for this purpose, see Chapters 26 and 27.

The explanatory note is written by the Department responsible for the content of an instrument, and submitted by them to Her Majesty's Stationery Office to be printed as an appendix to the instrument. Because these notes are generally very short, amounting generally to less than a page in length, the practice is not to print them separately from the instrument, as is the case for Bills and Acts,[26] but simply to append them. The notes may be written by departmental administrators rather than lawyers: but they will certainly have been considered and approved by the lawyers responsible for the drafting of the instrument itself.

Despite not being authoritative or comprehensive, it is obviously important that the explanatory note be accurate. A reader can be expected to consult the note before turning to the text of the instrument, and anything that seriously misleads him, and causes him to miss something in the instrument, could cause serious injustice. The Joint Committee on Statutory Instruments considers the substance of explanatory notes and has been known to criticise them and even to go to the lengths of demanding that they be corrected.[27]

Title, headings, footnotes, &c.

6.1.8 The title of an instrument is, as in the case of the short title of an Act, chosen by the draftsman so as to provide a convenient label by which to refer to an instrument, and a unique identification for it. It is common for the titles of instruments to be considerably longer than would be thought proper for Acts,[28] and the additional accuracy provided by a long title may be thought to justify the length, principally in cases where it is unlikely that it will often be necessary to make references or cross-references to the instrument. The principle remains,

---

[26] The policy for separate printing for Bills and Acts in hard copy is partly a matter of simple practicality, since it is increasingly difficult to print a Bill or Act as a single volume (and two volume Bills and Acts are now common for Finance Bills and Acts and not unprecedented for other cases) even without the Explanatory Notes. In part, however, the aim is to avoid forcing a reader to pay for a product that he does not want: separate printing and pricing makes it possible for the reader to choose to buy only the Act or the Act and the Notes (or, although this is unlikely, only the Notes).

[27] "The Committee considers that the Explanatory Note is extremely misleading . . . . The Committee considers that the Department of Trade and Industry . . . . miss the point when they seek to defend the omission of a vital qualification by reference to the user's ability to refer to the full provision in regulation 2(b). Trade and professional periodicals commonly reproduce the Explanatory Note of instruments relevant to their readers, who will have no reason to suspect such a material inaccuracy. In the Committee's view it calls for the issue of a correction slip."—Joint Committee on Statutory Instruments Session 1992–93 23rd Report March 9, 1993 (HL Paper 68 HC 51-xxiii); see also Joint Committee on Statutory Instruments, Session 1995–96, 19th Report, para.4 (HL Paper 72, HC 34-xix).

[28] See, for example, the following instruments from 2003: No. 3300—The Anti-social Behaviour Act 2003 (Commencement No. 1 and Transitional Provisions) Order 2003; No. 3308—The Tax Credits (Provision of Information) (Evaluation and Statistical Studies) Regulations 2003; No. 3319—The Conduct of Employment Agencies and Employment Businesses Regulations 2003; No.3339—The Watford and South of St Albans-Redbourn-Kidney Wood, Luton (Special Road Scheme 1957) (Park Street to Beechtrees Partial Revocation) Scheme 2004; and No. 3342—The Veterinary Surgeons and Veterinary Practitioners (Registration) Regulations Order of Council 2003.

however, that as a general rule shorter titles are likely to be more convenient for all concerned.

That the title of an instrument should be unique is clearly a necessity, and where by accident it happens that two instruments are made with the same title steps will be taken, probably involving the revocation and re-making of one instrument, to remedy the situation.[29]

It is common to have multiple exercises of an enabling power titled in the form of a numbered series. The most common example is commencement orders, which generally take the form of "The X Act (Commencement No. Y) Order [Year]". While it is for obvious reasons neither necessary nor always desirable to use No.1 in the title of what may prove to be the first of a series, it is not uncommon for draftsmen infused with a minor but certain spirit of prophecy to do so.[30]

Signature

Signature is to subordinate legislation as Royal Assent is to Acts: it is the formal **6.1.9** action which transforms the legislation from the prospective to the actual, without which any text is merely a draft. Before the text of an instrument has been signed by the Minister or other person purporting to legislate, nothing irrevocable has occurred and the instrument may be amended at will or abandoned. Once the text has been signed the law has been made and, subject to any provision for delayed commencement, has effect.

A Minister who thinks better of an item of legislation between its being signed and its being registered and printed has no power to abort it, although depending on the circumstances he is likely to have power to make another instrument revoking or amending the first.[31]

A Minister in whom a power to make subordinate legislation is vested may delegate to a junior Minister or to an official the function of signing (and therefore making) an instrument in the exercise of that power, in accordance with the general *Carltona* principle.[32] There are no rules for determining when an instrument may or should be signed on behalf of the senior Minister, nor for determining when the delegate should be a junior Minister and when an official, nor for determining what grade of official may properly act for this purpose. Examination of any recent batch of statutory instruments will demonstrate wide

---

[29] See, for example, the two commencement orders registered with identical titles (Criminal Justice and Public Order Act 1994 (Commencement No. 9) Order 1996) as a result of which one was remade as the (No. 10) Order (SI 1996/1608).

[30] For early examples see SI 1951/142 and 1964/1849; as to headings generally see further Chapter 3, Section 3.

[31] And there is nothing to prevent the revocation of an instrument before it has come into force.

[32] As to which see Chapter 12, Section 4.

diversity of practice, with no apparent distinguishing features of different cases.[33] It was once[34] widely thought that an instrument to be laid before Parliament should not be signed by an official for the Minister, but the convention is no longer observed: although in recent years signature by officials in any case has been little used for instruments of general significance.

Regulatory impact assessment

6.1.10 The rules for the production of a regulatory impact assessment, set out in Chapter 5, Section 1, are the same for subordinate legislation as for primary legislation.

Notification to European Commission

6.1.11 Certain statutory instruments require to be notified to the European Commission in draft.[35]

SECTION 2

PARLIAMENTARY SCRUTINY

Introduction

6.2.1 As a general rule, subordinate legislation is either subject to "affirmative resolution", to "negative resolution" or to no express form of Parliamentary scrutiny.

In the latter class the word "express" should be stressed. Subject to certain agreed self-denying principles in relation to cases before the courts and similarly sensitive matters, either House of Parliament may debate anything that it

---

[33] So, for example, the Scallop Fishing Order 2004 (SI 2004/12) is signed by the Parliamentary Under Secretary of State, Department for Environment, Food and Rural Affairs for his Secretary of State, but by the Secretary of State for Northern Ireland in person; the Bus Service Operators Grant (Amendment) (England) Regulations 2004 (SI 2004/9) is described as being signed "by authority of the Secretary of State for Transport" by a Parliamentary Under Secretary of State in the Department for Transport.

[34] Within the last three decades.

[35] Council Directive 83/189/EEC of 28 March 1983 (as amended) laying down a procedure for the provision of information in the field of technical standards and regulations Directive 83/189/EEC.

"... Whereas barriers to trade resulting from technical regulations relating to products may be allowed only where they are necessary in order to meet essential requirements and have an objective in the public interest of which they constitute the main guarantee;

"Whereas it is essential for the Commission to have the necessary information at its disposal before the adoption of technical provisions ; whereas, consequently, the Member States which are required to facilitate the achievement of its task pursuant to Article 5 of the Treaty must notify it of their projects in the field of technical regulations;

"Whereas all the Member States must also be informed of the technical regulations contemplated by any one Member State; ... " (Preamble).

chooses. So even in the case of an instrument where the primary legislation provided for no express form of Parliamentary scrutiny, it would be perfectly possible for the legislation to be debated in either House.[36] The principal difference between an informal scrutiny of this kind and one following a track laid down by the statute would be the absence of legal consequences of a majority vote disapproving of the legislation: but the political pressure could be considerable and might have much the same effect in practice as under the formal mechanisms for scrutiny.

Affirmative resolution

The affirmative resolution procedures are reserved for the more significant exercises of delegated power.[37]   **6.2.2**

Approval in draft

In the normal case of affirmative resolution procedure, Parliament requires an opportunity to approve each proposed exercise before it is made, by considering and passing a resolution in each House approving a draft of the instrument.   **6.2.3**

The House of Lords Select Committee on Delegated Powers and Regulatory Reform have opined that as a general rule this affirmative procedure should be used for any power that consists of or includes the power to amend primary legislation.[38] And in 1973 the Joint Committee on Delegated Legislation recommended[39] that affirmative resolution procedure was as a general rule appropriate for—

powers substantially affecting provisions of Acts of Parliament,

---

[36] While the time of the House in the House of Commons is for the most part at the disposal of the Government, the same is not true of the House of Lords. And even in the House of Commons the Standing Orders provide for a certain number of sittings to be placed at the disposal of the opposition parties. And there are a number of different ways in which a back-bench Member from any party can arrange to have a topic of particular interest debated.

[37] See further Chapter 1, Section 2.

[38] Session 2002–03 Third Report, December 16, 2002—"We note again with regard to the twelve appended examples [of "Henry VIII powers" to amend primary legislation by statutory instrument] that, as with their wording, the level of Parliamentary scrutiny varies.In some cases the negative procedure is used; in some the affirmative; and in others the affirmative procedure is used if an enactment is to be amended but otherwise negative. We are not surprised that this is the case. We recognise that in some instances the negative procedure provides a sufficient level of Parliamentary scrutiny. We take the view, however, that there should be a presumption in favour of the affirmative procedure and that reasons for any departure from the affirmative procedure should be set out in full in the Explanatory Notes accompanying a bill and in the memorandum submitted to this Committee." The Government have adopted the position that each case should be considered individually, but have appeared to accept the general presumption in the case of the amendment of primary legislation—see Lord Bassam of Brighton HL Deb. March 27, 2003 c.1020–21 speaking on the Courts Bill 2002–03.

[39] The "Brooke Report", para.78; cited in, for example, the memorandum by the Department for Constitutional Affairs given in the Written Evidence to the Joint Committee on Human Rights, 17th November 2003 (Session 2002–03, 19th Report) or the memorandum by the Department for Social Security to the Select Committee on Delegated Powers and Deregulation, printed with the 7th Report Session 1996–97 (HL Paper 16).

powers to impose or increase taxation, and

other powers of special importance, for example, those creating serious criminal offences.

The standard way of introducing a requirement for affirmative resolution is for the enabling statute to provide that a power may not be exercised unless each House (or, in certain financial contexts, the House of Commons alone) has passed a resolution approving of a draft of the instrument. In these cases the Government will table in each House a motion for the approval of the instrument and provide time to debate it. This still involves a considerable saving of Parliamentary time compared to the position if the provisions were included in a Bill, partly because a draft instrument is considered only once in each House[40] and partly because there is no equivalent of the Committee stage, and no opportunity to table and debate amendments to the instrument.[41]

An affirmative resolution sought by the Government is very rarely denied.[42]

---

[40] And in the House of Commons substantive consideration is likely to take place in Committee, and does not therefore take up time on the floor of the House—see Standing Order 118.

[41] The inability to amend a statutory instrument causes considerable frustration from time to time, and occasional suggestions are made to permit it, either generally or in specific contexts.

See, for example, the letter from the Chairman of Ways and Means to the House of Commons Select Committee on Procedure of the House, Appendix 2 to the Minutes of Evidence taken before the Committee, First Report Session 1999–2000, March 7, 2000.

See also "The bill, quite rightly in the Committee's view, requires the affirmative resolution procedure. This procedure, however, does not allow the House to amend an order. Given that the power has to be open-ended in order to meet any need that could arise, and that it might be used to make extensive changes to existing legislation, the House may wish to consider whether there is a case for developing a new procedure to scrutinise such orders modelled on that for the second stage parliamentary scrutiny of deregulation orders. Such a procedure could allow for a limited period in which the proposal to make a remedial order could be considered by both Houses of Parliament, with the opportunity that would give for amendments to be proposed."—Human Rights Bill 1997–98, Select Committee on Delegated Powers and Deregulation, Session 1997–98, 6th Report, November 5, 1997, para.24.

Note also that procedures such as that under the Transport and Works Act 1992 (as to which see Chapter 3, Section 8) in effect permit amendment of instruments, through the medium of draft proposals.

And note that the procedure for emergency regulations in Part 2 of the Civil Contingencies Bill 2003–04 permits actual amendment of regulations by the two Houses of Parliament.

Where an instrument cannot be amended, either House may attempt to make a specific point likely to lead to replacement of the instrument with an amended version by drawing attention to a specific defect in the course of a motion to annul or to approve—see, for example, the House of Lords attempt to approve an instrument while adding by amendment to the motion "that the draft order . . . be approved" the words "but that this House regrets that the proposed boundary does not enjoy full public support and note the clarity about arrangement which will be made for a number of matters, including the future of the Yorkshire Museum" (amendment defeated on Division) —North Yorkshire (District of York) (Structural and Boundary Changes) Order 1995—HL Deb. March 6, 1995 cc.109–10.

Note also the motion, taken immediately after a withdrawn motion for annulment of regulations, "that this House calls on Her Majesty's Government, following the implementation of the Social Security (Persons From Abroad) Miscellaneous Amendments Regulations 1996, to ensure that asylum seekers pursuing appeals have visible legal means of support pending the conclusion of their appeals"—HL Deb. January 30, 1996.

[42] But see footnote 56, below.

Affirmative resolution after instrument made

It can happen that a particular power is sufficiently serious for Parliament to wish **6.2.4** its exercise to be subject to affirmative resolution, while the Government fears that it may sometimes be necessary to exercise the power with greater rapidity than the constraints of the Parliamentary timetable allow.[43] In such cases a compromise is sometimes effected, whereby the power is granted subject to the condition that it be exercised following affirmative resolution approving a draft, but the Government is expressly permitted to exercise the power in case of urgency without first obtaining an affirmative resolution.[44]

The standard practice in such a case is as follows—

(1) The Minister exercising the power is required to declare that it is necessary by reason of urgency to exercise the power without approval of a draft.

(2) The declaration is included in the instrument, generally as part of the recital or preamble.

(3) The Minister is required to lay the instrument before both Houses after its being made.

(4) The instrument ceases to have effect if it is not approved by each House within a period of having been laid.

(5) The normal period is 40 days, calculated in accordance with section 7(1) of the Statutory Instruments Act 1946[45] (which allows periods of adjournment of more than four days, and periods when Parliament is prorogued[46] or dissolved,[47] to be ignored).

A similar arrangement can be provided as the normal course for the exercise of a particular power. See, for example, s.46 of the Agricultural Marketing Act 1958 (c.47).

Negative resolution

Normal procedure

The most common arrangement for Parliamentary scrutiny of subordinate **6.2.5** legislation is referred to colloquially simply as the "negative resolution"

---

[43] Particularly if the power may need to be exercised during the summer, when there can be an interval of several weeks during which Parliament does not sit and an affirmative resolution cannot therefore be obtained.

[44] See, for example, s.123(5) and (6) of the Terrorism Act 2000 (c.11).

[45] 1946 c.36.

[46] Prorogation is the process by which one Session of a Parliament is brought to an end and the time set for the beginning of the next.

[47] Dissolution is the process by which a Parliament is brought to an end and the process of a general election begun to determine the composition of the House of Commons at the beginning of the next Parliament.

procedure. The essence of this procedure is that the Minister or other person in whom the power is vested can exercise it without the approval of Parliament, but must inform Parliament of what he has done: Parliament then has a period within which to object. If no objection is made, the legislation stands. If an objection is made, the legislation is annulled, but without prejudice to transactions past and closed.

The standard way of introducing the negative resolution procedure is for the enabling statute to provide that a statutory instrument made under the power "is subject to annulment in pursuance of a resolution of either House of Parliament". For certain financial matters, only resolution of the House of Commons will be mentioned.[48]

That language reflects s.5(1) of the Statutory Instruments Act 1946[49] which is the principal provision dealing with the negative resolution procedure.

Amongst other things, knowledge of s.5 avoids a common misunderstanding in relation to laying before Parliament. It is common to find a requirement for a document to be laid before Parliament,[50] and the affirmative resolution procedure includes a requirement for laying. The provision appointing the negative resolution procedure for an instrument is silent about laying. But only because of s.5 of the 1946 Act, which imports an automatic requirement to lay before Parliament whenever the procedure is invoked.

6.2.6 The negative resolution procedure as established by s.5(1) of the 1946 Act is as follows—

(1) The instrument is laid before each House of Parliament after being made.

(2) Each House of Parliament has 40 days from the time when the instrument is laid to pass a resolution for the presentation to the Queen of an Address praying for the annulment of the instrument.[51]

(3) If that period expires without a resolution to that effect having been passed in either House, the procedure is at an end and the instrument continues to have effect.

---

[48] See, for example, s.22(2)(d) of the Government Resources and Accounts Act 2000 (c.20).

[49] 1946 c.36; "(1) Where by this Act or any Act passed after the commencement of this Act, it is provided that any statutory instrument shall be subject to annulment in pursuance of resolution of either House of Parliament, the instrument shall be laid before Parliament after being made and the provisions of the last foregoing section shall apply thereto accordingly, and if either House, within the period of forty days beginning with the day on which a copy thereof is laid before it, resolves that an Address be presented to His Majesty praying that the instrument be annulled, no further proceedings shall be taken thereunder after the date of the resolution, and His Majesty may by Order in Council revoke the instrument, so, however, that any such resolution and revocation shall be without prejudice to the validity of anything previously done under the instrument or to the making of a new statutory instrument."

[50] A requirement to lay a document before Parliament is a requirement to lay it before each House of Parliament—see Laying of Documents before Parliament (Interpretation) Act 1948 (c.59), s.1.

[51] In calculating the 40 day period "no account shall be taken of any time during which Parliament is dissolved or prorogued or during which both Houses are adjourned for more than four days"—1946 Act, s.7(1).

(4) If a resolution is passed to that effect during the 40 day period—

no further proceedings may be taken under the statutory instrument,

the Queen may revoke the instrument by Order in Council,

the revocation is without prejudice to "the validity of anything previously done under the instrument", and

the revocation does not prevent the making of a new instrument.

The Act is silent about how long a period may expire between the making of the instrument and its laying before Parliament. There is, however, an informal convention operated by the Joint Committee on Statutory Instruments to the effect that an instrument subject to the negative resolution procedure should not be made so as to come into force less than 21 days after laying.[52] There will frequently arise occasions on which this rule will have to be broken, but the Committee will expect each instance to be justified and, if not satisfied with the explanation, the Committee may draw an instrument to the special attention of each House on the grounds that the "21-day rule" had been broken without adequate justification.[53] [54]

Although the essence of the effect of annulment is specified by s.5 of the 1946 Act as explained above, the notion of preserving the validity of things already done may not always be entirely clear, and it will sometimes be thought necessary to be more explicit.[55]

There is a minor difficulty with s.5 of the 1946 Act in relation to instruments that are required to be scrutinised by the House of Commons only.   **6.2.7**

---

[52] Note the following statement of Baroness Blatch (Minister of State in the Home Office) HL Deb. May 23, 1995 c.1025—"I have to say that the 21-day rule is a rule of practice required by the Joint Committee on Statutory Instruments.It does not of course affect the 40-day time limit for the introduction of a negative resolution seeking to annul a statutory instrument. My understanding is that it is common for such instruments to come into force before the 40 days have expired."

[53] See, for example, paragraph 2 of the Sixteenth Report of the Committee for Session 2002–03 (April 8, 2003) on the Motor Vehicles (Compulsory Insurance) (Information Centre And Compensation Body) Regulations 2003 (SI 2003/37); see also "These regulations were laid before Parliament on 29th September 1994 and came into force two days later on 1st October 1994. The 21-day rule was therefore breached. In both memoranda printed in Appendix V the Department of Transport give 'pressure of work' as the reason for the breach of the rule. The Committee does not consider this to be an acceptable reason for breaching the rule, and so reports the instrument to both Houses."—Joint Committee on Statutory Instruments, Session 1994–95, 4th Report, para.6 (HL Paper 17, HC 8-iv); see also a report of unjustifiable breach of the rule because the department's memorandum "does not disclose any convincing reason for being unable to avoid the breach, and in particular does not indicate that the breach would have been unavoidable if preparation of the Regulations had begun earlier."—Joint Committee on Statutory Instruments, Session 1995–96, 23rd Report, para.3 (HL Paper 91, HC 34-xxiii).

[54] Note that the 21-day "rule" has been cited by Government as a reason why the Immigration Rules could not conveniently be required to be made by statutory instrument—see Chapter 3, Section 2, footnote 40.

[55] Along the lines, to take an example from a procedure where an instrument lapses if not affirmed, of s.4(4) of the Northern Ireland (Remission of Sentences) Act 1995 (c.47).

Section 7(2) of the 1946 Act provides that—

"In relation to any instrument required by any Act, whether passed before or after the commencement of this Act, to be laid before the House of Commons only, the provisions of the last three foregoing sections shall have effect as if references to that House were therein substituted for references to Parliament and for references to either House and each House thereof."

In other words, sections 4, 5 and 6 are to have effect in relation to Commons-only instruments with the obvious substitution of references to that House for references to both Houses.

Mostly that works without difficulty, and is indeed so obviously necessary that it might almost have been left to common sense.

But the difficulty is in the provision in s.5(1) for laying. That provision says that if an instrument is subject to annulment by resolution of either House then it also requires to be laid.

Section 7(2) is needed to operate on that provision so that the implied requirement to lay applies to Commons-only instruments, with laying before the Commons alone.

But there is nothing in s.7(2) sufficient to convert the opening reference in s.5(1) to annulment by resolution of either House of Parliament into a reference to annulment by the Commons. In other words, s.5(1) appears to apply only to dual-House instruments, although there can be no reason why that should have been intended.

Generally, it seems preferable to ignore this apparent difficulty and to read s.5(1) as if it applied to Commons-only instruments, taking the necessary modification equivalent to that of s.7(2) as being supplied by necessary implication.

Draft negative resolution procedure

6.2.8   The principal disadvantage of the negative resolution procedure is the practical difficulty that can be caused if an instrument is annulled.[56] In particular, although

---

[56] Annulment is very rare. It is common to have resolutions for annulment debated once or twice in a Session of Parliament, but they are very rarely passed. But it can happen—the most recent occurrence of this was on February 22, 2000, when the House of Lords rejected the Greater London Authority Elections Rules (SI 2000/208)—and the possibility cannot therefore be entirely ignored.

According to an answer given in the course of a starred question in 1995 (HL Deb. June 28, 1995, c.750), "since 1979 this House has rejected delegated legislation on only one occasion. In 1988 two special procedure orders relating to the harbour authorities of Harwich and Newport were annulled on motions moved by the Government and agreed to without Division, because they were found to be technically defective."

The possibility of annulment, however, remains live. Indeed the House of Lords passed a motion on October 20, 1994, at the instigation of Lord Simon of Glaisdale, "that this House affirms its unfettered freedom to vote on any subordinate legislation submitted for its consideration". The freedom relates both to motions to annul instruments already made and to motions to approve

s.5(1) of the 1946 Act expressly preserves "anything previously done under the instrument" it may not be entirely clear what this means in every context. The affirmative resolution procedure provides more certainty, but it also requires the provision by the Government of Parliamentary time, which is generally at a premium. Section 6(1) of the 1946 Act therefore provides an alternative negative procedure to the following effect—

The instrument is laid before each House of Parliament in draft.

(1) The instrument may not be made, or, in the case of an Order in Council, submitted to the Privy Council, until the period of 40 days[57] has elapsed since laying of the draft.

(2) If a resolution is passed by either House during that period that the draft should not be made or submitted for making, "no further proceedings shall be taken thereon".

instruments laid in draft for approval by affirmative resolution: as to those, although again it is extremely rare for either House to deny the Government its resolution it is possible to use various procedural devices to register opposition to particular aspects of the draft—see, for example, the motion in the name of Lord Lester of Herne Hill (HL Deb June 17, 2003 cc.751–785) "That this House invites Her Majesty's Government to withdraw the draft Employment Equality (Sexual Orientation) Regulations 2003 and to lay new regulations amending regulation 7(3) so as to conform with the E.C. Framework Directive 2000/78/EC."

As to the relationship between this freedom and the Salisbury/Addison Convention under which the unelected House of Lords does not block legislative proposals forming part of the manifesto on which the government was elected, see the observations of Lord Falconer of Thoroton HL Deb. March 29, 2000 c.839.

The general attitude of the Government to the House of Lords' reluctance to exercise the power to annul an instrument is encapsulated in the following observation of the Lord Privy Seal (Viscount Cranborne)—"Her Majesty's Government support the constructive way in which your Lordships have shown restraint in exercising the House's undoubted power to vote on subordinate legislation"—HL Deb. May 2, 1995 W.A. 113–114; see also HL Deb June 28, 1995 cc.750–751.

On occasion the House of Lords has expressed its concern at particular aspects of an instrument by passing or seeking to pass motions to that effect—see footnote 41 above: as to general disapproval of an instrument, the House of Lords has on at least one occasion expressed its concern in a strong way, but without breaching the convention against annulment, by passing a non-fatal motion—that is to say one not triggering the annulment provisions in the Statutory Instruments Act 1946—calling upon the Government to think again (see, in relation to the Beef Bones Regulations 1997 (SI 1997/2959), the motion carried against the Government on January 27, 1998. The Beef Bones Regulations 1997 were made under various powers in the Food Safety Act 1990 (c.16) and were subject to annulment pursuant to a resolution of either House of Parliament (s.48(3)). The Regulations were laid before the Lords on December 15, 1997. The motion was during the 40 day period for annulment but was not phrased as a resolution that an Address be presented to Her Majesty praying that the instrument be annulled, which would have satisfied s.5(1) of the 1946 Act and caused the instrument to cease to have effect. Instead it was phrased as a resolution calling on the Government to revoke the regulations to allow further consultation. The success of the motion, therefore, did not affect the validity of the regulations.Following the Division there was a brief exchange between the Government and Opposition front-benches (HL Deb. January 27, 1998 c.159). Viscount Cranborne referred to an occasion on which the last government "were defeated on what I think is technically a non-fatal Motion", when the present Leader of the House asked for the matter to be referred to a Select Committee. The Leader of the House replied, citing a number of precedents, that the Government in taking no further action would "be behaving precisely as the previous government did".)

[57] Again, ignoring long adjournments and prorogations—s.7(1).

(3) If no resolution is passed, the power can be exercised in the form of the draft in the safe knowledge that no further challenge is available.

This procedure is rarely used nowaday.

Mixed procedure

6.2.9   It is not possible to have a single instrument combining provisions that are required to be subjected to draft affirmative resolution and provisions that are subject to negative resolution.

It is, however, possible for Parliament to identify circumstances in which the exercise of a power will require affirmative resolution and circumstances in which the negative resolution procedure will suffice. Thus a provision may provide for affirmative resolution if an instrument amends primary legislation and negative otherwise.[58] Or it may provide that the first exercise of a power should be subject to affirmative resolution but later exercises should be subject to negative resolution.[59] And there are endless other theoretical possibilities, but none which routinely commends itself as practicable.[60]

---

[58] See, for example, s.94(4) and (5) of the Anti-social Behaviour Act 2003 (c.38); or s.108(2) and (3) of the Courts Act 2003 (c.39)—

> "(2) None of the orders and regulations mentioned in subsection (3) may be made unless a draft of the statutory instrument containing the order or regulations has been laid before, and approved by a resolution of, each House of Parliament.
>
> (3) The orders and regulations are—
>> (a) the first order to be made under section 4 (areas of courts boards);
>> (b) regulations under section 34(5) (costs in legal proceedings);
>> (c) an order under—
>>> (i) section 73 or 80 (powers to amend enactments in connection with Criminal Procedure Rules and Family Procedure Rules), or
>>> (ii) section 109 (power to make consequential provision etc), which contains any provision (whether alone or with other provisions) amending or repealing any Act or provision of an Act; . . . "

[59] See, for example, s.123(3) of the Terrorism Act 2000 (c.11) or s.7(5) of the Social Security (Incapacity for Work) Act 1994 (c.18).

[60] Note "The Committee considers that this is a proper case for the initial order to be subject to affirmative procedure. There is a difficulty with amendments (variations), since while minor variations may not justify that degree of scrutiny and expenditure of parliamentary time, in the case of substantial changes the affirmative procedure might be more appropriate. The House may therefore wish to consider whether the bill should be amended to allow Ministers the option of using either the affirmative or the negative resolution procedure for variations, thereby giving appropriate flexibility for the right amount of parliamentary control. There is a further possible cause for concern in that the subject mater of the bill is a highly sensitive area, where what to some people might seem 'minor' variations might to others be amendment of the utmost importance. In the event of the negative resolution procedure being used for variations it will be for members of the House to exercise vigilance in bringing areas of particular sensitivity to the attention of the House."—Competition Bill 1997–98, House of Lords Select Committee on Delegated Powers and Deregulation, Session 1997–98, 6th Report, (November 5, 1997, paras 17–18); and note the same suggestion made by the House of Lords Select Committee on Delegated Powers and Deregulation, Session 1997–98, 9th Report (HL Paper 54, December 17, 1997) para.6, in relation to the Teaching and Higher Education Bill 1997–98; and for conditional approval of a proposal to confer power to

As well as combining aspects of the negative and affirmative resolution procedures, it is possible to devise other kinds of variation on the standard procedures to fit the requirements of particular cases.[61]

Instruments to be laid only

In the case of certain statutory instruments no procedure, whether negative or affirmative, is prescribed by the enabling statute for their scrutiny by Parliament, but they are required to be laid before each House of Parliament.[62] Where this is required, the instrument should be laid before it comes into force, or where this cannot realistically be achieved the person making the instrument is obliged to write to the Lord Chancellor and the Speaker of the House of Commons, informing them of the occurrence and explaining it.[63]

6.2.10

Section 6(1) of the Statutory Instruments Act 1946[64] makes provision for instruments required to be laid in draft but that do not require an affirmative resolution before they can be made. The procedure (described in para.6.2.8) imposes an embargo during which the instrument may not be made, and prevents the making of the instrument if during the embargo a resolution against the instrument is passed by either House. This procedure is rarely applied nowadays.[65]

---

demote a first exercise from affirmative resolution to negative resolution if confined to implementing initiatives contained in a consultation paper, see the House of Lords Select Committee on Delegated Powers and Deregulation, Session 1997–98, 9th Report (HL Paper 54, December 17, 1997), para.39.

[61] See, for example, the special procedure, modelled on the procedure in the Deregulation and Contracting Out Act 1994 (as to which see Chapter 3, Section 9) but with variations for the sake of simplicity, in Part I of the Local Government Act 1999 (c.27); approved by the House of Lords Select Committee on Delegated Powers and Deregulation, Session 1998–99, 12th Report (HL Paper 51, April 14, 1999) para.5—"The additional provisions about consultation and laying before Parliament do not include the words in section 4(4) of the 1994 Act which require the minister to have regard to 'any resolution or report of or of any committee of, either House of Parliament with regard to the [proposal]'. The Committee considers that this departure from the 1994 Act is justified; the special arrangements in that Act were necessary because of the uncertain width of the powers, while in comparison, clause 15 has a clear and limited purpose."

[62] See, for example, s.108(4) of the Courts Act 2003 (c.39)—
"(4) A statutory instrument containing—
(a) the first order to be made under s.8 (local justice areas), or (1) (1) (a) regulations under s.40 (payments, accounting and banking by designated officers),
is to be laid before Parliament after being made."

[63] Statutory Instruments Act 1946 (c.36), s.4(1).

[64] 1946 c.36.

[65] Section 6(1) provides as follows—
"6 Statutory instruments of which drafts are to be laid before Parliament
(1) Where by this Act or any Act passed after the commencement of this Act it is provided that a draft of any statutory instrument shall be laid before Parliament, but the Act does not prohibit the making of the instrument without the approval of Parliament, then, in the case of an Order in Council the draft shall not be submitted to His Majesty in Council, and in any other case, the statutory instrument shall not be made, until after the expiration of a period of forty days beginning with the day on which a copy of the draft is laid before each House of Parliament, or, if such copies are laid on different days, with the later of the two days, and if within that period either House resolves that the draft be not submitted to His Majesty or that the statutory instrument be not made,

Instruments requiring no procedure or laying

6.2.11 In the case of some subordinate legislation, although it is required to be made by statutory instrument (which secures its printing and publication[66]) there is no requirement to lay it before either House of Parliament and no procedure for its scrutiny is prescribed. This is common practice for orders which do no more than appoint one or more days for provisions of an Act to come into force.

Choice of level of scrutiny

6.2.13 In general, the choice of what level of scrutiny to apply to the exercise of a particular power to legislate is made by the Government department responsible for the Bill for the Act which confers the power. In making the choice the department is likely to have regard to precedent and past expressions of opinion by Parliamentary Committees.[67] And the House of Lords Select Committee on Delegated Powers and Deregulation in examining the Bill[68] will expect the Government's memorandum to address the reasons for the choice in each case and will make recommendations for amendment to adopt a different level of scrutiny where they consider it appropriate.

21-day rule

6.2.14 See above, para.6.2.6.

Commons-only instruments

6.2.15 Certain instruments are subjected to scrutiny, whether by affirmative or negative resolution or by mere laying, in the House of Commons alone.[69] There is no hard and fast rule about whether an instrument should be made subject to negative or affirmative procedure in both Houses of Parliament or only in the Commons.

Instruments dealing only with taxation are normally subject to procedure in the Commons alone, because of the Commons' privilege relating to bills of aids and supplies.[70]

For other kinds of instruments the matter is one for political judgment, though reference to the precedents can be helpful and anything of a wholly financial nature is likely to be thought suitable for referral to the Commons alone. There are certainly many examples of instruments dealing with financial matters other than taxation which are subject to Commons procedure only. Examples (relating

---

as the case may be, no further proceedings shall be taken thereon, but without prejudice to the laying before Parliament of a new draft."

Section 6(2) can be ignored for modern purposes: it merely converts to the automatic procedure provided for by subsection (1) certain similar but slightly different procedures provided for by specific provisions of earlier Acts.

[66] See Chapter 9, Section 3.

[67] See, in particular, para.6.2.3.

[68] See Chapter 5, Section 2.

[69] See, for example, s.197(4) of the Transport Act 2000 (c.38).

[70] As to which see further Chapter 5, Section 2.

to borrowing) include orders under s.10(6) of the Civil Aviation Act 1982[71] (as amended by s.1(2) of the Civil Aviation Authority (Borrowing Powers) Act 1990[72]) and ss.9A(5) and 10(2) of the Commonwealth Development Corporation Act 1978.[73]

Many instruments relating to local government finance are subject to Commons-only procedure.[74]

Financial instruments with tangential reference to other matters may be made subject to Commons-only procedures.[75]

Joint Committee on Statutory Instruments

An important part in the scrutiny of subordinate legislation is played by the Joint Committee on Statutory Instruments.   **6.2.16**

The Joint Committee is established[76] by the Standing Orders of the two Houses.[77]

The terms of reference of the Committee are to consider subordinate legislation[78]—

"with a view to determining whether the special attention of the House should be drawn to it on any of the following grounds:

    i. that it imposes a charge on the public revenues or contains provisions requiring payments to be made to the Exchequer or any government department or to any local or public authority in consideration of any licence or consent or of any services to be rendered, or prescribes the amount of any such charge or payment;

    ii. that it is made in pursuance of any enactment containing specific provisions excluding it from challenge in the courts, either at all times or after the expiration of a specific period;

---

[71] 1982 c.16.

[72] 1990 c.2.

[73] 1978 c.2.

[74] See, for example, ss.5 and 11 of the Local Government Finance Act 1992 (c.14).

[75] So, for example, the Hong Kong Economic and Trade Office Act 1996 (c.63) includes power for Treasury orders which are mainly about relief from taxes and duties but tangentially also about granting relief from restrictions on imports; the orders are made subject to annulment by the House of Commons only.

[76] Although the Joint Committee has now been in existence for several decades, an early suggestion for the establishment of something along these lines was rejected by the Prime Minister in 1929 on the grounds (a) that it was impracticable and (b) that it was unnecessary, because the courts would reject *ultra vires* orders as such and because Members can move for annulment of instruments to which they object on technical or substantive grounds—HC Deb. February 26, 1929.

[77] See House of Commons Standing Order No. 151; House of Lords Standing Order No. 74.

[78] Specifically, "to consider—

    (A) every instrument which is laid before each House of Parliament and upon which proceedings may be or might have been taken in either House of Parliament, in pursuance of an Act of Parliament, being—

iii. that it purports to have retrospective effect where the parent statute confers no express authority so to provide;

iv. that there appears to have been unjustifiable delay in the publication or in the laying of it before Parliament;

v. that there appears to have been unjustifiable delay in sending a notification under the proviso to section 4(1) of the Statutory Instruments Act 1946, where an instrument has come into operation before it has been laid before Parliament;

vi. that there appears to be a doubt whether it is intra vires or that it appears to make some unusual or unexpected use of the powers conferred by the statute under which it is made;

vii. that for any special reason its form or purport calls for elucidation;

viii. that its drafting appears to be defective;

or on any other ground which does not impinge on its merits or on the policy behind it; and to report its decision with the reasons thereof in any particular case."[79]

6.2.17   The Joint Committee has no formal powers in relation to subordinate legislation[80] and the "worst" that it can do in relation to an instrument is bring it to the special attention of the two Houses in one of the Committee's regular written reports. But the strength of the Committee's influence should not be underestimated. The Committee is held in high esteem on all sides of both Houses.[81]

(a) a statutory instrument, or a draft statutory instrument;

(b) a scheme, or an amendment of a scheme, or a draft thereof, requiring approval by statutory instrument;

(c) any other instrument (whether or not in draft), where the proceedings in pursuance of an Act of Parliament are proceedings by way of an affirmative resolution; or

(d) an order subject to special parliamentary procedure;

but excluding any Order in Council or draft Order in Council made or proposed to be made under paragraph 1 of Schedule 1 to the Northern Ireland Act 2000, any draft order proposed to be made under section 1 of the Regulatory Reform Act 2001, or any subordinate provisions order made or proposed to be made under that Act, and any remedial order or draft remedial order under Schedule 2 to the Human Rights Act 1998;

(B) every general statutory instrument not within the foregoing classes, and not within paragraph (10) of this order [Commons-only instruments], but not including any statutory instrument made by a member of the Scottish Executive or by the National Assembly for Wales unless it is required to be laid before Parliament or either House of Parliament and not including measures under the Church of England Assembly (Powers) Act 1919 and instruments made under such measures" (Standing Order 151(1))."

[79] Standing Order 151(1).

[80] Except in so far as it can call for evidence and investigate the background of an instrument. In particular, "The committee and any sub-committee appointed by it shall have power to require any government department concerned to submit a memorandum explaining any instrument which may be under its consideration or to depute a representative to appear before it as a witness for the purpose of explaining any such instrument." (Standing Order 151(6)).

[81] The reasons for this are partly that it is a joint and largely non-party-political committee, and partly that it has an efficient and well-established system of work. See, for example, the following passage in the speech of Lord Lester of Herne Hill moving a motion in relation to the Employment Equality

The House of Lords has a rule of order requiring motions for the affirmation of statutory instruments not to be taken until the Joint Committee has reported.[82] While there is no such rule of order in the House of Commons, the timing of consideration of an affirmative instrument, or of debate of a resolution to annul, would be likely to be negotiated between the Usual Channels partly with the timing of the Joint Committee in mind.

Most of the Joint Committee's work is carried on by correspondence between the committee and departments, with meetings of the Committee being held in private to consider the correspondence. But the Committee does occasionally take and publish oral evidence from departments on particular matters.[83]

A typical report of the Committee, and there are several in each Parliamentary Session, contains a lengthy list of instruments to which the attention of the House is not brought, and a few pages giving reasons why particular instruments deserve to be brought to the attention of the House. Correspondence between the Committee and a department, in particular departmental memoranda elucidating or justifying aspects of an instrument, is commonly published in the Committee's report on the instrument, sometimes in relation to an instrument to which the Committee does not draw the special attention of the House.

There are no automatic proceedings on a report from the Committee, not even **6.2.18** where it is strongly adverse to an instrument. But the report may be referred to in proceedings on a motion for annulment or for approval of an affirmative instrument. And even where there are no proceedings on the instrument, an adverse report is likely to cause the department concerned to take another look at the matter to which the Committee draws attention and to brief the appropriate Minister on what action should be taken in the light of the Committee's criticism.

(Sexual Orientation) Regulations 2003 (SI 2003/1661) (HL Deb. June 17, 2003 c.751: "Parliament has the great benefit of an independent scrutiny committee—the Joint Select Committee on Statutory Instruments—one of whose main tasks is to draw to the special attention of each House its opinion that there appears to be a doubt whether delegated legislation for which parliamentary approval is being sought is *intra vires* or that it appears to make some unusual or unexpected use of the powers conferred by the statute under which it is made. Before doing so, the committee gives the Government the opportunity to explain their position. The committee receives not only expert advice but the most expert legal advice of senior Counsel. The committee is a vital safeguard and the executive and legislative arms of government would be wise to heed the committee's advice."

[82] House of Lords, Standing Order 73(1)—
   "(1) No Motion for a resolution of the House to approve an Affirmative Instrument shall be moved until:
      (a) except in the case of any Order in Council or draft Order in Council made or proposed to be made under paragraph 1 of the Schedule to the Northern Ireland Act 2000, or a draft remedial order or remedial order laid under Schedule 2 to the Human Rights Act 1998, or a draft order proposed to be made under section 1 of the Regulatory Reform Act 2001, or any subordinate provisions order made or proposed to be made under that Act, there has been laid before the House the report thereon of the Joint Committee on Statutory Instruments; . . . ".

[83] See, for example, Session 1994–95, 1st Report, Appendix II, Examination of Witnesses (HL Paper 3, HC 8-i) or Session 1994–95, 15th Report, p.14 (HL Paper 44, HC 8-xv).

A court considering a challenge to the instrument on grounds of *vires* might choose to have regard to comments in a report of the Joint Committee, although of course the report would in no way bind the court and might be regarded as being not even of persuasive value.

House of Commons Select Committee on Statutory Instruments

6.2.19 Standing Order 151(10) of the House of Commons requires the Select Committee of the House of Commons that joins with a Select Committee of the House of Lords for the purpose of forming the Joint Committee on Statutory Instruments also to constitute a separate Select Committee, to perform the same functions in relation to instruments laid before the Commons only.[84]

"Unusual use"

6.2.20 One of the matters against which the Joint Committee on Statutory Instruments test statutory instruments is "unusual use". While this is different from the question of whether or not an instrument is *intra vires* it addresses issues that would also be addressed by the High Court in considering a challenge against an instrument by way of judicial review.

Very often the concept of unusual use is not much distinguishable from the concept of *ultra vires*. The Joint Committee are likely to consider what has been previously effected by similar legislation, which is of course relevant to the determination of the likely contemplation of the legislature in conferring the power.

In relation to the Good Laboratory Practice Regulations 1999,[85] for example, the Joint Committee reported as follows—

> "The Committee was surprised that the list included at (d) 'a police force', that is all members of a force as defined in section 101(1) of the Police Act 1996, regardless of their position and functions. The committee is aware of at least ten Acts of Parliament since the Health and Safety at Work etc. Act 1974[86] in which similar disclosure recipients were defined and found no other example of a case in which disclosure to the police (or for purposes of criminal proceedings) was authorised in terms that included all members of a police force. In particular, section 28 of the 1974 Act authorises disclosure only to 'a constable authorised by a chief officer to receive it [the information]'. To the question whether they intended that disclosure should be authorised, in the case of the police force to all its members the department confirmed that this was the intention. Accordingly, the Committee report regulation 10(2) because it represents an unusually wide use of the

---

[84] As to which see para.6.2.15.
[85] SI 1999/3106.
[86] 1974 c.37.

power to authorise disclosure of confidential or commercially sensitive information obtained under statutory powers."[87]

House of Lords Select Committee on the merits of Statutory Instruments

This Committee was first established by the House of Lords on December 17, **6.2.21** 2003, pursuant to a recommendation of the House of Lords Select Committee on Liaison.[88] The terms of reference of the Committee are[89]—

"To consider every instrument which is laid before each House of Parliament and upon which proceedings may be or might have been taken in either House of Parliament, in pursuance of an Act of Parliament; being—

a statutory instrument, or a draft of a statutory instrument;

a scheme, or an amendment of a scheme, or a draft thereof, requiring approval by statutory instrument; or

any other instrument (whether or not in draft), where the proceedings in pursuance of an Act of Parliament are proceedings by way of an affirmative or negative resolution;

"but excluding any Order in Council or draft Order in Council made or proposed to be made under paragraph 1 of the Schedule to the Northern Ireland Act 2000 and any remedial order or draft remedial order under Schedule 2 to the Human Rights Act 1998 and any draft order proposed to be made under section 1 of the Regulatory Reform Act 2001, or any subordinate provisions order made or proposed to be made under that Act;

"with a view to determining whether the special attention of the House should be drawn to it on any of the following grounds—

(a) that it is politically or legally important or gives rise to issues of public policy likely to be of interest to the House;

(b) that it is inappropriate in view of the changed circumstances since the passage of the parent Act;

(c) that it inappropriately implements EU legislation;

(d) that it imperfectly achieves its policy objectives."

It will be seen from the generality of these terms of reference, and paragraphs (a) and (d) in particular, that the Committee is empowered to investigate widely

---

[87] Joint Committee on Statutory Instruments, Session 1999–00, 7th Report, para.21, (HL Paper 24, HC 47-vii).

[88] First Report, Session 2002–03, para.8.

[89] Pursuant to the recommendation of the House of Lords Select Committee on Procedure of the House, Third Report, Session 2003–03, para.4.

and to report on a practically unconstrained range of matters. While it is too early to comment on the political and wider impact of the Committee, it is clear that it is established in a manner which gives it the potential for profound and wide-ranging influence.[90]

House of Commons procedures for consideration of instruments

6.2.22 Since 1995[91] the Standing Orders of the House of Commons have provided for substantive proceedings on subordinate legislation to be taken in Standing Committee, saving the time of the Chamber. The present Standing Order on the matter[92] is as follows (with the practical effect of each provision being expounded in the footnotes)—

"(1) There shall be one or more standing committees,[93] to be called Standing Committees on Delegated Legislation, for the consideration of such instruments (whether or not in draft) as may be referred to them.

(2) Any Member, not being a member of such a standing committee, may take part in the deliberations of the committee, but shall not vote or make any motion or move any amendment or be counted in the quorum.

(3) Where a Minister of the Crown has given notice of a motion to the effect that an instrument (whether or not in draft) upon which proceedings may be taken in pursuance of an Act of Parliament (other than a draft regulatory reform order) be approved, the instrument shall stand referred to a Standing Committee on Delegated Legislation, unless—

(a) notice has been given by a Minister of the Crown of a motion that the instrument shall not so stand referred,[94] or

(b) the instrument is referred to the Scottish Grand Committee[95] or to the Northern Ireland Grand Committee.[96]

---

[90] When this work went to print an initial report on the working of the Committee was expected.

[91] See proceedings on the adoption of the "Jopling report" HC Deb. December 19, 1994 cc.1456 to 1509 and HC Deb. November 2, 1995 cc.405–450. Before that, consideration by Standing Committee was normal but not automatic.

[92] Standing Order 118.

[93] These are committees meeting in rooms along the Committee Corridor, composed of persons nominated by the Speaker following discussions in the Usual Channels. The Committee proceedings are presided over by a Chairman, who has most of the regulatory powers that the Speaker has in the Chamber. The proceedings are formal and are recorded in special issues of Hansard. The Committee sits according to party allegiance, as in the Chamber, and its composition is designed more or less to reflect the balance of power in the Chamber. A Committee may sit to consider an instrument at the same time as proceedings are being taken in the Chamber or at the same time as other Committees: provision is made by the rules for adjournment to allow Members to attend Divisions elsewhere.

[94] Where, for example, the Usual Channels have agreed that due to the special importance of an instrument it should be considered on the Floor of the House, whether in Government or Opposition time.

[95] For instruments of interest solely to Scotland; less commonly invoked since devolution.

[96] For instruments of interest solely to Northern Ireland; less commonly invoked during devolution.

(2) Where a Member has given notice of—

(a) a motion for an humble address to Her Majesty praying that a statutory instrument be annulled, or a motion of a similar character relating to a statutory instrument, or to any other instrument (whether or not in draft) which may be subject to proceedings in the House in pursuance of a statute, or a motion that the House takes note of a statutory instrument, or

(b) a motion that a measure under the Church of England Assembly (Powers) Act 1919 be presented to Her Majesty for her Royal Assent, or a motion relating to an instrument made under such a measure,

a motion may be made by a Minister of the Crown at the commencement of public business, that the instrument be referred to such a committee, and the question thereon shall be put forthwith; and if, on the question being put, not fewer than twenty Members rise in their places and signify their objection thereto, the Speaker shall declare that the noes have it.[97]

(5) Each committee shall consider each instrument referred to it on a motion, 'That the committee has considered the instrument'; and the chairman shall put any question necessary to dispose of the proceedings on such a motion, if not previously concluded, when the committee shall have sat for one and a half hours (or, in the case of an instrument relating exclusively to Northern Ireland, two and a half hours) after the commencement of those proceedings; and the committee shall thereupon report the instrument to the House without any further question being put.[98]

(6) If any motion is made in the House of the kind specified in paragraph (3) or (4) of this order, in relation to any instrument reported to the House in accordance with paragraph (5) of this order, the Speaker shall put forthwith the question thereon and such question may be decided at any hour, though opposed."[99]

It will be seen from this that the purpose of the Standing Committee is to take the substantive consideration and debate off the Floor of the Chamber in order to save the Chamber's time for other matters, but not to delegate to the Committee any decision on annulment or approval of the instrument. The decision is made by the House, on Division if need be,[1] for the purpose of which Members will

---

[97] In other words, twenty objections prevent referral to the committee.

[98] So the purpose of the committee is simply to consider and debate the substance of the order for up to one-and-a-half hours (two-and-a-half for Northern Ireland measures, which include lengthy Orders in Council replicating complicated Great Britain legislation—see Chapter 4, Section 3).

[99] The effect of this provision is simply that once the committee has debated the substance of the instrument, the vote returns to the Floor of the House, but is taken without any further substantive consideration.

[1] Nowadays this is likely to be by deferred Division in accordance with the Sessional Order of June 28, 2001, renewed for Session 2003–04 on November 6, 2003.

have such regard as they think fit to the debate in the Standing Committee[2] and to its report to the House. The Committee has no power to delay the instrument's progress or to remove it from consideration by the House.[3]

Hybrid instruments

6.2.23 Hybridity[4] has no relevance to subordinate legislation in the House of Commons.

In the House of Lords, where an instrument subject to the affirmative resolution procedure contains provisions which if contained in a Bill would render it hybrid, the instrument is subject to a petitioning procedure along the lines of that for hybrid Bills.[5]

The disapplication of the hybrid instruments procedure by express provision of the Act under which the instrument would come to be made is relatively common in recent times.[6]

---

[2] Which is made available in separate editions of Hansard.

[3] By voting in a particular way the Committee can, however, bring to the attention of the House the Committee's feelings about an instrument—see, for example, the vote of the Third Standing Committee on Statutory Instruments, Session 1994–95 July 12, 1995 on the Draft Broadcasting (Restrictions on the Holding of Licences) (Amendment) Order 1995, where the Chairman used his casting vote on the question "That the Committee has considered . . . " with the noes and said "I put the Question that the Committee had considered the draft instrument and it is that which will be reported to the House. The fact that a vote was registered makes the point that the Committee were unhappy, but the order is reported to the House in any event." (c.28)—see also Points of Order HC Deb. July 18, 1995 and the following ruling of Madam Speaker (cc.1485–1486) "When the statutory instrument went before the Committee, it did not reject it; it voted—on the Chairman's casting vote—that it had not considered the instrument. Standing Order No. 101 gives the Committee no power, once the vote has been taken, other than to report the matter to the House, and that is what is taking place. Nothing irregular has occurred. Although the motion may not be debated tonight, it must still be decided, and Hon. Members may vote against it if they wish."—the instrument was later approved on a motion made without debate (being taken after ten o'clock) on a division (112:39) (cc.1567–1570); for a similar episode in a Standing Committee considering a European Document where a motion to take note was negatived—see Points of Order HC Deb. November 20, 1996 cc.988–990.

[4] See Chapter 5, Section 4, Part (3).

[5] Standing Orders HL 216; see, for example, the Policing of Airports (Belfast City) Order 2003.

[6] See, for example, s.13(9) of the European Parliament (Representation) Act 2003 (c.7)—"(9) If, apart from this subsection, an order to which this section applies would be treated for the purposes of the standing orders of either House of Parliament as a hybrid instrument, it shall proceed as if it were not such an instrument."; or s.197(5) of the Licensing Act 2003 (c.17)—"(5) If a draft of an order within subsection (3)(d) would, apart from this subsection, be treated for the purposes of the Standing Orders of either House of Parliament as a hybrid instrument, it is to proceed in that House as if it were not such an instrument."

CHAPTER 7

DEVOLVED LEGISLATION

SECTION 1

SCOTLAND

Introduction

This section provides a brief outline of the procedures relating to legislation **7.1.1**
followed in the Scottish Parliament.

References to Standing Orders are to the Standing Orders of the Scottish
Parliament.[1]

Passage of Bills

The rules about introduction of a Bill are set out in Standing Order 9.2 as fol- **7.1.2**
lows—

"Rule 9.2 Form and introduction of Bills

1. A Bill may be introduced by any member on a sitting day. A Bill
   introduced by a member of the Scottish Executive is referred to as an
   'Executive Bill'.
2. A Bill shall be introduced by being lodged with the Clerk.
3. A Bill may not be introduced unless it is in proper form. The Presiding
   Officer shall determine the proper form of Bills and the Clerk shall
   arrange for the determinations of the Presiding Officer to be notified to
   the Parliament.

---

[1] Standing Orders are made in accordance with s.22 of and Sch.3 to the Scotland Act 1998 (c.46).
Section 22 provides as follows—
  "**22 Standing orders**
    (1) The proceedings of the Parliament shall be regulated by standing orders.
    (2) Schedule 3 (which makes provision as to how certain matters are to be dealt with by
        standing orders) shall have effect.";
(Sch.3 contains provisions not relevant to this work, except for paragraph 7 of the Schedule noted
below).
  The Orders were first adopted by resolution of the Parliament on December 9, 1999. References
are now to the 2nd Edition, September 2003.

4. A Bill must, before introduction, be signed by the member introducing it and may also be signed by any other member or members who support the Bill.
5. The Clerk shall ensure that notice of the introduction of a Bill in the Parliament is published in the Business Bulletin. Such notice shall set out the short and long titles of the Bill, the name of the member who has introduced it and the name of any member supporting the Bill and shall indicate what type of Bill it is.
6. No Bill, other than a Budget Bill, may be introduced in the Parliament if it contains any provision which would have the effect of authorising sums to be paid out of the Scottish Consolidated Fund (as opposed to a provision which charges expenditure on that Fund)."

7.1.3   While the Standing Order talks in terms of introduction by any Member, in practice a Bill may be introduced by—

(1) a Member on behalf of the Scottish Ministers[2] (an Executive Bill),

(2) a Member on behalf of a Parliamentary Committee[3] (a Committee Bill), or

(3) by a private Member on his or her own behalf (a Members' Bill).

The Scotland equivalent of the Westminster pre-legislative scrutiny initiative includes facilities for a Minister to advise a committee on a proposal for legislation. During consultation on proposes legislation a Minister may be asked to brief a committee and the committee may take other evidence on the proposals.

Bills as introduced are required to be accompanied by a variety of explanatory documents.[4]

---

[2] This is the Scottish equivalent of the Government—see Scotland Act 1998 (c.46), ss.44 to 47.

[3] The Parliament presently has the following subject committees (there are others established by Standing Orders for various administrative purposes): the Education Culture and Sport Committee; the Enterprise and Lifelong Learning Committee; the Health and Community Care Committee; the Justice 1 Committee; the Justice 2 Committee; the Local Government Committee; the Rural Development Committee; the Social Justice Committee; and the Transport and Environment Committee.

[4] Every Bill requires the following: (1) a written statement from the Presiding Officer as to whether the Bill is within the legislative competence of the Parliament (as to which see Chapter 4, Section 2); (2) a Financial Memorandum, estimating costs to the Scottish Executive, local authorities and other bodies, businesses and individuals of implementing and complying with the Bill's provisions; and (3) a report by the Auditor General, for any Bill charging expenditure to the Scottish Consolidated Fund, confirming whether the charge is appropriate. In addition, Executive Bills are required to be accompanied by; (4) a statement from the appropriate Minister that the Bill is within the legislative competence of the Parliament; (5) Explanatory Notes, summarising each provision of the Bill, without justifying it or containing other argumentative material; and (6) a Policy Memorandum setting out the Bill's policy objectives, consideration of any alternative approaches, details of consultation exercises and their outcome, assessments of any effect of the Bill on equal opportunities, human rights, islands communities, local government, sustainable development, and any other matter which the Executive considers relevant. (Standing Order 9.3); these requirements in part reflect s.31 of the Scotland Act 1998—

As to printing—

"As soon as a Bill has been introduced the Clerk shall arrange for the Bill, together with its accompanying documents, to be printed and published."[5]

While the Parliamentary process varies for different kinds of Bill,[6] the standard process[7] is described in Standing Orders as follows—

"Rule 9.5 Stages of Bills

1. The procedure for a Bill introduced in the Parliament shall be—

   (a) consideration of the Bill's general principles and a decision on whether to agree to them (Stage 1);
   (b) consideration of the details of the Bill (Stage 2); and
   (c) final consideration of the Bill and a decision whether to pass or reject it (Stage 3)."[8]

Stage 1 of a Bill is led by Committees.[9]

Each Bill is referred to the relevant subject committee which is known as "the lead committee" for the Bill. A Bill which authorises the making of subordinate legislation is also referred to the Subordinate Legislation Committee. Other committees (such as finance) may also become involved by expressing opinions to the lead committee.

"31 Scrutiny of Bills before introduction
    (1) A member of the Scottish Executive in charge of a Bill shall, on or before introduction of the Bill in the Parliament, state that in his view the provisions of the Bill would be within the legislative competence of the Parliament.
    (2) The Presiding Officer shall, on or before the introduction of a Bill in the Parliament, decide whether or not in his view the provisions of the Bill would be within the legislative competence of the Parliament and state his decision.
    (3) The form of any statement, and the manner in which it is to be made, shall be determined under standing orders, and standing orders may provide for any statement to be published."

[5] Standing Order 9.4.
[6] See in particular Standing Orders 9.14 (Members' Bills), 9.15 (Committee Bills), 9.16 (Budget Bills), 9.17 (private Bills (see also Standing Orders Chapter 9A)), 9.18 (Consolidation Bills), 9.19 (Statute Law Repeals Bills), 9.20 (Statute Law Revision Bills) and 9.21 (emergency Bills).
[7] As required by s.36 of the Scotland Act 1998.
[8] The Standing Order also deals with timing and programming of the stages.
[9] Standing Order 9.6.

The lead committee considers the Bill, in the course of which it may take evidence. It is required to shall "consider and report on the general principles of the Bill".[10]

Once the lead committee has reported on the Bill, the Parliament "shall consider the general principles of the Bill in the light of the lead committee's report and decide, on a motion of the member in charge of the Bill, whether to agree to those general principles."[11]

The Parliament may refer a Bill back to the lead committee for a further report on the principles of all or part of the Bill before reaching a decision.

Agreement by the Parliament to the general principles of a Bill sends it on to Stage 2. Failure to agree the general principles kills the Bill.

7.1.5   Stage 2 of a Bill roughly equates to the Westminster Parliament's Committee stage, involving consideration of the details of the Bill, provision by provision. Stage 2 may be taken in a number of ways[12]—

(1) entirely by the lead committee,

(2) entirely by a Committee of the Whole Parliament,

(3) entirely by a Parliamentary committee or committees other than the lead committee,

(4) partly by the lead committee and partly by a Committee of the Whole Parliament, or

(5) by a Parliamentary committee or committees other than the lead committee.

At Stage 2 each section and Schedule of and to the Bill is considered in turn. Amendments may be proposed.[13]

If amended in Stage 2, the Bill is printed as amended before the next stage.[14]

---

[10] Standing Order 9.6(1).
[11] Standing Order 9.6(4).
[12] Standing Order 9.7.
[13] If amendments add or substantially alter power to make delegated legislation, the amended Bill is referred to the Subordinate Legislation Committee for consideration and report—Standing Order 9.7(9).
[14] Standing Order 9.7(8).

Stage 3 of a Bill[15] involves consideration by the whole Parliament. As in the proceedings of the Westminster Parliament—

(1) amendments may be made,[16]

(2) parts of the Bill may be referred back for further Stage 2 consideration in committee, and

(3) there is then a debate and decision on the passing of the Bill in its final form.[17]

There may be a further reconsideration stage where certain kinds of technical questions as to competence have been raised.[18] **7.1.6**

On being passed, a Bill is submitted by the Presiding Officer to the Sovereign for Royal Assent.[19] On receiving Royal Assent it becomes an Act of the Scottish Parliament.

Provision for Queen's Consent is made in more or less the same way as for the Westminster Parliament.[20]

---

[15] Standing Order 9.8.

[16] The Presiding Officer has the power of selection—Standing Order 9.8(4).

[17] Standing Order 9.8(9) and (10)—"9. If there is a division at Stage 3 on the question whether the Bill be passed, the result is valid only if the number of members who voted is more than one quarter of the total number of seats for members of the Parliament. In calculating the number of members who voted for this purpose, account shall be taken not only of those voting for and against the motion but also of those voting to abstain. 10. If the result of such a division is not valid the Bill shall be treated as rejected."

[18] Standing Order 9.9.

[19] This is in accordance with section 32 of the Scotland Act 1998—

"**32 Submission of Bills for Royal Assent**

(1) It is for the Presiding Officer to submit Bills for Royal Assent.

(2) The Presiding Officer shall not submit a Bill for Royal Assent at any time when—

   (a) the Advocate General, the Lord Advocate or the Attorney General is entitled to make a reference in relation to the Bill under section 33,

   (b) any such reference has been made but has not been decided or otherwise disposed of by the Judicial Committee, or

   (c) an order may be made in relation to the Bill under section 35.

(3) The Presiding Officer shall not submit a Bill in its unamended form for Royal Assent if—

   (a) the Judicial Committee have decided that the Bill or any provision of it would not be within the legislative competence of the Parliament, or

   (b) a reference made in relation to the Bill under section 33 has been withdrawn following a request for withdrawal of the reference under section 34(2)(b).

(4) In this Act—

   "Advocate General" means the Advocate General for Scotland,

   "Judicial Committee" means the Judicial Committee of the Privy Council."

[20] This is a requirement of the Scotland Act 1998, para.7 of Sch.3 of which provides as follows: "The standing orders shall include provision for ensuring that a Bill containing provisions which would, if the Bill were a Bill for an Act of Parliament, require the consent of Her Majesty, the Prince and Steward of Scotland or the Duke of Cornwall shall not pass unless such consent has been signified to the Parliament." Standing Order 9.11 accordingly provides as follows—

"**Crown consent**

1. Where a Bill contains provisions, or is amended so as to include provisions, which would, if the Bill were a Bill for an Act of the United Kingdom Parliament, require the consent of Her Majesty, the Prince and Steward of Scotland or the Duke of Cornwall, the

Provision for financial resolutions is broadly along the same lines as that made in the Westminster Parliament.[21]

A Bill can be withdrawn by the Member in charge, but may not be withdrawn after completion of stage 1 without the leave of the Parliament.[22]

Scrutiny of instruments

7.1.7   The Standing Orders of the Scottish Parliament also make arrangements[23] for the scrutiny of subordinate legislation required[24] to be laid before the Parliament. The procedures, and in particular the choice of kinds of scrutiny procedure, are broadly the same as those adopted for the Westminster Parliament's scrutiny of subordinate legislation.[25]

The principal feature of the process is the use of the relevant subject committee

---

Parliament shall not debate any question whether the Bill be passed or approved unless such consent to those provisions has been signified by a member of the Scottish Executive during proceedings on the Bill at a meeting of the Parliament."

As to Consent in the Westminster Parliament see Chapter 5, Section 2.

[21] Standing Order 9.12—

    "Financial Resolutions

    " . . . 3. Where a Bill contains provisions—

        (a) which charge expenditure on the Scottish Consolidated Fund, or

        (b) the likely effect of which would be to—

            (i) increase significantly expenditure charged on that Fund;

            (ii) give rise to significant expenditure payable out of that Fund for a new purpose; or

            (iii) increase significantly expenditure payable out of that Fund for an existing purpose,

    no proceedings may be taken on the Bill at any Stage after Stage 1 unless the Parliament has by resolution agreed to the expenditure or the increase in expenditure being charged on or, as the case may be, payable out of that Fund.

    4. Where—

        (a) a Bill contains provisions which impose or increase (or confer a power to impose or increase) any charge, or otherwise require (or confer a power to require) any payment to be made; and

        (b) the person to whom the charge or payment is payable is required, by or under any enactment, to pay sums received into the Scottish Consolidated Fund (or would be so required but for any provision made by or under an Act of the Scottish Parliament),

    no proceedings may be taken on the Bill at any Stage after Stage 1 unless the Parliament has by resolution agreed to the charge, increase or payment.

    . . .

    7. Only a member of the Scottish Executive or a junior Scottish Minister may give notice of a motion for a Financial Resolution. The motion may be moved only by a member of the Scottish Executive or junior Scottish Minister, whether or not he or she has given notice of it or indicated support for it. Such a motion may not be amended."

[22] Standing Order 9.13.

[23] Standing Orders, Chapter 10.

[24] Principally by Act of the Scottish Parliament.

[25] See Chapter 6, Section 2.

and of the Subordinate Legislation Committee[26] for considering an instrument laid before the Parliament, except in cases of particular importance.[27]

Section 2

Northern Ireland

Introduction

This Section briefly describes the procedures followed in the Northern Ireland Assembly in relation to the making of legislation. **7.2.1**

References in this Section to Standing Orders are to the Standing Orders of the Northern Ireland Assembly.[28]

---

[26] The terms of reference of the Subordinate Legislation Committee—reminiscent of those for the Westminster Parliament's Joint Committee on Statutory Instruments—are established by Standing Order 10.3 as follows—

"1. In considering the instrument or draft instrument, the Subordinate Legislation Committee shall determine whether the attention of the Parliament should be drawn to the instrument on the grounds—

(a) that it imposes a charge on the Scottish Consolidated Fund or contains provisions requiring payments to be made to that Fund or any part of the Scottish Administration or to any local or public authority in consideration of any licence or consent or of any services to be rendered, or prescribes the amount of any such charge or payment;

(b) that it is made in pursuance of any enactment containing specific provisions excluding it from challenge in the courts, on all or certain grounds, either at all times or after the expiration of a specific period or that it contains such provisions;

(c) that it purports to have retrospective effect where the parent statute confers no express authority so to provide;

(d) that there appears to have been unjustifiable delay in the publication or in the laying of it before the Parliament;

(e) that there appears to be a doubt whether it is intra vires;

(f) that it raises a devolution issue;

(g) that it has been made by what appears to be an unusual or unexpected use of the powers conferred by the parent statute;

(h) that for any special reason its form or meaning could be clearer;

(i) that its drafting appears to be defective;

or on any other ground which does not impinge on its substance or on the policy behind it."

[27] Standing Order 10.1(3).

[28] Made under section 41 of the Northern Ireland Act 1998—

"**41 Standing orders**

(1) The proceedings of the Assembly shall be regulated by standing orders.

(2) Standing orders shall not be made, amended or repealed without cross-community support.

(3) Schedule 6 (which makes provision as to how certain matters are to be dealt with by standing orders) shall have effect."

Schedule 6 contains provisions not relevant for the purposes of this work.

Passage of Bill

7.2.2   A Bill may be introduced by any Member of the Assembly, whether a Minister or not, on notice to the Speaker.[29] Notice has to be given of the full text of the Bill (a significant departure from the process in the Westminster Parliament[30]). Standing Order 28(3) provides that—

> "No Bill shall be introduced in the Assembly if the Speaker decides that any provision that any provision of it would not be within the legislative competence of the Assembly."[31]

On introduction a Bill is required[32] to be accompanied by an Explanatory and Financial Memorandum which details the policy addressed by the Bill, consultation undertaken, other options considered and the financial implications of the provisions of the Bill.

---

[29] Standing Order 28.
[30] See Chapter 5, Section 2.
[31] This relates to ss.9 and 10 to of the Northern Ireland Act 1998—

"9 Scrutiny by Ministers
(1) A Minister in charge of a Bill shall, on or before introduction of it in the Assembly, make a statement to the effect that in his view the Bill would be within the legislative competence of the Assembly.
(2) The statement shall be in writing and shall be published in such manner as the Minister making the statement considers appropriate.

10 Scrutiny by Presiding Officer
(1) Standing orders shall ensure that a Bill is not introduced in the Assembly if the Presiding Officer decides that any provision of it would not be within the legislative competence of the Assembly.
(2) Subject to subsection (3)—
    (a) the Presiding Officer shall consider a Bill both on its introduction and before the Assembly enters on its final stage; and
    (b) if he considers that the Bill contains—
        (i) any provision which deals with an excepted matter and is ancillary to other provisions (whether in the Bill or previously enacted) dealing with reserved or transferred matters; or
        (ii) any provision which deals with a reserved matter,
    he shall refer it to the Secretary of State; and
    (c) the Assembly shall not proceed with the Bill or, as the case may be, enter on its final stage unless—
        (i) the Secretary of State's consent to the consideration of the Bill by the Assembly is signified; or
        (ii) the Assembly is informed that in his opinion the Bill does not contain any such provision as is mentioned in paragraph (b)(i) or (ii).
(3) Subsection (2)(b) and (c) shall not apply—
    (a) where, in the opinion of the Presiding Officer, each provision of the Bill which deals with an excepted or reserved matter is ancillary to other provisions (whether in the Bill or previously enacted) dealing with transferred matters only; or
    (b) on the introduction of a Bill, where the Bill has been endorsed with a statement that the Secretary of State has consented to the Assembly considering the Bill.
(4) In this section and section 14 "final stage", in relation to a Bill, means the stage in the Assembly's proceedings at which the Bill falls finally to be passed or rejected."
[32] Standing Order 39.

The standard stages for a Bill are as follows[33]—

(1) The First Stage is purely formal.[34]

(2) The Second Stage is "a general debate on the Bill, with an opportunity for Members to vote on its general principles".[35]

(3) The Committee Stage is a "detailed investigation by a Committee, followed by report to the Assembly".[36]

(4) The Consideration Stage is a "consideration of, and an opportunity for Members to vote on, the details of the Bill, including amendments proposed to the Bill".[37]

(5) The Further Consideration Stage is "an opportunity for Members to consider and vote on amendments proposed to the Bill".[38]

---

[33] As required by s.13 of the Northern Ireland Act 1998—

13 Stages of Bills

(1) Standing orders shall include provision—
 (a) for general debate on a Bill with an opportunity for members to vote on its general principles;
 (b) for the consideration of, and an opportunity for members to vote on, the details of a Bill; and
 (c) for a final stage at which a Bill can be passed or rejected but not amended.

(2) Standing orders may, in relation to different types of Bill, modify provisions made in pursuance of subsection (1)(a) or (b).

(3) Standing orders—
 (a) shall include provision for establishing such a committee as is mentioned in paragraph 11 of Strand One of the Belfast Agreement;
 (b) may include provision for the details of a Bill to be considered by the committee in such circumstances as may be specified in the orders.

(4) Standing orders shall include provision—
 (a) requiring the Presiding Officer to send a copy of each Bill, as soon as reasonably practicable after introduction, to the Northern Ireland Human Rights Commission; and
 (b) enabling the Assembly to ask the Commission, where the Assembly thinks fit, to advise whether a Bill is compatible with human rights (including the Convention rights).

(5) Standing orders shall provide for an opportunity for the reconsideration of a Bill after its passing if (and only if)—
 (a) the Judicial Committee decide that any provision of the Bill would not be within the legislative competence of the Assembly;
 (b) a reference made in relation to a provision of the Bill under section 11 has been withdrawn following a request for withdrawal under section 12;
 (c) a decision is made in relation to the Bill under section 14(4) or (5); or
 (d) a motion under section 15(1) is passed by either House of Parliament.

(6) Standing orders shall, in particular, ensure that any Bill amended on reconsideration is subject to a final stage at which it can be approved or rejected but not amended.

(7) References in subsection (5) and other provisions of this Act to the passing of a Bill shall, in the case of a Bill which has been amended on reconsideration, be read as references to the approval of the Bill."

[34] Standing Order 28(5).
[35] Standing Order 29(a).
[36] Standing Order 29(b).
[37] Standing Order 29(c).
[38] Standing Order 29(d).

(6) The Final Stage consists of the "passing or rejection of the Bill, without further amendment".[39]

The Committee Stage is held in the relevant Statutory Committee.[40]

There are procedures for determining questions relating to human rights issues or equality issues[41] on a Bill.

Scrutiny of subordinate legislation

7.2.3 The Standing Orders make provision for the scrutiny by the Assembly of subordinate legislation.[42]

The essence of the procedure is the use of referral to a Committee for examination and report. The Committee is required[43] to consider, in particular—

(1) financial implications,

(2) any ouster by the enabling legislation of the courts' jurisdiction to consider challenge to the instrument,

(3) unauthorised retrospection,

(4) delay in publication or laying,

(5) doubts as to vires,

(6) obscurity,

(7) defective drafting,

(8) any other matter which "does not on [the instrument's] merits or the policy behind it".

SECTION 3

THE NATIONAL ASSEMBLY FOR WALES

7.3.1 The procedures of the National Assembly for Wales make provision for the passage of subordinate legislation to be made by the Assembly and for the scrutiny of certain legislation not made by the Assembly.

---

[39] Standing Order 29(e).
[40] As to which see s.29 of the Northern Ireland Act 1998—
"(1) Standing orders shall make provision—
(a) for establishing committees of members of the Assembly ("statutory committees") to advise and assist each Northern Ireland Minister in the formulation of policy with respect to matters within his responsibilities as a Minister;
(b) for enabling a committee to be so established either in relation to a single Northern Ireland Minister or in relation to more than one; and
(c) conferring on the committees the powers described in paragraph 9 of Strand One of the Belfast Agreement. . . . ".
There are presently no committees of the Assembly, it being suspended.
[41] Standing Orders 32 and 33.
[42] Standing Order 41.
[43] Standing Order 41(6).

References to Standing Orders in this section are to the Standing Orders of the National Assembly.[44]

Subordinate legislation made by the Assembly

For most cases of general legislation to be made by the National Assembly for Wales, Standing Order 22 specifies the procedure to be followed.   **7.3.2**

The process begins with the preparation by a Minister of a proposal for an Assembly Order,[45] following which the Assembly Members are notified of the draft and have an opportunity to decide whether it merits consideration by a subject committee.

The Minister is generally obliged to prepare, having consulted appropriately, a regulatory appraisal of the likely costs and benefits of complying with the draft Order.[46] The appraisal and any consultation responses are published.

The Minister submits the draft, a memorandum explaining its intended effect and any financial implications, and any regulatory appraisal, to the Business Committee of the Assembly.

The Minister recommends whether the draft should be referred to the subject committee of which the Minister is a member. Assignment to subject committees is a function of the Deputy Presiding Officer, and he prescribes a timetable for the committee's deliberations.[47]

The subject committee considering a draft Order may recommend that it be—

(1) approved as submitted,

(2) approved with amendments, or

(3) rejected.

The subject committee may consult or take evidence, and makes a final report to the Assembly and the Minister who submitted the draft.

Following the committee consideration the Minister who prepared the draft (unless he decides to abandon it following committee) lays the draft before the Assembly, with amendments if desired, together with the explanatory memorandum and the regulatory appraisal. The draft Order is also submitted at this stage to the Legislation Committee of the Assembly.[48]

---

[44] Made under s.50(3) of the Government of Wales Act 1998 (c.38).
[45] Normally in both English and Welsh.
[46] See the passage on regulatory impact assessments in Chapter 5, Section 1.
[47] Assignment to committee is the rule, but there are exceptions: Standing Order 22.9.
[48] Constituted under Standing Order 11.

7.3.3   The Legislation Committee considers the draft and reports to the Assembly whether the draft deserves special attention on the grounds[49] that—

"(i)   there appears to be doubt whether the subordinate legislation is within the Assembly's powers or it appears to make unusual or unexpected use of the powers under which it is made;

(ii)   the Act of Parliament or other instrument which gives the Assembly the power to make the subordinate legislation contains specific provisions excluding it from challenge in the courts;

(iii)   it appears to have retrospective effect where the Act of Parliament or other authorising instrument does not give express authority for this;

(iv)   for any particular reason its form or meaning needs further explanation;

(v)   its drafting appears to be defective or the instrument fails to fulfil statutory or other legal requirements; or

(vi)   there appear to be inconsistencies between the English and Welsh texts."

At this stage the draft Order goes to the Assembly for approval, but—

" . . . the Assembly shall not approve such an Order until it has considered the report of the Legislation Committee relating to the draft Order, and the regulatory appraisal (if any) published in relation to it."[50]

In a manner similar to the arrangements of the Westminster Parliament in relation to money[51] the Standing Orders provide, in essence, a Government veto on proposals involving expenditure.[52]

Proceedings in the Assembly on the draft order follow in essence the proceedings in the Westminster Parliament for a Bill. Thus they open with consideration of "the principle of the draft Order, on a motion proposed by a Minister"[53] and then proceed to consideration of amendments tabled.[54] If the draft is not amended the Minister can invite the Assembly to approve the draft order. If the draft is amended, the Minister has to prepare a revised draft order, and some of the previous stages are re-applied.

---

[49] Standing Orders 22.10 and 11.5.

[50] Standing Order 22.12.

[51] See Chapter 5, Section 2.

[52] Standing Order 22.11—"A draft Assembly Order which may give rise to the payment of any sums by the Assembly, except in circumstances in which the sums are unlikely to be significant, shall not be considered by the Assembly unless the Assembly Cabinet has recommended that the Order be made."

[53] Standing Order 22.14.

[54] As to which arrangements for grouping and selection apply—Standing Order 22.18.

"When a draft Order has been approved by resolution of the Assembly it shall be made by being signed".[55]

The procedure described above can be modified and shortened in certain cases.[56]

7.3.4

In some cases instruments made by the Assembly are subject to scrutiny by the Westminster Parliament. The Assembly arrangements in relation to such instruments are set out in Standing Order 23, section 1.

In some cases instruments made by the Assembly provision require the consent of a Minister of Her Majesty's Government.[57] The Assembly arrangements in relation to such instruments are set out in Standing Order 23, section 2.

In some cases subordinate legislation is made by the National Assembly together with a Minister of Her Majesty's Government, a Government Department, the Scottish Executive or the Northern Ireland Executive. The Assembly arrangements in relation to such instruments are set out in Standing Order 23, section 3.

Standing Orders 25 and 26 make provision about special procedure orders and local instruments.

7.3.5

Standing Order 27 addresses subordinate legislation not made by statutory instrument.

Standing Order 28 addresses the confirmation or approval by the Assembly of legislation made by other bodies.

Standing Order 29 establishes, in effect, a system for private Members' proposals for subordinate legislation akin to the private Members' procedure in the Westminster Parliament.[58]

SECTION 4

WESTMINSTER SCRUTINY

One of the effects of the arrangements for devolution in relation to legislation is that a large number of matters previously legislated for by subordinate legislation made by a Minister under a power conferred by Act are now legislated for by the Scottish Parliament, the Northern Ireland Assembly[59] or the National Assembly for Wales, or under powers conferred by Act passed by either of the two former institutions.

7.4.1

---

[55] Standing Order 22.26(i).
[56] See in particular Standing Order 22.27.
[57] As distinct from any office-holder of or in relation to the Assembly. Section 56 of the Government of Wales Act 1998 refers to an executive committee of the Assembly, chaired by a First Secretary and composed of Assembly Secretaries. These have come colloquially to be referred to as the Cabinet, the First Minister and the Ministers.
[58] See Chapter 5, Section 2.
[59] When devolution in Northern Ireland is operative, as to which see Chapter 4, Section 3.

One of the results of this is that the arrangements for the scrutiny of subordinate legislation of this kind ceases to be as described in Chapter 6, Section 2, and the devolved legislatures are required to make their own arrangements for scrutiny.[60]

It is still, of course, open to Members of either House of Parliament to use the existing procedures for the initiation of debate relating to anything done by any of the devolved legislatures. But the essence of devolution is that anything done in relation to devolved matters is not routinely subject to the scrutiny or control of the Westminster Parliament.

In the House of Commons proceedings on a statutory instrument, whether for annulment, approval in draft or of any other kind, may on a Government motion be referred to the Scottish Grand Committee.[61] Similar arrangements exist in relation to Northern Ireland.[62]

---

[60] This was a matter of concern to the Joint Committee on Statutory Instruments when the Bills for devolution were in progress. Hence paragraph 1 of the 27th Report of the Joint Committee for Session 1997–98 (HL Paper 88, HC 33-xxvii)—"The Chairman of the Committee wrote to the President of the Council on 3rd February requesting a memorandum on the arrangements for the scrutiny of delegated legislation in the Welsh Assembly and the Scottish Parliament, and how areas of overlap or need for co-operation with Westminster are to be handled. This memorandum, received on 24th March, is printed in Appendix I."

[61] Standing Order 98.

[62] Standing Order 115.

302

Chapter 8

DRAFTING OF LEGISLATION

Introduction

It is impossible to give anything like an exhaustive account of how legislation **8.1.1** should be drafted. Apart from the impossibility of predicting all the difficulties and questions that may face the draftsman in the course of his work,[1] the only drafting matter on which it is wise to be dogmatic is that it is unwise to be dogmatic on any drafting matter. While there are occasional rules of thumb that may assist, they will do so only if applied flexibly and with an eye constantly on achieving the most clear, simple and effective result in each context. This is why the Office of the Parliamentary Counsel in the United Kingdom has never had such a thing as a drafting manual.[2]

This Section explores some general issues in relation to the drafting of legislation and offers some thoughts that may provide a useful background against which to take drafting decisions in specific contexts.

An important prefatory remark is that the way in which a person drafts a law or any other document must depend on the principles which will be applied by those reading it. In the context of United Kingdom legislation the point is expressed by Lord Bridge of Harwich in *Associated Newspapers Ltd v Wilson* as follows[3]—

---

[1] For simplicity this work adopts the practice of Acts of Parliament in relying on the implied inclusion within references to the masculine of references to the feminine (as to which see further Chapter 22). In the case of draftsmen, it is of course true that many are female. In some documents, particularly those from Australia or New Zealand, the neutral term "drafter" is preferred, and it has its adherents in the United Kingdom too. At present, the Office of the Parliamentary Counsel is composed of approximately equal numbers of men and women.

[2] The drafting establishments of certain Commonwealth, and probably other, jurisdictions do have drafting manuals of different kinds (see, for example, the 35th Report of the New Zealand Law Commission, May 1996). Provided that these are applied flexibly and intelligently there is no reason to doubt their usefulness, particularly for ensuring a desirable degree of consistency of approach to similar problems where a very large number of people are engaged in drafting legislation. And as noted below the Guidelines for Community drafting set out in the *Inter-institutional Agreement of 22nd December 1998 on common guidelines for the quality of drafting of Community legislation* are likely to be of interest to anyone involved in legislative (or indeed other) drafting, and are reproduced in the Appendix.

[3] [1995] 2 W.L.R. 354, 362 HL; there is nothing in the recent advances in purposivism—as to which see Chapter 18, to falsify this basic premise either in relation to drafting or in relation to construction.

"The courts' traditional approach to construction, giving primacy to the ordinary, grammatical meaning of statutory language, is reflected in the parliamentary draftsman's technique of using language with the utmost precision to express the legislative intent of his political masters and it remains the golden rule of construction that a statute means exactly what it says and does not mean what it does not say."

8.1.2   With this in mind, the increasing readiness of the courts to apply an overtly purposive construction eases the job of the draftsman considerably and facilitates economy and simplicity in drafting.[4]

Reliance on a purposive interpretation is not, however, an excuse for imprecision, for two reasons.

First, the main cause of imprecision in drafting is not that the draftsman cannot find or does not wish to trouble to find a precise way of expressing the concept in his mind, but rather that the concept in his mind is not sufficiently precise to admit of clear expression. The principal task in drafting is to refine and analyse the policy to the state of clarity in which the words for its expression suggest themselves naturally. When the draftsman struggles to find the words or structure to express a thought, it is generally time to abandon the struggle and return to analysis or refinement of the thought. All that being so, it is not sufficient to draft imprecisely and hope that the courts will supply the draftsman's deficiencies by adopting a purposive construction: if the thought behind the draft is unclear the courts will not be able to discern its purpose and will not be able to adopt a beneficial construction without trespassing on the legislature's province.[5]

Secondly, prediction of the likely results of a purposive construction is not a precise science. It will rarely be appropriate for the executive to substitute the certainty provided by a clear and precise provision for the hope that the courts' understanding of the general principles and purpose of the legislative scheme will correspond to the understanding of the executive.[6]

The same thoughts apply to deliberate reliance on the rule in *Pepper v Hart*.[7] While it may be tempting to leave a difficult point unresolved and invite a Minister to make an appropriate statement about the general purpose of the legislation, there is no guarantee that the statement will be relied upon by the courts[8] and used in the precise way expected by the executive.

By way of general guidance and provocation of thought, two European Community documents provide some very helpful material of general application in relation to general approaches to legislative (and indeed other) drafting: the

---

[4] See further Chapter 18.

[5] See further Chapter 17.

[6] That does not mean, however, that it is never appropriate to leave certain concepts to be applied by the courts: see, in particular, para.8.1.24 below.

[7] As to which see Chapter 28.

[8] Or, of course, that it will actually be made: political, procedural or other considerations may intervene between the time when the drafting process is forced to end and the opportunity for making *Pepper v Hart* statements was expected to arise.

Interinstitutional Agreement of 22nd December 1998 on common guidelines for the quality of drafting of Community legislation[9] and the *Joint Practical Guide for the Drafting of Community Legislation*[10] are likely to be of interest to anyone involved in drafting. Extracts of both are reproduced in the Appendix.[11]

Plain English

The use of clear language is not a luxury or a fad, but a fundamental necessity **8.1.3** of legislative drafting. If the meaning of a provision is not beyond doubt or argument then the law is not clear. As the Parliamentary Secretary in the Cabinet Office said in responding to an Adjournment Debate on Parliamentary Bills in 2000[12]—

> "The issue can be expressed quite succinctly: the essential need in legislation is law which is certain and which delivers the policy intention that underlies it."

It should not be thought that the desire for plain and clear language, not open to ingenious argument and tortuous construction, is a new preoccupation. Over the decades and indeed centuries pleas have been heard to the same effect.[13]

And in the words the founder of the Office of the Parliamentary Counsel, the first Parliamentary Counsel to the Treasury, Lord Thring[14]—

> " . . . the word best adapted to express a thought in ordinary composition will generally be found to be the best that can be used in an Act of Parliament."

The importance of using plain English in legislative drafting wherever possible is a recurring theme with Parliamentarians. A typical exchange on the point is appended to this work.[15]

---

[9] O.J. C. 73, 17.3.1999.
[10] Issued in Brussels on March 16, 2000 by the Legal Services of the European Parliament, of the Council and of the Commission.
[11] Appendix, Extracts 13 and 14.
[12] HC Deb. January 20, 2000 c.1100.
[13] Perhaps the earliest is a statute (28o Hen. VIII. c.7.—A.D. 1536)—"XVIII. This Act shall be construed most forcibly; without Derogation by any other Act made or to be made. And be it fynally enacted by auctorite aforsaid, that this p'sent acte and every clause article and sentence comprised in the same shall be taken and accepted accordyng to the playne wordes and sentences therin conteyned; and shall not be interpreted nor expounded by colour of any pretence or cause or by any subtill argumentes invencions or reasons to the hyndraunce disturbaunce or derogacion of this Acte or any parte therof; any thynge or thynges acte or actes of Parliamente hertofore made or herafter to be hadd done or made to the contrary therof notwithstandyng; and that ev'y acte statute lawe pvision thyng and thynges, hertofore hadd or made or herafter to be hadd done or made contrary to the effecte of this statute, shall be voyde and of no value nor force."
[14] *Practical Legislation*, London 1902.
[15] Appendix, Extract 15.

8.1.4   It is, however, often difficult to use plain English. For one thing, legislation often has to deal with concepts that are far from plain to most people and which cannot be made plain by the use of a reasonable number of words. A provision in a Finance Bill prohibiting rent-factoring, for example,[16] has to address concepts which combine the unreal world of accountancy and the unreal world of law and has to find some points of contact between those two and the real world. The result is inevitably something that will make no sense to anyone acquainted only with the real world. This is a reality understood by all lawyers and politicians of experience and wisdom.[17]

Even a relatively simple concept like betting, which is very much part of the real world, can give rise to considerable complexity when Parliament attempts to state rules for the taxation of betting profits, the notion of profit in that context proving surprisingly difficult to pin down.[18]

Clearly, when dealing with a relatively simple concept and imposing rules of relative simplicity, the draftsman ought to draft in a manner which will be easily penetrable by any class of reader. But when writing about matters of technical complexity, or imposing in relation to simple concepts rules of complexity, the draftsman will be forced to aim for clarity only in so far as he can assume his primary audience to be familiar both with the substantive area concerned and with the construction of legislation. And in that context the use of technical jargon will often be the most satisfactory way of proceeding: attempting to use "ordinary" words to define and recreate a concept already well understood by the audience at which the provision is primarily aimed is both pointless and likely to go wrong.[19]

8.1.5   Having said all that, the draftsman of legislation must bear in mind the advice given by Sir Alison Russell K.C.[20]—

> "The simplest English is the best for legislation. Sentences should be short. Do not use one word more than is necessary to make the meaning clear. The draftsman should bear in mind that his Act is supposed to be read and understood by the plain man. In any case, he may be sure that if he finds he can express his meaning in simple words all is going well with his draft: while if he finds himself driven to complicated expressions composed of

---

[16] See ss.43A to 43G of the Income and Corporation Taxes Act 1988 (c.1) as inserted by section 110 of the Finance Act 2000 (c.17).

[17] "I am afraid that, in order to achieve precision in legislation which is complex and often technical, it is not always possible to avoid an impression of obscurity."—Harold Macmillan in 1963, cited in *Tributes to the Earl of Stockton (Harold Macmillan)* HC Deb. January 12, 1987 cc.30–31.

[18] See ss.1 to 5 of the Betting and Gaming Duties Act 1981 (c.63) as substituted by Schedule 1 to the Finance Act 2001 (c.9).

[19] And technical language will be given an appropriately technical construction—see Chapter 20; but note the importance of avoiding the temptation to fall between two stools, by using "language neither wholly popular nor altogether technical, and which, therefore, is not to be interpreted readily either by a lawyer or a layman" (*R. v Yates* (1883) 11 Q.B.D. 750, 752 *per* Mathew J.). So if one is to use technical language it must be used precisely and aptly and with full knowledge of the connotations and nuances that it carries in its technical context.

[20] *Legislative Drafting and Forms*, London 1938, pp.12–13.

long words it is a sign that he is getting lost, and he should reconsider the form of the section. Of course, in Acts of a technical kind, he may find it necessary to use technical expressions: but such Acts will usually only affect readers who are qualified to understand them."

When confronted with a piece of legislation that does not appear to be as clear as it might have been, it is also sometimes helpful to remember some of the constraints of the system within which legislation is produced which may account for lack of clarity.[21] In the case of Acts, for example, the legislative timetable can exert extreme pressure, both before and after introduction, on the draftsman. And the need to accommodate amendments to reflect concessions by the Government after introduction may result in a structure that baffles the reader who is ignorant of the legislative history.[22] Indeed, it can happen that a non-Government amendment will be carried against the Government at a late stage in the process allowing no possibility of revision to reflect the structure of the Bill, to produce internal consistency within the Bill or to correct other defects.

Simplicity versus complexity

The draftsman's fundamental aim is as easy to describe as it is difficult to achieve: to produce legislation which is as clear and simple as possible, while achieving a reasonable level of certainty. In reality the requirements of certainty and clarity do not conflict. If the meaning of a law is not sufficiently clear for it to be possible to assume that the same meaning will be ascribed to it by each of its likely readers, the law cannot be said to be in a state of certainty. **8.1.6**

Two passages help to demonstrate the nature of the exercise—

" . . . the draftsman must never be forced to sacrifice certainty for simplicity, since the result may be to frustrate the legislative intention. An unfortunate subject may be driven to legislation because the meaning of an Act was obscure which could, by the use of a few extra words, have been made plain."[23]

---

[21] See paras 8.1.22 and 8.1.23 below.

[22] It is not, after all, possible to turn a hippopotamus into a giraffe, or vice versa, without breaking bones.But that is frequently what a draftsman is asked to do: to take a structure designed to deliver one policy and, in as few amendments as possible and therefore without breaking the essential design upon which that structure is based, to produce a completely different policy. Even the legislature are sometimes unaware of the difficulties produced by this process. When the chairman of a certain Joint Committee asked the draftsman of a Bill to guarantee that the draft placed before the Committee in working form would not later change, on being told that the draftsman could not guarantee that the words would not change he replied along the lines of "we understand that the words may have to change but can you promise not to change the meaning?".

[23] *The Preparation of Legislation*, Report of a Committee appointed by the Lord President of the Council, chaired by the Rt. Hon Sir (later Lord) David Renton, May 1975, Cmnd. 6053, para.11.5.

"Mr Justice Stephen said, speaking from his own experience: 'I think that my late friend, Mr.Mill, made a mistake upon the subject, probably because he was not accustomed to use language with that degree of precision which is essential to every one who has ever had, as I have had on many occasions, to draft Acts of Parliament, which, although they may be easy to understand, people continually try to misunderstand, and in which therefore it is not enough to attain to a degree of precision which a person reading in good faith can understand; but it is necessary to attain if possible to a degree of precision which a person reading in bad faith cannot misunderstand. It is all the better if he cannot pretend to misunderstand it."[24]

8.1.7   Of course, what amounts to an acceptable degree of simplicity and translucence depends on the nature of the likely reader of a piece of legislation. Legislation that imposes direct rights or obligations in respect of things done daily by citizens without special technical knowledge or experience requires, unless there is a good reason why this cannot be achieved, to be made sufficiently plain to be easily comprehended by those citizens. While legislation about, for example, the fiscal treatment of the surrender of a share option cannot sensibly be expected to made plain to anyone without knowledge and experience of both taxation and share options. It will therefore be defensible to use a number of technical terms rendering the meaning of the provision obscure to anyone without that knowledge and experience. Indeed, more than defensible, the use of technical terms will be indispensable, if the draftsman is to be sure that he has achieved a result that will have the requisite meaning to those in the habit of regulating themselves by reference to a technical professional jargon.

For Acts of Parliament, at least, this balancing process appears to work moderately satisfactorily for the most part. As Lord Bingham of Cornhill said in 2003—

"Such is the skill of parliamentary draftsmen that most statutory enactments are expressed in language which is clear and unambiguous and gives rise to no serious controversy."[25]

The drafting of statutory instruments has sometimes given cause for concern.[26] It is generally accepted that the need for clarity is no less urgent in the case of subordinate legislation than in the case of primary: indeed, it will often be the case that members of the public are more closely concerned with and directly

---

[24] Lord Thring, *Practical Legislation*, 1902 Ed., p.9 quoting Stephen J in *In re Castioni* (1891) 1 Q.B. 149, 167.

[25] *R. (Quintavalle) v Secretary of State for Health* [2003] 2 W.L.R. 692, 697.

[26] " . . . the Joint Committee is very concerned that instruments should be easy to understand by the general public. If you look at the provision with which we are concerned I am sure you will accept that it is not easy for members of the general public to read and, at a glance, understand what it says."—Joint Committee on Statutory Instruments, Session 1994–95, 1st Report, Appendix II, Examination of Witnesses, Chairman, para.1 (HL Paper 3, HC 8-i). Note also, more generally, "The Law Society said that the style of drafting used for delegated legislation is on the whole

affected by the terms of subordinate legislation regulating an activity conducted by them, than with the terms of the primary legislation conferring the powers.[27]

Departure from precedent

One of the difficulties in adopting plain English is caused by the need for legislative English to develop in a way that keeps pace with changes in colloquial English. If I use a word in casual conversation that is different from the word that I would naturally have used for the same concept in casual conversation two years previously, nobody is likely to analyse the two expressions looking for a subtle change in meaning. But that is precisely what will happen if a piece of legislation uses an expression that is different from, but apparently synonymous with, an expression used in an earlier piece of legislation, even if the draftsman's only motive for choosing the new expression is a desire to keep pace with developments in the vernacular. **8.1.8**

If legislative language is to develop at all, however, the draftsman simply has to adopt a robust attitude to this problem, in contexts that can sensibly bear it, and innovate without being too worried that people may seek to construe unintended changes of meaning into the innovation. Of course, particularly in post-*Pepper v Hart* days,[28] much can be done to assist by Ministers supporting the use of modern language and robustly denying any imputations of changed meaning.[29]

Useful legal archaisms

As explored above, where modern language can be introduced into legislative drafting, it should be. In other places, however, a phrase tried and tested and **8.1.9**

---

worse than that for primary legislation, possibly because the departmental lawyers had not had the opportunity to build up the necessary skill and expertise."—*Making the Law*, the Report of the Hansard Society Commission on the Legislative Process, The Hansard Society for Parliamentary Government, November 1992, para.172.

[27] Note the comments by the Chairman on the desirability of clarity—Joint Committee on Statutory Instruments, Session 1994–95, 15th Report, para.14 (HL Paper 44, HC 8-xv).

[28] As to which see Chapter 28.

[29] For two examples see: "It is the view of Parliamentary Counsel that 'clearly' and 'manifestly' mean the same. It is a view to which we accord the greatest of respect. I confirm that we will not argue that 'clearly' means anything different from 'manifestly'. That gives the noble Lord, Lord Kingsland, the assurance that he seeks. It is the view of Parliamentary Counsel that 'clearly' is a clearer word than 'manifestly', a view that I share. Our commitment to treat 'clearly' the same as 'manifestly' is unswerving." (Lord Falconer of Thoroton Q.C. (Minister of State, Home Office, and former Solicitor General) speaking for the Government in the Committee stage of the Nationality, Immigration and Asylum Bill, HL Deb. July 23, 2002 c.342 (on what became section 93)).

See also—"On the point raised by the noble Lord, Lord Berkeley, ["I have one comment on the phrase 'the Secretary of State thinks' . . . I suggest that 'think' is a slightly odd word. Perhaps 'consider' would have been a better word."] we are happy to engage Parliamentary Counsel who use ordinary English—what I would call demotic English—in the drafting of the Bill. I believe that 'think' says what it means and is the right word to use, rather than 'is of the opinion' or some more pompous phrase'. (Lord McIntosh of Haringey speaking for the Government on an amendment to the Railways and Transport Safety Bill 2002–03 HL Deb. July 10, 2003 c.432.)

upheld over a period of years by the courts is simply too precious a commodity to discard in the absence of an obvious modern equivalent, however archaic it appears. For example, it is hard to imagine encountering the phrase "without prejudice to the generality of" in any modern context outside the drafting of legislation: and yet there is no obvious current equivalent and the phrase is well understood by the courts and upheld for its—often very important—purpose.[30]

Similar questions arise in relation to the use of the legislative "shall"—as in "the Secretary of State shall make arrangements . . . ". There are respectable arguments both for retaining it and for disposing of it. But one of the arguments for its retention is that, while it is clearly and increasingly archaic, with few people outside the legislative context imposing requirements by the use of "shall", its meaning is still clearly understood and its very archaism helpfully indicates that it is a requirement imposed by a process that differs in character and effect from other non-legislative processes.[31]

The notion that certain expressions can helpfully wield a technical meaning in the context of legislative drafting is one that can be appreciated and supported even by those who may occasionally be misled or perplexed by a particular usage.[32]

Words that have been once in common usage and have ceased to be so, however, should be used even in legislation only with great caution, because their disuse may have obscured their meaning.[33]

Use of examples

8.1.10 There are distinct problems about the use of examples in legislation. But it is occasionally done.

---

[30] See *Homburg Houtimport B.V. v Agrosin Private Ltd, The Starsin* [2003] 2 All E.R. 785, 779–800, HL *per* Lord Bingham of Cornhill.

[31] And it does permit a useful distinction between provision included for the purpose of having legal effect and provision included merely to satisfy a convention—see Chapter 1, Section 6 and Chapter 11, Section 1, footnote 10.

[32] See, for example, the following exchange on an amendment to the Criminal Justice Bill 2002–03 (HL Deb. July 14, 2003 c.647)—

"Baroness Walmsley: At the end of discussion on these amendments in another place, the conclusion of the parliamentary draftsman was that they made no difference to the meaning of the provision in the Bill. We will therefore not be supporting them. Lord Goldsmith [Attorney General]: The noble Baroness, Lady Walmsley, makes my point for me. It is the view of parliamentary counsel that there is no difference between saying that a defendant may not be granted 'unless' and saying a defendant may only be granted 'if'. As it does not seem to us that this makes any difference, I, too, resist this amendment. I invite the noble Lord to withdraw it.

Lord Hodgson of Astley Abbotts: The world of parliamentary draftsmanship is always a strange one. To replace 'not' by 'only' and 'unless' by 'if' seems to me to make quite a difference in the way the clause will be interpreted. As the noble Baroness says, this has been raised once before. As it is now on the record again, I beg to leave to withdraw the amendment."

[33] See, for example, the debate about the meaning of "notwithstanding" *The Federal Huron* [1988] 1 Lloyd's Law Reports 289 Papua New Guinea Supreme Court of Justice January 20, 1986.

The most common instance, although it does not use the word example, is where a provision operates by reference to a list of specified matters followed by "or any other X".[34] It is also common when conferring powers to provide a list of things that may be done under the power, sometimes prefaced by "in particular": these will generally be presented not merely as examples but because they are the kind of thing that one cannot safely assume the legislature intends to permit without express power.[35]

Provisions expressly presented as examples are also found, although rarely.[36]

---

[34] See, for example (although statute abounds in equally useful examples), s.24(3) of the Finance Act 2003 (c.14)—" 'representative', in relation to any person, means—
    (a) his personal representative,
    (b) his trustee in bankruptcy or interim or permanent trustee,
    (c) any receiver or liquidator appointed in relation to that person or any of his property,
or any other person acting in a representative capacity in relation to that person."

[35] See, for example, s.141(3) of the Nationality, Immigration and Asylum Act 2002 (c.41) (European Economic Area ports: juxtaposed controls) which is almost a list of the kinds of the provision that subordinate legislation could not make without express *vires*—
"(3) In particular, an order under this section may—
    (a) provide for a law of England and Wales to have effect, with or without modification, in relation to a person in a specified area or anything done in a specified area;
    (b) provide for a law of England and Wales not to have effect in relation to a person in a specified area or anything done in a specified area;
    (c) provide for a law of England and Wales to be modified in its effect in relation to a person in a specified area or anything done in a specified area;
    (d) disapply or modify an enactment in relation to a person who has undergone a process in a specified area;
    (e) disapply or modify an enactment otherwise than under paragraph (b), (c) or (d);
    (f) make provision conferring a function (which may include—
        (i) provision conferring a discretionary function;
        (ii) provision conferring a function on a servant or agent of the government of a State other than the United Kingdom);
    (g) create or extend the application of an offence;
    (h) impose or permit the imposition of a penalty;
    (i) require the payment of, or enable a person to require the payment of, a charge or fee;
    (j) make provision about enforcement (which may include—
        (i) provision conferring a power of arrest, detention or removal from or to any place;
        (ii) provision for the purpose of enforcing the law of a State other than the United Kingdom);
    (k) confer jurisdiction on a court or tribunal;
    (l) confer immunity or provide for indemnity;
    (m) make provision about compensation;
    (n) impose a requirement, or enable a requirement to be imposed, for a person to co-operate with or to provide facilities for the use of another person who is performing a function under the order or under the international agreement (which may include a requirement to provide facilities without charge);
    (o) make provision about the disclosure of information."

[36] See, for examples, the Occupiers' Liability Act 1957 (c.31), s.2(3), the Courts and Legal Services Act 1990 (c.41), s.17(3)(c)(iii), the Sex Discrimination Act 1975 (c.65), s.29(2), the Race Relations Act 1976 (c.74), s.20(2) and sections 188 of and Schedule 2 to the Consumer Credit Act 1974 (c.39).

The principal difficulty of that kind of example is that the courts will assume that the general expression is to be construed to some extent by reference to the list of specific examples.[37] But there is also the danger that in working through an example the legislature will be seen (or argued[38]) to be qualifying, supplementing or contradicting the details already given of the provision itself.[39]

The advent of Explanatory Notes[40] has provided a home for examples which can be used helpfully to illustrate for the reader how a provision is intended to work, without risking the dangers outlined above.

In some cases it may be thought both safe and helpful to offer an example in parentheses in the text of legislation itself.[41]

Inability to repeat

8.1.11 Repetition plays an important and useful part in normal linguistic usage, written and oral. It is used to add emphasis.[42] It can also be an aid to clarity, since it becomes possible to put a difficult idea in a number of ways, each of which is likely to appeal to a different kind of audience, or the imperfect comprehension of each of which may result in sufficient comprehension of the whole. Legislation is forbidden this tool, because the courts will assume that each phrase is intended to have a discrete and complete legislative effect.[43]

Unnecessary words go septic

8.1.12 It is not only repeated words that cause trouble: any words included in a piece of legislation without having a clear legislative purpose and effect have a potential to go septic and cause trouble, whether in the context of that legislation or in another context. The reason is simply that the courts will assume that the words

---

[37] An instance of the maxim *expressio unius est exclusio alterius*—as to which see Chapter 20.

[38] See above, para.8.1.6.

[39] The Consumer Credit Act 1974 (c.39) attempts to avoid this difficulty by providing in s.188(3) that "In the case of conflict between Schedule 2 [which gives examples] and any other provision of this Act, that other provision shall prevail."

[40] See Chapter 9, Section 5.

[41] See, for example, the following paragraph of Part II of Schedule 5 to the Scotland Act 1998 (c.46) (reserved matters)—

"A1 Fiscal, economic and monetary policy

"Fiscal, economic and monetary policy, including the issue and circulation of money, taxes and excise duties, government borrowing and lending, control over United Kingdom public expenditure, the exchange rate and the Bank of England.

"Exception

Local taxes to fund local authority expenditure (for example, council tax and non-domestic rates)."

[42] The Bellman's plea of "What I tell you three times is true" (Lewis Carroll, *The Hunting of the Snark*, Fit the First) is a common assertion, though normally made less frankly: but while repetition can say nothing about the accuracy of a proposition it can say a good deal about its importance.

[43] See Chapter 20.

are intended to have legislative effect and will try to assign a meaning, which will necessarily be wrong since none at all is intended.

The nature of the problem is graphically illustrated in the context of savings provisions by the following passage of the speech of Lord Halsbury in *McLaughlin v Westgarth*[44]—

> "The misfortune in the framing of these statutes [private Acts] is that any body of persons, seeing a possibility of liability on their part, apply to Parliament to have special provisions inserted for their protection. That application is occasionally complied with and then the argument arises, which their Lordships have heard today—namely, that anybody who is not included in the enumeration of the particular persons so inserted must be taken to be excluded by the operation of the statute from protection, just because they are not included and others are. A great many things are put into a statute *ex abundanti cautela*."

For this reason the draftsman must resist pressures to add express words **8.1.13** dispelling a notion which in his opinion does not arise on a proper construction of the legislation as it stands. It is tempting to assuage concerns, whether they be legal or merely presentational and political, by adding extra words to a provision. But this should be done only if it is generally understood and accepted that sooner or later the extra words will go wrong. The eventual harm may take one of an unlimited number of forms, many of which will be unforeseeable. An express example of the use of a power may be taken to limit the breadth of the general words of grant[45] or the very interest that sought express protection in one context may omit to seek it in another context and find that the absence of the express protection is construed against that interest. The possibilities are endless and should lead the legislature to eschew extra words unless resisting the pressures to add them would itself inevitably lead to great harm.[46]

For similar reasons, words included merely in order to be helpful in assisting a reader to navigate around an Act or instrument need to be tested carefully to see whether they are likely to do more harm, in the way of creating confusion, than good.[47]

---

[44] (1906) 75 LJP.C. 117, 118 HL.

[45] As to which see Chapter 20.

[46] In the context of legislation with a high degree of political or social significance, for example, it may simply be impossible in practice to resist the inclusion of certain matter required for presentational purposes but not having distinct legislative effect.

[47] Hence—"Regulation 5(6) states 'Regulation 15 deals with circumstances in which contributions will be refunded to members who are not transferring members, and regulation 16 makes provision for a former holder of the office of Lord Chancellor'. The Committee asked the Lord Chancellor's Department what (if any) legal effect the provision has and, if it is merely explanatory, why it is included in the Regulations and not in the Explanatory Note. The Department accept in the memorandum printed in Appendix IV that regulation 5(6) is merely explanatory and has no legal effect. The provision was included to assist the reader by explaining the scheme of the regulations immediately before the operative regulations themselves. The Committee does not consider that this can justify the inclusion in a statutory instrument of material which lacks any legislative

As to when it is proper to include in legislation words which have a "genuine" declaratory effect, see Chapter 1, Section 7.

Incorporation of other legislation

8.1.14   A useful drafting device is to provide for provisions of earlier legislation to apply in relation to the present legislation as they apply in relation to the earlier.

For example, s.28 of the Railways and Transport Safety Act 2003[48] provides that a number of sections of the Police Reform Act 2002[49] "shall apply in relation to the [British Transport] Police Force as they apply in relation to other police forces". And in the same Act, Parts 4 and 5, which create offences of sea and air navigation while under the influence of drugs or alcohol, apply[50] a number of provisions of the Acts which deal with the taking of specimens in the context of the offences of driving while under the influence.

This device is also used very commonly to attract definitions from one piece of legislation to another, particularly where the definitions address concepts central to one piece of legislation and merely peripheral to the other.

8.1.15   The principal purpose of this device is, obviously, to avoid the need to repeat in full the provisions referred to. But the use of the device can exceed the saving of words. In some circumstances the device can ensure that changes to the law made in respect of a matter in its principal contexts will automatically apply to that matter in ancillary or subsidiary contexts.

As to the circumstances in which references will and will not have this kind of ambulatory effect, see Chapter 22, paras 22.1.23 and 22.1.24. The device may also be used to ensure (or make it more likely) that judicial decisions about the meaning or application of certain provisions will be applied to the provisions in their new context.

It is normal when applying other legislation to provide for application with such modifications as may be necessary, to set out a list of specific modifications, or (as the provisions of the Railways and Transport Safety Act 2003 mentioned above do) to do both. Even in the absence of provision for modifications, however, the courts will imply any that are indisputably necessary to make the application work.[51]

8.1.16   Despite its obvious advantages the practice of legislating by the application of provisions elsewhere has sometimes been criticised as making life more difficult for the reader of the legislation, since it requires reference to other documents

---

content and therefore reports regulation 5(6) on the ground that it is not in accord with proper legislative practice. The Committee, noting that there have been several recent examples of the practice, takes this opportunity to restate its view that non-legislative material should not be included in statutory instruments."—Joint Committee on Statutory Instruments, Session 1997–98, 37th Report, para.5 (HL Paper 119, HC 33-xxxvii).

[48] 2003 c.20.
[49] 2002 c.30.
[50] ss.83 and 96.
[51] See, for example, *R. v Whitehead* [1982] Q.B. 1272, 1282, CA.

(which may be in a wholly unrelated substantive field). Possibly the most trenchant criticism was expressed by Farwell L.J. in *Chislett v Macbeth & Co.*[52]—

> "Draftsmen of Acts of Parliament are only too ready to avail themselves of the pernicious practice of legislating by express reference to another Act. I should be sorry to give any encouragement to the view that such reference may be implied. It is bad draftsmanship enough to refer expressly; it would be far worse to refer by implication."

And the issue is a regular source of controversy among Parliamentarians.[53]   **8.1.17**
Certainly it would not generally be thought helpful to legislate by reference where the device saves few words and has no other benefits. But examination of the examples given above from the Railways and Transport Safety Act 2003 will show that in some cases the alternative to legislation by reference would be unwarrantable prolixity and possible confusion. Admittedly, the express modifications required in relation to Parts 4 and 5 of the 2003 Act are considerable: but being set out in a table as they are it is easy for the reader to see where the provisions for aviation and navigation depart from the provisions relating to road traffic, which would not be the case if the entire substance was repeated simply incorporating the modifications along the way.

So, again, the only rule of drafting is that there are no useful rules of drafting—the draftsman must set out the material in the most helpful way on each occasion. If incorporation is the most helpful way of proceeding, it should be used, and if not, not. Like other techniques, if used inappropriately merely because the draftsman has fallen into the habit of using it, the result will attract well-deserved criticism.[54]

---

[52] [1909] 2 K.B. 811, 815 CA.
[53] See HC Deb. March 6, 1924 c.1596; and see paras 11.27 to 11.31 of the Renton Report (*Report on the Preparation of Legislation*) (Cmnd. 6053)—in particular, "11.27—Our witnesses have been almost unanimous in condemning 'legislation by reference', or 'referential legislation', as a source of confusion and irritation both to legislators and to other users. They have not always, however, been very clear about what they mean by those terms."
[54] See, for example, the following report of the Joint Committee on Statutory Instruments—"Since the provisions referred to consist respectively of only three short paragraphs and one short sentence there appeared to the Committee to be no good reason for not repeating them with the two small adaptations required."—Joint Committee on Statutory Instruments, Session 1995–96, 15th Report, para.4, (HL Paper 60, HC 34-xv); or "The Committee draws the special attention of both Houses to these Regulations on the ground that they are drafted in a way which is unnecessarily referential. . . . the Home Office accept that, given the concise nature of the present Regulations and of the definitions contained in the 1983 Regulations, the definitions should have been set out in full."—Joint Committee on Statutory Instruments, Session 1995–96, 22nd Report, para.8, (HL Paper 89, HC 34-xxii); and similar objection was taken by the Committee to referential definitions in the Construction (Use of Explosives) Regulations (Northern Ireland) 1997 (S.R 1997/555)—Joint Committee on Statutory Instruments, Session 1997–98, 23rd Report, para.4, (HL Paper 70, HC 33-xxiii).

Exceptions, provisos, savings &c.

8.1.18 The draftsman is frequently required to give effect to a policy by applying a proposition to some but not all cases within a natural class. There is a variety of ways of achieving this.

The proviso ("X shall be the case; provided that Y and Z") has gradually given way to a variety of more modern forms of expression.

An exception can be provided for either by stating a proposition in general terms and then qualifying it, or by expressing the proposition only in limited terms. Which is appropriate will depend on the circumstances of the case. The draftsman should aim to present the material in the form and order which will most readily and easily enable the reader to build up a picture of the law. If the law is complicated, but there are certain fundamental principles that can helpfully be understood before proceeding to the detail, it is right to express the fundamental principles first and then qualify them. That will be particularly the case where the fundamental principles will be sufficient for the purposes of many readers, to whom the details are not relevant. Against that, however, is the need not to create a misleading impression in the mind of the reader which is then dispelled by later detailed provision.[55]

The principal context in which it matters whether a proposition amounts to an exception or a component of the underlying proposition is that of criminal offences.[56]

A saving is simply a provision which qualifies a proposition elsewhere in legislation so as to disapply it to certain matters (most commonly matters arising before the enactment of the proposition qualified). There is no particular form of words required to effect a saving. Savings are particularly common in relation to repeals, as to which see Chapter 14, Section 4.

"Subject to ... "

8.1.19 The question of when to use "subject to" follows from the previous discussion about qualifications. Opening a proposition with "Subject to ... " is a favourite gambit of persons caricaturing pompous or complicated legal drafting. The phrase should certainly be used only where necessary, and thought should be given to its placing to minimise its disruptive effect on the flow of the text.

As a general rule, it is most helpful first to tell the reader the substantive proposition that you are advancing, and then to warn him of any inconsistency between that and another proposition and to inform him how the inconsistency is

---

[55] So when providing for murderers to be hung it is not helpful to provide as follows—

"(1) All persons shall be hanged.

(2) But subsection (1) does not apply to a person who has not committed a murder."

If providing a general speed limit for roads of 60 miles per hour, however, with an express exemption for certain public-service vehicles, it is likely to be sensible to express the speed limit in general terms and follow it with express exceptions.

[56] See the discussion in Chapter 1, Section 5.

to be resolved. So the "subject to" proposition is generally best placed at the end of a subsection or paragraph.

The exception to this is a case where the inconsistency is so fundamental to the effect of the proposition being advanced that it would be positively misleading to allow the reader to absorb the proposition without first being aware of its relationship with the other inconsistent proposition.

Where the "subject to" proposition is mere clarification of what would probably be assumed in any event, it can, as well as being left to the end of the proposition, be made parenthetical. Where the resolution of the apparent inconsistency between two propositions is so clear as to be a matter of common sense, it is best to omit "subject to" altogether.[57]

Statements of purpose

An Act[58] may include, generally at the beginning of the Act or a Part, a section or subsection stating the purpose of the Act or Part or a statement of general principle setting the context for later provisions of the Act or Part. This is frequently referred to as a "purpose clause" (irrespective of whether it takes the form of a section or subsection).　　**8.1.20**

Opinions are sharply divided as to whether purpose clauses do, or may do, more harm than good. The arguments will be found rehearsed at length in recent Parliamentary debates on the subject as well as in recent publications.[59] The issues are summarised in the extracts from those debates appended to this work.[60] In essence, the question is whether the dangers of legislation in general terms—requiring the courts to supply the detailed application and making it impossible for the citizen to be sure in advance what application will be provided—outweigh the benefits of legislation that is shorter and the general purpose of which is much easier to comprehend and, in many cases, apply.

There is also a danger that later amendments to an Act will falsify a purpose clause or statement of principle, or will not be apt for its application, but that　　**8.1.21**

---

[57] For example, "subject to . . . " is redundant in the following—
　　　"(1) Subject to subsection (2), a person who takes a dog into a park must ensure that it wears a muzzle.
　　　(2) Subsection (1) shall not apply to a police officer."
　　The relationship between subsections (1) and (2) would be equally clear without the words "subject to . . . ", nor would anyone be seriously misled by the two propositions, because of their simplicity and contiguity. Some draftsmen would begin subsection (2) with the word "But".

[58] Or, theoretically, a piece of subordinate legislation. The notion does not arise for European legislation, in the case of which the purpose of the legislation is amply demonstrated by the preamble—see Chapter 31.

[59] HL Deb. November 11, 1997 cc.87–88; HL Deb. January 21, 1998 cc.1583–1602; Renton Report (*Report on the Preparation of Legislation*) (Cmnd. 6053) Recommendation 15; *Making the Law*, the Report of the Hansard Society Commission on the Legislative Process, The Hansard Society for Parliamentary Government, November 1992, paras 223 to 252.

[60] Appendix, Extract 16.

amendment or disapplication of the clause or statement will either be impracticable or overlooked.[61]

Whatever the rights and wrongs of the argument, the present practice of primary legislative drafting in the United Kingdom can be described as to make occasional but sparing and cautious use of the purpose clause or statement of principle.[62]

Both the Explanatory Notes prepared for Bills and Acts[63] and the courts' decision in *Pepper v Hart* to allow themselves to consider Parliamentary material in construing Acts[64] are relevant to the debate about purpose clauses, since both are alternative methods by which, to some extent, the underlying intention of Parliament in legislating can be made clear for the benefit of the courts without risking repetition or inconsistency within the legislative text itself.

The principles relating to purpose clauses are as relevant to the drafting of subordinate legislation as they are to the drafting of primary legislation.[65]

---

[61] The argument here is as for indices of defined expressions—see Chapter 24.

[62] Lord Renton in his speech cited in the Appendix gave three examples—

"A classic example is contained in Section 1 of the Children Act 1989, which states: 'When a court determines any question with respect to the upbringing of a child . . . the child's welfare shall be the court's paramount consideration'.

"That states the purpose of the Act. It is both a statement of principle and an interpretation clause, and later sections set out the detail. The Civil Liability (Contribution) Act 1978 states: 'A person is liable in respect of any damage for the purposes of this Act if the person who suffered it . . . is entitled to recover compensation from him in respect of that damage (whatever the legal basis of his liability, whether tort, breach of contract, breach of trust or otherwise)'. That is another clear statement of purpose. Best of all I like the example in the Transport Act 1978, which states: 'It shall be the duty of the Secretary of State to promote a national policy for the use of inland waterways for commercial transport'. It stood by itself. There was no detail to follow. That is a clear statement of what a Minister should do."

It is noticeable, however, that none of those examples expressly purports to be a statement of the purpose of the legislation. Such express provisions are occasionally found—see, for example, section 1 of the Legal Aid Act 1988 (c.34)—

"The purpose of this Act is to establish a framework for the provision under Parts II, III, IIIA, IV, V and VI of advice, assistance, mediation and representation which is publicly funded with a view to helping persons who might otherwise be unable to obtain advice, assistance, mediation or representation on account of their means."

See also s.1 of the Arbitration Act 1996 (c.23)—

"The provisions of this Part are founded on the following principles, and shall be construed accordingly—

(a) the object of arbitration is to obtain the fair resolution of disputes by an impartial tribunal without unnecessary delay or expense;

(b) the parties should be free to agree how their disputes are resolved, subject only to such safeguards as are necessary in the public interest;

(c) in matters governed by this Part the court should not intervene except as provided by this Part."

For another statement of purpose (described as a "statutory objective") applying only in relation to a Part of an Act see s.17 of the Courts and Legal Services Act 1990 (c.41).

For a provision expressly stating that the purpose of an Act is to enable effect to be given to a specified international agreement, see s.1 of the Nuclear Safeguards and Electricity (Finance) Act 1978 (c.25).

[63] See Chapter 9, Section 4.

[64] See Chapter 28.

[65] See, for example, the following trenchant observations of the Joint Committee on Statutory Instruments in relation to the Procurement of Air Navigation Equipment (Technical Specifications)

The question of the use of purpose clauses is of course relevant to the question of undue prolixity discussed below.

Prolixity

The draftsman of legislation in the United Kingdom generally aims to achieve the **8.1.22** stated policy as accurately and completely as possible.[66] But it is, of course, true that an attempt to foresee every possible kind of factual complication that may arise is bound to fail, and that an attempt to go beyond the more obvious cases is likely to result in a state of "false accuracy", whereby addressing one improbable case but failing to address another which is no less probable may either confuse the courts, causing them to read something unintended into the

---

Regulations 1997 (SI 1997/2329)—"The committee draws the special attention of both Houses to these regulations on the ground that they are defectively drafted. Regulation 2(2) provides that these regulations (made under section 2(2) of the European Communities Act 1972) are to have effect for the purpose of making such provision as is necessary to comply with the Directive and are to be construed accordingly. The Committee asked what is the purpose of each of the two propositions and, in relation to the second, which expressions used in the regulations are given a meaning in the Directive. The Department of the Environment, Transport and the regions reply in a memorandum printed in Appendix IX that the first proposition is declaratory of the purpose of the regulations and looks forward to the second proposition which is intended to ensure that any dispute as to the meaning of the regulations is resolved by reference to the Directive, in particular other expressions defined in or having an ascertainable meaning in the Directive. However, they acknowledge that 'the provision is unnecessary to the extent that it states the existing law' and that 'an alternative means of incorporating the definitions used in the Directive would have been more appropriate'. The Committee agrees with the department's conclusion and thinks it important to state why they do. As to the first proposition, the Committee agrees that it is an unnecessary provision—indeed considered it to be it to be subversive—because Member States are obliged by Directives and the jurisprudence of the European Court to make the provisions on their laws which are necessary to comply with the Directives and the Government are empowered by section 2(2) of the European Communities Act 1972 to make provision expressly for that purpose. As to the second proposition, the Committee considers that the appropriate way of incorporating expressions defined or used in a Directive is to state that the expression has the meaning given in the Directive or (where it is not defined but has an ascertainable meaning) that it has the same meaning as in the Directive. The Committee reports regulation 2(2) for defective drafting, acknowledged by the Department."—Joint Committee on Statutory Instruments, Session 1997–98, 14th Report, para.10 (HL Paper 42, HC 33-xiv).

[66] And their success as a general rule is noted in the passage of the speech of Lord Bingham of Cornhill in *R (Quintavalle) v Secretary of State for Health* cited above; and Lord Renton in his speech mentioned above in connection with purpose clauses (January 21, 1998 c.1583) said "Let me make clear at the outset that this Question is not an implied criticism of the Government. Indeed, much of their legislation is drafted with clarity and certainty of legal effect; but, as with previous governments, some of it is a mass of detail from which the underlying intention of Parliament has to be inferred. The detail can be incomplete and is sometimes uncertain in its legal effect or ambiguous in its meaning. Unlike European legislation, our legislation has traditionally been drafted in detail. That is inevitably so when dealing with taxes, social security and much of the criminal law. It has to be so in statutes which impose rights and duties upon the citizens; the provisions must be stated in detail. However, there has for years been a tendency to mention hypothetical cases to cover a subject in the hope that every circumstance that could arise has been covered, whereas in practice other cases arise which have not been covered by the detail. If examples were needed of that, one has only to look at the ancient and more recent sale of goods Acts, the theft Acts and other legislation."

failure, or simply leave a clear, but obviously unintended, gap in the law which the courts will feel themselves powerless to fill.[67]

A powerful argument against unreasonable prolixity is found in the following passage of a speech of Lord Simon of Glaisdale on the Access to Justice Bill 1998–99—

> "We come to the question of how far it is desirable to clutter up the statute book with unnecessary provisions that the existing law amply takes care of. My noble and learned friend the Lord Chancellor referred briefly to this matter in his speech on the previous amendment; namely, that if there was an unnecessary provision in one place it drew attention to, and founded an argument for, its absence from another.

> "Apart from that, it is expensive to add words to the statute book. We go on expanding and expanding. The Government are in favour of bearing down on inflation, quite rightly, but not when it comes to the inflation of statutory language. As to that, they tend to spread themselves. In addition to the expense of producing extra pages, drawing on the cost of secretaries, typists, civil servants, Ministers, printers and book-binders, enormous expenditure is involved if an extra volume is added to the statutes in force. They are extremely expensive. I indicated in Committee how the statute book had not only enlarged in format but increased in its number of volumes since the Renton Committee in 1975 drew attention to the prolixity and over-elaboration that had been the subject of criticism.

> "In addition, every unnecessary provision will found an argument. The noble and learned Lord, Lord Falconer, propounded what might be termed the Falconer syndrome; namely, that one had to think of every argument however far-fetched and fatuous and forestall it. If one places extra unnecessary words in a statute it merely gives greater scope to the Falconer syndrome."[68]

8.1.23   This is not a new problem or a new complaint. More than a century ago it was said that "the true objection to modern statutes is rather their prolixity than their want of perspicuity".[69]

In the end, the draftsman must effect a sensible compromise, so that the legislation deals clearly and concisely with the Government's policy, addressing

---

[67] For an example, see the footnote to the discussion of section 1 of the Laying of Documents before Parliament Act 1948 (c.59) in Chapter 14, Section 5.

[68] HL Deb. February 11, 1999 cc.354–55.

[69] Barrington, *Observations on Statutes*, 3rd ed. 175; earlier editions of this work include the helpful observation that the verbosity which began to be apparent in statutes from the fifteenth century may owe something to the change—doubtless intended to enhance clarity—from drafting in Latin and Norman French by committee to drafting in English by expert conveyancers: the suggestion is that "this may have been originally due to uncertainty as to which of several English words accurately rendered a Latin or Norman French law term".

all such cases as are thought reasonably likely to arise, without confusing the issue by attempting to deal with the improbable or far-fetched. The draftsman must always bear in mind the words of the *Renton Report* quoted above[70] about the importance of sparing the citizen from litigation that could have been avoided by the inclusion of a few additional words. But at the same time he must bear in mind that it will often be impossible to formulate cogent policy in relation to matters that are unlikely to arise, since the circumstances that would appertain if they were to arise cannot easily be conjectured.

Of course, the degree to which a compromise can sensibly be achieved depends to a considerable extent on the circumstances under which and constraints within which the draftsman has to operate.[71]

The question of the proper degree of complexity and particularity to attempt to attain is of course relevant to the question of the use of purposes clauses discussed above.

False accuracy

Despite what is said above about the importance of precision of thought and expression it is, as already noted, important to guard against appearing to be able to be more precise than is possible or advisable in the context. **8.1.24**

In many places, the appropriate form of the legislative provision is something that indicates to readers and the courts what is intended, but leaves it to the courts to apply the concept to particular cases in the light of their experience. An attempt to remove all element of discretion from the courts will sometimes produce more uncertainty and confusion than it removes.

For example, the draft Bill reforming the regulation of gambling taken for pre-legislative scrutiny by an ad hoc Joint Committee in Session 2003–04 contained the following clause—

> "**30 Cheating**
>
> (1) A person commits an offence if he—
>
> (a) cheats at gambling, or
> (b) does anything for the purpose of enabling or assisting another person to cheat at gambling.
>
> (2) For the purposes of subsection (1) it is immaterial whether a person who cheats—
>
> (a) improves his chances of winning anything, or
> (b) wins anything.

---

[70] Section 1.
[71] See paras 8.1.4 and 8.1.5 above.

(3) Without prejudice to the generality of subsection (1) cheating at gambling may, in particular, consist of actual or attempted deception or interference in connection with—

(a) the process by which gambling is conducted, or

(b) a real or virtual game, race or other event or process to which gambling relates.

[Provisions about kind of gambling to which the clause applies, penalties and repeal.]"

8.1.25   The essence of this clause is to leave it for the most part to the courts, in this case magistrates and juries, to determine what amounts to cheating. The concept is one used freely in colloquial conversation, and it depends so much on the particular circumstances of a case, including often complicated questions of who knew, did not know or should have known particular matters, that to try to go further in the production of a lengthy and complicated statutory definition of what it means to cheat at gambling would be unlikely to assist the courts very much and would be almost bound to create unintentional anomalies and infelicities. The only matters required to be expressed, in subs.(2) and (3), are that the offence applies whether or not the cheating has its intended effect and whether the interference is with the process of gambling or with the race or other event (in which latter case the people involved, apart from the cheat, might be unaware that any gambling was taking place at all): in relation to these matters the courts might hesitate to apply the offence without express support in the legislation. Because the courts will be bound to apply a colloquial and natural conversational construction to the term in this context, the reader will be in a reasonable position to determine the effect of the provision despite the fact that it deliberately leaves precise application to the courts.

Other drafting devices

8.1.26   For a discussion of the use of definitions of the "mere tag" variety to allow a long proposition to be broken up into a number of sub-propositions, see Chapter 24.

Subordinate legislation

8.1.27   The observations in this Section are equally true for primary and subordinate legislation. In the case of the latter, however, it can be added that there is an additional reason for precision. In the words of the Joint Committee on Statutory Instruments[72]—

---

[72] *First Special Report of the Joint Committee on Statutory Instruments*, Session 1977–78 (HL 51, HC 169).

"The Committee fully appreciate that the justification for the granting of delegated legislative powers is to remove subsidiary or procedural details from the Statute Book and to afford the Executive flexibility and the ability to alter detailed provisions to fit changing circumstances, without the need to enact a new Statute. The corollary of this, however, must be that the delegated legislation itself should be detailed, specific and self-explanatory and should not depend on the exercise of ministerial or departmental discretion unless provision to that effect is expressly contained in the enabling statute."

SECTION 2

SPECIFIC ISSUES

Introduction

The preceding Section adumbrated some general principles in relation to the drafting of legislation. This Section addresses a few specific issues that arise commonly and concerning which some general observations can helpfully be offered. **8.2.1**

"Above" and "below"

The use of references to "section X above" or "section X below" was at one time routine practice for Acts and for subordinate legislation. Practice now varies considerably, but it is possible to identify a trend towards using the words only where it is necessary in the context to distinguish a provision of the Act or instrument itself from a provision of another Act or instrument already referred to. So, for example, most draftsmen would wish to use either "above" or "of this Act" in the expression "an order under section X of the Y Act or under section Z above / below / of this Act". **8.2.2**

Under v by virtue of

It is common to find statutory references to things done "under [provision X]" or "by virtue of [provision X]", and sometimes to things done "under or by virtue of [provision X]". **8.2.3**

The distinction is based on the assumption that "by virtue of" is wider than "under", so that, for example, where regulation A made under section B permits an application to be made, the application might be described elsewhere in legislation as being made under regulation A but by virtue of section B. The result is that "anything done under or by virtue of section X" is intended to cover anything done under the section or under subordinate legislation made under it.

However, since "by virtue of" is wide enough to cover things done "under" as well, some draftsmen prefer to use "by virtue of" on its own. And some use only "under" and rely on its being construed in the context as having as wide a meaning as is necessary.

Numbering

8.2.4 The systems used for the numbering of Acts and subordinate legislation are described briefly above.[73]

The numbering of interpolated provisions presents difficulties. The normal, but not invariable, way of solving them is as follows.

A provision inserted between (1) and (2) is (1A) (followed by (1B), (1C) . . .). A provision inserted between (1A) and (1B) is (1AA) (followed by (1AB), (1AC) . . .). A provision inserted between (1) and (1A) is often numbered as (1ZA).[74]

A provision inserted between (a) and (b) is (aa) (followed by (ab), (ac) . . .). A provision inserted between (aa) and (ab) is (aaa) (followed by (aab), (aac) . . .). There is a particular danger in that (aa) is also commonly used in a series beginning (a) for the first entry after (z), in which case it is generally followed by (bb), (cc) and so on. So there is a certain potential for confusion, although perhaps more theoretical than real.[75]

8.2.5 The numbering system 1.1, 1.2 and so on[76] in theory assists interpolation, since it is always possible to start a new sub-series by the addition of .1 at whatever point in the number one wishes, eliminating the need for "A) and the like. And it can have other advantages.[77] But there is a disadvantage. A reference to s.134A(5B)(ba)(iA) would be both visually confusing and difficult to pronounce: but it is immediately apparent what order of provision is being referred to, namely a sub-paragraph of a paragraph of a subsection in s.134A.

---

[73] Chapter 2, Section 5 and Chapter 3, Section 3.

[74] This is, of course, both ugly and counter-intuitive—but there is no obvious alternative. Many draftsmen will, however, go to considerable lengths to avoid having to use this form of numbering. That may include renumbering a provision where appropriate, although there are of course dangers of renumbering, particularly where there are likely to be outlying cross-references that may be difficult or impossible to find.

[75] On other grounds many draftsmen would try to avoid such a long lettered series and to find some other way of presenting the material.

[76] Used for legislative drafting in some foreign jurisdictions.

[77] Note, for example, "The chosen method of numbering renders it immediately apparent that, for example, any regulation commencing with 2. relates to the pension scheme constituted under Part II of the Regulations. The Department point out that there are precedents for using this method of numbering. The Committee accepts that there are rare occasions, such as this one, when this method of numbering is acceptable. However, the Committee consider that the system set out in Statutory Instrument Practice should continue to be the one which is normally used, and that the system used in the present Regulations should be used only when there are good reasons for so doing."—Joint Committee on Statutory Instruments, Session 1994–95, 20th Report, para.9, (HL Paper 61, HC 8-xx).

That would not be true of s.134.1.5.2.2.1.1.1, which would be the strict equivalent.[78]

Vacant provisions

It frequently falls to the draftsman to place new material in a gap left by the omission of old material, whether or not the omission is part of the same exercise that inserts the new material. The question then arises whether to reuse the number of the old material.

8.2.6

The principal argument in favour is that it appears odd to place, say, a new subs.(2A) between subss.(2) and (4) where the number (3) is vacant.

The principal argument against, which is frequently the stronger, is that there may be outlying references, in the same Act or instrument or in other Acts or instruments, to the old subs.(3): despite the repeal of the old subs.(3) references to it may continue in force, being historical references to something done under the provision when it had force. Or the repeal may be subject to savings as a result of which the provision has or may have some effect for a considerable time. Re-using the number will result in, at best, confusion and, at worst, the falsification of necessary references.

Use of singular to be preferred to use of plural

It was once the generally applied rule in legislative drafting, and it is still a very serviceable rule although less widely adhered to, that one should for preference draft in the singular and rely on the principle, set out in section 6 of the Interpretation Act 1978,[79] to include the plural.

8.2.7

There is good reason for this rule of thumb, despite the fact that it is not in accordance with the natural tendency of common conversation.

> It would, for example, be natural to describe fox-hunting as the process of hunting foxes with dogs.
>
> But if drafting a law prohibiting fox-hunting it is better to say "a person commits an offence if he uses a dog to hunt a fox" than to say "if he uses dogs to hunt foxes".
>
> The reason is one of construction.
>
> If it is an offence to hunt one fox using one dog, there is no conceivable reason why Parliament should not intend it also to be an offence to hunt more than one fox with more than one dog, and of course a person who hunts foxes with dogs will, in the course of that, have satisfied literally the condition of hunting a fox with a dog.

---

[78] In practice, therefore, the use of A and the like is often combined with the 1.1 system.
[79] 1978 c.30; see Chapter 22.

But the other way around the construction is not nearly as clear. First, there may be reasons why the legislature intended to outlaw only the use of packs of dogs, not the use of single dogs by gamekeepers. Secondly, as a matter of strict construction a person who hunts one fox with one dog will not have hunted "foxes" with "dogs".

So for both reasons it is generally best to use the singular and to rely on the principle of s.6 of the Interpretation Act 1978 for the conversion to cover the plural as well.

There will be occasions when the rule is in itself insufficient to dispel possible doubt about the legislative intent. For example, when requiring a Minister to ensure that a particular statutory body includes a person with knowledge of the law, if one says merely "a person with knowledge of the law" one raises the question whether Parliament means "one and only one" or "at least one". Here too, the sense of the provision may suggest a contrary intention displacing the general application of s.6. So the draftsman is generally well advised to say "at least one" if that is what is meant, and to say "one (and not more than one)", or something along those lines, if that is what is meant.

Gender

8.2.8   As a general rule legislation uses "he" to mean "he or she" or sometimes "he, she or it". This has occasionally been the subject of controversy.[80] The Government's response to suggestions of a gender-free drafting policy has until now been that it would be perfectly possible to achieve, but only at the expense of a modest loss of simplicity.[81] Whether or not the assumption of masculinity causes increasing offence and leads to irresistible pressure to adopt a gender-free style, remains to be seen.

It is occasionally clear that to use anything other than a specifically feminine word would be to court ridicule. Provisions about maternity, for example, can

---

[80] See, for example, the Ten-Minute Rule Bill *Interpretation (Amendment)* HC Deb. May 9, 1995 cc.580–581 and the Adjournment Debate HC Deb. January 20, 2000 cc.1094–1100.

[81] See, in particular, the following Written Answer by the Prime Minister (HC Deb. October 29, 1998 W.A. 241)—"The most important objectives in the language used in legislation are clarity and legal certainty. In general, the use of gender-specific language is not necessary to meet these objectives. But there are occasions when, for example, the use of gender-specific pronouns makes it possible for legislation to be expressed more simply, and so more clearly, than it otherwise could be. In these cases, section 6 of the Interpretation Act 1978 applies. It provides that, unless the contrary intention applies, words importing the masculine gender include the feminine, and vice versa."

The loss of simplicity will be seen from those Commonwealth jurisdictions where gender-free drafting is the norm and the style accordingly requires either the frequent repetition of the noun concerned ("The Secretary of State may, if the Secretary of State thinks that the Secretary of State has been given insufficient notice", rather than "The Secretary of State may, if he thinks that he has been given insufficient notice") or some other, frequently inelegant and laborious, way of avoiding the pronoun.

obviously be drafted sensibly only by the use of feminine pronouns.[82] Equally, on occasion a reference to a specific office filled by a female should sensibly be made feminine.[83]

See also the discussion of section 6 of the Interpretation Act 1978 below.[84]

Disregarding the impossible

One of the ancient maxims of the common law is *lex non cogit ad impossibilia*.[85] As Broom's *Legal Maxims* puts it[86]—

    8.2.9

> "This maxim, or, as it is also expressed, *impotentia excusat legem*[87] . . . must be understood in this qualified sense, that *impotentia* excuses when there is a necessary or invincible disability to perform the mandatory part of the law, or to forbear the prohibitory. It is akin to the maxim of the Roman law, *nemo tenetur ad impossibilia*, which, derived from common sense and natural equity, has been adopted and applied by the law of England under various and dissimilar circumstances."

The result of the application of this maxim, which remains potent,[88] is that the draftsman need not expressly excuse that compliance which is obviously impossible. So, for example, if requiring a particular communication to take "the prescribed form" the draftsman need not generally state that the requirement can lawfully be ignored where no form has been prescribed for the purpose. There may be occasions, however, on which the sense of the legislation makes it arguable that the primary provisions are not to operate at all until certain mechanisms have been put into place by subordinate legislation: if the draftsman thinks it necessary in the context to avoid a suggestion of that kind he will

---

[82] Note, however, that a suggestion of drafting a provision about nurses by the use of feminine pronouns on the grounds that the overwhelming majority of nurses are female would be likely to be subject to criticism on the grounds of sexist stereotyping.

[83] See, for example, s.92 of the Scotland Act 1998 (c.46)—"There shall be a Queen's Printer for Scotland who shall—(a) exercise the Queen's Printer functions in relation to Acts of the Scottish Parliament and subordinate legislation to which this section applies, and (b) exercise any other functions conferred on her by this Act or any other enactment." The use of the feminine pronoun in paragraph (b) reflects the occupation of the post of Queen's Printer by a lady (see the speech of Baroness Ramsay of Cartvale on the provision that became section 92 of the 1998 Act—HL Deb. November 2, 1998 c.15). In contrast, legislation referring to the Secretary of State or another Minister is generally drafted by means of the masculine pronoun irrespective of the gender of the present occupant of the office, on the grounds that the occupants of these positions change so frequently.

[84] Chapter 22.

[85] Co. Litt. 231 b.

[86] Broom's *Legal Maxims*, 10th ed., London 1939, p.162.

[87] Co. Litt. 29 a—see *Eager v Furnivall* 17 Ch. D. 115, 121 *per* Jessel M.R.

[88] Particularly in the context of statutory duties—see *per* Chief Justice Vaughan in *Sheppard v Gosnold* (Vaughan, 159, 166)—"A duty impossible to be known can be no duty; for civilly, what cannot be known to be, is as that which is not." (See *Barrow v Arnaud* 1846 (8 Q.B. 595, 608)).

generally qualify a reference to prescription by "(if any)" or something of the kind.

Short sentences

8.2.10   It is generally accepted that, all else being equal, a series of short sentences is easier to comprehend than a single sentence, provided that the material be sensibly divided amongst the sentences. Whereas once it was common for statutory provisions to be drafted in long and turgid sentences with a vast number of subsidiary propositions,[89] anything in the way of a rambling or ill-structured sentence in legislative drafting today is liable to attract strong and well-deserved criticism.[90]

It should not be thought, however, that short sentences are a panacea for the avoidance of confusion. Sometimes, the reverse can be the case, and a proposition that can easily be assimilated as a single phrase becomes open to misunderstanding when sub-divided.[91]

---

[89] See, for an extreme but not unrepresentative example, s.3 of the Merchandise Marks Act 1862 (c.88)—"Every person who, with intent to defraud, or to enable another to defraud any person, shall apply or cause or procure to be applied any trade mark or any forged or counterfeited trade mark to an cask, bottle, stopper, vessel, case, cover, wrapper, band, reel, ticket, label, or other thing in, on, or with which any chattel or article shall be intended to be sold or shall be sold or uttered or exposed for sale, or intended for any purpose of trade or manufacture, or shall enclose or place any chattel or article, or cause or procure any chattel or article to be enclosed or placed, in, upon, under, or with any cask, bottle, stopper, vessel, case, cover, wrapper, band, reel, ticket, label, or other thing to which any trade mark shall have been falsely applied, or to which any forged or counterfeited trade mark shall have been applied, or shall apply or attach or cause or procure to be applied or attached to any chattel or article any case, cover, reel, ticket, label or other thing to which any trade mark shall have been falsely applied, or to which any forged or counterfeited trade mark shall have been applied, or shall enclose, place, or attach any chattel or article, or cause or procure any chattel or article to be enclosed, placed, or attached, in, upon, under, with or to any cask, bottle, stopper, vessel, case, cover, wrapper, band, reel, ticket, label, or other thing having thereon any trade mark of any other person, shall be guilty of a misdemeanour, and every person so committing a misdemeanour shall also forfeit to Her Majesty every such chattel and article, and also every such cask, bottle, stopper, vessel, case, cover, wrapper, band, reel, ticket, label, or other thing as aforesaid in the possession or power of such person; and every other similar cask, bottle, stopper, vessel, case, cover, wrapper, band, reel, ticket, label, or other thing made to be used in like manner as aforesaid, and every instrument in the possession or power of such person, and by means of which any such trade mark or forged or counterfeited trade mark as aforesaid shall have been applied, and also every instrument in the possession or power of such person for applying any such trade mark or forged or counterfeit trade mark as aforesaid, shall be forfeited to Her Majesty; and the court before which any such misdemeanour shall be tried may order such forfeited articles as aforesaid to be destroyed or otherwise disposed of as such court shall think fit."

[90] See, for example, "The Committee finds it hard to believe that dividing some of the longer provisions into sub-paragraphs, for example, would have confused users: on the contrary, it would have made the meaning much clearer. . . . In the Committee's view, the form of these Regulations is not in accordance with proper drafting practice and it accordingly reports them to both Houses." (Joint Committee on Statutory Instruments, Session 1994–95, 15th Report, para.3 (HL Paper 44, HC 8-xv); and for another instrument reported for drafting not in accordance with proper practice on account of a single sentence spanning 19 lines, see Joint Committee on Statutory Instruments, Session 1995–96, 10th Report, para.6 (HL Paper 43, HC 34-x).

[91] See, for example, s.19(1) of the Nationality, Immigration and Asylum Act 2002 (c.41)—"(1) Where a person has dependants, he and his dependants are destitute for the purpose of this Part if they do not have and cannot obtain both— (a) adequate accommodation, and (b) food and other

Equally, while short staccato subsections within a section are preferable to a long undivided section, too many subsections can itself be a source of confusion, making it difficult to follow the flow of the provisions.[92]

A helpful illustration of how practice in legislative drafting has improved over the years in the way in which material having similar effect is sub-divided and presented can be found by contrasting the following provisions, each of which is divided from the previous example by the passage of fifty years and each of which is concerned with the establishment of a statutory corporation—

Section XXII of the Poor Relief (Ireland) Act 1847.[93]

Sections 5 to 8 of the Public Health (Scotland) Act 1897.[94]

Section 1 of the Transport Act 1947.[95]

Sections 109 and 110 of, and Schedule 8 to, the Police Act 1997.[96]

Or

If one had to choose two words as being more difficult to use and understand in legislative drafting than any others they would be "or" and "any".[97]   **8.2.11**

As to "or", it is important to remember that it is not always, depending on the context, necessarily disjunctive. In the phrase, for example, "may proceed against him in the High Court for damages or such other relief as the court thinks appropriate" it would be perverse to argue that Parliament requires you to choose between compensation for past loss and curtailment of future loss. This is well understood in statutory construction.[98]

Where there would be a strong policy argument for construing "or" as necessarily disjunctive[99] the draftsman is well advised to add words to deal with the point, securing certainty at the expense of simplicity: but not otherwise.

---

essential items." As introduced into the House of Commons, the proposition did not have the word "both" before paragraph (a). The result was considerable confusion in the Standing Committee as to whether a person had to be without both accommodation and food in order to be considered destitute. The word "both" was added by Government amendment on Report in order to put the right construction beyond doubt: but it is possible that the doubt would never had arisen had the sentence simply read " . . . if they do not have and cannot obtain adequate accommodation, food and other essential items".

[92] For an example of a section containing 17 subsections see s.4 of the Olympic Symbol etc. (Protection) Act 1995 (c.32). And sections containing the same or a greater number of subsections are particularly common in Finance Acts.

[93] 1847 c.31.

[94] 1897 c.38.

[95] 1947 c.49.

[96] 1997 c.50.

[97] As to "any", see below.

[98] See, for example, *Simmons v Pizzey* [1979] A.C. 37, 61 HL *per* Lord Hailsham of St Marylebone.

[99] As, for example, in the case of a provision empowering a court to punish an offender with a fine or imprisonment: if it is intended to permit both a maximum fine and a maximum sentence of imprisonment, that should be specified.

Some draftsmen avoid the difficulties that can arise from the use of "or" and "and" by omitting any conjunction between paragraphs in certain contexts. In conferring powers, for example, it is common to avoid the suggestion that a power to do "(a) and (b)" is a power to do both things but not either, and the suggestion that a power to do "(a) or (b)" is a power to do either thing but not both, by separating paragraphs (a) and (b) with a semicolon but no conjunction. This requires each paragraph to be read as flowing independently from the chapeau and puts it beyond doubt that the power is to do either or both. This practice has the additional advantage that, by eliminating the conventional use of a conjunction in a place where it is clearly not intended to have its conjunctive (or disjunctive) effect, it will encourage the courts to give "or" and "and" their full disjunctive or conjunctive meanings where they are used.

As to the status of conjunctions between paragraphs see below.

Any

8.2.12   A large part of the problem in the construction and use of the word "any" in a legal document is that different people are accustomed to use it in different ways. Some draftsmen use the word almost in routine substitution for the use of the indefinite article. Others use it extremely sparingly.

The draftsman of a legal document which generally relies on the indefinite article can presumably expect the courts to give particular meaning to "any" on the rare occasions on which it is used. Equally, the more "any" is used in cases where "a" would have done the same job, the less the courts are likely to wish to assume that "any" means "any and every" in a context where the point is arguable.

In cases where "any" appears not have been used indiscriminately, therefore, the courts will decline to give to "any" its widest meaning where a more restrictive meaning appears more likely to have been intended.[1]

But in cases where "any" appears to have been used sparingly and deliberately, the courts will be more inclined to give it its widest possible meaning.[2]

---

[1] See, for example, "The word 'any' must thus, I think, be understood as indicating 'any such', or 'such a', confession as the applicant made."—*Re Proulx; R v Bow Street Magistrates' Court, ex parte Proulx* [2001] 1 All E.R. 57, 77 DC *per* Mance L.J.; or "When, therefore, in phrase 4 reference is made to '*any land not comprised in this lease*' (my emphasis), is it to be treated as referring to any land by whomsoever owned, or is it to be understood as referring only to the land of the landlord as in practice must be within the scope of phrase 3 and is expressed to be within the scope of phrase 2? I think [Counsel] is right to submit that the phrase must be construed restrictively and against the grantor."—*Paragon Finance plc v City of London Real Property Ltd* Ch. 16th July 2001 *per* Judge Rich Q.C.

[2] See, for example, "It appears to me that section 51 [of the Supreme Court Act 1981 (c.54)] is at least as capable of bearing a wider construction, to the effect that it is open to a litigant to seek a wasted costs order against the legal representatives of any party (including, but not limited to, himself) to the proceedings. In this connection, it is to be noted that section 51(7)(a) refers to 'any' representative, which, when read together with section 51(13), is at least capable of meaning, and in my view more naturally means, a representative of any party in the proceedings, and is not limited to the party making the claim for the wasted costs."—*Brown v Bennett* [2002] 2 All E.R. 273, 284 Ch. *per* Neuberger J.

Status of conjunctions between paragraphs

It is sometimes questioned whether a reference to paragraph (a) will include or exclude a conjunction appearing between paragraphs (a) and (b). The question frequently appears to confuse editors of publications of legislation. The better view is that the purpose of the conjunction is to indicate the relationship between the two paragraphs[3] and cannot therefore be regarded as falling within either. So the repeal of paragraph (a) in the case referred to above will leave the word "or" or "and" after it.[4] **8.2.13**

As to whether it is necessary to provide "and" or "or" between each pair of a series of paragraphs or only once, before the final paragraph in the series, the modern practice is generally to use the conjunction only once. But in older legislation, or where the conjunction or disjunction deserves special emphasis, the word may appear between each pair in the series.

The issues raised here are most commonly found in relation to paragraphs but are, of course, equally relevant to the relationship between other elements (principally sub-paragraphs).

Brackets

Propositions that have no legal effect are commonly found in parentheses in legislation, the most prominent example being the parenthetical explanation routinely included after a reference to a provision of an Act or instrument outside that in which the reference occurs. **8.2.14**

It is a sound practice, although not one invariably adopted, to reserve parentheses for material of this kind, having no legislative effect and being included merely to assist the reader. If following this practice, then in the case of a qualifying proposition that requires to be distinguished from its surrounding text but which has legislative effect, commas should be used.

So, for example, compare the following—

"The Minister in charge of a Government department, or a junior minister acting on his behalf, may make an order . . . ".[5]

"A Minister of the Crown (including a Minister of State or Parliamentary Under-Secretary[6]) may make an order . . . ".

---

[3] See above.

[4] Where the word is redundant as a result of the repeal of paragraph (a) it will frequently be repealed by mere addition to the Repeal Schedule without the repeal being founded—see Chapter 14, Section 4.

[5] As to why "or a junior minister acting on his behalf" might need to be said notwithstanding *Carltona*—as to which see Chapter 12, Section 4—the intention might be to empower only Ministers who either are in charge of a recognised Department or who are junior but departmental—excluding a Minister without Portfolio however senior and whether or not in the Cabinet (and possibly excluding certain other "sinecure" offices depending upon their departmental status at the time).

[6] In certain contexts it might be advisable to make it clear that even junior ministers were intended to be included: but they are within the strict ambit of the term "Minister of the Crown".

The legislative "shall"

8.2.15   As to the use of "shall" in legislation see Section 1 above, para.8.1.9.

Definitions

8.2.16   Some observations on the use of definitions within legislation will be found in Chapter 24.

Referential drafting

8.2.17   Some observations on the use of referential drafting will be found in Section 1 above.

Textual or non-textual amendment

8.2.18   Some observations on the choice between textual and non-textual amendment will be found in Chapter 14, Section 3.

Copy out

8.2.19   Some observations on the choice between copying out and replicating provisions of European legislation being implemented will be found in Chapter 3, Section 10.

CHAPTER 9

ACCESS TO LEGISLATION

SECTION 1

IMPORTANCE OF ACCESS

Ignorance of the law is no excuse

It is a well known and ancient principle of the law of the United Kingdom,[1] that **9.1.1** holds good even in these days of increasingly complex laws about an increasing range of human activity, that ignorance of the law is no excuse.[2] Nor is this a mere rebuttable presumption of knowledge of the law: rather, it is the principle that law binds the subject whether he be aware of it or not, unless an express excuse of ignorance is provided. In the absence of an express excuse of that kind, knowledge is neither relevant nor presumed. As Goddard L.J. put it in *Bowmaker v Tabor*[3]—

> "It is entirely fallacious to say that everyone is presumed to know the law. That fallacy was exposed once and for all by Lord Mansfield in *Jones v Randall*,[4] when he said: 'it would be very hard upon the profession, if the law was so certain, that everybody knew it; the misfortune is that it is so uncertain, that it costs much money to know what it is, even in the last resort.' Then in *Martindale v Falkner*,[5] Maule J. said: 'There is no presumption in this country that every person knows the law: it would be contrary to common sense and reason if it were so.' After citing *Jones v Randall*, the learned judge went on to say[6]: 'The rule is, that ignorance of the law shall not excuse a man, or relieve him from the consequences of a

---

[1] Broom's *Legal Maxims* (10th ed. Sweet & Maxwell Ltd., 1939, p.169) has it as follows: "*Ignorantia facti excusat—ignorantia juris non excusat. Ignorance of fact excuses—ignorance of the law does not excuse.*"; see also "First, the principle that ignorance of the law is no defence in crime is so fundamental that to construe the word 'knowingly' in a criminal statute as requiring not merely knowledge of the facts material to the offender's guilt, but also knowledge of the relevant law, would be revolutionary and, to my mind, wholly unacceptable."—*Grant v Borg* [1982] 2 All E.R. 257, 262 HL *per* Lord Bridge of Harwich.
[2] Note, however, s.3(2) of the Statutory Instruments Act 1946 (c.36), discussed in Chapter 1, Section 5.
[3] [1941] 2 K.B. 1, 5 CA.
[4] (1774) 1 Cowp. 37, 40.
[5] (1846) 2 C. B. 706, 719.
[6] At 720.

crime, or from liability upon a contract.' This judgment was cited with approval by Blackburn J. in *Reg. v Tewkesbury Corporation.*"[7]

The result is that it is of enormous importance that laws are made accessible to the public as soon as possible. The courts have deprecated difficulties experienced by citizens in obtaining authoritative copies of laws, whether or not the circumstances are such that one of the standard mechanisms for publication is available or apt.[8]

The idea that it is the subject's responsibility to become aware of the law, and that even a reasonable ignorance will afford him no protection from the law's effect, was affirmed by the Court of Appeal even in the extreme circumstances of parts of an Act[9] becoming law and acquiring significant practical significance before it was possible for Her Majesty's Stationery Office to make a complete text available to the public. In *Z.L. and V.L. v Secretary of State for the Home Department and Lord Chancellor's Department*[10] the Court of Appeal affirmed that "it is beyond argument that an Act of Parliament takes legal effect on the giving of the Royal Assent, irrespective of publication", but contrasted this with the jurisprudence of the European Court of Human Rights and laid considerable stress on the importance of laws being made accessible to the public as widely and as soon as possible.

9.1.2   This decision of the Court of Appeal was discussed in the House of Lords by way of an oral Parliamentary question[11] in the course of which the Government were asked, in particular, whether they would consider making the text of Acts available on the Internet in advance of publication of the Queen's Printer's hard copy by Her Majesty's Stationery Office. The Leader of the House of Lords replied for the Government as follows—

"My Lords, all Acts are published simultaneously on the Internet and in print as soon as possible after Royal Assent. It is important to ensure that an accurate approved text is published and that all users have access at the

---

[7] (1868) L.R. 3 Q.B. 629, 635.

[8] So, for example, "Before we come to consider those points, we consider that it is right to indicate that, if Mr. Bugg has achieved nothing else in consequences of this litigation, he has at least convinced us that over the last 30 years there has been a regrettable decline in the standards adopted by the Ministry of Defence in complying with their obligations in respect of byelaws made on different dates by the department. A quick perusal of those byelaws indicates the extent of the decline. Mr. Bugg would have liked us to have examined the various byelaws in detail in court, but time constraints did not permit this. However, we have, with his help and by our own researches, seen enough to satisfy ourselves that there is now an urgent need for the department to reassess its attitude towards the preparation of byelaws. It is not satisfactory that there can be in existence different editions of the same byelaws which refer to plans, which are annexed, which differ to a material extent. It cannot be right that members of the public should have such difficulty in obtaining copies of byelaws when the contravention of those byelaws can amount to an offence."—*Bugg v Director of Public Prosecutions* [1993] Q.B. 473, 490 DC *per* Woolf L.J.

[9] The Nationality, Immigration and Asylum Act 2002 (c.41).

[10] C2/2002/2644/2645.

[11] HL Deb. February 10, 2003 cc.464–466.

same time to the same text. To do otherwise might raise issues of fairness. When a Bill has been heavily amended during its final stages, there may be some delay between Royal Assent and the receipt of the final text by the Stationery Office."

The internet website of Her Majesty's Stationery Office presently contains the following statement in the introduction to that part of the site that makes available the text of Acts of Parliament—

> "The aim is to publish all new Acts of the UK Parliament on the Internet simultaneously with or, at least within 24 hours of their publication in printed form. However, any document which is especially complex in terms of its size or its typography may take longer to prepare."

SECTION 2

PUBLICATION OF PRIMARY LEGISLATION

Introduction

This Section explores the official methods by which it is possible for the public to obtain access to the text of primary legislation.   **9.2.1**

There are, of course, also a large number of commercial publications which provide access to the text of legislation, whether generally or in a specific area of law. In most cases the texts are periodically updated, and in some cases they are annotated.

Government's responsibility to provide access to legislation

Having established the importance of citizens having easy access to the text of laws made by or under the authority of Parliament, it is easy to see that this is a burden that can best be discharged by a combination of Government and Parliament. The Government's responsibility for this has been publicly acknowledged in a Written Answer given in the House of Commons by the Attorney General in 1991, in the following terms—   **9.2.2**

> "The Lord Chancellor recognises that he has a responsibility, on behalf of the Government, to ensure that satisfactory arrangements are made for the publication of the statute book, in order that the citizen may know by what laws he is bound. Since 1868, the Statute Law Committee, established by Lord Chancellor Cairns, has met periodically to consider issues relating to the publication of the statute book. In recent times it has been assisted by an editorial board to supervise the publication of statutes in force and by a secretariat. The Lord Chancellor has come to the conclusion that these

335

somewhat complex arrangements are not best suited, under modern conditions, for the effective discharge of this responsibility. He has, therefore,
decided to replace the committee, and its subordinate bodies, with a single
body to be known as the Advisory Committee on Statute Law. This body
will advise him as and when required on all matters relating to the
publication of the statute book, including the availability of up-to-date texts
in both printed and electronic form. It will meet under his chairmanship or
that of his Permanent Secretary, and its membership will comprise the Clerk
of the Parliaments, the Clerk of the House of Commons, the Chairman of the
Law Commission, the chairman of the Scottish Law Commission, First
Parliamentary Counsel, the legal secretary to the Lord Advocate and First
Scottish Parliamentary Counsel, First Legislative Counsel for Northern
Ireland, the Treasury Solicitor, the Solicitor to the Scottish Office, and
representatives from Her Majesty's Stationery Office and the Lord Chancellor's Department. In addition, it will be able to involve user and
consumer groups as necessary, either by way of consultation or by invitation
to attend meetings of the Committee."[12]

Proof of text of Act

9.2.3 Generally speaking, it is unnecessary for those seeking to take the benefit of or
enforce an Act of Parliament to prove its existence before the courts. It is now,
and has been for many decades, a rule[13] that "every Act is a public Act to be
judicially noticed as such, unless the contrary is expressly provided by the
Act".[14] This means that the courts will, once directed to an Act of Parliament,
assume its enactment in accordance with the terms exhibited in the Queen's
Printer's copy.[15] It is unnecessary for the party seeking to take the benefit of or
enforce a provision to prove its terms.

That is not true of an Act which declares itself to be only private and not
subject to the rule requiring judicial notice. Nor is it true of an Act passed before
1851 which does not contain an provision for judicial notice to be taken of it.
Even in these rare cases, however, specific arrangements for proof of authenticity
will be unnecessary, because anything printed by the Queen's Printer will have
the benefit of s.3 of the Evidence Act 1845,[16] which provides as follows—

> "All copies of private and local and personal Acts of Parliament not public
> Acts, if purporting to be printed by the Queen's printers ... shall be

---

[12] HC Deb. June 13, 1991 W.A. 613–614.
[13] Interpretation Act 1978 (c.30), s.3 (derived from the Interpretation Act 1889 (c.63)).
[14] As in, for example, s.9 of the Lucas Estate Act 1963 (c.1)—"This Act shall not be a public Act but
shall be printed by the several printers to the Queen's most Excellent Majesty duly authorised to
print the statutes of the United Kingdom and a copy thereof so printed by any of them shall be
admitted as evidence thereof by all judges, justices and others.". It is unclear what would be the
benefit of including a provision of this kind in an Act nowadays.
[15] As to which see below.
[16] 1845 c.113.

admitted as evidence thereof by all courts, judges, justices, and others without any proof being given that such copies were so printed."

Practical difficulties would arise only in the rare case of a right or duty deriving from an enactment of antiquity where real argument existed about the text or existence of the Act. In this connection it should be noticed that mere length of an assumed right or duty will not necessarily result in the courts assuming the existence of an Act.[17] **9.2.4**

Acts of the Scottish Parliament are to be judicially noticed in the same way as public Acts of Parliament.[18]

There is no provision requiring Acts of the Northern Ireland Assembly to be judicially noticed, but a similar effect is achieved by the provision that—

"The validity of any proceedings leading to the enactment of an Act of the Assembly shall not be called into question in any legal proceedings".[19]

Authoritative text

Despite the fact that it is unnecessary for almost all practical legal purposes to prove the authenticity of the text of an Act, for the reasons given above, it is of course important both for present political purposes and for the purposes of facilitating future historical research to ensure that arrangements are made for the production and preservation of an authoritative text of Acts. **9.2.5**

Ultimately, the only authoritative version of a modern Act of Parliament[20] is that which is preserved by the Clerks of the House of Lords[21] on the passing of an Act.[22] This is sometimes known as "the vellum" copy of an Act, being printed on vellum.[23] [24] It is now prepared on archival paper for private Acts but not for public Acts.[25]

---

[17] See, in particular, *Harper v Hedges* [1924] 1 K.B. 151 CA.
[18] Scotland Act 1998 (c.46), s.28(6).
[19] Northern Ireland Act 1998 (c.47), s.5(5).
[20] For information on the preservation and proof of ancient statutes see pages 44 to 50 of the 7th Edition of this work (1971).
[21] In the House of Lords Records Office. Duplicates were for some time kept in the Public Records Office.
[22] It is immaterial for this purpose whether the Bill for the Act originated in the House of Lords or the House of Commons. The senior official of the House of Lords is known as the Clerk of the Parliaments and he has a responsibility in respect of legislation emanating from Parliament, wherever it originated.
[23] Vellum is a light parchment, the most common choice for a wide range of public and private legal documents until around the end of the nineteenth century.
[24] For a full description of the process of the preparation of the vellum copy see Statute Law Review Vol.18, no.3, pp.177–207 (1997).
[25] The Second Report of the House of Commons Select Committee on Administration 1998–99, recommended—
"that from the first chapter of the year 2000 the record copy of public Acts preserved in the House of Lords Record Office should be preserved on archival paper and not on vellum, and both private and public Acts should have archival paper covers; and
that the deposit of duplicate record copies of both public and private Acts at the Public Record Office should be ended, with effect from the same date."

The recent history of the process is described in the text of the Second Report of the Select Committee on House of Lords Offices Session 1998–99[26]—

> "When the Parliament Rolls of Acts of Parliament[27] were discontinued in 1849, it was resolved by both Houses that two copies of every Act, whether Public or Private, should be printed in vellum, one to be stored in the Record Tower (now the House of Lords Record Office) and the other with the Master of the Rolls (now the Public Record Office). The former copy is authenticated by the Clerk of the Parliaments as the official authority for the published text of an Act. In 1956 vellum was replaced by archival paper for Private Acts."

9.2.6 Although historically the authoritative version of an Act has not always been preserved by the House of Lords' authorities, the most sensible starting point for a search for the authoritative text of an Act of any age is the House of Lords Records Office.

In preparing the authoritative text of an Act a limited editorial function is performed by the Clerks of the House of Lords. A minor error of a typographical kind may be rectified at this stage. But, broadly speaking, the Clerks will not make a change which would alter the legislative effect of a provision, even if there appears to be an obvious error in the form of the provision as it has been left following its passage through the two Houses. A wrong cross-reference, for example, will sometimes be a clear typographical error the rectification of which cannot alter the obvious sense that would have to be imparted to the provision in any event: but it may also be more problematic, where, for example, it is clear that a reference is incorrect but not beyond doubt or argument what the correct reference ought to be. The former kind of error is likely to be rectifiable at this stage, the latter not.

Recourse to the official and authoritative text of an Act is only likely to be necessary in occasional cases where it is necessary to establish beyond doubt the original text of an Act no longer available in ordinarily printed form. For most normal purposes, the text of the Act as produced and made available by the Queen's Printer suffices.

An account of the history of the preservation of the authoritative versions of Acts will be found in the note by the Clerk to the House of Commons of May 7, 1999 appended to the Select Committee's Report.

The recommendations of the Commons Select Committee and similar recommendations of the Lords' Select Committee on House of Lords Offices were approved by resolution of the House of Lords (June 16, 1999 c.288 and October 14, 1999 cc.516–19) but rejected by resolution of the House of Commons (November 1, 1999 c.49). They have therefore not as yet been implemented.

[26] HL Paper 65.

[27] The Parliament Rolls—so called because of being rolls of parchment—relate to the times when Acts were drafted by judges in response to petitions made to Parliament.

Queen's Printer's copies

The Queen's Printer is a civil servant appointed by the Queen, by virtue of **9.2.7** Letters Patent, on the advice of the Head of the Home Civil Service.[28] The function of the Queen's Printer in relation to Acts of Parliament is to arrange for their publication.

Acts of Parliament are published individually upon enactment, as are the enactment versions of Explanatory Notes.[29] Acts are also published in annual collections: the annual volumes are no more than a collection of the individual copies, except that they may incorporate the effect of any correction slips issued since enactment[30] and that they include, generally in a separate volume, some additional indexing information and tables of destinations and derivations for consolidations.[31]

Statutory authority is given to "the Acts printed by the Queen's Printer, or under the superintendence or authority of Her Majesty's Stationery Office" by s.19(1)(c) of the Interpretation Act 1978.[32]

The Annual Volumes of Acts of Parliament also include Church Measures.[33] **9.2.8** Measures are published in the public general series, appearing at the end of the Annual Volumes, with each Measure being assigned simply a number rather than a chapter number.[34]

The Queen's Printer for Scotland is appointed under s.92 of the Scotland Act 1998[35] with responsibility for acting as Queen's Printer in relation to Acts of the Scottish Parliament[36] and certain statutory instruments.

The present practice is for the Controller of Her Majesty's Stationery Office also to hold appointment as the Queen's Printer, as the Queen's Printer for Scotland and as the Government Printer for Northern Ireland.

An Act founded on a private Bill[37] is published in the same way as any other Act but in a separate series, omitted from the Annual Volumes of public general Acts but available from the Stationery Office in the ordinary way. The Local and Personal Acts series is distinguished from the public general Act series by the use of separate numbering sequences, the chapters being identified by small Roman chapter numerals in the case of private Acts and italicised Arabic numerals in the case of personal Acts.

---

[28] See HL Deb. November 2, 1998 cc.14–15.
[29] As to which see Chapter 9, Section 5.
[30] As to which see Chapter 2, Section 4.
[31] As to which see Chapter 1, Section 8.
[32] 1978 c.30.
[33] As to which see Chapter 3, Section 7.
[34] Since Measures do not form part of the notionally continuous statute book of each Session, as to which see Chapter 1, Section 1.
[35] 1998 c.46.
[36] As to which see Chapter 4, Section 2.
[37] As to which see Chapter 1, Section 3 and Chapter 5, Section 4.

Availability of Queen's Printer's version of Acts

9.2.9   Her Majesty's Stationery Office makes arrangements to ensure that supplies of an official version of legislation are available to the public as soon as is reasonably possible.[38] The Office also makes arrangements to ensure that supplies of an Act remain available throughout the time during which they might reasonably be wanted.[39]

Electronic text of Acts of Parliament is available on the internet website of Her Majesty's Stationery Office. The introduction to that part of the site that contains the text of Acts says as follows—

> "With effect from the first Public General Act of 1988, the full text of all new Public General Acts is available via this website. All Public General Acts appear as originally passed by the UK Parliament.

---

[38] As explained in Section 1 above Her Majesty's Stationery Office aim to publish the Acts as soon as possible after Royal Assent. In some cases the hard copy will be available from HMSO outlets within a day or two of Royal Assent. But some Acts will take several days, particularly if they are lengthy or otherwise technically complicated, or if a large number of Acts receive Royal Assent on one day, as frequently happens at or towards the end of a Session. As to electronic publication, the stated aim of HMSO as set out on their website is that "The aim is to publish all new Acts of the UK Parliament on the Internet simultaneously with or, at least within 24 hours of their publication in printed form. However, any document which is especially complex in terms of its size or its typography may take longer to prepare."

[39] The Government's policy is explained in the following two Written Answers in the House of Commons:

"Mr. Prentice: To ask the Chancellor of the Duchy of Lancaster if all extant legislation is currently available in print from Her Majesty's Stationery Office.

Mr. Freeman: Responsibility for the subject of the question has been delegated to HMSO under its chief executive, Mike Lynn. I have asked him to arrange for a reply to be given. Letter from Mike Lynn to Mr. Gordon Prentice, dated 1 July 1996: I have been asked by the Chancellor of the Duchy of Lancaster to reply to your Parliamentary Question (no. 109) about availability of legislation. Our general aim is to keep printed copies of Acts of Parliament available for at least five years, or longer where there is continuing demand. Several Acts from the early years of this century are still regularly reprinted. When printed copies are no longer available, arrangements can be made with the British Library to supply photocopies at a reasonable charge. We are also developing facilities to print 'on demand' facsimile copies of Acts, and hope to have this service operating later this year. We can also supply the Statutes in Force edition of extant Acts, which is of course confined to those sections of the Act which are still in force. However, Local and Personal Acts are not included. The position on secondary legislation is similar. Statutory Instruments are reprinted whilst in regular demand, and when printed copies cease to be available we offer customers the British Library photocopying service. There is no Statutes in Force equivalent for secondary legislation. . . . "

(HC Deb. July 2, 1996 c.390 W.A.).

"Mr. David Nicholson: To ask the Chancellor of the Duchy of Lancaster for how long published copies of individual Acts of Parliament are available; and whether he will consider more extensive publication as an initiative under the citizens charter.

Mr. Davis: HMSO aims as a minimum to keep all Acts of Parliament in print for at least three years.Thereafter individual acts are normally reprinted, provided there is sufficient demand. Where an Act goes out of print, HMSO can supply photocopies. In addition, HMSO can supply copies of any unrepealed Act in the version appearing in 'Statutes in Force'."

(HC Deb. December 15, 1993 c.635 W.A.).

"With effect from the first Local Act of 1991, the full text of all new Local Acts is available via this website. All Local Acts appear as originally passed by the UK Parliament."

The website also makes available the text of Explanatory Notes accompanying Acts.[40]

Availability of text before Royal Assent

Where early access to an authoritative text of legislation is thought important, it should be borne in mind that both the House of Commons and the House of Lords publish Bills before them on their websites. The websites carry not only the text of a Bill as introduced, but also as revised from time to time between stages. **9.2.10**

While these texts technically carry only the authority of Parliament and not, of course, of the Queen's Printer of Acts,[41] they are likely to be sufficiently reliable for many practical purposes. Before using them, however, the reader must either ascertain that there neither have been nor could yet be amendments not reflected in the version used (or which having been made in the second House may be disagreed to or varied by the first House) or that he has the full text of the amendments made (which are also published on the websites). The result is that for a Bill with a complicated Parliamentary passage this source may be insufficiently safe for some purposes: but for the large number of Bills which have achieved what is likely to be their final form early in their first or second House, this is a resource worth remembering.

Promulgation list

While the Queen's Printer's version of Acts of Parliament and subordinate legislation are available through a number of retail outlets, and over the internet, to any member of the public interested in a piece of legislation, Government acknowledges a specific duty to make all primary and certain subordinate legislation available to certain public officials. **9.2.11**

This duty originates in a resolution of the House of Commons in 1801 requiring the King's Printer to supply copies of Acts to certain specified judicial and other officers. This built on earlier arrangements for publication of statutes by sheriffs within their local jurisdictions[42] and for the provision of transcripts for

---

[40] As to which see Chapter 9, Section 5.
[41] Although in practice both the Parliamentary publication functions and the Queen's Printer's functions are handled, by arrangement, by Her Majesty's Stationery Office.
[42] Early English statutes were proclaimed by the sheriffs in the county courts by way of promulgation and exemplifications under the Great Seal were prepared and sent to them for this purpose. See *R. v Sutton* (1816) 4 M. & S. 532, 542, *per* Ellenborough C.J. Some Acts that have been relied upon as forming part of the statute-book are not found in the records of Parliament and were printed from these exemplifications. See, for example, 7 Edw. 2, forbidding the wearing of armour, 1 Stat. Rev. 3rd ed. p.55.

the use of the courts at Westminster and the justices of assize.[43] The original promulgation list arrangements were revised in 1881 by a departmental committee appointed on the recommendation of a Joint Committee appointed to consider the First Report of the Stationery Office.

This arrangement, known as the Promulgation List, continues to be implemented. The arrangements were described in two recent Written Answers in the House of Commons[44] in the following terms—

> "Under arrangements with HMSO, copies of all Acts of Parliament and certain subordinate legislation are sent to magistrates courts, a small number of circuit judges and to local authorities at [the Lord Chancellor's] Department's expense."

> "Existing arrangements for the provision of copies of legislation for the courts and others have been the subject of consultation with representatives of the parties affected and remain under consideration."

The Promulgation List arrangements may have become of less importance with the recent advances made in availability to the public of electronic versions of primary and secondary legislation.

Revised editions of statute published by authority

9.2.12 At one time the Government produced from time to time a publication known as the *Statutes Revised*. This was a series of volumes setting out the entirety of extant primary legislation in a form reflecting the most recent repeals and amendments.[45] The first edition was produced in 1885 and the last edition (the third) in 1950.[46] The *Statutes Revised* receives a limited degree of statutory recognition.[47]

The function of the *Statutes Revised* was superseded by a loose-leaf work entitled *Statutes in Force* which was also an official version of the statute book,

---

[43] See, for example, 10, 11, 14, 18 and 20 Hen. 6, 1 Stat. Rev. 3rd ed. pp.120–123.

[44] HC Deb. October 28, 1994 W.A. 869.

[45] As with all publications of this kind, however, whether commercial or official, it is necessary to exercise caution in reading it: an amendment or repeal which is in force for most purposes, and is therefore printed in the up-dated work, may be subject to a saving or qualification which is relevant to the very case that the reader happens to be interested in. There is never any substitute for building up the legislative history of a provision for oneself, working from the Queen's Printer's versions of the original legislation, each piece of amending or repealing legislation, and each relevant commencement order (in which savings and qualifications will often be set out).

[46] Although a later one was produced for Northern Ireland in 1981. As to the preparation of earlier editions note the Statute Law Revision Act (Northern Ireland) 1952 (1952 c.1) "An Act to authorise and facilitate the publication of a revised edition of the statutes affecting Northern Ireland, and to promote further the revision of the statute law by repealing enactments which have ceased to be in force or have become unnecessary, and for purposes connected with those matters."

[47] See s.19(1)(a) of the Interpretation Act 1978 (c.30), giving authority to "any revised edition of the statutes printed by authority" in the matter of citation.

arranged not by year as for *Statutes Revised* but by broad areas of substance. This was intended to be kept more or less continually accurate by means of the substitution of pages featuring amendments, repeals and additions. It is no longer maintained.

The Statutory Publications Office, an office within the Lord Chancellor's Department,[48] is working on the production of a Statute Law Database of United Kingdom legislation, both primary and subordinate. The aim is to include general and local legislation, and to apply the effects of amending legislation to primary legislation. The database is not yet[49] fully functional or generally accessible.

The history and state of these publications is discussed in the following written answer given in the House of Commons on February 6, 2002[50]—

9.2.13

> "Ms Rosie Winterton (Parliamentary Secretary, Lord Chancellor's Department): Responsibility for all hard copy publications previously processed by the Statutory Publications Office was, with one exception, transferred on 1 April 1997 to Her Majesty's Stationery Office within the Cabinet Office. The exception related to the publication 'Statutes in Force' (SIF) which contained the revised text of all in-force UK Acts and Measures. All revision work on SIF was suspended in September 1993 when the work had been revised to 1 February 1991. Work in relation to the issue of newly enacted Acts for inclusion in SIF continued until the end of 1999. Except as mentioned above, during the period mentioned in the question, the Statutory Publications Office has been concerned solely with the development of the Statute Law Database, a historical database of in-force statute law which represents the electronic successor to SIF."

As to the Statute Law Database, its nature and state of progress are illustrated by the following two written answers, one in each House—

Answer (1)

"Mr. Garnier: To ask the Parliamentary Secretary, Lord Chancellor's Department what progress is being made with the development of the statute law database; and what effect that work will have on the range of printed material published by Her Majesty's Stationery Office for the Statutory Publications Office.

"Mr. John M. Taylor: Good progress is being made with the development of the database, which is due to provide immediate access to up-to-date statute law by April 1995. In order to meet this target, the Lord Chancellor has authorised the suspension of work done by the Statutory Publications Office in providing certain material for publication by Her Majesty's Stationery

---

[48] Now the Department for Constitutional Affairs.
[49] At the time when this work went to print.
[50] HC Deb. February 6, 2002 c.1026 W.A.

Office. Newly enacted Acts in the 'Statutes in Force' series will continue to be available as at present, as will the annual volumes of public general acts and measures and of statutory instruments. However, work has been suspended on revised material for 'Statutes in Force' and on other tables and indexes. The Lord Chancellor and Her Majesty's Stationery Office will keep under review the balance between printed material and information available from the database, having regard to the potential for improved facilities which the database is expected to provide."[51]

Answer (2)

9.2.14 "Lord Goodhart asked Her Majesty's Government: Whether they have any plans to ensure that the publication of Acts of Parliament in the government website is of practical value to users by (a) incorporating in Acts as published on the website any amendments made by subsequent legislation; and (b) indicating which provisions of an Act are currently in force.

"Lord Williams of Mostyn: Acts of Parliament are published on the HMSO website in the form in which they are enacted. The website makes clear that no amendments are incorporated and that users should check the status of any piece of legislation. A notice on the website also draws attention to the development of the statute law database, which for any piece of legislation will indicate whether it is in force and the amendments which have been made by subsequent legislation. A new system for delivery of the statute law database is currently under development and scheduled to go live during July. The editorial team continue with the updating process, and it is forecast that by July the database will incorporate all amendments to the end of 2002. It is planned that a published version of the database will be made available to the Government Legal Service later this year and to the general public early next year."[52]

The present status of the Statute Law Database project[53] is indicated by the following announcement on the internet website of the Department for Constitutional Affairs—

"The Statutory Publications Office (SPO), an office within the Lord Chancellor's Department, is producing a Statute Law Database (SLD) of United Kingdom legislation.

"The database under development currently contains the text of all Acts that were in force on 1 February 1991, and all Acts and printed Statutory Instruments passed since then. It also contains local legislation, both

---

[51] HC Deb. June 9, 1993 c.245 W.A.
[52] HL Deb. February 19, 2003 cc.187–88.
[53] As at the time when this work went to print: the position may have changed since.

primary and printed secondary. The main task of the SPO editorial team is to apply the effects of amending legislation to primary legislation.

"The key feature of the central database being maintained by the SPO is that it will provide a historical view of primary legislation for any specific day from the base date of 1 February 1991 and any prospective legislation. Although secondary legislation is not being updated, the enquiry system will facilitate the identification of any legislation that amends or repeals it.

"The SPO is exploring various business and technical options for delivery of the service to users both inside and outside the public domain."

Copyright

The copyright in Acts of Parliament, Acts of the Scottish Parliament, Acts of the Northern Ireland Assembly and Church Measures is established by s.164 of the Copyright, Designs and Patents Act 1988[54] as follows— **9.2.15**

"164. Copyright in Acts and Measures

(1) Her Majesty is entitled to copyright in every Act of Parliament, Act of the Scottish Parliament, Act of the Northern Ireland Assembly or Measure of the General Synod of the Church of England.

(2) The copyright subsists from Royal Assent until the end of the period of 50 years from the end of the calendar year in which Royal Assent was given.

(3) References in this Part to Crown copyright (except in section 163) include copyright under this section; and, except as mentioned above, the provisions of this Part apply in relation to copyright under this section as to other Crown copyright.

(4) No other copyright, or right in the nature of copyright, subsists in an Act or Measure."

Despite the copyright, however, it is open to anyone to reproduce the text of any of these kinds of legislation in printed form, by virtue of a waiver of Copyright granted by the Crown shortly after the enactment of the 1988 Act.[55] It is no longer necessary, as it once was, to reproduce statutory material only in a "value-added" form. But it remains a requirement that the material be reproduced accurately.

---

[54] 1988 c.48.
[55] For the precise terms of the waiver see HMSO Guidance Note No.6 *Reproduction of United Kingdom, England, Wales and Northern Ireland Primary and Secondary Legislation* (October 27, 1999, as revised on November 6, 2000, August 10, 2001, and October 7, 2002).

Chronological tables

9.2.16 A publication entitled *Chronological Table of the Statutes* was first published in 1870 in pursuance of a suggestion made by Lord Chancellor Cairns. The tables were prepared under the general direction of the Statute Law Committee and are now published by the Statutory Publications Unit of Her Majesty's Stationery Office under the auspices of the Advisory Committee on Statute Law.[56]

The Chronological Table lists each Public General Act and annotates the entry for each Act to show amendment, extension, restriction, repeal or other effects of later enactments. This Chronological Table includes Acts of the Scottish Parliament and Church Assembly Measures.

A separate Chronological Table is published for Northern Ireland.

The regularly published Chronological Tables do not include local, private or personal Acts.[57] But the Law Commission and the Scottish Law Commission have prepared a Chronological Table of Local Legislation and a Chronological Table of Private and Personal Acts. These are published by Her Majesty's Stationery Office and are available in hard copy or, in a (slightly) more up-to-date version, over the internet.

Although an immensely useful resource, the principal disadvantage of the Chronological Tables is that the size and complexity of the task of preparing them result in considerable delay before publication. The Table for Public General Acts up to the year 2000 was, for instance, not published until 2003.

Indices

9.2.17 The annual volumes of statutes contain an index, nowadays normally published as a separate volume together with the destination and derivation tables for consolidations of that year. In earlier years the index was a valuable subject-based index. It is now little or nothing more than a collection of the arrangements of sections that appear at the beginning of each Act.

SECTION 3

PUBLICATION OF SUBORDINATE LEGISLATION

Statutory instruments

9.3.1 The arrangements for the printing and publication of statutory instruments are regulated by the Statutory Instruments Act 1946.[58] Section 2 of that Act provides as follows—

---

[56] The Advisory Committee on Statute Law is appointed by the Lord Chancellor and the names of its members are published in the annual Civil Service Year Book (published by the Stationery Office) and in other publications about Parliament and the civil service. For a review of its establishment and composition see the Written Answer given by the Attorney General in the House of Commons on June 13, 1991 (c.613) (see above, para.9.2.2).
[57] For definition, see Chapter 1, Section 3.
[58] 1946 c.36.

"(1) Immediately after the making of any statutory instrument, it shall be sent to the King's printer of Acts of Parliament and numbered in accordance with regulations made under this Act, and except in such cases as may be provided by any Act passed after the commencement of this Act or prescribed by regulations made under this Act,[59] copies thereof shall as soon as possible be printed and sold by or under the authority of[60] the King's printer of Acts of Parliament."

In addition to numbering in an annual series, some instruments are given a number in a sub-series of the statutory instruments.[61] This enables commencement orders, legislation relating to court fees or procedure, and legislation relating solely to a particular Part of the United Kingdom, to be readily identified.

Nowadays the authoritative version of a statutory instrument is not available only through the purchase of a hard copy from Her Majesty's Stationery Office, although that remains an option, but also electronically through the internet website of that Office.

9.3.2

What is meant by "immediately after the making" is, of course, open to question. In general the system appears to operate sufficiently to bring laws to the attention of those who need to know about them in good time, and it is likely that consultation or other administrative processes will result in those particularly affected by the terms of an instrument being made aware of its content considerably in advance of its being made: but there are occasional lapses of good practice, and this is one of the many aspects of the procedure which the Joint Committee on Statutory Instruments monitors.[62]

---

[59] This is used particularly to excuse printing of instruments whose effect is local or temporary in circumstances where it appears that all those with an interest in the substance of the instrument will already have been made sufficiently aware of its terms. It is designed merely to spare the expense to public funds of pursuing the standard arrangements for publication in a case where there is likely to be no demand.

[60] The words "or under the authority of" added, with retrospective effect, by the Statutory Instruments (Production and Sale) Act 1996 (c.54), s.1(1)(a), to confirm the legitimacy of the contracting-out arrangements of printing functions by Her Majesty's Stationery Office.

[61] See Chapter 3, Section 3.

[62] See, for example, "This instrument was laid before Parliament on 18th August 1994, came into force on 19th August 1994, and was published on 12th September 1994. It had therefore been in force for 24 days before it was publicly available. In a memorandum printed in Appendix IV the Ministry of Agriculture, Fisheries and Food explain that in order to close the necessary fisheries in time, the instrument had to be laid before Parliament in proof form. However, the Ministry admit that the delay between the instrument coming into force and being published was due to a clerical error on the part of the Ministry. The Committee therefore reports the instrument on the ground that there was an unjustifiable delay between the instrument coming into force and its being published."—Joint Committee on Statutory Instruments, Session 1994–95, 2nd Report, para.7 (HL Paper 11, HC 8-ii); or "The Order of Council was made on 11th September 1996, and came into force on that day. It was not sent for printing until 28th November 1996, and was not published until 4th December 1996. The Privy Council Office regret this delay and explain in their first memorandum, printed in Appendix I, that the delay was due to 'an administrative oversight'. The Committee therefore reports the instrument on the ground that there was an unjustifiable delay between its coming into force and its publication."—Joint Committee on Statutory Instruments, Session 1996–97, 9th Report, para.2 (HL Paper 33, HC 29-ix).

9.3.3   Section 8(1)(b) of the Statutory Instruments Act 1946 requires regulations to provide for the postponing of the numbering of an instrument which does not take effect until approved by Parliament. The intention "clearly was to avoid the confusion which could result if an instrument were to be numbered and then never take effect".[63]

There is power under the 1946 Act to make regulations about the numbering and printing of statutory instruments. In particular, the regulations may disapply the requirement to print and publish in certain cases. This power has been exercised so as to permit the Queen's Printer not to print certain instruments of purely local application, certain instruments which are regularly made available to interested parties in other ways, certain instruments that will have effect only for a short period of time and certain provisions of particular length.[64] There is also power to suppress certain instruments of a confidential nature, where publication would not be in the public interest, until they come into force.[65]

Statutory Instruments (Production and Sale) Act 1996[66]

9.3.4   The Statutory Instruments (Production and Sale) Act 1996 establishes that the functions of the Queen's Printer under the Statutory Instruments Act 1946[67] can be carried out either by the Queen's Printer or under the authority of the Queen's printer.[68]

Legislation of the Scottish Parliament and Administration

9.3.5   Section 92 of the Scotland Act 1998[69] established the office of Queen's Printer for Scotland and requires that officer to print Acts of the Scottish Parliament and devolved subordinate legislation. The office is held *ex officio* by the person who holds the office of the Queen's Printer of Acts of Parliament.[70] The website of Her Majesty's Stationery Office has a separate section for devolved Scottish legislation.

---

[63] Joint Committee on Statutory Instruments, Session 1997–98, 15th Report, para.10 (HL Paper 46, HC 33-xv) reporting an instrument in a case where this practice was not observed.
[64] Statutory Instruments Regulations 1947 (SI 1948/1), regs. 5 to 7.
[65] Regulation 8.
[66] 1996 c.54.
[67] 1946 c.36.
[68] It is of course distinctly arguable that the law of agency is sufficient to permit this in any event (particularly in the light of the *Carltona* principle—see Chapter 12, Section 4). But since the proposed use of agents was in the context of a privatisation exercise, it was apparently thought wise to avoid the possibility of arguments to the contrary.
[69] 1998 c.46.
[70] s.92(5).

Welsh subordinate legislation

Standing Order 30 of the National Assembly for Wales provides as follows— **9.3.6**

> **"STANDING ORDER 30 - Publication Of Subordinate Legislation (Other Than Assembly General Subordinate Legislation)**
>
> The Presiding Officer shall as soon as may be publish any subordinate legislation made or confirmed by the Assembly which is not otherwise published for sale under the Statutory Instruments Act 1946; and each Minister shall notify the Presiding Officer of any instruments he or she, or officials authorised by him or her, has made or confirmed. Subordinate legislation made by the Assembly which is not required to be made by statutory instrument shall be made in such form as the Presiding Officer may prescribe."

HMSO internet website

The internet website of Her Majesty's Stationery Office currently makes **9.3.7** available the text of—

Statutory Instruments and draft Statutory Instruments,[71]

Acts of the Scottish Parliament,[72]

---

[71] The introduction to the relevant part of the website states—

"With effect from the first printed Statutory Instrument of 1987, the full text of all published Statutory Instruments are available on the Internet via these Web Pages. Although numbered in the same Statutory Instrument series, non-print/unpublished Statutory Instruments which are generally of local application are not published on the internet.

"With effect from July 1999 those Statutory Instruments which have been made by the National Assembly for Wales have been published via the Wales Legislation Web Pages whilst the series of Scottish Statutory Instruments have been published via the Scottish Legislation Web Pages. All other Statutory Instruments continue to be available via these Web Pages.

"The aim is to publish all UK Statutory Instruments on the Internet simultaneously with or, at least within 24 hours of their publication in printed form. However, any document which is especially complex in terms of its size or its typography may take longer to prepare. . . .

"Published Draft Statutory Instruments are also available.";

The reference to draft statutory instruments is to those presented for formal consideration by Parliament—see Chapter 6, Section 2.

[72] The introduction to the relevant part of the website states—

"This website is managed by Her Majesty's Stationery Office on behalf of the Queen's Printer for Scotland. The site contains the full text of all Acts of the Scottish Parliament, the Explanatory Notes to the Acts of the Scottish Parliament and Scottish Statutory Instruments. The aim is to publish these documents on the Internet simultaneously or at least within 24 hours of their publication in printed form. However, any document which is especially complex in terms of its size or its typography may take longer to prepare."

Acts of the Northern Ireland Assembly,[73] and

Church Measures.[74]

Orders in Council

9.3.8 As has been stated above[75] not all Orders in Council are statutory instruments. Those made under the prerogative are therefore not published in accordance with the Statutory Instruments Act 1946. They are, however, readily available from the Privy Council Office.[76] Some are also printed at the end of the annual edition of statutory instruments published by Her Majesty's Stationery Office.

Copyright

9.3.9 As to copyright in Acts of the Scottish Parliament, Acts of the Northern Ireland Assembly and Church Measures, see Section 2 above.

Guidance, &c.

9.3.10 As is noted above,[77] there are an increasing number of powers to issue guidance, and to produce documents which while not directly producing rights and duties at law have a significant, and to some extent enforceable, effect on the way other functions at law are carried out.

In relation to these documents it is common to find a requirement to publish in such manner as the Minister thinks appropriate, or merely to publish (leaving the requirement of adequacy to be inferred in accordance with the normal principles of administrative law).[78]

---

[73] The introduction to the relevant part of the website states—
    "This website is managed by Her Majesty's Stationery Office on behalf of the Government Printer for Northern Ireland. The site contains the full text of Acts of the Northern Ireland Assembly, the Explanatory Notes to the Acts of the Northern Ireland Assembly and Statutory Rules of Northern Ireland.
    "The aim is to publish these documents on the Internet simultaneously or at least within 24 hours of their publication in printed form. However, any document which is especially complex in terms of its size or its typography may take longer to prepare."

[74] The introduction to the relevant part of the website states—
    "With effect from the first Church of England Measure of 1988, the full text of all new Church of England Measures is available via these Web Pages."

[75] Chapter 3, Section 2.

[76] See the Supplementary Memorandum to the Joint Committee on Statutory Instruments, December 1981 in relation to SI 1981/1670.

[77] Chapter 3, Section 7.

[78] S.33 of the Wildlife and Countryside Act 1981 (c.69), for example, which requires the production of a code about the exercise of certain statutory functions, requires that "the Ministers shall cause every code prepared or revised in pursuance of subsection (1) to be printed, and may cause copies of it to be put on sale to the public at such price as the Ministers may determine".

SECTION 4

EXPLANATORY NOTES: BILLS AND ACTS

Introduction

Until 1998 the long-standing practice[79] was for every Government Bill intro- **9.4.1**
duced in either House to be covered by an Explanatory and Financial Memorandum containing a brief explanation of the substantive provisions of the Bill and
giving details of the sources and estimated sums of expenditure from public
funds in connection with the provisions of the Bill if enacted. The memorandum
varied in length and degree of detail, but was in general perfunctory. It was
supplied by the Government with the Bill and printed under the auspices of the
Authorities of the House concerned.

In connection with the annual Finance Bill and certain other Bills the
Government produced a more detailed explanatory document known as Notes on
Clauses. Originally produced by way of internal Government briefing for
Ministers, the Notes on Clauses came increasingly frequently to be made
available to interested parties, particularly to members of the Standing Commit-
tee in the House of Commons.[80]

In 1997 the Select Committee on Modernisation of the House of Commons[81]
and the House of Lords Select Committee on Procedure of the House[82] gave their
approval to recommendations submitted by the First Parliamentary Counsel for
the introduction of a new system of explanatory material for Bills, and it is that
system which has effect now. The Committee said, in particular[83]—

"The Committee agreed to a proposal for 'Explanatory Notes' on Bills,
which was made by the Commons Modernisation Committee and has been
agreed to by the House of Commons. The Notes will be prepared by the
sponsoring Department and will combine in a single document accompanying the Bill the material provided at present in the Explanatory Memorandum and the Notes on Clauses, but will extend and improve it. There will
also be Explanatory Notes for Acts. The Committee believes that it is

---

[79] The practice, which was not confined to Government Bills, dates back at least to the Speaker's
instruction to the Public Bill Office on March 9, 1882—"A Member bringing in a Bill may prepare
a Memorandum explanatory of the contents and objects of the Bill, but containing nothing of an
argumentative character, which, when received at the Public Bill Office, will be printed and
circulated with the Bill."
[80] "The notes on clauses prepared for Ministers taking a Bill through the House are, by convention,
usually also made available to members of the relevant Standing Committee and to other interested
Members. They are not formally published, but are in the public domain and copies can be made
available to others on request."—Chancellor of the Duchy of Lancaster HC Deb. February 13,
1997 W.A. 296.
[81] Second Report, Session 1997–98, December 3, 1997; see also First Report *The Legislative Process*
1997–98 July 23, 1997.
[82] Second Report, Session 1997–98, November 19, 1997.
[83] Lords Report as agreed to HL Deb December 4, 1997 cc.1484–95.

desirable that, in order to establish that the Explanatory Notes cannot be amended in Parliament, the Notes should make clear that they had been drafted by the sponsoring Department and have not been authorised by Parliament; the Explanatory Notes should be neutral in tone and do not try to promote the Bill or the policy underlying it; the Explanatory Notes should be published separately from the Bill (and the subsequent Act), in order to avoid delay in publishing the Bill, to avoid the Bill being too bulky, and to give the public a choice of whether or not to buy the Notes."

Nature of the notes

9.4.2 Under this system the Government department[84] responsible for a Bill[85] being introduced in either House provides Explanatory Notes, following a standard form but allowing for variations as the case suggests. The Notes are published by the authorities of the relevant House as a separate document, normally on the same day as the Bill or a day or two later.[86] The Notes are revised when the Bill enters its second House, and again on Royal Assent,[87] to reflect amendments during the Bill's passage.[88]

The aim of the Notes is to "combine the material already provided in the explanatory memorandum and in notes on clauses, but extend and improve it".[89] Their format, although flexible, normally contains—

(1) an introduction,

(2) a summary and background explaining what the legislation does,

(3) an overview of the structure of the Bill and a summary of each Part,

(4) a section giving detail on each clause, and

(5) estimates of implications for the public finances, for the manpower of the public sector and for the costs of compliance by businesses with the legislation.

---

[84] As a general rule the notes are likely to be drafted by departmental administrators rather than lawyers, considered and approved by departmental lawyers and then submitted to the draftsman of the Bill for final approval: but the draftsman is unlikely to have much time at any of the critical points to consider the detail of the notes.

[85] The exceptions are Finance Bills (as to which the Government continues to produce a variety of explanatory materials), Consolidation Bills (as to the material accompanying which see Chapter 1, Section 8 and Chapter 5, Section 3) and Consolidated Fund and Appropriation Bills (as to which see Chapter 1, Section 6).

[86] But in the case of a large and technically complex Bill the delay can be considerable.

[87] Here too the delay can be considerable, even amounting to a matter of weeks in some cases.

[88] And the Modernisation Committee recommended the flexibility to permit revision of the Notes between stages in one House where appropriate—para.4.

[89] Memorandum by First Parliamentary Counsel (appended to the Modernisation Committee Report), para.9.

The notes can use a variety of expository techniques not available to the **9.4.3**
legislation itself. This is because—

> "Unlike other forms of writing, a Bill is not there to inform, to explain, to
> entertain or to perform any of the other usual functions of literature. A Bill's
> sole reason for existence is to change the law . . . A consequence of this
> unique function is that a Bill cannot set about communicating with the
> reader in the same way that other forms of writing do. It cannot use the same
> range of tools. In particular, it cannot repeat important points simply to
> emphasise their importance or safely explain itself by restating a proposition
> in different words. To do so would risk creating doubts and ambiguities that
> would fuel litigation. As a result, legislation speaks in a monotone and its
> language is compressed. It is less easy for readers to get their bearings and
> to assimilate quickly what they are being told than it would be if
> conventional methods of helping the reader were freely available to the
> drafter."[90]

So Explanatory Notes can and do make use of examples, diagrams, flow- **9.4.4**
charts, tables and versions of legislation annotated to show the effect of
amendments made by the Bill.

What Explanatory Notes may not do is seek to justify the policy underlying the
provisions of the Bill. The document is printed by the House itself, or in the case
of the notes for an Act by the Queen's Printer, for the purpose of assisting the
reader to understand what the Bill does. It is not intended to provide an
opportunity for the Government to persuade the reader of the case for legislating.
For this reason "the Explanatory Notes should be neutral in tone and [should] not
try to promote the bill or the policy underlying it".[91] A neutral reference to a
piece of factual background to the policy of a Bill, such as a Command Paper or
a report by some body outside Government, is normally permitted. But a
reference to a partisan document, such as a party's political manifesto, would not
be. The Government aims to abide by these rules which are enforced by the
authorities of each House, who scrutinise Explanatory Notes in draft before they
are published.[92]

---

[90] Memorandum submitted by the First Parliamentary Counsel to the Select Committee on
Modernisation of the House of Commons on June 23, 1997, appended to First Report of the
Committee, Session 1997–98, July 23, 1997.
[91] House of Lords Select Committee on the Procedure of the House, Second Report, Session
1997–98, November 19, 1997, para.2.
[92] For a rare criticism of the notes as having breached the rule against argumentative or debatable
material see Lord Donaldson of Lymington's observations on the notes for the Extradition Bill
2002–03 HL Deb. 1.v.03 c.867—"I find it slightly regrettable that paragraphs 6 to 11 of the
Explanatory Notes seem to be promotional material. When I wrote Explanatory Notes for a Private
Member's Bill, I hit against the fact that paragraph 6.21 of the *Companion* told me that I could not
use the Explanatory Notes to promote my Bill . . . the Home Office should have complied with the
rules if I have understood them correctly."

Status of the notes

9.4.5   Explanatory Notes routinely commence with an explanation of their status in the following terms—

> "These explanatory notes relate to the X Bill as introduced in the House of Commons/Lords on [date]. They have been prepared by the [Name of Department] in order to assist the reader of the Bill and to help inform the debate on it. They do not form part of the Bill and have not been endorsed by Parliament.

> "The notes need to be read in conjunction with the Bill. They are not, and are not meant to be, a comprehensive description of the Bill. So where a clause or part of a clause does not seem to require any explanation or comment, none is given."[93]

Explanatory Notes may be referred to in debate on the relevant Bill, and they are often are. But they may not be amended, not forming part of the text of the Bill.

The result is that Explanatory Notes cannot be regarded as an authoritative statement of Parliament's intention in enacting a piece of legislation. But they can be regarded as an authoritative statement of the Government's intention in proposing legislation.

For a discussion of the use that the courts permit themselves to make in construing legislation of Explanatory Notes to Acts and statutory instruments, see Chapter 27.

Private Members' or peers' Bills

9.4.6   Although there is no formal requirement for a private Member's or private peer's Bill to be accompanied by Explanatory Notes, the practice so far has been that where a Government department has provided support for the preparation of a Bill to be presented by a private Member or peer, the Department also provides Explanatory Notes. They are printed in the normal way and described in the opening statement as having been provided by the named department with the consent of the Member in Charge of the Bill.[94]

List of stages of Parliamentary process

9.4.7   The Explanatory Notes for an Act contain at the end a table listing the various stages of the Parliamentary process on the Bill for the Act and giving the dates

---

[93] This formula is used with minor and obvious variation in the case of the notes published for an Act after Royal Assent.

[94] "Member in Charge" is a significant term of art in Parliamentary procedure denoting ownership of, and therefore a degree of control over, a Bill.

for each stage. This provides a research tool of particular use for anyone faced with a perceived ambiguity in relation to which the rule in *Pepper v Hart*[95] might usefully be invoked. The list will enable the researcher to find easily those passages in Hansard most likely to be of relevance. The most promising areas to search are likely to be the Minister's introductory speech or winding-up speech at Second Reading of the Bill in either House or on the Clause Stand Part debate on the relevant provision in Committee in either House. In the case of a provision introduced during the passage of the Bill, the most likely source of illumination is the Minister's speech introducing the relevant amendment.

Human Rights

A particular function that can be performed by the Explanatory Notes to a Bill is to address issues relating to the European Convention on Human Rights,[96] explaining in a purely narrative way, the issues that might be thought to arise and some of the principal features of the legislation likely to be relevant to the resolution of those issues.[97]   **9.4.8**

SECTION 5

EXPLANATORY NOTES: SUBORDINATE LEGISLATION

Unlike the Explanatory Notes for Bills and Acts which are a recent innovation,[98] it has been the practice for many decades to append to a statutory instrument a note which describes its principal effects for the benefit of easy assimilation of the instrument's purport.   **9.5.1**

The preparation and use of explanatory notes for subordinate legislation are discussed in Chapter 6, Section 1.

---

[95] As to which see Chapter 28.

[96] The European Convention for the Protection of Human Rights and Fundamental Freedoms (Rome, November 4, 1950; TS 71 (1953); Cmd 8969).

[97] The Joint Committee on Human Rights, in its Third Report of Session 2002–03, approved (at para.4) as good practice guidance drawn up by the Lord Chancellor's Department in relation to the use of explanatory notes for the discussion of human rights issues. The key passage of that guidance, the entirety of which is appended to the Committee's report, reads as follows: "The Explanatory Notes should therefore not only record the fact that a section 19 statement has been made, but also briefly draw attention to the main Convention issues in the Bill. The Notes should describe, in general terms, the most significant Convention issues thought to arise on the Bill, together with the Minister's conclusions on compatibility. In some cases, it may be sufficient simply to state that an issue has been considered, and that a particular conclusion has been reached: for example, the Notes might record the Minister's conclusion that a provision should not be regarded, for the purpose of Article 6, as imposing a criminal charge. In other cases, Departments may refer to the policy justification for what is proposed, which will be central to any assessment of whether, for example, a possible interference with an Article 8(1) right is justified under Article 8(2). Departments are not expected to list every human rights point which could be taken on the Bill, or to cite case-law supporting the Minster's conclusion on compatibility. Legal advice should not be disclosed."

[98] See Section 5 above.

Part 3

THE EFFECT OF LEGISLATION

CHAPTER 10

TIMING

Introduction

Legislation does not necessarily have effect as law immediately after being **10.1.1** passed or made. Legislation may take effect—

(1) immediately upon being passed or made,[1]

(2) at a point in the future that is specified upon the legislation being passed or made,[2] or that can be determined in accordance with criteria specified upon the legislation being passed or made,[3]

(3) only if and when some future event occurs (which may be a real-world event or an event—such as the making of an order—designed for the purpose of commencing the legislation),[4]

(4) with retrospective effect from a past time,[5]

---

[1] This is the default position—see below.

[2] It being common to specify a date, or a period after the passing or making of the legislation—see, for an example of the use of a very common formula, art.1(1) of the European Parliamentary Elections (Returning Officers) Order 2003 (SI 2003/3362)—"This Order . . . shall come into force on the day after that on which it is made."

[3] The most obvious example being a fixed period after passing or making—see, for an example of the use of a very common formula, art.1(3) of the Regulatory Reform (Business Tenancies) (England and Wales) Order 2003 (SI 2003/3096)—"This Order shall come into force at the end of the period of 6 months beginning with the day on which it is made."

[4] While this is likely to be a commencement order, as to which see below, it may also be some *ad hoc* procedure devised for a particular purpose: see, for example, the following—

Regulation 1(2) of the Reporting of Savings Income Information Regulations 2003 (SI 2003/3297)—"These Regulations shall come into force on such date, being not earlier than 1st January 2005, as is determined by the Treasury and specified by notices in the London, Edinburgh and Belfast Gazettes."

Article 1 of the Merchant Shipping (Confirmation of Legislation) (Falkland Islands) Order 2003 (SI 2003/1877)—"This Order may be cited as the Merchant Shipping (Confirmation of Legislation) (Falkland Islands) Order 2003 and shall come into force on such date as the Governor of the Falkland Islands may appoint by proclamation published in the Falkland Islands Government Gazette."

[5] As to which see Section 3 below.

(5) not at a particular point in time, but in relation to things done or events occurring during a period specified upon the legislation being passed or made, with it being possible to specify either a single period for all purposes or different periods for different purposes.[6]

It should be noted at the outset that the terms "commencement", "coming into force", "taking effect", "coming into effect" and "coming into operation" are interchangeable and mean no more than the time when the legislation starts to have legal effect.

Status of legislation pending commencement

10.1.2 A frequently asked question is "what status in law does legislation have between the moment when it is enacted or made and the moment when it comes into force?"[7]

---

[6] See, for example, the following—

Section 3 of the Aviation (Offences) Act 2003 (c.19)—"This Act shall have effect in relation to an offence committed or alleged to have been committed after the end of the period of two months beginning with the day on which it is passed."

Section 162(3) to (5) of the Nationality, Immigration and Asylum Act 2002 (c.41)—

"(3) Section 5 shall have effect in relation to—

(a) an application made after the passing of this Act, and

(b) an application made, but not determined, before the passing of this Act.

(4) Section 8 shall have effect in relation to—

(a) an application made on or after a date appointed by the Secretary of State by order, and

(b) an application made, but not determined, before that date.

(5) Section 9 shall have effect in relation to a child born on or after a date appointed by the Secretary of State by order."

Section 2(1) and (2) of the Rating (Valuation) Act 1999 (c.6)—

"(1) Section 1 above shall have effect in relation to rating lists to be compiled on or after the day on which this Act was passed.

(2) Section 1 above shall be treated as having become effective on 1st April 1990 in relation to rating lists compiled before the day on which this Act was passed."

Regulation 1(2) of the Charitable Deductions (Approved Schemes) (Amendment) Regulations 2003 (SI 2003/1745)—"Regulations 3 and 4 to 7 shall have effect in relation to supplements payable under section 38 of the Finance Act 2000 in respect of sums withheld by an employer as mentioned in that section on or after 6th April 2003 and before 6th April 2004."

Regulation 1 of the Inheritance Tax (Delivery of Accounts) (Excepted Estates) (Amendment) Regulations 2003 (SI 2003/1658)—"These Regulations may be cited as the Inheritance Tax (Delivery of Accounts) (Excepted Estates) (Amendment) Regulations 2003, shall come into force on 1st August 2003, and shall have effect in relation to deaths occurring on or after 6th April 2003.".

Note, however, that it will rarely make sense to have a combination of a fixed commencement date and a provision for application in relation to events occurring at a specified time—as a general rule the latter will make the former both unnecessary and obscure.

[7] In particular one is sometimes asked whether prospective legislation—that is to say legislation that has not yet come into force—is part of the statute book or not. That is, of course, to put the question in a particularly meaningless form: there is no such thing as "the statute book" although it is a convenient notation by which to refer to the sum of legislation in the United Kingdom at any time—see further, Chapter 1, Section 1. Whether prospective legislation forms part of that notional statute book or not therefore depends simply on the purpose for which the question is asked. In so far as "the statute book" can be used to mean something along the lines of "the class of primary legislation presently in force" it is clear that prospective legislation is not "on the statute book".

The simple answer is that prospective legislation is merely an announcement by the legislator that the law will change at some point in the future and that until that point arises the law is unaffected by the announcement.

In particular, it is not open to the courts to act as if a prospective change in the law were already effected.[8] As to whether the courts or others may order their actions by reference to a prospective change in the law, see below.[9]

There are, of course, a number of qualifications required to the proposition that before commencement legislation has no effect.

(1) The first qualification is that the fact that a person has been given notice in this way of a prospective change in the law may in itself have a legal effect in relation to the change of law: the most obvious example is that a person will be less able to argue an unfairness as a matter of the law of human rights in relation to a change of law of which he has had due notice.[10]

(2) The second qualification relates to anticipatory exercise of powers and is discussed below.[11]

(3) The third qualification is that the existence on the statute book of prospective legislation may prevent the Executive from taking action of a

---

But if it is asked whether prospective legislation is sufficiently "on the statute book" to enable new legislation to operate by reference to amendment of the prospective legislation, the answer is that it is available for use in that way, and that the approach may often be the clearest and most helpful for the reader (depending upon the intended or expected differential commencement dates).

[8] "Parliament has unambiguously said that the Act is to come into operation on 1 August 1971. To my mind there is no ambiguity about that nor any doubt as to its effect. It means that Parliament has ordained that up to that date, 1 August 1971, the law is to remain as before. I do not know why Parliament so provided. But that it did so provide is beyond dispute. I should have thought it was also beyond dispute, as an essential part of the unwritten constitutional law of England, by which courts of law are ineluctably bound, that those courts must loyally give effect to what Parliament has provided, and not seek to give effect to what they may think that Parliament ought to have provided. If Parliament has made a mistake, it has full sovereign power to correct the mistake. It follows that in my judgment the learned judge could not lawfully treat section 4 of the Act as though it was already in force on 27th July."—*per* Megaw L.J. in *Wilson v Dagnall* [1972] 2 All E.R. 44, 52, CA.

[9] Para. 10.1.29, footnote 83.

[10] To give a specific example, take the question of expropriation without compensation. If a new law forbids the use of property for the performance of an activity which has previously been entirely lawful, the law of human rights may in certain circumstances require that compensation be paid to the persons who are no longer able to use their property for the purpose for which it was acquired. But if the legislature has given long notice of the intended change in the law, the argument for compensation may be less strong. For this purpose, notice of intention to legislate, whether given by the Government as notice of intention to invite Parliament to legislate or as the recipient of a power giving notice of intention to exercise it, may have some effect, although it is likely to be less effective than the notice provided by a period of delay between the passing or making of the law and its coming into force: a person may be entitled to ignore a notice of intention to legislate on the grounds that it may for political or other reasons be frustrated or abandoned, in circumstances where it would be unreasonable for him to ignore the impending commencement of legislation once passed or made.

[11] Para.10.1.32.

kind that would render it impracticable or undesirable to bring the legislation into force.[12]

10.1.3 At a technical level, it is common to find textual amendment made of a law which has not yet come into force, nor is there any reason to doubt that this is both proper and effective. The following fictitious example illustrates the point—

1. Legislation is passed reforming the law of insolvency. The old law is set out in Insolvency Act 1. The new law is set out in Insolvency Act 2 which is passed on 1st July and comes into force immediately upon passing.

2. A provision of Insolvency Act 1 is referred to in the law of immigration, in such a way that the reference will require to be changed consequential upon the enactment of Insolvency Act 2.

3. The immigration legislation is embodied in Immigration Act 1 which is replaced by Immigration Act 2 on 1st June. Immigration Act 2 is not to come into force until 1st August.

4. It is clearly essential for Insolvency Act 2 to make textual or other amendment both of Immigration Act 1 and of Immigration Act 2, so as to ensure that the reference to insolvency law will be effective both as the law of immigration operates between 1st July and 1st August and as it operates after 1st August.

5. It is therefore nothing untoward to find a piece of legislation making an amendment both of legislation that has been prospectively repealed and of legislation that has yet to come into force.[13]

Presumption of immediate commencement

10.1.4 The default rule about the commencement of legislation, to be applied in the absence of express provision to the contrary, is expressed in s.4 of the Interpretation Act 1978[14]—

---

[12] See below, paras 10.1.14—10.1.18.

[13] Rummer things than that, indeed, are done in the field of textual amendment as a result of the concept of commencement. For example, it is not unknown for commentators to announce triumphantly the discovery of an absurd error in a piece of legislation, namely the purported amendment or repeal of a provision of the legislation itself. But this is deliberate, although it is necessary only relatively infrequently. The need for it arises in the following way. Pt 1 of an Act is to come into force on Date 1 and Pt 2 on Date 2. When Pt 2 comes into force it will necessitate a consequential change in the law embodied in Part 1. A Schedule listing amendments consequential on the commencement of Pt 2 will therefore list an amendment of Pt 1, or possibly a partial repeal. Part 1 will operate in its enacted form until the commencement of Part 2. See, for example, Sch.4 to the Commonwealth Development Corporation Act 1999 (c.20) which repeals s.24 of that Act itself—s.24 confers powers on the Commonwealth Development Corporation to, in effect, prepare for its transformation into a Companies Act company, and when that transformation takes place the powers conferred are redundant and inappropriate, hence their inclusion in the repeals triggered by s.27 and set out in Sch.4.

[14] 1978 c.30.

"An Act or provision of an Act comes into force . . . where no provision is made for its coming into force, at the beginning of the day on which the Act receives the Royal Assent."

It will be seen that there is a slight element of retrospectivity in this rule, in the sense of back-dating the effect of an Act to the beginning of the day on which it receives Royal Assent. There is obviously no substantive unfairness in this very slight degree of retrospectivity, since the legislative procedure is such that a person affected can discover the effect of the intended change in the law well before Royal Assent.[15] But the rule is helpful in the case of the commencement of a power which is to be exercised on the day on which it comes into force, since it is unnecessary to inquire into the relative timings of the giving of Royal Assent and the exercise of the power.

The date of Royal Assent is endorsed on every Act when Royal Assent is signified[16] and appears printed immediately after the long title in the Queen's Printer's copy of the Act.[17] [18]

Unlike most of the Interpretation Act 1978, the default provision for commencement in section 3 does not apply to subordinate legislation.[19] It is the invariable rule for subordinate legislation to contain express provision for its coming into force.[20]

Two-month conventional interval before commencement

Despite the existence of the default provision for immediate commencement, **10.1.5** there is a convention that except in case of particular need arrangements will be made to ensure that primary legislation does not come into force less than two months after the date on which it is enacted. The obvious purpose of this

---

[15] But as to questions of late promulgation of statutes, see Chapter 9, Section 1. And as to the issue of retrospectivity generally, see Section 3 below.
[16] See Chapter 5, Section 2.
[17] See Chapter 9, Section 2.
[18] As to the origin of this practice and the situation that appertained before the predecessor of section 4, note Lord Alverstone C.J. in *R. v Smith* [1910] 1 K.B. 17, 24, CA—"At one time there was no date inserted in any Act of Parliament as the date of its receiving the Royal assent, and each Act was deemed to come into operation as from the first day of the session in which it was passed, unless some specific date was mentioned therein for its commencement. That was found to create injustice and it was altered by the Acts of Parliament (Commencement) Act, 1793, which provides that the date when each Act is passed and receives the Royal Assent is to be indorsed thereon, and that is to be the date of its commencement where no other commencement is provided therein. At the present time there are two well-known dates in many Acts of Parliament, the date of the Act passing and the date of its coming into operation. If, therefore, an Act is silent as to the date of its coming into operation, it comes into operation at the date of its passing."; as to the original rule of deemed commencement from the beginning of the Session see *Pylkington's case* (1452) Y.B. 33 Hen. VI pl. 8.
[19] s.23(1).
[20] There is no kind of restriction on the form which that provision can take, provided that it produces a clear result. In particular, an instrument can provide that it is to come into force on or immediately after some future event, such as the commencement of some other legislation, whether or not it is certain that the future event will in fact occur.

convention is that of giving those affected by new legislation time to acclimatise and adapt.[21]

This is, however, no more than a convention operated by successive Governments. It is not a law, and it is subject to the Government's open discretion to arrange for commencement with a shorter interval in appropriate cases.

For Consolidation Acts, the presumption is of a three month interval between enactment and commencement.[22]

10.1.6 The convention is often thought to have no application in relation to provisions which are wholly enabling and which therefore effect no change in the law upon their commencement.[23]

The origin of this convention as it presently exists is a letter from the Lord Privy Seal to the Secretary to the Law Society dated June 16, 1982. That letter was the culmination of correspondence between the Government and the Law Society's Law Reform Committee, and announced the agreement within Government of new guidance designed to "do much to overcome the difficulties which practitioners have experienced in the past".

There are two methods of effecting the two-month gap between enactment and commencement. The first method is for the Act to contain express provision for its commencement. The second method is for the Act to provide for its commencement by order.

Commencement provision

10.1.7 As mentioned above, despite the existence of the default rule for primary legislation mentioned above it is normal for a statute or piece of secondary legislation to make provision for its own commencement.

This is usually achieved by a single provision containing express propositions about when each substantive provision comes into force. This portmanteau

---

[21] Although the length of the legislative process generally has the effect that persons likely to be affected by a new law are on notice of its arrival much more than two months in advance, there are, or can be depending on the political situation, so many uncertainties about whether a piece of legislation will be enacted, or about the precise form that it will take, that it is frequently only natural for persons affected to delay making practical provision for compliance with the new law until its enactment and precise terms are beyond doubt. In particular, it is not uncommon for changes to be made to legislation by way of amendment at a late stage, not uncommonly during the to-and-fro stages (as to which see Chapter 5, Section 2) which may take place mere days or hours before Royal Assent, which could significantly alter the impact of the legislation on particular interests.

[22] Although the fact that a consolidation does not change the law might suggest that a lesser interval between enactment and commencement would suffice, the wholesale re-structuring of legislation occasioned by a consolidation measure can lead to a greater requirement for practical adjustments, particularly in the matter of changing references in documents to particular provisions of the legislation.

[23] But the convention will in such cases simply transfer to the exercise of the power conferred: in other words, the Government would be expected to provide the same justification for exercising a new power with effect from a time during the first two months of the power's life as it would be expected to provide had the entire practical result been achieved by primary legislation and not through the taking and exercise of a power.

provision is another device promised by the Government, for the purpose of aiding clarity and avoiding confusion, in the letter from the Lord Privy Seal mentioned above.[24]

The normal position for the commencement provision is towards the end in the case of an Act of Parliament and at the beginning in the case of subordinate legislation.

In form, a normal commencement provision of an Act may either fix a specified date which is expected to be more than two months after the date of Royal Assent[25] or it may provide for commencement after the expiry of a specified period after Royal Assent.[26] It is also feasible for a commencement provision to make commencement dependant upon the occurrence of a specified event, including one which may or may not happen at all.[27]

10.1.8

An interesting point arises on the standard form of commencement provision which provides for commencement "on the expiry of the period of two months beginning with the date on which this Act is passed" in the case of an Act which receives Royal Assent on the 30th or 31st day of a month (Month 1) if Month 3 has fewer days than Month 1. As a matter of common sense, it seems that in such a case the Act must be treated as commencing on the last day of Month 3, whether that be the 28th, 29th or 30th (despite the fact that in the case of Royal Assent on any other day of Month 1 one would have to wait for the corresponding day in Month 3). The only alternative, to wait until one, two or three days into Month 4, has nothing to recommend it.

Time of day of commencement

Section 4(a) of the Interpretation Act 1978[28] provides that where a day is specified for the commencement of legislation, commencement occurs at the

10.1.9

---

[24] There are cases, however, in which it most convenient for everyone to depart from this rule. Finance Acts are the best example: almost every provision of a Finance Act has specific rules for commencement, sometimes of greater length and complexity than the substantive change in the law: to group these together at the end of the Act would make it a great deal less easy for readers to understand the effect of each provision.

[25] Although this causes difficulty, of course, if Royal Assent is delayed because the Bill for the Act makes slower progress through Parliament than was originally expected.

[26] The traditional formula is (subject to minor variations) along the lines of "This Act shall come into force at the end of the period of two months beginning with the date on which it is passed". In that context a reference to the time when an Act is passed is a reference to "the time when the Royal Assent is given to a bill which has passed both Houses of Parliament"—*per* James L.J. in *Ex parte Rashleigh. In re Dalzell* (1875) 2 Ch. D. 9, 12, 13, and see *Coleridge-Taylor v Novello* [1938] Ch. 608 Ch. The date of Royal Assent is to be included in calculating the two months (see *Hare v Gocher* [1962] 2 Q.B. 641).

[27] As, for example, "This Order . . . . shall come into operation on the date on which the provisions of Article 5(2) of the Agreement between the Government of the United Kingdom and the Government of the Republic of Ireland concerning the International Fund for Ireland signed at Dublin and London on 18th September 1986 become effective for the two Governments. This date shall be notified in the London, Edinburgh and Belfast Gazettes."—International Fund for Ireland (Immunities and Privileges) Order 1986 (SI 1986/2017), art. 1.

[28] 1978 c.30.

beginning of that day. Unlike s.4(b), this principle applies to subordinate legislation as it does to primary legislation[29] (subject to contrary intention appearing in a particular context).

Despite the fact that commencement on a specified day is presumed in the absence of the expression of a contrary intention to occur at the beginning of a day, and in the case of primary legislation, is presumed to occur at the beginning of the day of Royal Assent,[30] it is by no means unheard of for legislation to provide for commencement at a particular time during a day.[31]

Appointed day provision—commencement orders

10.1.10 It is very common for primary legislation to be left to be commenced on a day appointed by a Minister of the Crown by order.[32]

These orders, known as "appointed day orders" or "commencement orders" are generally required to be made by statutory instrument, so as to attract the provisions about printing and publication.[33]

The provision conferring power to make provision for commencement routinely includes power to make different provision for different purposes. This can be used to commence different provisions of an Act on different days. But it can also be used to commence a provision for one purpose on one day and for remaining purposes on a later day.

10.1.11 It is not possible to state any rules about what can legitimately be regarded as a purpose in this context. The most that can helpfully be said at a level of generality is that like all other powers vested in the executive the exercise of the power is subject to the rules of administrative law (and therefore subject to control through the procedures of judicial review). So an attempt to exercise the power to make differential commencement in a manner that was arbitrary or

---

[29] s.23(1); note, therefore, that a point similar to that for Acts discussed in para.10.3.17 can arise where a statutory instrument appoints for commencement the same day as that on which the instrument is to be laid. Since in practice it is not possible to arrange for laying before some time around the middle of the morning of a day, it is bound to happen that the instrument comes into force a few hours before being laid, and the duty under section 4 of the Statutory Instruments Act 1946 (discussed below) is therefore attracted. See the 17th Report of the Joint Committee on Statutory Instruments, Session 1995–96, para.5 (HL Paper 66, HC 34-xvii) and the 15th Report of the Joint Committee on Statutory Instruments, Session 1997–98, para.4 (HL Paper 46, HC 33-xv).

[30] See para.10.1.4, footnote 18.

[31] See, for example, "This section shall be deemed to have come into force at six o'clock in the evening of 29th November 1994" (Finance Act 1995 (c.4), s.6(5)): for obvious reasons, propositions of this kind are found more frequently in relation to fiscal legislation than in relation to other matters. And for an example in relation to subordinate legislation see article 1 of the Food Protection (Emergency Prohibitions) (Scallops) (England) (Revocation) Order 2003 (SI 2003/2185)—"This Order may be cited as the Food Protection (Emergency Prohibitions) (Scallops) (England) (Revocation) Order 2003 and shall come into force at 14.25 hours on 22nd August 2003."

[32] And it is not unknown for subordinate legislation to be left to be commenced by act of the executive of some kind—see above.

[33] As to which see Chapter 9, Section 3.

unreasonable in some other way would be vulnerable to successful challenge in the courts.

What is arbitrary or unreasonable is, however, something that can be decided only in context. It might, for example, be arbitrary to decide to commence a provision first in relation to things done in London and only later in relation to things done elsewhere: but in certain contexts that might be thought unobjectionable.

It is certainly true that if at the time when the legislation is drafted it is known that anything unusual and possibly controversial is planned in respect of commencement, express provision is included to cover the point and to avoid argument. Hence, for example, s.162(6)(a) of the Nationality, Immigration and Asylum Act 2002[34] enables the commencement order to—

"make provision generally or for a specified purpose only (which may include the purpose of the application of a provision to or in relation to a particular place or area)".

The aim in that case is to permit beyond doubt experimental commencement **10.1.12** of certain provisions in certain areas of the country.

It is also common for a commencement power to include power to make transitional provision, and sometimes incidental or supplemental provision also. Where this is the case the commencement order is sometimes made expressly subject to Parliamentary scrutiny,[35] on the grounds that the transitional modification of a new provision or its disapplication to transitional cases could be a matter

---

[34] 2002 c.41.
[35] See, for example, the following—
Section 68(4) and (5) of the Coal Industry Act 1994 (c.21)—
"(4) Apart from [certain provisions] . . . this Act shall come into force on such day as the Secretary of State may by order made by statutory instrument appoint.
(5) An order under subsection (4) above may . . . (b) make any such transitional provision (including provision modifying for transitional purposes any of the provisions of this Act or of any enactment amended or repealed by this Act) as the Secretary of State considers appropriate in connection with the bringing into force of any provision of this Act;
but, where an order under that subsection makes any such provision as is mentioned in paragraph (b) above, the statutory instrument containing the order shall be subject to annulment in pursuance of a resolution of either House of Parliament."
Section 104(4) and (5) of the Police Act 1996 (c.16)—
"(4) The power to make orders under this section includes power to make such transitional provisions and savings as appear to the Secretary of State to be necessary or expedient.
(5) Where an order under this section contains provisions made by virtue of subsection (4), the statutory instrument containing that order shall be subject to annulment in pursuance of a resolution of either House of Parliament."
In the case of the Child Support, Pensions and Social Security Act 2000 (c.19) the transitional provisions are to be made by separate instrument subject to annulment—see s.86(5) and (6)—
"(5) The Secretary of State may by regulations make such transitional provision as he considers necessary or expedient in connection with the bringing into force of any of the following provisions of this Act . . .

367

of considerable practical importance and controversy, dispelling in that particular case the general feeling that the question of commencement is a minor administrative matter that can safely be left to the executive without special arrangements for Parliamentary supervision or control.[36]

In other cases Parliamentary scrutiny for a commencement order is unusual, but not by any means unheard of. Commencement orders are sometimes required to be laid before Parliament after being made but with no special procedure for scrutiny being prescribed.[37] In other cases they are subject to negative resolution,[38] and there are also a few instances of affirmative resolution.[39]

---

(6) Regulations under subsection (5) shall be made by statutory instrument subject to annulment in pursuance of a resolution of either House of Parliament."

A similar practice to that described above appears to be being adopted by the Scottish Parliament—see, for example, s.89(2) and (3) of the Adults with Incapacity (Scotland) Act 2000 (asp 4)—

"(2) This Act shall come into force on such day as the Scottish Ministers may by order made by statutory instrument appoint and different days may be appointed for different purposes.

(3) Without prejudice to the provisions of schedule 4, an order under subsection (2) may make such transitional provisions and savings as appear to the Scottish Ministers necessary or expedient in connection with any provision brought into force by the order; and where it does so, the statutory instrument under which it is made shall be subject to annulment in pursuance of a resolution of the Scottish Parliament."

See also, for affirmation of the principle of the suitability of scrutiny for powers including the power to make transitional provision, the House of Lords Select Committee on Delegated Powers and Deregulation, Session 1997–98, 27th Report (HL Paper 132—July 15, 1998) para.9, in relation to the Private Hire Vehicles (London) Bill 1997–98.

[36] See the House of Lords Select Committee on Delegated Powers and Deregulation, Session 1997–98, 27th Report (HL Paper 132) July 15, 1998.

[37] See, for example, s.7(5) of the Justices of the Peace Act 1968 (c.69)—"(5) Any statutory instrument containing an Order in Council or order under this section shall be laid before Parliament after being made."; see also, for further examples, ss.48(2) and 53(3) of the Police (Scotland) Act 1967 (c.77), s.3(3) of and para.1 of Sch.3 to, the Family Allowances and National Insurance Act 1968 (c.40), ss.18(2) and 23(2) of the Sea Fisheries Act 1968 (c.77), sections 16(2) and 22(9) of the Child Benefit Act 1975 (c.61) and s.5(3) of the Public Lending Right Act 1979 (c.10).

[38] See, for example, s.12(2) of the Adoption Act 1968 (c.53), s.59 of the Courts Act 1971 (c.23), s.3 of the Finance Act 1971 (c.68), ss.48(4) and 51(3) of the Housing (Scotland) Act 1974 (c.45), sections 15(5), 26(1) and 28(2) of the Scottish Development Agency Act 1975 (c.69) and s.94 of the Local Government, Planning and Land Act 1980 (c.65); for an example of negative resolution but with laying in draft see s.3(3) of the Horserace Totalisator and Betting Levy Boards Act 1972 (c.69).

[39] For example, see the following—

Section 2(2) of the Easter Act 1928 (c.35)—

"(2) This Act shall commence and come into operation on such date as may be fixed by Order of His Majesty in Council, provided that, before any such Order in Council is made, a draft thereof shall be laid before both Houses of Parliament, and the Order shall not be made unless both Houses by resolution approve the draft either without modification or with modifications to which both Houses agree, but upon such approval being given the order may be made in the form in which it has been so approved: Provided further that, before making such draft order, regard shall be had to any opinion officially expressed by any Church or other Christian body."

Section 3 of the Northern Ireland Act 1998 (c.47)—

"**Devolution order.**

(1) If it appears to the Secretary of State that sufficient progress has been made in implementing the Belfast Agreement, he shall lay before Parliament the draft of an

As a matter of standard practice a commencement order is accompanied by a **10.1.13**
note of previous commencement orders relating to the same Act, so that the
reader is able to form a picture as to the state of the Act as a whole.[40] It can
otherwise be difficult to keep track, because a lengthy Act may be commenced
in a series of ten or more orders.[41]

It seems clear that a commencement order can be revoked or amended prior to
the date which it appoints for commencement, and that in a straightforward case
after that date it is a spent force and can no longer be revoked or amended. But
where there are transitional or incidental provisions it may be clearly legitimate
to revoke or amend provisions of the order after the commencement date.[42]

Can the power to commence be or become a duty?

The question often arises whether a power vested in the executive is in fact, in **10.1.14**
the context of the rules of administrative law, a duty.[43] A specific instance arises
in relation to a power to commence primary legislation by order, following the
decision of the House of Lords in *R. v Secretary of State for the Home*

Order in Council appointing a day for the commencement of Parts II and III ('the appointed day').
(2) If the draft Order laid before Parliament under subsection (1) is approved by resolution of each House of Parliament, the Secretary of State shall submit it to Her Majesty in Council and Her Majesty in Council may make the Order."
Section 50(3) of the Consumer Protection Act 1987 (c.43)—
"(3) The Secretary of State shall not make an order under subsection (2) above bringing into force the repeal of the Trade Descriptions Act 1972, a repeal of any provision of that Act or a repeal of that Act or of any provision of it for any purposes, unless a draft of the order has been laid before, and approved by a resolution of, each House of Parliament."
Section 16(3) of the Electronic Communications Act 2000 (c.7)—
"(3) An order shall not be made for bringing any of Part I of this Act into force for any purpose unless a draft of the order has been laid before Parliament and approved by a resolution of each House."
For an example of the affirmative procedure where the commencement has provisional effect pending approval see s.25 of the Prices and Incomes Act 1966 (c.33)—
"(1) At any time in the period of twelve months beginning with the date of the passing of this Act Her Majesty may by Order in Council bring the provisions of this Part of this Act into force for the remainder of the said period of twelve months.
"An Order in Council made under this subsection shall cease to have effect at the expiration of a period of twenty-eight days beginning with the date on which it is made unless before the end of that period the Order has been approved by resolution of each House of Parliament. . . . "
For an example of the affirmative procedure for commencement using the House of Commons only see s.54(7) and (8) of the Finance Act 1985.
[40] And a number of commercial publications specify the commencement status of particular Acts from time to time.
[41] For example, the Control of Pollution Act 1974 (c.40) had twenty commencement orders. The Town and Country Act 1971 (c.78) had no fewer than 75 commencement orders, for unusual reasons of differential geographical commencement.
[42] See the Joint Committee on Statutory Instruments, 9th Report Session 1973–1974 June 13, 1974.
[43] See below, Chapter 1, Section 6.

Department, ex parte Fire Brigades Union.[44] That case can be summarised as follows—

A scheme for the compensation of victims of criminal violence, known as the Criminal Injuries Compensation Scheme, was established in 1964 without statute, relying simply on prerogative powers to make payments[45] calculated in a manner similar to the calculation of common law damages. The scheme was administered by a Board consisting of lawyers appointed again in reliance wholly on non-statutory powers.

In 1988 the non-statutory scheme was codified in ss.108 to 117 of, and Schs 6 and 7 to, the Criminal Justice Act 1988.[46] The Act provided for individual awards to be decided in accordance with the principles on which damages in tort are assessed.

Section 171(1) of the Act provided for these provisions of the 1988 Act to come into force on a day to be appointed by the Secretary of State by order made by statutory instrument. Pending commencement, the non-statutory scheme would remain in force.

10.1.15 In December 1993 the Government issued a White Paper[47] proposing the implementation of a new "tariff scheme" for the compensation of the victims of violent crime by reference to a flat-rate tariff. The tariff was graduated by reference to categories of injury and an award would be calculated by reference to those categories, without any consideration of the principles governing the award of damages as applied to the circumstances of each case. The establishment of the tariff scheme was to reduce the total cost of the compensation system. The White Paper stated that the compensation provisions of the 1988 Act would not be brought into force and would in due course be repealed.

In March 1994 the government announced the intention to implement the new tariff scheme from April 1.

The fire brigades' trade unions applied for judicial review of this decision, seeking a declaration that the decision not to bring the compensation provisions of the 1988 Act into force, but instead to establish the new tariff scheme, was unlawful.

The decision of the House of Lords was as follows[48]—

> On the one hand, there was no duty to commence the provisions of the 1988 Act, the power to appoint a day for commencement being an open discretion allowing the Home Secretary to determine when, if ever, the circumstances were right for commencement. In particular, it could be that circumstances

---

[44] [1995] 2 All E.R. 244, HL.
[45] As to which see Chapter 1, Section 6.
[46] 1988 c.33.
[47] A White Paper is simply a document representing Government policy published by the Government. It is generally made a Command Paper by a Parliamentary procedure which causes the paper to be laid before Parliament, the effect being to cause publication by Her Majesty's Stationery Office in a series of similar documents.
[48] With certain points being decided only by a majority.

arising since the enactment of the provisions would result in it never being right to implement the statutory scheme.

As Lord Browne-Wilkinson said, "in the absence of clear statutory words imposing a clear statutory duty, in my judgment, the court should hesitate long before holding that such a provision as section 171(1) imposes a legally enforceable statutory duty on the Secretary of State."

But, again in the words of Lord Browne-Wilkinson, "It does not follow that, because the Secretary of State is not under any duty to bring the section into effect, he has an absolute and unfettered discretion whether or not to do so. So to hold would lead to the conclusion that both Houses of Parliament had passed the Bill through all its stages and the Act received the Royal Assent merely to confer an enabling power on the executive to decide at will whether or not to make the parliamentary provisions a part of the law. Such a conclusion, drawn from a section to which the sidenote is 'Commencement', is not only constitutionally dangerous but flies in the face of common sense." **10.1.16**

The existence of the power to commence imposed, in effect, a duty to continue to keep the question of commencement under review. And, in particular, the Home Secretary could not lawfully fetter his own discretion in the matter of commencement of the statutory provisions, or do anything that would prejudice the issue of commencement.

Returning to the words of Lord Browne-Wilkinson, "the Secretary of State comes under a clear duty to keep under consideration from time to time the question whether or not to bring the section (and therefore the statutory scheme) into force. In my judgment he cannot lawfully surrender or release the power contained in section 171(1) so as to purport to exclude its future exercise either by himself or by his successors".

The exercise of non-statutory powers to establish an alternative scheme was an abuse or excess of power as pre-empting the decision on commencement and rendering the appointed-day power nugatory: "The Secretary of State cannot himself procure events to take place and rely on the occurrence of those events as the ground for not bringing the statutory scheme into force. In claiming that the introduction of the new tariff scheme renders it undesirable now to bring the statutory scheme into force, the Secretary of State is, in effect, claiming that the purpose of the statutory power has been frustrated by his own act in choosing to introduce a scheme inconsistent with the statutory scheme approved by Parliament." **10.1.17**

So the law on the exercise of a power to commence legislation can be summed up after the *Fire Brigades Unions* case as follows. The discretion to commence is precisely that, and cannot be converted into a duty. But the executive must accept responsibility for keeping under review the appropriateness of commencing the law as enacted by Parliament, and, in particular, may not do anything, or **10.1.18** omit to do anything, if the art of omission is designed to make provision in substitution for that made by Parliament and thereby to render otiose the question of commencement of the statute.

As with any other exercise of executive discretion, a decision to commence or not to commence a statute will be open to challenge in the courts and if contrary to the principles of administrative law will be overturned.[49]

If Parliament wishes a discretion to commence to be subject to specific constraints, such as a long-stop automatic commencement if the provisions are not brought into force earlier, it is of course possible to provide for that expressly.[50]

Controversy of delayed commencement

10.1.19 As the *Fire Brigades Union* case clearly demonstrates, considerable controversy is aroused from time to time in Parliament and elsewhere in relation to legislation which having been passed by Parliament is allowed by the executive to lie on the statute book without coming into force. Those who may have achieved a signal victory in securing the passage of an Act or a provision, perhaps in the face of considerable political difficulties, will feel understandable frustration at what may appear to be an attempt to deprive their victory of any practical effect.[51]

This issue has been debated from time to time in Parliament and the following extract of the Third Report of the House of Lords Select Committee on Procedure of the House[52] explores a number of relevant issues—

---

[49] And the reasons for any decision may be challenged and explored in the normal ways—see, for example, the Parliamentary Question relating to the failure to implement the Consumer Credit Act 1974—HL Deb. March 2, 1983 cc.1134–1135.

[50] See, for example, section 5(2) of the Domestic Violence and Matrimonial Proceedings Act 1976 (c.50)—"This Act shall come into force on such day as the Lord Chancellor may appoint . . . Provided that if any provision of this Act is not in force on 1st April 1977 the Lord Chancellor shall then make an order by statutory instrument bringing such provision into force."

[51] See, for example, the experiences culminating in the passage of the Divorce (Religious Marriages) Act 2002 (c.27) as described in the following passages (one about the Bill for that Act and one about a Bill to the same effect in the previous Session)—

"The result of the work carried out by that alliance was complete agreement and unanimous support for an amendment that was made to the Family Law Bill in 1996, which became what is now Section 9(3) of the Family Law Act 1996.

"It is because the Government feel unable to bring Part II of the 1996 Act, including Section 9(3), into force, that it was decided to introduce this Bill. It is designed to alleviate a real and pressing social injustice that inflicts acute distress and great hardship upon a small section of the Jewish community." (Lord Lester of Herne Hill—HL Deb. June 30, 2000 c.1241–1242)"This Bill is not a new idea—indeed, a very similar Bill was introduced in the previous Parliament by Lord Lester. It completed all its stages in another place, only to be blocked here in the end. I used the ten-minute procedure to bring in a Bill in the previous Session; it reached Second Reading but was talked out. This, therefore, is the third attempt in three years to introduce such a Bill. That shows how important the measure is, although it may also give the House a feeling of déjà vu.

"The terms of the Bill were in essence previously enacted in the Family Law Act 1996, part II, but those provisions have not been brought into force and are to be repealed for reasons wholly unconnected with this Bill." Andrew Dismore M.P.—HC Deb. October 23, 2001 c.146.

[52] Session 1995–96 (HL Paper 50); agreed HL Deb. March 27, 1996 cc.1705–1716.

"The Committee has considered the recommendation of the Delegated Powers Scrutiny Committee 'that the House seeks a mechanism to ensure that Acts passed by Parliament are brought into operation'.[53] The recommendation was made in the light of instances, such as the provisions of the Criminal Justice Act 1988 relating to criminal injuries compensation which were not brought into force.[54] Such instances can only arise because of the commencement provisions of the Act concerned, giving Ministers power to bring the Act, or parts of it, into operation. No recommendation by this Committee would override such provisions. It must be for the House in each case to decide whether commencement provisions in a bill are acceptable. In some cases it might be appropriate for a bill to lay down that the Act will come into force on a stated date if not brought into force earlier by means of a commencement order or orders. In others, it could be provided that the provisions of an Act would cease to have effect on a stated date if not previously brought into force. While no formula is likely to be suitable in all cases, the Committee considers that it would be useful for the House to be able to monitor the extent to which legislation has not been brought into force. The Committee recommends, therefore, that the Government should lay before the House (perhaps as a Command paper) an annual report listing all the Acts and provisions within Acts which have been neither repealed nor brought into force, giving reasons for the delay in each case. Initially, such a report might be limited to Acts which had been enacted before a certain date."[55]

For an example of a "sunset provision" of the kind mentioned by the Select Committee see s.16(4) of the Electronic Communications 2000[56]— **10.1.20**

"(4) If no order for bringing Part I of this Act into force has been made under subsection (2) by the end of the period of five years beginning with the day on which this Act is passed, that Part shall, by virtue of this subsection, be repealed at the end of that period."

In that case the expressed purpose of this approach to commencement was to allow a period during which it could be established whether a system of voluntary self-regulation could become sufficiently effective to make legislative control unnecessary.

A different kind of provision exerting some degree not of control but of supervision over the executive's progress in commencing legislation is found in s.87(5) of the Freedom of Information Act 2000[57]— **10.1.21**

---

[53] 12th Report, Session 1993–94, (HL Paper 90), paragraph 38.
[54] See above.
[55] For an example of a report made by the Government in pursuance of this recommendation see the Command Paper *Bringing Acts of Parliament into Force*, March 1997, Cm. 3595.
[56] 2000 c.7.
[57] 2000 c.36.

"(5) During the twelve months beginning with the day on which this Act is passed, and during each subsequent complete period of twelve months in the period beginning with that day and ending with the first day on which all the provisions of this Act are fully in force, the Secretary of State shall—

(a) prepare a report on his proposals for bringing fully into force those provisions of this Act which are not yet fully in force, and

(b) lay a copy of the report before each House of Parliament."

"The preceding provisions of this Act shall come into force"

10.1.22 In a number of recent Acts, the provision allowing the Act to be commenced by appointed-day order is limited to "the preceding provisions of this Act". The origin of this phrase lies in the conundrum that if an entire Act is left to be commenced by order, that could be thought to include the commencement provision itself, in which case the commencement provision itself cannot be brought into force until it has been brought into force.

The patent absurdity of that conclusion makes it reasonable to disregard it,[58] and many Acts provide simply that they are to come into force by order, leaving it to be inferred that the power to make the commencement order is intended to have immediate effect.

But in the case of an Act which is for other reasons bound to make complex and differential provision about commencement there seems to be no harm in remaining silent about the commencement provision itself, and sometimes other peripheral clauses such as those appointing the short title or specifying extent, with the result that they are treated as coming into force immediately in accordance with s.4 of the Interpretation Act 1978.[59]

---

[58] See—

"It is said for the applicants in the first instance that under the Act of 1947, standing alone, the Minister could never bring that Act into operation at all, and the argument is as follows:— Section 120 of the Town and Country Planning Act, 1947, provides: "(1.) This Act may be cited as the Town and Country Planning Act, 1947. (2.) This Act shall come into force on the appointed day: Provided that [certain sections which are there referred to] shall come into force on the date of the passing of this Act". The sections referred to as coming into force on the date of the passing of the Act do not include s.120, which is the section which provides for the appointed day, and it is accordingly said that the Minister cannot appoint a day until the Act has come into operation and the Act cannot come into operation until he has appointed a day, and the result is that the Act can never come into operation.

"That ingenious argument does not appeal to me because I think that the ordinary and natural interpretation must be given to the section which itself brings the Act into operation, namely, that it must necessarily come into operation with the passing of the Act, which was on August 6, 1947. Any other interpretation would really make nonsense of the provisions of the Act."

(*R. v Minister of Town and Country Planning, ex parte Montague Burton Ltd* [1951] 1 K.B. 1, 5, CA *per* Tucker L.J.)

[59] 1978 c.30.

Occasional difficulty of determining "when" legislation commences

It is sometimes assumed that it must be possible to state in relation to any given piece of legislation at what point in time it comes into force. But that is not the case. Apart from the fact that it is common for different provisions of a particular piece of primary or subordinate legislation to commence at different times for different purposes[60] (whether by virtue of a provision of the legislation itself or by virtue of the exercise of a power to commence) a commencement provision may be such that it is difficult to say that the legislation to which it relates comes into force at a particular time at all.

10.1.23

This is frequently true of provisions of tax law, which commonly assert in relation to commencement only that they have effect in relation to matters arising in or in respect of a particular tax year. That does not mean, of course, that they start to have legal effect at the beginning of that tax year and cease to have legal effect at its end. Their legal effect could begin for practical purposes immediately upon enactment and long before the commencement of the relevant tax year,[61] and it will certainly last after the end of the tax year, in relation to any matter arising during that year. So the best answer to the question "when does such a provision come into force?" is either to deny that it is a helpful question at all in the context of that provision or to assert that the provision comes into force immediately upon enactment but has limited effect.

To give a non-fiscal example, s.162(5) of the Nationality, Immigration and Asylum Act 2002[62] provides that—

> "Section 9 [effect of legitimacy of child in relation to certain nationality questions] shall have effect in relation to a child born on or after a date appointed by the Secretary of State by order."

Again this makes it difficult to answer the question "when does section 9 come into force" and probably renders the question meaningless. All that can helpfully be said is that from the day appointed by the Secretary of State under section 162(5) and onwards, section 9 will acquire some degree of practical effect in law, but only in relation to a limited class of persons. For some people, therefore, section 9 never "comes into force".

---

[60] See, for example, reg.1(2) and (3) of the Environmental Protection (Controls on Dangerous Substances) Regulations 2003 (SI 2003/3274)—

> "(2) Regulations 1, 2, 3, 4, 7 and 9(2) and regulation 8 insofar as it relates to regulations 4 and 7 shall come into force on 6th January 2004.
>
> (3) Regulations 5, 6 and 9(1) and regulation 8 insofar as it relates to regulations 5 and 6 shall come into force on 30th June 2004."

[61] For example, where a person takes advantage of a power to anticipate some matter relating to that tax year in an earlier tax year.

[62] 2002 c.41.

Different provision for different purposes

10.1.24   It is common for an Act to begin to have effect at different times for different purposes. This may be achieved by commencement provision in an Act,[63] or by provision in a commencement order.[64]

Different forms are used for the express power to achieve differential commencement. The forms have occasionally been a matter of Parliamentary controversy,[65] but as with all other matters of drafting it does not do to be dogmatic, rather one must use the form which imports the intention in each context as clearly as possible. So, for example, where commencement may have to be differentiated for particular cases, it is as well to say so rather than to rely on the more general concept of "different purposes". Similarly, if it is intended to have differential commencement geographically for the purpose of conducting pilot experiments of new procedures or systems, it is as well to authorise expressly different commencement for different areas.

During any period when an amending provision has been commenced for some purposes only, it follows that the provision amended by it will be in force in different versions for different purposes. This situation of having parallel texts of legislation, each text having force for a different purpose,[66] can cause considerable confusion, particularly where a reader incautiously assumes that the text which he first encounters has general effect, or where a legislator amending the text is unaware of all the parallel versions (or, perhaps, lacks the power to amend them all).

Conditional commencement

10.1.25   An Act may sometimes provide that it is to come into force only if and when something happens (other than the making of a commencement order).

A small number of Acts make their commencement conditional upon some kind of local resolution, vote or poll. This kind of conditional enactment is less common than it was, but the approach has not entirely disappeared.[67] And a number of provisions are, although not requiring the fulfilment of a condition for

---

[63] See, for example, s.28 of the European Parliament (Representation) Act 2003 (c.7).

[64] And powers to commence routinely confer power to appoint different days for different purposes.

[65] See, for example, HL Deb. July 21, 1994 cc.393–396 re the Deregulation and Contracting Out Bill 1993–94.

[66] Which also arises where different provision is made for different Parts of the United Kingdom—see also Chapter 11, para.11.1.9.

[67] See, for example, s.204(2)(c) of, and Schedule 15 to, the Highways Act 1980 (c.66) (advance payments code may be adopted by resolution of parish or community); s.2(1) of the Local Government (Miscellaneous Provisions) Act 1982 (c.30) (control of sex establishments) ("A local authority may resolve that Schedule 3 to this Act is to apply to their area; and if a local authority do so resolve, that Schedule shall come into force in their area on the day specified in that behalf in the resolution (which must not be before the expiration of the period of one month beginning with the day on which the resolution is passed).")

their commencement, are conditional for their effect in some degree on the results of a series of local referendums.[68]

Even where an Act or provision of an Act is to be commenced by commencement order, some pre-condition may be imposed in relation to the making of an order.[69]

Transitional provision

It is commonly necessary when one legislative system ends and another begins to enact special rules in relation to factual cases that straddle the transition. Sometimes the old law is continued for transitional cases, and sometimes the new law is applied; in either event, modifications may be necessary.

Transitional provisions may be relatively unimportant, in that by definition they affect relatively few cases, but they are frequently extremely complicated; and they can of course be of great importance to the cases affected. For an example of the kind of complication that can be required in transitional cases straddling two regimes each of which is relatively simple, see Sch.19 to the Enterprise Act 2003[70] (duration of bankruptcy: transitional provisions).

Sections 15 to 17 of the Interpretation Act 1978[71] set out a range of provisions designed to deal with specific transitional situations.[72]

Consolidation Acts frequently contain a particularly complex set of transitional provisions. See, for example, Sch.39 to the Education Act 1996.[73]

Transitional provisions should be treated as enacting only Parliament's intentions in relation to the specific cases concerned. Hence—

> " . . . I think that it would be very dangerous, in trying to get to the effect of the permanent provision, to attach too much weight to the particular wording of the transitional one."[74]

In the absence of express transitional provision the courts will have to attempt to discern what Parliament must have intended in respect of matters arising partly before and partly after the commencement of a provision, or which arose before commencement but fall to be addressed after commencement. This is not always easy.[75]

10.1.26

10.1.27

---

[68] See, for example, ss.25 to 36 of the Local Government Act 2000 (c.22) (executive arrangements).

[69] So, for example, s.7(5) of the Northern Ireland Arms Decommissioning Act 1997 (c.7): "This section shall come into force on such day as the Secretary of State, after consulting the Minister for Justice of the Republic of Ireland, may by order made by statutory instrument appoint".

[70] 2002 c.40.

[71] 1978 c.30.

[72] See Chapter 22.

[73] 1996 c.56.

[74] Nourse J. in *Inland Revenue Commissioners v Metrolands (Property Finance) Ltd* [1981] 2 All E.R. 166, 183 Ch.

[75] See for example, "The absence of any transitional provisions has made the construction of this section difficult because it is possible to argue in favour of more than one date."—*Cardshops Ltd v John Lewis Properties Ltd* [1963] 1 Q.B. 159, 165, CA *per* Waller L.J.

As mentioned above it is common for a power to bring an Act into force by order to confer also the power to make transitional provision. It can be difficult to know just how far the breadth of the vague term "transitional" can be relied on. The issue arose in the case of *Britnell v Secretary of State for Social Security*[76] in the course of which Lord Keith of Kinkel said[77]—

10.1.28   "As Staughton LJ observed in the Court of Appeal, it is not possible to give a definitive description of what constitutes a transitional provision. In Thornton on Legislative Drafting[78] it is said:

'The function of a transitional provision is to make special provision for the application of legislation to the circumstances which exist at the time when that legislation comes into force.'

One feature of a transitional provision is that its operation is expected to be temporary, in that it becomes spent when all the past circumstances with which it is designed to deal have been dealt with, while the primary legislation continues to deal indefinitely with the new circumstances which arise after its passage."

Transitional provisions, whether set out in an Act or in a commencement order, are easy to overlook. But they are as much part of the law as any other provision and the consequences of failing to find and apply them could be disastrous. In *R. v Folkestone and Hythe Juvenile Court, ex parte R (a juvenile)*[79] the High Court were able to overlook an erroneous statutory reference made in a committal document in ignorance of a provision "tucked away" in the transitional provisions of an Act, but only because the reference was held to be inessential as a matter of law.

Manipulation of "real world" events because of commencement arrangements

10.1.29   When legislation makes provision for its commencement, with or without transitional provision for matters already in progress when the legislation commences, it may be tempting for those likely to be affected by the legislation to order their actions with an eye on the commencement arrangements, either hurrying so as to avoid application of the new law or delaying so as to ensure it.

In many cases this will be unexceptionable behaviour. For example, if an individual becomes aware of a proposed change of the law about the taxation of profits and brings forward the realisation of a profit so as to be taxed under the

---

[76] [1991] 2 All E.R. 726, HL.
[77] At 730.
[78] 3rd ed. 1987, p.319.
[79] [1981] 1 W.L.R. 1501, QBD.

old law, he acts entirely properly so far as the law is concerned.[80] If the legislature wishes to avoid that kind of avoidance of the new law it must make arrangements either for the law to be prepared in secrecy and to have immediate effect on being made or, where that is impossible,[81] for the law to have a degree of retrospective effect.[82]

But there are limits. In particular, if a public authority deliberately delays acting so as to bring a particular matter within the scope of a new law of which it has notice, that may be challenged successfully as improper behaviour.[83]

Subordinate legislation

The principles explored above for the commencement of primary legislation apply for the most part in relation to subordinate legislation.   **10.1.30**

The convention requiring a two-month interval for preparation, however, applies only to primary legislation. Subordinate legislation is generally giving effect to some aspect of the primary legislation of which those affected will therefore have had general notice since the enactment of the primary legislation. And since it is usual, although not invariable, to consult interested parties during the preparation of secondary legislation, they are likely to be on notice of its terms well before it is made. So it is not unusual for subordinate legislation to come into effect immediately upon being made.[84] But where people might be taken by surprise if subordinate legislation were made with immediate effect one would expect the Government to act only with strong justification.

Despite the non-application of the two-month convention in the case of subordinate legislation, there are two relevant rules requiring delay in relation to the commencement of subordinate legislation.

The first rule is the "21-day rule" operated by the Joint Committee of Statutory Instruments: as discussed above,[85] this is, as a matter of law, merely an informal practice.

The second rule is a rule of law, being s.4(1) of the Statutory Instruments Act   **10.1.31**
1946[86] which applies to instruments which are required to be laid before Parliament and provides as follows—

---

[80] Assuming that he came by his advance knowledge properly.

[81] Which it always is for Acts of Parliament, except for the extremely exceptional emergency case.

[82] As to which see Section 3 below.

[83] See, for example, *R. v Walsall Justices, ex p. W. (a minor)* [1990] 1 Q.B. 253, DC, in which an attempt by justices to delay a trial for the purposes of taking advantage of a change in the law about the evidence of minors was defeated, as an attempt, in effect, to undermine Parliament's arrangements for the cases to which the new law should apply.

[84] But note the effect of the non-binding 21 day rule for certain instruments discussed above at Chapter 6, Section 2, para.6.2.6; for an example of a particularly precipitate commencement of an instrument affecting primary legislation see the Northern Ireland (Emergency Provisions) Act 1991 (Amendment) Order 1992 (SI 1992/1958) which was made on August 10, 1992 to come into force on the following day.

[85] para.6.2.6.

[86] 1946 c.36.

"(1) Where by this Act or any Act passed after the commencement of this Act any statutory instrument is required to be laid before Parliament after being made, a copy of the instrument shall be laid before each House of Parliament and, subject as hereinafter provided, shall be so laid before the instrument comes into operation:

"Provided that if it is essential that any such instrument should come into operation before copies thereof can be so laid as aforesaid, the instrument may be made so as to come into operation before it has been so laid; and where any statutory instrument comes into operation before it is laid before Parliament, notification shall forthwith be sent to the Lord Chancellor and to the Speaker of the House of Commons drawing attention to the fact that copies of the instrument have yet to be laid before Parliament and explaining why such copies were not so laid before the instrument came into operation."

As with the informal 21-day rule, compliance with this requirement is monitored by the Joint Committee on Statutory Instruments.[87]

Although there is nothing to stop a statutory instrument from having effect from a time before it is made available to the public, a person charged with an offence of failing to comply with a provision of a statutory instrument will have a defence if he can show that at the time of the alleged commission of the offence the instrument had not been printed and published and no reasonable steps had been taken to bring it to the attention of those likely to be affected by it.[88]

Anticipatory exercise of powers

10.1.32   Where an Act confers powers to make subordinate legislation, if the purpose of the subordinate legislation is to make detailed provision designed to support the general provisions of the Act, it may be essential that the detailed provision be in place before the general provisions come into force.

Section 13 of the Interpretation Act 1978[89] therefore provides—

"Where an Act which (or any provision of which) does not come into force immediately on its passing confers power to make subordinate legislation, or to make appointments, give notices, prescribe forms or do any other thing for the purposes of the Act, then, unless the contrary intention appears, the

---

[87] See, for example, the Joint Committee on Statutory Instruments, Session 1996–97, 5th Report, para.9 (HL Paper 21, HC 29-v).

[88] 1946 Act, s.3(2); and accordingly in *Simmonds v Newell (sub. nom. Defiant Cycle Co. v Newell)* [1953] 1 W.L.R. 826, DC the Divisional Court quashed a conviction for an offence under an Iron and Steel Prices Order because relevant Schedules had not been printed and there was no certificate under reg.7 of the Statutory Instruments Regulations 1947, nor had the prosecution proved reasonable publicity under s.3(2) of the 1946 Act. See also *R. v Sheer Metalcraft* [1954] 1 Q.B. 586.

[89] 1978 c.30.

power may be exercised, and any instrument made thereunder may be made so as to come into force, at any time after the passing of the Act so far as may be necessary or expedient for the purpose—

(a) of bringing the Act or any provision of the Act into force; or
(b) of giving full effect to the Act or any such provision at or after the time when it comes into force."

This establishes the general principle that in the period before the commencement of a provision certain things may be done under it[90] for the purpose of ensuring that when the provision comes into force it will be capable of having full effect. The constraints on this kind of anticipatory exercise are of frequent importance to Government departments but are unlikely to be of much general interest.[91]

Section 13 apart, it is of course open to a Minister who has a power to appoint a day for commencement of an Act to take advantage of the standard provision permitting the appointment of different days for different provisions or purposes so as to commence early a provision permitting the making of subordinate legislation[92] with a view to the subordinate legislation being made prior to the commencement of the remainder of the Act.

SECTION 2

DURATION

Introduction

Legislation may be permanent—in the sense that it is intended on being made to be of indefinitely prolonged effect—or designedly temporary. This Section discusses aspects of the duration of Acts. Many of the principles discussed are equally relevant to subordinate legislation.   **10.2.1**

Presumption of permanence

In general, when Parliament, or the executive using delegated powers, changes the law, the intention is to make a permanent change. In this sense "permanent"   **10.2.2**

---

[90] Principally the making of subordinate legislation but also the making of appointments and similar matters.
[91] The Joint Committee on Statutory Instruments has on occasion pronounced on the question of what may and may not be done in reliance on section 13. See, for example, "The Committee do not consider that the exercise of a power can be necessary or expedient for the purpose of giving full effect to the provision which confers it."—11th Report Session 1987–88, para.6; or 8th Report Session 1988–89.
[92] Or even, where the power and other matters are entwined in a single provision, to commence early an entire provision but expressly only for the purpose of enabling subordinate legislation to be made.

often turns out to mean for the space of only a few years, sometimes less. But it is permanent in the sense that upon enactment it is neither intended nor known that the law will cease to have effect at a particular time in the future or within a particular period of time.

Unless the legislature expressly repeals or revokes legislation, or in some other way makes express arrangements for it to cease to have effect, it will continue in force indefinitely.

In particular, a right or duty under an Act of Parliament is not extinguished by mere disuse.[93] So an Act could lie dormant for a number of years, even for centuries, and still be available for use.[94] (Note that the position in relation to Acts of the pre-Union Scottish Parliament may be different.[95])

10.2.3 While an Act of Parliament does not lapse for mere disuse, it is possible for the effect of an Act to lapse because it depends for its continuing effect on a state of affairs that has permanently ceased to exist. So, for example, the Agricultural Research Act 1956[96] had lapsed well before its formal repeal by the Statute Law (Repeals) Act 1998[97] because it concerned a Council established under a Charter, and the Council first changed its name (which probably did not interfere with the operation of Act, which would have been deemed to refer to the Council by its new name) and then surrendered its Charter.

Whether a long period of failure to exercise a right would give rise to a legitimate expectation on the part of a person against whom the right could be exercised that the right would not be exercised, and whether that legitimate expectation might found a successful challenge against, in particular, a public authority that sought to exercise the right, are open questions.[98]

---

[93] " . . . neither contrary practice nor disuse can repeal the positive enactment of a statute"—*Hebbert v Purchas* (1871) L.R. 3 P.C. 605, 650; " . . . the inhabitants must establish their right with clearness and certainty, but I must say they have done it. They have produced an Act of Parliament of the year 1799 and the inclosure award of 1803. Those clearly show the right of the inhabitants, and there is no reason to suppose they have lost it. I know of no way in which the inhabitants of a parish can lose a right of this kind once they have acquired it except by Act of Parliament. Mere disuse will not do." Lord Denning M.R. in *Wyld v Silver* [1963] Ch. 243, 255, CA.

[94] So, for example, Mr Gladstone exercised a power to appoint suffragan bishops of Dover and Nottingham under the Act 26 Hen. 8, c.14, no appointment having been made under the statute since the reign of Queen Elizabeth I (see *Life of Archbishop Parker*, by Dean Hook, p.450). And in *R. v Attorney General, ex parte Rusbridger* [2003] U.K.H.L. 38 it was generally accepted that the Treason Felony Act 1848, while not having been used for a long time, was available for use and could found a prosecution if the necessary ingredients of the crime were found (but see the footnote following).

[95] See *Brown v Magistrates of Edinburgh* 1931 S.L.T. 456, 458—but whether the doctrine of desuetude as applied in Scots law will apply in relation to modern Acts of the Scottish Parliament remains to be seen.

[96] 1956 c.28.

[97] 1998 c.43.

[98] The Human Rights Act 1998 (c.42) will in some instances make enforcement of an ancient statute impossible, as will other changes in the world—in the case of *R. v Attorney General, ex parte Rusbridger* [2003] U.K.H.L. 38 cited above the House of Lords was unanimously of the opinion that whatever the possible literal application of the words of the ancient criminal statute to an article in contemplation by a modern newspaper, both the application of the Human Rights Act 1998 and simple realism made it clear that the statute could not, in practice, be relied upon to found a prosecution—as Lord Scott of Foscote said (para.40) "It is plain as a pike staff to the respondents

Sometimes, it is known when a law is enacted that it is to be temporary.[99] There are a number of contexts in which this is common or to be expected, and this Section describes them.

It should be stated at the outset that in the context of legislation a temporary duration may mean anything from a fixed duration of as little as one year[1] to an initially uncertain duration that in the event spans a number of decades.[2]

Fixed term or "sunset" clause

A temporary enactment may have its life determined on its enactment.[3]   **10.2.4**

The principal alternative to a fixed term is to confer on a Minister of the Crown the power to repeal an enactment by subordinate legislation, usually an order.[4] The power may be expressed generally or so as to operate only if a future event occurs.[5]

It is possible to combine the two approaches. Some enactments, in particular, have both an initial life-span and a maximum life-span fixed on their enactment and specified in the relevant primary legislation, with power for a Minister of the Crown to provide for—

---

and everyone else that no one who advocates the peaceful abolition of the monarchy and its replacement by a republican form of government is at any risk of prosecution. Whatever may be the correct construction of section 3 [of the Treason Felony Act 1848], taken by itself, it is clear beyond any peradventure first, that the section would now be 'read down' as required by section 3 of the Human Rights Act 1998 so that the advocacy contemplated by the respondents could not constitute a criminal offence, and second, that no Attorney-General or Director of Public Prosecutions would or could authorize a prosecution for such advocacy without becoming a laughing stock."

[99] Many, but not all, will have the word "temporary" as part of their short title: see, for example, the Counter-Inflation (Temporary Provisions) Act 1972 (c.74), the Imprisonment (Temporary Provisions) Act 1980 (c.57), the Iran (Temporary Powers) Act 1980 (c.28) or the Stamp Duty (Temporary Provisions) Act 1992 (c.2).

[1] As is the case for income tax—see Chapter 1, Section 6. And the initial, although extendable, duration of Part I of the Imprisonment (Temporary Provisions) Act 1980 (c.57) was only one month (see s.8(1)).

[2] As in the case of the Deep Sea Mining (Temporary Provisions) Act 1981 (c.53) which has not yet been brought to an end. And the Population (Statistics) Act 1938 (c.12) was eventually converted into permanent legislation by s.1(1) of the Population (Statistics) Act 1960 (c.32).

[3] See, for example, section 29 of the Anti-terrorism, Crime and Security Act 2001 discussed below in this paragraph. For an example of a fixed sunset clause for subordinate legislation see reg.1(2) of the Fireworks Regulations 2003 (SI 2003/3085)—"These Regulations shall come into force on 22nd December 2003 and shall cease to have effect at the end of a period of twelve months beginning with that date."

[4] See, for example, s.7(6) of the Northern Ireland Arms Decommissioning Act 1997 (c.7) (The Commission): "This section shall cease to have effect at the end of such day as the Secretary of State, after consulting the Minister for Justice of the Republic of Ireland, may by order made by statutory instrument appoint; and an order under this subsection may include such transitional provisions as appear to the Secretary of State to be expedient."

[5] See, for example, s.18(3) of the Deep Sea Mining (Temporary Provisions) Act 1981 (c.53)—"If it appears to the Secretary of State that an international agreement on the law of the sea which has been adopted by a United Nations Conference on the Law of the Sea is to be given effect within the United Kingdom the Secretary of State may by order provide for the repeal of this Act."

(1) extension beyond the initial period,

(2) suspension,

(3) revival (subject to the overall maximum), and

(4) early repeal.[6]

A provision which sets a maximum life for an Act or part of an Act is frequently referred to as a "sunset clause". The Government's policy on the inclusion of sunset clauses has been expressed in a number of Written Answers in the House of Commons.[7]

10.2.5   An example of a sunset clause will be found in s.29 of the Anti-terrorism, Crime and Security Act 2001.[8] The provisions of ss.21 to 23 of that Act provide, in effect, for the detention in certain circumstances of persons based on certification by the Secretary of State that they are suspected of involvement in international terrorism. Not surprisingly, this provision was exceedingly controversial during its passage (being in part based on a derogation from the European Convention of Human Rights). The sunset clause was designed to reassure some of the provision's critics. It provides as follows—

"29 Duration of sections 21 to 23

(1) Sections 21 to 23 shall, subject to the following provisions of this section, expire at the end of the period of 15 months beginning with the day on which this Act is passed.

(2) The Secretary of State may by order—

(a) repeal sections 21 to 23;
(b) revive those sections for a period not exceeding one year;
(c) provide that those sections shall not expire in accordance with subsection (1) or an order under paragraph (b) or this paragraph, but shall continue in force for a period not exceeding one year.

(3) An order under subsection (2)—

---

[6] See, for example, s.1 of the Armed Forces Act 2001 (c.19) and section 112 of the Terrorism Act 2000 (c.11).

[7] See, for example, HC Deb. July 1, 2003 W.A. 217—

"Sunset Clauses

Bob Spink: To ask the Secretary of State for Trade and Industry if she will make it her policy to include a sunset clause in all new legislation unless a specific case can be made to exclude a sunset clause.

Ms Hewitt: Revised guidance on Regulatory Impact Assessments, 'Better Policy Making: A Guide to Regulatory Impact Assessment', was published by the Cabinet Office on 28 January 2003. It advises officials to consider time-limiting or a sunset clause at an early stage of policy development, and gives specific examples of where a sunset clause may be appropriate. The Department of Trade and Industry actively promotes the better regulation agenda and the use of sunset clauses where appropriate."

[8] 2001 c.24.

(a) must be made by statutory instrument, and

(b) may not be made unless a draft has been laid before and approved by resolution of each House of Parliament.

(4) An order may be made without compliance with subsection (3)(b) if it contains a declaration by the Secretary of State that by reason of urgency it is necessary to make the order without laying a draft before Parliament; in which case the order—

(a) must be laid before Parliament, and

(b) shall cease to have effect at the end of the period specified in subsection (5) unless the order is approved during that period by resolution of each House of Parliament.

(5) The period referred to in subsection (4)(b) is the period of 40 days—

(a) beginning with the day on which the order is made, and

(b) ignoring any period during which Parliament is dissolved or prorogued or during which both Houses are adjourned for more than four days.

(6) The fact that an order ceases to have effect by virtue of subsection (4)—

(a) shall not affect the lawfulness of anything done before the order ceases to have effect, and

(b) shall not prevent the making of a new order.

(7) Sections 21 to 23 shall by virtue of this subsection cease to have effect at the end of 10th November 2006."

The essence is therefore that there is an overall maximum of about five years, **10.2.6** within which the Secretary of State can turn the provisions on and off, but subject to Parliamentary control which except in cases of urgency must be exercised in advance.

At one time there was a series of Expiring Laws Continuance Acts.[9] The essence of these was to provide a mechanism by which time-limited enactments could be continued in effect for a specific period under a degree of Parliamentary control. As was said during debate on the Local Government Bill 1998–99 in the House of Commons[10]—

"So common was time limiting in our history—although many hon. Members present may have forgotten it—that it used to be the practice regularly to produce an Expiring Laws Continuance Act, as was done in

[9] See the Expiring Laws Continuance Acts 1928 to 1970.
[10] HC Deb. March 23, 1999 c.240–241—Oliver Letwin M.P.

1969 and 1970, to continue time-limited Acts for a further year. That was a splendid practice, because almost all the Acts that were time-limited contained powers of a highly intrusive nature. A parliamentary doctrine, repeated in debate over a century and a half, made it clear that if Acts gave exceptional and intrusive powers—or arbitrary and wide-ranging powers —to a Secretary of State, it was appropriate, unless there was an extraordinary argument to the contrary, that they should be time-limited."

Temporary provision within "permanent" Act

10.2.7 Within an Act that is intended to have permanent effect a particular provision may be assigned only temporary effect. So, for example, s.3(10) of the Health Authorities Act 1995[11] provides—

"This section (apart from subsection (8)) shall cease to have effect on 1st April 1996."

An alternative method of achieving the same policy would be to confer power on a Minister to repeal a provision of the Act by Order. Or where an Act provides for two regimes, one intended to have effect wholly or partly before the other, the provisions enacting the later regime might include amendments or repeals of provisions enacting the earlier regime, the amendments or repeals to be brought into force by a Minister when commencing the later regime.[12]

Income tax

10.2.8 The most significant example of temporary legislation—and, although the nature of the legislation is as well known as any other, few people are aware that it is technically temporary—is income tax. Because it was thought on its inception to be a radical notion—the expropriation of money earned by private citizens and its use for the welfare of the public—it became established that it required annual confirmation.[13] Income tax therefore requires express confirmation by Parliament each year in order to continue in force.[14]

---

[11] 1995 c.17: the Act received Royal Assent on June 28, 1995—so the intended life of the provision in question was short.
[12] See, for example, Schedule 4 to the Commonwealth Development Corporation Act 1999 (c.20).
[13] First introduced in 1799 by William Pitt the Younger as Prime Minister and Chancellor of the Exchequer, income tax was abolished in 1815 and later re-introduced by Prime Minister Sir Robert Peel in the 1842 Budget. Although expressed to be a temporary expedient it is still with us and appears likely to remain.
[14] Which is reflected in the formula used to enact it: see, for example, s.26 of the Finance Act 2002 (c.23): "Income tax shall be charged for the year 2002–03, and for that year [the rates shall be . . .]".

Emergency legislation

Although technically temporary, income tax is for all real purposes a permanent **10.2.9** feature of legislation. Genuinely temporary measures are enacted in response to situations thought to require legislative measures that could not be justified or maintained in ordinary circumstances.

A good example of this is the range of emergency measures thought to be necessary from time to time to deal with political and social volatilities in Northern Ireland. Part VII of the Terrorism Act 2000,[15] for example, (which replaced the powers previously conferred by a series of temporary Northern Ireland (Emergency Provisions) Acts, is temporary, having a maximum life of five years and being subject to extensions of one year at a time within that period.[16]

Other legislation aimed at making powers available to deal with emergencies should they arise is permanent, but dormant. That is to say the powers remain permanently on the statute book, but may be exercised only following a process begun in reaction to the occurrence of an emergency.[17]

It is also the case that, for obvious reasons, times of war tend to spawn a number of measures intended to have only temporary effect.[18]

Armed forces

The notion of a permanent army was historically a matter of great controversy.[19] **10.2.10** Questions of expense apart—although these were of considerable importance in times when the principal purposes of the raising of taxes were military—there are constitutional issues involved: the existence of a permanent army poses a potential threat to the freedom of the subject, if the army be tightly controlled by

---

[15] 2000 c.11. Part VII, which re-enacts a range of measures specific to Northern Ireland, was enacted so as (by virtue of s.112) to cease to have effect after one year, with power for the Secretary of State by order (subject to affirmative resolution—s.123(4)(f)) to continue a provision in force, or revive a provision, for up to one year at a time. For continuance orders see SI 2002/365, 2002/2141, 2003/427. S.112(4) places a long-stop on the continuance of these provisions by providing that "This Part shall, by virtue of this subsection, cease to have effect at the end of the period of five years beginning with the day on which it is brought into force", thereby necessitating another Act should the provisions still be thought necessary at that time.

[16] s.112; and see the Terrorism Act 2000 (Continuance of Part VII) Order 2002 (SI 2002/365), the Terrorism Act 2000 (Cessation of Effect of Section 76) Order 2002 (SI 2002/2141), the Terrorism Act 2000 (Continuance of Part VII) Order 2003 (SI 2003/427) and the Terrorism Act 2000 (Continuance of Part VII) Order 2004 (SI 2004/431).

[17] See, in particular, the Emergency Powers Act 1920 (c.55), expected as this work went to print to be replaced by the Act emerging from the Civil Contingencies Bill 2003–04.

[18] See, for example, the House of Commons Disqualification (Temporary Provisions) Acts 1941, 1943 and 1944, the Housing (Temporary Provisions) Act 1944 (c.33) and the Local Elections and Register of Electors (Temporary Provisions) Acts 1939, 1940, 1941, 1942, 1943 and 1944.

[19] See, for example, the preamble to the Bill of Rights 1688 (c.2)—"Whereas the late King James the Second by the assistance of diverse evil councillors judges and ministers employed by him did endeavour to subvert and extirpate the Protestant religion and the laws and liberties of this kingdom . . . By raising and keeping a standing army within this kingdom in time of peace without consent of Parliament and quartering soldiers contrary to law."

the Crown or the executive. And if the control is not tight, then the existence of a permanent and powerful army carries a potential threat of political instability.

The reality of the need for permanent armed forces is nowadays beyond dispute. But the constitutional considerations are preserved by the practice of having the armed forces legislated for by temporary legislation. Every five years an Armed Forces Act is passed,[20] and the normal arrangements made by each Armed Forces Act are[21]—

(1) that the Army Act 1955, the Air Force Act 1955 and the Naval Discipline Act 1957 are continued in force for an initial period of approximately one year, and

(2) that they can be further continued, for up to one year at a time, by Order in Council, which requires affirmative resolution of each House of Parliament, but

(3) that they may not be continued by that method after the expiry of the period of approximately five years from the passing of the Act, thus necessitating another quinquennial Act.

Subordinate legislation

10.2.11 There is nothing to stop the exercise of a delegated power to legislate from being exercised temporarily, where its indefinite protraction is likely to be unnecessary. The Government has affirmed as a general principle the use of temporary rather than permanent subordinate legislation where this can usefully reduce the regulatory burden on citizens.[22]

Effect of expiry

10.2.12 The provisions of the Interpretation Act 1978[23] which apply to the repeal of an enactment apply also to the expiry of a temporary enactment.[24]

---

[20] The current Act being the Armed Forces Act 2001 (c.19), the long title of which is "An Act to continue the Army Act 1955, the Air Force Act 1955 and the Naval Discipline Act 1957; to make further provision in relation to the armed forces and the Ministry of Defence Police; and for connected purposes."

[21] See, for example, s.1 of the 2001 Act.

[22] "Revised guidance on regulatory impact assessments was published on January 28, 2003, advising officials to consider time-limiting or sunsetting regulations and encouraging use of those tools where appropriate. . . . the sunset clause is only one of the tools available to advance the regulatory reform agenda that this Government are pursuing." Minister for the Cabinet Office and Chancellor of the Duchy of Lancaster, HC Deb. June 17, 2003 c.207.

[23] 1978 c.30.

[24] By virtue of s.16(2) of that Act—for a discussion of the effect of Section 15 see Chapter 14, Section 3.

A temporary enactment is likely, in particular, to have effects in relation to matters arising before its expiry which last for an indefinite period after expiry.[25]

Express separate provision

It is a rule of the House of Commons that where it is known on enactment that a provision will have effect only for a limited time, the intended duration be expressed in a separate provision.[26]   **10.2.13**

Act to continue temporary Act: deemed transitional effect

If a Bill is introduced in any Session of Parliament for the express purpose of continuing a temporary Act that is due to expire during that Session, then if the temporary Act expires before the continuing Act receives Royal Assent, the continuing Act is deemed, subject to express contrary provision of the continuing Act, to have effect from the date of the expiry of the temporary Act.[27] The deeming does not, however, extend to making a person liable for a penalty of any kind in respect of anything done or omitted to be done between the actual expiry of the temporary Act and the granting of Royal Assent to the continuing Act.   **10.2.14**

SECTION 3

RETROSPECTIVITY

Introduction

Legislation is retrospective if it has effect in relation to a matter arising before it was enacted or made. This definition is easy to state, but not always easy to apply.[28] This Section explores a little further the nature of retrospectivity in relation to legislation and enunciates some of the principles relating to it.   **10.3.1**

---

[25] So, for example, the repeal of the Stamp Duty (Temporary Provisions) Act 1992 (c.2) effects only instruments executed or issued on or after October 1, 1999.
[26] Standing Order No.81—"The precise duration of every temporary law or enactment shall be expressed in a distinct clause or subsection of the bill".
[27] Acts of Parliament (Expiration) Act 1808 (c.106).
[28] A more complex definition enunciated in the last edition of this work received judicial approval. The definition is "A statute is to be deemed to be retrospective, which takes away or impairs any vested right acquired under existing laws, or creates a new obligation, or imposes a new duty, or attaches a new disability in respect to transactions or considerations already past." The judicial approbation was given by Sir Thomas Bingham M.R. in *L'Office Cherifien des Phosphates and another v Yamashita-Shinnihon Steamship Co Ltd The Boucraa* [1993] 3 All E.R. 686 at 692, CA; further approved by Lord Mustill in the same case in the House of Lords ([1994] 1 All E.R. 20, HL).

The presumption against retrospectivity

10.3.2   The presumption against retrospectivity can be simply stated in the words of Lindley L.J. in *Lauri v Renad*[29]—

> "It is a fundamental rule of English law that no statute shall be construed so as to have a retrospective operation, unless its language is such as plainly to require such a construction. And the same rule involves another and subordinate rule, to the effect that a statute is not to be construed so as to have a greater retrospective operation than its language renders necessary."

A more recent exposition of the same principle was provided by Lord Reid in *Sunshine Porcelain Potteries Pty Ltd v Nash*[30]—

> "Generally, there is a strong presumption that a legislature does not intend to impose a new liability in respect of something that has already happened, because generally it would not be reasonable for a legislature to do that . . . But this presumption may be overcome not only by express words in the Act but also by circumstances sufficiently strong to displace it."

10.3.3   Not only is it a principle applied by the courts in construing legislation that retrospective application is to be rebuttably presumed not to be intended, but it is also a principle accepted by successive governments that retrospectivity should be avoided except where necessary.[31]

The seriousness with which the notion of retrospective legislation is approached is such that it is generally thought right to bring the retrospectivity to the attention of Parliamentarians and other readers in a prominent way. For example, the long title of a Bill has on occasion been used to draw attention to retrospective effect.[32]

The question of the fundamental injustice, as a general rule, of retrospective legislation has exercised the minds of lawyers and Parliamentarians for centuries. So, for example, the long title of the Acts of Parliament (Commencement) Act 1793[33] declared that it was "An Act to prevent Acts of Parliament from taking effect from a time prior to the passing thereof".

---

[29] [1892] 3 Ch. 402, 421.

[30] [1961] A.C. 927, 938.

[31] See, for example, the statement by Baroness Hollis of Heigham that "It is a general principle of English and Scottish law that retrospective legislation should be avoided wherever possible"—HL Deb. October 13, 1999 c.502.

[32] "An Act to make provision (with retrospective effect) . . . ."—Statutory Instruments (Production and Sale) Act 1996 (c.54).

[33] 1793 c.13; see further Chapter 5, Section 2.

Difficulties in applying the presumption

Although this rule is both fundamental and apparently straightforward, a number **10.3.4** of difficulties arise in determining its precise extent and how to apply it. The first difficulty lies in determining what is and is not retrospectivity.

Future action in relation to past events

A particular difficulty that arises in determining whether a statute is retrospective **10.3.5** concerns the possibility of action under a statute which has effect only for the future but is brought about in part by reference to past events (that is to say, events prior to the passing of the Act).

There is some judicial support for the suggestion that this is not retrospectivity. In the case of *Re A Solicitor's Clerk*[34] Lord Goddard C.J. said—

> "In my opinion, however, [the Solicitors Act 1941,[35] as amended by the Solicitors (Amendment) Act 1956[36]] is not in truth retrospective. It enables an order to be made disqualifying a person from acting as a solicitor's clerk in the future and what happened in the past is the cause or reason for the making of the order; but the order has no retrospective effect. It would be retrospective if the Act provided that anything done before the Act came into force or before the order was made should be void or voidable or if a penalty were inflicted for having acted in this or any other capacity before the Act came into force or before the order was made. This Act simply enables a disqualification to be imposed for the future which in no way affects anything done by the appellant in the past."

In a similar way, in *R. v Field*[37] the Court of Appeal held that a new system **10.3.6** for making orders disqualifying convicted persons from working with children could be applied to offences committed before the system came into force. The point was made in the following terms in submissions for the Secretary of State, quoted and approved by Kay L.J.[38]—

> "Assuming that a disqualification order is not a criminal penalty, the Secretary of State's interpretation does not offend against the presumption against retrospective legislation. That presumption is based on concepts of fairness and legal certainty, which dictate that accrued rights and the legal status of past acts should not be altered by subsequent legislation. But the

---

[34] [1957] 3 All E.R. 617, 619, QBD.
[35] 1941 c.46.
[36] 1956 c.41.
[37] [2003] 3 All E.R. 769, CA.
[38] At 782–783.

effect of a disqualification orders is entirely prospective, because it only affects future conduct. . . .

"Finally, the purpose of section 28 is plainly to protect children. That purpose would be severely undermined if a disqualification order could only be imposed in relation to offences committed after the section came into force. The courts should take a more relaxed approach to a potentially retro-active element in legislation where its intended purpose is to protect the public."

Despite this principle clearly emerging from the precedents, the legislature has sometimes thought it best to put the point beyond doubt where the intention was to allow future action to be influenced by pre-commencement events.[39]

Distinction between retrospectivity and affecting existing rights

10.3.7 A further necessary distinction between what is and is not retrospectivity is illustrated in the following passage of the judgment of Buckley L.J. in *West v Gwynne*[40]—

"Retrospective operation is one matter. Interference with existing rights is another. If an Act provides that as at a past date the law shall be taken to have been that which it was not, that Act I understand to be retrospective. That is not this case. . . . As a matter of principle an Act of Parliament is not without sufficient reason taken to be retrospective. There is, so to speak, a presumption that it speaks only as to the future. But there is no like presumption that an Act is not intended to interfere with existing rights. Most Acts of Parliament, in fact, do interfere with existing rights."

Application of the presumption

10.3.8 The principal difficulties in the application of the presumption against retro-spectivity are expounded in the passage of the speech of Lord Mustill in *L'Office Cherifien des Phosphates and another v Yamashita-Shinnihon Steamship Co Ltd, The Boucraa*[41] appended to this work.[42]

The essence of that decision is that the question of whether a statute is intended to have retrospective effect should be answered not by the application of any

---

[39] See, for example, s.4(4) of the Nationality, Immigration and Asylum Act 2002 (c.41)—"In exercising a power under section 40 of the British Nationality Act 1981 after the commencement of subsection (1) above the Secretary of State may have regard to anything which—
    (a) occurred before commencement, and
    (b) he could have relied on (whether on its own or with other matters) in making an order under section 40 before commencement."
[40] [1911] 2 Ch. 1, 11, CA.
[41] [1994] 1 All E.R. 20, HL.
[42] Appendix, Extract 17.

rigid criteria or distinctions between classes of enactment, but by considering, in the light of all the circumstances of each case—

> what degree of unfairness (if any) might be thought to be suffered if the provision were applied with retrospective effect, and

> that the greater the unfairness the stronger the presumption that Parliament would not have intended it, and therefore the greater the clarity of language required to rebut it.

This approach accords with a general trend of the courts[43] away from the rigid application of formulaic presumptions and the application of common sense in the search for the legislative intention in each context, by having regard to all relevant circumstances.[44]

Having denied the existence of rigid rules that can be applied in determining whether or not a provision is retrospective, it is certainly true that there are a number of special cases concerning which some particular considerations apply.

Special case (1): procedure

Although Lord Mustill warns against seeking a rigid rule in relation to retrospectivity of procedural provisions, he adds that the special distinction between procedural and substantive provisions for these purposes should be kept "well in view". It is therefore proper to say something of why it was thought right to treat procedural provisions differently in relation to retrospectivity, and the nature of the different treatment to be accorded.   **10.3.9**

The nature of the exception and its justification are clearly encapsulated in the following passage from the speech of Lord Brightman in *Yew Bon Tew Alias Yong Boon Tiew v Kenderaan Bas Mara*[45]—

> "Apart from the provisions of the interpretation statutes, there is at common law a prima facie rule of construction that a statute should not be interpreted retrospectively so as to impair an existing right or obligation unless that result is unavoidable on the language used. A statute is retrospective if it takes away or impairs a vested right acquired under existing laws, or creates a new obligation, or imposes a new duty, or attaches a new disability, in regard to events already past. There is, however, said to be an exception in the case of a statute which is purely procedural, because no person has a

---

[43] See, in particular, Chapter 18.
[44] See, for an example of the House of Lords accepting and applying this approach (in the case of considering the retrospectivity of s.3 of the Human Rights Act 1998 (c.42), *Wilson and others v Secretary of State for Trade and Industry, Wilson v First County Trust Ltd (No.2)* [2003] 3 W.L.R. 568, HL.
[45] [1983] 1 A.C. 553, 557, PC.

vested right in any particular course of procedure, but only a right to prosecute or defend a suit according to the rules for the conduct of an action for the time being prescribed."

The distinction between substance and procedure is, however, not always easy to ascertain or apply. As Lord Brightman continued[46]—

"But these expressions 'retrospective' and 'procedural,' though useful in a particular context, are equivocal and therefore can be misleading. A statute which is retrospective in relation to one aspect of a case (*e.g.* because it applies to a pre-statute cause of action) may at the same time be prospective in relation to another aspect of the same case (*e.g.* because it applies only to the post-statute commencement of proceedings to enforce that cause of action); and an Act which is procedural in one sense may in particular circumstances do far more than regulate the course of proceedings, because it may, on one interpretation, revive or destroy the cause of action itself."

10.3.10   The difficulty of knowing what amounts to a matter of procedure and what of substance arose in *Antonelli v Secretary of State for Trade and Industry*,[47] the specific issue being whether a notice could be served by the Secretary of State in relation to a conviction obtained before the commencement of the Act under which the notice was served. Beldam L.J. said[48]—

" . . . I start with the declared purpose of the [Estate Agents Act 1979[49]] and the policy behind its enactment that it is intended to make provision 'with respect to the carrying on of and the persons who carry on' estate agent's activities. The provisions giving the Director power to disqualify are intended for the protection of the public and it would be quixotic to suppose that Parliament intended that the public should be protected from the activities of a practitioner convicted a week after the Act came into force but not from those of the practitioner convicted a week before."

This approach supports the general proposition outlined above that whatever rules of thumb are used as starting-points for the consideration of retrospectivity, there is no substitute for consideration of the substance of the provision concerned and, taking all the circumstances into account, considering what results the legislature can reasonably be assumed to have wanted or not wanted to achieve.

The fact that a new law about procedure will often apply to proceedings begun before, or relating to matters arising before, the commencement of the new law,

---

[46] Same, 557–558.
[47] [1998] 2 W.L.R. 826, CA.
[48] At 835.
[49] 1979 c.38.

should not encourage public authorities to indulge in deliberate delay for the purpose of attracting to proceedings a prospective change in the law.[50]

Special case (2): tax

In the context of expropriating the private property of the citizen for the purposes of the state it requires absolutely clear words to make a provision of legislation retrospective.[51]   **10.3.11**

But it is not uncommon for Parliament to use clear words for that purpose.[52] In particular, it is clear that if the Government were not able to back-date provisions of the annual Finance Act to the date of the budget on which its provisions were first announced to the House of Commons, the intervening period between the budget and Royal Assent for the Bill brought in upon it would be filled with activity on the part of people trying to anticipate the eventual Act and to lessen its burden by transacting business as fast as possible in the interim. This is clearly undesirable. Not only is it therefore common for Parliament to provide for provisions to take effect as from the budget day on which they were announced, but the law enables the House of Commons by resolution to give provisional effect to specified provisions of the Finance Bill.[53]

More than this, it sometimes happens that the Government identify what they regard as an abusive or evasive practice in relation to a particular tax, in which case the Government may make an announcement, perhaps by way of a written ministerial statement in the House of Commons,[54] of an intention to prohibit the practice and close the particular loophole on which it is based. Where this occurs, it is generally regarded as acceptable for the legislation giving effect to the

---

[50] See *R. v Walsall Justices, Ex p. W. (a minor)* [1990] 1 Q.B. 253, DC, in which an attempt by justices to delay a trial for the purposes of taking advantage of a change in the law about the evidence of minors was defeated, as an attempt, in effect, to undermine Parliament's arrangements for the cases to which the new law should apply.

[51] See, for example, *Wijesureya v Amit* [1966] A.C. 372, PC; and note "the general principle that a Finance Act has no retrospective effect unless there are clear words to that effect"—*Greenberg v Inland Revenue* Commissioners [1972] A.C. 109, 145, HL *per* Lord Guest.

[52] That does not mean, however, that the presumption against using retrospectivity does not apply to tax: as to which it is interesting to note the following Ministerial answer given in the House of Lords on November 9, 1999—"Lord Chesham asked Her Majesty's Government: Whether the statement of the Baroness Hollis of Heigham that 'It is a general principle of English and Scottish law that retrospective legislation should be avoided wherever possible' applies to conditionally exempt items for inheritance tax purposes. Lord McIntosh of Haringey: Yes, my Lords, the presumption against retrospection applies to this as to all other legislation."

[53] See Chapter 3, Section 7.

[54] Until 2003 it was commonplace for the Government to make announcements in Parliament by instigating (or "planting") a question for written answer, normally tabled by a Government back-bencher. The artificiality of this process led to the introduction in 2003 of the written ministerial statement, whereby a Minister may merely make a statement on a particular matter and have it printed in Hansard, without going through the charade of asking a friendly Member to table a question in response to which the Minister can deliver his announcement. In the House of Lords the written ministerial statement has been available since January 1, 2004 (see HL Deb. December 17, 2004 cc.1159–1169): but it is not to be expected that it would be used in relation to fiscal matters.

announcement to have effect retrospectively as from the date of the announce-ment.[55] There is no unfairness provided that the announcement be given due publicity.

10.3.12   The common practice of legislating retrospectively in relation to fiscal matters was commented on by Lord Diplock in *Inland Revenue Commissioners v Joiner*[56] as follows—

> "The growing practice of back-dating the effect of statutes to the date of the first minatory announcement by the executive government of its intention to promote legislation to change the law does not weaken the presumption against retroactivity where there is no express provision in a statute to that effect. Rather it serves to confirm that the reason for the presumption is that in a civilised society which acknowledges the rule of law individual members of that society are entitled to know when they embark upon a course of conduct what the legal consequences of their doing so will be, so that they may regulate their conduct accordingly."

In accordance with the general principles of retrospectivity already outlined, even in a case where it might be thought unfair to legislate with retrospective effect on a fiscal matter it is open to the legislature to do so, but effect will be given to their intention by the courts only if it be indicated in a manner which leaves no room for doubt.[57]

As to the particular difficulties that can arise in determining whether fiscal legislation is truly to be regarded as retrospective or not, see *Greenberg v Inland Revenue Commissioners*.[58]

Special case (3): penal statutes

10.3.13   For obvious reasons, the presumption against retrospectivity will be particularly strong in relation to penal statutes, that is to say statutes creating criminal

---

[55] See, for example, s.102 of the Finance Act 1999 (c.16) (gifts with reservation). And for judicial approval of the practice, on the grounds that no practicable method of countering evasion exists, see the following passage of the judgment of Lord Greene M.R. in *Lord Howard de Walden v Inland Revenue Commissioners* [1942] 1 K.B. 389, 398, CA—"The fact that the section has to some extent a retroactive effect again appears to us of no importance when it is realized that the legislation is a move in a long and fiercely contested battle with individuals who well understand the rigour of the contest."

[56] [1975] 1 W.L.R. 1701, 1714, HL.

[57] "It is in my judgment clear that, as the constitutional law of England stands today, Parliament has the power to enact by statute any fiscal law, whether of a prospective or retrospective nature and whether or not it may be thought by some persons to cause injustice to individual citizens. If the wording of that legislation is clear, the court must give effect to it, even though it may have, or will have, a retrospective effect. It has no power, as the taxpayer submitted, to refuse to give effect to it on the ground that the protection of private citizens requires it."—*James v Inland Revenue Commissioners* [1977] 2 All E.R. 897, 901, Ch *per* Slade J.

[58] [1972] A.C. 109, HL.

offences.[59] To criminalise conduct which when committed was entirely lawful will as a general rule be unwarrantably unfair, the person committing the conduct having no reason to abstain from it at the time in question. This will apply not only to matters designated as criminal by the legislature but also to matters which have a penal effect.[60] It can therefore be said that "on general principles penal legislation is not retroactive in operation".[61]

Similarly, it will require strong evidence to rebut the presumption against retrospectivity in the case of a provision which has the effect of removing a defence formerly available in relation to a criminal matter.[62]

The European Convention on Human Rights enacts the principle of non-retrospectivity for criminal legislation in Art.7(1) of the Convention, which provides— **10.3.14**

"No one shall be held guilty of any criminal offence on account of any act or omission which did not constitute a criminal offence under national or international law at the time when it was committed. Nor shall a heavier penalty be imposed than the one that was applicable at the time the criminal offence was committed."[63]

This embodies both the principle that a new offence should not relate to past conduct and also that an increase of penalty should not relate to past offences.

---

[59] Certain other kinds of disadvantage may also be treated as penal. And the distinction between what is penal and what is, for example, for regulatory purposes or for purposes of public protection, may not always be an easy one—see, for example, *Re Pulborough Parish School Board Election, Bourke v Nutt* [1894] 1 Q.B. 725, CA and *The Queen, on the Prosecution Of Certain Justices Of Leeds v Vine* (1875) 10 Q.B. 195, DC. See also "There is no doubt, in our judgment, that these provisions [s.86 of the Powers of Criminal Courts (Sentencing) Act 2000 (c.6)] are punitive and are properly to be contrasted with purely preventative measures that do not invoke any principle against retrospective penalty: see *Ibbotson v United Kingdom* (1999) 27 E.H.R.R. C.D. 332, where, by contrast, the European Commission held that the registration requirements of the Sex Offenders Act 1997, which have a partially retrospective operation were preventative, rather than punitive in character, and did not therefore constitute a penalty for the purposes of article 7."—*R. v T.* [2003] 4 All E.R. 877, 881, CA, but compare and contrast the decision of the Court of Appeal rejecting *R. v T.* as *per incuriam* and finding that s.86 is preventive and not punitive—*R. v R.* [2003] 4 All E.R. 882, CA; see also *R. (Uttley) v Secretary of State* [2003] 4 All E.R. 891, CA.

[60] Hence the following passage from the judgment of Staughton L.J. in *Re Barretto* [1994] 1 All E.R. 446, CA: "[Counsel] submits that there is nothing unfair in requiring a drug trafficker to surrender gains which he has made in the past and concealed from the court on a previous occasion. But I do not think that one should go into detail to that extent. It will generally be unfair to increase the penalty for any past conduct however disreputable. . . . So the presumption [against retrospectivity] applies."

[61] *R. v Reah* [1968] 3 All E.R. 269, 271, CA *per* James J.

[62] "That conclusion is supported by the view that to give a retrospective effect to the statute would be to deprive the defendant of a defence upon which, at the time the acts complained of were committed, he was entitled to rely. It seems to me a very strong thing to hold that a defence which was open to a man at the time he did the acts complained of has been taken away by the retrospective operation of a subsequent statute."—*R. v Griffiths* [1891] 2 Q.B. 145, 148 *per* Lord Coleridge C.J.

[63] There is an exception in Art.7(2): "This Article shall not prejudice the trial and punishment of any person for any act or omission which, at the time when it was committed, was criminal according to the general principles of law recognised by civilised nations."

As to an enactment which makes permissible conduct which was formerly criminal, if it proceeds by repeal the provisions of s.16 of the Interpretation Act 1978[64] will apply, unless disapplied expressly or by clear implication, so as to preserve any accrued liability and permit its to be enforced.[65]

Special case (4): consolidation

10.3.15 In the case of a pure consolidation measure the question of retrospectivity does not, of course, arise. But it is common to have a measure which repeals an older measure and re-enacts it with modifications. The question of whether retrospectivity can be justified in such a case depends on the nature of the modifications as well as on all other relevant circumstances. But s.16 of the Interpretation Act 1978[66] can be used in that case to continue as much as necessary of the effect of the repealed Act in relation to matters arising before the repeal, to ensure that no injustice is done by failing to give the consolidation retrospective effect.[67]

Interference with contracts already concluded

10.3.16 While for obvious reasons the legislature is generally reluctant to interfere by legislation with rights or duties already conferred or imposed by contract before the passing of the legislation, it is sometimes thought proper to do so.[68]

Where a provision nominally interferes with accrued rights or duties, but in reality is merely declaratory or restorative of what was generally thought by all concerned to have been the position, retrospectivity is likely to be both unobjectionable and desirable or even essential for practical purposes.[69]

---

[64] 1978 c.30: as to s.16 see also Chapter 22.

[65] See also *R. v West London Stipendiary Magistrate, Ex p. Simeon* [1983] 1 A.C. 234.

[66] 1978 c.30: as to s.16 see also Chapter 22.

[67] For fuller discussion of the point see *Plewa v Chief Adjudication Officer* [1994] 3 W.L.R. 317, HL.

[68] See, for example, the National Economy Act 1931 (c.48), s.1(1)(d), the Agricultural Marketing Act 1933 (c.31), s.17(3), the Cinematograph Films Act 1938 (c.17), s.20(2) or the Landlord and Tenant (War Damage) Act 1939 (c.72), ss.1(1) and (7), 2(1), 4(1) and 2. There are also many instances of Acts imposing a penalty for doing something, without saying anything about contracts, though the result may well be that the performance of existing contracts becomes illegal and unenforceable. On other occasions an Act may expressly save performance of existing contracts: see, for example, s.4 of the Coal Mines Act 1930 (c.34) and s.8 of the Agricultural Marketing Act 1931 (c.42).

[69] See, for an extreme example, s.147 of the Education Act 2002 (c.32) (Application of pay-scale)—

"(1) This section—(a) applies to the construction of paragraph 18 of the document referred to in article 3 of the Education (School Teachers' Pay and Conditions) (No 2) Order 1999 (SI 1999/2160) (classroom teachers: criteria for position on pay spine) as it had effect from 1st September 1999 to 31st March 2000, and (b) shall be treated as having come into force on 1st September 1999 (for all purposes including the calculation of pensions). (2) Where a person is awarded one or more points, he shall be paid the salary shown for the spine point which equates to the number of points awarded. (3) Where a person is not awarded a point, he shall be paid the salary shown for the lowest spine point. (4) In paragraph 18.1.1 (good honours degree)—(a) paragraph (a) shall be ignored, (b) paragraph (b) shall be treated as applying irrespective of the date of a person's appointment to his first post following qualification as

Minor retrospectivity in default rule for commencement

It has already been noted[70] that the default rule for the commencement of primary   **10.3.17**
legislation involves a slight element of retrospectivity, going back only to the
beginning of the day on which the legislation is passed. The justification for this
element of retrospectivity is explained in para.10.1.4, footnote 18.).

Subordinate legislation

As a general rule, a power to make subordinate legislation does not confer the   **10.3.18**
power to make provision having retrospective effect unless it does so
expressly.[71]

But if the statutory scheme is clearly intended to have retrospective effect, and
certain details of the scheme are left to be supplied by subordinate legislation, the
subordinate legislation will be treated as having retrospective effect (and may be
so treated whether or not it contains express provision to that effect).[72]

---

a teacher, and (c) in paragraph (c) the words "before 1st September has been employed as a
qualified teacher and who" shall be ignored.".

Although this provision on its face has a radical retrospective effect on accrued private rights, the
reality of the position is expressed as follows in para.290 of the Explanatory Notes to the 2002
Act—

"With effect from 1 September 1999, point 0 [of the teachers' pay scale] was removed and
the differential for good honours degrees reduced to 1 point for new entrants. Subsequently,
the Department formed the view that the legal effect of the amendments was uncertain. The
Department sought to remedy this by means of a remedial order, which took effect on 1 April
2000. However the Department believes that the order did not resolve the matter fully. This
section now seeks to tidy up the way in which point 0 was removed in order to ensure that
all teachers' true lawful pay entitlement is clearly the entitlement intended in the 1999 and
subsequent School Teachers' Pay and Conditions Documents. The provisions should work in
practice by making no difference to teachers' pay."

[70] See Section 1 above.

[71] For an example of express power to make retrospective legislation see para.1(1)(b) of Sch.2 to the
Human Rights Act 1998 (c.42)—"A remedial order may . . . be made so as to have effect from a
date earlier than that on which it is made"; but note that paragraph 1(4) provides that "No person
is to be guilty of an offence solely as a result of the retrospective effect of a remedial order."

[72] See *Westminster City Council v Haywood (No.2)* [2000] 2 All E.R. 634, Ch.

CHAPTER 11

EXTENT AND APPLICATION

SECTION 1

EXTENT

Extent distinguished from application

It is important at the outset to distinguish between a proposition about the extent **11.1.1**
of a legislative provision and a proposition about the places to which it applies
or in respect of which it has effect.[1] A statement of the extent of a provision is
a statement that it forms part of the law of specified parts of the United Kingdom.
For this purpose there are three parts of the United Kingdom, that is to say that
there are three separate legal jurisdictions which together cover the entirety of the
United Kingdom. They are the law of England and Wales, the law of Scotland
and the law of Northern Ireland.

It should be noted in particular that there is no such thing as the law of England
or the law of Wales; there is a single jurisdiction governed by the law of England
and Wales.[2]

---

[1] See *Lawson v Serco* [2004] 2 All E.R. 200, 203 *per* Pill L.J.—
   "[14] Section 244(1) of the 1996 Act provides: ' . . . this Act extends to England and Wales
   and Scotland but not to Northern Ireland.'
   "[15] We do not accept the submission made by [Counsel], on behalf of the appellants, that
   the territorial limitation in s 244 concludes the present issue. That section defines the area
   within which the enactment is law, the first question, but does not define the persons and
   matters in relation to which the statute operates, the second question. The question to be
   decided is: on what employees does the law of England and Wales confer the right not to be
   unfairly dismissed? The distinction is illustrated by an example given by [Counsel], on behalf
   of the interested party, in a very different context. Section 10(4) of the Sex Offenders Act 1997
   provides that the Act 'extends to England and Wales and Northern Ireland', the first question,
   but s 7(1) provides that certain acts 'done by a person in a country or a territory outside the
   United Kingdom . . . shall constitute [a] sexual offence under the law of [the relevant] part of
   the United Kingdom', the second question."

[2] By way of expounding the reason for this one cannot do better than repeat the following
   impeccable analysis of the Chairman of the House of Commons Standing Committee F on the
   Community Charges (Substitute Setting) (December 18, 1990 c.68)—"Although clause 7 is
   entitled Citation and extent, an amendment to omit Wales from the clause would not, in fact,
   remove Wales from the operation of the Bill. That is because no separate Welsh legal system has
   existed since the Laws in Wales Act 1535 (c.26), which expressly provided that the only laws that
   are to operate in Wales are the 'laws, ordinances and statutes of this realm of England'. The Bill,
   therefore, if and when it is enacted, will apply in Wales even if its effect there is nil. To alter or
   negative its effects in Wales, amendments have to be made to the substantive clauses of the text.
   That is why amendments Nos.37 to 44 have been tabled and why I can select them. However,
   amendment No. 36 cannot be called for the reasons I have given previously."

A proposition that a provision extends to Wales is therefore meaningless. But a proposition that a provision applies only to persons in Wales, or things done in Wales, or premises in Wales, is perfectly reasonable, and indeed commonly found.[3] In the case of a provision of that kind, "England" and "Wales" are being used as geographical concepts not as references to legal jurisdictions.[4]

Note also that a proposition of the kind found in s.90 of the Railways and Transport Safety Act 2003[5]—which applies certain criminal offences in relation to mariners under the influence of drugs or alcohol to things done on ships registered in the United Kingdom wherever in the world they happen to be—has international application, but extends only to the United Kingdom.

The general rule

11.1.2 There is a presumption, which provides a serviceable starting point in considering the extent of an Act, to the effect that Acts passed by the Parliament of the United Kingdom are intended to extend to the whole of the United Kingdom but to no other place.[6] So if an Act is silent as to extent[7] it should be taken to apply to the whole of the United Kingdom and no further.

In the case of old Acts it may be necessary to consider whether the Westminster Parliament had at the relevant time power to legislate for Scotland or Northern Ireland. This is no longer a matter of frequent practical significance. The Westminster Parliament has had power to legislate for Scotland since the Union with Scotland Act 1706[8] and to legislate for

---

[3] See, for example, s.138 of the Education Act 2002 (c.32) which makes one kind of provision for institutions in England and another for institutions in Wales.

[4] As to the definition of England and of Wales, see Sch.1 to the Interpretation Act 1978 (c.30).

[5] 2003 c.20—
    "91 Territorial application
      (1) This Part shall have effect in relation to—
        (a) United Kingdom ships,
        (b) foreign ships in United Kingdom waters, and
        (c) un-registered ships in United Kingdom waters.
      (2) Section 86 shall not extend to Scotland.
      (3) Subsection (2) does not affect any rule of law or enactment concerning the right of a constable in Scotland to board a ship or enter any place for any purpose."

[6] *R. v Jameson* [1896] 2 Q.B. 425, 430, QBD, DC; *Attorney General for Alberta v Huggard Assets Ltd.* [1953] A.C. 420, 441, PC.

[7] There is a convention, not always applied, that a statute that extends to Northern Ireland will say so. That statement of extent is not strictly necessary because of the general presumption of United Kingdom extent. That explains why those draftsmen who still routinely use the legislative "shall" in making law may say "This Act extends to Northern Ireland", the proposition being one of convention and not of law, but "This Act shall not extend to Northern Ireland" (rather than merely "this Act does not extend to Northern Ireland), that being a proposition of law in the sense that it achieves that which would not otherwise be the case.

[8] 1706 c.11: "An Act for an Union of the Two Kingdoms of England and Scotland" (long title) the preamble of which recites the articles of union agreed between commissioners for England and for Scotland, Article III of which reads "That the United Kingdom of Great Britain be represented by one and the same Parliament to be stiled the Parliament of Great Britain."

(originally) Ireland or (latterly) Northern Ireland since the Union with Ireland Act 1800.[9]

Despite the general rule presuming extent to the whole of the United Kingdom in the event of silence, it is common for an Act to state expressly—although strictly unnecessarily—that it extends to Northern Ireland. The practice is thought to be for the convenience of lawyers in Northern Ireland, enabling them to find relatively easily those statutes that apply to them.[10]

In Acts that have complicated extent provisions it is sometimes thought helpful to the reader to give the complete picture by providing expressly—although strictly unnecessarily—for certain provisions to extend to England and Wales, Scotland and Northern Ireland.[11]

Extent outside United Kingdom

The United Kingdom Parliament is able to make legislation for a number of countries and territories outside the United Kingdom. But there will be no presumption of extent outside the United Kingdom and only clear words will suffice to effect it.[12] **11.1.3**

The most common procedure is for an Act to enable the Queen by Order in Council to direct that some or all of the Act's provisions are to extend, with or without modifications, outside the United Kingdom.[13]

It is rare but not unheard of for an Act of the United Kingdom Parliament to extend directly to places outside the United Kingdom. Large parts of the Nationality Act 1981[14] extend to the Channel Islands, the Isle of Man and a

---

[9] 1800 c.67: "An Act for the Union of Great Britain and Ireland" (long title) which recites the agreement between the Parliaments of Great Britain and of Ireland, the Third Article of which is "that the said United Kingdom be represented in one and the same Parliament, to be stiled the Parliament of the United Kingdom of Great Britain and Ireland". As of April 18, 1949 the Republic of Ireland has ceased to be part of Her Majesty's dominions—see s.1 of the Ireland Act 1949 (c.41).

[10] In the practice of some draftsmen the distinction between this statement of mere clarification but without legal effect and a statement having legal effect such as the exclusion of extent in relation to Northern Ireland is attended by a distinction of language: "This Act extends . . . " being used for the first proposition, with the legislative "shall" being reserved for the second proposition "This Act shall not extend . . . "—compare, for example, s.28(2) of the Commonwealth Development Corporation Act 1999 (c.20) and s.46(3) of the Employment Relations Act 1999 (c.26).

[11] See, for example, s.163(3) of the Nationality, Immigration and Asylum Act 2002 (c.41)—"A provision of this Act to which neither subs.(1) nor subs.(2) applies extends to—(a) England and Wales, (b) Scotland, and (c) Northern Ireland."

[12] The reason for this being quite simply, as put by Lord Davey in *New Zealand Loans and Mercantile Agency Co. v Christina* Morrison [1898] A.C. 349, 357 PC—"The Colonies possess and have exercised the power of legislating on these subjects for themselves, and there is every reason why legislation of the United Kingdom should not unnecessarily be held to extend to the Colonies and thereby overrule, qualify, or add to their own legislation on the same subject".

[13] The Channel Islands and the Isle of Man are the most frequently mentioned as places to which an Act can be applied by Order in Council. But a provision of this kind sometimes mentions other places as well: s.422 of the Insolvency Act 1986 (c.45), for example, enables application to "any colony".

[14] 1981 c.61.

number of listed overseas territories in accordance with express provision in s.53. Some statutes extend to some but not others of these places.[15] And the European Parliament (Representation) Act 2003[16] extends directly to Gibraltar.[17] The starting point, however, is a strong presumption that Parliament legislates only for the United Kingdom. The Isle of Man and other territories outside the United Kingdom have their own legislatures and, at least in domestic matters, generally make their own laws. For this reason, where Parliament does wish to legislate for the Isle of Man or others of the British Islands, it must make its intention clear beyond doubt.

11.1.4 An Act passed to have effect for a country outside the United Kingdom will generally be preceded by a recital that the legislature of the country has requested that provision be made for it.[18] As a matter of law, however, the doctrine of the sovereign supremacy of Parliament[19] enables Parliament to purport to legislate for any country and in any circumstances, with consent or without it, and while the courts and administrations of another country might well be disposed and able to ignore the enactment, the courts of this country would be bound to give it such effect as they were able to give. The situation is explained, as it had effect in relation to arguments about the validity of the Canada Act 1981 (c.11) by Sir Robert Megarry V.-C. in *Manuel v Attorney-General*[20] in the following terms—

> "It matters not if a convention had grown up that the United Kingdom Parliament would not legislate for that colony without the consent of the colony. Such a convention would not limit the powers of Parliament, and if Parliament legislated in breach of the convention, the courts could not hold the Act of Parliament invalid. . . . Similarly if the other country is a foreign state which has never been British, I do not think that any English court would or could declare the Act ultra vires and void. No doubt the Act would normally be ignored by the foreign state and would not be enforced by it, but that would not invalidate the Act in this country. Those who infringed it could not claim that it was void if proceedings within the jurisdiction were taken against them. Legal validity is one thing, enforceability is another. Thus a marriage in Nevada may constitute statutory bigamy punishable in

---

[15] For example, ss.6 and 7 of the Copyright, etc and Trade Marks (Offences and Enforcement) Act 2002 (c.25) extend to the Isle of Man but not to the Channel Islands.

[16] 2003 c.7.

[17] S.28(2); note also that legislation can be made directly for Gibraltar by Prerogative Order in Council—see Chapter 3, Section 2, footnote 22.

[18] See, for example, the Canada Act 1982 (c.11) (the preamble of which recites the fact that Parliament is legislating for Canada with the consent of and at the request of the Canadian legislatures).

[19] See Chapter 2, Sections 1 and 2.

[20] [1983] Ch. 77, 86–87, CA.

England,[21] just as acts in Germany may be punishable here as statutory treason.[22] Parliament in fact legislates only for British subjects in this way; but if it also legislated for others, I do not see how the English courts could hold the statute void, however impossible it was to enforce it, and no matter how strong the diplomatic protests.

"I do not think that countries which were once colonies but have since been granted independence are in any different position. Plainly once statute has granted independence to a country, the repeal of the statute will not make the country dependent once more; what is done is done, and is not undone by revoking the authority to do it. Heligoland did not in 1953 again become British. But if Parliament then passes an Act applying to such a country, I cannot see why that Act should not be in the some position as an Act applying to what has always been a foreign country, namely, an Act which the English courts will recognise and apply but one which the other country will in all probability ignore."

An Act may have to be promulgated in some manner before becoming law **11.1.5** outside the United Kingdom.[23]

It is common for Acts effecting or having effect in relation to the independence of former colonies or dependencies to assert the termination of the power of the Westminster Parliament to legislate for the country in question.[24] In accordance with the doctrine of the sovereign supremacy of Parliament, however, such a disclaimer cannot bind a future Parliament from attempting, with the freedom but subject to the constraints enunciated by Sir Robert Megarry above, to legislate again for any country.

For an example of legislation passed in relation to colonies of the United Kingdom see the South Africa Act 1909.[25]

---

[21] *Trial of Earl Russell* [1901] A.C. 446.

[22] *Joyce v Director of Public Prosecutions* [1946] A.C. 347.

[23] See, for example, s.3 of the Foreign Enlistment Act 1870 (c.90)—"This Act . . . shall be proclaimed in every British possession by the governor thereof as soon as may be after he receives notice of this Act, and shall come into operation in that British possession on the day of such proclamation, and the time at which this Act comes into operation in any place is, as respects such place, in this Act referred to as the commencement of this Act." S.2 of the Act provides that "This Act shall extend to all the dominions of Her Majesty, including the adjacent territorial waters." See also *R. v Jameson* [1896] 2 Q.B. 425, QBD, DC.

[24] See, for example, s.1 of the Australia Act 1986 (c.2)—"No Act of the Parliament of the United Kingdom passed after the commencement of this Act shall extend, or be deemed to extend, to the Commonwealth [of Australia], to a State or to a Territory as part of the law of the Commonwealth [of Australia], of the State or of the Territory."; although the Hong Kong Act 1985 (c.15) took a different form and asserted simply (in section 1) that "As from 1st July 1997 Her Majesty shall no longer have sovereignty or jurisdiction over any part of Hong Kong".

[25] 1909 c.9—"Whereas it is desirable for the welfare and future progress of South Africa that the several British Colonies therein should be united under one Government in a legislative union under the Crown of Great Britain and Ireland" (long title).

Scilly Isles

11.1.6   As a matter of law a reference to England will, in the absence of contrary intent, include a reference to the Isles of Scilly.[26] The Scilly Isles are unlike the Isle of Man and the Channel Islands, having neither a legislature nor a separate system of law. But on occasion it will be necessary to treat the Scilly Isles in a slightly different way from the rest of England, in which case this will be achieved expressly.[27]

Isle of Wight

11.1.7   Under the Local Government Act 1972[28] the Isle of Wight is an administrative county of England. At one time it was regarded for administrative purposes as being part of Hampshire, but it has always been part of England.

Caldey Island

11.1.8   Caldey Island forms part of Wales for all legislative purposes.[29] The Caldey Island Act 1990[30] provided for the Island to form part of the then District of South Pembrokeshire.

Parallel texts

11.1.9   In some instances the text of a single provision of an Act varies depending on whether the provision is being applied in relation to England and Wales, Scotland or Northern Ireland. This comes about principally as a result of amendment by a provision which only extends to one or two parts of the United Kingdom, or which makes differential provision. Some examples of this have always been available, but it is inevitably happening more frequently since devolution, because the devolved legislatures as a general rule can legislate only for their

---

[26] Interpretation Act 1978 (c.30), Sch.1.

[27] See, for example, s.344 of the Highways Act 1980 (c.66) which disapplies certain provisions of the Act to the Scilly Isles, provides a mechanism for application by order and makes arrangements for modification of certain provisions of the Act in so far as they apply to Scilly.

[28] 1972 c.70, Sch.1, Pt II.

[29] Wales is defined in the Interpretation Act 1978, Sch.1 (as amended by Sch.2, para.9 to the Local Government (Wales) Act 1994), as "the combined area of the counties which were created by s.20 of the Local Government Act 1972, as originally enacted, but subject to any alteration made under s.73 of that Act (consequential alteration of boundary following alteration of water course)". As Caldey Island was formerly in the County of Dyfed, it falls within the definition of Wales. Note also that the county of Pembrokeshire is defined in Pt 1 of Sch.4 to the Local Government Act 1972 (as substituted) as the districts of Preseli Pembrokeshire and South Pembrokeshire, together with Caldey Island and St Margaret's Island.

[30] 1990 c.44.

territory, although they may do so by amendment of a provision that formerly applied in a single way throughout the United Kingdom.[31]

Parallel texts can, of course, be very confusing for the reader, particularly because many commercial publications ignore aspects of provisions which do not have effect in relation to England and Wales or to the whole of the United Kingdom. There is also a particular trap in parallel texts for the legislator, because the draftsman amending a provision in consequence of something on which he is engaged may well overlook the fact that the provision takes different forms in its extent to different parts of the United Kingdom.

For this reason it is sometimes preferable to have a provision which extends generally but which is limited by its terms so that it expressly applies only in relation to one part of the United Kingdom.[32]

Extent of subordinate legislation

For subordinate legislation the initial presumption is that an instrument is intended to have the same extent as the enactment under which it is made. That can be displaced by express provision limiting the extent. There is, of course, no power for express provision to expand the extent of the instrument beyond that of the enabling enactment. **11.1.10**

But a power that extends to two or more parts of the United Kingdom may, subject to any express or implied limitation of vires, be exercised differently in relation to different parts, and this might be achieved by having different instruments each expressed to extend only to one part of the United Kingdom.

Extent of amending legislation

In the absence of express provision it can be assumed that silence as to the extent of one provision which amends another gives the amendment the same extent as that of the provision amended. **11.1.11**

It is common to find this position provided for expressly in a proposition along the lines that "an amendment made by this Act has the same extent as that of the enactment amended".[33] But a proposition as simple as that will not always produce a clear result where different provisions of the enactment being amended

---

[31] See, for example, s.70(2) of the Salmon and Freshwater Fisheries (Consolidation) (Scotland) Act 2003 (asp 15) (Consequential amendments, repeals and revocations); but note that the effect can be the reverse—so s.12 of the Protection of Children (Scotland) Act 2003 (asp 5) extends to Scotland certain amendments of the Police Act 1997 (c.50) that had previously not extended there.

[32] See, for example, the insertion of s.3(4A) of the Fire Services Act 1947 (c.41) by s.2 of the Marine Safety Act 2003 (c.16). For the most part, amendments made by Act of the Scottish Parliament appear to adopt this approach.

[33] See, for example, s.128(3) of the Anti-terrorism, Crime and Security Act 2001 (c.24)—

"(3) Except as provided in subsections (1) and (2), an amendment, repeal or revocation in this Act has the same extent as the enactment amended, repealed or revoked."

have different extent. Hence the modified proposition found[34] sometimes that an enactment has the same extent as the enactment or relevant part of the enactment being amended. Even this is not necessarily the end of what can be a serious trap for the draftsman: even the modified proposition would not produce a clear result in the case, for example, of provision A which inserts provision B into an earlier Act between provisions C and D, one of which extends to the whole of the United Kingdom and the other of which extends only to England and Wales.

SECTION 2

PERSONAL APPLICATION

Introduction

11.2.1 The question as to which persons a legislative proposition applies has become rapidly and considerably more complicated as the development of electronic and other technologies has increased the possibilities of actions being automated to different degrees and spread over a number of territories in a number of different ways.

A person may sit in front of a computer screen in London and send an electronic signal to a machine situated in the United States of America as a result of which a computer in France sends a message to a bank in Switzerland, crediting another person with a sum of money. It becomes increasingly difficult to answer the questions of where an action is performed or by whom is it performed, or how many actions are being performed. Traditional concepts require to be applied in an increasingly flexible way.[35]

The bewildering question of where an action is performed is of particular importance in relation to the law of contract, but it is also of fundamental importance in relation to statute law, in determining the range of activities to which a statutory proposition is addressed.

This Section discusses some issues about the persons to whom a legislative proposition applies, bearing in mind both the continued importance of the

---

[34] See, for example, s.121(2) of the Railways and Transport Safety Act 2003 (c.20)—

"(2) An amendment or repeal of an enactment effected by this Act shall have the same extent as the enactment (or the relevant part of the enactment) amended or repealed."

[35] In *Menashe Business Mercantile Ltd v William Hill Organisation Ltd* [2003] 1 W.L.R. 1462, 1471 Aldous L.J. said "If the host computer is situated in Antigua and the terminal computer is in the United Kingdom, it is pertinent to ask who uses the claimed gaming system. The answer must be the punter. Where does he use it? There can be no doubt that he uses his terminal in the united Kingdom and it is not a misuse of language to say that he uses the host computer in the United Kingdom. It is the input to and output of the host computer that is important to the punter and in a real sense the punter uses the host computer in the United Kingdom even though it is situated in Antigua and operates in Antigua. In those circumstances it is not straining the word 'use' to conclude that the United Kingdom punter will use the claimed gaming system in the United Kingdom, even if the host computer is situated in, say, Antigua." In other words, the modern technology has not changed the essential concepts of use, but it has made it more frequently possible for a person to use a thing that is physically located a long way away from him.

408

traditional doctrines and the degree to which their application is tested by recent technological development.

The basic rule

The starting point in determining to whom a legislative proposition is addressed **11.2.2** is that, in the absence of evidence to the contrary, it is addressed to anyone who is within the territory to which the proposition extends. This basic rule can be expressed in the words of Lord Russell of Killowen C.J. in *R. v Jameson*[36]—

> "It may be said generally that the area within which a statute is to operate, and the persons against whom it is to operate, are to be gathered from the language and purview of the particular statute. But there may be suggested some general rules - for instance, if there be nothing which points to a contrary intention, the statute will be taken to apply only to the United Kingdom. But whether it be confined in its operation to the United Kingdom, or whether, as is the case here, it be applied to the whole of the Queen's dominions, it will be taken to apply to all the persons in the United Kingdom or in the Queen's dominions, as the case may be, including foreigners who during their residence there owe temporary allegiance to Her Majesty. And, according to its context, it may be taken to apply to the Queen's subjects everywhere, whether within the Queen's dominions or without. One other general canon of construction is this - that if any construction otherwise be possible, an Act will not be construed as applying to foreigners in respect to acts done by them outside the dominions of the sovereign power enacting. That is a rule based on international law by which one sovereign power is bound to respect the subjects and the rights of all other sovereign powers outside its own territory."

Application to persons abroad and to actions performed abroad

Although application and extent are separate questions, as explained above, the **11.2.3** general presumption is that in the absence of express provision to the contrary an enactment will apply generally to things done and people in the territory to which it extends, and not further.[37]

It is, however, common for Parliament to purport to legislate for the actions of British citizens and others committed abroad, albeit that the ability to enforce the

---

[36] [1896] 2 Q.B. 425, 430, QBD.
[37] See *Clark v Oceanic Contractors Inc* [1983] 2 A.C. 130, 152 *per* Lord Wilberforce and *Lawson v Serco* [2004] 2 All E.R. 200, 204 *per* Pill L.J.

legislation will depend wholly or partly on a person's coming within the jurisdiction of courts within the United Kingdom.[38]

As to foreign persons, it remains true that as Lord Cranworth said in *Jefferys v Boosey*[39]—

> "Prima facie, the legislature of this country must be taken to make laws for its own subjects exclusively."

11.2.4   That requires the immediate qualification that when foreigners come within the jurisdiction of the law of the United Kingdom they are in general bound by it to the same extent as British citizens. The proposition therefore requires the qualifying observations of Lindley M.R. in *Re. A. B. & Co.*[40]—

> "This [the seriousness of the implications of bankruptcy] cannot be overlooked or forgotten when we are dealing with foreigners, who are not subject to our jurisdiction. What authority or right has the Court to alter in this way the status of foreigners who are not subject to our jurisdiction? If Parliament had conferred this power in express words, then, of course, the Court would be bound to exercise it. But the decisions go to this extent, and rightly, I think, in principle, that, unless Parliament has conferred upon the Court that power in language which is unmistakable, the Court is not to assume that Parliament intended to do that which might so seriously affect foreigners who are not resident here, and might give offence to foreign Governments.[41] Unless Parliament has used such plain terms as shew that they really intended us to do that, we ought not to do it."

This doctrine receives further useful qualification from the speech of Lord Porter, also in relation to bankruptcy, in *Theophile v Solicitor-General*[42]—

---

[38] For example, s.91 of the Railways and Transport Safety Act 2003 (c.20) provides for "territorial application" of the provisions about alcohol and drug-related offences in relation to shipping by providing that they shall "have effect in relation to—(a) United Kingdom ships, (b) foreign ships in United Kingdom waters, and (c) un-registered ships in United Kingdom waters"; s.101 of the same Act, which deals with similar provisions in relation to aviation, applies them "in relation to—(a) a function or activity performed or carried out in the United Kingdom, and (b) a flight function performed or flight activity carried out on a United Kingdom aircraft." (meaning any aircraft registered in the United Kingdom, irrespective of where it happens to be at the relevant time). See also Pt II of the Sex Offenders Act 1997 (c.51).

[39] (1854) 4 HLC. 815, 955.

[40] [1900] 1 Q.B. 541, 544–545, CA.

[41] This doctrine remains apposite despite the greater number of modern statutes which purport to apply to things done outside the jurisdiction wholly or partly by persons outside the jurisdiction, because they reflect the greater degree of international cooperation, particularly in economic and criminal matters, as a result of which legislation with extra-territorial effect is either implementing an international agreement of some kind or giving effect to agreements between governments. The notion of unilaterally asserting the will of the Westminster Parliament over persons living abroad and without any particular connection with the United Kingdom remains as dubious as it ever was (and, indeed, in some senses has become more so with the loss of Empire and the diminishing number of jurisdictions prepared to accept direct rule from the United Kingdom).

[42] [1950] A.C. 186, 195, HL.

"It would, [the appellant] says, be contrary to the comity of nations, and to the ordinary construction of Acts of Parliament, to decide that an act committed out of this country by a foreign national domiciled abroad should be held to come within the mischief of the Act.

" . . . If I am right [that on its face the Act applies to foreign persons] an invocation of the comity of nations is irrelevant. If the meaning of an Act of Parliament is ambiguous that doctrine may be prayed in aid, but where an English statute enacts a provision in plain terms no such principle applies. Any foreign nation of which the person affected is a member or with which such person is domiciled is free to disregard the provisions of the English enactment, but the person concerned cannot himself take exception to it, though it may be he will escape from compliance with its terms because he is out of the jurisdiction and cannot be reached by English process."

The presumption that Parliament does not intend to assert extra-territorial jurisdiction is, like other presumptions,[43] rebuttable by clear words or necessary implication. But mere generality of expression will not in this case be sufficient rebuttal. So, for example, Tindal C.J. said in *Thomson v Advocate-General*,[44] in relation to the construction of a provision of the Legacy Duty Act 1805 drafted in terms of "any person"— **11.2.5**

"The very general words of the statutes . . . must of necessity receive some limitation in their application, for they cannot in reason extend to every person everywhere, whether subjects of this kingdom or foreigners, and whether, at the time of their death, domiciled within the realm or abroad. . . . We think such necessary limitation is that the statute does not extend to the will of any person who at his death was domiciled out of Great Britain."[45]

The mere fact that an Act confers rights or duties in general terms will not suffice to suggest that it is intended to apply to activity anywhere in the world provided that there is a connection with the United Kingdom sufficient to found action for enforcement.[46]

---

[43] See Chapter 19.

[44] (1845) 4 H.L.C. 815.

[45] See also *Jefferys v Boosey* (1854) 4 HLC. 815 and *R. v Blane* (1849) 13 Q.B. 769; as to the latter decision, however, see *R. v Bow Road Justice, Ex p. Adedigba* [1968] 2 Q.B. 572, CA.

[46] See *Lawson v Serco* [2004] 2 All E.R. 200, 203 *per* Pill L.J.—

"We start on the basis that it is highly unlikely that Parliament intended to give this statutory right to all employees wherever they worked, subject to being able to serve proceedings on an employer in Great Britain. Far from it being inevitable that the repeal of s 196 produced that result, as found by the EAT, it would be necessary to find the plainest indications in the legislation, without s 196, before it could be concluded that Parliament intended to confer such a wide jurisdiction upon a domestic tribunal."

Justification for application to foreigners

11.2.6 The normal presumption about the circumstances in which legislation will and will not apply to persons other than British citizens is encapsulated in the following dictum of the James L.J.[47]—

> "It appears to me that the whole question is governed by the broad, general, universal principle that English legislation, unless the contrary is expressly enacted or so plainly implied as to make it the duty of an English court to give effect to an English statute, is applicable only to English subjects or to foreigners who by coming into this country, whether for a long or a short time, have made themselves during that time subject to English jurisdiction. Every foreigner who comes into this country, for however limited a time, is, during his residence here within the allegiance of the Sovereign, entitled to the protection of the Sovereign and subject to all the laws of the Sovereign. But, if a foreigner remains abroad, if he has never come into this country at all, it seems to me impossible to imagine that the English Legislature could have ever intended to make such a man subject to particular English legislation."[48]

Presumption of construction

11.2.7 Legislation is generally drafted in very wide terms. It is common to find a proposition relating to "any person" doing a specified action, that on its face purports to apply to any person throughout the world. The express provisions on territorial extent may limit the proposition expressly, but not always. In such a case the courts apply the following presumption—

> "There is a presumption that, in the absence of a contrary intention express or implied, United Kingdom legislation does not apply to foreign persons or corporations outside the United Kingdom whose acts are performed outside the United Kingdom. Some limitation of the general words of section 151 [of the Companies Act 1985[49]] is necessary in order to avoid imputing to Parliament an intention to create an exorbitant jurisdiction which is contrary to generally accepted principles of international law."[50]

Territorial sea

11.2.8 It is often important to know whether a piece of legislation applies to things done in the territorial sea of the United Kingdom.[51]

---

[47] *Ex p. Blain* 12 Ch, D. 522.
[48] Cited with approval by the Earl of Halsbury L.C. in *Cooke v The Charles A. Vogeler Co.* [1901] A.C. 102, HL.
[49] 1985 c.6.
[50] *Arab Bank plc v Merchantile Holdings Ltd* [1994] Ch 71, 82 *per* Millett J.
[51] For the definition of which see the Territorial Sea Act 1987 (c.49).

The first point to note is that extent is not determinative in this respect. An Act can have application outside the United Kingdom without extending (in the sense of being law of a jurisdiction) beyond the United Kingdom.[52]

Nor should undue weight be placed on the fact that a number of Acts mention the territorial sea expressly, so as to lead one to conclude that the absence of mention of the territorial sea results necessarily in a lack of application there. The fact that, for example, s.30 of the Police Act 1996[53] expressly confers powers in relation to the territorial sea does not imply that powers conferred without express reference to the territorial sea will not be available there. Section 30 is concerned to <u>limit</u> the exercise of constables' powers to those parts of the territorial sea of the United Kingdom which are adjacent to England or Wales.

As to whether a reference *simpliciter* to the United Kingdom in a statutory **11.2.9** provision applies the provision to things done in the territorial sea, the question can be determined only in the context of the enactment concerned. There are a number of judicial opinions expressed over the years on the application of particular enactments to the territorial sea, and it is not possible to distil from them either an answer that applies to all circumstances or even a rebuttable presumption.[54]

The result is that Acts in the case of which application to the territorial sea is of the essence, or is likely to be of practical importance, generally express the position,[55] although application could be effected by necessary implication.[56]

In determining whether a particular provision can be relied on as applying to things done in the territorial sea one should therefore start by asking, in the absence of express provision, whether the provision would be wholly or to a great extent nugatory if it did not apply to the territorial sea. If the answer is yes, it will be safe to assume that Parliament intended application there; and if not, not.

---

[52] See, for example, the Petroleum Act 1998 (c.17); and contrast ss.410 and 411 of the Communications Act 2003 (c.21).

[53] 1996 c.16.

[54] Note, in particular, that although much of the doubt relating to criminal offences and jurisdiction to try them created by the case of *The Queen v Keyn (The Franconia)* 1876–77 L.R. Ex. D. II 63 C.C.R. was dispelled by the Territorial Waters Jurisdiction Act 1878 (c.73), that Act left a number of questions unresolved, particularly in civil contexts; see also *Secretary of State for India v Rao* (1916) 32 T.L.R. 652, *Fagernes* [1927] P. 311, *R. v Kent Justices* [1967] 2 Q.B. 153, *Post Office v Estuary Radio Ltd* [1968] 2 Q.B. 740, CA, *R. v Liverpool Justices, Ex p. Molyneux* [1972] 2 Q.B. 384, and *The Earl of Lonsdale v Attorney-General* [1982] 1 W.L.R. 887.

[55] So, for example, s.91 of the Railways and Transport Safety Act 2003 (c.20) details the cases to which the marine offences apply, including things done by foreign and unregistered ships in United Kingdom waters and by United Kingdom ships anywhere in the world (and the question of extent is ignored, leaving United Kingdom extent to be presumed); and the Merchant Shipping Act 1995 (c.21) makes different provision in different contexts, legislating in some places expressly by reference to the territorial sea (through the definition of United Kingdom waters in s.313(2)), in other places by express extra-territorial jurisdiction (see, for example, s.3) and in other places by simple reliance on the notion of British registered ships.

[56] Indeed it is possible for jurisdiction to be inferred even beyond the territorial sea where the context of legislation clearly demands it—see, for example, *R. v Secretary of State for Trade and Industry, Ex p. Greenpeace Ltd* [2000] 2 C.M.L.R. 94.

SECTION 3

HUMAN RIGHTS

Introduction

11.3.1   For decades before the enactment of the Human Rights Act 1998,[57] which incorporated the European Convention on Human Rights[58] into the law of the United Kingdom, the Convention, to which the United Kingdom was a signatory, had a profound influence on legislation. Successive Governments paid considerable attention to the Convention and for the most part purported to frame their legislation in such a way as to comply with it.

The Human Rights Act 1998 formally incorporated the Convention into the law of the United Kingdom, and in relation to legislation did so by creating a number of procedures that can be used to ensure that the Convention rights are protected.

The Act has without a doubt immensely increased the importance of the effect of the Convention in the law of the United Kingdom. Cases in every area of the substantive law now routinely include claims based on a right protected under the Convention.[59] And in some areas of law, notably immigration and asylum, the framework of the law has been adapted to reflect the overwhelming importance of the Convention rights to the daily operation of the law.[60]

11.3.2   It should, however, be noted that while the European Convention is of enormous importance it is "not an exhaustive statement of fundamental rights under our system of law".[61] There are other fundamental rights not protected by the Convention that are protected by law in the United Kingdom. Some of these are protected by rebuttable presumptions of judicial construction of legislation and are addressed in that context in Chapter 19.

The position at common law and the effect of the Act

11.3.3   The rules of the ways in which Acts are and are not taken to have effect on human rights both at common law and under the 1998 Act are expounded in the

---

[57] 1998 c.42.

[58] The European Convention for the Protection of Human Rights and Fundamental Freedoms (Rome, November 4, 1950; TS 71 (1953); Cmd 8969).

[59] Early attempts by the courts to discourage the expansion of the emphasis on relatively trivial claims in relation to the Convention in the context of more serious substantive issues can be seen as having had limited success—see, for example, *Williams v Cowell* [2000] 1 W.L.R. 187, 198, CA, *per* Mummery L.J.

[60] See, for example, the Nationality, Immigration and Asylum Act 2002 (c.41) passim, and note particularly para.3 of Sch.3—"Paragraph 1 does not prevent the exercise of a power or the performance of a duty if, and to the extent that, its exercise or performance is necessary for the purpose of avoiding a breach of—(a) a person's Convention rights, . . . "

[61] *R. (Anufrijeva) v Secretary of State for the Home Department* [2003] 3 W.L.R. 252, 266, HL *per* Lord Steyn.

414

following passage of the speech of Lord Hoffmann in *R. v Secretary of State for the Home Department, Ex p. Simms*[62]—

"Parliamentary sovereignty means that Parliament can, if it chooses, legislate contrary to fundamental principles of human rights. The Human Rights Act 1998 will not detract from this power. The constraints upon its exercise by Parliament are ultimately political, not legal. But the principle of legality means that Parliament must squarely confront what it is doing and accept the political cost. Fundamental rights cannot be overridden by general or ambiguous words. This is because there is too great a risk that the full implications of their unqualified meaning may have passed unnoticed in the democratic process. In the absence of express language or necessary implication to the contrary, the courts therefore presume that even the most general words were intended to be subject to the basic rights of the individual. In this way the courts of the United Kingdom, though acknowledging the sovereignty of Parliament, apply principles of constitutionality little different from those which exist in countries where the power of the legislature is expressly limited by a constitutional document.

"The Human Rights Act 1998 will make three changes to this scheme of things.

"First, the principles of fundamental human rights which exist at common law will be supplemented by a specific text, namely the European Convention for the Protection of Human Rights and Fundamental Freedoms.[63] But much of the convention reflects the common law: see *Derbyshire County Council v Times Newspapers Ltd.*[64] That is why the United Kingdom government felt able in 1950 to accede to the convention without domestic legislative change. So the adoption of the text as part of domestic law is unlikely to involve radical change in our notions of fundamental human rights.

"Secondly, the principle of legality will be expressly enacted as a rule of construction in section 3 and will gain further support from the obligation of the Minister in charge of a Bill to make a statement of compatibility under section 19.

"Thirdly, in those unusual cases in which the legislative infringement of fundamental human rights is so clearly expressed as not to yield to the principle of legality, the courts will be able to draw this to the attention of Parliament by making a declaration of incompatibility. It will then be for the

[62] [1999] 3 All E.R. 400, 411–12, HL; note that this passage was cited with particular approval by Lord Steyn in *R. (Anufrijeva) v Secretary of State for the Home Department* [2003] 3 W.L.R. 252, 265, HL Note also the discussions of this case in relation to the sovereignty of Parliament (Chapter 2, Sections 1 and 2) and in relation to rebuttable presumptions of construction (Chapter 19).
[63] Rome, November 4, 1950; TS 71 (1953); Cmd 8969.
[64] [1993] 1 All E.R. 1011 at 1021, [1993] A.C. 534 at 551.

sovereign Parliament to decide whether or not to remove the incompatibility.

"What this case decides is that the principle of legality applies to subordinate legislation as much as to Acts of Parliament. Prison regulations expressed in general language are also presumed to be subject to fundamental human rights.The presumption enables them to be valid. But, it also means that properly construed, they do not authorise a blanket restriction which would curtail not merely the prisoner's right of free expression, but its use in a way which could provide him with access to justice."

Construction of legislation in accordance with Convention

11.3.4 Section 3 of the Human Rights Act 1998 creates a new rebuttable presumption to be applied in the construction of legislation. This is discussed in some detail in the context of the interpretation of legislation in Chapter 25.

Incompatibility: primary legislation

11.3.5 The doctrine of Parliamentary supremacy[65] makes it undesirable, indeed unconstitutional, for the courts to be placed in a position in which they are required or empowered to annul primary legislation on the grounds of incompatibility with the Convention.[66] But the effect of incorporating the Convention would be nugatory if Parliament were able to enact at will legislation that was incompatible with the Convention.

Section 4 of the 1998 Act[67] therefore provides what is, in effect, a mechanism by which the courts are enabled to bring to the attention of the public that a

---

[65] See above, Chapter 2, Section 1.

[66] It is true that the domestic courts occasionally have to do something tantamount to this in relation to obligations of the European Union—see *Factortame* as discussed above. But that is a result of the elaborate structure of the Union and, in particular, the relationship established in the Treaties between the domestic courts and the European Court of Justice. And the notion of Parliamentary supremacy is preserved in the thought that it is open to Parliament to resile from the propositions in the European Communities Act 1972 (c.68) that give supremacy to the law of the Communities.

[67] The full text of section 4 is as follows—

"4 Declaration of incompatibility

(1) Subsection (2) applies in any proceedings in which a court determines whether a provision of primary legislation is compatible with a Convention right.

(2) If the court is satisfied that the provision is incompatible with a Convention right, it may make a declaration of that incompatibility.

(3) Subsection (4) applies in any proceedings in which a court determines whether a provision of subordinate legislation, made in the exercise of a power conferred by primary legislation, is compatible with a Convention right.

(4) If the court is satisfied—

    (a) that the provision is incompatible with a Convention right, and

    (b) that (disregarding any possibility of revocation) the primary legislationconcerned prevents removal of the incompatibility,

it may make a declaration of that incompatibility.

(5) In this section "court" means—

    (a) the House of Lords;

provision of primary legislation is incompatible with a Convention right. The courts do this by making a declaration of incompatibility.[68]

A declaration under s.4 of the 1998 Act has no legal effect in the sense of affecting the validity of the legislation to which it refers, nor does it itself confer any right or obligation on the parties to the proceedings in which it is made.[69] But it triggers a power for the executive to take remedial action[70] and it would, presumably, be of considerable importance in proceedings either before the courts of the United Kingdom brought in reliance on s.7 of the 1998 Act or before a relevant international court or tribunal.

It is only the more senior courts that are able to issue a declaration of incompatibility. These are the High Court, the Court of Session,[71] the Courts-Martial Appeal Court, the Court of Appeal, the Privy Council and the House of Lords.[72] **11.3.6**

The principles applying to the making of a declaration of incompatibility and difficulties that can arise are illustrated by the following passage of the judgment of Stanley Burnton J. in *R. (D.) v Secretary of State for the Home Department*[73]—

> "A declaration of incompatibility is a last resort. Section 3 of the Human Rights Act requires legislation to be read and given effect to in a way that is compatible with Convention rights if it is possible to do so. The interesting and difficult question that raises in the present case concerns the degree of imperative imposed by section 3 and the matters to be taken into

---

      (b) the Judicial Committee of the Privy Council;

      (c) the Courts-Martial Appeal Court;

      (d) in Scotland, the High Court of Justiciary sitting otherwise than as a trial court or the Court of Session;

      (e) in England and Wales or Northern Ireland, the High Court or the Court of Appeal.

   (6) A declaration under this section ("a declaration of incompatibility")—

      (a) does not affect the validity, continuing operation or enforcement of the provision in respect of which it is given; and

      (b) is not binding on the parties to the proceedings in which it is made."

[68] For examples of declarations of incompatibility see: the declaration in *R. (Uttley) v Secretary of State for the Home Department* [2003] 4 All E.R. 891, CA—"A Declaration pursuant to s.4(2) of the Human Rights Acts 1998 that s.33(2) s.37(4)(a) and s.39 of the Criminal Justice Act 1991 is incompatible with the Claimant's rights under Art.7 of the European Convention for the Protection of Human Rights and Fundamental Freedoms in so far as it provides that he will be released at the two-thirds point of his sentence 'on licence with conditions and be liable to be recalled to prison' (he having committed the index offences before the Criminal Justice Act 1991 came into force, and at a time when he would have expected (subject to good behaviour) to be released at the two-thirds point of any sentence unconditionally, pursuant to the practice that had developed in implementing rule 5 of the Prison Rules 1964, SI 1964/388)."; and note that a declaration was made by the Court of Appeal in *Wilson v First County Trust Ltd* [2001] 3 All E.R. 229, CA but overturned by the House of Lords [2003] 3 W.L.R. 568, HL.

[69] s.4(6)(a) and (b).

[70] See below.

[71] Or the High Court of Justiciary when not sitting as a trial court—s.4(5)(d).

[72] s.4(5).

[73] [2003] 1 W.L.R. 1315, 1327, QBD.

account by the court in deciding whether a compatible interpretation of legislation is 'possible'. Clearly, in a sense a compatible interpretation is possible: the court could simply declare that *H's* case is, by reason of section 3, no longer good law. But the decision in *H's* case continues to make good sense in the vast majority of cases . . . It seems to me than in deciding whether an alternative interpretation of legislation is 'possible', the court must take account of the practical and negative consequences of that alternative interpretation. In these circumstances, I do not think that section 3 requires me to hold that *H's* case is now wholly abrogated. An alternative course would be to restrict the decision in *H's* case to lifers in respect of whom a mental health review tribunal has not expressed the opinion that their detention under the 1983 Act is no longer necessary. However, in my judgment to do so would involve judicial legislation, a re-writing of the statutory provisions, rather than an exercise in interpretation; and section 3 does not permit judicial legislation: see Lord Hope of Craighead in *R. v A. (No. 2)*[74]; *Poplar Housing and Regeneration Community Association Ltd. v Donoghue.*[75] . . . It seems to me that the resolution of these matters is for the legislature rather than the court. My conclusion, therefore, is that it is not possible to interpret the relevant legislation so as to avoid incompatibility with article 5."

Incompatibility: subordinate legislation

11.3.7 In relation to subordinate legislation it will in general be possible for the courts to do more than issue a declaration of incompatibility.[76] The normal way of approaching an allegation of incompatibility of subordinate legislation is to treat its making as an instance of action by a public authority that is incompatible with the Convention, which is made unlawful by s.6 of the 1998 Act.

Section 6 of the Act makes it "unlawful for a public authority to act in a way which is incompatible with a Convention right".[77] That includes the making of delegated legislation that breaches a person's Convention rights, or doing anything, under primary or delegated legislation, that breaches a person's Convention rights.[78]

Section 7 provides a right of action for a person adversely affected by action taken in breach of s.6, which would include the making if incompatible delegated legislation.

---

[74] [2002] 1 A.C. 45, 86–87.

[75] [2002] Q.B. 48, 72.

[76] The exception is where the legislation is made under a provision of primary legislation which "prevents removal of the incompatibility" (s.4(4)(b)): in such a case a procedure for declaration of incompatibility, of the same nature as is available for primary legislation, is provided by s.4(3) and (4).

[77] s.6(1).

[78] An express exception is made in s.6(1) for action which, one way or another, is unavoidably required by a provision of primary legislation.

A person aggrieved by delegated legislation on the grounds that it contravened his Convention rights could therefore challenge it, perhaps by way of proceedings for judicial review. Or the aggrieved person could choose simply to proceed in disregard of the legislation and, if civil or criminal proceedings were brought against him on that account, challenge the proceedings wholly or partly by reference to the illegality of the delegated legislation as contravening s.6 of the 1998 Act.[79]

Failure to legislate

A failure to introduce primary legislation that would have protected a person's **11.3.8** Convention rights is not actionable under the Human Rights Act 1998.[80] But where a power to make delegated legislation is vested in the executive and a Minister determines not to exercise that power, the failure could constitute an actionable breach of s.6.[81]

Remedial action

The Human Rights Act 1998 confers powers to amend legislation by order[82] for **11.3.9** the purpose of removing incompatibility with the Convention. For discussion of remedial orders see Chapter 3, Section 11.

Limitation of legislation by reference to Convention

It will sometimes be debatable whether a proposal for new legislation complies **11.3.10** with the Convention or not. Obviously, it is for the Government to take a view, acting on the legal advice available to them, about whether proposed legislation is compatible with the Convention, and they will not generally proceed with it if not satisfied as to compatibility. But there may be cases in which it is right to limit the doubt by including in legislation an express proposition to the effect that it is to have effect only in so far as is consistent with the Convention.

An early example of this is para.3 of Sch.2 to the Nationality, Immigration and Asylum Act 2002.[83] Paragraph 1 of the Schedule provides for the withdrawal of support from certain persons in certain immigration-related circumstances. Paragraph 3 qualifies the position as follows—

"3. Paragraph 1 does not prevent the exercise of a power or the performance of a duty if, and to the extent that, its exercise or performance is necessary for the purpose of avoiding a breach of—

[79] s.7(1)(b).
[80] s.6(6)(a).
[81] s.6(6).
[82] Or, in the case of legislation originally made by Order in Council, by Order in Council (s.10(5)).
[83] 2002 c.41.

(a) a person's Convention rights, or

(b) a person's rights under the Community Treaties."

Statements of compliance or non-compliance

11.3.11 Section 19 of the Human Rights Act 1998 requires the Government when proposing legislation to Parliament to certify the compatibility of the legislation with the Convention. The precise requirement is for the Minister in charge of a Bill in either House to state, before the second reading of the Bill, either—

(1) that in his view the provisions of the Bill are compatible with the Convention rights,[84] or

(2) that he is unable to make a statement of compatibility but that the government "nevertheless wishes the House to proceed with the Bill".[85]

There are no particular statutory requirements as to publication, beyond a general duty to publish. The practice that has developed, however, is for the cover-sheet to the first version of the Bill printed in each House to state that a specified Minister of the Crown has made one or other of the two possible kinds of statement under s.19 of the 1998 Act in relation to the Bill. In theory, if the statement were not available at the time when the Bill was introduced there is no reason why it could not be made and promulgated in some other manner before second reading.[86]

A Government Bill will therefore be certified for compatibility once on introduction into the first House and once when it is passed by the first House to the second. The obvious need for the second statement is to address amendments made to the Bill during its passage through the first House. There is no formal certification required in relation to amendments in the second House—in particular, there is no requirement to certify anything in respect of the Act as it receives Royal Assent.[87] But a Minister proposing an amendment to a Bill might consider it helpful to offer observations about its compatibility. And the Joint Committee on Human Rights[88] could take an interest, and conceivably report

---

[84] A s.19(1)(a) statement.

[85] A s.19(1)(b) statement.

[86] A Written Ministerial Statement in either House (the recent innovation to replace the old form of "planted" Written Question) would seem to be obviously acceptable methods.

[87] This contrasts with the non-statutory practice for Explanatory Notes, which are printed at the beginning of the Bill's life in each House and then on publication of the Act following Royal Assent.

[88] This is the committee of both Houses of Parliament established in the Session 2000–01 with the remit "to consider—(a) matters relating to human rights in the United Kingdom (but excluding consideration of individual cases), (b) proposals for remedial orders, draft remedial orders and remedial orders made under section 10 of and laid under Schedule 2 to the Human Rights Act 1998, and (c) in respect of draft remedial orders and remedial orders, whether the special attention of the House should be drawn to them on any of the grounds specified in Standing Order 73 (Joint Committee on Statutory Instruments)".

about, an amendment, whether on referral from an interested Member or peer or of its own motion.

Almost every Government Bill has since the commencement of s.19 of the 1998 Act been certified as compatible with the Convention.[89] **11.3.12**

A private Member's or private peer's Bill does not require a s.19 statement as a matter of law. But in the case of a Bill the policy of which is supported by the Government and in connection with which the Government have provided significant assistance it is now routine for Explanatory Notes to be produced by the relevant Department and published with the consent of the Member or peer in charge. Those notes generally include observations on the compatibility of the Bill with the Convention.

There is no formal procedure laid down by the 1998 Act for the certification of the compatibility of subordinate legislation with the Convention. But the Explanatory Note that is routinely appended to each statutory instrument could be used to advert to a question of the application of a Convention right, and in the case of an instrument laid before Parliament it would be possible to arrange for a statement of compatibility, or indeed incompatibility, to be made were it thought appropriate.[90]

Apart from the requirement for a statement of compatibility, the Explanatory Notes to a Bill can address human rights issues.[91]

Proportionality

In a number of instances the protection afforded by the Convention in relation to particular rights is not absolute, but is qualified so as to permit interference with a right where justified by reference to public interest of one kind or another.[92] Interference by the state with a qualified right is often effected by legislation, and it will be justifiable only if it can be shown to interfere with the right as little is as required for the purpose of protecting the public interest. **11.3.13**

The result of this is that legislation frequently contains limitations designed to limit interference with protected human rights to the minimum necessary to achieve the public policy underlying the legislation.

---

[89] Exceptions are the Local Government Bill 1999–00 (as to which see Point of Order, HC Deb. April 11, 2000 cc.197–198 and Second Reading debate HC Deb. April 11, 2000 c.214); and the Communications Bill 2002–03.

[90] The obvious route would again be a Written Ministerial Statement in either House of Parliament.

[91] For a discussion of the role that ought to be played by explanatory notes in this respect, see Chapter 9, Section 5.

[92] The right to respect for private and family life under Art.8 of the Convention, for example, is subject to provision permitting interference in so far as "necessary in a democratic society in the interests of national security, public safety or the economic well-being of the country, for the prevention of disorder or crime, for the protection of health or morals, or for the protection of the rights and freedoms of others". And the right to peaceful enjoyment of possessions under Art.1 to the First Protocol to the Convention (agreed at Paris on March 20, 1952) is qualified so as to preserve the right of the state to enforce laws "to control the use of property in accordance with the general interest".

A clear example is the case of rights of entry. Many enactments permit public servants of different kinds to enter private property, most frequently for the purpose of enforcing the law. These powers are generally crafted in such a way as to interfere with privacy as little as is necessary. In particular, it is common to exclude private dwelling-houses from a right of entry.[93] And sometimes a warrant is required[94] in order to ensure that the right is not used indiscriminately.

Derogation

11.3.14 The system of the European Convention on Human Rights makes allowance for the possibility that not every signatory state will feel able to secure total compliance with every aspect of the Convention all the time. In the United Kingdom's case there are some long-term reservations and derogations which have effect by virtue of and in accordance with ss.14 to 17 of the 1998 Act.

In cases of emergency, moreover, the United Kingdom may make a specific derogation from the Convention for the purpose of rendering lawful a piece of legislation that would otherwise be unlawful for incompatibility. This occurred in connection with ss.21 to 23 of the Anti-terrorism, Crime and Security Act 2002.[95]

SECTION 4

LEGISLATION CAUSING DAMAGE OR LOSS

Introduction

11.4.1 It will frequently happen that legislation, even where it is of a public general character and not aimed at a particular group or locality, will cause, particularly at its inception, loss or damage of some kind to a particular group of people. The question arises of what is to be done by way of compensating those people.

No inherent right to compensation

11.4.2 As a product of the principle of the supremacy of Parliament, no person has a right to demand compensation for something done by or under the authority of statute.[96]

---

[93] See, for example, s.2(1)(b) of the Armed Forces Act 2001 (c.19) (powers to stop and search persons, vehicles, &c.). Conversely, when the intention is to permit entry to a dwelling express power will normally be conferred—see, for example, s.8(1)(b) of the Railways and Transport Safety Act 2003 (c.20) (investigator's powers).

[94] See, for example, Sch.5 to the Terrorism Act 2000 (c.11) (terrorist investigations: information).

[95] 2002 c.24; the text of the derogation is set out in the Sch. to the Human Rights Act 1998 (Designated Derogation) Order 2001 (SI 2001/3644). That order designates the proposed derogation for the purposes of the 1998 Act.

[96] The principles of the procedure for private and hybrid legislation, discussed in Chapter 5, Section 4, are designed to ensure that this rule does not cause injustice, in effect requiring Parliament to consider the position of individuals who might be particularly affected before passing the legislation concerned.

The position is well illustrated by a combination of the following judicial pronouncements.

(1)

"Some things I think are no longer open to discussion. No action can be maintained for anything which is done under the authority of the legislature, though the Act is one which, if unauthorised by the legislature, would be injurious and actionable. The remedy of the party who suffers the loss is confined to recovering such compensation as the legislature has thought fit to give him (see *Hammersmith Railway v Brand*.[97] The Lands and Railways Clauses Acts of 1845 give some compensation . . . And it must now be considered settled that on the construction of those Acts, compensation is confined to damage arising from that which would, if done without authority from the legislature, have given rise to a cause of action."[98]

(2)

"Where the legislature directs that a thing shall at all events be done, the doing of which, if not authorised by the legislature, would give a right of action or suit to persons affected by the act or omission, the right of action is taken away. The legislature has very often interfered with the rights of private persons but in modern times it has generally given compensation to those injured; and if no compensation is given, it affords a reason, though not an exclusive one, for thinking that the intention of the legislature was, not that the thing should be done at all events, but only that it should be done, if it could be done, without injury to others. What was the intention of the legislature in any particular Act is a question of the construction of the Act."[99]

(3)

"30. A statute which authorises the construction of works like a reservoir, involving risk to others, may deal expressly with the liability of the undertakers.It may provide that they are to be strictly liable, liable only for negligence or not liable at all. But what if it contains no express provision? If the principle of *Rylands v Fletcher* is that costs should be internalised, the undertakers should be liable in the same way as private entrepreneurs.The fact that Parliament considered the construction and operation of the works to be in the public interest should make no difference. As Bramwell B. repeatedly explained, the risk should be borne by the public and not by the individual who happens to have been injured. But within a year of the decision of the House of Lords in *Rylands v Fletcher*, Blackburn J. advised the House that, in the absence of negligence, damage caused by operations

11.4.3

---

[97] (1869) 4 HL 171.

[98] Lord Blackburn in *Caledonian Railway v Walker's Trustees* (1882) 7 App. Cas.259, 293. Cited by Tucker L.J. in *Marriage v East Norfolk Rivers Catchment Board* [1950] 1 K.B. 284, 292–293.

[99] Lord Blackburn in *Metropolitan Asylums Board v Hill* (1881) 6 App. Cas.193, 203. Cited by Tucker L.J. in *Marriage v East Norfolk Rivers Catchment Board* [1950] 1 K.B. 284, 292–293.

authorised by statute is not compensatable unless the statute expressly so provides: see *Hammersmith and City Railway Co v Brand.*[1] The default position is that the owner of land injured by the operations "suffers a private loss for the public benefit". In *Geddis v Proprietors of Bann Reservoir*[2] Lord Blackburn summed up the law:

'It is now thoroughly well established that no action will lie for doing that which the legislature has authorised, if it be done without negligence, although it does occasion damage to anyone.'

"31. The effect of this principle was to exclude the application of the rule in *Rylands v Fletcher* to works constructed or conducted under statutory authority: see *Green v Chelsea Waterworks Co*[3]; *Dunne v North Western Gas Board.*[4]"[5]

(4)

"It is now well settled that where Parliament by express direction or by necessary implication has authorised the construction and use of an undertaking or works, that carries with it an authority to do what is authorised with immunity from any action based on nuisance."[6]

(5)

"When the legislature has sanctioned and authorised the use of a particular thing and it is used for the purpose for which it is authorised, and every precaution has been observed to prevent injury, the sanction of the legislature carries with it the consequence that if damage results from the use of such thing independent of negligence the party using it is not responsible."[7]

Incidental damage

11.4.4   Despite the position established above, that damage authorised by statute is not actionable, where a person is authorised by legislation to create what would otherwise amount to an actionable nuisance he is bound without any express enactment to do anything reasonably practicable to mitigate the nuisance and to diminish the annoyance.[8]

---

[1] (1869) L.R. 4 H.L. 171, 196.

[2] (1878) 3 App. Cas.430, 455.

[3] (1894) 70 L.T. 547.

[4] [1964] 2 Q.B. 806.

[5] *Transco plc (formerly BG plc and BG Transco plc) v Stockport Metropolitan Borough Council* [2003] 3 W.L.R. 1467 HL, *per* Lord Hoffmann.

[6] *Allen v Gulf Oil Refining Ltd* [1981] 1 All E.R. 353, 356, HL *per* Lord Wilberforce.

[7] *Vaughan v Taff Vale Railway* (1860) 5 H. & N. 679, 685. See also *R. v Pease* (1832) 4 B. & Ad. 30, *L.B. & S.C. Railway v Truman* (1885) 11 App. Cas. 45, 50n., *Cowper Essex v Acton L.B.* (1889) 14 App. Cas.153, *Municipality of Raleigh v Williams* [1893] A.C. 540, *Canadian Pacific Railway v Parke* [1889] A.C. 535 and *Shea v Reid-Newfoundland Railway* [1908] A.C. 520.

[8] See *Wilson v Delta Corporation* [1913] A.C. 181, 187 *per* Lord Moulton.

In *R. v Kerrison*[9] commissioners were authorised by statute to make a river navigable and to interfere with private rights for that purpose. Under this power they cut through a highway, rendering it impassable and making it necessary to build a bridge over the cut. The court found that the commissioners were liable to maintain the bridge.

> "The legislature intended that, so far as regards making the river navigable and cutting new channels for that purpose, neither public nor private rights should stand in their way; but still they must make good to the public in another shape the means of passage over such ways as they were empowered to cut through."[10]

Human rights

The incorporation into the law of the United Kingdom of the European **11.4.5** Convention on Human Rights significantly constrains the power described in the dictum of Lord Blackburn cited above. In particular, Art.1 of the First Protocol to the Convention provides as follows—

> "Every natural or legal person is entitled to the peaceful enjoyment of his possessions.No one shall be deprived of his possessions except in the public interest and subject to the conditions provided for by law and by the general principles of international law.

> "The preceding provisions shall not, however, in any way impair the right of a State to enforce such laws as it deems necessary to control the use of property in accordance with the general interest or to secure the payment of taxes or other contributions or penalties."

It is therefore necessary for the Government to ensure compliance with the European Convention both by justifying expropriation of property, or interference with the use of property, by reference to public policy and also, in at least some cases, by making appropriate arrangements for compensation.

Breach of right under European Community Treaties

There is a special case in which loss or damage caused by legislation is **11.4.6** actionable: the case where legislation produces a result which is contrary to the law of the European Communities. This is dealt with in Pt 5.[11]

Although this can be presented as a new constraint on the breadth of statute law and therefore on the supremacy of Parliament, it is of course itself dependant

---

[9] (1815) 3 M. & S. 526.
[10] *Per* Lord Ellenborough.
[11] Chapter 32, Section 4.

on statute for its effect, since the courts in giving effect to the European law in this respect are acting in accordance with s.2(1) of the European Communities Act 1972.[12] If Parliament were to repeal that Act and require the courts to ignore European law henceforth, the breach of European law would no longer be actionable in the courts of the United Kingdom.

Statutory compensation

11.4.7   Where legislation interferes with private property rights the question arises as to what compensation, if any, should be given to those whose interests are harmed by the effect of the legislation.

In relation to the compulsory purchase of a person's real property provision is routinely made for the assessment of compensation.[13] The compensation will fall to be paid as part of the expenses of the scheme of which the compulsory purchase forms part, which may be a scheme effected by public general Act,[14] by local Act[15] or by a Transport and Works Order.[16]

In certain other cases where Parliament has legislated so as to render unlawful the possession or use of certain kinds of property there has been express provision for compensation out of public funds.

11.4.8   For example, the Firearms Act 1997[17] made it unlawful to possess certain kinds of gun. Section 15(1) of the Act empowered the Secretary of State to make arrangements "to secure the orderly surrender at designated police stations of firearms or ammunition the possession of which will become or has become unlawful by virtue of section 1 or 9" of the Act. Section 16(1) then provided as follows—

> "The Secretary of State shall, in accordance with a scheme made by him, make payments in respect of firearms and ammunition surrendered at designated police stations in accordance with the arrangements made by him under section 15 above."

Section 17 of the 1997 Act also permitted compensatory payments in respect of certain ancillary equipment designed for use with the newly prohibited weapons.

See also s.1(3) of the Dangerous Dogs Act 1991[18] or s.5 of the Fur Farming (Prohibition) Act 2000.[19]

11.4.9   In some cases the legislature determines not to compensate those whose private interests would be harmed by new legislation but to provide a transitional

---

[12] 1972 c.68; see further Chapter 3, Section 10.

[13] See also the provision of a general kind made by the Compulsory Purchase Act 1965 (c.56).

[14] See Chapter 2, Section 2.

[15] See Chapter 1, Section 3.

[16] See Chapter 3, Section 8.

[17] 1997 c.5.

[18] 1991 c.65.

[19] 2000 c.33; and see the Fur Farming (Compensation Scheme) (England) Order 2002 (SI 2002/221) and the Fur Farming (Compensation Scheme) (England) Order 2001 (SI 2001/3853).

exemption for the protection of those interests. This is appropriate where it is thought acceptable for the new law to be phased in gradually.[20]

In other cases the legislature may determine that compensation is inappropriate, either because the opportunities for alternative use of property are sufficient to make it unnecessary to compensate owners for the fact that previously traditional uses have become unlawful, or because the kind of damage concerned is insufficiently direct.[21]

---

[20] See, for example, s.39(4) of the Anti-social Behaviour Act 2003 (c.38) (prohibition of certain air weapons)—

"(4) If at the time when subsection (3) comes into force a person has in his possession an air rifle, air gun or air pistol of the kind described in section 5(1)(af) of the Firearms Act 1968 (inserted by subsection (3) above)—
  (a) section 5(1) of that Act shall not prevent the person's continued possession of the air rifle, air gun or air pistol,
  (b) section 1 of that Act shall apply, and
  (c) a chief officer of police may not refuse to grant or renew, and may not revoke or partially revoke, a firearm certificate under Part II of that Act on the ground that the person does not have a good reason for having the air rifle, air gun or air pistol in his possession."

[21] In the case of the proposals to make it unlawful to hunt wild mammals with dogs, for example, a number of Government and non-Government Bills about which have passed through the House of Commons in recent years, so far without any reaching the statute book, the question of compensation has been raised and consistently resisted by the Government. The issue is summarised by the following passage of the speech of the Parliamentary Under-Secretary of State for the Home Department (Mr Mike O'Brien on Consideration of the Hunting Bill 2000–01 (HC Deb. February 27, 2001 c.785)—

"On grounds of practicality alone, I would not recommend that the House make either of the amendments. The Government, as guardians of the public purse—the taxpayer's money —could not, as a matter of principle, support them. The commitments in them would be completely open and would not allow the kind of controls on the public purse that I expect. "In the past, compensation has been paid to those who, as a consequence of legislation, have been deprived of their property. The most notable recent example was firearms compensation, following the tragedy at Dunblane. However, as I have already pointed out, certain dealers in firearms were not compensated for the loss of their profit. We generally have not paid compensation from public funds to those who may have lost their livelihoods as a result of legislation. To go down that route would set a precedent that might have unpredictable consequences if it were done in the way that the amendments propose. "The right hon. and learned Member for Sleaford and North Hykeham (Mr. Hogg) mentioned the compensation scheme for the fur farming industry, which was shut down as a result of the prohibition on fur farming. That case is hardly analogous. The Fur Farming (Prohibition) Act 2000 closed down an entire industry. The Bill, by contrast, simply restricts certain activities. Those who own hounds will still be able to use them for drag hunts, while those who own horses will be able to ride as part of an organised hunt or otherwise. Those who serve such people, such as the blacksmiths who shoe horses or the grooms, will still be required. "Hunt employees are precisely that—employees of individual hunts. It is open to those hunts, if they decide not to go in for drag hunting or some similar activity, to offer their staff appropriate payment. . . . "It has been suggested that the absence of provision for compensation renders the Bill incompatible with the European convention on human rights. Our legal advice is that that is not the case. We are not dealing with deprivation of property, but with control of the use of property. There is a requirement in all but exceptional cases to pay compensation for deprivation of property, but there is no such requirement in relation to measures constituting the control of the use of property. We are satisfied that the Bill, without any provision for compensation, is fully in accordance with article 1, Protocol 1 of the Convention."

Statutory liability

11.4.10 Compensation apart, a statute which confers powers or imposes duties, or which provides for the regulation of a service or industry, may make express provision for liability in the case of insufficient or negligent exercise or performance. So, for example, s.209 of the Water Industry Act 1991[22] provides—

> "(1) Where an escape of water, however caused, from a pipe vested in a water undertaker causes loss or damage, the undertaker shall be liable, except as otherwise provided in this section, for the loss or damage."[23]

As Lord Hoffmann said in *Transco plc (formerly BG plc and BG Transco plc) v Stockport Metropolitan Borough Council*[24]—

> "This provision is designed to avoid all argument over which insurers should bear the loss. Liability is far stricter than under the rule in *Rylands v Fletcher*. There is no exception for acts of third parties or natural events.The undertaker is liable for an escape 'however caused' and must insure accordingly. On the other hand, certain potential claimants like public gas suppliers (now called public gas transporters) must insure themselves. The irony of the present case is that if the leak had been from a high pressure water main, belonging to the North West Water Authority, a much more plausible high-risk activity, there could have been no dispute. Section 209(3)(b) would have excluded a statutory claim and the authority's statutory powers would have excluded the rule in *Rylands v Fletcher*."

SECTION 5

THE CROWN

Introduction

11.5.1 The question of the application of legislation to the Crown is of considerable importance and goes well beyond the question of the personal immunity of the Sovereign.[25] Whenever a private person has dealings with a public body in the context of legislation, it will be important to know both whether the public body

---

[22] 1991 c.56.
[23] The remaining provisions of the section qualify this proposition.
[24] [2003] 3 W.L.R. 1467, HL at para.42.
[25] The Sovereign's immunity is, indeed, of relatively little practical importance today, except perhaps in relation to land owned by the Sovereign in a private capacity. It is rare for the Sovereign's position to be addressed expressly in statute. But the notion of personal immunity from, in particular, criminal jurisdiction of the courts is so ingrained in the constitution of the United Kingdom that it would take more than express application of a statute to the Crown to admit the possibility of prosecution of the Sovereign personally.

is an emanation of the Crown for the purposes concerned and whether the legislation binds the Crown.

The basic rule

The essential rule is that the Crown is not bound by statute unless the contrary **11.5.2** is clearly intended. This is an immunity of ancient origin.[26] Chitty expresses it as follows—

> "The widest form in which the privilege is defined is to the effect that 'the general rule clearly is that, though the King may avail himself of any Acts of Parliament, he is not bound by such as do not particularly and expressly mention him".[27]

Although the immunity was not originally applied in Scotland[28] it is now to be applied uniformly in relation to all parts of the United Kingdom.[29]
It is possible to disapply the Crown exemption from statute by clear implication, but something very clear will be necessary. After an extensive review of the relevant cases Lord Keith of Kinkel puts the matter as follows in *Lord Advocate v Dumbarton District Council*[30]—

---

[26] " . . . the earliest formulation of the rule being expressed in the maxim: 'Roy n'est lie per ascun statute, si il ne soit expressement nosme' (Jenk. Cent. 307)"—*Lord Advocate v Dumbarton District Council* [1990] 2 A.C. 580, 588, HL *per* Lord Keith of Kinkel.

[27] Chitty's *Prerogative of the Crown*, (1820) ed. p.382; note that Chitty adds "To this rule, however, there is a most important exception, namely, that the King is impliedly bound by statutes passed for the public good; the release of the poor; the general advancement of learning, religion and justice; or to prevent fraud, injury or wrong." Chitty's list of exceptions is no longer an accurate reflection of the law but his formulation of the general principle is still sound.

[28] "It is to be observed at the outset that prior to the parliamentary union of England and Scotland in 1707 Scots law did not recognise any presumption that the Crown was not bound by general words in an Act of Parliament which were capable of applying to it. English law was to contrary effect, . . . English influence began to infiltrate the law of Scotland through the Court of Exchequer, set up under the Act 6 Anne c.26, which provided by section 6 that the court 'shall act, do and proceed . . . in any respect whatsoever . . . as the Court of Exchequer in England . . . has used or practised to do in the like cases in England.' Thus in Advocate-General v Garioch (1850) 12 D. 447 the Scottish Court of Exchequer held that the Crown was not liable for national taxation. Other cases decided that the Crown was exempt from local taxation."—*Lord Advocate v Dumbarton District Council* [1990] 2 A.C. 580, 588, HL *per* Lord Keith of Kinkel.

[29] "An Act of the United Kingdom Parliament may apply to the whole of the Kingdom or only to particular part of it. There would appear to be no rational grounds upon which a different approach to the construction of a statute might be adopted for the purpose of ascertaining whether or not the Crown is bound by it according to the jurisdiction where the matter is being considered. In the case of an Act in force over the whole of the United Kingdom the answer must be same whether its application to the Crown in Scotland or in England or in Northern Ireland is in issue. It is not conceivable that Parliament could have a different intention as regards the application of the Act to the Crown in the various parts of the Kingdom."—*Lord Advocate v Dumbarton District Council* [1990] 2 A.C. 580, 591, HL *per* Lord Keith of Kinkel.

[30] [1990] 2 A.C. 580, HL.

"I consider it to be no longer a tenable view that the Crown is in terms bound by general words in a statute but that the prerogative enables it to override the statute. As to the considerations which may be applicable for the purpose of finding a necessary implication that the Crown is bound, it is clear that the mere fact that the statute in question has been passed for the public benefit is not in itself sufficient for that purpose. . . .

"Accordingly it is preferable, in my view, to stick to the simple rule that the Crown is not bound by any statutory provision unless there can somehow be gathered from the terms of the relevant Act an intention to that effect. The Crown can be bound only by express words or necessary implication. The modern authorities do not, in my opinion, require that any gloss should be placed upon that formulation of the principle. However, as the very nature of these appeals demonstrates, it is most desirable that Acts of Parliament should always state explicitly whether or not the Crown is intended to be bound by any, and if so which, of their provisions."

11.5.3   The essential nature of and rationale for the doctrine of Crown immunity in relation to legislation is expressed by Diplock L.J in *British Broadcasting Corporation v Johns (Inspector of Taxes)*[31]—

"Since laws are made by rulers for subjects, a general expression in a statute such as 'any person,' descriptive of those upon whom the statute imposes obligations or restraints is not to be read as including the ruler himself. Under our more sophisticated constitution the concept of sovereignty has in the course of history come to be treated as comprising three distinct functions of a ruler: executive, legislative and judicial, though the distinction between these functions in the case, for instance, of prerogative powers and administrative tribunals is sometimes blurred.

"The modern rule of construction of statutes is that the Crown, which today personifies the executive government of the country and is also a party to all legislation, is not bound by a statute which imposes obligations or restraints on persons or in respect of property unless the statute says so expressly or by necessary implication. But to use the expression 'the Crown' as personifying the executive government of the country tends to conceal the fact that the executive functions of sovereignty are of necessity performed through the agency of persons other than the Queen herself. Such persons may be natural persons or, as has been increasingly the tendency over the last hundred years, fictitious persons—corporations.[32]"

---

[31] [1965] Ch. 32, 78, CA.
[32] In which context it is worth noting that most senior Ministers are now Corporations Sole, the only exceptions being the Home Secretary and non-Secretarial Ministers.

So the notion of Crown immunity can be put simply so far as legislation is concerned by stating that the Crown—and that concept includes the executive who act solely on behalf of the Crown—cannot be bound by anything done by Parliament (even by "The Queen in Parliament"[33]) except in so far as the Crown expresses itself as wishing to be bound.

The doctrine is further expounded and its origins and justification explored in the passage of the judgment of the Court of Appeal in *The Parlement Belge*[34] appended to this work.[35]

Basis of and justification for the rule

The nature of the rule of Crown immunity from statute law has been a matter of dispute from time to time, in particular as to whether it is— **11.5.4**

(a) an expression of a prerogative immunity subject to the possibility of express disapplication by Parliament, or

(b) simply a rule of statutory interpretation.

An authoritative view on this question is expressed by Lord MacDermott in *Madras Electric Supply Corporation Ltd v Boarland*[36]—

> "Whatever ideas may once have prevailed on the subject it is, in my opinion, today impossible to uphold the view that the Crown can find in the prerogative an immunity from tax if the statute in question, according to its true construction, includes the Crown amongst those made liable to the tax it imposes. The appropriate rule, as I understand it, is that in an Act of Parliament general words shall not bind the Crown to its prejudice unless by express provision or necessary implication. That, however, is and has long been regarded as a rule of construction, and such being its nature its application to the charging provisions of paragraph 1 of Schedule D seems to me to make an end of the respondent's submission on this aspect. In that paragraph the word 'person' is a general word capable of including the Crown, but there is no express provision and nothing by way of necessary implication to make it include the Crown, and so, as a matter of construction, it must be read in accordance with the rule as excluding the Crown."

The presumption of immunity is not one which attracts universal approval, and the courts are likely to have regard in applying it to the fairness of the result that **11.5.5**

---

[33] See Chapter 2, Section 1.
[34] (1880) 5 P.D. 197, 205–207, CA.
[35] Appendix, Extract 18.
[36] [1955] AC 667, 685, HL.

it would achieve in a particular case. Writing in *Criminal Law: The General Part*[37] the eminent jurist Professor Glanville Williams said[38]—

> "A second doctrine that has the effect of exempting State servants from the ordinary law is the presumption that the Crown is not bound by statutes. This presumption, as now applied by the courts, can be rebutted only by express words in the statute or necessary implication. The effect in a number of instances can only be described as pernicious. Under this doctrine it has been determined that Inspectors of Weights and Measures have no jurisdiction over the scales of Post Offices, though there is reason to believe that some are defective.

> " . . . the proper principle in the modern State should surely be that the Crown is bound by statute, unless expressly declared not to be bound, or unless public policy requires exemption. It seems that only legislation can now bring about this rule in England."

Who is the Crown?

11.5.6   The presumed immunity of the Crown from statute extends to persons acting on behalf of the Crown in the same way as do other immunities of the Crown. As Bankes L.J. said in *Public Works Commissioners v Pontypridd Masonic Hall Co.*[39]—

> "The defendants plead the Statute of Limitations. To that the plaintiffs answer that they are suing as the representatives of the Crown to recover this money, and that the Statute of Limitations does not apply as against the Crown. Two cases have been referred to, *Graham v Public Works Commissioners*[40] and *Roper v Public Works Commissioners*,[41] both of which make it clear that if a body, whether incorporated or not, is in fact acting in any particular matter as agents of the Crown, they are to be treated in law as such agents, and from that it follows that the Statute of Limitations does not apply to them. In this case I have no hesitation in coming to the conclusion that the plaintiffs are merely acting in their capacity as agents of the Crown in endeavouring to recover this money, although they possess a statutory right to bring the action in their own name."

A Crown servant acting in the course of his duties is not bound by, and therefore cannot be convicted of an offence under, a statute which does not expressly bind the Crown.[42]

---

[37] 2nd ed. London, 1961.
[38] pp.793–795.
[39] [1920] 2 K.B. 233, 233–234, KBD.
[40] [1901] 2 K.B. 781.
[41] [1915] 1 K.B. 45.
[42] *Cooper v Hawkins* [1904] 2 K.B. 164, DC.

While it is clear that the immunity of the Crown extends to persons acting on behalf of the Crown, who those persons are can be difficult to determine.

The fundamental position and the reasons for it are expressed in the speech of Lord Diplock in *Town Investments Ltd v Department of the Environment*[43]— **11.5.7**

> " . . . it is not private law but public law that governs the relationships between Her Majesty acting in her political capacity, the government departments among which the work of Her Majesty's government is distributed, the ministers of the Crown in charge of the various departments and civil servants of all grades who are employed in those departments. These relationships have in the course of centuries been transformed with the continuous evolution of the constitution of this country from that of personal rule by a feudal landowning monarch to the constitutional monarchy of today; but the vocabulary used by lawyers in the field of public law has not kept pace with this evolution and remains more apt to the constitutional realities of the Tudor or even the Norman monarchy than to the constitutional realities of the 20th century. To use as a metaphor the symbol of royalty, "the Crown," was no doubt a convenient way of denoting and distinguishing the monarch when doing acts of government in his political capacity from the monarch when doing private acts in his personal capacity, at a period when legislative and executive powers were exercised by him in accordance with his own will. But to continue nowadays to speak of 'the Crown' as doing legislative or executive acts of government, which, in reality as distinct from legal fiction, are decided on and done by human beings other than the Queen herself, involves risk of confusion. We very sensibly speak today of legislation being made by Act of Parliament—though the preamble to every statute still maintains the fiction that the maker was Her Majesty and that the participation of the members of the two Houses of Parliament had been restricted to advice and acquiescence. Where, as in the instant case, we are concerned with the legal nature of the exercise of executive powers of government, I believe that some of the more Athanasian-like features of the debate in your Lordships' House could have been eliminated if instead of speaking of 'the Crown' we were to speak of 'the government'—a term appropriate to embrace both collectively and individually all of the ministers of the Crown and parliamentary secretaries under whose direction the administrative work of government is carried on by the civil servants employed in the various government departments. It is through them that the executive powers of Her Majesty's government in the United Kingdom are exercised, sometimes in the more important administrative matters in Her Majesty's name, but most often under their own official designation. Executive acts of government that are done by any of them are acts done by 'the Crown' in the

---

[43] [1978] AC 359, 380.

fictional sense in which that expression is now used in English public law."

Difficulties will nevertheless persist in relation to the determination of who is and is not within the ambit of the Crown immunity.[44]

Statutory corporations

11.5.8   Where an Act creates a statutory corporation in respect of which it could be argued whether or not its functions are exercised on behalf of the Crown, it is common for the Act to specify either that the body is to be regarded as the servant or agent of the Crown[45] or that it is not to be so regarded.[46] Provisions providing for bodies not to be regarded as acting with Crown immunity are by far the more common.

Civil servants

11.5.9   The civil service is a large body of which everyone is aware but which is difficult or impossible to define. It is easy enough to identify large numbers of persons performing central government functions as members of the civil service. But there are many others at the periphery about whom it is difficult to be sure.[47]

For most legislative purposes membership of the civil service is not, however, the principal issue: what more often matters is whether a person is performing a function of the Crown.[48] Even here, however, the position will often be unclear.[49]

---

[44] See, in particular, *Tamlin v Hannaford* [1950] 1 K.B. 18 and *Trendtex Trading Corporation v Central Bank of Nigeria* [1976] 3 All E.R. 437.

[45] See, for example, s.3(5) of the National Heritage Act 2002 (c.14) "In relation to any matter as respects which the [Historic Buildings and Monuments Commission for England] act by virtue of a direction under this section, the Commission shall enjoy the same privileges, immunities and exemptions as those enjoyed in relation to that matter by the Secretary of State."

[46] See, for example, "The [British Transport Police] Authority shall not be regarded as the servant or agent of the Crown or as enjoying any status, immunity or privilege of the Crown."—Railways and Transport Safety Act 2003 (c.20), Sch.4, para.33(1).

[47] Even the Civil Service Orders in Council do not attempt clear and exhaustive definitions of what is simply referred to as Her Majesty's Home Civil Service.

[48] See *Graham* and *Roper*, cited above.

[49] A helpful analysis is provided in *Re Minotaur Data Systems Ltd* [1999] 3 All E.R. 122, CA where Aldous L.J. said (127–128)—

"The office of Official Receiver is not a prerogative office under the Crown, nor is it made, by statute, a Crown office. It is a statutory office. But although it is generally occupied, (we are told) by individuals who have until their appointment been civil servants within the Department of Trade and Industry, and although they continue by law to act at and under the direction of the Secretary of State, they cease on appointment to be civil servants in the proper sense of servants of the Crown employed in the business of government within (in this case) a department of state. In this they can be contrasted with immigration officers, who although originally appointed under statute, have become 'part of the Home Office' (see *Oladehinde v Secretary of State for the Home Dept, Alexander v Secretary of State for the Home Dept* [1990] 3 All E.R. 393, [1991] 1 A.C. 254); and compared with registrars of births, deaths and marriages who, despite similarities in some respects with local government employees, remain statutory office holders (see *Miles v Wakefield Metropolitan D.C.* [1987] 1 All E.R. 1089, [1987] A.C. 539). But as Beldam L.J. said in *Mond v Hyde* [1998] 3 All ER 833 at 849, [1999] 2 W.L.R. 499 at 515–516—

As is stated above in relation to statutory corporations, where doubt can be foreseen it is helpful for express provision to be made.

A small number of legislative provisions operate by reference to membership of the civil service.[50]

In cases of doubt, a number of legislative provisions make it clear whether employment of a particular kind is or is not to be treated as employment in the civil service.[51]

Executive Agencies

Following a Government report in 1988[52] it became common for arrangements to be made within individual Government departments for specified functions to be carried out by a group of officials with a degree of operational and administrative independence from the other functions of the department. These groups are known as Executive Agencies of the Department concerned, and are headed by a Chief Executive who is responsible directly to the senior Minister in charge of the Department.

As the Cabinet Office internet website explains—

11.5.10

'The official receiver is appointed by the DTI [Department of Trade and Industry] and acts subject to its direction and control. If the DTI were to be regarded in general as the employer of the official receiver and assistant official receiver, the statement in the rules that he is to be subject to the directions and control of the DTI would be unnecessary. I do not think that the relationship between the OR and the DTI [the Crown] is that of master and servant . . . '

"As the holder of a statutory office, each Official Receiver is empowered to bring proceedings, including disqualification proceedings, in his or her own name, and each is accorded by law a right of audience before the court to which he or she is attached. . . . ";

See also the reference in para. 12.4.5, footnote 71, to *Oladehinde*.

[50] See, for example, the following—

S.1(4) of the Superannuation Act 1972 (c.11) (Principal Civil Service Pension Scheme)—

"(4) This section applies to persons serving—

(a) in employment in the civil service of the State; or . . . "

Para.9 of Sch.4 to the Audit Commission Act 1998 (c.18)—

" . . . where a person employed in the civil service of the State became an officer or servant of the Commission . . . "

Para.3(1) of Sch.2 to the Environment Act 1995 (c.25)—

"(1) The rights and liabilities that may be transferred by and in accordance with a transfer scheme include (subject to the following provisions of this paragraph) any rights or liabilities of the employer under the contract of employment of any person—

(1) (1) (a) who is employed—

(i) in the civil service of the State . . . "

[51] See, for example, the following—

S.2(2) of the Courts Act 2003 (c.39) (court officers, staff and services)—"(2) The civil service pension arrangements for the time being in force apply (with any necessary adaptations) to persons appointed under subsection (1) as they apply to other persons employed in the civil service of the State."

S.103(8) of that Act (Official Solicitor for Northern Ireland)—"(8) Service as the Official Solicitor is employment in the civil service of the State for the purposes of section 1 of the Superannuation Act 1972 (Principal Civil Service Pension Scheme)."

[52] Sir Robin Ibbs' *Next Steps* Report.

"The intention was to hive off parts of government departments which were responsible for service delivery so that they would become more responsive to their customers, leaving the department to concentrate on policy development. Agencies have a chief executive who reports to the minister against specific targets. Agency operations are a charge on the parent department's budget and its accounts are normally consolidated into the parent department's accounts. Example: Prison Service".

The formation of an Executive Agency has no constitutional or other legal significance. The officials working within the Agency are officials of the Minister as much as any others within the Department. Where the officials are carrying out functions of the Crown, the presumed immunity from legislation will attach to the officials and the functions in the usual way.

Government Trading Funds

11.5.11 The principle behind the establishment of a Government Trading Fund is similar to that behind the establishment of Executive Agencies. Indeed, in policy terms the former can be seen as an extreme case of the latter. As the Cabinet Office internet website explains—

"Some Agencies have become Trading Funds.They must generate the cash they need to operate from their commercial business.Their accounts are presented separately from their parent department's.Example: Army Base Repair Organisation."

Unlike Agencies, however, Trading Funds are distinct legal entities, being established as such under the Government Trading Funds Act 1973.[53] Again, however, the degree of independence and separation from the parent Department does not prevent the activities of a Trading Fund from amounting to Crown activities and attracting the presumption of immunity from legislation.[54]

Express Crown application

11.5.12 If it is intended that a particular statute is to apply to the Crown it must displace the presumption of immunity by express words or clear implication, and the

---

[53] 1973 c.63.

[54] The long title of the 1973 Act ("An Act to enable certain services of the Crown to be financed by means of trading funds established in pursuance of orders made by the responsible Minister with Treasury concurrence . . . ") and the terms of s.1(1) (as amended by s.1 of the Government Trading Act 1990 (c.30)) ("If it appears to any Minister of the Crown—(a) that any operations of a department of the government for which he is responsible are suitable to be financed by means of a fund established under this Act . . . ") make it clear that the functions undertaken by a Government Trading Fund will be Crown functions.

former is preferable for obvious reasons.[55] As Lord Keith of Kinkel said in *Lord Advocate v Dumbarton District Council*[56]—

> "Accordingly it is preferable, in my view, to stick to the simple rule that the Crown is not bound by any statutory provision unless there can somehow be gathered from the terms of the relevant Act an intention to that effect. The Crown can be bound only by express words or necessary implication. The modern authorities do not, in my opinion, require that any gloss should be placed upon that formulation of the principle. However, as the very nature of these appeals demonstrates, it is most desirable that Acts of Parliament should always state explicitly whether or not the Crown is intended to be bound by any, and if so which, of their provisions."

The fact that express provision in relation to Crown application has become common in statutes generally, and may even have become the norm in relation to a particular area of the statute book, is not to be allowed to diminish the force of the general presumption of Crown immunity. As Lord Alverstone C.J. said in *Hornsey Urban District Council v Hennell*[57]—

> "The principle that Acts of Parliament do not impose pecuniary burdens upon Crown property unless the Crown is expressly named, or unless by necessary implication the Crown has agreed to be bound, is, in our opinion, still applicable to such a case. No doubt the insertion in many Acts of Parliament of clauses to protect the Crown, or save Crown rights, has given rise to the impression that this rule has to some extent been trenched upon, and we are far from saying that there may not be provisions in public Acts of Parliament so framed as to bind the Crown even though the Crown may not be specially named. But, in our opinion, the intention that the Crown shall be bound, or has agreed to be bound, must clearly appear either from the language used or from the nature of the enactments, and there is, in our opinion, nothing of the kind in the provisions of the Public Health Act applicable to this case which gives rise to any such presumption.

> " . . . Having regard to the above authorities, we cannot accept the argument that the limited exemption of certain Government lands in s.327 of the Public Health Act is sufficient to shew that all other interests of the Crown were intended to be affected by the provisions of the Act.

---

[55] Indeed, the ability to infer Crown application in particular kinds of statute from the public nature of the matters with which they deal may have been a rule once "but if the ancient rule ever had in fact the wide meaning claimed for it, we can only conclude that it has been 'eaten away' by exceptions."—*London County Territorial and Auxiliary Forces Association v Nichols* [1949] 1 K.B. 35, 45, CA *per* Scott L.J.

[56] [1990] 2 A.C. 580, 604, HL.

[57] [1902] 2 K.B. 73, 79–80, DC.

" . . . There is, in our opinion, no such general practice as to lead to the view that the original doctrine of Crown exemption has ceased to exist, or has been infringed upon, or that the insertion of a particular protecting clause is intended to shew that only that class of Crown property was intended to be exempt."

Crown land

11.5.13 The exemption of the Crown from statute applies in relation to land belonging to the Crown as it does in relation to things done by the Crown. But the exemption applies to Crown land only in so far as the Crown is affected. In the case of Crown land let to private tenants, therefore, there is no reason to apply the exemption in respect of the land, or anything done on the land, where neither the Crown nor its interest in the land in question will be adversely affected.

Can the Crown benefit from a statute by which it is not bound?

11.5.14 This has been a vexed question for a long time, at one stage thought to have been decided and later put back into doubt.[58] The question can now be regarded as settled, in the affirmative, at least in most of its aspects, partly by statute and partly by the weight of judicial opinion. Both are expounded in the following passage of the judgment of Lawton L.J. in *Town Investments Ltd. v Department of the Environment*[59]—

> "From the 18th century onwards it has been commonly believed amongst lawyers, first that an Act did not apply to the Crown unless there was an express provision in it to that effect and, secondly, that it can take the benefit of any statute although not specifically named in it: see *Blackstone's Commentaries*. 19th century text-book writers followed Blackstone: see *Stephen's Commentaries*. The courts did the same . . . In *Cayzer, Irvine & Co. Ltd. v Board of Trade* Rowlatt J. at first instance[60] had held that the Crown could take advantage of the Limitation Act 1923, but on appeal this court decided the case on another ground so it was unnecessary to decide whether the Crown could take advantage of that Act. . . . At the end of his judgment Scrutton L.J.[61] queried whether the statement of principle set out in Blackstone was well-founded. . . . I find it unnecessary to express any opinion about these foundations. By themselves they may not be of much value, but what has come about since is. First, there is the consensus of weighty legal opinion over two centuries and, secondly, and more importantly in my judgment, the Crown's rights in this respect have now been

---

[58] See *Cayzer, Irvine & Co v Board of Trade* [1927] 1 K.B. 269, CA and [1927] A.C. 610, HL.
[59] [1976] 3 All E.R. 479, 489–490, CA.
[60] (1925) 95 L.J.K.B. 134.
[61] [1927] 1 K.B. 269, 295.

recognised by Parliament. This came about under the Crown Proceedings Act 1947. . . . Section 31(1) provides as follows:

'This Act shall not prejudice the right of the Crown to take advantage of the provisions of an Act of Parliament although not named therein; and it is hereby declared that in any civil proceedings against the Crown the provisions of any Act of Parliament which could, if the proceedings were between subjects, be relied upon by the defendant as a defence to the proceedings, whether in whole or in part, or otherwise, may, subject to any express provision to the contrary, be so relied upon by the Crown.' "

Criminal liability

A fundamental principle in relation to the potential criminal liability of Crown servants is expressed by Anson[62] as follows— **11.5.15**

"The King's command is no excuse for a wrongful act, and whether the wrongful act takes place at the direct instance and instruction of the King, or is done in the course of the service, civil or military, of the Crown, he who has committed the crime or done the wrong is personally liable. Our constitution has never recognised any distinction between those citizens who are and those who are not officers of the State in respect of the law which governs their conduct or the jurisdiction which deals with them. Such exceptions to this general statement as may be found in our books depend on rules of statute or common law, limited in character and clear in principle."

Incidentally, this shows how the most important meaning of the maxim "the King can do no wrong"—that a Crown servant cannot excuse wrongdoing by reference to his office—is almost the opposite of what it is sometimes taken to mean.[63]

As to the personal immunity of the Sovereign from criminal prosecution, this is more a matter of procedure than anything else. The reason why the Sovereign cannot personally be prosecuted for a criminal offence is now generally agreed to be simply that there is no court in which to try him, his own courts being incompetent to do so. As Professor Glanville Williams puts it[64]—

"Blackstone ascribed the Sovereign's immunity to an imaginary imperfection of the will which rendered him incapable of mens rea. But the rule is

---

[62] *Law And Custom Of The Constitution*, (1907 ed.), Vol.II, Pt I, p.46.
[63] See Dicey, *Law of the Constitution* (1952 ed.), p.25.
[64] *Criminal Law, The General Part* (1961 ed.), para.257.

now recognised to be due not to any such absurd fiction, but to a lack of jurisdiction in the courts."

11.5.16   Clearly, it requires to be explored how the principle that (the Sovereign apart) there is no criminal immunity for the Crown relates to the presumption discussed above of non-application to the Crown in the context of criminal statutes. In particular—

(a) If a Crown servant cannot be prosecuted for committing an offence under a statute which does not expressly bind the Crown, that might be thought in practice significantly to erode the principle that service of the Crown is not in itself an excuse for the commission of wrong. Or is it to be assumed that the importance of the latter principle will sometimes give rise to the kind of necessary implication by which the Crown can be bound by statute even in the absence of express provision?

(b) A related, but subordinate, question is whether it is true that a Crown servant can never be prosecuted for the commission of a statutory offence once it is granted that the statute does not bind the Crown.

The difficulty can be clearly illustrated by considering the following case. If a servant of the Crown commits a common law offence of assault he will not be able to excuse himself by arguing that he was ordered to do so. But what if the common law offence is then codified and brought into the statute law without express Crown application? An obvious example is the Offences Against the Person Act 1861, which contains no express application to the Crown.

11.5.17   It might be tempting to argue that this is why Chitty excepts from the principle of Crown exemption statutes designed to suppress the commission of a wrong.[65] But that would beg the question. Whether it is "wrong" for Crown servants to commit a statutory offence depends, as in all other cases of construction, on whether Parliament intended the offence to apply to the Crown.

At first sight it might appear to be difficult to imagine that Parliament could possibly intend a statutory offence of assault not to apply to the Crown. But it might not be difficult to think of cases in which Crown servants of one kind or another might be wanted to perform actions which might technically amount to assault if performed by ordinary citizens without consent.

And apart from extreme cases like assault, in the case of most statutory offences it will not immediately be apparent whether Parliament could reasonably have expected to exempt Crown servants.

11.5.18   Obviously the rule that the Crown is not bound except by express enactment or necessary implication does not mean that a person is excepted from liability under a criminal statute because he is a civil servant. At the most it means that he is excepted in respect of what he does as such. On this view the question is

---

[65] See footnote 27 above.

usually academic because it is no part of any civil servant's duty to commit breaches of criminal enactments. But there are or may be exceptions.

In other words, an offence under a statute which does not expressly or by necessary implication bind the Crown will not apply to a Crown servant acting as such. But it will very often be impossible for a Crown servant charged with an offence to argue successfully that his commission of the offence was a necessary part of the performance of his duties as a Crown servant, rather than, to use the tort term, a frolic of his own.

How likely it is for a Crown servant not to be immune in respect of an offence will vary with the kind of offence: there are some which it will be almost impossible to imagine a Crown servant being required to commit, while others (disseminating confidential information, for example) may be commonplace.

This explains a number of apparent anomalies in criminal statute law.

The Offences Against the Person Act 1861,[66] for example, says nothing about Crown application because there is no intention to bind Crown servants in respect of actions committed in the course of their duties. But nor is there any intention to exempt Crown servants from actions performed outside their duties. So silence produces the right theoretical result, although the practical effect will vary from one offence to another. The s.64 offence, for example (making or having gunpowder, etc, with intent to commit or enable any person to commit any felony mentioned in this Act) will almost never fall to be committed by a Crown servant in the course of his employment because of the requirement as to intention (the only possible exception being the difficult question of entrapment).

11.5.19

In the case of the Firearms Act 1968,[67] however, there are clearly many cases in which Crown servants might be called upon to commit actions in the course of their duties which would amount to offences under the Act. And so s.54 of the Act applies a number of offences expressly, subject to specified modifications of the ordinary regime.[68]

---

[66] 1861 c.100.
[67] 1968 c.27.
[68] "**54 Application of Parts I and II to Crown servants**
(1) Sections 1, 2, 7 to 13 and 26A to 32 of this Act apply, subject to the modifications specified in subsection (2) of this section, to persons in the service of Her Majesty in their capacity as such so far as those provisions relate to the purchase and acquisition, but not so far as they relate to the possession, of firearms.
(2) The modifications referred to above are the following—
(a) a person in the service of Her Majesty duly authorised in writing in that behalf may purchase or acquire firearms and ammunition for the public service without holding a certificate under this Act;
(b) a person in the naval, military or air service of Her Majesty shall, if he satisfies the chief officer of police on an application under section 26A of this Act that he is required to purchase a firearm or ammunition for his own use in his capacity as such, be entitled without payment of any fee to the grant of a firearm certificate authorising the purchase or acquisition or, as the case may be, to the grant of a shot gun certificate.
(3) For the purposes of this section and of any rule of law whereby any provision of this Act does not bind the Crown, a person shall be deemed to be in the service of Her Majesty if he is—

The distinction between the statutory immunity of the Crown and the inability to prosecute a servant of the Crown who commits a wrong is illustrated by the judgments in *Cooper v Hawkins*.[69] This was the case of a person employed by the War Department as an engine driver who was prosecuted for the commission of an offence of speeding under s.4 of the Locomotives Act 1865.[70] The Act did not bind the Crown expressly.

11.5.20 On a case stated by the magistrate to the High Court, the court found that this was not a statute which applied to the Crown expressly or by implication. Having established that, in order to determine the accused's liability to prosecution it was necessary to establish that breach of the statute was something which a Crown servant could do in the course of his duties: that explains the following passages—

> "It is perfectly obvious that there must be many occasions when in the performance of military duties it would be absolutely necessary for locomotives to be driven at a greater speed than two miles an hour."[71]

> "Of course, that does not exhaust the case, because although it might perfectly well be that the Crown is not bound by [the Act], yet the circumstances might have been such that a man driving an engine which belongs to the Crown might be liable because the act of over-driving might be his own personal act. For instance, if the man were drunk, or under circumstances in which he was not performing a public duty, and was not acting in accordance with superior orders, he would be liable, although driving an engine belonging to the Crown; but in this case no such consideration arises. I understand from the case that the excess of speed was in conformity with orders. It may be that they were not orders specifically to go more than three miles an hour, but the driver was told, as I read it, that the coals were to be conveyed before nightfall to a particular place, and, as I understand, it was necessary in order that that should be done, that he should go at a pace which exceeded the limits imposed by the section. If so, this is a case, beyond all doubt, in which the act of the man is the act of the Crown. If so, there cannot be any question, assuming we are right in holding that this Act does not bind the Crown, that the conviction was wrong."[72]

      (a) a member of a police force, or
      (b) a person employed by a police authority who is under the direction and control of a chief officer of police, or
      (c) a member of the National Criminal Intelligence Service or the National Crime Squad. . . . "

[69] [1904] 2 KB 164.
[70] 28 & 29 Vict. c. 83.
[71] *Per* Lord Alverstone C.J. at 172.
[72] *Per* Wills J. at 173.

(Incidentally, the modern approach to a similar substantive issue is found in the Road Traffic Act 1988.[73] Section 183 provides for a number of provisions, including a number of offences, to apply to vehicles and persons in the public service of the Crown.)

There is one much-cited authority which deals expressly with the question whether a servant of the Crown can be prosecuted for the commission of an offence under a statute which does expressly bind the Crown. This is a decision of the High Court of Australia: *Cain v Doyle*.[74] The case is not generally given much weight in the texts or decided cases, which is not surprising when one looks at the basis upon which it was presented. As Glanville Williams says "the court occupied itself exclusively with the immunity of the Crown, and did not consider the question whether, granting such immunity, the secondary party could not be held responsible". In other words, the case principally considered whether an express provision binding the Crown in a statute has to be construed as including a minor provision within the statute which imposes criminal liability. **11.5.21**

So this has no relevance to the case of a statute which is primarily or significantly concerned with the creation of offences. And, more importantly, the more significant of the two meanings attributed by Dicey to the maxim "the King can do no wrong" was not considered. (Significantly, the case of *Cooper v Hawkins* was not discussed.)

As to the nature of the Sovereign's personal immunity from criminal liability, this is such a fundamental principle of law, deriving from the principles discussed in the opening of this Section, that it would take a great deal more to disapply it than to apply to the Crown in general terms a statute imposing criminal liability.

Tortious liability

As to the liability of the Crown and Crown servants in tort in relation to the performance of statutory functions, see the Crown Proceedings Act 1947.[75] **11.5.22**

Queen's Consent and Prince's Consent

The concepts of Queen's Consent and Prince's Consent refer to procedural requirements of the two Houses of Parliament in relation to the passing of Bills.[76] They are distinct from, and wholly irrelevant to, questions of application of legislation. In particular, much legislation that applies to the Crown does not require Consent. **11.5.23**

---

[73] 1988 c.52.
[74] (1946) 72 C.L.R. 409.
[75] 1947 c.44.
[76] See Chapter 5, Section 2, para.5.2.23.

Sovereign's opinion of Bill

11.5.24 Despite the special provision for Consent in relation to prerogative or private interests, it is a Parliamentary convention that the Sovereign's opinion on legislative proposals is neither sought nor referred to. The Lord Privy Seal expressed the rule and the reason for departing from it in speaking about the Succession to the Crown Bill 1997–98[77]—

> "No doubt the noble Lord had in mind the passage in Erskine May, which says: 'Her Majesty cannot be supposed to have a private opinion, apart from that of her responsible advisers; and any attempt to use her name in debate to influence the judgment of Parliament is immediately checked and censured'.... The advice that I have received is that, on a Bill which is so fundamentally personal to the sovereign and to her family, it would have been unhelpful to the House for the Government not to have made her view known to your Lordships. The procedure must always be applied with common sense and with due consideration of the circumstances. I am bound to say that the advice I received was both sensible and correct. Her Majesty's views would very soon have become apparent through other channels."

The Duke and Duchy of Cornwall

11.5.25 The special position of the land appertaining to the Duchy of Cornwall has already been mentioned and explained.[78] That apart, there is no prerogative right in the Duke or Duchy of Cornwall except as part of the Crown's prerogative; in all other respects the Sovereign's eldest son, though the Sovereign's first subject, is yet a subject and may be taxed like any other. The Duchy of Cornwall would probably be bound by an Act of Parliament expressed to bind the Crown and not mentioning the Duchy, while it is at least strongly arguable that an Act which did not bind the Crown would not bind the Duchy unless it was specially mentioned.

The Duchy of Lancaster

11.5.26 While there is no special prerogative consideration attaching to the Duchy of Lancaster, an Act may make special provision in relation to land belonging to the Crown in right of that Duchy; in particular for the purposes of requiring things to be done by or in relation to the Chancellor of the Duchy of Lancaster.[79]

---

[77] HL Deb. March 2, 1998 cc.954–958.
[78] Chapter 5, Section 2, para.5.2.23, footnote 95.
[79] See, for example, the Agricultural Tenancies Act 1995 (c.8), s.37(2)(c).

In keeping with the general acceptance of the desirability of being as clear as possible as to Crown application in modern statutes[80] it is common nowadays for a provision making express application of a statute to Crown land to make express provision for Duchy land both of Cornwall and of Lancaster.[81]

European and Europe-inspired legislation

The presumption about the immunity of the Crown is based on the nature of the Crown, and the relationship between the Crown and subjects, as a matter of domestic law. It therefore has no application to legislation emanating from the Communities. On the contrary—European Community rights will often have to be enforceable by citizens against the State—see further Chapter 32, Sections 3 and 4. **11.5.27**

Foreign governments

Crown immunity is a domestic rule of law, but it is also an international principal based upon comity of nations. The law of the United Kingdom also recognises immunities of foreign Sovereigns and governments, and their diplomatic emissaries. Those immunities will apply to obligations arising out of legislation as to other obligations.[82] **11.5.28**

SECTION 6

PARLIAMENT

The position of the two Houses of Parliament and their administrative machinery in the matter of the application of Acts of Parliament can be expressed concisely in three propositions— **11.6.1**

(1) The common law recognises a privilege of the two Houses of Parliament to regulate their own internal affairs in such manner as pleases them. Giving

---

[80] See para.11.5.12 above.

[81] See, for example, the Commonhold and Leasehold Reform Act 2002 (c.15), ss.108 and 172, the Licensing Act 2003 (c.17), s.195 and the Water Act 2003 (c.37), s.80.

[82] "It is a basic principle of international law that one sovereign state (the forum state) does not adjudicate on the conduct of a foreign state. The foreign state is entitled to procedural immunity from the processes of the forum state. This immunity extends to both criminal and civil liability. State immunity probably grew from the historical immunity of the person of the monarch. In any event, such personal immunity of the head of state persists to the present day: the head of state is entitled to the same immunity as the state itself. The diplomatic representative of the foreign state in the forum state is also afforded the same immunity in recognition of the dignity of the state which he represents. This immunity enjoyed by a head of state in power and an ambassador in post is a complete immunity attaching to the person of the head of state or ambassador and rendering him immune from all actions or prosecutions whether or not they relate to matters done for the benefit of the state. Such immunity is said to be granted ratione personae."—*R. v Bow Street Metropolitan Stipendiary Magistrate, Ex p. Pinochet Ugarte (No.3) (Amnesty International intervening)* [2000] 1 A.C. 147, 201–202 *per* Lord Browne-Wilkinson; see also the State Immunity Act 1978 (c.33), the Diplomatic Privileges Act 1964 (c.81) and the Consular Relations Act 1968 (c.18).

the concept of internal affairs a very wide construction, the courts will presume that an Act has no application in relation to the internal workings of the Houses of Parliament in the absence of express provision or necessary implication to the contrary.[83]

(2) Over the years it became increasingly common for the Houses to choose, while asserting as a matter of privilege the non-application of Acts to them, to subject themselves voluntarily to restrictions of the same kind as those imposed on them by others, particularly in matters such as employment law and health and safety and at least in so far as it was thought appropriate for those laws to bind the Crown.[84]

(3) In recent years a policy of voluntary application has ceded gradually to a policy of increasing express application.[85] The policy still applies primarily to employment and similar areas in which the Houses might be accused of double standards were they to legislate so as to impose standards of one kind on "ordinary employers" while exempting themselves: clearly, the potential accusation is stronger in cases where even the Crown as employer is required to abide by the statutory standards.

[83] See the leading case in which the courts refused to apply to the House of Commons provisions of licensing law, in *R. v Graham-Campbell Ex p. Herbert* [1935] 1 K.B. 594, DC; the leading cases establishing the privilege on which this leading ruling is based are cited in *Herbert*.

[84] See, for example, the following Written Answer given by the Chairman of Committees (Lord Boston of Faversham) on January 16, 1995 (HL Deb W.A. 33–34): "United Kingdom health and safety legislation is not considered as applying to the Palace of Westminster, having regard to the 1935 decision in *R. v Graham-Campbell Ex p. Herbert* [1 K.B. 594]. This decision indicates that the courts will not, in the absence of express provision or necessary implication, treat the provisions of an Act of Parliament as binding on the two Houses themselves, so far as those provisions would affect the internal affairs of the Houses. The authorities do, however, try to comply fully with the relevant legislation as if it were binding on them in the same way as on the Crown. The Government are committed to applying the provisions of the Health and Safety at Work etc. Act 1974 to the Palace of Westminster as soon as a suitable legislative opportunity arises. The House of Lords Offices Committee agreed to this in principle in its Sixth Report, Session 1992–93, HL Paper 109, to which the House agreed on July 27, 1993."

[85] Note "the Committee has agreed that the provisions of the Disability Discrimination Bill now going through Parliament would apply to the House of Lords. This is in line with the Committee's policy that the House should move from voluntary compliance to statutory application in the case of the Health and Safety at Work etc. Act 1974; and the Committee's recent acceptance of the removal of Crown Exemption from the Palace of Westminster in respect of Planning and Health and Safety legislation"—House of Lords Offices: Select Committee Report HL Deb. June 12, 1995 c.1540; note also House of Commons Commission Seventeenth Annual Report 1994–95, para.21—"Parliamentary Immunity: The Government's policy of ending Crown immunity in areas such as planning, health and safety and employment has caused the Commission to review its own approach. An explicit provision is required for any such legislation to apply to Parliament, and until now a policy of voluntary compliance has been operated. In the future, the Commission intends to agree to application whenever possible. In implementing this policy, it will wish to ensure that the right of Parliament to function effectively is not threatened, and that the special status of the Palace of Westminster as a historic royal place and seat of both Houses is taken into account."; for cases of express application to Parliament see s.65 of the Disability Discrimination Act 1995 (c.50), ss.194 and 195 of the Employment Rights Act 1996 (c.18), s.1(10A) and (10B) of the Equal Pay Act 1970 (c.41) (as inserted by the Trade Union and Labour Relations (Consolidation) Act 1992 (c.52) and the Trade Union Reform and Employment Rights Act 1993 (c.19)) and s.63A of the Data Protection Act 1998 (c.29) inserted by Sch.6 to the Freedom of Information Act 2000 (c.36).

CHAPTER 12

STATUTORY RIGHTS, POWERS AND DUTIES

INTRODUCTION

Law is a combination of rights (including powers) and duties. If a proposition **12.0.1** does not either require a person to do something or confer a power or other right on a person it cannot sensibly be described as a legislative proposition.[1]

    This Chapter explores some of the characteristics of rights, powers and duties conferred or imposed by legislation.

SECTION 1

CREATION AND REMOVAL

Requirement of clear creation

It has been said[2] that rights cannot be conferred by mere implication from the **12.1.1** language used in a statute, but only by clear and unequivocal language.

    While this is certainly true of the creation of a new right which represents a significant departure from the previous position,[3] it is not, or possibly no longer, true of more minor matters, particularly if necessary ancillaries of express provisions.[4] What remains true is that the courts will presume that legislation

---

[1] There are, however, a number of propositions in legislation that are not on this basis worthy of being described as legislative propositions. Some are there merely as supporting or facilitating the substantive propositions of law: examples of that class are indices of defined expressions (as to which see Chapter 24, para.24.1.6) or parenthetical explanations of the substance of provisions to which reference has been made. Some are there in accordance with an agreement or convention which requires the legislature to include in an enactment something that is not strictly necessary, or where the legislature has decided to do so to in order to help the reader: examples of that class are "sink clauses" and *Baldwin* provisions (as to which see Chapter 1, Section 6) and commencement or extent provisions that merely recite what would in any event be the law. There are also occasionally included propositions which are probably or certainly of no legal effect but are required to be included for political purposes. See also Chapter 1, Section 7.

[2] See the previous edition of this work (1971) at p.117.

[3] See *R. v Harrald* (1872) L.R. 7 Q.B. 361, 362 *per* Cockburn C.J. and *The Claim of the Viscountess Rhondda* [1922] 2 A.C. 339, HL.

[4] The obvious example is where a statute provides expressly that one person must comply with a requirement imposed by another, the clear, although implied and not express, corollary is that the second person acquires a right in the matter: see, for example, s.37(4) of the Nationality, Immigration and Asylum Act 2002 (c.41) ("The governing body of a maintained school shall comply with a requirement of the local education authority to admit to the school a child to whom this section applies.").

does not intend to create and confer a right unless it does so expressly or by clear implication.

As to the creation of obligations, similarly the courts will presume that legislation does not intend to impose an obligation unless it does so expressly or by clear implication.

12.1.2 In determining whether an Act has impliedly created a statutory duty the courts will consider, in part, whether the system established by the Act can properly work without the implied creation of the duty and in part whether the provisions of the Act have provided, in effect, a system for the enforcement of the duty that gives it sufficient meaning.[5] But the mere fact that Parliament had a motive or intention in enacting a system which will be frustrated unless a duty is implied in addition to any imposed by the statute is not sufficient to found the implication of a duty. As Lord Diplock said in *Director of Public Prosecutions v Bhagwan*[6]—

"My Lords, I know of no authority which would justify your Lordships in holding it to be a criminal offence for any person, whether or not acting in concert with others, to do acts which are neither prohibited by Act of Parliament nor at common law, and do not involve dishonesty or fraud or deception, merely because the object which Parliament hoped to achieve by the Act may be thereby thwarted. . . .

"Under our system of parliamentary government what Parliament enacts are not policies but means for giving effect to policies. Those means often involve imposing upon private citizens fresh obligations or restrictions on their liberties to which they were not previously subject at common law. The constitutional function of the courts in relation to enacted law is limited to interpreting and applying it. It is the duty of the judge to ascertain what are the means which Parliament has enacted by the Act. In construing the enacting words he may take account of what the Act discloses as the purpose that those means were intended to achieve and, in the case of ambiguity alone, he may interpret them in the sense in which they are more likely to promote than hinder its achievement. But it is no function of a judge to add to the means which Parliament has enacted in derogation of rights which citizens previously enjoyed at common law, because he thinks that the particular case in which he has to apply the Act demonstrates that those means are not adequate to achieve what he conceives to be the policy of the Act.

"To do so is not to carry out the intention of Parliament but to usurp its functions. The choice of means is itself part of the parliamentary choice of

---

[5] See Lord Diplock in *Director of Public Prosecutions v Bhagwan* [1972] A.C. 60, 77, HL. "I find some initial difficulty in the very concept of a statutory duty owed by the subject to the Crown which attracts no sanctions either penal or civil for its breach. . . . "
[6] [1972] A.C. 60, 80–82, HL.

policy. It represents the price, by way of deprivation of freedom to do or not to do as they wish, which Parliament is prepared to exact from individual citizens to promote those objects to which the Act is directed. To raise the price is to change the policy—not to give effect to it.

"If the policy is to be changed it is for Parliament not the courts to change it . . .

"It is no offence under the law of England to do or to agree with others to do acts which, though not prohibited by legislation nor criminal nor tortuous at common law, are considered by a judge or by a jury to be calculated to defeat, frustrate or evade the purpose or intention of an Act of Parliament. If it were otherwise, freedom under the law would be but an empty phrase."

Presumption against interference with rights

The courts will presume that legislation does not intend to remove an existing **12.1.3** right, whether of a public or a private nature, unless it does so expressly[7] or by clear implication.[8] The presumption will be particularly strong if the removal would otherwise be without compensation.[9] The presumption is expressed by Bowen L.J. in *Re Cuno*[10] in the following terms—

"In the construction of statutes you must not construe the words so as to take away rights which already existed before the statute was passed, unless you have plain words which indicate that such was the intention of the legislature."[11]

The presumption is strengthened since the passing of the Human Rights Act 1998[12] by the requirement of s.3 to construe legislation in a manner compatible with the Convention rights if possible. Article 1 of the First Protocol to the European Convention on Human Rights protects, subject to exceptions, the peaceful enjoyment of possessions, in which context the concept of possessions is to be given a wide construction.[13]

---

[7] See *Deeble v Robinson* [1954] 1 Q.B. 77.
[8] See *Edgington v Swindon Corporation* [1939] 1 K.B. 86.
[9] Express provision for compensation would, of course, put beyond doubt the intended removal of the right: but a case could arise in which contractual provisions would provide compensation of a kind in the case of the removal of the statutory right, in which case the presumption against statutory removal would be less strong than if there were no provision for compensation.
[10] (1889) 43 Ch. D. 12, 17.
[11] See also *Attorney-General v Horner* (1884) 43 Ch. D. 12, 17: "It is a proper rule of construction not to construe an Act of Parliament as interfering with or injuring persons' rights without compensation unless one is obliged to so construe it."
[12] 1998 c.42.
[13] See, for example, *Rowland v Environment Agency* [2003] 2 W.L.R. 1233 Ch.

12.1.4   In rebutting the presumption against the defeat of rights "it is not sufficient to show that the thing sanctioned by the Act, if done, will of sheer physical necessity put an end to the [exercise of the] right; it must also be shown that the legislature have authorised the thing to be done at all events, and irrespective of its possible interference with existing rights".[14] For examples of the application of this principle see *Forbes v Ecclesiastical Commissioners*[15] and *Gray v R.*[16]

The assumption that novel provision of legislation is not intended to defeat long-standing rights will sometimes cause the courts to find an exception to the rule against supplying *casus omissus*[17] and to "supply the omission of the legislature".[18]

Private rights are protected from casual interference by statute particularly strongly. See, for example, *Walsh v Secretary of State for India*[19] in which Lord Westbury said,[20] in holding that an Act did not remove a right of action under a covenant—

> "This result follows of necessity, consistently with every rule by which Acts of Parliament ought to be interpreted, especially the rule that they should be so interpreted as in no respect to interfere with or prejudice a clear private right or title, unless the private right or title is taken away *per directum.*"

SECTION 2

NATURE OF POWERS AND DUTIES

Status of statutory right as specialty

12.2.1   A statutory right is known technically as a specialty. The principal practical effect of this is that the limitation period for the enforcement of a statutory right is that for a specialty, presently 12 years.[21]

The nature of the statutory specialty, and the distinction between a case of an action on a statutory speciality and an action on a contract or other source of right subject to statutory qualification or interference, are expounded in the passage of the judgment of Oliver L.J. in *Collin v Duke of Westminster*[22] appended to this work.[23]

---

[14] *Western Counties Railway v Windsor, &c. Railway* (1882) 7 App. Cas. 178, 189, PC *per* Lord Watson.

[15] (1872) L.R. 15 Eq. 51, 53.

[16] (1844) 11 Cl. & F. 427, 480.

[17] As to which see Chapter 20.

[18] See *Cooper v Wandsworth Board of Works* (1863) 14 C.B. (N.S.) 180, 194 *per* Byles J. and the cases cited therein.

[19] (1863) 10 H.L.C. 367.

[20] At 386.

[21] Limitation Act 1980 (c.58), s.8(1).

[22] [1985] Q.B. 581, 600–01, CA.

[23] Appendix, Extract 19.

Can a power amount to a duty?

A frequent question is whether a statutory power can amount to a duty or, put **12.2.2** another way, whether there can arise a duty to exercise a statutory power.

The general answer to this question is no. Where a power is conferred in simple terms it amounts to a discretion enjoyed by the person on whom the power is conferred.[24]

In *R. v Commissioners of Inland Revenue, Ex p. Newfields Developments Ltd*[25] the House of Lords declined to construe the word "may" as conferring a power. But it was not imposing a duty either. Rather, it expressed a condition to be satisfied. As Lord Hoffmann said[26]—

> "Although the point may be merely verbal, I do not think it is right to say, as the parties appear to have done before Moses J., that 'may' confers a 'power'. It is true that there are powers which in certain circumstances must be exercised. But I think it is clearer, having regard to the impersonal use of 'may' in the subsection, to say that it expresses conditionality. If the force of the word 'may' is conditional, the next stage in the argument is to identify the conditions under which an attribution must be made."

The suggestion of a duty to exercise a power, and the constraints upon its **12.2.3** arising, are discussed in the following passage of the judgment of Mummery L.J. in *Pelling v Families Need Fathers Ltd*[27]—

> "In its ordinary and natural meaning the word 'may' is apt to confer a discretion or power. It is true that there are certain situations where a discretionary power is conferred for the purpose of enforcing a right and is coupled with an obligation or duty to exercise a power, when required to do so, for the benefit of the person who has the right (see *Julius v Lord Bishop of Oxford*[28]). This is not such a case. The use of 'may' in subsection (6) is in striking contrast to the mandatory force of 'shall' in other parts of the same section, such as subsection (3). In *O'Brien v Sporting Shooters Association of Australia (Victoria)*[29] Byrne J. rejected the submission that the court had no discretion under the similarly-worded provision in section 103 of the Australian Corporations Law. It was submitted to him that the

---

[24] The apparent exception in the case of a commencement power explored in the case of *R. v Secretary of State for the Home Department, Ex p. Fire Brigades Union* [1995] 2 All E.R. 244 (see also Chapter 10, Section 1) is not really an exception—the courts did not find that there was any compulsion on the Secretary of State to exercise a power of commencement, but rather that while he chose not to exercise the power of commencement he was unable to achieve the same object as that provided for in the un-commenced statute by the use of the prerogative.
[25] [2001] 4 All E.R. 400, HL.
[26] Paras 22 & 23.
[27] [2002] 2 All E.R. 440, CA.
[28] (1880) 5 App. Cas. 214, 233, 241.
[29] [1999] 3 V.R. 251, 255.

word 'may' in that section was not permissive, but merely signified that the jurisdiction of the court to make an order did not arise unless there had been a refusal or contravention of the Corporations Law. He held[30] that the drafting of the Law was such that—

> 'the word "may" means exactly that. It means that the court is empowered to make the order where a refusal in contravention of the Law has been established, as in the present case. Whether the power will be exercised must depend upon the proper discretionary considerations affecting the power in the light of the facts as are found by the court.'

"We agree."

12.2.4 This leaves open the possibility noted in earlier cases that while "may" always confers a power and not a duty, a duty will sometimes arise to exercise a power. A significant and helpful example is provided by the judgment of Talbot J. in *Sheffield Corporation v Luxford*[31]—

> "Now, it is quite true that the language of the Act is permissive and not compulsory. It has often been said, and it is possibly a convenient abbreviation, but like all inaccurate expressions it often leads to mis-understanding, that in many statutes the word 'may' means 'must.' I think it has been pointed out once for all in *Julius v Bishop of Oxford*[32] that that is an inaccurate expression. 'May' always means may. 'May' is a permissive or enabling expression; but there are cases in which, for various reasons, as soon as the person who is within the statute is entrusted with the power it becomes his duty to exercise it. One of those cases is where he is applied to to use the power which the Act gives him in order to enforce the legal right of the applicant. I think this is such a case.

> "On the information before us, the legal right of the plaintiffs, the landlords, was complete as soon as the notice to quit had expired, and the tenant's right to remain in occupation of this house had absolutely ceased. . . . I think that, as soon as the application is made to the judge for an order for possession, the latter being clothed by the Act of Parliament with the power to make such an order, it becomes his duty to make it. And if the Act contained no more than that, it would be his duty to make the order then and there without any qualification. But the Act does undoubtedly give him, in terms, a certain discretion, because after the words 'the judge may order that posses-sion . . . . be given,' the section continues: 'either forthwith or on or before such day as the judge shall think fit to name.'

---

[30] At 255.
[31] [1929] 2 K.B. 180, 183–185.
[32] 5 App. Cas. 214, 222, 229, 235, 241.

" . . . I think that a postponement of the operation of the order for twelve months is not, at any rate unless there are some circumstances quite other than those that appear in this case, permissible in exercising discretion under this Act.

"I recognize that this is a somewhat difficult question . . . But I think that to postpone possession for a period of twelve months, even apart from the other conditions, is not such an exercise of discretion as the Act of Parliament, in spite of its unlimited terms, contemplates or permits.It is, of course, to some extent a question of degree . . . ".

As to the specific question of whether a power to commence a statute can amount to a duty, see Chapter 10, Section 1.

As to the incidence of the imposition of a duty to legislate, rather than a power, see Chapter 3, Section 1.

Limitations on discretionary statutory power

In many cases a statute confers a power in terms which leave an apparently unfettered discretion to the recipient of the power as to what use he chooses to make of the power. The law, however, constrains these apparently open powers in a number of ways. A helpful statement of the position, and reference to the earlier leading authorities, is found in the following passage of the judgment of Stuart-Smith L.J. in the Court of Appeal in *R. v Secretary of State for the Environment, Transport and the Regions and another, Ex p. Spath Holme Ltd*[33]—   **12.2.5**

> "30. Statutory power conferred for public purposes is conferred as it were upon trust, not absolutely—that is to say, it can validly be used only in the right and proper way which Parliament, when conferring it, is presumed to have intended. Although the Crown's lawyers have argued in numerous cases that unrestricted permissive language confers unfettered discretion, the truth is that, in a system based on the rule of law, unfettered governmental discretion is a contradiction in terms: see *Tower Hamlets London BC v Chetnik Developments Ltd.*[34]

> "31. The minister exceeds his jurisdiction where: (1) he acts outside the powers which, upon the true construction of the enabling Act, are expressly or impliedly conferred as to the terms of the subordinate legislation; (2) he seeks to achieve a purpose which, upon the true construction of the enabling

---

[33] [2000] 1 All E.R. 884, 893, CA: the decision of the Court of Appeal was reversed by the House of Lords ([2001] 2 A.C. 349) on issues relevant to the fundamental nature of statutory construction—as to which a number of references to the case are made elsewhere in this work—but which do not affect the authority of this exposition of implied constraints on *vires*.

[34] [1988] A.C. 858, 872, HL.

Act, is outside the express or implied object of the power; and (3) he takes irrelevant considerations, or does not take relevant considerations, into account in the exercise of the power: see *Associated Provincial Picture Houses Ltd v Wednesbury Corp*,[35] *Padfield v Minister of Agriculture Fisheries and Food*,[36] *Tower Hamlets London Borough Council v Chetnik Developments Ltd*,[37] *Hammersmith and Fulham London Borough Council v Secretary of State for the Environment*[38] and *Brind v Secretary of State for the Home Department*.[39]"

12.2.6   Even where Parliament does not fetter a discretion that it confers by reference to express considerations, constraints and limitations arise both from the rules of administrative law and also from the requirement to construe a broad discretion in the context in which it is conferred. As Ward L.J. said in *R. (C) v Lewisham London Borough Council*[40]—

> "The discretion conferred by s 202(3) is unfettered in the sense that Parliament has not stipulated, as it often does, the factors to be taken into account in the exercise of the discretion which it confers. In the absence of such a statutory checklist, the discretion is wide. The question is: how wide? The answer is given by Lord Bridge of Harwich in *Tower Hamlets London BC v Chetnik Developments Ltd*[41]—
>
> > 'Thus, before deciding whether a discretion has been exercised for good or bad reasons, the court must first construe the enactment by which the discretion is conferred. Some statutory discretions may be so wide that they can, for practical purposes, only be challenged if shown to have been exercised irrationally or in bad faith. But if the purpose which the discretion is intended to serve is clear, the discretion can only be validly exercised for reasons relevant to the achievement of that purpose.' "

12.2.7   It will also be presumed by the courts that a power conferred is to be exercised only in accordance with, and subject to, the ordinary rules and principles of the common law. As Lord Browne-Wilkinson said in *Pierson v Secretary of State for the Home Department*[42]—

> "I consider first whether there is any principle of construction which requires the court, in certain cases, to construe general words contained in the statute as being impliedly limited. In my judgment there is such a principle. It is well established that Parliament does not legislate in a

---

[35] [1948] 1 K.B. 223, 228–231.
[36] [1968] A.C. 997 at 1030, 1032–1033, 1046, 1052, 1054, 1058 and 1061.
[37] [1988] A.C. 858, 872–873.
[38] [1991] 1 A.C. 521, 597.
[39] [1991] 1 A.C. 696 at 756, 761.
[40] [2003] 3 All E.R. 1277, 1291, CA.
[41] [1988] 1 A.C. 858, 873, HL.
[42] [1998] A.C. 539, 573–574, HL.

vacuum: statutes are drafted on the basis that the ordinary rules and principles of the common law will apply to the express statutory provisions: . . . As a result, Parliament is presumed not to have intended to change the common law unless it has clearly indicated such intention either expressly or by necessary implication: . . . This presumption has been applied in many different fields including the construction of statutory provisions conferring wide powers on the executive.

"Where wide powers of decision-making are conferred by statute, it is presumed that Parliament implicitly requires the decision to be made in accordance with the rules of natural justice: . . . However widely the power is expressed in the statute, it does not authorise that power to be exercised otherwise than in accordance with fair procedures."[43]

When can additional powers be implied?

Where a statutory function is conferred on a Minister or any other person, it is **12.2.8** implicit that they may do anything necessary for the performance of that function. If the function is conferred in very broad terms, the powers available for its performance will be implied in very broad terms, subject to the presumptions specified in Chapter 19.

The more detailed the statutory provisions are as to how the function conferred is to be exercised, the slower the courts will be to grant the implication of powers to supplement the details of the statute. As Neill L.J. said in *Crédit Suisse v Waltham Forest London Borough Council*[44]—

" . . . where Parliament has made detailed provisions as to how certain statutory functions are to be carried out there is no scope for implying the existence of additional powers which lie wholly outside the statutory code."[45]

SECTION 3

EXERCISE OF POWERS AND DUTIES

Exercise from time to time

Section 12 of the Interpretation Act 1978[46] provides— **12.3.1**

"(1) Where an Act confers a power or imposes a duty it is implied, unless the contrary intention appears, that the power may be exercised, or the duty is to be performed, from time to time as occasion requires.

---

[43] See also *M. v Secretary of State for Education* [2001] EWCA Civ 332, *R (X) v Chief Constable of West Midlands Police* [2004] 2 All E.R. 1, QBD and cases cited by Lord Browne-Wilkinson in *Pierson*.

[44] [1997] Q.B. 363, 374, CA.

[45] Cited by Brooke L.J. in *R. (Khan) v Secretary of State for Health* [2003] 4 All E.R. 1239, 1261, CA; see also *Crédit Suisse v Allerdale Borough Council* [1997] Q.B. 306.

[46] 1978 c.30.

(2) Where an Act confers a power or imposes a duty on the holder of an office as such, it is implied, unless the contrary intention appears, that the power may be exercised, or the duty is to be performed, by the holder for the time being of the office."

These rules, which again might be thought generally to stand to reason, are of particular significance in relation to the power to make subordinate legislation.

In certain circumstances it is clear that a power is intended to be available as a once-off power and the presumption in s.12(1) is rebutted. The most obvious example of this is a power to bring primary legislation into force: that is a power to pull a trigger, which once pulled ceases have any effect.[47]

Delegation

12.3.2   As a general principle, the recipient of a statutory power cannot delegate it to anyone else unless the authority to delegate arises by express provision or necessary implication.[48]

A question arising frequently in relation to the nature of delegation is whether the delegate assumes sole and exclusive power to act or whether the power to act is shared between the delegate and the person in whom the power originally vested. As to this the following can be said—

(1) There are conflicting authorities as to whether in the absence of special determinative factors a delegation implies a denuding of the authority delegated by the person making the delegation.[49]

(2) The better modern view is that all else being equal a delegation does denude the person making it of the power delegated except in so far as an express reservation is made.[50]

---

[47] But as to the case where there is power to make transitional provision and as to revocation of the commencement provision before it has taken effect see Chapter 10, para.10.1.13.

[48] See also Chapter 3, Section 13, and Chapter 13; and see para.12.4.3 below.

[49] Compare, in particular, *Huth v Clarke* [1890] 25 QBD 391, *Gordon, Dadds & Co v Morris* [1945] 2 All E.R. 616, *Manton v Brighton Corporation* [1951] 2 K.B. 393 and *Blackpool Corporation v Locker* [1948] 1 K.B. 49.

[50] *Department for Environment, Food and Rural Affairs v Robertson* (2003) E.A.T. (UKEAT/ 0273/03/DM) in which Burton J. said—

"45 In any event we are of the view that, in ordinary parlance, delegation does imply denudation and that ordinarily (leaving aside instruction of a non-exclusive estate agent) it will not be regarded as appropriate for a delegor to go off and do himself, without notice to the delegate, what he has just delegated. There are dangers and uncertainties, in our judgment, in such concurrent authority. Mr Ford sought to distinguish a concept of transfer (such as is referred to in the 1975 Act), which he accepts does divest the transferor of powers, from that of delegation which he submits does not. We do not see that distinction. In our judgment a transfer would ordinarily imply an irrevocable horizontal transfer of powers, whereas delegation would imply a vertical transfer, very often, if not normally, accompanied by an express or implied retention of powers, but not so as a matter of course."

(3) It will in any case be important for the avoidance of doubt that in making a delegation provision is made expressly as to whether the delegation is intended to be exclusive or not.

Waiver, &c.

Despite the principle that the courts will not interfere to relieve against the effect of legislation[51] there is some ancient support for the proposition that people may contract out of, agree not to rely on, waive or establish an estoppel in relation to statutory rights, unless the contrary is expressly provided by the legislation concerned.[52] As Goddard L.J. put it in *Bowmaker v Tabor*[53]— **12.3.3**

> " . . . whether it be a case of contracting out or of waiver the same principles apply. The maxim which sanctions the non-observance of a statutory provision is *cuilibet licet renuntiare juri pro se introducto*. Everyone may waive the advantage of a law made solely for the benefit or protection of him as an individual in his private capacity, but this cannot be done if the waiver would infringe a public right or public policy: see *MacAllister v Bishop of Rochester*.[54] A good illustration of a protection that can be waived is afforded by the Statute of Limitations which a debtor can waive if he chooses: *East India Co. v Paul*."[55]

That being the case, it is common for modern statutes to provide expressly that rights and duties conferred or imposed may or may not be disapplied or waived by express agreement between the parties most closely concerned.

So, for example, s.73 of the Companies Act 1985[56] provided as follows— **12.3.4**

> "A condition requiring or binding an applicant for shares or debentures to waive compliance with any requirement imposed—
>
> (a) by subsection (2) of section 72, as regards the particulars to be contained in the prospectus, or
>
> (b) by subsection (3) of that section, as regards compliance with Schedule 3,

---

[51] See Chapter 17.

[52] See *Wright v Bagnall* [1900] 2 Q.B. 240; *East India Company v Paul* (1849) 7 Moore P.C. 85; *Supple v Cann* (1858) 9 Ir. Ch. R. 1; *Wilson v M'Intosh* [1894] A.C. 129; *Taylor v Clemson* (1844) 11 Cl. & F. 610, 643; *Mackenzie v Lord Powis* (1737) 7 Brown P.C. 282. But note that there may be unwaiveable rights as a matter of public policy, and that a right amounting to a rule of procedure or jurisdiction may not be at the disposal of either party to waive: see the various considerations discussed in *Kammins Ballrooms Co. Ltd v Zenith Investments (Torquay) Ltd* [1971] A.C. 850, HL and in *Equitable Life Assurance Society of the United States v Reed* [1914] A.C. 587, PC.

[53] [1941] 2 K.B. 1, 6, CA.

[54] (1880) 5 C.P.D. 194.

[55] (1849) 7 Moo. (P.C.) 85.

[56] 1985 c.6.

or purporting to affect an applicant with notice of any contract, document or matter not specifically referred to in the prospectus, is void."

And s.203(1) of the Employment Rights Act 1996[57] provides, subject to certain express exceptions, that—

"Any provision in an agreement (whether a contract of employment or not) is void in so far as it purports—

(1) to exclude or limit the operation of any provision of this Act, or
(2) to preclude a person from bringing any proceedings under this Act before an [employment tribunal]."

As to what amounts to waiver, what is required is some kind of behaviour that shows both that a person is aware of a right accruing under statute and that he has decided not to insist upon that right. Mere delay in enforcement does not amount to a waiver, although delay in circumstances in which it would be otherwise unaccountable may be evidence of a decision to waive.[58]

Duty to keep strictly within power

12.3.5 Where legislation authorises interference with property the power will be construed strictly against those exercising it, and the person authorised to interfere must adhere strictly to the power and proceed by the method, if there is one, indicated by the legislation.

If this duty is breached, however, it will be actionable only by someone who directly suffers loss or damage of a kind which gives rise to a cause of action (which will not, in this instance, be defeated by the legislation). Action in defence of the public right generally could, however, be taken by the Attorney General.[59]

Joint and concurrent exercise

12.3.6 For discussion of the difference between joint and concurrent exercise of a statutory power see Chapter 3, Section 12.

---

[57] 1986 c.18.

[58] "The question is, Has he waived it? In other words, is there evidence from which it may fairly be inferred that he consented to dispense with the notice? Bowen L.J. in *Selwyn v Garfit* ((1888) 38 Ch. D. 273, 284) says: 'What is waiver? Delay is not waiver. Inaction is not waiver, though it may be evidence of waiver. Waiver is consent to dispense with the notice. If it could be shewn that the mortgagor had power to waive the notice, and that he knew that the notice had not been served, but said nothing before the sale and nothing after it, although this would not be conclusive, there would be a case which required to be answered.'"—*Toronto Corporation v Russell* [1908] A.C. 493 at 500, 499, PC *per* Lord Atkinson.

[59] *Mayor of Liverpool v Chorley Waterworks Co.* (1852) 2 De G. M. & G. 852.

SECTION 4

MINISTERIAL POWERS AND DUTIES

Introduction

In relation to statutory powers conferred on Ministers of the Crown a number of **12.4.1** considerations apply that do not apply to the performance of powers and duties by private individuals.

Challenge

The first and most important, the availability of judicial review, has already been **12.4.2** adverted to.[60] Details of the criteria to be applied, and the remedies available, on the review of administrative action will be found in specialist works on administrative law. Details of the procedures to be followed in seeking judicial review will be found in specialist works on civil procedure.

Carltona

The other principal distinctive feature of a power vested in Ministers is the **12.4.3** assumption that they are entitled to exercise the power through the medium of their civil servants. This is known as the *Carltona* rule, having been established in the case of *Carltona Ltd v Commissioners of Works*[61] in the following words of the judgment of Lord Greene M.R.[62]—

"In the administration of government in this country the functions which are given to ministers (and constitutionally properly given to ministers because they are constitutionally responsible) are functions so multifarious that no minister could ever personally attend to them. To take the example of the present case no doubt there have been thousands of requisitions in this country by individual ministers. It cannot be supposed that this regulation meant that, in each case, the minister in person should direct his mind to the matter. The duties imposed upon ministers and the powers given to ministers are normally exercised under the authority of the ministers by responsible officials of the department. Public business could not be carried on if that were not the case. Constitutionally, the decision of such an official is, of course, the decision of the minister. The minister is responsible. It is he who must answer before Parliament for anything that his officials have done under his authority, and, if for an important matter he selected an official of such junior standing that he could not be expected competently to

---

[60] Chapter 3, Section 6.
[61] [1943] 2 All E.R. 560, CA.
[62] At 563.

perform the work, the minister would have to answer for that in Parliament. The whole system of departmental organisation and administration is based on the view that ministers, being responsible to Parliament, will see that important duties are committed to experienced officials. If they do not do that, Parliament is the place where complaint must be made against them."

The principle in *Carltona* is a specific exception to the rule that a recipient of delegated power cannot assume the authority to pass on the delegation by sub-delegating the power,[63] the rationale for the general rule being that the donor of the power may have conferred it specifically in reliance on confidence in the judgment of the recipient as to its exercise, but he may not wish to repose the same degree of confidence in a variety of people of whose identity he is unaware. The *Carltona* exception arises only because it is clear beyond doubt that in conferring a power on a Ministerial office the legislature cannot possibly intend the holder of the office to exercise it personally, there being such a plethora of executive functions of each ministerial office.

12.4.4   For this reason the *Carltona* principle, although principally developed in and associated with the context of Ministerial functions, will also apply where Parliament confers functions on a person or body who or which cannot realistically be expected to perform those functions without both the use of staff and the delegation to staff of certain discretionary decisions.[64] Because of the limited circumstances in which the courts will be prepared to extend *Carltona*, however, delegation is normally provided for expressly.[65]

The principle in *Carltona* is not without its exceptions.

---

[63] *Delegatus non potest delegare.*

[64] But the courts will imply a power to delegate only sparingly and in the face of practical absurdity in its absence. See, for leading example, *Attorney-General ex rel. McWhirter v Independent Broadcasting Authority* [1973] Q.B. 629, CA—"At that stage it seems to me that the authority, in order to do their duty properly as the statute requires, should have seen it and satisfied themselves personally that nothing in it was likely to be offensive to public feeling. They may, of course, delegate many things to the staff, but occasions may arise—and this may be one—when no delegation will suffice. They must satisfy themselves personally." (*per* Lord Denning M.R. at 636).

[65] See, for example, the following—
The Railways and Transport Safety Act 2003 (c.20), Sch.1, para.7 (Office of Rail Regulation)—
  "7 The Office may delegate a function to—
      (1) (a) the Chief Executive or another employee, or
      (2) (b) a committee.".
The Private Security Industry Act 2001 (c.12), Sch.1, para.9 (the Security Industry Authority)—
  "9 (1) The Authority may, to such extent as it may determine, delegate any of its functions to any committee of the Authority or to any employee of the Authority.
    (2) Any such committee may, to such extent as it may determine, delegate any function conferred on it to any of its sub-committees or to any employee of the Authority.
    (3) Any sub-committee of the Authority may, to such extent as the sub-committee may determine, delegate any functions conferred on the sub-committee to any employee of the Authority."

On some specific occasions when *Carltona* would otherwise apply, Parliament does intend that a Minister should exercise a power personally—and when that is the intention Parliament provides for it expressly.[66]

Generally, a power to make subordinate legislation conferred on a Minister does not confer the power to sub-delegate.[67]

As to who are proper recipients of a delegated power under the rule in **12.4.5** *Carltona*, the normal case is of delegation to established civil servants in the department of the Minister in whom the power is vested.

The question arises from time to time whether a Minister in another Department, or an official of a Minister in another Department, is a proper *Carltona* delegate of statutory powers. What is clear is that where a power vests in one Minister he is not entitled simply to transfer it informally[68] to another Minister. He is entitled "to have regard to the policies of the Government generally and to consult the department of state most closely connected with any particular subject".[69] And a Minister may have officials who work principally in another minister's Department advice him in relation to a particular matter. But he may not simply hand over the decision to another department and "rubber stamp" its decisions. The matter is of course of less practical importance than it was now that statutory functions are mostly vested in the Secretary of State at large.[70]

It is clear that an individual who is a civil servant but also the holder of a statutory office implying some degree of operational independence may nevertheless, in appropriate circumstances, be the proper recipient of a *Carltona* delegation from the senior Minister of the department to which he belongs or with which his functions are most closely associated.[71]

---

[66] See, for example, s.48(3) of the Anti-terrorism, Crime and Security Act 2001 (c.24), s.1(3) of the Nuclear Explosions (Prohibition and Inspections) Act 1998 (c.7) or s.25B(2) of the Immigration Act 1971 (c.77) as inserted by s.143 of the Nationality, Immigration and Asylum Act 2002 (c.41) ("Subsection (3) applies where the Secretary of State personally directs that the exclusion from the United Kingdom of an individual who is a citizen of the European Union is conducive to the public good."); see also s.13(5) of the Immigration Act 1971 as originally enacted—" . . . if the Secretary of Sate certifies that directions have been given by the Secretary of State (and not by a person acting under his authority) . . . "—in which case it was presumably permissible for a *Carltona* delegate to act in certifying that directions were given but not in giving directions!

[67] See Chapter 3, Section 5.

[68] As opposed to arranging transfer by Transfer of Functions Order, as to which see Chapter 3, Section 12.

[69] *R. v Secretary of Sate for Trade, Ex p. Chris International Foods Limited* (Case CO/1020/82, Friday March 4, 1983 QBD—the "bananas case"), *per* Hodgson J.

[70] See further para.3.12.8.

[71] See the decision of the House of Lords in *R v Secretary of State for the Home Department, Ex p. Oladehinde* [1991] 1 A.C. 254, HL—Lord Griffiths said (at 301–302)—

"The appellants submit that immigration officers are the holders of a statutory office and as such they are independent of the executive arm of government and cannot have devolved upon them any of the executive's powers. Therefore it is said the Carltona principle cannot extend to cover the exercise of the Secretary of State's powers by an immigration inspector.

"Alternatively it is submitted that if immigration officers are civil servants in the Home Office the structure of the Act, which differentiates between the powers of the immigration

Transfer of powers

12.4.6 As to the transfer of powers among Ministers, see Chapter 3, Section 12.

Executive agencies and Government Trading Funds

12.4.7 As to the position of Executive Agencies and Government Trading Funds, see Chapter 11, Section 5.

Liability in relation to performance of functions

12.4.8 In the case of powers vested in Ministers, the principles outlined in Sections 3 above and 5 and 6 below must be approached in the light of the Crown Proceedings Act 1947.[72] [73]

Joint and concurrent exercise

12.4.9 For explanation of the difference between joint and concurrent exercise of powers, see Chapter 3, Section 12.

Subjectivity, reasonableness, &c.

12.4.10 For discussion of the subjectivity of *vires* and the extent to which a requirement of reasonableness will be required see Chapter 3, Section 4, paras 3.4.6—3.4.9.

---

officers which are primarily concerned with entry control and subsequent policing of illegal immigrants, and the powers of the Secretary of State in relation to deportation carries with it a clear statutory implication that the powers of the Secretary of State are not to be exercised by immigration officers.

"I cannot accept either of these submissions. I have no doubt in my mind that immigration officers have been civil servants since they were first employed under the Aliens Act 1905. The fact that nowhere in the Act of 1971 is there any reference to an immigration service, or the structure of such a service, is only explicable in terms that it was recognised that it had evolved as part of the Home Office expanding over the years. The status of immigration officers is not that of statutory office holders such as adjudicators or members of appeal tribunals who are referred to in the Act as office holders: see Schedule 3, paragraphs 2 and 8. Immigration officers are civil servants in the Home Office to whom are assigned specific statutory duties under the Act. Apart from a small pay lead in recognition of their statutory responsibilities their conditions of service and grading are in all respects comparable to other Home Office civil servants. The Act makes no provision for the management of the immigration service for that is the function of the Home Office of which the service is a part.

Immigration inspectors are senior line managers and as such will rarely exercise the specific powers given to immigration officers by the Act.";

This decision shows that in determining the status of a particular office-holder, and the permissibility of a Carltona delegation, a rigorous analysis of the circumstances within which he operates is required.

See also the reference in para.11.5.9, footnote 49, to *Re Minotaur Data Systems Ltd.*

[72] 1947 c.44; see, in particular, the provisions cited in para.14.5.8.

[73] See also, in cases relating to depreciation of land-values caused by public works, the Land Compensation Act 1973 (c.26) and, in particular, the cumulative effect of ss.1(6) and 17.

Recipients of power

For discussion of which Ministerial offices are appropriate recipients of legis- **12.4.11**
lative power see Chapter 6, Section 1.

Obligation to comply with statutory duty

There is an obligation on all to whom a statutory duty applies to comply with **12.5.1**
it.[74]

Generally speaking this obligation will be supported by an express sanction,
whether by breach of the duty being made an offence or by some other
consequence of breach being specified. But sometimes it is acceptable for the
legislation imposing a duty to be silent as to the consequences of breach, either
because in the context the consequences are obvious[75] or because the duty is
addressed to a public authority as to whom no consequence but those provided
by the rules of administrative law is necessary or appropriate.

Excuses for failing to discharge statutory duty

Although ignorance of the law is in general no excuse for failing to comply with **12.5.2**
it,[76] there are a number of circumstances in which the legislature does not intend
to expose a person to criminal or other punishment for failure to comply with a
requirement of which he could not reasonably have been aware.

In the criminal context this is frequently avoided by legislation making it an
offence to do something "without reasonable excuse".[77] The same approach is
also used in other contexts.[78]

The qualification "without reasonable excuse" is designed to admit possibilities other than ignorance of the law. Where it is only that situation which it is

---

[74] Ignorance is no excuse—see Chapter 9, Section 1.
[75] As, for example, where an applicant is under a duty to include some information in the application,
or to pay a fee, and the consequence of failure to do so is that his application will not be
entertained. In such a context it is common for the statute simply to say that an application must
contain specified information or be accompanied by a fee, leaving the consequence of failure to be
inferred. See, for example, s.2(2) of the Commonhold and Leasehold Reform Act 2002
(c.15)—"(2) An application under this section must be accompanied by the documents listed in
Schedule 1."
[76] See Chapter 9, Section 1.
[77] See, for example, s.8(3) of the Railways and Transport Safety Act 2003 (c.20).
[78] Such as the imposition of a civil penalty (see para.141A of Sch.6 to the Finance Act 2000 (c.17))
or the triggering of a Minister's default power (see s.14(1) of the Adoption and Children Act 2002
(c.38)).

designed to cover, the legislature is sometimes more specific.[79] Again, this can be used outside criminal provisions.[80]

Evasion and avoidance of statutory duties

12.5.3 The courts will not interfere to prevent an evasion of a statutory duty. The nature and extent of this principle is expounded by Lindley L.J. in *Yorkshire Railway Wagon Company v Maclure*[81]—

> "There is always an ambiguity about the expression 'evading an Act of Parliament'; in one sense you cannot evade an Act of Parliament; that is to say, the court is bound so to construe every Act of Parliament, as to take care that that which is really prohibited may be held void. On the other hand, you may avoid doing that which is prohibited by the Act of Parliament, and you may do something else equally advantageous to you which is not prohibited by the Act of Parliament."

In similar vein Lord Cranworth said in *Edwards v Hall*[82]—

> "I never understood what is meant by an evasion of an Act of Parliament; either you are within the Act of Parliament or not within the Act of Parliament: if you are not within it you have a right to avoid it, to keep out of the prohibition."[83]

The essence of what is permissible and impermissible is expressed by Lord Sumner in *Levene v Inland Revenue Commissioners*[84]—

> "It is trite law that His Majesty's subjects are free if they can to make their own arrangements so that their cases fall outside the scope of the taxing Acts. They incur no legal penalties and, strictly speaking, no moral censure if, having considered the lines drawn by the legislature for the imposition of the taxes, they make it their business to walk outside them."

---

[79] See, for example, s.89(6) of the Care Standards Act 2000 (c.14).

[80] See, for example, s.7E(6) of the Industrial and Provident Societies Act 1965 (c.12) inserted by s.3 of the Co-operatives and Community Benefit Societies Act 2003 (c.15).

[81] (1882) 21 Ch. D. 309, 318.

[82] (1855) 25 L.J. Ch. 82, 84.

[83] See also Willes J. in *Jefferies v Alexander* (1860) 8 H.L.C. 594, 637—"To say that what was done is an evasion of the law is idle, unless it means that, though in apparent accordance with it, it really was in contravention of the law." And Grove J. said in *Attorney-General v Noyes* (1881) 8 Q.B.D. 125, 133—"The word 'evasion' may mean either of two things.It may mean an evasion of the Act by something which, while it evades the Act, is within the sense of it, or it may mean an evading of the Act by doing something to which the Act does not apply."

[84] [1928] A.C. 217, 227, HL.

Again in the fiscal context, Lord Tomlin said in *Inland Revenue Commis-* **12.5.4**
sioners v Westminster (Duke)[85]—

> "Every man is entitled, if he can, to order his affairs so that tax attaching
> under appropriate Acts is less than it otherwise would be. If he succeeds in
> ordering them so as to secure this result, then, however unappreciative the
> Commissioners of Inland Revenue or his fellow taxpayers may be of his
> ingenuity, he cannot be compelled to pay an increased tax. The so-called
> doctrine of 'the substance' seems to me to be nothing more than an attempt
> to make a man pay notwithstanding that he has so ordered his affairs that the
> amount of tax sought from him is not legally claimable."

One of the most helpful recent authoritative statements of the difference
between lawful evasion and unlawful avoidance occurs in the context not of tax
but of leasehold, and is found in a passage of an academic treatise on the topic
cited with approval in *Jones v Wrotham Park Settled Estates*[86]—

> "In the second place Counsel . . . relied on the distinction drawn in decided
> cases in relation to the Rent Acts between, on the one hand, attempted
> exclusion of those Acts, and on the other the parties' bona fide entering into
> a situation where those Acts have no application; a distinction which is
> clearly stated in the following passages in *Megarry on the Rent Acts*[87]:
>
>> '(a) Genuine Transactions. There is nothing, however, to prevent the
>> parties from so arranging matters that there is nothing to which the Acts
>> can apply, provided the transaction in question is a genuine transaction
>> and not a mere sham, such as a tenancy disguised as a contract for sale;
>> "real and lawful intentions cannot be dismissed as shams merely because
>> they are disliked." The difference is between on the one hand a provision
>> attempting to exclude the Acts from a transaction to which they apply,
>> and on the other hand entering into a bona fide transaction to which the
>> Acts have no application.
>>
>> '(b) Evasion and avoidance. "There is every difference between evasion
>> and avoidance." "You do not evade an Act by doing something which is
>> not forbidden by the Act, but you do evade the Act by doing something
>> which is prohibited under the guise of doing something else.' "

It will be seen from all this that the essence of the distinction between what is **12.5.5**
lawful and what is unlawful is the presence or absence of dishonesty in the sense
of an attempt to mislead and to present a transaction as having a purpose other

---

[85] [1936] A.C. 1, 19; *c.f.* Lord Simon's suggestion in *Latilla v Inland Revenue Commissioners* [1943]
A.C. 377, 381 that there is no reason why the efforts of persons to avoid tax "should be regarded
as a commendable exercise of ingenuity or as a discharge of the duties of good citizenship".
[86] [1978] 3 All ER 527, 533, CA *per* Orr L.J.
[87] 10th edn. (1967), pp.19–20.

than that which it has. This is the concept of the "mere sham" which is much litigated in the fiscal context.

> If a person gives his children his property not because he is motivated by a desire to transfer it now but merely because he wishes to avoid the eventual transfer on his death from being liable to tax, he does nothing unlawful.

> If he pretends to give his children his property, for the purpose of avoiding a statutory duty to pay tax, but intending to keep the property actually for his own use, he is guilty of an avoidance.

> If he enters into a transaction which is real so far as it goes but partakes of the character of no kind of transaction that a person would enter into but for the desire to evade a liability to tax, he and the Inland Revenue are likely to disagree.[88]

12.5.6   This last case comes into the context of what is sometimes described as a fraud upon an Act, the idea being that a contract, for example, which is framed so as entirely to defeat the object of an Act of Parliament may be held to be impliedly forbidden despite not coming within its express prohibition.[89]

Where legitimate evasion ends and fraudulent avoidance begins is, however, generally open to debate. As Turner L.J. said in *Alexander v Brame*[90]—

> "[there is] perhaps no question of law more difficult to determine than the question, what particular acts, not expressly prohibited, shall be deemed to be void as being against the policy of a statute. It is not doubt the duty of the courts so to construe statutes as to suppress the mischief against which they are directed, and to advance the remedy which they are intended to provide; but it is one thing to construe the words of a statute, and another to extend its operation beyond what the words of it express."

This passage of the Turner L.J.'s judgment helpfully refers to the notion of the mischief at which legislation is directed. In determining whether activity is evasion or avoidance it will be appropriate to apply the rules in *Heydon's Case*[91] for the purposes of determining the mischief at which the legislation aims and of endeavouring to "suppress subtle inventions and evasions for the continuance of the mischief".[92]

---

[88] See the case of *Ingram v Inland Revenue Commissioners* [2000] 1 A.C. 293, HL and the resultant s.102A of the Finance Act 1986 (c.41) (gifts with reservation: interest in land) as inserted by s.104 of the Finance Act 1999 (c.16).
[89] See *Wright v Davies* (1876) 1 C.P.D. 638 and *Fox v Bishop of Chester* (1829) 1 Dow & Cl. 416.
[90] (1855) 7 De G.M. & G. 525, 539.
[91] See Chapter 20.
[92] Same.

Occasional express prohibitions of and references to evasion are found in **12.5.7**
statute, the principal example being the Value Added Tax Act 1994.[93] [94]

As to whether an action can be within the letter of the law but not within the
spirit of the law—

> It is clear from the discussion above that the courts will give effect only to
> the letter of the law, that is to say what the legislature has enacted rather than
> what it might have enacted had it thought about it.

> But it is equally clear that in determining what the letter of the law means,
> and what is intended to be encompassed by language capable of a breadth
> of construction, the courts will have regard to the spirit of the law, meaning
> the obvious intention with which the letter of the law was framed.

In this context Sir Roundell Palmer said in 1872[95]—   **12.5.8**

> "Nothing is better settled than that a statute is to be expounded, not
> according to the letter, but according to the meaning and spirit of it. What
> is within the true meaning and spirit of the statute is as much law as what
> is within the very letter of it, and that which is not within the meaning and
> spirit, though it seems to be within the letter, is not the law, and is not the
> statute. That effect should be given to the object, spirit, and meaning of a
> statute is a rule of legal construction, but the object, spirit, and meaning
> must be collected from the words used in the statute. It must be such an
> intention as the legislature has used fit words to express."

On the question of whether the law has a spirit for practical purposes, the
exception proves the rule: in the case of taxing enactments the determination of
the courts not to permit themselves to prefer the apparent underlying intention of

---

[93] 1994 c.23: see ss.60, 61, 72, 76 and 84. And see *R v Dealy* [1995] 1 W.L.R. 658, CA.

[94] See also what were, when this work went to print, clause 19 and Pt 7 of the Finance Bill 2003–04
and which will have become sections of the Finance Act 2004 by the time this work is published.
Clause 19 deals with tax avoidance in relation to Value Added Tax, while Pt 7, entitled Disclosure
of Tax Avoidance Schemes, establishes a requirement of notification for schemes which—
> "(a) fall within any description prescribed by the Treasury by regulations,
> (b) enable any person to obtain an advantage in relation to any tax that is so prescribed in
>   relation to arrangements of that description, and
> (c) are such that the main benefit, or one of the main benefits, that might be expected to
>   arise from the arrangements is the obtaining of that advantage."

[95] 209 Hansard, Parl. Deb. (3rd Series) 685. This speech was made in the context of the appointment
of Sir Robert Collier in November 1871 as a member of the Judicial Committee of the Privy
Council. That incident was a classic case of the letter of the law being complied with in a manner
that appeared to undermine the legislative intention. An Act (34 & 35 Vict. c.91) required
appointees to the Judicial Committee to be or have been judges of a superior court. Sir Robert, who
was Attorney-General, was made a judge of the Court of Common Pleas and, one week later and
without ever having sat as a judge, was appointed to the Judicial Committee. A motion in the
House of Commons condemning the appointment was narrowly defeated. As to the use of context
of an Act generally and recourse to its apparent purpose as an aid to its construction, see Chapters
18 to 20.

an enactment to its letter is often forcibly contrasted by the courts with the greater latitude that they might permit themselves in other contexts.[96] As Lord Reid said[97]—

> "It is sometimes said that we should apply the spirit and not the letter of the law so as to bring in cases which, though not within the letter of the law, are within the mischief at which the law is aimed. But it has long been recognised that our courts cannot so apply taxing Acts."[98]

The fact that a statutory regime has a clear social purpose does not mean that the courts will always feel able to act so as to prevent a course of conduct which is clearly designed to circumvent the statute and undermine its intention. In *In re C (A Minor) (Adoption: Illegality)*,[99] for example, the High Court found that although the statutory regime of adoption law, with its rigorous screening processes, was being consistently and deliberately circumvented by people obtaining foreign adoption orders and seeking to have them confirmed here, the courts were nevertheless powerless to refuse confirmation where it was in the best interests of the child *post facto*.

See also Chapter 2, Section 3.

SECTION 6

ENFORCEMENT

Duty of courts to give effect to legislative rights and duties

12.6.1   The essential duty of the courts in relation to rights and duties emanating from legislation has been established in relation to the general duty to give effect to Acts (and powers delegated under an Act).[1]

The requirement for certainty that applies in relation to the validity of subordinate legislation[2] is equally relevant to the enforceability of statutory duties.[3]

---

[96] For an example of another context, see "The provision which we have found not to be complied with is not one . . . that is in the Act. Indeed, it is in a sense not one which is laid down by law at all. But it is a requirement which, in our judgment, certainly ought to be fulfilled, that the spirit of the requirements of the first schedule should be complied with."—*R v Salt* [1996] 8 Admin L.R. 429, 434, CA, *per* Staughton L.J.

[97] *Inland Revenue Commissioners v Saunders* [1958] A.C. 285, HL.

[98] The clear implication being that they can so apply certain other enactments—as to which see Chapter 20, paras 20.1.4 and 20.1.5.

[99] [1999] 2 W.L.R. 203 F.

[1] See Chapter 2, Section 3.

[2] See Chapter 3, Sections 4 and 6.

[3] As Chief Justice Vaughan put it in *Sheppard v Gosnold* (Vaughan, 159, 166)—"A duty impossible to be known can be no duty; for civilly, what cannot be known to be, is as that which is not." See *Barrow v Arnaud* 1846 (8 Q.B. 595, 608).

Mandatory or directory?

There is a fundamental distinction to be drawn between duties that are intended **12.6.2**
to be enforceable as such by the courts and duties that, while not entirely without
legal effect, are not attended by any sanction and are not therefore intended to be
directly enforceable by the courts.

The distinction has sometimes, although not entirely consistently, been
encapsulated in the expressions "mandatory duty" and "directory duty".

The nature of the distinction was discussed by Millett L.J. in *Petch v Gurney
(Inspector of Taxes)*[4]—

> "The difficulty arises from the common practice of the legislature of stating
> that something 'shall' be done (which means that it 'must' be done) without
> stating what are to be the consequences if it is not done. The court has dealt
> with the problem by devising a distinction between those requirements
> which are said to be 'mandatory' (or 'imperative' or 'obligatory') and those
> which are said to be merely 'directory' (a curious use of the word which in
> this context is taken as equivalent to 'permissive'). Where the requirement
> is mandatory, it must be strictly complied with; failure to comply invalidates
> everything that follows. Where it is merely directory, it should still be
> complied with, and there may be sanctions for disobedience; but failure to
> comply does not invalidate what follows.

> "The principles upon which this question should be decided are well **12.6.3**
> established. The court must attempt to discern the legislative intention. In
> *Liverpool Borough Bank v Turner*[5] Lord Campbell L.C. said:

>> 'No universal rule can be laid down for the construction of statutes, as to
>> whether mandatory enactments shall be considered directory only or
>> obligatory, with an implied nullification for disobedience. It is the duty of
>> Courts of justice to try to get at the real intention of the legislature, by
>> carefully attending to the whole scope of the statute to be construed.'

> "In a well-known passage of his judgment in *Howard v Bodington*[6] Lord
> Penzance said:

>> 'I believe, as far as any rule is concerned, you cannot safely go further
>> than that in each case you must look to the subject-matter; consider the
>> importance of the provision that has been disregarded, and the relation of
>> that provision to the general object intended to be secured by the Act; and
>> upon a review of the case in that aspect decide whether the matter is what
>> is called imperative or only directory.' "

---

[4] [1994] 3 All E.R. 731, 735–36, CA.
[5] (1861) 30 L.J. Ch 379, 380.
[6] (1877) 2 P.D. 203, 211.

12.6.4   It will be noted that Millett L.J.'s remarks are principally of relevance in the context of a duty that is a subordinate feature of a larger process, where validity or invalidity of other things forming part of the process is relevant.

In other contexts the distinction between directory and mandatory may be less helpful. In *Woodhouse v Consignia plc*,[7] for example, Brooke L.J. said[8] that "such expressions as 'bound', 'required' and obligatory' are in a very strict sense inappropriate when used in the explanation of a rule which deploys the directory word 'will' rather than the mandatory word 'must'." But Brooke L.J. does not in this context expand on what is the difference between legislation "directing" me to do something and "mandating" me to do it. If "will" is used otherwise than in a merely predictory sense—its most common use in conversation—but in a sense which has some degree of imperative, it is hard to see that there can be degrees. In essence, if Parliament instructs a person—whether of a public or private nature—to do something, it matters not whether Parliament says "shall", "must", "will" or "is to"[9]: the person is obliged to do the thing, and the courts will find methods of enforcement.[10]

The same distinction is sometimes expressed as being between procedural irregularities and substantive deficiencies[11]; the former being waiveable and the latter not.

Public enforcement of statutory duty

12.6.5   Very often the legislature will provide a sanction for breach of a public duty by creating a criminal offence that exposes a person to a criminal penalty.[12]

Where the legislature imposes a duty on a public body it frequently provides for no express sanction of any kind, relying on the existence of the administrative law system to provide the sanction. The availability of judicial review of

---

[7] [2003] 2 All E.R. 738, CA.

[8] Para.41.

[9] The reason for the choice between, in particular, "shall" and "must" varies. Some draftsmen routinely eschew the legislative "shall" on the grounds of alleged archaism. Others use it exclusively. Still others use sometimes one and sometimes the other. There is, for example, a school of thought that it is convenient to use "shall" when imposing an obligation on a person and "must" when stating a condition precedent without which an act or thing is invalid. It will be noticed that the latter distinction conveniently matches the distinction between mandatory and directory propositions in Millett L.J.'s judgment cited above.

[10] Although fines and imprisonment are available only where statutory power so provides, even where other remedies are used first—such as injunctive or even merely declaratory remedies—in the event of continued non-compliance the courts will be able to use fines or imprisonment in reliance on the law of contempt of court, and even where the person under the original statutory duty is a legal person and not a natural person, there will be always individuals (even in the case of public entities) who can be acted against if the legal person's non-compliance is directly attributable to the individuals' will.

[11] See, for example, *Hargreaves v Alderson* [1964] 2 Q.B. 159, QBD or *Elsden v Pick* [1980] 3 All E.R. 235, CA.

[12] See further Chapter 1, Section 5, and, in particular, as to the notion that there is not, or at least is no longer, any common law criminal sanction for breach of statutory duty, see para.1.5.4.

administrative action through the High Court means that public bodies of all kinds, from relatively minor administrative bodies to senior Ministers, are susceptible to challenge in the High Court, which has a range of remedies available to require or prohibit action.[13]

The High Court will also on occasion exercise its equitable jurisdiction for the purposes of retraining the breach of a statutory duty or for the purpose of compelling the performance of a statutory duty. As Farwell J. established in *Stevens v Chown*[14]—

"In my opinion, there was nothing to prevent the old Court of Chancery from granting an injunction to restrain the infringement of a newly created statutory right, unless the Act of Parliament creating the right provided a remedy which it enacted should be the only remedy—subject only to this, that the right so created was such a right as the Court under its original jurisdiction would take cognizance of."

It is probable that the growth of the scope of judicial review has reduced the likely area of application of the High Court's equitable jurisdiction in relation to the enforcement of statutory duties.

As a general rule, therefore, it is considered acceptable to impose a statutory duty on any body susceptible to judicial review without creating an express sanction of any kind.[15]

Private right of action

Legislation in all areas of the law places duties of various kinds on various kinds of legal person. The question frequently arises, in the case where a duty is placed on a person who is of a public character in some way, whether breach of the duty is intended to give rise to a cause of action at the instance of a person who suffers loss or harm as a result of the breach, or whether only public remedies are intended to be available (which would, broadly, be competent to prevent repetition of the breach but might not be able to achieve much or anything in relation to the consequences of the breach that has already occurred).

12.6.6

---

[13] As Lloyd L.J. said in *R. v Horseferry Road Justices, Ex p. Independent Broadcasting Authority* [1987] Q.B. 54, DC—"If the applicants neglect or refuse to perform their duty under that subsection, it would be open to the Attorney-General or perhaps an individual, to apply for an order of mandamus, to compel them to do so. I say, 'perhaps an individual,' because the point was left open in *Reg. v Independent Broadcasting Authority, Ex p. Whitehouse.*" (T.L.R. April 4, 1985 CA).

[14] [1901] 1 Ch. 894, 904.

[15] An extreme example is s.64 of the Police and Criminal Evidence Act 1984 (c.60), which imposes negative and positive duties in relation to certain fingerprints taken by the police, without specifying either any sanction for non-compliance or even on precisely whom, or even on which police force, the duty falls. The assumption is that the trail of responsibility will be capable of being sufficiently established as a result of statutory and other rules for apportionment of responsibility between and within police forces, to enable any necessary action to be taken to compel compliance through the administrative law system.

The background to the question as it is presently approached[16] appears from the following passage of the speech of Lord Atkin in *East Suffolk Rivers Catchment Board v Kent*[17]—

"The duty imposed by statute is primarily a duty owed to the State. Occasionally penalties are imposed by the statute for breach; and, speaking generally, in the absence of special sanctions imposed by the statute the breach of duty amounts to a common law misdemeanour. The duty is not necessarily a duty owed to a private citizen. The duty may, however, be imposed for the protection of particular citizens or class of citizens, in which case a person of the protected class can sue for injury to him due to the breach. The cases as to breach of the Factory or Coal Mines Act are instances. . . .

"But apart from the existence of a public duty to the public, every person whether discharging a public duty or not is under a common law obligation to some persons in some circumstances to conduct himself with reasonable care so as not to injure those persons likely to be affected by his want of care. This duty exists whether a person is performing a public duty, or merely exercising a power which he possesses either under statutory authority or in pursuance of his ordinary rights as a citizen. To whom the obligation is owed is, as I see it, the principal question in the present case."

12.6.7   So—

(1) Statute may impose a pure public duty (as to which no private interests are intended to arise), a pure private duty or a hybrid.

(2) Even in the case of a pure public duty, a common law duty arises to perform it in a way which is not injurious to private interests (except where the injury is clearly contemplated by the legislature).

A test for determining whether a statutory duty gives rise to a private right of action was stated by Lord Browne-Wilkinson in the case of *X (Minors) v Bedfordshire County Council*[18]—

"The principles applicable in determining whether such statutory cause of action exist are now well established, although the application of those principles in any particular case remains difficult. The basic proposition is that in the ordinary case a breach of statutory duty does not, by itself, give

---

[16] For some historical observations on the issue see the Final Report of Departmental Committee on Alternative Remedies (Ministry of National Insurance) July 1946 Cmd. 6860.

[17] [1941] A.C. 74, 87–88, HL.

[18] [1995] 2 A.C. 633, 731.

rise to any private law cause of action. However a private law cause of action will arise if it can be shown, as a matter of construction of the statute, that the statutory duty was imposed for the protection of a limited class of the public and that Parliament intended to confer on members of that class a private right of action for breach of the duty. There is no general rule by reference to which it can be decided whether a statute does create such a right of action by there are a number of indicators. If the statute provides no other remedy for its breach and the Parliamentary intention to protect a limited class is shown, that indicates that there may be a private right of action since otherwise there is no method of securing the protection the statute was intended to confer. If the statute does provide some other means of enforcing the duty that will normally indicate that the statutory right was intended to be enforceable by those means and not by private right of action: *Cutler v Wandsworth Stadium Ltd*[19]; *Lonrho Ltd v Shell Petroleum Co. Ltd (No.2)*.[20] However, the mere existence of some other statutory remedy is not necessarily decisive. It is still possible to show that on the true construction of the statute the protected class was intended by Parliament to have a private remedy. Thus the specific duties imposed on employers in relation to factory premises are enforceable by an action for damages, notwithstanding the imposition by the statutes of criminal penalties for breach: see *Groves v Wimborne (Lord)*.[21]"

A number of cases since *X (Minors)* have had to apply the principles set out by Lord Browne-Wilkinson. The essence of the tests specified are that they have to be applied in each case by reference to the circumstances of the legislation, so it is inevitable that the application of the test will fall to be litigated regularly. It is not possible to distil principles of general application beyond those specified above. **12.6.8**

There are, however, cases that illustrate the nature of the balancing exercise to be undertaken in attempting to apply the principles to new sets of circumstances.

In *Roe v Sheffield City Council*[22] the Court of Appeal had to address a provision of the Tramways Act 1870[23] which authorised an interference with the highway by the grant of specific rights to a tramway company but required the company to take certain steps in relation to the work. Pill L.J. said—

"It is, in my judgment, likely that, having authorised an interference with the highway, Parliament intended to create a private cause of action where the duties imposed on the tramway company in the statute conferring the

---

[19] [1949] A.C. 398.
[20] [1982] A.C. 173.
[21] [1898] 2 Q.B. 402.
[22] [2003] 2 W.L.R. 848, CA.
[23] 1870 c.78.

right are breached. The situation is much more akin to the statutes imposing duties on employers than to the schemes of social welfare considered in cases such as *X (Minors) v Bedfordshire County Council*. The duty is limited to the physical construction and maintenance of works and is quite specific. As to the alleged, though in context somewhat nebulous, requirement for a limited class, road users will be very numerous but are, in my judgment, sufficiently a class for present purposes."[24]

12.6.9 In *Barrett v Enfield London Borough Council*[25] the House of Lords restored a claim previously struck out as disclosing no reasonable cause of action and discussed *X (Minors)* in the light of the possibility that an authority faced with possible private legal proceedings in respect of its performance of its care functions for children might come to be over-cautious. Lord Slynn affirmed[26] the following dictum of Evans L.J. in the Court of Appeal in *Barrett*—

> "I would agree that what is said to be a 'policy' consideration, namely that imposing a duty of care might lead to defensive conduct on the part of the person concerned and might require him to spend time or resources on keeping full records or otherwise providing for self-justification, if called upon to do so, should normally be a factor of little, if any, weight. If the conduct in question is of a kind which can be measured against the standards of the reasonable man, placed as the defendant was, then I do not see why the law in the public interest should not require those standards to be observed."

Where legislation is clearly creating a right or duty in circumstances in which the question of private enforcement or liability is likely to arise, it will obviously be in the interests of clarity for the legislation to make express provision either confirming or denying the right of private action.[27]

12.6.10 The Court of Appeal in *D. v East Berkshire National Health Service Trust*[28] reviewed a number of post-*X (Minors)* cases and, without disturbing the essence of the tests adumbrated in that case, found that a number of decisions since *X (Minors)* have reduced the breadth of the range of cases in which application of those tests would preclude the existence of a duty of care. The Court also considered the effect of the Human Rights Act 1998[29] and concluded that in a number of instances, the investigation of child abuse being that concerned in *East*

---

[24] At 864.
[25] [2001] 2 A.C. 550, HL.
[26] At 568–569.
[27] See, for example, s.70(a) of the Water Resources Act 1991 (c.57)—" . . . the restrictions imposed by ss.24, 25 and 30 above shall not be construed as— (a) conferring a right of action in any civil proceedings (other than proceedings for the recovery of a fine) in respect of any contravention of those restrictions".
[28] [2003] 4 All E.R. 796.
[29] 1998 c.42.

Berkshire itself, the Convention would make it impossible to deny a duty of care.[30]

Given the uncertainty of the application to particular cases of the tests outlined by the courts above[31] it is of course desirable for legislation to make specific provision, where appropriate, about the possibility or impossibility of private action to enforce a duty or to recover loss. That provision may simply assert or deny a cause of action or may make provision acknowledging a cause of action but limiting its prosecution in specified ways or making some other proposition about it.[32]

---

[30] See also *R. (A) v Lambeth London Borough Council* [2004] 1 All E.R. 97, HL.

[31] For an understanding of the possible complexities of determining the application of the different tests see, by way of an illustrative but not exhaustive selection, *Mid Kent Holdings plc v General Utilities plc* [1996] 3 All E.R. 132, Ch; *E (a minor) v Dorset County Council* [1994] 3 W.L.R. 853, CA; *Richardson v Pitt-Stanley* [1995] 1 All E.R. 460, CA; *Melton Medes Ltd v Securities and Investments Board* [1995] 3 All E.R. 880, Ch; *R. v Ealing London Borough Council Ex p. Parkinson* [1996] 8 Admin. L.R. 281, QBD; *North Cornwall District Council v Welton and Welton* [1997] 9 Admin. L.R. 45, CA; and *Issa v Hackney London Borough Council* [1997] 1 All E.R. 999, CA.

[32] See, for example, the Mineral Workings (Off-shore Installations) 1971 (c.61), s.11—"*Civil liability for breach of statutory duty* (1) This section has effect as respects— (a) a duty imposed on any person by any provision of this Act, or (b) a duty imposed on any person by any provision of regulations made under this Act which expressly applies the provisions of this section. (2) Breach of any such duty shall be actionable so far, and only so far, as it causes personal injury, and references in s.1 of the Fatal Accidents Act 1846, as it applies in England and Wales, and in Northern Ireland, to a wrongful act, neglect or default shall include references to any breach of a duty which is so actionable. (3) Subsection (2) above is without prejudice to any action which lies apart from the provisions of this Act. . . . "; also "(5) Failure to comply with any requirement of subs.(4) above in respect of any sale, while actionable as against the aerodrome authority concerned at the suit of any person suffering loss in consequence thereof, shall not, after the sale has taken place, be a ground for impugning its validity" (Civil Aviation Act 1982 (c.16), s.88(5)); also "(3) Breach of a duty imposed by subs.(2) shall be actionable" (Clean Air Act 1993 (c.11), s.34); see also the Airports Act 1986 (c.31), s.49(6)(b); see also (in relation to liability for any breach which causes loss or damage) the Telecommunications Act 1984 (c.12), s.18(6), the Airports Act 1986 (c.31), s.49(6), the Gas Act 1986 (c.44), ss.22(2), 30(6) and 63(5), the Electricity Act 1989 (c.29), ss.27(5) and 58(5) and Sch.6, para.2(4), the Water Industry Act 1991 (c.56), ss.22(2), 41(4), 45(5), 54(2), 60(5), 98(4), 112(5) and 174(6), the Water Resources Act 1991 (c.57), s.176(5) and the Railways Act 1993 (c.43); (as to express provision for injunctive relief) the Northern Ireland Constitution Act 1973 (c.36), s.19(3), the Restrictive Trade Practices Act 1976 (c.34), s.35(3), the Resale Prices Act 1976 (c.53), s.25(3), the Telecommunications Act 1984 (c.12), s.18(8), the Airports Act 1986 (c.31), s.49(8), the Gas Act 1986 (c.44), ss.22(4), 30(8) and 63(7), the Electricity Act 1989 (c.29), ss.27(7) and 58(7) and Sch.6, para.2(6), the Fair Employment (Northern Ireland) Act 1989 (c.32), s.42(1), the Water Industry Act 1991 (c.56), s.22(4) and the Railways Act 1993 (c.43), s.57(7); (as to provision for action by a person who suffers loss) the Health and Safety at Work etc. Act 1974 (c.37), s.47(2), the Civil Aviation Act 1982 (c.16), s.88(5), the Financial Services Act 1986 (c.60), ss.62(1), 131, 171 and 185 and Sch.11, para.22(4), the Local Government Act 1988 (c.9), s.19 and the Fair Employment (Northern Ireland) Act 1989 (c.32), s.42(2); (as to creation of a general cause of action in relation to personal injury) the Mineral Workings (Offshore Installations) Act 1971 (c.61), s.11, the Petroleum and Submarine Pipe-lines Act 1975 (c.74), s.30(1), the Deep Sea Mining (Temporary Provisions) Act 1981 (c.53), s.15(1) and the Antartic Minerals Act 1989 (c.21), s.13(1); (as to action without specification of loss or damage) the Northern Ireland Constitution Act 1973 (c.36), s.19(2), the Restrictive Trade Practices Act 1976 (c.34), s.35(2), the Resale Prices Act 1976 (c.53), s.25(3), the Copyright, Designs and Patents Act 1988 (c.48), s.229(1) and (2), and the Trade Union and Labour Relations (Consolidation) Act 1992 (c.52), ss.145(5) and 187(3).

Apart from the possibility of a private duty of care being created by and relied upon for the enforcement of a statutory duty, it is possible for a statutory and a common law duty of care to co-exist in close proximity. So in *B. v Attorney General of New Zealand*[33] the Privy Council held that the social work authorities could owe a common law duty of care to children in respect of whom a statutory duty to arrange for a prompt inquiry applied, and that the duties could be temporally co-extensive.

Action for breach of statutory duty

12.6.11   Breach of statutory duty is a tort.[34] So an injured person may sue for damages or other relief for breach of statutory duty in the same way as he might sue for damages or other relief for nuisance or negligence[35]: but only in a case where in the context of the legislation imposing the duty it appears the intention of the legislature to give a private right of action for breach.[36] Where the legislation provides criminal sanctions or some other form of enforcement mechanism of a public nature,[37] it may well be concluded that private enforcement in relation to a breach of statutory duty is not available, albeit that a statutory duty has been breached and that loss has been suffered as a result.[38]

---

[33] [2003] 4 All E.R. 833, PC.

[34] Sometimes referred to as breach of statutory duty simpliciter to distinguish it from other cases in which breach of statutory duty is part, but not the whole of, the grounds on which an action might be brought: see the following analysis in the speech of Lord Browne Wilkinson in *X (Minors) v Bedfordshire County Council* [1995] 2 A.C. 633, 730, HL—"Private law claims for damages can be classified into four different categories, *viz*: (A) actions for breach of statutory duty simpliciter (*i.e.* irrespective of carelessness); (B) actions based solely on the careless performance of a statutory duty in the absence of any other common law right of action; (C) actions based on a common law duty of care arising either from the imposition of the statutory duty or from the performance of it; and (D) misfeasance in public office, *i.e.* the failure to exercise, or the exercise of, statutory powers either with the intention to injure the plaintiff or in the knowledge that the conduct is unlawful."

[35] For a recent example of a case in which the defendant (a statutory sewerage undertaker) was sued in negligence, nuisance and breach of statutory duty see *Marcic v Thames Water Utilities Ltd* [2003] 3 W.L.R. 1603, HL.

[36] See the judgment of Lord Browne-Wilkinson in *X (Minors) v Bedfordshire County Council* [1995] 2 A.C. 633 and especially the passage cited above; see also *Cocks v Thanet District Council* [1983] 2 A.C. 286 and *O'Rourke v Camden London Borough Council* [1988] A.C. 188 HL.

[37] And even where no mechanism is expressly provided, the public law remedies will be available through action for judicial review.

[38] See, for example, the following passage of the judgment of Sir Richard Scott V-C in *Attorney General v Blake (Jonathan Cape Ltd, third party)* [1996] 3 All E.R. 903, 910, Ch—"It seems to me clear that the submission by the defendant of his manuscript to Jonathan Cape Ltd constituted the disclosure of information which was in his possession by virtue of his work as a member of SIS and that he thereby committed an offence under sub-s (1). He has, therefore, committed a breach of statutory duty. This action has not, however, been based on any breach by Mr Blake of statutory duty under the 1989 Act. There is no mention of the Act in the pleadings. The reason for this is, I imagine, that breach of statutory duty under the 1989 Act would not lead to any of the remedies sought in this action. Criminal penalties are prescribed for offences under the 1989 Act. Conviction of any such offence could be followed, I am told, by a confiscation order depriving the offender of the fruits of his crime. But long-established principles of statutory construction preclude the civil law remedies sought in this action being added to the statutory remedies prescribed by the 1989 Act. . . . Accordingly, the circumstance that Mr Blake's activities on which the present action is

Action for judicial review will always be available where there has been a breach of statutory duty, and it has distinct advantages over private action whether or not the circumstances are such that a private action would lie: in particular, while the courts have no difficulty in acceding the request of even a single private citizen to investigate the conduct of even the most powerful Minister of the Crown, there are procedural safeguards against the misuse of judicial review of a kind not similarly developed in relation to private actions. As Lord Denning M.R. said in *O'Reilly v Mackman*[39]—

> "Now that judicial review is available to give every kind of remedy, I think it should be the normal recourse in all cases of public law where a private person is challenging the conduct of a public authority or a public body, or of anyone acting in the exercise of a public duty. I am glad to see that in *Reg. v Inland Revenue Commissioners, Ex p. National Federation of Self-Employed and Small Businesses Ltd.*[40] Lord Diplock has endorsed the principle which I ventured to set out in *Reg. v Greater London Council, Ex p. Blackburn*[41]—
>
>> 'I regard it as a matter of high constitutional principle that if there is good ground for supposing that a government department or a public authority is transgressing the law, or is about to transgress it, in a way which offends or injures thousands of Her Majesty's subjects, then any one of those offended or injured can draw it to the attention of the courts of law and seek to have the law enforced, and the courts in their discretion can grant whatever remedy is appropriate.' "

12.6.12

The three safeguards identified by Lord Denning M.R. in that case as being of particular importance in preventing abusive actions were the requirement for leave (now permission) and the limitation of discovery and cross-examination.[42]

As to the remedies available on an action for judicial review, see s.31 of the Supreme Court Act 1981.[43]

---

founded appear to constitute an offence under s 1(1) of the 1989 Act does not assist the Crown to establish a breach of duty under the civil law for which the civil law remedies sought in this action can be claimed."; or, as Scott Baker J. put it in *T (a minor) v Surrey County Council* [1994] 4 All ER 577, 596, QBD—"It by no means follows that because the local authority failed to meet its obligations under the Act, an action lies against it for breach of statutory duty. It is a question of the true construction of the Act whether an action lies with a private individual for breach of its provisions . . . ".

[39] [1983] 2 A.C. 237, 256, CA (also HL).
[40] [1981] 2 W.L.R. 722, 737, HL.
[41] [1976] 1 W.L.R. 550, 559, CA.
[42] At 257.
[43] 1981 c.54.
  "**31 Application for judicial review**
  (1) An application to the High Court for one or more of the following forms of relief, namely—
    (a) an order of mandamus, prohibition or certiorari;

Enforcement of right by public authority

12.6.13 As to the enforcement of a right by a public authority, it will generally be open to the authority to consider whether to take action to enforce the right will be in the public interest, bearing in mind all the circumstances.

As to extra-statutory concessions, see Chapter 3, Section 7.

In certain cases it may be necessary for the legislature to confer an express right of action to enforce a public right or duty of some kind, where it would not otherwise be clear that a particular body had sufficient interest to bring proceedings.[44]

Limitation of action

12.6.14 See Section 2 above.

     (b) a declaration or injunction under subs.(2); or
     (c) an injunction under s.30 restraining a person not entitled to do so from acting in an office to which that section applies,
    shall be made in accordance with rules of court by a procedure to be known as an application for judicial review.
  (2) A declaration may be made or an injunction granted under this subsection in any case where an application for judicial review, seeking that relief, has been made and the High Court considers that, having regard to—
     (a) the nature of the matters in respect of which relief may be granted by orders of mandamus, prohibition or certiorari;
     (b) the nature of the persons and bodies against whom relief may be granted by such orders; and
     (c) all the circumstances of the case,
    it would be just and convenient for the declaration to be made or of the injunction to be granted, as the case may be.
  (3) No application for judicial review shall be made unless the leave of the High Court has been obtained in accordance with rules of court; and the court shall not grant leave to make such an application unless it considers that the applicant has a sufficient interest in the matter to which the application relates.
  (4) On an application for judicial review the High Court may award damages to the applicant if—
     (a) he has joined with his application a claim for damages arising from any matter to which the application relates; and
     (b) the court is satisfied that, if the claim had been made in an action begun by the applicant at the time of making his application, he would have been awarded damages. . . . "

[44] See, for example, s.14(2) of the Betting, Gaming and Lotteries Act 1963 (c.2)—"Any infringement of the right conferred on the Totalisator Board by the foregoing subsection shall be actionable at the suit of the Board . . . ", s.10A(14) of the National Lottery etc. Act 1993 (c.39)—"A financial penalty imposed on any person, and any interest accrued under subs.(13) in respect of the penalty, shall be recoverable from that person as a debt due to the Secretary of State from that person" or s.54(3) of the Cable and Broadcasting Act 1984 (c.46).

Chapter 13

STATUTORY CORPORATIONS

Introduction

A statutory corporation is a body which is either established by statute as a
corporation or, having been established in some other way, is incorporated by
statute. The principal purpose of a body being incorporated is to acquire a legal
personality distinct from the personalities of the members, and perpetual
succession; without these attributes it is difficult or impossible for a body to carry
on business.[1]

13.1.1

There are several thousand extant provisions on the statute book incorporating
entities ranging in size and importance from specialised boards and commissions
to local authorities. An Act can establish a single small incorporated board for a
specific purpose, or it can incorporate a whole swathe of bodies by a single
provision.[2]

It is rare, but not unheard of, for a statutory corporation to owe its existence
to subordinate rather than primary legislation.[3]

Constraints on action

A corporation created by statute possesses all the attributes of a corporation at
common law (or, now, under the Companies Acts)[4] unless any of those attributes
is expressly taken away by the statute which creates it.[5] "When once you have
given being to such a body as this, you must be taken to have given to it all the
consequences of its being called into existence, unless by express negative words
in the statute you have restricted the operation of the acts of the being you have
so created."[6]

13.1.2

---

[1] It should be noted, however, that although an unincorporated association lacks legal personality, a
statutory reference to "person" will, unless the contrary intention is implied, include a reference
to "a body of persons corporate or unincorporated" (Interpretation Act 1978 (c.30), Sch.1).

[2] Possibly the most striking examples are ss.15 and 16 of the Further and Higher Education Act 1992
(c.13) (incorporation of bodies to operate existing educational institutions) and s.238 of the
Education Act 1993 (c.35) (incorporation of existing governing bodies of certain schools).

[3] See, for example, the Local Government Residuary Body (England) Order 1995 (SI 1995/401)
made under the Local Government Act 1992 (c.19), ss.22 and 26(4).

[4] *Riche v Ashbury Carriage Co.* (1874) L.R. 9 Ex. 224.

[5] A fairly common example of an express limitation of this kind is a proviso preventing the statutory
corporation from borrowing money—see, for example, the Railways and Transport Safety Act
2003 (c.20), Sch.11, para.16.

[6] *Riche* above, but in the House of Lords, *per* Lord Hatherley, (1875) L.R. 7, HL 653, 685.

But although a statutory corporation has very wide capacity to act, it may exercise that capacity only in pursuance of the legislative purposes entrusted to it. As Lord Hatherley said in *Campbell's Trustees v Police Commissioners of Leith*[7]—

> "In all matters regarding their jurisdiction they are, of course, allowed to exercise those powers according to their judgment and discretion; but where they exceed those powers they are immediately arrested by interdict and by injunction, it not being a sufficient answer on their part to say, 'You have your remedy at law'. The courts will hold a strict hand over those to whom the legislature has entrusted large powers, and take care that no injury is done by an extravagant assertion of them."

13.1.3 A statutory body will have a number of implied powers as necessary incidents of its creation and of the functions conferred upon it. For example, the power to act to enforce: as Lord Woolf M.R. said in *Broadmoor Special Health Authority v Robinson*[8]—

> "In relation to many statutory functions the power to bring proceedings can be implicit. The statutes only rarely provide expressly that a particular public body may institute proceedings in protection of specific public interests.It is usually a matter of implication. If a public body is given responsibility for performing public functions in a particular area of activity, then usually it will be implicit that it is entitled to bring proceedings seeking the assistance of the courts in protecting its special interests in the performance of those functions."

Ultra vires actions

13.1.4 If a statute confers power on a statutory corporation to make contracts for certain specified purposes, clear words are required to place any limitation on the contractual rights conferred.[9] But if a statutory corporation makes a contract which is *ultra vires* it will be invalid and cannot be made valid by action on the part of the members.[10] As Lord Cairns said in *Riche*—

> "Now I am clearly of opinion that this contract was entirely, as I have said, beyond the objects in the memorandum of association. If so, it was thereby placed beyond the power of the company to make the contract. If so, my Lords, it is not a question whether the contract was ever ratified or was not

---

[7] (1870) L.R. 2, H.L. (Sc.) 1, 3.
[8] [2000] Q.B. 775, 779, CA.
[9] *Morris & Bastert Ltd. v Loughborough Corporation* [1908] 1 K.B. 205, 216, *per* Lord Alverstone C.J. and at 219 *per* Buckley L.J.
[10] See *Riche* cited above.

ratified; if it was a contract void at its beginning, it was void because the company could not make the contract. If every shareholder had been in the room and every shareholder of the company had said 'That is a contract which we desire to make, which we authorise the directors to make, to which we sanction the placing of the seal of the company,' the case would not have stood in any different position from that in which it stands now. The shareholders would thereby by unanimous consent have been attempting to do the very thing which by the Act of Parliament they were prohibited from doing."

The doctrine of *ultra vires* actions on the part of statutory corporations receives both historical exposition and practical modern analysis in the case of *Crédit Suisse v Allerdale Borough Council*.[11] In that case a local authority purported to establish a company for the purposes of borrowing money which was in turn for the purpose of providing recreational facilities. It also purported to guarantee a related loan to another entity. The Court of Appeal held that a local authority had no express statutory power to act in this way. Despite a "catch-all" subsidiary power under statute to "do any thing (whether or not involving the . . . borrowing . . . of money . . .) which is calculated to facilitate, or is conducive or incidental to" the discharge of the authority's functions, this power was to be construed in the context of the relevant statutory functions and circumstances, paying particular attention to the fact that a comprehensive code for local authorities' power to borrow was established elsewhere in statute. Since the purported use of the company and the giving of the guarantee were therefore *ultra vires*, the contract of guarantee entered into by the local authority was void and unenforceable. This shows that the doctrine is not merely an ancient theory but a powerful modern force capable of producing results of enormous financial and political importance.

Implied ancillary powers

Despite the strictures of the doctrine of *ultra vires* discussed above, as with a statute doing any other thing, a statute establishing a corporation can expect to receive from the courts a favourable interpretation in order to ensure that the purpose of the statute is not frustrated. The doctrine of *ultra vires* "ought to be reasonably, and not unreasonably, understood and applied [so that] whatever may be fairly regarded as incidental to, or consequential upon, those things which the legislature has authorised ought not (unless expressly prohibited) to be held by judicial construction, to be *ultra vires*."[12]

So, as Lord Watson said in *Baroness Wenlock v River Dee Co.*[13]—

13.1.5

---

[11] [1996] 4 All E.R. 129, CA.
[12] *Attorney General v Great Eastern Railway* (1880) 5 App. Cas. 473, 478 *per* Lord Selborne.
[13] (1885) 10 App. Cas. 354, 362.

"Whenever a corporation is created by Act of Parliament with reference to the purposes of the Act, and solely with a view to carrying these purposes into execution, I am of opinion not only that the objects which the corporation may legitimately pursue must be ascertained from the Act itself, but that the powers which the corporation may lawfully use in furtherance of these objects must either be expressly conferred or derived by reasonable implication from its provisions."

Note, however, that the more detailed the scheme provided by statute for a corporation the less likely the courts are to imply the grant of additional powers.[14]

Constitutional and procedural provision

13.1.6 An Act establishing a statutory corporation provides for a number of matters in relation to its constitution and procedures. Frequently these are mostly relegated to a Schedule, with only principal provisions about membership and functions set out in the sections.

The standard provisions have changed a little over the decades, but their essence remains the same. Some provisions found frequently in earlier Acts are now rarely or never included,[15] because they were designed to address doubts or matters that no longer arise. Some of these are identified below.

For recent paradigm provisions making constitutional and procedural provision in relation to statutory corporations see: Schs.1 and 4 to the Railways and Transport Safety Act 2003[16] (Office of Rail Regulation and British Transport Police Authority); s.201 of and Sch.14 to the Transport Act 2000[17] (Strategic Rail Authority); and s.109 of and Sch.8 to the Police Act 1997[18] (Police Information Technology Organisation).

13.1.7 A helpful illustration[19] of how practice in the drafting of provisions for the establishment of statutory corporations has improved and simplified over the years can be found by contrasting the following provisions, each of which is divided from the previous example by the passage of fifty years and each of which is concerned with the establishment of a statutory corporation—

Section XXII of the Poor Relief (Ireland) Act 1847.[20]

---

[14] See Chapter 12, Sections 1 and 2.

[15] In particular, it was once common to provide expressly when establishing a statutory corporation for it to have perpetual succession and a common seal. These both being natural incidents of incorporation (although the possession of a seal is not always a necessary incident—see para.[]) it is common although not invariable to omit either or both in modern drafting.

[16] 2003 c.20.

[17] 2000 c.38.

[18] 1997 c.50.

[19] Also given earlier as an illustration of improvements in the presentation of legislative material generally—see Chapter 8.

[20] 1847 c.31.

Sections 5 to 8 of the Public Health (Scotland) Act 1897.[21]

Section 1 of the Transport Act 1947.[22]

Sections 109 and 110 of, and Sch.8 to, the Police Act 1997.[23]

Perpetual succession and common seal

It used to be commonplace for an Act establishing a statutory corporation to provide for it to "be a body corporate with perpetual succession and a common seal".[24] Modern practice favours the omission of both elements of this proposition.[25] **13.1.8**

> The notion of perpetual succession is the essence of incorporation, and is one of the two principal reasons for it. It is impossible to imagine a situation in which the legislature would wish to incorporate a body and to provide for its membership to change but not to provide for succession.
>
> As to a common seal, if a body corporate finds it conducive to the conduct of its business to possess a seal,[26] it does not require the authority of the legislature to go out and buy one.

For these reasons, the provision for perpetual succession and a common seal have sometimes been omitted from older enactments during the process of consolidation.[27]

Membership

Legislation establishing a statutory corporation must, of course, make provision for its membership. Members are normally appointed by the Secretary of State or another Minister. **13.1.9**

---

[21] 1897 c.38.

[22] 1947 c.49.

[23] 1997 c.50.

[24] See, for example, the Gaming Act 1968 (c.65), Sch.1, para.1.

[25] They may have been helpful in the early days of the establishment of statutory corporations to clarify the intended nature of a new class of legal person.

[26] There is less occasion today than there was once to use a seal, due to changes in both law and practice. For details of the evolution of the law relating to the use of seals and of certain further changes recommended, see the Law Commission's report *The Execution of Deeds and Documents by or on behalf of Bodies Corporate* (Law Commission Report 253) (1998). Contrast, however, the position years ago when it was thought that a statutory corporation was obliged by law to possess and use a common seal for the authentication of its documents: hence s.13(5) of the Local Government Act 1972 (c.70)—"(5) Notwithstanding anything in any rule of law the parish trustees need not have a common seal, but where they have no seal any act of theirs which requires to be signified by an instrument under seal may be signified by an instrument signed and sealed by the persons who are the parish trustees."

[27] Compare, for example, s.3 of the Independent Broadcasting Authority Act 1973 (c.19) and Sch.1 to the Broadcasting Act 1981 (c.68); and note that the latter retains provisions about the authentication of use of the seal that might today be thought possible to omit, depending on the circumstances. As to consolidation generally, see Chapter 1, Section 8.

The legislation may appoint a minimum and maximum number of members and leave it to the appointing Minister to determine how many members to have at any time within that prescribed range.[28] Or it may appoint only a minimum number of members.[29] Or it may leave the number of members entirely at the discretion of the appointing Minister.[30]

The appointing Minister is sometimes required to ensure that particular interests are represented among the membership of the body.[31] Sometimes all or part of the membership is to be selected by the Minister from amongst persons nominated by specified organisations.[32] Where it is intended that a single individual may be appointed as a member in more than one capacity—so that his membership counts towards satisfying more than one requirement for representation—the legislation will permit this expressly.[33]

Tenure

13.1.10   It is usual for the legislation to include express provision for resignation, and it is common (although not invariable) to find express provision for dismissal by the appointing Minister on various grounds (normally misbehaviour and incapacity of various kinds). Provision for retirement is sometimes made. Apart from whatever of these specific matters is dealt with expressly, it is usual for the legislation to provide for tenure to be "in accordance with the terms and conditions of appointment".

Whether terms and conditions of appointment could provide a power for the appointing Minister or someone else to dismiss (in a case where no express power of dismissal is provided by the legislation) must be doubtful. In a case where the purpose of a statutory corporation is to provide for the exercise of a public function with a degree of independence from the Minister (as will certainly be the case in the establishment of a tribunal or other quasi-judicial body and may be the case in other instances also) it may be thought unlikely that Parliament intends to empower a Minister to empower himself, through terms and conditions, to dismiss at will. But in other contexts it may be less

---

[28] See, for example, s.1(2) of the Further and Higher Education Act 1992 (c.13) (Further Education Funding Council for England).

[29] See, for example, the Railways and Transport Safety Act 2003 (c.20) Sch.1, para.1(1) (Office of Rail Regulation).

[30] This is the norm for statutory bodies created in the form of or with the functions of a tribunal expected to sit in several divisions at once: see, for example, Schedule 3 to the Terrorism Act 2000 (c.11) (Proscribed Organisations Appeal Commission)—and note that that Schedule does not expressly incorporate the Commission, it not being expected to be required to enter into commercial transactions.

[31] See, for example, the Railways and Transport Safety Act 2003 (c.20) Sch.4, para.2(1) (British Transport Police Authority).

[32] See para.2(1)(d) of that Schedule; or, for a more general example, see the Police Act 1997 (c.50), Sch.8, para.1(3) (Police Information Technology Organisation).

[33] See, for example, the Railways and Transport Safety Act 2003 (c.20) Sch.4, para.2(2) (British Transport Police Authority).

contentious. Where the doubt is real and likely to prove important, the legislature is likely to wish to dispel it by express words.[34]

Bankruptcy

As part of provision about disqualification for membership or dismissal it was **13.1.11** once common to find reference to bankruptcy. The Enterprise Act 2002,[35] in addition to making a number of changes to the system of bankruptcy, "downgraded" a number of express statutory disqualifications so that they apply only in cases in respect of which a bankruptcy restrictions order is made[36] and conferred a power to make the same or similar provision in respect of other statutory disqualifications relating to bankruptcy.[37]

Creation of statutory corporation outside statute

Not all statutory corporations are created by a provision of an Act. An Act may **13.1.12** delegate the power to confer the status of a body corporate on a specified entity.[38]

Quasi-corporations

An Act may, without conferring the status of a body corporate on a specified **13.1.13** entity, confer on it specified capacities and incidents of incorporation.[39]

---

[34] See, for example, but in the context of a statutory unincorporated body, s.33(5) of the Nationality, Immigration and Asylum Act 2002 (c.41).

[35] 2002 c.40.

[36] ss.266 and 267: despite its name, a bankruptcy restrictions order marks cases thought proper for particularly severe treatment, by extending certain restrictions beyond the point of discharge.

[37] s.268.

[38] See, for example, s.7(2) of the Northern Ireland Arms Decommissioning Act 1997 (c.7) (the Decommissioning Commission). In that case the body was to have legal personality in the United Kingdom and in the Republic of Ireland and was, for obvious political reasons, to be "an independent organisation established by an agreement, made in connection with the affairs of Northern Ireland between Her Majesty's Government in the United Kingdom and the Government of the Republic of Ireland, to facilitate the decommissioning of firearms, ammunition and explosives". So the body was established by agreement, but the Secretary of State was empowered by statute to confer upon the body certain status and capacity as a matter of United Kingdom law: "The Secretary of State may by order—(a) confer on the Commission the legal capacities of a body corporate; (b) confer on the Commission, in such cases, to such extent and with such modifications as the order may specify, any of the privileges and immunities set out in Part I of Schedule 1 to the International Organisations Act 1968; . . . "

[39] See, for example, s.10 of the Trade Union and Labour Relations (Consolidation) 1992 (c.52) "(1) A trade union is not a body corporate but—(a) it is capable of making contracts; (b) it is capable of suing and being sued in its own name, whether in proceedings relating to property or founded on contract or tort or any other cause of action; and (c) proceedings for an offence alleged to have been committed by it or on its behalf may be brought against it in its own name. (2) A trade union shall not be treated as if it were a body corporate except to the extent authorised by the provisions of this Part."

Liability

13.1.14   Statutory corporations have the same exposure to criminal[40] and civil liability as other persons.

Corporation sole

13.1.15   It is possible for a person other than a body to incorporated as a corporation sole. The effect is to confer legal personality[41] and the attribute of perpetual succession.

The principal modern use of the corporation sole is for Ministerial offices. Almost all senior Ministers (that is to say Ministers in charge of Departments[42]) are now corporations sole. The provision making an office a corporation sole may be made in an order under s.2(1)(a) of the Ministers of the Crown Act 1975[43] or in an Act.[44]

---

[40] As to which note—"A corporation that commits a criminal act leading to the death of an individual may be prosecuted for a range of possible offences, depending on the circumstances of the case. The possible offences include manslaughter.The Crown Prosecution Service does not record statistics for different categories of defendant, but, in the past three years, there have been two prosecutions for manslaughter against corporations. The first of those resulted in a conviction of the company itself and the second in the conviction of its managing agent."—Attorney General HC Deb. June 17, 1996 c.520.

[41] Although, of course, legislation is able to make provision by reference to an entity without legal personality for other purposes, such as an unincorporated association—see Chapter 22, para. 22.1.7.

[42] As to which see Chapter 3, Section 12, Chapter 11, Section 5 and Chapter 12, Section 4.

[43] 1975 c.26: "Her Majesty may in connection with any change in the departments of the office of Secretary of State, or any change in the functions of a Secretary of State, by Order in Council make such incidental, consequential and supplemental provisions as may be necessary or expedient in connection with the change, including provisions—(a) for making a Secretary of State a corporation sole, ... ". See further Chapter 3, Section 12.

[44] See, for example, s.2 of the Defence (Transfer of Functions) Act 1964 (c.15)—

"2 Incorporation of Secretary of State for Defence, and vesting etc. of property, rights and liabilities.

(1) If Her Majesty is pleased to make the arrangements described in section 1(1) above, the person appointed Secretary of State with general responsibility for defence and his successors shall be, by the name of the Secretary of State for Defence, a corporation sole (with a corporate seal) for all purposes relating to the acquisition, holding, management or disposal of property ... "

Ministerial corporations sole benefit, in the case of Secretaries of State, from provision allowing certain actions to be carried out by one on behalf of the other.[45]

There are also occasional non-Ministerial uses of the corporation sole.[46]

---

[45] s.3 of the Ministers of the Crown Act 1975 (c.26)—

3 Transfer of property etc by or to Secretary of State

(1) This section applies where any enactment (including an order under this Act) provides that a named Secretary of State and his successors shall be a corporation sole, and applies whether or not the office of corporation sole is for the time being vacant.

(2) Anything done by or in relation to any other Secretary of State for the named Secretary of State as a corporation sole shall have effect as if done by or in relation to the named Secretary of State.

(3) Without prejudice to the preceding provisions of this section, any deed, contract or other instrument to be executed by or on behalf of the named Secretary of State as a corporation sole shall be valid if under the corporate seal of that Secretary of State authenticated by the signature of any other Secretary of State, or of a Secretary to any department of a Secretary of State, or of a person authorised by any Secretary of State to act in that behalf."

[46] See, for example, the following—

Section 2(1) of the Charities Act 1993 (c.10)—

2 The official custodian for charities.

(1) There shall continue to be an officer known as the official custodian for charities (in this Act referred to as "the official custodian") whose function it shall be to act as trustee for charities in the cases provided for by this Act; and the official custodian shall be by that name a corporation sole having perpetual succession and using an official seal which shall be officially and judicially noticed."

Section 90 of the Government of Wales Act 1998 (c.38)—

90 Auditor General for Wales.

(1) There shall be an office of Auditor General for Wales or Archwilydd Cyffredinol Cymru.

(2) The person for the time being holding that office shall by the name of that office be a corporation sole. . . . "

Section 225 of the Greater London Authority Act 1999 (c.29)—

225 The PPP arbiter.

(1) The Secretary of State may appoint a person to an office to be known as 'the Public-Private Partnership Agreement Arbiter' (in this Chapter referred to as the 'PPP arbiter').

(2) The PPP arbiter shall have the functions conferred or imposed on him by or under this Act.

(3) The PPP arbiter shall be a corporation sole by the name of 'the Public- Private Partnership Agreement Arbiter'. . . . "

CHAPTER 14

EFFECT ON OTHER LAW

SECTION 1

EFFECT ON COMMON LAW

Introduction

This Section considers the relationship between legislation (whether primary or **14.1.1** subordinate) and the common law.

For this purpose there are three aspects of non-legislative law to be considered under the general heading of the common law—

(1) all that body of law which, being enunciated by the higher courts in reported cases, forms part of the common law of any part of the United Kingdom,[1]

(2) the law developed by the higher courts in accordance with the principles of equity,[2] and

(3) decisions of any of the courts or tribunals of the United Kingdom in construing legislation.

Balance between case law and legislation

The balance of importance between legislation and case law has shifted **14.1.2** significantly over the centuries. This gradual process accelerated considerably in the twentieth century, with the result that there are now few if any significant

---

[1] What the common law is and when and how it developed is a matter of common controversy. But note "By the common law we mean here the settled law of the king's court, common to all free men in the sense that it is available to them in civil causes if they will have it, and applicable against them in serious criminal causes whether they like it or not. It is easy and fruitless to argue about the details of such a definition, and about the exact date at which there can first be said to be a common law: what is clear is that it is a product of the twelfth century."—*Glanvill—The Treatise on the Laws and Customs of the Realm of England Commonly Called Glanvill* (Oxford Medieval Texts, Edited and Translated by G.D.G. Hall, 1993 reprint of 1965 Edition) introduction p.xi.

[2] The supremacy of equity over pure common law is established by s.44 of the Supreme Court of Judicature (Consolidation) Act 1925 (c.49). For present purposes it is unnecessary to distinguish between the two kinds of law.

areas of law that are not the subject of statutory codes, many of which were originally attempts to codify the existing common law.

As a result, while the courts retain a position of critical significance in the preservation of the rule of law, their role is less about the independent control of areas of life in accordance with long-standing principle, or even about filling in significant gaps in the legislative landscape, and more and more about—

(1) construing legislation in accordance with the perceived intention of the legislature (sometimes relying on principles of the pre-existing common law for illumination of what was intended), and

(2) exercising discretion expressly or impliedly conferred on the courts by the legislature.[3]

There are still fields in which common law controls much of the ground, offences against the person being perhaps the most significant example.[4] Another area where the incursion of statute is relatively recent is the law of charities.[5] And a recent, although relatively insignificant, case of statute being used to codify and simplify an area of the common law that had become insupportably complicated is the Animals Act 1971[6]: see the comments of Lord Nicholls of Birkenhead in *Mirvahedy v Henley*.[7]

Increasing judicial reluctance to make new law

14.1.3 The fact that the legislature has invaded so many fields of the common law and converted them into areas regulated by statute has made the judges increasingly reluctant, even in fields where development is still technically open to them, to make significant legal change themselves. There is a temptation to feel that if Parliament wanted significant change in the area, Parliament would arrange for it. As Lord Rodger of Earlsferry said in *R. v Mirza*[8] in relation to the privacy of jurors' deliberations—

> "The unpalatable truth is that there is no sure touchstone for deciding whether the allegation of a juror, considered in isolation, is truly cogent. What at first appeared cogent might look very different if the matter were

---

[3] And it will sometimes be better to confer a discretion in relation to the application of a necessarily wide concept than to true to achieve a false accuracy by the use of spurious detail—see further Chapter 8, para.8.1.24.

[4] As to the law commission act and plans for codification of the criminal code see para.14.1.15 below. And, of course, even in this area a good deal of the field was occupied by statute long ago, notably by the Offences of the Person Act 1861 (c.100).

[5] Piecemeal provisions for certain aspects were made in the Charitable Trusts Act 1853 to 1939, being replaced by a general regulating Act only in the Charities Act 1960 (c.58).

[6] 1971 c.22.

[7] [2003] 2 W.L.R. 882, 884, HL.

[8] [2004] 2 W.L.R. 201, 257–258, HL.

fully investigated and evidence taken from the other jurors.Conversely, the allegation of a less articulate juror, which at first appeared weak, might look more cogent after investigation. . . .

"If it were indeed possible to devise a workable exception which would not eat up the rule, then that might be the ideal solution. But over the years judges of the highest authority have considered the matter and have not found such a solution. They have therefore affirmed the rule that evidence about jurors' deliberations should not be admitted. . . . Unfortunately, in formulating the law judges today can claim no greater skill or knowledge than their distinguished predecessors. They cannot draw lines or make distinctions which those predecessors rightly felt unable to draw or to make. Significantly, when Parliament stepped into the arena in section 8 of the Contempt of Court Act 1981, it was to strengthen, rather than to water down, the protection for the confidentiality of jurors' deliberations. . . .

"The law on this matter is well settled. But, of course, despite the **14.1.4** endorsement of their approach by Parliament and by the European Court, it may be that the courts have attached undue weight to the confidentiality of jurors' deliberations. Or, for some other reason, the law as laid down in the authorities may not be well suited to conditions today. If that is found to be so, it should, of course, be changed—as some respected critics have indeed suggested. Notably, in the Report of his Review of the Criminal Courts of England and Wales (2001), Chapter 5, para 98 Lord Justice Auld recommended that the Court of Appeal should be able to inquire into alleged impropriety by a jury, whether in the course of their deliberations or otherwise. This would involve a substantial, if not complete, departure from the present law and from its underlying policies. There is, as yet, no sign that the Government intend to bring forward legislation to implement the recommendation. Any such far-reaching reform of the law on this topic must, however, be a matter for Parliament rather than for this House in its judicial capacity. Only Parliament is in a position to weigh the competing policy arguments and, if so advised, to produce a new and suitably sophisticated solution. Unless and until that happens, the existing law must be applied."

As to an area which has been extensively regulated, the reluctance to continue or supply rules of common law in the area is particularly pronounced. As Lord Nicholls of Birkenhead said in *Re McKerr*[9]—

"The courts have always been slow to develop the common law by entering, or re-entering, a field regulated by legislation. Rightly so, because otherwise

---

[9] [2004] 2 All E.R. 409, 419, HL.

there would inevitably be the prospect of the common law shaping powers and duties and provisions inconsistent with those prescribed by Parliament."

14.1.5   See also *R. v Lyons*[10] and Lord Hoffmann's observations about the development of the law of privacy in *Wainwright v Home Office*.[11]

However, the courts' reluctance to be drawn into legislating by supplying apparent deficiencies of the legislature does not imply a reluctance to continue to expound and develop the common law in all areas not, or not yet, invaded by legislation.[12]

As to the effect of the invasion by statute of an area previously regulated by the common law, Lindley L.J. expressed the effect of the change in discussing s.35 of the Divorce Act 1859[13]—

"[The section] enacts that the court may make such provision as it may deem just and proper with respect to the custody, maintenance and education of the children the marriage of whose parents is the subject of the suit. The language is express and unmistakable, and clearly gives to the judge of the Divorce Court a wide discretion as to the custody of the children, though not a discretion which cannot be the subject of an appeal. This discretion, in my

---

[10] [2003] 1 A.C. 976, HL.

[11] [2003] 3 W.L.R. 1137, 1141–1150, HL.

[12] So, for what can arguably be seen as the creation of a new criminal offence, despite the protestations to the contrary, see the following passage of the speech of Viscount Simonds in *Shaw v Director of Public Prosecutions* [1962] A.C. 220, 266–267, HL—"My Lords, as I have already said, the first count in the indictment is 'Conspiracy to corrupt public morals,' and the particulars of offence will have sufficiently appeared. I am concerned only to assert what was vigorously denied by counsel for the appellant, that such an offence is known to the common law, and that it was open to the jury to find on the facts of this case that the appellant was guilty of such an offence. I must say categorically that, if it were not so, Her Majesty's courts would strangely have failed in their duty as servants and guardians of the common law. Need I say, My Lords, that I am no advocate of the right of the judges to create new criminal offences? I will repeat well known words: 'Amongst many other points of happiness and freedom which your Majesty's subjects have enjoyed there is none which they have accounted more dear and precious that this, to be guided and governed by certain rules of law which giveth both to the head and members that which of right belongeth to them and not by any arbitrary or uncertain form of government.' These words are as true today as they were in the seventeenth century and command the allegiance of us all. But I am at a loss to understand how it can be said either that the law does not recognise a conspiracy to corrupt public morals or that, though there may not be an exact precedent for such a conspiracy as this case reveals, it does not fall fairly within the general words by which it is described."; note also "It is now clearly established that the courts have not now power to create new offences *(Knuller (Publishing, Printing and Promotions) Ltd v Director of Public Prosecutions)* but as late as 1801 a different view appears to have been held. On the demise of the Star Chamber the Court of King's Bench assumed its mantle and the power to declare conduct to be criminal which had not before been so treated. In those days Parliament met but seldom and concerned itself less than now with the criminal law."—*DPP v Withers* [1974] 3 All E.R. 984, HL.

[13] 1859 c.85.

opinion, overrules both the common law rules and the Chancery rules as to the custody of children which were in force when the Act was passed. The judge is not bound to follow any of these rules, though he will have regard to them in exercising his discretion; but he will be mainly guided by the particular circumstances of the case before him."[14]

Possible range of effects of legislation on common law

In essence, legislation may do one of three things in relation to a rule of case law—   **14.1.6**

(1) It may modify the rule in some way.

(2) It may reverse or abolish the rule.

(3) It may codify the rule and bring it within the statute law.

As will be explained, the inter-relationship between legislation and other forms of law is of less frequent importance today than it once was, and this Section therefore omits a number of details that are no longer likely to be of practical interest, except perhaps occasionally in a historical context or in the context of local legislation.[15]

Presumption against legislative interference with common law

Despite the increasing shift towards control by legislation, there remains a   **14.1.7**
rebuttable presumption that the legislature does not intend to alter a clearly established principle of law—

> "Statutes are not presumed to make any alteration in the common law further or otherwise than the Act does expressly declare."[16]

---

[14] *Handley v Handley* [1891] P. 124, 127.

[15] Some expansion will be found in Chapter 14 of the 7th Edition, 1971.

[16] *Arthur v Bokenham* (1708) 11 Mod. 148, 150 CCP; see also *Rolfe v Flower* (1866) L.R. 1, PC 27, 48 and *Leach v R.* [1912] A.C. 305; see also "It is a well-established principle of construction that a statute is not to be taken as effecting a fundamental alteration in the general law unless it uses words that point unmistakably to that conclusion. Accordingly, if the words 'a man shall be liable to maintain his wife' in section 42 of the National Assistance Act, 1948, stood by themselves, I should read them subject to the common law, and should not conclude that they were intended to disturb the principle that a wife forfeited her right to maintenance by the commission of a matrimonial offence. Against this it is argued that the initial phrase 'for the purposes of this Act' makes it possible to give the wide words that follow their full meaning without altering the general law. The same sort of wide words was, however, used in the Poor Law Act, 1927, s.41 (1), which provides that it shall be the duty of a husband of a poor person to maintain her. These words are not subject to any limitation of the purposes of the Act, and they are moreover contained in a consolidating Act. I could not, therefore, hold that the Act of 1927 altered the common law; and it is noteworthy that no one has in 20 years ever suggested that it did. But if words of this sort are not to be widely and literally construed in 1927, why should they in 1948? The qualifying phrase 'for the purposes of this Act' is not, in my judgment, sufficient to effect the alteration. The use of

So in many cases the courts have rejected a possible interpretation of legislation on the grounds that it would involve a significant departure from pre-existing common law, without the departure being expressly provided for or a necessary implication from the context of the provision.[17]

---

the phrase is sufficiently explained by the inclusion in the section of a novel liability in the case of women, and by a wish to avoid the consequences, as demonstrated in *Middlesex. C.C. v Nathan*, of the unrestricted words in the Act of 1927."—*National Assistance Board v Wilkinson* [1952] 2 Q.B. 648, 661, DC *per* Devlin J.

[17] See, for a stirring but dated example, the following extracts of speeches in *Leach v R.* [1912] A.C. 305, HL Earl Loreburn L.C. (At 310)—"Now, my Lords, if it had not been for that 4th section the wife could not have been allowed to give evidence, and the result of that was that the wife could not have been compelled to do so and was protected against compulsion. The difference between leave to give evidence and compulsion to give evidence is recognized in a series of Acts of Parliament. Does then the 4th section, which I have read, deprive the wife of this protection? It is capable of being construed in different ways, and it may hereafter lead, for all I know, to various other difficulties, but the present question is, does it deprive this woman of this protection? My Lords, it says in effect that the wife can be allowed to give evidence, even if her husband objects. It does not say she must give evidence against her own will. It seems to me that we must have a definite change of the law in this respect, definitely stated in an Act of Parliament, before the right of this woman can be affected, and therefore I consider that this appeal ought to be allowed, with what consequences, or how that may be conformable to what is in the true interests of society or the public in this particular case, we are not concerned and are not at liberty to inquire." Earl of Halsbury (at 310–311): "Now, dealing with that question, I should have thought that it would occur not only to a lawyer, but to almost every Englishman, that a wife ought not to be allowed to be called against her husband, and that those who are under the responsibility of passing Acts of Parliament would recognize a matter of that supreme importance as one to be dealt with specifically and definitely and not to be left to inference. I think that observation is true also for this reason: that when you are dealing with a question of this kind you cannot leave out of sight the different enactments that have been passed upon this subject with a sort of nomenclature of their own; and speaking for myself, as an ordinary person, I should have asked, when it was proposed to call the wife against the husband, 'Will you shew me an Act of Parliament that definitely says you may compel her to give evidence? because since the foundations of the common law it has been recognized that that is contrary to the course of the law.' If you want to alter the law which has lasted for centuries and which is almost ingrained in the English Constitution, in the sense that everybody would say, 'To call a wife against her husband is a thing that cannot be heard of,'—to suggest that that is to be dealt with by inference, and that you should introduce a new system of law without any specific enactment of it, seems to me to be perfectly monstrous. The result is that I entirely concur with the judgment of the Lord Chancellor, and particularly with that part of it in which he said that such an alteration of the law as this ought to be by definite and certain language." Lord Atkinson (At 311)—"The principle that a wife is not to be compelled to give evidence against her husband is deep seated in the common law of this country, and I think if it is to be overturned it must be overturned by a clear, definite, and positive enactment, not by an ambiguous one such as the section relied upon in this case."; see also *Société Co-operative Sidmetal v Titan International Ltd* [1966] 1 Q.B. 828, 847, QBD *per* Widgery J.—"But, in the end, I do feel bound to take the view that one ought not to assume that this Act has made a substantial alteration in the common law approach to the enforcement of foreign judgments unless that intention can be found in express terms or by necessary implication. In my judgment the intention cannot be found, and ought not lightly to be assumed. In any case, it seems to me that, if Parliament had intended that jurisdiction for the purposes of section 4(1)(a) should be based on comity and not in any way upon common law rules, section 4(2) must have taken a very different form. I cannot really understand how the draftsman could have indulged in the complexity, and, on [Counsel's] approach, the irrelevancy, of section 4(2) if he really had in mind that comity and reciprocity should be the basic test upon which jurisdiction had to be determined"; see also *Rolfe and Bank of Australasia v Flower, Salting & Co* (1865) L.R. 1, PC 27 and *Burge v Ashley and Smith* [1900] 1 Q.B. 744, CA.

By express provision or necessary implication, however, it is open to Parliament to abolish or modify ancient principles of the common law.[18]

It is sometimes the sole intent of a legislative initiative to reverse the effect of a decision of the courts.[19] Whether or not the intention is achieved can sometimes, however, be a matter of debate.[20]

14.1.8

---

[18] See, for example, s.34 of the Crime and Disorder Act 1998 (c.37) *"Abolition of rebuttable presumption that a child is doli incapax.* The rebuttable presumption of criminal law that a child aged 10 or over is incapable of committing an offence is hereby abolished."; or s.1 of the Law Reform (Year and a Day Rule) Act 1996 (c.19)—"The rule known as the 'year and a day rule' (that is, the rule that, for the purposes of offences involving death and of suicide, an act or omission is conclusively presumed not to have caused a person's death if more than a year and a day elapsed before he died) is abolished for all purposes."; and where the precise nature or even existence of the rule of law is open to question it is possible to use more general abrogating words—as in s.13(5) of the Local Government Act 1972 (c.70)—"(5) Notwithstanding anything in any rule of law the parish trustees need not have a common seal, but where they have no seal any act of theirs which requires to be signified by an instrument under seal may be signified by an instrument signed and sealed by the persons who are the parish trustees."; as to the abrogation of an inherent jurisdiction by the establishment of a statutory scheme (subject to the inherent jurisdiction remaining in relation to "lacunas" in the new scheme) see *A. v Liverpool City Council* [1982] A.C. 363, 373, *In re C. (A Minor) (Adoption: Freeing Order)* [1999] Fam. 240 and *In re O. (A Minor) (Blood Tests: Constraints)* [2000] Fam. 139 F.; but compare, for example, *Bhamjee v Forsdick (Practice Note)* [2004] 1 W.L.R. 88, CA where the court's inherent jurisdiction in relation to preventing vexatious litigation appeared able to co-exist alongside the statutory system under s.42 of the Supreme Court Act 1981 (c.54). See also, for an example expressly referring to the common law, s.6 of the Criminal Attempts Act 1981 (c.47)—

"6 Effect of Part I on common law

(1) The offence of attempt at common law and any offence at common law of procuring materials for crime are hereby abolished for all purposes not relating to acts done before the commencement of this Act.

(2) Except as regards offences committed before the commencement of this Act, references in any enactment passed before this Act which fall to be construed as references to the offence of attempt at common law shall be construed as references to the offence under section 1 above."; (and see footnote [simeon quote] below).

[19] See, for example, the Bill for the Social Security (Overpayments) Act 1996 (c.51) and the speech on the Second Reading of the Bill by The Minister of State, Department of Social Security (Lord Mackay of Ardbrecknish) HL Deb. July 15, 1996 c.724. In that case the Bill was designed to reverse a decision of a Social Security Commissioner; or see the following observation of Lord McIntosh of Haringey in moving the Second Reading of the Insolvency Bill 1999–2000 (HL Deb. April 4, 2000 c.1252)—"When the Administration of Insolvent Estates of Deceased Persons Order was brought into effect at the end of 1986, it was generally believed that all the assets that a debtor owned immediately before his death would be available to his creditors in any insolvency proceedings which took place after his death. It was also believed that that would include his share in any jointly-owned property. That would have provided a level playing field for the treatment of the estates of all insolvents, whether living or deceased; otherwise, the assets available to creditors would have differed, depending on whether the debtor was alive or dead. However, a decision in the Court Appeal in the case of Palmer (deceased) has established that the order-making power contained in Section 421 of the Insolvency Act is not sufficient to bring about that result. The consequence is that the provisions in the 1986 Order are ineffective. As a result, in some cases what may appear to be the main, if not the only, asset—namely, the deceased debtor's interest in the matrimonial home—passes under the survivorship rules to the joint owner and is therefore beyond the reach of his creditors. We are taking this opportunity to amend the order-making power in Section 421 and by so doing we will, as far as is possible, restore a level playing field and give a certainty of outcome for creditors irrespective of whether the insolvent is living or deceased."

[20] See the following exchange between the Home Secretary and the Opposition in proceedings on the Bill for the Human Rights Act 1998 (c.42)—HC Deb. June 3, 1998 c.422: Home Secretary " . . . I come back to the point about parliamentary sovereignty. If the higher courts come up with

Alternatively, legislation may leave a principle or procedure of the common law in place, but expressly control it in some way.[21]

The fact that interference with the common law must be by express provision does not necessarily mean that the legislature is aware of or has the correct understanding of the common law that it is changing. The courts will presume that it is not intended to alter the pre-existing common law if that is consistent with a natural construction of the words used by the legislature: but if not, the courts will have to give effect to the new law even if they suspect that the legislature would not have enacted it had it been aware of or properly understood the state of the law as it then was.[22]

Implied disapplication of common law by establishment of statutory scheme

14.1.9 Where a detailed legislative scheme imposes duties on persons engaged in a particular kind of undertaking, there may be an implied modification of the common law obligations of those persons in relation to that undertaking. So, for example, the House of Lords found[23] that an action for nuisance brought against statutory sewerage undertakers was in effect inconsistent with the statutory scheme imposed on those undertakers by the Water Industry Act 1991,[24] since the claim for nuisance could only be made out by implying obligations in

---

an interpretation that makes the intention of Parliament risible and means that legislation is applied in a way that is unreasonable and has ridiculous results, it is open to the House to change the decision. For example, in the Crime and Disorder Bill we are overturning the decision of the court in *Regina v Khan* . . . " Mr. Clappison: "No, you are not." Mr. Straw: "With great respect, we are; we are abolishing the concept of *doli incapax*—[Interruption.] I hope that we are overturning Khan, but I will not go any further into that—[Interruption.] It is open to the House—it is its ultimate right—to change a decision."

[21] See, for example, Children Act 1989 (c.41), s.100 (restrictions on use of wardship jurisdiction); and note *Devon County Council v S. (Inherent Jurisdiction)* [1994] Fam. 169 F.

[22] For an example of a reference to the unwitting change of the pre-existing law see the following passage from the speech of Lord Upjohn in *Beswick v Beswick* [1968] A.C. 58, 105–106, HL—"Bearing in mind the wide import of the word 'property' apart from any definition, I find it difficult in the context to limit that word to an interest in real property. Without expressing any concluded view, I think it may be that the true answer is that Parliament (as sometimes happens in consolidation statutes) inadvertently did alter the law in section 56 by abrogating the old common law rule in respect of contracts affecting personal property as well as real property. But it cannot have done more. Parliament, per incuriam it may be, went back to the position under the Act of 1844 but I am convinced it never intended to alter the fundamental rule laid down in *Tweddle v Atkinson*. The real difficulty is as to the true scope and ambit of the section. My present views, though obiter and tentative, are these. Section 56, like its predecessors, was only intended to sweep away the old common law rule that in an indenture inter partes the covenantee must be named as a party to the indenture to take the benefit of an immediate grant or the benefit of a covenant; it intended no more. So that for the section to have any application it must be to relieve from the consequences of the common law, and in my opinion three conditions must be satisfied. If all of them are not satisfied then the section has no application and the parties are left to their remedies at common law."; see also Chapter 1, Section 7, para.1.7.4.

[23] *Marcic v Thames Water Utilities Ltd* [2003] 3 W.L.R. 1603, HL.

[24] 1991 c.56.

addition to those imposed by the statute. There was, therefore, "no room"[25] for a common law cause of action.[26]

Similarly, in *B. v Forsey*[27] the House of Lords found that the powers of detention conferred on hospital authorities by the Mental Health (Scotland) Act 1984[28] were clearly intended to be exhaustive, so that the common law powers could not survive so as to fill an apparent lacuna in the statutory regime. As Lord Keith of Kinkel said[29]—

> "In my opinion it is impossible to reach any other conclusion than that the powers of detention conferred upon hospital authorities by the scheme were intended to be exhaustive. Procedure is laid down for emergency, short term and long term detention. The period of short term detention might reasonably be expected to be long enough for an application for long term detention to be submitted to and approved by the sheriff under s.18. What happened in this case was that the petitioner's condition appeared initially to be improving, so that an application under s.18 was not thought appropriate. Dr Mackay was of opinion that an application which turned out to be unnecessary would be upsetting and harmful to the patient. The petitioner's condition suddenly and unexpectedly deteriorated, and by then it was too late to have an application submitted and approved before the expiry of the short term detention. That would appear to be a situation which was not in the contemplation of the framers of the legislation. However, I am of opinion that the provisions of ss.24 (6), 25 (5) and 26 (7) are absolutely inconsistent with a possible view that the legislature intended that a hospital authority should have a common law power to detain a patient otherwise than in accordance with the statutory scheme. That scheme contains a number of safeguards designed to protect the liberty of the individual. It is not conceivable that the legislature, in prohibiting any successive period of detention under provisions containing such safeguards, should have intended to leave open the possibility of successive periods of detention not subject to such safeguards. I would therefore hold that any common law power of detention which a hospital authority might otherwise have possessed has been impliedly removed."

For instances of the existence in parallel of common law and statutory powers, however, see the cases of *Bhamjee v Forsdick (Practice Note)*[30] and *B. v Attorney General of New Zealand*.[31]

---

[25] *Per* Lord Nicholls of Birkenhead at 1614.
[26] See also the principles discussed in Chapter 11, Section 4.
[27] [1988] S.L.T. 572.
[28] 1984 c.36.
[29] At 576; cited in *R (B) v Ashworth Hospital Authority* [2003] 4 All E.R. 319, 330, CA *per* Dyson L.J.
[30] Discussed in footnote 18 above.
[31] Discussed in para.14.1.12 below.

Clear conflict between common law and legislation

14.1.10 Once a clear conflict has been established, and the presumption against interference has thereby been rebutted, the principle is easy to state: the supremacy of Parliament requires that case law must always yield to legislation.[32] The dictum of Coke C.J. that an Act of Parliament cannot overrule the principles of the common law has long ago been rejected.[33] Although "The common law has no controller in any part of it but the High Court of Parliament, and if it be not abrogated or altered by Parliament it remains still",[34] once the clear intention of Parliament in passing a statute is to abrogate the previous common law on the subject, that law must give way and the statute must prevail.

As Lord Browne-Wilkinson put it in the case of *R. v Secretary of State for the Home Department, Ex p. Fire Brigades Union*[35]—

> "The constitutional history of this country is the history of the prerogative powers of the Crown being made subject to the overriding powers of the democratically elected legislature as the sovereign body. The prerogative powers of the Crown remain in existence to the extent that Parliament has not expressly or by implication extinguished them. But under the principle in *Attorney-General v De Keyser's Royal Hotel Ltd*[36] if Parliament has conferred on the executive statutory powers to do a particular act, that act can only thereafter be done under the statutory powers so conferred: any pre-existing prerogative power to do the same act is pro tanto excluded."

So legislation overrides the common law in a case of clear conflict: but in a case of debatable conflict one is driven back to the presumption that "it is a well-established principle of construction that a statute is not to be taken as effecting a fundamental alteration in the general law unless it uses words that point unmistakeably to that conclusion".[37]

Doubtful effect on common law

14.1.11 Although there are now fewer cases than there once were concentrating on determining the effect on the common law of particular elements of legislation where the legislation invades an area that remains primarily controlled by the common law, when this does happen, it is not always easy to determine whether, to what extent or in precisely what way a provision of legislation has altered the

---

[32] See, in particular, the cases cited in Chapter 2, Sections 1 and 3.
[33] See Maine, Hist. Early Inst., p.381; Dicey, *Constitution*, (10th ed.), 41, 61, n.2.
[34] 1 Co. Inst. 115b.
[35] [1995] 2 All E.R. 244: see also Chapter 10, Section 1.
[36] [1920] A.C. 508.
[37] *National Assistance Board v Wilkinson* [1952] 2 Q.B. 648, DC *per* Devlin J.

pre-existing case law. See, for example, *Moore v Knight*[38] where Stirling J. had to determine whether the decision in *Blair v Bromley*[39] was affected by s.8 of the Trustee Act 1888,[40] which extended the Statutes of Limitations to certain breaches of trust.[41]

It is common practice where a statute is designed to overrule a principle of the common law to say so expressly.[42]

Effect on common law right or duty

The creation of a statutory duty to do something does not of itself abrogate a common law duty to do that thing, unless there is something about the form or content of the statutory duty which is repugnant to the continuation of the common law duty.[43]

14.1.12

Legislation which might appear to impinge on a common law right or duty may expressly preserve it.[44]

It is possible for a statutory and a common law duty of care to co-exist in close proximity. So in *B. v Attorney General of New Zealand*[45] the Privy Council held that the social work authorities could owe a common law duty of care to children in respect of whom a statutory duty to arrange for a prompt inquiry applied, and that the duties could be temporally co-extensive.

Continuing to have regard to pre-legislative law

The notion that the courts will have regard to the rules of the pre-existing case law in construing and applying the provisions of the legislation which replace those rules is an important one, although obviously it can be displaced by a clearly expressed intention of the legislature. Although the notion is of less and less importance as there are fewer and fewer areas of law where the displacement of case law by legislation is sufficiently recent for the common law rules to be both well-remembered and capable of application in modern circumstances, it

14.1.13

---

[38] [1891] 1 Ch. 547.
[39] (1848) 2 Ph. 354; 5 Hare 542.
[40] 1888 c.59.
[41] For older cases considering whether and to what extent a statute intended to override principles of the common law see *National Assistance Board v Wilkinson* [1952] 2 Q.B. 648, DC, *R. v Scott* (1856) 25 L.J.M.C. 128, *Morris & Bastert v Loughborough Corporation* [1908] 1 K.B. 205, *R. v Morris* (1867) L.R. 1 C.C.R. 90, *Warden of St. Paul's v Dean of St. Paul's* (1817) 4 Price 65, *Leach v R.* [1912] A.C. 305 and *Re Ludmore* (1884) 13 Q.B.D. 415.
[42] See, for example, s.29B(1) of the Industrial and Provident Societies Act 1965 (c.12) inserted by s.5 of the Co-operatives and Community Benefit Societies Act 2003 (c.15) (Execution of deeds and other documents)—
"(1) Notwithstanding any enactment or rule of law, a registered society need not have a common seal."; and see the other examples cited in footnotes 18–20 above.
[43] See *Barnes v Irwell Valley Water Board* [1939] 1 K.B. 21, 32, CA *per* Slesser L.J.
[44] See, for example, s.70(c) of the Water Resources Act 1991 (c.57).
[45] [2003] 4 All E.R. 833, PC.

retains importance in connection with long-standing concepts of law which pervade a number of different areas of substance. The injunction is a good example. Speaking of s.187B(2) of the Town and Country Planning Act 1990[46]—which permits the court to grant "such an injunction as the court thinks appropriate for the purpose of restraining the breach"—Lord Clyde said—

> "It may be noted at the outset that the section is talking about an injunction. This is not a new remedy created by Parliament but a familiar and long-established form of remedy in England law. What the section did was to give an express statutory power for local planning authorities to apply to the court for that remedy and a discretion in the court to grant it. The power was given expressly to local planning authorities, so that this remedy may not be sought under the statute by anyone else."[47]

The idea is that by choosing to retain a concept of long-standing legal usage, the injunction, Parliament is both enabling and encouraging the courts to apply the rules and principles that govern their use of this remedy, subject to any express constraints and glosses specified by Parliament, and not to regard this in the light of a new form of statutory remedy to which the "old" rules cannot be applied.[48]

Effect on transitional cases

14.1.14 It should be noted, as it was by Lord Roskill in *R. v West London Stipendiary Magistrate, Ex p. Simeon*,[49] that the provisions of the Interpretation Act 1978[50] that deal with the effect of repeal are confined to the effect of the repeal of an enactment and do not apply in the case of the repeal by an enactment of a rule of the common law. The effect on transitional cases must therefore be set out expressly by the repealing enactment.

---

[46] 1990 c.8.

[47] *South Buckinghamshire District Council v Porter* [2003] 3 All E.R. 1, 27, HL.

[48] Nowadays the terminology of the injunction is, of course, no longer favoured: but the principle is unaffected.

[49] [1983] 1 A.C. 234, 243, HL—"My Lords, as regards section 3 (6) [of the Criminal Attempts Act 1981 (c.47)—'Subsections (2) to (5) above shall not have effect in relation to an act done before the commencement of this Act.'], the Interpretation Act 1978 only applies to repeals, and does not deal with the retrospective effect of legislation which is not achieving a repeal. On any view section 3(6) may well have been included *ex abundanti cautela*. Section 5(2) is clearly necessary because conspiracy is a continuing offence. Section 6(1) is necessary because the Interpretation Act 1978, so far as relevant, is not concerned with common law offences but only with statutory offences."

[50] 1978 c.30; see further Chapter 22.

Codification

The process of bringing ancient law within the code of statute law is a process **14.1.15**
that began a long time ago[51] but has developed gradually, and it is not until
relatively recently that it has been possible to say that there are few areas of
important law still governed wholly or mainly by non-statute law.

There are still many areas of the criminal law, such as offences against the
person, where common law offences are still of enormous importance. There too,
however, there is a certain amount of pressure to codify and bring the offences
within a statutory scheme. As the Attorney General said in the House of Lords
on December 10, 2003[52]—

> " . . . the Government are committed to modernising and consolidating the
> criminal law with the eventual production of a criminal code in four parts as
> proposed by Sir Robin Auld. We are currently considering how best that
> work should be taken forward . . . ".

It should also be noted that the Tax Law Rewrite project, discussed in detail in
Chapter 1, Section 10, as well as consolidating and improving the form of tax
legislation also takes the occasional opportunity to codify certain aspects of the
application of the legislation not previously apparent on its face, notably judicial
decisions and extra-statutory concessions.

It should be noted that the courts will assume that an Act which supplants an **14.1.16**
area of the common law is intended to be purely codificatory in nature in the
absence of good reason to believe that a substantive change in the law was
intended, particularly where an aspect of the common law has been given careful
attention by the courts. So, for example, Brooke L.J. in *Donoghue v Folkestone
Properties*[53]—

> "I can see no evidence that in 1984 Parliament intended to alter the general
> philosophy of the law relating to trespasses which the House of Lords
> articulated in differing terms in *Herrington's* case.[54] The mischief the Act
> was enacted to remedy was the one identified by the Law Commission at the
> start of its report . . . and nothing more."

It will sometimes be unclear to what extent a statute intends to replace the
common law and to what it extent it intends merely to modify its effect. In *R. v*

---

[51] For example, what had previously been an ecclesiastical jurisdiction in relation to certain family
matters was codified the Matrimonial Causes Act 1857 (c.85), with certain long-standing concepts
being renamed and reshaped—see s.26 of the Supreme Court Act 1981 (c.54) which notes, in
particular, the earlier refashioning by the 1857 Act (see section VII) of "divorce a mensa et thoro"
as "judicial separation".
[52] HL Deb. December 10, 2003 c.749.
[53] [2003] 2 W.L.R. 1138, CA at 1159.
[54] [1972] A.C. 877.

Harrow Justices, Ex p. Osaseri[55] the High Court considered the effect of the Offences against the Person Act 1861[56] on pre-existing common law offences and found the resulting position confusing and standing in serious need of legislative clarification.

SECTION 2

EFFECT ON OTHER NON-LEGISLATIVE LAW

Introduction

14.2.1 Custom and prescription were once of considerable importance as a source of legal rights and duties in the law of the United Kingdom. They are much less so today, although there remain significant traces of their force, particularly in relation to the law of real property.[57]

As to Royal Charters as a source of law, see Chapter 3, Section 7.

Effect of legislation on custom or prescription

14.2.2 The position is encapsulated in the following dicta—

> "It is therefore clear to my mind beyond question that the nature of the right [of customary tolls] is completely altered by turning it into a statutory right and that the right must continue—if it does continue—by virtue of the statute without any power of revival or reverter back to its original nature."[58]

> "I hold it to be an indisputable proposition of law that where an Act of Parliament has according to its true construction, to use the language of Littledale J.,[59] 'embraced and confirmed' a right which had previously existed by custom or prescription, that right becomes thenceforward a statutory right, and that the lower title by custom or prescription is merged in and extinguished by the higher title derived from the Act of Parliament."[60]

The idea in this doctrine is that the former right is completely subsumed within and extinguished by its statutory successor. The result is that repeal of the statute would not be sufficient without express saving words to revive the original

---

[55] [1986] Q.B. 589.
[56] 1861 c.100.
[57] Common land, adverse title by prescription, customary rights of way.
[58] Lord Chancellor Halsbury in *New Windsor Corporation v Taylor* [1899] A.C. 41, 45.
[59] In *The Islington Market Bill* (1835) 3 Cl. & F. 513.
[60] Lord Davey in *New Windsor Corporation v Taylor* [1899] A.C. 41, 49.

right.[61] If the legislation superseding the original right was clearly of a temporary character it is uncertain whether the lapse of the legislation revives the right.[62]

Effect on Royal Charters and franchises

The doctrine expressed above in relation to rights by custom or prescription holds good for rights created by grant from the Crown, whether by Charter or franchise.[63]   **14.2.3**

Legislation may make express provision in relation to provision of a Charter.[64]

Effect on contracts

For obvious reasons, the legislature will be reluctant to interfere by legislation with rights or duties created by contract concluded before the passing of the legislation. But there are cases in which this is considered proper.[65]   **14.2.4**

There have also been occasional instances of legislation giving effect to contractual provisions that would otherwise be of no, or doubtful, validity.[66]

---

[61] An idea given statutory expression by s.16(1)(a) of the Interpretation Act 1978 (c.30)—note in particular "the repeal does not unless the contrary intention appears revive anything not in force or existing at the time at which the repeal takes effect".

[62] *New Windsor Corporation v Taylor* [1899] A.C. 41; *Gwynne v Drewitt* [1894] 2 Ch. 616.

[63] Franchise was used, for example, to give rights in respect of the holding of a market: and in *Mayor of Manchester v Lyons* (1882) 22 Ch. D. 287 an ancient franchise market was held to have been extinguished by a series of statutes creating a statutory market in its place.

[64] See, for example, Disability (Grants) Act 1993, s.1 "The Secretary of State may make grants to . . . (c) Motability (a body corporate constituted by Royal Charter), for such purposes as the Secretary of State may determine".

[65] See Chapter 10, Section 3.

[66] So, for example, The Manchester Ship Canal Company was incorporated under the Manchester Ship Canal Act, 1885 (48 & 49 Vict. c.clxxxviii.), for the construction of a canal and docks, and the Manchester Racecourse Company was a limited company whose racecourse adjoined the canal. Prior to March, 1893, there were certain disputes between the canal company and the racecourse company with reference to a variety of matters, and on March 7 1893, an agreement under seal was entered into between the two companies in order to settle those disputes. This agreement was scheduled to the Manchester Ship Canal (Surplus Lands) Act, 1893 (56 & 57 Vict. c.lxxiii.), whereby, after reciting that the companies had entered into the agreement, and that it was expedient that the agreement should be confirmed, which object could not be obtained without the authority of Parliament, the agreement was "confirmed and declared to be valid and binding upon the parties thereto." Held, "Now, it has been argued that it merely gives the parties power to enter into the agreement, that is to say, it gives them a contracting capacity which they had not got before, irrespective of the terms contained in the particular contract. It appears to me that that would lead to a somewhat extraordinary result. If the Legislature has given the parties merely a right to enter into the contract and the contract is one which is altogether void, the Legislature has solemnly empowered them to enter into a contract which is void. That is a reductio ad absurdum. I cannot impute that intention to the Legislature. I think when the Act of Parliament confirms the scheduled agreement and declares it to be valid and binding upon the parties, it means what it says and gives it validity."—*Manchester Ship Canal Co. v Manchester Racecourse Co.* [1900] 2 Ch. 352, 359 *per* Farwell J., affirmed [1901] 2 Ch. 37, CA; see also *Pyx Granite Co. Ltd v Ministry of Housing and Local Government* [1960] A.C. 260, HL.

Effect on the prerogative

14.2.5   The Crown can do anything by way of governing the country that it chooses. This broad power is generally dignified by the description of the Royal Prerogative.

The range of areas of law still open to regulation and control under the Royal Prerogative is extensive and includes some matters of fundamental importance.[67]

The extent of the prerogative in so far as Ministerial powers was discussed in an opinion of a former First Parliamentary Counsel which has recently received judicial recognition in the following passage of the speech of Lord Phillips of Worth Matravers M.R. in *R. (Hooper) v Secretary of State for Work and Pensions*[68]—

> "[132] On 2 November 1945 Mr Granville Ram, First Parliamentary Counsel, produced a memorandum setting out what has become known as 'The Ram Doctrine' and which is, we understand, still treated by ministers as setting out the position in respect of the question of 'how far legislation is necessary to authorise any extension of the existing powers of a Government Department'? Mr Ram commented that it was necessary to draw a sharp distinction between what was legally possible and what was permissible having regard to established practice. He referred to the exchange of views in 1932, to which we have referred above. He reached the following conclusions:
>
> > 'a. Legislation is not legally necessary to authorise an extension of the existing powers of a Government Department except where such an extension is precluded by a previous statute either expressly or by necessary implication.
> >
> > 'b. If the extended powers involve an annual charge extended over a period of years legislation though not required by law, is required by established practice formally recorded in the transactions between the Public Accounts Committee and the Treasury.' "[69]

14.2.6   The situation where an area of the prerogative is addressed by legislation, and the extent to which this ousts the prerogative and replaces it with a new statutory jurisdiction, is discussed by Lord Phillips MR in the same judgment[70]—

> "[127] [Counsel for the Crown] accepted that where Parliament has legislated in such a way as to occupy an entire field, any prerogative or

---

[67] A list of prerogative powers was prepared as a Government Paper submitted to and published by the House of Commons Select Committee on Public Administration (Session 2002–03, Press Notice No.19 of October 27, 2003).

[68] [2003] 1 W.L.R. 2623, 2669, CA; note that as this work went to press *Hooper* was pending appeal to the House of Lords.

[69] See further Chapter 1, Section 6.

[70] At 705–706.

common law right of the Crown to act within that field will be displaced. He contended, however, (against his interest in this appeal) that the 1992 and 1999 Acts did not occupy the field in relation to bereavement benefits so as to preclude the common law power of the Crown to pay these to widowers. . . .

"[128] The starting point is *A-G v De Keyser's Royal Hotel Ltd*.[71] In that case the House of Lords held that a statutory power to requisition property displaced the prerogative power to do this that the Crown would otherwise have enjoyed. Lord Dunedin observed[72] 'if the whole ground of something which could be done by the prerogative is covered by the statute, it is the statute that rules'. Lord Atkinson said[73] 'after the statute has been passed, and while it is in force, the thing it empowers the Crown to do can thenceforth only be done under the statute'."

That issue in *Hooper* was decided on the basis that the introduction of the Human Rights Act 1998[74] had imposed duties on the Crown which "altered the restraint upon the Secretary of State which resulted from the principle in *A-G v De Keyser's Royal Hotel Ltd*" (see para.136 of Lord Phillips of Worth Matravers M.R.'s judgment in *Hooper*).

The position was summarised in a government paper presented to a House of **14.2.7** Commons Select Committee in the following terms—

"10. It is long established law that Parliament can override and displace the prerogative by statute. Where the Crown is empowered by statute to do something that it could previously do under the prerogative, it can no longer act under the prerogative but must act within the statutory scheme. The statute can, however, expressly preserve the prerogative. For example the Crown Proceedings Act 1947 contains an express saving at section 11 that the provisions of the Act shall not extinguish or abridge pre-existing prerogative powers (as well as powers conferred on the Crown by statute).

"11. It is not altogether clear what happens where a prerogative power has been superseded by statute and the statutory provision is later repealed but it is likely to be the case that the prerogative will not revive unless the repealing enactment makes specific provision to that effect. And in practical terms, it seems virtually unthinkable that the Government would seek to rely on the prerogative to replace an Act of Parliament, except perhaps in a grave national emergency.

---

[71] [1920] A.C. 508.
[72] At 526.
[73] At 540.
[74] 1998 c.42.

"12. As the prerogative is a residual power it cannot be used to amend the general law. This is of particular interest in relation to international treaties. Although the Executive can commit the United Kingdom to obligations under international law, if a change to domestic law is required, it will only take effect if Parliament passes the necessary legislation."[75]

SECTION 3

AMENDMENT OF EARLIER LEGISLATION

Introduction

14.3.1 Parliament can legislate in any fashion that it chooses. And a person exercising power to make subordinate legislation can also legislate in any fashion that he chooses provided that he does not exceed his delegated authority.

The convenience of legislators and readers has caused the invention and increasing use of a device for changing the law which supposes the existence of a notional book of legislation[76] and gives instructions to a notional editor as to its amendment.

Opinions are divided as to the degree of use of this device that is desirable.[77] About the extremes it is fairly easy to agree: for example, the shortest and clearest way of changing the law about a tax where the only change to be made is to reduce the rate by 1 per cent is to make a short textual amendment. To rewrite the entire law about the tax not only adds to the pages requiring scrutiny by the legislature but actually obscures the limited nature of the change being made. At the other extreme, there are occasions on which anything other than

---

[75] Government Paper submitted to and published by the House of Commons Select Committee on Public Administration (Session 2002–03, Press Notice No.19 of October 27, 2003).

[76] As for primary legislation and the notional "statute book" see Chapter 1, Section 1.

[77] For a thorough discussion of the issues see Chapter XIII of the Renton Report (*Report on the Preparation of Legislation*) (Cmnd. 6053)—note, in particular, para.13.17—"In so far as there is a conflict between the respective needs of the legislator and of the eventual user of the statutes, we have concluded that the needs of the user must be given priority when proposals for amending previous legislation are being framed. Many statutes are already difficult enough to understand in themselves without making their sense even more abstruse by amending them in a manner which further perplexes the user. There is no doubt that the non-textual amendment of existing legislation often adds to the burdens of the user, particularly when the consolidation of heavily amended Acts is held up for one reason or another. However, it is also clear that in present circumstances the adoption of a rule that amendments to existing legislation should always be made textually would create difficulties. Apart from the fact that there are many cases where the amendment of existing law can be achieved more compendiously by non-textual amendment, the present state of the statute book is far from conducive to the exclusive practice of textual amendment. An inflexible rule requiring this system always to be adopted would not be in the interests of the user, nor would it be workable . . . ".

wholesale repeal and re-enactment would clearly result in unnecessary confusion.[78] It is the large range of cases between the two extremes that give rise to debate.[79]

In part, the efficacy of textual amendment depends on the ease with which a copy of the legislation as amended can be obtained. Now that it is relatively easy to obtain up-dated legislation the benefits of textual amendments are considerable, since they "make complex legislation more manageable, so that instead of having to assemble the original statute and all the amending Acts and then piece them together the reader need do no more than obtain a copy of the Act as amended".[80]

This Section explores certain aspects of amending legislation.

Form of amendment

In general, an amending provision performs one or more of three kinds of notional function in relation to the legislation being amended—   **14.3.2**

(1) The addition of words.[81]

(2) The removal of words.

(3) The substitution of some words for other words.

It is also possible for a provision to "gloss" an earlier provision without purporting to alter its text. As in "section X shall be read / treated or shall have effect as if for references to dogs there were substituted references to cats". This is particularly suitable for amendments of a transitory nature or which affect only a sub-class of the matters affected by the provision being addressed: the gloss is left in the legislation most relevant to the matter to which the gloss relates, and does not alter the text of the principal provision either after the relevant time or in relation to more general matters.

It is not always easy to know whether the draftsman intends a gloss or a textual amendment. The forms commonly used nowadays when a mere gloss is intended were once used routinely for textual amendment.[82]

---

[78] See, for example, s.4 of the Nationality, Immigration and Asylum Act 2002 (c.41).

[79] As to which, of course, the needs of different classes of reader may conflict. The Legislature handling proposed legislation may find the form that emphasises the changes of the law easiest to absorb (and there may be technical scope-related disadvantages of repeal and re-enactment). Those to whom the legislation is addressed may find that its form matters little, since they are unlikely to use the Queen's Printer's version of Acts to build up the legislative history of a provision, relying instead on commercial publications which present an amended text of the legislation.

[80] Lord Mustill in *L'Office Cherifien v Yamashita Ltd* [1994] 2 W.L.R. 39, 47G, HL.

[81] The traditional formula refers to the "insertion" of words or a provision into the notional text of the statute being amended. Some draftsmen use "add" in place of "insert" when adding words at the beginning or end of a section or other element: compare, for example, s.56(2)(a) and (b) of the Nationality, Immigration and Asylum Act 2002 (c.41).

[82] See, for example, art.3(2) of SI 1964/490 which provides for enactments referring to the Minister for Education to have effect as if there were substituted a reference to the Secretary of State for Education and Science. In the drafting language of the day this was probably intended to be a textual amendment.

When is an amendment a repeal?

14.3.3 An amendment which removes words from a provision or a provision from an Act may do so by providing for the words or provision to "cease to have effect", the traditional language of repeal, or by using the notion of omission or deletion. In either case the effect is to repeal part of an Act.

By convention, a substitution is not treated as a repeal for the purposes of being entered in the Repeal Schedule. But whether or not a substitution is in essence a repeal depends, of course, on whether the words being substituted merely modify the effect of the provision or remove one proposition and replace it with a wholly different one—

> Imagine a provision "A person may not take a dog, cat or elephant into a public park".
>
> A draftsman is instructed that the prohibition is to be lifted in relation to elephants and, perhaps for entirely different policy reasons, to be introduced in relation to giraffes.
>
> He is likely to draft something along the lines of "In [the provision] for 'elephant' substitute 'giraffe', that being a simple way of demonstrating to the reader the nature of the change being made.
>
> But the simplicity of the change hides the fact that what is being effected is really two entirely separate changes of policy, the repeal of the reference to elephants and the introduction of a reference to giraffes.
>
> Logically, the amendment should be treated as being in part a repeal and in part the addition of a new proposition.
>
> The position would arguably be different if the only change was to exclude Indian elephants from the application of the provision.
>
> Be that as it may, the convention is not to treat the substitution as a repeal for the purposes of having it listed in the Repeal Schedule.

14.3.4 The idea expressed in the previous two paragraphs that what is and is not a repeal depends, for all practical legal purposes, on the substance of what is being achieved and not on form or terminology is irrefutable as a matter of common sense and has judicial support—

> "Now it appears to me that when an Act of Parliament not using the word 'repealed' contains a provision which alters the provisions of a previous Act it repeals that provision. It is not necessary that the word 'repeal' should be used, or that the Act repealed should be in the schedule to the second Act.

You may easily have a repeal which is not made by using the word 'repeal' and is not effected by putting the Act into shape."[83]

Section 4 below explores a number of matters which are specific to repeals, whether of entire Acts or of words or provisions within an Act.

Speaking amendments

Textual amendments are sometimes described as being "always speaking". This **14.3.5** means that where Act A says "In section X of Act Y for 'dogs' substitute 'cats'" we treat section X of Act Y as continuing to have an underlying effect as referring to dogs, but being constantly modified by Act A, while it has effect, so as to refer to cats. Act A is not a mere trigger which effects a once-for-all change in Act Y, but requires to be kept in force as long as the change is to have effect.

Vacant provisions

As to the replacement of a provision with a new provision dealing with a wholly **14.3.6** or partly different matter, see Chapter 8, Section 2.

Enactment and amendment in same Session

Section 2 of the Interpretation Act 1978[84] provides that— **14.3.7**

"Any Act may be amended or repealed in the Session of Parliament in which it is passed."[85]

Short title

It is rare for an Act to amend the short title of an earlier Act (simply because the **14.3.8** short title has no legal effect): but it has been known. For example, when the Industrial Tribunals were renamed Employment Tribunals by the Employment

---

[83] *Moakes v Blackwell Colliery Company Ltd* [1925] 2 K.B. 64, 70, CA *per* Scrutton L.J.: it may, of course, be that a provision which merely modifies slightly an earlier provision is best regarded not as a repeal (as to which see above).
[84] 1978 c.30.
[85] This has been the position for many decades and would now be thought to stand to reason. The origin for the necessity of such a rule, however, is the situation that appertained prior to 1793 whereby all Acts of one Session were treated as having received Royal Assent on the same day (*Coke* 4 Inst. 25 and *Attorney-General v Panter* (1772) 6 Bro. P.C. 486). It was therefore impossible to know which of two mutually repugnant Acts ought to prevail—see *R. v Middlesex Justices* (1831) 2 B. & Ad. 818, 821 *per* Lord Tenterden. Therefore the Acts of Parliament (Commencement) Act 1793 was passed with the effect that each Act is treated as enacted, and is presumed in the absence of express contrary provision to come into force, on the day on which Royal Assent is signified.

Rights (Dispute Resolution) Act 1998[86] it was thought that it would result in less confusion if the Industrial Tribunals Act 1996[87] were renamed—this was achieved by s.1(2)(c) of the 1998 Act.[88]

Extent

14.3.9   For a discussion of the extent of amending enactments, see Chapter 11, Section 1.

Implied amendment

14.3.10   The doctrine of Parliamentary supremacy means that the power of the Parliament that exists at any time is not constrained by anything done by a previous Parliament or by the same Parliament.[89] Therefore, if a provision of one Act is inconsistent with a provision of an earlier Act one has to construe the later Act as containing an implied amendment, or repeal, of the earlier Act. This idea, and its disapplication in relation the principal qualification on it relating to constitutional enactments, is discussed in Chapter 1, Sections 2 and 4.

Consequential amendments

14.3.11   It is common for an Act in one substantive context to require a number of consequential amendments to be made in other contexts. The consequential amendments are frequently set out in a Schedule introduced by a section or subsection towards the end of the Act.[90] Sometimes an Act confers power to make consequential amendments by subordinate legislation.[91] Sometimes a combination is used, with the Act specifying all those consequential amendments that at the time of enactment can (or can reasonably conveniently) be identified amendments, but with power being taken to make other amendments of provisions in respect of which the need for amendment arises or is discovered only after enactment.[92]

As a general rule, consequential amendments of subordinate legislation occasioned by primary legislation are effected neither by the primary legislation

---

[86] 1998 c.8.

[87] 1996 c.17.

[88] Technically, however, s.1(2)(c) provides for an additional permissible citation and does not displace the earlier short title.

[89] See further Chapter 2, Sections 1 and 2.

[90] See, for example, Sch.5 to the Commonhold and Leasehold Reform Act 2002 (c.15).

[91] See, for example, s.157 of the Nationality, Immigration and Asylum Act 2002 (c.41); note, however, that provisions of this kind are of considerable political sensitivity—see, in particular, HL Deb. January 14, 2003 cc.165–188, a debate based on the Third Report of the House of Lords Select Committee on Delegated Powers and Regulatory Reform, Session 2002–03, HL Paper 21, which in turn arose out of controversy during the Third Reading in the House of Lords where the clause which became s.157 was introduced.

[92] See, for example, ss.277 and 278 of the Enterprise Act 2002 (c.40).

nor by powers under it but by eventual exercise of the individual powers under which the subordinate legislation was originally made.[93]

Where a provision is amended and it is clear that the purpose of the amendment is not to make a substantive change to the policy of the area of law underlying the provision but merely to make a technical adjustment to that provision in order to reflect a substantive change to another area of law, the courts will be reluctant to construe the change as altering the substance of the amended provision.[94]

Use of original text to construe amended Act

The text of an Act as it was prior to being amended may still be of use in determining what the intention of the legislature was. A common example of this is the case where words are removed, whether by straight repeal or by way of substitution, because the policy enacted by them is abandoned, but their original inclusion implies a restriction on the intended meaning of an apparently wide expression used elsewhere in the Act.[95]

14.3.12

---

[93] As to the dangers of mixing primary and subordinate legislation, see Chapter 1, Section 2. But this is, of course, a rule with exceptions; see, for example, para.9 of Sch.21 to the Political Parties, Elections and Referendums Act 2000 (c.41) (consequential amendment of the Representation of the People Regulations 1986 (SI 1986/1081) and of the Representation of the People (Scotland) Regulations 1986 (SI 1986/1111)). Note also that it is common to treat Northern Ireland Orders in Council under para.1 of Sch.1 to the Northern Ireland Act 1974 (c.28) as primary legislation for this purpose—see, for example, Sch.16 to the Terrorism Act 2000 (c.11) (repeals and revocations).

[94] See, for example, "The question, it seems to me, is whether Parliament can have intended that subject to that procedural change the rights of the landlord and tenant should have been changed as the result of something merely consequential on the repeal of Schedule 4 to the Customs and Excise Act 1952. In my judgment, it is most improbable that Parliament ever intended to change the substantive rights enjoyed by tenants under the 1954 Act in the course of making merely a procedural modification. I would expect the underlying rights of the parties to have remained the same and be unaffected save to the extent necessary to replace the machinery formerly contained in the Customs and Excise Act 1952."—*Ye Olde Cheshire Cheese Ltd v Daily Telegraph plc* [1988] 3 All E.R. 217, 323, Ch *per* Sir Nicolas Browne-Wilkinson V.-C.

[95] See, for example, *Attorney General v Lamplough* (1877–78) L.R. 3 Ex. D. 214, 227–228, CA *per* Bramwell L.J.: "Then it is argued that you cannot look at the repealed portion of the Act of Parliament to see what is the meaning of what remains of the Act. I know that is not the argument of the Solicitor-General, but that opinion has been expressed. I, however, dissent from it; if it were an accurate opinion, this consequence would follow, that an Act of Parliament which at one time had one meaning would by the repeal of some one clause in it have some other meaning. Thus, a duty is imposed upon race-horses, carriage-horses, riding-horses, and all other horses, then if the Act is repealed as regards race-horses, it is said that nevertheless you must look at the Act as though the words imposing the tax on race-horses had never been in at all, and that you must take in race-horses under the words all 'other horses.' I will apply these observations not to this Act, but to another Act. Suppose there was another Act which said So and so shall be the law, and then there was a subsequent Act which said that the old Act should not apply to certain matters, but that a new law should be created, and that there was no particular naming of the matters, so that you could only make sense of the second Act by looking at the first: according to the argument which has been used you could not look at the first Act; you must really regard the words in the first Act as obliterated. I should say that where an Act of Parliament has been repealed it is as to all matters completed and ended at the time of its repeal, as though it had never existed as a governing law with respect to these subject-matters. Now of course we ought to interpret the words which are used, first by forming an opinion as to what the intention of the legislature was, and then whether

References to amended legislation

14.3.13 For principles relating to the construction of references to amended legislation see Chapters 22, 26 and 29.

Subordinate legislation

14.3.14 The provisions of this Chapter are as relevant to the notion of amendment within subordinate legislation as within primary legislation.[96]

SECTION 4

REPEAL OF EARLIER LEGISLATION

Introduction

14.4.1 It is part of the doctrine of supremacy of Parliament, and vital to the flexibility of the constitution, that no one Parliament can fetter the discretion either of itself or of a later Parliament.[97] There is therefore no law that cannot be repealed by Parliament, although of course this freedom as a matter of legal theory is not always matched by the political reality.[98]

   Repeal of part of an Act is a specific instance of one of the ways in which that Act can be amended. Much of Section 3 above is therefore relevant to partial repeals and should be consulted in that connection.

Terminology

14.4.2 The standard way to provide for the repeal of a provision of legislation is to provide that it "shall cease to have effect". But the expression "[provision X] is hereby repealed" is also found. There is no substantive difference between saying that a provision shall cease to have effect and saying that it is repealed.[99]

---

the words bear it out."; see also "These provisions for revision have since been amended by the Countryside Act 1968; but this cannot affect the construction of the National Parks and Access to the Countryside Act 1949 as it was originally enacted."—*Suffolk County Council v Mason* [1979] 2 All E.R. 369, 375, HL *per* Lord Diplock; and "The original section 21(2) of the Act of 1926 is no longer law, since it has been replaced by section 23(3) of the Births and Deaths Registration Act 1953. Nevertheless, the original subsection is admissible in construing the section as a whole and, in our judgment, throws light on its construction."—*R. v Greater Manchester North District Coroner, Ex p. Worch* [1988] Q.B. 513, 528, CA *per* Slade L.J.

[96] Except for para.14.3.7.

[97] See further Chapter 2, Sections 1 and 2.

[98] It would not, for example, be possible in practice to repeal the European Communities Act 1972 (c.68) without first renouncing membership of the European Communities.

[99] See further below.

A temporary enactment which ceases to have effect at a predetermined time is said to have expired or lapsed.[1]

Secondary legislation is said to be revoked rather than repealed.[2]

"Double" repeal

The traditional approach in an Act of any length is for the substantive provisions of the Act to provide in their place for provisions of earlier enactments to cease to have effect and for a Schedule at the end of the Act, introduced by a provision providing for the repeal of the provisions listed in the Schedule, to list all the repeals in a single place. The cumulative effect is sometimes described by referring to the substantive provisions as killing the repealed enactments and the Repeal Schedule as burying the bodies. **14.4.3**

Readers of Acts should be wary, however, because not every entry in the Repeal Schedule is necessarily founded on a substantive "shall cease to have effect" provision earlier in the Act. In particular, take the case where provision A is amended by provisions B and C and finally repealed by Act D. Commonly, and for the purpose of avoiding too much unnecessary detail in the body of Acts, Act D will confine the substantive proposition to "provision A shall cease to have effect". Provisions B and C are thereby rendered devoid of content. It is unnecessary to say anything about their ceasing to have effect, but they will nevertheless be included, as a matter of good practice in keeping the statute book "tidy", in the Repeal Schedule.

This practice of "double repeal" came under scrutiny in *Commissioner of Police of the Metropolis v Simeon*.[3] The argument advanced in the Divisional Court was, as Lord Roskill put it in the House of Lords—

> "that, because there was what was called in argument before your Lordships' House a 'double repeal' provision in sections 8 and 10 and the Schedule, it must have been the intention of section 8, worded as it was, to have the further effect of abolishing the relevant part of section 4 of the 1824 Act so as to prevent future prosecutions for offences against that part of section 4 which had already been allegedly committed".

Lord Roskill rejected this suggestion and held, in giving the single speech, that there is no substantive significance in the presence or absence of this double form of repeal on any particular occasion.[4]

---

[1] See, for example, s.62(1) of the Northern Ireland (Emergency Provisions) Act 1996 (c.22).

[2] The idea is that the Minister or other person in whom the power is vested "recalls" his earlier exercise of it.

[3] [1982] 2 All E.R. 813, HL.

[4] See also Chapter 18, para.18.1.2, footnote 8.

Implied repeal

14.4.4   Where a provision of an Act is inconsistent with a provision of earlier legislation, the earlier provision is impliedly repealed by the later. The rule was stated by North J. in *Re Williams*[5]—

> "The provisions of an earlier Act may be revoked or abrogated in particular cases by a subsequent Act, either from the express language used being addressed to the particular point, or from implication or inference from the language used."

The question whether two Acts are inconsistent will not always be clear, which is why most repeal these days is effected expressly (that being one part of the purpose of the Repeal Schedule). In the case of statutes passed about the same time[6] the question can be particularly difficult. So on s.8 of the Real Property Limitation Act 1874[7] Cotton L.J. said—

> "One difficulty I have felt has been in consequence of the case of *Hunter v Nockolds*,[8] decided by Lord Cottenham in which he expressed an opinion that, although in actions brought to recover money issuing out of the lands, only six years' interest could be allowed, yet he based his decision on this ground, that one must take the two statutes, 3 & 4 Will. 4, c.27[9] and 3 & 4 Will. 4, c.42[10] together. That might be right under the circumstances. He was driven to that by this consideration, that the one Act was passed three weeks before the other and therefore he said you must read the two together, and take the later one only as an explanation of the other Act."[11]

Based on that decision Bray J. said—

> "The result of that decision was in terms to say that though the two Acts of 1833 were to be read together, there was not the same necessity to read the Act of 1874 and the Civil Procedure Act of 1833 together and that in effect

---

[5] (1887) 36 Ch. D. 573, 578.

[6] It was once a rule that a statute of one Session could not repeal or amend an Act of the same Session. The rule originated with the pre-1793 rule that all Acts came into force in the absence of express contrary provision as of the first day of the Session in which they were passed. So until 1850 Acts routinely contained express empowerment to amend, alter or repeal an enactment of the same Session. In 1850 the notion was embodied in s.1 of Brougham's Act 13 & 14 Vict. c.21. It is now found in s.2 of the Interpretation Act 1978 (c.30) ("Any Act may be amended or repealed in the Session of Parliament in which it is passed.").

[7] 1874 c.57.

[8] (1850) 1 Macn. & G. 640.

[9] Real Property Limitation Act 1833 (no action after six years for rent or interest on money charged on land).

[10] Civil Procedure Act 1833 (no action after 20 years for rent or money secured by specialty).

[11] *Sutton v Sutton* (1882) 22 Ch. D. 511, 518–519.

section 8 of the Act of 1874 did not qualify section 3 of the earlier Act."[12]

When considerable time elapses between the passing of two Acts the nature of an **14.4.5** implied repeal is more likely to be apparent. The general rule is stated by Fletcher Moulton L.J. in *Macmillan v Dent*[13] with reference to the Copyright Act 1842[14]—

> "The Act of 1842 did two things. It established a new copyright law and it wiped out all the old statutes relating to copyrights. For the sake of clearness I will use the phrase 'it had an enacting part and it had a repealing part'. The enacting part must have full force given to it whatever be the pre-existing statutes. If those provisions are contrary to those of the Act of Anne, these provisions being in a later Act override and *pro tanto* extinguish the provisions of the earlier Act. But apart from this, the repealing part wiped these earlier Acts off the statute book. The consequence of this would have been that all the rights which had been created under them and had not expired would have been wiped out. The enabling part of the Act of 1842 applies only to books published after that date, but it the preceding statutes had been wiped out *simpliciter*, all the books published before that date which were then in the enjoyment of copyright would have lost their privilege."[15]

The doctrine of implied repeal is as relevant to subordinate legislation as it is to primary, the notion being simply that a provision of a later instrument inconsistent with a provision of an earlier instrument is assumed to be revoking the earlier provision, in so far as it has power to do so. It is these last words "in so far as it has power to do so" that contain the principal difference between implied repeal and implied revocation. The main effect of this modification is that in so far as an instrument is inconsistent with earlier primary legislation it will be ineffective, unless it both has power under the enabling legislation to modify primary legislation and is clearly exercising that power. Another major effect is that inconsistency with a provision made under another enabling power will generally be ineffective, again unless the instrument both has power under the enabling legislation to interfere with other subordinate enactments and is clearly exercising that power.[16]

---

[12] *Shaw v Crompton* [1910] 2 K.B. 370, 377.

[13] [1907] 1 Ch. 107, 124.

[14] 1842 c.45.

[15] But s.1 of the Act of 1842 preserved the older Act so far as necessary to secure rights already acquired under them and not expired.

[16] For an instance of the effect of implied revocation being apparently overlooked by the draftsman of subordinate legislation note the following extract of the 5th Report of the Joint Committee on Statutory Instruments, Session 1996–97, para.10 (HL Paper 21, HC 29-v)—" 'Subject to any statutory provision in that behalf . . . '—In the Committee's view, the words italicised above are wrongly inserted and might be misleading. In so far as 'statutory provision' means the provision of an Act of Parliament, it is unnecessary to include the italicised words because subordinate

No implied repeal of constitutional statutes

14.4.6   Certain statutes alter the constitutional arrangements of the United Kingdom in such a way as create a new framework within which later legislation is to be construed and applied. That does not, of course, preclude a later statute from expressly repealing or amending those new arrangements, for it is of the essence of the notion of Parliament's sovereign supremacy[17] that no one Parliament can fetter the scope of action of a later Parliament. But it does mean that the courts will assume—in accordance with the wish of the Parliament enacting the constitutional statute—that no future Parliament intends to depart from or contravene any aspect of the new constitutional arrangements unless it does so in clear and unambiguous words.

The position is explained in great detail in connection with s.2(1) of the European Communities Act 1972,[18] which gave force of law within the United Kingdom to the laws of the European Communities and was on its terms clearly intended to be an entrenched constitutional statute, by Laws L.J. in *Thoburn v Sunderland City Council*.[19] A considerable portion of his judgment—dealing both with the notion of constitutional statutes in the context of implied repeal and with other matters—is appended to this work.[20]

The list of statutes offered by Laws L.J. is not and could not be complete. In compiling and up-dating a complete list one would probably need to look for those statutes which have the flavour of laying down rules, or establishing systems, which are likely and intended to affect the way in which laws of a general kind are made or applied or in which public or private business is effected. In one sense, this development perhaps reflects the fact that much of the fabric of law and constitution has moved from the common law to statute,[21] and that the presumptions of durability operated in relation to the common law[22] now have to be operated in relation to statutes that appear to be laying down principles or establishing systems intended to be enduring.[23]

---

legislation must give way to primary legislation, and it is misleading in suggesting that, without such express words, the legal position might be otherwise. In so far as 'statutory provision' is meant to include the provisions of earlier statutory instruments, it cannot be effective in these unspecific terms, earlier instruments being subject to later ones."

[17] See Chapter 2, Sections 1 and 2.

[18] 1972 c.68.

[19] [2003] Q.B. 151.

[20] Appendix, Extract 4: and see also Chapter 1, Section 4.

[21] See Section 1 above.

[22] See Sections 1 and 2 above, and also Chapter 19.

[23] Certainly the tenor of Laws L.J.'s judgment is reminiscent of the following passage from the speech of the Earl of Halsbury in *Leach v R.* [1912] A.C. 305, HL (cited, with other speeches in that case, more extensively in Section 1 above)—"Now, dealing with that question, I should have thought that it would occur not only to a lawyer, but to almost every Englishman, that a wife ought not to be allowed to be called against her husband, and that those who are under the responsibility of passing Acts of Parliament would recognize a matter of that supreme importance as one to be dealt with specifically and definitely and not to be left to inference. . . . If you want to alter the law

Subordinate legislation repealing legislation

There is of course no general power for subordinate legislation to override or repeal earlier inconsistent legislation, whether primary or subordinate. But s.14 of the Interpretation Act 1978[24] confers implied power on most kinds of subordinate legislation to revoke and re-enact.[25] And it is common for a Henry VIII power[26] to confer express power to repeal an enactment. **14.4.7**

General savings

The effect of a repeal unless savings are made is expressed in the following dicta— **14.4.8**

> "I take the effect of repealing a statute to be to obliterate it as completely from the records of the Parliament as if it had never been passed; and it must be considered as a law that never existed except for the purpose of those actions which were commenced, prosecuted and concluded whilst it was an existing law."[27]

> "It has long been established that, when an Act of Parliament is repealed, it must be considered (except as to transactions past and closed) as if it had never existed."[28]

The result was that an offence committed against a penal Act while it was in force could not be prosecuted after the repeal of the Act.[29] And pending proceedings could not be further continued after the repeal, even to the extent of applying for a certificate of costs.[30]

The position is altered by the Interpretation Act 1978,[31] ss.15 and 16 of which deal with the construction and application of one provision which repeals another. **14.4.9**

Section 15 resolves a conundrum about the repeal of a repealing provision. It provides—

> "Where an Act repeals a repealing enactment, the repeal does not revive any enactment previously repealed unless words are inserted reviving it."

---

which has lasted for centuries and which is almost ingrained in the English Constitution, in the sense that everybody would say, 'To call a wife against her husband is a thing that cannot be heard of,'—to suggest that that is to be dealt with by inference, and that you should introduce a new system of law without any specific enactment of it, seems to me to be perfectly monstrous."

[24] 1978 c.30.
[25] See Chapter 22.
[26] As to which see Chapter 1, Section 2.
[27] Tindal C.J. in *Kay v Goodwin* (1830) 6 Bing. 576, 582.
[28] Lord Tenterden in *Surtees v Ellison* (1829) 9 B. & C. 750, 752.
[29] *R. v M'Kenzie* (1820) Russ. & R. 429.
[30] *Morgan v Thorne* (1841) 7 M. & W. 400; *Butcher v Henderson* (1868) L.R. 3 Q.B. 335.
[31] 1978 c.30; and similar provisions were included in the Interpretation Act 1889 c.63.

Although this conundrum would normally fall to be resolved in the way which s.15 requires as a matter of common sense, it is useful to have the doubt avoided. In this respect it is interesting to note that s.15 is not subject to the normal qualifying notion of applying only if the contrary intention appears: so it would have to be displaced by very clear words indeed. The proposition laid down by s.15 is the simple one that the repeal by provision A of provision B which itself repealed provision C, does not revive provision C unless provision A expressly says that it does.

Section 16, which unlike s.15 is subject to the usual qualification about the absence of contrary intention, in essence preserves transactions past and closed from the effect of a repeal.

14.4.10   The provisions of s.16 are as follows—

> "(1) Without prejudice to section 15, where an Act repeals an enactment, the repeal does not, unless the contrary intention appears,—
>
> > (a) revive anything not in force or existing at the time at which the repeal takes effect;
> > (b) affect the previous operation of the enactment repealed or anything duly done or suffered under that enactment;
> > (c) affect any right, privilege, obligation or liability acquired, accrued or incurred under that enactment;
> > (d) affect any penalty, forfeiture or punishment incurred in respect of any offence committed against that enactment;
> > (e) affect any investigation, legal proceeding or remedy in respect of any such right, privilege, obligation, liability, penalty, forfeiture or punishment;
> >
> > and any such investigation, legal proceeding or remedy may be instituted, continued or enforced, and any such penalty, forfeiture or punishment may be imposed, as if the repealing Act had not been passed.
>
> (2) This section applies to the expiry of a temporary enactment as if it were repealed by an Act."

So, for example, a person who has become liable to some penalty as a result of contravening a requirement imposed by a provision is not saved from liability for the penalty by later repeal of the provision, and can be proceeded against by way of enforcement of the penalty after the repeal. This principle is really the corollary of the presumption against retrospectivity[32]: just as we assume, in the absence of very clear evidence to the contrary, that the legislature does not intend to introduce a new law in relation to past events, so too we assume that the abolition of a particular law for the future is not intended to prevent the due

---

[32] Discussed in Chapter 10, Section 3.

operation of the rule of law as it stood prior to the abolition's taking effect. Section 16 is a very broad set of propositions and the courts will give it an appropriately wide construction, so as not to frustrate the underlying intention of allowing matters arising before the repeal of an enactment to be followed through to their conclusion as if the repeal had not happened.[33]

The cumulative effect of ss.15 and 16 of that Act is that, in the absence of **14.4.11** express contrary intention, a repeal—

(1) does not revive an enactment that was itself repealed by the provision that is now repealed[34] (s.15),

(2) does not revive anything not in force or existing when the repeal takes effect (s.16(1)(a)),

(3) does not affect the previous operation of the enactment repealed or anything fully done or suffered under that enactment (s.16(1)(b)),

(4) does not affect any right, privilege, obligation or liability acquired, accrued or incurred under the enactment repealed (s.16(1)(c)),

(5) does not affect any penalty, forfeiture or punishment incurred in respect of any offence committed under the enactment repealed (s.16(1)(d)), and

(6) does not affect an investigation, legal proceeding or remedy in respect of a right, privilege, obligation, liability, penalty, forfeiture or punishment accruing or incurring prior to the repeal of the enactment (s.16(1)(e)).

By way of an example of a thing "duly done" under a repealed enactment for the purposes of s.16(1)(b), it was held in *Heston and Isleworth Urban Council v Grout*[35] that notice given to frontagers to pave and make up a street under a provision of the Public Health Act 1875[36] survived the partial repeal of the provision by the adoption for the relevant district of the Private Streets Works Act 1892.[37]

The notion of a right accrued in s.16(1)(c) requires a little exposition. In **14.4.12** particular, the saving does not apply to a mere right to take advantage of a repealed enactment (clearly, since that would deprive the notion of a repeal of much of its obvious significance). Something must have been done or have occurred to cause a particular right to accrue under a repealed enactment. So where under the Agricultural Holdings Act 1908[38] a tenant had become entitled

---

[33] See, for example, *Aitken v South Hams District Council* [1995] 1 A.C. 262, HL, and *Floor v Davis* [1980] A.C. 695, HL.

[34] But note that this principle does not apply to prevent the revival of principles of the common law—see Section 1 above.

[35] [1897] 2 Ch. 306, distinguished in *Director of Public Works v Ho Po Sang* [1961] A.C. 901. This is a case on the equivalent proposition in the Interpretation Act 1889 (c.63).

[36] 1875 c.55.

[37] 1892 c.57.

[38] 1908 c.28.

to compensation by his landlord's having given him notice to quit, he acquired a right to compensation which was not lost by the repeal of the Act, so he was entitled to continue after the repeal the proceedings necessary for the recovery of compensation.[39]

A contrary intention for the purpose of displacing s.16 of the Interpretation Act must be very clear, although it could in theory arise by very strong implication. Early cases discounting the use of "cease to have effect" rather than "repeal" as a contrary intention are overtaken by *Simeon*.[40]

Ad hoc savings

14.4.13   It is common for one provision of legislation repealing another to do so subject to express savings designed to meet the particular circumstances, in addition to those implied by ss.15 and 16 of the Interpretation Act 1978.[41]

These may be imposed by the legislation that effects the repeal. But it is common for the order appointing a time for commencement of a piece of legislation to be empowered to impose savings on the effect of any repeal commenced. This can be a trap for the reader. Act A may contain a simple proposition that Act B is repealed. But Act A comes into force by appointed day order. And the appointed day order provides that the repeal of Act B comes into force on day X "but shall have no effect in relation to persons born before day X". The result is that while the face of the statute book presents Act B as repealed, it continues to have legal effect in relation to a large class of people for a number of years. Nor is this a far-fetched example: in the context of tax legislation, for example, almost all commencement and repeal is in relation to particular tax-years, and the practical effects of a tax-year can be felt for a number of years afterwards (and sometimes, by retrospective application, before).

The inclusion of ad hoc savings also explains an apparent oddity that sometimes appears, whereby provision A has three subsections each of which is repealed by one of provisions B, C, and D, and provision E finally repeals the entirety of provision A. What may be thought to be a mere oversight by the draftsman of provision E, who is thought to have overlooked the cumulative repeal of the entire substance of provision A by Acts B, C and D, may actually reflect the fact that each of provisions B, to D contained significant savings that have now ceased to have practical significance (or have ceased to be desirable as

---

[39] *Hamilton Gell v White* [1922] 2 K.B. 422, CA. *cf. Falcon v Famous Players Film Co.* [1926] 1 K.B. 393, [1926] 2 K.B. 474 and *Re a Debtor (No.490 of 1935)* [1936] Ch. 237.
[40] See above.
[41] For example, see s.406(7) of and Notes 1 to 6 to Sch.19 to the Communications Act 2003 (c.21) (repeals).

a matter of policy) with the result that it is now right to "bury the body" by a final repeal of the entire provision without savings.[42]

Revival

Although it is fairly rare, it is possible for a provision repealed by one piece of legislation to be revived by a later one. Nowadays one would expect a revival to be in clear and precise terms.[43]

14.4.14

Calculation of portion of enactment repealed

In early repealing enactments it was sometimes unclear how much of the enactment to be repealed was intended to be referred to. The Interpretation Act 1889[44] codified a rule of construction to the effect that "a description or citation of a portion of another Act shall, unless the contrary intention appears, be construed as including the word, section, or other part mentioned or referred to as forming the beginning and as forming the end of the portion comprised in the description or citation".[45] The rule is replicated in s.20(1) of the Interpretation Act 1978.[46]

14.4.15

Repeal and re-enactment

Section 17 of the Interpretation Act 1978[47] provides—

14.4.16

"(1) Where an Act repeals a previous enactment and substitutes provisions for the enactment repealed, the repealed enactment remains in force until the substituted provisions come into force.

(2) Where an Act repeals and re-enacts, with or without modification, a previous enactment then, unless the contrary intention appears,—

(a) any reference in any other enactment to the enactment so repealed shall be construed as a reference to the provision re-enacted;

(b) in so far as any subordinate legislation made or other thing done under the enactment so repealed, or having effect as if so made or

---

[42] Much of the work of the Statute Law (Reform) Acts, in particular, consists in the repeal of provisions which, while nominally and formally still wholly or partly in force, or repealed subject to savings that nominally and formally continue, have long since ceased to be of any conceivable practical significance. See further Chapter 1, Section 9.

[43] That has not always been the case, however: see *Northam Bridge Co. v R.* (1886) 55 L.T. 759.

[44] 1889 c.63.

[45] s.35(3).

[46] 1978 c.30: it should be noted that the obverse rule—whereby the cited words are excluded—applies in the case of the framing of amendments to Bills in either House of Parliament.

[47] 1978 c.30.

> done, could have been made or done under the provision re-enac-
> ted, it shall have effect as if made or done under that provi-
> sion."

From this may be distilled three propositions in the case where a provision is repealed and its substance re-enacted—

(1) It is to be assumed that the repeal takes effect only when the re-enactment comes into force. This is of limited practical significance these days, the practice being to make express provision as to the timing both of the repeal and of the re-enactment.

(2) A reference in any primary or subordinate legislation to the repealed provision is to be construed as a reference to the re-enacted provision. The difficulty here is that the conversion may not always be sufficiently clear. Reference to the destination and derivation tables for a Consolidation Bill show that on re-enactment the substance of what was previously a single proposition may have to be wholly or partially reproduced in several different places. Section 17(2)(a) therefore provides a rule of thumb that will suffice in comparatively simple cases: but where the conversion of references is at all complicated the re-enacting legislation will be well advised to make express provision about the conversion of references (or to give power for consequential provision of that kind to be made).

(3) Anything (including the making of subordinate legislation) that can be done under the repealed provision, or that has effect as if done under the repealed provision, has effect as if done under the re-enacted provision. This is one of the many places in which it is important to have regard to substance rather than form. In the case of subordinate legislation one must ask not could precisely the same words be used to embody legislation under the two primary provisions, but whether the substance of what was done under the old provision could be replicated under the new. Section 17(2)(b) does not preserve anything which is radically different in substance and effect to what may be done under the old legislation, merely because the form is preserved. Equally, s.17(2)(b) will be sufficient to preserve something the effect and substance of which may be reproduced under the new legislation, irrespective of whether the old form could survive under the new scheme.

14.4.17 Simple as those propositions appear at first, they can be immensely troublesome to apply. The principal difficulty lies in knowing what amounts to a re-enactment. Obviously[48] the section is not confined to cases where an old law is re-enacted in precisely the same substantive terms. The section also applies where a

---

[48] And, in the case of s.17(2), expressly.

provision is re-enacted with modifications, which could amount to significant differences of substance. But presumably at some point a new law ceases to be a re-enactment of the old and becomes the imposition of an entirely new regime.

The result of this uncertainty is that s.17 can safely be relied on only where it amounts to little or nothing more than a statement of the obvious. So where, for example, there is real doubt as to how one should convert a reference to a provision of the old law into a reference to the new law, because there is insufficiently precise correspondence between the two sets of provisions, the answer is that s.17 should not be relied on to support the conversion at all. This limitation is the reason why it is common to find detailed transitional provisions in the context of anything that amounts to a consolidation with modifications, providing expressly for conversion of references and the like.[49]

Extent of repeal

It is possible for a repealing provision to be more limited in extent than is the provision repealed. In which case the provision retains the full force of law in the territory to which the repealing provision does not extend.[50]   **14.4.18**

Short title

A short title may be used to refer to an Act despite the fact that the entire Act (including the provision appointing the short title) has been repealed.[51]   **14.4.19**

Statute Law Repeal Acts

The Acts used to remove obsolete Acts from the statute book are discussed in Chapter 1, Section 9.   **14.4.20**

Enactment and amendment in same Session

Section 2 of the Interpretation Act 1978[52] provides that—   **14.4.21**

> "Any Act may be amended or repealed in the Session of Parliament in which it is passed."[53]

---

[49] See, for example, s.63(2) of, and Sch.5 to, the Northern Ireland Emergency Provisions Act 1996 (c.22).

[50] See, for example, s.109 of the Railways and Transport Safety Act 2003 (c.20).

[51] Interpretation Act 1978 (c.30), s.19(2).

[52] 1978 c.30.

[53] This has been the position for many decades and would now be thought to stand to reason. The origin for the necessity of such a rule, however, is the situation that appertained prior to 1793 whereby all Acts of one Session were treated as having received Royal Assent on the same day (*Coke* 4 Inst. 25 and *Attorney-General v Panter* (1772) 6 Bro. P.C. 486). It was therefore impossible to know which of two mutually repugnant Acts ought to prevail—see *R. v Middlesex*

Implied power to revoke, &c.

14.4.22   Section 14 of the Interpretation Act 1978[54] creates a presumption that power to legislate "implies, unless the contrary intention appears, a power, exercisable in the same manner and subject to the same conditions or limitations, to revoke, amend or re-enact any instrument made under the power".

This presumption applies to rules, regulations, byelaws and Orders in Council in any event and, but only if to be made by statutory instrument, orders and other forms of subordinate legislation.[55] This creates a minor heffalump trap for primary legislators, having to remember when conferring, for example, a power to give directions or to make executive orders other than by statutory instrument, to confer express power to revoke and amend.[56]

Of course, it is probable that in appropriate cases the courts would infer the power to revoke and amend administrative and other directions where it was not seriously likely that Parliament had intended to enable a single and invariable exercise of the power. The concept of *functus officio*, according to which a power once exercised is spent and the person in whom the power is vested has no further power, is properly confined to those powers that can sensibly have been intended to be treated in that way. The obvious example is a power to appoint a day for the commencement of a provision.[57]

Even in relation to commencement, however, the better view[58] is that although it in effect confers a power to pull a trigger, the power does not become spent until the bullet has left the gun, that is to say until the commencement day has arrived: until that day there is good reason to say that the Minster appointing the day can revoke the first order and appoint a new day, otherwise early appointment of a future day would penalise a Minister by reducing his flexibility, which would

---

Justices (1831) 2 B. & Ad. 818, 821 *per* Lord Tenterden. Therefore the Acts of Parliament (Commencement) Act 1793 was passed with the effect that each Act is treated as enacted, and is presumed in the absence of express contrary provision to come into force, on the day on which Royal Assent is signified.

[54] 1978 c.30.

[55] s.14(a) and (b).

[56] See, for example, s.23 of the Government Resources and Accounts Act 2000 (c.20) (Treasury directions).

[57] See further Chapter 10, Section 1.

[58] See, in particular, the following passage of a memorandum from the Department of Health and Social Security to the Joint Committee on Statutory Instruments, printed as the Appendix to the Ninth Report of the Committee for Session 1974 (HL 66, HC 51-X)—

"5. Moreover, it is clear that Parliament takes the view that revocation and variation of commencement orders may be desirable, because in many Acts in which a general provision for revocation and variation of orders is inappropriate *[NB—this passage ante-dates the Interpretation Act 1978, s.14]* Parliament has included a specific provision expressly empowering the revocation and variation of commencement orders. . . .

6. The Committee has itself drawn attention to the distinction between an order which revokes or varies a commencement order after the date appointed by the latter has come, bringing into operation the statutory provision affected by it, and one which (like the present Order) is made before that date has come. It is not entirely clear what would be the effect of revoking a commencement order after it had already operated to bring statutory provisions into force; indeed the practice of revoking or varying such an order after it has taken effect

be both illogical and inconvenient for all concerned. Even after the appointed day has arrived, it is arguable in the normal case of a power to appoint a day that also confers power to make transitional provision, that the transitional provision could be amended or supplemented after the appointed day.

Lapse

Subordinate legislation lapses automatically when the enabling power ceases to have effect, unless saved expressly. **14.4.23**

This proposition is, however, subject to ss.16 and 17 of the Interpretation Act 1978.[59]

Section 16 provides for a number of savings on the repeal of legislation, some of which are relevant to the exercise of powers under the legislation, and is discussed in more detail elsewhere in this work.[60]

Section 17(2)(b) provides that where primary legislation is repealed and re-enacted, with or without modification,[61] then unless the contrary intention appears—

> "(b) in so far as any subordinate legislation made or other thing done under the enactment so repealed, or having effect as if so made or done, could have been made or done under the provision re-enacted, it shall have effect as it made or done under that provision."

In determining the effect of s.17(2)(b) it is important to apply a test of substance and not of form. In other words, it does not matter whether the precise words of the early subordinate legislation could be used to have effect under the new enabling power[62]: what matters is whether the substance of the old provision could equally well be enacted under the new.

---

is one which Parliament ahs sometimes forbidden (for example in section 16(2) of the Family Income Supplements Act 1970 and section 56(3) of the National Health Service Reorganisation Act 1973, both cited above). No such prohibition, or even criticism, of the practice of revoking or varying a commencement order before it has taken effect has been discovered and it will be noted that in this instance the revocation order was made almost 11 months before the provisions revoked and varied were to take effect."

[59] 1978 c.30.

[60] See above.

[61] It may not always be easy to discern when a new enactment that occupies the same substantive area as an enactment repealed amounts to a re-enactment with modifications rather than a completely fresh start.

[62] This test works both ways: that is to say, the mere fact that a new power could be exercised in the same words as the old will not be sufficient to preserve subordinate legislation under the old as if made under the new, if the substantive effect of the two is different.

SECTION 5

EFFECT ON LATER LEGISLATION

Introduction

14.5.1   The principle has already been established[63] that Parliament cannot fetter its own discretion or that of a later Parliament. But that does not prevent legislation from establishing presumptions that are to be given effect to in later legislation, unless the later legislation expressly provides to the contrary.

   The principal instances have been encountered earlier in this work, some of them frequently. They are—

(1) The European Communities Act 1972,[64] s.2(1) of which has the effect of requiring later legislation to be read in such a way as to make it compatible with the obligations of the United Kingdom under the Community Treaties.[65]

(2) The Human Rights Act 1998,[66] s.3 of which performs a similar, and more direct, function in relation to the European Convention on Human Rights.[67]

(3) The Interpretation Act 1978,[68] which establishes a number of rebuttable presumptions.[69]

There are others of less general significance but which can nevertheless be of importance in their context. And since the later legislation has no need to refer to these presumptions or propositions, because of their automatic application in the absence of contrary intention, they can be something of a trap for the reader, particularly for someone relatively unused to construing legislation.

Definitions

14.5.2   A number of these propositions amount to definitions established by one piece of legislation that are to have effect in relation to future provisions unless overridden expressly. Some of the most significant are listed in Chapter 23.

Other provisions

14.5.3   Apart from definitions there are many provisions which, in one way or another, are intended to inform or affect the construction of later enactments. It is not

---

[63] Chapter 2, Section 2.
[64] 1972 c.68.
[65] See further Chapter 32, Section 3.
[66] 1998 c.42.
[67] See further Chapter 25.
[68] 1978 c.30.
[69] See Chapter 22.

practicable to give an exhaustive list in this work, but it is possible to mention some that are particularly likely to be of particular, if only occasional, importance.

Scottish legislative competence

Section 101 of the Scotland Act 1998[70] requires an Act of the Scottish Parliament or devolved Scottish subordinate legislation "to be read as narrowly as is required for it to be within competence, if such a reading is possible". In other words, the courts are required to apply the presumption that the Scottish Parliament or executive intended to limit themselves to what they had power to do. Only if the words used defy any explanation or construction that would be within legislative competence are the courts to declare the legislation to be unlawful. If they can save the legislation by construing it in a way which, even if not the natural construction or that most likely actually to have been intended by the draftsman, they are to do so.

14.5.4

Welsh expressions

The National Assembly for Wales is enabled to make provision by order under which where a Welsh word or phrase appears in the Welsh text of subordinate legislation made by the Assembly "it is to be taken as having the same meaning as the English word or phrase specified in relation to it in the order".[71]

14.5.5

Oaths

It is reasonably common to find a legislative requirement for a person to make an oath of veracity in relation to a statement made by him or a document signed by him.[72] Any reference to an oath must be read as including a reference to a statutory affirmation, by virtue of s.5 of the Oaths Act 1978.[73]

14.5.6

---

[70] 1998 c.46.

[71] s.122(2).

[72] It is, however, less common than it was. It is common nowadays simply to require a statement to be made, without saying anything about an oath or other formality, but to enforce truthfulness by making it a statutory offence to give information that the person does not believe to be true.

[73] 1978 c.19.

"**5 Making of solemn affirmations**

(1) Any person who objects to being sworn shall be permitted to make his solemn affirmation instead of taking an oath.

(2) Subsection (1) above shall apply in relation to a person to whom it is not reasonably practicable without inconvenience or delay to administer an oath in the manner appropriate to his religious belief as it applies in relation to a person objecting to be sworn.

(3) A person who may be permitted under subsection (2) above to make his solemn affirmation may also be required to do so.

(4) A solemn affirmation shall be of the same force and effect as an oath."

See also Schedule 1 to the Interpretation Act 1978 (c.30).

Rehabilitation of offenders

14.5.7 Legislation may make reference to whether a person has convictions for a criminal offence. Section 4 of the Rehabilitation of Offenders Act 1974[74] has effect so as to require those references, in the absence of express provision to the contrary, as excluding references to convictions spent in accordance with the earlier provisions of that Act.[75]

Crown Proceedings

14.5.8 The Crown Proceedings Act 1947[76] establishes a number of rules that have effect in relation to later provisions about, or potentially giving rise to, tortious and other kinds of liability.[77]

---

[74] 1974 c.53.

[75] **"4 Effect of rehabilitation**

(1) Subject to sections 7 and 8 below, a person who has become a rehabilitated person for the purposes of this Act in respect of a conviction shall be treated for all purposes in law as a person who has not committed or been charged with or prosecuted for or convicted of or sentenced for the offence or offences which were the subject of that conviction; and, notwithstanding the provisions of any other enactment or rule of law to the contrary, but subject as aforesaid—

  (a) no evidence shall be admissible in any proceedings before a judicial authority exercising its jurisdiction or functions in Great Britain to prove that any such person has committed or been charged with or prosecuted for or convicted of or sentenced for any offence which was the subject of a spent conviction; and

  (b) a person shall not, in any such proceedings, be asked, and, if asked, shall not be required to answer, any question relating to his past which cannot be answered without acknowledging or referring to a spent conviction or spent convictions or any circumstances ancillary thereto. . . . "

[76] 1947 c.44.

[77] See, in particular, the following—

s.2(2) and (3)—

"(2) Where the Crown is bound by a statutory duty which is binding also upon persons other than the Crown and its officers, then, subject to the provisions of this Act, the Crown shall, in respect of a failure to comply with that duty, be subject to all those liabilities in tort (if any) to which it would be so subject if it were a private person of full age and capacity.

(2) Where any functions are conferred or imposed upon an officer of the Crown as such either by any rule of the common law or by statute, and that officer commits a tort while performing or purporting to perform those functions, the liabilities of the Crown in respect of the tort shall be such as they would have been if those functions had been conferred or imposed solely by virtue of instructions lawfully given by the Crown."

Section 11—

"11 Saving in respect of acts done under prerogative and statutory powers

(1) Nothing in Part I of this Act shall extinguish or abridge any powers or authorities which, if this Act had not been passed, would have been exercisable by virtue of the prerogative of the Crown, or any powers or authorities conferred on the Crown by any statute, and, in particular, nothing in the said Part I shall extinguish or abridge any powers or authorities exercisable by the Crown, whether in time of peace or of war, for the purpose of the defence of the realm or of training, or maintaining the efficiency of, any of the armed forces of the Crown.

(2) Where in any proceedings under this Act it is material to determine whether anything was properly done or omitted to be done in the exercise of the prerogative of the

Acquisition of land, &c.

Provisions about the compulsory acquisition of land will need to be read in the light of, in particular, the Land Compensation Acts 1961[78] and 1973[79] and the Acquisition of Land Act 1981.[80] **14.5.9**

Limitation of actions

Legislation conferring rights of action will be affected by the rules of limitation established by the Limitation Act 1980.[81] In particular, s.9(1) provides as follows— **14.5.10**

> "(1) An action to recover any sum recoverable by virtue of any enactment shall not be brought after the expiration of six years from the date on which the cause of action accrued."[82]

Laying before Parliament

Section 1 of the Laying of Documents before Parliament Act 1948[83] provides that— **14.5.11**

> "a reference in any Act of Parliament or subordinate legislation, whether passed or made before or after the passing of this Act, to the laying of any instrument, report, account or other document before either House of Parliament is, unless the contrary intention appears, to be construed as a reference to the taking, during the existence of a Parliament, of such action as is directed by virtue of any Standing Order, Sessional Order or other direction of that House for the time being in force[84] to constitute the laying

---

Crown, . . . a Secretary of State may, if satisfied that the act or omission was necessary for any such purpose as is mentioned in the last preceding subsection, issue a certificate to the effect that the act or omission was necessary for that purpose; and the certificate shall, in those proceedings, be conclusive as to the matter so certified."

[78] 1961 c.33.

[79] 1973 c.26.

[80] 1981 c.67.

[81] 1980 c.58.

[82] Subject to the rules in section 10 about claiming of contributions—see s.9(2).

[83] 1948 c.59.

[84] An excellent example of the kind of false accuracy warned against in Chapter 8, Section 1 (under the sub-heading "prolixity"). By attempting to cover the whole field in express detail the draftsman has omitted—probably because of the Parliamentary practice prevailing in 1948—to mention the possibility of an order that is neither Sessional nor Standing, but appertains for the remainder of a Parliament (see, for example, the Order as to Liaison Committee (Membership) of November 5, 2001). While one might be able to stretch the expression "other direction" to cover an Order of this kind, that would require disregard of the distinction between the concepts of Orders and directions (the latter being used, for example, under the Parliament Act 1911—see Chapter 5, Section 2). A more general reference to the practice of the House would have shortened this provision considerably and removed the possibility of argument and misunderstanding.

of that document before that House, or as is accepted by virtue of the practice of that House for the time being as constituting such laying, notwithstanding that the action so directed or accepted consists in part or wholly in action capable of being taken otherwise than at or during the time of a sitting of that House; and that a reference in any such Act or subordinate legislation to the laying of any instrument, report, account or other document before Parliament is, unless the contrary intention appears, to be construed accordingly as a reference (construed in accordance with the preceding declaration) to the laying of the document before each House of Parliament."

Parliamentary control of statutory instruments

14.5.12   Sections 4 to 6 of the Statutory Instruments Act 1946[85] establish rules to be applied where a later Act makes provision requiring an instrument or draft instrument to be laid before Parliament.[86]

---

[85] 1946 c.36.
[86] Discussion of the detail of the various kinds of procedure is found in Chapter 6, Section 2.

CHAPTER 15

ERRORS IN LEGISLATION

Introduction

For a variety of reasons and in a variety of ways, it sometimes happens that **15.1.1** legislation is enacted or made in a form that incorporates errors of form or substance. This Chapter addresses, or refers the reader to passages elsewhere in this work that consider, a number of different aspects of that issue.

Corrective legislation

From time to time it is thought either necessary or presentationally desirable both **15.1.2** to use legislation to correct faults in earlier legislation and also to make the corrective purpose of the later legislation clear. In 1835, for example, an Act was passed[1] the long title of which was "An Act to amend Two clerical Errors contained in an Act passed in the Ninth Year of the Reign of His late Majesty King George the Fourth, intituled An Act for consolidating and amending the Laws in Ireland relative to Larceny and other Offences connected therewith". And in 1862 an Act was passed the long title of which was "An Act for rectifying a clerical error in the Act of the present Session, Chapter Forty, with respect to the African Slave Trade Treaty".[2]

Ambiguity in statute: *Pepper v Hart*

Where a statute leaves an area of ambiguity the rule in *Pepper v Hart* may be **15.1.3** applied to resolve the ambiguity. See Chapter 28.

Correction slips

It sometimes happens that the version of an Act printed by the Queen's Printer **15.1.4** contains a typographical error, such as a wrong cross-reference or something of that kind, that does not obscure the sense of the legislative intent but ought to be corrected so as to avoid misleading readers. The standard practice is for the Queen's Printer to issue a correction slip, which is circulated with new sales of the Act and to those known to have purchased it already, drawing attention to the

---

[1] 1835 c.34.
[2] African Slave Trade Treaty Act (No.2) 1862 c.90.

error and the correction. The correction is then made in the version of the Act as it appears in the annual volumes of Acts published by Her Majesty's Stationery Office.

A similar procedure operates for subordinate legislation.

The correction slip procedure is, however, designed only to achieve consistency between the law as enacted or made and the law as published. It is not designed to correct substantive errors, however small, in the former.[3]

As to making minor corrections directly in the form of the legislation as to be published, while common sense must prevail in the case of trivial but confusing typographical errors, the following words of the House of Commons Select Committee on Statutory Instruments express the position accurately and authoritatively—

> "The Committee notes that the Department have arranged for this error[4] to be corrected in the published copies of the Order. Although the Committee has no objection to such a minor correction in this instance, it would emphasise to all Departments that it is not acceptable unilaterally to correct errors that have been made in instruments made and laid."[5]

Sleeping dogs

15.1.5   In the case of a minor error where what is intended is clear beyond doubt and there is no room for misunderstanding or for serious confusion, it is often best simply to allow sleeping dogs to lie. Corrective legislation involves large expenditure of public money, and even the administrative costs associated with the issue of a correction slip are considerable.[6]

There are therefore a number of instances in which trivial errors have simply been allowed to remain.[7]

---

[3] Note "The Privy Council Office's memorandum acknowledges that the references in the Schedule and the Table of Fees are incorrect, and indicates that the corrections will be made by means of a printer's correction slip. However, this would not be the correct way of proceeding, since issuing a correction slip is only appropriate where the discrepancy is between the original instrument and the printed copy. The Privy Council have subsequently indicated that these corrections will now be made when the Regulations are consolidated next year."—Joint Committee on Statutory Instruments, Session 1998–99, 3rd Report, para.12 (HL Paper 10, HC 47-iii).

[4] A wrong section in the recital of powers.

[5] House of Commons Select Committee on Statutory Instruments, Session 1994–95, 1st Report, para.3 (HC 16-i).

[6] And an insignificant error can be corrected when the Annual Volumes of statutes or statutory instruments are published.

[7] For example, s.20 of the Commonwealth Development Corporation Act 1999 (c.20) says "Schedule 20 shall have effect", although it is abundantly clear from the parenthetical description and general context that what is meant is a reference to Sch.3 (there is no Sch.20). It did not seem worth the trouble and expense to public funds of issuing a correction slip for an error which could not mislead anyone. The annual volume has the correct version. See also the Offensive Weapons Act 1996 (c.26), ss.2(4) and 3(2); the Police and Criminal Evidence Act 1984 (c.60), ss.120(9) before renumbering by the Criminal Justice Act 1988, Sch.15, para.101; Criminal Justice

Beneficial construction to repair obvious error

While taking great care to avoid trespassing on the legislature's area of **15.1.6**
responsibility, the courts will sometimes be prepared to use their powers of
construction to mend what are beyond any doubt clerical or administrative errors,
although more than merely typographical errors, in the preparation of legislation.

In relation to primary legislation, the position is as described in and
exemplified by the following passage of the speech of Lord Nicholls of
Birkenhead in *Inco Europe Ltd v First Choice Distribution*[8]—

> "Several features make it plain beyond a peradventure that on this occasion
> Homer, in the person of the draftsman of Schedule 3 to the Act of 1996,
> nodded. Something went awry in the drafting of paragraph 37(2) of
> Schedule 3. Paragraph 37(2) is the paragraph which set out the amendment
> made to section 18(1)(g) of the Act of 1981. Moreover, what paragraph
> 37(2) was seeking to do, but on a literal reading of the language failed to
> achieve, is also abundantly plain. . . .

> "I am left in no doubt that, for once, the draftsman slipped up. The sole
> object of paragraph 37(2) in Schedule 3 was to amend section 18(1)(g) by
> substituting a new paragraph (g) that would serve the same purpose
> regarding the Act of 1996 as the original paragraph (g) had served regarding
> the Act of 1979. The language used was not apt to achieve this result. Given
> that the intended object of paragraph 37(2) is so plain, the paragraph should
> be read in a manner which gives effect to the parliamentary intention. Thus
> the new section 18(1)(g), substituted by paragraph 37(2), should be read as
> confined to decisions of the High Court under sections of Part I which make
> provision regarding an appeal from such decisions. In other words, 'from
> any decision of the High Court under that Part' is to be read as meaning
> 'from any decision of the High Court under a section in that Part which
> provides for an appeal from such decision'.

> "I freely acknowledge that this interpretation of section 18(1)(g) involves
> reading words into the paragraph. It has long been established that the role
> of the courts in construing legislation is not confined to resolving ambi-
> guities in statutory language. The court must be able to correct obvious
> drafting errors."[9]

(Terrorism and Conspiracy) 1998, s.6(2) (in which the obvious error was rectified by judicial
construction in Pringle J's judgment in the case of *R. v Maguid & Green* (Crown Court in Northern
Ireland, Case 261/98, Crown application for preliminary ruling); and Trade Union and Labour
Relations (Consolidation) 1992, s.262(3).

[8] [2000] 1 W.L.R. 586, 592, HL.

[9] See further Chapter 20, paras 20.1.9—20.1.16.

15.1.7   The point arose in relation to secondary legislation in the case of *Confederation of Passenger Transport UK v The Humber Bridge Board (Secretary of State for Transport, Local Government and the Regions, interested party).*[10] The Court of Appeal was faced with a challenge to the charging of tolls on the Humber Bridge in respect of large buses using the bridge, on the simple ground that none of the orders under which the charges are levied[11] prescribed a toll for that category of transport. Clarke L.J. held that this was simply a mistake of the draftsman and that it could be repaired by reference to a combination of the Explanatory Notes to the instruments, a decision letter of the Secretary of State and the report of an inspector. It was plain from the language used that a mistake was made by the maker of the 1997 Order and the Order was neither clear nor unambiguous on its face. Without adding a reference to large buses, the Order was an absurdity. The explanatory note, the decision letter and the inspector's report into the bridge tolls were all legitimate extraneous aids to identify the purpose of the Order, which should on its true construction include the words "large bus". The 2002 Order as drafted was also ambiguous or obscure and productive of absurdity. Its intended purpose was to increase maximum tolls across the board, including for large buses. A failure to provide a maximum toll for large buses could only have been inadvertent or perhaps incompetent or inept. The draftsman could not have intended that the Board should not be permitted to charge for large buses at all.[12]

It should be noted that the degree of strain which the courts are now prepared to place upon the literal meaning of words in legislation for the purpose of rectifying what is obviously an error, as illustrated in the cases cited above, places an important qualification on the rules for determining whether an anomaly can be rectified by beneficial construction enunciated by the House of Lords in *Stock v Frank Jones (Tipton) Ltd.*[13]

For cases other than those of clear error in which the courts will adopt a beneficial construction, see Chapters 17 to 19.

Suspected errors

15.1.8   When in doubt as to whether the published text of legislation is entirely accurate the courts will consult the Parliamentary or other legislative authorities.[14]

---

[10] [2004] Q.B. 310, CA.
[11] The Humber Bridge (Revision of Tolls and Vehicle Classification) Orders 1997, 2000 and 2002.
[12] See, and compare, other cases cited under *casus omissus* rule at Chapter 20, paras 20.1.9—20.1.16.
[13] [1978] 1 W.L.R. 231, HL—as to which see Chapter 17, para.17.1.8. The qualification is recognised in the speech of Lord Scarman as noted in para.17.1.8, footnote 24.
[14] So, for example, "A more substantial point is that section 361 only has two subsections, and it is difficult to see why the draftsman did not simply refer to 'section 361'. A suspicion even rose in the course of argument that '361(1)(2)' might have been a misprint but I am satisfied that that is not so. We have confirmed with the Clerk of the Parliaments that section 45(3) is printed exactly as it was enacted."—*Gubay v Kington (Inspector of Taxes)* [1984] 1 All E.R. 513, 516, HL *per* Lord Fraser of Tullybelton.

Part 4

INTERPRETATION OF LEGISLATION

CHAPTER 16

INTRODUCTION TO STATUTORY INTERPRETATION

Rules of construction theoretically unnecessary and undesirable

Ideally, there would be no need to have any rules as to the interpretation of **16.1.1** statutes or other legislation.

First, the intended meaning of every legislative proposition would be clear beyond doubt from the natural meaning of the words used.

Secondly, those words would put beyond doubt the legislature's intention in respect of the application of the proposition to every possible practical case.

At the first of these standards it is both possible and proper to aim, although the success rate is bound to be less than total.[1]

At the second of these standards, however, it is often unreasonable even to aim—

"It seldom happens that the framer of an Act of Parliament has in contemplation all the cases that are likely to arise under it, therefore the language used seldom fits every possible case."[2]

---

[1] For a brief discussion of some of the principal reasons why draftsmen are likely to fail in this aim, see Chapter 8, Section 1.

[2] *Scott v Legg* (1876) Ex. D. 39, 42 *per curiam*; and the attempt to prepare for all conceivably possible applications often results in obscurity and inevitably results in prolixity of a kind that can mislead the courts as much as or more than it assists. See, also—"My Lords, let me make clear at the outset that this Question is not an implied criticism of the Government. Indeed, much of their legislation is drafted with clarity and certainty of legal effect; but, as with previous governments, some of it is a mass of detail from which the underlying intention of Parliament has to be inferred. The detail can be incomplete and is sometimes uncertain in its legal effect or ambiguous in its meaning.

"Unlike European legislation, our legislation has traditionally been drafted in detail. That is inevitably so when dealing with taxes, social security and much of the criminal law. It has to be so in statutes which impose rights and duties upon the citizens; the provisions must be stated in detail. However, there has for years been a tendency to mention hypothetical cases to cover a subject in the hope that every circumstance that could arise has been covered, whereas in practice other cases arise which have not been covered by the detail. If examples were needed of that, one has only to look at the ancient and more recent Sale of Goods Acts, the Theft Acts and other legislation." (HL Deb. January 21, 1998 c.1583, Lord Renton).

537

16.1.2 So while draftsmen do aim to address clearly all the principal cases actually in the contemplation of the legislature when the legislation is enacted or made—and they frequently attract criticism for the perceived prolixity that the attempt inevitably produces[3]—the courts will still be faced with matters arising which were either too subsidiary or apparently obvious to be worth addressing expressly or which for some reason or another were not actually within the contemplation of the legislature. In those cases the courts have to apply rules of construction to determine the meaning of the legislation.

It is still the case, however, that the basic enterprise is to determine the intention of the legislature, meaning what the legislature intended in relation to cases of the kind concerned.[4]

16.1.3 So far as possible, that should be achieved by a simple application of the normal and natural meaning of the words used in the statute. Although this is commonly propounded as the cardinal rule of statutory construction,[5] it is more properly understood as the rule that judicial construction of and elaboration upon the natural meaning of the words used is to be avoided so far as possible. As Lord Evershed M.R. said in *Bewlay (Tobacconists) Ltd v British Bata Shoe Co. Ltd*[6]—

> "I prefer to avoid exegeses of the statutory language unless they are absolutely necessary; for the result would otherwise tend thereafter to substitute for the problem of construction of parliamentary language the problem of the construction of the judgments of the court."[7]

Having said that, it remains the case that for the reasons given above the courts will frequently be obliged to look beyond the surface of the text of the Act to establish its meaning in or application to a particular case. That is where the many rules of construction, developed over many decades, have a role to play. In fact, it will be rare that the cardinal rule will be sufficient for the courts on its own in any case that has given genuine cause for dissent between interested parties: as Lord Reid said in *Kammins Ballrooms Co Ltd v Zenith Investments (Torquay) Ltd*[8]—

---

[3] See below, and also Chapter 8, Sections 1 and 2.

[4] Sometimes this process has more the character of discovering what the legislature would have certainly intended had they been able to contemplate the case at the time of enacting or making the legislation: but this is subject to the courts' consciousness that while they may be able to mend or circumvent technical errors in the drafting of legislation it is not their role to supply deficiencies in the policy intentions of the legislature. For fuller discussion of these two ideas and the tension between them, and for discussion of the meaning of the intention of the legislature, see below and also see Chapter 18.

[5] See Chapter 17.

[6] [1959] 1 W.L.R. 45, 49.

[7] For a recent application of this approach see *Ivorygrove Ltd v Global Grange Ltd* [2003] 1 W.L.R. 2090, Ch.

[8] [1970] 2 All E.R. 871, 873, HL.

"If the words of an Act are so inflexible that they are incapable in any context of having any but one meaning, then the court must apply that meaning, no matter how unreasonable the result—it cannot insert other words. But such cases are rare because the English language is a flexible instrument."

The concept of the "intention of the legislature"

While the purpose of construction is said to be the search for the intention of the legislature, it is important to remember that this is to some extent an artificial concept, and is certainly to be kept distinct from the search from the motive or aims of individual players, however important, in the legislative process.   **16.1.4**

As Lord Nicholls of Birkenhead put it in *R. v Secretary of State for the Environment, Transport and the Regions and another, Ex p. Spath Holme Ltd*[9]—

"The task of the court is often said to be to ascertain the intention of Parliament expressed in the language under consideration. This is correct and may be helpful, so long as it is remembered that the 'intention of Parliament' is an objective concept, not subjective. The phrase is a shorthand reference to the intention which the court reasonably imputes to Parliament in respect of the language used. It is not the subjective intention of the minister or other persons who promoted the legislation. Nor is it the subjective intention of the draftsman, or of individual members or even of a majority of individual members of either House. These individuals will often have widely varying intentions. Their understanding of the legislation and the words used may be impressively complete or woefully inadequate. Thus, when courts say that such-and-such a meaning 'cannot be what Parliament intended', they are saying only that the words under consideration cannot reasonably be taken as used by Parliament with that meaning."

A similar point was expressed much earlier by Lord Watson in *Salomon v A. Salomon & Co. Ltd*[10] as follows—

" 'Intention of the legislature' is a common but very slippery phrase, which, popularly understood, may signify anything from intention embodied in positive enactment to speculative opinion as to what the legislature probably would have meant, although there has been an omission to enact it. In a court of law or equity, what the legislature intended to be done or not to be

---

[9] [2001] 2 A.C. 349, 395, HL; a longer extract of Lord Nicholls' speech is appended to this work—Appendix, Extract 21.
[10] [1897] A.C. 22, 38, HL.

done can only be legitimately ascertained from what it has chosen to enact, either in express words or by reasonable and necessary implication."

Gradual trend towards more flexible approach to construction

16.1.5   The following Chapters of this work will consider a number of rules and principles of the construction of statutes, many of which are of ancient origin, a few of which are more recent. And the two immediately following Chapters will address the key question of how far legislation is to be given an effect outside the literal meaning of the words used. While those Chapters, and in particular the second, will identify a gradual shift in one direction, although not perhaps as radical a change as is sometimes thought, it is right to note at the outset that there has been a general trend towards a more flexible application of all the rules and principles of construction. Put simply, the courts are less willing than they once were to allow the application to a rule to frustrate what can loosely be described as the obvious legislative intent. This theme will recur throughout this work's exposition of the statutory rules of construction—but it can perhaps be seen at its most extreme in relation to the erosion of the long-standing rule of *casus omissus*.[11]

Meaning and effect distinguished

16.1.6   It is important at the outset to distinguish between questions about what a legislative provision means and questions about what its effect is. As Lindley L.J. said in *Chatenay v Brazilian Submarine Telegraph Co.*[12]—

> "The expression 'construction,' as applied to a document, at all events as used by English lawyers, includes two things: first, the meaning of the words; and, secondly, their legal effect, or the effect which is to be given to them. The meaning of the words I take to be a question of fact in all cases, whether we are dealing with a poem or a legal document. The effect of the words is a question of law."

This underlies the fundamental principle set out above. Ideally, the courts would require no legal rules for the construction of legislation—in the sense of determining the meaning of the legislature—because that is a question of fact to be determined by the ordinary principles of the English language, and ought to be immediately apparent from the expressions used. In practice, of course, and for any one of a number of reasons, the natural meaning of legislative language is often obscure or arguable, and it is then that the rules of construction are

---

[11] See Chapter 15.
[12] [1891] 1 Q.B. 79, 85, CA.

required and applied. As to the effect which legislation has, however, there do have to be legal rules, and they are explored above.[13]

Authority for construction of legislation

Ultimately, all interpretations put upon legislation, whether by established **16.1.7** professional usage, by the Crown, by Parliament or by subordinate judicial authorities must yield to any construction established by the Supreme Court[14] or, if the case is taken there, by the House of Lords.[15]

Government departments may offer guidance as to the meaning and application of legislation.[16] But that guidance is of no authority whatsoever.[17] Even where a department or other public authority possesses an unfettered discretion in respect of the determination of disputes or any other matter, if the exercise of the discretion can be shown to be based on an erroneous understanding of the meaning of a provision of legislation the courts will interfere and, if necessary, quash the exercise of the discretion and require the authority to start again.[18]

Where disputes in a particular area are delegated by express legislation to an inferior tribunal (whether established for the purpose or pre-existing) the tribunal will, of course, have power to determine questions of law authoritatively. But unless the legislation provides for the tribunal's decision to be final in the sense not only of being subject to no appeal but also of being excluded from the general supervisory jurisdiction of the High Court, that court and, ultimately, the House of Lords will be competent to verify or modify the tribunal's opinion.[19]

---

[13] In Part 3.

[14] That is to say, for the present, the system of jurisdictions confirmed by the Supreme Court Act 1981 (c.54). But the Government has announced intentions to abolish the judicial jurisdiction of the House of Lords and to establish a Supreme Court. When this work went to print the future of the proposals was uncertain.

[15] *Home v Lord Camden* (1795) 6 Bro. Parl. Cas. 203; 1 H. Bl. 476; 2 *ibid.* 533.

[16] A modern and particular form of which is the Explanatory Notes discussed in Chapter 9, Section 4 and elsewhere.

[17] Although—

    (1) the expression of an intention by a Minister during the passage of a Bill may be of later use to the courts in the case of ambiguity—see the rule in *Pepper v Hart* explored in Chapter 28, and

    (2) background policy material may be of assistance in discovering the legislative intention—see Chapter 27.

[18] See *Board of Education v Rice* [1911] A.C. 179, HL, *Wilford v West Riding of Yorkshire County Council* [1908] 1 K.B. 685, *R. v Treasury* [1909] 2 K.B. 183 and *Re Weir Hospital* [1910] 2 Ch. 124.

[19] It is common to find appeals from *ad* hoc or inferior tribunals limited to questions of law—see, for example, the Railways and Transport Safety Act 2003 (c.20), s.35 (arbitration by Secretary of State) or the Nationality, Immigration and Asylum Act 2002 (c.41), ss.101 and 103 (appeal from adjudicator to Tribunal and from Tribunal to High Court). It is rare to find the supervisory jurisdiction excluded altogether, but it is reasonably common to find provision for a decision to be final (which does not, or does not necessarily, oust all supervisory jurisdiction)—see, for example, s.39B of the Electricity Act 1989 (c.29) (decisions of Gas and Electricity Markets Authority in relation to application of provisions about standards of performance).

    Note also Chapter 19, para.19.1.19.

CHAPTER 17

THE CARDINAL RULE: CONSTRUCTION ACCORDING TO PLAIN MEANING

The traditional rule

The cardinal rule for the construction of legislation is that it should be construed **17.1.1** according to the intention expressed in the language used. So the function of the court is to interpret legislation "according to the intent of them that made it"[1] and that intent is to be deduced from the language used.[2]

Ideally, as stated above,[3] the words of the legislation will be precise and unambiguous; and wherever they are they are the best and only true means of declaring the intention of the legislature.[4] As Tindal C.J. said in *Warburton v Loveland*[5]—

> "Where the language of an Act is clear and explicit, we must give effect to it, whatever may be the consequences, for in that case the words of the statute speak the intention of the legislature."

This cardinal rule, which is of ancient origin,[6] is given different names by different judges; the epithets "natural", "ordinary", "literal", "grammatical", "popular" and "primary" are all found.

This rule is also sometimes described as the "golden rule" of construction,[7] **17.1.2** the nature and original limitations of which are propounded in the following

---

[1] 4 Co. Inst. 330.

[2] See *per* Lord Parker C.J. in *Capper v Baldwin* [1965] 2 Q.B. 53, 61.

[3] Chapter 16.

[4] *Sussex Peerage Claim* (1844) 11 Cl. & F. 85, 143. See also *Cargo ex Argos* (1873) L.R. 5 P.C. 134, 153.

[5] (1832) 2 D. & Cl. (HL) 480, 489.

[6] Perhaps the earliest expression of it is found in a statute (28o Hen. VIII. c.7.—A.D. 1536)—"XVIII. This Act shall be construed most forcibly; without Derogation by any other Act made or to be made. And be it fynally enacted by auctorite aforsaid, that this p'sent acte and every clause article and sentence comprised in the same shall be taken and accepted accordyng to the playne wordes and sentences therin conteyned; and shall not be interpreted nor expounded by colour of eny pretence or cause or by any subtill argumentes invencions or reasons to the hyndraunce disturbaunce or derogacion of this Acte or any parte therof; any thynge or thynges acte or actes of Parliamente hertofore made or herafter to be hadd done or made to the contrary therof notwithstandyng; and that ev'y acte statute lawe pvision thyng and thynges, hertofore hadd or made or herafter to be hadd done or made contrary to the effecte of this statute, shall be voyde and of no value nor force."

[7] See, for example, "The courts' traditional approach to construction, giving primacy to the ordinary, grammatical meaning of statutory language, is reflected in the parliamentary draftsman's technique

543

passage of the speech of Lord Blackburn in *Caledonian Railway v North British Railway*[8]—

> "There is not much doubt about the general principle of construction. Lord Wensleydale used to enunciate (I have heard him many and many a time) that which he called the golden rule for construing all written engagements. I find that he stated it very clearly and accurately in *Grey v Pearson*[9] in the following terms:
>
> > 'I have been long and deeply impressed with the wisdom of the rule, now, I believe, universally adopted—at least in the courts of law in West-minster Hall—that in construing wills, and indeed statutes and all written instruments, the grammatical and ordinary sense of the words is to be adhered to, unless that would lead to some absurdity, or some repugnance or inconsistency with the rest of the instrument, in which case the grammatical and ordinary sense of the words may be modified so as to avoid the absurdity and inconsistency, but no further.'
>
> "I agree in that completely, but in the cases in which there is a real difficulty this does not help us much, because the cases in which there is a real difficulty are those in which there is a controversy as to what the grammatical and ordinary sense of the words used with reference to the subject-matter is. To one mind it may appear that the most that can be said is that the sense may be what is contended by the other side, and that the inconsistency and repugnancy is very great, that you should make a great stretch to avoid such absurdity, and that what is required to avoid it is a very little stretch or none at all. To another mind it may appear that the words are perfectly clear—that they can bear no other meaning at all, and that to substitute any other meaning would be not to interpret the words used, but to make an instrument for the parties—and that the supposed inconsistency or repugnancy is perhaps a hardship—a thing which perhaps it would have been better to have avoided, but which we have no power to deal with."

Basis for rule

17.1.3 The application of the cardinal rule rests upon the assumption that words used in legislation are used with precision. As Lord Hewart C.J. said in *Spillers Ltd Cardiff Assessment Committee*[10]—

---

of using language with the utmost precision to express the legislative intent of his political masters and it remains the golden rule of construction that a statute means exactly what it says and does not mean what it does not say."—*Associated Newspapers Ltd v Wilson* [1995] 2 W.L.R. 354, 362, HL *per* Lord Bridge of Harwich.

[8] (1881) 6 App. Cas. 114, 131.
[9] (1857) 6 H.L.C. 61, 106.
[10] [1931] 2 K.B. 21, 42–43.

"Another argument was hinted at, though the various Counsel had not the hardihood to advance it—namely, that in the use of any language by the Legislature one should expect the loose and inexact, rather than the correct and exact. It is true that one who spends much time in this Court might be tempted in his haste to make some such assertion. But if he allowed cynicism to be tempered with sympathy for the harassed Parliamentary draftsman, he would reflect that it is only in regard to phrases of doubtful import that this Court is called upon to apply a toilsome scrutiny.

"The task is pathological, and too much immersion in it may well induce oblivion of the fact that in comparison with the vast bulk of our legislation these difficult passages are rare. It ought to be the rule, and we are glad to think that it is the rule, that words are used in an Act of Parliament correctly and exactly, and not loosely and inexactly. Upon those who assert that that rule has been broken the burden of establishing their proposition lies heavily. And they can discharge it only by pointing to something in the context which goes to show that the loose and inexact meaning must be preferred."

This assumption of precision remains the same today. As Lord Bingham of Cornhill said in *R (Quintavalle) v Secretary of State for Health*[11]—

"Such is the skill of parliamentary draftsmen that most statutory enactments are expressed in language which is clear and unambiguous and gives rise to no serious controversy. But these are not the provisions which reach the courts, or at any rate the appellate courts."

Effect of rule (1): unintended consequences of clear language

The principal effect of the cardinal rule, subject to the restrictions and modifications explored below, is that a court is bound to give effect to clear legislative language even if the consequences in the instant case are such that the legislature did not contemplate and would not have countenanced. As Jervis C.J. said in *Abley v Dale*[12]— **17.1.4**

"If the precise words used are plain and unambiguous, we are bound to construe them in their ordinary sense, even though it does lead to an absurdity or manifest injustice. Words may be modified or varied where their import is doubtful or obscure, but we assume the functions of legislators when we depart from the ordinary meaning of the precise words used, merely because we see, or fancy we see, an absurdity or manifest injustice from an adherence to their literal meaning."

---

[11] [2003] 2 W.L.R. 692, HL.
[12] (1850) 20 L.J.C.P. 33, 35.

So, for example, the following dictum of Lord Herschell in *Cox v Hakes*[13] remains valid today—

> "It is not easy to exaggerate the magnitude of this change[14]; nevertheless, it must be admitted that, if the language of the legislature, interpreted according to the recognised canons of construction, involves this result, your lordships must frankly yield to it, even if you should be satisfied that it was not in the contemplation of the legislature."

17.1.5   The only difference in the application of this dictum today and when it was said is that the "recognised canons of construction" leave greater flexibility today, as will be seen below,[15] for the use of matters outside the language of the text, where it is not clear, in order to discern the legislative intent.

This principal effect of the rule requires to be considered in the light of the principal qualification, mentioned in the quotation from Lord Wensleydale above and considered further below. The distinction requires to be drawn between a result which appears absurd merely in the sense that it hard to believe that the legislature would have wanted it and one which is absurd in the sense that it falsifies or produces inconsistency in the legislation, so that even looking at nothing but the literal meaning of the text as a whole a difficulty emerges.

As to the unintended consequences of using language which clearly excludes on its face something that was clearly intended to be included, see Chapter 15 and Chapter 20, paras 20.1.9—20.1.16.

Effect of rule (2): no judicial relief against clear provision

17.1.6   It follows from the cardinal rule that the courts will decline to interfere for the assistance of persons who seek judicial aid to relieve them against the effect of express legislative provision. The leading statement of this effect is found in the judgment of Mellish L.J. in *Edwards v Edwards*[16] in the following terms—

> "If the legislature says that a deed shall be 'null and void to all intents and purposes whatsoever,' how can a court of equity say that in certain circumstances it shall be valid. The courts of equity have given relief on equitable grounds from provisions in old Acts of Parliament, but this has not been done in the case of modern Acts, which are framed with a view to equitable as well as legal doctrines."

---

[13] (1890) 15 App. Cas. 506, 528, HL.
[14] That discharge from custody by a court of competent jurisdiction does not protect from further proceedings.
[15] See Chapters 20 and 27.
[16] (1876) 2 Ch. D. 291, 297; *cf. Partington v Attorney-General* (1869) L.R. 4, HL 100, 122 *per* Lord Cairns.

This is really just one aspect of the principle of the supremacy of Parliament (including the supremacy of the powers of Parliament as delegated to subordinate law-makers) discussed above.[17]

As to the potential use of statute as an instrument of fraud, and the corresponding reaction of the courts, see *Maddison v Alderson*.[18]

This principle does not mean that the regulation of an aspect of law by statute will necessarily defeat any role that the rules of equity have to play in that area. For an example of the co-existence of a statutory code and the pre-existing rules of equity see *Midland Bank Trust Co. Ltd v Green*.[19]

Effect of rule (3): evasion not restrained by courts

A further consequence of the rule requiring statutes to be given a straight-forward construction is that the courts will not prevent evasion: if the citizen can find a way of avoiding the probable intention of Parliament while complying with the rules that Parliament has enacted,[20] so be it. The extent of this principle, and the difference between evasion and avoidance, is discussed in Chapter 12, Section 6 at paras 12.5.3—12.5.8.   **17.1.7**

Qualification of rule: avoidance of absurdity, &c.

The principle that the literal meaning of legislation must be applied even if it appears unjust does not prevent a construction which does more justice or appears more desirable from being preferred to an unjust or undesirable construction, where both are equally supported by the words used. As Finnemore J. said in *Holmes v Bradfield R.D.C.*[21]—   **17.1.8**

> "The mere fact that the results of a statute may be unjust or absurd does not entitle this court to refuse to give it effect, but if there are two different interpretations of the words in an Act, the court will adopt that which is just, reasonable and sensible rather than that which is none of those things."

In *Stock v Frank Jones (Tipton) Ltd*[22] the House of Lords considered the extent to which the literal meaning might be qualified for the purposes of rectifying anomaly. Lord Simon of Glaisdale said[23]—

---

[17] Chapter 2, Sections 1 and 2; and as to the waiver, &c.of statutory rights and duties see Chapter 12, Sections 2 and 6.

[18] (1883) 8 App. Cas. 467, 474 *per* Lord Selborne.

[19] [1981] A.C. 513, 528, HL *per* Lord Wilberforce; see also *Corbett v Halifax plc* [2003] 4 All E.R. 180, 194–195, CA *per* Pumfrey J. See also para.14.1.7, footnote 18.

[20] "Getting away from the remedial operation of the statute while complying with the words of the statute"—*Ramsden v Luption* (1873) L.R. 9 Q.B. 17, 32 *per* Grove J.

[21] [1949] 2 K.B. 1, 7.

[22] [1978] 1 W.L.R. 231, HL.

[23] At 237.

" . . . a court would only be justified in departing from the plain words of the statute were it satisfied that: (1) there is clear and gross balance of anomaly; (2) Parliament, the legislative promoters and the draftsman could not have envisaged such anomaly and could not have been prepared to accept it in the interest of a supervening legislative objective; (3) the anomaly can be obviated without detriment to such legislative objective; (4) the language of the statute is susceptible of the modification required to obviate the anomaly."[24]

17.1.9   For early examples of the latitude available for the avoidance of manifest absurdity see *Simms v Registrar of Probates,*[25] *R. v Tonbridge Overseers,*[26] *Gover's Case,*[27] *River Wear Commissioners v Adamson*[28] and *Ex p. St. Sepulchre's.*[29] For recent cases on the point see *Omar Parks Ltd v Elkington,*[30] *Baker v The Queen,*[31] *In re Pantmaenog Timber Co. Ltd,*[32] *Cranfield v Bridgegrove Ltd*[33] and *Lewis v Eliades.*[34]

The latitude to have regard to justice and common sense in choosing in which of the various ways, each of which is possible as a matter of grammar and syntax, to read a particular legislative expression, does not, however, amount to permission for the courts to modify express legislative language for the same purpose.[35] As Willes J. said in *Abel v Lee*[36]—

"No doubt the general rule is that the language of an Act is to be read according to its ordinary grammatical construction unless so reading it

---

[24] But in cases of clear error the latter condition may not apply—see above, paras 15.1.6—15.1.7; and note also Lord Scarman in *Stock* at 239—"If the words used by Parliament are plain, there is no room for the 'anomalies' test, unless the consequences are so absurd that, without going outside the statute, one can see that Parliament must have made a drafting mistake. If words 'have been inadvertently used', it is legitimate for the court to substitute what is apt to avoid the intention of the legislature being defeated: *per* MacKinnon L.J. in *Sutherland Publishing Co Ltd v Caxton Publishing Co Ltd (No.2)* ([1938] Ch. 174 at 201). This is an acceptable exception to the general rule that plain language excludes a consideration of 'anomalies', *i.e.* mischievous or absurd consequences. If a study of the statute as a whole leads inexorably to the conclusion that Parliament has erred in its choice of words, *e.g.* used 'and' when 'or' was clearly intended, the courts can, and must, eliminate the error by interpretation. But mere 'manifest absurdity' is not enough: it must be an error (of commission or omission) which in its context defeats the intention of the Act."

[25] [1900] A.C. 323, 335.

[26] (1884) 13 Q.B.D. 339, 342.

[27] (1875) 1 Ch. D. 182, 198.

[28] (1876) 1 Q.B.D. 546, 549.

[29] (1864) 33 L.J. Ch. 372, 375.

[30] [1993] 1 All E.R. 282, CA.

[31] [1975] 3 All E.R. 55, PC.

[32] [2003] 3 W.L.R. 767, HL.

[33] [2003] 1 W.L.R. 2441, 2453, CA.

[34] [2004] 1 W.L.R. 692, 706, CA *per* Jacob L.J.—"To choose between the possible meanings I think it sufficient to apply a purposive construction and the well-known principle that one leans against absurd conclusions, leaning harder the more absurd the conclusion."

[35] But, now, see Chapter 25 as to cases in which the Human Rights Act 1998 (c.42) may, in effect require legislative language to be considerably strained in order to produce a meaning compatible with the European Convention on Human Rights.

[36] (1871) L.R. 6 C.P. 365, 371.

would entail some absurdity, repugnancy or injustice. . . . But I utterly repudiate the notion that it is competent to a judge to modify the language of an Act in order to bring it in accordance with his views of what is right or reasonable."

In accordance with this principle in *Young & Co. v Mayor, &c. of Lea-* **17.1.10** *mington*[37] the Court of Appeal declared one party not bound by a contract that failed to comply with the formal requirements of s.174 of the Public Health Act 1875[38] despite the fact that the party had received the benefit of the contract, on the ground that otherwise the section would be deprived of all effect. Lindley L.J. said[39]—

> "It may be that this is a hard and narrow view of the law; but my answer is, that Parliament has thought it expedient to require this view to be taken, and it is not for this or any other court to decline to give effect to a clearly expressed statute because it may lead to apparent hardship."

It will often be difficult to know whether a construction that avoids absurdity does or does not do too much violence to the plain language of the provision to be permitted. In *Customs and Excise Commissioners v Zielinski Baker,*[40] for example, the House of Lords was divided in construing Note (I) to Group 6 of Sch.8 to the Value Added Tax Act 1994.[41] Lord Nicholls said[42] "I decline to attribute to Parliament such a strange intention as is involved in the commissioners' case." But Lord Hoffmann found the language of the statute "too clear to admit contradiction or need support from such tenuous inferences".[43] Lord Hope of Craighead apparently sympathised with the wish to avoid what he acknowledged as an unreasonable construction but felt the ordinary meaning too plain to be set aside: as he said[44]—

---

[37] (1882) 8 Q.B.D. 579; (1883) 8 App. Cas.517.
[38] 1875 c.55.
[39] At 585.
[40] [2004] 1 W.L.R. 707, HL.
[41] 1994 c.23—"(1) "Protected building" means a building which is designed to remain as or become a dwelling or number of dwellings (as defined in Note (2) below) or is intended for use solely for a relevant residential purpose or a relevant charitable purpose after the reconstruction or alteration and which, in either case, is—
  (a) a listed building, within the meaning of—
      (i) the Planning (Listed Buildings and Conservation Areas) Act 1990; or
      (ii) the Planning (Listed Buildings and Conservation Areas) (Scotland) Act 1997; or
      (iii) the Planning (Northern Ireland) Order 1991; or
  (b) a scheduled monument, within the meaning of—
      (i) the Ancient Monuments and Archaeological Areas Act 1979; or
      (ii) the Historic Monuments and Archaeological Objects (Northern Ireland) Order 1995."
[42] At 709.
[43] At 710.
[44] At 712–713.

"The consequences of this approach to the definition may be to produce results which appear odd and unreasonable. The facts of the present case can perhaps be said to fall into that category. The house and the outbuilding are in the same occupation, they are occupied together as a single dwelling and both buildings fall within the definition of a listed building for the purposes of the 1990 Act. Prior to the abolition of the rating system for domestic properties by the Local Government Finance Act 1988 they would have been entered in the valuation list as a single hereditament. But there is no getting away from the fact that it is only the outbuilding and not the house that is being altered, and it is the house and not the outbuilding that has been listed. We must take the definition in note (1) as it stands, and we must construe it as we find it. In my opinion the ordinary meaning of the words used, taken in the order in which they are set out in the definition, leads inevitably to the result contended for by the commissioners."

17.1.11   The result is that it is agreed by all that there is a limit to what the judges can properly do to supply the deficiencies of the draftsman in making plain the intention of the legislature: but precisely where that limit comes will be perceived differently by different judges. Any temptation to rely upon a purposive approach to judicial construction so as to leave an admitted ambiguity or lack of clarity in the text of legislation should be evaluated having regard to this difference of judicial opinion: one cannot safely leave to the judges a task which some at least of them will think it their constitutional duty to decline.[45]

In Lord Simon of Glaisdale's speech in *Stock* he discusses the jurisprudential justifications for and limitations on this qualification of the golden rule, in the context of the judicial role generally. The relevant passage of his speech is appended to this work.[46]

Original limitations of traditional rule

17.1.12   The cardinal rule has always been subject to limitations and qualifications, even apart from those many cases in which it is incapable of being applied owing to ambiguity or obscurity of the legislative language. Indeed, as soon as the rule is stated it is normally qualified in some such way as appears from the following words of Lord Blackburn in *Direct US Cable Co. v Anglo-American Telegraph Co.*[47]—

"The tribunal that has to construe an Act of a legislature, or indeed any other document, has to determine the intention as expressed by the words used. And in order to understand these words it is natural to inquire what is the

---

[45] See further Chapter 14, Section 1, paras 14.1.3 and 14.1.4.
[46] Appendix, Extract 20.
[47] (1877) 2 App. Cas. 394, 412, HL—cited by Lord Atkinson in *London and India Docks Co. v Thames Steam Tug, etc. Co.* [1909] A.C. 15, 23, HL.

subject-matter with respect to which they are used and the object in view."

Put another way—

"A certain amount of common sense must be applied in construing statutes. The object of the Act has to be considered."[48]

And having expounded the cardinal rule in *Spillers Ltd Cardiff Assessment Committee*[49] as quoted above Lord Hewart C.J. went on as follows—   **17.1.13**

" . . . they can discharge [the rule] only by pointing to something in the context which goes to show that the loose and inexact meaning must be preferred.

"This, indeed, must be not merely the legal, but also the literary canon of interpretation. No person of education or intelligence would understand, or suspect, that a writer or speaker was using the word 'contiguous' in its loose sense of 'neighbouring,' unless there was something in the context that compelled that conclusion. If a man spoke or wrote of 'contiguous islands' he must necessarily mean 'neighbouring,' because one island must be separated by water from another. But if he spoke of 'contiguous houses' it would be difficult to suppose that he meant anything but houses touching each other.

"The legal canon is the same."

Just as people naturally and colloquially use words which have a literal   **17.1.14**
meaning which nobody for a single moment confuses with their actual meaning, so does the legislature; and for similar reasons and in similar circumstances.[50]

A person may say "all trains stop at Crewe" without there being any risk that anyone will assume that he is actually making the patently absurd assertion embodied in the literal meaning of the words spoken: his words will automatically be construed in the light of their obvious context.

If he said "all trains that leave from this platform while in public service (and not merely going to the depot) stop at Crewe but only once they have arrived there and subject to the fact that they then leave Crewe whether to come back again or to go further or to go to the depot" he would rightly be regarded as an obsessive lunatic with a pedantic neurosis.

---

[48] *Barnes v Jarvis* [1953] 1 W.L.R. 649, QBD, DC.
[49] [1931] 2 K.B. 21, 42–43.
[50] Although not to the same extent: it is hard, for example, to imagine Lord Hewart C.J.'s example of contiguous islands being used in legislation, while as he says it would be both imaginable in a colloquial context and also generally sufficiently precise for that purpose.

The same is true of the legislature.

So, for example, a subsection within a section about applications for registration in a statutory register held by local authorities may state "a local authority may reject an application if . . . " without it being remotely arguable that the proposition is intended to apply to anything other than applications under the section concerned, whatever its literal meaning.[51]

17.1.15   More than this, the legislature is always conscious that it is writing in the context of the law of the United Kingdom[52] as a whole. Certain expressions will be used which are intended to have a meaning either more or less extensive than they would acquire if used in the course of common conversation. For example, any proposition conferring a discretion on a public body may be expressed in the widest of terms, knowing that certain limitations will automatically be implied by the principles of administrative law. It is well established that if there is a conflict between the superficial and literal meaning of expressions used in legislation and their "legal meaning", that is to say the meaning which those expressions obviously acquire when used in a legislative context, the latter must prevail.[53] And when reading plain words of a statute one must be prepared to give them the flavour that they would naturally have in the context of the statute.[54]

The courts will, moreover, be reluctant to assume that a statute has modified or abolished a rule of the common law by a side wind, merely because that would

---

[51] As to the extent of reliance on the common sense construction of legislation in its drafting, see Chapter 18, para.18.1.10.

[52] Or of those parts of the United Kingdom to which the relevant legislation extends.

[53] So Burton J. in *Warburton v Loveland* ((1828) 1 Hud. & Bro. 632, 648) (cited with approval by Lord Fitzgerald in *Bradlaugh v Clarke* (1883) 8 App. Cas. 354, 384)—"I apprehend it is a rule in the construction of statutes that in the first instance the grammatical sense of the words is to be adhered to. If that is contrary to, or inconsistent with, any expressed intention or declared purpose of the statutes, or if it would involve any absurdity, repugnance or inconsistency, the grammatical sense must then be modified, extended, or abridged, so far as to avoid such an inconvenience, but not further."; and Lord Selborne in *Caledonian Railway v North British Railway* ((1881) 6 App. Cas. 114, 131)—"The mere literal construction of a statute ought not to prevail if it is opposed to the intentions of the legislature as apparent by the statute, and if the words are sufficiently flexible to admit of some other construction by which that intention can be better effectuated."

[54] Note, for example, "What [Counsel] says in a nutshell is that it is not necessary to read any words of restriction into the subsection. . . . . He says that the words must be given their ordinary and natural meaning. On the other hand, when construing the section in an Act of Parliament it must be construed in the context in which it appears. This is a road traffic matter and the section . . . . appears (as amended) in the Road Traffic Regulation Act 1994. Simply looking at the section and construing these words I have to say at once that I am wholly convinced that they do not cover the situation envisaged by the applicants. What is envisaged by s.14 in my judgment is a restriction upon the use of a road because of the likelihood of danger to the public from traffic ordinarily using it. Using ordinary principles of construction and indeed common sense, this section was not designed to allow local authorities temporarily to close roads because either they or somebody else concluded that the air levels were polluted by vehicles using the road. What was envisaged, simply as a matter of common sense again, was the sort of occasion mentioned by [Counsel], when for example oil upon the road made the use of the road dangerous to the public . . . ."—*R. v London Borough of Greenwich Ex p. W* [1996] 8 Admin. L.R. 423, QBD *per* Macpherson J.

be the logical result of a literal reading of the words used.[55] So, as Lord Loreburn L.C. said in *Nairn v University of St. Andrews*[56]—

> "I will only add this much as to the case of the appellants in general. It proceeds upon the supposition that the word 'person' in the Act of 1868 did include women, though not then giving them the vote, so that at some later date an Act purporting to deal only with education might enable commissioners to admit them to the degree, and thereby also indirectly confer upon them the franchise. It would require a convincing demonstration to satisfy me that Parliament intended to effect a constitutional change so momentous and far-reaching by so furtive a process."

Apart from literal inexactitude permissible in, and therefore to be construed in the light of, a particular context, the courts have to remember that while the legislature and its draftsmen strive for precision and accuracy they will necessarily on occasions fall short of their target, either through simple lack of skill or attention or because of the impossibility of stating expressly all the possible applications of a particular rule. So, as Lord Loreburn L.C. said in *Nairn v University of St. Andrews*[57]— **17.1.16**

> "It is a dangerous assumption to suppose that the Legislature foresees every possible result that may ensue from the unguarded use of a single word, or that the language used in statutes is so precisely accurate that you can pick out from various Acts this and that expression and, skilfully piecing them together, lay a safe foundation for some remote inference. Your Lordships are aware that from early times courts of law have been continuously obliged, in endeavouring loyally to carry out the intentions of Parliament, to observe a series of familiar precautions for interpreting statutes, so imperfect and obscure as they often are. Learned volumes have been written on this single subject. It is not, in my opinion, necessary in the present case to apply any of those canons of construction. The Act invoked by the appellants is plain enough to repel their contentions."

See also paras 20.1.20 and 20.1.21.

Additional modern limitations of traditional rule

The statement by Tindal C.J. of the traditional rule cited above speaks of giving effect to the clear and explicit language of an Act "whatever may be the consequences". But this has to be qualified in the light of the new class of what have sometimes been described as "constitutional" statutes.[58] **17.1.17**

---

[55] See Chapter 14, Section 1 and Chapter 19.
[56] [1909] A.C. 147, 161.
[57] [1909] A.C. 147, 161.
[58] As to which see Chapter 1, Section 4.

In particular, the effect of the European Communities Act 1972[59] and the Human Rights Act 1998[60] is that if the consequences of giving effect to the literal meaning of an Act would be to place it in contravention of the United Kingdom's obligations as a member of the European Union or as a signatory to the European Convention on Human Rights, the courts will not automatically disregard those consequences, unless the consequences are clearly identified and expressly confirmed by the Act in question.

Subordinate legislation

17.1.18   While the cardinal rule explained in this Chapter is no less applicable to the construction of subordinate legislation than it is to primary legislation,[61] an additional factor to be borne in mind in determining whether to disregard consequences of the literal interpretation, as discussed in the previous paragraphs, is the extent of the *vires* conferred by the primary legislation, which again has to be determined by reference to the general context and purpose of that legislation.

---

[59] See Chapter 14, Section 5 and Chapter 32.
[60] See Chapter 14, Section 5 and Chapter 25.
[61] See *R. v Dowling* (1857) 8 E. & B. 605 and *The Fanny M. Carvill* (1875) 13 App. Cas. 455n. (PC) approved in *The Glamorganshire* (1888) 13 App. Cas. 454 (HL).

CHAPTER 18

LITERAL OR PURPOSIVE INTERPRETATION

Introduction

Discussions of statutory construction often focus on whether a court should look **18.1.1** strictly and exclusively at the words employed by the legislature or whether they should be prepared to apply a construction which, without doing actual violence to the clear meaning of any of the words used, will reflect the underlying political and social purposes of the legislation in its application to new cases, by elucidating what the words are intended to mean, by supplying technical deficiencies[1] or by resolving ambiguities.

But the argument between the literal and purposive approaches is often more academic and semantic than of substantial practical relevance. In particular—

> In advocating the literal approach one is quickly forced to concede a great many exceptions and qualifications.[2] The most important exception, which emanates entirely from common sense, is that however literal one wishes to be, if the natural construction of the words does not answer the question being asked, the courts are forced to look outside the strict letter of the legislation for its intention. So, for example, Lord Wilberforce said in *Fothergill v Monarch Airlines*[3]—
>
> > "I start by considering the purpose of article 26, and I do not think that in doing so I am infringing any 'golden rule.' Consideration of the purpose of an enactment is always a legitimate part of the process of interpretation, and if it is usual—and indeed correct—to look first for a clear meaning of the words used, it is certain, in the present case, both on a first look at the relevant text, and from the judgments in the courts below, that no 'golden rule' meaning can be ascribed."
>
> In advocating the purposive school of thought, on the other hand, one is quickly forced to concede that the fundamental principle of the Sovereignty and supremacy of Parliament require clear and unambiguous words to be given their clear and unambiguous meaning, even in cases where one

---

[1] For the tension between *casus omissus* and purposive construction, see Chapter 20.
[2] See, for example, *Maxwell on The Interpretation of Statutes*, (2nd ed., 1969), Chap.2 and ff.
[3] [1981] A.C. 251, 271, HL.

suspects that the legislature might have provided differently had a particular question or issue been exposed to them.[4]

Area of agreement and scope for disagreement

18.1.2   The following propositions may serve to illustrate both the degree of necessary agreement in the matter of the correct approach to construction and the limited scope for disagreement.

(1) It is beyond doubt that what the courts must do, and always have done, in construing legislation is to seek the true intention of the legislature.[5]

(2) It is equally beyond doubt that the starting-point, and very often the end-point, for the search is the natural meaning of the clear language used by the legislature.[6]

(3) If the words used import a clear and unequivocal meaning, the courts must give effect to that meaning, even if they suspect that it turns upon a mistake of fact or law but for which the legislature would not have wished to legislate in those terms.[7]

---

[4] See Chapter 17.

[5] See, for example, the following dictum of the Earl of Halsbury L.C. in *the Eastman Photographic Materials Company, Ltd v the Comptroller-General of Patents, Designs and Trade-Marks* [1898] A.C. 571, 575: "Turner L.J. in *Hawktins v Gathercole* ((1855) 6 D. M. & G. 1, 21), and adding his own high authority to that of the judges in *Stradling v Morgan* ((1584) 1 Plowd. 204), after enforcing the proposition that the intention of the Legislature must be regarded, quotes at length the judgment in that case: that the judges have collected the intention 'sometimes by considering the cause and necessity of making the Act . . . . sometimes by foreign circumstances' (thereby meaning extraneous circumstances), 'so that they have ever been guided by the intent of the Legislature, which they have always taken according to the necessity of the matter, and according to that which is consonant to reason and good discretion.' And he adds: 'We have therefore to consider not merely the words of this Act of Parliament, but the intent of the Legislature, to be collected from the cause and necessity of the Act being made, from a comparison of its several parts, and from foreign (meaning extraneous) circumstances so far as they can justly be considered to throw light upon the subject.' Lord Blackburn in *River Wear Commissioners v Adamson* ((1877) 2 App. Cas. 743, 763) says: 'In all cases the object is to see what is the intention expressed by the words used. But, from the imperfection of language, it is impossible to know what that intention is without inquiring further, and seeing what the circumstances were with reference to which the words were used, and what was the object, appearing from those circumstances, which the person using them had in view.' My Lords, it appears to me that to construe the statute now in question, it is not only legitimate but highly convenient to refer both to the former Act and to the ascertained evils to which the former Act had given rise, and to the later Act which provided the remedy. These three things being compared, I cannot doubt the conclusion."; but as to the meaning of "the intention of the legislature" see Chapters 16 and 17.

[6] See Chapters 16 and 17.

[7] See Upjohn J. in *Re County of London (Devons Road, Poplar) Housing Confirmation Order, 1945* [1956] 1 All E.R. 818, 820, Ch—"If the section proceeds on an erroneous view of the law it cannot be construed otherwise than in its ordinary meaning so as to attain the result which it is thought was achieved by registration under the Land Charges Act, 1925; if the view be truly erroneous the section has misfired: *Ayrshire Employers Mutual Insurance Association Ltd v Inland Revenue Commissioners* ((1946) (27 Tax Cas 331)) and *Inland Revenue Commissioners v Dowdall, O'Mahoney & Co Ltd* (([1952] 1 All E.R. 531))." The reason for not interfering in these circumstances is stated succinctly by Lord Reid in *Inland Revenue Commissioners v Dowdell O'Mahoney & Co Ltd* [1952] 1 All E.R. 531, 541, HL—"Paragraph 5 is very misleading, but to

(4) But it has always been generally accepted that legislation is to be drafted in a fluid and not a ritualistic or formalistic way,[8] and that inference therefore has a legitimate and significant part to play in construction.[9]

(5) Inferences are of various kinds, one of which is an inference from context and presumed purpose.

(6) The principal point of disagreement over the years is how far it is permissible to go in presuming the underlying policy intention for the purposes of drawing from it inferences that qualify or strain the words used, in cases of doubt as to their literal application.

(7) A subordinate question is that of the evidence that may be considered in forming those inferences.[10]

In practice, therefore, the argument between literal and purposive inter- **18.1.3** pretation may never have had much substance except as a purely academic exercise,[11] and it is now probably wholly futile. Recent developments, a number of which are explored elsewhere in this work[12] combine both to produce and reflect a situation in which it is now beyond doubt that the courts will go to any sensible length to discern and give effect to the underlying policy intention of legislation, and that in construing a statute they will use all kinds of material available to them as tools to discover that intention.[13]

The illusory nature of the tension between purposive and literal construction can lead to an apparent frustration in judges who are pressed by Counsel to

---

mislead a taxpayer is not the same thing as to entitle him to relief. It may well be that these paragraphs show that Parliament was under a misapprehension as to the existing law at the time, but it does not necessarily follow that if Parliament had been correctly informed it would have altered the law."; see also *Birmingham City Corporation v West Midland Baptist (Trust) Association (Incorporated)* [1969] 3 All E.R. 172. Note also Chapter 1, Section 7, para.19.7.4.

[8] More than 200 years ago the 12 judges in *Longmead's Case* (1795) Leach C. C. 694, 696 said "The legislature, when they intend to pass, to continue, or to repeal a law, are not bound to use any precise form of words."

[9] "When we are seeking the intention of Parliament that may appear from express words but it may also appear by irresistible inference from the statute read as a whole."—Lord Reid, in the context of the presumption against expropriation, in the case of *Westminster Bank Ltd v Minister of Housing and Local Government* [1971] A.C. 508, 529, HL (discussed in Chapter 19, para.19.1.4).

[10] See, in particular, Chapters 26 to 28.

[11] The wisest judges have always admitted that any attempt at formalism in relation to statutory interpretation is unlikely to be helpful and that it is best to treat the construction of statutes as no more exact a science as any of the other functions performed by the judiciary. As Lord Hobart said about four hundred years ago—"If you ask me by what rules the judges guided themselves in diverse expositions of the self-same word and sentence, I answer, it is by that liberty and authority which judges have over statute laws according to reason and best convenience to mould them to the truest and best use." (*Sheffield v Ractcliffe* (1616) Hob. 334, 346.).

[12] In particular the Human Rights Act 1998 (c.42) (as to which see Chapter 25), the impact of European legislation (see Chapter 32, Section 4) and the rule in *Pepper v Hart* (see Chapter 28).

[13] See, for a particularly significant example, the following words of Lord Griffiths in *Pepper (Inspector of Taxes) v Hart* [1993] 1 All E.R. 42, HL, discussed below in Chapter 28: "The days have long passed when the courts adopted a strict constructionist view of interpretation which

decide expressly for or against a literal or purposive construction, where what the courts want to do is simply to find the proper meaning of the legislation in its application to the case before them without settling questions of theoretical dogma. Particularly worthy of note is the following passage of the judgment of Laws L.J. in *Oliver Ashworth (Holdings) Ltd v Ballard (Kent) Ltd*[14]—

> "By way of introduction to the issue of statutory construction I should say that in my judgment it is nowadays misleading—and perhaps it always was—to seek to draw a rigid distinction between literal and purposive approaches to the interpretation of Acts of Parliament. The difference between purposive and literal construction is in truth one of degree only. On received doctrine we spend our professional lives construing legislation purposively, inasmuch as we are enjoined at every turn to ascertain the intention of Parliament. The real distinction lies in the balance to be struck, in the particular case, between the literal meaning of the words on the one hand and the context and purpose of the measure in which they appear on the other. Frequently there will be no opposition between the two, and then no difficulty arises. Where there is a potential clash, the conventional English approach has been to give at least very great and often decisive weight to the literal meaning of the enacting words. This is a tradition which I think is weakening, in face of the more purposive approach enjoined for the interpretation of legislative measures of the European Union and in light of the House of Lords' decision in *Pepper (Inspector of Taxes) v Hart*.[15] I will not here go into the details or merits of this shift of emphasis; save broadly to recognise its virtue and its vice. Its virtue is that the legislator's true purpose may be more accurately ascertained. Its vice is that the certainty and accessibility of the law may be reduced or compromised. The common law, which regulates the interpretation of legislation, has to balance these considerations."

The present position

18.1.4 The issues and the present state of the judges' approach to the question, as adumbrated above, are succinctly exposed in the following two passages from the House of Lords' decision in *R (Quintavalle) v Secretary of State for Health*[16]—

---

required them to adopt the literal meaning of the language. The courts now adopt a purposive approach which seeks to give effect to the true purpose of legislation and are prepared to look at much extraneous material that bears on the background against which the legislation was enacted."

[14] [1999] 2 All E.R. 791, 805, CA.
[15] [1993] A.C. 593, HL; see further Chapter 28.
[16] [2003] 2 W.L.R. 692, HL.

Speech of Lord Bingham of Cornhill

"Such is the skill of parliamentary draftsmen that most statutory enactments are expressed in language which is clear and unambiguous and gives rise to no serious controversy. But these are not the provisions which reach the courts, or at any rate the appellate courts. Where parties expend substantial resources arguing about the effect of a statutory provision it is usually because the provision is, or is said to be, capable of bearing two or more different meanings, or to be of doubtful application to the particular case which has now arisen, perhaps because the statutory language is said to be inapt to apply to it, sometimes because the situation which has arisen is one which the draftsman could not have foreseen and for which he has accordingly made no express provision.

"The basic task of the court is to ascertain and give effect to the true meaning of what Parliament has said in the enactment to be construed. But that is not to say that attention should be confined and a literal interpretation given to the particular provisions which give rise to difficulty. Such an approach not only encourages immense prolixity in drafting, since the draftsman will feel obliged to provide expressly for every contingency which may possibly arise. It may also (under the banner of loyalty to the will of Parliament) lead to the frustration of that will, because undue concentration on the minutiae of the enactment may lead the court to neglect the purpose which Parliament intended to achieve when it enacted the statute. Every statute other than a pure consolidating statute is, after all, enacted to make some change, or address some problem, or remove some blemish, or effect some improvement in the national life. The court's task, within the permissible bounds of interpretation, is to give effect to Parliament's purpose. So the controversial provisions should be read in the context of the statute as a whole, and the statute as a whole should be read in the historical context of the situation which led to its enactment.[17]

" . . . Limited help is in my opinion to be derived from statements made in **18.1.5** cases where there is said to be an omission in a statute attributable to the oversight or inadvertence of the draftsman . . . This is not such a case. More pertinent is the guidance given by the late Lord Wilberforce in his dissenting opinion in *Royal College of Nursing of the United Kingdom v Department of Health and Social Security*.[18] The case concerned the Abortion Act 1967 and the issue which divided the House was whether nurses could lawfully take part in a termination procedure not known when the Act was passed. Lord Wilberforce said, at p.822:

'In interpreting an Act of Parliament it is proper, and indeed necessary, to have regard to the state of affairs existing, and known by Parliament to be

---

[17] For an example of this passage being cited and applied see *Evans v Amicus Healthcare Ltd* [2003] 4 All E.R. 903, 913 Fam.
[18] [1981] A.C. 800, HL.

existing, at the time. It is a fair presumption that Parliament's policy or intention is directed to that state of affairs. Leaving aside cases of omission by inadvertence, this being not such a case, when a new state of affairs, or a fresh set of facts bearing on policy, comes into existence, the courts have to consider whether they fall within the parliamentary intention. They may be held to do so, if they fall within the same genus of facts as those to which the expressed policy has been formulated. They may also be held to do so if there can be detected a clear purpose in the legislation which can only be fulfilled if the extension is made. How liberally these principles may be applied must depend upon the nature of the enactment, and the strictness or otherwise of the words in which it has been expressed. The courts should be less willing to extend expressed meanings if it is clear that the Act in question was designed to be restrictive or circumscribed in its operation rather than liberal or permissive. They will be much less willing to do so where the subject matter is different in kind or dimension from that for which the legislation was passed. In any event there is one course which the courts cannot take, under the law of this country; they cannot fill gaps; they cannot by asking the question "What would Parliament have done in this current case—not being one in contemplation—if the facts had been before it?" attempt themselves to supply the answer, if the answer is not to be found in the terms of the Act itself.'

"Both parties relied on this passage, which may now be treated as authoritative."

Speech of Lord Steyn

18.1.6 "In reaching a conclusion that cell nuclear replacement is a process covered by section 1(1) of the Human Fertilisation and Embryology Act 1990, the Court of Appeal adopted a purposive approach ... The extensive interpretation adopted by the Court of Appeal could only be justified by a purposive approach. It was a necessary step in the reasoning of the Court of Appeal but not a sufficient one. ... the adoption of a purposive approach to construction of statutes generally, and the 1990 Act in particular, is amply justified on wider grounds [than the application of the Human Rights Act 1998]. In *Cabell v Markham*[19] Learned Hand J. explained the merits of purposive interpretation:

'Of course it is true that the words used, even in their literal sense, are the primary, and ordinarily the most reliable, source of interpreting the meaning of any writing: be it a statute, a contract, or anything else. But it is one of the surest indexes of a mature and developed jurisprudence not to make a fortress out of the dictionary; but to remember that statutes

---

[19] 1945 F. 2d. 737, 739.

always have some purpose or object to accomplish, whose sympathetic and imaginative discovery is the surest guide to their meaning.'

"The pendulum has swung towards purposive methods of construction. This change was not initiated by the teleological approach of European Community jurisprudence, and the influence of European legal culture generally, but it has been accelerated by European ideas: see, however, a classic early statement of the purposive approach by Lord Blackburn in *River Wear Commissioners v Adamson*.[20] In any event, nowadays the shift towards purposive interpretation is not in doubt. The qualification is that the degree of liberality permitted is influenced by the context, *e.g.* social welfare legislation and tax statutes may have to be approached somewhat differently."

So the essence is that while the courts regard it is important to attempt to discover the intention of the legislator by reference to the legislative context and underlying policy, the attempt will start—and generally and ideally finish—by applying the most natural construction to the words actually used.[21]

Subliminal application of both approaches

A large part of the reason why it has never been particularly helpful to argue either for literalism or for purposivism in a rigid way is that in reality judges construing legislation always have and always will instinctively look both at the strict and superficial meaning of the words used and at the underlying purpose of the legislation, normally as a single, and largely subliminal, mental process. It is only in the rare cases where there is a tension between the two that the court needs to turn its mind actively to which should prevail, and in that context it is now possible to say that the purposive interpretation will generally prevail where it provides a clear answer,[22] but that otherwise the strict meaning will have to

18.1.7

---

[20] (1877) 2 App. Cas. 743, 763.

[21] In particular, the courts still assume that the draftsman weighs every word with care and neither changes language without a change of meaning nor includes superfluities for emphasis. So, for example, the refutation of the suggestion that "premises" was intended to mean all or part of premises, on the grounds that the wider expression was found elsewhere in the relevant statute, was rejected by Mackay J. on the grounds that "the draftsman could have said so, and would have said so, as he did in two other places in this very section" (*Westminster City Council v O'Reilly* [2003] 1 W.L.R. 1411, QBD).

[22] For two recent examples see the decision of the Divisional Court in *Talbot v Director of Public Prosecutions* [2000] 1 W.L.R. 1102, QBD ("enclosed area" in s.4 of the Vagrancy Act 1824 held not to include a room in a building—although in a literal sense a room is by definition enclosed, in the context of the 1824 Act the use of the term "enclosed" was as a natural colloquial expression clearly intended to exclude a room) and of the House of Lords in *Birmingham City Council v Oakley* [2001] 1 A.C. 617, HL ("Taken literally, it can be said that 'the state of the premises' is capable of a broad meaning to include a consideration of the layout, even unavoidable use within the layout. But a narrower meaning is equally possible. One must therefore look at the purpose of the legislation and for that consider the history of the legislation and the context of these words in the [Environmental Protection Act 1990 (c.43)] together with previous judicial interpretations." —*per* Lord Slynn of Hadley at 623).

prevail, even if the court is uncomfortable with the result. The application of both approaches is very likely to be automatic and subconscious in many cases, but one can occasionally find it expressed.[23]

This balancing process is not new. Consider, for example, the following passage of Horridge J. in *Newman Manufacturing Co. v Marrable*[24]—

> " . . . I think that I ought to look at the object of this section. I think it was intended to protect the English button trade. To protect that trade against the importation of completed buttons it would only be necessary for the definition and the sub-section to use the word 'buttons.' But in my view the statute was directed against those who imported goods which were not quite buttons, but upon which the bulk of the work had been done abroad, and very little remained to be done by the manufacturer in England. I think that was the reason why the words 'buttons . . . . whether finished or unfinished' were used in this section.
>
> "In my judgment these articles were unfinished buttons; they were going to be buttons, and they were going to have a shank put into them. The insertion of that shank only involved one-seventh of the total cost of the finished button. This article with a hole ready to have a shank put into it was an unfinished button within the meaning of section 9 of the Finance Act, 1928. I think therefore that these articles were dutiable under the section, and that my judgment must be for the defendant."

So even in a taxing statute, where it is a long-established rule to begin by construing the statute strictly against the Crown,[25] it has always been more important to apply common sense to construction of the intention of the statute and its overall purpose than to apply any strict rules.

Limitation of purposive construction: danger of speculating on legislative intent

18.1.8   Although it is clear that those judicial pronouncements that strongly resisted any interpretative approach that involved the court attempting "to find out the

---

[23] See, for example the judgment of Lloyd J. in *Re B.R.A.C. Rent-A-Car* [2003] 2 All E.R. 201, Ch, a case involving the construction of subordinate legislation; and note "I have reached the conclusion that the situation here under consideration is not capable of giving rise to a statutory nuisance within section 79(1)(a) of the Act of 1990. I accept the general thrust of [Counsel's] submissions that this statutory regime is not intended to apply in cases where the sole concern is that, by reason of the state of the premises, there is a likelihood of an accident causing personal injury. In reaching that conclusion, I am influenced more by the legislative background and apparent legislative purpose of the provisions than by their actual language."—*R. v Bristol City Council Ex p. Everett* [1999] 1 W.L.R. 92, QBD, Richards J. (appeal dismissed [1999] 1 W.L.R. 1170, CA).

[24] [1931] 2 K.B. 297, 304–305 K.B.; based on *Powell Lane Manufacturing Co v Putnam* (see Note at end of the report).

[25] See Chapter 19.

intention of parliament"[26] have been relegated to history,[27] it remains true that the courts are aware of the dangers of speculation about the legislative intent, as distinct from deducing it in accordance with established principles and in reliance on clear signs.[28]

So even in those cases where the courts are prepared to supply the deficiencies of the legislature by inferring the making of provision which was not in fact made[29] they do so not because they are assuming the role of the legislature, and enacting what they think the legislature would have wished to do enact had it thought of a case, but only because they consider it plain from what is provided that the legislature actually intended to do something, the parameters of which are beyond doubt or argument, that it in fact neglected or failed to do.

The result of this is that the courts will be at their boldest in applying a purposive interpretation to legislation in cases where there is ample and clear evidence of what the legislation was actually intended to achieve by all those involved. A notable example of an insistence on a purposive approach based on judicial determination not to see an expressed purpose fail for arguably insufficient implementation of an expressed policy is found in the following passage of the Court of Appeal's judgment in *Harrods Ltd v Remick*[30]—

> "If [Counsel's] approach to the construction of section 7 is right, these ladies will be victims of injustice without redress. The legislation will have failed to achieve the purpose set for it by para 25 of the White Paper. . . .
>
> "Accordingly, in approaching the construction of section 7(1) we should, in my judgment, give a construction to the statutory language that is not only consistent with the actual words used but also would achieve the statutory purpose of providing a remedy to victims of discrimination who would otherwise be without one."

There are, however, many examples of recent cases where the courts have felt **18.1.9** compelled to resist the temptation to repair an apparent substantive deficiency in legislation on the grounds that the necessary extension would exceed a purposive construction of what is said and amount to judicial legislation.[31]

Of course, it is easy to assert that the courts must, and have always tried to, chart a course between the Scylla of senseless literalism and the Charybdis of irresponsible speculation: it is much more difficult to do it. The higher courts

---

[26] See, for example, *Magor and St. Mellons R.D.C. v Newport Corporation* [1952] A.C. 189, 191, HL *per* Lord Simonds responding to a strongly pro-purposive statement of Denning L.J. in the same case in the Court of Appeal ([1950] 2 All E.R. 1226, 1236); and see the Law Commissions' report *The Interpretation of Statutes* (Law Com. No.21 of 1969), p.32—now to be taken in the light of *Pepper v Hart*, as to which see Chapter 28.

[27] See above, para.18.1.3.

[28] See, in particular, the dicta cited above about the dangers of the meaning of "the legislative intent".

[29] See, for example, para.20.1.11 below.

[30] [1998] 1 All E.R. 52, 57, CA, *per* Sir Richard Scott V.C.

[31] See, for example, para.20.1.16 below.

cannot lay down any rules for what has to be a sensitive exercise of judicial power: but they occasionally offer warnings of the dangers and advice as to how they should be approached. See, for example, the following dictum of Lord Clyde in *Cutter v Eagle Star*[32]—

> "It may be perfectly proper to adopt even a strained construction to enable the object and purpose of legislation to be fulfilled. But it cannot be taken to the length of applying unnatural meanings to familiar words or of so stretching the language that its former shape is transformed into something which is not only significantly different but has a name of its own. This must particularly be so where the language has no evident ambiguity or uncertainty about it. While I have recognised that there could be some exceptional cases where what can reasonable be described as a car park may also qualify as a road, it is the unusual character of such cases which would justify such a result in the application of the statutory language rather than any distortion of the language itself. . . . Against the employment of a broad approach to express the purpose of the Act must be put the undesirability of adopting anything beyond a strict construction of provisions which have penal consequences."

Practical result of the present position (1): brevity of drafting

18.1.10   Whether the balance has really changed towards a more purposive approach to statutory interpretation or whether the purposive element is merely more openly acknowledged, in either case an important practical result is that the draftsman of primary or subordinate legislation is able to assume to a greater degree than was once the case that his words will be given a construction by reference to their context.

In particular, the temptation to pepper provisions with confusing verbiage for the sake of literal accuracy is much less strong than it was.

Imagine a section beginning with the following subs.(1)—

> "(1) A person may apply to a local authority to be registered in a register kept by the authority."

The following version of a possible subs.(2) adopts a style, once common, which ensures total literal accuracy and deflects even the most fanciful or even untenable arguments of ambiguity—

> "(2) An application under subsection (1) above shall specify the name of the applicant for registration and such other details (if any) as the local authority to whom the application is made may require."

---

[32] [1998] 4 All E.R. 417, 425, HL.

Relying on the common sense discussed above,[33] however, it is possible to make provision which can be relied upon to have the same effect, but with relative brevity and euphony, along the following lines— **18.1.11**

> "(2) An application must specify the applicant's name and any other details that the authority may require."

In other words, the ability to assume a broadly purposive approach to construction encourages brevity in legislative drafting,[34] which in turn enhances clarity for the reader.

Incidentally, both formulations leave room for argument about the effect of a failure to comply with the subsection in respect of an application, whether it makes it void, voidable or neither.[35] In either case it is possible to avoid the argument, if it seems necessary in the context, with a few additional words.

Practical result of the present position (2): exposition

Another practical result of the present position is that in pursuing an obviously fair and just result it is less often necessary to establish or appeal to a rule or presumption of construction and more often possible to appeal simply to the purpose of the provision in question. So, for example, in *Karpavicius v The Queen*[36] Lord Steyn said[37]— **18.1.12**

> "In a more literalist age it may have been said that the words of section 6(2A)(c) [of the New Zealand Misuse of Drugs Act 1975] are capable of bearing either a wide or a narrow meaning and that the fact that a criminal statute is involved requires the narrower interpretation to be adopted. Nowadays an approach concentrating on the purpose of the statutory provision is generally to be preferred ... ".

Substance over form

Both as a component or corollary of the trend towards purposive interpretation and as a matter of common sense, the courts try not to allow questions of form to interfere with the application of principles of substance. While an expression used in legislation may be susceptible of a technical meaning, therefore, the **18.1.13**

---

[33] Chapter 17, para.17.1.14.
[34] The saving in this case is only 17 words, but it is also just over 50%: so it will be seen that the potential saving in the overall volume of annual legislation to be achieved by individually relatively minor and easy economies of words is enormous.
[35] See Chapter 12, Section 6.
[36] [2003] 1 W.L.R. 169, PC.
[37] para.15.

courts will concentrate in construing the provision not on whether the technicalities are satisfied but on whether the obvious intention behind the use of the expression has been met.

So in *In re Ismail*,[38] for example, the House of Lords declined to concentrate on whether the requirement in section 1 of the Extradition Act 1989[39] for a person to have been "accused" abroad of a crime had been met in a technical sense according to the use in the relevant foreign jurisdiction of the notion of accusation: the term required a broad and purposive construction according to which the clear meaning of the Act was to require only that the foreign authorities should have taken a step which could fairly be described, as a matter of substance rather than of form, as the commencement of a prosecution.

Conclusion

18.1.14   From the cases drawn on in this Chapter can be distilled the following principles—

(1) Legislation is always to be understood first in accordance with its plain meaning.

(2) Where the plain meaning is in doubt, the courts will start the process of construction by attempting to discover, from the provisions enacted, the broad purpose of the legislation.

(3) Where a particular reading would advance the purpose identified, and would do no violence to the plain meaning of the provisions enacted, the courts will be prepared to adopt that reading.

(4) Where a particular reading would advance the purpose identified but would strain the plain meaning of the provisions enacted, the result will depend on the context and, in particular, on a balance of the clarity of the purpose identified and the degree of strain on the language.

(5) Where the courts conclude that the underlying purpose of the legislation is insufficiently plain, or cannot be advanced without an unacceptable degree of violence to the language used, they will be obliged, however regretfully in the circumstances of a particular case, to leave to the legislature the task of extending or modifying the legislation.

These principles should be read in the light, in particular, of the discussions of s.3 of the Human Rights Act 1998 in Chapter 25, of the mischief rule, the *casus omissus* rule and other canons in Chapter 20 and of s.2(1) of the European Communities Act 1972 in Chapter 32, Section 3.

---

[38] [1998] 3 W.L.R. 495, HL.
[39] 1989 c.33.

CHAPTER 19

REBUTTABLE PRESUMPTIONS OF CONSTRUCTION

Introduction

Once the meaning of legislation has been found sufficiently unclear on the **19.1.1** surface to make it necessary to embark upon the task of statutory construction, the courts will apply, in addition to the elucidatory rules already discussed,[1] a number of presumptions.

While these presumptions are various and each deals with a different aspect of the law, they have one thing in common: each rests on the assumption that the legislature (whether Parliament or the recipient of a delegated power) has no intention to encroach upon what are fundamental rights or principles of law. As Lord Scott of Foscote said in *R. (Edison) v Central Valuation Officer*[2]—

> "My Lords, as an aid to construction of statutes, presumptions are from time to time invoked. This is particularly so where rights of citizens regarded as of fundamental importance appear to be encroached upon by a particular application of a statute. In such a case it is presumed that Parliament, if it intended the statute to encroach upon the important fundamental right, would have expressly said so. If Parliament has not expressly said so, and if the statute is capable of being given sensible effect without encroaching upon the fundamental right, a construction of the statutory language may be adopted that would leave unimpeded the right in question."

The general justification for the approach is explained by Lord Hoffmann in *R.* **19.1.2** *v Secretary of State for the Home Department, Ex p. Simms*[3]—

> "Fundamental rights cannot be overridden by general or ambiguous words. This is because there is too great a risk that the full implications of their unqualified meaning may have passed unnoticed in the democratic process. In the absence of express language or necessary implication to the contrary, the courts therefore presume that even the most general words were intended to be subject to the basic rights of the individual."

---

[1] Chapters 16 to 18.
[2] [2003] 4 All E.R. 209, 243, HL.
[3] [2000] 2 A.C. 115, 131, HL; cited in *Edison*.

It has been suggested that some of these presumptions owe their origin to the age of literal construction and the need to find a method of departing from the literal meaning of a provision where justice clearly demanded departure: the implication being that in a more purposive climate of statutory construction some of these presumptions have outlived their usefulness and can be dispensed with, or at least relied upon less.[4]

19.1.3   This Chapter explores a number of presumptions that the courts apply in construing legislation. Others have been addressed earlier in this work. The following table lists the presumptions and where they are discussed—

Presumption against unfairness	Para. 19.1.5
Presumption against double taxation	Para. 19.1.6
Presumption against double jeopardy	Para. 19.1.7
Presumption against expropriation	Para. 19.1.8
Presumtion of protection of human rights	Paras 19.1.9—19.1.11
Presumption against absurdity	Para. 19.1.12
Presumption against double recovery	Para. 19.1.13
Presumption against penalty	Paras 19.1.14
Presumption against unusual imposition	Para. 19.1.15
Presumption of fairness and convenience	Para. 19.1.16
Presumption against creating or removing judicial jurisdiction	Paras 19.1.17—19.1.22
Presumption of notice	Para. 19.1.23
Presumption of privilege	Para. 19.1.24
Presumption against territorial limitation	Para. 19.1.25
Presumption against creation of rights and duties	Chapter 12, Section 1.
Presumption against removal of rights and duties	Same
Presumption against altering legal principle	Chapter 14, Sections 1 & 2.
Presumption against strict liability for offence	Chapter 1, Section 5.

---

[4] See Chapter 18, para.18.1.12; but see also para.18.1.12.

Presumption against taxation	Chapter 1, Section 6.
Presumption against expenditure	Chapter 1, Section 6.
Presumption against retrospectivity	Chapter 10, Section 3.

Rebuttal of presumption

The presumptions listed above are all rebuttable. They will be displaced **19.1.4** whenever it is the clear intention of the legislature that they should be, in accordance with the principle of the Sovereign supremacy of Parliament.[5]

It should be noted at the outset that although it is sometimes said that these presumptions can be rebutted only by express words, what is actually required is clarity of intention to rebut. Although that will most normally (and safely) be achieved by express words, a clear implication is sufficient. The point is expounded as follows by Lord Reid, in the context of the presumption against expropriation, in the case of *Westminster Bank Ltd v Minister of Housing and Local Government*[6]—

> "The appellants' argument is really founded on the principle that 'a statute should not be held to take away private rights of property without compensation unless the intention to do so is expressed in clear and unambiguous terms' (per Lord Warrington in *Colonial Sugar Refining Co Ltd v Melbourne Harbour Trust Commissioners*[7]).
>
> "I entirely accept the principle. It flows from the fact that Parliament seldom intends to do that and therefore before attributing such an intention to Parliament we should be sure that that was really intended. I would only query the last words of the quotation. When we are seeking the intention of Parliament that may appear from express words but it may also appear by irresistible inference from the statute read as a whole. But I would agree that, if there is reasonable doubt, the subject should be given the benefit of the doubt."

In other words, an inference will do by way of rebuttal, if it be a clear one.[8]

---

[5] See Chapter 2, Section 2; even where the legislation being construed is subordinate, provided the necessary *vires* have been clearly conferred to rebut a presumption, the courts will be obliged to.

[6] [1971] A.C. 508, 529, HL.

[7] [1927] A.C. 343, 359.

[8] The same idea applies in relation to all rebuttals of presumption, including those introduced by language along the lines of "except where the contrary appears". So, in the case of *Chorlton v Lings* (1868) L.R. 4 C.P. 374, Willes J. dealt (at 387), in relation to a presumption of the statute 13 & 14 Vict. c.21—a forerunner of the Interpretation Act 1978 (c.30), s.6—which provided that "in all Acts, words importing the masculine gender shall be deemed and taken to include females, and the singular to include the plural, and the plural the singular, unless the contrary as to gender or number is expressly provided."; despite the word "expressly" he said as follows: "The application of the Act, 13 & 14 Vict. c.21, contended for by the appellant is a strained one. It is not easy to conceive that the framer of that Act, when he used the word 'expressly,' meant to

Presumption against unfairness

19.1.5   There is a general presumption that the legislature does not intend to achieve a result that is manifestly unfair, unreasonable or arbitrary.[9]

The breadth of the presumption is expounded by Lord Reid in *Inland Revenue Commissioners v Hinchy*[10]—

> "One is entitled and, indeed, bound to assume that Parliament intends to act reasonably and, therefore, to prefer a reasonable interpretation of a statutory provision if there is any choice."

A number of matters sometimes expressed as separate presumptions do not arise out of specific fundamental rights to be guarded by the courts but are simply particular manifestations of this general rule.[11]

The presumption extends to the nature of powers conferred by Acts of Parliament and their exercise. As Lord Diplock said in *Hillingdon London Borough Council v Commission for Racial Equality*[12]—

> "Where an Act of Parliament confers upon an administrative body functions which involve its making decisions which affect to their detriment the rights of other persons or curtail their liberty to do as they please, there is a presumption that Parliament intended that the administrative body should act fairly towards those persons who will be affected by their decision."

Presumption against double taxation

19.1.6   A first example of a presumption often talked of as if it were a *sui generis* technicality, but in reality emanating from the general presumption against unfairness, is illustrated by the following passage of the speech of Lord Scott of Foscote in *R. (Edison) v Central Valuation Officer*[13]—

> "There are no doubt other rights whose fundamental importance may justify similar reverence but I need not try and identify them for it is surely clear

---

suggest that what is necessarily or properly implied by language is not expressed by such language. It is quite clear that whatever the language used necessarily or even naturally implies is expressed thereby. Still less did the framer of the Act intend to exclude the rule alike of good sense and grammar and law, that general words are to be restrained to the subject-matter with which the speaker or writer is dealing."

[9] "It is another principle of statutory construction that the court leans against an interpretation which produces unjust and arbitrary consequences. I think it would be unjust if a husband were compelled to support a wife in open and admitted adultery; and it would be arbitrary if the amount of money he had to spend on her depended on the speed with which he was able to obtain his decree absolute"—*National Assistance Board v Wilkinson* [1952] 2 Q.B. 648, 661, DC *per* Devlin J.

[10] [1960] A.C. 748, 768, HL.

[11] See below.

[12] [1982] A.C. 779, 787, HL.

[13] [2003] 4 All E.R. 209, 243, HL.

that the so-called presumption against double taxation or double recovery does not derive from a fundamental right of that character. There is no fundamental right not to be taxed,[14] or not to be taxed in a particular way or at a particular time. The so-called presumption against double taxation is in reality no more, and no less, than the formulation in a taxation context of the broader interpretative presumption that Parliament does not intend that legislation should bring about results that are unreasonable or unfair or arbitrary."

It is not only the presumption against double taxation that can be traced to this general presumption.

Presumption against double jeopardy

The presumption against double jeopardy is another example of a rule sometimes cited as if it were a separate principle of law, whereas in reality it emanates only from the general presumption against unfairness. There are important practical consequences of this. In particular, it is not to be presumed that double jeopardy is unintended by the legislature unless there would be something inherently unfair about it. In the case, for example, where commission of an offence could also make a person susceptible to the exercise of disciplinary action by a professional or other regulatory body, there is no reason to assume that the legislature would have wished to avoid exposing a person both to prosecution and to disciplinary action: the former results in punishment for the offence, the latter may be used to protect the public for the future. Although either power could be used in a way that resulted in unfair double punishment, that is not inevitable.[15]

19.1.7

In relation to double jeopardy it is important also to bear in mind s.18 of the Interpretation Act 1978.[16]

Presumption against expropriation

With the general principle in mind, that many specific presumptions are merely emanations from a general presumption of fairness, it will become apparent that certain things will be treated as unlikely to have been intended by the legislature if done in one way, but not necessarily if done in a different way.

19.1.8

---

[14] But, as has been seen (Chapter 1, Section 6) the courts will assume no intention to tax unless it be expressed by clear words or implication.

[15] And, indeed, one finds a number of places where both professional and criminal sanctions are available in respect of the same matter.So, for example, the power to disqualify under s.62 of the Merchant Shipping Act 1995 (c.21) applies "Where it appears to the Secretary of State that a person who is the holder of a certificate to which this section applies is unfit to be the holder of such a certificate, whether by reason of incompetence or misconduct or for any other reason," (subs.(1))—the mere commission of an offence of a certain kind or in certain circumstances might suffice to justify the imposition of this additional penalty.

[16] 1978 c.30: see Chapter 1, Section 5.

An obvious example is that of expropriation of or interference with property. The courts will assume that legislation does not intend simply to deprive persons of property or to interfere with the enjoyment of property, but if done in such a way as to ensure that there would be due compensation for any deprivation or interference, the presumption may be rebutted[17]: not merely because unless the deprivation or compensation were intended the provision for compensation would be redundant[18] but also because the availability of compensation may redress such inherent unfairness as would otherwise be exhibited by the deprivation or interference.[19]

Presumption of protection of human rights

19.1.9 Another manifestation of the general principle against unfairness adumbrated above is the common law presumption that the courts will apply in favour of construing all legislation as intending, in the absence of express contrary provision, as intending to respect basic human rights.

This was an active principle of construction before the enactment of the Human Rights Act 1998.[20]

The effect of the presumption, the manner of its rebuttal and the effect of the enactment of the 1998 Act are expounded in the following passage of the speech of Lord Hoffmann in *R. v Secretary of State for the Home Department, Ex p. Simms*[21]—

"I add only a few words of my own about the importance of the principle of legality in a constitution which, like ours, acknowledges the sovereignty of Parliament.

19.1.10 "Parliamentary sovereignty means that Parliament can, if it chooses, legislate contrary to fundamental principles of human rights.The Human Rights Act 1998 will not detract from this power.The constraints upon its exercise by Parliament are ultimately political, not legal. But the principle

---

[17] "The absence of compensation clauses from an Act conferring powers affords an important indication that the Act was not intended to authorise interference with private rights ... But the indication is not conclusive"—*Allen v Gulf Oil Refining Ltd* [1981] 1 All E.R. 353, 359, HL *per* Lord Edmund-Davies.

[18] Which consideration would not apply if the provision were compensation were either implied or merely the automatic application of an external system.

[19] See further Chapter 11, Section 4.

[20] 1998 c.42; see, for example, the discussion in Lord Steyn's speech in *Ex p. Simms* (cited in the next footnote) at 124–125. And see, in general, the following passage of the speech of Lord Browne-Wilkinson in *Pierson v Secretary of State for the Home Department* [1998] A.C. 539, 575—

"A power conferred by Parliament in general terms is not to be taken to authorise the doing of acts by the donee of the power which adversely affect the legal rights of the citizen or the basic principles on which the law of the United Kingdom is based unless the statute conferring the power makes it clear that such was the intention of Parliament."

[21] [2000] 2 A.C. 115, 131, HL; and note that this passage was cited with particular approval by Lord Steyn in *R. (Anufrijeva) v Secretary of State for the Home Department* [2003] 3 W.L.R. 252, 265, HL.

of legality means that Parliament must squarely confront what it is doing and accept the political cost. Fundamental rights cannot be overridden by general or ambiguous words. This is because there is too great a risk that the full implications of their unqualified meaning may have passed unnoticed in the democratic process.In the absence of express language or necessary implication to the contrary, the courts therefore presume that even the most general words were intended to be subject to the basic rights of the individual. In this way the courts of the United Kingdom, though acknowledging the sovereignty of Parliament, apply principles of constitutionality little different from those which exist in countries where the power of the legislature is expressly limited by a constitutional document.

"The Human Rights Act 1998 will make three changes to this scheme of things.

"First, the principles of fundamental human rights which exist at common law will be supplemented by a specific text, namely the European Convention for the Protection of Human Rights and Fundamental Freedoms.[22] But much of the convention reflects the common law: see *Derbyshire County Council v Times Newspapers Ltd.*[23] That is why the United Kingdom government felt able in 1950 to accede to the convention without domestic legislative change. So the adoption of the text as part of domestic law is unlikely to involve radical change in our notions of fundamental human rights.

"Secondly, the principle of legality will be expressly enacted as a rule of construction in section 3 and will gain further support from the obligation of the Minister in charge of a Bill to make a statement of compatibility under section 19. **19.1.11**

"Thirdly, in those unusual cases in which the legislative infringement of fundamental human rights is so clearly expressed as not to yield to the principle of legality, the courts will be able to draw this to the attention of Parliament by making a declaration of incompatibility. It will then be for the sovereign Parliament to decide whether or not to remove the incompatibility.

"What this case decides is that the principle of legality applies to subordinate legislation as much as to Acts of Parliament. Prison regulations expressed in general language are also presumed to be subject to fundamental human rights.The presumption enables them to be valid. But, it also means that properly construed, they do not authorise a blanket restriction which would curtail not merely the prisoner's right of free expression, but its use in a way which could provide him with access to justice."

---

[22] Rome, November 4, 1950; TS 71 (1953); Cmd 8969.
[23] [1993] 1 All E.R. 1011 at 1021, [1993] A.C. 534 at 551.

It should, however, be noted that while the European Convention is of enormous importance it is "not an exhaustive statement of fundamental rights under our system of law".[24] There are certain other fundamental rights that are addressed by particular presumptions of judicial construction.

Presumption against absurdity

19.1.12   While it is not for the courts to reject or refuse to give effect to legislation merely on the grounds that the clear meaning of the legislation appears absurd to the judiciary,[25] when forced to construe a provision the meaning of which is open to question they will lean against any construction that would produce a result which appears to them to be absurd or unjust. As the majority held in *R. v Skeen*[26]—

> "If the language employed admit of two constructions, and according to one of them the enactment would be absurd and mischievous, and according to the other it would be reasonable and wholesome, we surely ought to put the latter construction upon it as that which the legislature intended. . . . For can it be supposed that the legislature intended wantonly to extend the indemnity to cases where there is no merit whatever in the accused, where he states only what he knows to be already notorious, and where neither civil nor criminal justice can be at all advanced by the alleged disclosure?"

Presumption against double recovery

19.1.13   While again being a particular manifestation of the general presumption that Parliament intends to do only that which is fair and proper, the presumption against double recovery is worthy of separate mention because of its wide-ranging and various implications.

The most obvious application of the presumption is in relation to remedies for loss, in which it will be assumed that, for example, liability of a number of persons is joint and several to the extent only that it permits the person who suffered loss to recover from whichever of those who caused the loss is easiest

---

[24] *R. (Anufrijeva) v Secretary of State for the Home Department* [2003] 3 W.L.R. 252, 266, HL *per* Lord Steyn.

[25] See Chapter 17; and note "Where by the use of clear and unequivocal language capable of only one construction anything is enacted by the legislature, we must enforce it, though in our own opinion it is absurd or mischievous."—*R. v Skeen* (1859) 28 L.J.M.C. 91 (adopted by Farwell L.J. in *Sadler v Whiteman* [1910] 1 K.B. 868, 892).

[26] (1859) 28 L.J.M.C. 91.

to pursue: but it does not permit him to pursue more than one in such a way as to end up recovering more than the amount of his loss.

The presumption applies in many other situations. In the context of rating, for example, much will be learned about the nature and strength of the presumption from the speeches of both majority and minority in the House of Lords in *R. (on the application of Edison First Power Ltd) v Central Valuation Officer*.[27]

Presumption against penalty

The imposition of a penalty on a person must be achieved by clear legislative words, and in the absence of clear words the courts will assume that no penalty is intended.[28]

19.1.14

Presumption against unusual imposition

In the same way that the Joint Committee on Statutory Instruments scrutinises subordinate legislation for, amongst other things, unusual exercises of the power, the courts will be put on their guard by Parliament's setting out in an Act, or the executive setting out in subordinate legislation, to do anything out of the ordinary run of the legislative course. Parliament can, of course, do anything that it wishes,[29] but the courts will apply the constraint that the more unusual or unlikely the thing that Parliament wishes to do, the more clearly it must do it.

19.1.15

This is a principle of general application that will be found in all areas of the law. An example of its application can be found in the judgment of Hale L.J. in *Re R (a child)*[30]—

> "We start from the proposition ... that section 28(3) [of the Human Fertilisation and Embryology Act 1990[31]] is an unusual provision, conferring the relationship of parent and child on people who are related neither by blood nor by marriage. Conferring such relationships is a serious matter, involving as it does not only the relationship between father and child but also between the whole of the father's family and the child. The rule should only apply to those cases which clearly fall within the footprint of the statutory language."

---

[27] [2003] 4 All E.R. 209.
[28] For recent statements of this long-standing principle see *R. v Bristol Magistrates' Court, Ex p.* E [1999] 1 W.L.R. 390, 397 CA and *Massey v Boulden* [2003] 2 All E.R. 87, 93, CA both *per* Simon Brown L.J.
[29] See Chapter 2, Section 2.
[30] [2003] 2 All E.R. 131, 137, CA.
[31] 1990 c.37.

Presumption of fairness and convenience

19.1.16　The nature of this presumption and the constraints upon its application can best be demonstrated by the following passage from the judgment of Pill L.J. in *R. (Tagoe-Thompson) v Mental Health NHS Trust*[32]—

> "It was, however, submitted that consideration of equality, fairness and convenience can and should be used in favour of the construction of section 23(4) [of the Mental Health Act 1983[33]] that [Counsel] advocated. [Counsel] referred to the speech of Lord Shaw in *Shannon Realties Ltd. v Ville de St Michel*[34]:
>
> > 'Where the words of a statute are clear they must, of course, be followed; but, in their Lordships' opinion, where alternative constructions are equally open, that alternative is to be chosen which will be consistent with the smooth working of the system which the statute purports to be regulation; and that alternative is to be rejected which will introduce uncertainty, friction or confusion into the working of the system.'
>
> "It was submitted that a procedure which permits continued detention when only a minority of members oppose release leads to inequality, uncertainty, delay and inconvenience and may be arbitrary. I can give little weight to these submissions in the context of this issue. A procedure requiring unanimity is not arbitrary and is no less certain than one permitting a majority . . . "

Presumption against creating or removing judicial jurisdiction

19.1.17　To confer jurisdiction on a court of law or to remove jurisdiction from a court of law requires express words or the clearest of implications.[35] The following statements suffice to elucidate the essence of the presumption—

> "The creation of a new right of appeal is plainly an act which requires [distinct] legislative authority."[36]

> "The general rule undoubtedly is that the jurisdiction of superior courts is not taken away except by express words or necessary implication".[37]

---

[32] [2003] 1 W.L.R. 1272, 1278–9, CA.

[33] 1983 c.20.

[34] [1924] A.C. 185, 192–193.

[35] For example, a power to make provision for the determination of disputes in relation to a particular matter would clearly be sufficient to enable jurisdiction to be conferred on a court or tribunal. It is, however, common for statutes to gloss an enabling power so as expressly to permit the conferring of jurisdiction—see, for example, s.37(3) of the Commonhold and Leasehold Reform Act 2002 (c.15).

[36] *Attorney-General v Sillem* (1864) 10 H.L.C. 704, 720, HL *per* Lord Westbury.

[37] *Albon v Pyke* (1842) 4 M. & G. 421, 424 *per* Tindal C.J.

"The jurisdiction of the King's courts must not be taken to be excluded unless there is clear language in the statute which is alleged to have that effect."[38]

While these statements are generally either expressed to be about the superior courts or occur in relation to those courts, the situation in relation to the inferior courts is in essence the same. Conferring a discretion on a court amounts to sub-delegation of power, and the courts will always lean against that in the absence of strong reason to the contrary. But lesser forms of implication may suffice for the implied conferring of jurisdiction on lower courts.[39]

The presumption is particularly strong in relation to subtraction from the supervisory jurisdiction of the High Court. Since it is this jurisdiction that has to be relied upon for the purpose of determining the lawfulness of purported exercises of legislative power, the relationship between the legislature and the courts in this context is one of particularly extreme sensitivity.

The presumption as it affects the supervisory jurisdiction is expressed by Lord **19.1.18** Reid in the leading case of *Anisminic Ltd v Foreign Compensation Commission*[40]—

"It is a well established principle that a provision ousting the ordinary jurisdiction of the court must be construed strictly—meaning, I think, that, if such a provision is reasonably capable of having two meanings, that meaning shall be taken which preserves the ordinary jurisdiction of the court."

In that case Lord Reid established that the strength of words required to rebut the presumption would, as normal, depend on the circumstances, and that at one extreme, the case where the court was asked to refrain even from examining even whether something was valid as what it purported to be, very plain language indeed would be required—

"Statutory provisions which seek to limit the ordinary jurisdiction of the court have a long history. No case has been cited in which any other form of words limiting the jurisdiction of the court has been held to protect a nullity. If the draftsman or Parliament had intended to introduce a new kind of ouster clause so as to prevent any inquiry even as to whether the document relied on was a forgery, I would have expected to find something

---

[38] *Goldsack v Shore* [1950] 1 All E.R. 276, 277 *per* Evershed M.R.

[39] It was, for example, common for statutes to confer jurisdiction on the county courts indirectly by providing for a sum to be recoverable as a simple contract debt. With the generalisation of the county courts' statutory jurisdiction this formula began to fall into disuse, but it may have been rejuvenated by the decision of the Court of Appeal in *Agodzo v Bristol City Council* [1999] 1 W.L.R. 1971, CA. See the entry for *Simple Contract Debt* in the latest supplement to *Stroud's Judicial Dictionary*, (6th ed.).

[40] [1969] 2 A.C. 147, 170, HL.

much more specific than the bald statement that a determination shall not be called in question in any court of law. Undoubtedly such a provision protects every determination which is not a nullity. But I do not think that it is necessary or even reasonable to construe the word 'determination' as including everything which purports to be a determination but which is in fact no determination at all. And there are no degrees of nullity. There are a number of reasons why the law will hold a purported decision to be a nullity. I do not see how it could be said that such a provision protects some kinds of nullity but not others: if that were intended it would be easy to say so."[41]

19.1.19   As Lord Irvine of Lairg L.C. said in *Boddington v British Transport Police*[42]—

"However, in approaching the issue of statutory construction the courts proceed from a strong appreciation that ours is a country subject to the rule of law. This means that it is well recognised to be important for the maintenance of the rule of law and the preservation of liberty that individuals affected by legal measures promulgated by executive public bodies should have a fair opportunity to challenge these measures and to vindicate their rights in court proceedings. There is a strong presumption that Parliament will not legislate to prevent individuals from doing so:

'It is a principle not by any means to be whittled down that the subject's recourse to Her Majesty's courts for the determination of his rights is not to be excluded except by clear words' *Pyx Granite Co. Ltd v Ministry of Housing and Local Government*[43]; cited by Lord Fraser of Tullybelton in *Wandsworth London Borough Council v Winder.*[44] [45]

"As Lord Diplock put it in *F. Hoffmann-La Roche & Co. Ltd. v Secretary of State for Trade and Industry*[46]:

'the courts lean very heavily against a construction of an Act which would have this effect' (*cf. Anisminic Ltd v Foreign Compensation Commission*[47])."

---

[41] Same.
[42] [1999] 2 A.C. 143, 161, HL.
[43] [1960] A.C. 260, 286, *per* Viscount Simonds.
[44] [1969] A.C. 461, 510.
[45] See also McNair J. in *Francis v Yiewsley and West Drayton Urban District Council* [1957] 2 Q.B. 136.
[46] [1975] A.C. 295, 366C.
[47] [1969] 2 A.C. 147.

The application of the presumption has been considered in a number of recent cases.[48] **19.1.20**

Despite the strength of this presumption it is sometimes rebutted expressly.[49] Ouster clauses, as they are sometimes called, are found in a number of forms, from a relatively uncontentious proposition making a particular decision final to an express ouster of all supervisory jurisdiction. To give two extreme examples[50]—

---

[48] See, in particular, *Attorney-General v Ryan* [1980] A.C. 718, HL and *R. v Monopolies and Mergers Commission, Ex p. South Yorkshire Transport Ltd* [1993] 1 W.L.R. 23.

[49] See, for example, ss.30 and 33 of the Anti-terrorism, Crime and Security Act 2001 (c.24); and note that two provisions which were, in part, ousters of review were repealed by s.7 of the Nationality, Immigration and Asylum Act 2002 (c.41). And the notion of ousting supervisory jurisdiction is not a recent invention: see, for example, s.39 of the Small Holdings and Allotments Act 1908 (c.36) and *Ex p. Ringer* (1909) 25 T.L.R. 718.

[50] An even more extreme example was contained in clause 14 of the Asylum and Immigration (Treatment of Claimants, etc.) Bill 2003–04 as sent from the House of Commons to the House of Lords on March 3, 2004.
The relevant part of that clause provided as follows—
"(1) No court shall have any supervisory or other jurisdiction (whether statutory or inherent) in relation to the Tribunal.
(2) No court may entertain proceedings for questioning (whether by way of appeal or otherwise)—
    (a) any determination, decision or other action of the Tribunal (including a decision about jurisdiction and a decision under section 105A), . . .
(3) Subsections (1) and (2)—
    (a) prevent a court, in particular, from entertaining proceedings to determine whether a purported determination, decision or action of the Tribunal was a nullity by reason of—
        (i) lack of jurisdiction,
        (ii) irregularity,
        (iii) error of law,
        (iv) breach of natural justice, or
        (v) any other matter, but
    (b) do not prevent a court from—
        (i) reviewing a decision to issue a certificate under section 94 or 96 of this Act or under Schedule 3 to the Asylum and Immigration (Treatment of Claimants, etc.) Act 2004 (removal to safe country),
        (ii) entertaining proceedings to determine whether the Tribunal has acted in a way which is incompatible with a person's rights under Article 5 of the Human Rights Convention (liberty and security), or
        (iii) considering whether a member of the Tribunal has acted in bad faith.
(4) A court may consider whether a member of the Tribunal has acted in bad faith, in reliance on subsection (3)(b)(iii), only if satisfied that significant evidence has been adduced of—
    (a) dishonesty,
    (b) corruption, or
    (c) bias.
(5) Section 7(1) of the Human Rights Act 1998 (c.42) (claim that public authority has infringed Convention right) is subject to subsections (1) to (3) above.
(6) Nothing in this section shall prevent an appeal under section 2, 2B or 7 of the Special Immigration Appeals Commission Act 1997 (c.68) (appeals to and from Commission)."
Following criticism from the judiciary and others, however, the Government determined to withdraw and recast the provision. On introducing the Second Reading of the Bill the Lord Chancellor, Lord Falconer of Thoroton, said (HL Deb. March 15, 2004 cc.50–51)—
"As noble Lords will know, the central part of this Bill is Clause 14, which creates a unified

Section 44(2) of the British Nationality Act 1981[51] (which replicated s.26 of the British Nationality Act 1948[52]) provided—

"(2) The Secretary of State . . . shall not be required to assign any reason for the grant or refusal of any application under this Act the decision on which is at his discretion; and the decision of the Secretary of State . . . on any such application shall not be subject to appeal to, or review in, any court."

In s.33 of the Anti-terrorism, Crime and Security Act 2001[53] (certificate of Secretary of State that Refugee Convention does not apply to an appellant) subss.(8) and (9) provide—

"(8) No court may entertain proceedings for questioning—

(a) a decision or action of the Secretary of State in connection with certification under subsection (1),

(b) a decision of the Secretary of State in connection with an asylum claim (within the meaning given by section 113(1) of the Nationality, Immigration and Asylum Act 2002) in a case in respect of which he issues a certificate under subsection (1) above, or

(c) a decision or action of the Secretary of State taken as a consequence of the dismissal of all or part of an asylum appeal in pursuance of subsection (4).

---

appellate structure for asylum and immigration appeals.It is important that the appeals system is fair, but it must also provide speed and finality. . . .

"There remains considerable scope for delay. We have reduced delay in the initial decision process . . . but delays still exist in the appeals process. . . . Of course, people are able to exploit that delay; . . .

"I have listened carefully to the arguments put by the senior judiciary, including those of the Lord Chief Justice, the noble and learned Lord, Lord Woolf. I have also talked to my predecessor, my noble and learned friend Lord Irvine of Lairg, who has forcibly made representations about the Bill. I have read closely the arguments advanced in debate in another place, as well as the report by the Select Committee for Constitutional Affairs and by the Joint Committee on Human Rights.

"I believe that we can have the necessary judicial oversight of the system by the higher courts and obtain the aims of speed and reduction in abuse. These are aims which I believe we share. There are a variety of ways in which we could achieve this, and I am confident that we can find a solution which meets the needs of all. I am sure that noble Lords will want to work with us.

"In those circumstances, I am prepared to bring forward amendments to replace the judicial review ouster with a new system allowing oversight by the administrative court in those decisions.That system must ensure speed is increased and abuse is reduced. We need to concentrate on how these objectives should be achieved. The relationship between the single tier and the administrative court is important in this respect. No one disagrees that we should aim for a system where very few cases go to the High Court."

When this work went to print the final form of clause 14 of the Bill had not emerged.

[51] 1981 c.61.
[52] 1948 c.56.
[53] 2001 c.24.

"(9) Subsection (8) shall not prevent an appeal under section 7 of the Special Immigration Appeals Commission Act 1997 (appeal on point of law)."

A provision of that kind will have the effect of preventing the courts from adjudicating on a decision in certain circumstances in which they would otherwise have done so. It cannot, however, guarantee that the courts will not become involved—   **19.1.21**

(1) It takes a hearing before a judicial officer of some kind for a court to decline jurisdiction.

(2) Without calling into question the exercise of the discretion, there may be other aspects of the decision-making process upon which the courts may feel competent to adjudicate. So, for example, in *Gowa v Attorney General*[54] the court was prepared to examine the administrative circumstances as a result of which the Secretary of State claimed not to be in a position to exercise discretion under the 1948 Act.

(3) The courts have sometimes held that a provision preventing them from questioning a determination does not prevent them from deciding that something which purports to be a determination is in fact a nullity. See, for example, the leading case of *Anisminic Ltd v Foreign Compensation Commission*.[55]

A statutory provision for determining a particular class of dispute by arbitration impliedly ousts the jurisdiction of the High Court in relation to such disputes.[56]   **19.1.22**
The requirement of express words to confer or remove jurisdiction does not prevent the courts from exercising certain inherent jurisdictions in relation to certain matters. As Farwell J said in *Stevens v Chown*[57]—

"There is nothing, even when a statute creates an entirely new right and gives a special remedy, to prevent a court having equitable jurisdiction from granting an injunction to restrain the infringement of a newly created statutory right, unless the Act of Parliament creating the right provides a remedy which it enacts shall be the only remedy, subject only to this, that the right so created is such a right as the court under its original jurisdiction would take cognisance of."[58]

---

[54] [1985] 1 W.L.R. 1003, HL.
[55] [1969] 2 A.C. 147, HL.
[56] *Crisp v Bunbury* (1832) 8 Bing. 394, *Norwich Corporation v Norwich Tramways Co.* [1906] 2 K.B. 119, and *Re Kellner's Will Trusts* [1949] 2 All E.R. 43, 47.
[57] [1901] 1 Ch. 894, 904.
[58] But see Chapter 14, Section 1.

Presumption of notice

19.1.23 This presumption is expounded by Lord Steyn in *R. (Anufrijeva) v Secretary of State for the Home Department*[59] as follows—

> "Notice of a decision is required before it can have the character of a determination with legal effect because the individual concerned must be in a position to challenge the decision in the courts if he or she wises to do so. This is not a technical rule. It is simply an application of the right of access to justice. That is a fundamental and constitutional principle of our legal system . . .

> "This view is reinforced by the constitutional principle requiring the rule of law to be observed. That principle too requires that a constitutional state must accord to individuals the right to know of a decision before their rights can be adversely affected. The antithesis of such a state was described by Kafka: a state where the rights of individuals are overridden by hole in the corner decisions or knocks on doors in the early hours. That is not our system. I accept, of course, that there must be exceptions to this approach, notably in the criminal field, *e.g.* arrests and search warrants, where notification is not possible. . . .

> "Until the decision in *Ex parte Salem*[60] it had never been suggested that an uncommunicated administrative decision can bind an individual. It is an astonishingly unjust proposition. In our system of law surprise is regarded as the enemy of justice. Fairness is the guiding principle of our public law."

In summary, the courts will presume that a decision—particularly, but not necessarily exclusively, of a public authority—is not to have legal effect in relation to a person unless and until he has notice of it, and this presumption can be rebutted only by clear legislative language.[61]

Presumption of privilege

19.1.24 In *R. (Morgan Grenfell & Co. Ltd) v Special Commissioners of Income Tax*[62] the House of Lords decided that the right of citizens and companies to seek legal

---

[59] [2003] 3 W.L.R. 252, 265, HL.

[60] *R. v Secretary of State for the Home Department, Ex p. Salem* [1999] Q.B. 805, CA.

[61] Compare, however, *C. A. Webber (Transport) Ltd v Railtrack plc* [2004] 1 W.L.R. 320, CA in which the Court of Appeal found that s.23 of the Landlord and Tenant Act 1927 (c.36) created an irrebuttable presumption of service and was not subject to s.7 of the Interpretation Act 1978 (as to which see Chapter 22, para.22.1.12). While capable of causing injustice, the irrebuttable presumption was thought to be justifiable, both by reference to the Human Rights Act 1998 and generally, on the grounds of amounting to "a fair allocation of the risk of any failure of communication" and it being "neither unreasonable nor disproportionate to achieve certainty for landlords and tenants alike" (at 337, *per* Peter Gibson L.J.).

[62] [2002] 2 W.L.R. 1299.

advice in secure privacy is of sufficiently fundamental importance to require express statutory language or an unavoidable implication if it is to be overruled by statute.

Presumption of territorial limitation

The rebuttable presumption that an Act is not intended to apply to persons other than British citizens outside the United Kingdom is discussed in Chapter 11, Sections 1 and 2. **19.1.25**

Secondary legislation

The presumptions set out in this Chapter apply as much to secondary legislation as they do to primary legislation. **19.1.26**

The presumptions not only apply to subordinate legislation, but they are also relevant to the question of *vires*.[63] If it is to be presumed that primary legislation does not intend to do a particular thing unless express words are used, it can also be presumed that primary legislation may not permit subordinate legislation to do that thing, again unless the permission is expressed.

---

[63] See Chapter 3, Section 4.

CHAPTER 20

OTHER CANONS AND PRINCIPLES OF CONSTRUCTION

Introduction

Despite the clear move away from rigid application of rules towards a more **20.1.1** general and teleological search for the legislature's intention, a number of the canons of construction that have been in use for centuries by courts in the United Kingdom are of undoubted value as rules of thumb for exposing the legislative intention. This Chapter sets out these canons and explains something both of their original scope and of their recent application.

Some thoughts on the construction of certain common words and expressions will also be found in Chapter 8, Section 2.

The following rules and principles are expounded in this Chapter—

Purpose of canons

20.1.2 It is important to note at the outset that even in the times in which these canons were constructed and first applied, they were never intended to do more than elucidate the intention of the legislature in cases of doubt. They have no application, and have never had any application, in a case where the intention of the legislature is clear on its face.[1] This was acknowledged decades ago by the very judges who developed and applied these doctrines. Lord Russell of Killowen C.J., for example, said in *The Queen v Titterton*,[2] putting into context the rule of construction by reference to other Acts deemed to be in *pari materia*[3]—

> "The duty of the Court when called upon to construe an Act of Parliament is, I conceive, to read the Act itself, and if its language is clear to give effect to what the legislature has said. It is to my mind proper to refer to earlier Acts *in pari materia* only where there is ambiguity. And I can see no ambiguity here. The scheme of the Act of 1875 seems to me perfectly intelligible and coherent; and if one is to look beyond the language itself for justification in reason and principle for what the legislature has said, I think the explanation is in every way complete and satisfactory."[4]

Authority for canons

20.1.3 As to the authority for these canons and principles *Prestcold (Central) Ltd v Minister of Labour*[5] *per* Lord Diplock —

> "Modern statutes are drafted by professional legal draftsmen and intended to be read and understood by professional lawyers. As they create legal rights and liabilities, their meaning should be unambiguous and precise, and to aid precision certain habits of composition have been acquired by Parliamentary draftsmen which are familiar to professional lawyers and to the courts. These habits obtain recognition in the canons of statutory construction, though many of them are general rules of composition which any writer seeking clarity of expression is likely to follow, such as *expressio unius exclusio alterius*, *ejusdem generis*, and *noscitur a sociis*, though, unlike lawyers, he does not express them in the arcane obscurity of the Latin tongue. As regards rules of composition of this kind the main difference between a professional legal draftsman and any other kind of writer is that

---

[1] To follow a contrary approach would, of course, be to detract from the sovereign supremacy of Parliament, discussed in Chapter 1, Sections 1 and 2, by preferring a principle of common law to Parliament's express wish.

[2] [1895] 2 Q.B. 61.

[3] Discussed below.

[4] In other words, not only is there no ambiguity but nor is there any substantive anomaly.

[5] [1969] 1 All E.R. 69, 75, HL.

the Parliamentary draftsman is less likely to depart from them. But there are other habits of professional legal draftsmen which are less widely shared by other kinds of writers or not shared by them at all. Some expressions in common use in documents dealing with legal rights or obligations acquire in a legal context a special meaning different from, or more precise than, their meaning in common speech—they become 'terms of art'. Again, the habit of a legal draftsman is to eschew synonyms. He uses the same words throughout the document to express the same thing or concept, and consequently if he uses different words the presumption is that he means a different thing or concept. Another habit, relevant to this case, is that a legal draftsman aims at uniformity in the structure of his draft. If he has thought it desirable to qualify what he has stated in one part of the document and has omitted to qualify a statement of a similar kind in another part of the document, the presumption is that the latter statement is to be understood as not being subject to a similar qualification, even though the natural meaning of the second statement would otherwise have been understood, *sub silentio*, as subject to it.

"As the Standard Industrial Classification was prepared by statisticians to be read and understood, not primarily by lawyers but by those engaged in managing industrial and commercial establishments, these distinctions between legal and non-legal draftsmanship must be borne in mind . . . "

It is interesting to note that whether or not these canons emerged in their traditional form as a result of formalistic drafting and construction, their substantive foundation in justice and sense is evidenced by the degree to which they, or something to the same purpose, are found in other judicial systems.[6]

The Mischief Rule—The rules in *Heydon's Case*

The most firmly established rules for construing an obscure enactment are those laid down by the Barons of the Exchequer in *Heydon's case*.[7] These rules have for centuries been cited with approval and acted upon.[8]

The rules are as follows—

20.1.4

---

[6] One of the earliest of which is the system of Biblical exegesis developed by the ancient Rabbis for the purpose of the judicial development and application of principles of the Bible—see the *Beraiso d'Rebbi Yishmoel* in the introduction to the Midrashic writing known as the *Sifro*: and note that the principles stated in that place include *expressio unius, ejusdem generis, pari materia* and others.
[7] (1584) 3 Co. Rep. 7a. See 1 Bl. Com. Ed. Hargrave, p.87, note 38.
[8] For helpful and explicit examples of the application of these rules see *Salkeld v Johnson* (1848) 2 Ex. 256, 272, *Gartside v Inland Revenue* Commissioners [1968] A.C. 553, 612 *per* Lord Reid, *Coutts & Co. v Inland Revenue Commissioners* [1964] A.C. 1393. For recent examples see *R. v Secretary of State for the Environment, Transport and the Regions and another, Ex p. Spath Holme Ltd* [2001] 2 A.C. 349, HL (and in particular that part of the opinion of Lord Nicholls of Birkenhead appended to this work—Appendix, Extract 21); *Maclaine Watson & Co Ltd v Department of Trade and Industry and related appeals* [1988] 3 All E.R. 257, 337, CA.

"That for the sure and true interpretation of all statutes in general (be they penal[9] or beneficial, restrictive or enlarging of the common law), four things are to be discerned and considered—

(1) What was the common law before the making of the Act.
(2) What was the mischief and defect for which the common law did not provide.
(3) What remedy the Parliament hath resolved and appointed to cure the disease of the commonwealth.[10]
(4) The true reason of the remedy.

"And then the office of all the judges is always to make such construction as shall suppress the mischief and advance the remedy, and to suppress subtle inventions and evasions for the continuance of the mischief and *pro privato commodo*, and to add force and life to the cure and remedy according to the true intent of the makers of the Act *pro bono publico*."

20.1.5 These rules are still in full force and effect, with the addition that regard must now be had not only to the common law but also to prior legislation and its judicial interpretation. As Lindley M.R. said in *Re Mayfair Property Co.*[11]—

"In order properly to interpret any statute it is as necessary now as it was when Lord Coke reported *Heydon's Case* to consider how the law stood when the statute to be construed was passed, what the mischief was for which the old law did not provide, and the remedy provided by the statute to cure that mischief."

The concept of the mischief at which legislation is aimed is of considerable antiquity and while the word "mischief" has an antique flavour the concept is still of great service in statutory construction. While the same concept is sometimes put into different and more modern language, the expression is still found in the language of the law and is found in many modern decided cases.[12]

Supporting legislative intent

20.1.6 The rule requiring that *verba ita sunt intelligenda ut res magis valeat quam pereat*[13] requires that where possible the intention of the legislature is not to be treated as vain or left to operate in the air. The result is that if two constructions of a provision are possible on its face, and one would clearly advance the

---

[9] In *Attorney-General v Sillem* (1864) 2 H. & C. 431, 509 Pollock C.B. held that 'penal' in *Heydon's Case* meant creating a disability or forfeiture.
[10] Meaning here no more than something along the lines of "the public good".
[11] [1898] 2 Ch. 28, 35.
[12] See, for a recent example, Brooke L.J. in *Donoghue v Folkestone Properties* [2003] 2 W.L.R. 1138, 1159, CA.
[13] See *Curtis v Stovin* (1889) 22 Q.B.D. 513, 517 *per* Bowen L.J.

legislative purpose and the other would clearly achieve little or nothing, the former is to be preferred.

This is a particular example of a presumption in favour of validity that the courts apply to the construction of any document. Both the nature of the rule and its original limitations are expressed as follows by Lord Greene M.R. in *Hankey v Clavering*[14]—

> "It is perfectly true that in construing such a document,[15] as in construing all documents, the court in a case of ambiguity will lean in favour of reading the document in such a way as to give it validity, but I dissent entirely from the proposition that, where a document is clear and specific, but inaccurate on some matter, such as that of date, it is possible to ignore the inaccuracy and substitute the correct date or other particular because it appears that the error was inserted by a slip."

The rule has been expressly applied in hundreds of cases over the decades, and has doubtless influenced thousands of decisions in which it has not been expressly referred to. It is, after all, little more than that which common sense would anyway demand, as is the case for many canons and principles of construction. Of the importance and effect of the rule Stephenson L.J. said in *Thames Water Authority v Elmbridge Borough Council*[16]— **20.1.7**

> "For some centuries our courts have been applying to the benevolent interpretation of written instruments of all kinds, including statutes, the common sense principle preserved in Latin as 'ut res magis valeat quam pereat': Coke upon Littleton 36a; *Broom's Legal Maxims*, 10th ed. (1939), p.361.
>
> "By applying that principle they have been able, not only to make sense of near nonsense but also to give effect to what is good and enforce what is valid, while refusing to enforce what is bad and giving no effect to what is invalid."

This approach requires the construer of legislation to consider what is intended to be achieved by the legislation, and to this extent it goes together with the rules in *Heydon's Case*.[17] To achieve the obvious intent the courts will be prepared even to apply that interpretation of the words used which is less linguistically apparent. As Lord Simon L.C. said in *Nokes v Doncaster Amalgamated Collieries Ltd*[18]—

---

[14] [1942] 2 K.B. 326, 330.
[15] A leasehold termination notice.
[16] [1983] Q.B. 570, 585.
[17] See below.
[18] [1940] A.C. 1014, 1022, HL; see also *Shannon Realties Ltd v Ville de St Michael* [1924] A.C. 185, 192, *I.T.C. v Gibbs* [1942] A.C. 402, 414 and *Gill v Donald Humberstone & Co. Ltd* [1963] 1 W.L.R. 929, 933–934 *per* Lord Reid.

"If the choice is between two interpretations, the narrower of which would fail to achieve the manifest purpose of the legislation, we should avoid a construction which would reduce the legislation to futility and should rather accept the bolder construction based on the view that Parliament would legislate only for the purpose of bringing about an effective result."

Public policy

20.1.8   It is sometimes said that where a provision falls to be construed as a result of its terms being insufficiently clear to establish a single meaning without an application of the rules of construction, matters of public policy may be considered.

In so far as what is meant by "public policy" in this context is the policy intention of the legislature, recourse to public policy is both uncontentious and clearly supported by precedent.[19]

But in so far as what is meant by "public policy" is the courts' understanding of the public's or the legislature's general intentions in relation to social matters, recourse to public policy would lead to the kind of judicial legislation that the courts strain so hard to avoid, as has been shown elsewhere in this work.[20] As Taunton J. said in *R. v St. Gregory*[21] speaking of an earlier decision—

"In that case the judgment was rested partly on the consideration of public policy, a very questionable and unsatisfactory ground, because men's minds differ so much on the nature and extent of public policy."[22]

The balance to be struck in this respect between judicial legislation on general social grounds and giving full effect to the intention of the legislature is expressed by Lord Selborne in *Hardy v Fothergill*[23]—

"It is not, I conceive, for your lordships or for any other court to decide such questions as this under the influence of considerations of policy, except so far as that policy may be apparent from, or at least consistent with, the

---

[19] See Chapter 17; see also *R. v Hipswell* (1828) 8 B. & C. 466, 471, *Lord Provost etc.of Glasgow v Hillhead* (1885) 12 R. (Sc.) 864, 872, *R. B. Policies at Lloyd's v Butler* [1949] 2 All E.R. 226, 227, *Duncan v Aberdeen County Council* (1936) 106 L.J.P.C. 1, *Powell Lane Manufacturing Co. v Putnam* [1931] 2 K.B. 305, *Newman Manufacturing Co. v Marrables* [1931] 2 K.B. 297, *Gardiner v Sevenoaks R.D.C.* (1950) 66 T.L.R. (Pt. 1) 1091, and *Caledonian Railway v North British Railway* (1881) 6 App. Cas. 114.

[20] See, in particular, Chapter 14, Section 1 and Chapters 17 and 18.

[21] (1834) 2 A. & E. 99, 107.

[22] See also "Public policy is always an unsafe and treacherous ground for judicial decision"—*Janson v Driefontein Consolidated Mines Ltd* [1902] A.C. 484, 500 *per* Lord Davey; or "Public policy is a restive horse, and when you get astride of it, there is no knowing where it will carry you."—*Amicable Society v Bolland (Fauntleroy's Case)* (1830) 4 Bligh. (N.S.) 194; 2 Dow. & Cl. 1 *per* Burroughs J.

[23] (1888) 13 App. Cas.351, 358.

language of the legislature in the statute or statutes upon which the question depends."[24]

Casus omissus

The passage of Lord Greene's speech in *Hankey v Clavering* cited above records **20.1.9** that the desirability of supporting the legislative purpose does not permit the courts to supply actual deficiencies and remedy actual errors. This was originally the general approach of the courts to ensure that they did not stray into usurping the legislative function. A specific instance of this approach is the rule that a *casus omissus* is not to be created or supplied, so that a statute may not be extended to meet a case for which provision has clearly and undoubtedly not been made.

This rule could once be stated in very strong and broad terms. Lord Halsbury said in *Mersey Docks v Henderson*[25]—

"No case can be found to authorise any court to alter a word so as to produce a *casus omissus*."

And the Judicial Committee of the Privy Council said in *Crawford v Spooner*[26]—

"We cannot aid the legislature's defective phrasing of an Act, we cannot add and mend, and, by construction, make up deficiencies which are left there".

The reason for this traditional refusal to supply deficiencies, even where their **20.1.10** cause is obviously error or inattention and even where they cause injustice, is expounded by Lord Brougham in *Gwynne v Burnell*[27]—

"If we depart from the plain and obvious meaning . . . we do not in truth construe the Act, but alter it. We add words to it, or vary the words in which its provisions are couched. We supply a defect which the legislature could easily have supplied, and are making the law, not interpreting it. That becomes peculiarly improper in dealing with a modern statute, because the extreme conciseness of the ancient statutes was the only ground for the sort of legislative interpretation frequently put upon their words by the judges.

---

[24] See, therefore, Barton J. in the Australian case of *Tasmania v Commonwealth* (1904) 1 C.L.R. 329, 349—"The intention of an instrument is to be gathered from the obvious facts of its history—if we at all go outside the four corners of the instrument itself and the policy logically to be deduced from its express words."

[25] (1888) 13 App. Cas.595, 602.

[26] (1846) 6 Moore P. C. 1, 8–9.

[27] (1840) 7 Cl. & F. 572, 696.

The prolixity of modern statutes, so very remarkable of late, affords no grounds to justify such a sort of interpretation."

The thought is put simply in the Latin tag *boni judicis est dicere, non jus dare.*

Although *casus omissus* is still a rule of considerable importance, and the judges' reluctance to usurp the legislative function is as real as ever,[28] the courts are nowadays prepared to go a little further than was once the case in supplying deficiencies, where there is no reason to doubt what the legislature's intention really was, whether or not they have accurately achieved it. This will be seen by contrasting with the statements of Lords Halsbury and Brougham cited above the following relatively modern statement of the rule of *casus omissus* by Scarman L.J. in *Western Bank Ltd v Schindler*[29]—

"Judicial legislation is not an option open to an English judge. Our courts are not required, as are, for instance, the Swiss courts (see the Swiss Civil Code, articles 1 and 2), to declare and insert into legislation rules which the judge would have put there, had he been the legislator. But our courts do have the duty of giving effect to the intention of Parliament, if it be possible, even though the process requires a strained construction of the language used or the insertion of some words in order to do so: see *Luke v Inland Revenue Commissioners*.[30] The line between judicial legislation, which our law does not permit, and judicial interpretation in a way best designed to give effect to the intention of Parliament is not an easy one to draw. Suffice it to say that before our courts can imply words into an Act the statutory intention must be plain and the insertion not too big, or too much at variance with the language in fact used by the legislature. The courts will strain against having to take the first of the three courses I mentioned; that is to say, leaving unfilled the 'casus omissus'."

20.1.11 The phrase "will strain against" is particularly telling when contrasted with Lord Halsbury's words.

The decreased reluctance of the courts to supply deficiencies, and the range of techniques that they will employ for that purpose, is well illustrated in the case of *Confederation of Passenger Transport UK v The Humber Bridge Board (Secretary of State for Transport, Local Government and the Regions, interested party).*[31]

(1) The Court of Appeal was faced with a challenge to the charging of tolls on the Humber Bridge in respect of large buses using the bridge, on the simple

---

[28] Or, indeed, stronger than it used to be—see Chapter 14, para.14.1.3.
[29] [1977] 1 Ch. 18–19, CA.
[30] [1963] A.C. 557, 577, HL *per* Lord Reid.
[31] [2004] Q.B. 310, CA.

ground that none of the orders under which the charges are levied[32] prescribed a toll for that category of transport.

(2) Clarke L.J. held that this was simply a mistake of the draftsman and that it could be repaired by reference to a combination of the Explanatory Notes to the instruments, a decision letter of the Secretary of State and the report of an inspector.

(3) It was plain from the language used that a mistake was made by the maker of the 1997 Order and the Order was neither clear nor unambiguous on its face.

(4) Without adding a reference to large buses, the Order was an absurdity.

(5) The explanatory note, the decision letter and the inspector's report into the bridge tolls were all legitimate extraneous aids to identify the purpose of the Order, which should on its true construction include the words "large bus".

(6) The 2002 Order as drafted was also ambiguous or obscure and productive of absurdity. Its intended purpose was to increase maximum tolls across the board, including for large buses. A failure to provide a maximum toll for large buses could only have been inadvertent or perhaps incompetent or inept.

(7) The draftsman could not have intended that the Board should not be permitted to charge for large buses at all.[33]

In reaching his decision Clarke L.J. relied on a recent decision of the House of Lords—*Inco Europe Limited v First Choice Distribution (A Firm)*[34]—and, in particular, on the following passages of the opinion of Lord Nicholls of Birkenhead— **20.1.12**

"I am left in no doubt that, for once, the draftsman slipped up. The sole object of paragraph 37(2) in Schedule 3 was to amend s.18(1)(g) by substituting a new paragraph (g) that would serve the same purpose regarding the Act of 1996 as the original paragraph (g) had served regarding the Act of 1979. The language used was not apt to achieve this result. Given that the intended object of paragraph 37(2) is so plain, the paragraph should

---

[32] The Humber Bridge (Revision of Tolls and Vehicle Classification) Orders 1997, 2000 and 2002.
[33] "There can, to my mind, be no doubt that the draftsman omitted a reference to 'large bus' by mistake, not only because of the reference to 'large bus' in the definition but also because of its historical context (to which I return below) and because the Explanatory Note states that one of the 'changes now made' is '(c) the toll for good (sic) vehicles over 7.5 tonnes maximum weight with 2 axles and buses and coaches with 17 or more seats is increased from £6.50 to £9.20.' To my mind that makes it clear beyond a peradventure that the draftsman omitted a reference to large buses by mistake and that, had he not made a mistake, he would have included them in class 4 with a new maximum toll of £9.20." (para.19).
[34] [2000] 1 W.L.R. 586.

be read in a manner which gives effect to the parliamentary intention. Thus the new s.18(1)(g), substituted by paragraph 37(2), should be read as confined to decisions of the High Court under sections of Part I which make provision regarding an appeal from such decisions.In other words, 'from any decision of the High Court under that Part' is to be read as meaning 'from any decision of the High Court under a section in that Part which provides for an appeal from such decision'.

"I freely acknowledge that this interpretation of s.18(1)(g) involves reading words into the paragraph. It has long been established that the role of the courts in construing legislation is not confined to resolving ambiguities in statutory language. The court must be able to correct obvious drafting errors. In suitable cases, in discharging its interpretative function the court will add words, or omit words or substitute words. Some notable instances are given in Professor Sir Rupert Cross' admirable opuscule, Statutory Interpretation, 3rd ed., pp. 93–105. He comments, at page 103:

> 'In omitting or inserting words the judge is not really engaged in a hypothetical reconstruction of the intentions of the drafter or the legislature, but is simply making as much sense as he can of the text of the statutory provision read in its appropriate context and within the limits of the judicial role.'

20.1.13   "This power is confined to plain cases of drafting mistakes.The courts are ever mindful that their constitutional role in this field is interpretative. They must abstain from any course which might have the appearance of judicial legislation. A statute is expressed in language approved and enacted by the legislature. So the courts exercise considerable caution before adding or omitting or substituting words.Before interpreting a statute in this way the court must be abundantly sure of three matters: (1) the intended purpose of the statute or provision in question; (2) that by inadvertence the draftsman and Parliament failed to give effect to that purpose in the provision in question; and (3) the substance of the provision Parliament would have made, although not necessarily the precise words Parliament would have used, had the error in the Bill been noticed. The third of these conditions is of crucial importance. Otherwise any attempt to determine the meaning of the enactment would cross the boundary between construction and legislation: see Lord Diplock in *Jones v Wrotham Park Settled Estates*.[35] In the present case these three conditions are fulfilled.

"Sometimes, even when these conditions are met, the court may find itself inhibited from interpreting the statutory provision in accordance with what it is satisfied was the underlying intention of Parliament. The alteration in language may be too far-reaching. In *Western Bank Ltd v Schindler*,[36]

---

[35] [1980] A.C. 74, 105.
[36] [1977] Ch. 1, 18.

Scarman L.J. observed that the insertion must not be too big, or too much at variance with the language used by the legislature. Or the subject matter may call for a strict interpretation of the statutory language, as in penal legislation. None of these considerations apply in the present case. Here, the court is able to give effect to a construction of the statute which accords with the intention of the legislature."

What emerges from this is that, in essence, where it is inconceivable that the legislature did not contemplate a particular case, but it is clear that the draftsman simply inadvertently omitted it, the *casus omissus* rule will not prevent the courts from supplying the deficiency. Whether this is a statement of what has always been the case or, as seems likely, a significant modification of the *casus omissus* rule, is of academic interest only.[37] What matters for present purposes is only that this important qualification of the rule exists and, as will immediately be seen, has the potential to be applied both widely and flexibly, since the difference between a case which the legislature did contemplate and one which they did not but would have provided for had they thought of it is more distinct in theory than in the light of what one knows about the realities of the legislative process.

For a particular class of case in which other desiderata will erode or modify the *casus omissus* rule see Chapter 12, para.12.1.4 (deprivation of long-standing right to be avoided in the absence of express words or clear implication, by supply of an omission if necessary). **20.1.14**

While there is a clear line of recent authority permitting the courts to supply what is clearly a deficiency, in the sense of a case for which it can be clearly presumed the legislature intended to provide, that is a very far cry from permitting the courts to add words to legislation wherever they think something has been left out that could well have been included. The following dictum of Lord Bridge of Harwich in *Holden & Co. v Crown Prosecution Service (No.2)*[38] remains true[39]—

"The rule of general application which limits the court's power to read into legislation words which the draftsman has not used is, even in today's

---

[37] It is, for example, debatable whether *R. v Dyott* (1882) 9 Q.B.D. 47 would be decided differently today in accordance with the three principles enunciated by Lord Nicholls: but it is quite possible that in attempting to supply the legislature's deficiencies in that case one would fall at the third hurdle, being unsure of what provision for notice the legislature would have chosen to make in the absence of a church or chapel. Less debatable, however, is the case of *North Eastern Railway v Leadgate* (1870) L.R. 5 Q.B. 157: the comments of Cockburn C.J. at 161 suggest that all three conditions were satisfied. There are, however, cases of antiquity in which the courts have been prepared to supply a deficiency of detail where the omission appeared both unlikely to have been intended and likely to frustrate the operation of the statute—see, for example, *Cookson v Lee* (1854) 23 L.J. Ch. 473, 475, HL *per* Lord Cranworth L.C.

[38] [1994] 1 A.C. 22, 33, HL.

[39] See, for recent application, *R. v Moore* [2003] 1 W.L.R. 2170, 2173, CA *per* Rose J.

climate of purposive construction, still an important rule which cannot be disregarded.

> 'It is a strong thing to read into an Act of Parliament words which are not there, and in the absence of clear necessity it is a wrong thing to do' *Thompson v Goold & Co.*[40] *per* Lord Mersey.
> 'We are not entitled to read words into an Act of Parliament unless clear reason for it is to be found within the four corners of the Act itself' *Vickers, Sons & Maxim Ltd v Evans*[41] *per* Lord Loreburn L.C."

20.1.15   The distinction to be drawn is between supplying a deficiency without which the Act is incomplete in its own terms ("within its four corners") and seeking to expand the policy of the Act so as to deal with an ancillary matter for which the legislature did not provide, although they might have chosen to do so had they thought of it. Contrasting *Inco Europe* with *Holden* makes the point clear: a system for the regulation of traffic that operates by reference to classes of transport must not be allowed to fail because one class has not been provided for in one respect, provided that it is clear what provision can be presumed to have been intended for that class. But it is not integral to the efficacy of the system of prosecutions that a particular class of costs should be paid from central funds, however desirable it might be that they should be so paid.

20.1.16   A good example of the distinction is provided by *R. v Roberts*[42] in which the Court of Appeal refused to allow land adjacent to areas where the public have access to be construed as being within the expression "public place" for the purposes of s.139 of the Criminal Justice Act 1988,[43] despite the fact that harm of the kind designed to be prevented by the section could be caused from that place (and therefore Parliament might well have wished to expand the section to include adjacent areas had the point been raised during the passage of the legislation).

The reluctance of the courts to be drawn into legislating in the guise of construing will be particularly acute where the substance of the legislation is politically or socially sensitive and where the words used by the legislation imply that Parliament has already set the lines to be observed to the best of its ability. Note, for example, the following passage of the judgment of Wall J. in *Evans v Amicus Healthcare Ltd*[44]—

> "In my judgment, this is pre-eminently an area in which it is for Parliament to legislate, and in relation to which a generous margin of appreciation is appropriate. . . .

---

[40] [1910] A.C. 409, 420, HL.
[41] [1910] A.C. 444, 445, HL.
[42] [2004] 1 W.L.R. 181, CA.
[43] 1988 c.33.
[44] [2003] 3 All E.R. 903, 955–956 Fam.

"In my judgment, in this sensitive area of the law, it is for Parliament to legislate. It is an area in which the courts have only a limited role to play. Parliament has chosen a carefully structured system of regulation, with clear rules based on mutual consent and the interests of the unborn child. The approach to statutory construction set out by Lord Bingham of Cornhill in *Quintavalle C.N.R....* and Lord Hope of Craighead in *Ex parte Kebeline* ... applies. If any changes in the law are appropriate, it is for Parliament to make them."

See also Chapter 15.

Ejusdem generis or *noscitur a sociis*

The rule of law known as *ejusdem generis* or *noscitur a sociis* can be expounded   **20.1.17** through the following dictum of Lord Campbell in *R. v Edmundson*[45]—

"I accede to the principle laid down . . . that, where there are general words following particular and specific words, the general words must be confined to things of the same kind as those specified."[46]

A helpful early example of the application of this rule is found in *Scales v Pickering*.[47] A private Act empowered a water company to "break up the soil and pavement of roads, highways, footways, commons, streets, lanes, alleys, passages and public places," provided that they did not enter on private land without the consent of the owner. To the contention that this authorised the company to break up the soil of a private field in which there was a public footway Best C.J. said—

"Construing the word 'footway' from the company in which it is found . . . the legislature appear to have meant those paved footways in large towns which are too narrow to admit of horses and carriages."

Park J. added "The word 'footway' here *noscitur a sociis*".

---

[45] (1859) 28 LJM.C. 213, 215.
[46] Note that in the last edition of this work the dictum of Lord Campbell was given to supplement the following dictum of Lord Bramwell in *Great Western Railway v Swindon, &c. Railway* (1884) 9 App. Cas. 787, 808—"As a matter of ordinary construction, where several words are followed by a general expression which is as much applicable to the first and other words as to the last, that expression is not limited to the last, but applies to all. For instance, 'horses, oxen, pigs and sheep, from whatever country they may come'—the latter words would apply to horses as much as to sheep.". But this is either a distinct variant of the *ejusdem generis* rule or a different rule altogether, namely that general qualifying words apply to all that goes before them, and it is of doubtful application to modern legislative practice: the example given by Lord Bramwell would be regarded today as distinctly poor drafting.
[47] (1828) 4 Bing. 448, 452–453.

20.1.18   It will be seen from this example that the rule, by whichever maxim it is known, is like so many other rules of construction a mere application of common sense. If Parliament legislates that "A landlord may not prevent a tenant from keeping in the leased premises a dog, cat or other animal" it is reasonable to assume that in providing for the keeping of an "other animal" Parliament contemplated only those that were reasonably similar in their relevant characteristics to those specified, and that a fully grown crocodile would not, for example, be within the obvious legislative intention.

Being an application of sense the rule has to be applied with common sense and with proper caution. As Lord Diplock said in *Customs and Excise Commissioners v Viva Gas Appliances Ltd*[48]—

> "The maxim *noscitur a sociis* may be a useful aid to statutory interpretation, but the contexts in which it is applicable are limited. In the case of a word which is capable of bearing various shades of meaning, the fact that it is included in a list of words of greater precision in which some common characteristic can be discerned may enable one to say that the chameleon word takes its colour from those other words and of its possible meanings bears that which shares the characteristic that is common to the other."[49]

Of course nowadays the legislature would be likely to attempt some kind of qualifying description for the residual category, such as "or other domesticated animal": a description of that kind, however, may restrict the grey area but is unlikely to dispel it entirely. Were a court to reject the suggestion that a crocodile that had been to some extent tamed was within the meaning of "domesticated animal" for these purposes, it would in effect be applying the *ejusdem generis* notion, whether by name or not.[50]

The inclusion of words along the lines of "or <u>any</u> other" will sometimes be sufficient to exclude the *eiusdem generis* construction.[51]

---

[48] [1984] 1 All E.R. 112, 116, HL.

[49] See also "Unless you can find a category, there is no room for the application of the *ejusdem generis* doctrine"—*Tillmans & Co. v S.S. Knutsford* [1908] 2 K.B. 385, 403 *per* Farwell L.J.

[50] For recent express applications of the principle see *Shamoon v Chief Constable of the Royal Ulster Constabulary* [2003] 2 All E.R. 26, 37, HL, *Skenderaj v Secretary of State for the Home Department* [2002] 4 All E.R. 555, 561, CA and *Adan v Secretary of State for the Home Department* [1997] 2 All E.R. 723, CA; note also "In my view, in the end, having tried to bear in mind what in 1921 a man might be thinking when he sat down to draft this appointment and to make this reservation, I have to go back to the precise words of it and try to understand those words in the light of such general history as I can gather and the natural meaning of the words. The phrase, I repeat, was 'all game woodcocks snipe and other wild fowl hares rabbits and fish'. To my mind, there is a plain implication in the first eight words of noscitur a sociis: phrase 'other wild fowl', attached as it is to the end of the phrase 'game woodcocks snipe', gives one a feeling that in that collocation of words the draftsman was speaking about feathered creatures. The way he goes on by referring next to 'hares rabbits', being things which are mammals as apart from 'game woodcocks snipe and other fowl', gives to my mind a flavour that the whole of the first phrase of that reservation has to do with birds."—*Inglewood Investment Co Ltd v Forestry Commission* [1988] 1 All E.R. 783, 789–90, Ch. *per* Harman J.

[51] See the House of Lords' decision in *Larsen v Sylvester & Co.* [1908] A.C. 295 as discussed in *Massey v Boulden* [2003] 2 All E.R. 87, CA.

Precedent

In pursuance of the application of the common law requiring certain courts to follow decisions of certain other courts, the question sometimes arises whether a court is bound to follow a decision of an equal or superior court in relation to the interpretation of a provision which has been repealed an re-enacted. In *R. v Muhamad*[52] the Court of Appeal affirmed that the re-enactment of a provision which has been the subject of a decided case is merely a reason why the courts should be more than ordinarily cautious in overruling the earlier interpretation.

20.1.19

Use of context

An obvious but important rule for approaching the construction of a piece of legislation is to look at the provision concerned in the context of the legislation as a whole.[53] This is a rule of ancient origin, and one which owes its authority to common sense.[54]

20.1.20

As Coke said—

> "The office of a good expositor of an Act of Parliament is to make construction on all parts together, and not of one part only by itself—*nemo enim aliquam partem recte intelligere potest antequam totum iterum atque iterum perlegerit*".[55]

> "It is the most natural and genuine exposition of a statute to construe one part of a statute by another part of the same statute, for that best expresseth the meaning of the makers ... and this exposition is *ex visceribus actus*."[56]

---

[52] [2003] 2 W.L.R. 1050, 1057 CA.

[53] As for the extent to which the context establishes a spirit of the law transcending the letter, see Chapter 12, paras 12.5.3—12.5.8 and, in particular, the quotation from Sir Roundell Palmer in relation to the Collier appointment. The reason, of course, why the obvious undermining of the spirit of the law was not the basis of a successful challenge to the appointment was that no question of construction arose: the law clearly made certain judges eligible for appointment to the Judicial Committee and Collier was undoubtedly appointed as a judge of the relevant class. It is an open question whether a challenge might be founded today in similar circumstances questioning, on *Wednesbury* grounds, the legality of the decision to appoint a judge purely in order to translate him immediately to another office. But as a matter of statutory construction no point arises. See also in the context of the notion of the spirit of an enactment, Jessel M.R. in *Re Bethlem Hospital* (1875) L.R. 19 Eq. 457, 459—"[There is still] such a thing as construing an Act according to its intent, though not according to its words.", a concept applied by Scott L.J. in *Barber v Pigden* [1937] 1 K.B. 664, 677.

[54] One of the earliest exponents of the rule of construction by reference to context is said to have been Sir Thomas Moore—"Here I will remark, that no one ever lived who did not at first ascertain the meaning of words, and from them gather the meaning of the sentences which they compose—no one, I say, with one single exception, and that is our own Thomas Moore. For he is wont to gather the force of the words from the sentences in which they occur, especially in his study of Greek. This is not contrary to grammar, but above it, and an instinct of genius." (*Pace*, quoted in Bridgett's *Life of More*, p.12).

[55] *The Lincoln College Case* (1595) 3 Co. Rep. 58b.

[56] I Inst. 381, 1 b.

As in the case of all these rules, however, the use of context is designed only for the elucidation of what the legislature has said where there is any doubt about its meaning. It is not a method of changing or undermining the clear meaning of words used.[57]

The rule advocating the use of context for the elucidation of meaning is sometimes referred to as the rule of exposition *ex visceribus actus*, construction within the four corners of the Act.

This rule has been cited and acted upon in a large number of cases, ancient and modern.[58]

20.1.21   When statutes were fashioned out of a small number of long sentences, or even one long sentence, the context had to be fashioned from more or less the whole statute. Now that statutes are divided into short sections, one should start to assess the context from the section in which the relevant expression occurs, and then move gradually out into the surrounding provisions.[59]

Immediate context, meaning immediately contingent words, can often have a contextual meaning wholly different to that which either word would bear on its own. As Somervell L.J. said in *Lee v Showmen's Guild of Great Britain*[60]—

> "I do not think that if the words 'unfair competition' stood alone they are apt to describe what happened here. It is often fallacious in considering the meaning of a phrase consisting of two words to find a meaning which each has separately and then infer that the two together cover the combination so arrived at. The two together may, as here, have acquired a special meaning of their own. In any event, the phrase here has to be read in the context of the rule . . . ".

See also paras 17.1.12—17.1.16.

---

[57] See Chapter 17; and note *Warburton v Loveland* (1832) 2 D. & Cl. 480, 500, HL—"No rule of construction can require that when the words of one part of a statute convey a clear meaning it shall be necessary to introduce another part of a statute for the purpose of controlling or diminishing the efficacy of the first part."

[58] For some older cases see *Brett v Brett* (1826) 3 Addams 210, 216, *Bywater v Brandling* (1828) 7 B. & C. 643, 660, *R. v Mallow Union Guardians* (1860) 12 Ir.C.L.R. 35, 40, *Ex p. St. Sepulchre's* (1864) 33 L.J. Ch. 372, 375, *Colquhoun v Brooks* (1889) 14 App. Cas. 493, 506, *Mersey Docks, &c. Board v Henderson* (1888) 13 App. Cas. 595, 599 and *Attorney-General v Prince Ernest Augustus of Hanover* [1957] A.C. 436, 473 *per* Lord Somerville—"It is unreal to proceed as if the court looked first at the provision in dispute without knowing whether it was contained in a Finance Act or a Public Health Act. The title and general scope of the Act constitute the background of the context. When a court comes to the Act itself, bearing in mind any relevant extraneous matters, there is, in my opinion, one compelling rule. The whole or any part of the Act may be referred to and relied on." For a recent cases, which does not refer to the rule by its Latin tag but rather discusses the question of the use of context in construing legislation, see *Oliver Ashworth (Holdings) Ltd v Ballard (Kent) Ltd* [1999] 2 All E.R. 791, CA.

[59] *Spencer v Metropolitan Board of Works* (1882) 22 Ch. D. 142, 162 *per* Jessel M.R.

[60] [1952] 2 Q.B. 329, 338, CA.

Presumption of clear language

The rule has been stated above[61] that where the meaning of the language of legislation is clear, effect is to be given to that meaning, without it being necessary or proper to consider further the desirability of the result or the application of any other rule of construction.

20.1.22

It can happen that there are two ways to express a particular intention, one of which will convey the intention more clearly than the other but both of which are linguistically adequate. If so, it is proper to conclude that if the legislature uses the less clear expression it does so because it is not trying to convey the intention concerned at all. At that point, one concludes that the intention of the legislature is not clear on the face of the language used (despite the fact that the language would have been considered sufficiently clear to express the intention had no more obvious route been available) and it therefore becomes appropriate to apply the canons and rules of construction set out in this Chapter and elsewhere.[62]

Presumption of meaning

In approaching statutory construction the courts will generally assume that every word used by the legislature is intended to have some legislative effect.[63]

20.1.23

This is not, however, a rule without exceptions. Nor is it one given equal weight by all judges.[64]

For one thing, it has always been common to include a certain amount of material in legislation that is purely and clearly explanatory.[65]

---

[61] Chapter 17.

[62] See *Attorney-General v Sillem* (1864) 2 H. & C. 431, 515 & 526 *per* Pollock C.B.—especially: "If this had been the object of our legislature it might have been accomplished by the simplest possible piece of legislation; it might have been expressed in language so clear that no human being could entertain a doubt about it, instead of the awkward, difficult, and doubtful clause which it is admitted on the party of the prosecution we have to deal with"; see also *Waugh v Middleton* (1853) 8 Ex. 352, 358 and *Dover Gaslight Co. v Mayor, &c. of Dover* (1855) I Jur.(N.S.) 813.

[63] *R. v Berchet* (1690) 1 Show. 108 (as cited in *R. v Bishop of Oxford* (1879) 4 Q.B.D. 245, 261) and *Harcourt v Fox* (1693) 1 Show. 506, 532. See also *Cooper v Slade* (1858) 6 HLC. 672, 675 *per* Bramwell B. and *East London Railway v Whitechurch* (1874) L.R. 7 H.L. 81, 91. For recent cases applying this rule see *Securities and Investments Board and another v Financial Intermediaries Managers and Brokers Regulatory Association Ltd* 409 *per* Morritt J. [1991] 4 All E.R. 398 Ch., *Newham London Borough Council v Skingle* [2002] 3 All ER 287, 290 *per* Jacob J. (a case on subordinate legislation), *Pearlman v Keepers and Governors of Harrow School* [1979] 1 All E.R. 365, 373, CA *per* Geoffrey Lane L.J. and *Re Pantmaenog Timber Co Ltd (in liquidation)* [2003] 4 All E.R. 418, HL; note also "The construction which [Counsel] advances gives no meaning whatever to the word 'other' in paragraph 6. If that word were excluded, it would leave the meaning of the phrase exactly that for which [Counsel] contends. [But] It is elementary that one must seek to give meaning to every word used in a statute."—*Secretary of State for Defence v Spencer* [2003] 1 W.L.R. 2701, 2710 CA *per* Peter Gibson L.J.

[64] Note, for example, "My Lords, I seldom think that an argument from redundancy carries great weight, even in a Finance Act. It is not unusual for Parliament to say expressly what the courts would have inferred anyway."—*Walker (Inspector of Taxes) v Centaur Clothes* [2000] 2 All E.R. 589, 595, HL *per* Lord Hoffmann.

[65] References to provisions of other legislation are routinely followed by parenthetical explanations of the provisions cited which are intended to have no legal effect. The index clause in an Act, as

Leaving aside those parts of legislation that are not intended to have legal effect, it has been said long ago that—

"nor is surplusage, or even tautology, wholly unknown in the language of the legislature. It is not so very uncommon in an Act of Parliament to find special exemptions which are already covered by a general exemption."[66]

20.1.24 Whether this has become less a feature of modern legislation is open to doubt: but it remains undoubtedly true that in the matter of specific exemptions, or specific instances of the ways in which a power may be exercised—

"such specific exemptions are often introduced *ex majori cautela* to quiet the fears of those whose interests are engaged or sympathies aroused in favour of some particular institution, and who are apprehensive that it may not be held to fall within a general exemption".[67]

Anyone with significant experience of the passage of primary or secondary legislation knows well that there will be matters which, while they are or clearly could be covered by general words, are thought to be of too great presentational or political significance not to be stated expressly.

20.1.25 In essence, therefore, the rule that every provision of an enactment is intended to have separate effect is treated much like the rebuttable presumptions expounded in Chapter 19. The point was expressed by Viscount Simon in *Hill v William Hill (Park Lane) Ltd*[68]—

" ... it is to be observed that though a Parliamentary enactment (like parliamentary eloquence) is capable of saying the same thing twice over without adding anything to what has already been said once, this repetition in the case of an Act of Parliament is not to be assumed. When the legislature enacts a particular phrase in a statute the presumption is that it is saying something which has not been said immediately before. The rule that a meaning should, if possible, be given to every word in the statute implies that, unless there is good reason to the contrary, the words add something which would not be there if the words were left out."

Since the fundamental enterprise is to give meaning to the legislation being construed as a whole, if to attach meaning to a particular word or expression

---

to which see Chapter 24, has no legal effect. Nor does the financial sink clause, as to which see Chapter 1, Section 6. And propositions about commencement or extent may also be devoid of legislative content where they only state the position that would anyway appertain—see Chapters 10 and 11.

[66] *Income Tax Commissioners v Pemsel* [1891] A.C. 531, 589, HL *per* Lord Macnaghten.

[67] *Income Tax Commissioners v Pemsel* [1891] A.C. 531, 574, HL *per* Lord Herschell.

[68] [1949] A.C. 530, 546–547.

would deprive the surrounding provision of meaning, or render its meaning absurd, the courts will disregard the word or expression as surplusage.[69]

Statutes *in pari materia*

Two Acts are said to be *in pari materia* if taking all their circumstances into account it is natural to construe them as if they formed part of a single code on a particular matter. Where this is found to be the case the result is that definitions in one may be applied to expressions found in another, and decided cases setting out principles of application to one will be applied to the other. **20.1.26**

The fact that two statutes have the same titles may be indicative of their being *in pari materia*. As Bridge L.J. said in *R. v Wheatley*[70]—

> "Looking at the two statutes [the Explosives Act 1875 and the Explosive Substances Act 1883], at the nature of the provisions which they both contain, and in particular at the short and long titles of both statutes, it appears to this court that clearly they are in pari materia, and that conclusion alone would seem to us to be sufficient to justify the conclusion which the judge reached that the definition of the word 'explosive' found in the 1875 Act is available to be adopted and applied under the provisions of the 1883 Act."

There is no reason why similar principles should not be applied to subordinate legislation. **20.1.27**

The construction of two pieces of legislation as being *in pari materia* is, however, something to be used to elicit the legislative intention not to override it. As with other canons of construction, therefore, it comes into play only where a doubt or ambiguity would otherwise arise.[71]

Expressio unius est exclusio alterius

This rule, which is no more than a particular application of common sense to legislative interpretation,[72] means that where legislation goes out of its way **20.1.28**

---

[69] *R. v East Ardsley (Inhabitants)* (1850) 14 Q.B. 793, 801 *per* Coleridge J.; see also *Fisher v Val de Travers Asphalte Co.* (1875) 1 C.D.P. 259 and *Stone v Yeovil Corporation* (1876) 1 C.P.D. 691, 701 *per* Brett J.—"The word 'such' in the second branch of that clause would seem at first sight to apply to lands purchased or taken; but if so read, it is insensible. It is a canon of construction that, if it be possible, effect must be given to every word of an Act of Parliament or other document, but that if there be a word or a phrase therein to which no sensible meaning can be given, it must be eliminated. It seems to me therefore that the word 'such' must be eliminated from this part of the clause."; and *Hollyhomes v Hind* [1944] K.B. 571. For a case in which an entire phrase was disregarded as surplusage which would otherwise defeat the meaning of the entire provision see *Salmon v Duncombe* (1886) 11 App. Cas. 627, 634, PC.

[70] [1979] 1 All E.R. 954, 956, CA.

[71] See the quotation from Lord Russell of Killowen C.J. above (para.20.1.2).

[72] See the quotation from Lord Diplock's speech in *Prestcold* in para.20.1.29 below.

expressly to include one thing, it can be assumed that it did not intend to include other things of the same kind. By "of the same kind" in this context must be meant anything which would be included by implication no more easily than the thing which has been expressly included.

This is a rule of long standing, expressed succinctly by Lord Dunedin in *Whiteman v Sadler* in the following terms—

> "It seems to me that express enactment shuts the door to further implication. '*Expressio unius est exclusio alterius*'."[73]

While this is a useful rule of thumb, it is like other canons and principles of construction not to be applied rigidly or without careful thought for the context: and it can be particularly dangerous if applied prescriptively. As Lopes L.J. said of this rule in *Colquhoun v Brooks*[74]—

> "It is often a valuable servant, but a dangerous master to follow in the construction of statutes or documents. The *exclusio* is often the result of inadvertence or accident, and the maxim ought not to be applied, when its application, having regard to the subject-matter to which it is to be applied, leads to inconsistency or injustice."[75]

20.1.29   The rule is likely to be at its most serviceable in the case of express exceptions. Where the legislature has gone out of its way expressly to cut down a power or other proposition in a particular way it will often be reasonable to assume that other restrictions of a similar order were not intended.[76]

It is usual for legislative draftsmen to avoid possible application of the *exclusion unius* rule by express provision. This varies from the full-blown "without prejudice to the generality of X, ... " to the more modest and modern ", in particular,", with a number of variants being found. These too are not without their difficulties. As Lord Diplock said in *Prestcold (Central) Ltd v Minister of Labour*[77]—

---

[73] [1910] A.C. 514, 527, HL.

[74] (1888) 21 Q.B.D. 52, 65.

[75] A caution often cited and acted upon—see, for recent example, *Re B-J (a child) (non-molestation order: power of arrest)* [2001] 1 All E.R. 235, 244 Hale L.J.; see also "This is an argument of the *expressio unius* variety. I think that such arguments are often perilous, especially when applied to a patchwork document like the pension scheme. The fact that a specific provision is made in one place may throw very little light on whether general words in another place include the power to do something similar. The proviso deals with the correction of specific overpayments, whether the fund is in surplus or not. It does not help one to decide whether the employer can appropriate a surplus to the discharge of what would otherwise have been his accrued obligations. In any case, the proviso was introduced by amendment in 1988 and cannot have changed the meaning of cl 14(5), which has been in the scheme since its inception."—*National Grid Co. plc v Mayes* [2001] 2 All E.R. 417, 431, HL *per* Lord Hoffmann.

[76] For an application of the rule of this kind see *Re O (a child) (blood tests: constraint)* [2000] 2 All E.R. 29 Fam.—and note, in particular, "The *expressio unius* rule gives the word 'may' in s 21(3) the meaning of 'may only' (a meaning which it is well able to bear) ... " (at 37).

[77] [1969] 1 All E.R. 69, 76, HL.

"I have already pointed out . . . that the rule of construction '*expressio unius exclusio alterius*' is not appropriate where that which is expressed is introduced by a phrase such as 'such as'. And that applies whether the draftsmanship is legal or non-legal. But before one includes in the expression introduced by 'such as' an activity which is not expressly described, one must discover from the context in which the expression appears what are the relevant common characteristics of the activities expressly described, and then decide whether the undescribed activity shares those characteristics."

Looked at another way, preventing express words from reducing the applica- **20.1.30** tion of a provision will neither expand it beyond its own natural meaning in its context nor give the courts guidance as to how wide a construction to give it, beyond not cutting it down artificially by reference to the express inclusions or exclusions. And even the grand "without prejudice to the generality of X . . . " can be nothing more than a pious, and often false, hope: since the meaning of a word is to be construed from its context, and the context will include any express inclusions or exclusions, it is inevitable that an express reference to one thing will impliedly exclude something in circumstances where one would have expected the legislature to be as concerned to ensure its inclusion or exclusion as they were to ensure the inclusion or exclusion of the matter expressly provided for.

None of this means that it is pointless to attempt to disapply *expressio unius* with a suitable phrase. The use of "in particular", for example, can be safely relied upon to prevent a list of examples from being taken as an exhaustive list (although for the reasons given above any list will inevitably have some limiting effect on the general expression which precedes it). For example, in *R. City of Westminster Housing Benefit Review Board, Ex p. Mehanne*[78] the House of Lords rejected the suggestion that a statutory instrument which required a local authority to reduce a person's rent by such amount as it considered appropriate "having regard in particular to the cost of suitable alternative accommodation" excluded consideration of factors other than the one particularised.

Note that a phrase requiring a deciding authority to have regard "in particular" to specified matters does not necessarily require those matters to be given more weight than other matters.[79]

Note also that the use of a purely general expression without any *expressio* **20.1.31** *unius* at all will not necessarily result in the general expression being given its fullest literal meaning. Indeed the wider an expression used the less safe it may be to expect the courts not to imply some limitations in it. For example, in the case of a statutory power to amend any enactment, cast in such wide terms, it is inconceivable that the legislature did not intend any restrictions on the exercise of the power at all. And if, for example, it were desired to use the power to make

---

[78] [2001] 2 All E.R. 690, HL.
[79] See *Ashdown v Telegraph Group* [2001] 2 All E.R. 370. 383, Ch.

substantive amendment of an enactment of particular importance, such as one of those enactments identified by Laws L.J. as constitutional enactments,[80] it would certainly be unwise not to take express power to do so.[81]

The general point was expressed by Lord Herschell in *Cox v Hakes*[82]—

"It cannot, I think, be denied that, for the purpose of construing any enactment, it is right to look, not only at the provision immediately under construction, but at any others found in connection with it which may throw light upon it, and afford an indication that general words employed in it were not intended to be applied without some limitation."

As to how to cut down general words where their full generality cannot be intended, the Privy Council said in *Blackwood v R.*[83]—

"One of the safest guides to the construction of sweeping general words which it is difficult to apply in their full literal sense is to examine other words of like import in the same instrument, and to see what limitations

---

[80] See Chapter 1, Section 4.

[81] Hence the following passage of the Government's Response to the Report of the Joint Committee on the Draft Civil Contingencies Bill (January 2004, Cm. 6078, para.34)—"We have sought advice from Parliamentary Counsel as to the scope of the power to "modify or disapply an enactment", and in particular whether it would permit regulations under Part 2 of the Bill to modify an enactment which has constitutional importance—such as the Human Rights Act 1998 or the Bill of Rights Act 1689. They have advised that each proposed exercise of such a power must be assessed by reference to whether or not it is within the class of action that Parliament must have contemplated when conferring the power. There are certain rebuttable presumptions as to what Parliament must have intended in conferring a power of this kind. These may be presumptions of common law (for example, the presumption against the imposition of taxation) or presumptions based on statute (for example, s.2 of the European Communities Act 1972 or s.3 of the Human Rights Act 1998). These presumptions apply even where Parliament has used general language. The courts have also suggested rules in relation to provisions of particular constitutional importance, requiring statutory modification to be express. The Bill does not contain any express provision that enables regulations under Part 2 of the Bill to modify or disapply a constitutional enactment. While the specific powers listed in the Bill are very wideranging, they are capable of being exercised without interfering with a constitutional enactment. In particular, they are capable of being exercised in accordance with the Convention rights. Nor is the permission to do anything that an Act could do sufficiently precise to displace the general approach detailed above. In light of this, Parliamentary Counsel have advised that, in exercising the power conferred under Part 2 of the Bill, in the unlikely event of needing to use this power, Parliament will not permit interference either with a general presumption or with a "constitutional" enactment. However, it may be safe to assume that Parliament intended to confer the power to interfere with such a statute if the interference is trivial in so far as it concerns the substance of the presumption or the constitutional enactment. Given the inherent limits on the scope of the power, Parliamentary Counsel have advised that if we wished to be able to modify or disapply a constitutional enactment, we should take an express power to do so. We do not propose to do this. Without such an express power, we cannot presently envisage circumstances in which this power would lawfully enable us to make a substantive amendment to a constitutional enactment. In light of this, the Government does not consider that it is appropriate expressly to protect the enactments cited by the Committee from modification or disapplication. The effect of the current drafting appears to achieve the right result in a less inflexible way."

[82] (1890) 15 App. Cas. 506, 529.

[83] (1882) 8 App. Cas. 82, 94.

must be imposed on them. If it is found that a number of such expressions have to be subjected to limitations or qualification, and that such limitations or qualifications are of the same nature, that forms a strong argument for subjecting the expression in dispute to a like limitation or qualification."

To give an example, in *Burge v Ashley & Smith Ltd*[84] the words "money paid" in the Gaming Act 1892[85] were held not to include money deposited by way of stakes on a wager. Collins L.J. said—

20.1.32

"I agree that the words looked at by themselves might cover the case. But I think we have to consider something more than the mere words. The Act was passed, after a long chain or authorities, establishing that a sum deposited, as in the present case, might be recovered. If it had been intended to alter the law as established by these decisions, I should have expected to find a clear expression of that intention, which I do not find in this Act."

Natural versus technical meaning

There is a principle of general application that while a technical legal expression should be construed in a technical way, a word that has a natural meaning in ordinary English conversation should be given that meaning and not a restrictive technical one. As Lord Tenterden said in *Attorney General v Winstanley*[86]—

20.1.33

"the words of an Act of Parliament which are not applied to any particular science or art" are to be construed "as they are understood in common language".

This gives rise to the assertion of Lord Reid in *Cozens v Brutus*[87] that—

"The meaning of an ordinary word of the English language is not a question of law. The proper construction of a statute is a question of law. If the context shows that a word is used in an unusual sense the court will determine in other words what that unusual sense is."

It is possible to misunderstand this statement. It should not be taken to mean more than that where a word has a natural colloquial meaning that must be presumed to be its intended meaning in statute unless the contrary is apparent. The meaning intended by the legislature in using any word remains a question of law.[88]

20.1.34

---

[84] [1900] 1 Q.B. 744, 750.
[85] 1892 c.9.
[86] (1831) 2 D. & Cl. 302, 310.
[87] [1973] A.C. 854, 861, HL.
[88] See *Moyna v Secretary of State for Work and Pensions* [2003] 1 W.L.R. 1929, 1935, HL *per* Lord Hoffmann.

So where a word used in legislation has an ordinary colloquial meaning, the courts will require good reason to depart from that plain meaning and to ascribe a technical meaning the word in a particular context.[89] If in legislation in a particular technical context, however, a word has a clearly understood meaning different to that which it has when used in non-technical conversation, the courts will incline towards giving it its technical meaning.

As to the construction of technical expressions in a technical context, as Fry J said in *Holt & Co. v Collyer*[90]—

> "If it is a word which is of a technical or scientific character then it must be construed according to that which is its primary meaning, namely, its technical or scientific meaning".

20.1.35   And as Farwell L.J. said in *Mason v Bolton's Library*[91]—

> "The proviso is expressed in terms of art; technical phrases are used. It is a stringent rule of construction that in construing an Act of Parliament or a deed containing technical words those words must be given their technical meaning."

In this context technical does not mean only scientific or appertaining to some branch of trade or learning that develops its own jargon; it can refer to any meaning of the term designed to evoke specific ideas or bear specific connotations in a particular legal context. As Lord Halsbury said in *Income Tax Commissions v Pemsel*[92]—

> "Now, before proceeding to discuss the words themselves, I somewhat protest against the assumption that the alternative is to be between a popular and what is called a technical meaning, unless the word 'technical' itself receives a construction different from that which is its ordinary use. There are, doubtless, some words to which the law had attached in the stricter sense a technical meaning; but the word 'charitable' is not one of those words, though I do not deny that the old Court of Chancery, in enforcing the performance of charitable trusts, included in that phrase a number of subjects which undoubtedly no one outside the Court of Chancery would have supposed to be comprehended within that term. The alternative, therefore, to my mind may be more accurately stated as lying between the popular and ordinary interpretation of the word 'charitable,' and the

---

[89] See, for examples of cases where the courts resisted temptation to depart from the ordinary meaning of an expression, *Anyanwu v South Bank Student's Union* [2001] 1 All E.R. 1, CA ("aids") and *A. E. Beckett & Sons v Midland Electricity plc* [2001] 1 W.L.R. 291, CA ("economic loss").
[90] (1881) 16 Ch. D. 718, 720.
[91] [1913] 1 K.B. 83, 90.
[92] [1891] A.C. 531, 542, HL.

interpretation given by the Court of Chancery to the use of those words in the statute of 43 Elizabeth."

No change of meaning without change of language

The first lesson learned by aspiring legislative draftsmen is that in legislative drafting one should not change language from one context to another unless a change of meaning is intended, and that the courts will assume that a change of language indicates a change of meaning. But—

20.1.36

> "70. Whilst I agree that ordinarily a word appearing in more than one place in the same statute should be given the same meaning wherever it appears and particularly so when it appears in the same section or subsection this, like all rules of construction, is but a guide to achieve the overriding objective which is to ascertain the intention of Parliament."[93]

The principle remains, therefore, that what is meant by a word in one context should be judged in the light of that context, and decisions relating to usage elsewhere should be used only as a starting-point or to provide assistance where none can be gained from the context.

On occasion, the decision to change words in similar contexts, or even in one provision, will so clearly be governed by presentational considerations that it will be reasonable to expect the reader not to presume any intended change of meaning.[94]

Presumption of correct law

In construing legislation the courts will "assume that the legislature knows the existing state of the law".[95] [96]

20.1.37

This assumption as an aid to construction can be seen at work in a number of leading cases on statutory interpretation.[97]

---

[93] *London Borough of Hounslow v Thames Water Utilities Ltd* [2003] 3 W.L.R. 1243, QBD, DC, *per* Scott Baker L.J.

[94] See, for example, "It is perfectly true—and this is really what the argument for the plaintiff turned on—that the word 'property' is used as well as the word 'premises' in s.23 (1), but I think that the draftsman changed the language because he thought it would be inelegant to use the word 'property' twice over. If one said 'where the property impressed in the tenancy is or unloads property which is occupied by the tenant,' that would be a little cumbrous, and I think the draftsman thought it would sound better to say 'where the property impressed in the tenancy is or unloads premises which are occupied by the tenant.' I do not think he contemplated that 'premises' would have the strict meaning which it is argued on behalf of the plaintiff that it does have."—*Bracey v Read* [1962] 3 W.L.R. 1194, 1198, Ch.

[95] *Young & Co. v Mayor, &c.of Leamington* (1883) 8 App. Cas.517, 526.

[96] But the courts will not defer to a clearly deficient understanding on the part of the legislature—see Chapter 1, Section 7, para.1.7.4.

[97] See *Bradlough v Clarke* (1883) 8 App. Cas. 354, 373, 375; *Carter v Molson* (1883) 8 App. Cas. 530, 536, 541, *The Claim of the Viscountess Rhondda* [1922] 2 A.C. 339 (relying on *Stradling v Morgan* (1560) 1 Plowden 199), *Eastman Photographic Co. v Comptroller-General of Patents* [1898] A.C. 571, 575 and *Avery v L. & N. E. Ry.* [1938] A.C. 606, 612, 617.

This rule is in part an adjunct of the rules in *Heydon's Case*, since it guides the courts in the task appointed by those rules of determining the change of the state of the law that the legislature intended to effect.

Cross-contextual use of judicial and statutory definitions

20.1.38   It is clear from the foregoing that where the same expression is used in two similar contexts, a statutory definition in one context may be persuasive in the other. The same is true of a judicial definition.[98]

What amounts to a sufficient similarity of context may, of course, be difficult to determine. And the problem is the same whether one is deciding whether to adopt a judicial definition of words in one context for words used also in another context, or whether one is deciding whether to adopt an express statutory definition of words defined in one context to illuminate the legislative use of the words in another context.

No rules can be offered—and it should not be assume that there is any presumption that a definition in one place will necessarily have any implication whatsoever for the use of the defined expression in another place[99]—but two contrasting cases may serve to illustrate how the problem requires to be addressed.

(1) In *Parkinson v St James and Seacroft University Hospital NHS Trust*[1] in seeking a "solution to the problem of degree: how disabled does a child have to be for the parents to be able to make a claim?" Hale L.J. borrowed a statutory definition of disability from another context, s.17 of the Children Act 1989.[2] She relied on the use of a definition in these or similar terms in a number of legislative contexts, and was influenced by the fact that "local social services authorities are used to operating it".

(2) But in *R. (Eliot) v Crown Court at Reading*[3] the court declined to apply criteria for determining whether there was good and sufficient cause in relation to the grant of bail in determining whether there was good and sufficient cause for extending a custody time limit.

20.1.39   The obvious difference between these two cases is that the definition in *Parkinson* is a definition of a concept which has a natural and substantive existence outside the legislative context in which it is defined. So one might wish to adopt a particular definition of disability from one particular context and at least to use it as a starting point in defining the same concept in another context,

---

[98] See Chapter 29, paras 29.1.6—29.1.10.

[99] "Even although the Act of 1925 repeated the Act of 1922 (which in 1925 was split up into its component divisions), the Agricultural Holdings Act, 1923, is not to be construed by reference to a definition in an entirely different Act inserted solely for the interpretation of words in the other Act."—*Land Settlement Association v Carr* [1944] K.B. 657, 663, CA *per* Scott L.J.

[1] [2001] 3 All E.R. 97, CA.

[2] 1989 c.41.

[3] [2001] 4 All E.R. 625, QBD, DC.

having regard to whether the natural meaning requires modification in the second context or may have been subject to modification in the first context. But a concept like "good and sufficient cause" has no substance or meaning outside the context in which it is used. The term being wholly context-specific, there is no reason to assume that criteria used in defining it in one context will provide even a useful starting point in another context.

In any event, a definition in one context, whether judicial or statutory, should be never be seen as more than a starting point for construction in another context, unless the definition is expressly applied to that other context. The courts have long rejected any attempt to force them to regard cross-contextual applications of definitions as more than persuasive.[4]

Where an expression is defined in relation to one section of an Act but not in relation to another, it will sometimes, but not always, be appropriate to draw an inference from the absence of definition in the second place.[5] But in general there is a presumption that a word used in different parts of an Act will bear the same meaning in each place.[6]

Where a distinction has been drawn in legislation between the uses of two expressions, it is to be presumed in the absence of evidence to the contrary that in later legislation, whether or not in the same context, the same distinction is intended.[7]

Construction of Act: whether private or public

There is a slight difference in the approach to construction of an Act of Parliament according to whether it be public or private.[8] The position is as stated by Bray J. in *Stewart (Surveyor of Taxes) v Conservators of River Thames*[9]—

20.1.40

---

[4] See, for example, Lord Loreburn L.C. in *Macbeth v Chislett* [1910] A.C. 220, 223, HL—"The statute we are concerned with does not say that you are to apply the Act of 1854; and it would be a new terror in the construction of Acts of Parliament if we were required to limit a word to an unnatural sense because in some Act which is not incorporated or referred to such an interpretation is given to it for the purposes of that Act alone."

[5] *Camden London Borough Council v Gunby* [2000] 1 W.L.R. 465, QBD; and note *Derby Specialist Fabrication Ltd v Burton* [2001] 2 All E.R. 840 EAT where the court declined to assume that the express inclusion of constructive dismissal within the expression "dismissal" in one context prevented an implied inclusion in another, quite similar, context.

[6] "It is a sound rule of construction to give the same meaning to the same words occurring in different parts of an Act of Parliament."—*Courtauld v Legh* (1869) L.R. 4 Ex. 126, 130.; but the rule gives way readily to other considerations (such as, for example, the fact that the contexts in which the word is used derive from different earlier enactments consolidated into one)—see *Re Moody and Yates' Contract* (1885) 30 Ch. D. 344, 349, *Re National Savings Bank* (1866) L.R. 1 Ch. App. 547, 550, *R. v Burt, Ex p. Pressburg* [1960] 1 Q.B. 625, *Re Smith, Green v Smith* (1883) 24 Ch. D. 672, 678, and *R. v Allen* (1872) 1 C.C.R. 367, 374. On the other hand, note, "While s 259(1)(b) has a different statutory origin, as explained by Hale L.J., I cannot accept that the draftsman intended it to bear a completely different meaning in two paragraphs of the same subsection."—*R. v Falmouth and Truro Port Health Authority, Ex p. South West Water Ltd* [2000] 3 All E.R. 306, 337, CA *per* Pill L.J.

[7] See, for example, *Smith v Brown* (1871) L.R. 6 Q.B. 729, 732 *per* Cockburn C.J.

[8] As to which distinction, see Chapter 1, Section 3.

[9] [1908] 1 K.B. 893, 900–901.

"In *Altrincham Union Assessment Committee v Cheshire Lines Committee*[10] Lord Esher M.R. said: 'Now it is quite true that there is some difference between a private Act of Parliament and a public one, but the only difference which I am aware of is as to the strictness of the construction to be given to it, when there is any doubt as to the meaning. In the case of a public Act you construe it keeping in view the fact that it must be taken to have been passed for the public advantage, and you apply certain fixed canons to its construction. In the case of a private Act, which is obtained by persons for their own benefit, you construe more strictly provisions which they allege to be in their favour, because the persons who obtain a private Act ought to take care that it is so worded that that which they desire to obtain for themselves is plainly stated in it. But when the construction is perfectly clear, there is no difference between the modes of construing a private Act and a public Act.'

"Therefore, according to Lord Esher, a private Act must be construed strictly, and so as not to give the promoters any greater advantage than is clearly given by the language used. It must be remembered, however, that, although this is a private Act, it is not the ordinary case of promoters who are going to make a profit by means of the acquisition of parliamentary powers, for, as is stated in the preamble to the Thames Conservancy Act, 1857, the preservation and improvement of the navigation of the river Thames is a matter of great national importance. Therefore, although I have to look very carefully at the provisions of this Act to see whether they do give the exemption claimed by the respondents, I do not think that the fact that the Act is a local and personal Act is one which ought to have very great weight with me."

So the position is that, as so often, when the legislative words are clear there is neither need nor authority to depart from them, but where there is ambiguity it is to be construed more strictly against someone seeking a private benefit than against the Crown enacting what is thought to be a public benefit.

Uniformity of interpretation

20.1.41 In construing statutes the House of Lords and the Privy Council[11] have regard to the desirability of uniformity of practice in relation to the construction of statutes

---

[10] 15 Q.B.D. 597, 602.

[11] As well as its recent acquisition of jurisdiction in relation to devolution, through a variety of routes the Privy Council routinely acts as the final court of appeal in relation to appeals from the British Islands, from the United Kingdom Overseas Territories, from a number of Commonwealth countries, and from a number of other countries, territories and bodies. The Judicial Committee of the Privy Council is served for the most part by Lords of Appeal in Ordinary, so that in general practice there is a good deal of parity between the approach taken in the Judicial Committee of the Privy Council and that taken in the Judicial Committee of the House of Lords.

throughout the territories, and in relation to all the matters, in respect of which they have jurisdiction.[12]

Decisions of a court in one part of the United Kingdom will be persuasive but not authoritative in courts in other parts.[13] Comity is likely to be a powerful force influencing any court's decision on construction of legislation. But comity can give way to other factors, such as moral sentiment: hence the contrasting decisions on the application of s.2 of the Cruelty to Animals Act 1849[14] made by courts in different places.[15]

Where decisions of forums in different parts of the United Kingdom differ in relation to the construction of the same enactment it will be, ultimately, for the House of Lords to reconcile or select from the conflicting decisions so as to produce uniformity.[16]

Comity of nations

While the courts will have particular recourse to international law in the case of legislation designed to implement international obligations arising out of Treaties and the like,[17] they will to a limited extent have regard to international law, and the laws of other jurisdictions, in construing United Kingdom law. As was said in *Bloxam v Favre*[18]— **20.1.42**

"Sir Benson Maxwell says, in his work on the Interpretation of Statutes, p.122, that 'every statute is to be so interpreted and applied, as far as its language admits, as not to be inconsistent with the comity of nations or with the established rules of international law.' This passage expresses the rule of construction which is applicable to the present case."

---

[12] See *Income Tax Commissioners v Pemsel* [1891] A.C. 531, 557, 577 *per* Lords Watson and Macnaghten; *Duncan v Findlater* (1839) 6 Cl. & F. 894, 902, 909 *per* Lords Cottenham and Brougham; and *Cooper v Cooper* (1888) 13 App. Cas. 88, 104 *per* Lord Watson.

[13] See *Blake v Midland Railway* (1852) 18 Q.B. 93, 109 *per* Coleridge J, *Ford v Wiley* (1889) 23 Q.B.D. 203, 216, *per* Coleridge CJ, *Cantiare San Rocco v Clyde Shipbuilding Company* [1924] A.C. 226, 247, 248, *Chandler v Webster* [1904] 1 K.B. 493 (as to the substance of the last of which see *Fibrosa Spolka Akcyjna v Fairbairn Lawson Combe Barbour Ltd* [1943] A.C. 32, HL).

[14] Since repealed by the Protection of Animals Act 1911 (c.27).

[15] See *Ford v Wiley* (1889) 23 Q.B.D. 203, *R. v M'Donagh* (1891) 28 L.r. Ir. 204, *Renton v Wilson* (1885) 15 Rettie (Justiciary Sc.) 84 and *Todrick v Wilson* (1891) 18 R. (Justiciary Sc.) 41.

[16] See *Income Tax Commissioners v Gibbs* [1942] A.C. 402.

[17] See Chapter 29.

[18] (1883) 8 P.D. 101, 104 *per* Sir J. Hannen.

CHAPTER 21

EXPRESSIONS WHICH CHANGE MEANING OVER TIME

The question frequently arises of how to construe an expression which has changed its meaning since the time when the statute or instrument in which it appears was enacted or made. **21.1.1**

Put simply, while the rule was once to give effect to legislation as when it was passed or made,[1] the rule now is to allow legislation to have an "always speaking" meaning.[2]

But, as with all questions of statutory interpretation, the correct approach (or, at least, the correct modern approach) depends not on the application of a fixed doctrine but on determining what the legislature can best be taken to have meant in the particular context. Sometimes the courts will take the view that Parliament must have intended to use an expression in an ambulatory way, encompassing not only a class as at the time of enactment but also anything that might come to fall within that class in the future. This will, of course, be of particular importance when dealing with a class which refers to or depends upon technology.

So, for example, in *Victor Chandler International v Customs and Excise Commissioners*[3] the Court of Appeal concluded that although when enacting a provision about advertisements in 1952 Parliament could not have contemplated the means by which advertisements can now be distributed electronically, in order to prevent the provision being undermined it was necessary and appropriate to give the expression "advertisement" an "always speaking" or ambulatory construction to take account of developments since the provision was originally enacted. This breadth of construction is particularly significant given that the provision in question created a criminal offence. **21.1.2**

---

[1] The rule was first laid down by Coke (2 Inst., ed. Thomas, p.2, n.(1)) in speaking of Magna Carta in the following terms: "This and the like were the forms of ancient Acts and graunts, and the ancient Acts and graunts must be construed and taken as the law was holden at that time when they were made." This became developed into the doctrine expressed by Lord Esher in *Sharpe v Wakefield* ((1889) 22 Q.B.D. 239, 241, affirmed [1891] A.C. 173): the words of a statute must be construed as they would have been the day after the statute was passed, unless some subsequent Act has declared that some other construction is to be adopted or has altered the previous statute". This is sometimes referred to as the rule of *contemporanea expositio*.

[2] But note the resolution of the two approaches offered by Lord Bingham of Cornhill in *Quintavalle* discussed below.

[3] [2000] 2 All E.R. 315, CA.

The case of *Fitzpatrick v Sterling Housing Association Ltd*[4] provided a particularly important development of this approach. The House of Lords, reversing the Court of Appeal, decided that while a homosexual partner is not included in a reference to a person's spouse, he can be included in a modern construction of a reference to a person's family.[5]

The limits beyond which the courts will not go in expanding the meaning of an expression by reference to changing social patterns and notions are helpfully expounded in *R. v Pearce*.[6] Faced with the word "wife" in a statute the court considered developments in social policy of the kind discussed in *Fitzpatrick* but declined to extend the word to cover unmarried partners.[7] Similarly, in *MacDonald v Advocate-General for Scotland*[8] the House of Lords declined to construe the Sex Discrimination Act 1975[9] as applying to discrimination on grounds of homosexuality: Lord Hope, having found it impossible to find support for the extension from the European jurisprudence, said[10]—

> "So we must take the 1975 Act as we find it. As [Counsel] said at the outset of his submissions in Ms Pearce's case, it is an unfortunate fact that human beings discriminate against each other all the time. But this is unlawful only when the law proscribes such conduct. All we can do is apply to the facts the ordinary and natural meaning of the words which Parliament used when it was describing the circumstances in which the statutory remedy was to be available. There is no escape from the conclusion that the lack of insight into homosexuality which was current when the statutory framework within which the appellants' cases lie was being laid down casts a shadow over these proceedings which is not capable of being lifted by the more recent developments."

21.1.3   Or, as Lord Hobhouse put the same point[11]—

> " . . . proper regard must be had in construing an Act of Parliament to the words actually used. It is they which define the effect of the legislation. The

---

[4] [1999] 3 W.L.R. 1113, HL.

[5] For a critique of *Fitzpatrick v Sterling* see Statute Law Review, Vol.22, no.2 pp.154–56 (2001). This explores the tension between the need for the judges to avoid usurping the role of the legislature in sensitive and controversial areas of social policy and the obvious desirability of technical words being construed as having been intended to include any later reasonably foreseeable extension of meaning (and obvious example being the development of new forms of communication).

[6] [2002] 1 W.L.R. 1553, CA.

[7] For a case in which, interestingly, the courts were invited on human rights grounds, and declined, to read the word "spouse" more narrowly than its natural meaning, so as to exclude marriages of convenience for the purposes of the Witholding and Withdrawal of Support (Travel Assistance and Temporary Accommodation) Regulations 2002 (SI 2002/3078), see *R. (Kimani) v Lambeth London Borough Council* [2004] 1 W.L.R. 272, CA.

[8] [2004] 1 All E.R. 339, HL.

[9] 1975 c.65.

[10] At 359.

[11] At 374.

now abandoned argument that the phrase 'on the ground of her sex' can mean 'on the ground of her sexual orientation' fails to respect the language of the statute. The two things are not the same. The use of different words give the phrases different meanings. To disregard this simple fact is to fall into the error rightly, and memorably, condemned by Lord Atkin as long ago as 1941 (see *Liversidge v Anderson*[12]).

The emerging distinction is between concepts which do not do violence to the words used in legislation, although they may expand the scope of an expression beyond anything likely to have been in the contemplation of the legislature when the expression was used, and concepts which whether or not the legislature would have wished to include them had it thought of them are outside the plain meaning of the words used, a case of *casus omissus*.[13]

Fitzpatrick was relied on in *R. (Smeaton) v Secretary of State for Health*[14] where the court insisted that "miscarriage", in the context of an offence under the Offences against the Person Act 1861,[15] must be construed in accordance with current medical opinion and without reference to what opinion might have been when the provision was enacted. The court therefore concluded that the term is

---

[12] [1942] A.C. 206 at 244–245: the relevant passage is as follows—"I view with apprehension the attitude of judges who on a mere question of construction when face to face with claims involving the liberty of the subject show themselves more executive minded than the executive. Their function is to give words their natural meaning, not, perhaps, in war time leaning towards liberty, but following the dictum of Pollock C.B. in *Bowditch v Balchin* ((1850) 5 Ex. 378), cited with approval by my noble and learned friend Lord Wright in *Barnard v Gorman* ([1941] A.C. 378, 393): 'In a case in which the liberty of the subject is concerned, we cannot go beyond the natural construction of the statute.' In this country, amid the clash of arms, the laws are not silent. They may be changed, but they speak the same language in war as in peace. It has always been one of the pillars of freedom, one of the principles of liberty for which on recent authority we are now fighting, that the judges are no respecters of persons and stand between the subject and any attempted encroachments on his liberty by the executive, alert to see that any coercive action is justified in law. In this case I have listened to arguments which might have been addressed acceptably to the Court of King's Bench in the time of Charles I.'
"I protest, even if I do it alone, against a strained construction put on words with the effect of giving an uncontrolled power of imprisonment to the minister. To recapitulate: The words have only one meaning. They are used with that meaning in statements of the common law and in statutes. They have never been used in the sense now imputed to them. They are used in the Defence Regulations in the natural meaning, and, when it is intended to express the meaning now imputed to them, different and apt words are used in the regulations generally and in this regulation in particular. Even if it were relevant, which it is not, there is no absurdity or no such degree of public mischief as would lead to a non-natural construction.
"I know of only one authority which might justify the suggested method of construction: "'When I use a word," Humpty Dumpty said in rather a scornful tone, "it means just what I choose it to mean, neither more nor less." "The question is," said Alice, "whether you can make words mean so many different things." "The question is," said Humpty Dumpty, "which is to be master—that's all.'" (*Through the Looking Glass*, c.vi.) After all this long discussion the question is whether the words 'If a man has' can mean 'If a man thinks he has.' I am of opinion that they cannot, and that the case should be decided accordingly."
[13] As to which see Chapter 20.
[14] [2002] EWHC 610 (Admin).
[15] 1861 c.100.

properly construed nowadays as referring only to post-implantation termination.

21.1.4   The fundamental difficulty in addressing the problem of language that changes in meaning over time is that the courts wish to continue to give effect to the cardinal rule of interpretation[16] by giving the language used the fullest meaning that the legislature could have intended, but it is difficult or impossible to know how far that intention embraced the possibility of future developments in a particular context and a particular direction.

The problem and the modern approach to its solution are expounded by Lord Bingham of Cornhill in *R. (Quintavalle) v Secretary of State for Health*[17] in the following terms—

> "8. The basic task of the court is to ascertain and give effect to the true meaning of what Parliament has said in the enactment to be construed. But that is not to say that attention should be confined and a literal interpretation given to the particular provisions which give rise to difficulty. Such an approach not only encourages immense prolixity in drafting, since the draftsman will feel obliged to provide expressly for every contingency which may possibly arise. It may also (under the banner of loyalty to the will of Parliament) lead to the frustration of that will, because undue concentration on the minutiae of the enactment may lead the court to neglect the purpose which Parliament intended to achieve when it enacted the statute. Every statute other than a pure consolidating statute is, after all, enacted to make some change, or address some problem, or remove some blemish, or effect some improvement in the national life. The court's task, within the permissible bounds of interpretation, is to give effect to Parliament's purpose. So the controversial provisions should be read in the context of the statute as a whole, and the statute as a whole should be read in the historical context of the situation which led to its enactment.

> "9. There is, I think, no inconsistency between the rule that statutory language retains the meaning it had when Parliament used it and the rule that a statute is always speaking. If Parliament, however long ago, passed an Act applicable to dogs, it could not properly be interpreted to apply to cats; but it could properly be held to apply to animals which were not regarded as dogs when the Act was passed but are so regarded now. The meaning of 'cruel and unusual punishments' has not changed over the years since 1689, but many punishments which were not then thought to fall within that category would now be held to do so. . . . A revealing example [of the courts' task in this respect] is found in *Grant v Southwestern and County Properties Ltd.*[18] where Walton J. had to decide whether a tape recording

---

[16] See Chapter 17.
[17] [2003] 2 W.L.R. 692, HL.
[18] [1975] Ch. 185.

fell within the expression 'document' in the Rules of the Supreme Court. Pointing out[19] that the furnishing of information had been treated as one of the main functions of a document, the judge concluded that the tape recording was a document.

"10. Limited help is in my opinion to be derived from statements made in cases where there is said to be an omission in a statute attributable to the oversight or inadvertence of the draftsman: see *Jones v Wrotham Park Settled Estates*[20]; *Inco Europe Ltd. v First Choice Distribution.*[21] This is not such a case. More pertinent is the guidance given by the late Lord Wilberforce in his dissenting opinion in *Royal College of Nursing of the United Kingdom v Department of Health and Social Security.*[22] The case concerned the Abortion Act 1967[23] and the issue which divided the House was whether nurses could lawfully take part in a termination procedure not known when the Act was passed. At page 822 Lord Wilberforce said:

'In interpreting an Act of Parliament it is proper, and indeed necessary, to **21.1.5** have regard to the state of affairs existing, and known by Parliament to be existing, at the time. It is a fair presumption that Parliament's policy or intention is directed to that state of affairs. Leaving aside cases of omission by inadvertence, this being not such a case, when a new state of affairs, or a fresh set of facts bearing on policy, comes into existence, the courts have to consider whether they fall within the Parliamentary intention. They may be held to do so, if they fall within the same genus of facts as those to which the expressed policy has been formulated. They may also be held to do so if there can be detected a clear purpose in the legislation which can only be fulfilled if the extension is made. How liberally these principles may be applied must depend upon the nature of the enactment, and the strictness or otherwise of the words in which it has been expressed. The courts should be less willing to extend expressed meanings if it is clear that the Act in question was designed to be restrictive or circumscribed in its operation rather than liberal or permissive. They will be much less willing to do so where the subject matter is different in kind or dimension from that for which the legislation was passed. In any event there is one course which the courts cannot take, under the law of this country; they cannot fill gaps; they cannot by asking the question 'What would Parliament have done in this current case—not being one in contemplation—if the facts had been before it?' attempt themselves to supply the answer, if the answer is not to be found in the terms of the Act itself."

---

[19] At 190.
[20] [1980] A.C. 74, 105.
[21] [2000] 1 W.L.R. 586.
[22] [1981] A.C. 800.
[23] 1967 c.87.

"Both parties relied on this passage, which may now be treated as authoritative. . . . .

"While it is impermissible to ask what Parliament would have done if the facts had been before it, there is one important question which may permissibly be asked: it is whether Parliament, faced with the taxing task of enacting a legislative solution to the difficult religious, moral and scientific issues mentioned above, could rationally have intended to leave live human embryos created by cell nuclear replacement outside the scope of regulation had it known of them as a scientific possibility. There is only one possible answer to this question and it is negative."

21.1.6   The same lack of inconsistency between the notion of an Act as always speaking and the meaning of an expression not changing is concisely explained by Lord Bingham of Cornhill in *R. v G.*[24]—

"Since a statute is always speaking, the context or application of a statutory expression may change over time, but the meaning of the expression itself cannot change. So the starting point is to ascertain what Parliament meant by 'reckless' in 1971 . . . "

As a final thought on this problem, it should be noted that the approach in *Fitzpatrick*, which focused on developments in the natural use of language and not on the non-discrimination requirements of the European Convention on Human Rights, has been superseded in cases to which the Convention is relevant by the case of *Ghaidan v Godin-Mendoza*.[25] The Court of Appeal concluded that the requirements of the Human Rights Act 1998[26] are such that the reference "the surviving spouse of the late partner" in para.2 of Sch.1 to the Rent Act 1977[27] should be extended so as to include a reference to a homosexual male partner, irrespective of the degree of violence thereby occasioned to the language used.

---

[24] [2003] 3 W.L.R. 1060, 1078, HL.
[25] [2003] Ch. 380, CA.
[26] 1998 c.42; see Chapter 25.
[27] 1977 c.42.

CHAPTER 22

THE INTERPRETATION ACT 1978

Introduction

The principal statute laying down rules for the interpretation of legislation is the **22.1.1** Interpretation Act 1978. It replaced an earlier Act, the Interpretation Act 1889, and was founded on a report by the two Law Commissions.[1] The essential features of the Act should be committed to memory by anyone who is regularly required to consult legislation, because it contains principles which amount to unspoken assumptions upon which every other provision of legislation rests. This Chapter expounds some of the principal features of the Act.[2]

The Act is expressed throughout in propositions about Acts. But in fact most of the critical provisions of the Act apply not only to other Acts but to almost all legislation.[3] And it is likely that the courts would regard most of the principles of the Act as being indicative of the proper approach to construing other forms of legislation also.[4]

The Interpretation Act 1978 contains provisions of two kinds. First, provisions codifying and thereby putting beyond doubt principles which are largely a matter of common sense and which would probably be applied in the absence of the Act. Secondly, rules which, having been set out once in the Act, enable the draftsman of other legislation to use shortened forms of expression in the knowledge that they will be construed in the light of the principles laid down in the 1978 Act.

Most of the provisions of the Interpretation Act have already fitted naturally **22.1.2** into the consideration of particular features of legislation and have been so fully addressed in the appropriate place that they are omitted here. They are listed in

---

[1] *Report on the Interpretation Act 1889 and certain other Enactments Relating to the Construction and Operation of Acts of Parliament and other Instruments*, June 1978, Cmnd. 7235. The Report is a useful source of illumination as to the intention underlying, and the expected limitations of the effect of, a number of provisions of the 1978 Act.

[2] This Chapter pays little attention to those provisions of the Act which were included to address points which while they may once have been sufficiently in doubt to require express provision are no longer in doubt at all. For example, s.1 which provides that a section of an enactment is treated as an enactment despite itself containing "introductory words", and s.2 which permits an Act to be amended in the Session in which it is passed.

[3] Most of the Act is expressly extended to most pre-1978 Acts (s.22(1)), Measures of the Church of England (s.22(3)) and subordinate legislation (s.23(2)). To a limited extent specified in ss.23 and 24, the Act's provisions also apply to Acts of the Scottish Parliament and instruments made under them and to Acts of the Northern Ireland Assembly.

[4] Two provisions are expressly applied to non-legislative documents ("deeds and other instruments and documents") by s.23(3): the provision construing references to time as references to Greenwich Mean Time, subject to summer time, and the provision for citation of Acts.

the table below (which for ease of reference also shows the paragraphs in this Chapter dealing with the remaining sections).

22.1.3

Section	Topic	Place addressed
1	Every section of Act to take effect as substantive enactment without introductory words.	Chapter 1, Section 7.
2	Act may be amended or repealed in Session in which passed.	Chapter 14, Section 3.
3	Every Act to be judicially noticed as public Act unless providing expressly to the contrary.	Chapter 1, Section 3.
4	Time of commencement.	Chapter 10, Section 1.
5	Particular definitions.	This Chapter, paras 22.1.4—22.1.8.
6	Gender and number.	This Chapter, paras 22.1.9—22.1.11.
7	Service by post.	This Chapter, para. 22.1.12.
8	Distance.	This Chapter, para. 22.1.13.
9	Time.	This Chapter, para. 22.1.14.
10	Sovereign.	This Chapter, para. 22.1.15.
11	References in subordinate legislation to bear same meaning as in parent Act.	This Chapter, para. 22.1.16.
12	Continuity of powers and duties.	Chapter 12, Section 3.
13	Anticipatory exercise of powers.	Chapter 10, Section 1.
14	Implied power to amend and revoke.	Chapter 14, Section 3.
15	Repeal of repeal not reviving.	Chapter 14, Section 4.
16	Repeals: savings.	Chapter 14, Section 4.
17	Repeal and re-enactment.	Chapter 14, Section 4.
18	Duplicated offences.	Chapter 1, Section 5.

Section	Topic	Place addressed
19	Citation of one Act by another.	This Chapter, para. 22.1.22.
20	Reference in one Act to another.	This Chapter, paras 22.1.23—22.1.27.
21	Meaning of "Act" and "subordinate legislation" in Interpretation Act 1978.	This Chapter, para. 22.1.28.
22–24	Application of Interpretation Act 1978.	This Chapter, para. 22.1.29.
25–27	Repeals, savings, commencement and short title.	

Section 5: particular definitions

Section 5 of, and Sch.1 to, the Interpretation Act 1978 ascribe fixed meanings to a number of listed words and expressions. Like the rest of the Act, there are a number of these defining provisions which can safely be ignored on the grounds that one would assume them to be the case anyway.[5] But some give a precise and unexpectedly technical meaning to an expression, ignorance of which could lead to serious misunderstanding of a provision of legislation.[6] The following table distils from the Schedule a number of definitions which are likely to be of particular importance relatively frequently.

22.1.4

Expression	Definition
Affidavit	Includes affirmation and declaration.[7]
British Islands	The United Kingdom, the Channel Islands and the Isle of Man.

22.1.5

---

[5] For example " 'Act' means Act of Parliament" or " 'commencement' in relation to an Act or enactment, means the time when the Act or enactment comes into force". And many of the definitions in the Schedule are in effect giving the full technical title of an office or source for an expression (such as "county court", "Crown Estate Commissioners" or "Lord Chancellor") which will be sufficiently understood for the purposes of most readers of legislation without expansion.

[6] For example, " 'Associated state' means a territory maintaining a status of association with the United Kingdom in accordance with the West Indies Act 1967".

[7] See also Chapter 14, para.14.5.6.

Expression	Definition
British overseas territory[8]	As defined in the British Nationality Act 1981 (c.61).[9]
Central funds	In an enactment providing in relation to England and Wales for the payment of costs out of central funds, means money provided by Parliament.[10]
The Communities, &c.	As defined in s.1 of and Sch.1 to the European Communities Act 1972 (c.68). Other defined expressions from that Act include "the Treaties", "the Community Treaties" and "Member State".
The Corporation Tax Acts	The enactments relating to the taxation of the income and chargeable gains of companies and of company distributions (including provisions relating to income tax).
Enactment	Not including enactment comprised in, or in an instrument made under, an Act of Scottish Parliament—see Chapter 1, Section 1 and Chapter 4, Section 2.
England	The area consisting of the counties established by s.1 of the Local Government Act 1972 (c.70), Greater London and the Isles of Scilly (subject to alterations in the boundaries under Pt IV of the 1972 Act).
Financial year	In relation to, broadly speaking, public money, the period of 12 months ending with March 31.
High Court	Her Majesty's High Court of Justice in England, in relation to England, or Her Majesty's High Court of Justice in Northern Ireland, in relation to Northern Ireland.
The Income Tax Acts	All enactments relating to income tax, including any provisions of the Corporation Tax Acts which relate to income tax.
Land	Includes buildings and other structures, land covered with water, and any estate, interest, easement, servitude or right in or over land.
Month	Calendar month.

---

[8] Definitions will also be found for "British possession" and "colony".

[9] Formerly known as British Dependent Territories, but that term was replaced by the British Overseas Territories Act 2002 (c.8).

[10] In other words, money voted out of the Consolidated Fund in accordance with the House of Commons' supply procedure (see Chapter 1, Section 6).

Expression	Definition
Oath	Includes affirmation and declaration.[11]
Person	Includes a body of persons corporate or unincorporated.
Secretary of State	One of Her Majesty's Principal Secretaries of State.[12]
The standard scale	For summary-only offences, the scale established for England and Wales by s.37 of the Criminal Justice Act 1982 (c.48), for Scotland by s.225(1) of the Criminal Procedure (Scotland) Act 1995 (c.46) and for Northern Ireland by art.5 of the Fines and Penalties (Northern Ireland) Order 1984 (SI 1984/703 (NI 3)).
Statutory declaration	Declaration made by virtue of the Statutory Declarations Act 1835.
Statutory maximum	For summary conviction of either-way offences, the prescribed sum for England and Wales within the meaning of s.32 of the Magistrates Courts Act 1980 (c.43), the prescribed sum for Scotland within the meaning of s.225(8) of the Criminal Procedure (Scotland) Act 1995 (c.46) and the prescribed sum for Northern Ireland within the meaning of art.4 of the Fines and Penalties (Northern Ireland) Order 1984 (SI 1984/703 (NI 3)).[13]
Swear	Includes affirmation and declaration.[14]
United Kingdom	Great Britain and Northern Ireland.

[11] For further information see Oaths Act 1978 (c.19).
[12] It is common to confer statutory powers simply on "the Secretary of State". It was once normal to specify a particular Secretary of State, but this is normally reserved now for Charters, non-legislative instruments or provisions of very specific or local application. Originally two in number (Home Secretary and Foreign Secretary) there are now so many Secretaries of State, and their numbers, titles and division of responsibilities change so frequently, that the phrase "Secretary of State" as well as being a convenient shorthand avoids the need for frequent orders under the Ministers of the Crown Act 1975 (c.26), by in effect vesting the function concurrently in each holder of the office of Secretary of State.
[13] It is commonly assumed that just as "the standard scale" is meaningless in relation to offences triable summarily or on indictment, so too "the statutory maximum" is meaningless in relation to summary-only offences. But the definition of "statutory maximum" is in fact confined to summary conviction, which could in theory include summary conviction for an offence triable either way.
[14] For further information see Oaths Act 1978 (c.19).

Expression	Definition
Wales	The combined area of the counties created by s.20 of the Local Government Act 1972 (c.70) as originally enacted but subject to any alteration made under s.73 (consequential alteration of boundary following alteration of watercourse).
Writing	Includes typing, printing, lithography, photography and other modes of representing or reproducing words in a visible form, and expressions referring to writing are to be construed accordingly.[15]

22.1.6

It should be noted that, as with many of the rules in the Interpretation Act 1978, these definitions are subject to the caveat that they apply only "unless the contrary intention appears".

It is often unclear what does or might amount to a contrary intention for this purpose. So the draftsman of legislation is unlikely to risk putting too great weight on any of these definitions, and if in doubt will include an express definition or make the application of the expression clear in some other way.

For example, although the expression "land" is defined so as to include buildings, in conferring a power to enter land one would fear that the courts might consider the presumption in favour the liberty of the subject and the protection of privacy a sufficient contrary intention to prevent the automatic inclusion of buildings in the power. So "buildings" or "premises" would normally be mentioned separately (and, where necessary, it would be usual to make express provision permitting the entry of dwelling-houses, on the grounds again that power to enter premises might, depending on the context, be construed as falling short of a power to enter private homes).

22.1.7   If one of these definitions deserves singling out for special notice it is "person". Much of legislation is drafted by reference to persons, which expression is generally intended to cover both individuals (or natural persons)

---

[15] The development of electronic technology has created considerable problems, not addressed by this limited definition, in relation to legislative references to writing. For example, is a requirement that a notice be in writing satisfied by sending a fax or an electronic message? There is no definitive answer at law to these questions yet, and perhaps there neither will nor should be. At present everything depends on a construction of the provision concerned and consideration of all the relevant circumstances, and perhaps that is how the position ought to remain. Generally speaking, however, it can be said that the normal legislative intention in requiring writing is to ensure formality and to assist evidence. Faxes and electronic messages are likely to satisfy the requirements of formality. As to reliability of evidence, it is likely to remain true that a person who want to send a message in such a way as to make it impossible for the recipient to argue plausibly that he did not both receive it and become aware of its nature will find few if any methods as satisfactory as having a paper document delivered and the delivery attested or recorded.

and entities which owe their individual existence not to nature but to a rule of statutory or other law (or legal persons, the body corporate being the principal example[16]). However the definition of "person" covers bodies unincorporated with the result that a club, for example, would be included. Whether a particular provision that applies to persons is apt for application without modification to an unincorporated association is, of course, a matter of fact to be determined in the circumstances. Where the fluidity of membership of the group makes the application of the provision inoperable in practice, that might amount to a sufficient contrary indication to displace the Interpretation Act definition.

Schedule 1 to the Interpretation Act 1978 also refers to a number of Acts which establish principles or definitions of general application.

For the most part these are the sources to which the reader would naturally turn without the sign-post in the 1978 Act.[17]

Less obvious and more important is the provision directing the reader to s.1 of the Family Law Reform Act 1987 (c.42) for construction of references to relationships, the principal point being that references to relationships are now generally to be treated as not depending on legitimacy.[18] **22.1.8**

It should also be noted that certain fields of expression that were once defined in the Interpretation Act 1978 have now been relegated to the principal enactments dealing with the relevant field generally: so, for example, expressions

---

[16] Others of occasional significance are statutory corporations, corporations sole, and limited liability partnerships.

[17] For example, it would not be difficult for someone anxious to construe a reference to a water undertaker to find the Water Industry Act 1991 (c.56).

[18] **"General principle**

(1) In this Act and enactments passed and instruments made after the coming into force of this section, references (however expressed) to any relationship between two persons shall, unless the contrary intention appears, be construed without regard to whether or not the father and mother of either of them, or the father and mother of any person through whom the relationship is deduced, have or had been married to each other at any time.

(2) In this Act and enactments passed after the coming into force of this section, unless the contrary intention appears—
   (a) references to a person whose father and mother were married to each other at the time of his birth include; and
   (b) references to a person whose father and mother were not married to each other at the time of his birth do not include,
   references to any person to whom subsection (3) below applies, and cognate references shall be construed accordingly.

(3) This subsection applies to any person who—
   (a) is treated as legitimate by virtue of section 1 of the Legitimacy Act 1976;
   (b) is a legitimated person within the meaning of section 10 of that Act;
   (c) is an adopted person within the meaning of Chapter 4 of Part 1 of the Adoption and Children Act 2002; or
   (d) is otherwise treated in law as legitimate.

(4) For the purpose of construing references falling within subsection (2) above, the time of a person's birth shall be taken to include any time during the period beginning with—
   (a) the insemination resulting in his birth; or
   (b) where there was no such insemination, his conception,
   and (in either case) ending with his birth."

relating to rights and duties in relation to children will generally be found in the Children Act 1989 (c.41).

Section 6(a) and (b): gender

22.1.9   Section 6(a) and (b) of the Interpretation Act 1978 provide—

"In any Act, unless the contrary intention appears—

(a) words importing the masculine gender include the feminine;

(b) words importing the feminine gender include the masculine;"

So as a matter of law a male reference ("he", "him", and the like) includes the equivalent female reference, and vice versa.

As to the policy and other considerations in relation to gender-free drafting, see Chapter 8, Section 2.

In the present state of legislative drafting where the masculine gender is used routinely in reliance on s.6 of the Interpretation Act, it follows that any departure from the practice by way of the use of a feminine expression will require little or nothing by way of supporting evidence to evince a contrary intention, since the use of the feminine is so rare.[19] Equally, deliberate exclusion of the feminine by use of a masculine expression will require considerable supporting evidence.

22.1.10   In certain contexts it will be clear that there is a risk of a contrary indication being found displacing s.6(a), in which case the legislation will make express provision.[20]

For a case in which the Court of Appeal held that a legislative reference to the feminine gender was too clearly intended to be specific to permit of the application of s.6, even in the light of pressure from s.3 of the Human Rights Act 1998,[21] see the judgment of Lord Phillips of Worth Matravers M.R. in *R. (Hooper) v Secretary of State for Work and Pensions*.[22]

Section 6(c): number

22.1.11   Section 6(c) of the Interpretation Act 1978 provides—

"In any Act, unless the contrary intention appears,— . . .

---

[19] For occasions on which the feminine is likely to be used see Chapter 8, Section 2.

[20] See, for example, para.1(1) of Sch.3 to the Armed Forces Act 1981 (c.55)—"(1) Every enactment which refers to the armed forces or the naval, military or air forces of the Crown shall have effect as if the reference included a reference to the women's services of those forces administered by the Defence Council and any enactment containing the words 'men', 'soldiers', 'seamen', 'airmen' or other word importing a reference to persons of the male sex only as, or as having been, or as capable of being members of the naval, military or air forces of the Crown shall have effect as if for such word there had been substituted therein words having a like meaning in other respects but importing a reference to persons of either sex."

[21] As to which see Chapter 25.

[22] [2003] 1 W.L.R. 2623, CA; note that as this work went to press *Hooper* was pending appeal to the House of Lords.

(c) words in the singular include the plural and words in the plural include the singular."

As to the preference in drafting for the singular over the plural, see Chapter 8, Section 2.

For an instance of a Government department drafting a provision by reference to "regulation or regulations" to avoid the possibility of a contrary indication displacing s.6, in circumstances where the Joint Committee on Statutory Instruments were not convinced that any contrary indication could be found, see the 17th Report of the Joint Committee for Session 1995–96.[23]

Section 7: service by post

Section 7 of the Interpretation Act 1978 provides—

22.1.12

"Where an Act authorises or requires any document to be served by post (whether the expression 'serve' or the expression 'give' or 'send' or any other expression is used) then, unless the contrary intention appears, the service is deemed to be effected by properly addressing, pre-paying and posting a letter containing the document and, unless the contrary is proved, to have been effected at the time at which the letter would be delivered in the ordinary course of post."

This creates two presumptions. First, that where a document is expressly authorised or required to be served by post "service is deemed to be effected by properly addressing, preparing and posting a letter containing the document". Secondly, that where this method is used the document is received "at the time at which the letter would be delivered in the ordinary course of post".

The use of the expression "serve" is less common in modern legislative drafting, although the expression is still found. More frequent is reference to "sending a document" or "giving a notice". The presumptions in s.7 are expressly applied irrespective of the expression used.

It is increasingly common to find express presumptions along the lines of s.7, but adding something that would not otherwise be supplied by that section.[24]

---

[23] HL Paper 66, HC 34-xvii, para.3.

[24] See, for example, s.21(4) of the Nationality, Immigration and Asylum Act 2002 (c.41)—"(4) A notice under subsection (3)(a)—(a) must be in writing, and (b) if sent by first class post to the claimant's last known address or to the claimant's representative, shall be treated as being received by the claimant on the second day after the day of posting." While this presumption is not expressed to be rebuttable, it is likely that the courts would treat the possibility of rebuttal as implied, so that in the case of, for example, a postal strike, the courts would probably not regard Parliament as intending to regard as received that which the person sending the notice knew for certain would not have been received.

The presumption of effective service by post is rebuttable in the case of the presumption created by s.7.[25] But other express presumptions of service may be irrebuttable.[26]

Section 8: references to distance

22.1.13   Section 8 of the Interpretation Act 1978 provides—

> "In the measurement of any distance for the purposes of an Act, that distance shall, unless the contrary intention appears, be measured in a straight line on a horizontal plane."

It is likely that rebuttal of this presumption would be implied in most circumstances in which the presumption would not itself be supplied by common sense.[27]

---

[25] That is to say, it can be displaced by evidence to the contrary: but it is, of course, difficult or impossible to prove a negative—so it will generally be impossible to prove that a document was not delivered, and it will be possible to prove that it was not delivered at a particular time only by positive proof that it was delivered at a different time.

[26] See *C. A. Webber (Transport) Ltd v Railtrack plc* [2004] 1 W.L.R. 320, CA in which the Court of Appeal found that s.23 of the Landlord and Tenant Act 1927 (c.36) ("(1) Any notice, request, demand or other instrument under this Act shall be in writing and may be served on the person on whom it is to be served either personally, or by leaving it for him at his last known place of abode in England or Wales, or by sending it through the post in a registered letter addressed to him there, or, in the case of a local or public authority or a statutory or a public utility company, to the secretary or other proper officer at the principal office of such authority or company, and in the case of a notice to a landlord, the person on whom it is to be served shall include any agent of the landlord duly authorised in that behalf. (2) Unless or until a tenant of a holding shall have received notice that the person theretofore entitled to the rents and profits of the holding (hereinafter referred to as 'the original landlord') has ceased to be so entitled, and also notice of the name and address of the person who has become entitled to such rents and profits, any claim, notice, request, demand, or other instrument, which the tenant shall serve upon or deliver to the original landlord shall be deemed to have been served upon or delivered to the landlord of such holding.") created an irrebuttable presumption of service and was not subject to s.7 of the Interpretation Act 1978. While capable of causing injustice, the irrebuttable presumption was thought to be justifiable, both by reference to the Human Rights Act 1998 and generally, on the grounds of amounting to "a fair allocation of the risk of any failure of communication" and it being "neither unreasonable nor disproportionate to achieve certainty for landlords and tenants alike" (at 337, *per* Peter Gibson L.J.).

[27] Take, for example, the much litigated provision now found in s.444(4) and (5) of the Education Act 1996 (c.56) (offence of failure to secure regular attendance at school of registered pupil)—"(4) The child shall not be taken to have failed to attend regularly at the school if the parent proves—(a) that the school at which the child is a registered pupil is not within walking distance of the child's home, and . . . (5) In subsection (4) 'walking distance'—(a) in relation to a child who is under the age of eight, means 3.218688 kilometres (two miles), and (b) in relation to a child who has attained the age of eight, means 4.828032 kilometres (three miles), in each case measured by the nearest available route." Even without the final words, which contain a clear although not explicit rebuttal of s.8 of the Interpretation Act 1978, the rebuttal would be implied from the sense of the provision, since what is clearly intended to be referred to is the distance which the child has to walk, which cannot be determined by the calculation contained in s.8. Contrast this case with that of s.76(3) of the Anti-terrorism, Crime and Security Act 2001 (c.24) (Atomic Energy Authority special

Section 9: references to time of day

Section 9 of the Interpretation Act 1978 provides—

22.1.14

"Subject to section 3 of the Summer Time Act 1972 (construction of references to points of time during the period of summer time), whenever an expression of time occurs in an Act, the time referred to shall, unless it is otherwise specifically stated, be held to be Greenwich mean time."

Section 3 of the Summer Time Act 1972[28] provides—

"(1) Subject to subsection (2) below, wherever any reference to a point of time occurs in any enactment, Order in Council, order, regulation, rule, byelaw, deed, notice or other document whatsoever, the time referred to shall, during the period of summer time, be taken to be the time as fixed for general purposes by this Act.

(2) Nothing in this Act shall affect the use of Greenwich mean time for purposes of astronomy, meteorology, or navigation, or affect the construction of any document mentioning or referring to a point of time in connection with any of those purposes."

The combined result of these propositions is that a legislative reference to a time of day is to British Summer Time while it applies and otherwise to Greenwich mean time. While this is expressed as a proposition about Acts, it applies to subordinate legislation[29] and is more relevant in that context: an Act rarely[30] descends to details of times of day, but regulations are much more likely to do so.[31]

Section 10: references to the Sovereign

Section 10 of the Interpretation Act 1978 provides—

22.1.15

"In any Act a reference to the Sovereign reigning at the time of the passing of the Act is to be construed, unless the contrary intention appears, as a reference to the Sovereign for the time being."

---

constables)—"(3) An A.E.A. constable shall have the powers and privileges (and be liable to the duties and responsibilities) of a constable anywhere within 5 kilometres of the limits of the nuclear sites to which subsection (1) applies.": in that case the courts would be likely to apply the calculation contained in s.8 of the 1978 Act as a matter of common sense.

[28] 1972 c.6.

[29] See below.

[30] But the principal exception, and a common one at that, is in relation to changes of duty—see, for example, s.1(2) or 3(3) of the Finance Act 2003 (c.14). There are also some instances in relation to licensing.

[31] See, for example, regs 3 and 14 of the Electricity (Standards of Performance) Regulations 2001 (SI 2001/3265), reg.8 of the Gaming Duty Regulations 1997 (SI 1997/2196) or reg.7 of the Distress for Customs and Excise Duties and Other Indirect Taxes Regulations 1997 (SI 1997/1431).

This provision, which again would stand to reason were it not expressed, simply allows legislation to operate by reference to "Her Majesty" or "the Queen" and to have effect irrespective of changes in the occupant of the throne (including changes from Queen to King).

Section 11: expressions in subordinate legislation

22.1.16 Section 11 of the Interpretation Act 1978 provides—

> "Where an Act confers power to make subordinate legislation, expressions used in that legislation have, unless the contrary intention appears, the meaning which they bear in the Act."

This establishes the useful principle that, unless the contrary intention appears, an expression found in subordinate legislation has the meaning that it bears in the parent Act. So the reader of subordinate legislation has to be aware of, and take for granted in construing the legislation, any interpretation provision in the parent Act.

This has the potential to be a significant trap for the unwary reader of subordinate legislation. In particular, although many Acts have a single interpretation provision (or one for each Part) that both assigns meaning to expressions and sign-posts significant definitions set out elsewhere, and some Acts contain their own indices of defined expressions, there are many cases where significant definitions that apply for the purposes of the Act as a whole, and therefore by virtue of s.11 of the 1978 Act for any subordinate legislation under the Act, are stated in a relatively inconspicuous place.

Section 12: continuity of powers and duties

22.1.17 See Chapter 12, Section 3.

Section 13: anticipatory exercise of powers

22.1.18 See Chapter 10, Section 1.

Section 14: implied power to amend, revoke and re-enact

22.1.19 Section 14 of the Interpretation Act 1978 provides—

> "Where an Act confers power to make—
>
>   (a) rules, regulations or byelaws; or
>   (b) Orders in Council, orders or other subordinate legislation to be made by statutory instrument,

632

it implies, unless the contrary intention appears, a power, exercisable in the same manner and subject to the same conditions or limitations, to revoke, amend or re-enact any instrument made under the power."

This rebuttable presumption—that a power to legislate includes an implied power to revoke, amend and re-enact legislation—does not apply to every kind of subordinate legislation but only to a list which, as well as appearing somewhat capricious in the modern context, covers enough of the available ground to make exceptions unusual and therefore easy for the unwary to overlook.

The section applies to any power to make rules, regulations, byelaws and Orders in Council. But it applies to other orders and subordinate legislation only if made by statutory instrument.

The result is that a power to make orders about a minor, transitory or administrative matter where it is thought best not to engage the rules applying to statutory instruments, or a power to legislate in some relatively unusual form—directions being a relatively common example—does not benefit from s.14 and requires an express power to vary, revoke and re-enact.[32]

Sections 15 to 17: repeal

See Chapter 14, Section 4.   **22.1.20**

Section 18: duplicated offences

See Chapter 1, Section 5.   **22.1.21**

Section 19: citation of one Act by another

Section 19 of the Interpretation Act 1978 provides—   **22.1.22**

"(1) Where an Act cites another Act by year, statute, session or chapter, or a section or other portion of another Act by number or letter, the reference shall, unless the contrary intention appears, be read as referring—

(a) in the case of Acts included in any revised edition of the statutes printed by authority, to that edition;

(b) in the case of Acts not so included but included in the edition prepared under the direction of the Record Commission, to that edition;

(c) in any other case, to the Acts printed by the Queen's Printer, or under the superintendence or authority of Her Majesty's Stationery Office.

---

[32] Although the power to re-enact will frequently be impliedly conferred by s.12 of the Act, which applies to powers generally and implies the ability to exercise the power "from time to time as occasion requires".

(2) An Act may continue to be cited by the short title authorised by any enactment notwithstanding the repeal of that enactment."

The effects of this section are self-explanatory and are alluded to elsewhere in this work.[33]

Section 20: references in one enactment to another

22.1.23   Section 20 of the Interpretation Act 1978 provides—

"(1) Where an Act describes or cites a portion of an enactment by referring to words, sections or other parts from or to which (or from and to which) the portion extends, the portion described or cited includes the words, sections or other parts referred to unless the contrary intention appears.

(2) Where an Act refers to an enactment, the reference, unless the contrary intention appears, is a reference to that enactment as amended, and includes a reference thereto as extended or applied, by or under any other enactment, including any other provision of that Act."

Of these two rules the first (subs.(1)) might be thought to stand entirely to reason: a reference to "the words from 'house' to 'bat'" includes the words house and bat. The only reason for mentioning the rule here is to note that the authorities in each House of Parliament apply the reverse rule in the construction of amendments to Bills. The result is that the words cited in an amendment leaving out a passage of a Bill often give a very misleading description of the effect of the amendment, since the words themselves are to remain.[34]

22.1.24   The second rule (subs.(2)) provides that, subject to the usual caveat about contrary intention, a reference in enactment A to enactment B include a reference to enactment B as amended, extended or applied by any other enactment. Take, therefore, the case in which Act A is amended by Act B, and Act C says that something shall be determined "in accordance with Act A": the reference in Act C is to be construed as a reference to Act A as amended by Act B.

The question is often asked whether this rule applies to "future" amendments.

Suppose the following case: Act A refers to Act B, and Act C, which is passed after Acts A and B, amends Act B.

---

[33] See Chapter 9, Section 2 and Chapter 14, Section 4.

[34] So, for example, in seeking to remove the reference to cats in the proposition "a person may not take a dog into a public park and may not enter a public park while he is or purports to be in control of a dog, and may not do anything to encourage a cat to follow or accompany him while he is walking in a public park, unless he has a licence for the purpose issued by a local authority", the correct form of amendment would read "leave out from 'dog' to 'park'", which would certainly mislead the reader into thinking that the words to be removed related to dogs.

Does s.20(2) mean that the reference in Act A to Act B is deemed to include a reference to Act B as amended by Act C?

The simple answer is that it would be absurd to suggest that as a general rule Parliament is taken when referring to Act B to have included a reference to amendments that nobody at that time could possibly have known about.[35]

That does not, however, mean that the reference in Act A will necessarily exclude the amendment made by Act C: that has to be determined by looking at all the circumstances and construing, in particular, the nature of the amendment made by Act C and the probable intention of Parliament in passing it, as well as the nature of the reference made by Act A and whether Parliament probably expected it to be ambulatory.

For example, a reference to "local authorities within the meaning of {a provision elsewhere listing them and conferring power to amend the list}" is likely to be expected to be ambulatory, since it locks into a fluid system.

22.1.25

While on the other hand, where an enactment about cats adopts a definition of mouse in an Act about mice, and the law of mice is then thoroughly overhauled by a later enactment, it may not be safe to assume that the legislature in amending the law about mice had in mind an obscure application elsewhere in the statute book.

The care that needs to be taken in applying s.20(2) is therefore an excellent example of the principle that the only rule about construction that can be applied dogmatically in all circumstances is that no rule of construction can be applied dogmatically in all circumstances.

The point arose in the case of *Willows v Lewis*,[36] the judgment of Nourse J. in which supports the proposition that the question whether a statutory reference is ambulatory, in the sense of incorporating amendments made after the date of the reference, can be answered only by a construction of the enactment which makes the reference and the enactment which makes the later amendment.

22.1.26

As to a reference in domestic legislation to European legislation, there may be particular reason to assume that a reference is intending to lock into the European legislative system in an ambulatory way. That may be true even in the case of referential legislation that has the effect of creating or extending a criminal

---

[35] Where Parliament does mean that in a particular case, it may say so—see for example, "references to particular provisions of the Council Regulation shall be construed as references to those provisions, or provisions of an Community instrument replacing them, as amended from time to time" (Plant Varieties Act 1997 c.66, s.38(1)) or leave the point to be inferred from the context (as, arguably, it would have been had the Plant Varieties Act been silent).

[36] [1982] S.T.C. 141.

offence. As Lord Nicholls of Birkenhead said in *Department for Environment, Food and Rural Affairs v Asda Stores Ltd*[37]—

> "26. I agree that offence-creating provisions must always be expressed with sufficient clarity and precision. But the mechanism chosen by Parliament for implementing Community obligations is a matter of legislative choice for Parliament. Particularly where Community legislation may be changed frequently, Parliament may choose to adopt an approach which does not involve making new implementing regulations whenever Community legislation changes. Courts should not approach the interpretation of implementing statutes or regulations as though there were a presumption that they do not embrace future changes in Community legislation. There is no such presumption. There might have been a place for such a presumption if it were inherently unlikely that implementing statutes or implementing statutory instruments would be intended to embrace future changes in Community legislation, but that is not always so. Rather, in each case the court is seeking to find, with the assistance of the usual interpretative aids, the intention reasonably to be attributed to Parliament in enacting the relevant legislation or to the minister in making the relevant statutory instrument.

22.1.27

> "27. In the present case, for the reasons given above, I consider there is no room for doubt on the proper interpretation of section 11(3) of the 1964 Act and the 1973 regulations. The contrary interpretation of these provisions, I might add in passing, would involve rejecting the assumption universally held since 1973. It would also mean that for many years this country has been in breach of its Community law obligation to penalise contraventions of Community grading rules introduced after 1972.

> "28. [Counsel], toiling valiantly to make bricks without straw, stressed the importance of legal certainty. Persons affected by these sanctions and their advisers need to have ready access to the relevant regulations. Today there is no difficulty because the text of Community grading rules is readily accessible on the website of the Horticultural Marketing Inspectorate. But this was not so in 1972. In those days high street solicitors had ready access to statutory instruments but not, it is said, to Community regulations. A preferable legislative approach, promoting increased legal certainty in practical terms, would have been for each change in Community grading rules to have been followed by a corresponding statutory instrument.

> "I am not impressed by this argument as an aid to interpretation in the present case. No doubt such an alternative way of setting about things could have been adopted by Parliament. Whether it would have made much difference in practice is not clear. In particular, there is no reason to suppose that in practice those affected have ever had difficulty in obtaining adequate

---

[37] [2004] 1 W.L.R. 105, 111, HL.

information about the scope and terms of current Community grading rules."

Section 21

Section 21 of the Interpretation Act 1978 provides—   **22.1.28**

"(1) In this Act 'Act' includes a local and personal or private Act; and 'subordinate legislation' means Orders in Council, orders, rules, regulations, schemes, warrants, byelaws and other instruments made or to be made under any Act.

(2) This Act binds the Crown."

While the definitions in subs.(1) apply only to the Interpretation Act 1978 itself, the definition of subordinate legislation may provide a useful checklist for other purposes.

Sections 22 to 24: application of Interpretation Act 1978

The result of ss.22 to 24 of the 1978 Act is that the rules of the Act apply   **22.1.29**
to—

Acts passed after January 1, 1979 (s.22(1)).

Acts passed before that date (s.22(1)—subject to the rules in Sch.2).

Church Measures[38] (s.22(3)).

Subordinate legislation (except for ss.1 to 3 and 4(b)) (s.23(1)).

Deeds, instruments documents—ss.9 and 19 only (s.23(3)).

Acts of the Scottish Parliament and instruments under them, to the extent provided for by s.23A.

Northern Ireland legislation (s.24).

---

[38] As to which see Chapter 3, Section 7.

CHAPTER 23

OTHER GENERAL INTERPRETATION PROVISIONS

A number of Acts contain provisions which are of an Interpretation Act **23.1.1** character, in the sense that they are expected to be born in mind by the reader of legislation generally (whether or not they are expressly formed as propositions about construction).

Of these, some will be more or less obvious from their context. So, for example, it will not be difficult for a reader of a statute about land law to work out that a proposition about commonhold land is likely to require to be construed by reference to the Commonhold and Leasehold Reform Act 2002.[1]

It is not practicable to give a complete list in this work of definitions included in one Act which are intended to have effect in relation to later legislation. But the following are particularly worthy of note.

Definition	*Source*	**23.1.2**
Alien.	British Nationality Act 1981 (c.61), s.51(4).	
Expressions relating to the armed forces.	Army Act 1955 (c.18), Air Force Act 1955 (c.19) and the Naval Discipline Act 1957 (c.53).	
British subject.	British Nationality Act 1981 (c.61), s.51(2).	
Family relationships (father, mother, &c.).	Human Fertilisation and Embryology Act 1990 (c.37).	
Post, &c.	Postal Services Act 2000 (c.26).	
Territorial sea.	Territorial Sea Act 1987 (c.49).	

---

[1] 2002 c.15.

Certain other provisions which do not have the character of definitions but which the reader of legislation would do well generally to bear in mind are noted in Chapter 14, Section 5.

CHAPTER 24

OTHER SPECIFIC INTERPRETATION PROVISIONS

Introduction

Almost every item of legislation, whether primary or subordinate, contains a **24.1.1** number of provisions that serve only to define expressions found elsewhere in the legislation. This Chapter makes some observations about provisions of this kind.

Legislative definitions frequently represent the result of considerable thought about cases that might need to be included in or excluded from the meaning of an expression in a particular context; they can therefore be of interest to practitioners for use in non-legislative documents in similar contexts.[1]

As to what amounts to a definition, see below.

Position

By convention, the general rule is that in primary legislation definitions appear **24.1.2** at the end, while in subordinate legislation it is the general rule for definitions to be grouped near the beginning. But these rules have their exceptions. In particular, it is common—and was once the general rule—for Schedules to Acts to group defined terms at the beginning. And even where a statutory instrument, for example, groups a number of defined terms at the beginning, individual provisions throughout the instrument are likely to make use of additional definitions, in which case they are likely to be found at or near the end of the provisions to which they relate.

The rationale for neither of these two general rules is easy to state. They serve together to illustrate the only useful rule of legislative drafting, namely that there are no useful rules of legislative drafting, the only correct approach being to consider what is best for clarity of the law or the convenience of the reader on each occasion.

There will be occasions on which it is most helpful to have definitions, or at least some definitions, at the outset, because without them the reader will have no real understanding of the effect of the substantive provisions. The Terrorism Act

---

[1] *Stroud's Judicial Dictionary*, as well as digesting decided cases in which particular legislative expressions are construed, lists definitions from primary and subordinate legislation that are thought likely to be of particular use to practitioners.

2000[2] opens with a section dedicated to the definition of terrorism, a concept which is so fundamental to the provisions of the Act that the reader could not very well be expected to proceed without knowing it.

Very often, however, a definition is included not because there is likely to be any real doubt in the mind of the reader of the substantive provision as to the principal cases intended to be caught by a particular expression, but only because there are marginal cases which a reader could be unsure about, or could affect to be unsure about. In these cases it is clearly most sensible to allow the reader to penetrate to the essence of the section immediately, without first wading through a set of technical provisions, and in such cases the definitions are best left to the end.[3]

Inclusive and exclusive definitions

24.1.3 There are three kinds of definition—

(1) An exhaustive definition of an expression.

(2) Provision ensuring that an expression is treated as covering something which is not (or more usually may not be) within its ordinary meaning.

(3) Provision ensuring that an expression does not cover something which is or may be within the ordinary meaning.

It is normal drafting practice to use "means" for the first kind of definition, "includes" for the second and "does not include" for the third.

It is also common not to define an expression, but to attract a definition that appears elsewhere. This approach is particularly useful if the definition is lengthy or if it is helpful for the reader to have his attention drawn to the provision which contains the primary definition. It is also important if the definition may change and the intention is to attract it not only as it is now but including future changes.[4] The usual form for an approach of this kind is to say "In this section X has the meaning given in section A of Act B" or "In this section X has the same meaning

---

[2] 2000 c.11.

[3] So, for example, s.13 of the Employment Relations Act 1999 (c.26) defines for a small group of earlier provisions the concept of "worker": that being a common enough concept of the real world, a reader will have no difficulty in learning the essence of the provisions without having the term defined, but there are real marginal doubts in relation to persons working from home, for example, which need to be dealt with at some stage and are thus addressed after the substantive provisions have been set out.

[4] See the general discussion of s.20(2) of the Interpretation Act 1978 (c.30) in Chapter 22. A definition is a case where the ambulatory intention is likely to be sufficiently apparent. If Act A says "'large dog' has the same meaning as in Act B" and Act B contains both a definition and a power for a Minister to alter the definition from time to time, it is unlikely (in the absence of anything suggesting the contrary) that Act A intends to attract the definition only as it happens to stand at a particular time.

as in section A of Act B".[5] The concept of "X shall be construed in accordance with Y" is also useful where Y is not a straight definition of an expression but some kind of a gloss on its meaning in a particular context.

Many definitions take the form of "In this [Act or instrument] X means . . . ". **24.1.4** This is the method for setting out an exhaustive definition which rigidly defines the class of matter to be caught by and excluded from the meaning of the expression as used.

Often, however, an expression has a readily understood "central" range of meanings, which it would be unnecessary, and quite possible dangerous, to try to set out in a definition. But there are matters at either end of the range as to the intended inclusion of which the reader could not be certain. In those cases it is proper to leave the central meaning of the term to have its natural meaning, but to address the extreme so the range and put them beyond doubt by a provision along the lines of "X includes . . . " or "X does not include".[6]

Although definitions of this kind are expressly non-exhaustive, there is a risk in setting out a list of things included by a term that the natural range of its meanings will come to be construed with some reference to the express list. This is simply a particular instance of the application of the rule *expressio unius est exclusio alterius* discussed in detail elsewhere in this work.[7]

"Tag" definitions

One of the points emerging from the discussion above about the positioning of **24.1.5** definitions is that definitions are of different kinds and do different things. An important distinction can be made between "substantive definitions" and "mere tags".

Substantive definitions are those which have a substantive legal effect, being designed to change the law by dispelling doubt in relation to marginal cases, or in relation to matters that for some reason or another one would not otherwise expect to be included or excluded from a particular expression.[8]

Other definitions are sometimes used as mere drafting devices, by way of tags to make it easier to break up a proposition into a number of more readily assimilated sub-propositions. Although these come in many different forms,

---

[5] The different forms are largely a matter of taste: but the latter will be apt for a case where the most helpful provision to refer the reader to is not the provision in which the expression is defined, but perhaps where it is first used or from which its nature is most readily apparent. And the latter form will also be used where the expression is not expressly defined in Act B at all: this is common where referring to an expression having the meaning which it has in a European Directive, in a case where the Directive does not contain an express definition but does impart a distinct flavour to the expression, and it is imperative to attract that flavour (see the debate about copy-out in Chapter 3, Section 10).

[6] See, for example, s.39(5)(c) of the Commonhold and Leasehold Reform Act 2002 (c.15)—"the reference to a judgment debt includes a reference to any interest payable on a judgment debt"; and s.20(6) of that Act—"(6) In this section "interest" does not include—(a) a charge, or (b) an interest which arises by virtue of a charge."

[7] See Chapter 20.

[8] As in the case of s.13 of the Employment Relations Act 1999, mentioned above.

perhaps the most common is the use of "the relevant X" followed by "in this provision 'relevant' means . . . ".[9] So, to take a notional example, instead of saying "A person may make an application under this section to whichever district council, county council, London borough council, or borough council is responsible for the collection of waste in the area where a person lives or, if he lives in more than one area, the area in which he lives for most of the time", the draftsman might prefer to say—

"(1) A person may make an application under this section to the relevant local authority.
(2) In subsection (1) 'local authority' means . . .
(3) The relevant local authority for a person's application is that which is responsible for the collection of waste in his home area.
(4) A person's home area is—

(a) the area in which he habitually lives, or
(b) if he lives in more than one area, the area in which he habitually lives for the majority of each year."

That provision uses three definitions of the "tag" variety simply in order to break up a proposition.

Index of defined terms

24.1.6   A number of Acts contain, either at the end of the Act or at the end of each Part that contains a number of defined terms, a provision setting out an index of the defined terms in that Act or Part.[10]

This is a relatively recent innovation and has been welcomed, in particular, by Parliamentarians. For example, in speaking to an amendment on the Licensing Bill 2002–03 Lord Brightman said[11]—

"I applaud the Minister's drafting team for including Clause 189, on page 104, which is an index of specially defined words and expressions used in the Bill. It is of great convenience to the reader. By referring to the left-hand column of the index, the reader can discover at a glance whether a word or expression has or has not a special statutory meaning. If so, the right-hand column tells the reader at a glance where the meaning is to be found. Once rarely found in Bills, an index is becoming a feature of a number of well drafted Bills.

---

[9] Also in the Employment Relations Act 1999, see the considerable use of this device made in para.14 of Sch.1.
[10] See, for example, s.70 of the Commonhold and Leasehold Reform Act 2002 (c.15).
[11] HL Deb. January 20, 2003 c.473.

"The Health Minister, the noble Lord, Lord Hunt of Kings Heath, at a closing stage of the Adoption and Children Bill last October, said that—

'having an easy-to-understand glossary is of use to a Minister as it is to every other Member of your Lordships' House. I commend that very good practice of my own department to other government departments'.[12]

"I hope that, in time, every long Bill will have an index of defined expressions to help the reader."[13]

There are, however, potential difficulties associated with indices of defined phrases. Apart from the danger of readers being misled by the inadvertent omission of an item from the index—which could be a result of the difficulty in deciding what amounts to a definition[14]—there is the impossibility of ensuring that the index is properly maintained when the substantive provisions come to be amended, either during the passage of the Bill through Parliament or by amending primary or subordinate legislation at a later time.[15] There is therefore a school of thought that the benefits of these indices are outweighed by the dangers of their misleading. An alternative approach is to include an index in the Explanatory Notes, in which context it is expected to reflect the Bill only as introduced in each House: since it is not expected to be updated during the passage of a Bill through each House or after enactment, it is less likely to mislead.

Designation of definitions

In some of the discussions about possible devices to improve the clarity and ease of understanding of legislative drafting, it is sometimes suggested that all defined terms should be underlined or distinguished in some other way. The principal difficulty with this approach is, as with the index of defined expressions, that omissions would be likely to mislead a reader, possibly with serious consequences.

24.1.7

Inadvertent omissions apart, the draftsman's conception of what is and is not a definition might not coincide with that of every reader. By no means all definitions are introduced with "X means . . . " or "X includes . . . ". Some are

---

[12] HL Deb. October 30, 2002 c.251.

[13] For a House of Commons example see Standing Committee D c.298 on the Terrorism Bill 1999–2000.

[14] As to which see below.

[15] It is, in particular, not reasonable to expect that non-Government amendments will be in a technically perfect form, and it is usual to find that the necessary consequential amendments, which might include an amendment of the index of defined expressions, are omitted. While the Government will normally try to remedy technical defects of non-Government amendments carried with or without Government support by tabling supplementary amendments at a later stage, this is not always reasonably practicable, particularly if the non-Government amendment is carried at a late stage.

couched in terms along the lines of "A reference to X includes a reference to Y", while others may be almost imperceptibly interpolated by way of a subordinate proposition—perhaps along the lines of "Where an X (including a Y) . . . ".[16] And an infinite range of other possibilities exists.

Apart from the possibility of misleading, in some Acts of a technical nature the number of words requiring some kind of gloss or qualification that is or might be thought to be a definition is so great that underlining or another form of other distinguishing mark would greatly disturb the flow of the text and might become more of a distraction than an assistance.

Different meanings in different parts of Act or instrument

24.1.8 It is common for a particular expression to be required to mean different things in different provisions of one Act or instrument.[17]

For the cross-contextual application of definitions within Acts and between Acts, see Chapter 20, paras 20.1.38 and 20.1.39.

Construction of Act "as one" with another

24.1.9 Where a code in relation to a particular area of law takes the form of a number of different Acts, it is common—and was once more common—for a later Act in the series to contain a provision requiring it to be read as one with an earlier Act in the series.[18]

The same device can be used in relation to one part of an Act, requiring just that part to be read as one with an earlier Act.[19]

The purpose of this device is simply to require the reader to approach the provisions of the later Act or part as if it formed part of the earlier Act, thereby applying automatically all the general provisions of the earlier Act, such as definitions and requirements as to the making of orders and regulations.

A classic expression of the effect of this device is found in the judgment of Lord Selborne L.C. in *Canada Southern Railway Company v International Bridge Company*[20]—

"It is to be observed that those two Acts are to be read together by the express provision of the seventh and concluding section of the amending

---

[16] See, for example, s.31(5)(g) of the Commonhold and Leasehold Reform Act 2002 (c.15): "to refrain from undertaking works (including alterations) of a specified kind".

[17] For example, expressions relating to employment ("worker", "employee" and the like) have a number of different defined meanings in legislative provisions about employment, and variations will be found within most lengthy Acts or instruments—see, for example, the Employment Relations Act 1999 (c.26).

[18] For example, s.56(2) of the Education Act 1997 (c.44) provides that "This Act shall be construed as one with the Education Act 1996".

[19] For example, s.4(3) of the Education (schools) Act 1997 (c.59) provides that: "Sections 1 to 3 shall be construed as one with the Education Act 1996."

[20] (1883) 8 App. Cas. 723, 727.

Act; and therefore we must construe every part of each of them as if it had been contained in one Act, unless there is some manifest discrepancy, making it necessary to hold that the later Act has to some extent modified something found in the earlier Act."

Even where the device is not used, its effect may be created automatically where two Acts have very similar subject matters.[21]

---

[21] See the discussion of the construction of Acts *in pari materia* in Chapter 20.

CHAPTER 25

SECTION 3 OF THE HUMAN RIGHTS ACT 1998

Introduction

The Human Rights Act 1998[1] is discussed elsewhere in this work.[2] Section 3 **25.1.1** requires particular examination in the context of statutory interpretation. That section provides[3]—

> "So far as it is possible to do so, primary legislation and subordinate legislation must be read and given effect in a way which is compatible with the Convention rights".

Section 3 is the third of the changes of the law in relation to the effect of legislation on human rights mentioned by Lord Hoffmann in his speech in *R. v Secretary of State for the Home Department, ex parte Simms*.[4]

This Chapter discusses the application of s.3.

Scope of the rule

The rule requiring legislation to be read in a manner compatible with the **25.1.2** European Convention on Human Rights applies to legislation whether passed before or after the Human Rights Act 1998.[5] It is reasonable to hope that for legislation drafted after the coming into force of that Act it will rarely be

---

[1] 1998 c.42.
[2] See, in particular, Chapter 11, Section 3.
[3] The full text is as follows—
"3 Interpretation of legislation
  (1) So far as it is possible to do so, primary legislation and subordinate legislation must be read and given effect in a way which is compatible with the Convention rights.
  (2) This section—
    (a) applies to primary legislation and subordinate legislation whenever enacted;
    (b) does not affect the validity, continuing operation or enforcement of any incompatible primary legislation; and
    (c) does not affect the validity, continuing operation or enforcement of any incompatible subordinate legislation if (disregarding any possibility of revocation) primary legislation prevents removal of the incompatibility."
[4] [1999] 3 All E.R. 400, 411–12 HL, discussed elsewhere in this work in relation to the sovereignty of Parliament (Chapter 2, Sections 1 and 2), in relation to the effect of legislation on human rights (Chapter 11, Section 3) and in relation to rebuttable presumptions of construction (Chapter 19).
[5] s.3(2)(a).

necessary to do much violence to the language of the legislation to ensure compatibility, although doubtless cases will arise where an aspect of the legislation later gives rise to a human rights difficulty that could not reasonably have been foreseen when it was drafted.

The alternative to the application of the rule, where the courts are simply unable to read the legislation in a compatible way, is to make a declaration of incompatibility under s.4 of the Human Rights Act 1998, in the case of primary legislation, or to quash the legislation under s.6 of the Act in the case of subordinate legislation.[6]

The requirement is that "so far as it is possible to do so, primary legislation and subordinate legislation must be read and given effect in a way which is compatible with the Convention rights".[7]

25.1.3   An early instance of the application of this rule was the case of *Ghaidan v Godin-Mendoza*.[8] For some time there had been uncertainty about how to construe references in legislation to various kinds of family relationship in the light of changing social practice and, in particular, the increasing incidence of persons of the same sex living together in a manner reminiscent of a married relationship. In *Fitzpatrick v Sterling Housing Association Ltd*[9] the courts had, on the ordinary domestic rules of statutory construction in relation to language changing its meaning over time,[10] felt unable to stretch the meaning of a reference to a person living "as his or her wife or husband" in relation to a statutory tenancy so as to include a partner of the same sex. But in *Mendoza*, the added impetus of s.3 of the Human Rights Act 1998 gave the courts the additional support necessary to enable them to go that far, on the grounds that whether or not same-sex relationships were within the reasonable contemplation of the terms as originally used by Parliament, to exclude those relationships would now result in a provision that discriminated contrary to the provisions of the Convention, so obliging the courts to read the terms in an extended way for the purposes of ensuring compliance with the Convention.

There will of course be occasions on which the terms of legislation cannot sensibly be construed, even at the expense of violence to the language of minor or technical aspects, as having an effect that complies with the Convention. Section 3 expressly acknowledges that, and affirms the doctrine of the supremacy of Parliament by stating that the new rule of construction—

(1) "does not affect the validity, continuing operation or enforcement of any incompatible primary legislation",[11] and

---

[6] Except in the rare case where the incompatibility of the subordinate legislation is required by a provision of primary legislation—see ss.4(3) and (4) and 6(2) of the 1998 Act.
[7] s.3(1).
[8] [2003] Ch. 380, CA.
[9] [2001] 1 A.C. 27, HL.
[10] See Chapter 21.
[11] s.3(2)(b).

(2) "does not affect the validity, continuing operation or enforcement of any incompatible subordinate legislation if (disregarding any possibility of revocation) primary legislation prevents removal of the incompatibility".[12]

The effect of this saving in relation to subordinate legislation is that if Parliament were to wish not to enact a provision of law contrary to the Convention but to enable the executive to enact such a provision, it could achieve this by framing the power in such a way as expressly to require the executive to act in that way. But in the absence of such an express requirement, the new rule of construction is sufficiently strong to require the courts to assume, even in the face of overwhelming evidence to the contrary, that the executive (as distinct from Parliament) could not have meant to legislate in a manner incompatible with the Convention.

Application of the rule

The way in which the rule is to be applied, and the limits on its application, are **25.1.4** discussed in a number of cases.

It is clear that in order to give effect to s.3 the courts will be prepared to imply into a legislative expression limitations or conditions that were clearly not within the contemplation of Parliament at the time of enactment. So, for example—

> "In my judgment the provisions of article 5(1) [of the European Convention on Human Rights] are not met if the language of section 4A [of the Criminal Justice Act 1991[13]—recall of prisoner to custody, release required where 'it is no longer necessary for the protection of the public'] is to be construed in the ordinary way. The Parole Board needs to be satisfied that the risk to the public cannot be dealt with appropriately by leaving the prisoner in the community. ... I do not accept that it is consistent with the original sentence to deprive someone of his liberty, which is a more draconian penalty, unless it is shown that the initial objective has failed. ... The question which then arises is whether it is possible to give section 44A a construction which is compatible with these Convention rights in accordance with section 3 of the Human Rights Act 1998, or whether it is necessary to make a declaration of incompatibility under section 4. Both the claimant and the Secretary of State submit that it is possible to adopt the section 3 route. This can be done, it is submitted, by construing the word 'necessary' in a sufficiently flexible way. I agree that it is possible to achieve consistency with the Convention in this manner. It involves interpreting the phrase 'no longer necessary for the protection of the public interest' in section 44A in such a way that the board must reach that conclusion unless

---

[12] s.3(2)(c).
[13] 1991 c.53.

positively satisfied that continuing detention is necessary in the public interest. It is not necessary to add to or amend the language of the section to achieve this result."[14]

25.1.5   There have been cases where a relatively minor straining of the language of an expression in reliance on s.3 of the Human Rights Act 1998, and certainly a straining which appears in harmony with the probable original legislative intentions, has had a significant effect on the courts' ability to produce a satisfying result. For example, in *Cachia v Faluyi*[15] merely construing a reference to "action" as a reference to served process caused Brooke L.J. to say the following[16]—

> "Since 2 October 2000 we have been under a duty not to act in a way which is incompatible with a convention right (s.6(1) of the 1998 Act), and so far as it is possible to do so, primary legislation must be read and given effect in a way which is compatible with the convention rights (s.3(1)). It is certainly possible to interpret the word 'action' as meaning 'served process' in order to give effect to the convention rights of these three children. Until the present writ was served in July 1997, no process had been served which asserted a claim to compensation by these children for their mother's death. Section 2(3) of the 1976 Act therefore presents no artificial bar to this claim.
>
> "This is a very good example of the way in which the enactment of the 1998 Act now enables English judges to do justice in a way which was not previously open to us."

In similar vein in *Goode v Martin*[17] Brooke L.J. said—

> " . . . without the encouragement of s.3(1) of the 1998 Act, I could see no way of interpreting the language of the rule so as to produce a just result.
>
> "The 1998 Act, however, does in my judgment alter the position. I can detect no sound policy reason why the claimant should not add to her claim in the present action the alternative plea which she now proposes. No new facts are being introduced: she merely wants to say that if the defendant succeeds in establishing his version of the facts, she will still win because those facts, too, show that he was negligent and should pay her compensation.
>
> "In these circumstances it seems to me that to prevent her from putting this case before the court in this action would impose an impediment on her access to the court which would require justification."

---

[14] *R. (Sim) v Parole Board* [2003] 2 W.L.R. 1374, 1396–7, QBD, *per* Elias J.
[15] [2002] 1 All E.R. 192, CA.
[16] At 197.
[17] [2002] 1 All E.R. 620, 629, CA.

The limits to which the courts will be prepared to go in straining the natural **25.1.6**
meaning of legislative language in the application of s.3[18] are explored by Lord
Phillips of Worth Matravers M.R. in *R. (Hooper) v Secretary of State for Work
and Pensions*[19]—

> "26 We agree with Moses J. that the principles to be applied when
> considering the effect of section 3 of the 1998 Act are encapsulated in the
> following statements. In *R v A (No.2)*[20] Lord Steyn said—
>
>> 'In accordance with the will of Parliament as reflected in section 3, it will
>> sometimes be necessary to adopt an interpretation which linguistically
>> may appear strained. The techniques to be used will not only involve the
>> reading down of express language in the statute, but also the implication
>> of provisions. A declaration of incompatibility is a measure of last resort.
>> It must be avoided unless it is plainly impossible to do so. If a clear
>> limitation on convention rights is stated in terms, such an impossibility
>> will arise.'
>
> "However, in *R. v Lambert*,[21] decided about one-and-a-half months after *R.
> v A.*, Lord Hope observed that section 3(1) preserves the sovereignty of
> Parliament: 'It does not give power to the judges to overrule decisions,
> which the language of the statute shows have been taken on the very point
> at issue by the legislature.' Later he observed (at 81)—
>
>> 'But the interpretation of the statute by reading words in to give effect to
>> the presumed intention must always be distinguished carefully from
>> amendment. Amendment is a legislative act. It is an exercise which must
>> be reserved to Parliament.' "

As a result, Lord Phillips of Worth Matravers M.R. declined to read references **25.1.7**
to the feminine gender in ss.36 to 38 of the Contributions and Benefits Act 1992[22]
as including references to the masculine, despite both s.3 of the Human Rights
Act 1998 and s.6 of the Interpretation Act 1978.[23]

In *R. (O) v Crown Court at Harrow*[24] the court held that compliance with the
European Convention on Human Rights required the concept that in relation to
the grant of bail the court must be satisfied of the existence of exceptional
circumstances (in s.25(1) of the Criminal Justice and Public Order Act 1994[25]) to
be read down so as to impose only an evidential burden on the defendant.

---

[18] As to the same limits without reference to s.3, see Chapter 18.
[19] [2003] 1 W.L.R. 2623, CA; note that as this work went to press *Hooper* was pending appeal to the
House of Lords.
[20] [2002] 1 A.C. 45, HL.
[21] [2002] 2 A.C. 545, HL.
[22] 1992 c.4.
[23] 1978 c.30: see also Chapter 22.
[24] [2003] 1 W.L.R. 2756 QBD.
[25] 1994 c.33.

Impact of the rule

25.1.8   While s.3 of the 1998 Act is clearly a powerful weapon in the courts' armoury in construing legislation, and one which they are obliged by statute to use whenever it would affect the result, it may be less significant than it appears at first. Given the trend of the courts towards giving a purposive construction based upon what the legislature should be presumed to have intended in accordance with principle, even without s.3 and even before the enactment of the 1998 Act the courts were prepared to give considerable weight to arguments for a construction based upon the Convention on Human Rights.[26] Of course, they were not able to reach a result at clear variance with the words of the statute, but that is still the case.[27] What s.3 has done is given the courts support for the adoption of a construction which, while right on a purposive approach, places a mild strain upon the legislative language.[28]

Retrospectivity of section 3

25.1.9   The question whether s.3 applies retrospectively to legislation passed before the Human Rights Act 1998 is likely to be of occasional practical importance for some time. In *Wilson and others v Secretary of State for Trade and Industry, Wilson v First County Trust Ltd (No.2)*[29] the House of Lords decided that, as with retrospectivity generally,[30] the question will depend on what Parliament must be presumed to have intended in relation to each case, which will in turn depend on

---

[26] See, in particular, the following passage of the speech of Lord Bridge of Harwich in *Brind and others v Secretary of State for the Home Department* [1991] 1 All E.R. 720, 722–723, HL—

"It is accepted, of course, by the appellants that, like any other treaty obligations which have not been embodied in the law by statute, the convention is not part of the domestic law, that the courts accordingly have no power to enforce convention rights directly and that, if domestic legislation conflicts with the convention, the courts must nevertheless enforce it. But it is already well settled that, in construing any provision in domestic legislation which is ambiguous in the sense that it is capable of a meaning which either conforms to or conflicts with the convention, the courts will presume that Parliament intended to legislate in conformity with the convention, not in conflict with it."

See also the approach of the Court of Appeal in *Derbyshire County Council v Times Newspapers Ltd* [1993] A.C. 534, but noting that the House of Lords found it possible to reach the same conclusion on the basis solely of the common law (see, in particular, the speech of Lord Keith of Kinkel); see also *R v Secretary of State for the Home Department, Ex p. Wynne* [1992] 2 All E.R. 301, 307, CA.

[27] See para.25.1.26 above.

[28] So in *P. W. & Co. v Milton Gate Investments Ltd* [2004] 2 W.L.R. 443, 474–475, Ch, for example, Neuberger J., having construed s.141 of the Law of Property Act 1925 (c.20) in a manner that "would not technically fall within the words" of the statute but which was "capable of falling within those words as a matter of ordinary language", concluded that "I am persuaded that, in light of the provisions of s.3 and . . . the 1925 Act could, in this case, be construed, if possible, in such a way as to enable the covenants in a subtenancy to be enforceable as between head landlord and subtenant, in the event of the head tenancy being determined by a notice, and that this result can be achieved through the medium of a modern and purposive construction of section 141 [editor's emphasis]."

[29] [2003] 3 W.L.R. 568, HL.

[30] See Chapter 10, Section 3.

what is fair or unfair in the circumstances. Lord Nicholls of Birkenhead said[31]—

> "20 . . . I agree with Mummery L.J. in *Wainwright v Home Office*,[32] para.61, that in general the principle of interpretation set out in section 3(1) does not apply to causes of action accruing before the section came into force. The principle does not apply because to apply it in such cases, and thereby change the interpretation and effect of existing legislation, might well produce an unfair result for one party or the other.The Human Rights Act was not intended to have this effect.
>
> "21. I emphasise that this conclusion does not mean that section 3 never applies to pre-Act events.Whether section 3 applies to pre-Act events depends upon the application of the principle identified by Staughton L.J. in the context of the particular issue before the court. To give one important instance: different considerations apply to post-Act criminal trials in respect of pre-Act happenings.The prosecution does not have an accrued or vested right in any relevant sense."

Later cases of the Court of Appeal have suggested that despite Lord Nicholls' caution in not ruling out any retrospective application of s.3 the courts will be very reluctant to find any room for such application.[33]

---

[31] Para.20.

[32] [2001] EWCA Civ 2081.

[33] Note, in particular, the judgment of Mummery L.J. in *Wainwright v Home Office* [2003] 3 All E.R. 943, 956–57, CA.

Chapter 26

USE OF PARTS OF LEGISLATION OTHER THAN TEXT FOR CONSTRUCTION

Introduction

All legislation routinely includes a number of things that are not simply **26.1.1** propositions of law in the text. There are, in particular, preambles, titles and headings of different kinds and in different positions.[1] This Chapter considers what use may be made of these aspects of legislation in construing it.

Preamble

As has been said above, the use of the preamble in Acts of Parliament is now **26.1.2** rare.[2]

A short preamble is routinely given prior to the opening text of a statutory instrument: but it is confined to identifying the person making the instrument, the authority under which the instrument is made and reciting the satisfaction of any statutory conditions precedent to the making of the instrument, such as the affirmation of Parliament or the carrying out of consultation. It does not provide any material which could be used to elicit the purpose or meaning of the instrument.

European legislation routinely includes an extensive preamble, sometimes as long as or even longer than the text of the instrument itself. This frequently addresses both the political and factual background to the passing of a Directive or other piece of legislation and also the agreed motives in enacting it. It is thus a re-creation, and even an extension, of the way in which preambles were used in early Acts, and is accorded the same kind of treatment by the courts as were those early preambles.

The abandonment of preambles in Acts has been regretted by the courts. In *LCC v Bermondsey Bioscope Co*[3] Lord Alverstone C.J. said: "I quite recognise that the title of an Act is part of the Act and that it is of importance as showing the purview of the Act: and I may express in this connection my regret that the practice of inserting preambles in Acts of Parliament has been discontinued as they were often of great assistance to the courts in construing the Acts". And in

---

[1] See Chapter 2, Section 5 and Chapter 3, Section 3.
[2] See Chapter 2, Section 5.
[3] [1911] 1 K.B. 445, 451.

Vacher v London Society of Compositors[4] Lord Macnaghten said: "Nowadays, when it is a rare thing to find a preamble in any public general statute, the field of inquiry is even narrower than it was in former times." And it was certainly the case that the judges used to rely heavily on the preamble to expose the underlying policy of an Act, even in days when the theory of the purposive construction of legislation was less openly recognised (although probably no less important in practice) than it is now.[5]

26.1.3   The abandonment of preambles has also occasionally been regretted by Parliamentarians.[6]

To some extent it can be argued that the loss caused by the disuse of the preamble has been repaired to some extent by the advent of Explanatory Notes. Certainly, the following description from the original First Parliamentary Counsel, Lord Thring, of the proper function of a preamble in an Act would serve as an equally satisfactory description of one of the functions of Explanatory Notes for both primary and subordinate legislation—

> "The proper function of a preamble is to explain certain facts which are necessary to be explained before the enactments contained in the Act can be understood; for example, the Courts of Justice Building Act 1865 proposed to apply certain funds to the payment of the expenses of constructing new courts of justice. Accordingly, a long preamble was prefixed to the Act, explaining the origin of these funds, for without such a preamble it would have been impossible for Parliament to have understood the subject-matter of the Act."[7]

It is still the practice for a private Act to be preceded by a preamble, and the courts routinely have regard to the preamble in construing a private Act.[8]

It is a matter for academic debate whether a preamble forms part of the legislation or not. When substantive preambles were commonly used in relation to Acts different opinions were held as to whether they should be regarded as

---

[4] [1013] A.C. 107, 118.

[5] "The preamble of the statute is a good means to find out the meaning of the statute, and as it were a key to open the understanding thereof." (Coke, 1 Inst. 79a). "From statutes his [Littleton's] arguments and proof are drawn first from the rehearsal or preamble of the statute." (Coke, 1 Litt. 11b.); see also and *Att-Gen v Prince Ernest Augustus of Hanover* [1957] A.C. 436 *per* Lord Normand.

[6] For example, an amendment was tabled that would have added a preamble to the House of Lords Bill 1998–99, opposed by the Government with the Leader of the House, Baroness Jay of Paddington, speaking to it in the following terms—"We have already been round this course several times in relation to purpose clauses. . . . Acts of Parliament are legislative vehicles that are supposed to do something. They are not places for uttering aspirations. I accept [that there were preambles in the past-1911 Act and Parliament (No.2) Bill in 1968]. But, on the whole, in 1999 that is not how legislation is drafted. We reply on the operative words of an Act to tell us what the legislation means, while the Long Title informs Peers and Members of parliament about its subject-matter and purpose. Words that do not mean anything have no place in modern legislation, and that practice certainly predates the present Government."—HL Deb. October 26, 1999 cc.275–76.

[7] Lord Thring, *Practical Legislation*, 1902 ed., p.92.

[8] See, for example, *Allen v Gulf Oil Refining Ltd* [1981] 1 All E.R. 353, HL.

forming part of the Act, a decisive majority holding that they should be.[9] But this debate probably neither is nor even was of much importance, since it is generally agreed both—

> that a preamble cannot be given preference over the clear text of the legislation, and

> that the courts are entitled to have regard to the preamble in construing unclear aspects of the text.[10]

In this sense the permissible use of the preamble corresponds to the **26.1.4** permissible use of extraneous material of other kinds, such as statements in Hansard[11] and Explanatory Notes.[12]

The most important difference between ancient practice in relation to preambles and modern practice in relation to explanatory material is that preambles were undoubtedly part of an Act in the sense that they were open to amendment in the passage of the Bill through Parliament, and could therefore be presumed to represent the settled will and intention of Parliament in enacting the legislation. Explanatory Notes, whether for primary or subordinate legislation, are not open to amendment by Parliament, and must therefore be approached with greater circumspection even in cases where it is clearly permissible to look to them for assistance.

In European legislation, where preambles are the norm, it is certainly permissible to have regard to the preamble in construing the text.[13] Indeed it is often impossible to do otherwise, with definitions and other essential aspects of the legislation being addressed only in the preamble.

Long title

It is clearly established that the long title of an Act may be considered for the **26.1.5** purpose of resolving an ambiguity but will not be used to displace the clear meaning of the text.[14] The position is stated as follows by Donovan J.—

> "In many cases the long title may supply the key to the meaning. The principle, as I understand it, is that where something is doubtful or

---

[9] See Pollock C.B. in *Salkeld v Johnson* (1848) 2 Ex. 256, 283—"The preamble is undoubtedly part of the Act."

[10] See the Earl of Halsbury in *Powell v Kempton Park Racecourse Co* [1899] A.C. 143, 157: "Two propositions are quite clear, one that a preamble may afford useful light as to what a statute intends to reach, and the other that if an enactment is itself clear and unambiguous, no preamble can qualify or cut down the enactment".

[11] See Chapter 28.

[12] See Chapter 27.

[13] A large number of cases each year demonstrate the routine use of the preamble for the construction of Community instruments of all kinds. For random recent examples, see *Saatgut-Treuhandverwaltungsgesellschaft mbH v Werner Jäger* (Case C-182/01) and *Koninklijke KPN Nederland NV v Benelux-Merkenbureau* (Case C-363/99).

[14] See *Fisher v Raven* [1964] A.C. 210, HL, *Brown v Brown* [1967] P. 105, 110, *Haines v Herbert* [1963] 1 W.L.R. 1401, 1404, *Ward v Holman* [1964] 2 Q.B. 580, and *Re Wykes* [1961] 1 Ch. 229,

ambiguous the long title may be looked to to resolve the doubt or ambiguity, but, in the absence of doubt or ambiguity, the passage under construction must be taken to mean what it says, so that, if its meaning be clear, that meaning is not to be narrowed or restricted by reference to the long title."[15]

In *Cornwall County Council v Baker*[16] Toulson J. was able, citing the passage above from Donovan J., to gain support from the long title of the Protection of Animals (Amendment) Act 2000[17] for the notion that the Act "was to enable provision to be made for the care, disposal or slaughter of animals to which section 1 of the 1911 Act relates, and not to make provision for the welfare of animals unrelated to such proceedings".

But the occasions on which the long title will be decisive or even of assistance are certainly few and may become still fewer. The long title is drafted not with the aim of assisting the construction of an Act—as to which the draftsman relies only on the words used in the Act itself—but for purposes related to Parliamentary procedure and, sometimes and to some extent, wider presentational issues.

26.1.6 In the House of Lords in particular, the long title was once considered paramount in determining the area of relevance of a Bill,[18] in the sense that an amendment which was covered by the long title would certainly be relevant, although the converse was not necessarily true. Nowadays both Houses adopt a more purposive approach in determining relevance (or, in the House of Commons, scope): and so one reason for a lengthy and precise long title has disappeared. In addition, there has been some pressure from within Parliament[19] for the reduction of the length of long titles. It is generally thought helpful to readers both within Parliament and without for a long title to do no more than give a concise flavour of the principal purpose of the Bill, and that is unlikely to be of much assistance in cases of detailed construction.[20]

There is no equivalent for subordinate legislation of the long title. But the long title of a parent Act may be used as an aid to the construction of subordinate legislation.[21]

---

242 *per* Buckley J. ("It is well established that the language of a statute must primarily be construed according to its natural meaning. If the language is ambiguous the long title of the Act may be looked at to help resolve the ambiguity: it may not be looked at to modify the interpretation of plain language.").

[15] *R. v Bates* [1952] 2 All E.R. 842, 844.

[16] [2003] 1 W.L.R. 1813, 1818, QBD.

[17] 2000 c.40.

[18] Within which amendments may be tabled, and outside which they may not be tabled.

[19] See, in particular, HL Deb. June 21, 1994 cc.200–204.

[20] Although occasionally lengthy long titles are still inevitable, particularly in the case of Bills desiring to make fairly limited provision in areas of law that are otherwise almost illimitable—see, for example, the long title to the Criminal Justice Act 1993 (c.36).

[21] *Jacks v Wilkie* [1961] P. 135.

Short title

It is clear from what has been said about the manner in which the short title of an Act is chosen and the function which it is designed to perform[22] that it is unlikely to be a reliable tool for the construction of the Act. In this respect it is wholly unlike the long title, which is framed with greater attention both to accuracy and to comprehensiveness. As Lord Moulton said in *Vacher and Sons Ltd v London Society of Compositors*[23]— **26.1.7**

> "The [long] title of an Act is undoubtedly part of the Act itself, and it is legitimate to use it for the purpose of interpreting the Act as a whole and ascertaining its scope. This is not the case with the short title, which in this instance is 'The Trade Disputes Act, 1906.' That is a title given to the Act solely for the purpose of facility of reference. If I may use the phrase, it is a statutory nickname to obviate the necessity of always referring to the Act under its full and descriptive title. It is not legitimate, in my opinion, to use it for the purpose of ascertaining the scope of the Act. Its object is identification and not description."

Headings

Legislation is now routinely divided for the assistance of the reader by headings of different kinds. In the case of Acts each section has a heading,[24] Parts into which the Act may be divided have headings,[25] Chapters within Parts have headings, italic cross-headings may be used as informal headings to blocks of sections within a Part or Chapter and extensive use is made of italic headings in Schedules.[26] **26.1.8**

The use of headings was not found in the early days of statute law. The origin of the practice is generally ascribed to the Clauses Consolidation Acts in 1845.[27]

---

[22] See Chapter 2, Section 5.

[23] [1913] A.C. 107, 127–128, HL.

[24] Until 2001 this heading was placed as a marginal sidenote. The format of the printing of Bills and Acts was changed in 2000 (see Chapter 2, Section 5, para.2.5.1) and one of the most significant changes to the layout of a page of legislation was to move clause and section headings from the margin into the text. The marginal nature of headings previously made it clear that they were not part of the text: in particular, there was no question whether they could be amended, since they were printed in a font not conforming to the line numbers of the page, making it impossible to frame amendments to them in accordance with the procedures of either House. That has changed with the move to headings in the body of the text, removing any technical obstacle to their amendment: but for the present no moves appear to have been made towards permitting amendments to headings to be tabled.

[25] Parts used to be numbered with capital Roman numerals, but since 2001 Arabic numerals have been used.

[26] As to other divisions, see Chapter 2, Section 5.

[27] See Lord Thring, *Practical Legislation*, 1902 ed., p.58.

Some of the early headings took the form of introductory words set apart from the text but capable grammatically of being read into it. In essence these were more of a preamble to a group of sections designed to connect them one to the other. These headings therefore partake in part of the character of provisions of the text itself.

26.1.9 The conclusive proof that the kind of heading used in Acts nowadays neither is nor should be treated as part of the text of an Act is that the authorities of both Houses do not regard them as part of the Bill before the House, and therefore permit their informal amendment more or less at the will of the draftsman. As the Bill progresses through Parliament amendment of a section may falsify the heading of the section or of a Part or Chapter of which it forms part. The normal procedure in that case is for the draftsman to request the authorities of the relevant House to make an appropriate change, specified by the draftsman, when the Bill is next reprinted. And it is not permissible within the rules of either House of Parliament for Members to table amendments to headings. It would therefore be quite wrong to regard a heading as part of the text that expresses the settled will and intention of Parliament.

That does not, however, mean that it is never appropriate for the courts to have regard to headings. It is probably fair to say that a court will have regard to a heading to obtain support for a construction that is indicated by other factors but would be unlikely to rely on a heading to found a construction which was without other support and was contradicted or disturbed by other factors.[28]

This approach is in accordance with the decision of the Court of Appeal in *In Re Woking Urban District Council (Basingstoke Canal) Act 1911.*[29] That decision concerned marginal notes describing provisions,[30] the process for which was similar to that for headings. Phillimore L.J. said[31]—

> "I need not go any further, but if one may look at the marginal note to section 11, it would seem clear that the Legislature considered that the original canal company was still in existence. I am aware of the general rule of law as to marginal notes, at any rate in public general Acts of Parliament; but that rule is founded, as will be seen on reference to the cases, upon the principle that those notes are inserted not by Parliament nor under the authority of Parliament, but by irresponsible persons. Where, however, as in section 10 of this Act, and in some other recent local and personal Acts

---

[28] In *R. (Quintavalle) v Human Fertilisation and Embryology Authority* [2003] 2 All E.R. 105, QBD. Maurice Kay J. in construing the term "use" in relation to embryonic tissue testing found four reasons, including a general contextual and purposive reason, to favour a particular construction. As one of them he says "Secondly, section 3 is headed 'Prohibitions in connection with embryos'. The words 'in connection with' militate against a narrow construction." (para.12); note that the case went to appeal in the Court of Appeal ([2003] 3 W.L.R. 878, CA) and was pending appeal to the House of Lords when this work went to print. See also *Re Carlton* [1945] Ch. 280, 284, Ch *per* Cohen J.

[29] [1914] 1 Ch. 300, CA.

[30] Now replaced by bold headings within the main page, see Chapter 2, Section 5.

[31] Pp. 320–321.

which have come under my cognizance, the marginal notes are mentioned as already existing and established, it may well be that they do form a part of the Act of Parliament. I do not, however, decide the case upon this ground."

And the position is summarised by Lord Goddard C.J. in *R v Surrey (North-Eastern Area) Assessment Committee Ex p. Surrey County Valuation Committee*[32]— **26.1.10**

"But while the court is entitled to look at the headings in an Act of Parliament to resolve any doubt they may have as to ambiguous words, the law is quite clear that you cannot use such headings to give a different effect to clear words in the section where there cannot be any doubt as to their ordinary meaning. The leading authority is *Hammersmith & City Ry Co v Brand*[33] and the matter has been more recently considered in *Fletcher v Birkenhead Corporation*.[34] There Collins M.R. said[35]: 'The head-note to the report of the case of *Hammersmith & City Ry Co v Brand* seems to me to state fairly the result of that decision, as being that "the headings of different portions of a statute are to be referred to, to determine the sense of any doubtful expression in a section ranged under any particular heading." Lord Chelmsford said, in giving judgment: "The sections of the Railways Clauses Acts are, as your Lordships know, arranged in order under different heads, which indicate the general object of the provisions immediately following: and these may be usefully referred to, to determine the sense of any doubtful expression in a section ranged under a particular heading".' Their Lordships in the House of Lords and the Court of Appeal emphasized that reference can be made to these headings only where the construction is doubtful, and what doubt can there be with regard to such words as 'the institution, carrying on or defence of any proceedings in relation to the valuation list?' "

It would follow from the informal approach to headings in the passage of a Bill through Parliament that an equally informal approach would be taken to them following enactment. But the draftsman of Act A that amends Act B and thereby falsifies a heading in Act B does not have any opportunity informally to arrange for the amendment of that heading. This is one of the effects of the entirely fictitious nature of what is referred to as "the statute book": because it does not actually exist, it is not possible to make informal alterations to it. Even in the official versions of statute mentioned in Chapter 9, Section 2 there was no mechanism by which headings in one Act could be changed informally to reflect

---

[32] [1948] 1 K.B. 28, 31–32, DC.
[33] L. R. 4, H.L. 171.
[34] [1907] 1 K.B. 205.
[35] At 213.

its later amendment by another Act. There is no reason why commercial editors should not make appropriate amendments of headings that have become falsified by later amendment, marking and explaining the nature of the change that they have made. But this does not seem to be the practice.

26.1.11   The result is that a number of provisions are printed both in the Queen's Printer's version and in commercial publications with headings that no longer adequately reflect their content, as a result of later amendment. It is therefore tempting for the draftsman of Act A amending Act B to include an express amendment of any heading within Act B that is falsified by Act A. Originally it was the general rule to resist this temptation, but the exceptions to the rule appear to be becoming increasingly frequent.[36] The danger of making these amendment is that they appear to ascribe greater legislative importance to the headings than was formerly the case, which could lead to abandonment of the practice whereby they can be altered purely informally during the Bill's passage.

Arguably that would be just as well, since it is beyond doubt that, whether or not headings are described as forming part of the text placed before and approved by Parliament, the courts will certainly have regard to them where it seems helpful in elucidating a provision. The same rule applies here as for preambles: a heading may be used to enhance certainty or resolve ambiguity, but it will not be used to override the clear meaning of the text.[37]

As to headings in statutory instruments, in *R. (on the application of Toth) v Solicitors Disciplinary Tribunal*[38] Stanley Burnton said—

> "The heading of Pt III of the 1994 rules is 'General'. It does not indicate that the 1994 rules in Pt III apply other than generally. It is permissible to have regard to such headings in a statutory instrument . . . "[39]

Punctuation

26.1.12   The correct modern approach to the use of punctuation of an Act (or an instrument) as an aid to its construction is explained in the following passage of Lord Lowry's speech in *Hanlon v The Law Society*[40]—

---

[36] See, for example, s.172(2) of the Finance Act 2003 (c.14) ("Accordingly, in the heading before paragraph 12 of that Schedule, for "mortality risk" substitute "risk of death or disability"") and s.62(10)(b) of the Nationality, Immigration and Asylum Act 2002 (2002 c.41) ("in the heading of section 53 (supplemental provision) the reference to the Immigration Act 1971 becomes a reference to the Immigration Acts")—note that in each of these examples the non-legislative nature of the change to the heading is alluded to (by "accordingly" in the first example and by "becomes" in the second): but that is not the universal practice.
[37] See the dictum of Lord Goddard above.
[38] [2001] 3 All E.R. 180, 189, QBD.
[39] Not, presumably, implying that a heading in a statutory instrument is any more to be relied on than a heading in a statute.
[40] [1981] A.C. 124, 196–197, HL.

"Before 1850 Acts of Parliament were not punctuated; even after that punctuation was left to the draftsman and not scrutinised by Parliament. And sometimes a clause would be amended in debate but the punctuation might not be altered to take account of the amendment. Lord Esher M.R. proclaimed the old doctrine in *Duke of Devonshire v O'Connor*[41] when he said, at p.478: ' . . . it is perfectly clear that in an Act of Parliament there are no such things as brackets any more than there are such things as stops.' But I respectfully adopt what Lord Jamieson said in *Alexander v Mackenzie*[42]:

'I am not prepared to hold that in construing a modern Act of Parliament a court may not have regard to punctuation. Bills when introduced in Parliament have punctuation, and without such would be unintelligible to the legislators, who pass them into law as punctuated. There appears to me no valid reason why regard should be denied to punctuation in construing a statute so passed, when effect may be given to it in a punctuated writing under the hand of a testator, as was held in *Houston v Burns*.[43] While notice may, therefore, in my view be taken of punctuation in construing a statute, a comma or the absence of a comma must, I think, be disregarded if to give effect to it would so alter the sense as to be contrary to the plain intention of the statute.'

"I refer to a note in (1959) 75 L.Q.R. 29 which the learned author was able to endow with judicial authority in *Slaney v Kean*.[44] And Lord Reid's cautious attitude to punctuation in *Inland Revenue Commissioners v Hinchy*[45] (which was concerned with an Act of 1842), seems to be more than offset by his observations in *Reg. v Schildkamp*.[46]

"I consider that not to take account of punctuation disregards the reality that literate people, such as Parliamentary draftsmen, punctuate what they write, if not identically, at least in accordance with grammatical principles. Why should not other literate people, such as judges, look at the punctuation in order to interpret the meaning of the legislation as accepted by Parliament?"

---

[41] (1890) 24 Q.B.D. 468, CA.
[42] 1947 J.C. 155, 166.
[43] [1918] A.C. 337.
[44] [1970] Ch. 243, *per* Megarry J., at p.252F.
[45] [1960] A.C. 748, 763.
[46] [1971] A.C. 1, 10.

CHAPTER 27

USE OF EXTRANEOUS MATERIAL IN CONSTRUING LEGISLATION

Introduction

The principles discussed in this Chapter should be read alongside and in the light **27.1.1**
of Chapter 26 (the use of parts of legislation other than text for construing
legislation) and Chapter 28 (the rule in *Pepper v Hart*).

A helpful introduction to the modern position on, and a word of caution about,
the practice of using extraneous material for the construction of legislation is
found in the passage from the opinion of Lord Nicholls of Birkenhead in *R. v
Secretary of State for the Environment, Transport and the Regions and another,
Ex p. Spath Holme Ltd*[1] appended to this work.[2]

Dictionaries

Since, as has been said,[3] the starting point for statutory construction is to give **27.1.2**
each word its natural meaning, a dictionary is likely to be a useful source of
reference.[4] As Lord Coleridge said in *R. v Peters*[5]—

"I am quite aware that dictionaries are not to be taken as authoritative
exponents of the meanings of words used in Acts of Parliament, but it is a
well-known rule of courts of law that words should be taken to be used in
their ordinary sense, and we are therefore sent for instruction to these
books."

---

[1] [2001] 2 A.C. 349, HL.
[2] Appendix, Extract 21.
[3] Chapter 17.
[4] In several reported cases each year some reference is made to a dictionary for the purposes of
providing at least a starting point in establishing the meaning of a word or phrase. For recent
examples see *Miah v Secretary of State for Work and Pensions* [2003] 4 All E.R. 702, CA, *Football
Association Premier League Ltd and others v Panini UK Ltd* [2003] 4 All E.R. 1290, CA, *Sepet
v Secretary of State for the Home Department* [2003] 3 All E.R. 304, HL, *Director of Public
Prosecutions v Stoke-on-Trent Magistrates' Court* [2003] 3 All E.R. 1086, QBD and *Cream
Holdings Ltd v Banerjee* [2003] 2 All E.R. 318, CA.
[5] (1886) 16 Q.B.D. 636, 641.

But dictionaries are compiled by persons using evidence from colloquial and published usage of various kinds,[6] which may result in their attributing to a word a meaning which is not apt in any legal context,[7] or in any legislative context, or perhaps in a specific legislative context. The judges will trust their own legal intuition as to the most natural meaning of an expression, whether or not a technical legal expression, in the context of an Act, more than they will trust the opinion of the editor of a dictionary as to the "average" meaning of the expression in general literature. As Lord Macnaghten said in *Midland Railway v Robinson*,[8] in rebuffing a citation of Dr Johnson's dictionary by Lord Herschell in defining "quarry" as a "stone mine" (and therefore bringing it within a reference to "mine" in s.77 of the Railways Clauses Act 1845[9])—

> "I continue to think that the word [mine] was used both in the heading and in the section in the sense in which, if I am not mistaken, every English judge who had occasion to consider the meaning of the word before *Farie's* case[10] was decided, took to be its ordinary signification. It seems to me that on such a point the opinions of such judges as Kindersley V.-C., Turner L.J. and Sir George Jessel are probably a safer guide than any definitions or illustrations to be found in dictionaries."[11]

For guidance as to the meaning of specialised or technical words, specialist or technical dictionaries may be consulted. So, the expression "political crime" has been judicially construed by reference to Mill's and Stephen's discussions of its meaning, and the expression "direct taxation" has been judicially construed by reference to works on political economy.[12]

---

[6] The *Oxford English Dictionary* is compiled by editors exercising no normative function but merely the function of assessing as wide as possible a collection of evidence from published works (and nowadays from certain other media) as to the sense in which words are used.

[7] For an example of a phrase which has acquired a legal meaning almost the opposite of its non-legal meaning, see the following dictum of Sedley L.J. in *Fawdry & Co. (a firm) v Murfitt (Lord Chancellor intervening)* [2003] 4 All E.R. 60, 73—"The expression 'colourable authority', upon which some of the decided cases turn, I find opaque. The adjective itself, which (so far as it is used at all) ordinarily connotes something specious and therefore false (see the Oxford English Dictionary entry), has acquired a legal meaning which is almost the opposite: 'Capable of being presented as true or right; having at least a prima facie aspect of justice or validity' (definition 2.b.). This too tends to collapse reality into appearance."

[8] (1890) 15 App. Cas. 19, 34.

[9] 1845 c.20.

[10] *Provost, etc. of Glasgow v Farie* (1888) 13 App. Cas. 657.

[11] For a more recent example see "But in seeking for the true meaning of 'ethnic' in the statute, we are not tied to the precise definition in any dictionary."—*Mandla v Dowell Lee* [1983] 1 All E.R. 1062, 1066, HL *per* Lord Fraser of Tullybelton.

[12] *Bank of Toronto v Lambe* (1887) 12 App. Cas. 575, 581; *Brewers, etc. Association of Ontario v Attorney General for Ontario* [1897] A.C. 231, 236.

Legislation implementing international agreement: travaux preparatoires

It has long been established that, where the acknowledged[13] purpose of a piece **27.1.3**
of legislation is to give effect to an international agreement in accordance with
the obligations of the United Kingdom as a party to the agreement, it is
permissible for the courts to have regard to the intent of the agreement itself, and
to use the *travaux preparatoires* or any other appropriate background documents
as a way of eliciting that intention. The nature and history of the practice is
described in the following passage of the judgment of Rix L.J. in *J.I. MacWilliam
Co. Inc v. Mediterranean Shipping Co. SA, The Rafaela S*[14]—

> "It is by now well recognised that English statutes which give effect to
> international conventions need to be interpreted with the international origin
> of the rules well in mind. In *Stag Line Ltd v Foscolo, Mango & Co Ltd*,[15]
> with reference to the Hague Rules themselves as incorporated into the 1924
> Act, Lord Atkin said[16]—
>
>> 'It will be remembered that the Act only applies to contracts of carriage
>> of goods outwards from ports of the United Kingdom: and the rules will
>> often have to be interpreted in the courts of the foreign consignees. For
>> the purpose of uniformity it is, therefore, important that the Courts should
>> apply themselves without any predilection for the former law, always
>> preserving the right to say that words used in the English language which
>> have already in the particular context received judicial interpretation may
>> be presumed to be used in the sense already judicially imputed to
>> them.'
>
> "And Lord MacMillan famously said[17]—
>
>> 'As these rules must come under the consideration of foreign Courts it is
>> desirable in the interests of uniformity that their interpretation should not
>> be rigidly controlled by domestic precedents of antecedent date, but
>> rather that the language of the rules should be construed on broad
>> principles of general acceptance.'"

---

[13] The normal manner in which this purpose is acknowledged officially is to have a reference to
implementation of the agreement in the long title of the Act, in the Explanatory Notes to the Act
or to the statutory instrument, or by some kind of reference in the text of the legislation itself
(which frequently exhibits the international agreement as an Annex). But these methods are not
necessarily the only ones that would suffice. And for a substantive provision expressly stating that
the purpose of an Act is to enable effect to be given to a specified international agreement, see s.1
of the Nuclear Safeguards and Electricity (Finance) Act 1978 (c.25).
[14] [2003] 3 All E.R. 369, 388–389, CA.
[15] [1932] A.C. 328.
[16] At 342–343.
[17] At 350.

27.1.4   For other recent examples of the application of this principle—

(1) In *Insured Financial Structures Ltd v Elektrocieplownia Tychy SA*[18] the Court of Appeal sought the intention of the contracting parties by reference to "the general intention" of the Lugano Convention on Jurisdiction and the Enforcement of Judgments in Civil and Commercial Matters.[19]

(2) In *Menashe Business Mercantile Ltd v William Hill Organisation Ltd*[20] the Court of Appeal supported a construction of a section of the Patents Act 1977[21] by reference to the records of the Luxembourg Conference on the Community Patent 1975, and augmented that support by reference to other language versions of the European Patent Convention.

There are, however, a number of constraints upon the circumstances in which it is considered proper to have regard to travaux preparatoires and also upon the kinds of use that may properly be made of them. The relevant considerations, and in particular the issues of comity by reference to the practices of foreign courts, are discussed in the passage of the speech of Lord Wilberforce in *Fothergill v Monarch Airlines*[22] appended to this work.[23]

27.1.5   It is possible that the general relaxation that the courts have permitted themselves recently in relation to the use of extraneous documents of various kinds may have led to some qualification of the rules enunciated by Lord Wilberforce in *Fothergill*, and the lessons learned from international practice may have to be modified from time to time in accordance with development in the jurisprudence of foreign courts: but the considerations of principle set out in that case will remain relevant.

Apart from specific preparatory documents, the courts will also take account of general principles of international law in construing legislation giving effect to an international obligation, subject to express provisions of the Act.[24] As Sir John Donaldson M.R. said in *Alcom Ltd v Republic of Colombia*[25]—

> "I agree that if the Act is ambiguous, a court is entitled to have regard to the general principles of international law and to resolve that ambiguity in the way most consistent with those principles."

There are, however, limits to the latitude that the courts will allow themselves in referring to underlying international obligations in construing implementing

---

[18] [2003] 2 W.L.R. 656, CA.
[19] See in particular paras 10 to 15 of Lord Woolf C.J.'s judgment.
[20] [2003] 1 W.L.R. 1462, CA.
[21] 1977 c.37.
[22] [1981] A.C. 251, HL.
[23] Appendix, Extract 22.
[24] And even, to some extent, in the case of other legislation—see Chapter 3, para.3.7.19 and Chapter 20, para.20.1.42.
[25] 1984 A.C. 580, 588, CA (also HL).

legislation. So, for example, in *In re S (Child Abduction: Asylum Appeal)*[26] Laws L.J. said—

> "Since section 15 [of the Immigration and Asylum Act 1999[27]] is the domestic statutory expression of article 33 [of the 1951 Refugee Convention] it is submitted that it must have general effect . . . But this argument . . . contains a false premise. It is that the scope of section 15 must be as wide as the scope of article 33. The importance, or the generality, or the fundamental nature of article 33 cannot, in my judgment, afford a justification for a construction of section 15 of the 1999 Act which is wider than its terms or context will bear."[28]

Legislation implementing European obligation: European legislative text

An example of particular importance and frequent recurrence of the general rule in relation to legislation implementing international obligations is legislation inspired by the many obligations arising out of the United Kingdom's membership of the European Communities. **27.1.6**

Indeed, even where the implementation of an obligation involves the production of an apparently free-standing and self-sufficient text, it will often be impossible properly to understand the text without some appreciation of the European obligation underpinning it.

Note, in particular, the following passage from the opinion of Lord Walker of Gestingthorpe in *Royal and Sun Alliance v Customs and Excise Commissioners*[29]—

> "My Lords, value added tax is essentially a European Union tax, imposed by member states in compliance with European Union legislation, of which the most important is Council Directive (EEC) 77/388 (on the harmonisation of the laws of the member states relating to turnover taxes—common system of value added tax: uniform basis of assessment (O.J. 1977 L145 p.1) (the Sixth Directive)). Member states give effect to the European Union legislation . . . by national legislation, in the case of the United Kingdom the Value Added Tax Act 1994 and the Value Added Tax Regulations 1995, SI 1995/2518. In this appeal neither side has suggested that the United Kingdom government has failed to implement the Sixth Directive correctly. Nevertheless it is convenient to make some references to it (as well as to the 1994 Act and the 1995 regulations) since the general scheme of the national

---

[26] [2002] 1 W.L.R. 2548, CA.
[27] 1999 c.33.
[28] In other words, like all other principles of construction this principle of having regard to the underlying obligation is to come into use only when there is a job of construction to be effected, not when the cardinal rule itself suffices (see Chapter 17) because the meaning of the legislation is beyond doubt on its face.
[29] [2003] 2 All E.R. 1073, 1090, HL.

legislation can sometimes be better understood by reference to the Sixth Directive. Moreover decisions of the Court of Justice of the European Communities naturally refer principally to the European Union legislation in laying down some general principles (in particular the principle of fiscal neutrality, and the concept of the 'direct and immediate link') which inform the interpretation of the legislation."

Explanatory notes to Acts[30]

27.1.7 Explanatory Notes to Acts may be referred to in debate on the relevant Bill, and they are often are. But they may not be amended, not forming part of the text of the Bill. The result is that Explanatory Notes cannot be regarded as an authoritative statement of Parliament's intention in enacting a piece of legislation. But they can be regarded as an authoritative statement of the Government's intention in proposing legislation. The same is true of explanatory notes to statutory instruments.

In accordance with the principle underlying the decision in *Pepper v Hart*,[31] therefore it is reasonable to expect the courts to permit themselves to have regard to the Explanatory Notes for the purpose of ascertaining the legislative intent when attempting to resolve an ambiguity, on the grounds that it is improbable, in the absence of strong indications in the Official Report of the debate on the Bill, that Parliament's intention in enacting it will be significantly different from the Government's in proposing it.

Indeed in one respect at least the courts have so far been prepared to go further in their use of Explanatory Notes than the mere resolution of ambiguity—

> "In so far as the Explanatory Notes case light on the objective setting or contextual scene of the statute, and the mischief at which it is aimed, such materials are therefore always admissible aids to construction. They may be admitted for what logical value they have. . . . If exceptionally there is found in Explanatory Notes a clear assurance by the executive to Parliament about the meaning of a clause, or the circumstances in which a power will or will not be used, that assurance may in principle be admitted against the executive in proceedings in which the executive places a contrary contention before a court. . . . What is impermissible is to treat the wishes and desires of the Government about the scope of the statutory language as reflecting the will of Parliament. The aims of the Government in respect of the meaning of clauses as revealed in Explanatory Notes cannot be attributed to Parliament. The object is to see what is the intention expressed by the words enacted."[32]

---

[30] See Chapter 9, Section 5.
[31] [1991] 2 All E.R. 824, CA; see Chapter 28.
[32] Lord Steyn in *R.(Westminster City Council) v National Asylum Support Service* [2002] 1 W.L.R. 2956, HL.

Explanatory notes to statutory instruments[33]

Explanatory notes to statutory instruments may be used by courts to identify the   **27.1.8**
mischief which the instrument was attempting to remedy.[34]

As to the use of explanatory notes to statutory instruments, and other
background materials, for the resolution of errors, see *Confederation of Passenger Transport UK v The Humber Bridge Board (Secretary of State for
Transport, Local Government and the Regions, interested party).*[35]

Background policy material

Where legislation is introduced not for the purpose of implementing an   **27.1.9**
international obligation but with the intention of pursuing recommendations of or
ideas in a report of a public body or a similar document, the recommendation or
idea as expressed in that report or document will often afford a valuable insight
to the legislative intention.[36] The theoretical rule is against using a background
policy document of this kind for the purpose of construing legislation. But the
courts have developed ways of adhering to the rule without entirely depriving
themselves of the assistance which the report or other document can provide.

In particular, it is established that a founding report or other document will be
good evidence of the mischief at which an Act is aimed, where the court comes
to apply the mischief rule.[37] As Lord Diplock said in *Fothergill v Monarch
Airlines Ltd*[38]—

> "Where the Act has been preceded by a report of some official commission
> or committee that has been laid before Parliament and the legislation is
> introduced in consequence of that report, the report itself may be looked at
> by the court for the limited purpose of identifying the 'mischief' that the Act

---

[33] Chapter 9, Section 6.

[34] "It is worth noting that the explanatory note (which is not, of course, part of the Regulations
but is of use in identifying the mischief which the Regulations were attempting to remedy)
states . . . "—*Pickstone v Freemans plc* [1989] A.C. 66, 127, HL *per* Lord Oliver of Aylmerton;
see also *Westminster City Council v Haywood (No.2)* [2000] 2 All E.R. 634, 645, Ch; and see "'In
my opinion an explanatory note may be referred to as an aid to construction where the statutory
instrument to which it is attached is ambiguous. In *Pickstone v Freemans plc* [1989] A.C. 66, 127
Lord Oliver of Aylmerton said that the explanatory note attached to a statutory instrument,
although it was not of course part of the instrument, could be used to identify the mischief which
it was attempting to remedy. The problem in this case is that the explanatory note is itself
ambiguous, because of similar inconsistencies in its use of language to those which appear in the
order which it seeks to explain. But the explanation which it gives for the amendment to paragraph
(ii) of article 3(2)(a) is a simple one, and it seems to me to be perfectly intelligible."—*Coventry
Waste Ltd v Russell* [1999] 1 W.L.R. 2093, 2103 *per* Lord Hope of Craighead; see also para.27.1.12
below.

[35] [2004] Q.B. 310, CA; discussed in Chapters 15 and 20.

[36] And may be used to support a purposive construction that would otherwise be impossible: see, for
example, Chapter 18, para.18.1.8.

[37] As to which see Chapter 20.

[38] [1981] A.C. 251, 281, HL.

was intended to remedy, and for such assistance as is derivable from this knowledge in giving the right purposive construction to the Act. Only to this limited extent are what would in continental legal systems be classified as 'travaux préparatoires' legitimate aids to the construction of an Act of Parliament of the United Kingdom which deals with what is purely domestic legislation."

27.1.10   Hence, for example, the following observation of Lord Steyn in *South Buckinghamshire District Council v Porter*[39]—

"The starting point must be the language of section 187B [of the Town and Country Planning Act 1990] read in the context of its purpose viz. In the words of the Carnwath Report that 'use of the course ensures that both sides are fully protected' . . . ".

Where appropriate the courts will look not only at background material to a provision before them but also at background material to a provision that has been replaced and re-enacted, possibly with considerable modification, by the provision before them. So, for example, in *Société Eram v Compagnie Internationale*[40] Lord Hoffmann said[41]—

"So despite its very recent enactment and modern language, the third party debt order is a process of execution which goes back far into English legal history. R.S.C. Order 49 is derived from the provisions of sections 61 to 70 of the Common Law Procedure Act 1854. These provisions were enacted on the recommendation of the *Second Report of the Royal Commission on the Superior Courts of Common Law* (1853), which included Jervis C.J., Martin B., Sir Alexander Cockburn and the future Bramwell B. and Willes J. The commissioners said . . . "

In the case of legislation preceded by and presented as implementing a report of the Law Commission the courts will presume that the intention of the legislature was the same as the intention displayed in the report.[42]

---

[39] [2003] 3 All E.R.1, 24.
[40] [2003] 3 All E.R. 465, HL.
[41] At p.480.
[42] See, for example, Lord Bingham of Cornhill in *R. v G.* [2003] 3 W.L.R. 1060, 1078, HL—"It cannot be supposed that by 'reckless' Parliament meant anything different from the Law Commission. The Law Commission's meaning was made plain both in its Report . . . "; see also *R v Bow Street Metropolitan Stipendiary Magistrate, Ex p. Government of the United States of America; R. v Governor of Brixton Prison, Ex p. Allison* [1999] Q.B. 847, DC; note also "Where a Bill is based wholly or partly on a Law Commission recommendation, it is appropriate to take account of the Report to find the mischief to which the provision was directed: see *Pepper v Hart* [1993] A.C. 593, 633–635"—*Cooke v United Bristol Healthcare NHS Trust* [2004] 1 W.L.R. 251, 270, CA *per* Carnwath L.J.

Consultation paper prior to legislation

There is no difference of kind between material produced by a government **27.1.11** department presenting issues and inviting views as a preparatory step towards legislation and materials produced by the Law Commission for the same purpose.[43]

Departmental consultation papers are therefore relevant evidence for the construction of legislation, although of their nature it will be rare that they point conclusively to a particular interpretation. As Lord Steyn said in his dissenting speech in *R. (on the application of Edison First Power Ltd) v Central Valuation Officer*[44]—

> "In the end the problem before the House is one of vires. The text of the statute must be the starting point. The question is how far, on a contextual reading of the statute, the language is capable of stretching. While I accept that all relevant contextual material must be taken into account, not all the material deployed by the Secretary of State can affect the point of statutory construction. Thus while I accept that the consultation process in this case is admissible, it ultimately does not warrant an interpretation which attributes to the language used by Parliament a meaning which displaces the presumption."

Departmental guidance

The theoretical rules would again clearly dictate that guidance issued by a **27.1.12** government department as to the meaning of legislation cannot be effective to establish or change the natural meaning of the words as enacted, nor is it a reliable indication of the legislative intention of the legislature as a whole, or even of the government at the time when they introduced the legislation. But, again, the courts find ways of giving such weight to guidance of this kind as the circumstances appear to warrant. Hence the following observation of Lord Bingham of Cornhill in *South Buckinghamshire District Council v Porter*[45]—

> "Since the enactment of the section the Department of the Environment has given guidance to local planning authorities on the exercise of enforcement powers which, although inadmissible to construe the section, throws light on what was officially understood to be its effect. . . . "

---

[43] There will, however, be different weight to be attached to a paper which merely consults without proposing solutions (the old "green paper") and one which advances considered legislative proposals and invites reactions (the old "white paper"). Nowadays most consultation papers issued by Government departments are a whitey-green. Similarly there will be a different weight attached to a Law Commission investigative paper inviting ideas and a formal Law Commission report attached to draft legislation and intended as a distinct legislative proposal.

[44] [2003] 4 All E.R. 209.

[45] [2003] 3 All E.R. 1, 11.

Letters, &c. from draftsman

27.1.13 Superficially it might seem attractive to have regard to what the draftsman of a provision says was his intention in drafting. But the attraction soon recedes when one considers the implications of such a proceeding. Apart from the impropriety and unfairness of giving, in effect, the executive[46] a second chance to say what was meant the first time around, and the arbitrariness of whether the draftsman happens to be available and able or willing to recall and assert his intention in drafting, the intention of the draftsman is not strictly relevant: what matters is the notional intention of Parliament or, in the case of subordinate legislation, the Minister, which can be determined only by reference to the words as offered to Parliament or to the Minister by the draftsman. It is the legislature's notional intention which matters, not the actual intention of the person who wrote the words.[47]

The point was expressed as follows by Lord Steyn in *R. v Hinks*[48]—

> "While this anecdote is an interesting bit of legal history, it is not relevant to the question before the House. Given Counsel's use of it, as well as aspects of Sir John Smith's writing on the point in question, which have played such a large role in the present case, it is necessary to state quite firmly how the issue of interpretation should be approached.

> "In *Black-Clawson International Ltd v Papierwerke Waldhoff-Anschaffenburg A.G.*[49] Lord Reid observed:

>> 'We often say that we are looking for the intention of Parliament, but that is not quite accurate. We are seeking the meaning of the words which Parliament used. We are seeking not what Parliament meant but the true meaning of what they said.'

> "This does not rule out or diminish relevant contextual material. But it is the critical point of departure of statutory interpretation. It also sets logical limits to what may be called in aid of statutory interpretation. Thus the published *Eighth Report of the Criminal Law Revision Committee on Theft and Related Offences*,[50] and in particular paragraph 35, may arguably be relevant as part of the background against which Parliament enacted the Bill which became the 1968 Act. ... Relevant publicly available contextual materials are readily admitted in aid of the construction of statutes. On the other hand, to delve into the intentions of individual members of the Committee, and their communications, would be to rely on material which

---

[46] The draftsman (whether Parliamentary Counsel or, in the case of subordinate legislation, a departmental lawyer) generally being a civil servant.

[47] See also Chapter 12, Section 2.

[48] [2000] 3 W.L.R. 1590, 1596, HL.

[49] [1975] A.C. 595, 613, HL.

[50] (1966) (Cmnd 2977).

cannot conceivably be relevant. If statutory interpretation is to be a rational and coherent process a line has to be drawn somewhere. And what Mr Fiennes[51] wrote to the Larceny Sub-Committee was demonstrably on the wrong side of the line."

Repealed and amended text

For the use of repealed or amended text in construing the original intention of the legislature in relation to unrepealed or unamended text, see Chapter 14, Section 4.

27.1.14

Acts emanating from hybrid Bills

It is common for the text of an Act emanating from a hybrid Bill to make reference to a "book of reference" deposited in relation to the Bill, regard to which is to be had in construing the Act.[52]

27.1.15

---

[51] The Parliamentary Draftsman, later Sir John Fiennes K.C.B., Q.C., First Parliamentary Counsel.
[52] See, for example, the Channel Tunnel Rail Link Act 1996 (c.61), s.53(6)—"In this section, 'book of reference' means the book deposited in connection with the Channel Tunnel Rail Link Bill in the office of the Clerk of the Parliaments and the Private Bill Office of the House of Commons in November 1994 together with the books so deposited in November and December 1995."

677

CHAPTER 28

THE RULE IN *PEPPER v HART*

Introduction

Until 1992 it was generally accepted[1] that statements of underlying policy **28.1.1**
intention on the part of the government could not be used by the courts for the
purpose of construing legislation.[2] The words enacted by Parliament were to be
taken and interpreted at face value, to discover what Parliament in fact enacted
not what it would probably have wanted to enact had it thought about the point
at issue more carefully. This was not so much part of the debate about whether
construction should be literal or purposive[3] as about the evidential weight that
could properly be given in discovering the purpose of legislation, or the mischief
at which it was aimed, to a particular kind of material.

In 1990 the Court of Appeal in deciding the case of *Pepper (Inspector of
Taxes) v Hart*[4] were faced with construing an ambiguity in tax legislation.
Working only with the text of the statute the court felt forced towards one
conclusion. But there was a clear feeling that had the point been considered
expressly by Parliament it would have been provided for in the contrary way.[5]

The case went to the House of Lords, and on its becoming apparent that
recourse to the Parliamentary proceedings might cause the provision at issue to
be construed in a different way, the case was remitted to a seven-man House for
an authoritative determination on the permissibility of using Parliamentary

---

[1] The relevant leading cases are referred to in the extract of Lord Browne-Wilkinson's speech in
Pepper v Hart set out in the Appendix (Extract 23).

[2] There were, however, certain well-established exceptions, the principal one being statutes giving
effect to international obligations in which case not only the relevant international obligation but
even its travaux preparatoires could be made available to the court for the purposes of construction.
The difference being that in that case Parliament's declared intention was to give effect to
obligations arising out of a pre-existing document.

[3] As to which see Chapter 18.

[4] [1991] 2 All E.R. 824, CA.

[5] *Per* Slade L.J.: "I have an uneasy suspicion that the legislature, in drafting s.63(2), was simply not
directing its mind to the case where an employer, whose business consists of the provision of
services to the public or a section of the public, confers on his employees a benefit consisting of
the use of surplus capacity in the services supplied by him for his customers. If the legislature's
attention had been directed to this case, I suspect that it might have provided for it in a somewhat
different manner. For all that, we have to apply the subsections as they stand, and I agree with
Vinelott J that his interpretation of their effect is inescapable. With some misgivings, I would
therefore concur in dismissing these appeals."

papers as an aid to interpretation.[6] The House of Lords held[7] that the practice should be permitted.

The principles at issue

28.1.2 The nature of the constitutional issues raised by the case as presented to the House of Lords are explored in detail in the passages of the speech of Lord Browne-Wilkinson appended to this work.[8] The essence of the argument is whether instead of merely elucidating the intention of Parliament by reference to its proceedings, the use of *Hansard* in these circumstances amounts to an attempt to question the proceedings of the House of Commons contrary to the Bill of Rights. The views of the Government and of the House authorities emerge from documents cited in the appended passages of Lord Browne-Wilkinson's speech.

The scope of the decision

28.1.3 The other issues involved in the decision of the House of Lords, its justification and its precise parameters are fully set out in the passages of the speeches of Lord Browne-Wilkinson, Lord Bridge of Harwich, Lord Griffiths and Lord Oliver of Aylmerton appended to this work.[9]

The effect of the decision can be effectively summarised in the following short passage from the speech of Lord Browne-Wilkinson—

> "I therefore reach the conclusion, subject to any question of parliamentary privilege, that the exclusionary rule should be relaxed so as to permit reference to parliamentary materials where: (a) legislation is ambiguous or obscure, or leads to an absurdity; (b) the material relied on consists of one or more statements by a minister or other promoter of the Bill together if necessary with such other parliamentary material as is necessary to

---

[6] [1993] 1 All E.R. 42, HL: note in particular the opening of the judgment of Lord Bridge of Harwich: "My Lords, I was one of those who were in the majority at the conclusion of the first hearing of this appeal in holding the opinion that s.63 of the Finance Act 1976, construed by conventional criteria, supported the assessments to income tax made by the Revenue on the taxpayers which had been upheld by Vinelott J. (see [1990] S.T.C. 6, [1990] 1 W.L.R. 204) and the Court of Appeal (see [1991] 2 All E.R. 824, [1991] Ch. 203). If it were not permissible to take account of the parliamentary history of the relevant legislation and of ministerial statements of its intended effect, I should remain of that opinion. But, once the parliamentary material was brought to our attention, it seemed to me, as, I believe, to others of your Lordships who had heard the appeal first argued, to raise an acute question as to whether it could possibly be right to give effect to taxing legislation in such a way as to impose a tax which the Financial Secretary to the Treasury, during the passage of the Bill containing the relevant provision, had, in effect, assured the House of Commons it was not intended to impose. It was this which led to the appeal being reargued before the Appellate Committee of seven which now reports to the House."

[7] With the sole, but significant, dissent of the Lord Chancellor, Lord Mackay of Clashfern.

[8] Appendix, Extract 23.

[9] Same.

understand such statements and their effect; (c) the statements relied on are clear. Further than this, I would not at present go. ... "

As to what amounts to ambiguity, it has been suggested that any difference of judicial opinion as to the proper construction of a provision will be sufficient evidence of ambiguity to permit recourse to Hansard.[10]

The use made of the rule

When the case of *Pepper v Hart* was first decided some commentators predicted[11] an avalanche of cases in which recourse to Hansard would be decisive. That has not happened. Discussing the advent and use made of the new rule Lord Nicholls of Birkenhead said in *R. v Secretary of State for the Environment, Transport and the Regions and another, Ex p. Spath Holme Ltd*[12]— **28.1.4**

"Experience has shown that the occasions on which reference to parliamentary proceedings is of assistance are rare".

Despite the gravity with which the proceedings in the case were conducted and the weight of the constitutional issues considered and determined, the rule has been relied on to permit consulting Hansard in relatively few cases.[13] Even when it is consulted, Hansard rarely appears to have been decisive and is frequently dismissed as not being of assistance[14]: but it is certainly seen as one of the useful tools for resolving ambiguity, even if it normally does no more than support conclusions already suggested by other factors, and the courts themselves encourage reliance on the rule in *Pepper v Hart* where appropriate.[15]

The courts have so far resisted attempts to make *Pepper v Hart* an excuse to give general effect to Ministerial pronouncements during the passage of

---

[10] See *Restick v Crickmore* [1994] 1 W.L.R. 420 *per* Stuart-Smith L.J. and *Chief Adjudication Officer v Foster* [1993] A.C. 754, 772 *per* Lord Bridge of Harwich.

[11] And indeed it was argued by Counsel in *Pepper v Hart* itself, as is noted in Lord Browne-Wilkinson's judgment; see also HL Deb. December 8, 1993 cc.942—945.

[12] [2001] 2 A.C. 397, HL.

[13] The case has been referred to in about 100 other cases, but often only very peripherally.

[14] See, for example, Lord Scott of Foscote in *Mirvahedy v Henley* [2003] 2 All E.R. 401, HL: "Your Lordships have been given a *Pepper v Hart* invitation . . . and taken to passages in Hansard recording comments about the Bill made in 1969 and 1970 during its progress through Parliament. My Lords, the passages in question are, in my opinion, inconclusive and do not provide any clear answer to the question as to the intended function of the concluding words of para (b). That being so, the Hansard passages should be set aside and the statutory words in question given a function consistent with the language used, with the general scheme of the 1971 Act and with the reasonable presumption that Parliament does not intend absurd results."

[15] In *Cream Holdings v Banerjee* [2003] 2 All E.R. 318, CA the Court of Appeal itself suggested to Counsel that the Parliamentary history of a provision should be researched and submissions made based on Hansard—see Simon Brown L.J. at para.41.

legislation, and have applied strictly the constraints on the use of Hansard specified by Lord Browne-Wilkinson.

28.1.5   The most significant of these constraints is that the courts should have recourse to Hansard only where the strict words of the legislation are not entirely clear but leave an ambiguity to be resolved. Temptations to go further than this are routinely resisted in strong terms: in *Thoburn v Sunderland City Council*,[16] for example, Laws L.J. said—

> "76. If this is not a *Pepper v Hart* case, as it is not, I question the propriety of any reliance on the Parliamentary material. I acknowledge without cavil that there are many circumstances in which such references are perfectly proper, and, in general terms, one sees in modern litigation appeal being made to the text of Hansard altogether more frequently than happened not very long ago. ... But absent a *Pepper v Hart* argument the only purpose [for a submission based on Hansard] can have been to invite us to give effect, in deciding the legality of the amendments to the 1985 Act, to statements suggesting that the section 2(2) power [of the European Communities Act 1972[17]] would, or perhaps could, only be used to effect minor amendments. Looking at the Parliamentary material as a whole, I do not think that is their overall effect. But even if it were so, I would not base an enforceable legitimate expectation (for that is what would be involved) purely on what was said in Parliament. I think that would infringe article 9 of the Bill of Rights 1689. If a minister gives the House a false impression of the potential effect of a Bill's provisions (and I do not say that was done here), the cost and the sanction are political. The relationship between Parliament and the courts is one of mutual respect: not only out of habit of mind, but by convention and by law. So long as that is so, I think we should be strict about such matters."

For a recent example in which recourse to Hansard under the rule in *Pepper v Hart* was of particularly significant assistance, see the following passages of the judgment of the Court of Appeal (*per* Lord Phillips M.R.) in the case of *A E Beckett & Sons (Lyndons) Ltd v Midlands Electricity plc*[18]—

> "33. The possibility that 'economic loss' in section 21 [of the Electricity Act 1989[19]] might mean 'pure economic loss' had not been canvassed in argument. We invited Counsel to address this possibility, either in written argument or in a further hearing. They provided written submissions which they elaborated in a short further hearing. These submissions we have found of great assistance.

---

[16] [2003] Q.B. 151.
[17] 1972 c.68.
[18] [2001] 1 W.L.R. 281, CA.
[19] 1989 c.29.

"34. In accordance with *Pepper v Hart* Counsel referred us to passages of   **28.1.6**
parliamentary debate in relation to the clause in the Bill which was to
become section 21. These immediately made clear what had previously
been obscure. . . .

"38. These passages [cited earlier] do not support the proposition that
'economic loss' in section 21 is restricted to pure economic loss, for as
[Counsel] demonstrated by reference to subsequent case law, loss of
information from a computer as a result of the interruption of supply of
electricity may be consequent upon a degree of physical damage. What they
demonstrate quite clearly, however, is that section 21 was introduced to
permit exclusion of liability in negligence for economic loss resulting from
the interruption or variation of the supply of electricity.

"39. We have concluded that this is a rare case where material admitted
under *Pepper v Hart* has resolved an ambiguity in the statute being
construed. Clause 21 permits terms restricting liability for economic loss to
be imposed only in relation to loss resulting from the effect upon the supply
of current that results from the negligence in question. We anticipate that
this conclusion is likely to lead to the resolution of this litigation."

Additional constraints on the use of the rule

In addition to the constraints enunciated when *Pepper v Hart* was decided, the   **28.1.7**
courts have since suggested other limitations on the use of the rule.

It has been doubted, though not conclusively, whether *Pepper v Hart* may be
invoked in a criminal context, because of the policy that doubt should be resolved
in favour of the citizen in a context where the statute seeks to penalise him.[20]

Again, although in theory there is no reason why the rule in *Pepper v Hart*
should not be applied to a private Member's Bill or private peer's Bill, the
absence of detailed briefing notes prepared by administrative and legal officials
from within the Government department responsible for the subject matter of the
Bill makes it even less likely that a statement by the private promoter of a Bill
will amount to a clear indication of Parliamentary intention sufficient to satisfy
the requirements of the rule.[21]

An additional constraint is expressed by Laws L.J. in the case of *Thoburn v
Sunderland City Council*[22]—

"I should add that in my judgment general words could not be supplemented, so as to effect a repeal or significant amendment to a constitutional

---

[20] *Massey v Boulden* [2003] 2 All E.R. 87, CA *per* Simon Brown L.J. paras 18 to 20.
[21] See, for example, *Cornwall County Council v Baker* [2003] 2 All E.R. 178, 183, QBD *per* Toulson
J.
[22] [2003] Q.B. 151.

statute, by reference to what was said in Parliament by the minister promoting the Bill pursuant to *Pepper (Inspector of Taxes) v Hart*."[23]

Possible extension of *Pepper v Hart*: **Human Rights compatibility**

28.1.8   The use made of the rule in *Pepper v Hart*, and its relevance in matters raising questions under the Human Rights Act 1998[24] came under close scrutiny in the case of *Wilson and others v Secretary of State for Trade and Industry, Wilson v First County Trust Ltd (No.2)*.[25] A passage from the speech of Lord Nicholls of Birkenhead is appended to this work.[26]

In summary, the suggestion was that use might be made of statements in Hansard during the passage of a Bill not for the purpose of resolving ambiguity but in order to determine whether or not the underlying policy objective rendered the legislation compatible with the European Convention on Human Rights, since compatibility in some cases can be determined only by balancing the effect of the legislation and its policy justification. This appeared to alarm the Parliamentary authorities even more than was the case in relation to *Pepper v Hart* itself.

The House of Lords concluded that there was no reason why Hansard should be excluded in the search for background material elucidating the social and practical circumstances surrounding the introduction of legislation, where that is critical to the issue of compatibility. Although not expecting frequent use to be made in this context, their Lordships did not feel that it would be rational for the courts to deny themselves any source of potentially illuminating background material. The enterprise is, however, slightly different from that involved in the rule in *Pepper v Hart* itself: in the *Wilson* case, the courts are using Hansard not to discover the legislature's intention, but simply to set the legislation into its social and practical context.

28.1.9   The *Wilson* discussion was alluded to in a later House of Lords decision, *McDonnell (FC) v Congregation of Christian Brothers Trustees (Formerly Irish Christian Brothers)*[27]—

> "It is permissible to use Hansard to identify the mischief at which a statute is aimed. It is, therefore, unobjectionable to use ministerial and other promoters' statements to identify the objective background to the legislation. To the extent that *Pepper v Hart* permits such use of Hansard the point is uncontroversial. A difficulty has, however, arisen about the true ratio of *Pepper v Hart*. It is certainly at least authority for the proposition that a categorical assurance given by the government in debates as to the meaning

---

[23] [2001] EWHC Admin 934; see also Chapter 1, Section 4.
[24] 1998 c.42.
[25] [2003] 3 W.L.R. 568, HL.
[26] Appendix, Extract 24.
[27] [2003] 3 W.L.R. 1627, 1641–1642, HL.

of the legislation may preclude the government *vis-à-vis* an individual from contending to the contrary. This may be seen as an estoppel or simply a principle of fairness. This view of *Pepper v Hart* restricts its ratio to the material facts of that case. There is, however, a possible broader interpretation of *Pepper v Hart, viz.* that it may be permissible to treat the intentions of the government revealed in debates as reflecting the will of Parliament. This interpretation gives rise to serious conceptual and constitutional difficulties which I summarised elsewhere: *Pepper v Hart: A Re-examination.*[28] In *Wilson v First County Trust Ltd (No.2),*[29] Lord Nicholls of Birkenhead discussed this distinction. In my view the narrower interpretation of *Pepper v Hart* ought to be preferred."

Practical application of the rule

It may be helpful to include a few words about how a person faced with a perceived ambiguity in an Act should go about trying to invoke the rule in *Pepper v Hart*. The Explanatory Notes for the Act in question will contain at the end a table listing each of the Parliamentary stages of the Bill for the Act and giving dates for each. That will enable the researcher to find easily those passages in Hansard most likely to be of relevance.   **28.1.10**

As a starting point, the most promising areas to search are likely to be the Minister's introductory speech or winding-up speech at Second Reading of the Bill in either House or on the Clause Stand Part debate on the relevant provision in Committee in either House. In the case of a provision introduced during the passage of the Bill, the most likely source of illumination is the Minister's speech introducing the relevant amendment. If there is no clear statement of intention in any of those places, or in the relevant passage of the Explanatory Notes themselves, it is unlikely (although not, of course, impossible) that there will be one anywhere else. But if the provision concerned was amended during the passage of the Bill, and if the amendment might be thought relevant to the question being considered, it would certainly be worth checking the speech of the Minister introducing the relevant amendment, at whatever stage and in whichever House it was passed.

As appears from the passages of the judgment in *Pepper v Hart* cited, it is only a clear and unequivocal statement that will be of assistance. Where an explanation given by the Minister falls short to any extent of absolute clarity, it is unlikely to be regarded by the courts as being of any assistance.

Generally speaking, it is only statements of Ministers that will be considered under the rule in *Pepper v Hart*. But since the purpose of the rule is to elicit the intention of Parliament in enacting legislation—and not strictly to elicit the intention of the Government in proposing legislation to Parliament for enactment—there will be exceptions to this rule.   **28.1.11**

---

[28] (2001) 21 O.J.L.S. 59.
[29] [2003] 3 W.L.R. 568, 586.

For example, where a non-Government Member of either House makes an assertion in clear terms about the effect of a provision, and the assertion is not challenged by a Minister, if the circumstances are such that one would expect the assertion to have been challenged were it not to accord with the Minister's own views,[30] the courts might well be prepared to accept the Minister's silence as acquiescence in the proposition asserted.

The other obvious exception is the case where a particular provision is added to the Bill, or amended, by an amendment or motion tabled by a non-Government member of either House.[31] In that case a statement made by the non-Government member as to the intended effect of the new provision might well be taken as being of the same evidential weight in illustrating the will of Parliament as is accorded to a Ministerial explanation of a Government provision or amendment.

Consequences of the rule for legislative practice

28.1.12 Among the various lines of speculation that arose when the rule in *Pepper v Hart* was pronounced was the question whether it would change the style of legislative drafting. Those, in particular, who urge a greater reliance on broad statements of principle[32] may have been encouraged to hope that draftsmen would feel able to use less precision in the knowledge that the courts would construe in accordance with statements of principle expressed during the passage of legislation.

That has not happened and would clearly be undesirable. It is as important after *Pepper v Hart* for the citizen to be able to determine the extent of his rights and obligations from the text of legislation as it was before that decision. It is uncertain whether the appropriate Ministerial pronouncements will be found and cited during a case on a legislative provision and whether they will be given the same weight and effect that the Government had intended. But even more uncertain is it whether the citizen reading legislation will be in a position to have regard to Ministerial pronouncements made during its passage.

The practice of the Government has, however, had to change in certain respects. The position is expressed in the following Written Answer[33]—

---

[30] For example, where advantage was being taken of the relative informality of the Standing Committee procedure in the House of Commons to have a detailed exchange of views about a particular provision.

[31] Although the Government by definition has a majority in the House of Commons, that does not, of course, mean that they never lose votes there, although as a general rule it is rare. But it is perfectly possible, and by no means uncommon, for an amendment moved by a non-Government Member, whether on the Government side or not, to find sufficient favour with the Government either to be accepted as it stands or for the Government to undertake to bring forward at a later stage in the Bill an amendment in more technically accurate form achieving the substantive wishes of the Member concerned. And in the House of Lords it is both more common for Governments to be defeated on Divisions and (possibly as a result) for Governments to concede amendments.

[32] As to which see Chapter 8, Section 1.

[33] HL Deb. April 5, 1995 W.A. 25; see also HL Deb. February 1, 1996 W.A. 118.

"Textual clarity and precision, and the avoidance of ambiguity, will continue to be high priorities in drafting legislation. Nonetheless, in the light of the ruling, administrative procedures are being put into place for avoiding or correcting any errors or ambiguities arising out of Ministerial statements during the passage of legislation. In particular: speeches and speaking notes will generally be reviewed by a department's legal adviser for possible influence on interpretation; the Hansard record of Ministers' contributions to debates on legislation will similarly be reviewed to consider whether there is any inaccuracy; and, where it seems sensible to do so, Ministers may more frequently offer to reflect and take further advice on points of interpretation that are raised in a debate. If it does prove necessary to correct a Ministerial statement, the aim will be to do this as promptly as possible at an appropriate point during the further consideration of the Bills."

Privilege

One of the objections, historically, to consulting the official report of Parliamentary proceedings in the course of legal proceedings was the fear of breaching the privilege of each House, asserted in the Bill of Rights, not to have its proceedings "impeached or questioned in any court or place out of Parliament". While that privilege is still alive, and is sometimes invoked for significant practical purposes,[34] it is no longer considered a bar to the production to the courts of published reports of proceedings, nor is formal waiver of privilege any longer required to be sought.[35]

28.1.13

---

[34] Note, for example, Madam Speaker's Statement "I have requested the Law Officers to intervene in the case [certain defamation proceedings] on behalf of the House, to assert the House's right that its proceedings should not—to quote the Bill of Rights—be 'impeached or questioned in any court or place out of Parliament'." (HC Deb. March 10, 1999 c.382).

[35] Note the First Report of the Committee of Privileges Session 1978–79 (December 7, 1978) recommending that the requirement for leave to refer to the Official Report be discontinued, and the consequent resolution of the House of Commons on October 31, 1980 "That this House, while re-affirming the status of proceedings in Parliament, confirmed by Article 9 of the Bill of Rights, gives leave for reference to be made in future Court proceedings to the Official Report of Debate and to the published Reports and evidence of Committees in any case in which, under the practice of the House, it is required that a petition for leave should be presented and the practice of presenting petitions for leave to refer to parliamentary papers be discontinued".

CHAPTER 29

INTERPRETATION OF SPECIAL KINDS OF LEGISLATION

Introduction

In the case of certain legislation principles apply that do not apply to the construction of other kinds of legislation. This Chapter explores those principles. **29.1.1**

Legislation implementing international obligation

Certain special principles applied in construing legislation[1] implementing an international obligation are discussed in Chapter 27. **29.1.2**

European, or Europe related, legislation

Certain principles applied in construing legislation implementing a Community obligation, or in construing legislation in an area of law in which Community obligations are inextricably entwined, are discussed in Chapter 27 and in Chapter 32, Section 5. **29.1.3**

As a general principle, it is important to reflect in reading national legislation designed to implement European law that an expression or concept with a technical or established meaning at national law may be required to be given a construction for the purpose of the implementing legislation that derives from the use of the expression or concept in European law.[2]

As to the construction for domestic purposes of Community instruments underlying implementing legislation, s.3 of the European Communities Act 1972[3] establishes the following principles in relation to the interpretation of Community Treaties and instruments—

---

[1] Although international obligations are often implemented by Act, they are also often implemented by delegated legislation—s.2(2) of the European Communities Act 1972 (c.68) is the obvious example of a general power for this purpose, while specific powers are also sometimes conferred—see, for example, s.103 of and Sch.6 to the Railways and Transport Safety Act 2003 (c.20) (Convention on International Carriage by Rail).

[2] So, for example, the concepts of a rest period and of working time for the purposes of Directive 93/104 and legislation implementing it are concepts of Community law requiring to be defined by reference to the Directive—*Landeshauptstadt Kiel v Jaeger* [2003] 3 C.M.L.R. 16, ECJ.

[3] 1972 c.68.

"3 Decisions on, and proof of, Treaties and Community instruments, etc

29.1.4

(1) For the purposes of all legal proceedings any question as to the meaning or effect of any of the Treaties, or as to the validity, meaning or effect of any Community instrument, shall be treated as a question of law (and, if not referred to the European Court, be for determination as such in accordance with the principles laid down by and any relevant decision of the European Court or any court attached thereto).

(2) Judicial notice shall be taken of the Treaties, of the Official Journal of the Communities and of any decision of, or expression of opinion by, the European Court or any court attached thereto on any such question as aforesaid; and the Official Journal shall be admissible as evidence of any instrument or other act thereby communicated of any of the Communities or of any Community institution.

(3) Evidence of any instrument issued by a Community institution, including any judgment or order of the European Court or any court attached thereto, or of any document in the custody of a Community institution, or any entry in or extract from such a document, may be given in any legal proceedings by production of a copy certified as a true copy by an official of that institution; and any document purporting to be such a copy shall be received in evidence without proof of the official position or handwriting of the person signing the certificate.

29.1.5

(4) Evidence of any Community instrument may also be given in any legal proceedings—

(a) by production of a copy purporting to be printed by the Queen's Printer;

(b) where the instrument is in the custody of a government department (including a department of the Government of Northern Ireland), by production of a copy certified on behalf of the department to be a true copy by an officer of the department generally or specially authorised so to do;

and any document purporting to be such a copy as is mentioned in paragraph (b) above of an instrument in the custody of a department shall be received in evidence without proof of the official position or handwriting of the person signing the certificate, or of his authority to do so, or of the document being in the custody of the department."

Consolidation and replicating legislation

29.1.6 Where legislation consolidates former law which has been judicially construed the courts will sometimes pay attention to case law on the enactments consolidated. This is justified on the grounds that, as Lord Reid said in *Beswick v Beswick*[4]—

> "That Act was a consolidation Act and it is the invariable practice of Parliament to require from those who have prepared a consolidation Bill an assurance that it will make no substantial change in the law and to have that checked by a committee. On this assurance the Bill is then passed into law, no amendment being permissible."

The nature and extent of this principle is helpfully expounded in the following passage of the judgment of Taylor J. in *Champion v Maughan*[5]—

> "Finally, Counsel for the respondents prays in aid the principle that since this Act is expressed to be a consolidating statute one ought not to conclude that it introduces that which was not there previously, namely an absolute offence, without proof of *mens rea*. So far as that is concerned it is relevant to look at a recent authority in relation to the construction of statutes, and in particular of a consolidating statute. The authority which was drawn to our attention by counsel for the appellant is *R. v West Yorkshire Coroner Ex p. Smith*.[6] That was a case concerned with the Coroners Act 1887.[7] Lord Lane C.J. said[8]—

>> 'The Coroners Act 1887 is expressed to be a consolidating statute, though, it is fair to say, one has to look no further than section 6 of the Act (which provides a whole new method of redress) to realise that consolidation was not the only aim of the statute. I start off by examining *Bank of England v Vagliano Bros*[9] where Lord Herschell said:

>>> "I think the proper course is in the first instance to examine the language of the statute and to ask what is its natural meaning, uninfluenced by any considerations derived from the previous state of the law, and not to start with inquiring how the law previously stood, and then, assuming that it was probably intended to leave it unaltered, to see if the words of the enactment will bear an interpretation in conformity with this view . . . ' "

> "Lord Lane C.J. continued his citation from Lord Herschell and then referred to a number of other authorities on the interpretation of statutes. He said finally on this matter[10]:

29.1.7

---

[4] [1968] A.C. 58, 73, HL.
[5] [1984] 1 All E.R. 680, 683, QBD.
[6] [1983] Q.B. 335.
[7] 1887 c.71.
[8] At 352.
[9] [1891] A.C. 107, 144–145, HL.
[10] At 354–355.

'Applying those various considerations then to the words of section 3, I am unable to find any ambiguity or obscurity. I do not think that the words used are fairly susceptible of bearing more than one meaning in their context. Consequently it is not permissible to have regard, in my judgment, to any earlier statutory enactment as an aid to construction. No aid is required save the words themselves. It should perhaps be added that the interpretation of section 3 suggested by Counsel as *amicus* would itself require extensive wording being read into the section, which, on its own, perhaps provides an argument against such an interpretation being adopted.'

29.1.8   "Applying those observations to the present case, in my judgment the words of section 6(1)(a) of the [Salmon and Freshwater Fisheries Act 1975[11]] are plain and unambiguous. They clearly indicate an absolute offence. Counsel for the respondents very frankly conceded at the beginning of his argument that it was necessary to import into section 6(1)(a) the qualifying words contained in para (b). Lord Lane C.J. in the passage that I have just cited indicated that such a need was in itself perhaps an argument against such an interpretation being adopted, and I consider that in the present case the same argument holds good."

As with other principles of construction, the principle of looking to the pre-consolidation legislation comes into play only where some difficulty or ambiguity arises on the face of the consolidating legislation.[12]

The principle of assuming the same meaning in the case of a consolidating provision is not restricted to straight consolidation. Where legislation uses an

---

[11] 1975 c.51.

[12] See Lord Diplock in *Inland Revenue Commissioners v Joiner* [1975] 1 W.L.R. 1701, 1711, HL "The purpose of a consolidation Act is to remove this difficulty [large numbers of textual amendments] by bringing together in a single statute all the existing statute law dealing with the same subject matter which forms the general context in which the particular provisions of the Act fall to be construed, so that it will be no longer necessary to seek that context in a whole series of amended and re-amended provisions appearing piecemeal in earlier statutes. That is the only purpose of a consolidation Act; this is the only 'mischief' it is designed to cure. It is true that a consolidation Act is not intended to alter the law as it existed immediately before the Act was passed, but to treat this absence of intention as justifying recourse to the previous legislation repealed by the consolidation Act in order to ascribe to any of the provisions of that Act a meaning different from that which it would naturally bear when read only in the context of the other provisions of the consolidation Act itself would be to defeat the whole purpose of this type of legislation—to allow the absence of a tail to wag the dog. So the primary rule of construction of a consolidation Act is to examine the actual language used in the Act itself without reference to any of the statutes which it has repealed."; hence, for example, Lord Bridge of Harwich in *Associated Newspapers Ltd v Wilson* [1995] 2 A.C. 454, 472, HL—"To put it no higher, the question whether section 23(1) should be rewritten in some way so as to spell out expressly the meaning of 'action' as including omission, or whether the context requires that the definition be not applied, gives rise to a 'real and substantial difficulty' in the interpretation of the statute 'which classical methods of construction cannot resolve' and thus entitles us to go behind the consolidating Act of 1978 to derive whatever assistance we can in resolving the difficulty from the legislative history: see *Farrell v Alexander* [1977] A.C. 59, 73, *per* Lord Wilberforce."

expression that has been used in earlier legislation in a similar context and has received judicial interpretation, the courts will have regard to that interpretation in the new context—

> "It has long been a well established principle to be applied in the consideration of Acts of Parliament that where a word of doubtful meaning has received a clear judicial interpretation, the subsequent statute which incorporates the same word or the same phrase in a similar context, must be construed so that the word or phrase is interpreted according to the meaning that has previously been assigned to it.

> "James L.J. in the case of *Ex parte Campbell*[13] expresses this rule in the following terms: **29.1.9**

>> 'Where once certain words in an Act of Parliament have received a judicial construction in one of the Superior Courts, and the Legislature has repeated them without alteration in a subsequent statute, I conceive that the Legislature must be taken to have used them according to the meaning which a Court of competent jurisdiction has given to them.'

> "And this opinion was expressed in a case where the learned Lord Justice himself said it was difficult to bring the interpretation within the words of the Act. The same opinion was expressed by Lord Halsbury in delivering the opinion of the Judicial Committee in the case of *Webb v Outrim*,[14] and I know of no authority that has in any way weakened the effect of this pronouncement."[15]

> "Decisions of the court on the meanings of phrases used in Acts of Parliament may come in the course of time to give them the quality of terms of art which Parliament may well be assumed to have intended them to bring with them when used in subsequent legislation."[16]

For further discussion on what counts as a similar context for the purposes of   **29.1.10**
this principle see the discussion of cross-contextual application of statutory definitions in Chapter 20, paras 20.1.38 and 20.1.39.

Note, however, that in deciding what weight, if any, to give to judicial decisions in relation to a legislative regime repealed and re-enacted, the courts must determine how far the re-enactment was intended to replace the principles upon which the scheme operated. This can, except in cases of pure consolidation, be a far-from-easy exercise.[17]

---

[13] L.R. 5 Ch. 703, 706.
[14] [1907] A.C. 81, 89.
[15] *Barras v Aberdeen Steam Trawling and Fishing Co* [1933] A.C. 402, 411 *per* Lord Buckmaster.
[16] *Re a debtor (No 784 of 1991)* [1992] Ch 554, 558–559 *per* Hoffmann J.
[17] For an example of the tests and approaches to be applied in determining it, see *Woodland-Ferrari v U.C.L.* [2002] 3 All E.R. 670, Ch.

Note also that among the limitations of the doctrine of having regard to decisions on the meaning of legislation from which the current legislation derives is the principle that the courts will not regard themselves as being prevented from reversing an earlier error merely because it relates to legislation that has now been reworked. As Denning L.J. said in *Royal Crown Derby Porcelain Co Ltd v Russell*[18]—

> "I do not believe that whenever Parliament re-enacts a provision of a statute it thereby gives statutory authority to every erroneous interpretation which has been put upon it. The true view is that the court will be slow to overrule a previous decision on the interpretation of a statute when it has long been acted on, and it will be more than usually slow to do so when Parliament has, since the decision, re-enacted the statute in the same terms. But if a decision is, in fact, shown to be erroneous, there is no rule of law which prevents it being overruled."

Subordinate legislation

29.1.11 While the principles expounded elsewhere in this Part are, except where the contrary is stated, as true and sufficient for subordinate legislation as they are for primary, there is one additional matter that needs to be stated in relation to the construction of subordinate legislation.

There is a statutory presumption that expressions used in subordinate legislation have the same meaning as that given to them in the primary legislation under which the subordinate legislation is made.[19] This is a rebuttable presumption, so the true position remains as stated by Grove J. in *Blashill v Chambers*[20]—

> "I do not say that there may not be words in by-laws which are so obviously used in a different sense to the same words in the Act that the Court may properly, reading them with the context, put a different construction upon them; but primâ facie I should say that the proper mode of construction is to apply the same interpretation to terms used in a by-law which is applied to the same terms in the Act under the powers of which the by-law is framed."

---

[18] [1949] 2 K.B. 417, 429, CA.
[19] Interpretation Act 1978 (c.30), s.11.
[20] (1885) 14 Q.B.D. 479, 485; see also *Potts or Riddell v Reid* [1943] A.C. 1, HL.

Part 5

EUROPEAN LEGISLATION

CHAPTER 30

NATURE OF EUROPEAN LEGISLATION

SECTION 1

INTRODUCTION

The European Union has of course become of fundamental importance in almost **30.1.1** every area of the law of the United Kingdom. And its influence appears to grow continually, both in respect of the areas to which it is relevant and in respect of the extent of its influence in those areas.

A work on legislation in the United Kingdom needs to approach the topic of the European Union from two aspects—

(1) First, it is necessary to say something about the kinds of legislation that emanate from the institutions of the Communities that form the Union.[1] Some legislation of this kind will, by virtue of the United Kingdom's membership of the European Union,[2] create of itself legal rights and obligations that are enforceable and binding within the United Kingdom. And in relation to the greater part of European legislation that requires to be transposed into law within the United Kingdom in some way it will be helpful for the reader encountering the transposing legislation to have some small acquaintance with the nature of the European legislation to which it gives effect.[3]

(2) Secondly, it is frequently necessary when dealing with general matters relating to the form, process and effect of legislation to make specific

---

[1] The European Union is "founded on the European Communities"—Treaty on European Union, Maastricht, February 7, 1992, as amended by the Treaty of Amsterdam, Art.1.

[2] As implemented by s.2(1) of the European Communities Act 1972 (c.68).

[3] Sometimes, indeed, where an area of legislation is entirely underpinned by European obligations more than a slight familiarity with the European law is desirable. Note, in particular, the following passage from the speech of Lord Walker of Gestingthorpe in *Royal and Sun Alliance v Customs and Excise Commissioners* [2003] 2 All E.R. 1073, 1090, HL—"My Lords, value added tax is essentially a European Union tax, imposed by member states in compliance with European Union legislation, of which the most important is Council Directive (EEC) 77/388 (on the harmonisation of the laws of the member states relating to turnover taxes—common system of value added tax: uniform basis of assessment (O.J. 1977 L145 p.1)) (the Sixth Directive). Member states give effect to the European Union legislation . . . by national legislation, in the case of the United Kingdom the Value Added Tax Act 1994 and the Value Added Tax Regulations 1995, SI 1995/2518. In this appeal neither side has suggested that the United Kingdom government has failed to implement the Sixth Directive correctly. Nevertheless it is convenient to make some references to it (as well as to the 1994 Act and the 1995 regulations) since the general scheme of the national legislation can sometimes be better understood by reference to the Sixth Directive. Moreover decisions of the

reference to legislation designed to give effect to obligations imposed by, or in some other way to reflect, the United Kingdom's membership of the European Union. This has been done in earlier Chapters.[4]

30.1.2 This Chapter will go some way towards achieving the first of these two objectives. The description of the forms of European legislation will, however, be brief and cursory. Those who have a need for a detailed and authoritative guide to the legislative process within the European Communities will find no shortage of other works purporting to provide just that. A reader needing to acquire a profound understanding of the nature and effect of legislation emanating from the European Communities and how to approach it will not find his purpose answered by any part of this work. This Chapter, and other related passages of this work, aim only to give sufficient background to alert readers to some fundamental issues relating to European legislation that regularly affect legal practitioners within the United Kingdom (other than those whose concerns are primarily international) and to put into context that part of our domestic legislation which is primarily inspired by our membership of the European Union.

There is, of course, room for theoretical argument whether any document emanating from the European Communities deserves to be described in relation to the United Kingdom as legislation. There is only one primary legislature for the United Kingdom, the Westminster Parliament, and this form of "European legislation" is made neither by nor with the authority of Parliament. Nor can this kind of "European legislation" properly be described in relation to the United Kingdom as secondary legislation, since the European institutions owe no kind of allegiance to Parliament and take neither instructions nor permission from it.

But the argument is of little or no practical importance. The institutions of the European Communities purport to legislate in accordance with the Treaty establishing the European Community, and their legislation is given legal effect within the United Kingdom by s.2(1) of the European Communities Act 1972.[5]

A reference in this Chapter to the Treaty establishing the European Community is a reference to the treaty made at Rome on March 25, 1957 as amended, in particular, by the Treaty on European Union signed at Maastricht on February 7, 1992 and the Treaty signed at Amsterdam on October 2, 1997.

Court of Justice of the European Communities naturally refer principally to the European Union legislation in laying down some general principles (in particular the principle of fiscal neutrality, and the concept of the 'direct and immediate link') which inform the interpretation of the legislation."

[4] See, in particular, Chapter 3, Section 10.
[5] 1972 c.68.

European Economic Area

The European Economic Area was established under the Agreement signed at **30.1.3**
Oporto on May 2, 1992.[6] In essence, it amounts to a range of countries that, while
not part of the European Union, have a close relationship with it involving
mutual recognition of the principal rights and freedoms arising under the
Community Treaties, being therefore a relationship closer than that forged with
various other non-EU countries by *ad hoc* Treaties.

The European Economic Area Act 1993[7] has the effect of extending in relation
to the European Economic Area the legal and legislative mechanisms appertaining within the United Kingdom to membership of the European Union.

Preservation of Parliamentary Sovereignty and supremacy

A frequently discussed question is whether and to what extent the incorporation **30.1.4**
into the law of the United Kingdom of the Community Treaties, and the strength
of rule in s.2(1) of the European Communities Act 1972, have undermined the
powers of the Westminster Parliament and transferred legislative supremacy to
the institutions of the European Union.

As a question of political realities, the question is of course complicated. But
as a matter of legal theory it is relatively simple. Section 2(1) of the European
Communities Act 1972 does place European law in a place of supremacy to
which the powers of the executive and Parliament itself are subject. Even an Act
of Parliament requires to be measured against the requirements of the United
Kingdom's obligations under the European Treaties, and if it fails to be
compatible it will be overridden by the domestic courts,[8] preference being given
to the need to give effect to the European obligation.

But this supremacy of European law within the law of the United Kingdom
owes its existence to, and is dependent upon, the Sovereignty of Parliament and
its enactment of the 1972 Act. Whatever the political realities, as a matter of legal
theory it is open to Parliament to repeal the European Communities Act 1972:
and were that done, European Community law would cease to have any effect
within the courts of the United Kingdom.[9]

So the "new legal order of international law" described by the European Court **30.1.5**
of Justice in the leading case of *Algemene Transport-en Expeditie Onderneming
van Gend en Loos NV v Nederlandse Belastingadministratie*[10] is an accurate

---

[6] As adjusted by the Protocol signed at Brussels on March 17, 1993.
[7] 1993 c.51.
[8] As happened in *Factortame*—as to which see Chapter 32, Section 4.
[9] Although, of course, if the United Kingdom remained part of the European Union the failure to
have a mechanism for giving effect to European law would amount to a breach of our international
obligations and would have legal consequences at that level. And even as a wholly foreign
institution the law of the Communities might continue to have effect in the courts of the United
Kingdom, in the same way as other foreign laws, in accordance with the principles of private
international law.
[10] [1963] C.M.L.R. 105, ECJ.

account of how European law and domestic law inter-relate, while the former is given effect in and by the latter: it does not of itself imply either that the situation is not revocable for a Member State at the will of its domestic legislature or that European law enjoys any inherent authority founded on a situation or principle outside the control of the Member States.

The point of legal theory, and the extent to which political and practical realities can be seen to affect the theory, are well expounded in the passages of the judgment of Lord Denning in *Blackburn v Attorney-General*[11] and of Laws L.J. in *Thoburn v Sunderland City Council*,[12] both appended to this work.[13]

The general effect on Parliamentary supremacy of "entrenched" enactments, of which s.2(1) of the European Communities Act 1972 is just one, has already been touched in the general context of those enactments.[14] The entrenched position in relation to the European Union is that legislation emanating from the Communities binds the United Kingdom and has effect in United Kingdom law automatically, by virtue of the 1972 Act. Without repeal of that Act, the position can be regarded as entrenched. But, again, repeal of that Act is always a legal possibility, whatever the practical and political realities.

30.1.6   The political position was expressed in the following Written Question and Answer in the House of Lords[15]—

> <u>Lord Tebbit</u> "Whether the United Kingdom's membership of the European Union is irrevocable."

> <u>Baroness Chalker of Wallasey</u> "It remains open to Parliament to repeal the European Communities Act 1972 and for the United Kingdom to withdraw from the European Union. The terms of that withdrawal would have to be negotiated with the other member states. The government believe, that the future prosperity and security of the United Kingdom depends on our membership of the European Union."

SECTION 2

PRIMARY LEGISLATION

The primary sources of European law

30.2.1   The entirety of the European Union and the Communities which form it depend upon international treaties, agreed as a result of direction negotiations between the governments of the Member States. The original treaty made at Rome on March 25, 1957 has since been amended and supplemented by a long series of

---

[11] [1971] 2 All E.R. 1380, 1381–82, CA.
[12] [2003] Q.B. 151.
[13] Appendix, extracts 1 and 2: see also Chapter 2, Section 2.
[14] See Chapter 1, Section 4.
[15] HL Deb. March 23, 1995 W.A. 76.

treaties. These are listed in s.1(2) of and Sch.1 to the European Communities Act 1972[16] and are the ultimate source of all rights and obligations in relation to the European Union and its constituent Communities.

The principal treaties establishing the European Communities have been revised in ways of particular importance by—

(1) the Single European Act in 1987,

(2) the Treaty on European Union (the "Maastricht Treaty") in 1992, and

(3) the Treaty of Amsterdam in 1997.

The Treaties are given force of law within the United Kingdom by s.2(1) of the European Communities Act 1972[17] which provides as follows—

> "All such rights, powers, liabilities, obligations and restrictions from time to time created or arising by or under the Treaties, and all such remedies and procedures from time to time provided for by or under the Treaties, as in accordance with the Treaties are without further enactment to be given legal effect or used in the United Kingdom shall be recognised and available in law, and be enforced, allowed and followed accordingly".

The Treaty of principal practical importance is that establishing the European Community, under which almost all of the subordinate European legislation affecting Member States generally is made. Legislation is also made under the treaties establishing the European Coal and Steel Community and Euratom, and the same considerations as those described in this Chapter in relation to the European Community will apply. In addition, the Maastricht Treaty on European Union creates procedures for the adoption of legislation (in the sense of binding instruments) in relation to foreign policy, security and crime.

Framework legislation

The term "framework legislation" is used in European law to refer to legislation that establishes general rules or principles on a subject, which may themselves be sufficient to require and found specific implementing domestic legislation, but which may also be followed by further European legislation imposing more specific rules. It is a rule of construction of European law that a provision of specific legislation (*lex specialis*) prevails over a provision of the framework legislation from which it arises.[18]   **30.2.2**

---

[16] 1972 c.68: and there is power to add to the list by Order in Council—see s.1(3).
[17] 1972 c.68.
[18] *R. v Environment Agency, Ex p. Mayer Parry Recycling Ltd* [2003] 3 C.M.L.R. 8, ECJ.

There is nothing quite akin to this in the context of United Kingdom legislation. While primary legislation frequently leaves details to be provided by subordinate legislation, the rights or duties provided by the primary legislation are in general incomplete and ineffective until the subordinate legislation is enacted. Similarly, although purpose clauses of the kind discussed in Chapter 8, Section 1 establish principles underpinning the specific rules that follow, they are not sufficient on their own to impose rights or duties.

SECTION 3

SUBORDINATE LEGISLATION

30.3.1   A number of provisions of the Treaty establishing the European Community empower one or other of the institutions of the Communities to make legislation of different kinds. The three principal kinds and their natures are described in Art.249 of that Treaty—

> "In order to carry out their task and in accordance with the provisions of this a Treaty, the European Parliament acting jointly with the Council, the Council and the Commission shall make regulations and issue directives, take decisions, make recommendations or deliver opinions.

> "A regulation shall have general application. It shall be binding in its entirety and directly applicable in all Member States.

> "A directive shall be binding, as to the result to be achieved, upon each Member State to which it is addressed, but shall leave to the national authorities the choice of form and methods.

> "A decision shall be binding in its entirety upon those to whom it is addressed.

> "Recommendations and opinions shall have no binding force."

The result is that it is the Directive that is most frequently responsible for inspiring domestic implementing legislation.

Implementation of Directives, &c. by domestic subordinate legislation

30.3.2   The principal method by which a Directive will be given legal effect in the United Kingdom is the use of the power conferred by s.2(2) of the European Communities Act 1972.[19] That power is also available for use for the purpose of making such domestic legislative change as may be required by any form of European legislation other than a Directive. Chapter 3, Section 10 discusses in a little detail instruments under s.2(2).

---

[19] 1972 c.68.

Parliamentary scrutiny of European legislation

Chapter 31, Section 2 details the processes by which the Westminster Parliament **30.3.3** exercises a (self-imposed) function of scrutinising legislation emanating from the institutions of the European Communities.

SECTION 4

FUNDAMENTAL PRINCIPLES

Introduction

This Section briefly describes some fundamental principles of European law **30.4.1** relating to legislation.

Legality of legislation

Unlike the law of the United Kingdom,[20] every European law is open to be tested **30.4.2** for legality. The EC Treaty permits[21] an action to be brought[22] for the annulment of any binding legal instruments of the Council, the Commission, the Parliament or the European Central Bank.

Articles 230 and 231 of the Treaty[23] provide as follows—

> **"Article 230**
>
> "The Court of Justice shall review the legality of acts adopted jointly by the European Parliament and the Council, of acts of the Council, of the Commission and of the ECB, other than recommendations and opinions, and of acts of the European Parliament intended to produce legal effects vis-à-vis third parties.
>
> "It shall for this purpose have jurisdiction in actions brought by a Member State, the European Parliament, the Council or the Commission on grounds of lack of competence, infringement of an essential procedural requirement, infringement of this Treaty or of any rule of law relating to its application, or misuse of powers.
>
> "The Court of Justice shall have jurisdiction under the same conditions in actions brought by the Court of Auditors and by the ECB for the purpose of protecting their prerogatives.

---

[20] As to which Acts of Parliament are beyond judicial testing, except in so far as Parliament has provided to the contrary—see Chapter 2, Section 3.
[21] Art.230.
[22] In the European Court of Justice (or, sometimes, in the Court of First Instance).
[23] As amended by the Treaty of Nice.

"Any natural or legal person may, under the same conditions, institute proceedings against a decision addressed to that person or against a decision which, although in the form of a regulation or a decision addressed to another person, is of direct and individual concern to the former.

"The proceedings provided for in this article shall be instituted within two months of the publication of the measure, or of its notification to the plaintiff, or, in the absence thereof, of the day on which it came to the knowledge of the latter, as the case may be.

Article 231

30.4.3   "If the action is well founded, the Court of Justice shall declare the act concerned to be void.

"In the case of a regulation, however, the Court of Justice shall, if it considers this necessary, state which of the effects of the regulation which it has declared void shall be considered as definitive."

An action for annulment may be brought on the grounds that European legislation—

(1) is ultra vires,

(2) violates essential procedural requirements,

(3) infringes the Treaties legislation under them, or

(4) amounts to an abuse of discretionary powers.

If the action succeeds, the court may declare legislation void either with retrospective effect or with effect from the date of the judgment.

Subsidiarity

30.4.4 The principle of subsidiarity is encapsulated in Art.5 of the EC Treaty (as amended) as follows—

"The Community shall act within the limits of the powers conferred upon it by this Treaty and of the objectives assigned to it therein.

"In areas which do not fall within its exclusive competence, the Community shall take action, in accordance with the principle of subsidiarity, only if and in so far as the objectives of the proposed action cannot be sufficiently achieved by the Member States and can therefore, by reason of the scale or effects of the proposed action, be better achieved by the Community."

A useful test to be applied in determining whether the principle of subsidiarity is observed in relation to proposed legislation is to determine 180 "whether the objective of the proposed action could be better achieved at Community level".[24]

A protocol on the application of the principles of subsidiarity and proportionality was adopted as an annexe to the EC Treaty in 1997.[25]

Proportionality

The principle of proportionality is encapsulated in Art.5 of the EC Treaty (as amended) as follows— **30.4.5**

> "Any action by the Community shall not go beyond what is necessary to achieve the objectives of this Treaty."

A protocol on the application of the principles of subsidiarity and proportionality was adopted as an annexe to the EC Treaty in 1997.[26]

Other fundamental principles

The European Court of Justice recognises a number of fundamental principles of **30.4.6** Community law which it will apply in the construction and application of European law.

One of the most significant is that of legitimate expectation,[27] also recognised by the courts of the United Kingdom as a principle to be applied in administrative law.

---

[24] *British American Tobacco Investments and Imperial Tobacco* (C-491/01) ECJ.

[25] The substantive provisions of the protocol are reproduced in the Appendix to this work as Extract 25.

[26] The substantive provisions of the protocol are reproduced in the Appendix to this work as Extract 25.

[27] See, for example, "With regard to infringement of legitimate expectations, it is settled case-law that the right to rely on the principle of the protection of legitimate expectations, which is one of the fundamental principles of the Community, extends to any individual who is in a situation in which it is apparent that the Community administration has led him to entertain reasonable expectations by giving him precise assurances (see, to that effect, Case T-266/97 *Vlaamse Televisie Maatschappij v Commission* [1999] ECR II-2329, para.71, and Joined Cases T-485/93, T-491/93, T-494/93 and T-61/98 *Dreyfus and Others v Commission* [2000] ECR II-3659, paragraph 85)."—*Van den Bergh Foods Ltd, formerly HB Ice Cream Ltd v Commission of the European Communities* (Case T-65/98) C.F.I. para.192.

CHAPTER 31

THE LEGISLATIVE PROCESS

SECTION 1

PASSAGE OF EUROPEAN LEGISLATION

Introduction

As has already been made clear it is beyond the scope of this work to give a   **31.1.1**
thorough exposition of matters relating to legislation emanating from the
institutions of the European Union. Instead, this work provides only a cursory
introduction sufficient to explain in general terms the principal effects of that
legislation within the law of the United Kingdom and to set into context domestic
legislation that is wholly or partly inspired by European legislation.

This Section will accordingly provide a brief overview of the way in which
legislation is made by the institutions of the European institutions.

The categories of legislation and their effects have already been described.[1]

The key to understanding the process of legislating within the European Union
is to understand the distinct role of each of the three major institutions involved
in it.

The Council of the European Union

The Council[2] is, amongst its other responsibilities, the principal legislative body   **31.1.2**
of the Communities. In some substantive areas it discharges that function jointly
with the European Parliament. It is also the Council which makes international
agreements on behalf of the Communities, again sometimes acting with the
express consent of the Parliament.

The Council's legislative role is expounded helpfully in the following
passage[3]—

---

[1] See Chapter 30.
[2] This institution, which is normally referred to in the context of European legislation simply as "the
Council", requires to be distinguished both from the "European Council", a political forum
consisting of the Heads of State or Government of the Member States of the European Union and
the President of the European Commission, and from the "Council of Europe" which is an
international organisation.
[3] Taken from *Europa*, an on-line information service maintained by the European Commission.

707

"The role of the Council as the main decision-making institution in Community activities is defined in terms of the three 'pillars' set out in the Treaty on European Union (the Treaty of Maastricht).

"The first pillar—covering a wide range of Community policies such as agriculture, transport, environment, energy, research and development—is designed and implemented according to a well-proven decision-making process which starts with a Commission proposal. Following detailed examination by experts and at the political level, the Council may either adopt the Commission proposal, amend it or ignore it. The Treaty of Maastricht strengthened the role of the European Parliament in this context by creating a co-decision procedure. As a consequence, a wide range of legislation (such as that pertaining to the single market, consumer affairs, trans-European networks, education and health) is adopted by both the Parliament and the Council. The 'social partners' and other interest groups are consulted via the Economic and Social Committee and local and regional authorities represented in the Committee of the Regions in a number of fields.

"The Treaties lay down that, depending on the subject, the Council acts by a simple majority of its members, by a qualified majority or by unanimous decision. Where the Council acts by a qualified majority, the votes of each of its members are weighted. In the Community sphere, a large proportion of legislative decisions are taken by qualified majority. The policy areas in the first pillar which remain subject to unanimity include taxation, industry, culture, regional and social funds and the framework programme for research and technology development. For the other two pillars created by the Treaty on European Union, the Council is the decision-maker as well as the promoter of initiatives. On common foreign and security policy the Council takes the decisions necessary for defining and implementing this policy, on the basis of general guidelines specified by the European Council. It recommends common strategies to the European Council and implements them, particularly by deciding on joint actions and common positions. On police and judicial cooperation in criminal matters, the Council, at the initiative of a Member State or of the Commission, decides on common positions, framework decisions and decisions, and draws up conventions. Unanimity is the rule in both pillars, except for the implementation of a joint action, which can be decided by qualified majority.

31.1.3 "In the framework of the Treaty establishing the European Community, Community law, adopted by the Council—or by the Parliament and the Council in the framework of the co-decision procedure—may take the following forms:

> Regulations
> Directives
> Decisions

Recommendations and opinions.

"The Council may also adopt conclusions of a political nature or other types of acts such as Declarations or Resolutions. Furthermore, the Council establishes requirements for exercising the implementing powers conferred on the Commission or reserved to the Council itself."

The European Commission

Amongst its other responsibilities, the Commission of the European Union is the only body able formally to initiate proposals for legislation within the Communities. The Commission starts the legislative process by making a proposal for a regulation or a directive, for the purpose of expanding or improving the implementation of a feature of the Community Treaties. **31.1.4**

Rules of the Communities require that before the Commission makes a formal proposal it must—

(1) identifying the Community interest in the matter concerned,

(2) consult as it thinks appropriate, and

(3) have regard to the principle of subsidiarity.[4]

The process is described by the Commission as follows[5]—

"Once the Commission has formally sent a proposal for legislation to the Council and the Parliament, the Union's law-making process is dependent on effective cooperation between three institutions—the Council, the Commission and the European Parliament. In agreement with the Commission, the Council can amend a proposal by a qualified majority (if the Commission does not agree, the change requires unanimity). The European Parliament shares the power of co-decision with the Council in most areas and has to be consulted in others. When revising its proposals, the Commission is required to take amendments of the Parliament into consideration."

In the two areas of intergovernmental cooperation covered by the Treaty on European Union—common foreign and security policy and cooperation on justice and home affairs—the Commission does not enjoy a monopoly of the right to propose a decision: but it may submit a proposal and participate in discussions of it.

---

[4] As to which see Chapter 30, Section 4.
[5] On *Europa*, an online information system maintained by the European Commission.

The European Parliament

31.1.5 The role of the European Parliament in the legislative processes within the European Union is described in the following passage[6]—

> "Originally, the Treaty of Rome (1957) gave the European Parliament a consultative role only, whereas the Commission was entitled to propose and the Council of Ministers to decide legislation. Subsequent Treaties have extended the European Parliament's influence from a purely advisory role to full involvement in the Community's legislative process. The European Parliament is now empowered to amend and even adopt legislation. Thus, in a large number of areas the power of decision is shared by the Council and the European Parliament. Depending on the individual legal basis, the European Parliament takes part, to varying degrees, in the drafting of Community legislation. The different legal bases and associated procedures defined in the Treaties are as follows.

> *"Co-decision procedure*

> "According to the Amsterdam Treaty, the simplified co-decision procedure shares decision-making power equally between the European Parliament and the Council. A legal act is adopted if Council and European Parliament agree at first reading. If these institutions disagree, a "conciliation committee"—made up of equal numbers of Members of Parliament and of the Council, with the Commission present—convenes, seeking a compromise on a text that the Council and Parliament can both subsequently endorse. If this conciliation does not result in an agreement, the Parliament can reject the proposal outright by an absolute majority. The co-decision procedure, which strengthens the role of the EP as co-legislator, applies to a wide range of issues (39 legal bases in the EC Treaty), such as the free movement of workers, consumer protection, education, culture, health and trans-European networks.

> *"Consultation procedure*

> The consultation procedure requires an opinion from the European Parliament before the Council can adopt a legislative proposal from the Commission. Neither the Commission nor the Council is obliged to accept the amendments listed in the opinion of the European Parliament. Once the European Parliament has given its opinion, the Council can adopt the proposal without amendments or adopt it in an amended form. However, the European Parliament can refuse to give an opinion. The consultation procedure applies to agriculture (price review), taxation, competition,

---

[6] Taken from *Europa*, an online information system maintained by the European Commission.

harmonisation of legislation not related to the single market, industrial policy, aspects of social and environmental policy (subject to unanimity), most aspects pertaining to the creation of an area of freedom, security and justice, and adoption of general rules and principles for comitology. For the purpose of the approximation of laws and regulations, this procedure also applies to a new framework-decision instrument created by the Amsterdam Treaty under the third pillar.

"Cooperation procedure

"The cooperation procedure allows the European Parliament to improve **31.1.6** proposed legislation by amendment. This requires an opinion and involves two readings by the European Parliament, giving its members ample opportunity to review and amend the Commission's proposal as well as the Council's preliminary position. The Commission indicates which amendments it accepts before forwarding its proposal to the Council. This results in a 'common position' of the Council. At second reading the Council is obliged to take into account those amendments of the European Parliament that were adopted by an absolute majority in so far as they have been taken on board by the Commission. The Treaty of Amsterdam has simplified the various legislative procedures by significantly extending the co-decision procedure, which is in practice almost replacing the cooperation procedure. As a consequence, the cooperation procedure applies to very few cases (two European Monetary Union provisions).

"Assent procedure

"The assent procedure applies to those legislative areas in which the Council acts by unanimous decision, limited, since the Amsterdam Treaty, to the organisation and objectives of the Structural and Cohesion Funds. The European Parliament's assent is also required for important international agreements concluded between the Union and a non-member country or group of countries, such as the accession of new Member States and association agreements with third countries (absolute majority of the European Parliament's total membership required).

"The right of initiative

"Since the Maastricht Treaty, the European Parliament has a limited right of legislative initiative in that it has the possibility of asking the Commission to put forward a proposal."

Consultation

The essential features of the European legislative process are those contained in **31.1.7** the responsibilities of the three key institutions, the Council, the Commission and the Parliament, as described above. There are, however, other aspects of the process worthy of mention. In particular, the concept of pre-legislative consultation is, as a reflection of the political realities of negotiation amongst a number of independent States, highly formalised within the European context. In some cases it is a required part of the procedure as a matter of law, while in other cases it is, while not a legal requirement, practically unavoidable.

The consultative role of two bodies requires particular mention.

The Economic and Social Committee

31.1.8 The Economic and Social Committee is a non-political advisory body designed to give employers, workers, trade unions, consumers and others directly effected by the European Union's social and economic polices, an opportunity to express a formal opinion on those policies.

In addition to its other more general responsibilities, the Committee has a role in the legislative process consisting of advising the Commission, the Council and the European Parliament by informing them of the Committee's opinion on particular issues.

The formalities of the process are described in the following passage[7]—

"There are three different types of opinions the ESC may issue.

"Mandatory consultation

"In certain areas, a decision can only be taken after the Council or the Commission have consulted the Economic and Social Committee. This applies for agricultural policy; free movement of persons and services; transport policy; harmonisation of indirect taxation; approximation of laws for the single market; employment policy; social policy; education, vocational training and youth employment policy; public health; consumer protection; trans-European networks; industrial policy; economic and social cohesion; research and technological development; and environment.

"Voluntary consultation

31.1.9 "The ESC may also draw up exploratory opinions if the Commission, the Council or the European Parliament ask the Committee to consider specific issues with a view to future action.

"Own-initiative opinions

"The ESC may decide to express its views by issuing an opinion on any subject it considers of interest.

---

[7] Taken from *Europa*, an online information service maintained by the European Commission.

"All ESC opinions are published in the European Union's Official Journal after having been forwarded to the Communities' decision-making bodies."

The Committee of the Regions

The Committee of the Regions was created, in the form of an independent **31.1.10** advisory body, by the Maastricht Treaty, with the principal objective of defending the common interests of local and regional bodies, and European Union citizens, in the Community policy-making process. The Committee has a particular responsibility for safe-guarding the principle of subsidiarity.

In addition to its general responsibilities the Committee has an advisory role in the legislative process which is described in the following passage[8]—

"The Committee of the Regions can adopt different types of opinions which are sent to the Council, the Commission and the European Parliament and are published in the Official Journal of the European Communities:

"opinions issued at the request of other institutions (mandatory or voluntary consultation);

"opinions issued on the initiative of the Committee of the Regions.

"*Opinions issued at the request of other institutions*

"According to the European Union Treaty, the Council and the Commission are obliged to consult the Committee of the Regions on certain issues before taking a decision. These cover specific areas, falling within the responsibilities of local and regional authorities:

"*(a) Mandatory consultation*

"Economic and social cohesion (specific actions; defining the tasks, priorities and organisation of the Structural Funds; implementing decisions relating to the European Regional Development Fund);
"trans-European transport, telecommunications and energy networks;
public health;
education, vocational training and youth;
culture.

"Following the Amsterdam Treaty, the position of the Committee of the Regions as a consultative body has been extended by five additional areas of mandatory consultation: employment; social issues; environment; training; and transport. Furthermore, the European Parliament may now consult the Committee of the Regions on matters of mutual interest."

[8] Taken from *Europa*, an online information system maintained by the European Commission.

"(b) Voluntary consultation

31.1.11   "The Committee of the Regions may also be consulted by the Commission, the Council or the EP on any other matter they see fit.

"Issuing an opinion on its own initiative

"(a) ESC

"When the Council consults the Economic and Social Committee or the Commission the Committee of the Regions must also be informed. It may then also issue an opinion on the matter if it considers that regional interests are affected.

"(b) General practice

The Committee of the Regions may issue an opinion in other areas whenever it sees fit."

Overview of process

31.1.12   The EC legislative process operates in different ways according to the nature of the legislation. Instruments of general validity (regulations and Directives) have to pass through—

(1) the consultation procedure,

(2) the cooperation procedure,

(3) the co-decision procedure, and

(4) the approval procedure.

In other cases the procedure is varied or simplified.[9]

The consultation procedure[10]

31.1.13   Under the consultation procedure the Commission submits proposals and the Council makes decisions, having first completed stages which involve, depending on the case, the European Parliament, the Economic and Social Committee and the Committee of the Regions.

---

[9] Measures implementing other legislation are adopted by specified procedures; there is a simplified procedure for binding individual decisions and non-mandatory instruments; and E.C.S.C. instruments are subject to their own specific procedures.

[10] The consultation procedure was originally the central legislative process within the Community, but has given way in importance to the cooperation and co-decisions procedures.It is now principally of importance only in cases where neither of the other two procedures is specifically required (for example, anti-discrimination provision under Art.13 EC, certain common agricultural policy provisions under Art.37(2) EC and certain competition provisions under Arts 83 and 89 EC).

The Commission draws up a proposal for the measure in question (under its "right of initiative"). The proposal will be prepared, under the authority of a Member of the Commission, by the Commission department dealing with the relevant substantive field. In the course of the preparation of the proposal it is common to consult national experts, whether individually or through the convening of committees.

A draft is adopted by the Commission (for which purpose a simple majority suffices) and becomes a Commission proposal. The proposal is then submitted to the Council for a decision.

Before deciding on a proposal the Council may need to consult other Community bodies. Consultation is a right under the treaties, and failure to comply can amount to a material irregularity leading to annulment.[11] Even where it is not required, consultation at this stage is common.   **31.1.14**

Following consultation, and following any amendment thought necessary by the Commission in the light of consultation, a proposal is put before the Council for decision. If adopted by the Council the proposal becomes law. The final text, in all official languages of the Community is adopted by the Council, signed by the President of the Council, and then published or notified to the person to whom it is addressed.[12]

The cooperation procedure

The cooperation procedure[13] provides a more important role for the European Parliament in the decision-making process than the consultation procedure. It is   **31.1.15**

---

[11] See Chapter 30, Section 4.
[12] Art.254(1) and (3) EC.
[13] Which is established by Art.252 EC as follows—
    "Article 252
    Where reference is made in this Treaty to this Article for the adoption of an act, the following procedure shall apply.
    (a) The Council, acting by a qualified majority on a proposal from the Commission and after obtaining the opinion of the European Parliament, shall adopt a common position.
    (b) The Council's common position shall be communicated to the European Parliament. The Council and the Commission shall inform the European Parliament fully of the reasons which led the Council to adopt its common position and also of the Commission's position. If, within three months of such communication, the European Parliament approves this common position or has not taken a decision within that period, the Council shall definitively adopt the act in question in accordance with the common position.
    (c) The European Parliament may, within the period of three months referred to in point (b), by an absolute majority of its component Members, propose amendments to the Council's common position. The European Parliament may also, by the same majority, reject the Council's common position. The result of the proceedings shall be transmitted to the Council and the Commission. If the European Parliament has rejected the Council's common position, unanimity shall be required for the Council to act on a second reading.
    (d) The Commission shall, within a period of one month, re-examine the proposal on the basis of which the Council adopted its common position, by taking into account the amendments proposed by the European Parliament. The Commission shall forward to

also generally quicker. The procedure is used now principally for matters relating to economic and monetary union.[14]

As with the consultation procedure the process begins with a Commission proposal, but it is sent to the Parliament as well as to the Council. The Parliament in a "first reading" process expresses views to the Council, which then adopts a common position (by qualified majority).

The Parliament then considers, in a second reading process, the Council's common position. Within three months Parliament accepts the common position or gives no response, in which case the Council adopts the common position.

If the Parliament rejects the common position or, as is usual, proposes amendments the Council may either—

(1) adopt the common position unanimously, or

(2) accept any amendments proposed by the Parliament, and then adopt the instrument by qualified majority.

It is rare for the Parliament to seek to block a measure entirely.

The co-decision procedure (Art.251 EC)

31.1.16 The co-decision procedure[15] gives the Parliament yet more control over the legislative process. The essence of the process is that the Council, whether acting

---

the Council, at the same time as its re-examined proposal, the amendments of the European Parliament which it has not accepted, and shall express its opinion on them. The Council may adopt these amendments unanimously.

(e) The Council, acting by a qualified majority, shall adopt the proposal as re-examined by the Commission. Unanimity shall be required for the Council to amend the proposal as re-examined by the Commission.

(f) In the cases referred to in points (c), (d) and (e), the Council shall be required to act within a period of three months. If no decision is taken within this period, the Commission proposal shall bedeemed not to have been adopted.

(g) The periods referred to in points (b) and (f) may be extended by a maximum of one month by common accord between the Council and the European Parliament."

[14] Arts 99(5) and 106(2) EC.

[15] This procedure is established by Art.251 EC as follows—

"Article 251

1. Where reference is made in this Treaty to this Article for the adoption of an act, the following procedure shall apply.

2. The Commission shall submit a proposal to the European Parliament and the Council. The Council, acting by a qualified majority after obtaining the opinion of the European Parliament:

— if it approves all the amendments contained in the European Parliament's opinion, may adopt the proposed act thus amended,

— if the European Parliament does not propose any amendments, may adopt the proposed act,

— shall otherwise adopt a common position and communicate it to the European Parliament.

The Council shall inform the European Parliament fully of the reasons which led it to adopt its common position. The Commission shall inform the European Parliament fully of its position.

unanimously or not, has no veto over the Parliament, and the two are equal partners in the decision-making. In practical political terms, the co-decision procedure makes negotiation and compromise between the two decisive institutions indispensable.

The co-decision procedure is now used in connection with a large number of significant matters.[16]

As in the cases of the other procedures, the Commission initiates the process with a proposal, which in this case is submitted to the Council and to the Parliament (and to any committees requiring to be consulted). The Parliament forms an opinion at a first reading and notifies the Council.

If the Parliament makes no amendment of the proposal, or any amendment proposed is acceptable to the Commission, the instrument may become law without any further process.

31.1.17

If, within three months of such communication, the European Parliament:
    (a) approves the common position or has not taken a decision, the act in question shall be deemed to have been adopted in accordance with that common position;
    (b) rejects, by an absolute majority of its component members, the common position, the proposed act shall be deemed not to have been adopted;
    (c) proposes amendments to the common position by an absolute majority of its componentmembers, the amended text shall be forwarded to the Council and to the Commission, which shall deliver an opinion on those amendments.
    3. If, within three months of the matter being referred to it, the Council, acting by a qualified majority, approves all the amendments of the European Parliament, the act in question shall be deemed to have been adopted in the form of the common position thus amended; however, the Council shall act unanimously on the amendments on which the Commission has delivered a negative opinion. If the Council does not approve all the amendments, the President of the Council, in agreement with the President of the European Parliament, shall within six weeks convene a meeting of the Conciliation Committee.
    4. The Conciliation Committee, which shall be composed of the Members of the Council or their representatives and an equal number of representatives of the European Parliament, shall have the task of reaching agreement on a joint text, by a qualified majority of the Members of the Council or their representatives and by a majority of the representatives of the European Parliament. The Commission shall take part in the Conciliation Committee's proceedings and shall take all the necessary initiatives with a view to reconciling the positions of the European Parliament and the Council. In fulfilling this task, the Conciliation Committee shall address the common position on the basis of the amendments proposed by the European Parliament.
    5. If, within six weeks of its being convened, the Conciliation Committee approves a joint text, the European Parliament, acting by an absolute majority of the votes cast, and the Council, acting by aqualified majority, shall each have a period of six weeks from that approval in which to adopt the act in question in accordance with the joint text. If either of the two institutions fails to approve the proposed act within that period, it shall be deemed not to have been adopted.
    6. Where the Conciliation Committee does not approve a joint text, the proposed act shall be deemed not to have been adopted.
    7. The periods of three months and six weeks referred to in this Article shall be extended by a maximum of one month and two weeks respectively at the initiative of the European Parliament or the Council."
[16] For example, in connection with national discrimination (Art.12 E.C.), freedom of movement (Art.40 EC), social security (Art.42 EC), freedom of establishment (Arts 44(2) and 47(1) EC), social policy, including measures to bring about equality of the sexes (Arts 137, 141 and 148 EC), consumer protection (Art.153 EC).

Having regard to all opinions expressed by this stage of the process the Council then adopts a common position (by qualified majority). That common position is then sent to the Parliament for its second reading. In the next three months the Parliament must—

(1) accept or ignore the common position, in which case the instrument is adopted as set out in the common position,

(2) reject the common position (by absolute majority), in which case the proposal dies, or

(3) propose amendments to the common position.

31.1.18   Where the Parliament proposes amendments, the Council may accept them. Failing that, a conciliation committee is established containing representatives of the Council and the Parliament with the aim of achieving a compromise.

If the conciliation committee produces a compromise draft instrument the Council and the Parliament have six weeks to accept it (at a third reading). If they do so the instrument is adopted as a joint instrument of the two institutions. Otherwise, the proposal dies.

It will be seen from the above that the co-decision procedure, both in its aim to achieve agreement between the Council and the Parliament and in the methods by which it achieves this aim, shares something in common with the procedures for achieving agreement between the two Houses of the Westminster Parliament.[17] The principal difference is that instead of a protracted correspondence between the two sides, a forum for joint consideration of the proposal is used at a certain stage.

The approval procedure

31.1.19   Under the approval procedure, an instrument can be adopted only with the approval of the Parliament. This gives Parliament a veto, but not an opportunity to influence the early formal stages or to propose amendments. It is therefore like the Westminster Parliament's affirmative resolution procedure for statutory instruments.[18]

The approval procedure is required for a number of significant constitutional matters.[19]

---

[17] See Chapter 5, paras 5.2.24 and 5.2.25.

[18] See Chapter 6, Section 2.

[19] Notably in connection with the accession of new Member States (Art.49 EU), the conclusion of association agreements with non-member countries (Art.300(3) EC), the transfer of tasks to the E.C.B. (Art.105(6) EC), amendments to the Statute of E.S.C.B. (Art.107(5) EC) and the appointment of the President of the Commission and the members of the Commission as a body (Art.214(2) EC).

The simplified procedure

There is also available a simplified procedure, the most important feature of **31.1.20** which is that it does not require initiation by a Commission proposal.

Drafting principles and practice

European legislation is framed in a very different way to United Kingdom **31.1.21** legislation. Whether out of principle or political necessity, the text of legislation is arrived at through a process of political compromise, and individual words may be chosen less for their legal certainty than for their political acceptability.

Once negotiated and passed, however, legislation from the Communities has to be applied and implemented within each Member State, and despite the additional freedom imparted by a purposive approach to construction,[20] it must have sufficient legal certainty to enable consistent application and implementation. The difficulties in drafting style resulting from the political process by which Community legislation is constructed were acknowledged for many years, and resulted in the establishment on December 22, 1998 of an *Interinstitutional Agreement on common guidelines for the quality of drafting of Community legislation.*[21] While these guidelines are to be regarded as instruments for internal use by the institutions and are not legally binding,[22] they are noteworthy and likely to be helpful for all engaged in legislative (or indeed other) drafting, whether international or national: the guidelines are therefore reproduced in the Appendix.[23]

SECTION 2

WESTMINSTER SCRUTINY

Introduction

Legislation emanating from the European Union is not, of course, within the gift **31.2.1** or subject to the control of the United Kingdom Parliament. Equally of course, the enormous and increasing impact that European legislation has on the daily lives of citizens of the United Kingdom makes it necessary that Parliament should exercise some kind of monitoring function, partly for the simple purpose of maintaining awareness of the continuing and changing effect of the legal implications of the United Kingdom's membership of the European Union, but also because in relation to certain proposed measures Parliament will be able to

---

[20] See Chapter 18.
[21] O.J.C. 73, 17.3.1999.
[22] Preamble (7).
[23] Extract 13.

influence their development, through the actions of the United Kingdom's ministerial representatives in the European institutions.

For both these reasons the need for "effective parliamentary scrutiny of the European Union's activities"[24] in relation to the production of legislation is generally thought essential.

The Scrutiny Committees

31.2.2   Each House of Parliament has a European Scrutiny Select Committee.

In the House of Commons the primary role of the European Scrutiny Committee[25] is "to examine each European Union document deposited and to assess the legal and political importance of each and whether it should be debated".[26]

The practical operation of the work of the Committee is arranged in the following way. The Government arranges for the deposit in the offices of Parliament of relevant European documents as soon as reasonably practicable after their arrival from the relevant European institution.[27] The Committee then receives an Explanatory Memorandum on each document from the Minister responsible for the relevant area of substance. The Committee then considers each document and does one or more of the following things—

(1) discards it,

(2) reports it to the House as being of importance,

(3) recommends a debate in a European Standing Committee,

(4) exceptionally, recommends a debate on the Floor of the House, or

(5) does not recommend a debate, but notes the document as being relevant to a debate due to take place in the House or a Committee.[28]

31.2.3   In particular, the Committee aims "to ensure that Ministers do not agree to proposals in the Council of Ministers in advance of scrutiny clearance" by the Committee[29] or before a debate recommended by the Committee has taken place.

---

[24] Lord Grenfell introducing a debate on the Scrutiny of European Legislation, HL Deb. May 9, 2003 cc.1313–69.

[25] Which is appointed under Standing Order No. 143 and has 16 members.

[26] Eighth Report of Session 2002–03, January 15, 2003, para.2.

[27] The Committee has frequently criticised as inadequate the time allowed by the European institutions for consideration by Member States' institutions of proposals for legislation—see, for example, the report cited above, para.7—"The main underlying problem continues to be European Union Presidencies pressing for agreement on controversial proposals without allowing sufficient time for scrutiny by national parliaments and others."

[28] As a rule of thumb, more than a thousand documents are deposited before the Committee each year, of which approximately half will be the subject of a report by the Committee, with a handful being recommended for debate in Standing Committee and only one or two for debate on the Floor of the House.

[29] Same, para.7.

This is designed to give effect to a resolution of the House of Commons, known as the Scrutiny Reserve Resolution"[30] which provided, amongst other things, that a Minister of the Crown should not give agreement in the European Council to a proposal for European Community legislation while the proposal has not been completely scrutinised by the European Scrutiny Committee or while it is awaiting a debate pursuant to a recommendation of the Committee. There are express exceptions from this rule for confidential, routine or trivial legislative proposals. And the resolution allows the Scrutiny Committee to permit a Minister to proceed without waiting for the Committee to conclude its consideration of a proposal. The resolution also recognises that there will be other circumstances in which Ministers find it necessary to depart from the general rule, but in such a case the Minister is required by the resolution to give an explanation to the Scrutiny Committee or to the House of Commons at the first reasonable opportunity.

As has already been observed[31] a resolution of the House of Commons does not create law. The Scrutiny Reserve Resolution does not therefore affect the legal competence of Her Majesty's Government to enter into, in effect, binding international agreements, by supporting or acquiescing in the passing of European legislation without waiting for the completion of scrutiny by the European Scrutiny Committee. And even once the Committee has recommended a debate and the House has passed a resolution on the subject of a proposal for European legislation, the result is not to place any kind of legal restriction or obligation on Ministers. How seriously they will take the opinion of the Committee or the House in relation to a particular legislative proposal will doubtless depend on a whole range of circumstances, both general and specific.

Debates recommended by the Committee take place either in a European **31.2.4** Standing Committee or (more rarely) on the Floor of the House. The House of Commons has a number of Standing Committees[32] whose role is to receive referrals for consideration of European Union documents recommended for consideration by the European Scrutiny Committee. The motion on which a particular document is considered is tabled by the Government. Once the document ahs been considered in the Standing Committee a report is made to the House and a motion on the report is decided by a vote.[33]

As a general rule it is rare for legislation made by the European Commission on its own authority to be scrutinised by the Scrutiny Committee, on the grounds that it is mostly ephemeral and of little practical significance.

The House of Lords also has a Select Committee on the European Union which, with a system of sub-committees, performs a similar function to the Commons committee but in a slightly different way. In essence, the House of

---

[30] November 17, 1998.
[31] Chapter 3, Section 7.
[32] Established under Standing Order No.119.
[33] But not debated—Standing Order No.119(9).

Lords system tends to promote detailed inquiries, each one of which can take a considerable time to conclude, into proposals and issues of particular importance, leaving the House of Commons to provide a briefer scrutiny of a wider range of documents.

SECTION 3

PUBLICATION

31.3.1 Community legislation as well as the Council's common positions forwarded to the European Parliament are published in the Official Journal of the European Communities in all the official EC languages. The requirements are as stated in Art.254 of the Treaty Establishing the European Community—

> "Article 254
>
> 1. Regulations, directives and decisions adopted in accordance with the procedure referred to in Article 251 shall be signed by the President of the European Parliament and by the President of the Council and published in the Official Journal of the European Union. They shall enter into force on the date specified in them or, in the absence thereof, on the 20th day following that of their publication.
> 2. Regulations of the Council and of the Commission, as well as directives of those institutions which are addressed to all Member States, shall be published in the Official Journal of the European Union.
>
>   They shall enter into force on the date specified in them or, in the absence thereof, on the 20th day following that of their publication.
> 3. Other directives, and decisions, shall be notified to those to whom they are addressed and shall take effect upon such notification."

In addition to the Official Journal there are also a number of online sources of European legislation, both commercial and official. The official sources are summarised in the following passage[34]—

> "Recognising the complexity of European Union law, several information products and services have been developed to ensure that vital information sources are easily accessible for consultation online. These aim to offer a comprehensive picture of European Union legislation and the decision-making procedures from concept to conclusion.

---

[34] Taken from *Europa*, an online information system maintained by the European Commission.

722

"(a) CELEX

"This multilingual database service offers users solutions to the problems associated with legal research by ensuring full coverage of ever-expanding volumes of source material such as the Treaties, secondary legislation, international agreements and supplementary legislation, case-law, preparatory documents and parliamentary questions. Hypertext links are provided to related acts including subsequent modifications, earlier acts and even references to national implementing legislation.   **31.3.2**

"Registration is required for access to Celex.

"(b) EUR-Lex

This service was set up by the European Union institutions to make European Union law available to members of the public.Here can be found, in all the official European Union working languages, the latest issues of the Official Journal of the European Union (OJ) L and C series, together with those only published in electronic format. This collection is updated daily.   **31.3.3**

"The site also offers the Treaties, European Union legislation in force and the texts of consolidated legislation, proposals for legislation and a link to recent judgments and orders of the European Court of Justice and the Court of First Instance.

"(c) CURIA

"This is the multilingual website of the European Court of Justice and the Court of First Instance. Links to this site offer the possibility of searching for judgments and orders of the Courts.   **31.3.4**

"(d) Oeil—The Legislative Observatory of the European Parliament

"This is an information, monitoring, forecasting and research tool for inter-institutional legislative procedures, activities of the institutions and part-sessions of the European Parliament. ... The information contained is in English and French.

"(e) PreLex—the database on inter-institutional procedures

"Pre-Lex follows the major steps of the decision-making process between the Commission and the other institutions by providing information on: **31.3.5**

    "stage of the procedure;
    "decisions of the institutions;
    "contact names;
    "responsible institutional services;
    "references of documents, etc.

"Pre-Lex, managed by the Secretariat-General of the Commission, monitors the work of the various institutions involved (European Parliament, Council, Economic and Social Committee, Committee of the

Regions, Court of Justice, etc.). It follows all Commission proposals (legislative and budgetary files, and conclusions of international agreements) and communications from their transmission to the Council or to the European Parliament until their adoption or their rejection by the Council, their adoption by Parliament or their withdrawal by the Commission.

"While Pre-Lex does not itself contain the documents, links connect directly to the texts which are available electronically (COM documents, Official Journal, Bulletin of the European Union, documents of the European Parliament, press releases, etc.)."

Different language texts

31.3.6 While most European legislation is produced in a number of authoritative texts of different language, of which English is always one, there are occasions on which it is necessary or desirable to refer to one of the other texts. Schedule 1A to the Carriage by Air Act 1961[35] annexes the text of the Warsaw Convention for the Unification of Certain Rules Relating to International Carriage by Air in both the English and the French versions.[36]

SECTION 4

CONSOLIDATION

31.4.1 The institutions of the European Union do not produce formal consolidation legislation in the way that the Westminster Parliament sometimes does. But the authorities within the institutions operate a project for the production of informal consolidations for the assistance of those affected by areas of law that have become complicated as a result of a series of related pieces of legislation. The aim of the project is—

"the integration of basic instruments of Community legislation, their amendments and corrections in single, non-official documents [which] aim to provide more transparency and easier access to European Union law."[37]

The project is implemented by a unit known as the "Office for Official Publications of the European Communities". That office takes a number of texts

---

[35] 1961 c.27.
[36] By amendment made by the Carriage by Air Acts (Implementation of Protocol No. 4 of Montreal, 1975) Order 1999 SI 1999/1312, art.2.
[37] As explained in *Europa*, an online information service maintained by the European Commission.

officially published in different issues of the Official Journal of the European Communities and produces out of them a single combined document.

The project is intended to be a continuous operation, making new consolida- **31.4.2** tions, and revised consolidations, available from time to time. But the collection of neither complete nor authoritative, and only the original documents as published in the Official Journal may be relied upon.[38]

Since the project results in unofficial, purely declaratory consolidations of legislation and simplifications of legal instruments, the consolidations, whether amounting simply to the incorporation of amendments into the amended text or to something more complex, are not formally adopted as a new instrument. But despite having no legal effect the consolidated texts may be published in the Official Journal of the European Communities.[39]

---

[38] But each consolidated text contains a list of the texts on which it is based, so it should be possible relatively easily to ascertain whether it is likely to be out of date in respect of a particular matter.

[39] In the C Series.

CHAPTER 32

EFFECT AND INTERPRETATION

Introduction

Much of European legislation requires to be transposed into domestic legislation **32.1.1**
within each of the Member states. The nature of this requirement and the
methods by which it is fulfilled in the United Kingdom are discussed elsewhere
in this work.[1]

But some European legislation is required, as a matter of European law, to
have direct effect, that is to say that it is required to be treated as directly
conferring enforceable rights and duties. This Chapter discusses the nature of the
direct effect of European legislation.

While much of European law takes the form of Directives requiring to be
implemented, regulations have direct effect.[2] For an example of a recent
regulation likely to have considerable effect on the legal and social situation in
the United Kingdom, see Council Regulation (EC) No. 2157/2001 of October 8,
2001 on the Statute for a European company (SE[3]).

Parliamentary sanction for direct effect

Whatever the position at European law, legislation enacted by the European **32.1.2**
Communities could not, of course, have any kind of effect in creating legal rights
and duties enforceable by courts in the United Kingdom without the express

---

[1] See Chapter 3, Section 10.
[2] See Art.249 EC—

> **"Article 249**
>
> In order to carry out their task and in accordance with the provisions of this Treaty, the
> European Parliament acting jointly with the Council, the Council and the Commission shall
> make regulations and issue directives, take decisions, make recommendations or deliver
> opinions.
>
> A regulation shall have general application. It shall be binding in its entirety and directly
> applicable in all Member States.
>
> A directive shall be binding, as to the result to be achieved, upon each Member State to
> which it is addressed, but shall leave to the national authorities the choice of form and
> methods. A decision shall be binding in its entirety upon those to whom it is addressed.
>
> Recommendations and opinions shall have no binding force."

[3] Societas Europaea.

sanction of Parliament. That sanction is provided by s.2(1) of the European Communities Act 1972[4] in the following terms—

> "(1) All such rights, powers, liabilities, obligations and restrictions from time to time created or arising by or under the Treaties, and all such remedies and procedures from time to time provided for by or under the Treaties, as in accordance with the Treaties are without further enactment to be given legal effect or used in the United Kingdom shall be recognised and available in law, and be enforced, allowed and followed accordingly;".

Criteria for determining whether legislation has direct effect

32.1.3   Once Parliament has given as stated above the necessary authority for the direct effect of certain Community laws, the question of whether a particular Community law has direct effect becomes itself a question of Community law, not one to be determined solely by the domestic courts in accordance with domestic constitutional law.[5]

Although it can be difficult to apply the criteria for determining whether a provision of European legislation has direct effect, the criteria are simple to state. The traditional formula proceeds along the following lines—

> "Provisions are to be regarded as being directly applicable when, regard being had to their wording and to the purpose and nature of the agreement itself, they contain a clear and precise obligation which is not subject, in its implementation, to the adoption of any subsequent measure."[6]

32.1.4   A law which confers a discretion on the Member States, or which leaves them a number of options for attainment of a precisely specified objective, will not have direct effect. But—

> (1) if the law confers minimum rights of a non-discretionary nature the law may be directly effective to the extent that it confers those rights.[7] And a marginal discretion, such as the ability to exclude a right in certain cases for reasons of security or public policy, will not prevent direct effect.[8]

---

[4] 1972 c.68.

[5] *Van Gend en Loos* (Case 26/62) [1963] E.C.R. 1.

[6] Taken from the opinion of the Advocate General in *R. v Secretary of State for the Home Department, Ex p. Gloszczuk* [2002] All E.R. (EC) 353 E.C.J. ([2001] 3 C.M.L.R. 1035, [2001] E.C.R. I–6369) (citing *Sürül v Bundesanstalt für Arbeit* [1999] E.C.R. I–2685 (para.60) and further references therein). The *Van Gend en Loos* case was an early instance of the formulation of a test along very much these lines.

[7] *Francovich v Italy* (Cases C–6, 9/90).

[8] Compare *Van Duyn v Home Office* (Case 41/74) [1974] E.C.R. 1337 with *Von Colson and Kamann v Land Nordrhein-Westfalen* (Case 14/83) [1984] E.C.R. 1891.

(2) The application of the criteria for determining whether legislation is intended to have direct effect is not dissimilar to the application of the criteria used for determining whether United Kingdom legislation is intended to confer actionable rights on individuals.[9]

(3) Where a period is provided for implementing action in respect of certain rights, they may become directly effective if that period expires without the necessary action having been taken.[10]

Extent of doctrine of direct effect

The doctrine of direct effect requires Community law to be given fullest effect in relation to all matters of and proceedings at domestic law. The extent of the doctrine and the protection which it affords to citizens of the European Union against governments of their own States is illustrated by the following passage from the judgment of Buxton L.J. in *R. v Searby*[11]— **32.1.5**

"16. The national court is bound to give full effect to directly applicable Community law by disapplying provisions of national law that conflict with it. That is the principle in *Simmenthal*,[12] somewhat obscured in that case by its setting in the rules of Italian constitutional law, but clearly enunciated in general terms by the E.C.J. in Case C-358 *Morellato* [1997].[13] Therefore if the criminal court reaches the conclusion that the Control Arrangements involve a disproportionate interference with the right to import goods from other member states, it is bound to act on that conclusion by treating the Control Arrangements as not being part of English law.

"17. The prosecution argued that this principle was indeed honoured in domestic law, but by giving the appellants the ability to have the Control Arrangements set aside in Judicial Review proceedings.We cannot agree. We have in mind what was said by Lord Woolf M.R. in *Ex p Pharma Nord*[14]: once a question as to compatibility with Community law is raised in criminal proceedings, the court has no alternative but to become involved. For the reasons set out in particular by Jacobs A-G in §§ 19–20 of his opinion in *Joined Cases C430 and 431–93 Van Schijndel*[15] that involvement requires an immediate response to a finding of incompatibility. The

---

[9] As to which see Chapter 12, paras 12.6.6—12.6.12.
[10] *Defrenne v Sabena* (Case 43/75) [1976] E.C.R. 455.
[11] [2003] 3 C.M.L.R. 15, CA paras 16 and 17.
[12] A reference to the leading case of *Amministrazione delle Finanze dello Stato v Simmenthal SpA* [1978] 3 C.M.L.R. 263, in which the European Court of Justice held that Community law was able to "preclude the valid adoption" of domestic legislation that was not compatible or consistent with the Community law.
[13] E.C.R. I–1431[18].
[14] (1998) 10 Admin. L.R. 646, 660.
[15] [1995] E.C.R. I–4961.

Advocate General referred to the observations of the House of Lords in the *Factortame* case,[16] and in particular Lord Bridge of Harwich at p 659D, that to require proceedings to set aside the infringing national rule before relief is granted will involve at least the risk that a breach of Community law will go uncompensated. But the present case is stronger still: if, as we have to assume, the Control Arrangements are in breach of Community law then, if proceedings to set them aside are a necessary precursor to asserting that invalidity in a criminal trial, the appellants will have no remedy at all in respect of an invalidity that, under the *Simmenthal* principle, the court should have asserted of its own motion."

Implementation in support of direct effect

32.1.6 The fact that a piece of Community legislation has direct effect does not mean that it may not be expedient, or even necessary for all practical purposes, to make changes of the law of the United Kingdom to accommodate the changes imposed directly.[17] This action must, however, avoid interfering or appearing to interfere with the application of the directly effective legislation, whether by way of imposing a construction upon it or otherwise.[18]

---

[16] [1991] A.C. 603, HL.

[17] See, for example, "In this respect, although, by virtue of the very nature of regulations and of their function in the system of sources of Community law, the provisions of those regulations generally have immediate effect in the national legal systems without its being necessary for the national authorities to adopt measures of application, some of their provisions may none the less necessitate, for their implementation, the adoption of measures of application by the Member States." —*Azienda Agricola Monte Arcosu Srl v Regione Autonoma della Sardegna* (Case C–403/98) ECJ, para.26.

[18] See, for example, the following passage of the consultation paper *Implementation of the European Company Statute: The European Public Limited-Liability Company Regulations 2004*, issued by the Department for Trade and Industry in October 2003—

"2.4 The Regulation is freestanding and will have direct effect in the Member States and GB does not need, as such, to 'implement' it. On many matters, it applies to SEs the national legislation applicable to public companies in the Member State where the SE is registered. However, the Regulation includes a number of options and new domestic legislation will be required to ensure the effective application of the Regulation where a decision on a specific option in the Regulation has to be made, and also to provide for sanctions and penalties for contraventions of the Regulation. The Regulation has been included as an annex to the draft Statutory Instrument at Annex B.

2.5 The Statutory Instrument cannot state which parts of GB company (and insolvency) law apply to SEs, since this is determined by the Regulation itself. Neither is it permissible for a Member State, through its own legislation, to seek to interpret (or to amend or 'improve') through legislative action the effect of the Regulation. It should also be noted that, except where specifically allowed by the Regulation, it is not permissible to apply special provisions of national law only to SEs. Anyone registering an SE in GB or transferring an SE from another Member State to GB will need to determine, together with legal advisers, what law applies.Interpretation of the legislation (and the Regulation) will, ultimately, be a matter for the Courts who may seek interpretative rulings from the European Court of Justice on appropriate points."

Direct effect in lieu of full or proper implementation

It is a basic concept of European Community jurisprudence that European **32.1.7**
legislation comprises two classes, that which takes effect directly and that which
requires Member States to take legislative or other action by way of implementation. As has been seen, the Treaties themselves acknowledge this as a fundamental distinction.[19]

In fact, however, as Community jurisprudence has developed the distinction
has become less sharp. In particular, a single piece of European legislation is
capable both of requiring implementation within the Member States and of
having direct effect. As the European Court put it—

> "the adoption of national measures correctly implementing a directive does
> not exhaust the effects of the directive. Member states remain bound
> actually to ensure full application of the directive even after the adoption of
> those measures. Individuals are therefore entitled to rely before the national
> courts, against the state, on the provisions of a directive which appear, so far
> as their subject matter is concerned, to be unconditional and sufficiently
> precise whenever the full application of the directive is not in fact secured,
> that is to say, not only where the directive has not been implemented or has
> been implemented incorrectly, but also where the national measures
> correctly implementing the directive are not being applied in such a way as
> to achieve the result sought by it."[20]

For that reason in construing implementing legislation it is always necessary to
have regard to the underlying European legislation being implemented. A narrow
construction of the implementing legislation may result only in the conclusion
that the underlying obligation has been improperly implemented, it cannot affect
the scope of that obligation.

Timing of direct effect

Where a Directive requires that the implementing domestic legislation be in place **32.1.8**
by Date 1 but that it should be in force only by a later Date 2, the legislation will
have no default direct effect until Date 2.[21]

Vertical and horizontal direct effect

The concept of vertical direct effect is that of directly conferring rights on **32.1.9**
individuals against the State. The concept of horizontal direct effect is that of

---

[19] See Chapter 30, para.30.3.1.
[20] *Marks & Spencer v Customs and Excise Commissioners* [2003] 2 W.L.R. 665, ECJ, judgment
para.27.
[21] *Vaneetveld v Sa Le Foyer* [1994] 2 C.M.L.R. 852, ECJ.

directly conferring on individuals obligations owed to the State or to other individuals. Regulations and provisions of the Treaties may have horizontal direct effect.[22] Directives may not.[23]

Direct effect of agreement between European Union and others

32.1.10 It is not only the legislation of the European Union itself that is capable of having direct effect in the United Kingdom. The European Union and its component Communities act in certain matters as organisations with international legal personality, in the course of which they may conclude agreements with other entities. The effect of the Treaties is to require those agreements to be given the same effect as internal legislation of the communities.

As the European Court of Justice said in *Wahlergruppe "Gemeinsam Zajedno/ Birlikte Alternative und Grune Gewerkschafterinnen/UG*[24]—

> "According to the settled case law of the Court, a provision in an agreement concluded by the Community with a non-member country must be regarded as being directly applicable when, regard being had to its wording and to the purpose and nature of the agreement, the provision contains a clear and precise obligation which is not subject, in its implementation or effects, to the adoption of any subsequent measure."

SECTION 2

OTHER ASPECTS OF EFFECT

Introduction

32.2.1 This Section explores some effects of European legislation other than direct effect and the requirement to implement.

Commencement

32.2.2 The rules for the commencement of European legislation are as stated in art.254 of the Treaty establishing the European Community—

---

[22] This being the concept of direct applicability provided for in Art.249 of the EC Treaty as quoted above.

[23] *Marshall v Southampton and South West Hampshire Area Health Authority (Teaching)* (Case 152/84) [1986] E.C.R. 723. But the principle is obscured by the occasional difficulty of distinguishing between individuals and emanations of the State—see, for example, *Johnston v Chief Constable of the Royal Ulster Constabulary* (Case 222/84) [1986] E.C.R. 1651 and *Foster v British Gas* (Case C–188/189) [1990] E.C.R. I–3313.

[24] [2003] 2 C.M.L.R. 29, para.54.

"Article 254

1. Regulations, directives and decisions adopted in accordance with the procedure referred to in Article 251 shall be signed by the President of the European Parliament and by the President of the Council and published in the Official Journal of the European Union. They shall enter into force on the date specified in them or, in the absence thereof, on the 20th day following that of their publication.

2. Regulations of the Council and of the Commission, as well as directives of those institutions which are addressed to all Member States, shall be published in the Official Journal of the European Union. They shall enter into force on the date specified in them or, in the absence thereof, on the 20th day following that of their publication.

3. Other directives, and decisions, shall be notified to those to whom they are addressed and shall take effect upon such notification."

As to the possibility of retrospective commencement, it can be stated in broad terms that the European legislatures and the domestic and other courts construing European legislation will apply a similar approach to the issue of retrospectivity to that outlined in relation to domestic legislation in Chapter 10, Section 3. **32.2.3**

In particular, the attitude of the European Court of Justice to retrospectivity in the case of penal legislation is set out in the following passage of the Court's judgment in *R. v Kirk*[25]—

"The principle that penal provisions may not have retroactive effect is one which is common to all the legal orders of the member states and is enshrined in article 7 of the European Convention for the Protection of Human Rights and Fundamental Freedoms[26] as a fundamental right; it takes its place among the general principles of law whose observance is ensured by the Court of Justice."

Challenges to European legislation

See Chapter 30, paras 30.4.2 and 30.4.3. **32.2.4**

Occupied field doctrine

Once the European Community has occupied a field of policy by legislating about a particular subject, it is no longer open to domestic legislatures to legislate in that area.[27] **32.2.5**

---

[25] [1985] 1 All E.R. 453, para.22.
[26] Rome, November 4, 1950; TS 71 (1953); Cmd 8969.
[27] See for example, *Spitta & Co. v Hauptzollampt Frankfurt am Main-Ost* [1986] 2 C.M.L.R. 686, ECJ.

A similar doctrine arises in relation to other cases of, in effect, primary and subordinate legislatures[28]; and the issue is similar to that discussed in Chapter 14, Section 1 of the relationship between legislation and the pre-existing common law.

Extent

32.2.6   Of its nature European legislation generally has effect in relation to all the territories of the Member States. It does not apply to States that are not Members of the Union, merely because a Member State has some degree of constitutional relationship with it, or even the residual ability to legislate for it.

As to territorial seas and areas of the continental shelf, European legislation and domestic legislation implementing it will be construed as having such territorial extent as is necessary in the context. So the Conservation (Natural Habitats, etc.) Regulations 1994 implementing a Directive were to be construed in the context as applying to an area outside United Kingdom territorial waters but within the continental shelf on a purposive construction since the Directive could only achieve its aims if applied beyond territorial waters.[29]

32.2.7   Where legislation emanating from an institution of the European Communities has legal effect in the United Kingdom, it does so by virtue of the international obligations of the United Kingdom as implemented through the European Communities Act 1972 and will therefore extend to the whole of the United Kingdom.

The principal complexity for the United Kingdom in relation to the extent of European legislation concerns Gibraltar. The position is stated clearly by the Government of Gibraltar internet website under the heading *Gibraltar's Status in the European Union—*

> "Gibraltar is a dependent territory of the UK with a separate Constitution granted to it by the British Parliament. The Government of Gibraltar exercises self government except in matters of defence, internal security and foreign affairs which are reserved to the UK. Gibraltar laws are promulgated by its own elected parliament (House of Assembly).

32.2.8   "Gibraltar entered the EU together with the United Kingdom upon its accession in 1973. It is a European territory for whose external relations a Member State (UK) is responsible and accordingly Article 227(4) of the EC Treaty applies.

> "Article 28 of the UK Accession Act provides that there shall be certain exceptions from Community measures with respect to Gibraltar *i.e.* (the

---

[28] See *Attorney-General of Alberta v Attorney-General of Canada* [1943] 1 All E.R. 240, PC and *Forbes v The Attorney-General of Manitoba* [1937] 1 All E.R. 249, PC.

[29] *R v Secretary of State for Trade and Industry, Ex p. Greenpeace Ltd* [2000] 2 C.M.L.R. 94, QBD.

CAP, VAT and CCT) the Common Agricultural Policy, Value Added Tax and the Common Customs Tariff do not apply. Subject to these explicit exceptions, all legislation adopted by the Community since 1973 has been applicable to Gibraltar and Gibraltar's parliament (House of Assembly) has transposed applicable Directives.

"Accordingly although Gibraltar is obviously not a separate Member State, since its membership derives as part of the Member State UK, it is none the less a separate legal jurisdiction for the purpose of Government legislation and judicial authority.

"The citizens of Gibraltar, although British Dependent Territory Citizens (as opposed to British Citizens), are UK Nationals for Community purposes with all consequential rights and entitlements. **32.2.9**

"All the Treaty provisions on the free movement of capital, services and persons apply to Gibraltar. The fourth 'freedom'—movement of goods—is restricted by Gibraltar's position outside the Customs territory."

The Crown

As is said above,[30] the doctrine impliedly exempting the Crown from constraints **32.2.10** and duties imposed by legislation arises from the nature of the Crown as a matter of domestic law and is not relevant to Community legislation. Community legislation rests on Treaties which Her Majesty's Government have signed, thereby binding themselves to comply, albeit that implementation of the Treaty obligations is achieved in large part by the passage of domestic legislation.

One therefore starts to approach Community legislation with the assumption that it applies to the Crown unless it states otherwise expressly or by necessary implication: indeed Community legislation is frequently addressed only to governments.

Similarly, and for the same reason, domestic legislation implementing a Treaty obligation or an obligation arising out of European legislation, can be assumed to bind the Crown unless the contrary is provided expressly or by necessary implication.

European legislation ceasing to have effect

If European legislation ceases to have effect, whether as a result of substantive **32.2.11** repeal by later legislation or by a process of European administrative law,[31] then any United Kingdom legislation which relies solely on s.2(2) of the European

---

[30] Chapter 11, para.11.5.27.
[31] See, for example, the annulment of a Directive because the European Parliament had not been properly consulted: *Re Road Taxes: European Parliament v EU Council* [1996] 1 C.M.L.R. 94, ECJ.

Communities Act 1972[32] ceases to have effect, as in any other case of lapsing as a result of the removal of vires.[33]

There would be no similar automatic effect in the case of primary implementing legislation, although s.2(2) would be available to amend or repeal the primary legislation where this was necessary to reflect the altered state of the United Kingdom's European obligations as a result of the original European legislation ceasing to have effect.

As to the question of damages for loss arising on the annulment of European legislation, see *Industrie-En Handelsonderneming Vreugdenhil BV v EC Commission* and later cases citing it.[34]

SECTION 3

IMPLEMENTATION

Introduction

32.3.1 This Section considers some matters relating to the implementation and enforcement of European legislation. It should be read with Chapter 3, Section 10, which addresses domestic aspects of instruments made under s.2(2) of the European Communities Act 1972.[35]

Since for the most part it is Directives which require to be implemented by legislation in each of the Member States this Section refers throughout to Directives. But the principles are equally applicable to any other form of European legislation in so far as it requires transposition or implementation in or by domestic legislation.

The basic duty

32.3.2 The fundamental duty on each Member State in the matter of implementation is asserted by Art.10 of the EC Treaty[36] in the following terms—

> "Member States shall take all appropriate measures, whether general or particular, to ensure fulfilment of the obligations arising out of this Treaty or resulting from action taken by the institutions of the Community. They shall facilitate the achievement of the Community's tasks.

> "They shall abstain from any measure which could jeopardise the attainment of the objectives of this Treaty."

---

[32] 1972 c.68.
[33] See Chapter 3, Section 4.
[34] [1994] 2 C.M.L.R. 803, ECJ.
[35] 1972 c.68.
[36] As amended.

736

This basic duty is approached as a very broad requirement not merely to give technical effect to the obligations imposed, but to ensure that they receive full practical effect in such a way as to secure so far as possible their stated objectives.[37]

Effect of section 2(1) of European Communities Act 1972[38]

Section 2(1) of the European Communities Act 1972 provides as follows—   **32.3.3**

> "All such rights, powers, liabilities, obligations and restrictions from time to time created or arising by or under the Treaties, and all such remedies and procedures from time to time provided for by or under the Treaties, as in accordance with the Treaties are without further enactment to be given legal effect or used in the United Kingdom shall be recognised and available in law, and be enforced, allowed and followed accordingly;".

The result of the breadth of this proposition is that as a general rule it is unnecessary for provisions of United Kingdom legislation, whether primary or subordinate, to be made expressly subject to principles of Community law. The effect of s.2(1) is that any legislative proposition will automatically be read as subject to, and construed in accordance with, the Community obligations as to, for example, freedom of movement, freedom of establishment and the like. Express legislative provision is therefore mostly required only for the occasions on which new legislation is required to implement a Directive, or another item of European legislation, that does not have direct effect.

Be that as it may, it is occasionally thought right for legislation to include express reference to the primacy or precise application of Community law, for the avoidance of doubt and to provide additionally clarity for the reader.[39]

Adequacy of implementation

There are many different ways of implementing a Directive, from merely   **32.3.4**
enacting a proposition that a specified Directive is to have the force of law, at one extreme, to reproducing as free-standing propositions the entirety of the

---

[37] "The national courts, whose task it is to apply the provisions of Community law in areas within their jurisdiction, must ensure that they take full effect (see, *inter alia, Amministrazione delle Finanze dello Stato v Simmenthal SpA* Case 106/77 [1978] E.C.R. 629 (para.16), *Factortame Ltd v Secretary of State for Transport (No 2)* Case C–213/89 [1991] 1 All E.R. 70 at 105, [1990] E.C.R. I–2433 at 2473 (para.19) and *Courage Ltd v Crehan* Case C–453/99 [2001] All E.R. (EC) 886 at 900, [2001] E.C.R. I–6297 (para.25))."—*Antonio Munoz y Cia SA v Frumar Ltd* [2003] Ch. 328, ECJ (judgment, para.28).

[38] 1972 c.68.

[39] See, for example, s.106 of the Government of Wales Act 1998 (c.38), s.24 of the Northern Ireland Act 1998 (c.47), s.56 of the Scotland Act 1998 (c.46) and s.3(4) of the Trade Marks Act 1994 (c.26) ("A trade mark shall not be registered if or to the extent that its use is prohibited in the United Kingdom by any enactment or rule of law or by any provision of Community law").

Directive, at the other extreme, with many possibilities between the two extremes.

As a matter of European law it does not matter which method is used.[40] What matters is not only that the implementation should be sufficient in the sense of covering the entire breadth of the Directive but also that it should be sufficient in the sense of conferring and imposing rights and obligations that are directly enforceable at domestic law, without any further implementing steps having to be taken. While the national implementing measures require further implementing provisions in order to have direct legal effects, the Directive will not as a matter of European law be treated as having been transposed into domestic law.[41]

In many cases it will theoretically be possible to implement a Directive without any kind of legislation, merely through administrative action. Even so, legislation is generally preferable because administrative action will tend to lack the attributes of clarity, certainty and adequate publicity. As a general rule, therefore, merely adopting a policy as to administrative action to be taken will not constitute sufficient implementation.[42] However, it may be sufficient to confer on subordinate authorities the power to make the required arrangements for implementation, so long as the satisfactory nature of those arrangements is guaranteed by the enabling legislation.[43]

32.3.5   Obviously, it will sometimes be tempting for Member States to prevent any question of liability for inadequate implementation of Community legislation by going much further than the legislation demands. As a matter of Community law, it will generally be permissible for a national government to determine to over-implement[44] but the result may be to impose unnecessary burdens on those required to comply with the implementing legislation. The United Kingdom's policy on implementation was stated by the Chancellor of the Duchy of Lancaster in 1996 as follows—

> "The Government's policy is to implement EC legislation in a way that fully meets our legal obligations while imposing the least possible burden on business and others affected. I am today publishing a new 'Implementing European Law' Checklist, which will assist Ministers and officials in avoiding any over-implementation of EC legislation. Ministers will certify personally that they have applied the checklist."[45]

Over-implementation will not be lawful as a matter of European law if it amounts to imposing restrictions contrary to Community rules on freedom of

---

[40] Although note that one of the dangers of the non-copy-out route is that of inadequate implementation—see Chapter 3, Section 10.

[41] *Re Midwives: EC Commission v Spain* [1991] 1 C.M.L.R. 256, ECJ Lenz A-G, 263–264.

[42] *Re Protection of Wild Birds, EC Commission v Netherlands* [1993] C.M.L.R. 360, ECJ.

[43] *Association pour la protection des animaux sauvages v Prefet de Maine-et-Loire (wild birds)* [1994] 3 C.M.L.R. 685, ECJ.

[44] Except where that amounts to creating a barrier to intra-Union competition, movement or the like.

[45] HC Deb. May 16, 1996 W.A. 512.

movement or the like, or if it amounts to contravention of the occupied field doctrine.[46]

The European Commission makes an annual report to the European Parliament on the adequacy of implementation of European law.

Enforcement

Where a Directive does not provide a penalty for infringement, Art.5 EEC requires Member States to take necessary measures to guarantee the application and effectiveness of Community law. This will require them to include in their implementing legislation sanctions and penalties which are analogous to those applicable to infringements of similar national laws and which, in any event, make the penalty effective, proportionate and dissuasive.[47]

32.3.6

A Directive will sometimes specify methods of enforcement that are required to be adopted. Whether it does so or not, however, it is open to Member States to provide criminal sanctions for the enforcement of obligations under a Directive.[48]

Application of national laws and principles

Where the Community legislation does not make provision for or about a particular aspect of its enforcement, and there are no relevant principles or rules of the jurisprudence built up by the European Court of Justice, it is open to Member Sates in implementing European legislation to apply and adopt such of their own rules and principles as they think fit.

32.3.7

So, for example, in the absence of Community rules, national rules relating to time limits for bringing actions can be applied to actions based on Community law, provided that they are not less favourable than for similar rights of a domestic nature and do not render the exercise of rights conferred by Community law impossible in practice.[49]

Timing

Where a Directive is not implemented by the time specified for its transposition into national law, it is possible that a Member State may be able to retrieve the position by passing legislation with retrospective effect. Whether this is entirely effective as a matter of European law will depend upon whether a person can demonstrate specific loss caused by the failure to implement on time.[50]

32.3.8

---

[46] As to which see Chapter 32, para.32.2.5.

[47] *E.C. Commission v United Kingdom (Re business transfers)* [1995] 1 C.M.L.R. 345.

[48] *Gallotti* [1997] 1 C.M.L.R. 32, ECJ.

[49] *Preston and Others v Wolverhampton Healthcare Trust and the Secretary of State for Health; Fletcher and Others v Midland Bank PLC* [1997] 2 C.M.L.R. 754, CA.

[50] *Maso and Gazzetta v Instituto Nazionale della Prevedenza Sociale and Italy* [1997] 3 C.M.L.R. 1244, ECJ.

SECTION 4

ENFORCEMENT

Introduction

32.4.1 This Section considers some basic principles in relation to the enforcement of European law, including remedies for breach of a requirement of European law and remedies for inadequate or ineffective implementation.

Invalidity of incompatible domestic law

32.4.2 So absolute are the obligations conferred by the European Treaties on the signatory Governments, and so complete is the legal effect given to those obligations in United Kingdom law by the European Communities Act 1972,[51] that the European and domestic courts will be prepared to go to any necessary lengths to enforce the obligations.

In the extreme case of the *Factortame*[52] litigation, the courts were prepared to do the previously unthinkable and declare an Act of Parliament to be unlawful,[53] in the sense that without expressly or by necessary implication declaring an intention to repeal the European Communities Act 1972 it nevertheless enacted legislation that produced a situation contrary to the Community obligations of the United Kingdom.

---

[51] 1972 c.68.

[52] A protracted series of proceedings, of which *R. v Secretary of State for Transport, Ex p. Factortame Ltd (No. 3)* [1991] 3 C.M.L.R. 589, ECJ and *R. v Secretary of State for Transport, Ex p. Factortame Ltd (No. 2)* [1991] 1 A.C. 603, HL and *R. v Secretary of State for Transport, Ex p. Factortame Ltd* [2000] 1 A.C. 524, HL are the key stages for these purposes.

[53] As to the constitutional implications for the supremacy of Parliament see, as well as the considerations in Chapter 30, paras 30.1.4—30.1.6, the following passage of the judgment in *Factortame* of Lord Bridge of Harwich (at 658–659)—"Some public comments on the decision of the European Court of Justice, affirming the jurisdiction of the courts of member states to override national legislation if necessary to enable interim relief to be granted in protection of rights under Community law, have suggested that this was a novel and dangerous invasion by a Community institution of the sovereignty of the United Kingdom Parliament. But such comments are based on a misconception. If the supremacy within the European Community of Community law over the national law of member states was not always inherent in the E.E.C. Treaty (Cmnd. 5179-II) it was certainly well established in the jurisprudence of the European Court of Justice long before the United Kingdom joined the Community. Thus, whatever limitation of its sovereignty Parliament accepted when it enacted the European Communities Act 1972 was entirely voluntary. Under the terms of the Act of 1972 it has always been clear that it was the duty of a United Kingdom court, when delivering final judgment, to override any rule of national law found to be in conflict with any directly enforceable rule of Community law. Similarly, when decisions of the European Court of Justice have exposed areas of United Kingdom statute law which failed to implement Council directives, Parliament has always loyally accepted the obligation to make appropriate and prompt amendments. Thus there is nothing in any way novel in according supremacy to rules of Community law in those areas to which they apply and to insist that, in the protection of rights under Community law, national courts must not be inhibited by rules of national law from granting interim relief in appropriate cases is no more than a logical recognition of that supremacy."

The critical part of the judgment of the European Court of Justice, replying to **32.4.3** questions referred to it by the High Court, is as follows—

"(1) As Community law stands at present, it is for the member states to determine, in accordance with the general rules of international law, the conditions which must be fulfilled in order for a vessel to be registered in their registers and granted the right to fly their flag, but, in exercising that power, the member states must comply with the rules of Community law.

"(2) It is contrary to the provisions of Community law and, in particular, to article 52 of the E.E.C. Treaty for a member state to stipulate as conditions for the registration of a fishing vessel in its national register: (a) that the legal owners and beneficial owners and the charterers, managers and operators of the vessel must be nationals of that member state or companies incorporated in that member state, and that, in the latter case, at least 75 per cent. of the shares in the company must be owned by nationals of that member state or by companies fulfilling the same requirements and 75 per cent. of the directors of the company must be nationals of that member state; and (b) that the said legal owners and beneficial owners, charterers, managers, operators, shareholders and directors, as the case may be, must be resident and domiciled in that member state. . . . "

On referral of questions from the House of Lords on the structural issues **32.4.4** involved the European Court of Justice observed as follows—

"20. The Court of Justice has also held that any provision of a national legal system and any legislative, administrative or judicial practice which might impair the effectiveness of Community law by withholding from the national court having jurisdiction to apply such law the power to do everything necessary at the moment of its application to set aside national legislative provisions which might prevent, even temporarily, Community rules from having full force and effect are incompatible with those requirements, which are the very essence of Community law: see the judgment in the *Simmenthal* case.[54]

"21. It must be added that the full effectiveness of Community law would be just as much impaired if a rule of national law could prevent a court seised of a dispute governed by Community law from granting interim relief in order to ensure the full effectiveness of the judgment to be given on the existence of the rights claimed under Community law. It follows that a court which in those circumstances would grant interim relief, if it were not for a rule of national law, is obliged to set aside that rule.

---

[54] [1978] E.C.R. 629, 644, paras 22 and 23.

"22. That interpretation is reinforced by the system established by article 177 of the E.E.C. Treaty whose effectiveness would be impaired if a national court, having stayed proceedings pending the reply by the Court of Justice to the question referred to it for a preliminary ruling, were not able to grant interim relief until it delivered its judgment following the reply given by the Court of Justice.

"23. Consequently, the reply to the question raised should be that Community law must be interpreted as meaning that a national court which, in a case before it concerning Community law, considers that the sole obstacle which precludes it from granting interim relief is a rule of national law must set aside that rule."

In accordance with this ruling the House of Lords held that the Merchant Shipping Act 1988[55] was a breach of the EC Treaty, since it discriminated on grounds of nationality, and that those who had suffered loss as a result of the passing of the Act were entitled to damages from Her Majesty's Government, despite the fact that the Government had acted in good faith and in accordance with their legal advice (although in knowing disregard of the Commission's opinion).

Damages for inadequate or ineffective implementation

32.4.5   As a result of the *Factortame* case and of the joined case of *Brasserie du pêcheur*[56] it is established as a principle of European law that a Member State, that is to say the government of a Member State, will be liable to compensate individuals for loss suffered as a result of the State's failure to implement or apply European law.

Whether or not liability arises in a particular case depends on a number of criteria[57]—

The infringed provision of Community law must have the purpose of granting rights to the individual who claims to have suffered harm.

---

[55] 1988 c.12.

[56] Cases C–48/93 and C–46/93: judgment March 5, 1996. See in particular *Brasserie du Pecheur SA v Federal Republic of Germany, R. v Secretary of State for Transport, Ex p. Factortame Ltd and Others (No.4)* [1996] 2 W.L.R. 506, ECJ, [1996] 1 C.M.L.R. 889, ECJ, [1997] 1 C.M.L.R. 971, German Federal Supreme Court, [1998] 10 Admin L.R 107, QBD, [1999] 3 C.M.L.R. 597, HL, [1999] 4 All E.R. 906, HL and (No.5) [1999] 3 W.L.R. 1062, HL. See also *Francovich* and *Bonifaci*. Before *Factortame* there was a concept of State liability for failure to implement, but the criteria for eligibility for compensation were much tighter.

[57] Which are distinctly reminiscent of the criteria established in United Kingdom law for individual action to enforce a statutory duty, as to which see Chapter 12, paras 12.6.5—12.6.10.

The infringement must be sufficiently serious to merit an award of damages.[58]

A direct causal link must exist between the infringement of the obligation of the Member State and the harm suffered by the injured party.

It is not necessary to prove that the failure to implement European law was intentional or even negligent, although what the relevant Member State's government knew or should have known will often be relevant, and may be critical, to the question of seriousness of the breach.

It is open to a Member State to impose upon proceedings in respect of inadequate or ineffective implementation certain of the rules and characteristics of their own domestic legal proceedings, even where these in effect constrain the availability of the remedy.[59]

32.4.6

SECTION 5

INTERPRETATION

Introduction

European legislation has never lent itself to the application of rigid rules of construction. As has been mentioned[60] many legislative instruments within the European Communities are necessarily formed more by a process of political negotiation than by a process of accurate drafting for the purposes of meeting an agreed policy. It is therefore unnecessary to attempt—and any attempt would be doomed to failure—to set out canons for construction or even principles at the same level of detail as has been done for our own domestic legislation earlier in this work.

But one or two things can helpfully be said about the construction of European legislation, and of domestic legislation that is closely connected to Community

32.5.1

---

[58] The question of seriousness is to be decided by the national courts: the European Court of Justice offered the following guidelines in *Factortame*: "The factors which the competent court may take into consideration include the clarity and precision of the rule breached, the measure of discretion left by that rule to the national or Community authorities, whether the infringement and the damage caused was intentional or involuntary, whether any error of law was excusable or inexcusable, the fact that the position taken by a Community institution may have contributed towards the omission, and the adoption or retention of national measures or practices contrary to Community law. On any view, a breach of Community law will clearly be sufficiently serious if it has persisted despite a judgment finding the infringement in question to be established, or a preliminary ruling or settled case-law of the Court on the matter from which it is clear that the conduct in question constituted an infringement." For an example of a breach of European law not considered sufficiently serious to give rise to damages see Case C–392/93 *The Queen v HM Treasury Ex p. British Telecommunications plc* (26.iii.96).

[59] So, for example, a national limitation period for action may be imposed provided that it is not less favourable than the limits for similar domestic claims—*Palmisani v Instituto Nazionale Della Previdenza Sociale* [1997] 3 C.M.L.R. 1356, ECJ; and see *Apriole SRI (In Liquidation) v Administrazione Delle Finanze Dello Stato (No.2)* [2000] 1 W.L.R. 126, ECJ.

[60] See Chapter 31, para.31.1.21.

obligations. That is the purpose of this Section. Some relevant principles are also discussed in Chapter 29.

The basic approach

32.5.2 The normal approach of the European Court of Justice to the construction of a European legislative instrument is[61]—

(1) to start with the terms of the instrument in question, including its pre-amble,

(2) if the matter is not resolved by that, to turn to preparatory documents,

(3) if the matter is not resolved by that, to consider the usual meaning of expressions used and to consider, in particular, comparison of different language texts of the instrument, and

(4) if the matter is not resolved by that, to consider the purpose and general scheme of the instrument to be construed.

It will be seen from this that the fundamental approach is not greatly different from that which is applied to the construction of United Kingdom legislation by the courts of the United Kingdom. It is, however, true that the European Court of Justice has never experienced the kind of debate that has taken place in the United Kingdom[62] about whether to apply a literal or purposive approach. It has always applied the latter, in accordance with the long-standing jurisprudential practice of the majority of the Member States, and is forced to do so comparatively frequently by the lesser exactitude with which European legislative instruments are habitually drafted.

The European Court of Justice has also never had any difficulty in looking at preparatory materials for the purpose of aiding construction. Interestingly, however, since the European institutions have so many ways both in the preambles to legislation and in legislation itself of making its purpose clear and, in particular, referring to supporting material, the courts will sometimes be reluctant to have regard to preparatory material to supply an intention which could have been made clear in the usual way and was not. So, for example, the European Court of Justice said in *The Queen v The Immigration Appeal Tribunal, Ex p. Gustaff Desiderius Antonissen*[63]—

---

[61] For an example of the Court expressly passing through these stages see *R.T.L. Television v N.L.M.* [2004] 1 C.M.L.R. 5, judgment, paras 97–108.

[62] See Chapter 18.

[63] Case C–292/89, European Court Reports 1991 I–745, ECJ, judgment paras 17 & 18: compare, now, the arguably more liberal practice of the courts in relation to United Kingdom domestic legislation.

"The national court referred to the declaration recorded in the Council minutes at the time of the adoption of the aforesaid Regulation . . . and of Council Directive . . . However, such a declaration cannot be used for the purpose of interpreting a provision of secondary legislation where, as in this case, no reference is made to the content of the declaration in the wording of the provision in question. The declaration therefore has no legal significance."

Construing implementing legislation

As has already been stated,[64] it is always necessary in construing legislation inspired by a European obligation to have regard to the terms and purpose of that obligation. That is true even in a case where nobody disputes that the domestic legislation effects full and proper implementation of the underlying European obligation. It is common in such a case to find a court that has to construe a piece of implementing legislation applying a purposive construction to the underlying European Directive as the principal thrust of its decision, with the terms of the implementing legislation being used as secondary support (or, if incompatible with the fundamental purpose revealed by examination of the European legislation, ignored).[65]

32.5.3

Note also that domestic legislation implementing European legislation may well have to be construed in a more ambulatory or otherwise flexible way than would be the case with other domestic legislation.[66]

In construing European legislation or implementing legislation it will be permissible, and often necessary, to have regard to the preamble (the inclusion of which in European legislation is, unlike in United Kingdom legislation, the invariable rule) in construing the text.[67] Apart from clarifying the political context within which the legislation falls to be construed, definitions and other essential aspects of the legislation may be addressed only in the preamble.

Principles of European law

In approaching the construction of European law underpinning United Kingdom legislation, or the construction of United Kingdom legislation giving effect to European law, it can be assumed that most of the fundamental principles of

32.5.4

---

[64] See para.27.1.6.

[65] See, for example, the case of *R. (Hoverspeed Ltd) v Customs and Excise Commissioners* [2003] 2 W.L.R. 950, CA in which the Court of Appeal had to determine the extent of the powers under ss.163 and 163A of the Customs and Excise Management Act 1979 in relation to the import of tobacco and alcohol, where the argument related entirely to the extent of the purpose underlying Council Directive 92/12/EEC.

[66] See the dictum of Lord Nicholls of Birkenhead cited in para.1.5.5.

[67] A large number of cases each year demonstrate the routine use of the preamble for the construction of Community instruments of all kinds. For random recent examples, see *Saatgut-Treuhandverwaltungsgesellschaft mbH v Werner Jäger* (Case C–182/01) and *Koninklijke KPN Nederland NV v Benelux-Merkenbureau* (Case C–363/99).

European law with regard to which the construction process is performed are also principles of the law of the United Kingdom, whether because of identical origins or because legal comity within the European Union has caused national law to adopt and embrace concepts of Community law.[68]

So, for example, principles such as that of not allowing a person to defeat a legitimate expectation that he has created, are shared by Community law and our law.[69]

Consistency of construction

32.5.5   In an area of law fundamental to the nature of the European Union, it is obviously important that a consistent approach is taken throughout the Union to the construction of legislation.

Where the legislation is European legislation having direct effect, the courts of this country will necessarily have regard to the interpretations given by the European Court of Justice, as required by s.3 of the 1972 Act.[70] And they will use

---

[68] Proportionality being the obvious example. While the notion expressed in this principle may have been part of the notion of reasonableness at United Kingdom law for some time, it has come to be given expression by reference to this term as a result of the influence of European law.

[69] "It is quite clear from these judgments that the principle of the protection of legitimate expectation is one of the fundamental principles of the Community"—*Carberry Milk Products Ltd v Minister for Agriculture* [1994] 3 C.M.L.R. 914, Irish High Court.

[70] The text of s.3 is as follows—

> **"3 Decisions on, and proof of, Treaties and Community instruments, etc**
>
> (1)   For the purposes of all legal proceedings any question as to the meaning or effect of any of the Treaties, or as to the validity, meaning or effect of any Community instrument, shall be treated as a question of law (and, if not referred to the European Court, be for determination as such in accordance with the principles laid down by and any relevant decision of the European Court or any court attached thereto).
>
> (2)   Judicial notice shall be taken of the Treaties, of the Official Journal of the Communities and of any decision of, or expression of opinion by, the European Court or any court attached thereto on any such question as aforesaid; and the Official Journal shall be admissible as evidence of any instrument or other act thereby communicated of any of the Communities or of any Community institution.
>
> (3)   Evidence of any instrument issued by a Community institution, including any judgment or order of the European Court or any court attached thereto, or of any document in the custody of a Community institution, or any entry in or extract from such a document, may be given in any legal proceedings by production of a copy certified as a true copy by an official of that institution; and any document purporting to be such a copy shall be received in evidence without proof of the official position or handwriting of the person signing the certificate.
>
> (4)   Evidence of any Community instrument may also be given in any legal proceedings—
>
> > (a)   by production of a copy purporting to be printed by the Queen's Printer;
> >
> > (b)   where the instrument is in the custody of a government department (including a department of the Government of Northern Ireland), by production of a copy certified on behalf of the department to be a true copy by an officer of the department generally or specially authorised so to do;
>
> and any document purporting to be such a copy as is mentioned in paragraph (b) above of an instrument in the custody of a department shall be received in evidence without proof of the official position or handwriting of the person signing the certificate, or of his authority to do so, or of the document being in the custody of the department."

the mechanism in Art.234 of the EC Treaty to obtain an opinion of the Court wherever necessary.[71]

Where the legislation is domestic legislation directly inspired by, and implementing, European legislation, as has already been said[72] the courts will have regard to the European legislation. And they will be encouraged to go as far as is possible in giving effect to the underlying European obligations.[73]

Occasionally, however, in relation to domestic legislation that is not directly implementing European legislation it would be undesirable to have disparity of   **32.5.6**

---

[71] **"Article 234**

The Court of Justice shall have jurisdiction to give preliminary rulings concerning:

    (a) the interpretation of this Treaty;

    (b) the validity and interpretation of acts of the institutions of the Community and of the ECB;

    (c) the interpretation of the statutes of bodies established by an act of the Council, where those statutes so provide.

Where such a question is raised before any court or tribunal of a Member State, that court or tribunal may, if it considers that a decision on the question is necessary to enable it to give judgment, request the Court of Justice to give a ruling thereon.

Where any such question is raised in a case pending before a court or tribunal of a Member State against whose decisions there is no judicial remedy under national law, that court or tribunal shall bring the matter before the Court of Justice."

[72] Chapter 29.

[73] See, for example, the following passage of the judgment of Lord Phillips of Worth Matravers M.R. in *Alderson v Secretary of State for Trade and Industry* [2004] 1 C.M.L.R. 36, CA—

"The approach to construction

Newman J observed at paragraph 21 of his judgment that "some regard can be paid to the principle that the court should attempt to interpret the offending exception so far as possible to accord with the purposes of the Directive". [Counsel] challenged this proposition. He submitted that it was plain that the words in italics restricted the ambit of TUPE so that it did not have as wide a scope as the ARD. It was not possible to give to the words in italics a meaning that accorded with the Directive. In these circumstances the correct approach was to give the words their natural meaning.

We do not accept [Counsel's] submission. Nor do we think that Newman J put the matter sufficiently strongly. The Court is under an obligation, in so far as the language of TUPE permits, to construe TUPE in a manner which accords with the ADR. If it is not possible to give the two the same scope, the Court must go as far towards this as is possible. An example of just how far this purposive approach can legitimately go is provided by the decision of the House of Lords in *Litster v Forth Dry Dock and Engineering Co Ltd* [1990] 1 A.C. 546. In that case the House implied into a clause which defined a person protected by TUPE as "a person so employed immediately before the transfer" the additional words "or would have been so employed if he had not been unfairly dismissed in the circumstances described by regulation 8(1)".

The jurisprudence of the European Court of Justice has led to 'undertaking' in the ARD acquiring the definition of "an organised grouping of resources which has the objective of pursuing an economic activity". The question that has concerned us is whether it is not possible, without stretching the meaning of the phrase to breaking point, to give an undertaking "in the nature of a commercial venture" precisely the same meaning. If so, it is the duty of the court to do so. It does not seem to us that the concession that appears to have been made in the enforcement proceedings that the words in italics meant 'non-profit making' can preclude such an approach.

Our conclusion is that the words "in the nature of a commercial venture" are sufficiently imprecise and elastic to enable TUPE in its original form to be construed as having the same scope as the ARD. We do not, however, have to go this far in order to decide this appeal."

construction, because the area of substance concerned so closely impinges upon matters fundamental to the Communities.

Competition law is one of the most obvious examples, and in relation to that area of law consistency is achieved by express legislative provision in section 60 of the Competition Act 1998[74] which provides as follows—

32.5.7 **"60 Principles to be applied in determining questions**

"(1) The purpose of this section is to ensure that so far as is possible (having regard to any relevant differences between the provisions concerned), questions arising under this Part in relation to competition within the United Kingdom are dealt with in a manner which is consistent with the treatment of corresponding questions arising in Community law in relation to competition within the Community.

(2) At any time when the court determines a question arising under this Part, it must act (so far as is compatible with the provisions of this Part and whether or not it would otherwise be required to do so) with a view to securing that there is no inconsistency between—

the principles applied, and decision reached, by the court in determining that question; and
the principles laid down by the Treaty and the European Court, and any relevant decision of that Court, as applicable at that time in determining any corresponding question arising in Community law.

"(3) The court must, in addition, have regard to any relevant decision or statement of the Commission. . . . "

Other cases where uniformity of construction is desirable arise and are noted as such by the European Court of Justice.[75]

Pepper v Hart

32.5.8 There is some authority for the suggestion that the rule in *Pepper v Hart* should be applied particularly generously when construing legislation designed to implement a European obligation.[76]

---

[74] 1998 c.41.
[75] See, for example, paras 39 to 45 of the judgment of the Court in *Mau v Bundestanstalt Fur Arbeit* [2004] 1 C.M.L.R. 34, ECJ on the importance of a uniform interpretation of the concept of an employment relationship for the purposes of Directive 80/987.
[76] *Three Rivers District Council and others v Bank of England (No. 2)* [1996] 2 All E.R. 363, QBD.

APPENDIX

KEY PASSAGES OF RELEVANT
JUDGMENTS AND OTHER DOCUMENTS

THE QUEEN ON THE PROSECUTION OF THE ST. GILES BOARD OF WORK AND OTHERS v LONDON COUNTY COUNCIL[1]

DISTINCTION BETWEEN PUBLIC AND PRIVATE ACT

SEE CHAPTER 1, SECTION 3

(a) Extract of judgment of Lord Esher M.R.

"I have very considerable doubt whether prohibition is the right remedy if the county council have no power to make the order, and whether they are such a body as ought to be prohibited in such a case. That however becomes immaterial if we are of opinion that the question of their right to proceed in the matter is raised with regard to an Act of Parliament that is local and personal. If the question is raised in respect of such an Act, there is no doubt that the county council have power to deal with the matter under the Local Government Act, 1888, so that the substantial question is whether we are of opinion that the Acts which it is sought to amend are local and personal Acts, within the meaning of s.59 of the Local Government Act, 1888.   **A.1.1**

The Acts on which the question arises are 9 Anne, c.22, and 10 Anne, c.11. It is said that both Acts are public Acts and that neither is of a local and personal nature, and, considering the subject-matter of the Acts, that they deal with the building of fifty new churches in and about the metropolis, and the adapting of these and other churches and chapels for the requirements of public service, and that they deal with the purchasing of houses for the habitation of the ministers and with matters that to my mind are clearly public objects, namely, the maintenance of Westminster Abbey and Greenwich Hospital, I can have no doubt but that, taking the Acts as a whole, they are of a public character. Taking their main object, it would appear to be for the welfare of the whole kingdom, and they cannot be said to be local and personal in their nature.

But that does not solve the whole question, because though the main object of the Act may be of a public nature there may be parts of them which are of a local and personal nature, and, if so, I think that the county council would have power

---

[1] [1893] 2 Q.B. 454, 458–60, CA.

under sub-s.6 to amend such parts. Considering the matter now in dispute, we find in the Acts that power is given to purchase land for a cemetery in a parish other than that for which a cemetery is required, and such land when purchased and consecrated is to be taken to be part of the parish for the use of which it is purchased.

In determining whether that part of the Acts is local and personal we have to find out what is the meaning of that expression, and if we find that a Court has given a definition of the phrase 'local and personal' when used in an Act of Parliament, we should not be anxious to differ from such definition even if we thought we could give a better one.

Such a definition we find in the case of *Richards v Easto*.[2] From the judgment of Parke, B., it appears that the words to be considered were, 'so much of any clause or provision in any Act or Acts commonly called public local and personal, or local and personal, or in any Acts of a local and personal nature, whereby any party or parties are entitled or permitted to plead the general issue only, and to give any special matter in evidence without specially pleading the same, shall be repeated.' The judgment continues—

'The Act 14 Geo.3, c.78, was not an Act commonly called public local and personal, for that designation did not take place till long after the statute passed. On May 1, 1797, the House of Lords resolved that the King's printer should class the general statutes and special, the public local, and private, in separate volumes; and on May 8, 1801, there was a resolution of the House of Commons, agreed to by the House of Lords, that the general statutes and the 'public local and personal' in each session should be classed in separate volumes. The question, however, is whether the Act does not fall under the description of an Act of a local and personal nature. It seems singular that the new Act, 7 & 8 Vict. c.84, should not be classed amongst public local and personal Acts, for it is confined in its operation to the district in and about the metropolis, with power to Her Majesty to extend its limits. How this has happened cannot be explained, for it is clearly of a local and personal nature.'

Then there is the definition which describes it as 'local, as being confined to local limits; personal, as affecting particular descriptions of persons only, as distinguished from all the Queen's subjects.' It seems to me that that is the best definition that could be proposed, and acting only on that case I should be prepared to adopt it.

But the matter was before the Exchequer Chamber in *Shepherd v Sharp*,[3] who considered the case, and to my mind adopted the definition laid down, though I

---

[2] 15 M. & W. 244.
[3] 25 L. J. (Ex.) 254.

752

do not say they did so in terms. These are strong authorities in favour of the definition, and if it is a good one the latter part of s.4 of 10 Anne, c.11, comes within it. The enactment of that part of the statute is local as to place, for it is manifest to my mind that land at that time could only be bought for use as a cemetery within a limited range and distance from the parish for which it was bought. It was personal as applying to such part only of the Queen's subjects as should happen to die within the particular parish as distinguished from the rest of the Queen's subjects. The question whether the money is to be raised from all or from a portion only of the Queen's subjects is to my mind immaterial in the solution of the point before us.

Under these circumstances, I think the enactment which it is proposed to amend is of a local and personal nature within the meaning of subs.6 of s.59 of the Local Government Act, 1888, and that the county council have power to make the amendment which they have been asked to make, and therefore this appeal must be dismissed."

(b) Extract of judgment of Bowen L.J.

"The history of the nomenclature of Acts of Parliament is given in two books, **A.1.2** which are valuable for the purpose of reference. . . . I am not going through the history of this nomenclature; but it is important to remark that it has altered very much, and that part of the obscurity which has been introduced into the subject is due to the alterations which have been made at different times.

There was a time when public and general Acts were distinguished from private and special; but that is not the division which has obtained in later times, and the more modern division has been between general Acts and local and personal; for it is to be observed (and this is essential for recollecting the point of our decision in the present instance), that 'general,' and not 'public,' is opposed to 'local and personal'; and the division, therefore, lies between public and general Acts on the one side, and public local and personal Acts on the other; because, of course, a local and personal Act may be public without losing its character of local and personal.

The question, therefore, really is, not so much whether this section, or the Act of Parliament to which it belongs, is a public Act, but whether it is a public and general Act. Is it a general Act, or is it a local and personal Act?

Now, a general Act, *prima facie*, is that which applies to the whole community. In the natural meaning of the term it means an Act of Parliament which is unlimited both in its area and, as regards the individual, in its effects; and as opposed to that you get statutes which may well be public because of the importance of the subjects with which they deal and their general interest to the community, but which are limited in respect of area—a limitation which makes them local—or limited in respect of individuals or persons—a limitation which makes them personal.

753

The statutes of the 9th and 10th of Anne certainly deal with matters of public importance and objects which certainly affect the community at large; but that only goes to shew that the Acts are public, and does not solve the question which we have to decide. We still have to ask ourselves whether they are general Acts, or whether they are local and personal."

O. CYPRIAN WILLIAMS, C.B., M.C., D.C.L.,

THE HISTORICAL DEVELOPMENT OF PRIVATE BILL PROCEDURE AND STANDING ORDERS IN THE HOUSE OF COMMONS[1]

See Chapter 1, Section 3

"Every citizen of this country, whenever he mounts an omnibus or tram or gets into a railway train, whenever he turns on a water tap supplied from a company's main, ignites a gas burner or switches on a company's electric current, whenever he walks in a well paved and lighted street, saunters on an esplanade, or listens to a band playing in a municipal bandstand, and in many other actions of his daily life, is profiting from the results of private bill legislation. Equally, when his land or his right of way is compulsorily purchased by a corporation or company, when the street in which he lives is temporarily broken up, when he is compelled to notify infectious disease, when he is forced to observe by-laws relating to the storage of food or the manufacture of ice-cream, or when he is fined £5 for unjustifiably pulling a communication cord, and so forth, be is being affected, inconvenienced or hampered, in part if not exclusively, through the results of private bill legislation. And the statutes which embody this legislation, printed every session as the 'local and personal' Acts, are part of the public law of the land. Yet the average citizen is comparatively ignorant of the process by which these local and personal acts become law, and still more ignorant of the parliamentary procedure involved in the process."

A.2.1

---

[1] His Majesty's Stationery Office, 1948, p.1.

STATUTE LAW REVISION: REPORT ON THE CHRONOLOGICAL TABLE OF PRIVATE AND PERSONAL ACTS

LAW COMMISSION (No.256) AND SCOTTISH LAW COMMISSION (No.170)

SEE CHAPTER 1, SECTION 3

The Importance of Private and Personal Legislation

7. In the Report[1] we pointed out that "Local legislation has played a crucial part **A.3.1** in the process whereby the United Kingdom has since the eighteenth century been changed from a predominantly agricultural and rural society into one that is predominantly urban and suburban."

Private and personal Acts have not, in general, played such an important part in that process and they do not have the continuing relevance which many local Acts have for some of the recently privatised statutory undertakings. But they have nevertheless made a significant contribution to the development of the United Kingdom over the past 460 years and they are, in certain important areas of the law, the precursors of local Acts.

8. Of the 11,000 Acts listed in the Table the most numerous appear to have been those relating to inclosures and landed estates. Inclosure Acts played a central part in modernising the country's agricultural system by authorising the inclosure of open and commonable fields, consolidating small, scattered, landholdings into single, larger, units and "substituting individual interests in place of common interests . . . as a means of furthering agriculture."

Estate Acts enabled landowners to exploit their estates by freeing them from the restrictions of the settlements and other legal impediments to which both the estates and their owners were often subject and some of them, by authorising the granting of building leases, led to important urban developments.

Some of the less numerous private Acts such as those relating to bridges, canals, docks, ports and harbours, local government (including poor law and public health), roads and water supply were precursors of later local Acts. Other Acts related to such matters as charities, the church and ecclesiastical affairs,

---

[1] A reference to an earlier report by the Commission to the Advisory Committee on Statute Law.

hospitals, schools and Oxford and Cambridge universities and their individual colleges.

On a more personal level private Acts related to attainders and their annulment and reversal, restitutions in blood and the restoration of honours, property and titles to those who had been deprived of them. They also authorised changes of surname, so enabling those concerned to inherit in accordance with testators' wishes, divorce and the naturalization of foreigners as British subjects, a notable example being the naturalization of George Frederick Handel by an Act of 1726.

THOBURN v SUNDERLAND CITY COUNCIL[1]

(A) PARLIAMENTARY SUPREMACY AND THE EUROPEAN UNION

(B) THE DOCTRINE OF IMPLIED REPEAL AND CONSTITUTIONAL STATUTES

SEE CHAPTER 1, SECTION 4 AND CHAPTER 30, PARA.30.1.4

Extract of judgment of Laws L.J.

"58. . . . [Counsel's argument] proceeds on the assumption that the incorporation **A.4.1** of European law effected by the European Communities Act 1972[2] must have included not only the whole corpus of European law upon substantive matters such as (by way of example) the free movement of goods and services, but also any jurisprudence of the Court of Justice, or other rule of Community law, which purports to touch the constitutional preconditions upon which the sovereign legislative power belonging to a member State may be exercised.

59. Whatever may be the position elsewhere, the law of England disallows any such assumption. Parliament cannot bind its successors by stipulating against repeal, wholly or partly, of the European Communities Act 1972. It cannot stipulate as to the manner and form of any subsequent legislation. It cannot stipulate against implied repeal any more than it can stipulate against express repeal. Thus there is nothing in the European Communities Act 1972 which allows the Court of Justice, or any other institutions of the European Union, to touch or qualify the conditions of Parliament's legislative supremacy in the United Kingdom. Not because the legislature chose not to allow it; because by our law it could not allow it. That being so, the legislative and judicial institutions of the European Union cannot intrude upon those conditions. The British Parliament has not the authority to authorise any such thing. Being sovereign, it cannot abandon its sovereignty. Accordingly there are no circumstances in which

---

[1] [2003] Q.B. 151.
[2] 1972 c.68.

the jurisprudence of the Court of Justice can elevate Community law to a status within the corpus of English domestic law to which it could not aspire by any route of English law itself. This is, of course, the traditional doctrine of sovereignty. If is to be modified, it certainly cannot be done by the incorporation of external texts. The conditions of Parliament's legislative supremacy in the United Kingdom necessarily remain in the United Kingdom's hands. But the traditional doctrine has in my judgment been modified. It has been done by the common law, wholly consistently with constitutional principle. . . .

60. The common law has in recent years allowed, or rather created, exceptions to the doctrine of implied repeal: a doctrine which was always the common law's own creature. There are now classes or types of legislative provision which cannot be repealed by mere implication. These instances are given, and can only be given, by our own courts, to which the scope and nature of Parliamentary sovereignty are ultimately confided. The courts may say—have said—that there are certain circumstances in which the legislature may only enact what it desires to enact if it does so by express, or at any rate specific, provision. The courts have in effect so held in the field of European law itself, in the *Factortame* case, and this is critical for the present discussion. By this means, as I shall seek to explain, the courts have found their way through the impasse seemingly created by two supremacies, the supremacy of European law and the supremacy of Parliament.

61. The present state of our domestic law is such that substantive Community rights prevail over the express terms of any domestic law, including primary legislation, made or passed after the coming into force of the European Communities Act 1972, even in the face of plain inconsistency between the two. This is the effect of *Factortame (No.1)*.[3] To understand the critical passage in Lord Bridge's speech it is first convenient to repeat part of European Communities Act 1972 section 2(4):

'The provision that may be made under subsection (2) above includes . . . any such provision (of any such extent) as might be made by Act of Parliament, and any enactment passed or to be passed, other than one contained in this Part of this Act, shall be construed and have effect subject to the foregoing provisions of the section.'

In *Factortame (No.1)* Lord Bridge said this at 140:

'By virtue of section 2(4) of the Act of 1972 Part II of the [Merchant Shipping] Act of 1988 is to be construed and take effect subject to directly enforceable Community rights . . . This has precisely the same effect as if a section were incorporated in Part II of the Act of 1988 which in terms enacted that the provisions with respect to registration of British fishing

---

[3] [1990] 2 A.C. 85.

vessels were to be without prejudice to the directly enforceable Community rights of nationals of any member state of the EEC.'

So there was no question of an implied pro tanto repeal of the European Communities Act 1972 by the later Act of 1988; on the contrary the Act of 1988 took effect subject to Community rights incorporated into our law by the European Communities Act 1972. In Factortame no argument was advanced by the Crown in their Lordships' House to suggest that such an implied repeal might have been effected. It is easy to see what the argument might have been: Parliament in 1972 could not bind Parliament in 1988, and s.2(4) was therefore ineffective to do so. It seems to me that there is no doubt but that in *Factortame (No.1)* the House of Lords effectively accepted that s.2(4) could not be impliedly repealed, albeit the point was not argued.

62. Where does this leave the constitutional position which I have stated? **A.4.2** [Counsel] would say that *Factortame (No.1)* was wrongly decided; and since the point was not argued, there is scope, within the limits of our law of precedent, to depart from it and to hold that implied repeal may bite on the European Communities Act 1972 as readily as upon any other statute. I think that would be a wrong turning. My reasons are these. In the present state of its maturity the common law has come to recognise that there exist rights which should properly be classified as constitutional or fundamental: see for example such cases as *Simms*[4] per Lord Hoffmann at 131, *Pierson v Secretary of State*,[5] *Leech*,[6] *Derbyshire County Council v Times Newspapers Ltd*,[7] and *Witham*.[8] And from this a further insight follows. We should recognise a hierarchy of Acts of Parliament: as it were 'ordinary' statutes and 'constitutional' statutes. The two categories must be distinguished on a principled basis. In my opinion a constitutional statute is one which (a) conditions the legal relationship between citizen and State in some general, overarching manner, or (b) enlarges or diminishes the scope of what we would now regard as fundamental constitutional rights. (a) and (b) are of necessity closely related: it is difficult to think of an instance of (a) that is not also an instance of (b). The special status of constitutional statutes follows the special status of constitutional rights. Examples are the Magna Carta, the Bill of Rights 1689, the Act of Union,[9] the Reform Acts which distributed and enlarged the franchise, the Human Rights Act 1998, the Scotland Act 1998 and the Government of Wales Act 1998. The European Communities Act 1972 clearly belongs in this family. It incorporated the whole corpus of substantive Community rights and obligations, and gave overriding

---

[4] [2000] 2 A.C. 115.
[5] [1998] A.C. 539.
[6] [1994] Q.B. 198.
[7] [1993] A.C. 534.
[8] [1998] Q.B. 575.
[9] Which is no longer to be treated as a treaty in international law (see proceedings in House of Lords Committee for Privileges in respect of Lord Gray's Motion on the House of Lords Bill 1999–2000 [2000] 2 W.L.R. 664 HL Committee for Privileges).

domestic effect to the judicial and administrative machinery of Community law. It may be there has never been a statute having such profound effects on so many dimensions of our daily lives. The European Communities Act 1972 is, by force of the common law, a constitutional statute.

63. Ordinary statutes may be impliedly repealed. Constitutional statutes may not. For the repeal of a constitutional Act or the abrogation of a fundamental right to be effected by statute, the court would apply this test: is it shown that the legislature's actual—not imputed, constructive or presumed—intention was to effect the repeal or abrogation? I think the test could only be met by express words in the later statute, or by words so specific that the inference of an actual determination to effect the result contended for was irresistible. The ordinary rule of implied repeal does not satisfy this test. Accordingly, it has no application to constitutional statutes. I should add that in my judgment general words could not be supplemented, so as to effect a repeal or significant amendment to a constitutional statute, by reference to what was said in Parliament by the minister promoting the Bill pursuant to *Pepper v Hart*.[10] A constitutional statute can only be repealed, or amended in a way which significantly affects its provisions touching fundamental rights or otherwise the relation between citizen and State, by unambiguous words on the face of the later statute.

64. This development of the common law regarding constitutional rights, and as I would say constitutional statutes, is highly beneficial. It gives us most of the benefits of a written constitution, in which fundamental rights are accorded special respect. But it preserves the sovereignty of the legislature and the flexibility of our uncodified constitution. It accepts the relation between legislative supremacy and fundamental rights is not fixed or brittle: rather the courts (in interpreting statutes, and now, applying the Human Rights Act 1998) will pay more or less deference to the legislature, or other public decision-maker, according to the subject in hand. Nothing is plainer than that this benign development involves, as I have said, the recognition of the European Communities Act 1972 as a constitutional statute.

65. In dealing with this part of the case I should refer to a passage from the speech of Lord Bridge of Harwich in *Factortame (No.2)*,[11] on which [Counsel] relies:

'Some public comments on the decision of the European Court of Justice, affirming the jurisdiction of the courts of member states to override national legislation if necessary to enable interim relief to be granted in protection of rights under Community law, have suggested that this was a novel and dangerous invasion by a Community institution of the sovereignty of the United Kingdom Parliament. But such comments are based on a misconception. If the supremacy within the European Community of Community law over the national law of member states was not always inherent in the

---

[10] [1993] A.C. 593.
[11] [1991] 1 A.C. 603, 658–659.

E.E.C. Treaty . . . it was certainly well established in the jurisprudence of the European Court of Justice long before the United Kingdom joined the Community. Thus, whatever limitation of its sovereignty Parliament accepted when it enacted the European Communities Act 1972 was entirely voluntary. Under the terms of the Act of 1972 it has always been clear that it was the duty of a United Kingdom court, when delivering final judgment, to override any rule of national law found to be in conflict with any directly enforceable rule of Community law. Similarly, when decisions of the European Court of Justice have exposed areas of United Kingdom statute law which failed to implement Council directives, Parliament has always loyally accepted the obligation to make appropriate and prompt amendments. Thus there is nothing in any way novel in according supremacy to rules of Community law in those areas to which they apply and to insist that, in the protection of rights under Community law, national courts must not be inhibited by rules of national law from granting interim relief in appropriate cases is no more than a logical recognition of that supremacy.'

66. This reasoning does not, I think, touch the conclusions which I have **A.4.3** expressed. As Lord Bridge makes crystal clear, its context was the requirement (stated by the Court of Justice on a reference under Article 177) that the courts of member states must posses the power to override national legislation, as necessary, to enable interim relief to be granted in protection of rights under Community law. The 'limitation of sovereignty' to which Lord Bridge referred arises only in the context of Community law's substantive provisions. The case is concerned with the primacy of those substantive provisions. It has no application where the question is, what is the legal foundation within which those substantive provisions enjoy their primacy, and by which the relation between the law and institutions of the European Union law and the British State ultimately rests. The foundation is English law. . . .

68. On this part of the case, then, I would reject [Counsel's] submissions. At the same time I would recognise for reasons I have given that the common law has in effect stipulated that the principal executive measures of the European Communities Act 1972 may only be repealed in the United Kingdom by specific provision, and not impliedly. It might be suggested that it matters little whether that result is given by the law of the European Union (as [Counsel] submits) or by the law of England untouched by Community law (as I would hold). But the difference is vital to a proper understanding of the relationship between European Union and domestic law.

69. In my judgment (as will by now be clear) the correct analysis of that relationship involves and requires these following four propositions.

"(1) All the specific rights and obligations which European Union law creates are by the European Communities Act 1972 incorporated into our domestic law and rank supreme: that is, anything in our substantive law inconsistent with any of these rights and obligations is abrogated or must be modified to avoid the inconsistency. This is true even where the inconsistent municipal provision is contained in primary legislation.

(2) The European Communities Act 1972 is a constitutional statute: that is, it cannot be impliedly repealed.

(3) The truth of (2) is derived, not from European Union law, but purely from the law of England: the common law recognises a category of constitutional statutes.

(4) The fundamental legal basis of the United Kingdom's relationship with the European Union rests with the domestic, not the European, legal powers. In the event, which no doubt would never happen in the real world, that a European measure was seen to be repugnant to a fundamental or constitutional right guaranteed by the law of England, a question would arise whether the general words of the European Communities Act 1972 were sufficient to incorporate the measure and give it overriding effect in domestic law. But that is very far from this case.

70. I consider that the balance struck by these four propositions gives full weight both to the proper supremacy of Community law and to the proper supremacy of the United Kingdom Parliament. By the former, I mean the supremacy of substantive Community law. By the latter, I mean the supremacy of the legal foundation within which those substantive provisions enjoy their primacy. The former is guaranteed by propositions (1) and (2). The latter is guaranteed by propositions (3) and (4). If this balance is understood, it will be seen that these two supremacies are in harmony, and not in conflict."

R. (McCANN) v MANCHESTER CROWN COURT[1]

DISTINCTION BETWEEN CRIMINAL AND CIVIL PROCEEDINGS

See Chapter 1, Section 5

Extract of the speech of Lord Steyn

"The Legislative Technique.

17. The aim of the criminal law is not punishment for its own sake but to permit   **A.5.1**
everyone to go about their daily lives without fear of harm to person or property.
Unfortunately, by intimidating people the culprits, usually small in number,
sometimes effectively silenced communities. Fear of the consequences of
complaining to the police dominated the thoughts of people: reporting incidents
to the police entailed a serious risk of reprisals. The criminal law by itself offered
inadequate protection to them. There was a model available for remedial
legislation. Before 1998 Parliament had, on a number of occasions, already used
the technique of prohibiting by statutory injunction conduct deemed to be
unacceptable and making a breach of the injunction punishable by penalties. It
may be that the Company Directors Disqualification Act 1986 was the precedent
for subsequent use of the technique. The civil remedy of disqualification enabled
the court to prohibit a person from acting as a director: s.1(1) of the 1985 Act:
R v Secretary of State for Trade and Industry, Ex p. McCormick[2]; *Official
Receiver v Stern*.[3] Breach of the order made available criminal penalties: ss.13
and 14 of the 1986 Act. In 1994 Parliament created the power to prohibit
trespassory assemblies which could result in serious disruption affecting communities, movements, and so forth: see s.70 of the Criminal Justice and Public Order
Act 1994 which amended Part II of the Public Order Act 1986 by inserting s.14A.
Section 14B which was introduced by the 1994 Act, created criminal offences in
respect of breaches. In the field of family law, statute created the power to make
residence orders, requiring a defendant to leave a dwelling house; or non

---

[1] [2002] 3 W.L.R. 131, HL.
[2] [1998] B.C.C. 379, 395C–F.
[3] [2000] 1 W.L.R. 2230.

molestation orders, requiring a defendant to abstain from threatening an associated person: ss.33(3) and (4) and s.42 of the Family Law Act 1996. The penalty for breach is punishment for contempt of court. The Housing Act 1996 created the power to grant injunctions against anti-social behaviour: s.152; s.153 (breach). This was, however, a power severely restricted in respect of locality. A broadly similar technique was adopted in the Protection from Harassment Act 1997: s.3; s.3(6) (breach). Post-dating the Crime and Disorder Act 1998, which is the subject matter of the present appeals, Parliament adopted a similar model in ss.14A and 14J (breach) of the Football Spectators Act 1989, inserted by s.1(1) of the Football (Disorder) Act 2000: *Gough v Chief Constable of the Derbyshire Constabulary*.[4] In all these cases the requirements for the granting of the statutory injunction depend on the criteria specified in the particular statute. The unifying element is, however, the use of the civil remedy of an injunction to prohibit conduct considered to be utterly unacceptable, with a remedy of criminal penalties in the event of disobedience.

18. There is no doubt that Parliament intended to adopt the model of a civil remedy of an injunction, backed up by criminal penalties, when it enacted s.1 of the Crime and Disorder Act 1998. The view was taken that the proceedings for an anti-social behaviour order would be civil and would not attract the rigour of the inflexible and sometimes absurdly technical hearsay rule which applies in criminal cases. If this supposition was wrong, in the sense that Parliament did not objectively achieve its aim, it would inevitably follow that the procedure for obtaining anti-social behaviour orders is completely or virtually unworkable and useless. If that is what the law decrees, so be it. My starting point is, however, an initial scepticism of an outcome which would deprive communities of their fundamental rights: see *Brown v Stott*[5]; per Lord Bingham of Cornhill, at p.836D; *per* Lord Hope of Craighead, at pp.850D and 850G; my judgment, at p.839E–F.

19. It is necessary to consider whether under domestic law proceedings under the first part of s.1 should be classified as criminal or civil proceedings. In law it is always essential to ask for what purpose a classification is to be made or a definition is to be attempted. It is necessary in order to decide whether the provisions of the Civil Evidence Act 1995, which permits the admission of hearsay evidence in civil proceedings, and the Magistrates' Courts (Hearsay Evidence in Civil Proceedings) Rules 1999, are available to establish the requirements of s.1(1). It is also relevant to the appropriate standard of proof to be adopted.

20. In a classic passage in *Proprietary Articles Trade Association v Attorney General for Canada*[6] Lord Atkin observed:

---

[4] [2001] 3 W.L.R. 1392.
[5] [2001] 2 W.L.R. 817.
[6] [1931] A.C. 310, 324.

'Criminal law connotes only the quality of such acts or omissions as are prohibited under appropriate penal provisions by authority of the state. The criminal quality of an act cannot be discerned by intuition; nor can it be discovered by reference to any standard but one: Is the act prohibited with penal consequences?'

In *Customs and Excise Commissioners v City of London Magistrates' Courts*[7] Lord Bingham of Cornhill C.J., expressed himself in similar vein:

'It is in my judgment the general understanding that criminal proceedings involve a formal accusation made on behalf of the state or by a private prosecutor that a defendant has committed a breach of the criminal law, and the state or the private prosecutor has instituted proceedings which may culminate in the conviction and condemnation of the defendant.'

21. Absent any special statutory definition, in the relevant contexts, this **A.5.2** general understanding must be controlling. Counsel for Clingham invited the House to approach the question from the point of view of the meaning given in decided cases to the words "criminal cause or matter" which appear in s.1(1)(a) of the Administration of Justice Act 1960 and s.18(1)(a) of the Supreme Court Act 1981. The decided cases on both sides of the line are helpfully summarised in *Taylor On Appeals*.[8] The cases were decided in the context of regulating and determining the appropriate appeal route. Often pragmatic considerations played a role. These cases do not help the true inquiry before the House and distract attention from the ordinary meaning of civil proceedings which must prevail. Similarly, the fact that proceedings under the first part of s.1 of the Act are classified as criminal in order to ensure the availability to defendants of legal assistance is in my view entirely neutral: see s.12(2) of the Access to Justice Act 1999 and para.1(2) of the Access to Justice Act 1999 (Commencement No.3, Transitional Provisions and Savings) Order 2000.[9] I would approach the matter by applying the tests enunciated by Lord Atkin and Lord Bingham of Cornhill, C.J.

22. Counsel for the defendants accepted that the purpose of Parliament was to cast proceedings under the first part of s.1, as opposed to proceedings for breach, in a civil mould. However, counsel submitted that objectively considered the objective was not achieved. They argued that in reality and in substance such proceedings are criminal in character. This is an important argument which must be carefully examined. The starting point is that in proceedings under the first part of s.1 the Crown Prosecution Service is not involved at all. At that stage there is no formal accusation of a breach of criminal law. The proceedings are

---

[7] [2000] 1 W.L.R. 2020, 2025.
[8] (2000) pp.515–518, paras 14–020—14–021.
[9] SI 2000/774.

initiated by the civil process of a complaint. Under s.1(1)(a) all that has to be established is that the person has acted:

> 'in an anti-social manner, that is to say, in a manner that caused or was likely to cause harassment, alarm or distress to one or more persons not of the same household as himself;'

This is an objective inquiry: mens rea as an ingredient of particular offences need not be proved. It is unnecessary to establish criminal liability. The true purpose of the proceedings is preventative. This appears from the heading of Pt 1. It is also clearly brought out by the requirement of s.1(1)(b):

> 'that such an order is necessary to protect persons in the local government area in which the harassment, alarm or distress was caused or was likely to be caused from further anti-social acts by him;'

It follows that the making of an anti-social behaviour order is not a conviction or condemnation that the person is guilty of an offence. It results in no penalty whatever. It cannot be entered on a defendant's record as a conviction. It is also not a recordable offence for the purpose of taking fingerprints: see s.27 of the Police and Criminal Evidence Act 1984.

23. Counsel for the defendants sought to avoid the consequences of this analysis by various arguments. First, they argued that the procedure leading to the making of an order under s.1(4) must be considered together with the proceedings for breach under s.1(10), the latter being undoubtedly criminal in character. I do not agree. These are separate and independent procedures. The making of the order will presumably sometimes serve its purpose and there will be no proceedings for breach. It is in principle necessary to consider the two stages separately.

24. Counsel next made a comparison between the requirements of s.1(1) and the ingredients of an offence under s.4A of the Public Order Act 1986. They submitted that there was a striking similarity. This proposition was not made good. It is sufficient to point out that s.4A of the 1986 Act requires proof of mens rea whereas s.1(1) does not. In any event, this is a barren exercise. It elides the critical point that s.1(1) itself does not prohibit any act. An anti-social behaviour order under s.1(4) does prohibit conduct specified in the order but by itself does not amount to a condemnation of guilt. It results in no penal sanction.

25. Counsel for the defendants also emphasised the consequences which an anti-social behaviour order may have for a defendant. This is an important factor. Section 1 is not meant to be used in cases of minor unacceptable behaviour but in cases which satisfy the threshold of persistent and serious anti-social behaviour. Given the threshold requirements of s.1(1) it can readily be accepted that the making of such an order against a person inevitably reflects seriously on

his character. In response to this argument Lord Phillips of Worth Matravers M.R. observed[10]:

> 'Many injunctions in civil proceedings operate severely upon those against whom they are ordered. In matrimonial proceedings a husband may be ordered to leave his home and not to have contact with his children. Such an order may be made as a consequence of violence which amounted to criminal conduct. But such an order is imposed not for the purpose of punishment but for protection of the family. This demonstrates that, when considering whether an order imposes a penalty or punishment, it is necessary to look beyond its consequence and to consider its purpose.'

Similarly, Mareva injunctions, which are notified to a defendant's bank, may have serious consequences. An Anton Piller order operates in some ways like a civil search warrant and may be particularly intrusive in its operation. Breach of such orders may result in penalties. Nevertheless, the injunctions are unquestionably civil.

26. The view that proceedings for an anti-social behaviour order under section 1 are civil in character is further supported by two important decisions. In *B v Chief Constable of Avon and Somerset Constabulary*[11] the question arose whether proceedings for a sex offender order under s.2 of the Act are civil. Section 2 is different in conception from section 1 in as much as an order can only be made in respect of a person who has already been convicted as a sex offender. On the other hand, its purpose is preventative "to protect the public from serious harm from him". Lord Bingham of Cornhill C.J. held[12]:   **A.5.3**

> 'The rationale of section 2 was, by means of an injunctive order, to seek to avoid the contingency of any further suffering by any further victim. It would also of course be to the advantage of a defendant if he were to be saved from further offending. As in the case of a civil injunction, a breach of the court's order may attract a sanction. But, also as in the case of a civil injunction, the order, although restraining the defendant from doing that which is prohibited, imposes no penalty or disability upon him. I am accordingly satisfied that, as a matter of English domestic law, the application is a civil proceeding, as Parliament undoubtedly intended it to be.'

To the same effect was the detailed reasoning in *Gough v Chief Constable of the Derbyshire Constabulary.*[13] It was held that a football banning order under

---

[10] [2001] 1 W.L.R. 1084, 1094–1095, para.39.
[11] [2001] 1 W.L.R. 340.
[12] At p.352, para.25.
[13] [2002] Q.B. 459; and on appeal at [2002] 3 W.L.R. 289.

ss.14A and 14B of the Football Spectators Act 1989 do not involve criminal penalties and are therefore civil character.

27. I conclude that proceedings to obtain an anti-social behaviour order are civil proceedings under domestic law.

IX. *The Classification Under Article 6.*

28. The question now arises whether, despite its domestic classification, an anti-social behaviour order nevertheless has a criminal character in accordance with the autonomous concepts of art.6. The fair trial guarantee under art.6(1) applies to both 'the determination of a (person's) civil rights' and 'the determination of any criminal charge'. On the other hand, only the latter attract the additional protections under arts 6(2) and 6(3). Insofar as the latter provisions apply to 'everyone charged with a criminal offence' it is well established in the jurisprudence of the European Court of Human Rights that this concept is co-extensive with the concept of the determination of any criminal charge: *Lutz v Germany*.[14] Germane to the present case is the minimum right under art.6(3)(d) of everyone charged with a criminal offence to examine or have examined witnesses against him or to obtain the attendance and examination of witnesses on his behalf under the same conditions as witnesses against him. If the proceedings under s.1 of the Act are criminal within the meaning of art.6, this provision is applicable. If it is civil, art.6(3)(d) is inapplicable.

29. Before I examine directly in the light of European jurisprudence the question whether proceedings involve a criminal charge, it is necessary to make clear that this is not one of those cases where the proceedings may fall outside art.6 altogether. Examples of such cases are given by *Emmerson and Ashworth, Human Rights and Criminal Justice*.[15] In the cases before the House the two principal respondents accept that the proceedings are civil in character and that they attract the fair trial guarantee under art.6(1). Counsel for the Secretary of State in the *McCann* case reserved his position. For my part, in the light of the particular use of the civil remedy of an injunction, as well as the defendant's right under art.8 to respect for his private and family life, it is clear that a defendant has the benefit of the guarantee applicable to civil proceedings under art.6.1. Moreover, under domestic English law they undoubtedly have a constitutional right to a fair hearing in respect of such proceedings.

30. In *Engel v The Netherlands (No.1)*,[16] the European Court established three criteria for determining whether proceedings are 'criminal' within the meaning of the Convention, namely (a) the domestic classification, (b) the nature of the offence, and (c) the severity of the potential penalty which the defendant risks incurring. The character and attributes of the proceedings for an anti-social behaviour order have been outlined. Domestically, they are properly classified as

---

[14] (1987) 10 E.H.R.R. 182.
[15] (2001) pp.152–166.
[16] (1976) 1 E.H.R.R. 647, 678–679, para.82.

civil. That is, however, only a starting point. Turning to factor (b), the position is that the order under the first part of section 1 does not constitute a finding that an offence has been committed: contrast the community charge decision in *Benham v United Kingdom*.[17] It is right, however, to observe that the third factor is the most important. Here the position is that the order itself involves no penalty. The established criteria suggest that the proceedings were not in respect of a criminal charge.

31. The House has been taken on a tour d'horizon of the leading decisions of the European Court: see the judgment of Potter L.J. in *Han v Customs and Excise Commissioners*[18] for a recent review of the European case law. It will serve no purpose to review again decisions far removed from the present case. What does emerge, however, is that there is, as Lord Bingham of Cornhill C.J. pointed out in *B v Chief Constable of Avon and Somerset Constabulary*,[19] no case in which the European Court has held proceedings to be criminal even though an adverse outcome for the defendant cannot result in any penalty. It could be said, of course, that there is scope for the law to be developed in this direction. On the other hand, an extensive interpretation of what is a criminal charge under art.6(1) would, by rendering the injunctive process ineffectual, prejudice the freedom of liberal democracies to maintain the rule of law by the use of civil injunctions. **A.5.4**

32. The closest case in support of the defendants' submission is *Steel v The United Kingdom*,[20] which is authority for the proposition that proceedings whereby in England and Wales a person may be bound over to keep the peace involve the determination of a criminal charge for the purposes of art.6. This power goes back many centuries: see *Percy v Director of Public Prosecutions*.[21] It is in a very real sense a judicial power sui generis. The European Court found a punitive element in the fact that the magistrates may commit to prison any person who refuses to be bound over not to breach the peace where there is evidence beyond reasonable doubt that his or her conduct caused or was likely to cause a breach of the peace and that he would otherwise cause a breach of the peace: para.48. There was an immediate and obvious penal consequence. Properly analysed this case does not assist the defendant's argument.

33. The conclusion I have reached is reinforced by a cogently reasoned judgment on the interpretation of art.6 by the Lord President (Rodger) in *S v Miller*.[22] Section 52(2) of the Children (Scotland) Act 1995 provides that a child may have to be subjected to compulsory measures of supervision when he 'has committed an offence'. The question arose whether in such proceedings art.6 is applicable. The Lord President observed, at pp.989–990:

---

[17] (1996) 22 E.H.R.R. 293.
[18] [2001] 1 W.L.R. 2253, 2269–2273, paras 55–64.
[19] [2001] 1 W.L.R. 340.
[20] (1998) 28 E.H.R.R. 603, 636, paras 48–49.
[21] [1995] 1 W.L.R. 1382, 1389H–1390H.
[22] 2001 S.C. 977.

'23 ... at the stage when S was arrested and charged by the police on 31 October, he was indeed 'charged with a criminal offence' in terms of article 6, since he was liable to be brought before a criminal court in proceedings which could have resulted in the imposition of a penalty. He remained "charged with a criminal offence" in terms of article 6 until the procurator fiscal decided the following day—in the language of section 43(5) of the Criminal Procedure Act—"not to proceed with the charge". At that point the criminal proceedings came to an end and the reporter initiated the procedures under the 1995 Act by arranging a hearing in terms of section 63(1). In my view, once the procurator fiscal has decided not to proceed with the charge against a child and so there is no longer any possibility of proceedings resulting in a penalty, any subsequent proceedings under the 1995 Act are not criminal for the purposes of article 6. Although the reporter does indeed intend to show that the child concerned committed an offence, this is not for the purpose of punishing him but in order to establish a basis for taking appropriate measures for his welfare. That being so, the child who is notified of grounds for referral setting out the offence in question is not thereby "charged with a criminal offence" in terms of article 6.

24 It is not now disputed, of course, that the children's hearing proceedings involve the determination of civil rights and obligations. Article 6 therefore applies. But, since the proceedings are not criminal, the specific guarantees in article 6(2) and (3) do not apply.'

I am in complete agreement with this reasoning as correctly reflecting the purpose of art.6. And it applies a fortiori to proceedings under s.1. After all, s.1(1) does not require proof of a criminal offence.

34. In my view an application for an anti-social behaviour order does not involve the determination of a criminal charge."

ATTORNEY-GENERAL'S REFERENCE (No.4 OF 2000)[1]

BURDENS OF PROOF ON THE ACCUSED IN CRIMINAL LEGISLATION

SEE CHAPTER 1, SECTION 5

Extract of the judgment of Latham L.J.[2]

"At the Crown Court, counsel for the Crown accepted that the acquitted person only bore an evidential burden in relation to the defence under s.11(2) of the Act. In other words he accepted that as the defendant was able to raise upon the evidence a real issue as to whether or not he had become a member of Hamas, or professed to be a member of Hamas, before it was a proscribed organisation, it was for the prosecution to establish to the criminal standard of proof that either his membership or professed membership had been after Hamas had been proscribed, or that he had taken part in the activities of the organisation after it had been proscribed. ... The Attorney General, in referring the matter to this court, is principally concerned with whether or not counsel for the prosecution was correct to concede that the acquitted person only had an evidential, as opposed to a legal burden of establishing the defence under s.11(2) of the Act.

A.6.1

Counsel for the Crown clearly made his concession on the belief that s.11(2) if construed so as to impose a legal burden of proof, that is the task of proving the defence on the balance of probabilities, would conflict with the presumption of innocence, and would accordingly be a breach of Art.6(2) of the Convention for the Protection of Human Rights and Fundamental Freedoms (the Convention). He did so on the basis of the decision of the House of Lords in *R. v Lambert*,[3] in which the House, strictly speaking obiter, determined, by a majority, that the provision with which the House was concerned, apparently imposing a legal burden on a defendant to establish a defence would, so construed, amount to a breach of Art.6(2); but their Lordships concluded that the provision could, in accordance with s.3(1) of the Human Rights Act 1998, be construed so as to

---

[1] [2003] 3 W.L.R. 1153, CA.
[2] At 1157–1166 (with omissions).
[3] [2002] 2 A.C. 545, HL.

impose an evidential burden only and would be proportionate and accordingly compatible with the Convention.

Since the case of Lambert there have been a number of cases in which the courts have grappled with the issue of how to deal as a result with statutory provisions providing for a defence to a charge. In *R v Drummond*[4] and *Sheldrake v Director of Public Prosecutions*[5] the courts considered provisions of the Road Traffic Acts. In *R. v Carass*[6] and *R. v Daniel*,[7] the courts considered provisions of the Insolvency Act 1966. In *R. v Halton Division Magistrates' Court and the Forestry Commission*[8] the court considered provisions of the Forestry Act 1967. This is not an exhaustive list of the cases in which the ambit of the decision of the House of Lords in *Lambert* has been considered. But they highlight a number of difficulties that are arising in practice, and indeed an apparent divergence of views that have emerged as to the right approach to this problem. In *Drummond* and the *Halton Magistrates* cases the courts held that the statutory provisions in question imposed a legal burden of proof on a defendant which was justified and proportionate in the public interest in its context, albeit prima facie in conflict with the presumption of innocence. In *Carass* and *Sheldrake* the courts applied the reasoning of the House of Lords in Lambert to construe what was apparently the imposition of a legal burden of proof as imposing merely an evidential burden of proof. In *Daniel*, the court held that it was bound by the decision in *Carass* but had clear reservations about the ability of the court to construe words which on their face appeared to impose a legal burden of proof as imposing merely an evidential one.

The varying consequences of the application of the views of the House of Lords in *Lambert* in these cases makes it clear to us that the first task of the court in this type of case is to determine the meaning of the statutory provision in question on ordinary canons of construction and to identify the context in terms of the mischief to which the statutory provisions are directed before turning to determine the effect of the Human Rights Act and the Convention.

... There is no dispute before us as to the proper interpretation of s.11 if the ordinary principles of construction of a statute are applied. The requirement for a person charged with the offence under subs.(2) to 'prove' the matters set out in (a) and (b) impose on him a legal burden of establishing both of those matters on the balance of probabilities. ... The purpose of the section, it seems to us is clear. ...

The reason for the defence was given by Lord Bassam in the House of Lords in the course of the debate on the second reading as follows:

'Clause 11(2) contains a defence to cover the very rare and specific set of circumstances in which a person becomes a member of an organisation

---

[4] [2001] 2 Cr. App. Rep. 25.
[5] [2003] EWHC Admin. 273 (QB).
[6] [2002] 2 Cr. App. Rep. 77.
[7] [2002] EWCA Crim. 959.
[8] [2003] EWHC Admin 272 (QB).

before it is proscribed and has played no part in it after its proscription. . . .
Having made an exception to the general rule that membership per se is an
offence, it seems reasonable that the onus should be on the defendant to
make the case that he or she has not played an active part in the organisation.'

This statement of the purpose of the provision underlines what seems to us to **A.6.2**
be the inescapable meaning and effect of s.11 taken as a whole. The offence itself
is complete on proof that the defendant belongs to the organisation or has
professed that he belongs to the organisation. The defence is only available to
two limited categories of persons. As to the first, that is the person who belonged
before the date of proscription and played no part in its activities after
proscription, there is no difficulty in understanding the rationale of excluding
such a person from the criminal consequences of the section. There would
otherwise be a real danger of giving to the section a retrospective effect. It is less
easy to see the justification for excluding the second category, namely a person
who professes membership. He could only be charged with an offence under
s.11(1) if he professed membership at some time after proscription. It follows
that the defence will be available to him if he first professed membership before
proscription but repeated it afterwards in circumstances where he played no
active part in the organisation. It might be thought that professing membership in
such circumstances would carry with it the same vice as professing membership
for the first time after proscription. Be that as it may, Parliament has determined
that the defence should be available to that category of person. What is of
particular significance is that the defence will inevitably be available to fewer and
fewer persons charged with the offence with the passage of time.

On that construction of the section, subs.11(2) involves no infringement of the
presumption of innocence. It provides an exception in a limited number of cases.
The effect of the judge's decision in the present case, is that wherever a defendant
raises on the evidence an issue as to his belonging to one of the two excluded
categories, the prosecution has to disprove that issue. That can only be justified
if s.11(2) involves an infringement of the defendant's Article 6(2) rights; in other
words it can only be right if in addition to proving membership or professed
membership of the proscribed organisation, there is a further necessary ingredient
of the offence, namely, that the defendant was not a member of the organisation
or a person who professed membership before proscription and had not taken part
in the activities of the organisation after it had been proscribed. If that element
is not a necessary ingredient of the offence, it is difficult to see how s.11(2) could
be said to interfere with the presumption of innocence.

. . . It is in our judgment quite clear that Parliament intended that a person
should be guilty of an offence under s.11(1) irrespective of whether or not he had
played any active part in the organisation. Section 11(2) therefore does not
infringe the presumption of innocence so as to breach Art.6(2) of the Convention.

Although we have referred in this judgment to the defence in s.11(2) of the Act as amounting to an exception, it is not an exception of the same sort as was considered in the cases of *Edwards* and *Hunt* referred to by Lord Steyn in *Lambert*. The courts in those cases discussed provisions of Acts which did not expressly impose on the defendant any burden, but which were held to have done so on the construction of the Act in question. A typical case of this type involves an allegation that a particular activity has been carried on without a licence. The Divisional Court considered this problem in the *Halton Magistrates* case to which we have already referred. It was a court again presided over by Clarke L.J., and the judgment was handed down on the same day as *Sheldrake*. Clarke L.J. giving the leading judgment, considered that in such cases the question was not whether or not the presumption of innocence had been infringed, if the burden of proving that the activity was carried out in accordance with the licence was a legal burden, because it clearly was. The question was whether or not the imposition of that burden was both justified and proportionate. He held that in the context of the Forestry Act 1967, it was.

That type of statutory provision is clearly different from the one under consideration in this case. In particular the context of those cases was that the statutory provisions were regulatory in nature.

HOUSE OF LORDS WRITTEN ANSWERS ON THE *RAM* DOCTRINE

MINISTERIAL ACTION AND EXPENDITURE WITHOUT EXPRESS STATUTORY AUTHORITY

SEE CHAPTER 1, SECTION 6

Written Answer January 22, 2003[1]

Lord Lester of Herne Hill asked Her Majesty's Government:

Whether, in the light of the Performance and Innovation Unit's report *Privacy*   **A.7.1**
and data-sharing: The way forward for public services (April 2002), they will
publish the Ram doctrine.

The Parliamentary Secretary, Lord Chancellor's Department (Baroness
Scotland of Asthal):

The Ram doctrine, which is set out in a memorandum dated November 2, 1945
from the then First Parliamentary Counsel, Granville Ram, states that a Minister
of the Crown may exercise any powers that the Crown has power to exercise,
except in so far as the Minister is precluded by statute from so doing, either
expressly or by necessary implication. Generally, legally privileged advice to
government is not disclosed but, given the age of the advice, we are content to
do so in this case and the text of the memorandum has been made available in the
Library.

Written Answer February 25, 2003[2]

Lord Lester of Herne Hill asked Her Majesty's Government:

Whether they consider it to be in accordance with contemporary principles of
British parliamentary democracy for legislation to be necessary (in a political, if

---

[1] HL Deb. January 22, 2003 WA 98–99.
[2] HL Deb. February 25, 2003 WA 12.

not a legal sense) to authorise an extension of Ministers' powers; and, if not, why not; and

Further to the Written Answer by Baroness Scotland of Asthal on 22 January (WA 98), whether reliance on the so-called Ram doctrine is compatible with a modern system of public law, including the principles of legality and legal certainty; and, if so, how; and

In what circumstances and upon how many occasions during the past five years Ministers of the Crown and their departments have relied upon the Ram doctrine as the legal basis for the exercise of their public powers; and

What were the circumstances that gave rise to the Ram doctrine.

The Parliamentary Secretary, Lord Chancellor's Department (Baroness Scotland of Asthal):

The Ram doctrine reflects a well-established principle of constitutional law. Like many other persons, Ministers and their departments have common law powers which derive from the Crown's status as a corporation sole. Ministers and their departments also exercise prerogative powers of the Crown. Common law and prerogative powers may be limited by statute either expressly or by necessary implication and in this respect are subject to direct parliamentary control. The courts have recognised the legitimacy of these principles.

Whether legislation is necessary or appropriate to authorise government actions depends on the circumstances and the matters in issue. Sometimes it will be clear that legislation is needed, for example, when the proposed action might substantially interfere with human rights. In such cases a clear and reasonably accessible legal framework is required in order to comply with human rights law. At other times, the legal necessity for legislation will not be clear, in which case a political as well as a legal judgment has to be made as to whether legislation is desirable. Such a judgment may take into account a number of factors, including whether the proposed action is a priority and whether authorising that action by legislating represents a good use of Parliamentary time.

The principles governing the use of the annual Appropriation Act to provide authority for the exercise of functions by government departments where such functions may involve financial liabilities extending beyond a year are stated in the Public Accounts Committee Concordant, 1932 (see Annex 2.1 of Government Accounting 2000).

During the past five years, as in previous periods, the common law powers of the Crown have often been relied upon as the legal basis for government action. Common law powers form the basis of such governmental actions as entering into contracts, employing staff, conveying property and other management functions not provided for by statute either expressly or by implication. To require parliamentary authority for every exercise of the common law powers exercisable by the Crown either would impose upon Parliament an impossible burden or produce legislation in terms that simply reproduced the common law.

Finally, the circumstances that gave rise to the Ram doctrine are that the Ram opinion (the text of which was made available when an earlier Question was answered on 22 January 2003) was given when the Ministers of the Crown (Transfer of Functions) Bill was being considered. This Bill later became the Ministers of the Crown (Transfer of Functions) Act 1946. The opinion addresses the need for legislation to confer power to add new functions to existing government departments by order. At that time Ministers were considering machinery of government changes following the Second World War.

Written Answer March 24, 2003[3]

Lord Lester of Herne Hill asked Her Majesty's Government:

Further to the Written Answer by Baroness Scotland of Asthal on 25 February **A.7.2**
(WA 12–13), whether the courts have recognised the legitimacy of the principles stated in the second paragraph of the Answer; and, if so, whether they will identify the reported cases in respect of each principle; and

Further to the Written Answer by Baroness Scotland of Asthal on 25 February (WA 12–13), whether the reference to "human rights law" includes the obligations imposed upon the United Kingdom by international treaties other than the European Convention on Human Rights, including the International Covenant on Civil and Political Rights, the International Covenant on Economic Social and Cultural Rights and the International Labour Organisation Conventions; and, if not, why not; and

Further to the Written Answer by Baroness Scotland of Asthal on 25 February (WA 12–13), what criteria are used, in cases not involving the need to comply with human rights law, to decide whether there is legal need for legislation to authorise an extension of Ministers' powers; and

Further to the Written Answer by Baroness Scotland of Asthal on 25 February (WA 12–13), whether they consider that the common law principles of legality and legal certainty extend beyond circumstances where proposed action might substantially interfere with human rights; and if so, what are those circumstances; and

Further to the Written Answer by Baroness Scotland of Asthal on 25 February (WA 12–13), what were the instances during the past five years in which they decided that legislation was undesirable to authorise an extension of Ministers' powers; and

Further to the Written Answer by Baroness Scotland of Asthal on 25 February (WA 12–13), which powers of Ministers have been extended without legislative authority during the past five years.

---

[3] HL Deb. March 24, 2003 WA 59–60.

Baroness Scotland of Asthal:

Ministers can act only within the law. It follows that an extension of ministerial power will always require legislation (or, conceivably, a change in the common law). Legislation will also be necessary where what is proposed requires not only the exercise of powers but also, for example, the imposition of legal obligations, the creation of offences, or the raising of taxes.

If, however, it is proposed that Ministers exercise powers that are already available at common law to private individuals, or to the Crown by virtue of the prerogative, there is no legal requirement for legislation.

The case for putting existing powers onto a statutory footing will therefore depend not on strict law but on the matters of convention, good governance and practicality discussed in the previous Answer. These include the considerations of propriety addressed by the Public Accounts Committee Concordat mentioned in that Answer. They include also the principles of legal certainty, accessibility and clarity, which the Government regard as important in their own right, quite apart from human rights considerations.

In considering the possibility of legislation, the Government indeed have in mind all their international treaty obligations. As well as the European Convention on Human Rights, these include the International Covenant on Civil and Political Rights, the International Covenant on Economic Social and Cultural Rights and the International Labour Organisation Conventions.

The use of non-statutory powers was discussed by the House of Lords in the *Fire Brigade Union* case [1995] 2 A.C. 513.[4] The Ram doctrine is being considered by the Court of Appeal in a current case, *R. (Hooper) v Secretary of State for Work and Pensions.*[5]

Written Answer April 9, 2003[6]

Lord Lester of Herne Hill asked Her Majesty's Government:

A.7.3   Further to the Written Answer by Baroness Scotland of Asthal on 24 March (WA 59–60), whether they will give the main examples of circumstances during the past five years in which they decided, in accordance with the Ram doctrine, that legislation was undesirable.

Baroness Scotland of Asthal:

Occasions on which the Government have chosen not to legislate in order to provide statutory authority for an action that is in any event lawful at common law are necessarily difficult to categorise. No list is maintained.

---

[4] See Chapter 10, para.10.1.14.
[5] See Chapter 1, Section 6.
[6] HL Deb. April 9, 2003 WA 38.

However, the Government recognise limits to the reliance that should be placed on non-statutory authority. For example, in accordance with Government Accounting, paragraph 11.3.33, departmental estimates should identify expenditure which rests on the sole authority of the appropriation Act. This is done by the use of symbols in the notes to the estimates. Departments are also required constantly to review continuing provision to ensure that it complies with the 1932 concordat[7] (referred to in previous Written Answers) so far as possible.

It follows that scrutiny of the estimates for each year should disclose the main cases in which expenditure rested on the appropriation Act, without other statutory provision.

---

[7] See Chapter 1, Section 6.

BLACKBURN v ATTORNEY-GENERAL[1]

PRACTICAL CONSTRAINTS ON PARLIAMENTARY SOVEREIGNTY

SEE CHAPTER 1, SECTIONS 1 AND 2

Extract of judgment of Lord Denning M.R.

"We have all been brought up to believe that, in legal theory, one Parliament **A.8.1** cannot bind another and that no Act is irreversible. But legal theory does not always march alongside political reality. Take the Statute of Westminster 1931, which takes away the power of Parliament to legislate for the dominions. Can anyone imagine that Parliament could or would reverse that statute? Take the Acts which have granted independence to the dominions and territories overseas. Can anyone imagine that Parliament could or would reverse those laws and take away their independence? Most clearly not. Freedom once given cannot be taken away. Legal theory must give way to practical politics. It is as well to remember the remark of Lord Sankey L.C. in *British Coal Corporation v Regem*[2]—

' . . . the Imperial Parliament could, as a matter of abstract law, repeal or disregard s.4 of the Statute [of Westminster]. But that is theory and has no relation to realities.'

What are the realities here? If Her Majesty's Ministers sign this treaty [to join the Common Market, as it then was, now the European Union] and Parliament enacts provisions to implement it, I do not envisage that Parliament would afterwards go back on it and try to withdraw from it. But, if Parliament should do so, then I say we will consider that event when it happens. We will then say whether Parliament can lawfully do it or not.

Both sides referred us to the valuable article by Professor H. W. R. Wade in the Cambridge Law Journal[3] in which he said that 'sovereignty is a political fact for which no purely legal authority can be constituted'. That is true. We must wait

---

[1] [1971] 2 All E.R. 1380, 1381–82, CA.
[2] [1935] A.C. 500, 520, HL.
[3] [1954–55] C.L.J. at p.196.

to see what happens before we pronounce on sovereignty in the Common Market.

So, whilst in theory Mr Blackburn is quite right in saying that no Parliament can bind another, and that any Parliament can reverse what a previous Parliament has done, nevertheless so far as this court is concerned, I think we will wait until that day comes. We will not pronounce on it today."

SPEECH[1] OF THE MINISTER OF STATE FOR THE CABINET OFFICE[2] ON INTRODUCING SECOND READING OF THE BILL FOR THE REGULATORY REFORM ACT 2001[3]

PURPOSE OF REGULATORY REFORM ORDERS

SEE CHAPTER 3, SECTION 9

Extract of Minister's speech

"The Bill will provide a major tool for this and future governments to reform   **A.9.1**
entire regulatory regimes and to tackle unnecessary, overlapping, over-complex
and over-burdensome legislation. It builds on the acknowledged strengths of the
deregulation order-making procedure,[4] including the rigorous parliamentary
scrutiny of proposed orders, and provides additional safeguards. It facilitates
reducing the burden of regulation. . . .

---

[1] HL Deb. December 21, 2000 cc.850–851.
[2] Lord Falconer of Thoroton.
[3] 2001 c.6.
[4] This is a reference to the system of deregulation orders under the Deregulation and Contracting Out Act 1994, the fore-runner to the 2001 Act, which permitted orders to be made relaxing certain kinds of regulation, but in a more limited way than is permitted by the 2001 Act. Although there are a few Deregulation Orders which continue to have effect, they are effectively outmoded by the 2001 Act and can be disregarded as a continuing form of legislation. In the course of the same speech on the Second Reading of the Bill for the 2001 Act the Minster of State addressed the previous system in the following terms: "There have been some notable successes. The Bills of Exchange Order (1996/2993) saved the banking industry tens of millions of pounds in costs by removing an unnecessary statutory requirement for the processing of cheques; and the check-off order (1998/129) removed the need for three-yearly re-authorisation of deduction of trade union subscriptions from pay, thereby reducing costs for business. Although the process has worked well, limitations identified in the power mean that, with only 46 orders to date, it has been something of a disappointment in terms of the scale of the deregulation delivered. The peak year of activity was 1996 with 23 orders, tailing off ever since—but not because of lack of will; rather, the supply of simple statutory burdens on business that the 1994 Act was designed to remove is drying up. We can only fish for deregulation orders in the pool of pre-1994 legislation. We want to do more and we need the right tools for the job."

Our Bill is evolutionary in approach, building on two propositions. I refer first to the deregulation order-making power in Sections 1 to 4 of the Deregulation and Contracting Out Act 1994. . . . Experience has taught us the value of the new kind of amendable secondary legislation created by the 1994 Act.

. . . Regulation is important. Getting it right first time is important, as is ensuring that the benefits must justify the costs. But the ability to change legislation subsequently to reflect changes in the world around us is just as important.

We intend preserving the strengths of the existing deregulation process. First, thorough and effective consultation will remain the gateway to the order-making process; secondly, the two Houses will be true co-equals in the scrutiny process—highly controversial or party-political measures will naturally remain more suited to debate on the Floor of the House; and, thirdly, the rigours of the scrutiny process will also be preserved and enhanced. Each proposed order must undergo an intense scrutiny. After consultation, it has to go before a committee in each House not once, but twice, with Ministers required to provide detailed explanatory material in justification.

. . . It is not only business that will benefit, but also individuals, the voluntary sector, charities and the wider public sector too.

The ability to remove burdens from the wider public sector should not be seen as a charter for the Government to abrogate their responsibilities. Neither we nor the committees have found a satisfactory way to differentiate between proposals that would remove minor administrative burdens from government and those that would, for instance, remove a Minister's duty to provide essential public services. The Bill therefore provides that Ministers will not be able to remove burdens that fall solely on themselves or their departments. Somebody else would have to benefit too.

We should like to see a shift in gear. Until now the deregulation process has produced generally small, but significant, proposals. We should like to see this high quality scrutiny process used for more substantial items, such as reform of fire safety legislation currently spread over 120 Acts; or reform of weights and measures legislation. Those are the sorts of worthwhile reforms that are well overdue and may not otherwise see the light of day. . . .

The Bill redefines 'burden' to include any limit on the statutory powers of any person. This is an important change. We envisage that regulatory reform orders should be able to deal with circumstances where people do not have the legal authority to do perfectly sensible things. In line with our National Childcare Strategy, for example, we propose to enable school governing bodies to offer after-hours childcare, which at present they can do only if they provide education at the same time. This is something for which many schools have asked."

ABSTRACT OF SCHEDULE 4 TO THE SCOTLAND ACT 1998[1]

ENACTMENTS, &c. PROTECTED FROM MODIFICATION

SEE CHAPTER 4, SECTION 2

Part I

The Protected Provisions

Particular enactments

1(1) An Act of the Scottish Parliament cannot modify, or confer power by **A.10.1**
subordinate legislation to modify, any of the following provisions.
(2) The provisions are—

    (a) Articles 4 and 6 of the Union with Scotland Act 1706 and of the Union
        with England Act 1707 so far as they relate to freedom of trade,

    (b) the Private Legislation Procedure (Scotland) Act 1936,

    (c) the following provisions of the European Communities Act 1972—
        Section 1 and Schedule 1,
        Section 2, other than . . . ,
        Section 3(1) and (2),
        Section 11(2),

    (d) . . .

    (f) the Human Rights Act 1998.

The law on reserved matters

2(1) An Act of the Scottish Parliament cannot modify, or confer power by
subordinate legislation to modify, the law on reserved matters.

---

[1] 1998 c.46.

(2) In this paragraph, "the law on reserved matters" means—

    (a) any enactment the subject-matter of which is a reserved matter and which is comprised in an Act of Parliament or subordinate legislation under an Act of Parliament, and

    (b) any rule of law which is not contained in an enactment and the subject-matter of which is a reserved matter,
    and in this sub-paragraph "Act of Parliament" does not include this Act.

(3) Sub-paragraph (1) applies in relation to a rule of Scots private law or Scots criminal law (whether or not contained in an enactment) only to the extent that the rule in question is special to a reserved matter or the subject-matter of the rule is—

    (a) interest on sums due in respect of taxes or excise duties and refunds of such taxes or duties . . . ,

3(1) Paragraph 2 does not apply to modifications which—

    (a) are incidental to, or consequential on, provision made (whether by virtue of the Act in question or another enactment) which does not relate to reserved matters, and

    (b) do not have a greater effect on reserved matters than is necessary to give effect to the purpose of the provision.

(2) In determining for the purposes of sub-paragraph (1)(b) what is necessary to give effect to the purpose of a provision, any power to make laws other than the power of the Parliament is to be disregarded.

This Act

4(1) An Act of the Scottish Parliament cannot modify, or confer power by subordinate legislation to modify, this Act.
(2) This paragraph does not apply to modifying sections . . .

Enactments modified by this Act

. . .

Shared powers

6 An Act of the Scottish Parliament cannot modify, or confer power by subordinate legislation to modify, any enactment so far as the enactment relates to powers exercisable by a Minister of the Crown by virtue of section 56.

788

Part II

General Exceptions

Restatement, etc.

7(1) Part I of this Schedule does not prevent an Act of the Scottish Parliament—   **A.10.2**

    (a) restating the law (or restating it with such modifications as are not prevented by that Part), or

    (b) repealing any spent enactment,
       or conferring power by subordinate legislation to do so.

(2) For the purposes of paragraph 2, the law on reserved matters includes any restatement in an Act of the Scottish Parliament, or subordinate legislation under such an Act, of the law on reserved matters if the subject-matter of the restatement is a reserved matter.

Effect of Interpretation Act 1978

8 Part I of this Schedule does not prevent the operation of any provision of the Interpretation Act 1978.

Change of title etc

. . .

Accounts and audit and maladministration

Subordinate legislation

11 (1) Part I of this Schedule does not prevent an Act of the Scottish Parliament modifying, or conferring power by subordinate legislation to modify, any enactment for or in connection with any of the following purposes.
(2) Those purposes are—

    (a) making different provision in respect of the document by which a power to make subordinate legislation within sub-paragraph (3) is to be exercised,

    (b) making different provision (or no provision) for the procedure, in relation to the Parliament, to which legislation made in the exercise of such a power (or the instrument or other document in which it is contained) is to be subject,

(c) applying any enactment comprised in or made under an Act of the Scottish Parliament relating to the documents by which such powers may be exercised.

(3) The power to make the subordinate legislation, or a power to confirm or approve the legislation, must be exercisable by—

(a) a member of the Scottish Executive,

(b) any Scottish public authority with mixed functions or no reserved functions,

(c) any other person (not being a Minister of the Crown) within devolved competence.

. . .

EXTRACT OF *BETTER POLICY MAKING: A GUIDE TO REGULATORY IMPACT ASSESSMENT*[1]

THE NATURE AND PURPOSE OF THE REGULATORY IMPACT ASSESSMENT

See Chapter 5, Section 1

What is an RIA?

1.1 A Regulatory Impact Assessment (RIA) is a tool which informs policy decisions. It is an assessment of the impact of policy options in terms of the costs, benefits and risks of a proposal. It is not specific to the UK Civil Service—many countries use a similar analysis to assess their proposed regulations and large organisations appraise their investment decisions in similar ways too. . . .   **A.11.1**

4.2 The full RIA will accompany legislation when it is presented to Parliament. It becomes a final RIA when it is signed by the responsible Minister and placed in the House library. It should also be placed on your departmental website.

4.3 The contents of a full/final RIA:

- identify the policy objectives;

- identify and quantify the risks that the proposal is addressing;

- describe the remaining options, explain how each option would fit with existing requirements and describe the key risks associated with the options, and how these can be mitigated;

- identify the business sectors affected;

- set out any issues of equity and fairness;

- compare the benefits and costs for each option considered in the partial RIA.

---

[1] *Better Policy Making: A guide to Regulatory Impact Assessment*—a Cabinet Office publication published in January 2003 and available on the Cabinet Office website.

At this stage the estimates of costs and benefits should be much more precise,[2] as you will have the information from the consultation as well as from further data collection and analysis being done within your department. Where there are uncertainties about the impacts, use ranges rather than being spuriously accurate (*e.g.* "£1–2 million"). Always spell out your assumptions underlying the analysis of costs and benefits, and provide references to data sources and data analysis methodologies used. And undertake sensitivity analysis on those assumptions where there is uncertainty. The estimates of costs and benefits should be on a per annum basis and, where necessary, discounted.

Costs should be split between policy and implementation costs. . . . By now[3] it should be possible to quantify and place a monetary value on all impacts. In the few cases where this is not possible then quantify what you can and provide detailed qualitative analysis where you cannot. Remember that there needs to be enough analysis of impacts to enable Ministers to decide whether or not the benefits justify the costs and for any external scrutiny to take place;

- also consider other costs and benefits—*i.e.* not just those to firms, charities and the voluntary sector but also to consumers/individuals, the public sector and to the economy at large, taking in the economic, social and environmental effects. These costs should be recorded separately from the costs to business, charities and the voluntary sector;

- consider any distributional impacts, clearly identifying both the positive and negative aspects of any transfers of income or redistribution of opportunities;

- summarise who or what sectors bear the costs and benefits of each option;

- address any unintended consequences and indirect costs;

- include a simple or a detailed Competition Assessment according to the result of the filter test . . . ;

- include details of the Small Firms' Impact Test and any comments from the Small Business Service;

- set out the enforcement arrangements for securing compliance with each of the proposed options, as well as a consideration of the risks involved with this, and include your plans for guidance;

- say how the policy will be monitored and evaluated/reviewed, *e.g.* set an appropriate point at which to look back at what the actual costs and benefits were;

- provide a summary of the results of the consultation exercise, responses received from different sectors or types of business/body (where these vary)

---

[2] Than in the initial assessment produced at the stage of policy development.
[3] When legislation comes to be prepared and introduced.

and set out how/whether you have changed the assumptions, costings and recommendations following consultation;

■ summarise the impacts, including the impact of each option on small firms and any measures for helping then comply; and

■ recommend a preferred option, giving reasons based on the elements of the RIA, in particular the analysis of the benefit and costs.

Implementation

4.4 Consider any other changes that are coming in at the same time. Would it make sense to have a common starting date, or would it help businesses if you staggered the start dates? Generally, businesses prefer changes to happen in a co-ordinated way—for example, all payroll changes to be effective from April. If there are changes happening throughout the year, businesses will have to continually watch out for changes. There is a danger that they may miss the changes, or may ignore them completely."

FIRST REPORT OF SESSION 2002–03 OF THE HOUSE OF COMMONS SELECT COMMITTEE ON MODERNISATION OF THE HOUSE OF COMMONS (*PROGRAMMING OF BILLS*)[1]

ADVANTAGES AND DISADVANTAGES OF PROGRAMMING OF BILLS

SEE CHAPTER 5, SECTION 2

Extract of Report of the Committee

"Benefits of programming

12. There are a number of ways in which programming, when it is done well, assists the scrutiny of legislation. It provides Members with a clear idea of which parts of a bill will be debated when, allowing them to concentrate on those parts of a bill in which they are most interested. By providing greater certainty of voting times in the House, it also enables Members and committees to plan their work overall more effectively. The greater certainty of timing is also beneficial for outside groups. Often it is the case that a pressure group will be interested in only one part of a bill, particularly in the case of lengthy and complex bills which deal with a wide range of areas, such as the Finance Bill. Knowing, at the beginning of the committee stage, when that part of the bill will be debated makes it easier for them to plan the delivery of briefing material to members of a standing committee. **A.12.1**

13. Programming should allow the House and committees to plan their consideration of a bill more effectively so that more time is made available to consider those parts of a bill which are of interest to the Opposition and backbenchers, while less time may be devoted to those parts of the bill which are more straightforward and less controversial. The Government will inevitably get its legislation, subject to the agreement of the House. Lengthy debates, motivated largely by the desire of the Opposition or groups of backbenchers—of whatever

---

[1] H.C. 1222—November 3, 2003.

party—to obstruct legislation are ultimately fruitless, but are part of our democratic process. Such debates can reflect very poorly on the House as a whole and do little to persuade the public that Parliament is enhancing the legislative process by debating bills in a mature and thoughtful way.

14. It is nonetheless vitally important that sufficient time is made available for debating those parts of a bill to which the Opposition genuinely attach importance, and programming can be an effective vehicle for achieving this.

15. In tandem with programming, the Government has introduced greater pre-legislative scrutiny of bills. Pre-legislative scrutiny has been incorporated into the core tasks for select committees, and the number of bills which are laid in draft for consideration by a select or joint committee continues to grow. During the 2000–01 Session, three draft bills were published for pre-legislative scrutiny; in 2001–02, there were five such bills. In the current Session (2002–03), there have been ten: six were considered by departmental select committees one by the Human Rights Committee and three by joint committees specially appointed for the purpose. Pre-legislative scrutiny provides a vehicle for the careful, planned consideration of bills before they reach the floor of the House. In some cases, Committees have had to begin pre-legislative scrutiny before a draft bill has been available.

Drawbacks of programming

A.12.2   16. One important concern which has been raised about the programming process is the extent to which certain groups of amendments, clauses and schedules are passed with no debate, the relevant questions being put forthwith when an internal knife falls. In the current Session, 23 Government bills have been subject to a programme order in standing committee. Of these: a) in six cases, the committee ran ahead of the timetable throughout proceedings, so the knives never fell, the programme order thus had no effect at all on the length of debate; b)in nine cases, the knives fell in such a way as to leave a significant number of clauses and schedules undebated. c)in the remaining cases, some knives fell and some did not, leaving only a few clauses or schedules undebated.

17. The total number of clauses and schedules which are not debated in standing committee is not always a reliable indicator of the extent to which a bill was or was not properly considered. It may be that the programme order has had the undesirable effect of curtailing debate on controversial matters on which Members wished to speak; it may or may not be that the clauses or schedules which went undebated would not have been the subject of prolonged scrutiny by the standing committee anyway. Most bills contain some minor or technical matters—schedules of minor and consequential amendments and repeals, for example—which rarely excite much interest in committee. It was not unusual, before the advent of programming, for parts of bills to go through at both committee and report stage without any debate, either because nobody had anything to say about them or because of deliberate attempts to filibuster.

18. Furthermore, it is worth noting that, of the nine cases this Session where significant parts of a bill went through committee without debate, three had been the subject of pre-legislative scrutiny. In another, the Planning and Compulsory Purchase Bill, was re-committed and carried-over, allowing time for another standing committee stage and further consideration in the next Session.

19. Nonetheless, concern about the volume of legislation which passes undebated is entirely legitimate, whether the lack of scrutiny is the result of a programme order or the absence of a programme order. There is a danger that, where programme orders specify unnecessarily short timetables, or where time is badly allocated within the overall limits set out in the original programme order, programming will be seen as only a convenience for the Government, allowing it to get legislation through the House in a hurry. . . .

Responsibility for the effective use of programming

28. It is important for all sides to recognise that programming is here to stay and, **A.12.3** if it is implemented correctly, can help to enhance the legislative process in a number of ways. It is not simply a tool of Government, to be invoked only at its convenience and in its own interests; it is a set of procedures of the House and, as such, Members in all parts of the House bear responsibility for its efficient operation. We believe that the Government, in the form of the Ministers and Whips responsible for each bill, bears the primary responsibility for ensuring that programming works effectively.

However, it is also incumbent on the Opposition and backbench Members to engage constructively in the process to ensure that bills receive proper scrutiny. One aim of programming is to allow the House to devote more time to those parts of bills to which the Opposition, or groups of backbenchers, attach importance. Failure to engage with the process undermines this objective in a way which is helpful to nobody."

INTERINSTITUTIONAL AGREEMENT OF DECEMBER 22, 1998 ON COMMON GUIDELINES FOR THE QUALITY OF DRAFTING OF COMMUNITY LEGISLATION.[1]

QUALITY OF DRAFTING OF EUROPEAN LEGISLATION

See Chapter 8, Section 1

Extract of the Agreement

General principles

1. Community legislative acts shall be drafted clearly, simply and precisely. **A.13.1**

2. The drafting of Community acts shall be appropriate to the type of act concerned and, in particular, to whether or not it is binding (Regulation, Directive, Decision, recommendation or other act).

3. The drafting of acts shall take account of the persons to whom they are intended to apply, with a view to enabling them to identify their rights and obligations unambiguously, and of the persons responsible for putting the acts into effect.

4. Provisions of acts shall be concise and their content should be as homogeneous as possible. Overly long articles and sentences, unnecessarily convoluted wording and excessive use of abbreviations should be avoided.

5. Throughout the process leading to their adoption, draft acts shall be framed in terms and sentence structures which respect the multilingual nature of Community legislation; concepts or terminology specific to any one national legal system are to be used with care.

6. The terminology used in a given act shall be consistent both internally and with acts already in force, especially in the same field.

Identical concepts shall be expressed in the same terms, as far as possible without departing from their meaning in ordinary, legal or technical language.

---

[1] O.J.C. 73, 17.3.1999.

Different parts of the act

A.13.2   7. All Community acts of general application shall be drafted according to a standard structure (title—preamble—enacting terms—annexes, where necessary).

8. The title of an act shall give as succinct and full an indication as possible of the subject matter which does not mislead the reader as to the content of the enacting terms. Where appropriate, the full title of the act may be followed by a short title.

9. The purpose of the citations is to set out the legal basis of the act and the main steps in the procedure leading to its adoption.

10. The purpose of the recitals is to set out concise reasons for the chief provisions of the enacting terms, without reproducing or paraphrasing them. They shall not contain normative provisions or political exhortations.

11. Each recital shall be numbered.

12. The enacting terms of a binding act shall not include provisions of a non-normative nature, such as wishes or political declarations, or those which repeat or paraphrase passages or articles from the Treaties or those which restate legal provisions already in force.

Acts shall not include provisions which enunciate the content of other articles or repeat the title of the act.

13. Where appropriate, an article shall be included at the beginning of the enacting terms to define the subject matter and scope of the act.

14. Where the terms used in the act are not unambiguous, they should be defined together in a single article at the beginning of the act. The definitions shall not contain autonomous normative provisions.

15. As far as possible, the enacting terms shall have a standard structure (subject matter and scope—definitions—rights and obligations—provisions conferring implementing powers—procedural provisions—implementing measures—transitional and final provisions).

The enacting terms shall be subdivided into articles and, depending on their length and complexity, titles, chapters and sections. When an article contains a list, each item on the list should be identified by a number or a letter rather than an indent.

Internal and external references

16. References to other acts should be kept to a minimum. References shall indicate precisely the act or provision to which they refer. Circular references (references to an act or an article which itself refers back to the initial provision) and serial references (references to a provision which itself refers to another provision) shall also be avoided.

17. A reference made in the enacting terms of a binding act to a non-binding act shall not have the effect of making the latter binding. Should the drafters wish

to render binding the whole or part of the content of the non-binding act, its terms should as far as possible be set forth as part of the binding act.

Amending acts

18. Every amendment of an act shall be clearly expressed. Amendments shall take the form of a text to be inserted in the act to be amended. Preference shall be given to replacing whole provisions (articles or subdivisions of articles) rather than inserting or deleting individual sentences, phrases or words. **A.13.3**

An amending act shall not contain autonomous substantive provisions which are not inserted in the act to be amended.

19. An act not primarily intended to amend another act may set out, at the end, amendments of other acts which are a consequence of changes which it introduces. Where the consequential amendments are substantial, a separate amending act should be adopted.

Final provisions, repeals and annexes

20. Provisions laying down dates, time limits, exceptions, derogations and extensions, transitional provisions (in particular those relating to the effects of the act on existing situations) and final provisions (entry into force, deadline for transposition and temporal application of the act) shall be drawn up in precise terms. **A.13.4**

Provisions on deadlines for the transposition and application of acts shall specify a date expressed as day/month/year. In the case of Directives, those deadlines shall be expressed in such a way as to guarantee an adequate period for transposition.

21. Obsolete acts and provisions shall be expressly repealed. The adoption of a new act should result in the express repeal of any act or provision rendered inapplicable or redundant by virtue of the new act.

22. Technical aspects of the act shall be contained in the annexes, to which individual reference shall be made in the enacting terms of the act and which shall not embody any new right or obligation not set forth in the enacting terms.

Annexes shall be drawn up in accordance with a standardised format."

JOINT PRACTICAL GUIDE FOR THE DRAFTING OF COMMUNITY LEGISLATION[1]

QUALITY OF DRAFTING OF EUROPEAN LEGISLATION

See Chapter 8, Section 1

Extract of the Guide

1. COMMUNITY LEGISLATIVE ACTS SHALL BE DRAFTED CLEARLY, SIMPLY AND PRECISELY. **A.14.1**

1.1. The drafting of a legislative act must be:

clear, easy to understand and unambiguous;

simple, concise, containing no unnecessary elements;

precise, leaving no uncertainty in the mind of the reader.

1.2. This common-sense principle is also the expression of general principles of law, such as:

the equality of citizens before the law, in the sense that the law should be accessible and comprehensible for all;

legal certainty, in that it should be possible to foresee how the law will be applied.

. . .

1.3. Provisions that are not clear may be interpreted restrictively by the Community courts. If that happens, the result will be just the opposite of what was intended by the incorporation into the text of grey areas intended to resolve problems in negotiating the provision (see Case C–6/98 *ARD v Pro Sieben*[2]).

---

[1] Issued in Brussels on March 16, 2000 by the Legal Services of the European Parliament, of the Council and of the Commission.

[2] [1999] E.C.R. 1–7599.

1.4. There may obviously be a conflict between the requirement of simplicity and that of precision. Simplification is often achieved at the expense of precision and vice versa. In practice, a balance must be struck so that the provision is as precise as possible, without becoming too difficult to understand. That balance may vary according to the addressees of the provision (see Guideline 3).
. . .

A.14.2   2. THE DRAFTING OF COMMUNITY ACTS SHALL BE APPROPRIATE TO THE TYPE OF ACT CONCERNED AND, IN PARTICULAR, TO WHETHER OR NOT IT IS BINDING (REGULATION, DIRECTIVE, DECISION, RECOMMENDATION OR OTHER ACT).

2.1. The various acts each have their own standard presentation and standard formulas (see Guideline 15). . . .

2.2. The drafting style should take account of the type of act.

2.2.1. Since regulations have direct application and are binding in their entirety, their provisions should be drafted in such a way that the addressees have no doubts as to the rights and obligations resulting from them: references to intermediary national authorities should therefore be avoided, except where the act provides for complementary action by the Member States.
. . .

A.14.3   3. THE DRAFTING OF ACTS SHALL TAKE ACCOUNT OF THE PERSONS TO WHOM THEY ARE INTENDED TO APPLY, WITH A VIEW TO ENABLING THEM TO IDENTIFY THEIR RIGHTS AND OBLIGATIONS UNAMBIGUOUSLY, AND OF THE PERSONS RESPONSIBLE FOR PUTTING THE ACTS INTO EFFECT.

3.1. There are different categories of addressees of legislative acts, ranging from the population at large to specialists in specific fields. Each category is entitled to expect that legislation will use language that they can understand.

3.2. The fact that account is taken of the different categories of person to whom the acts are addressed results in differences in both the statement of reasons and the enacting terms of those acts.

3.3. Ease of transposition also depends on it.

3.4. In addition to the addressees, acts entail intervention by the national authority at different levels, for example, civil servants, scientists and judges. The language of the act should take account of that; texts may include technical requirements whose implementation falls to specialised officials in that field.
. . .

A.14.4   4. PROVISIONS OF ACTS SHALL BE CONCISE AND THEIR CONTENT SHOULD BE AS HOMOGENEOUS AS POSSIBLE. OVERLY LONG ARTICLES AND SENTENCES, UNNECESSARILY CONVOLUTED WORDING AND EXCESSIVE USE OF ABBREVIATIONS SHOULD BE AVOIDED.

4.1 The characteristic of good legislative style is the succinct expression of the key ideas of the text. Illustrative clauses, intended to make the text clearer for the reader, may give rise to problems in interpretation.

4.2 The text should be internally consistent.

4.2.1. The scope must be respected throughout the act. Rights and obligations must not go beyond those stated to be covered by the act in question, nor extend to other fields.

4.2.2. Rights and obligations must be coherent and not contradictory.

4.2.3. A text that is essentially temporary must not comprise provisions of a permanent nature.

4.2.4. A basic act must not contain detailed provisions, which could be placed in an implementing measure.

4.3. Acts should also be consistent with regard to other acts of Community legislation.

4.3.1. In particular, it is necessary to avoid overlap and contradictions with respect to other acts within a given field.

4.3.2. Doubts as to the applicability of other acts must also be avoided (see also Guideline 21).

4.4. Sentences should express just one idea, whilst an article must group together a number of ideas having a logical link between them. The text must be split into easily assimilated subdivisions (see table in Guideline 15) following the progression of the reasoning, since an excessively compact block of text is hard for both the eye and the mind to take in. This must not, however, result in sentences being artificially and unduly broken up.

4.5 Each article should contain a single provision or rule. Its structure must be as simple as possible.

4.5.1 It is not necessary for interpretation, nor desirable in the interest of clarity, for a single article to cover an entire aspect of the rules laid down in an act. It would be far better to deal with that aspect in several articles grouped together in a single section (see Guideline 15).

4.5.2. Particularly in the initial stages of drafting an act, articles should not be too complex in structure. Drafts and proposals for acts will be subject to deliberations and negotiations throughout the adoption procedure which, in most cases, will result in further additions and refinements. Subsequent amendments of the act, which are often numerous, will also be difficult to insert if the articles are already overloaded.

. . .

4.6 It is sometimes easier to draft complicated sentences than make the effort of synthesis necessary to achieve clear wording. However, this effort is essential in order to achieve a text which can be easily understood and translated.

4.7 The extent to which abbreviations should be used depends on the potential addressees. The abbreviation should be familiar to them or be clearly defined when first used (for example: 'European Central Bank, hereinafter "ECB").

5. THROUGHOUT THE PROCESS LEADING TO THEIR ADOPTION, **A.14.5** DRAFT ACTS SHALL BE FRAMED IN TERMS AND SENTENCE STRUCTURES WHICH RESPECT THE MULTILINGUAL NATURE OF COMMUNITY LEGISLATION; CONCEPTS OR TERMINOLOGY SPECIFIC TO ANY ONE NATIONAL LEGAL SYSTEM ARE TO BE USED WITH CARE

. . .

A.14.6   6. THE TERMINOLOGY USED IN A GIVEN ACT SHALL BE CONSISTENT BOTH INTERNALLY AND WITH ACTS ALREADY IN FORCE, ESPECIALLY IN THE SAME FIELD.

IDENTICAL CONCEPTS SHALL BE EXPRESSED IN THE SAME TERMS, AS FAR AS POSSIBLE WITHOUT DEPARTING FROM THEIR MEANING IN ORDINARY, LEGAL OR TECHNICAL LANGUAGE.

6.1. In order to aid comprehension and interpretation of a legislative act, the text must be consistent. A distinction can be drawn between formal consistency, concerning only questions of terminology, and substantive consistency, in a broader sense, concerning the logic of the act as a whole.

Formal consistency

6.2. Consistency of terminology means that the same terms are to be used to express the same concepts and that identical terms must not be used to express different concepts. The aim is to leave no ambiguities, contradictions or doubts as to the meaning of a term. Any given term is therefore to be used in a uniform manner to refer to the same thing and another term must be chosen to express a different concept.

6.2.1. This applies not only to the provisions of a single act, including the annexes, but also to provisions of related acts, in particular implementing acts and all other acts in the same area. In general, terminology must be consistent with the legislation in force.

6.2.2. Words must be used in their ordinary sense. If a word has one meaning in everyday or technical language, but a different meaning in legal language, the phrase must be formulated in such a way as to avoid any ambiguity.

6.2.3. In the interests of precision and to avoid problems of interpretation, it may be necessary to define a term (see Guideline 14).

Substantive consistency

6.3. Consistency of terminology must also be checked with regard to the content of the act itself. There must be no contradictions inherent in the act.

6.4 Definitions must be respected throughout the act. Defined terms must be used in a uniform manner and their content must not diverge from the definitions given. . . . "

EXTRACTS FROM HANSARD[1]

IMPORTANCE OF PLAIN ENGLISH IN LEGISLATIVE DRAFTING

See Chapter 8, Section 1

Extract of speech of Lord Brightman[2]

"My Lords, I believe that plain English should be used in the drafting of Acts of   **A.15.1** Parliament. . . .

I suggested to the Minister in Committee that the wording of the Notes on Clauses should be used instead of the obscure wording of the Bill. My suggestion received a partial blessing. The noble Baroness said that I raised:

'an interesting and sensible point'.

She helpfully added:

'anything which adds clarity in that way and simplifies the drafting is entirely to be welcomed'[3]

However, I am told that my wording—the wording in the Notes on Clauses—has been turned down by the parliamentary draftsman.[4]

All I ask now is that your Lordships should say which is plainer English, the provision in the Bill, which states that an uncertified agreement is valid if it would have been an externally financed development agreement if it had been certified as an externally financed development agreement or the Notes on Clauses, and my amendment, which say that."

---

[1] [1985] Q.B. 581, 600–02, CA.
[2] HL Deb. June 26, 1997 cc.1647–48—Lord Brightman, speaking on the National Health Service (Private Finance) Bill [HL].
[3] HL Deb. June 19, 1997 c.1366.
[4] As to the ability to use a colloquial form of expression in Explanatory Notes that cannot be used in legislation, and for the reasons, see Chapter 9, Section 4.

Extract of speech of Lord Simon of Glaisdale[5]

A.15.2   "We have simply no right to legislate in a manner that is incomprehensible to the people to whom the legislation is addressed and who are primarily concerned, particularly if the matter can be put in lucid and plain terms as it has been by my noble and learned friend, to whom we are deeply indebted. Like many great Chancery lawyers, my noble and learned friend is a gifted draftsman. It behoves us all, including parliamentary counsel, to show a little humility in the face of that.

This is not a new style of drafting. It is a form of drafting based on hypothesis. When I gave evidence to the Renton Committee on the preparation of legislation, I drew attention to a provision in a national insurance Act which went very much on the same lines. I venture to read it:

> 'For the purpose of this Part of the Schedule a person over pensionable age, not being an insured person, shall be treated as an employed person if he would be an insured person were he under pensionable age and would be an employed person were he an insured person'.

Your Lordships will see the relationship between the two styles of drafting.

The matter was put very plainly by my noble and learned friend. It is extremely important because the legislation is a vital part of the process whereby democratic society frames rules which bind of themselves. If the rules are incomprehensible, then the process of democratic legislation has broken down."

---

[5] HL Deb. June 26, 1997 cc.1648–49—Lord Simon of Glaisdale, following the speech cited above of Lord Brightman, speaking on the National Health Service (Private Finance) Bill [HL].

EXTRACTS FROM HANSARD

ADVANTAGES AND DISADVANTAGES OF PURPOSE CLAUSES

See Chapter 8, Section 1

Lord McIntosh of Haringey[1]: "Legislation should be as clear as possible, **A.16.1** including a statement of purpose, which may sometimes assist clarity but not always. There are dangers. If the statement has legal effect and covers the same ground as later detailed provisions, there is a risk of real or apparent inconsistency. If the statement is not intended to have legal effect, the courts may give it some effect with unintended results. The Renton Report therefore concluded that purpose clauses should be used only 'selectively and with caution' and the Hansard Society's 1992 report concluded that they should, 'not be adopted as a general practice'."[2]

Lord Renton: "A few people, including some members of the Hansard committee, have expressed doubt about statements of purpose and of principle. But I challenge anyone to mention any such statement which has done harm. In practice, all statements of purpose and of principle have been useful in helping people to understand and interpret the legislation. I discussed that with various judges and Law Lords and not one of them mentioned a statement of purpose or of principle which has caused any problem. . . .

I have never taken the view that the aim of purpose clauses was to dispense with detail. It was to lead to a better understanding of detail that such clauses have, within my knowledge, always been recommended."[3]

Lord McIntosh of Haringey: "As to guiding principles, the danger is that they may be open to interpretation in many ways. The result is vague law: citizens cannot know with any certainty how it affects them in their particular circumstances. That approach can have a place, but it must be used with great caution and in appropriate cases, where Parliament wishes to condition the discretion it gives to the courts.

As to statements of principle, the problem arises from duplication. There is a real risk of inconsistency between the statement of principles and the detailed

---

[1] A Minister of the Crown answering for the Government.
[2] HL Deb. November 11, 1997 c.87.
[3] HL Deb. January 21, 1998 cc.1584–85 and 1598.

provisions in the Act, because the same thing is being said twice in different words. That view has been taken by successive Governments and they have been supported by the two major reports on the law-making process to which reference has been made."[4]

Parliamentary Secretary, Cabinet Office: "By 'purpose clauses' people some-times mean guiding principles for interpreting the text, and sometimes statements of principle on which the detail of legislation is based. In either case, the statements are intended to have legal effect. It is wrong to think that using those techniques in all Bills would be an advance; they would often create confu-sion.

Guiding principles may be open to interpretation in many ways. The result is vague law: citizens cannot know with any certainty how the law affects them in their particular circumstances. That approach can have a place, but it must be used with the utmost caution.

With statements of principle, the problem is duplication. There is a real risk of inconsistency between statements of principle and the detailed provisions of an Act, because the same thing is said twice in different words. That can create a dilemma in deciding where the balance lies between the general principle and the specific rule, and which of them matters most in specific circumstances. Those views have been taken by successive Governments and are supported by the two main modern reports on the law-making process—the Renton report of 1975 and the Hansard Society report of 1992.

Both types of material have their uses, and examples can be found in various Acts in recent years. There are good reasons not to include such statements in Acts as a routine practice, but we shall continue to use the techniques where it is helpful to do so.

It is highly desirable that the purpose of a Bill be explained, but it should be explained alongside the legislation and not in the legislation itself. As part of the modernisation programme, the Government took up a proposal by the Office of Parliamentary Counsel for explanatory notes and introduced them from the beginning of last Session. They are published alongside Bills and are available to the general public from the Stationery Office and on the internet. They are prepared when the Bill is first introduced; revised when the Bill enters its Second House; and revised again when the Bill receives Royal Assent.

The new notes do not form part of the Bill and do not claim to be authoritative or to have received Parliament's approval."[5]

Lord Renton: (speaking on an amendment to the Security Service Bill 1995–96 moved by Lord McIntosh of Haringey[6] (citing recent precedent of the Family Law Bill 1995–96)) "I do not doubt the good intentions of the noble Lord, Lord McIntosh, in moving this amendment, but frankly I do not think it is suitable for legislation. It states opinions and does not enact law with any precision which

---

[4] HL Deb. January 21, 1998 cc.1599.
[5] HC Deb. January 20, 2000 c.1100.
[6] Before he became a Minister.

would be considered binding on those who have to observe the law and, indeed, upon the courts. Different judges would take different views as to what should be the application of some of these phrases. . . . There again, it is good guidance to give to the Security Service in years to come, but to try to tie them down in law to a statement of this kind does not seem to me to be a way to legislate."[7]

[7] HL Deb. June 27, 1996 cc.1026–1027.

L'OFFICE CHERIFIEN DES PHOSPHATES AND ANOTHER v YAMASHITA-SHINNIHON STEAMSHIP CO LTD, THE BOUCRAA[1]

RETROSPECTIVITY OF LEGISLATION

SEE CHAPTER 10, SECTION 3

Extract of the speech of Lord Mustill

"My Lords, it would be impossible now to doubt that the court is required to **A.17.1** approach questions of statutory interpretation with a disposition, and in some cases a very strong disposition, to assume that a statute is not intended to have retrospective effect. Nor indeed would I wish to cast any doubt on the validity of this approach for it ensures that the courts are constantly on the alert for the kind of unfairness which is found in, for example, the characterisation as criminal of past conduct which was lawful when it took place, or in alterations to the antecedent natural, civil or familial status of individuals. Nevertheless, I must own to reservations about the reliability of generalised presumptions and maxims when engaged in the task of finding out what Parliament intended by a particular form of words, for they too readily confine the court to a perspective which treats all statutes, and all situations to which they apply, as if they were the same. This is misleading, for the basis of the rule is no more than simple fairness, which ought to be the basis of every legal rule. True it is that to change the legal character of a person's acts or omissions after an event will very often be unfair; and since it is rightly taken for granted that Parliament will rarely wish to act in a way which seems unfair it is sensible to look very hard at a statute which appears to have this effect, to make sure that this is what Parliament really intended. This is, however, no more than common sense, the application of which may be impeded rather than helped by recourse to formulae which do not adapt themselves to individual circumstances, and which tend themselves to become the subject of minute analysis, whereas what ought to be analysed is the statute itself.

---

[1] [1994] 1 All E.R. 20, 29–30 HL.

My Lords, my purpose in stressing this point is not to suggest that the courts below approached the question in a mechanistic way. Their careful judgments show that this was not the case. It is simply to explain why I do not find it necessary to cite and analyse the numerous authorities on retrospective effect, but prefer to proceed directly to the ascertainment of the intention which Parliament intended s.13A to achieve, by a reference to the following statement by Staughton L.J. in *Secretary of State for Social Security v Tunnicliffe*[2] (quoted by Sir Thomas Bingham M.R. in the present case)[3]:

> 'In my judgment the true principle is that Parliament is presumed not to have intended to alter the law applicable to past events and transactions in a manner which is unfair to those concerned in them, unless a contrary intention appears. It is not simply a question of classifying an enactment as retrospective or not retrospective. Rather it may well be a matter of degree—the greater the unfairness, the more it is to be expected that Parliament will make it clear if that is intended.'

A.17.2   Precisely how the single question of fairness will be answered in respect of a particular statute will depend on the interaction of several factors, each of them capable of varying from case to case. ... Again, the unfairness of adversely affecting the rights, and hence the degree of unlikelihood that this is what Parliament intended, will vary from case to case. So also will the clarity of the language used by Parliament, and the light shed on it by consideration of the circumstances in which the legislation was enacted. All these factors must be weighed together to provide a direct answer to the question whether the consequences of reading the statute with the suggested degree of retrospectivity is so unfair that the words used by Parliament cannot have been intended to mean what they might appear to say. ...

My Lords, the problem of a statute which creates powers exercisable in the future by reference to a continuous period of time antecedent to their exercise, and which comes into force whilst that period is running is not new ... The cases show that the presumption against retrospectivity does not necessarily entail that the period antecedent to the statute should be left out of account. ... [The cases do not point to a single clear conclusion] but they do demonstrate that where an intermediate type of retrospectivity is in issue the purpose of the legislation and the hardship of the result contended for are of particular importance. ...

My Lords, at this point a strictly orthodox approach to the problem of retrospection would call up a line of authority ... which applies different rules for ascertaining the retrospective effect of statutes by reference to a distinction between accrued substantive and procedural rights. This distinction is so firmly embedded in the law as to lead easily to an assumption that every right can be

---

[2] [1991] 2 All E.R. 712 at 724.
[3] [1993] 3 All E.R. 686 at 693.

characterised uniquely as either substantive or procedural, and that the assignment of a particular right to one category rather than the other will automatically
yield an answer to the question whether a particular statute can bear upon it
retrospectively.

   ... My Lords, I believe that such a discussion would be unprofitable, partly
because the distinction just mentioned is misleading, since it leaves out of the
account the fact that some procedural rights are more valuable than some
substantive rights, and partly because I doubt whether it is possible to assign
rights such as the present unequivocally to one category rather than another.
Thus, whilst keeping the distinction well in view, I prefer to look to the practical
value and nature of the rights presently involved as a step towards an assessment
of the unfairness of taking them away after the event."

THE PARLEMENT BELGE[1]

THE ORIGIN AND NATURE OF THE DOCTRINE OF CROWN IMMUNITY

SEE CHAPTER 11, SECTION 5

Extract of the judgment of Brett L.J.

"What is the principle on which the exemption of the person of sovereigns and of certain public properties has been recognised?   **A.18.1**

> 'Our king,' says Blackstone[2], 'owes no kind of subjection to any other potentate on earth. Hence it is that no suit or action can be brought against the king, even in civil matters, because no Court can have jurisdiction over him. For all jurisdiction implies superiority of power; authority to try would be vain and idle without an authority to redress, and the sentence of a Court would be contemptible unless the Court had power to command the execution of it, but who shall command the king?'

In this passage, which has been often cited and relied on, the reason of the exemption is the character of the sovereign authority, its high dignity, whereby it is not subject to any superior authority of any kind.

 . . . it seems to us, although other reasons have sometimes been suggested, that the real principle on which the exemption of every sovereign from the jurisdiction of every Court has been deduced is that the exercise of such jurisdiction would be incompatible with his regal dignity—that is to say, with his absolute independence of every superior authority."

---

[1] (1880) 5 P.D. 197, 205–207, CA.
[2] B.1, c.7.

EXTRACT 19

COLIN v DUKE OF WESTMINSTER[1]

STATUTORY RIGHT AS A SPECIALTY

SEE CHAPTER 12, SECTION 2

Extract of judgment of Oliver L.J.

"The obvious and most common case of an action upon a specialty is an action **A.19.1**
based on a contract under seal, but it is clear that 'specialty' was not originally
confined to such contracts but extended also to obligations imposed by statute.
Under the Statute of Limitations of 1623[2] no limit was prescribed for actions on
a specialty and it was not until the Civil Procedure Act of 1833[3] that a time limit
of 20 years was introduced for actions of debt 'upon any bond or other specialty':
s.3.

There was no statutory definition of a specialty but it was established in *Cork
and Bandon Railway Co. v Goode*[4] that (to adopt the words of Lord Hanworth
M.R. in *Aylott v West Ham Corporation*[5])—

> 'where a plaintiff relies and has to rely upon the terms of a statute so that
> his claim is under the statute the nature of the claim is one of specialty and
> the 20 years applies.'

Goode's case was an action for calls and a similar principle was applied to an
action for interest on debenture stock (*In re Cornwall Minerals Railway Co.*[6])
and to an action for recovery of rates and duties imposed by statute: *Shepherd v
Hills*.[7] A distinction, however, was drawn between the case where all that the
statute did was to make binding a contract which otherwise would not be binding
or to vary one term of a contract (see *Aylott's case*[8] and *Gutsell v Reeve*[9]) and the
case where the action rested on the statute and only on the statute: see, for

---

[1] [1985] Q.B. 581, 600–02, CA.
[2] 21 Jac.1, c.16.
[3] 3 & 4 Will 4, c.42.
[4] (1853) 13 C.B. 826.
[5] [1927] 1 Ch. 30, 50.
[6] [1897] 2 Ch. 74.
[7] (1855) 11 Exch. 55.
[8] [1927] 1 Ch. 30.
[9] [1936] 1 K.B. 272.

instance, *Pratt v Cook, Son & Co. (St. Paul's) Ltd.*[10] Broadly the test is whether any cause of action exists apart from the statute: *per* Lord Atkin at p.446.

It seems to me to be quite clear that in the instant case any cause of action which the applicant has derived from the statute and from the statute alone. Apart from the statutory provisions he could have no claim and it is only by virtue of the statute and the regulations made thereunder that there can be ascertained the amount of the price to be paid under the statutory contract the terms of which can be gathered only from the sections of the Act and the Schedules. Subject, therefore, to one question, namely whether the word 'specialty' as used in the Limitation Act 1939 and the Act of 1980 has assumed a more limited meaning than it originally bore, I have no doubt at all that the applicant's claim is a claim on a specialty.

The doubt, if it be a doubt, arises from the way in which sums recoverable under statute were dealt with in the Limitation Act 1939 and from certain observations of Goddard L.J. and Lord Maugham in two cases referred to below. The provisions which now appear as s.8 of the Act of 1980 were contained in substantially the same form in s.2(3) of the Act of 1939 save that what is now subsection (2) of s.8 there appeared as a proviso. Sums of money payable under statute were however dealt with specifically in s.2(1)(d) of the Act of 1939 which provided a period of six years for 'actions to recover any sum recoverable by virtue of any enactment, other than a penalty or forfeiture or sum by way of penalty or forfeiture'. Now on the face of it this did not and could not affect the meaning of the word 'specialty' in s.2(3). Indeed the reference to an action for which a shorter period of limitation is prescribed in the proviso rather underlines that such an action is an action on a specialty but one for which a special limitation period is prescribed elsewhere in the Act. However, in *Leivers v Barber, Walker & Co. Ltd*,[11] Goddard L.J., in the course of reviewing the history of the statutory provisions and referring to *Goode's case* observed—

> 'The Act of 1939 has, however, effected a material change in the law in this respect. Debts recoverable by virtue of an enactment are now subject to the same period of limitation as those arising from simple contract, while a different period is prescribed for specialties. In my opinion, therefore, "specialties" must now be confined to deeds or contracts under seal.'

A.19.2   These observations were obiter but they have been adopted by textbook writers as an authoritative exposition of the meaning of the word in s.2(3) of the Act of 1939: . . .

Undoubtedly the effect of the combination of subss.(1)(d) and (3) of s.2 of the Act of 1939 was that the period of limitation of 12 years for the recovery of debts or sums of money was restricted to contracts under seal, so that to that extent what Goddard L.J. said was not inaccurate; but with respect, I do not for my part

---

[10] [1940] A.C. 437.
[11] [1943] K.B. 385, 398.

see that it follows that the ancient and accepted meaning of 'specialty' as including causes of action based on statute was in any way altered. Undoubtedly the word immediately suggests a contract under seal and, no doubt, the word is used loosely as connoting a specialty debt. Thus in *Rex v Williams*,[12] Viscount Maugham giving the opinion of the Judicial Committee said—

> 'The word "specialty" is sometimes used to denote any contract under seal, but it is more often used in the sense of meaning a specialty debt, that is, an obligation under seal securing a debt, or a debt due from the Crown or under statute . . . '

Nevertheless it would, in my judgment, be wrong to deduce from this that the word 'specialty' where it is used in the Limitation Acts is, as a matter of construction, confined to specialty debts much less to obligations arising specifically under contracts under seal and in no other way. . . .

In my judgment, if and so far as the Limitation Act 1980 applies to a cause of action arising out of the enfranchisement provisions of the Leasehold Reform Act, the applicable provisions are those contained in s.8 and the appropriate period of limitation is 12 years."

---

[12] [1942] A.C. 541, 555.

STOCK v FRANK JONES (TIPTON) LTD[1]

DEPARTURE FROM CARDINAL RULE OF STATUTORY CONSTRUCTION IN ORDER TO RECTIFY ANOMALY

SEE CHAPTER 17

Extract of the speech of Lord Simon of Glaisdale

"In his argument based on alleged anomaly counsel for the appellants was founding himself on the rider in what has become to be known as 'Lord Wensleydale's golden rule'[2] of statutory construction, namely one is to apply statutory words and phrases according to their natural and ordinary meaning without addition or subtraction, unless that meaning produces injustice, absurdity, anomaly or contradiction, in which case one may modify the natural and ordinary meaning so as to obviate such injustice etc but no further. (Nowadays we should add to 'natural and ordinary meaning' the words 'in their context and according to the appropriate linguistic register.)' Counsel for the appellants urged your Lordships, as he did the Court of Appeal, to modify the natural and ordinary meaning of the statutory language, in effect, to add words which are not in the statute in order to obviate what he claimed were the absurd and anomalous consequences of taking the words literally. **A.20.1**

The rider to Lord Wensleydale's golden rule may seem to be at variance with the citations of high authority contained in the speeches of my noble and learned friends. But this is not really so. The clue to their reconciliation is to be found in the frequently cited passage on statutory construction in Lord Blackburn's speech in *River Wear Comrs v Adamson* ((1877) 2 App. Cas. 743 at 763, [1874–80] All E.R. Rep. 1 at 11):

'In all cases the object is to see what is the intention expressed by the words used. But, from the imperfection of language, it is impossible to know what that intention is without inquiring farther, and seeing what the circumstances were with reference to which the words were used, and what was the object,

---

[1] [1978] 1 W.L.R. 231 HL.
[2] *Caledonian Railway Co v North British Railway Co* (1881) 6 App. Cas. 114 at 131, *per* Lord Blackburn.

appearing from those circumstances, which the person using them had in view . . . '

Words and phrases of the English language have an extraordinary range of meaning. This has been a rich resource in English poetry (which makes fruitful use of the resonances, overtones and ambiguities), but it has a concomitant disadvantage in English law (which seeks unambiguous precision, with the aim that every citizen shall know, as exactly as possible, where he stands under the law). The first way, says Lord Blackburn, of eliminating legally irrelevant meanings is to look to the statutory objective. This is the well-known canon of construction referred to by my noble and learned friend, Viscount Dilhorne, which goes by the name of 'the rule in *Heydon's Case* ((1584) 3 Co. Rep. 7a at 7b)'. (Nowadays we speak of the 'purposive' or 'functional' construction of a statute.)

A.20.2   But it is essential to bear in mind what the court is doing. It is not declaring 'Parliament has said X: but it obviously meant Y; so we will take Y as the effect of the statute'. Nor is it declaring 'Parliament has said X, having situation A in mind', but if Parliament had had our own forensic situation, B, in mind, the legislative objective indicates that it would have said Y; so we will take Y as the effect of the statute as regards B'. What the court is declaring is 'Parliament has used words which are capable of meaning either X or Y; although X may be the primary, natural and ordinary meaning of the words, the purpose of the provision shows that the secondary sense, Y, should be given to the words'. So too when X produces injustice, absurdity, anomaly or contradiction. The final task of construction is still, as always, to ascertain the meaning of what the draftsman has said, rather than to ascertain what the draftsman meant to say. But if the draftsmanship is correct these should coincide. So that if the words are capable of more than one meaning it is a perfectly legitimate intermediate step in construction to choose between potential meanings by various tests (statutory, objective, justice, anomaly, etc.) which throw light on what the draftsman meant to say.

It is idle to debate whether, in so acting, the court is making law. As has been cogently observed, it depends on what you mean by 'make' and 'law' in this context. What is incontestible is that the court is a mediating influence between the executive and the legislature on the one hand and the citizen on the other. Nevertheless it is essential to the proper judicial function in the constitution to bear in mind: (1) that modern legislation is a difficult and complicated process, in which, even before a bill is introduced in a House of Parliament, successive drafts are considered and their possible repercussions on all envisageable situations are weighed by people bringing to bear a very wide range of experience; the judge cannot match such experience or envisage all such repercussions, either by training or by specific forensic aid; (2) that the bill is liable to be modified in a Parliament dominated by a House of Commons whose members are answerable to the citizens who will be affected by the legislation;

an English judge is not so answerable; (3) that in a society living under the rule of law citizens are entitled to regulate their conduct according to what a statute has said, rather than by what it was meant to say or by what it would have otherwise said if a newly considered situation had been envisaged; (4) that a stark contradistinction between the letter and the spirit of the law may be very well in the sphere of ethics, but in the forensic process St John is a safer guide than St Paul, the logos being the informing spirit; and it should be left to peoples' courts in totalitarian regimes to stretch the law to meet the forensic situation in response to a gut reaction; (5) that Parliament may well be prepared to tolerate some anomaly in the interest of an overriding objective; (6) that what strikes the lawyer as an injustice may well have seemed to the legislature as no more than the correction of a now unjustifiable privilege or as a particular misfortune necessarily or acceptably involved in the vindication of some supervening general social benefit; (7) that the Parliamentary draftsmen knows what objective the legislative promotor wishes to attain, and he will normally and desirably try to achieve that objective by using language of the appropriate register in its natural, ordinary and primary sense; to reject such an approach on the ground that it gives rise to an anomaly is liable to encourage complication and anfractuosity in drafting; (8) that Parliament is nowadays in continuous session, so that an unlooked-for and unsupportable injustice or anomaly can be readily rectified by legislation; this is far preferable to judicial contortion of the law to meet apparently hard cases with the result that ordinary citizens and their advisers hardly know where they stand.

All this is not to advocate judicial supineness: it is merely respectfully to commend a self-knowledge of judicial limitations, both personal and constitutional. To apply it to the argument on behalf of the appellant based on anomaly, a court would only be justified in departing from the plain words of the statute were it satisfied that: (1) there is clear and gross balance of anomaly; (2) Parliament, the legislative promoters and the draftsman could not have envisaged such anomaly and could not have been prepared to accept it in the interest of a supervening legislative objective; (3) the anomaly can be obviated without detriment to such legislative objective; (4) the language of the statute is susceptible of the modification required to obviate the anomaly."[3]

---

[3] But as to the fourth condition note the passage of Lord Scarman's speech in *Stock* referred to in Chapter 17, para.17.1.9, foonote 24.

R. v SECRETARY OF STATE FOR THE ENVIRONMENT, TRANSPORT AND THE REGIONS AND ANOTHER, EX P. SPATH HOLME LTD[1]

AIM OF CONSTRUING INTENTION OF PARLIAMENT; AND USE OF EXTRANEOUS MATERIAL

SEE CHAPTERS 20 AND 27

Extract of speech of Lord Nicholls of Birkenhead

"Statutory interpretation is an exercise which requires the court to identify the meaning borne by the words in question in the particular context. The task of the court is often said to be to ascertain the intention of Parliament expressed in the language under consideration. This is correct and may be helpful, so long as it is remembered that the 'intention of Parliament' is an objective concept, not subjective. The phrase is a shorthand reference to the intention which the court reasonably imputes to Parliament in respect of the language used. It is not the subjective intention of the minister or other persons who promoted the legislation. Nor is it the subjective intention of the draftsman, or of individual members or even of a majority of individual members of either House. These individuals will often have widely varying intentions. Their understanding of the legislation and the words used may be impressively complete or woefully inadequate. Thus, when courts say that such-and-such a meaning 'cannot be what Parliament intended', they are saying only that the words under consideration cannot reasonably be taken as used by Parliament with that meaning. As Lord Reid said in *Black-Clawson International Ltd v Papierwerke Waldhof-Aschaffenburg AG*[2]—

  'We often say that we are looking for the intention of Parliament, but that is not quite accurate. We are seeking the meaning of the words which Parliament used'.

A.21.1

---

[1] [2001] 2 A.C. 349, 395–398, HL.
[2] [1975] A.C. 591, 613, HL.

In identifying the meaning of the words used, the courts employ accepted principles of interpretation as useful guides. For instance, an appropriate starting point is that language is to be taken to bear its ordinary meaning in the general context of the statute. Another, recently enacted, principle is that so far as possible legislation must be read in a way which is compatible with human rights and fundamental freedoms: see section 3 of the Human Rights Act 1998. The principles of interpretation include also certain presumptions. To take a familiar instance, the courts presume that a mental ingredient is an essential element in every statutory offence unless Parliament has indicated a contrary intention expressly or by necessary implication.

Additionally, the courts employ other recognised aids. They may be internal aids. Other provisions in the same statute may shed light on the meaning of the words under consideration. Or the aids may be external to the statute, such as its background setting and its legislative history. This extraneous material includes reports of Royal Commissions and advisory committees, reports of the Law Commission (with or without a draft Bill attached), and a statute's legislative antecedents.

Use of non-statutory materials as an aid to interpretation is not a new development. As long ago as 1584 the Barons of the Exchequer enunciated the so-called mischief rule. In interpreting statutes courts should take into account, among other matters, 'the mischief and defect for which the common law did not provide': *Heydon's Case*.[3] Nowadays the courts look at external aids for more than merely identifying the mischief the statute is intended to cure. In adopting a purposive approach to the interpretation of statutory language, courts seek to identify and give effect to the purpose of the legislation. To the extent that extraneous material assists in identifying the purpose of the legislation, it is a useful tool.

A.21.2　　This is subject to an important caveat. External aids differ significantly from internal aids. Unlike internal aids, external aids are not found within the statute in which Parliament has expressed its intention in the words in question. This difference is of constitutional importance. Citizens, with the assistance of their advisers, are intended to be able to understand parliamentary enactments, so that they can regulate their conduct accordingly. They should be able to rely upon what they read in an Act of Parliament. This gives rise to a tension between the need for legal certainty, which is one of the fundamental elements of the rule of law, and the need to give effect to the intention of Parliament, from whatever source that (objectively assessed) intention can be gleaned. Lord Diplock drew attention to the importance of this aspect of the rule of law in *Fothergill v Monarch Airlines Ltd*[4]—

'The source to which Parliament must have intended the citizen to refer is the language of the Act itself. These are the words which Parliament has

[3] (1584) 3 Co. Rep. 7a, 7b.
[4] [1981] A.C. 251, 279–280.

itself approved as accurately expressing its intentions. If the meaning of those words is clear and unambiguous and does not lead to a result that is manifestly absurd or unreasonable, it would be a confidence trick by Parliament and destructive of all legal certainty if the private citizen could not rely upon that meaning but was required to search through all that had happened before and in the course of the legislative process in order to see whether there was anything to be found from which it could be inferred that Parliament's real intention had not been accurately expressed by the actual words that Parliament had adopted to communicate it to those affected by the legislation.'

This constitutional consideration does not mean that when deciding whether statutory language is clear and unambiguous and not productive of absurdity, the courts are confined to looking solely at the language in question in its context within the statute. That would impose on the courts much too restrictive an approach. No legislation is enacted in a vacuum. Regard may also be had to extraneous material, such as the setting in which the legislation was enacted. This is a matter of everyday occurrence.

That said, courts should nevertheless approach the use of external aids with circumspection. Judges frequently turn to external aids for confirmation of views reached without their assistance. That is unobjectionable. But the constitutional implications point to a need for courts to be slow to permit external aids to displace meanings which are otherwise clear and unambiguous and not pro-ductive of absurdity. Sometimes external aids may properly operate in this way. In other cases, the requirements of legal certainty might be undermined to an unacceptable extent if the court were to adopt, as the intention to be imputed to Parliament in using the words in question, the meaning suggested by an external aid. Thus, when interpreting statutory language courts have to strike a balance between conflicting considerations."

FOTHERGILL v MONARCH AIRLINES LTD.[1]

USE OF TRAVAUX PREPARATOIRES IN CONSTRUING LEGISLATION IMPLEMENTING INTERNATIONAL TREATY

SEE CHAPTER 27

Extract of speech of Lord Wilberforce

"This conclusion, that a complaint was necessary within seven days makes it   **A.22.1**
strictly unnecessary to decide whether reliance may be placed on travaux
préparatoires and, if so, to what effect. But as these matters were relied on in the
Court of Appeal by the learned Master of the Rolls, Browne and Geoffrey Lane
L.JJ. taking the contrary view, I think that I must add some observations. I make
it clear that they relate solely to the use of travaux préparatoires in the
interpretation of treaties, and do not relate to interpretation of domestic
legislation, rules as to which have been recently laid down by this House[2] . . .

There is little firm authority in English law supporting the use of travaux
préparatoires in the interpretation of treaties or conventions. The passage usually
cited in support of such use is from the judgment of Lord Reading C.J. in *Porter
v Freudenberg*[3] when reference was made to statements made in a committee of
the conference which prepared the Hague Convention of 1907 upon the Laws and
Customs of War on Land. The judgment contains no reasoning in support of this
approach, and the case was decided upon the wording of the relevant article in
its context in preference to the (inconsistent) statements. There is a passing
reference to travaux préparatoires in relation to an international convention in
Post Office v Estuary Radio Ltd.,[4] but even this is tentatively expressed. When
dealing with an international treaty or convention I think that there is no doubt
that international courts and tribunals (I exclude from this category the Court of
Justice of the European Communities which stands in a class apart) do in general

---

[1] [1981] A.C. 251, 275–278, HL.
[2] In a case which is no longer good law, following *Pepper v Hart*—as to which see Chapter 28.
[3] [1915] 1 K.B. 857, 876.
[4] [1968] 2 Q.B. 740, *per* Diplock L.J., at 761.

make use of travaux préparatoires as an aid to interpretation: see O'Connell, International Law, 2nd ed. (1970), vol.1, p.262, Brownlie, Principles of Public International Law, 3rd ed. (1979), pp.627–628. This practice is cautiously endorsed by the Vienna Convention on the Law of Treaties (1969) (Cmnd. 4140), article 32. We are here concerned with what is in effect a private law convention likely to be litigated primarily in municipal courts. In the interest of uniformity of application we ought, in considering whether to use travaux préparatoires, to have regard to the general practice applied, or likely to be applied, in the courts of other contracting states. Professor A. Dumon (First Advocate-General of the Cour de Cassation of Belgium and the Benelux Court of Justice) in his comprehensive examination of the subject of interpretation, delivered to the Court of Justice of the European Communities in 1976[5] states as follows, at p.III–101:

> 'It may be stated that in the Federal Republic of Germany, France, Italy, Luxembourg, the Netherlands and Belgium both "administrative" and other courts have recourse in varying degrees, but generally with prudence and caution, to preparatory work of the laws of the legislature.'

Professor Dumon here is dealing primarily with domestic laws but a footnote indicates that this approach has been used in interpreting an international treaty.

An example of this can be found in the United States of America: see *Day v Trans World Airlines Inc.*,[6] a decision of the second circuit of the United States Court of Appeals, on the Warsaw Convention. That Court took into account the preparatory work prior to the Warsaw Conference done by the Comité Internationale Technique d'Experts Juridiques Aériens ("C.I.T.E.J.A.") and the minutes of the Warsaw Conference. It is no doubt true that United States courts are in general more liberal in recourse to legislative history than are courts in this country, but the decision in question is one which I would cautiously follow.

A.22.2   A second important illustration is provided by a decision in 1977 of the French Cour de Cassation sitting in assemblée plénière—in a case on the Warsaw Convention, article 29—*Consorts Lorans v Air France*, January 14, 1977.[7] In his 'conclusion' the Advocate-General M. R. Schmelck said this (my translation):

> 'I shall not take up time upon the old dispute concerning the general scope of travaux préparatoires. I shall limit myself to the observation that when one is concerned with the travaux préparatoires for an international convention, there may be special reasons for not placing too much reliance on them. The first is that although for a French lawyer these travaux préparatoires may be of some value at least by way of guidance, they have

---

[5] *The case-law of the Court of Justice—a critical examination of the method of interpretation* (Luxembourg, 1976).
[6] (1975) 528 F. 2d 31.
[7] Revue Française de Droit Aérien (Jurisprudence), vols 31–32, p.268.

none for a lawyer brought up on the principles of Anglo-Saxon law. Moreover, international tribunals, no doubt under British influence, in general take no account of them. Your court itself does not attribute to them decisive force because when there is a serious doubt upon the interpretation of a treaty, it considers it necessary to consult the Ministry of Foreign Affairs in order to ascertain the intention of the High Contracting Parties.'

He continues by referring to the case (such as the Warsaw Convention itself) of an open convention which may be acceded to by states not parties to the negotiations.

The travaux préparatoires of the Warsaw Convention, he concludes, ought not to be treated as gospel truth.

The court, in its decision, did not deal directly with these submissions. However, it referred to the decision appealed from as having reached an interpretation of article 29 of the Warsaw Convention by reference, inter alia, to the travaux préparatoires without expressing disagreement with the procedure, and reversed it upon another ground, *viz.* that the Convention contains no express derogation from the rules of French domestic law.

My Lords, if one accepts that this reflects a recognition on the part of French **A.22.3** law that in the interest of uniformity with English tendencies (perhaps rather overstated by the Advocate-General) the use of travaux préparatoires in the interpretation of treaties should be cautious, I think that it would be proper for us, in the same interest, to recognise that there may be cases where such travaux préparatoires can profitably be used. These cases should be rare, and only where two conditions are fulfilled, first, that the material involved is public and accessible, and secondly, that the travaux préparatoires clearly and indisputably point to a definite legislative intention. It would I think be unnecessarily restrictive to exclude from consideration, as travaux préparatoires, the work of the Paris Conference of 1925, and the work of the C.I.T.E.J.A. before 1929, both of which are well known to those concerned with air law, in any case where a clear intention were to be revealed. If the use of travaux préparatoires is limited in this way, that would largely overcome the two objections which may properly be made: first, that relating to later acceding states—as to this see Brownlie, Principles of Public International Law, 3rd ed., p. 628, citing the International Law Commission—and secondly, the general objection that individuals ought not to be bound by discussions or negotiations of which they may never have heard.

The presently relevant travaux préparatoires are contained in the minutes of the Hague Conference of 1955, published by the International Civil Aviation Organisation and available for sale in a number of places including Her Majesty's Stationery Office, and so accessible to legislators, text-book writers, airlines and insurers. I would therefore be in favour of a cautious use of work leading up to the Warsaw Convention and the Hague Protocol."

PEPPER (INSPECTOR OF TAXES) v HART[1]

USE OF HANSARD IN CONSTRUING LEGISLATION

SEE CHAPTER 28

Extract of the speech of Lord Browne-Wilkinson

" . . . the appeals have also raised two questions of much wider importance. The first is whether in construing ambiguous or obscure statutory provisions your Lordships should relax the historic rule that the courts must not look at the parliamentary history of legislation or Hansard for the purpose of construing such legislation. The second is whether, if reference to such materials would otherwise be appropriate, it would contravene section 1, article 9 of the Bill of Rights (1688) or parliamentary privilege so to do. . . .   **A.23.1**

The case was originally argued before a committee of five of your Lordships without reference to any parliamentary proceedings. After the conclusion of the first hearing, it came to your Lordships' attention that an examination of the proceedings in Parliament in 1976 which led to the enactment of ss.61 and 63 of the 1976 Act [Finance Act 1976[2]] might give a clear indication which of the two rival contentions represented the intention of Parliament in using the statutory words. Your Lordships then invited the parties to consider whether they wished to present further argument on the question whether it was appropriate for the House (under Note[3]) to depart from previous authority of this House which forbids reference to such material in construing statutory provisions and, if so, what guidance such material provided in deciding the present appeal. The taxpayers indicated that they wished to present further argument on these points. The case was listed for rehearing before a committee of seven members not all of whom sat on the original committee.

At the start of the further hearing, the Attorney General, who appeared for the Crown, drew our attention to a letter addressed to him by the Clerk of the House of Commons suggesting that any reference to Hansard for the purpose of construing the 1976 Act might breach the privileges of that House. Until October

---

[1] [1991] 2 All E.R. 824 CA
[2] 1976 c.40.
[3] [1966] 3 All E.R. 77, [1966] 1 W.L.R. 1234.

31, 1980 the House of Commons took the view that any reference to Hansard in court proceedings would constitute a breach of its privileges and required a petition for leave to use Hansard to be presented in each case. On October 31, 1980 the House of Commons resolved as follows:

> 'That this House, while re-affirming the status of proceedings in Parliament confirmed by article 9 of the Bill of Rights, gives leave for reference to be made in future court proceedings to the Official Report of Debates and to the published Reports and evidence of Committees in any case in which, under the practice of the House, it is required that a petition for leave should be presented and that the practice of presenting petitions for leave to refer to Parliamentary papers be discontinued.'

The letter of June 5, 1992 from the Clerk of the House of Commons starts by saying:

> 'My attention has been drawn to the fact that the House of Lords may be asked to hear argument in this case based on the meaning or significance of words spoken during proceedings on a Bill in the House of Commons.'

A.23.2   The letter then sets out the text of the resolution of October 31, 1980, and continues:

> 'In my opinion, the use proposed for the Official Report of Debates in this case is beyond the meaning of the "reference" contemplated in the Resolution of October 1980. If a court were minded in particular circumstances to permit the questioning of the proceedings of the House in the way proposed, it would be proper for the leave of the House to be sought first by way of petition so that, if leave were granted, no question would arise of the House regarding its Privileges as having been breached.'

The reference in that letter to 'questioning' the proceedings of the House of Commons plainly raised the issue whether the proposed use of parliamentary materials without the leave of the House of Commons would breach section 1, article 9 of the Bill of Rights, which provides:

> 'That the freedome of speech and debates or proceedings in Parlyament ought not to be impeached or questioned in any court or place out of Parlyament.'

The Attorney General, while submitting that such use of parliamentary material would breach article 9, accepted that it was for the courts to determine the legal meaning and effect of article 9. However, the Attorney General warned your Lordships that, even if reference in this case to parliamentary materials did not infringe article 9, the House of Commons might take the view the House enjoyed some wider privilege which we would be infringing and might well regret that its views on the point had not been sought before a decision was reached by your Lordships. Whilst strictly maintaining the privileges of the House of Commons, the Attorney General used the parliamentary materials in this case as an illustration of the dangers of so doing. Moreover, in order to assist us, whilst still maintaining the privileges of the House of Commons, he made submissions as to the effect of such material on the construction of s.63 if, contrary to his contentions and advice, we decided this appeal with the assistance of such material.

In the result, the following issues arise. (1) Should the existing rule prohibiting any reference to Hansard in construing legislation be relaxed and, if so, to what extent? (2) If so, does this case fall within the category of cases where reference to parliamentary proceedings should be permitted? (3) If reference to parliamentary proceedings is permissible, what is the true construction of the statutory provisions? (4) If reference to the parliamentary proceedings is not permissible, what is the true construction of the statutory provisions? (5) If the outcome of this case depends on whether or not reference is made to Hansard, how should the matter proceed in the face of the warnings of the Attorney General that such references might constitute a breach of parliamentary privilege?

. . .

Under present law, there is a general rule that reference to parliamentary **A.23.3** material as an aid to statutory construction is not permissible (the exclusionary rule) (see *Davis v Johnson*[4] and *Hadmor Productions Ltd v Hamilton*[5]). This rule did not always apply but was judge-made. Thus, in *Ash v Abdy*[6] Lord Nottingham L.C. took judicial notice of his own experience when introducing the Bill in the House of Lords. The exclusionary rule was probably first stated by Willes J. in *Millar v Taylor.*[7] However, *Re Mew and Thorne*[8] shows that even in the middle of the last century the rule was not absolute: in that case Lord Westbury L.C. in construing an Act had regard to its parliamentary history and drew an inference as to Parliament's intention in passing the legislation from the making of an amendment striking out certain words.

The exclusionary rule was later extended so as to prohibit the court from looking even at reports made by commissioners on which legislation was based (see *Salkeld v Johnson*[9]). This rule has now been relaxed so as to permit reports of commissioners, including Law Commissioners, and white papers to be looked

---

[4] [1978] 1 All E.R. 1132, [1979] A.C. 264.
[5] [1981] 2 All E.R. 724, [1983] 1 A.C. 191.
[6] (1678) 3 Swan 664, 36 E.R. 1014.
[7] (1769) 4 Burr 2303 at 2332, 98 E.R. 201 at 217.
[8] (1862) 31 L.J. Bcy. 87.
[9] (1848) 2 Exch. 256 at 273, 154 E.R. 487 at 495.

at for the purpose solely of ascertaining the mischief which the statute is intended to cure but not for the purpose of discovering the meaning of the words used by Parliament to effect such cure (see *Eastman Photographic Materials Co Ltd v Comptroller-General of Patents Designs and Trade-marks*[10] and *Assam Railways and Trading Co Ltd v IRC*[11]). Indeed, in *Factortame Ltd v Secretary of State for Transport*[12] your Lordships' House went further than this and had regard to a Law Commission report not only for the purpose of ascertaining the mischief but also for the purpose of drawing an inference as to parliamentary intention from the fact that Parliament had not expressly implemented one of the Law Commission's recommendations.

Although the courts' attitude to reports leading to legislation has varied, until recently there was no modern case in which the court had looked at parliamentary debates as an aid to construction. However, in *Pickstone v Freemans plc*[13] this House, in construing a statutory instrument, did have regard to what was said by the minister who initiated the debate on the regulations. Lord Keith after pointing out that the draft regulations were not capable of being amended when presented to Parliament, said that it was 'entirely legitimate for the purpose of ascertaining the intention of Parliament to take into account the terms in which the draft was presented by the responsible minister and which formed the basis of its acceptance'.[14] Lord Templeman also referred to the minister's speech, although possibly only by way of support for a conclusion he had reached on other grounds.[15] Lord Brandon and Lord Jauncey agreed with both those speeches. This case therefore represents a major inroad on the exclusionary rule (see also *Owens Bank Ltd v Bracco*[16]).

A.23.4   [Counsel] for the taxpayers, did not urge us to abandon the exclusionary rule completely. His submission was that where the words of a statute were ambiguous or obscure or were capable of giving rise to an absurd conclusion it should be legitimate to look at the parliamentary history, including the debates in Parliament, for the purpose of identifying the intention of Parliament in using the words it did use. He accepted that the function of the court was to construe the actual words enacted by Parliament so that in no circumstances could the court attach to words a meaning that they were incapable of bearing. He further accepted that the court should only attach importance to clear statements showing the intention of the promoter of the Bill, whether a minister or private member; there could be no dredging through conflicting statements of intention with a

---

[10] [1898] A.C. 571.
[11] [1935] A.C. 445 at 457–458, [1934] All E.R. Rep. 646 at 655.
[12] [1989] 2 All E.R. 692, [1990] 2 A.C. 85.
[13] [1988] 2 All E.R. 803, [1989] A.C. 66.
[14] See [1988] 2 All E.R. 803 at 807, [1989] A.C. 66 at 112.
[15] See [1988] 2 All E.R. 803 at 814, [1989] A.C. 66 at 121–122.
[16] [1992] 2 All E.R. 193, [1992] 2 A.C. 443.

view to discovering the true intention of Parliament in using the statutory words. . . . [17]

[Counsel] submitted that the time has come to relax the rule to the extent which I have mentioned. He points out that the courts have departed from the old literal approach of statutory construction and now adopt a purposive approach, seeking to discover the parliamentary intention lying behind the words used and construing the legislation so as to give effect to, rather than thwart, the intentions of Parliament. Where the words used by Parliament are obscure or ambiguous, the parliamentary material may throw considerable light not only on the mischief which the Act was designed to remedy but also on the purpose of the legislation and its anticipated effect. If there are statements by the minister or other promoter of the Bill, these may throw as much light on the 'mischief' which the Bill seeks to remedy as do the white papers, reports of official committees and Law Commission reports to which the courts already have regard for that purpose. If a minister clearly states the effect of a provision and there is no subsequent relevant amendment to the Bill or withdrawal of the statement it is reasonable to assume that Parliament passed the Bill on the basis that the provision would have the effect stated. There is no logical distinction between the use of ministerial statements introducing subordinate legislation (to which recourse was had in *Pickstone's case*[18]) and such statements made in relation to other statutory provisions which are not in fact subsequently amended. Other common law jurisdictions have abandoned the rule without adverse consequences. Although the practical reasons for the rule (difficulty in getting access to parliamentary materials and the cost and delay in researching it) are not without substance, they can be greatly exaggerated: experience in Commonwealth countries which have abandoned the rule does not suggest that the drawbacks are substantial, provided that the court keeps a tight control on the circumstances in which references to parliamentary material are allowed.

---

[17] Lord Browne-Wilkinson then rehearsed the principal authorities against the use of parliamentary material for interpreting statute: *Beswick v Beswick* [1967] 2 E.R. 1197 at 1202, [1968] A.C. 58 at 74 *per* Lord Reid; *Black-Clawson International Ltd v Papierwerke Waldhof-Aschaffenburg A.G.* [1975] All E.R. 810 at 814–815, [1975] A.C. 591 at 613–615 *per* Lord Reid and *per* Lord Wilberforce at 828 and 629; *Fothergill v Monarch Airlines Ltd* [1980] 2 All E.R. 696 at 705, [1981] A.C. 251 at 279 *per* Lord Diplock; *Davis v Johnson* [1978] 1 All E.R. 1132 at 1157, [1979] A.C. 264 at 350 *per* Lord Scarman. He then summarised as follows: "Thus the reasons put forward for the present rule are, first, that it preserves the constitutional proprieties, leaving Parliament to legislate in words and the courts (not parliamentary speakers) to construe the meaning of the words finally enacted, second, the practical difficulty of the expense of researching parliamentary material which would arise if the material could be looked at, third the need for the citizen to have access to a known defined text which regulates his legal rights and, fourth, the improbability of finding helpful guidance from Hansard. The Law Commissions of England and Scotland in their joint report on Interpretation of Statutes (Law. Com. No.21; Scot. Law. Com. No.11 (1969)) and the Renton Committee on Preparation of Legislation (Cmnd. 6053 (1975)) both recognised that there was much to be said in principle for relaxing the rule but advised against a relaxation at present on the same practical grounds as are reflected in the authorities. However, both bodies recommended changes in the form of legislation which would, if implemented, have assisted the court in its search for the true parliamentary intention in using the statutory words."

[18] [1988] 2 All E.R. 803, [1989] A.C. 66.

A.23.5   On the other side, the Attorney General submitted that the existing rule had a sound constitutional and practical basis. If statements by ministers as to the intent or effect of an Act were allowed to prevail, this would contravene the constitutional rule that Parliament is 'sovereign only in respect of what it expresses by the words used in the legislation it has passed' (see the *Black-Clawson case*[19]). It is for the courts alone to construe such legislation. It may be unwise to attach importance to ministerial explanations which are made to satisfy the political requirements of persuasion and debate, often under pressure of time and business. Moreover, in order to establish the significance to be attached to any particular statement, it is necessary both to consider and to understand the context in which it was made. For the courts to have regard to parliamentary material might necessitate changes in parliamentary procedures to ensure that ministerial statements are sufficiently detailed to be taken into account. In addition, there are all the practical difficulties as to the accessibility of parliamentary material, the cost of researching it and the use of court time in analysing it, which are good reasons for maintaining the rule. Finally, to use what is said in Parliament for the purpose of construing legislation would be a breach of s.1, art.9 of the Bill of Rights as being an impeachment or questioning of the freedom of speech in debates in proceedings in Parliament.

My Lords, I have come to the conclusion that, as a matter of law, there are sound reasons for making a limited modification to the existing rule (subject to strict safeguards) unless there are constitutional or practical reasons which outweigh them. In my judgment, subject to the questions of the privileges of the House of Commons, reference to parliamentary material should be permitted as an aid to the construction of legislation which is ambiguous or obscure or the literal meaning of which leads to an absurdity. Even in such cases references in court to parliamentary material should only be permitted where such material clearly discloses the mischief aimed at or the legislative intention lying behind the ambiguous or obscure words. In the case of statements made in Parliament, as at present advised I cannot foresee that any statement other than the statement of the minister or other promoter of the Bill is likely to meet these criteria.

A.23.6   I accept [Counsel's] submissions, but my main reason for reaching this conclusion is based on principle. Statute law consists of the words that Parliament has enacted. It is for the courts to construe those words and it is the court's duty in so doing to give effect to the intention of Parliament in using those words. It is an inescapable fact that, despite all the care taken in passing legislation, some statutory provisions when applied to the circumstances under consideration in any specific case are found to be ambiguous. One of the reasons for such ambiguity is that the members of the legislature in enacting the statutory provision may have been told what result those words are intended to achieve. Faced with a given set of words which are capable of conveying that meaning it is not surprising if the words are accepted as having that meaning. Parliament

---

[19] [1975] 1 All E.R. 810 at 836, [1975] A.C. 591 at 638 *per* Lord Diplock.

never intends to enact an ambiguity. Contrast with that the position of the courts. The courts are faced simply with a set of words which are in fact capable of bearing two meanings. The courts are ignorant of the underlying parliamentary purpose. Unless something in other parts of the legislation discloses such purpose, the courts are forced to adopt one of the two possible meanings using highly technical rules of construction. In many, I suspect most, cases references to parliamentary materials will not throw any light on the matter. But in a few cases it may emerge that the very question was considered by Parliament in passing the legislation. Why in such a case should the courts blind themselves to a clear indication of what Parliament intended in using those words? The court cannot attach a meaning to words which they cannot bear, but if the words are capable of bearing more than one meaning why should not Parliament's true intention be enforced rather than thwarted?

A number of other factors support this view. As I have said, the courts can now look at white papers and official reports for the purpose of finding the 'mischief' sought to be corrected, although not at draft clauses or proposals for the remedying of such mischief. A ministerial statement made in Parliament is an equally authoritative source of such information; why should the courts be cut off from this source of information as to the mischief aimed at? In any event, the distinction between looking at reports to identify the mischief aimed at but not to find the intention of Parliament in enacting the legislation is highly artificial. Take the normal Law Commission report which analyses the problem and then annexes a draft Bill to remedy it. It is now permissible to look at the report to find the mischief and at the draft Bill to see that a provision in the draft was not included in the legislation enacted (see *Factortame v Secretary of State for Transport*[20]). There can be no logical distinction between that case and looking at the draft Bill to see that the statute as enacted reproduced, often in the same words, the provision in the Law Commission's draft. Given the purposive approach to construction now adopted by the courts in order to give effect to the true intentions of the legislature, the fine distinctions between looking for the mischief and looking for the intention in using words to provide the remedy are technical and inappropriate. Clear and unambiguous statements made by ministers in Parliament are as much the background to the enactment of legislation as white papers and parliamentary reports. . . .

Against these considerations, there have to be weighed the practical and **A.23.7** constitutional matters urged by the Attorney General, many of which have been relied on in the past in the courts in upholding the exclusionary rule. I will first consider the practical difficulties.

It is said that parliamentary materials are not readily available to, and understandable by, the citizen and his lawyers, who should be entitled to rely on the words of Parliament alone to discover his position. It is undoubtedly true that Hansard and particularly records of committee debates are not widely held by

---

[20] [1989] 2 All E.R. 692, [1990] 2 A.C. 85.

libraries outside London and that the lack of satisfactory indexing of committee stages makes it difficult to trace the passage of a clause after it is redrafted or renumbered. But such practical difficulties can easily be overstated.[21] It is possible to obtain parliamentary materials and it is possible to trace the history. The problem is one of expense and effort in doing so, not the availability of the material. In considering the right of the individual to know the law by simply looking at legislation, it is a fallacy to start from the position that all legislation is available in a readily understandable form in any event: the very large number of statutory instruments made every year are not available in an indexed form for well over a year after they have been passed. Yet, the practitioner manages to deal with the problem, albeit at considerable expense. Moreover, experience in New Zealand and Australia (where the strict rule has been relaxed for some years) has not shown that the non-availability of materials has raised these practical problems.

Next, it is said that lawyers and judges are not familiar with parliamentary procedures and will therefore have difficulty in giving proper weight to the parliamentary materials. Although, of course, lawyers do not have the same experience of these matters as members of the legislature, they are not wholly ignorant of them. If, as I think, significance should only be attached to the clear statements made by a minister or other promoter of the Bill, the difficulty of knowing what weight to attach to such statements is not overwhelming. In the present case, there were numerous statements of view by members in the course of the debate which plainly do not throw any light on the true construction of section 63. What is persuasive in this case is a consistent series of answers given by the minister, after opportunities for taking advice from his officials, all of which point the same way and which were not withdrawn or varied prior to the enactment of the Bill.

A.23.8   Then it is said that court time will be taken up by considering a mass of parliamentary material and long arguments about its significance, thereby increasing the expense of litigation. In my judgment, though the introduction of further admissible material will inevitably involve some increase in the use of time, this will not be significant as long as courts insist that parliamentary material should only be introduced in the limited cases I have mentioned and where such material contains a clear indication from the minister of the mischief aimed at, or the nature of the cure intended, by the legislation. Attempts to introduce material which does not satisfy those tests should be met by orders for costs made against those who have improperly introduced the material. Experience in the United States of America, where legislative history has for many years been much more generally admissible than I am now suggesting, shows how important it is to maintain strict control over the use of such material. That position is to be contrasted with what has happened in New Zealand and

---

[21] Lord Browne-Wilkinson was speaking before the development of the internet as a primary tool of legal research and the routine inclusion on the Parliamentary website of debates and indices to them: it is therefore reasonable to assume that his views would be all the stronger today.

Australia (which have relaxed the rule to approximately the extent that I favour): there is no evidence of any complaints of this nature coming from those countries.

There is one further practical objection which, in my view, has real substance. If the rule is relaxed legal advisers faced with an ambiguous statutory provision may feel that they have to research the materials to see whether they yield the crock of gold, *i.e.* a clear indication of Parliament's intentions. In very many cases the crock of gold will not be discovered and the expenditure on the research wasted. This is a real objection to changing the rule. However, again it is easy to overestimate the cost of such research: if a reading of Hansard shows that there is nothing of significance said by the minister in relation to the clause in question, further research will become pointless.

In sum, I do not think that the practical difficulties arising from a limited relaxation of the rule are sufficient to outweigh the basic need for the courts to give effect to the words enacted by Parliament in the sense that they were intended by Parliament to bear. Courts are frequently criticised for their failure to do that. This failure is due not to cussedness but to ignorance of what Parliament intended by the obscure words of the legislation. The courts should not deny themselves the light which parliamentary materials may shed on the meaning of the words Parliament has used and thereby risk subjecting the individual to a law which Parliament never intended to enact.

Is there, then, any constitutional objection to a relaxation of the rule? The main constitutional ground urged by the Attorney General is that the use of such material will infringe s.1, art.9 of the Bill of Rights as being a questioning in any court of freedom of speech and debates in Parliament. As I understood the submission, the Attorney General was not contending that the use of parliamentary material by the courts for the purposes of construction would constitute an 'impeachment' of freedom of speech since impeachment is limited to cases where a member of Parliament is sought to be made liable, either in criminal or civil proceedings, for what he has said in Parliament, *e.g.* by criminal prosecution, by action for libel or by seeking to prove malice on the basis of such words. The submission was that the use of Hansard for the purpose of construing an Act would constitute a 'questioning' of the freedom of speech or debate. The process, it is said, would involve an investigation of what the minister meant by the words he used and would inhibit the minister in what he says by attaching legislative effect to his words. This, it was submitted, constituted 'questioning' the freedom of speech or debate.

Article 9 is a provision of the highest constitutional importance and should not **A.23.9** be narrowly construed. It ensures the ability of democratically elected members of Parliament to discuss what they will (freedom of debate) and to say what they will (freedom of speech). But, even given a generous approach to this construction, I find it impossible to attach the breadth of meaning to the word 'question' which the Attorney General urges. It must be remembered that art.9 prohibits questioning not only 'in any court' but also in any 'place out of

Parliament'. If the Attorney General's submission is correct, any comment in the media or elsewhere on what is said in Parliament would constitute 'questioning' since all members of Parliament must speak and act taking into account what political commentators and others will say. Plainly article 9 cannot have effect so as to stifle the freedom of all to comment on what is said in Parliament, even though such comment may influence members in what they say.

In my judgment, the plain meaning of art.9, viewed against the historical background in which it was enacted, was to ensure that members of Parliament were not subjected to any penalty, civil or criminal, for what they said and were able, contrary to the previous assertions of the Stuart monarchy, to discuss what they, as opposed to the monarch, chose to have discussed. Relaxation of the rule will not involve the courts in criticising what is said in Parliament. The purpose of looking at Hansard will not be to construe the words used by the minister but to give effect to the words used so long as they are clear. Far from questioning the independence of Parliament and its debates, the courts would be giving effect to what is said and done there.

Moreover, the Attorney General's contentions are inconsistent with the practice which has now continued over a number of years in cases of judicial review. In such cases, Hansard has frequently been referred to with a view to ascertaining whether a statutory power has been improperly exercised for an alien purpose or in a wholly unreasonable manner. . . .

A.23.10 The Attorney General raised a further constitutional point, namely that for the court to use parliamentary material in construing legislation would be to confuse the respective roles of Parliament as the maker of law and the courts as the interpreter. I am not impressed by this argument. The law, as I have said, is to be found in the words in which Parliament has enacted. It is for the courts to interpret those words so as to give effect to that purpose. The question is whether, in addition to other aids to the construction of statutory words, the courts should have regard to a further source. Recourse is already had to white papers and official reports not because they determine the meaning of the statutory words but because they assist the court to make its own determination. I can see no constitutional impropriety in this.

Finally on this aspect of the case, the Attorney General relied on considerations of comity: the relaxation of the rule would have a direct effect on the rights and privileges of Parliament. To the extent that such rights and privileges are to be found in the Bill of Rights, in my judgment they will not be infringed for the reasons which I have given. I deal below with any other parliamentary privileges there may be (see 5. Parliamentary privilege, *post*).

I therefore reach the conclusion, subject to any question of parliamentary privilege, that the exclusionary rule should be relaxed so as to permit reference to parliamentary materials where: (a) legislation is ambiguous or obscure, or leads to an absurdity; (b) the material relied on consists of one or more statements by a minister or other promoter of the Bill together if necessary with such other parliamentary material as is necessary to understand such statements and their effect; (c) the statements relied on are clear. Further than this, I would not at present go. . . .

It follows from what I have said that in my view the outcome of this appeal depends on whether or not the court can look at parliamentary material: if it can, the appeal should be allowed; if it cannot, the appeal should be dismissed. For the reasons I have given, as a matter of pure law this House should look at Hansard and give effect to the parliamentary intention it discloses in deciding the appeal. The problem is the indication given by the Attorney General that, if this House does so, your Lordships may be infringing the privileges of the House of Commons.

For the reasons I have given, in my judgment reference to parliamentary materials for the purpose of construing legislation does not breach section 1, art.9 of the Bill of Rights. However, the Attorney General courteously but firmly warned your Lordships that this did not conclude the question. He said that art.9 was an illustration of the right that the House of Commons had won by 1688 to exclusive cognisance of its own proceedings. He continued:

'I remain convinced . . . that the House of Commons would regard a decision by your Lordships to use Hansard to construe a statute as a grave step and that the House of Commons may well regret that its views were not sought on such an important matter before your Lordships reached a decision.'

My Lords, this House and the courts have always been, and I trust will always **A.23.11** continue to be, zealous in protecting parliamentary privileges. I have therefore tried to discover some way in which this House can fulfil its duty to decide the case before it without trespassing on the sensibilities of the House of Commons. But I can find no middle course. Although for a considerable time before the resumed hearing it was known that this House was to consider whether to permit Hansard to be used as an aid to construction, there was no suggestion from the Crown or anyone else that such a course might breach parliamentary privilege until the Attorney General raised the point at the start of the rehearing. Even then, the Attorney General did not ask for an adjournment to enable the House of Commons to consider the matter. Your Lordships therefore heard the case through to the end of the argument.

Although in the past the courts and the House of Commons both claimed the exclusive right to determine whether or not a privilege existed, it is now apparently accepted that it is for the courts to decide whether a privilege exists and for the House to decide whether such privilege has been infringed (see *Erskine May Parliamentary Practice*[22]). . . .

I trust that, when the House of Commons comes to consider the decision in this case, it will be appreciated that there is no desire to impeach its privileges in any

---

[22] 21st edn. (1989) pp.147–160.

way. Your Lordships are motivated by a desire to carry out the intentions of Parliament in enacting legislation and have no intention or desire to question the processes by which such legislation was enacted or of criticising anything said by anyone in Parliament in the course of enacting it. The purpose is to give effect to, not thwart, the intentions of Parliament."

Extract of the speech of Lord Bridge of Harwich

A.23.12   "It should, in my opinion, only be in the rare cases, where the very issue of interpretation which the courts are called on to resolve has been addressed in parliamentary debate and where the promoter of the legislation has made a clear statement directed to that very issue, that reference to Hansard should be permitted. Indeed, it is only in such cases that reference to Hansard is likely to be of any assistance to the courts. Provided the relaxation of the previous exclusionary rule is so limited, I find it difficult to suppose that the additional cost of litigation or any other ground of objection can justify the court continuing to wear blinkers which, in such a case as this, conceal the vital clue to the intended meaning of an enactment. I recognise that practitioners will in some cases incur fruitless costs in the search for such a vital clue where none exists. But, on the other hand, where Hansard does provide the answer, it should be so clear to both parties that they will avoid the cost of litigation."

Extract of the speech of Lord Griffiths

A.23.13   "I have long thought that the time had come to change the self-imposed judicial rule that forbade any reference to the legislative history of an enactment as an aid to its interpretation. The ever-increasing volume of legislation must inevitably result in ambiguities of statutory language which are not perceived at the time the legislation is enacted. The object of the court in interpreting legislation is to give effect so far as the language permits to the intention of the legislature. If the language proves to be ambiguous I can see no sound reason not to consult Hansard to see if there is a clear statement of the meaning that the words were intended to carry. The days have long passed when the courts adopted a strict constructionist view of interpretation which required them to adopt the literal meaning of the language. The courts now adopt a purposive approach which seeks to give effect to the true purpose of legislation and are prepared to look at much extraneous material that bears on the background against which the legislation was enacted. Why then cut ourselves off from the one source in which may be found an authoritative statement of the intention with which the legislation is placed before Parliament. ... I agree that the use of Hansard as an aid to assist the court to give effect to the true intention of Parliament is not 'questioning' within the meaning of section 1, article 9 of the Bill of Rights (1688). I agree that the House is not inhibited by any parliamentary privilege in deciding this appeal.

I cannot agree with the view that consulting Hansard will add so greatly to the cost of litigation that on this ground alone we should refuse to do so. Modern technology greatly facilitates the recall and display of material held centrally. I have to confess that on many occasions I have had recourse to Hansard, of course only to check if my interpretation had conflicted with an express parliamentary intention, but I can say that it does not take long to recall and assemble the relevant passages in which the particular section was dealt with in Parliament, nor does it take long to see if anything relevant was said. Furthermore if the search resolves the ambiguity it will in future save all the expense that would otherwise be incurred in fighting the rival interpretations through the courts. We have heard no suggestion that recourse to parliamentary history has significantly increased the cost of litigation in Australia or New Zealand and I do not believe that it will do so in this country."

Extract of the speech of Lord Oliver of Aylmerton

"I venture to add a few observations of my own only because I have to confess **A.23.14** to having been a somewhat reluctant convert to the notion that the words which Parliament has chosen to use in a statute for the expression of its will may fall to be construed or modified by reference to what individual members of Parliament may have said in the course of debate or discussion preceding the passage of the Bill into law. A statute is, after all, the formal and complete intimation to the citizen of a particular rule of the law which he is enjoined, sometimes under penalty, to obey and by which he is both expected and entitled to regulate his conduct. We must, therefore, I believe, be very cautious in opening the door to the reception of material not readily or ordinarily accessible to the citizen whose rights and duties are to be affected by the words in which the legislature has elected to express its will.

But experience shows that language—and, particularly, language adopted or concurred in under the pressure of a tight parliamentary timetable is not always a reliable vehicle for the complete or accurate translation of legislative intention; and I have been persuaded, for the reasons so cogently deployed in the speech of my noble and learned friend [Lord Browne-Wilkinson], that the circumstances of this case demonstrate that there is both the room and the necessity for a limited relaxation of the previously well-settled rule which excludes reference to parliamentary history as an aid to statutory construction.

It is, however, important to stress the limits within which such a relaxation is permissible and which are set out in the speech of my noble and learned friend. It can apply only where the expression of the legislative intention is genuinely ambiguous or obscure or where a literal or prima facie construction leads to a manifest absurdity and where the difficulty can be resolved by a clear statement directed to the matter in issue. Ingenuity can sometimes suggest ambiguity or obscurity where none exists in fact, and, if the instant case were to be thought to justify the exercise of combing through reports of parliamentary proceedings in the hope of unearthing some perhaps incautious expression of opinion in support of an improbable secondary meaning, the relaxation of the rule might indeed lead to the fruitless expense and labour which has been prayed in aid in the past as one of the reasons justifying its maintenance. But so long as the three conditions expressed in the speech of my noble and learned friend are understood and observed, I do not, for my part, consider that the relaxation of the rule which he has proposed will lead to any significant increase in the cost of litigation or in the burden of research required to be undertaken by legal advisers."

WILSON AND OTHERS v SECRETARY OF STATE FOR TRADE AND INDUSTRY, WILSON v FIRST COUNTY TRUST LTD. (NO.2).[1]

USE OF HANSARD IN DETERMINING COMPATIBILITY OF LEGISLATION WITH EUROPEAN CONVENTION ON HUMAN RIGHTS

SEE CHAPTER 28

Extract of the speech of Lord Nicholls of Birkenhead

"55. The starting point for any consideration of the matters raised by these **A.24.1** submissions [on behalf of the Parliamentary authorities] is, indeed, the respective roles of Parliament and the courts. Parliament enacts legislation, the courts interpret and apply it. The enactment of legislation, and the process by which legislation is enacted, are matters for Parliament, not the courts. Thus, art.9 of the Bill of Rights 1689 provides, in modern spelling, that 'the freedom of speech and debates or proceedings in Parliament ought not to be impeached or questioned in any court or place out of Parliament.' . . .

56. The decision in *Pepper v Hart* removed from the law an irrational exception. When a court is carrying out its constitutional task of interpreting legislation it is seeking to identify the intention of Parliament expressed in the language used. This is an objective concept. In this context the intention of Parliament is the intention the court reasonably imputes to Parliament in respect of the language used. In seeking this intention the courts have recourse to recognised principles of interpretation and also a variety of aids, some internal, found within the statute itself, some external, found outside the statute. External aids include the background to the legislation, because no legislation is enacted in a vacuum. It has long been established that the courts may look outside a statute in order to identify the 'mischief' Parliament was seeking to remedy. Lord Simon of Glaisdale noted it is 'rare indeed' that a statute can be properly

---

[1] [2003] 3 W.L.R. 568, HL.

interpreted without knowing the legislative object: *Black-Clawson International Ltd v Papierwerke Waldhof-Aschaffenburg AG.*[2] Reports of the Law Commission or advisory committees, and government white papers, are everyday examples of background material which may assist in understanding the purpose and scope of legislation.

57. Before the decision in *Pepper v Hart* a self-imposed judicial rule excluded use of parliamentary materials as an external aid. The courts drew a veil around everything said in Parliament. This had the consequence that a statement made in a government white paper, issued by the relevant government department before legislation was introduced, could be used as an external aid. But if the same statement were made by a minister of the department in Parliament when promoting the Bill in one or other House, the courts were strictly unable to take cognisance of the minister's statement.

58. In relaxing this self-imposed rule the House enunciated some practical safeguards in *Pepper v Hart*. These were intended to keep references to Hansard within reasonable bounds. . . .

59. Suggestions have been made that unequivocal ministerial statements made in Parliament regarding an ambiguous provision in a Bill may have a more exalted role. In his influential article *Pepper v Hart; A Re-examination,*[3] Lord Steyn noted it may be unobjectionable for a judge to use Hansard to identify the mischief at which a statute is aimed. But he rightly drew attention to the conceptual and constitutional difficulties in treating the intentions of the government revealed in debates as reflecting the will of Parliament, as distinct from the possibility that they may give rise to an estoppel or the like against the government.

A.24.2   60. In the present case [Counsel] did not submit that *Pepper v Hart* was wrongly decided. Nor is it necessary to decide whether *Pepper v Hart* does more than permit courts, when ascertaining the intention of Parliament, to have regard to ministerial statements made in Parliament in the same way as they may have regard to ministerial statements made outside Parliament. What is important is to recognise there are occasions when courts may properly have regard to ministerial and other statements made in Parliament without in any way 'questioning' what has been said in Parliament, without giving rise to difficulties inherent in treating such statements as indicative of the will of Parliament, and without in any other way encroaching upon parliamentary privilege by interfering in matters properly for consideration and regulation by Parliament alone. The use by courts of ministerial and other promoters' statements as part of the background of legislation, pursuant to *Pepper v Hart*, is one instance. Another instance is the established practice by which courts, when adjudicating upon an application for judicial review of a ministerial decision, may have regard to a ministerial statement made in Parliament. . . . I now turn to consider whether a challenge to the compatibility of legislation with Convention rights may be a

---

[2] [1975] A.C. 591, 647.
[3] (2001) 21 O.J.L.S. 59.

further instance of the innocuous use by courts of statements made in Parliament.

61. The Human Rights Act 1998 requires the court to exercise a new role in respect of primary legislation. This new role is fundamentally different from interpreting and applying legislation. The courts are now required to evaluate the effect of primary legislation in terms of Convention rights and, where appropriate, make a formal declaration of incompatibility. In carrying out this evaluation the court has to compare the effect of the legislation with the Convention right. If the legislation impinges upon a Convention right the court must then compare the policy objective of the legislation with the policy objective which under the Convention may justify a prima facie infringement of the Convention right. When making these two comparisons the court will look primarily at the legislation, but not exclusively so. Convention rights are concerned with practicalities. When identifying the practical effect of an impugned statutory provision the court may need to look outside the statute in order to see the complete picture, as already instanced in the present case regarding the possible availability of a restitutionary remedy. As to the objective of the statute, at one level this will be coincident with its effect. At this level, the object of s.127(3) is to prevent an enforcement order being made when the circumstances specified in that provision apply. But that is not the relevant level for Convention purposes. What is relevant is the underlying social purpose sought to be achieved by the statutory provision. Frequently that purpose will be self-evident, but this will not always be so.

62. The legislation must not only have a legitimate policy objective. It must also satisfy a 'proportionality' test. The court must decide whether the means employed by the statute to achieve the policy objective is appropriate and not disproportionate in its adverse effect. This involves a 'value judgment' by the court, made by reference to the circumstances prevailing when the issue has to be decided. It is the current effect and impact of the legislation which matter, not the position when the legislation was enacted or came into force. (I interpose that in the present case no suggestion was made that there has been any relevant change of circumstances since the Consumer Credit Act was enacted.)

63. When a court makes this value judgment the facts will often speak for **A.24.3** themselves. But sometimes the court may need additional background information tending to show, for instance, the likely practical impact of the statutory measure and why the course adopted by the legislature is or is not appropriate. Moreover, as when interpreting a statute, so when identifying the policy objective of a statutory provision or assessing the 'proportionality' of a statutory provision, the court may need enlightenment on the nature and extent of the social problem (the 'mischief') at which the legislation is aimed. This may throw light on the rationale underlying the legislation.

64. This additional background material may be found in published documents, such as a government white paper. If relevant information is provided by a minister or, indeed, any other member of either House in the course of a debate

on a Bill, the courts must also be able to take this into account. The courts, similarly, must be able to have regard to information contained in explanatory notes prepared by the relevant government department and published with a Bill. The courts would be failing in the due discharge of the new role assigned to them by Parliament if they were to exclude from consideration relevant background information whose only source was a ministerial statement in Parliament or an explanatory note prepared by his department while the Bill was proceeding through Parliament. By having regard to such material the court would not be 'questioning' proceedings in Parliament or intruding improperly into the legislative process or ascribing to Parliament the views expressed by a minister. The court would merely be placing itself in a better position to understand the legislation.

65. To that limited extent there may be occasion for the courts, when conducting the statutory 'compatibility' exercise, to have regard to matters stated in Parliament. It is a consequence flowing from the Human Rights Act. The constitutionally unexceptionable nature of this consequence receives some confirmation from the view expressed in the unanimous report of the parliamentary Joint Committee on Parliamentary Privilege,[4] that it is difficult to see how there could be any objection to the court taking account of something said in Parliament when there is no suggestion the statement was inspired by improper motives or was untrue or misleading and there is no question of legal liability.

66. I expect that occasions when resort to Hansard is necessary as part of the statutory 'compatibility' exercise will seldom arise. The present case is not such an occasion. Should such an occasion arise the courts must be careful not to treat the ministerial or other statement as indicative of the objective intention of Parliament. Nor should the courts give a ministerial statement, whether made inside or outside Parliament, determinative weight. It should not be supposed that members necessarily agreed with the minister's reasoning or his conclusions.

A.24.4   67. Beyond this use of Hansard as a source of background information, the content of parliamentary debates has no direct relevance to the issues the court is called upon to decide in compatibility cases and, hence, these debates are not a proper matter for investigation or consideration by the courts. In particular, it is a cardinal constitutional principle that the will of Parliament is expressed in the language used by it in its enactments. The proportionality of legislation is to be judged on that basis. The courts are to have due regard to the legislation as an expression of the will of Parliament. The proportionality of a statutory measure is not to be judged by the quality of the reasons advanced in support of it in the course of parliamentary debate, or by the subjective state of mind of individual ministers or other members. Different members may well have different reasons, not expressed in debates, for approving particular statutory provisions. They may have different perceptions of the desirability or likely effect of the legislation. Ministerial statements, especially if made ex tempore in response to questions,

---

[4] (1999) (HL Paper 43–I, HC 214–I), p.28, para.86.

may sometimes lack clarity or be misdirected. Lack of cogent justification in the course of parliamentary debate is not a matter which 'counts against' the legislation on issues of proportionality. The court is called upon to evaluate the proportionality of the legislation, not the adequacy of the minister's exploration of the policy options or of his explanations to Parliament. The latter would contravene art.9 of the Bill of Rights. The court would then be presuming to evaluate the sufficiency of the legislative process leading up to the enactment of the statute. I agree with Laws L.J.'s observations on this in *International Transport Roth GmbH v Secretary of State for the Home Department*.[5]"

---

[5] [2002] 3 W.L.R. 344, 386, paras 113–114.

EXTRACT 25

PROTOCOL ON THE APPLICATION OF THE PRINCIPLES OF SUBSIDIARITY AND PROPORTIONALITY[1]

JUSTIFICATION OF EUROPEAN LEGISLATION

SEE CHAPTER 30, SECTION 4

"1. In exercising the powers conferred on it, each institution shall ensure that the principle of subsidiarity is complied with. It shall also ensure compliance with the principle of proportionality, according to which any action by the Community shall not go beyond what is necessary to achieve the objectives of the Treaty.

A.25.1

2. The application of the principles of subsidiarity and proportionality shall respect the general provisions and the objectives of the Treaty, particularly as regards the maintaining in full of the acquis communautaire and the institutional balance; it shall not affect the principles developed by the Court of Justice regarding the relationship between national and Community law, and it should take into account Art.6(4) of the Treaty on European Union, according to which 'the Union shall provide itself with the means necessary to attain its objectives and carry through its policies'.

3. The principle of subsidiarity does not call into question the powers conferred on the European Community by the Treaty, as interpreted by the Court of Justice. The criteria referred to in the second paragraph of Art.5 of the Treaty shall relate to areas for which the Community does not have exclusive competence. The principle of subsidiarity provides a guide as to how those powers are to be exercised at the Community level. Subsidiarity is a dynamic concept and should be applied in the light of the objectives set out in the Treaty. It allows Community action within the limits of its powers to be expanded where circumstances so require, and conversely, to be restricted or discontinued where it is no longer justified.

4. For any proposed Community legislation, the reasons on which it is based shall be stated with a view to justifying its compliance with the principles of subsidiarity and proportionality; the reasons for concluding that a Community

---

[1] Adopted as an Annex to the EC Treaty in 1997.

objective can be better achieved by the Community must be substantiated by qualitative or, wherever possible, quantitative indicators.

5. For Community action to be justified, both aspects of the subsidiarity principle shall be met: the objectives of the proposed action cannot be sufficiently achieved by Member States' action in the framework of their national constitutional system and can therefore be better achieved by action on the part of the Community.

The following guidelines should be used in examining whether the above-mentioned condition is fulfilled:

— the issue under consideration has transnational aspects which cannot be satisfactorily regulated by action by Member States;

— actions by Member States alone or lack of Community action would conflict with the requirements of the Treaty (such as the need to correct distortion of competition or avoid disguised restrictions on trade or strengthen economic and social cohesion) or would otherwise significantly damage Member States' interests;

— action at Community level would produce clear benefits by reason of its scale or effects compared with action at the level of the Member States.

6. The form of Community action shall be as simple as possible, consistent with satisfactory achievement of the objective of the measure and the need for effective enforcement. The Community shall legislate only to the extent necessary. Other things being equal, directives should be preferred to regulations and framework directives to detailed measures. Directives as provided for in Article 249 of the Treaty, while binding upon each Member State to which they are addressed as to the result to be achieved, shall leave to the national authorities the choice of form and methods.

7. Regarding the nature and the extent of Community action, Community measures should leave as much scope for national decision as possible, consistent with securing the aim of the measure and observing the requirements of the Treaty. While respecting Community law, care should be taken to respect well established national arrangements and the organisation and working of Member States' legal systems. Where appropriate and subject to the need for proper enforcement, Community measures should provide Member States with alternative ways to achieve the objectives of the measures.

8. Where the application of the principle of subsidiarity leads to no action being taken by the Community, Member States are required in their action to comply with the general rules laid down in Article 10 of the Treaty, by taking all appropriate measures to ensure fulfilment of their obligations under the Treaty and by abstaining from any measure which could jeopardise the attainment of the objectives of the Treaty.

9. Without prejudice to its right of initiative, the Commission should:

— except in cases of particular urgency or confidentiality, consult widely before proposing legislation and, wherever appropriate, publish consultation documents;

— justify the relevance of its proposals with regard to the principle of subsidiarity; whenever necessary, the explanatory memorandum accompanying a proposal will give details in this respect. The financing of Community action in whole or in part from the Community budget shall require an explanation;

— take duly into account the need for any burden, whether financial or administrative, falling upon the Community, national governments, local authorities, economic operators and citizens, to be minimised and proportionate to the objective to be achieved;

— submit an annual report to the European Council, the European Parliament and the Council on the application of Article 5 of the Treaty. This annual report shall also be sent to the Committee of the Regions and to the Economic and Social Committee.

10. The European Council shall take account of the Commission report referred to in the fourth indent of point 9 within the report on the progress achieved by the Union which it is required to submit to the European Parliament in accordance with Article 4 of the Treaty on European Union.

11. While fully observing the procedures applicable, the European Parliament and the Council shall, as an integral part of the overall examination of Commission proposals, consider their consistency with Article 5 of the Treaty. This concerns the original Commission proposal as well as amendments which the European Parliament and the Council envisage making to the proposal.

12. In the course of the procedures referred to in Articles 251 and 252 of the Treaty, the European Parliament shall be informed of the Council's position on the application of Article 5 of the Treaty, by way of a statement of the reasons which led the Council to adopt its common position. The Council shall inform the European Parliament of the reasons on the basis of which all or part of a Commission proposal is deemed to be inconsistent with Article 5 of the Treaty.

13. Compliance with the principle of subsidiarity shall be reviewed in accordance with the rules laid down by the Treaty."

INDEX

(All references are to paragraph number)